ISBN 0-89820-129-2

Record Research Inc.
P.O. Box 200
Menomonee Falls, Wisconsin 53052-0200   U.S.A.

Phone:	414-251-5408
Fax:	414-251-9452
E-Mail:	record@execpc.com
Web site:	http://www.recordresearch.com

Joel Whitburn's

Top Country Singles

4th Edition

1944-1997

Billboard.

Chart Data Compiled From *Billboard's* Country Singles Charts, 1944-1997.

Dedicated to...

...my mother-in-law, Doña Luisa Morales Mudgett (1917-1997). What
a privilege it was to know this sweet lady of quiet strength, grace
and modesty. She is missed by a great many.

The author wishes to extend a special note of thanks to:

The staff of Record Research — Bill Hathaway, Kim Bloxdorf, Paul Haney, Troy Kluess,
Jeanne Olynick, Brent Olynick, Kay Boehlke, Bobby DeSai and Fran Whitburn.

Otto Kitsinger — I am deeply grateful for Otto's contributions to my Country research.
I could always rely upon him to supply the facts. We mourn his untimely passing
on April 15, 1998.

George Lockwood — for supplying various missing B-sides and picture sleeve information.

CONTENTS

Most Chart Hits	Most Consecutive #1 Hits
Most Top 40 Hits	Most Consecutive Top 10 Hits
Most Top 10 Hits	Artists With Longest Chart Careers
Most #1 Hits	Artists With Longest Span Between Chart Hits
Most Weeks At The #1 Position	Top Artists Who Never Hit #1
Most Crossover Hits	Artist's First Hit Is Their Biggest Hit
	One-Hit Wonders

Single of the Year
Song of the Year
A chronological listing, by peak date, of every title to top
Billboard's Country singles charts.

AUTHOR'S NOTE

Johnny Cash. Marty Robbins. Jim Reeves. Don Gibson. Sonny James. These artists brought me into Country record collecting. As a teenager during the early years of rock 'n' roll, my record collecting had focused mainly on rock 'n' roll and pop music. The Country-Pop crossover hits of these five gentlemen introduced me to the whole wide world of Country music. Soon I added the hits of Webb Pierce, Hank Snow and Faron Young to my collection.

Years later, when I began publishing my chart research, I made the *Top Country & Western Records 1949-1971* book my second project. I was delighted to put together the bountiful chart histories of Buck Owens, Kitty Wells and George Jones. Mixed in with these stars were the sole chartings of Wes Buchanan, Geraldine Stevens and June Webb. In studying this research, I was struck by two things: the popular longevity of many Country artists and the allegiance between the labels and artists. (Very few artists in the Pop music world consistently charted hits year after year, from the early 1950s through the early '70s, much less remained with one label.) Having that first Country book on hand not only made the trends and nature of Country music more obvious but supplied hours of fun reading and trivia.

Top Country Singles 1944-1997 is the fourth edition of that original book. With each edition, I have aimed to not only bring the history of *Billboard's* Country singles chart up to date, but to present as much information as possible on each record. This book is bursting with more than double the amount of information as any previous edition.

Perhaps the most significant new feature is the inclusion of all B-sides of the records. Now preserved in print, these many songs are no longer forgotten.

Another useful addition is the handy record price guide. As with any price guide, the values are subjective but my determinations, based on several factors, reflect median asking prices. Keep in mind that prices can vary widely depending on demand, location and condition.

Collectors will appreciate the new picture sleeve and picture box guide. Symbols appear in the new "Pic" column indicating which records and cassette singles were released with special packaging.

Of any of my books that highlight the top recordings and prolific eras of major artists, I have found these new format features are most helpful in this book. Since there are many Country artists whose chart careers span several decades and scores of hits, it is now easier to find their hot streaks (debut dates shaded in a box) and biggest hit (underlined). Several other additions serve to indicate an artist's special achievements.

For the first time, the histories of *Billboard's Hot Country Singles Sales* and *Hot Country Singles Airplay* charts are now completely chronicled. A song's peak position attained on either of these charts is listed to the right of the A-side title. Every title that appeared on these two charts also hit *Billboard's Hot Country Singles* chart.

I added all of these new features in order to deepen the presentation of my chart research and the recorded history of these songs. As always, in the process of researching the *Billboard* Country charts, I've learned a great deal about America's favorite music, from its first commercial surge in the '40s through its mainstream dominance in the '90s. And still through these many years, Johnny, Marty, Jim, Don and Sonny remain the top five artists among my ever-growing list of favorite artists that spans the decades.

JOEL WHITBURN

SYNOPSIS OF BILLBOARD'S COUNTRY SINGLES CHARTS
1944-1997

JUKE BOX

Date	Positions	Chart Title
1/8/44	2-8	Most Played Juke Box Folk Records
		(9/6/47-11/1/47 shown as Most-Played Juke Box Hillbilly Records)
1/31/48	9-15	Most Played Juke Box Folk Records
6/25/49	7-15	Most Played Juke Box (Country & Western) Records
11/4/50	6-10	Most Played Juke Box Folk (Country & Western) Records
11/15/52	8-10	Most Played in Juke Boxes
6/30/56	9-10	Most Played C&W in Juke Boxes
6/17/57	final chart	

BEST SELLERS

5/15/48	10-15	Best Selling Retail Folk Records
6/25/49	5-15	Best Selling Retail Folk (Country & Western) Records
11/15/52	8-10	National Best Sellers
2/20/54	9-15	Best Sellers in Stores
6/30/56	13-20	C&W Best Sellers in Stores
10/13/58	final chart	

JOCKEYS

12/10/49	8-10	Country & Western Records Most Played By Folk Disk Jockeys
11/15/52	9-15	Most Played by Jockeys
6/30/56	12-15	Most Played C&W by Jockeys
10/13/58	final chart	

HOT COUNTRY SINGLES

10/20/58	30	Hot C&W Sides
11/3/62	30	Hot Country Singles
1/11/64	50	Hot Country Singles
10/15/66	75	Hot Country Singles
7/14/73	100	Hot Country Singles
1/20/90*	75	Hot Country Singles
2/17/90	75	Hot Country Singles & Tracks

*Billboard begins compiling chart with information provided by Broadcast Data Systems (BDS), which electronically monitors actual radio airplay. Songs are ranked by their gross impressions, which multiplied each play by the Arbitron-estimated audience for the station at the time of the play. On December 5, 1992, Billboard began compiling the chart strictly on the number of detections or plays registered by each song according to BDS.

HOT COUNTRY SINGLES SALES

10/20/84	30	Hot Country Singles Sales
5/31/86	40	Hot Country Singles Sales
8/2/86	30	Hot Country Singles Sales
1/21/89–6/24/95		No chart published
7/1/95*	25	Top Country Singles Sales

*Billboard began compiling chart from a national sample of retail store and rack sales reports collected, compiled, and provided by SoundScan; this data is not a factor in the *Hot Country Singles & Tracks* chart.

HOT COUNTRY SINGLES AIRPLAY

10/20/84	30	Hot Country Singles Airplay
5/31/86	40	Hot Country Singles Airplay
8/2/86	30	Hot Country Singles Airplay
5/16/87	final chart	

This book covers the entire history of *Billboard* magazine's Country singles charts from 1944 through 1997. Over 16,700 charted hits and over 2,100 artists are listed in all.

MULTIPLE COUNTRY SINGLES CHARTS, 1948-1958

Billboard published its first Country singles chart, *Juke Box Folk Records*, on January 8, 1944. All chart data from 1944 through May 8, 1948, refers to the Juke Box chart. On May 15, 1948, *Billboard* introduced another Country singles chart, *Best Selling Retail Folk Records*. A third Country singles chart, *Most Played by Folk Disk Jockeys,* made its debut on December 10, 1949. All of these charts were published on a weekly basis and each focused on specific areas of the music trade. The *Juke Box* chart was discontinued on June 17, 1957. On October 20, 1958, the *Best Seller* and *Disk Jockey* charts were replaced by one all-encompassing Top 30 Country singles chart titled *Hot C&W Sides*. This chart has changed in name and size over the past 40 years and is known, today, as *Hot Country Singles & Tracks*. For a more detailed history of all of *Billboard's* Country singles charts, see the "Synopsis of *Billboard's* Country Singles Charts" on the previous page.

During the years of multiple charts, 1948-1958, many singles hit more than one chart. In our research, the single's debut date is taken from the chart on which it first appeared. The single's peak position is taken from the chart on which it achieved its highest ranking. Listed to the right of the title (before the listing of the B-side) is an indication of the chart(s) and peak position on which it hit. (See "Peak Position Attained On Various Country Charts" in the USER'S GUIDE for a further explanation.) The single's weeks charted and weeks at positions #1 or #2 are taken from the chart on which it achieved its highest total.

CHART METHODOLOGIES

For decades, *Billboard's* Country singles charts were compiled from playlists reported by radio stations and sales reports reported by stores. These airplay and sales reports established the weekly rankings on *Billboard's* airplay charts (*Jockeys, Hot Country Singles Airplay*) and sales charts (*Best Sellers, Hot Country Singles Sales*), and were combined for the compilation of the *Hot Country Singles* charts. On January 20, 1990, *Billboard* began basing their chart entirely on airplay with information gathered by Broadcast Data Systems (BDS). BDS is a subsidiary of *Billboard* that electronically monitors actual radio airplay. They have installed monitors throughout the country that track the airplay of songs 24 hours a day, seven days a week. These monitors can identify each song played by an encoded audio "fingerprint." *Billboard* determined weekly rankings according to gross impressions, which multiplied each play by the Arbitron-estimated audience for the station at the time of the play.

Since not all songs played on Country radio are available as singles, *Billboard* began including album tracks on the revised chart, renaming it *Hot Country Singles & Tracks* to reflect this change. In this book, all charted album tracks are identified by the words "album cut" in the "Label & Number" column; the album that the track is from is noted below the song title.

On December 5, 1992, *Billboard* began compiling the Country singles chart strictly on the number of detections or plays registered by each song according to BDS.

COUNTRY SINGLES SALES AND AIRPLAY

Billboard began publication of the *Hot Country Singles Sales and Airplay* charts on October 20, 1984. These charts were the two ingredients that made up the *Hot Country Singles* chart. The airplay chart was discontinued in 1987; the *Hot Country Singles* chart essentially became the airplay chart after *Billboard* began compiling that chart with BDS data. The sales chart experienced a six-year hiatus beginning in 1989; when it returned in July of 1995, it was not figured into the compilation of the *Hot Country Singles* chart.

ISSUE DATE vs. COLLECTION DATE

All dates within *Top Country Singles* refer to the issue dates of *Billboard* magazine and not the "week ending" dates as shown on the various charts when they were originally published. The issue and week ending dates were different until January 13, 1962, when *Billboard* began using one date system for both the issue and the charts inside. *Billboard's* issue dates were all Saturdays, except from April 29, 1957 to December 25, 1961, when they changed to a Monday issue date. On January 6, 1962, *Billboard* reverted to a permanent Saturday issue date.

Keep in mind that the *Hot Country Singles & Tracks* reports on singles activity from the seven-day period ending 12 days prior. For example, *Billboard* compiled the *Hot Country Singles & Tracks* chart dated October 25, 1997 (Saturday) on October 13 (Monday). The radio airplay reports for this chart covered a seven-day period beginning at 12:01 a.m. on October 6 (Monday) and ending at midnight on October 12 (Sunday). Delivery of the October 25 issue began on October 17 (Friday). *Billboard's* timing has changed slightly over the years.

In our continuing efforts to improve each subsequent edition of *Top Country Singles*, we have added several new features to this fourth edition.

B-SIDES

We are thrilled to introduce all of the B-sides, thus doubling the number of titles listed in any previous edition. All flip sides are shown for all charted vinyl singles, as are additional tracks on charted cassette singles and compact disc singles.

RECORD PRICE GUIDE

Included for the first time in *Top Country Singles* is a price column that lists the current average price for all singles. This column will give you a general idea of the asking prices for these records.

PICTURE SLEEVE AND PICTURE BOX GUIDE

The new "Pic" column shows picture sleeve and picture box symbols for the records and cassette singles which were released with this special packaging.

BIG HITS & HOT STREAKS HIGHLIGHTED

The biggest hits and hottest streaks of each major artist are easy to spot instantly with new special symbols and highlighting.

All #1 singles are identified by a special #1 symbol (❶).

All Top 10 hits are shaded with a gray background.

The biggest hit of an artist with five or more hits is underlined.

The Top 3 or 5 hits of every artist with 10 or more charted hits appear below the artist's bio.

The chart debut dates of an artist's string of five or more consecutive Top 10 hits are shaded in a box.

MULTIPLE COUNTRY CHART POSITIONS NEXT TO TITLE

The peak positions attained on the *Best Sellers In Stores*, *Most Played By Jockeys*, *Most Played In Juke Boxes*, *Hot Country Singles Sales* and *Hot Country Singles Airplay* are now conveniently listed directly across from the A-side title. This is the first-ever publication of the peak positions on the *Hot Country Singles Sales* and *Hot Country Singles Airplay* charts. All titles that appeared on these two charts also hit *Billboard's Hot Country Singles* chart.

The artist section lists each artist's charted hits in chronological order. Each of an artist's song titles is sequentially numbered. All Top 10 hits are shaded for quick identification.

EXPLANATION OF COLUMNAR HEADINGS

DEBUT: Date first charted

PEAK: Highest charted position (highlighted in bold type). All #1 singles are identified by a special #1 symbol (❶).

WKS: Total weeks charted

Gold: ● Gold single*

▲ Platinum single* (additional million units sold are indicated by a numeral following the symbol)

A-side: Song title of chart hit

B-side: Flip side of vinyl single or additional track(s) on a charted cassette or CD single

POP: Peak position achieved on *Billboard's Hot 100* or *Bubbling Under The Hot 100* Pop charts

$: Current value of near-mint commercial copy

Pic: ■ Indicates a custom picture sleeve was originally issued commercially with the record.

☐ Indicates a promotional picture sleeve was distributed to radio stations and the press.

▮ Indicates a custom picture box was originally issued commercially with the cassette single.

LABEL & NUMBER: Original record label and number of single when charted. For songs not released as singles, "album cut" is shown in the label column and the album from which the track attained its airplay is noted below the title along with its label and number.

*The primary source used to determine gold and platinum singles is the Recording Industry Association of America (RIAA), which began certifying gold singles in 1958 and platinum singles in 1976. From 1958 through 1988, RIAA required sales of one million units for a gold single and two million units for a platinum single; however, as of January 1, 1989, RIAA lowered the certification requirements for gold singles to sales of 500,000 units and for platinum to one million units. Please keep in mind that some record labels have never requested RIAA certifications for their hits. In order to fill in the gaps, especially during the period prior to 1958, various other trade publications and reports were used to supplement RIAA's certifications.

EXPLANATION OF SYMBOLS

★21★   Number next to an artist name denotes an artist's ranking among the Top 400 Country Artists of All Time (see ranking on page 498).

1   Superior number to the right of the #1 or #2 peak position is the total weeks the single held that position — also used in POP column for #1 hits.

+   Indicates single peaked in the year after it first charted.

/   Divides a two-sided hit. Complete chart data (debut date, peak position, etc.) is shown for both sides if each side achieved its own peak position. If a title was shown only as the B-side, then only the weeks it was shown as a "tag along" are listed.

LETTER(S) IN BRACKETS AFTER TITLES

C - Comedy
F - Foreign language
I - Instrumental
N - Novelty

R - Re-entry, reissue, remix or re-release of a previously recorded single by that artist
S - Spoken
X - Christmas

PEAK POSITIONS ATTAINED ON VARIOUS POP CHARTS

Prior to publishing the all-encompassing *Hot C&W Sides* chart in 1958, *Billboard* published three weekly Country singles charts: *Best Sellers In Stores*, *Most Played By Jockeys* and *Most Played In Juke Boxes*. The peak position shown in the Peak column for these charts is taken from the chart on which it achieved its highest position. The individual peak positions attained on these three charts is listed to the right of the A-side title. Also, the peak positions attained on the *Hot Country Singles Sales* and *Hot Country Singles Airplay* charts are listed to the right of the A-side titles. All of the Country singles charts consulted are listed below. The following letter designations precede the peak position attained on these charts:

A: Airplay (*Most Played By Jockeys* and *Hot Country Singles Airplay*)
S: Sales (*Best Sellers In Stores* and *Hot Country Singles Sales*)
J: *Most Played In Juke Boxes*

CONSECUTIVE TOP 10 HITS

The peak positions of an artist's string of five or more consecutive Top 10 hits are underlined in a box, so you can quickly spot their hot streaks. Reissues or early label affiliation releases, EP releases, B-side chart hits, recordings with other artists, or a group member's solo releases that did not hit the Top 10 do not break a string nor count within a string. The peak position of a non-Top 10 B-side chart hit (of a Top 10 A-side chart hit) is shaded in a string even if it appears at the end of a string.

B-SIDES

If an A-side is recorded by a duo and its B-side is recorded by a solo artist, then the solo artist's name is shown in parentheses after the B-side.

If a B-side hit *Billboard's Hot 100* or *Bubbling Under the Hot 100* pop singles charts, its peak position is shown in parentheses to the right of the B-side.

The B-sides of cassette singles often contain one or more mixes of the A-side along with another title that may also include one or more mixes. Mixes are shown in parentheses in small letters in the B-side column — ex.: (instrumental), (live), (remix), (album version). Often an A-side and a B-side are on the same side of the cassette single. Usually cassette singles repeat the same program on both sides of the cassette.

RECORD PRICE GUIDE

This is the first edition of *Top Country Singles* to feature a price guide. The prices reflect the current estimated value of an original commercial copy in near-mint condition. You will note that the very collectable records such as rockabilly singles reflect a much higher price than most. When evaluating the more common singles, the age of the record is a major determining factor. Generally, older records are more scarce and more difficult to find in good condition and thus command a higher value.

Often, the prices within this book for near-mint copies of high- and low-charting records of the same era are very close. Although it may be easier to find a copy of a million-selling hit of the past, it is difficult to find one in near-mint condition; because popular records are usually played more, they sustain more scratching and damage. Lower-charting and less popular records are, generally, handled significantly less, thereby remaining in great condition.

Granted, everyone's estimate of value is different, especially when considering geographics. An $8 record in this book may be worth $12 in Nashville, but only $4 in Pittsburgh. Also, variations of the original commercial release, such as promotional copies, mistakes or differentiations on the label, colored vinyl, etc. can vastly increase, or in rare cases, decrease the price of a record. The purpose of this guide is to give a ballpark figure to aid in determining the value of chart hits.

The current price of a single's earlier release is noted below the title along with its label and number. Also noted are the current prices of valuable versions of that song by different artists; usually such versions are rare originals and never charted.

PICTURES OF THE TOP 200 ARTISTS

A picture of each of the Top 200 artists is shown next to their listing in the artist section and their overall ranking is listed to the right of their name. (Ranking positions of the Top 201-400 artists appear to the left of the artist name.)

ARTIST'S TOP YEAR

The year of an artist's peak popularity (based on yearly chart performance) is listed to the right of the artist's name. The same point system used to determine an artist's overall rank (see page 497) is also used to determine their top year. The year of a record's popularity is based on its peak year and not the year it first charted. For example, an artist may chart a record with a debut date of 11/28/64+. The plus sign after the date indicates the record peaked in 1965; and therefore, the record is considered a 1965 hit.

Although the year from which an artist generates the most points is generally considered the top year, some exceptions are made. For example, if an artist had a lone major hit in one year, and a few minor hits in another year which collectively accumulated more points, the year of the major hit is considered the artist's top year.

ARTIST & TITLE NOTES

Below nearly every artist name are brief notes about the artist. Directly under some song titles are notes indicating backing vocalists, guest instrumentalists, the title of the movie in which the song was featured, the name of a famous songwriter or producer, etc. Duets and other important name variations are shown in bold capital letters. Names of artists mentioned in the artist and title notes of others, who have their own chart hits elsewhere in this book, are highlighted in bold type; a name is shown bold the first time it appears in an artist's biography. All movie, TV and album titles, and other major works, are shown in italics. To conserve space in some artist biographies, the abbreviation "b:" for "born on" or "born in" and the abbreviation "d:" for "died on" are used.

A note beneath the title shows if a Country hit was also recorded by another artist and that recording made the Pop and/or R&B charts but not the Country charts. However, if another recording of a Country hit made the Pop and/or R&B charts and hit the Country charts (and therefore appears in this book), we do not show a note beneath the title. If you have any questions about such hits, refer to the title section where you will see all versions of the hit including the crossover version.

As always, we gladly welcome any corrections/updates to our artist biographies or title trivia notes. Please include solid evidence.

CMA AWARDS

The Country Music Association (CMA) began giving yearly awards to Country music artists in 1967. The CMA Awards are very prestigious and we thought it was important to show the winners of the major categories listed below. The following information is shown in the artist and title notes of each winner:

Entertainer Of The Year   Musician Of The Year
Male and Female Vocalist Of The Year   Horizon Award
Vocal Group Of The Year   Single Of The Year
Vocal Duo Of The Year

ARTIST'S BIGGEST HITS

Listed in bold type right below the artist's biography in rank order are:
    the Top 3 hits of every artist with 10 to 19 charted hits and
    the Top 5 hits of every artist with 20 or more charted hits.

Underlined is the highest-charting title for an artist who charted five or more titles. The top hit is a reflection of chart performance only and may or may not relate to an artist's best seller or most popular song over the years. A tie is broken based on total weeks at the peak position, total weeks in the Top 10, total weeks in the Top 40, and finally, total weeks charted.

ARTIST SECTION

Lists, alphabetically by artist name, every song in chronological sequence that charted on *Billboard's* Country Singles charts from January 1, 1944 through December 27, 1997.

A

ABBOTT, Jerry '78
Singer/songwriter from Dallas.

4/29/78	63	7		1 I Want A Little Cowboy .... When It Comes To Cowgirls (I Just Can't Say "No")		$5		Churchill 7712
9/9/78	80	6		2 I Owe It All To You ....Jack Of All Trades		$5		Churchill 7715
1/9/82	82	4		3 One Night Stanley ....(Love Is Still) The Main Attraction		$6		Dallas Star 102581

ABERNATHY, Mack '89
Singer/songwriter from Austin, Texas.

11/12/88	98	2		1 Slippin' Around ....Pocket Rocket Ranger		$6		CMI 1988-8
2/18/89	80	3		2 Different Situations ....Dos Hermanos Cantina		$6		CMI 1988-9

★265★ ACUFF, Roy '44
Born on 9/15/03 in Maynardville, Tennessee. Died of heart failure on 11/23/92 (age 89). Joined the *Grand Ole Opry* in 1937. The Smoky Mountain Boys consisted of Pete "Bashful Brother Oswald" Kirby (dobro), Howdy Forrester (fiddle) and Jimmie Riddle (piano). Formed Acuff-Rose music publishing company in 1942 and the Hickory record label in 1953 with *Fred Rose*. Twice ran for governor of Tennessee. Elected to the Country Music Hall of Fame in 1962. Won Grammy's Lifetime Achievement Award in 1987. Known as "The King Of Country Music."

1)I'll Forgive You But I Can't Forget 2)Jole Blon 3)The Prodigal Son

ROY ACUFF and his Smoky Mountain Boys:

2/12/44	4	2		1 The Prodigal Son ....Not A Word From Home	13	$25		Okeh 6716
11/4/44	3	8		2 I'll Forgive You But I Can't Forget/	21			
11/11/44	6	4		3 Write Me Sweetheart		$25		Okeh 6723
4/19/47	4	6		4 (Our Own) Jole Blon ....Tennessee Central (Number 9)		$20		Columbia 37287
2/7/48	8	5		5 The Waltz Of The Wind ....J:8 / S:13 The Songbirds Are Singing In Heaven		$20		Columbia 38042
6/19/48	14	2		6 Unloved And Unclaimed ....S:14 I Had A Dream		$20		Columbia 20425
8/7/48	12	1		7 This World Can't Stand Long ....S:12 It's So Hard To Smile		$20		Columbia 20454
11/6/48	12	1		8 Tennessee Waltz ....J:12 Sweeter Than The Flowers		$20		Columbia 20551
12/18/48	14	1		9 A Sinner's Death ....S:14 The Midnight Train		$20		Columbia 20475
3/31/58	8	7		10 Once More ....A:8 I Don't Care (If You Don't Love Me)		$15		Hickory 1073
12/29/58+	16	11		11 So Many Times ....They'll Never Take Her Love From Me		$15		Hickory 1090
6/15/59	20	3		12 Come And Knock (On The Door Of My Heart) ....My Love Came Back To Me		$15		Hickory 1097

ROY ACUFF:

5/15/65	45	5		13 Freight Train Blues ....All The World Is Lonely Now		$10		Hickory 1291
11/27/71	56	6		14 I Saw The Light ....The Precious Jewel		$8		United Artists 50849

NITTY GRITTY DIRT BAND with ROY ACUFF

2/16/74	51	11		15 Back In The Country ....(Our Own) Jole Blon		$6		Hickory/MGM 314
6/22/74	97	3		16 Old Time Sunshine Song ....This World Can't Stand Long		$6		Hickory/MGM 319
6/17/89	87	2		17 The Precious Jewel ....Buried Alive		$7		Hal Kat 63058

CHARLIE LOUVIN - ROY ACUFF

ADAMS, Don '74
Born on 1/4/41 in Ross County, Ohio.

4/1/67	64	4		1 Two Of The Usual..........................Wake Me 100 Years From Now		$10		Jack O'Diam. 1002
7/14/73	91	5		2 I'll Be Satisfied ....All For The Love Of A Girl		$5		Atlantic 4002
				#20 Pop hit for Jackie Wilson in 1959				
11/24/73+	34	12		3 I've Already Stayed Too Long ....Oh What A Future She Had		$5		Atlantic 4009
4/27/74	80	4		4 Baby Let Your Long Hair Down..........................Little Girl Blue		$5		Atlantic 4017
				DON ADAMS AND THE GREENFIELD EXPRESS				
8/17/74	52	9		5 That's Love ....I Just Lost My Favorite Girl		$5		Atlantic 4027

ADAMS, Kay '66
Born Princetta Kay Adams on 4/9/41 in Knox City, Texas.

10/15/66	30	7		Little Pink Mack ....That'll Be The Day		$12		Tower 269
				KAY ADAMS with The Cliffie Stone Group				

ADAMS, Kaylee '86
Born in Navarre, Ohio. Female session/jingle singer.

10/18/86	68	4		I Can't Help The Way I Don't Feel..........................Love You 'Til It Hurts		$3		Warner 28567

ADAMS, Peggy Jo — see McCLINTON, O.B.

ADEN, Terry '82
Born on 8/11/52 in Poplar Bluff, Missouri. Male singer.

10/31/81	81	3		1 What's So Good About Goodbye ....I'm Here		$6		B&B 21
4/3/82	73	5		2 She Doesn't Belong To You..........................What's So Good About Goodbye		$5		AMI 1303

ADKINS, Trace '97
Born Tracy Adkins on 1/13/62 in Sarepta, Louisiana. Male singer/songwriter/guitarist.

4/13/96	20	20		1 There's A Girl In Texas ....S:7 A Bad Way Of Saying Goodbye		$3	▌	Capitol 58562
8/24/96	3	21		2 Every Light In The House ....S:2 If I Fall (You're Goin' With Me)	78	$3	▌	Capitol 58574
1/25/97	❶[1]	20		3 (This Ain't) No Thinkin' Thing 634-5789		$3		Capitol 19524
4/26/97	2[2]	20		4 I Left Something Turned On At Home ....I Can Only Love You Like A Man		$3		Capitol 19579
9/6/97	4	22		5 The Rest Of Mine ....S:6 Dreamin' Out Loud	70	$3	▌	Capitol 58680

ADKINS, Wendel　'77
Born in 1946 in Kentucky.

DEBUT	PEAK	WKS		A-side / B-side	Pop	$	Pic	Label & Number
2/19/77	80	4		1 I Will .... *Show Me The Way*		$5		Hitsville 6050
4/30/77	91	3		2 Laid Back Country Picker .... *Texas Moon*		$5		Hitsville 6055
11/26/77	98	2		3 Julieanne (Where Are You Tonight)?................ *She Gives Me Love*		$5		MC/Curb 5002

AKINS, Rhett　★365★　'96
Born on 10/13/69 in Valdosta, Georgia. Singer/songwriter/guitarist.

DEBUT	PEAK	WKS		A-side / B-side	Pop	$	Pic	Label & Number
10/1/94	35	20		1 What They're Talkin' About .... *Heart To Heart*		$3	▌	Decca 54910
1/21/95	36	14		2 I Brake For Brunettes .... *(dance mix)*		$3	▌	Decca 54974
5/13/95	3	21		3 That Ain't My Truck　　　　S:15 *Same Ol' Story*		$3	▌	Decca 55034
10/21/95+	17	22		4 She Said Yes .... *Old Dirt Road*		$3		Decca 55085
3/30/96	❶¹	21		5 Don't Get Me Started　　　　*I Was Wrong*		$3		Decca 55166
9/7/96	38	13		6 Love You Back.............................. *No Match (For That Old Flame)*		$3		Decca 55223
12/7/96+	51	10		7 Every Cowboy's Dream .... *Carolina Line*		$3		Decca 55291
3/22/97	69	1		8 Somebody Knew				album cut
				from the album *Somebody New* on Decca 11424				
10/4/97	41	20		9 More Than Everything...................S:16 *Better Than It Used To Be*	121	$3	▌	Decca 72022

ALABAMA　★20★　'85
Group formed as Young Country in 1969 in Fort Payne, Alabama. Changed name to Wildcountry in 1972, then to Alabama in 1977. Consisted of Randy Owen (vocals, guitar), Jeff Cook (keyboards, guitar, fiddle), Teddy Gentry (bass) and Bennett Vartanian (drums). Owen, Cook and Gentry are cousins. Jackie Owen (another cousin) replaced Vartanian briefly in 1976; Rick Scott then took over as drummer later that same year. Mark Herndon replaced Scott as drummer in 1979. CMA Awards: 1981, 1982 & 1983 Vocal Group of the Year; 1982, 1983 & 1984 Entertainer of the Year.

1)Jukebox In My Mind　2)Down Home　3)I'm In A Hurry　4)Love In The First Degree　5)Feels So Right

DEBUT	PEAK	WKS		A-side / B-side	Pop	$	Pic	Label & Number
7/23/77	78	8		1 I Wanna Be With You Tonight .... *Lovin' You Is Killing Me*		$15	■	GRT 129
9/29/79	33	12		2 I Wanna' Come Over .... *Get It While It's Hot*		$12		MDJ 7906
2/2/80	17	13		3 My Home's In Alabama .... *Some Other Time, Some Other Place / Why, Lady, Why*		$12		MDJ 1002
				shorter version later released on RCA 12008 with a picture sleeve ($4)				
5/31/80	❶¹	17		4 Tennessee River　　　　*Can't Forget About You*		$4		RCA 12018
9/20/80	❶¹	19		5 Why Lady Why　　　　*I Wanna Come Over*		$4	■	RCA 12091
2/14/81	❶¹	14		6 Old Flame　　　　*I'm Stoned*	103	$4		RCA 12169
5/23/81	❶²	13		7 Feels So Right　　　　*See The Embers, Feel The Flame*	20	$4		RCA 12236
10/24/81	❶²	16		8 Love In The First Degree　　　　*Ride The Train*	15	$4		RCA 12288
3/6/82	❶¹	18		9 Mountain Music　　　　*Never Be One*	101	$4	■	RCA 13019
5/29/82	❶¹	17		10 Take Me Down　　　　*Lovin' You Is Killin' Me*	18	$4		RCA 13210
8/28/82	❶¹	17		11 Close Enough To Perfect　　　　*Fantasy*	65	$4		RCA 13294
12/11/82	35	7		12 Christmas In Dixie .... *Christmas Is Just A Song For Us This Year* [X]		$4		RCA 13358
2/12/83	❶¹	16		13 Dixieland Delight　　-　　*Very Special Love*		$4		RCA 13446
5/14/83	❶¹	17		14 The Closer You Get　　　　*You Turn Me On*	38	$4		RCA 13524
				#103 Pop hit for **Rita Coolidge** in 1981				
8/20/83	❶¹	20		15 Lady Down On Love　　　　*Lovin' Man*	76	$4		RCA 13590
1/21/84	❶¹	17		16 Roll On (Eighteen Wheeler)　　　　*Food On The Table*		$4		RCA 13716
4/21/84	❶¹	19		17 When We Make Love　　　　*Carolina Mountain Dewe*	72	$4		RCA 13763
8/4/84				18 If You're Gonna Play In Texas (You Gotta Have A Fiddle		$4		RCA 13840
				In The Band)/　　　　　S:❶¹ / A:2				
	❶¹	2		19　I'm Not That Way Anymore				
11/10/84+	❶¹	19		20 (There's A) Fire In The Night　　A:❶¹ / S:2 *Rock On The Bayou*		$4		RCA 13926
2/9/85	❶¹	21		21 There's No Way　　　　S:❶¹ / A:❶¹ *The Boy*		$4		RCA 13992
5/18/85	❶¹	19		22 Forty Hour Week (For A Livin')　A:❶¹ / S:2 *As Right Now*		$4	■	RCA 14085
8/24/85	❶¹	22		23 Can't Keep A Good Man Down　S:❶¹ / A:❶¹ *If It Ain't Dixie (It Won't Do)*		$4		RCA 14165
1/25/86	❶¹	21		24 She And I　　　　A:❶² / S:❶¹ *The Fans*		$4	■	RCA 14281
9/20/86	❶¹	20		25 Touch Me When We're Dancing　S:❶¹ / A:❶¹ *Hanging Up My Travelin' Shoes*		$3		RCA 5003
				#16 Pop hit for the **Carpenters** in 1981				
12/6/86+	10	15		26 Deep River Woman　　S:❶¹ / A:10 *Ballerina Girl (Pop #7)*	71	$3	■	Motown 1873
				LIONEL RICHIE with Alabama				
1/24/87	❶¹	22		27 "You've Got" The Touch　　A:❶¹ / S:3 *True, True Housewife*		$3		RCA 5081
8/22/87	7	17		28 Tar Top　　　　S:5 *If I Could Just See You Now*		$3	❑	RCA 5222
12/5/87+	❶¹	22		29 Face To Face　　　　S:3 *Vacation*		$3		RCA 5328
				K.T. Oslin (guest vocal)				
4/23/88	❶¹	17		30 Fallin' Again　　　　S:3 *I Saw The Time*		$3		RCA 6902
11/26/88+	❶¹	19		31 Song Of The South　　S:10 *(I Wish It Could Always Be) '55*		$3		RCA 8744
3/11/89	❶¹	19		32 If I Had You　　　　*I Showed Her*		$3		RCA 8817
8/12/89	❶¹	24		33 High Cotton　　　　*"Ole" Baugh Road*		$3		RCA 8948
12/9/89+	❶¹	26		34 Southern Star　　　　*Barefootin'*		$3		RCA 9083
4/28/90	3	21		35 Pass It On Down　　　　*The Borderline*		$3	▌	RCA 2519
7/28/90	❶⁴	20		36 Jukebox In My Mind　　　　*Fire On Fire*		$3		RCA 2643
11/17/90+	❶¹	20		37 Forever's As Far As I'll Go　　　　*Starting Tonight*		$3		RCA 2706
3/2/91	❶³	20		38 Down Home　　　　*Goodbye (Kelly's Song)*		$3		RCA 2778
6/8/91	2¹	20		39 Here We Are　　　　*Gulf Of Mexico*		$3		RCA 2828

| --- | --- | --- | --- | --- | --- | --- | --- | --- |

ALABAMA — Cont'd

DEBUT	PEAK	WKS		A-side / B-side	Pop	$	Pic	Label & Number
9/28/91	4	20		40 **Then Again** · *Hats Off*		$3		RCA 62059
1/11/92	2¹	20		41 **Born Country** · *Until It Happens To You*		$3		RCA 62168
6/6/92	2¹	20		42 **Take A Little Trip** · *Pictures And Memories*		$3		RCA 62253
9/26/92	❶²	20		43 **I'm In A Hurry (And Don't Know Why)** · *Sometimes Out Of Touch*		$3		RCA 62336
12/26/92+	3	20		44 **Once Upon A Lifetime** · *American Pride*		$3		RCA 62428
4/10/93	3	20		45 **Hometown Honeymoon** · *Homesick Fever*		$3		RCA 62495
9/11/93	❶¹	20		46 **Reckless** · *Clear Water Blues*	123	$3	∎	RCA 62636
12/18/93+	7	20		47 **T.L.C. A.S.A.P.** · *That Feeling*		$3		RCA 62712
12/25/93	51	6		48 **Angels Among Us** .... S:6 *Santa Claus (I Still Believe In You)* [X]	122	$3	∎	RCA 62643
4/16/94	13	20		49 **The Cheap Seats** · *This Love's On Me*		$3		RCA 62623
9/10/94	6	20		50 **We Can't Love Like This Anymore** · *Still Goin' Strong*		$3	∎	RCA 62897
12/31/94	28	14		51 **Angels Among Us** · *Santa Claus (I Still Believe In You)* [X-R]		$3	∎	RCA 62643
1/28/95	75	1		52 **Sweet Home Alabama**				album cut
				#8 Pop hit for Lynyrd Skynyrd in 1974; from the album *Skynyrd Frynds* on MCA 11097				
2/11/95	3	20		53 **Give Me One More Shot** · *Jukebox In My Mind*		$3		RCA 64273
7/1/95	2¹	20		54 **She Ain't Your Ordinary Girl** · S:21 *Heartbreak Express*		$3	∎	RCA 64346
9/30/95	4	20		55 **In Pictures** · S:6 *Between The Two Of Them*	118	$3	∎	RCA 64419
1/13/96	19	20		56 **It Works** .... S:18 *Katy Brought My Guitar Back Today*		$3	∎	RCA 64473
5/18/96	38	7		57 **Say I** .... *My Love Belongs To You*		$3		RCA 64543
7/20/96	4	20		58 **The Maker Said Take Her** · *Nothing Comes Close*		$3		RCA 64588
12/28/96	72	2		59 **The Blessings** .... [X]				album cut
				from the album *Christmas Volume II* on RCA 66927				
3/1/97	2¹	20		60 **Sad Lookin' Moon** · S:14 *Give Me One More Shot*		$3	∎	RCA 64775
6/28/97	3	20		61 **Dancin', Shaggin' On The Boulevard** · *Very Special Love*		$3		RCA 64849
10/11/97	22	20		62 **Of Course I'm Alright** .... *(I Wish It Could Always Be) '55*		$3		RCA 64965
12/27/97	47	3		63 **Christmas In Dixie** .... *Santa Claus (I Still Believe In You)* [X-R]		$3		RCA 64436
				same version as #12 above				

★254★ ALAN, Buddy '68

Born Alvis Alan Owens on 5/23/48 in Mesa, Arizona. Singer/songwriter/guitarist. Son of **Buck Owens** and **Bonnie Owens**.

1)Let The World Keep On A Turnin' 2)Cowboy Convention 3)Big Mama's Medicine Show 4)Lodi
5)Too Old To Cut The Mustard

DEBUT	PEAK	WKS		A-side / B-side		$	Pic	Label & Number
7/27/68	7	15		1 **Let The World Keep On A Turnin'** · *I'll Love You Forever And Ever*		$10	∎	Capitol 2237
				BUCK OWENS AND BUDDY ALAN AND THE BUCKAROOS				
11/23/68	54	6		2 **When I Turn Twenty-One**.................... *Adios, Farewell, Goodbye, Good Luck, So Long*		$8	∎	Capitol 2305
				written by **Merle Haggard**				
10/25/69	23	10		3 **Lodi** .... *I Wanna Be Wild And Free*		$8		Capitol 2653
				#52 Pop hit for **Creedence Clearwater Revival** in 1969				
2/7/70	23	8		4 **Big Mama's Medicine Show** .... *When A Man Can't Call His Home A Home*		$8		Capitol 2715
5/2/70	38	9		5 **Down In New Orleans** .... *I've Never Had A Dream Come True Before*		$8		Capitol 2784
8/8/70	57	7		6 **Santo Domingo** .... *That's Quite A Ride*		$8		Capitol 2852
				#1, 5 & 6: written by **Buck Owens**				
11/7/70	19	12		7 **Cowboy Convention** .... *We're All Gonna Get Together*		$8		Capitol 2928
				BUDDY ALAN & DON RICH				
1/16/71	37	9		8 **Lookin' Out My Back Door** .... *Corn Liquor*		$8		Capitol 3010
				#2 Pop hit for **Creedence Clearwater Revival** in 1970				
3/6/71	54	5		9 **I'm On The Road To Memphis** .... *I'll Be Swingin' Too*		$8		Capitol 3040
				BUDDY ALAN & DON RICH				
6/5/71	48	9		10 **Fishin' On The Mississippi**................. *If I Could Love You More*		$8		Capitol 3110
8/21/71	46	9		11 **I Will Drink Your Wine** .... *Doin' The Best I Can*		$8		Capitol 3146
12/4/71+	29	10		12 **Too Old To Cut The Mustard** .... *Wham Bam*		$7	∎	Capitol 3215
				BUCK & BUDDY				
3/4/72	68	4		13 **White Line Fever** .... *Another By Your Side*		$7		Capitol 3266
				written by **Merle Haggard**				
6/24/72	47	10		14 **I'm In Love** .... *The Happiness Song*		$7		Capitol 3346
				written by **Freddie Hart**				
9/23/72	49	7		15 **Things** .... *One Good Woman*		$7		Capitol 3427
				#3 Pop hit for **Bobby Darin** in 1962				
12/30/72+	60	6		16 **Move It On Over** .... *Magic Man*		$6		Capitol 3485
4/7/73	64	4		17 **Why, Because I Love You** .... *She's Been On My Mind For So Long*		$6		Capitol 3555
5/19/73	67	4		18 **Caribbean** .... *Please, Friend, Take Me Home*		$6		Capitol 3598
8/11/73	68	6		19 **Summer Afternoons** .... *Maybe Things Would Be Better That Way*		$6		Capitol 3680
11/24/73+	67	8		20 **All Around Cowboy Of 1964** .... *You Are My Everything*		$6		Capitol 3749
5/4/74	70	8		21 **I Never Had It So Good** .... *She Always Wears A Yellow Rose*		$6		Capitol 3861
2/15/75	35	11		22 **Chains** .... *A Whole Lot Of Somethin!*		$5		Capitol 4019
				#17 Pop hit for **The Cookies** in 1962				
6/7/75	88	5		23 **Another Saturday Night** .... *Nickles, Dimes And Quarters*		$5		Capitol 4075
				#10 Pop hit for **Sam Cooke** in 1963				

ALBERT, Urel '73

Male comedian/impressionist.

DEBUT	PEAK	WKS		A-side / B-side		$	Pic	Label & Number
10/13/73	97	2		**Country And Pop Music** .... *Just Wait* [N]		$15		Toast 311
				"live" effects are dubbed-in				

DEBUT	PEAK	WKS	Gold	A-side (Chart Hit)..B-side	Pop	$	Pic	Label & Number
				ALEXANDER, Daniele '89				
				Born on 12/2/54 in Fort Worth, Texas. Female singer/songwriter.				
7/22/89	19	20		1 She's There .... *Goodbye Me*		$3		Mercury 874330
11/11/89	53	8		2 Where Did The Moon Go Wrong .... *First Move*		$3		Mercury 876228
12/1/90+	56	9		3 It Wasn't You, It Wasn't Me .... *Fairytale Fool*		$3	■	Mercury 878256
				DANIELE ALEXANDER & BUTCH BAKER				
				ALEXANDER, Wyvon '82				
				Born in Weaverville, California. Male singer.				
2/14/81	90	2		1 Frustration .... *Old Familiar Feeling*		$5		Gervasi 633
4/18/81	86	2		2 Old Familiar Feeling		$5		Gervasi 644
8/15/81	74	4		3 Women/				
1/16/82	83	3		4 Don't Lead Me On		$5		Gervasi 659
8/28/82	69	6		5 Alice In Dallas (Sweet Texas) .... *Hungry Man's Dream*		$5		Gervasi 660
				co-written by Merle Haggard				
11/27/82	76	4		6 Midnight Cabaret .... *Same Old Song*		$5		Gervasi 661
12/10/83+	68	8		7 The Look Of A Lovin' Lady .... *High Time*		$5		Gervasi 663
				co-written by Bill Anderson				
				ALIBI '88				
				Vocal group from Canada.				
10/3/87	84	2		1 Roller Coaster		$6		Comstock 1856
5/21/88	61	6		2 Do You Have Any Doubts		$6		Comstock 1884
				ALLAN, Gary '97				
				Born on 12/5/67 in California.				
8/24/96+	7	23		1 Her Man *Wake Up Screaming*		$3		Decca 55227
12/28/96	70	1		2 Please Come Home For Christmas..................*(no B-side)* [X]		$10		Decca 3864 (CD)
				#18 Pop hit for the **Eagles** in 1978; available only as a promotional CD single				
1/18/97	44	11		3 Forever And A Day .... *Living In A House Full Of Love*		$3		Decca 55289
4/12/97	43	15		4 From Where I'm Sitting .... *Wine Me Up*		$3		Decca 72003
8/23/97	43	12		5 Living In A House Full Of Love .... *Of All The Hearts*		$3		Decca 72018
★264★				**ALLANSON, Susie** '78				
				Born on 3/17/52 in Las Vegas. Singer/actress. Performed in the musical *Hair* and both the musical and movie version of *Jesus Christ Superstar*. Formerly married to music executive Ray Ruff.				
				1)We Belong Together 2)Two Steps Forward And Three Steps Back 3)Maybe Baby				
7/9/77	23	14		1 Baby, Don't Keep Me Hangin' On .... *It's Gone*		$7		Oak 1001
				later released on Warner/Curb 8429 ($5)				
11/5/77+	20	14		2 Baby, Last Night Made My Day .... *Will There Really Be A Morning*		$5		Warner/Curb 8473
3/4/78	7	13		3 Maybe Baby *Hide Me In Your Love*		$5		Warner/Curb 8534
				#17 Pop hit for Buddy Holly in 1958				
6/24/78	2²	13		4 We Belong Together *I Don't Want To Cry Anymore*		$5		Warner/Curb 8597
10/28/78	17	11		5 Back To The Love..................*I Want This Feeling To Last*		$5		Warner/Curb 8686
2/3/79	8	11		6 Words *We Can Make It Up To Each Other*		$5		Elektra/Curb 46009
				#15 Pop hit for the **Bee Gees** in 1968				
4/28/79	6	12		7 Two Steps Forward And Three Steps Back *I Will Never Leave You*		$5		Elektra/Curb 46036
8/18/79	79	4		8 Without You .... *Heart To Heart*		$5		Elektra/Curb 46503
				#1 Pop hit for Nilsson in 1972				
12/1/79+	38	10		9 I Must Be Crazy .... *I Can't See Me Without You*		$5		Elektra/Curb 46565
8/2/80	31	12		10 While I Was Makin' Love To You .... *Michael*		$4		United Artists 1365
11/8/80+	23	14		11 Dance The Two Step .... *You Never Told Me About Goodbye*		$4		Liberty 1383
5/30/81	53	7		12 Run To Her .... *Send Me Somebody To Love*		$4		Liberty/Curb 1408
				#2 Pop hit for Bobby Vee in 1961				
9/5/81	44	8		13 Love Is Knockin' At My Door (Here Comes Forever Again) .... *Lay A Little Lovin' On Me*		$4		Liberty/Curb 1425
12/5/81	60	7		14 Hearts (Our Hearts) .... *Dreamin' Again*		$4		Liberty/Curb 1422
4/24/82	62	6		15 Wasn't That Love ....*Falling In Love For The Last Time*		$4		Liberty/Curb 1460
12/27/86+	67	7		16 Where's The Fire		$6		TNP 75001
6/20/87	70	5		17 She Don't Love You		$6		TNP 75005
★305★				**ALLEN, Deborah** '84				
				Born Deborah Lynn Thurmond on 9/30/53 in Memphis. Singer/songwriter. Formerly married to songwriter Rafe Van Hoy. Regular on TV's *The Jim Stafford Show* in 1975.				
				1)I've Been Wrong Before 2)Baby I Lied 3)Take Me In Your Arms And Hold Me				
4/12/80	10	16		1 Take Me In Your Arms And Hold Me *Missing Angel*		$5		RCA 11946
				JIM REEVES/DEBORAH ALLEN				
11/22/80+	24	15		2 Nobody's Fool .... *Let Me Down*		$4		Capitol 4945
8/15/81	20	11		3 You (Make Me Wonder Why) .... *Next To You*		$4		Capitol 5014
1/9/82	33	10		4 You Look Like The One I Love .... *It's Cold Inside*		$4		Capitol 5080
5/29/82	82	3		5 After Tonight..................*Don't Worry 'Bout Me Baby*		$4		Capitol 5110
8/20/83	4	24		6 Baby I Lied *Time Is Taking You Away From Me*	26	$4	■	RCA 13600
1/28/84	2²	24		7 I've Been Wrong Before *Fool's Paradise*		$4		RCA 13694
5/26/84	10	20		8 I Hurt For You *Cheat The Night*		$4		RCA 13776
10/20/84	23	17		9 Heartache And A Half .... *A:20 / S:26 It Makes Me Cry*		$4	■	RCA 13921
12/5/92+	29	20		10 Rock Me (In The Cradle Of Love) .... *Natural Tears*		$3		Giant 18566
4/17/93	44	13		11 If You're Not Gonna Love Me .... *Long Time Lovin' You*		$3		Giant 18530
5/7/94	66	2		12 Break These Chains .... *Talkin' To My Heart*		$3	■	Giant 18199

ALLEN, Joe '75
Born in Aspen, Colorado. Singer/session musician.

1/25/75	83	5		1 Should I Come Home (Or Should I Go Crazy) .... *What Kind Of A Fool*		$5		Warner 8052
7/5/75	88	8		2 Carolyn At The Broken Wheel Inn..*Again*		$5		Warner 8098

ALLEN, Judy '78

| 1/28/78 | 94 | 4 | | Sweet Little Devil .... *He Was Fire* | | $5 | | Polydor 14440 |

ALLEN, Melody '75

| 2/1/75 | 91 | 6 | | 1 Once Again I Go To Sleep With Lovin' On My Mind .. *You've Got A Way With Love* | | $5 | | Mercury 73638 |
| 5/10/75 | 68 | 8 | | 2 May You Rest In Peace........................... *When Someone Wants To Leave* | | $5 | | Mercury 73674 |

ALLEN, Red — see OSBORNE BROTHERS

ALLEN, Rex '53
Born on 12/31/20 in Willcox, Arizona. Singer/guitarist/actor. Professional rodeo rider as a teenager. Acted in several western movies. Narrator for several Disney nature movies. Played "Bill Baxter" on TV's *Frontier Doctor*. Father of **Rex Allen Jr.**

9/3/49	14	1		1 Afraid..J:14 *Cottage In The Clouds*		$15		Mercury 6192
				REX ALLEN and The Arizona Wranglers with Jerry Byrd				
4/21/51	10	1		2 Sparrow In The Tree Top J:10 *Always You*	28	$20		Mercury 5597-X45
				Harry Geller (orch.); Jud Conlin Singers (backing vocals)				
8/8/53	4	13		3 Crying In The Chapel S:4 / J:4 / A:6 *I Thank The Lord*	8	$15		Decca 28758
				#3 Pop hit for **Elvis Presley** in 1965				
8/14/61	21	4		4 Marines, Let's Go ....*Heartaches Of A Fool*		$10		Mercury 71844
9/29/62	4	13		5 Don't Go Near The Indians *Touched So Deeply*	17	$10		Mercury 71997
				The Merry Melody Singers (backing vocals)				
1/11/64	44	3		6 Tear After Tear ....*I'm Just Killin' Time (Till This Heartache Kills Me)*		$8	■	Mercury 72205
6/22/68	71	5		7 Tiny Bubbles .... *Jose Villa Lobo Alfredo Thomaso Vincente Lopez*		$6		Decca 32322
				#57 Pop hit for Don Ho in 1967				

ALLEN, Rex Jr. ★144★ '77
Born on 8/23/47 in Chicago. Singer/songwriter/guitarist. Son of **Rex Allen**. Traveled with his father from age six. Formed the groups the Townsmen and Saturday's Children. Served in the U.S. Army from 1967-69. Hosted TNN's *Nashville On The Road* and worked as a regular performer on *The Statler Brothers Show*.

1)Two Less Lonely People 2)Lonely Street 3)No, No, No 4)Me And My Broken Heart 5)With Love

12/29/73+	63	10		1 The Great Mail Robbery....................................*Start Again*		$6		Warner 7753
4/20/74	19	14		2 Goodbye ....*The Same Old Way*		$6		Warner 7788
8/24/74	31	14		3 Another Goodbye Song ....*Yes We Have Love*		$6		Warner 8000
12/7/74+	36	11		4 Never Coming Back Again ....*I Can See Clearly Now*		$6		Warner 8046
5/31/75	70	7		5 Lying In My Arms ....*She Just Said Goodbye*		$5		Warner 8095
1/24/76	34	9		6 Play Me No Sad Songs ....*She Just Said Goodbye*		$5		Warner 8171
5/1/76	17	12		7 Can You Hear Those Pioneers ....*Streets Of Laredo*		$5		Warner 8204
				Rex Allen and The Sons of The Pioneers (guest vocals)				
8/7/76	18	13		8 Teardrops In My Heart ....*Home-Made Love*		$5		Warner 8236
12/11/76+	8	16		9 Two Less Lonely People *I Gotta Remember To Forget You*		$5		Warner 8297
4/9/77	10	12		10 I'm Getting Good At Missing You (Solitaire) *Don't Say Goodbye*		$5		Warner 8354
8/6/77	15	11		11 Don't Say Goodbye ....*There's No Use Hanging On*		$5		Warner 8418
11/12/77+	8	15		12 Lonely Street *Don't It Make You Want To Go Home*		$5		Warner 8482
				#5 Pop hit for Andy Williams in 1959				
3/25/78	8	15		13 No, No, No (I'd Rather Be Free) *I Got A Name*		$5		Warner 8541
7/29/78	10	12		14 With Love *You Turned It On Again Last Night*		$5		Warner 8608
11/25/78+	12	14		15 It's Time We Talk Things Over ....*Watch Me Cry*		$5		Warner 8697
				REX ALLEN, JR. AND THE BOYS				
4/14/79	9	12		16 Me And My Broken Heart *Lovin' You Is Everything To Me*		$5		Warner 8786
8/4/79	18	12		17 If I Fell In Love With You ....*Pick Up The Pieces*		$4		Warner 49020
2/16/80	25	10		18 Yippy Cry Yi ....*She Has My Heart*		$4		Warner 49168
5/24/80	14	13		19 It's Over..............................*Why Did You Stop Lovin' Me*		$4		Warner 49128
9/27/80	25	12		20 Drink It Down, Lady ....*What Was Your Name?*		$4		Warner 49562
12/20/80+	12	14		21 Cup Of Tea ....*Goodbye*		$4		Warner 49626
				REX ALLEN, JR. AND MARGO SMITH				
3/14/81	35	9		22 Just A Country Boy ....*Cat's In The Cradle*		$4		Warner 49682
6/13/81	26	12		23 While The Feeling's Good ....*Watered Down Love*		$4		Warner 49738
				REX ALLEN, JR. & MARGO SMITH				
3/27/82	43	10		24 Last Of The Silver Screen Cowboys ....*Round Up Time*		$4	■	Warner 50035
				Rex Allen and Roy Rogers (guest vocals)				
7/10/82	44	10		25 Cowboy In A Three Piece Business Suit ....*Round Up Time*		$4		Warner 29968
11/27/82	85	3		26 Ride Cowboy Ride ....*Three Friends Have I*		$4		Warner 29890
10/22/83	37	15		27 The Air That I Breathe...........................*Whiskey Cheer*		$5		Moon Shine 3017
				#6 Pop hit for The Hollies in 1974				
3/10/84	44	9		28 Sweet Rosanna ....*You Sure Could Have Fooled Me*		$5		Moon Shine 3022
7/14/84	18	16		29 Dream On Texas Ladies		$5		Moon Shine 3030
11/10/84+	24	19		30 Running Down Memory Lane ....S:17 / A:26 *Shameless Love*		$5		Moon Shine 3034
4/20/85	62	7		31 When You Held Me In Your Arms.............................		$5		Moon Shine 3036
11/14/87	59	8		32 We're Staying Together ....*Diamond In The Rough*		$6		TNP 75010

ALLEN, Rosalie '46
Born Julie Marlene Bedra on 6/27/24 in Old Forge, Pennsylvania. Hosted own TV show in New York City from 1949-53. Known as "The Prairie Star" and "Queen of The Yodelers."

8/17/46	3	4		1 Guitar Polka (Old Monterey)/				
8/10/46	5	1		2 I Want To Be A Cowboy's Sweetheart		$20		RCA Victor 20-1924
2/4/50	7	4		3 Beyond The Sunset A:7 The Game Of Broken Hearts		$30		RCA Victor 47-3105
				THE THREE SUNS with ROSALIE ALLEN and ELTON BRITT				
				78 rpm: 20-3599; #71 Pop hit for Pat Boone in 1959				
2/25/50	3	10		4 Quicksilver A:3 / J:6 / S:9 The Yodel Blues		$30		RCA Victor 48-0168
				ELTON BRITT and ROSALIE ALLEN with The Skytoppers				
				78 rpm: 21-0157				

ALLEY, Jim '68
Born in Hemphill, West Virginia. Singer/guitarist.

1/20/68	73	2		1 Only Daddy That'll Walk The Line..................................When You Were Here		$15		Dot 17051
3/15/75	96	2		2 Her Memory's Gonna Kill Me..................................If I Didn't Have A Dime		$8		Avco 606

ALMOST BROTHERS, The '86
Duo from New York City: guitarist/songwriter/producer Mike Ragogna and guitarist/pianist Steve Mosto.

8/17/85	55	7		1 Don't Tell Me Love Is Kind..................................Nighttime Fantasy		$4		MTM 72053
2/22/86	63	6		2 Birds Of A Feather..................................I Wanna Kiss The Bride		$4		MTM 72062
8/9/86	72	6		3 What's Your Name..................................Adventures In Love		$4		MTM 72072
				#7 Pop hit for Don & Juan in 1962				
11/22/86	52	8		4 I Don't Love Her Anymore ....Nighttime Fantasy		$4		MTM 72079

ALVIN & THE CHIPMUNKS — see CHIPMUNKS, The

AMARILLO — see GRANT, Barry

AMAZING RHYTHM ACES '76
Country-rock group from Memphis: **Russell Smith** (vocals, guitar), Barry "Byrd" Burton (guitar, dobro), Billy Earhart III (keyboards), James Hooker (piano), Jeff Davis (bass) and Butch McDade (drums). Burton left in 1977; replaced by Duncan Cameron. Disbanded in 1980. Earhart joined **The Bama Band** in 1986. Cameron joined **Sawyer Brown** in 1992.

7/5/75	11	14		1 Third Rate Romance..................................Mystery Train	14	$5		ABC 12078
11/29/75+	9	14		2 Amazing Grace (Used To Be Her Favorite Song) The Beautiful Lie	72	$5		ABC 12142
8/7/76	12	14		3 The End Is Not In Sight (The Cowboy Tune) ....Same Ole' Me	42	$5		ABC 12202
7/15/78	100	1		4 Ashes Of Love ....All That I Had Left (With You)		$5		ABC 12369
3/24/79	88	4		5 Lipstick Traces (On A Cigarette)..................................Whispering In The Night	104	$5		ABC 12454
				#48 Pop hit for The O'Jays in 1965				
11/29/80	77	6		6 I Musta Died And Gone To Texas ....Give Me Flowers While I'm Living		$4		Warner 49600

AMES, Durelle '87
Born Durelle Upchurch on 5/4/65 in Gaffney, South Carolina. Female singer. Also recorded as **De De Ames**.

8/15/87	72	5		1 Dancin' In The Moonlight..................................		$6		Advantage 175
1/16/88	75	4		2 Break Down The Walls		$6		Advantage 185
				DE DE AMES				

AMY '79

2/3/79	76	4		Please Be Gentle ....Jump Into My Love		$6		Scorpion 0570
				written by Mac Davis				

ANDERSON, Bill ★27★ '62
Born James William Anderson III on 11/1/37 in Columbia, South Carolina. Singer/songwriter/actor. Worked as a sportswriter in Atlanta and as a DJ in Commerce, Georgia. Joined the *Grand Ole Opry* in 1961. Appeared in such movies as *Las Vegas Hillbillies*, *Forty Acre Feud* and *Road To Nashville*. Hosted own TV show in 1966. Hosted TV game shows *The Better Sex* and *Fandango*. Host of TNN's *Opry Backstage*. Known as "Whispering Bill."

1)*Mama Sang A Song* 2)*Still* 3)*For Loving You* 4)*My Life* 5)*I Get The Fever*

12/29/58+	12	17		1 That's What It's Like To Be Lonesome..................................Thrill Of My Life		$15		Decca 30773
7/6/59	13	19		2 Ninety-Nine..................................Back Where I Started From		$15		Decca 30914
12/28/59+	19	8		3 Dead Or Alive..................................It's Not The End Of Everything		$15		Decca 30993
6/20/60	7	18		4 The Tip Of My Fingers No Man's Land		$12		Decca 31092
12/26/60+	9	14		5 Walk Out Backwards The Best Of Strangers		$12		Decca 31168
7/10/61	9	19		6 Po' Folks Goodbye Cruel World		$12		Decca 31262
4/21/62	14	10		7 Get A Little Dirt On Your Hands..................................Down Came The Rain		$12		Decca 31358
				also see #63 below				
7/28/62	❶⁷	27		8 Mama Sang A Song On And On And On [S]	89	$10		Decca 31404
2/23/63	❶⁷	27		9 Still You Made It Easy	8	$10		Decca 31458
8/24/63	2²	23		10 8 X 10 One Mile Over - Two Miles Back	53	$10	■	Decca 31521
1/25/64	5	18		11 Five Little Fingers/	118			
2/15/64	14	20		12 Easy Come-Easy Go		$10		Decca 31577
7/25/64	8	16		13 Me Cincinnati, Ohio [S]		$10		Decca 31630
11/14/64+	8	18		14 Three A.M./				
11/7/64	38	5		15 In Case You Ever Change Your Mind..................................		$10		Decca 31681
4/3/65	12	17		16 Certain You Can Have Her		$10		Decca 31743
9/4/65	11	16		17 Bright Lights And Country Music Born		$10		Decca 31825
2/12/66	4	24		18 I Love You Drops/		$10		Decca 31825
				#30 Pop hit for Vic Dana in 1966				
1/22/66	11	13		19 Golden Guitar ....[S]		$10		Decca 31890

ANDERSON, Bill — Cont'd

DEBUT	PEAK	WKS	A-side (Chart Hit) / B-side	Pop	$	Label & Number
2/19/66	29	8	20 I Know You're Married (But I Love You Still)/			
3/12/66	44	1	21 Time Out..		$10	Decca 31884
			BILL ANDERSON AND JAN HOWARD (above 2)			
8/27/66	❶¹	20	22 I Get The Fever The First Mrs. Jones		$8	Decca 31999
1/14/67	5	19	23 Get While The Gettin's Good Something To Believe In		$8	Decca 32077
7/1/67	10	19	24 No One's Gonna Hurt You Anymore/		$8	Decca 32146
7/15/67	64	5	25 Papa...[S]		$8	Decca 32146
10/28/67	❶⁴	20	26 For Loving You The Untouchables [S]		$8	Decca 32197
			BILL ANDERSON And JAN HOWARD			
11/11/67	42	9	27 Stranger On The Run................. Happiness		$8	Decca 32215
3/16/68	2¹	18	28 Wild Week-End Fun While It Lasted		$8	Decca 32276
8/17/68	2²	16	29 Happy State Of Mind Time's Been Good To Me		$8	Decca 32360
3/1/69	❶²	19	30 My Life (Throw It Away If I Want To) To Be Alone		$8	Decca 32445
7/12/69	2³	15	31 But You Know I Love You A Picture From Life's Other Side		$8	Decca 32514
			#19 Pop hit for Kenny Rogers & The First Edition in 1969			
11/15/69+	2¹	15	32 If It's All The Same To You I Thank God For You		$8	Decca 32511
			BILL ANDERSON And JAN HOWARD			
3/14/70	5	15	33 Love Is A Sometimes Thing And I'm Still Missing You		$8	Decca 32643
			BILL ANDERSON And The Po' Boys			
			"live" recording			
6/20/70	4	15	34 Someday We'll Be Together Who Is The Biggest Fool		$8	Decca 32689
			BILL ANDERSON And JAN HOWARD			
			#1 Pop hit for Diana Ross & The Supremes in 1969			
10/24/70	6	14	35 Where Have All Our Heroes Gone Loving A Memory [S]	93	$8	Decca 32744
3/13/71	6	15	36 Always Remember You Can Change My World	111	$8	Decca 32793
7/24/71	3	17	37 Quits I'll Live For You		$8	Decca 32850
10/9/71	4	15	38 Dis-Satisfied Knowing You're Mine		$8	Decca 32877
			BILL ANDERSON AND JAN HOWARD			
3/18/72	5	15	39 All The Lonely Women In The World It Was Time For Me To Move On Anyway		$8	Decca 32930
9/9/72	2²	16	40 Don't She Look Good I'm Just Gone		$8	Decca 33002
2/24/73	2¹	14	41 If You Can Live With It (I Can Live Without It) Let's Fall Apart		$5	MCA 40004
7/7/73	2³	15	42 The Corner Of My Life Home And Things		$5	MCA 40070
12/15/73+	❶¹	15	43 World Of Make Believe Gonna Shine It On Again		$5	MCA 40164
6/1/74	24	14	44 Can I Come Home To You .... I'm Happily Married (And Planning On Staying That Way)		$5	MCA 40243
10/5/74	7	13	45 Every Time I Turn The Radio On You Are My Story (You Are My Song)		$5	MCA 40304
2/8/75	14	11	46 I Still Feel The Same About You .... Talk To Me Ohio		$5	MCA 40351
5/10/75	36	11	47 Country D.J................................ We Made Love (But Where's The Love We Made)		$5	MCA 40404
8/23/75	24	11	48 Thanks....................................Why'd The Last Time Have To Be The Best		$5	MCA 40443
11/29/75+	❶¹	16	49 Sometimes Circle In A Triangle		$5	MCA 40488
			BILL ANDERSON and MARY LOU TURNER			
3/27/76	7	12	50 That's What Made Me Love You Can We Still Be Friends		$5	MCA 40533
			BILL ANDERSON and MARY LOU TURNER			
8/14/76	10	14	51 Peanuts And Diamonds Your Love Blows Me Away		$5	MCA 40595
12/4/76+	6	14	52 Liars One, Believers Zero Let Me Whisper Darling One More Time		$5	MCA 40661
5/7/77	7	13	53 Head To Toe Love Song For Jackie		$5	MCA 40713
7/16/77	18	12	54 Where Are You Going, Billy Boy .... Sad Ole Shade Of Gray		$5	MCA 40753
			BILL ANDERSON and MARY LOU TURNER			
10/1/77	11	12	55 Still The One .... This Ole Suitcase		$5	MCA 40794
			#5 Pop hit for Orleans in 1976			
1/28/78	25	10	56 I'm Way Ahead Of You.................Just Enough To Make Me Want It All		$5	MCA 40852
			BILL ANDERSON & MARY LOU TURNER			
4/29/78	4	14	57 I Can't Wait Any Longer Joanna	80	$5	MCA 40893
11/11/78	30	9	58 Double S ....Married Lady [S]		$5	MCA 40964
2/17/79	20	13	59 This Is A Love Song................................. Remembering The Good		$5	MCA 40992
7/21/79	40	9	60 The Dream Never Dies .... One More Sexy Lady		$5	MCA 41060
			BILL ANDERSON & THE PO' FOLKS			
			#48 Pop hit for The Cooper Brothers in 1978			
12/8/79+	51	8	61 More Than A Bedroom Thing .... Love Me And I'll Be Your Best Friend		$5	MCA 41150
4/12/80	35	9	62 Make Mine Night Time The Old Me And You		$5	MCA 41212
6/21/80	46	7	63 Get A Little Dirt On Your Hands .... What Can I Do [R]		$5	Columbia 11277
			DAVID ALLAN COE AND BILL ANDERSON			
			new version of #7 above			
8/23/80	58	7	64 Rock 'N' Roll To Rock Of Ages................ I'm Used To The Rain		$4	MCA 41297
11/22/80	83	3	65 I Want That Feelin' Again .... She Made Me Remember		$4	MCA 51017
2/21/81	44	8	66 Mister Peepers .... How Married Are You, Mary Ann?		$4	MCA 51052
8/15/81	74	4	67 Homebody .... (Her Wedding Ring's A) One Man Band		$4	MCA 51150
			Whispering BILL ANDERSON			
12/26/81+	76	4	68 Whiskey Made Me Stumble (The Devil Made Me Fall) ....All That Keeps Me Goin'		$4	MCA 51204
8/21/82	42	10	69 Southern Fried You Turn The Light On		$5	Southern Tracks 1007
12/25/82+	82	5	70 Laid Off .... Lovin' Tonight		$5	Southern Tracks 1011
3/12/83	70	6	71 Thank You Darling ....Lovin' Tonight [S]		$5	Southern Tracks 1014
7/9/83	71	6	72 Son Of The South/			
		6	73 20th Century Fox		$5	Southern Tracks 1021
5/12/84	76	7	74 Your Eyes .... I Never Get Enough Of You		$5	Southern Tracks 1026
2/9/85	58	7	75 Wino The Clown Wild Weekend		$5	Swanee 4013
4/27/85	62	6	76 Pity Party Don't She Look Good		$5	Swanee 5015
8/17/85	75	5	77 When You Leave That Way You Can Never Go Back.......................Quits		$5	Swanee 5018

ANDERSON, Bill — Cont'd

DEBUT	PEAK	WKS		A-side	B-side	Pop	$	Pic	Label & Number
12/27/86+	80	5		78 Sheet Music.. *Maybe Go Down*			$5		Southern Tracks 1067
5/9/87	78	5		79 No Ordinary Memory .... *Sheet Music*			$5		Southern Tracks 1077
2/9/91	60	6		80 Deck Of Cards .... *Thank You Darling* [S]			$3	▌	Curb 76855

ANDERSON, Ivie '44

Born on 7/10/05 in Gilroy, California. Died of asthma on 12/28/49 (age 44). Female vocalist with Duke Ellington's band from 1931-42.

DEBUT	PEAK	WKS		A-side	B-side	Pop	$	Pic	Label & Number
4/8/44	4	2		Mexico Joe *When The Ships Come Sailing Home Again*		16	$50		Exclusive 3113

IVIE ANDERSON with CEELLE BURKE'S ORCH.

ANDERSON, John ★57★ '83

Born on 12/13/54 in Orlando, Florida; raised in Apopka, Florida. Singer/songwriter/guitarist. While a teenager led the groups the Weed Seeds and the Living End. Sang with sister Donna in the early '70s. Moved to Nashville in 1971. Worked construction on the new Grand Ole Opry building. Worked as a staff writer with Gallico Music. CMA Award: 1983 Horizon Award.

1)Wild And Blue 2)Black Sheep 3)Money In The Bank 4)Straight Tequila Night 5)Swingin'

DEBUT	PEAK	WKS		A-side	B-side	Pop	$	Pic	Label & Number
12/10/77+	62	8		1 I've Got A Feelin' (Somebody Stealin').......................... *It's All The Way Together*			$5		Warner 8480
6/24/78	69	5		2 Whine, Whistle, Whine .... *If There Were No Memories*			$5		Warner 8585
11/25/78	40	9		3 The Girl At The End Of The Bar .... *You're Pleasin' Me*			$5		Warner 8705
3/24/79	41	8		4 My Pledge Of Love .... *Why Baby Why*			$5		Warner 8770
				#14 Pop hit for The Joe Jeffrey Group in 1969					
7/14/79	31	11		5 Low Dog Blues .... *Girl, For You*			$5		Warner 8863
10/27/79+	15	16		6 Your Lying Blue Eyes .... *Mountain High, Valley Low*			$4		Warner 49089
3/15/80	13	15		7 She Just Started Liking Cheatin' Songs .....*I Wish I Could Write You A Song*			$4		Warner 49191
7/26/80	21	14		8 If There Were No Memories .... *Shoot Low Sheriff!*			$4		Warner 49275
11/22/80+	7	17		9 1959 .... *It Looks Like The Party Is Over*			$4		Warner 49582
3/28/81	4	16		10 I'm Just An Old Chunk Of Coal (But I'm Gonna Be A Diamond Someday) *Havin' Hard Times*			$4		Warner 49699
8/1/81	8	15		11 Chicken Truck/			$4		Warner 49772
8/1/81	54	15		12 I Love You A Thousand Ways			$4		
11/21/81+	7	18		13 I Just Came Home To Count The Memories .... *Girl, For You*			$4		Warner 49860
4/17/82	6	19		14 Would You Catch A Falling Star .... *I Danced With San Antonio Rose*			$4		Warner 50043
9/25/82	❶²	20		15 Wild And Blue .... *Honky Tonk Hearts*			$4		Warner 29917
1/15/83	❶¹	22	●	16 Swingin' .... *A Honky Tonk Saturday Night*		43	$4		Warner 29788
				CMA Award: Single of the Year					
6/25/83	5	17		17 Goin' Down Hill .... *If A Broken Heart Could Kill*			$4		Warner 29585
9/24/83	❶¹	21		18 Black Sheep .... *Call On Me*			$4		Warner 29497
1/14/84	10	16		19 Let Somebody Else Drive .... *Old Mexico*			$4		Warner 29385
5/12/84	14	17		20 I Wish I Could Write You A Song .... *The Sun's Gonna Shine (On Our Back Door)*			$4		Warner 29276
8/18/84	3	25		21 She Sure Got Away With My Heart *S:3 / A:3 Lonely Is Another State*			$4		Warner 29207
12/8/84+	20	17		22 Eye Of A Hurricane................................ *S:18 / A:21 Chicken Truck*			$4		Warner 29127
5/4/85	15	17		23 It's All Over Now .... *A:14 / S:15 Only Your Love*			$4		Warner 29002
				#26 Pop hit for The Rolling Stones in 1964					
8/24/85	30	14		24 Tokyo, Oklahoma .... *A:29 / S:30 Willie's Gone*			$4		Warner 28916
11/16/85+	12	22		25 Down In Tennessee .... *S:11 / A:14 I've Got Me A Woman*			$4		Warner 28855
3/22/86	31	11		26 You Can't Keep A Good Memory Down .... *What's So Different About You*			$4		Warner 28748
8/16/86	10	22		27 Honky Tonk Crowd .... *S:4 / A:11 If I Could Have My Way*			$4		Warner 28639
12/6/86+	44	12		28 Countrified .... *Yellow Creek*			$4		Warner 28502
3/7/87	55	8		29 What's So Different About You .... *Wife's Little Pleasures*			$4		Warner 28433
9/5/87	48	8		30 When Your Yellow Brick Road Turns Blue .... *Lying In Her Arms*			$3		MCA 53155
12/5/87+	23	15		31 Somewhere Between Ragged And Right .... *Just For You*			$3		MCA 53226
				Waylon Jennings (guest vocal)					
4/23/88	65	4		32 It's Hard To Keep This Ship Together *There's Nothing Left For Me To Take For Granted*			$3		MCA 53307
7/9/88	35	12		33 If It Ain't Broke Don't Fix It .... *Just To Hold A Little Hand*			$3		MCA 53366
11/5/88	68	4		34 Down In The Orange Grove .... *The Will Of God*			$3		MCA 53441
2/11/89	73	4		35 Lower On The Hog .... *The Ballad Of Zero And The Tramp*			$3		MCA 53485
10/14/89	66	5		36 Who's Lovin' My Baby .... *There Was A Time When I Was Alone*			$3		Universal 66020
9/28/91	67	3		37 Who Got Our Love .... *Steamy Windows*			$3	▌	BNA 62062
12/21/91+	❶¹	20		38 Straight Tequila Night .... *Seminole Wind*			$3		BNA 62140
4/18/92	3	20		39 When It Comes To You .... *Cold Day In Hell*			$3	▌	BNA 62235
				first recorded by Dire Straits on their 1991 album *On Every Street*					
8/15/92	2²	20		40 Seminole Wind .... *Steamy Windows*			$3		BNA 62312
11/28/92+	7	20		41 Let Go Of The Stone .... *Look Away*			$3		BNA 62410
5/1/93	❶¹	20		42 Money In The Bank .... *Nashville Tears*			$3	▌	BNA 62443
8/28/93	13	20		43 I Fell In The Water.................................. *All Things To All Things*			$3		BNA 62621
12/11/93+	3	20		44 I've Got It Made .... *Can't Get Away From You*			$3		BNA 62709
4/23/94	4	20		45 I Wish I Could Have Been There .... *Solid Ground*			$3		BNA 62795
10/1/94	35	10		46 Country 'Til I Die .... *Swingin'*			$3	▌	BNA 62935
12/10/94+	3	20		47 Bend It Until It Breaks .... *Keep Your Hands To Yourself*			$3		BNA 64260
12/31/94	57	2		48 Christmas Time...[X]					album cut
				from the album *Christmas Time* on BNA 66411					

ANDERSON, John — Cont'd

DEBUT	PEAK	WKS		A-side / B-side	Pop	$	Pic	Label & Number
4/22/95	15	20		49 **Mississippi Moon** ....*It Ain't Pneumonia, It's The Blues*		$3		BNA 64274
12/9/95+	26	20		50 **Paradise** ....*Bad Weather*		$3	▮	BNA 64465
3/9/96	51	10		51 **Long Hard Lesson Learned** ....*Paradise*		$3		BNA 64498
6/22/96	67	4		52 **My Kind Of Crazy** ....*Long Hard Lesson Learned*		$3		BNA 64573
7/5/97	22	20		53 **Somebody Slap Me** ....S:11 *We've Got A Good Thing Goin'*	115	$3	▮	Mercury 574640
9/27/97	44	11		54 **Small Town** ....*The Fall*		$3		Mercury 574948

ANDERSON, Liz ★276★ '67

Born Elizabeth Jane Haaby on 3/13/30 in Roseau, Minnesota; raised in Grand Forks, North Dakota. Singer/songwriter/guitarist. Mother of Lynn Anderson.

1)Mama Spank 2)The Game Of Triangles 3)Mother, May I

DEBUT	PEAK	WKS		A-side / B-side	Pop	$	Pic	Label & Number
4/2/66	23	10		1 **Go Now Pay Later** ....*The Bottle Turned Into A Blonde*		$10		RCA Victor 8778
7/30/66	45	4		2 **So Much For Me, So Much For You** ....*Release Me*		$10		RCA Victor 8861
10/15/66	5	17		3 **The Game Of Triangles** *Bye Bye, Love*		$10		RCA Victor 8963
				BOBBY BARE, NORMA JEAN, LIZ ANDERSON				
12/3/66+	22	12		4 **The Wife Of The Party** ....*Fairytale*		$10		RCA Victor 8999
4/22/67	5	17		5 **Mama Spank** *To The Landlord*		$8		RCA Victor 9163
9/2/67	24	13		6 **Tiny Tears** ....*Grandma's House*		$8		RCA Victor 9271
12/23/67+	40	12		7 **Thanks A Lot For Tryin' Anyway** ....*Come Walk In My Shoes*		$8		RCA Victor 9378
2/24/68	21	12		8 **Mother, May I** ....*Better Than Life Without You*		$8		RCA Victor 9445
				LIZ ANDERSON AND LYNN ANDERSON				
5/11/68	43	9		9 **Like A Merry-Go-Round** ....*Thanks, But No Thanks*		$8		RCA Victor 9508
8/31/68	58	4		10 **Cry, Cry Again/**				
8/24/68	65	7		11 **Me, Me, Me, Me, Me**		$8		RCA Victor 9586
11/23/68	51	5		12 **Love Is Ending** ....*Blue Are The Violets*		$8		RCA Victor 9650
2/14/70	26	8		13 **Husband Hunting** ....*All You Add Is Love*		$8		RCA Victor 9796
8/15/70	64	6		14 **All Day Sucker** ....*Wonder If I'll Feel This Bad Tomorrow*		$8		RCA Victor 9876
12/19/70	75	2		15 **When I'm Not Lookin'** ....*Only For Me*		$8		RCA Victor 9924
10/23/71	69	3		16 **It Don't Do No Good To Be A Good Girl** ... *That's What Loving You Has Meant To Me*		$6		Epic 10782
4/8/72	56	7		17 **I'll Never Fall In Love Again** ....*You Buy The Wine*		$6		Epic 10840
				#6 Pop hit for Dionne Warwick in 1970				
8/12/72	67	4		18 **Astrology** ....*Living One Day At A Time*		$6		Epic 10896
3/17/73	72	2		19 **Time To Love Again** ....*Wearing A Smile*		$6		Epic 10952

ANDERSON, Lynn ★49★ '70

Born on 9/26/47 in Grand Forks, North Dakota; raised in Sacramento, California. Singer/songwriter/guitarist/actress. Daughter of **Liz Anderson**. An accomplished equestrian, she was the California Horse Show Queen in 1966. Regular on TV's *The Lawrence Welk Show* from 1968. Acted in the movie *Country Gold*. Formerly married to **Glenn Sutton**. CMA Award: 1971 Female Vocalist of the Year.

1)Rose Garden 2)How Can I Unlove You 3)You're My Man 4)Keep Me In Mind 5)What A Man, My Man Is

DEBUT	PEAK	WKS		A-side / B-side	Pop	$	Pic	Label & Number
10/29/66+	36	17		1 **Ride, Ride, Ride** ....*Tear By Tear*		$8		Chart 1375
3/18/67	5	19		2 **If I Kiss You (Will You Go Away)** *Then Go*		$8		Chart 1430
7/1/67	49	6		3 **Keeping Up Appearances** ....*You've Gotta Be The Greatest*		$8		Chart 1425
				LYNN ANDERSON & JERRY LANE				
8/12/67	28	13		4 **Too Much Of You** ....*If This Is Love*		$8		Chart 1475
12/2/67+	4	18		5 **Promises, Promises** *It Makes You Happy*		$8		Chart 1010
2/24/68	21	12		6 **Mother, May I** ....*Better Than Life Without You*		$8		RCA Victor 9445
				LIZ ANDERSON AND LYNN ANDERSON				
3/30/68	8	14		7 **No Another Time** ....*The Worst Is Yet To Come*		$8		Chart 1026
8/3/68	12	14		8 **Big Girls Don't Cry** ....*I Keep Forgettin' (That I Forgot About You)*		$8		Chart 1042
11/30/68+	11	14		9 **Flattery Will Get You Everywhere** ....*A Million Shades Of Blue*		$8		Chart 1059
3/8/69	18	12		10 **Our House Is Not A Home (If It's Never Been Loved In)** ....*Wave Bye Bye To The Man*		$8		Chart 5001
8/2/69	2²	15		11 **That's A No No** *If Silence Is Golden*		$8		Chart 5021
11/22/69+	15	12		12 **He'd Still Love Me** ....*All You Add Is Love*		$8		Chart 5040
2/14/70	16	10		13 **I've Been Everywhere** ....*A Penny For Your Thoughts*		$8		Chart 5053
3/21/70	7	16		14 **Stay There 'Til I Get There** *I'd Run A Mile To You*		$5		Columbia 45101
6/6/70	17	10		15 **Rocky Top** ....*Take Me Home*		$7		Chart 5068
8/1/70	15	12		16 **No Love At All/**				
				#16 Pop hit for B.J. Thomas in 1971				
		12		17 **I Found You Just In Time**		$5		Columbia 45190
10/31/70	20	11		18 **I'm Alright** ....*Pick Of The Week*	112	$7		Chart 5098
11/7/70	❶⁵	20	●	19 **Rose Garden** *Nothing Between Us*	3	$5		Columbia 45252
2/6/71	20	13		20 **It Wasn't God Who Made Honky Tonk Angels** ....*Be Quiet Mind*		$7		Chart 5113
5/8/71	❶²	15		21 **You're My Man** *I'm Gonna Write A Song*	63	$5		Columbia 45356
5/15/71	74	3		22 **Jim Dandy** ....*Strangers*		$7		Chart 5125
				#17 Pop hit for LaVern Baker in 1957				
7/24/71	54	5		23 **He Even Woke Me Up To Say Goodbye** ....*The Pillow That Whispers*		$7		Chart 5136
8/21/71	❶³	16		24 **How Can I Unlove You** *Don't Say Things You Don't Mean*	63	$5		Columbia 45429
1/29/72	3	16		25 **Cry** *Simple Words*	71	$5		Columbia 45529
				#1 Pop hit for Johnnie Ray in 1951				

DEBUT	PEAK	WKS	Gold	A-side (Chart Hit)..B-side	Pop	$	Pic	Label & Number
				ANDERSON, Lynn — Cont'd				
6/10/72	4	13		26 Listen To A Country Song _That's What Loving You Has Meant To Me_	107	$5		Columbia 45615
10/14/72	4	14		27 Fool Me _What's Made Milwaukee Famous_	101	$5		Columbia 45692
				#78 Pop hit for **Joe South** in 1971				
1/13/73	❶¹	16		28 Keep Me In Mind _Rodeo Cowboy_	104	$5		Columbia 45768
6/2/73	2¹	15		29 Top Of The World _I Wish I Was A Little Boy Again_	74	$5		Columbia 45857
				#1 Pop hit for the **Carpenters** in 1973				
9/15/73	3	17		30 Sing About Love _Fickle Fortune_		$5		Columbia 45918
3/9/74	15	13		31 Smile For Me _A Man Like Your Daddy_		$5		Columbia 46009
6/29/74	7	14		32 Talkin' To The Wall _I Want To Be A Part Of You_		$5		Columbia 46056
10/26/74	❶¹	13		33 What A Man, My Man Is _Everything's Falling In Place (For Me And You)_	93	$4		Columbia 10041
3/8/75	13	12		34 He Turns It Into Love Again.........................Someone To Finish What You Started		$4		Columbia 10100
6/28/75	14	14		35 I've Never Loved Anyone More ....He Worshiped Me		$4		Columbia 10160
11/22/75+	26	11		36 Paradise..We've Got It All Together Now		$4		Columbia 10240
2/7/76	20	14		37 All The King's Horses ....If All I Have To Do Is Just Love You		$4		Columbia 10280
6/5/76	44	9		38 Rodeo Cowboy/		$4		
		3		39 Dixieland, You Will Never Die		$4		Columbia 10337
9/25/76	23	11		40 Sweet Talkin' Man...A Good Old Country Song		$4		Columbia 10401
1/22/77	12	14		41 Wrap Your Love All Around Your Man......_I Couldn't Be Lonely (Even If I Wanted To)_		$4		Columbia 10467
5/28/77	22	10		42 I Love What Love Is Doing To Me ....Will I Ever Hear Those Church Bells Ring?		$4		Columbia 10545
9/3/77	19	12		43 He Ain't You ....It's Your Love That Keeps Me Going		$4		Columbia 10597
12/3/77+	26	13		44 We Got Love ....Sunshine Man		$4		Columbia 10650
4/29/78	44	9		45 Rising Above It All...............................My World Begins And Ends With You		$4		Columbia 10721
9/2/78	43	8		46 Last Love Of My Life ....When You Marry For Money		$4		Columbia 10809
3/10/79	10	13		47 Isn't It Always Love _A Child With You Tonight_		$4		Columbia 10909
6/23/79	18	12		48 I Love How You Love Me ....Come As You Are		$4		Columbia 11006
				#5 Pop hit for The Paris Sisters in 1961				
10/13/79	33	9		49 Sea Of Heartbreak ....Say You Will		$4		Columbia 11104
7/5/80	26	13		50 Even Cowgirls Get The Blues ....See Through Me		$4		Columbia 11296
10/25/80	27	13		51 Blue Baby Blue ....The Lonely Hearts Cafe		$4		Columbia 11374
4/9/83	42	11		52 You Can't Lose What You Never Had ....This Time The Heartbreak Wins		$4		Permian 82000
7/16/83	18	16		53 What I Learned From Loving You ....Mr. Sundown		$4		Permian 82001
12/17/83+	9	23		54 You're Welcome To Tonight _Your Kisses Lied_		$4		Permian 82003
				LYNN ANDERSON & GARY MORRIS				
9/13/86	49	9		55 Fools For Each Other ....S:28 _Memphis Roots_		$3		RCA 5005
				ED BRUCE with Lynn Anderson				
12/20/86+	45	9		56 Didn't We Shine ....We Must Be Doing It Right		$3		Mercury 888209
9/19/87	38	12		57 Read Between The Lines ....If This Ain't Love		$3		Mercury 888839
7/30/88	24	17		58 Under The Boardwalk ....S:24 _Turn The Page_		$3		Mercury 870528
				#4 Pop hit for The Drifters in 1964				
12/3/88+	50	10		59 What He Does Best ....It Goes Without Saying		$3		Mercury 872220
3/11/89	69	6		60 How Many Hearts _(long version)_		$3		Mercury 872602
				ANDI AND THE BROWN SISTERS '89				
				Vocal trio from Albany, Oregon: Andi Brown and her sister Robin, with Darby Huffman.				
10/8/88	94	2		1 I'd Do Anything For You, Baby		$6		Killer 1013
2/4/89	90	2		2 This Old Feeling		$6		Killer 115
				ANDY & THE BROWN SISTERS (above 2)				
5/6/89	79	4		3 Labor Of Love		$5		Door Knob 323
7/8/89	84	3		4 Gently Hold Me		$5		Door Knob 329
9/30/89	90	2		5 Lighter Shade Of Blue		$5		Door Knob 331
11/25/89	70	6		6 Shows You What I Know _Lighter Shade Of Blue_		$5		Door Knob 337
				ANDREWS, Sheila '80				
				Born in Alabama; raised in Ohio.				
12/16/78+	88	4		1 Too Fast For Rapid City ....Bigger Fool Than I Am		$5		Ovation 1116
9/22/79	88	3		2 I Gotta Get Back The Feeling ....Diggin' And A Grindin' For His Love		$5		Ovation 1128
1/26/80	48	7		3 What I Had With You ....I Gotta Get Back The Feeling		$5		Ovation 1138
				SHEILA ANDREWS with Joe Sun				
7/26/80	42	10		4 It Don't Get Better Than This _The Softer You Touch Me The Harder I Fall_		$5		Ovation 1146
11/29/80	58	8		5 Where Could You Take Me ....Pretty Lies		$5		Ovation 1160
				ANDREWS SISTERS '44				
				Vocal trio from Minneapolis: sisters Patty, Maxene and LaVerne Andrews. Charted 69 pop hits from 1940-51. LaVerne died on 5/8/67 (age 52). Maxene died on 10/21/95 (age 79). The trio appeared in several movies.				
1/8/44	❶⁵	11	●	1 Pistol Packin' Mama _Vict'ry Polka (Pop #6)_	2⁴	$20		Decca 23277
				BING CROSBY and ANDREWS SISTERS				
4/9/49	2¹	16		2 I'm Bitin' My Fingernails And Thinking Of You/ _J:2 / S:4_	30			
				ANDREWS SISTERS and ERNEST TUBB with The Texas Troubadors				
4/16/49	6	5		3 Don't Rob Another Man's Castle _J:6 / S:10_		$20		Decca 24592
				ERNEST TUBB and ANDREWS SISTERS with The Texas Troubadors				
				ANGELLE, Lisa '85				
				Born near New Orleans. Singer/songwriter.				
4/6/85	78	4		1 Love, It's The Pits ....Biloxi Blue		$3	■	EMI America 8258
11/16/85	96	3		2 Bring Back Love ....Poor Baby		$3		EMI America 8294

ANTHONY, Rayburn '79
Born in Jackson, Tennessee. Singer/songwriter/bassist.

DEBUT	PEAK	WKS		A-side / B-side	Pop	$	Pic	Label & Number
10/9/76	84	5		1 Crazy Again .... *Mother Country Music*		$5		Polydor 14346
3/26/77	39	9		2 Lonely Eyes .... *Walkin'*		$5		Polydor 14380
6/25/77	57	8		3 Hold Me .... *Don't Fall In Love*		$5		Polydor 14398
10/15/77	75	5		4 She Keeps Hangin' On .... *Talk About A Feeling*		$5		Polydor 14423
3/25/78	31	9		5 Maybe I Should've Been Listenin' .... *This Time Marie*		$5		Polydor 14457
10/21/78	75	5		6 I Thought You Were Easy .... *This One's For You*		$4		Mercury 55042
2/3/79	28	11		7 Shadows Of Love .... *Fire In The Night*		$4		Mercury 55053
6/23/79	79	3		8 It Won't Go Away .... *Baby Take It From Me*		$4		Mercury 55063
10/6/79	60	6		9 The Wild Side Of Life .... *I Don't Believe I'll Fall In Love Today*		$4		Mercury 57006

RAYBURN ANTHONY WITH KITTY WELLS

ANTHONY, Vince '82
Singer from Berwick, Louisiana.

DEBUT	PEAK	WKS		A-side / B-side	Pop	$	Pic	Label & Number
3/6/82	82	3		Call Me Friend .... *Leave Me Tonight*		$8		Midnight Gold 160

VINCE ANTHONY with The "Country" Blue Notes

ANTON, Susan — see KNOBLOCK, Fred

ARATA, Tony '85
Born on 10/10/57 in Savannah, Georgia. Singer/songwriter/guitarist.

DEBUT	PEAK	WKS		A-side / B-side	Pop	$	Pic	Label & Number
9/22/84	76	4		1 Come On Home .... *Maybe I'm Over You*		$5		Noble Vision 106
2/9/85	65	7		2 Sure Thing		$5		Noble Vision 108

ARCHER PARK '94
Duo of Randy Archer (from Swainsboro, Georgia) and Johnny Park (from Arlington, Texas).

DEBUT	PEAK	WKS		A-side / B-side	Pop	$	Pic	Label & Number
8/20/94	29	14		1 Where There's Smoke .... *'Til Something Better Comes Along*		$3	▌	Atlantic 87211
12/3/94	63	6		2 We Got A Lot In Common .... *I Still Wanna Jump Your Bones*		$3	▌	Atlantic 87181

ARGO, Judy '79

DEBUT	PEAK	WKS		A-side / B-side	Pop	$	Pic	Label & Number
4/7/79	83	6		1 Night Time Music Man .... *Country Hall Of Shame*		$6		ASI 1019
8/11/79	95	3		2 He's A Good Man .... *Why Me*		$5	■	MDJ 51379
9/29/79	55	7		3 Hide Me (In The Shadow Of Your Love) .... *Millionaire Lover*		$5		MDJ 4633

ARMSTRONG, Wayne '80

DEBUT	PEAK	WKS		A-side / B-side	Pop	$	Pic	Label & Number
8/9/80	59	8		Hot Sunday Morning .... *I Don't Want To Be Alone*		$5		NSD 57

ARNOLD, Eddy ★1★ '48
Born Richard Edward Arnold on 5/15/18 in Madisonville, Tennessee. Singer/songwriter/guitarist. Own radio show on WMPS in Memphis from 1934-39. Lead singer of **Pee Wee King's** Golden West Cowboys from 1940-43. Hosted own TV show from 1952-56. Hosted TV's *Out On The Farm* in 1954. Hosted TV's *Today On The Farm* in 1960. Once known as "The Tennessee Plowboy." Elected to the Country Music Hall of Fame in 1966. CMA Award: 1967 Entertainer of the Year.

1)I'll Hold You In My Heart 2)Bouquet of Roses 3)Don't Rob Another Man's Castle
4)I Wanna Play House With You 5)There's Been A Change In Me

EDDY ARNOLD and his Tennessee Plowboys:

DEBUT	PEAK	WKS		A-side / B-side	Pop	$	Pic	Label & Number
6/30/45	5	2		1 Each Minute Seems A Million Years — *The Cattle Call*		$60		Bluebird 33-0527
7/13/46	7	1		2 All Alone In This World Without You — *Can't Win, Can't Place, Can't Show*		$30		RCA Victor 20-1855
10/12/46	2^4	17		3 That's How Much I Love You/				
10/12/46	3	2		4 Chained To A Memory		$30		RCA Victor 20-1948
3/1/47	$❶^1$	22		5 What Is Life Without Love — *Be Sure There's No Mistake*		$30		RCA Victor 20-2058
5/31/47	$❶^5$	38		6 It's A Sin/				
6/21/47	4	2		7 I Couldn't Believe It Was True 45 rpm: 48-0198		$30		RCA Victor 20-2241
8/23/47	$❶^{21}$	46		8 I'll Hold You In My Heart (Till I Can Hold You In My Arms) — J:$❶^{21}$ / S:7 *Don't Bother To Cry* 45 rpm: 48-0030		$30		RCA Victor 20-2332
11/8/47	2^2	15		9 To My Sorrow — J:2 *Easy Rocking Chair* 45 rpm: 48-0197		$30		RCA Victor 20-2481
2/7/48	10	2		10 Molly Darling — J:10 / S:14 *It Makes No Difference Now* 45 rpm: 48-0017		$30		RCA Victor 20-2489
3/20/48	$❶^9$	39		11 Anytime/ — J:$❶^9$ / S:$❶^3$ #2 Pop hit for Eddie Fisher in 1952	17			
3/27/48	2^5	21		12 What A Fool I Was — J:2 / S:7 45 rpm: 48-0002	29	$30		RCA Victor 20-2700
5/15/48	$❶^{19}$	54	●	13 Bouquet Of Roses/ — S:$❶^{19}$ / J:$❶^{15}$	13			
5/15/48	$❶^3$	26		14 Texarkana Baby — J:$❶^3$ / S:$❶^1$ 45 rpm: 48-0001	18	$30		RCA Victor 20-2806

EDDY ARNOLD, The Tennessee Plowboy and his Guitar:

DEBUT	PEAK	WKS		A-side / B-side	Pop	$	Pic	Label & Number
8/28/48	$❶^8$	32		15 Just A Little Lovin' (Will Go A Long, Long Way)/ — J:$❶^8$ / S:$❶^4$	13			
8/28/48	5	19		16 My Daddy Is Only A Picture — S:5 / J:6 45 rpm: 48-0026		$30		RCA Victor 20-3013
11/20/48	$❶^1$	21		17 A Heart Full Of Love (For A Handful Of Kisses)/ — S:$❶^1$ / J:3	23			
11/20/48+	2^1	17		18 Then I Turned And Walked Slowly Away — J:2 / S:4 45 rpm: 48-0025	30	$30		RCA Victor 20-3174
2/5/49	10	1		19 Many Tears Ago — J:10 *Mommy Please Stay Home With Me*		$30		RCA Victor 20-1871

EDDY ARNOLD and his Tennessee Plowboys
recorded and released in 1946

DEBUT	PEAK	WKS	Gold	A-side (Chart Hit)..B-side	Pop	$	Pic	Label & Number
				ARNOLD, Eddy — Cont'd				
2/19/49	❶¹²	31		20 Don't Rob Another Man's Castle/ J:❶¹² / S:❶⁶	23			
2/12/49	3	10		21 There's Not A Thing (I Wouldn't Do For You) J:3 / S:7		$30		RCA Victor 21-0002
				45 rpm: 48-0042				
5/14/49	❶³	22		22 One Kiss Too Many/ J:❶³ / S:2	23			
5/21/49	2³	19		23 The Echo Of Your Footsteps S:2 / J:3		$30		RCA Victor 21-0051
				45 rpm: 48-0083				
7/2/49	❶⁴	22		24 I'm Throwing Rice (At The Girl That I Love)/ S:❶⁴ / J:❶³	18			
7/16/49	7	4		25 Show Me The Way Back To Your Heart S:7 / J:11		$30		RCA Victor 21-0083
				45 rpm: 48-0080				
12/10/49	5	4		26 Will Santy Come To Shanty Town/ A:5 / J:6 / S:8 [X]		$30		RCA Victor 21-0124
11/19/49	7	8		27 C-H-R-I-S-T-M-A-S S:7 / A:7 / J:9 [X]		$30		
				45 rpm: 48-0127				
12/17/49+	6	2		28 There's No Wings On My Angel J:8 / S:11 *You Know How Talk Gets Around*		$35		RCA Victor 48-0137
				from the movie *Feudin' Rhythm* starring Arnold; 78 rpm: 21-0134				
12/31/49+	❶¹	17		29 Take Me In Your Arms And Hold Me/ J:❶¹ / A:4 / S:5				
				answer to #8 above				
1/14/50	6	7		30 Mama And Daddy Broke My Heart S:6 / J:8		$35		RCA Victor 48-0150
				78 rpm: 21-0146				
4/15/50	3	12		31 Little Angel With The Dirty Face/ S:3 / J:7 / A:10				
4/22/50	3	13		32 Why Should I Cry? J:3 / A:5 / S:5		$35		RCA Victor 48-0300
7/1/50	2²	17		33 Cuddle Buggin' Baby/ S:2 / J:3 / A:4				
7/1/50	6	12		34 Enclosed, One Broken Heart J:6 / A:7 / S:7		$35		RCA Victor 48-0342
9/30/50	2⁸	16		35 The Lovebug Itch/ S:2 / A:2 / J:2				
12/9/50	10	1		36 A Prison Without Walls J:10		$35		RCA Victor 48-0382
1/13/51	❶¹¹	23		37 There's Been A Change In Me A:❶¹¹ / S:❶⁴ / J:2 *Tie Me To Your Apron Strings Again*		$30		RCA Victor 48-0412
2/24/51	8	5		38 May The Good Lord Bless And Keep You S:8 / A:10 *I'm Writing A Letter To The Lord*		$30		RCA Victor 48-0425
4/14/51	❶³	17		39 Kentucky Waltz S:❶³ / J:❶³ / A:4 *A Million Miles From Your Heart*		$30		RCA Victor 48-0444
6/23/51	❶¹¹	24		40 I Wanna Play House With You/ J:❶¹¹ / S:❶⁶ / A:2				
7/7/51	4	9		41 Something Old, Something New J:4 / S:7		$30		RCA Victor 48-0476
10/27/51	2¹	16		42 Somebody's Been Beatin' My Time/ J:2 / A:3 / S:5				
10/27/51	5	12		43 Heart Strings S:5 / J:8		$25		RCA Victor 47-4273
1/26/52	4	12		44 Bundle Of Southern Sunshine/ S:4 / J:4 / A:5				
2/23/52	9	1		45 Call Her Your Sweetheart A:9		$25		RCA Victor 47-4413
4/5/52	❶¹	14		46 Easy On The Eyes S:❶¹ / A:4 / J:6 *Anything That's Part Of You*		$25		RCA Victor 47-4569
7/19/52	❶⁴	18		47 A Full Time Job A:❶⁴ / S:3 / J:3 *Shepherd Of My Heart*		$25		RCA Victor 47-4787
10/25/52	3	11		48 Older And Bolder/ S:3 / J:4 / A:7				
12/6/52	9	1		49 I'd Trade All Of My Tomorrows (For Just One Yesterday) J:9		$25		RCA Victor 47-4954
1/24/53	❶³	13		50 Eddy's Song S:❶³ / J:2 / A:5 *Condemned Without Trial*		$20		RCA Victor 5108
6/20/53	4	9		51 Free Home Demonstration/ S:4 / A:5 / J:5				
7/18/53	4	10		52 How's The World Treating You A:4 / J:7		$20		RCA Victor 5305
10/3/53	4	10		53 Mama, Come Get Your Baby Boy A:4 / S:9 / J:9 *If I Never Get To Heaven*		$20		RCA Victor 5415
1/9/54	❶¹	37		54 I Really Don't Want To Know J:❶¹ / A:2 / S:2 *I'll Never Get Over You*		$20		RCA Victor 5525
4/10/54	7	9		55 My Everything S:7 / A:7 *Second Fling*		$20		RCA Victor 5634
8/28/54	3	23		56 This Is The Thanks I Get (For Loving You)/ S:3 / A:3 / J:3				
8/21/54	7	14		57 Hep Cat Baby J:7 / S:9 / A:14		$20		RCA Victor 5805
				EDDY ARNOLD and his Guitar:				
12/18/54	12	3		58 Christmas Can't Be Far Away ....A:12 *I'm Your Private Santa Claus* [X]		$20		RCA Victor 5905
1/29/55	2⁴	25		59 I've Been Thinking/ J:2 / S:3 / A:4				
2/5/55	12	7		60 Don't Forget..S:12		$20		RCA Victor 6000
4/23/55	6	9		61 In Time/ A:8 / S:7				
4/23/55	9	8		62 Two Kinds Of Love S:9 / J:9		$20		RCA Victor 6069
6/25/55	❶²	26		63 The Cattle Call/ S:❶² / J:2 / A:4	69			
				new version of the B-side of #1 above				
7/9/55	8	7		64 The Kentuckian Song J:8		$20		RCA Victor 6139
				from the movie *The Kentuckian* starring Burt Lancaster				
8/20/55	❶²	15		65 That Do Make It Nice/ J:❶² / A:4 / S:11				
8/20/55	2⁷	31		66 Just Call Me Lonesome S:2 / A:2 / J:2		$20		RCA Victor 6198
11/26/55	6	8		67 I Walked Alone Last Night/ S:6				
11/12/55	10	10		68 The Richest Man (In The World) S:10 / A:14	99	$20		RCA Victor 6290
1/28/56	7	3		69 Trouble In Mind S:7 *When You Said Goodbye*		$20		RCA Victor 6365
				EDDY ARNOLD:				
8/25/56	15	1		70 Casey Jones (The Brave Engineer) ....A:15 *You Were Mine For Awhile*		$20		RCA Victor 6601
9/1/56	10	8		71 You Don't Know Me S:10 / A:15 *The Rockin' Mockin' Bird*		$20		RCA Victor 6502
5/27/57	12	3		72 Gonna Find Me A Bluebird ....A:12 / S:15 *Little Bit*	51	$20		RCA Victor 6905
3/16/59	12	9		73 Chip Off The Old Block ....*I'll Hold You In My Heart*	97	$15		RCA Victor 7435
6/22/59	5	19		74 Tennessee Stud *What's The Good (Of All This Love)*	48	$15		RCA Victor 7542
1/9/61	23	3		75 Before This Day Ends ....*Just Out Of Reach*		$15		RCA Victor 7794
5/29/61	27	1		76 (Jim) I Wore A Tie Today ....*Just Call Me Lonesome*		$15		RCA Victor 7861
10/16/61	17	10		77 One Grain Of Sand *The Worst Night Of My Life*	107	$12		RCA Victor 7926
3/17/62	7	10		78 Tears Broke Out On Me *I'll Do As Much For You Someday*	102	$12		RCA Victor 7984
6/30/62	3	19		79 A Little Heartache/	103			
8/4/62	7	19		80 After Loving You	112	$10		RCA Victor 8048
12/8/62+	5	15		81 Does He Mean That Much To You? *Tender Touch*	98	$10	■	RCA Victor 8102

DEBUT	PEAK	WKS	Gold	A-side (Chart Hit)..B-side	Pop	$	Pic	Label & Number
				ARNOLD, Eddy — Cont'd				
4/27/63	11	10		82 Yesterday's Memories .... *Lonely Balladeer*		$10	■	RCA Victor 8160
8/10/63	13	12		83 A Million Years Or So .... *Just A Ribbon*		$10	■	RCA Victor 8207
12/7/63+	12	12		84 Jealous Hearted Me .... *I Met Her Today*		$10		RCA Victor 8253
2/1/64	5	20		85 Molly .... *The Song Of The Coo Coo*		$10		RCA Victor 8296
				EDDY ARNOLD and The Needmore Creek Singers				
7/18/64	26	13		86 Sweet Adorable You .... *Why*		$10		RCA Victor 8363
11/7/64+	8	19		87 I Thank My Lucky Stars .... *I Don't Cry No More*		$10		RCA Victor 8445
3/27/65	❶²	25		88 What's He Doing In My World .... *Laura Lee*	60	$8		RCA Victor 8516
9/18/65	15	9		89 I'm Letting You Go .... *The Days Gone By*	135	$8		RCA Victor 8632
10/9/65	❶³	25		90 Make The World Go Away .... *The Easy Way*	6	$8	■	RCA Victor 8679
2/12/66	❶⁶	19		91 I Want To Go With You .... *You'd Better Stop Tellin' Lies (About Me)*	36	$8		RCA Victor 8749
5/14/66	2¹	16		92 The Last Word In Lonesome Is Me .... *Mary Claire Melvina Rebecca Jane*	40	$8	■	RCA Victor 8818
7/23/66	3	15		93 The Tip Of My Fingers .... *Long, Long Friendship*	43	$8	■	RCA Victor 8869
10/15/66	❶⁴	19		94 Somebody Like Me .... *Taking Chances*	53	$8	■	RCA Victor 8965
12/24/66+	51	8		95 The First Word .... *The Angel And The Stranger*		$7		RCA Victor 9027
2/18/67	❶²	16		96 Lonely Again .... *Love On My Mind*	87	$7		RCA Victor 9080
5/6/67	3	16		97 Misty Blue .... *Calling Mary Names*	57	$7		RCA Victor 9182
				#3 Pop hit for Dorothy Moore in 1976				
8/26/67	❶¹	16		98 Turn The World Around .... *The Long Ride Home*	66	$7		RCA Victor 9265
12/2/67+	2²	15		99 Here Comes Heaven .... *Baby That's Living*	91	$7		RCA Victor 9368
2/17/68	4	14		100 Here Comes The Rain, Baby .... *The World I Used To Know*	74	$7		RCA Victor 9437
6/1/68	4	12		101 It's Over .... *No Matter Whose Baby You Are*	74	$7		RCA Victor 9525
				#37 Pop hit for **Jimmie Rodgers** in 1966				
8/31/68	❶²	14		102 Then You Can Tell Me Goodbye .... *Apples, Raisins And Roses*	84	$7		RCA Victor 9606
				#6 Pop hit for The Casinos in 1967				
11/23/68+	10	14		103 They Don't Make Love Like They Used To .... *What A Wonderful World*	99	$7		RCA Victor 9667
3/29/69	10	13		104 Please Don't Go .... *Heaven Below*	129	$6		RCA Victor 0120
6/28/69	19	12		105 But For Love .... *My Lady Of Love*	125	$6		RCA Victor 0175
				#69 Pop hit for **Jerry Naylor** in 1970				
9/27/69	69	2		106 You Fool .... *You Don't Need Me Anymore*		$6		RCA Victor 0226
12/27/69+	73	2		107 Since December .... *Morning Of My Mind*		$6		RCA Victor 0282
2/28/70	22	11		108 Soul Deep .... *(Today) I Started Loving You Again*		$6		RCA Victor 9801
				#18 Pop hit for The Box Tops in 1969				
6/13/70	28	11		109 A Man's Kind Of Woman/				
		10		110 Living Under Pressure		$6		RCA Victor 9848
9/12/70	22	9		111 From Heaven To Heartache .... *Ten Times Forever More*		$6		RCA Victor 9889
1/2/71	26	12		112 Portrait Of My Woman .... *I Really Don't Want To Know*		$6		RCA Victor 9935
5/1/71	49	8		113 A Part Of America Died .... *Call Me* [S]		$6		RCA Victor 9968
7/3/71	34	9		114 Welcome To My World .... *It Ain't No Big Thing (But It's Growing)*		$6		RCA Victor 9993
11/13/71	55	7		115 I Love You Dear .... *Long Life, Lots Of Happiness*		$6		RCA Victor 0559
2/26/72	38	9		116 Lonely People .... *If It's Alright With You*		$6		RCA Victor 0641
8/5/72	62	4		117 Lucy .... *The Last Letter*		$6		RCA Victor 0747
1/20/73	28	12		118 So Many Ways .... *Once In A While*		$5		MGM 14478
				#6 Pop hit for **Brook Benton** in 1959				
5/19/73	56	9		119 If The Whole World Stopped Lovin' .... *My Son I Wish You Everything*		$5		MGM 14535
8/18/73	29	11		120 Oh, Oh, I'm Falling In Love Again .... *Anyway You Want Me*		$5		MGM 14600
12/8/73+	24	13		121 She's Got Everything I Need .... *I'm Glad You Happened To Me*		$5		MGM 14672
3/30/74	56	9		122 Just For Old Times Sake .... *I Got This Thing About You*		$5		MGM 14711
				#20 Pop hit for The McGuire Sisters in 1961				
8/3/74	19	12		123 I Wish That I Had Loved You Better .... *Let It Be Love*		$5		MGM 14734
12/28/74+	47	9		124 Butterfly .... *If You Could Only Love Me Now*		$5		MGM 14769
				#78 Pop hit for **Danyel Gerard** in 1972				
6/7/75	60	12		125 Red Roses For A Blue Lady .... *I Will*		$5		MGM 14780
				#10 Pop hit for **Vic Dana** in 1965				
10/11/75	86	6		126 Middle Of A Memory .... *I Just Had You On My Mind*		$5		MGM 14827
6/19/76	13	13		127 Cowboy .... *Don't Let The Good Times Roll Away*		$4		RCA Victor 10701
10/23/76	43	9		128 Put Me Back Into Your World .... *Goodnight, Irene*		$4		RCA 10794
3/5/77	22	13		129 (I Need You) All The Time .... *I've Never Loved Anyone More*		$4		RCA 10899
7/23/77	53	7		130 Freedom Ain't The Same As Being Free .... *Till You Can Make It On Your Own*		$4		RCA 11031
11/12/77	83	3		131 Where Lonely People Go .... *Penny Arcade*		$4		RCA 11133
4/22/78	23	12		132 Country Lovin' .... *Feelings/Dime (Samba Soul)*		$4		RCA 11257
8/5/78	91	2		133 I'm The South .... *You Are My Sunshine*		$4		RCA 11319
12/9/78+	13	14		134 If Everyone Had Someone Like You .... *You're A Beautiful Place To Be*		$4		RCA 11422
4/14/79	21	11		135 What In Her World Did I Do .... *The Love Of My Life*		$4		RCA 11537
8/4/79	22	11		136 Goodbye .... *You're So Good At Lovin' Me*		$4		RCA 11668
11/17/79+	28	13		137 If I Ever Had To Say Goodbye To You .... *The Love Of My Life*		$4		RCA 11752
3/8/80	6	13		138 Let's Get It While The Gettin's Good .... *You Cared Enough (To Give Your Very Best)*		$4		RCA 11918
6/28/80	10	15		139 That's What I Get For Loving You .... *Undivided Love*		$4		RCA 12039
12/6/80+	11	16		140 Don't Look Now (But We Just Fell In Love) .... *There Are Women*		$4		RCA 12136
5/16/81	32	10		141 Bally-Hoo Days/				
		5		142 Two Hearts Beat Better Than One		$3		RCA 12226
12/12/81+	30	11		143 All I'm Missing Is You .... *Don't It Break Your Heart*		$3		RCA 13000
4/24/82	73	5		144 Don't Give Up On Me .... *In Love With Loving You*		$3		RCA 13094
3/19/83	76	6		145 The Blues Don't Care Who's Got 'Em .... *Wooden Heart*		$3		RCA 13452

ARNOLD, Rick   '89

| 9/16/89 | 89 | 2 | | I Must Be Crazy .... | | $6 | | Lynn 51088 |

★385★ **ASHLEY, Leon**   '67

Born Leon Walton on 5/18/36 in Newton County, Georgia. Singer/songwriter/guitarist. Married **Margie Singleton** in 1965. Formed own Ashley record label in 1967.

7/29/67	❶¹	18		1 Laura What's He Got That I Ain't Got *With The Help Of The Wine*	120	$10		Ashley 2003
11/11/67	54	7		2 Hangin' On .... *Four O'Clock*		$10		Ashley 2015
				LEON ASHLEY & MARGIE SINGLETON				
12/2/67+	28	12		3 Anna, I'm Taking You Home ....*Curtain Of Sadness*		$10		Ashley 2025
3/30/68	14	14		4 Mental Journey .... *All I Can Stand*		$10		Ashley 2075
5/11/68	55	6		5 You'll Never Be Lonely Again ....*Parting Of The Ways*		$10		Ashley 3000
				LEON ASHLEY - MARGIE SINGLETON				
7/27/68	8	15		6 Flower Of Love *Prayers Can't Reach Me*		$10		Ashley 4000
1/11/69	25	9		7 While Your Lover Sleeps ....*That's Alright*		$10		Ashley 7000
4/19/69	23	10		8 Walkin' Back To Birmingham ....*It's All Over But The Crying*		$10		Ashley 9000
8/16/69	55	7		9 Ain't Gonna Worry .... *Illusions Of Life*		$10		Ashley 22

★201★ **ASHWORTH, Ernest**   '63

Born on 12/15/28 in Huntsville, Alabama. Singer/songwriter/guitarist. Joined the *Grand Ole Opry* in 1964. Appeared in movie *The Farmer's Other Daughter.*

1)Talk Back Trembling Lips 2)Everybody But Me 3)Each Moment 4)I Love To Dance With Annie 5)I Take The Chance

5/30/60	4	16		1 Each Moment ('Spent With You) *Night Time Is Cry Time*		$12		Decca 31085
10/24/60	8	20		2 You Can't Pick A Rose In December *You'll Hear My Heart Break*		$12		Decca 31156
5/15/61	15	2		3 Forever Gone ....*Life Of The Party*		$12		Decca 31237
6/30/62	3	20		4 Everybody But Me *(I Just Spent) Another Sleepless Night*		$10		Hickory 1170
12/29/62+	7	15		5 I Take The Chance *King Of The Blues*		$10		Hickory 1189
6/22/63	❶¹	36		6 Talk Back Trembling Lips *That's How Much I Care*	101	$10		Hickory 1214
				#7 Pop hit for **Johnny Tillotson** in 1964				
2/1/64	10	20		7 A Week In The Country *Heartbreak Avenue*		$10		Hickory 1237
6/20/64	4	23		8 I Love To Dance With Annie *My Heart Would Know*		$10		Hickory 1265
11/7/64+	11	21		9 Pushed In A Corner ....*Gooder Than Good*		$10		Hickory 1281
5/15/65	18	13		10 Because I Cared ....*Love Has Come My Way*		$10		Hickory 1304
8/7/65	8	20		11 The DJ Cried *Scene Of Destruction*		$10		Hickory 1325
				ERNIE ASHWORTH:				
1/29/66	28	11		12 I Wish ....*Crazy Me, Foolish You*		$10		Hickory 1358
7/16/66	13	17		13 At Ease Heart ....*The Nearest Thing To Heaven*		$10		Hickory 1400
12/3/66+	31	9		14 Sad Face ....*I'm From Missouri*		$10		Hickory 1428
4/1/67	63	4		15 Just An Empty Place ....*Just One Time*		$10		Hickory 1445
8/5/67	48	10		16 My Love For You (Is Like A Mountain Range)..........*You're Tearing My Heart Out*		$10		Hickory 1466
11/25/67	48	7		17 Tender And True ....*Back On My Mind Again*		$10		Hickory 1484
5/25/68	39	8		18 A New Heart ....*The Next Ones (You Love)*		$10		Hickory 1503
3/29/69	69	4		19 Where Do You Go (When You Don't Go With Me) ....*Hocus-Pocus*		$10		Hickory 1528
7/12/69	72	3		20 Love, I Finally Found It ....*King Of The Blues*		$10		Hickory 1538
7/18/70	72	1		21 That Look Of Good-Bye ....*A Woman's Touch*		$10		Hickory 1570

★295★ **ASLEEP AT THE WHEEL**   '75

Group from Paw Paw, West Virginia: **Ray Benson** (male vocals, guitar), Chris O'Connell (female vocals, guitar) Reuben "Lucky Oceans" Gosfield (steel guitar), Danny Levin (fiddle, mandolin) and Jim "Floyd Domino" Haber (piano). Numerous personnel changes with Benson the only constant. **Jann Browne** was a member from 1981-83. **Rosie Flores** joined in 1997.

1)The Letter That Johnny Walker Read 2)House Of Blue Lights 3)Bump Bounce Boogie

12/21/74+	69	8		1 Choo Choo Ch'Boogie ....*Our Names Aren't Mentioned (Together Anymore)*		$5		Epic 50045
				#1 R&B hit for **Louis Jordan** in 1946				
8/9/75	10	18		2 The Letter That Johnny Walker Read *Part Two*		$5		Capitol 4115
12/13/75+	31	11		3 Bump Bounce Boogie ....*Fat Boy Rag*		$5		Capitol 4187
4/3/76	35	11		4 Nothin' Takes The Place Of You ....*Tonight The Bartender Is On The Wrong Side Of The Bar*		$5		Capitol 4238
8/28/76	48	8		5 Route 66 ....*Shout Wa Hey*		$5		Capitol 4319
				#11 Pop hit for **Nat King Cole** in 1946				
11/20/76+	38	10		6 Miles And Miles Of Texas ....*Blues For Dixie*		$5		Capitol 4357
3/19/77	42	9		7 The Trouble With Lovin' Today ....*Ragtime Annie*		$5		Capitol 4393
12/2/78	75	6		8 Texas Me & You ....*One O'Clock Jump*		$5		Capitol 4659
2/28/87	39	14		9 Way Down Texas Way ....S:27 *String Of Pars*		$3	■	Epic 06671
5/30/87	17	18		10 House Of Blue Lights ....S:10 *Big Foot Stomp*		$3		Epic 07125
				#9 Pop hit for **Chuck Miller** in 1955				
10/17/87	53	7		11 Boogie Back To Texas ....*Tulsa Straight Ahead*		$3		Epic 07610
1/9/88	59	9		12 Blowin' Like A Bandit ....*String Of Pars*		$3		Epic 07659
7/23/88	55	6		13 Walk On By ....*Sugarfoot Rag*		$3		Epic 07966
10/29/88	65	11		14 Hot Rod Lincoln ....S:29 *String Of Pars*		$3		Epic 08087
				#26 Pop hit for **Johnny Bond** in 1960				
9/1/90	54	4		15 Keepin' Me Up Nights ....*Pedernales Stroll*		$3		Arista 2045
12/1/90+	60	14		16 That's The Way Love Is ....*Beat Me Daddy (Eight To The Bar)*		$3	▮	Arista 2122
3/16/91	71	2		17 Dance With Who Brung You...............*Quittin' Time*		$3		Arista 2178
9/21/91	67	4		18 Four Scores And Seven Beers Ago ....*Eyes*		$3	▮	Arista 12340
				RAY BENSON				
3/19/94	73	1		19 Corine, Corina				album cut
				ASLEEP AT THE WHEEL Featuring Brooks & Dunn				
				#9 Pop hit for **Ray Peterson** in 1961; from the album *Tribute To Bob Wills* on Liberty 81470				

ATCHER, Bob '48
Born James Robert Owen Atcher on 5/11/14 in Hardin County, Kentucky. Died on 10/31/93 (age 79). Singer/guitarist/fiddler. Joined the WLS *National Barn Dance* in 1948. Mayor of Schaumburg, Illinois, from 1959-75.

7/13/46	7	1		1 **I Must Have Been Wrong** *I Want To Be Wanted*		$15		Columbia 36983
1/31/48	6	11		2 **Signed, Sealed And Delivered** *Mountain Maw*		$15		Columbia 37991
5/7/49	12	1		3 Tennessee Border...J:12 *Don't Rob Another Man's Castle*		$15		Columbia 20557
10/8/49	9	2		4 **Why Don't You Haul Off And Love Me** J:9 *The Warm Red Wine*		$15		Columbia 20611

ATKINS, Big Ben '78
Born in 1943 in Vernon, Alabama.

5/13/78	72	4		We Don't Live Here, We Just Love Here .... *Baby Blue Eyes*		$5		GRT 161

ATKINS, Chet '65
Born Chester Burton Atkins on 6/20/24 in Luttrell, Tennessee. Moved to Nashville in 1950 and became a prolific studio guitarist and producer. RCA's A&R manager in Nashville from 1960-68; RCA vice president from 1968-82. Elected to the Country Music Hall of Fame in 1973. Won Grammy's Lifetime Achievement Award in 1993. Recipient of *Billboard's* Century Award in 1997. CMA Awards: 1967, 1968, 1969, 1981, 1982, 1983, 1984, 1985 & 1988 Musician of the Year. Also see **Some Of Chet's Friends**.
1)Yakety Axe 2)We Didn't See A Thing 3)Mister Sandman

1/15/55	13	2		1 Mister Sandman .... A:13 / S:15 *Set A Spell* [I]		$15		RCA Victor 5956
				CHET ATKINS and his Gallopin' Guitar #1 Pop hit for The Chordettes in 1954				
4/2/55	15	1		2 Silver Bell...S:15 *The Old Spinning Wheel* [I]		$15		RCA Victor 5995
				HANK SNOW and CHET ATKINS				
6/26/65	4	19		3 Yakety Axe *Letter Edged In Black* [I]	98	$8		RCA Victor 8590
10/15/66	30	10		4 Prissy .... *La Fiesta* [I]		$8		RCA Victor 8927
12/1/73	75	6		5 Fiddlin' Around .... *Paramaribo* [I]		$5		RCA Victor 0146
9/20/75	77	5		6 The Night Atlanta Burned.................... *The Odd Folks Of Okracoke* [I]		$5	■	RCA Victor 10346
				THE ATKINS STRING COMPANY				
6/12/76	40	12		7 Frog Kissin' .... *Bill Cheatham* [N]		$5		RCA Victor 10614
3/1/80	83	3		8 Blind Willie .... *Dance With Me*		$4		RCA 11892
				above 2 are "live" recordings				
8/23/80	83	4		9 I Can Hear Kentucky Calling Me .... *Strawberry Man*		$4		RCA 12064
12/17/83+	6	18		10 We Didn't See A Thing *I Wish You Were Here Tonight*		$3		Columbia 04297
				RAY CHARLES & GEORGE JONES (Featuring Chet Atkins)				

ATKINS, Rodney '97
Singer/songwriter from Tennessee.

8/30/97	74	1		In A Heartbeat... *God Only Knows*		$3		Curb 73026

ATLANTA '84
Group from Atlanta: Brad Griffis and Bill Davidson (vocals), Tony Ingram (vocals, fiddle; **Spurzz**), Alan David (guitar), Allen Collay and Bill Packard (keyboards), Jeff Baker (harmonica), Dick Stevens (bass) and John Holder (drums).

5/21/83	9	17		1 **Atlanta Burned Again Last Night** *Tumblin' Tumbleweeds*		$5		MDJ 4831
9/10/83	11	19		2 Dixie Dreaming .... *Orange Blossom Special/Rocky Top*		$5	■	MDJ 4832
2/18/84	5	23		3 **Sweet Country Music** *Seven Bridges Road*		$4		MCA 52336
6/16/84	35	12		4 Pictures....................*Long Cool Woman (In A Black Dress)*		$4		MCA 52391
9/15/84	22	16		5 Wishful Drinkin'........................S:17 / A:27 *Blue Side Of The Grey*		$4		MCA 52452
				from the movie *Ellie* starring Shelley Winters				
4/6/85	57	10		6 My Sweet-Eyed Georgia Girl .... *Dancin' On The Bayou*		$4		MCA 52552
6/22/85	58	7		7 Why Not Tonight .... *Dancin' On The Bayou*		$4		MCA 52603
1/31/87	75	6		8 We Always Agree On Love.................... *Close Enough For Country*		$5		Southern Tracks 1074
1/23/88	70	5		9 Sad Cliches .... *We Always Agree On Love*		$5		Southern Tracks 1091

ATLANTA POPS — see COLEMAN, Albert

ATLANTA RHYTHM SECTION '80
Group from Doraville, Georgia: Ronnie Hammond (vocals), Barry Bailey and J.R. Cobb (guitars), Dean Daughtry (keyboards), Paul Goddard (bass) and Robert Nix (drums; replaced by Roy Yeager in 1980). Charted 14 pop hits from 1974-81.

7/7/79	92	3		1 Do It Or Die .... *My Song*	19	$5		Polydor 14568
12/6/80	75	7		2 Silver Eagle.................... *Strictly R & R*	101	$5		Polydor 2142

AUSTIN, Bobby '66
Born on 5/5/33 in Wenatchee, Washington. Singer/songwriter/bassist.

10/8/66	21	14		1 Apartment #9 *Gone Home To Momma*		$15		Tally 500
4/8/67	59	6		2 Cupid's Last Arrow ....*Mary's Merry-Go-Round*		$8		Capitol 5867
12/30/67+	68	5		3 This Song Is Just For You....................*Do-Die*		$8		Capitol 2039
12/27/69+	65	4		4 For Your Love ....*(Leaning On) Your Everlasting Love*		$8		Capitol 2681
				#13 Pop hit for Ed Townsend in 1958				
11/11/72	39	8		5 Knoxville Station ....*Bitter Chill Of Lonely*		$5		Atlantic 2913

AUSTIN, Bryan '94
Born on 9/12/67 in Pass Christian, Mississippi. Singer/songwriter.

5/28/94	62	9		Radio Active ....*Limo Driver*		$5	▌	Patriot 58176

AUSTIN, Chris '89
Born in Boone, North Carolina. Male singer/guitarist/fiddler. Backing singer for **Reba McEntire**. Died on 3/16/91 (age 27) in the plane crash that killed seven of McEntire's band members.

7/30/88	62	5		1 Lonesome For You .... *The Reason*		$3	■	Warner 27815
12/10/88	89	6		2 I Know There's A Heart In There Somewhere ....*Somehow Tonight*		$3		Warner 27661
4/1/89	54	7		3 Blues Stay Away From Me ....*We Will Take A Lot Of Memories When We Go*		$3		Warner 27531

DEBUT	PEAK	WKS	Gold	A-side (Chart Hit)..B-side	Pop	$	Pic	Label & Number
				AUSTIN, Darlene '87				
				Born in Salina, Kansas. Female singer.				
6/26/82	68	6		1 Sunday Go To Cheatin' Clothes...		$6		Myrtle 1002
10/9/82	75	5		2 Take Me Tonight		$6		Myrtle 1003
3/12/83	79	4		3 I'm On The Outside Looking In .... *Heartaches By The Number*		$6		Myrtle 1004
				#15 Pop hit for Little Anthony & The Imperials in 1964				
7/5/86	81	4		4 Guilty Eyes..*When Do We Stop Starting Over*		$6	■	CBT 4146
9/12/87	63	6		5 I Had A Heart		$6		Magi 4444
				AUSTIN, Kay '80				
				Born in Long Beach, California. Female singer.				
5/31/80	86	3		1 The Rest Of Your Life..		$5		e.i.o. 1122
9/13/80	75	4		2 Two Hearts Beat (Better Than One) .... *Like The Seasons*		$5		e.i.o. 1127
				AUSTIN, Sherrié '97				
				Born on 8/28/70 in Sydney, Australia; raised in Townsville, Australia. Moved to Los Angeles in 1988.				
5/24/97	34	20		1 Lucky In Love .... S:12 *Put Your Heart Into It*		$3	▍	Arista 13083
9/13/97	41	15		2 One Solitary Tear................................... S:19 *I Want To Fall In Love (So Hard It Hurts)*		$3	▍	Arista 13099

AUTRY, Gene ★122★   '45

Born Orvon Gene Autry on 9/29/07 in Tioga, Texas. Died on 10/2/98 (age 91). Singer/songwriter/guitarist/actor. Worked as a cowboy and telegraph operator for the Frisco Railroad. Played saxophone and guitar with the Fields Brothers Marvelous Medicine Show. Sang on KVOO in Tulsa in 1929 as "The Oklahoma Yodeling Cowboy." Joined the WLS *National Barn Dance* in 1930. Hosted own *Melody Ranch* radio series. Acted in several western movies. Starred in own TV western from 1950-56. Later owned several businesses (including the California Angels major league baseball team). Elected to the Country Music Hall of Fame in 1969.

1)At Mail Call Today 2)Rudolph, The Red-Nosed Reindeer 3)Gonna Build A Big Fence Around Texas
4)Have I Told You Lately That I Love You 5)I Wish I Had Never Met Sunshine

DEBUT	PEAK	WKS	Gold	A-side	B-side	Pop	$	Pic	Label & Number
1/29/44	3	9		1 I'm Thinking Tonight Of My Blue Eyes	*I'll Be True While You're Gone*		$25		Okeh 6648
4/29/44	4	1		2 I Hang My Head And Cry	*You'll Be Sorry*		$25		Okeh 6627
2/10/45	2¹	8		3 Gonna Build A Big Fence Around Texas/					
2/17/45	4	3		4 Don't Fence Me In			$25		Okeh 6728
				from the movie *Hollywood Canteen* starring Bette Davis					
4/28/45	❶⁸	22		5 At Mail Call Today/					
4/28/45	7	2		6 I'll Be Back			$25		Okeh 6737
10/27/45	4	2		7 Don't Hang Around Me Anymore	*Address Unknown*		$20		Columbia 36840
12/29/45	4	1		8 Don't Live A Lie/					
12/29/45	4	1		9 I Want To Be Sure			$20		Columbia 36880
2/23/46	4	5		10 Silver Spurs (On The Golden Stairs)	*Good Old Fashioned Hoedown*		$20		Columbia 36904
5/25/46	3	7		11 I Wish I Had Never Met Sunshine			$20		Columbia 36970
7/6/46	7	1		12 You Only Want Me When You're Lonely			$20		
6/15/46	4	8		13 Wave To Me, My Lady	*Over And Over Again*		$20		Columbia 36984
10/19/46	3	12		14 Have I Told You Lately That I Love You/					
10/26/46	4	3		15 Someday You'll Want Me To Want You			$20		Columbia 37079
3/8/47	3	2		16 You're Not My Darlin' Anymore	*Here's To The Ladies*		$20		Columbia 37201
12/27/47	5	1	●	17 Here Comes Santa Claus (Down Santa Claus Lane) *An Old-Fashioned Tree* [X]		9	$20		Columbia 37942
10/9/48	6	12		18 Buttons And Bows S:6 / J:6 *Can't Shake The Sands Of Texas From My Shoes*		17	$20		Columbia 20469
				from the movie *The Paleface* starring Bob Hope					
11/27/48	4	7		19 Here Comes Santa Claus (Down Santa Claus Lane) S:4 / J:7 *An Old-Fashioned Tree* [X-R]		8	$20		Columbia 20377
12/10/49	8	3		20 Here Comes Santa Claus (Down Santa Claus Lane) A:8 / S:13 *An Old-Fashioned Tree* [X-R]		24	$20		Columbia 20377
12/10/49	❶¹	5	●	21 Rudolph, The Red-Nosed Reindeer A:❶¹ / S:4 / J:7 *If It Doesn't Snow On Christmas* [X]		❶¹	$15		Columbia 38610
				7" 33 1/3 rpm: 1-375					
12/16/50	5	3		22 Rudolph, The Red-Nosed Reindeer S:5 / A:5 / J:5 *If It Doesn't Snow On Christmas* [X-R]		3	$15		Columbia 38610
				GENE AUTRY and The Pinafores (above 2)					
4/8/50	3	4	●	23 Peter Cottontail S:3 / A:5 / J:7 *The Funny Little Bunny (With The Powder Puff Tail)*		5	$20		Columbia 38750
				7" 33 1/3 rpm: 1-575					
12/9/50	4	4	●	24 Frosty The Snow Man S:4 *When Santa Claus Gets Your Letter* [X]		7	$20		Columbia 6-742
				GENE AUTRY and The Cass County Boys					
				78 rpm: 38907					
6/9/51	9	1		25 Old Soldiers Never Die	*A:9 God Bless America*		$25		Columbia 4-39405

DEBUT	PEAK	WKS	Gold	A-side	B-side	Pop	$	Pic	Label & Number
	★335★			**AXTON, Hoyt** '74					
				Born on 3/25/38 in Camanche, Oklahoma. Singer/songwriter/guitarist/actor. Son of songwriter Mae Axton ("Heartbreak Hotel"). Started own Jeremiah label in 1978. Acted in such movies as *The Black Stallion* and *Gremlins*.					
				1)Boney Fingers 2)When The Morning Comes 3)A Rusty Old Halo					
3/30/74	10	15		1 When The Morning Comes	*Billie's Theme*	54	$6		A&M 1497
				Linda Ronstadt (guest vocal)					
8/24/74	8	16		2 Boney Fingers	*Life Machine*		$6	■	A&M 1607
				Renee Armand (female vocal)					
2/8/75	61	9		3 Nashville.. *Speed Trap* (Pop #105)		106	$6		A&M 1657

AXTON, Hoyt — Con'd

DEBUT	PEAK	WKS	A-side / B-side	$	Pic	Label & Number
5/10/75	57	7	4 Lion In The Winter.. *No No Song*	$6		A&M 1683
			Linda Ronstadt (guest vocal)			
5/15/76	18	14	5 Flash Of Fire .... *Paid In Advance*	$6		A&M 1811
4/16/77	57	7	6 You're The Hangnail In My Life .... *Never Been To Spain*	$5		MCA 40711
6/18/77	65	6	7 Little White Moon .... *Funeral Of The King*	$5		MCA 40731
5/12/79	17	15	8 Della And The Dealer .... *In A Young Girls Mind*	$5		Jeremiah 1000
10/6/79	14	14	9 A Rusty Old Halo .... *Gotta Keep Rollin'*	$5		Jeremiah 1001
1/12/80	21	12	10 Wild Bull Rider .... *Torpedo*	$5		Jeremiah 1003
4/12/80	37	12	11 Evangelina .... *So Hard To Give It All Up*	$5		Jeremiah 1005
10/11/80	80	3	12 Where Did The Money Go .... *Smile As You Go By*	$5		Jeremiah 1008
5/9/81	78	3	13 Flo's Yellow Rose .... *Lion In The Winter*	$5		Elektra 47133
			from the TV series *Flo* starring Polly Holliday			
7/25/81	86	4	14 The Devil .... *Jealous Man*	$5		Jeremiah 1011

AZAR, Steve   '96
Born on 4/11/64 in Greenville, Mississippi. Singer/songwriter/guitarist.

DEBUT	PEAK	WKS	A-side / B-side	$	Pic	Label & Number
3/16/96	51	10	1 Someday .... *Thunderbird*	$3	▌	River North 3008
7/6/96	50	15	2 I Never Stopped Lovin' You .... *Heartbreak Town*	$3	▌	River North 3013

B

BACKROADS   '83

DEBUT	PEAK	WKS	A-side / B-side	$	Pic	Label & Number
2/19/83	72	5	So Close.. *Gonna Stay All Night*	$5		Soundwaves 4698

BACKTRACK   '85

| 4/6/85 | 94 | 3 | Mexico .... *I'm On The Outside* | $6 | | Goldmine 11 |

BACKTRACK Featuring John Hunt

BADALE, Andy   '80
Born Angelo Daniel Badalamenti on 3/22/37 in Brooklyn. Wrote several TV and movie scores.

| 1/26/80 | 93 | 4 | Nashville Beer Garden.. *Finger Pickin' Good* [I] | $6 | | GP 577 |

BAILES, Eddy   '76

| 2/21/76 | 93 | 3 | Love Isn't Love (Till You Give It Away) .... *Houston* | $5 | | Cin Kay 101 |

BAILEY, Glen   '82
Born in 1952 in Thunder Bay, Ontario, Canada.

| 3/6/82 | 87 | 3 | 1 Stompin' On My Heart .... | $5 | | Yatahey 1221 |
| 6/26/82 | 85 | 3 | 2 Designer Jeans .... | $5 | ■ | Yatahey 3024 |

BAILEY, Johnny   '83

| 2/5/83 | 86 | 2 | 1 What's She Doing To My Mind/ | | | |
| | | 2 | 2 This Country Music's Driving Me Crazy .... | $5 | | Soundwaves 4695 |

BAILEY, Judy   '81
Born on 1/6/55 in Winchester, Kentucky.

11/29/80+	10	14	1 Following The Feeling *Mexico Winter*	$4		Columbia 11395
			MOE BANDY Featuring Judy Bailey			
5/9/81	56	7	2 Slow Country Dancin' .... *Anything You Can Do (I Can Do Worse)*	$4		Columbia 02045
10/3/81	54	7	3 The Best Bedroom In Town .... *I'm Guilty Of Loving You*	$4		Columbia 02505
2/12/83	72	4	4 Tender Lovin' Lies .... *Trying Hard Not To Be Easy*	$4		Warner 29799
2/9/85	96	3	5 There's A Lot Of Good About Goodbye .... *Comfort*	$5		White Gold 22249

BAILEY, Lynn   '80
Born on 4/18/42 in Indianapolis. Female singer.

| 4/5/80 | 94 | 2 | Cheater Fever .... *Small Talk* | $6 | | Wartrace 613 |

BAILEY, Mary   '81
Born in 1945 in Toronto.

| 8/15/81 | 84 | 3 | Too Much, Too Little, Too Late .... | $6 | | E & R 8101 |

BAILEY, Razzy   ★138★   '81
Born Rasie Michael Bailey on 2/14/39 in Five Points, Alabama. Singer/songwriter/guitarist. First recorded for B&K label in 1949. Worked as a truck driver, insurance salesman and furniture salesman during the early '60s. Formed the group Daily Bread in 1968. Formed the Aquarians in 1972. Recorded as Razzy for MGM in 1974.

1)She Left Love All Over Me   2)Friends   3)Loving Up A Storm   4)I Keep Coming Back   5)Midnight Hauler

10/30/76	99	2	1 Keepin' Rosie Proud Of Me..	$6		Erastus 526
8/12/78	9	15	2 What Time Do You Have To Be Back To Heaven *That's The Way A Cowboy Rocks And Rolls*	$4		RCA 11338
12/23/78+	6	14	3 Tonight She's Gonna Love Me (Like There Was No Tomorrow) *Your Old Love Letters (Always Get The Better Of Me)*	$4		RCA 11446

DEBUT	PEAK	WKS	Gold	A-side (Chart Hit) .... B-side	Pop	$	Pic	Label & Number
				BAILEY, Razzy — Cont'd				
4/21/79	6	13		4 If Love Had A Face *Natural Love*		$4		RCA 11536
8/18/79	10	14		5 I Ain't Got No Business Doin' Business Today *Conchita*		$4		RCA 11682
12/22/79+	5	14		6 I Can't Get Enough Of You *The North Won The War Again Last Night*		$4		RCA 11885
4/19/80	13	14		7 Too Old To Play Cowboy .... *9,999,999 Tears*		$4		RCA 11954
8/2/80	❶¹	15		8 Loving Up A Storm *What's A Little Love Between Friends*		$4	■	RCA 12062
11/22/80+	❶¹	17		9 I Keep Coming Back/				
		17		10 True Life Country Music		$4	■	RCA 12120
3/28/81	❶¹	16		11 Friends/				
		16		12 Anywhere There's A Jukebox		$4		RCA 12199
7/11/81	❶¹	18		13 Midnight Hauler/				
7/11/81	8	18		14 Scratch My Back (And Whisper In My Ear)		$4		RCA 12268
12/19/81+	❶¹	20		15 She Left Love All Over Me *Blaze Of Glory*		$4		RCA 13007
4/10/82	10	15		16 Everytime You Cross My Mind (You Break My Heart) *Tonight She's Gonna Love Me (Like There Was No Tomorrow)*		$4		RCA 13084
8/21/82	8	17		17 Love's Gonna Fall Here Tonight *Singin' Other People's Songs*		$4		RCA 13290
12/4/82+	30	14		18 Poor Boy .... *What Time Do You Have To Be Back To Heaven*		$4		RCA 13383
4/30/83	19	13		19 After The Great Depression .... *Guess Who's Gonna Be A Dad*		$4		RCA 13512
10/29/83	62	10		20 This Is Just The First Day .... *Night Life*		$4		RCA 13630
2/25/84	14	17		21 In The Midnight Hour .... *Mr. Melody Man*		$4		RCA 13718
				#21 Pop hit for Wilson Pickett in 1965				
8/4/84	29	14		22 Knock On Wood .... *If You Happen To See My Baby*		$3		MCA 52421
				#1 Pop hit for Amii Stewart in 1979				
12/8/84+	43	13		23 Touchy Situation .... *Music Takes Me Past The Point*		$3		MCA 52500
3/23/85	51	10		24 Modern Day Marriages .... *New Orleans When It Rains*		$3		MCA 52547
7/27/85	78	4		25 Fightin' Fire With Fire .... *To Write A Sad Song*		$3		MCA 52628
12/14/85+	48	9		26 Old Blue Yodeler .... *To Write A Sad Song*		$3		MCA 52701
6/28/86	63	7		27 Rockin' In The Parkin' Lot .... *Baby My Baby*		$3		MCA 52851
10/31/87	69	5		28 If Love Ever Made A Fool		$5		SOA 001
1/23/88	58	6		29 Unattended Fire .... *Lover Please*		$5		SOA 002
12/24/88+	73	6		30 Starting All Over Again		$5		SOA 003
				#19 Pop hit for Mel & Tim in 1972				
4/29/89	65	5		31 But You Will		$5		SOA 006
	★293★			**BAILLIE AND THE BOYS** '89				
				Trio of songwriters/session singers: Kathie Baillie and husband Michael Bonagura with Alan LeBoeuf. LeBoeuf starred as **Paul McCartney** in Broadway show *Beatlemania.* Group became a duo when LeBoeuf left in January 1989.				
				1)*Heart Of Stone* 2)*Fool Such As I* 3)*Long Shot*				
4/18/87	9	21		1 Oh Heart S:18 *Waitin' Out The Storm*		$3	☐	RCA 5130
8/8/87	18	16		2 He's Letting Go S:29 *Heartless Night*		$3		RCA 5227
12/19/87+	9	18		3 Wilder Days S:23 *You Fool*		$3		RCA 5327
10/1/88+	5	27		4 Long Shot S:9 *You Fool*		$3		RCA 8631
2/4/89	8	21		5 She Deserves You *The Only Lonely One*		$3		RCA 8796
7/1/89	4	24		6 (I Wish I Had A) Heart Of Stone *Heartache In Motion*		$3		RCA 8944
11/4/89+	9	26		7 I Can't Turn The Tide *The Only Lonely One*		$3		RCA 9076
4/14/90	23	14		8 Perfect *Lovin' By Numbers*		$3		RCA 2500
8/11/90	5	21		9 Fool Such As I		$3		RCA 2641
1/5/91	18	20		10 Treat Me Like A Stranger .... *I'd Love To*		$3		RCA 2720
				BAKER, Adam '86				
				Born on 5/26/64 in Oklahoma City; raised in Edmond, Oklahoma.				
3/9/85	97	3		1 I Can See Him In Her Eyes		$6		Signature 22484
2/8/86	48	10		2 In Love With Her .... *They Come And They Go*		$5		Avista 8610
10/18/86	46	9		3 Weren't You Listening *Dixie Nightlife*		$5		Avista 8602
2/7/87	54	7		4 You've Got A Right		$5		Avista 8703
10/31/87	63	4		5 Standing Invitation .... *Dixie Nightlife*		$5		Avista 8704
				BAKER, Butch '86				
				Born on 10/22/58 in Sweetwater, Tennessee. Singer/songwriter/guitarist. Acted in the movie *Country Gold.*				
				1)*That's What Her Memory Is For* 2)*Don't It Make You Wanta Go Home* 3)*Your Loving Side*				
8/4/84	80	3		1 Burn Georgia Burn (There's A Fire In Your Soul) *Bury My Heart (In The Smoky Mountains)*		$3		Mercury 880020
10/27/84	56	7		2 Thinking 'Bout Leaving .... *Bury My Heart (In The Smoky Mountains)*		$3		Mercury 880256
8/9/86	41	14		3 That's What Her Memory Is For *After Losing You*		$3		Mercury 884857
11/15/86	53	9		4 Your Loving Side .... *After Losing You*		$3		Mercury 888133
5/16/87	51	10		5 Don't It Make You Wanta Go Home .... *Your Loving Side*		$3		Mercury 888543
11/28/87	60	10		6 I'll Fall In Love Again .... *After Losing You*		$3		Mercury 888926
7/2/88	69	5		7 Party People .... *After Losing You*		$3		Mercury 870486
9/2/89	64	6		8 Our Little Corner .... *Party People*		$3		Mercury 874746
11/18/89	66	9		9 Wonderful Tonight .... *Party People*		$3		Mercury 876226
				#16 Pop hit for Eric Clapton in 1978				
12/1/90+	56	9		10 It Wasn't You, It Wasn't Me .... *Fairytale Fool*		$3	▮	Mercury 878256
				DANIELE ALEXANDER & BUTCH BAKER				

BAKER, Carroll   '81
Born on 3/4/49 in Port Medway, Nova Scotia, Canada. Singer/songwriter. Hosted TV show *Sounds Good Country* in Canada.

| 7/4/81 | 82 | 3 | | 1 Mama What Does Cheatin' Mean.......................................*Lover On The Shelf* | | $6 | | Excelsior 1013 |
| 7/6/85 | 95 | 1 | | 2 It Always Hurts Like The First Time .... | | $6 | | Tembo 8520 |

BAKER, George   '76
Born Johannes Bouwens on 12/9/44 in Holland.

| 1/10/76 | 33 | 15 | | Paloma Blanca ....*Dreamboat* | 26 | $5 | | Warner 8115 |

GEORGE BAKER SELECTION

BAKER, Two Ton — see HOOSIER HOT SHOTS

BAKER & MYERS   '96
Songwriting team of Gary Baker and Frank Myers. Baker was a member of **The Shooters**.

2/10/96	48	17		1 Years From Here/				
9/30/95	67	6		2 These Arms		$3	∎	Curb 76967
8/24/96	71	1		3 A Little Bit Of Honey				album cut

from the album *Baker & Myers* on Curb 77806

★388★   **BALL, David**   '94
Born on 7/9/53 in Rock Hill, South Carolina. Singer/songwriter/guitarist.
1)Thinkin' Problem 2)When The Thought Of You Catches Up With Me 3)Look What Followed Me Home

5/7/88	46	10		1 Steppin' Out....................................*I Wish He Was Me (And She Was You)*		$4		RCA 6899
8/20/88	55	7		2 You Go, You're Gone...........................*I Wish He Was Me (And She Was You)*		$4		RCA 8636
9/2/89	64	4		3 Gift Of Love ....*I Wish He Was Me (And She Was You)*		$4		RCA 8975
4/16/94	2[1]	20		4 Thinkin' Problem *Down At The Bottom Of A Broken Heart*	40	$3	∎	Warner 18250
9/10/94	7	20		5 When The Thought Of You Catches Up With Me *Don't Think Twice*	107	$3	∎	Warner 18081
1/14/95	11	20		6 Look What Followed Me Home...........................*What Do You Want With His Love*		$3	∎	Warner 17977
5/20/95	48	10		7 What Do You Want With His Love		$3		album cut

from the album *Thinkin' Problem* on Warner 45562

9/16/95	50	9		8 Honky Tonk Healin'..*Blowin' Smoke*		$3		Warner 17785
5/4/96	49	9		9 Circle Of Friends ....S:18 *No More Lonely*		$3	∎	Warner 17639
8/10/96	67	3		10 Hangin' In And Hangin' On ....*If You'd Like Some Lovin'*		$3	∎	Warner 17574

BALL, Marcia   '78
Born Marcia Mouton on 3/20/49 in Orange, Texas; raised in Vinton, Louisiana.

| 11/18/78 | 91 | 2 | | I'm A Fool To Care ....*50 Words Or Less* | | $5 | | Capitol 4633 |

#24 Pop hit for Joe Barry in 1961

BALLARD, Roger   '93
Born in Kentwood, Louisiana.

| 9/25/93 | 68 | 3 | | Two Steps In The Right Direction .... *A Little Piece Of Heaven* | | $3 | ∎ | Atlantic 87313 |

BALLEW, Michael   '81

| 11/7/81 | 67 | 6 | | 1 Your Daddy Don't Live In Heaven (He's In Houston)...................*Blue Water* | | $4 | | Liberty 1437 |
| 2/13/82 | 71 | 5 | | 2 Pretending Fool ....*Ain't No Future In Loving You* | | $4 | | Liberty 1447 |

BAMA BAND, The   '83
Backing band for **Hank Williams, Jr.**: Lamar Morris (vocals, guitar), Wayne "Animal" Turner (guitar), Edward "Cowboy" Long (steel guitar), Paul Eugene "Dixie" Hatfield (keyboards), Jerry McKinney (sax), Vernon Derrick (fiddle), Ray Barrickman (bass) and William Claude Marshall (drums). Billy Earhart (of **Amazing Rhythm Aces**) replaced Hatfield in 1986.

| 12/18/82+ | 54 | 9 | | 1 Dallas ....*A Cowboy's Welcome Home* | | $6 | | Oasis 1 |
| 5/7/83 | 56 | 9 | | 2 Tijuana Sunrise ....*It Sure Feels Like Love Tonight* | | $5 | | Soundwaves 4707 |

first released on Oasis 2 in 1983

7/20/85	60	8		3 What Used To Be Crazy.............................*White Cadillac*		$4	∎	Compleat 144
3/29/86	70	4		4 I've Changed My Mind ....*Stone Cold And Country*		$4		Compleat 152
1/31/87	64	7		5 Suddenly Single ....*Save That Dress*		$4		Compleat 163
8/27/88	71	5		6 Southern Accent ....*It's Gotta Be Love*		$3		Mercury 870603
12/24/88+	69	6		7 Real Old-Fashioned Broken Heart ....*Ellen B.*		$3		Mercury 872150
3/18/89	87	3		8 When We Get Back To The Farm		$3		Mercury 872650

★397★   **BANDANA**   '82
Group from Nashville: Lon Wilson (vocals), **Tim Mensy** and Joe Van Dyke (guitars), Jerry Fox (bass) and Jerry Ray Johnston (drums). In 1986 Mensy, Van Dyke and Johnston left, replaced by Michael Black and Billy Kemp (guitars) and Bob Mummert (drums). Disbanded in 1987.
1)The Killin' Kind 2)Outside Lookin' In 3)Better Our Hearts Should Bend

1/9/82	37	12		1 Guilty Eyes ....*Whatta I Gotta Do?*		$4		Warner 49872
5/1/82	61	7		2 Cheatin' State Of Mind.............................*They Call It Love*		$4		Warner 50045
8/21/82	17	18		3 The Killin' Kind *Whatta I Gotta Do?*		$4		Warner 29936
12/11/82+	29	15		4 I Can't Get Over You (Getting Over Me)................................*Come To Me*		$4		Warner 29831
9/3/83	18	18		5 Outside Lookin' In...................................*Ocean Of Love*		$4		Warner 29524
4/14/84	26	13		6 Better Our Hearts Should Bend (Than Break)......................*Ocean Of Love*		$4		Warner 29315
8/18/84	52	12		7 All I Wanna Do (Is Make Love To You)...............................*Outside Lookin' In*		$4		Warner 29226
5/4/85	46	13		8 It's Just Another Heartache ....*Heat Of The Night*		$4		Warner 29029
9/14/85	37	12		9 Lovin' Up A Storm.................................*Good Groove*		$4		Warner 28939
5/17/86	54	9		10 Touch Me ....*Heat Of The Night*		$4		Warner 28721

BANDIT BAND, The   '87
Group from Lexington, Kentucky.

| 4/4/87 | 73 | 4 | | Do You Wanna Fall In Love.. | | $6 | | Pegasus 108 |

DEBUT	PEAK	WKS	Gold	A-side (Chart Hit)..B-side	Pop	$	Pic	Label & Number

BANDIT BROTHERS '91

| 4/6/91 | 57 | 5 | | Women...*(instrumental)* [N]
 parody of "Men" by **The Forester Sisters** | | $3 | ▮ | Curb 76867 |

BANDY, Charlie '84
Born in 1954 in Grundy, Virginia.

| 7/28/84 | 95 | 2 | | Tenamock Georgia .... *All I See Is You* | | $6 | | RCI 2386 |

BANDY, Moe ★64★ '79
Born Marion Bandy on 2/12/44 in Meridian, Mississippi; raised in San Antonio, Texas. Singer/guitarist. Played in his father's band, the Mission City Playboys, in San Antonio; also worked as a rodeo rider. Regular on the local San Antonio TV show *Country Corner* in 1973. Started his own theater in Branson, Missouri. CMA Award: 1980 Vocal Duo of the Year (with **Joe Stampley**).

> 1)*Just Good Ol' Boys* 2)*I Cheated Me Right Out Of You* 3)*Hank Williams, You Wrote My Life*
> 4)*It's A Cheating Situation* 5)*She's Not Really Cheatin'*

3/30/74	17	15		1 I Just Started Hatin' Cheatin' Songs Today ... *How Far Do You Think We Would Go* first released on Footprint 1006 ($10)		$6		GRC 2006
8/3/74	24	11		2 Honky Tonk Amnesia .... *Cowboys And Playboys*		$6		GRC 2024
11/23/74+	7	14		3 It Was Always So Easy (To Find An Unhappy Woman) *I Wouldn't Cheat On Her If She Was Mine*		$6		GRC 2036
3/22/75	13	11		4 Don't Anyone Make Love At Home Anymore .... *Somebody That Good*		$6		GRC 2055
6/28/75	7	16		5 Bandy The Rodeo Clown *I'm Looking For A New Way To Love You*		$6		GRC 2070
12/20/75+	2²	15		6 Hank Williams, You Wrote My Life *I'm The Honky-Tonk On Loser's Avenue*		$5		Columbia 10265
4/17/76	27	10		7 The Biggest Airport In The World .... *I Think I've Got A Love On For You*		$5		Columbia 10313
7/4/76	11	14		8 Here I Am Drunk Again .... *What Happened To Our Love*		$5		Columbia 10361
10/30/76+	11	15		9 She Took More Than Her Share .... *Then You Can Let Me Go (Out Of Your Mind)*		$5		Columbia 10428
3/5/77	9	14		10 I'm Sorry For You, My Friend *A Four Letter Fool* written by Hank Williams		$5		Columbia 10487
6/18/77	13	12		11 Cowboys Ain't Supposed To Cry......................................*Till I Stop Needing You*		$5		Columbia 10558
10/8/77	11	14		12 She Just Loved The Cheatin' Out Of Me *Up To Now I've Wanted Everything But You*		$5		Columbia 10619
1/28/78	13	14		13 Soft Lights And Hard Country Music *There's Nobody Home On The Range Anymore*		$5		Columbia 10671
5/20/78	11	14		14 That's What Makes The Juke Box Play *Are We Making Love Or Just Making Friends*		$5		Columbia 10735
9/16/78	7	13		15 Two Lonely People *I Never Miss A Day (Missing You)*		$5		Columbia 10820
1/27/79	2²	15		16 It's A Cheating Situation *Try My Love On For Size* Janie Fricke (backing vocal)		$5		Columbia 10889
6/16/79	9	14		17 Barstool Mountain *To Cheat Or Not To Cheat*		$5		Columbia 10974
7/14/79	❶¹	16		18 Just Good Ol' Boys *Make A Little Love Each Day* **MOE BANDY & JOE STAMPLEY**		$5		Columbia 11027
10/6/79	❶¹	14		19 I Cheated Me Right Out Of You *Honky Tonk Merry Go Round*		$5		Columbia 11090
11/17/79+	7	14		20 Holding The Bag *When It Comes To Cowgirls (We Just Can't Say No)* **MOE BANDY & JOE STAMPLEY**		$5		Columbia 11147
2/2/80	13	12		21 One Of A Kind .... *The Bitter With The Sweet*		$5		Columbia 11184
4/12/80	11	15		22 Tell Ole I Ain't Here, He Better Get On Home.................................... *Only The Names Have Been Changed* **MOE BANDY & JOE STAMPLEY**		$5		Columbia 11244
4/26/80	22	12		23 The Champ.................................. *She Took Out The Outlaw In Me*		$5		Columbia 11255
8/2/80	10	15		24 Yesterday Once More *I Just Can't Leave Those Honky Tonks Alone*		$5		Columbia 11305
11/29/80+	10	14		25 Following The Feeling *Mexico Winter* **MOE BANDY Featuring Judy Bailey**		$4		Columbia 11395
3/14/81	10	15		26 Hey Joe (Hey Moe) *Two Beers Away* **MOE BANDY & JOE STAMPLEY**		$4		Columbia 60508
4/18/81	15	14		27 My Woman Loves The Devil Out Of Me............ *Today I Almost Stopped Loving You*		$4		Columbia 02039
8/1/81	12	14		28 Honky Tonk Queen ....*Partners In Rhyme* **MOE BANDY & JOE STAMPLEY**		$4		Columbia 02198
10/17/81+	10	17		29 Rodeo Romeo *There's Nothing More Desperate (Than An Old Desperado)*		$4		Columbia 02532
2/27/82	21	16		30 Someday Soon .... *She's Playin' Hard To Forget*		$4		Columbia 02735
6/19/82	4	18		31 She's Not Really Cheatin' (She's Just Gettin' Even) *The All American Dream*		$4		Columbia 02966
10/23/82+	12	19		32 Only If There Is Another You .... *Your Memory Is Showing All Over Me*		$4		Columbia 03309
3/5/83	19	15		33 I Still Love You In The Same Ol' Way .... *Drivin' My Love Back To You*		$4		Columbia 03625
6/25/83	10	18		34 Let's Get Over Them Together *In Love* **MOE BANDY (Featuring Becky Hobbs)**		$4		Columbia 03970
11/5/83	34	16		35 You're Gonna Lose Her Like That........................... *One More Port*		$4		Columbia 04204
2/18/84	31	13		36 It Took A Lot Of Drinkin' (To Get That Woman Over Me) .... *In Mexico*		$4		Columbia 04353
6/2/84	8	16		37 Where's The Dress *Wildlife Sanctuary* [N] **MOE BANDY & JOE STAMPLEY**		$4		Columbia 04477
8/4/84	12	22		38 Woman Your Love................................A:8 / S:12 *Texas Saturday Night*		$4	▪	Columbia 04466
10/13/84	36	10		39 The Boy's Night Out .... *Alive And Well* **MOE BANDY and JOE STAMPLEY**		$4	▪	Columbia 04601
1/26/85	48	10		40 Daddy's Honky Tonk ....*Wild And Crazy Guys* **MOE BANDY and JOE STAMPLEY**		$4		Columbia 04756
4/20/85	58	8		41 Still On A Roll.. *He's Back In Texas* **MOE BANDY and JOE STAMPLEY**		$4		Columbia 04843
8/10/85	45	14		42 Barroom Roses .... *That's All She Needed To Hear*		$4		Columbia 05438

BANDY, Moe — Cont'd

DEBUT	PEAK	WKS	A-side (Chart Hit) / B-side	Pop	$	Label & Number
11/15/86	42	14	43 One Man Band .... *Ridin' Her Memory Down*		$3	MCA/Curb 52950
2/28/87	6	27	44 Till I'm Too Old To Die Young A:10 / S:11 *You Can't Straddle The Fence Anymore*		$3	MCA/Curb 53033
8/1/87	11	27	45 You Haven't Heard The Last Of Me ...... S:14 *I Forgot That I Don't Live Here Anymore*		$3	MCA/Curb 53132
1/30/88	8	21	46 Americana S:11 *What Goes Around*		$3	Curb 10504
6/25/88	47	10	47 Ashes In The Wind .... *Hittin' Close To Home*		$3	Curb 10510
9/10/88	21	19	48 I Just Can't Say No To You .... *Nobody Gets Off In This Town*		$3	Curb 10513
			#42 Pop hit for Parker McGee in 1977			
2/25/89	34	13	49 Many Mansions .... *Yuppie Love*		$3	Curb 10524
6/10/89	53	8	50 Brotherly Love .... *Charlie*		$3	Curb 10537
9/16/89	49	10	51 This Night Won't Last Forever .... *Ain't Nothin' Gonna Slow This Train Down*		$3	Curb 10555
			#19 Pop hit for Michael Johnson in 1979			

★339★ BANNON, R.C. '79

Born Daniel Shipley on 5/2/45 in Dallas. Singer/songwriter/guitarist. Married to **Louise Mandrell** from 1979-91.

1)Reunited 2)Winners And Losers 3)It Doesn't Matter Anymore

DEBUT	PEAK	WKS	A-side (Chart Hit) / B-side	Pop	$	Label & Number
7/30/77	99	1	1 Southbound .... *You Make All The Difference In The World*		$5	Columbia 10570
10/1/77	90	4	2 Rainbows And Horseshoes .... *You Make All The Difference In The World*		$5	Columbia 10612
12/24/77+	33	12	3 It Doesn't Matter Anymore .... *All Of The Best*		$5	Columbia 10655
			#13 Pop hit for Buddy Holly in 1959			
4/22/78	64	7	4 (The Truth Is) We're Livin' A Lie .... *Love At First Sight*		$5	Columbia 10714
11/11/78	64	5	5 Somebody's Gonna Do It Tonight .... *Got That Lookin' Feelin'*		$5	Columbia 10847
3/10/79	46	8	6 I Thought You'd Never Ask .... *Yes, I Do* LOUISE MANDRELL & R.C. BANNON		$4	Epic 50668
6/2/79	13	12	7 Reunited *Hello There Stranger* LOUISE MANDRELL & R.C. BANNON		$4	Epic 50717
			#1 Pop hit for Peaches & Herb in 1979			
9/22/79	26	11	8 Winners And Losers .... *Cheatin' On Him, Lovin' On Me*		$4	Columbia 11081
11/17/79	48	8	9 We Love Each Other ....*I Want To (Do Everything For You)* LOUISE MANDRELL & R.C. BANNON		$4	Epic 50789
3/1/80	65	5	10 Lovely Lonely Lady ....*I've Never Gone To Bed With An Ugly Woman*		$4	Columbia 11210
5/24/80	61	7	11 If You're Serious About Cheatin' .... *What's A Nice Girl Like You Doing (Living In A Place Like This)*		$4	Columbia 11267
9/13/80	36	10	12 Never Be Anyone Else .... *What's A Nice Girl Like You Doing (Living In A Place Like This)*		$4	Columbia 11346
			#6 Pop hit for Ricky Nelson in 1959			
11/28/81+	35	11	13 Where There's Smoke There's Fire ....*Before You* LOUISE MANDRELL AND R.C. BANNON		$4	RCA 12359
1/23/82	46	11	14 Til Something Better Comes Along .... *You're Bring Out The Fool In Me*		$4	RCA 13029
6/5/82	56	7	15 Our Wedding Band/			
		7	16 Just Married .... *(above 2)* LOUISE MANDRELL AND R.C. BANNON		$4	RCA 13095
12/11/82	35	7	17 Christmas Is Just A Song For Us This Year .... *Christmas In Dixie* [X] LOUISE MANDRELL/R.C. BANNON		$4	RCA 13358

BARBER, Ava '78

Born on 6/28/54 in Knoxville, Tennessee. Singer/pianist. Regular on TV's *The Lawrence Welk Show* from 1974-82.

DEBUT	PEAK	WKS	A-side (Chart Hit) / B-side	Pop	$	Label & Number
2/12/77	70	8	1 Waitin' At The End Of Your Run .... *Blue Eyes Crying In The Rain/Remember Me*		$5	Ranwood 1071
6/18/77	92	2	2 Your Love Is My Refuge .... *I'll Do It All Over Again*		$5	Ranwood 1077
8/13/77	69	8	3 Don't Take My Sunshine Away ....*There's More Love Where That Came From*		$5	Ranwood 1080
2/4/78	14	14	4 Bucket To The South *There's More Love Where That Came From*		$5	Ranwood 1083
6/17/78	44	7	5 You're Gonna Love Love........................*I'm Gonna Make It After All*		$5	Ranwood 1085
10/28/78	75	6	6 Healin' ....*I Never Will Get Over You*		$5	Ranwood 1087
2/28/81	70	5	7 I Think I Could Love You Better Than She Did ....*That's How Much I Love You*		$5	Oak 1029

BARBER, Debra '75

Born on 11/3/53 in Tupelo, Mississippi.

DEBUT	PEAK	WKS	A-side (Chart Hit) / B-side	Pop	$	Label & Number
3/29/75	97	1	1 Help Yourself To Me/			
3/22/75	98	1	2 You Can't Follow Where He's Been...		$5	RCA Victor 10190

★284★ BARBER, Glenn '72

Born Martin Glenn Barber on 2/2/35 in Hollis, Oklahoma; raised in Pasadena, Texas. Singer/multi-instrumentalist.

1)Unexpected Goodbye 2)Kissed By The Rain, Warmed By The Sun 3)Stronger Than Dirt 4)Love Songs Just For You 5)I'm The Man On Susie's Mind

DEBUT	PEAK	WKS	A-side (Chart Hit) / B-side	Pop	$	Label & Number
1/25/64	48	2	1 How Can I Forget You.............................. *Rain Check*		$15	Sims 148
8/29/64	27	9	2 Stronger Than Dirt/			
8/22/64	42	7	3 If Anyone Can Show Cause .... *(Just Load The Wagon)*		$12	Starday 676
11/9/68	41	8	4 Don't Worry 'Bout The Mule (Just Load The Wagon) .... *Reflex Reaction*		$8	Hickory 1517
9/20/69	24	11	5 Kissed By The Rain, Warmed By The Sun .... *My World Is Square*		$8	Hickory 1545
1/10/70	28	11	6 She Cheats On Me .... *Who's Taking The Picture*		$8	Hickory 1557
6/20/70	72	2	7 Poison Red Berries .... *Abilene*		$8	Hickory 1568
1/16/71	75	2	8 Yes, Dear, There Is A Virginia .... *I'm Only Company*		$8	Hickory 1585
3/25/72	28	12	9 I'm The Man On Susie's Mind .... *Satan's Painted Woman*		$8	Hickory 1626
8/5/72	23	12	10 Unexpected Goodbye *Blue Bayou*		$8	Hickory 1645
1/6/73	67	4	11 Yes Ma'm (I Found Her In A Honky Tonk) ....*Who In The World*		$8	Hickory 1653
9/8/73	61	8	12 Country Girl (I Love You Still) .... *Watching You Go*		$7	Hickory/MGM 302
12/29/73+	45	11	13 Daddy Number Two .... *We Let That Lovely Flame Die*		$7	Hickory/MGM 311
4/13/74	65	7	14 You Only Live Once (In Awhile) .... *Sweet On My Mind*		$7	Hickory/MGM 316
11/26/77	79	6	15 (You Better Be) One Hell Of A Woman .... *Is Another Man's Woman Worth Another Man's Life*		$7	Groovy 102

BARBER, Glenn — Cont'd

DEBUT	PEAK	WKS	A-side / B-side	Pop	$	Label & Number
1/14/78	67	6	16 Cry, Cry Darling .... *Has It Been So Long*		$7	Groovy 103
9/30/78	30	10	17 What's The Name Of That Song? .... *I Can't Find A Way (To Be Free)*		$6	Century 21 100
1/6/79	27	10	18 Love Songs Just For You .... *Go Home Little Girl*		$6	Century 21 101
4/14/79	76	2	19 Everybody Wants To Disco .... *Most Wanted Man In Tennessee*		$6	MMI 1029
6/23/79	70	4	20 Woman's Touch .... *Most Wanted Man In Tennessee*		$6	MMI 1031
8/16/80	74	5	21 First Love Feelings .... *What's The Name Of That Song*		$5	Sunbird 7551

BARBER, Bobby ★45★ '74

Born on 4/7/35 in Ironton, Ohio. Singer/songwriter/guitarist. Recorded the song "The All American Boy" which hit #2 on the pop charts in 1959, credited to the song's co-writer Bill Parsons. Served in the U.S. Army from 1958-61. Acted in the movie *A Distant Trumpet*. Hosted TNN's *Bobby Bare and Friends*. His daughter Cari, heard on "Singin' In The Kitchen," died of heart failure in 1976 at age 15.

1)Marie Laveau 2)Daddy What If 3)Four Strong Winds 4)How I Got To Memphis 5)The Lincoln Park Inn

DEBUT	PEAK	WKS	A-side / B-side	Pop	$	Pic	Label & Number
9/15/62	18	8	1 Shame On Me .... *Above And Beyond*	23	$12		RCA Victor 8032
7/6/63	6	18	2 Detroit City .... *Heart Of Ice*	16	$10	■	RCA Victor 8183
10/26/63+	5	16	3 500 Miles Away From Home .... *It All Depends On Linda*	10	$10		RCA Victor 8238
2/8/64	4	17	4 Miller's Cave .... *Jeannie's Last Kiss*	33	$10		RCA Victor 8294
6/6/64	47	3	5 Have I Stayed Away Too Long .... *More Than A Poor Boy Can Give*	94	$10		RCA Victor 8358
			#14 Pop hit for Perry Como in 1944				
11/14/64+	3	19	6 Four Strong Winds .... *Take Me Home*	60	$10		RCA Victor 8443
3/13/65	11	12	7 A Dear John Letter .... *Too Used To Being With You*	114	$10		RCA Victor 8496
			SKEETER DAVIS & BOBBY BARE				
			#44 Pop hit for Pat Boone in 1960				
3/27/65	30	8	8 Times Are Gettin' Hard .... *One Day At A Time*		$10		RCA Victor 8509
6/5/65	7	16	9 It's Alright .... *She Picked A Perfect Day*	122	$10		RCA Victor 8571
10/2/65	31	6	10 Just To Satisfy You .... *Memories*		$10		RCA Victor 8654
11/20/65+	26	12	11 Talk Me Some Sense .... *Delia's Gone*		$10		RCA Victor 8699
3/12/66	34	6	12 In The Same Old Way .... *The Long Black Veil*	131	$10	*	RCA Victor 8758
6/25/66	5	20	13 The Streets Of Baltimore .... *She Took My Sunshine Away*	124	$10		RCA Victor 8851
10/15/66	5	17	14 The Game Of Triangles .... *Bye Bye, Love*		$10		RCA Victor 8963
			BOBBY BARE, NORMA JEAN, LIZ ANDERSON				
11/5/66	38	11	15 Homesick .... *Guess I'll Move On Down The Line*		$8		RCA Victor 8988
3/4/67	16	13	16 Charleston Railroad Tavern .... *Vincennes*		$8		RCA Victor 9098
5/20/67	14	16	17 Come Kiss Me Love .... *Sandy's Crying Again*		$8		RCA Victor 9191
10/7/67	15	13	18 The Piney Wood Hills .... *They Covered Up The Old Swimmin' Hole*		$8		RCA Victor 9314
3/2/68	15	11	19 Find Out What's Happening .... *When Am I Ever Gonna Settle Down*		$8		RCA Victor 9450
7/27/68	14	13	20 A Little Bit Later On Down The Line ... *Don't Do Like I Done Son (Do Like I Say)*		$8		RCA Victor 9568
10/26/68	16	12	21 The Town That Broke My Heart ...... *My Baby*		$8		RCA Victor 9643
3/15/69	4	17	22 (Margie's At) The Lincoln Park Inn ... *Rainy Day In Richmond*		$7		RCA Victor 0110
8/2/69	19	11	23 Which One Will It Be .... *My Frame Of Mind*		$7		RCA Victor 0202
11/15/69	16	12	24 God Bless America Again .... *Baby, What Else Can I Do*		$7		RCA Victor 0264
1/24/70	22	7	25 Your Husband, My Wife .... *Before The Sunrise*		$6		RCA Victor 9789
			BOBBY BARE AND SKEETER DAVIS				
8/8/70	3	16	26 How I Got To Memphis .... *It's Freezing In El Paso*		$6		Mercury 73097
12/26/70+	7	17	27 Come Sundown .... *Woman, You Have Been A Friend To Me*	122	$6		Mercury 73148
5/15/71	8	15	28 Please Don't Tell Me How The Story Ends ... *Where Have All The Seasons Gone*		$6		Mercury 73203
9/25/71	57	9	29 Short And Sweet .... *A Million Miles To The City*		$6		Mercury 73236
4/1/72	13	14	30 What Am I Gonna Do .... *Love Forever*		$6		Mercury 73279
8/26/72	12	14	31 Sylvia's Mother .... *Music City U.S.A.*		$6		Mercury 73317
			#5 Pop hit for Dr. Hook in 1972				
1/6/73	25	11	32 I Hate Goodbyes .... *Fallin' Apart*		$6		RCA Victor 0866
4/14/73	11	15	33 Ride Me Down Easy .... *A Train That Never Runs*		$6		RCA Victor 0918
9/8/73	30	13	34 You Know Who .... *Send Tomorrow To The Moon*		$6		RCA Victor 0063
12/22/73+	2²	16	35 Daddy What If .... *A Restless Wind* [N]	41	$6		RCA Victor 0197
			with 5-year-old son, Bobby, Jr.				
5/4/74	❶¹	18	36 Marie Laveau .... *The Mermaid*		$6		RCA Victor 0261
			"live" recording				
9/7/74	41	8	37 Where'd I Come From .... *Scarlet Ribbons (Jeannie Bare)* [N]		$5		RCA Victor 10037
			BOBBY BARE, JR. & MAMA (his son and wife, Jeannie)				
11/16/74+	29	13	38 Singin' In The Kitchen .... *You Are* [N]		$5		RCA Victor 10096
			BOBBY BARE AND THE FAMILY				
3/15/75	23	11	39 Back In Huntsville Again .... *Warm And Free*		$5		RCA Victor 10223
7/19/75	18	12	40 Alimony .... *Daddy's Been Around The House Too Long*		$5		RCA Victor 10318
10/25/75	29	11	41 Cowboys And Daddys .... *High Plains Jamboree*		$5		RCA Victor 10409
3/13/76	13	14	42 The Winner .... *Up Against The Wall Redneck Mother*		$5		RCA Victor 10556
7/10/76	23	11	43 Put A Little Lovin' On Me .... *Those City Lights*		$5		RCA Victor 10718
10/9/76	17	11	44 Dropkick Me, Jesus .... *Baby Wants To Boogie*		$5		RCA 10790
1/8/77	30	9	45 Vegas .... *The Shelter Of Your Eyes*		$5		RCA 10852
			BOBBY AND JEANNIE BARE				

BARE, Bobby — Cont'd

DEBUT	PEAK	WKS	A-side	B-side	$	Label & Number
3/12/77	21	14	46 Look Who I'm Cheating On Tonight/			
		14	47 If You Think I'm Crazy Now (You Should Have Seen Me When I Was A Kid)		$5	RCA 10902
7/30/77	85	3	48 Red-Neck Hippie Romance	Bottom Dollar	$5	RCA 11037
4/15/78	29	11	49 Too Many Nights Alone	Yard Full Of Rusty Cars	$4	Columbia 10690
10/14/78	11	12	50 Sleep Tight, Good Night Man	Hot Afternoon (Arizona Desert)	$4	Columbia 10831
1/27/79	23	11	51 Healin'	Love Is A Cold Wind	$4	Columbia 10891
6/9/79	42	8	52 Till I Gain Control Again	I'll Feel A Whole Lot Better	$4	Columbia 10998
9/8/79	17	12	53 No Memories Hangin' Round	This Has Happened Before	$4	Columbia 11045
			ROSANNE CASH with BOBBY BARE			
1/5/80	11	14	54 Numbers	When Hippies Get Older [N]	$4	Columbia 11170
4/26/80	31	12	55 Tequila Sheila	Qualudes Again	$4	Columbia 11259
			above 2 are "live" recordings			
10/4/80	41	8	56 Food Blues	Used Cars	$4	Columbia 11365
12/20/80+	19	12	57 Willie Jones	If That Ain't Love	$4	Columbia 11408
			Charlie Daniels (backing vocal)			
4/25/81	28	13	58 Learning To Live Again	Appaloosa Rider	$4	Columbia 02038
8/8/81	28	11	59 Take Me As I Am (Or Let Me Go)	White Freight Liner Blues	$4	Columbia 02414
11/7/81	35	11	60 Dropping Out Of Sight	She Is Gone	$4	Columbia 02577
1/30/82	18	16	61 New Cut Road	Let Him Roll	$4	Columbia 02690
5/29/82	31	11	62 If You Ain't Got Nothin' (You Ain't Got Nothin' To Lose)....	Golden Memories	$4	Columbia 02895
8/21/82	37	11	63 (I'm Not) A Candle In The Wind	Cold Day In Hell	$4	Columbia 03149
11/20/82	83	3	64 Praise The Lord And Send Me The Money	I've Been Rained On Too	$4	Columbia 03334
3/12/83	30	14	65 It's A Dirty Job	Caught In The Spotlight	$4	Columbia 03628
			BOBBY BARE & LACY J. DALTON			
5/28/83	29	15	66 The Jogger	Gravy Train [N]	$4	Columbia 03809
10/1/83	69	7	67 Diet Song	Stacy Brown Got Two	$4	Columbia 04092
8/10/85	53	9	68 When I Get Home	Party Of The First Part	$3	EMI America 8279
11/23/85	76	4	69 Reno And Me	Party Of The First Part	$3	EMI America 8296
8/2/86	67	6	70 Real Good	Wait Until Tomorrow	$3	EMI America 8333

BAREFOOT JERRY — see McCOY, Charlie

BARKER, Aaron   '92
Singer/songwriter from Texas.

DEBUT	PEAK	WKS	A-side		Label & Number
7/18/92	73	2	The Taste Of Freedom		album cut
			from the album *Taste Of Freedom* on Atlantic 82354		

BARLOW, Jack   '72
Born Jack Butcher in Muscatine, Iowa. Singer/songwriter/guitarist. Also recorded as Zoot Fenster.

DEBUT	PEAK	WKS	A-side	B-side	$	Label & Number
10/26/68	40	4	1 Baby, Ain't That Love	It Ain't No Big Thing	$8	Dot 17139
5/3/69	55	6	2 Birmingham Blues	Papa Didn't Give Me No Love	$8	Dot 17212
12/13/69+	68	5	3 Nobody Wants To Hear It Like It Is	No Time For Roses	$8	Dot 17317
1/23/71	59	4	4 Dayton, Ohio	Where There Ain't No Fools (There Ain't No Fun)	$8	Dot 17366
11/6/71+	26	13	5 Catch The Wind	Again Tonight I'm Wantin' You	$8	Dot 17396
5/13/72	58	7	6 They Call The Wind Maria	It's A Long Way Back To Georgia	$8	Dot 17414
			from the movie *Paint Your Wagon* starring Clint Eastwood			
8/4/73	55	9	7 Oh Woman	Wake Up Anna	$8	Dot 17468
11/8/75	30	10	8 The Man On Page 602	Vinegar In My Wine [N]	$8	Antique 106
			ZOOT FENSTER			

BARLOW, Randy   '78

★244★

Born on 3/29/43 in Detroit. Singer/songwriter/guitarist.
1)No Sleep Tonight 2)Sweet Melinda 3)Fall In Love With Me Tonight 4)Slow And Easy 5)Love Dies Hard

DEBUT	PEAK	WKS	A-side	B-side	$	Label & Number
7/20/74	80	6	1 Throw Away The Pages	Hello Pawnshop	$6	Capitol 3883
2/14/76	74	6	2 Johnny Orphan	We're Crazy	$6	Gazelle 153
5/15/76	53	9	3 Goodnight My Love	Don't Worry I'm Okay	$6	Gazelle 217
			#27 Pop hit for Paul Anka in 1969			
8/21/76	46	9	4 Lonely Eyes	One Night Stand	$6	Gazelle 280
11/27/76+	18	14	5 Twenty-Four Hours From Tulsa	The Bottle Took His Mother (And My Wife)	$6	Gazelle 330
			#10 Pop hit for Gene Pitney in 1963			
3/26/77	26	11	6 Kentucky Woman	I'm A Swinger	$6	Gazelle 381
			#22 Pop hit for Neil Diamond in 1967			
6/25/77	31	9	7 California Lady	We're Crazy	$6	Gazelle 413
10/1/77	48	8	8 Walk Away With Me	Johnny Orphan	$6	Gazelle 427
4/1/78	10	17	9 Slow And Easy	Stranger I'm Married	$5	Republic 017
8/12/78	10	13	10 No Sleep Tonight	Burning Bridges	$5	Republic 024
12/9/78+	10	14	11 Fall In Love With Me Tonight	One More Time	$5	Republic 034
4/7/79	10	12	12 Sweet Melinda	Heaven Here We Come	$5	Republic 039
8/11/79	25	10	13 Another Easy Lovin' Night	Louisiana Delta	$5	Republic 044
11/3/79+	13	14	14 Lay Back In The Arms Of Someone	Musical Hearts	$5	Republic 049
10/25/80	46	8	15 Willow Run	Can't Believe I Fell For That Line	$5	Paid 110
1/24/81	25	10	16 Dixie Man	Don't Give Up On Me	$5	Paid 116
4/18/81	13	13	17 Love Dies Hard	New York City Cowboys/Deep In The Heart Of Texas	$5	Paid 133
9/12/81	32	10	18 Try Me	Why Go Searchin' For Something More	$5	Paid 144
12/19/81+	30	13	19 Love Was Born	Cheater's Eyes	$6	Jamex 002
10/29/83	67	6	20 Don't Leave Me Lonely Loving You	For A Few Dollars More	$5	Gazelle 001

BARMBY, Shane   '89
Born in Sacramento, California. Male singer.

| 5/13/89 | 77 | 3 | | 1 Let's Talk About Us... | | $3 | | Mercury 874168 |
| 11/4/89 | 77 | 3 | | 2 A Rainbow Of Our Own... | | $3 | | Mercury 876020 |

BARNES, Benny   '56
Born in 1934 in Beaumont, Texas. Died in 1985 (age 51). Singer/guitarist.

9/29/56	2[1]	17		1 Poor Man's Riches *J:2 / A:8 / S:15 Those Who Know*		$30		Starday 262
6/12/61	22	4		2 Yearning..*Go On, Go On*		$20		Mercury 71806
7/30/77	94	2		3 I've Got Some Gettin' Over You To Do........................*I'll Drink To That*		$8		Playboy 5808

BARNES, Kathy   '77
Born in Henderson, Kentucky. Female singer.
    1)Good 'N' Country 2)Someday Soon 3)Catch The Wind

4/26/75	64	9		1 I'm Available (For You To Hold Me Tight)..................*Come To Me*		$6		MGM 14797
				#9 Pop hit for Margie Rayburn in 1957				
8/30/75	94	3		2 Shhh...*I Will*		$6		MGM 14822
12/6/75	92	5		3 Be Honest With Me...*Paper Cups*		$6		MGM 14836
				written by Gene Autry and Fred Rose				
5/15/76	73	6		4 Sleeping With A Memory...............*I Hang My Head And Cry*		$5	■	Republic 223
9/11/76	39	11		5 Someday Soon.............*Your Love (Makes Our Love So Easy)*		$5		Republic 293
1/8/77	37	9		6 Good 'N' Country *One A Day Heartaches*		$5		Republic 338
3/26/77	92	3		7 If We Can't Do It Right...		$5		Republic 369
				KATHY and LARRY BARNES (her brother)				
4/2/77	50	8		8 Catch The Wind..*Starve A Fever*		$5		Republic 376
				#23 Pop hit for Donovan in 1965				
7/9/77	88	3		9 Tweedle-O-Twill.......................*There You Go Doin' It Again*		$5		Republic 389
				written by Gene Autry and Fred Rose				
10/8/77	62	7		10 The Sun In Dixie...................*I Can't Make It Without You*		$5		Republic 005
12/24/77+	81	5		11 Something's Burning.............................*Take It And Go*		$5		Republic 012
				#11 Pop hit for Kenny Rogers & The First Edition in 1970				

BARNES, Max D.   '80
Born Max Duane Barnes on 7/24/36 in Hardscratch, Iowa. Singer/songwriter/guitarist.

10/22/77	97	1		1 Allegheny Lady.................................*All The Way In*		$6		Polydor 14419
1/5/80	88	5		2 Dear Mr. President......................*Patricia* [S]		$5		Ovation 1139
3/8/80	79	4		3 Mean Woman Blues...........*Too Far Gone To Find*		$5		Ovation 1142
6/28/80	68	6		4 Cowboys Are Common As Sin *Only For You*		$5		Ovation 1149
11/22/80	88	3		5 Heaven On A Freight Train.................*Patricia*		$5		Ovation 1158
3/7/81	84	2		6 Don't Ever Leave Me Again.........*Singer Of Sad Songs*		$5		Ovation 1164

BARNETT, Bobby   '68
Born on 2/15/36 in Cushing, Oklahoma. Singer/songwriter.

10/10/60	24	1		1 This Old Heart..		$20		Razorback 306
2/22/64	47	2		2 Worst Of Luck....................................*Working Man*		$15		Sims 159
5/20/67	52	12		3 Down, Down, Came The World.........*Too Tough To Die*		$10		K-Ark 741
10/14/67	74	2		4 The Losing Kind........................*A Long Way To Go*		$10		K-Ark 766
8/10/68	14	14		5 Love Me, Love Me.................*The End Of The Lyin'*		$6		Columbia 44589
1/4/69	44	10		6 Your Sweet Love Lifted Me..............*You'll Fly Away*		$6		Columbia 44716
6/21/69	59	8		7 Drink Canada Dry.................*Image On Your Mind*		$6		Columbia 44861
3/18/78	97	3		8 Burn Atlanta Down.................*Pody And Barbara*		$5		Cin Kay 128

BARNETT, Mandy   '96
Born on 9/28/75 in Crossville, Tennessee. Singer/actress. Portrayed **Patsy Cline** in the Nashville musical *Always Patsy Cline*.

1/13/96	43	16		1 Now That's All Right With Me............*What's Good For You*		$3	■	Asylum 64308
5/18/96	65	6		2 Maybe.................................*Wayfaring Stranger*		$3	■	Asylum 64280
8/31/96	72	4		3 A Simple I Love You...				album cut
				from the album *Mandy Barnett* on Asylum 61810				

BARNHILL, Joe   '89
Born in Turkey, Texas; raised in California and Tennessee. Son of Joe Bob Barnhill, leader of **Joe Bob's Nashville Sound Company**.

| 7/15/89 | 56 | 7 | | 1 Your Old Flame's Goin' Out Tonite.........*For Cryin' Out Loud* | | $3 | | Universal 66014 |
| 12/2/89+ | 57 | 7 | | 2 Good As Gone...........*Becky Morgan (Cotton Pickin' Time)* | | $3 | | Universal 66032 |

BARNHILL, Leslee   '79

| 2/25/78 | 92 | 2 | | 1 Let's Call It A Day (And Get On With The Night)..................*I Love The Way You Do What You Do* | | $5 | | Republic 014 |
| 5/19/79 | 62 | 6 | | 2 Bad Day For A Breakup.............*I'm Still In Love With You* | | $5 | | Republic 040 |

BASS, Sam D.   '80
Born in Oklahoma. Joined the backing bands of **Tommy Duncan**, **Tex Ritter**, **T. Texas Tyler** and **Moon Mullican**.

| 7/5/80 | 92 | 2 | | How Could I Do This To Me.........*Get Ready For The Blues* | | $6 | | 3J 1003 |

BAUER, Kathy   '83
Born in League City, Texas.

| 4/23/83 | 82 | 4 | | Hold Me Till The Last Waltz Is Over..........*What's A Couple More* | | $5 | | NSD 164 |

BAUGH, Phil   '65
Born in 1936 in Marysville, California. Died of heart failure on 11/4/90 (age 54). Session guitarist. Member of **Nashville Superpickers**. Former owner of the Soundwaves record label.

6/12/65	16	15		1 Country Guitar................................*Chattanooga* [N]		$15		Longhorn 559
				Vern Stovall (vocal)				
11/6/65	27	7		2 One Man Band.................................*Live Wire* [N]		$15		Longhorn 563

BAXTER, BAXTER & BAXTER '81
Trio of brothers from Rockford, Illinois: Rick, Mark and Duncan Baxter.

| 2/28/81 | 76 | 4 | | Take Me Back To The Country .... *John* | | $4 | | Sun 1160 |

BEACH BOYS, The '96
Surf-rock group from Hawthorne, California. Lineup in 1996: brothers Brian and Carl Wilson, their cousin Mike Love, Al Jardine and Bruce Johnston. Carl Wilson died of cancer on 2/6/98 (age 51). Group charted 59 pop hits from 1962-89. Inducted into the Rock and Roll Hall of Fame in 1988.

8/24/96	69	1		1 Little Deuce Coupe .... *(no B-side)*		$5	∎	River North 3014
				THE BEACH BOYS Featuring James House #15 Pop hit for The Beach Boys in 1963				
9/7/96	73	1		2 Don't Worry Baby..				album cut
				THE BEACH BOYS Featuring Lorrie Morgan #24 Pop hit for The Beach Boys in 1964				
10/12/96	69	1		3 Long Tall Texan				album cut
				THE BEACH BOYS Featuring Doug Supernaw #51 Pop hit for Murry Kellum in 1963; above 2 from the album *Stars And Stripes Vol. 1* on River North 1205				

BEAN, Jim '88

| 9/17/88 | 96 | 1 | | Lay, Lady Lay .... | | $6 | | Hub 47 |
| | | | | #7 Pop hit for Bob Dylan in 1969 | | | | |

BEAR CREEK BAND '88

| 10/22/88 | 99 | 1 | | Falling In Love Right & Left .... *I've Had Enough (Of Romance)* | | $6 | | Bear Creek 103 |
| | | | | **BEAR CREEK BAND Featuring Leonda** | | | | |

BEARDS, The '88
Brothers Randy (guitar, vocals) and Ronnie (drums, vocals) Beard from Indiana.

| 5/14/88 | 75 | 4 | | 1 Stone Cold Love... *Fearless Heart* | | $6 | | Beardo 001 |
| 11/26/88 | 71 | 6 | | 2 Fearless Heart .... *Stone Cold Love* | | $6 | | Beardo 002 |

BEATTY, Susi '90
Born on 6/1/62 in Alexandria, Virginia.

| 9/30/89 | 71 | 5 | | 1 Hard Baby To Rock .... *Down Home Jubilee* | | $6 | | Starway 1205 |
| 12/9/89+ | 65 | 6 | | 2 Heart From A Stone .... *Down Home Jubilee* | | $6 | | Starway 1206 |

BEAVERS, Clyde '60
Born on 6/8/32 in Tennega, Georgia.

10/24/60	13	15		1 Here I Am Drunk Again.. *My Love Is Real*		$15		Decca 31173
3/16/63	27	2		2 Still Loving You .... *Happy Times*		$10		Tempwood V 1039
8/3/63	21	1		3 Sukiyaki (I Look Up When I Walk) ...... *Handprints On The Window*		$10		Tempwood V 1044
				#1 Pop hit for Kyu Sakamoto in 1963				
3/12/66	47	3		4 That's You (And What's Left Of Me)............................... *Old Tree*		$8		Hickory 1346

BECKHAM, Bob '67
Born on 7/8/27 in Stratford, Oklahoma.

| 9/2/67 | 73 | 2 | | Cherokee Strip .... *You Really Know How To Hurt A Guy* | | $8 | | Monument 1018 |

BECKHAM, Charlie '88

| 6/18/88 | 84 | 3 | | Think I'll Go Home .... | | $6 | | Oak 1048 |

BEE, Kathy '88
Born in Bloomingburg, Ohio.

| 10/8/88 | 100 | 1 | | Let's Go Party .... | | $6 | | Lilac 1213 |

BEE, Molly '74
Born Molly Beachboard on 8/18/39 in Oklahoma City. Singer/actress. Regular on **Rex Allen**'s radio show in 1950 and **Cliffie Stone**'s TV show in 1951. Appeared in the musicals *The Boy Friend, Paint Your Wagon* and *Finian's Rainbow*. Acted in the movies *The Chartreuse Caboose* and *The Young Swingers*.

| 9/21/74 | 55 | 8 | | 1 She Kept On Talkin' .... *Baby You Got It* | | $7 | | Granite 509 |
| 2/22/75 | 83 | 7 | | 2 Right Or Left At Oak Street .... *I Got A Man* | | $7 | | Granite 515 |

BEE GEES '79
Trio of brothers from Manchester, England: Barry and twins Robin and Maurice Gibb. Charted 43 pop hits from 1967-97. Inducted into the Rock and Roll Hall of Fame in 1997.

| 11/25/78+ | 39 | 12 | ▲ | Rest Your Love On Me............................. *Too Much Heaven (Pop #1)* | | $4 | | RSO 913 |

BEESON, Marc '94
Born on 12/20/54 in Champaign, Illinois. Singer/songwriter/guitarist. Founding member of **Burnin' Daylight**.

| 9/3/94 | 70 | 2 | | A Wing And A Prayer .... *We'll Get By* | | $3 | ∎ | BNA 62794 |

BELEW, Carl '62
Born on 4/21/31 in Salina, Oklahoma. Died of cancer on 10/31/90 (age 59). Singer/songwriter/guitarist.
1)Hello Out There 2)Am I That Easy To Forget 3)Crystal Chandelier

	★380★							
4/6/59	9	20		1 Am I That Easy To Forget	*Such Is Life*		$12		Decca 30842
				#25 Pop hit for Debbie Reynolds in 1960				
6/13/60	19	15		2 Too Much To Lose .... *That's What I Get For Loving You*		$12		Decca 31086
9/29/62	8	12		3 Hello Out There	*Together We Stand*	120	$10		RCA Victor 8058
9/26/64	23	13		4 In The Middle Of A Memory .... *Cheaters Never Prosper*		$10		RCA Victor 8406
8/7/65	12	18		5 Crystal Chandelier .... *Lonely Hearts Do Foolish Things*		$10		RCA Victor 8633
2/5/66	43	4		6 Boston Jail .... *I Spent A Week There One Day*		$10		RCA Victor 8744
11/26/66	64	3		7 Walking Shadow, Talking Memory .... *I'm Lonesome*		$10		RCA Victor 8996
9/9/67	65	2		8 Girl Crazy .... *Turnabout*		$10		RCA Victor 9272
3/16/68	68	2		9 Mary's Little Lamb .... *Once*		$10		RCA Victor 9446
4/24/71	51	10		10 All I Need Is You .... *Funny What A Pair Of Fool Will Do*		$8		Decca 32802
				CARL BELEW & BETTY JEAN ROBINSON				
9/14/74	56	11		11 Welcome Back To My World .... *Turn Out The Lights And Turn Me On*		$6		MCA 40276

BELL, Delia '83
Born in Bonham, Texas; raised in Hugo, Oklahoma. Female singer.

DEBUT	PEAK	WKS			Pop	$	Pic	Label & Number
5/7/83	45	11		1 Flame In My Heart .... *Good Lord A'Mighty*		$4		Warner 29653
8/13/83	82	3		2 Coyote Song .... *Lone Pilgrim*		$4		Warner 29550

BELL, James '68
Born James Mullins.

5/4/68	51	7		He Ain't Country .... *A Friendly Place To Cry*		$8		Bell 710

BELL, Tommy '82
Born in 1950 in Lansing, Michigan.

10/2/82	83	3		1 Georgiana.. *Untangle My Mind*		$6	■	Gold Sound 8013
9/24/83	97	2		2 Honky Tonk Crazy		$6		Gold Sound 8016

BELL, Vivian '77

3/19/77	71	7		The Angel In Your Arms .... *What In The Name Of Love*		$5		GRT 118

#6 Pop hit for Hot in 1977

BELLAMY BROTHERS ★58★ '79
Duo of brothers Howard and David Bellamy. Howard was born on 2/2/46 in Darby, Florida. David was born on 9/16/50 in Darby, Florida. Both graduated from the University of Florida; Howard with a degree in veterinary medicine and David with a degree in psychology. David was a member of the Accidents in 1967. Both were members of Jericho from 1968-71. Moved to Los Angeles 1975. Started own Bellamy Brothers record label in 1992.

1)If I Said You Have A Beautiful Body Would You Hold It Against Me 2)Too Much Is Not Enough
3)Dancin' Cowboys 4)When I'm Away From You 5)Sugar Daddy

DEBUT	PEAK	WKS			Pop	$	Pic	Label & Number
3/13/76	21	12		1 Let Your Love Flow .... *Inside Of My Guitar*	❶¹	$4		Warner/Curb 8169
2/18/78	86	4		2 Bird Dog .... *Make Me Over*		$4		Warner/Curb 8521
4/29/78	19	12		3 Slippin' Away .... *Let's Give Love A Go*		$4		Warner/Curb 8558
9/16/78	99	2		4 Wild Honey .... *Tumbleweed & Rosalee*		$4		Warner/Curb 8627
11/18/78+	16	14		5 Lovin' On .... *My Shy Anne*		$4		Warner/Curb 8692
3/24/79	❶³	15		6 If I Said You Have A Beautiful Body Would You Hold It Against Me *Make Me Over*	39	$4		Warner/Curb 8790
8/18/79	5	13		7 You Ain't Just Whistlin' Dixie *Blue Ribbons*		$4		Warner/Curb 49032
2/2/80	❶¹	14		8 Sugar Daddy *I Could Be Makin' Love To You*		$4		Warner/Curb 49160
5/24/80	❶¹	17		9 Dancin' Cowboys *Dead Aim*		$4		Warner/Curb 49241
10/11/80	3	15		10 Lovers Live Longer *Classic Case Of The Blues*		$4		Warner/Curb 49573
1/17/81	❶¹	13		11 Do You Love As Good As You Look *Givin' Into Love Again*		$4		Warner/Curb 49639
6/6/81	12	13		12 They Could Put Me In Jail *Endangered Species*		$4		Warner/Curb 49729
10/10/81	7	17		13 You're My Favorite Star *It's Hard To Be A Cowboy These Days*		$4		Warner/Curb 49815
12/19/81	62	7		14 It's So Close To Christmas (And I'm So Far From Home) *Let Me Walk Into Your Life* [X]		$4		Warner/Curb 49875
3/27/82	❶¹	18		15 For All The Wrong Reasons *This Time*		$3		Elektra/Curb 47431
7/17/82	21	13		16 Get Into Reggae Cowboy *We're Just A Little Ole Country Band*		$3		Elektra/Curb 69999
9/25/82	❶¹	18		17 Redneck Girl *Let Your Love Flow*		$3		Warner/Curb 29923
1/15/83	❶¹	18		18 When I'm Away From You *Long Distance Love Affair*		$3		Elektra/Curb 69850
5/21/83	4	17		19 I Love Her Mind *Lazy Eyes*		$3		Warner/Curb 29645
9/10/83	15	15		20 Strong Weakness *Doin' It The Hard Way*		$3		Warner/Curb 29514
6/2/84	5	18		21 Forget About Me *We're Having Some Fun Now*		$3		Curb/MCA 52380
9/22/84	6	21		22 World's Greatest Lover *A:5 / S:6 Rock-A-Billy*		$3		Curb/MCA 52446
1/19/85	❶¹	20		23 I Need More Of You *S:❶¹ / A:❶¹ Diesel Cafe*		$3		Curb/MCA 52518
5/4/85	2²	20		24 Old Hippie *S:❶¹ / A:2 Wheels*		$3		Curb/MCA 52579
9/14/85	2¹	22		25 Lie To You For Your Love *S:2 / A:2 Season Of The Wind*		$3		Curb/MCA 52668
2/8/86	2¹	20		26 Feelin' The Feelin' *S:2 / A:2 The Single Man And His Wife*		$3		Curb/MCA 52747
9/27/86	❶¹	20		27 Too Much Is Not Enough *S:❶¹ / A:❶¹ Restless*		$3		Curb/MCA 52917
				THE BELLAMY BROTHERS with The Forester Sisters				
1/24/87	❶¹	22		28 Kids Of The Baby Boom *A:❶¹/S:7 Hard On A Heart*		$3		Curb/MCA 53018
5/9/87	31	10		29 Country Rap *S:30 One Too Many Times*		$3		Curb/MCA 52834
8/15/87	3	24		30 Crazy From The Heart *S:9 White Trash*		$3		Curb/MCA 53154
1/9/88	5	21		31 Santa Fe *S:8 White Trash*		$3		Curb/MCA 53222
5/7/88	6	21		32 I'll Give You All My Love Tonight *S:16 Ying Yang*		$3		Curb/MCA 53310
9/3/88	9	19		33 Rebels Without A Clue *S:8 A Little Naive*		$3		Curb/MCA 53399
1/7/89	5	20		34 Big Love *The Courthouse*		$3		Curb/MCA 53478
5/6/89	51	7		35 Hillbilly Hell *You're My Favorite Star*		$3		Curb/MCA 53642
7/1/89	10	27		36 You'll Never Be Sorry *Hillbilly Hell*		$3		Curb/MCA 53672
11/11/89	37	12		37 The Center Of My Universe *Hillbilly Hell*		$3		Curb/MCA 53719
4/14/90	63	7		38 Drive South *You Can't Have A Good Time Without Me*		$3		Warner 19874
				THE FORESTER SISTERS with The Bellamy Brothers				
6/30/90	7	21		39 I Could Be Persuaded *(album snippets)*		$3	■	Curb/MCA 53824
3/23/91	46	18		40 She Don't Know That She's Perfect *I Make Her Laugh*		$3	■	Atlantic 87748
8/17/91	74	2		41 All In The Name Of Love *Anyway I Can*		$3		Atlantic 87650
6/6/92	23	20		42 Cowboy Beat		$3		album cut
10/17/92	64	6		43 Can I Come On Home To You				album cut
3/13/93	62	7		44 Hard Way To Make An Easy Livin'...............................				album cut

above 3 from the album *The Latest And The Greatest* on Bellamy Brothers 9108

BELLAMY BROTHERS — Cont'd

DEBUT	PEAK	WKS	A-side / B-side	Pop	$	Pic	Label & Number
8/7/93	66	6	45 Rip Off The Knob				album cut
1/15/94	71	3	46 Not				album cut
			above 2 from the album *Rip Off The Knob* on Bellamy Brothers 9109				

BENEDICT, Ernie   '49

10/8/49	15	1	Over Three Hills .... J:15 *Red Lips And Red Wine*		$25		RCA Victor 20-3389
			ERNIE BENEDICT and His Polkateers				

BENONI, Arne   '89

Male singer from Norway.

6/24/89	96	1	1 Southern Lady .... *Those Evening Bells*		$6	■	Round Robin 1879
10/7/89	88	2	2 If I Live To Be A Hundred (I'll Die Young)		$6		Round Robin 1881

BENSON, Matt   '89

7/29/89	63	5	When Will The Fires End .... *America*		$3		Step One 406

BENTLEY, Stephanie   '96

Born in Thomasville, Georgia.

10/14/95+	21	20	1 Heart Half Empty .... S:10 *Love At 90 Miles An Hour*		$3	▌	Epic 78073
			TY HERNDON Featuring Stephanie Bentley				
2/3/96	32	20	2 Who's That Girl .... *The Hopechest Song*		$3	▌	Epic 78234
7/27/96	60	16	3 Once I Was The Light Of Your Life .... *What's Wrong With You*		$3		Epic 78336
2/22/97	47	11	4 The Hopechest Song				album cut
			from the album *Hopechest* on Epic 66877				

BENTON, Barbi   '75

Born Barbara Klein on 1/28/50 in Sacramento, California. Singer/actress/model. Regular on TV's *Hee Haw* and *Sugar Time*.

3/15/75	5	14	1 Brass Buckles .... *Put A Little Bit On Me*		$5		Playboy 6032
8/16/75	61	8	2 Movie Magazine, Stars In Her Eyes .... *He Looks Just Like His Daddy*		$5		Playboy 6043
10/18/75	32	9	3 Roll You Like A Wheel .... *Let's Sing A Song Together*		$5	■	Playboy 6045
			MICKEY GILLEY & BARBI BENTON				
12/27/75+	74	5	4 The Reverend Bob .... *Ain't That Just The Way (That Life Goes Down)*		$5		Playboy 6056

BERG, Matraca   '90

Pronounced: Muh-TRAY-suh. Born on 2/3/64 in Nashville. Singer/songwriter. Daughter of Nashville session singer/songwriter Icee Berg. Married to Jeff Hanna of Nitty Gritty Dirt Band.

6/9/90	36	10	1 Baby, Walk On		$3	▌	RCA 2584
9/8/90	36	15	2 The Things You Left Undone .... *Dancin' On The Wire*		$3		RCA 2644
1/12/91	43	16	3 I Got It Bad .... *Calico Plains*		$3		RCA 2710
5/25/91	55	13	4 I Must Have Been Crazy .... *Alice In The Looking Glass*		$3		RCA 2827
11/16/91	66	5	5 It's Easy To Tell .... *Baby, Walk On*		$3		RCA 62060
9/13/97	59	4	6 That Train Don't Run .... *Here You Come Raining On Me*		$3	▌	Rising Tide 56047

BERNARD, Crystal   '96

Born on 9/30/61 in Houston. Singer/actress. Played "Helen Chapel" on TV's *Wings*.

11/2/96	57	15	1 Have We Forgotten What Love Is .... S:13 *Eleven Roses*		$3	▌	River North 3015
			Billy Dean (backing vocal)				
3/15/97	70	3	2 State Of Mind .... S:14 *Have We Forgotten What Love Is*		$3	▌	River North 3016

BERRY, John   ★240★   '94

Born on 9/14/59 in Aiken, South Carolina; raised in Atlanta. Singer/songwriter.
1)Your Love Amazes Me 2)She's Taken A Shine 3)Standing On The Edge Of Goodbye

6/5/93	51	11	1 A Mind Of Her Own				album cut
			from the album *John Berry* on Liberty 80472				
9/25/93	22	20	2 Kiss Me In The Car .... *More Than Just A Little*		$3		Liberty 17518
2/12/94	❶[1]	20	3 Your Love Amazes Me/				
6/25/94	5	20	4 What's In It For Me	120	$3	▌	Liberty 58212
10/15/94+	4	20	5 You And Only You .... *More Sorry Than You'll Ever Know*		$3		Liberty 18137
3/4/95	2[1]	20	6 Standing On The Edge Of Goodbye .... *Ninety Miles An Hour*		$3		Patriot 18401
7/8/95	4	20	7 I Think About It All The Time				album cut
			from the album *Standing On The Edge Of Goodbye* on Patriot 28495				
10/21/95	25	20	8 If I Had Any Pride Left At All .... *What Are We Fighting For*		$3	▌	Capitol 58465
12/30/95	55	2	9 O Holy Night .... *O Come Emmanuel* [X]		$3		Capitol 18910
2/17/96	34	11	10 Every Time My Heart Calls Your Name				album cut
			from the album *Standing On The Edge Of Goodbye* on Patriot 28495				
7/27/96	10	20	11 Change My Mind .... S:5 *Standing On The Edge Of Goodbye*	103	$3	▌	Capitol 58577
12/7/96+	2[2]	20	12 She's Taken A Shine .... S:10 *Time To Be A Man*	117	$3	▌	Capitol 58624
4/19/97	19	20	13 I Will, If You Will .... *Love Is Everything*		$3		Capitol 19511
9/20/97	59	6	14 The Stone .... *Livin' On Love*		$3		Capitol 19724
12/27/97	63	1	15 O Holy Night .... *O Come Emmanuel* [X-R]		$3		Capitol 18910

BICKHARDT, Craig   '84

Singer/songwriter. Joined Schuyler, Knobloch & Bickhardt in 1987.

5/26/84	86	4	You Are What Love Means To Me .... *Overnight Sensations*		$3		Liberty 1518
			from the movie *Tender Mercies* starring Robert Duvall				

BIG HOUSE   '97

Group from Bakersfield, California: brothers Monty (vocals) and Tanner (drums) Byrom, David Neuhauser and Chuck Seaton (guitars), Sonny California (harmonica) and Ron Mitchell (bass).

2/8/97	30	20	1 Cold Outside .... S:21 (album snippets)		$3	▌	MCA 55253
5/24/97	57	11	2 You Ain't Lonely Yet .... *The Tables Are Turned*		$3		MCA 72005
10/11/97	71	4	3 Love Ain't Easy		$3		MCA 72020

DEBUG	PEAK	WKS	Gold	A-side (Chart Hit) ....B-side	Pop	$	Pic	Label & Number

BILLY HILL '89

Group from Nashville: **Dennis Robbins** (vocals), Bob DiPiero and John Scott Sherrill (guitars), Reno Kling (bass) and Martin Parker (drums). DiPiero married **Pam Tillis**.

7/8/89	**25**	17	1 Too Much Month At The End Of The Money..............................*Rollin' Dice*	$3	Reprise 22942
12/9/89+	**58**	6	2 I Can't Help Myself (Sugar Pie Honey Bunch) .....*Just In Case You Want To Know*	$3	Reprise 22746
			#1 Pop hit for the Four Tops in 1965		

BILLY THE KID '79

6/16/79	**50**	7	What I Feel Is You...*Songpainter*	$6	Cyclone 103

BIRD, Vicki '88

Born on 7/9/55 in Bird's Hollow, West Virginia. Regular on TV's *Hee Haw* from 1989-91.

10/24/87	**64**	6	1 I've Got Ways Of Making You Talk ....*I Need A Real Good Love Real Bad*	$4	16th Avenue 70405
4/23/88	**61**	6	2 A Little Bit Of Lovin' (Goes A Long Long Way) ....*I've Got Ways Of Making You Talk*	$4	16th Avenue 70413
			same song as "Just A Little Bit" by The Diamonds		
4/8/89	**73**	4	3 Mem'ries ....*A Little Bit Of Lovin' (Goes A Long Long Way)*	$4	16th Avenue 70421
10/14/89	**87**	2	4 Moanin' The Blues.......................................*Mem'ries*	$4	16th Avenue 70431

BISHOP, Bob '68

Born Bishop Milton Sykes on 8/6/28 in Henry County, Tennessee. Guitarist with **Marty Robbins** and Hank Snow.

11/9/68	**42**	6	Roses To Reno ....*It's Gonna Hurt You More Than Me*	$7	ABC 11132

BISHOP, Joni '87

8/1/87	**71**	4	Heart Out Of Control ....*Walls, Doors, Windows And Floors*	$3	Columbia 07225

BISHOP, Terri '78

7/22/78	**97**	3	One More Kiss ....*My Memories*	$6	United Artists 1194

BLACK, Bill '75

Born on 9/17/26 in Memphis. Died of a brain tumor on 10/21/65 (age 39). Bass guitarist. Backed **Elvis Presley** on most of his early records. Formed own band in 1959. Larry Rogers and Bob Tucker led group after Black's death.

BILL BLACK'S COMBO:

4/5/75	**29**	13	1 Boilin' Cabbage ....*Truck Stop* [l]	$6	Hi 2283
9/20/75	**84**	5	2 Back Up And Push ....*Almost Persuaded* [l]	$6	Hi 2291
1/24/76	**57**	8	3 Fire On The Bayou ....*Memphis Stroll* [l]	$6	Hi 2301
7/24/76	**100**	2	4 Jump Back Joe Joe ....*I Can Help* [l]	$6	Hi 2311
11/20/76	**89**	7	5 Redneck Rock.......................*Yakety Sax* [l]	$6	Hi 2317
			"live" recording		
4/8/78	**96**	4	6 Cashin' In (A Tribute To Luther Perkins) ...............*L.A. Blues* [l]	$6	Hi 78508

BLACK, Clint ★71★ '90

Born on 2/4/62 in Long Branch, New Jersey; raised in Houston. Singer/songwriter/guitarist. Began singing professionally in 1981 at the Benton Springs Club in Houston. Married actress Lisa Hartman on 10/20/91. Joined the *Grand Ole Opry* in 1991. CMA Awards: 1989 Horizon Award; 1990 Male Vocalist of the Year.

1)Like The Rain 2)Nobody's Home 3)Summer's Comin' 4)Walkin' Away 5)Nothin' But The Taillights

2/18/89	**❶¹**	24	1 A Better Man ....*Winding Down*		$3		RCA 8781
7/15/89	**❶¹**	21	2 Killin' Time ....*A Better Man*		$3		RCA 8945
11/18/89+	**❶³**	26	3 Nobody's Home ....*Winding Down*		$3		RCA 9078
3/10/90	**❶²**	25	4 Walkin' Away ....*Straight From The Factory*		$3		RCA 2520
7/7/90	**3**	21	5 Nothing's News ....*Live And Learn*		$3	∎	RCA 2596
10/27/90	**4**	20	6 Put Yourself In My Shoes ....*Live And Learn*		$3		RCA 2678
2/2/91	**❶²**	20	7 Loving Blind ....*Muddy Water*		$3		RCA 2749
4/27/91	**7**	20	8 One More Payment ....*You're Gonna Leave Me Again*		$3		RCA 2819
7/27/91	**❶²**	20	9 Where Are You Now ....*Muddy Water*		$3		RCA 62016
11/2/91	**42**	10	10 Hold On Partner ....*Alive And Kickin'*		$3		RCA 62061
			ROY ROGERS & CLINT BLACK				
4/25/92	**61**	8	11 This Nightlife				album cut
			from the album *Put Yourself In My Shoes* on RCA 2372				
6/20/92	**2²**	20	12 We Tell Ourselves ....*There Never Was A Train*		$3		RCA 62194
9/26/92	**4**	20	13 Burn One Down ....*Wake Up Yesterday*		$3		RCA 62337
1/16/93	**❶²**	20	14 When My Ship Comes In ....*Buying Time*		$3		RCA 62429
5/15/93	**2¹**	20	15 A Bad Goodbye ....*The Hard Way*	43	$3	∎	RCA 62503
			CLINT BLACK (with Wynonna)				
8/14/93	**3**	20	16 No Time To Kill ....*Happiness Alone*		$3		RCA 62609
10/30/93	**54**	20	17 Desperado				album cut
			from the album *Common Thread* on Giant 24531				
11/20/93+	**2²**	20	18 State Of Mind/	102			
2/5/94	**74**	1	19 Tuckered Out......................		$3		RCA 62700
3/5/94	**❶¹**	20	20 A Good Run Of Bad Luck ....*Half The Man*		$3	∎	RCA 62762
6/4/94	**4**	20	21 Half The Man ....*Back To Back*		$3		RCA 62878
9/24/94	**4**	20	22 Untanglin' My Mind ....*I Can Get By*		$3	∎	RCA 62933
12/31/94+	**3**	20	23 Wherever You Go ....*You Walked By*		$3		RCA 64267
4/8/95	**❶³**	20	24 Summer's Comin' ....*Hey Hot Rod*		$3		RCA 64281
7/8/95	**2²**	20	25 One Emotion ....*You Made Me Feel*		$3		RCA 64381

BLACK, Clint — Cont'd

DEBUT	PEAK	WKS	A-side / B-side	Pop	$	Pic	Label & Number
10/14/95	**4**	20	26 Life Gets Away _The Kid_		$3		RCA 64442
12/16/95	58	4	27 Til' Santa's Gone (Milk And Cookies) [X]				album cut
12/30/95	71	1	28 The Kid [X]				album cut
			above 2 from the album _Looking For Christmas_ on RCA 66593				
9/7/96	**❶**[3]	20	29 Like The Rain _Desperado_		$3		RCA 64603
11/30/96+	**6**	20	30 Half Way Up _Cadillac Jack Favor_		$3		RCA 64724
12/28/96	65	2	31 Til' Santa's Gone (Milk And Cookies) [X-R]				album cut
			from the album _Looking For Christmas_ on RCA 66593				
6/14/97	11	20	32 Still Holding On _(long version)_		$3		RCA 64850
			CLINT BLACK & MARTINA McBRIDE				
8/30/97	**2**[3]	21	33 Something That We Do _S:6 Bitter Side Of Sweet_	76	$3	▮	RCA 64961
10/18/97+	**❶**[2]	29	34 Nothin' But The Taillights _S:18 Cadillac Jack Favor_	116	$3	▮	RCA 65350
12/27/97	40	2	35 Til' Santa's Gone (Milk And Cookies) [X-R]				album cut
			from the album _Looking For Christmas_ on RCA 66593				

BLACK, Jeanne '60
Born Gloria Jeanne Black on 10/25/37 in Pomona, California. Regular on **Cliffie Stone**'s TV show.

5/2/60	6	12	●	He'll Have To Stay _Under Your Spell Again_	4	$12		Capitol 4368
				answer to "He'll Have To Go" by **Jim Reeves**				

★256★ BLACKHAWK '95
Trio of music veterans Henry Paul (member of Southern-rock bands The Outlaws and Henry Paul Band) with the songwriting team of Dave Robbins and Van Stephenson.
1)I'm Not Strong Enough To Say No 2)Every Once In A While 3)Like There Ain't No Yesterday

DEBUT	PEAK	WKS	A-side / B-side	Pop	$	Pic	Label & Number
11/20/93+	11	20	1 Goodbye Says It All _Let 'Em Whirl_	111	$3	▮	Arista 12568
4/16/94	**2**[1]	20	2 Every Once In A While _One More Heartache_		$3	▮	Arista 12668
8/20/94	9	20	3 I Sure Can Smell The Rain _Stone By Stone_		$3		Arista 12718
12/17/94+	10	20	4 Down In Flames _Between Ragged And Wrong_		$3		Arista 12769
4/15/95	7	20	5 That's Just About Right _Love Like This_		$3		Arista 12813
7/29/95	**2**[2]	20	6 I'm Not Strong Enough To Say No _S:3 A Kiss Is Worth A Thousand Words_	104	$3	▮	Arista 12857
11/11/95+	3	20	7 Like There Ain't No Yesterday _A Kiss Is Worth A Thousand Words_		$3	▮	Arista 12897
2/24/96	11	20	8 Almost A Memory Now _Cast Iron Heart_		$3	▮	Arista 12975
6/15/96	17	20	9 Big Guitar _S:24 Any Man With A Heartbeat_		$3	▮	Arista 13017
10/26/96	49	9	10 King Of The World _Bad Love Gone Good_		$3		Arista 13049
6/28/97	31	20	11 Hole In My Heart _S:13 She Dances With Her Shadow_	123	$3	▮	Arista 13092
10/18/97	37	17	12 Postmarked Birmingham _It Ain't About Love Anymore_		$3		Arista 13109
12/27/97	75	1	13 We Three Kings (Star Of Wonder) _Rudolph The Red-Nosed Reindeer_ [X]		$3		Arista 13060

BLACKJACK — see GRAYSON, Jack

BLACK TIE '91
All-star trio: Jimmy Griffin (Bread; **The Remingtons**), Randy Meisner (**Eagles**; **Poco**) and Billy Swan.

12/15/90+	59	8	Learning The Game		$6		Bench 27
			written by Buddy Holly				

BLACKWELL, Karon '77
Pronounced: KAY-ron. Born in Ellisville, Mississippi. Female singer.

1/22/77	93	3	Blue Skies And Roses _I Wanna Love You_		$7		Blackland 254

BLACKWOOD, R.W. '76

8/7/76	32	10	1 Sunday Afternoon Boatride In The Park On The Lake _Lookin' At The World Through The Eyes Of Love_		$6		Capitol 4302
11/13/76	91	4	2 Memory Go Round _Freedom Lives In A Country Song_		$6		Capitol 4346
			R.W. BLACKWOOD and The Blackwood Singers (above 2)				
10/28/78	57	6	3 Dolly _Counterfeit Cowboy_		$6		Scorpion 0561
			tribute to Dolly Parton				

BLAIR, Kenny '88

7/2/88	84	2	Lost In Austin		$6		Awesome 119

BLAKE & BRIAN '97
Duo of Blake Weldon (b: 9/13/66 in Lufkin, Texas) and Brian Gowen (b: 1/7/69 in Temple, Texas).

7/19/97	45	16	1 Another Perfect Day _Straight To You_		$3	▮	Curb 73024
11/22/97+	62	8	2 The Wish				album cut
			from the album _Blake & Brian_ on Curb 77900				

BLAKER, Clay '88
Male singer from San Antonio.

5/16/87	91	2	1 South Of The Border _Lonesome Rodeo Cowboy_		$7		Texas Musik 6153
2/27/88	75	5	2 A Honky Tonk Heart (And A Hillbilly Soul) _The Only Thing I Have Left_		$7		Rain Forest 120187
			CLAY BLAKER and The Texas Honky-Tonk Band (above 2)				

BLANCH, Arthur '78
Born in Tamworth, New South Wales, Australia. Singer/songwriter/guitarist. Father of **Jewel Blanch**.

9/16/78	73	4	1 The Little Man's Got The Biggest Smile In Town _Another Pretty Country Song_		$5		MC/Curb 5015
9/1/79	82	7	2 Maybe I'll Cry Over You		$5		Ridgetop 00479

BLANCH, Jewel '79
Born in Australia. Singer/actress. Daughter of **Arthur Blanch**. Acted in the movie _Against A Crooked Sky_.

9/30/78	68	6	1 So Good _Roses Ain't Red_		$4		RCA 11329
2/10/79	33	12	2 Can I See You Tonight _When A Love Ain't Right_		$4		RCA 11464

	★299★			**BLANCHARD, Jack, & Misty Morgan** '70				
				Blanchard was born on 5/8/42 in Buffalo. Morgan was born on 5/23/45 in Buffalo. Married in 1963.				
				1)Tennessee Bird Walk 2)Humphrey The Camel 3)Somewhere In Virginia In The Rain				
3/1/69	59	4		1 Big Black Bird (Spirit Of Our Love) ....The Autumn Song (On a Yellow Day)		$6		Wayside 1028
2/7/70	❶²	19		2 Tennessee Bird Walk ....The Clock Of St. James [N]	23	$6		Wayside 010
6/20/70	5	13		3 Humphrey The Camel ....A Place In My Mind [N]	78	$6		Wayside 013
9/26/70	27	11		4 You've Got Your Troubles (I've Got Mine) ....How I Lost 31 Pounds In 17 Days		$6		Wayside 015
				#7 Pop hit for The Fortunes in 1965				
7/24/71	25	13		5 There Must Be More To Life (Than Growing Old)/				
7/24/71	46	13		6 Fire Hydrant #79		$5		Mega 0031
11/6/71+	15	14		7 Somewhere In Virginia In The Rain ....If Eggs Had Legs		$5		Mega 0046
3/25/72	38	11		8 The Legendary Chicken Fairy ....The Night We Heard The Voice [N]		$5		Mega 0063
9/30/72	60	7		9 Second Tuesday In December ....Don't It Make You Wanta Go Home		$5		Mega 0089
3/10/73	65	4		10 A Handful Of Dimes ....It Seems Like There Ain't No Going Home		$5		Mega 0101
12/1/73+	23	13		11 Just One More Song ....Why Did I Sleep So Long		$4		Epic 11058
5/11/74	53	10		12 Something On Your Mind ....Here Today And Gone Tomorrow		$4		Epic 11097
9/28/74	41	12		13 Down To The End Of The Wine ....You Can't Say I Didn't Try		$4		Epic 50023
7/26/75	74	7		14 Because We Love ....It's Me		$4		Epic 50122
12/27/75+	68	6		15 I'm High On You ....Let's Pretend		$4		Epic 50181
				BLANTON, Loy '85				
				Born in Victoria, Texas. Male singer.				
6/15/85	77	4		1 California Sleeping ....I Wrote The Book		$5		Soundwaves 4750
9/7/85	63	11		2 Sailing Home To Me ....Run For Your Life Love Affair		$5		Soundwaves 4760
				BLIXSETH, Tim '85				
5/4/85	91	2		It Can't Be Done ....Sometimes I Wish You Didn't Love Me		$5		Compleat 141
				TIM BLIXSETH (with Kathy Walker)				
				BLOCK, Doug '84				
				Singer from New York.				
1/31/81	82	3		1 Have Another Drink ....It's Only A Matter Of Time		$6		Door Knob 143
				DOUGLAS				
				first recorded by The Kinks on their 1975 album Soap Opera				
12/22/84	73	4		2 Have Another Drink ....It's Only A Matter Of Time [R]		$6		Revolver 005
				above 2 are the same version				
				BLUE, Bobby '86				
				Born in Los Angeles.				
2/1/86	80	3		Once Upon A Time		$6	■	Nite 108
				BLUE BOYS, The '68				
				Backing band for Jim Reeves: Bud Logan (vocals, bass), Leo Jackson (guitar), Bunky Keels (piano) and Jimmy Orr (drums).				
7/15/67	63	3		1 My Cup Runneth Over ....Cry For The Lady		$10		RCA Victor 9201
				#8 Pop hit for Ed Ames in 1967; from the musical I Do! I Do! starring Mary Martin and Robert Preston				
2/3/68	58	6		2 I'm Not Ready Yet ....My Heart's With You		$10		RCA Victor 9418
				THE BLUE BOYS Featuring Bud Logan (above 2)				
				BLUE RIDGE RANGERS — see FOGERTY, John				
				BLUESTONE '80				
				Duo of Ray Pennington and Jerry McBee.				
2/9/80	84	3		Haven't I Loved You Somewhere Before ....A Little Thing Like A Golden Ring		$5		Dimension 1002
				BOARDO, Liz '87				
				Born on 10/22/62 in Dorchester, Massachusetts.				
2/7/87	58	6		1 There's Still Enough Of Us ....Hangin' On By A Heartache		$5		Master 02
6/27/87	65	5		2 I Need To Be Loved Again		$5		Master 03
	★224★			**BOGGUSS, Suzy** '93				
				Born Susan Kay Bogguss on 12/30/56 in Aledo, Illinois. Singer/songwriter/guitarist. Married to songwriter/engineer Doug Crider. CMA Award: 1992 Horizon Award. Also see The Red Hots.				
				1)Drive South 2)Hey Cinderella 3)Just Like The Weather 4)Letting Go 5)Outbound Plane				
3/14/87	68	6		1 I Don't Want To Set The World On Fire ....Hopeless Romantic		$3		Capitol 5669
				#1 Pop hit for Horace Heidt & His Orchestra in 1941				
8/15/87	69	6		2 Love Will Never Slip Away ....True North		$3		Capitol 44045
8/13/88	77	2		3 I Want To Be A Cowboy's Sweetheart ....I Still Love You		$3		Capitol 44187
3/11/89	46	13		4 Somewhere Between ....I'm At Home On The Range		$3		Capitol 44270
6/3/89	14	26		5 Cross My Broken Heart ....Hopeless Romantic		$3		Capitol 44399
10/14/89	38	13		6 My Sweet Love Ain't Around				album cut
				from the album Somewhere Between on Capitol 90237				
9/1/90	72	1		7 Under The Gun				album cut
12/15/90	72	4		8 All Things Made New Again				album cut
				above 2 from the album Moment Of Truth on Capitol 92653				
5/11/91	12	20		9 Hopelessly Yours				album cut
				LEE GREENWOOD with Suzy Bogguss				
				from the album A Perfect 10 on Capitol 95541				
9/14/91	12	20		10 Someday Soon ....Fear Of Flying		$3		Capitol 44772
1/4/92	9	20		11 Outbound Plane ....Yellow River Road		$3		Liberty 57753
4/4/92	9	20		12 Aces ....Hopelessly Yours		$3		Liberty 57764
8/15/92	6	20		13 Letting Go ....Music On The Wind		$3		Liberty 57801
12/5/92+	2¹	20		14 Drive South ....In The Day		$3		Liberty 56786
3/27/93	23	15		15 Heartache ....Lovin' A Hurricane		$3		Liberty 56972

DEBUT	PEAK	WKS	Gold	A-side	B-side	Pop	$	Pic	Label & Number
				BOGGUSS, Suzy — Cont'd					
8/7/93	5	20		16 Just Like The Weather	*No Green Eyes*		$3		Liberty 17495
12/4/93+	5	20		17 Hey Cinderella	*You'd Be The One*		$3		Liberty 17641
5/7/94	43	9		18 You Wouldn't Say That To A Stranger .... *Something Up My Sleeve*			$3		Liberty 17907
8/27/94	65	3		19 Souvenirs	*You'd Be The One*		$3		Liberty 18091
6/1/96	60	6		20 Give Me Some Wheels .... *Far And Away*			$3	▍	Capitol 58564
9/14/96	53	9		21 No Way Out .... *Letting Go*			$3	▍	Capitol 58590
3/22/97	57	9		22 She Said, He Heard .... *Feeling 'Bout You*			$3		Capitol 19508
				BOLT, Al **'76**					
				Born Almos Bolt in 1940 in Atlanta, Texas.					
2/28/76	85	6		1 I'm In Love With My Pet Rock .... *Paint Your World Happy* [N]			$5		Cin Kay 102
6/12/76	92	3		2 Family Man .... *If Today Were A Fish*			$5		Cin Kay 103
				BONAMY, James **'96**					
				Born on 4/29/72 in Winter Park, Florida; raised in Daytona Beach, Florida. Singer/songwriter/guitarist.					
11/11/95	64	4		1 Dog On A Toolbox .... *She's Got A Mind Of Her Own*			$3	▍	Epic 78090
12/16/95+	26	20		2 She's Got A Mind Of Her Own .... *Amy Jane*			$3	▍	Epic 78220
5/11/96	2¹	21		3 I Don't Think I Will	*Heartbreak School*		$3		Epic 78298
10/26/96+	27	20		4 All I Do Is Love Her .... *Jimmy And Jesus*			$3	▍	Epic 78396
4/5/97	31	20		5 The Swing .... *S:22 (dance mix)*			$3	▍	Epic 78560
8/16/97	65	6		6 Naked To The Pain .... *I Don't Think I Will*			$3	▍	Epic 78675
11/22/97	63	4		7 Little Blue Dot.. *(remix)*			$3	▍	Epic 78742
				BOND, Bobby **'72**					
				Born in Grand Rapids, Michigan.					
9/30/72	66	7		You Don't Mess Around With Jim .... *Looking For My Tracks*			$8		Hickory 1649
				#8 Pop hit for **Jim Croce** in 1972					
	★314★			**BOND, Johnny** **'65**					
				Born Cyrus Whitfield Bond on 6/1/15 in Enville, Oklahoma. Died of a heart attack on 6/22/78 (age 63). Singer/songwriter/guitarist. Regular on radio shows *Melody Ranch, Hollywood Barn Dance* and *Town Hall Party.* Acted in several western movies. Wrote book *The **Tex Ritter** Story.*					
				1)10 Little Bottles 2)So Round, So Firm, So Fully Packed 3)The Daughter Of Jole Blon					
2/22/47	4	1		1 Divorce Me C.O.D.	*Rainbow At Midnight*		$20		Columbia 37217
3/8/47	3	5		2 So Round, So Firm, So Fully Packed	*You Brought Sorrow To My Heart*		$20		Columbia 37255
8/16/47	4	3		3 The Daughter Of Jole Blon	*It's A Sin*		$20		Columbia 37566
				JOHNNY BOND and his Red River Valley Boys (above 3)					
6/12/48	9	6		4 Oklahoma Waltz .... *J:9 John's Other Wife*			$20		Columbia 38160
4/9/49	12	2		5 Till The End Of The World ....*J:12 Take It Or Leave It Baby*			$20		Columbia 20549
7/23/49	11	1		6 Tennessee Saturday Night.............. *J:11 A Heart Full Of Love (For A Handful Of Kisses)*			$20		Columbia 20545
4/15/50	8	2		7 Love Song In 32 Bars .... *J:8 Tennessee, Kentucky And Alabam'*			$20		Columbia 20671
				JOHNNY BOND and his Red River Valley Boys					
8/4/51	7	3		8 Sick, Sober And Sorry .... *J:7 Tennessee Walking Horse*			$25		Columbia 4-20808
11/2/63	30	1		9 Three Sheets In The Wind .... *Let The Tears Begin*			$12		Starday 649
2/6/65	2⁴	21		10 10 Little Bottles	*Let It Be Me* [N]	43	$12		Starday 704
2/20/71	59	6		11 Here Come The Elephants .... *Take Me Back To Tulsa* [N]			$10		Starday 916
				BONNERS, The **'88**					
				Black vocal group from Cucamonga, California: Jim and wife Edith Bonner, with children Teresa, Cheryl, Kenny and Jim Jr.					
9/10/88	99	1		Way Beyond The Blue .... *You Haven't Tried Me*			$6		OL 126
				BONNIE & BUDDY — see GUITAR, Bonnie					
				BONNIE LOU **'53**					
				Born Mary Kath on 10/27/24 in Towanda, Illinois. Singer/guitarist. Regular on the WLW *Midwestern Hayride.*					
5/9/53	7	5		1 Seven Lonely Days .... *A:7 / S:8 / J:9 Just Out Of Reach*			$40		King 1192
				#5 Pop hit for **Georgia Gibbs** in 1953					
9/19/53	6	9		2 Tennessee Wig Walk .... *S:8 / J:6 Hand-Me-Down Heart*			$40		King 1237
				BONSALL, "Cat" Joe — see SAWYER BROWN					
				BOOKER, Jay **'87**					
				Born in Pensacola, Florida. Singer/songwriter/guitarist.					
5/2/87	61	8		Hot Red Sweater .... *Mary Mandolin*			$3		EMI America 8379
	★311★			**BOONE, Debby** **'80**					
				Born on 9/22/56 in Leonia, New Jersey. Daughter of **Pat Boone** and granddaughter of **Red Foley**. Worked with the Boone Family from 1969; sang with her sisters in gospel quartet. Went solo in 1977. Won the 1977 Best New Artist Grammy Award. Married Gabriel Ferrer, the son of singer Rosemary Clooney and actor Jose Ferrer, on 9/1/79.					
				1)Are You On The Road To Lovin' Me Again 2)You Light Up My Life 3)My Heart Has A Mind Of Its Own					
10/22/77	4	14	▲	1 You Light Up My Life	*Hasta Mañana*	❶¹⁰	$4		Warner/Curb 8455
				from the movie starring Didi Conn					
5/20/78	22	8		2 God Knows/		74			
4/29/78	33	11		3 Baby, I'm Yours		flip	$4	■	Warner/Curb 8554
11/18/78	61	4		4 In Memory Of Your Love .... *When You're Loved*			$4		Warner/Curb 8700
1/13/79	11	13		5 My Heart Has A Mind Of Its Own .... *I'd Rather Leave While I'm In Love*			$4		Warner/Curb 8739
				#1 Pop hit for **Connie Francis** in 1960					
5/26/79	25	10		6 Breakin' In A Brand New Broken Heart .... *When You're Loved*			$4		Warner/Curb 8814
				#7 Pop hit for **Connie Francis** in 1961					
9/1/79	41	7		7 See You In September .... *Jamie*			$4		Warner/Curb 49042
				#3 Pop hit for The Happenings in 1966					
11/10/79	48	6		8 Everybody's Somebody's Fool .... *I'll Never Say Goodbye*			$4		Warner/Curb 49107
				#1 Pop hit for **Connie Francis** in 1960					

DEBUT	PEAK	WKS	Gold	A-side (Chart Hit) ... B-side	Pop	$	Pic	Label & Number
				BOONE, Debby — Cont'd				
2/16/80	**❶**[1]	15		9 Are Are You On The Road To Lovin' Me Again _When It's Just You And Me_		$4		Warner/Curb 49176
7/26/80	**14**	13		10 Free To Be Lonely Again _Love Put A Song In My Heart_		$4		Warner/Curb 49281
11/8/80	**44**	10		11 Take It Like A Woman _I Wish I Could Hurt That Way Again_		$4		Warner/Curb 49585
2/7/81	**23**	12		12 Perfect Fool _Every Day I Have To Cry_		$4		Warner/Curb 49652
6/27/81	**46**	7		13 It'll Be Him _Too Many Rivers_		$4		Warner/Curb 49720
	★329★			**BOONE, Larry** **'88** Born on 6/7/56 in Cooper City, Florida. Singer/songwriter/guitarist. 1)Don't Give Candy To A Stranger 2)I Just Called To Say Goodbye Again 3)Wine Me Up				
7/26/86	**64**	9		1 Stranger Things Have Happened _Our Paths May Never Cross_		$3		Mercury 884858
10/25/86	**52**	9		2 She's The Trip That I've Been On _Honky Tonk Song_		$3		Mercury 888044
3/21/87	**48**	10		3 Back In The Swing Of Things Again _Bottom Dollar_		$3		Mercury 888427
6/6/87	**52**	8		4 I Talked A Lot About Leaving _I Don't Feel Much Like A Cowboy Tonight_		$3		Mercury 888598
12/19/87+	**44**	19		5 Roses In December _It's Too Late Now_		$3	■	Mercury 870086
4/9/88	**48**	10		6 Stop Me (If You've Heard This One Before) _Back In The Swing Of Things Again_		$3		Mercury 870267
6/18/88	**10**	19		7 Don't Give Candy To A Stranger _S:18 Back In The Swing Of Things Again_		$3		Mercury 870454
11/19/88+	**16**	21		8 I Just Called To Say Goodbye Again _A Reason For The Rain_		$3		Mercury 872046
3/25/89	**19**	14		9 Wine Me Up _Old Coyote Town_		$3		Mercury 872728
7/8/89	**39**	9		10 Fool's Paradise _Under A Lone Star Moon_		$3		Mercury 874538
3/17/90	**75**	1		11 Everybody Wants To Be Hank Williams _Lovesick Blues_		$3		Mercury 876426
3/9/91	**57**	8		12 I Need A Miracle _Rock On The Road_		$3	▌	Columbia 73710
5/25/91	**34**	20		13 To Be With You _I Still Do_		$3		Columbia 73813
4/24/93	**65**	5		14 Get In Line _Watermelon Time In Georgia_ "live" recording		$3	▌	Columbia 74913
				BOONE, Pat **'76** Born Charles Eugene Boone on 6/1/34 in Jacksonville, Florida. Married Red Foley's daughter, Shirley, in 1954. Charted 60 pop hits from 1955-69. Father of Debby Boone.				
4/5/75	**72**	7		1 Indiana Girl _Young Girl_		$5		Melodyland 6005
9/27/75	**84**	6		2 I'd Do It With You _Yester-Me, Yester-You, Yesterday_ PAT BOONE with SHIRLEY BOONE		$5		Melodyland 6018
7/17/76	**34**	10		3 Texas Woman _It's Gone_		$5		Hitsville 6037
10/16/76	**86**	4		4 Oklahoma Sunshine _Won't Be Home Tonight_		$5		Hitsville 6042
11/15/80	**60**	6		5 Colorado Country Morning _What Ever Happened To Good Old Honky Tonk_		$4		Warner/Curb 49596
				BOOTH, Larry **'78** Singer/songwriter/bassist. Brother of Tony Booth. Member of Gene Watson's band.				
5/27/78	**99**	2		I See Love In Your Eyes _Cheater_		$7		Cream 7823
	★351★			**BOOTH, Tony** **'72** Born on 2/7/43 in Tampa, Florida. Singer/songwriter/guitarist. Brother of Larry Booth. Member of Gene Watson's band. 1)The Key's In The Mailbox 2)Lonesome 7-7203 3)A Whole Lot Of Somethin'				
3/28/70	**67**	3		1 Irma Jackson _One Too Many Times_ written by Merle Haggard		$7		MGM 14112
12/4/71+	**45**	12		2 Cinderella _Somebody Called L.A._		$6		Capitol 3214
3/25/72	**15**	15		3 The Key's In The Mailbox _The Devil Made Me Do That_		$6		Capitol 3269
7/8/72	**18**	12		4 A Whole Lot Of Somethin' _Nobody's Fool But Yours_		$6		Capitol 3356
9/30/72	**16**	13		5 Lonesome 7-7203 _Congratulations, You're Absolutely Right_		$6		Capitol 3441
1/27/73	**32**	10		6 When A Man Loves A Woman (The Way That I Love You) _Just A Man_		$5		Capitol 3515
4/28/73	**41**	8		7 Loving You _What A Liar I Am_		$5		Capitol 3582
7/7/73	**49**	6		8 Old Faithful _Don't Let True Love Slip Away_		$5		Capitol 3639
10/6/73	**47**	11		9 Secret Love _Someday I'm Gonna Go To Mexico_ #1 Pop hit for Doris Day in 1954		$5		Capitol 3723
12/29/73+	**49**	11		10 Happy Hour _Midnight Race_ #6-8 & 10: written by Buck Owens		$5		Capitol 3795
4/20/74	**84**	6		11 Lonely Street _It Never Will Be Over For Me_ #5 Pop hit for Andy Williams in 1959		$5		Capitol 3853
8/31/74	**27**	13		12 Workin' At The Car Wash Blues _That Loving Feeling_ #32 Pop hit for Jim Croce in 1974		$5		Capitol 3943
12/28/74+	**72**	8		13 Watch Out For Lucy _Good As Gone_		$5		Capitol 3994
5/21/77	**95**	2		14 Letting Go _Nothing Seems To Work Anymore_		$4		United Artists 962
	★350★			**BORCHERS, Bobby** **'77** Born in Cincinnati; raised in Kentucky. Singer/songwriter. 1)Cheap Perfume And Candlelight 2)Whispers 3)What A Way To Go				
3/6/76	**29**	10		1 Someone's With Your Wife Tonight, Mister _Hobo's Delight_		$5		Playboy 6065
8/21/76	**32**	9		2 They Don't Make 'Em Like That Anymore _I Can't Keep My Hands Off Of You_		$5		Playboy 6083
12/4/76+	**12**	15		3 Whispers _Just For A Minute_		$5		Playboy 6092
5/14/77	**7**	14		4 Cheap Perfume And Candlelight _Hobo's Delight_		$5		Playboy 5803
9/3/77	**18**	11		5 What A Way To Go _Lunch-Time Lovers_		$5		Playboy 5816
12/10/77+	**18**	13		6 I Promised Her A Rainbow _Brass Buckles_		$5		Playboy 5823
4/8/78	**23**	10		7 I Like Ladies In Long Black Dresses _Shawn_		$5		Playboy 5827
8/12/78	**20**	11		8 Sweet Fantasy _You Are Merely_		$4		Epic 50585
1/13/79	**32**	8		9 Wishing I Had Listened To Your Song _I've Had A Lovely Time_		$4		Epic 50650
5/5/79	**43**	8		10 I Just Wanna Feel The Magic _Old Emotional Me_		$4		Epic 50687
2/21/87	**80**	3		11 It Was Love What It Was		$6		Longhorn 3002
5/2/87	**86**	2		12 (I Remember When I Thought) Whiskey Was A River _It Was Love What It Was_		$6		Longhorn 3003

BOTTOMS, Dennis '85
Born on 8/28/54 in Springfield, Illinois. Singer/songwriter/banjo player.

DEBUT	PEAK	WKS		A-side / B-side	$	Label & Number
4/27/85	74	7	1	Did I Stay Too Long .... *Pick A Little Boogie*	$3	Warner 29035
8/3/85	80	5	2	Bring On The Sunshine .... *Gone But Not Forgotten*	$3	Warner 28944

BOUCHER, Jessica — see MERRILL and JESSICA / STAMPLEY, Joe

BOWES, Margie '59
Born on 3/18/41 in Roxboro, North Carolina. Singer/actress. Acted in the movie *The Gold Guitar*. Once married to Doyle Wilburn of the Wilburn Brothers.

3/23/59	10	16	1	Poor Old Heartsick Me *Blue Dream*	$15	Hickory 1094
8/31/59	15	14	2	My Love And Little Me .... *Sweet Night Of Love*	$15	Hickory 1102
7/24/61	21	6	3	Little Miss Belong To No One .... *Bitter Sweet Kisses*	$10	Mercury 71845
1/11/64	33	4	4	Our Things.. *There's Gotta Be A Way*	$8	Decca 31557
5/23/64	26	7	5	Understand Your Gal .... *You Can Be Replaced*	$8	Decca 31606
				answer to "Understand Your Man" by **Johnny Cash**		

BOWLING, Roger '81
Born in Harlan, Kentucky. Died on 12/26/82 (age 38). Singer/songwriter/guitarist.

6/10/78	96	5	1	Dance With Me Molly	$7	Louisiana Hay. 783
9/16/78	90	5	2	A Loser's Just A Learner (On His Way To Better Things)...................... *Lucille*	$7	Louisiana Hay. 784
2/23/80	55	7	3	Friday Night Fool .... *There'll Never Be A Love Song (As Beautiful As You)*	$5	NSD 37
5/31/80	78	3	4	The Diplomat .... *I'm Looking For A Lonely Woman*	$5	NSD 46
8/23/80	52	8	5	Long Arm Of The Law.. *I Can't Get Over You*	$5	NSD 58
11/29/80+	30	15	6	Yellow Pages *I Don't Feel At Home (At Home Anymore)*	$5	NSD 71
				later released on Mercury 57042 ($4)		
4/11/81	50	8	7	A Little Bit Of Heaven .... *She Can't Break It To Her Heart*	$4	Mercury 57049

BOWMAN, Billy Bob '72
Pseudonym for producer/DJ Biff Collie. Born Hiram Abiff Collie on 11/25/26 in Little Rock, Arkansas; raised in San Antonio, Texas. Died on 2/19/92 (age 65). Formerly married to **Shirley Collie**.

11/4/72	55	5		Miss Pauline .... *Showers*	$6	United Artists 50957
				BILLY BOB BOWMAN and The Beaumont Bag & Burlap Company		

BOWMAN, Don '64
Born on 8/26/37 in Lubbock, Texas. Singer/songwriter/guitarist/comedian. Discovered by **Chet Atkins**. Original host of radio's *American Country Countdown*.

7/25/64	14	16	1	Chit Akins, Make Me A Star *I Never Did Finish That Song* [N]	$8	RCA Victor 8384
6/18/66	49	2	2	Giddyup Do-Nut...*Freda On The Freeway* [N]	$8	RCA Victor 8811
				parody of "Giddyup Go" by **Red Sovine**		
12/3/66	73	2	3	Surely Not...*Dear Sister* [N]	$8	RCA Victor 8990
2/24/68	72	2	4	For Loving You .... *Baby It's Cold Outside* [N]	$8	RCA Victor 9415
				SKEETER DAVIS AND DON BOWMAN		
10/5/68	74	2	5	Folsom Prison Blues #2 .... *House Of The Setting Sun* [N]	$8	RCA Victor 9617
				parody of "Folsom Prison Blues" by **Johnny Cash**		
5/17/69	70	5	6	Poor Old Ugly Gladys Jones.................................*Boll Weevil Air Lines* [N]	$8	RCA Victor 0133
				DON BOWMAN AND FRIENDS		
				Bobby Bare, Waylon Jennings and Willie Nelson (guest vocals)		

BOWSER, Donnie '89
Male singer from Miami.

9/16/89	90	1		Falling For You .... *You've Got My Arms To Come Back To*	$6	Ridgewood 3002

BOXCAR WILLIE '82
Born Lecil Travis Martin on 9/1/31 in Sterratt, Texas. Singer/songwriter/guitarist. Adopted his on-stage hobo attire in 1976. Joined the *Grand Ole Opry* in 1981.
1)Bad News 2)The Man I Used To Be 3)Train Medley

4/26/80	95	3	1	Train Medley ....*Lonesome Hobo*	$7	Column One 1012
				Fireball Mail/Train of Love/Walking Cane/Wreck of the Old #97/Orange Blossom Special/Wabash Cannonball/Night Train to Memphis; also see #6 below		
3/13/82	36	12	2	Bad News *Lefty Left Us Lonely*	$5	Main Street 951
7/10/82	77	5	3	We Made Memories.. *To My Baby I'm A Big Star All The Time*	$5	Main Street 952
				BOXCAR WILLIE and PENNY DeHAVEN		
11/13/82	70	6	4	Keep On Rollin' Down The Line/		
9/11/82	80	4	5	Last Train To Heaven	$5	Main Street 953
4/16/83	61	8	6	Train Medley/ [R]		
				same version as #1 above		
2/5/83	76	6	7	Country Music Nightmare...[N]	$5	Main Street 954
12/24/83+	44	12	8	The Man I Used To Be.. *No More Trains To Ride*	$5	Main Street 93017
5/5/84	87	3	9	Not On The Bottom Yet .... *It Ain't No Record*	$5	Main Street 93020
7/14/84	69	6	10	Luther .... *(long version)*	$5	Main Street 93021

BOYD, Bill '45
Born on 9/28/14 in Fannin County, Texas. Died on 12/7/77 (age 63). Singer/guitarist. Not to be confused with William "Hopalong Cassidy" Boyd. The Cowboy Ramblers included his younger brother Jim Boyd (guitar), Ken Pitts (fiddle), Knocky Parker (piano) and Marvin "Smoky" Montgomery (banjo). Group appeared in several western movies.

9/8/45	4	2	1	Shame On You *Home Coming Waltz*	$30	Bluebird 33-0530
8/24/46	5	1	2	New Steel Guitar Rag *New Spanish Two-Step*	$20	RCA Victor 20-1907
				BILL BOYD and his Cowboy Ramblers (above 2)		

BOYD, Jimmy '52
Born on 1/9/40 in McComb, Mississippi. Played "Howard Meachum" on TV's *Bachelor Father*.

12/20/52	7	3	●	I Saw Mommy Kissing Santa Claus *A:7 / J:7 Thumbelina* [X-N]	**❶²** $20	Columbia 4-39871

| --- | --- | --- | --- | --- | --- | --- | --- | --- |
				BOYD, Mike **'78**				
				Male singer from Houston.				
5/22/76	98	2		1 The Leaving Was Easy .... *Time Wounds All Heels*		$6		Claridge 417
8/20/77	93	6		2 Stop And Think It Over .... *Whiskey*		$6		MBI 4816
				#8 Pop hit for Dale & Grace in 1964				
2/11/78	80	5		3 Love And Hate .... *Birds And Bees*		$6		Inergi 305
				BOYER TWINS, The **'80**				
				Twin brothers Gene and Dean Boyer.				
2/9/80	91	4		Three Little Words		$6		Sabre 4516
				BOY HOWDY **'94**				
				Group from Los Angeles: brothers Cary and Larry Parks (guitars), **Jeffrey Steele** (vocals, bass) and Hugh Wright (drums). Cary and Larry are the sons of noted bluegrass fiddler Ray Parks.				
7/4/92	43	16		1 Our Love Was Meant To Be				album cut
6/19/93	12	20		2 A Cowboy's Born With A Broken Heart				album cut
				above 2 from the album *Welcome To Howdywood* on Curb 77562				
11/6/93+	4	20		3 She'd Give Anything				album cut
				#28 Pop hit for Gerald Levert in 1994				
4/2/94	2[1]	20		4 They Don't Make 'Em Like That Anymore				album cut
				above 2 from the album *She'd Give Anything* on Curb 77656				
12/10/94+	23	20		5 True To His Word .... *I'm Already Lovin' You Too Much*		$3	■	Curb 76934
7/1/95	48	10		6 She Can't Love You/				
				from the album *Born That Way* on Curb 77691				
4/8/95	57	6		7 Bigger Fish To Fry		$3	■	Curb 76940
				BRADDOCK, Bobby **'79**				
				Born on 8/5/40 in Lakeland, Florida. Singer/songwriter/pianist.				
7/29/67	74	4		1 I Know How To Do It .... *Get Along*		$7		MGM 13737
1/11/69	62	6		2 The Girls In Country Music .... *Put Me Back Together Again*		$7		MGM 14017
6/2/79	58	5		3 Between The Lines .... *The Happy Hour*		$5		Elektra 46038
2/9/80	87	3		4 Nag, Nag, Nag .... *Rainy Florida Afternoon* [N]		$5		Elektra 46585
				BRADFORD, Keith **'78**				
				Born Arthur Guilbeault in Burrillville, Rhode Island.				
6/17/78	83	4		1 Lonely People .... *A Whole Lot Of Crying*		$6		Mu-Sound 421
3/17/79	86	2		2 Lonely Coming Down .... *A Whole Lot Of Crying*		$6		Scorpion 0572
				BRADING, Susie **'84**				
				Born Susan Storment in Lincoln, Illinois.				
2/4/84	94	3		Dream Lover .... *Standing On The Outside*		$6		Riddle 1010
				BRADLEY, Owen **'50**				
				Born on 10/15/15 in Westmoreland, Tennessee. Died on 1/7/98 (age 82). Music director at WSM-Nashville from 1940-58. Nashville producer for Decca from 1947. Country A&R director for Decca from 1958-68. Vice president of MCA from 1968. Elected to the Country Music Hall of Fame in 1974.				
12/3/49+	7	4		Blues Stay Away From Me A:7 / J:8 / S:9 *Fairy Tales* **OWEN BRADLEY QUINTET** Jack Shook and Dottie Dillard (vocals); #36 Pop hit for **Ace Cannon** in 1962	11	$15		Coral 60107 (**78**)
				BRADSHAW, Carolyn **'53**				
8/22/53	10	1		Marriage Of Mexican Joe J:10 *Baby, Then You're Catchin' On* sequel to "Mexican Joe" by Jim Reeves		$30		Abbott 141
				BRADSHAW, Terry **'76**				
				Born on 9/2/48 in Shreveport, Louisiana. Pro football quarterback with the Pittsburgh Steelers from 1970-83. Acted in the movies *Hooper, Smokey and The Bandit II* and *Cannonball Run*.				
1/31/76	17	13		1 I'm So Lonesome I Could Cry .... *Making Plans*	91	$5		Mercury 73760
7/10/76	90	4		2 The Last Word In Lonesome Is Me .... *Less And Less*		$5		Mercury 73808
4/26/80	73	5		3 Until You .... *Dimestore Jesus*		$6	■	Benson 2001
				BRANDON, T.C. **'89**				
				Born in Fullerton, California. Female singer.				
9/2/89	93	1		You Belong To Me		$6	■	Bear 2006
				#1 Pop hit for Jo Stafford in 1952				
				BRANDT, Paul **'96**				
				Born on 7/21/72 in Calgary, Alberta, Canada. Singer/songwriter.				
3/9/96	5	22		1 My Heart Has A History S:10 *Calm Before The Storm*		$3	■	Reprise 17683
6/8/96	2[2]	23		2 I Do S:3 *(instrumental)*	102	$3	■	Reprise 17616
11/16/96+	39	20		3 I Meant To Do That .... *All Over Me*		$3		Reprise 17493
3/29/97	38	15		4 Take It From Me .... *12 Step Recovery*		$3		Reprise 17381
10/18/97	45	10		5 A Little In Love				album cut
				from the album *Outside The Frame* on Reprise 46635				
				BRANE, Sherry **'79**				
12/9/78+	56	7		1 It's My Party		$6		Oak 1013
				#1 Pop hit for Lesley Gore in 1963				
5/17/80	83	2		2 Little Girls Need Daddies .... *I'm Gonna Make You Love Me*		$6		Tejas 1015
10/11/80	86	2		3 Falling In Trouble Again .... *I'm Gonna Make You Love Me*		$6		e.i.o. 1129
				BRANNON, Kippi **'81**				
				Born Kippi Brinkley in 1966 in Goodlettsville, Tennessee. Female singer.				
9/26/81	37	11		1 Slowly .... *Dreamin*		$4		MCA 51166
4/3/82	55	7		2 If I Could See You Tonight .... *I'm So Afraid Of Losing You Again*		$4		MCA 52023
9/11/82	87	4		3 He Don't Make Me Cry .... *Piece Of My Heart*		$4		MCA 52096

BRANNON, Kippi — Cont'd

| 2/1/97 | 42 | 20 | 4 Daddy's Little Girl/ | S:6 | 120 | | | |
| 6/28/97 | 53 | 8 | 5 I'd Be With You .... S:8 | 120 | $3 | ▪ | Curb/Universal 56092 |

BREAKFAST BARRY — see GRANT, Barry

BRENNAN, Walter   '62
Born on 7/25/1894 in Swampscott, Massachusetts. Died on 9/21/74 (age 80). Acted in several movies. Played "Grandpa" on TV's *The Real McCoys*.

| 5/5/62 | 3 | 13 | Old Rivers   *The Epic Ride Of John H. Glenn* [S] | 5 | $10 | | Liberty 55436 |

The Johnny Mann Singers (backing vocals)

BRENTWOOD   '84
Vocal trio from Nashville: Jay Kencke, Kenny Wrinn and Ron Freeman.

| 10/1/83 | 96 | 1 | 1 Love The One You're With .... | | $6 | | Hot Schatz 0051 |

#14 Pop hit for Stephen Stills in 1971

| 3/17/84 | 80 | 3 | 2 Anything For Your Love .... | | $6 | | Hot Schatz 0052 |

BRESH, Tom   '76
Born on 2/23/48 in Hollywood. Singer/songwriter/guitarist/actor. Son of **Merle Travis**. Worked as a stuntman as a child. Member of **Hank Penny**'s band. Appeared in the musicals *Finian's Rainbow, Harvey* and *The Music Man*.

4/24/76	6	16	1 Home Made Love *California Old Time Song*		$6		Farr 004
8/14/76	17	11	2 Sad Country Love Song .... *While We Make Love Together*		$6		Farr 009
11/20/76+	33	11	3 Hey Daisy (Where Have All The Good Times Gone) .... *Where Was I*		$6		Farr 012
6/11/77	57	7	4 Until I Met You .... *Wonder What It's Like*		$4		ABC/Dot 17703
9/24/77	48	7	5 That Old Cold Shoulder .... *Start All Over Again*		$4		ABC/Dot 17720
1/28/78	78	4	6 Smoke! Smoke! Smoke! (That Cigarette) .... *My Lickskillet, Indiana Home*		$4		ABC/Dot 17738
4/29/78	74	6	7 Ways Of A Woman In Love .... *Huckleberry Week-End*		$4		ABC 12352
8/12/78	84	4	8 First Encounter Of A Close Kind .... *Woman Who Will*		$4		ABC 12389
12/11/82	77	5	9 When It Comes To Love .... *Somebody Like You*		$4	▪	Liberty 1487

THOM BRESH & LANE BRODY

BR5-49   '96
Group based in Nashville: Gary Bennett (vocals, guitar), Chuck Mead (guitar), Don Herron (mandolin), "Smilin'" Jay McDowell (bass) and "Hawk" Shaw Wilson (drums). Group named after the fictional telephone number used by **Junior Samples** on TV's *Hee-Haw*.

9/21/96	44	20	1 Cherokee Boogie .... *I Ain't Never*		$3		Arista 13039
1/18/97	68	1	2 Even If It's Wrong .... *Crazy Arms*		$3		Arista 13061
2/22/97	61	6	3 Little Ramona (Gone Hillbilly Nuts) .... *Hickory Wind*		$3		Arista 13046

BRICKMAN, Jim — see McBRIDE, Martina / RAYE, Collin

BRILEY, Jebry Lee   '82
Featured female singer with Harry James's big band as Judy Branch.

| 10/13/79 | 89 | 3 | 1 I Just Wonder Where He Could Be Tonight .... *(And) Robin Danced* | | $6 | | IBC 0004 |

HILKA & JEBRY

| 2/13/82 | 80 | 4 | 2 Let Your Fingers Do The Walkin' .... *Riders & Drivers* | | $6 | | Paid 141 |

★259★   **BRITT, Elton**   '46
Born James Britt Baker on 6/27/13 in Marshall, Arkansas. Died on 6/23/72 (age 58). Singer/songwriter/guitarist. Appeared in the movies *Laramie, The Last Doggie* and *The Prodigal Son*.
1)*Someday* 2)*Quicksilver* 3)*Wave To Me, My Lady*

1/27/45	7	1	1 I'm A Convict With Old Glory In My Heart *The Best Part Of Travel*		$30		Bluebird 33-0517
1/26/46	2⁵	18	2 Someday *Weep No More, My Darlin'*		$30		Bluebird 33-0521
3/16/46	3	9	3 Wave To Me, My Lady/	19			
4/13/46	4	1	4 Blueberry Lane		$25		Victor 20-1789
5/11/46	5	1	5 Detour *Make Room In Your Heart For A Friend*		$20		RCA Victor 20-1817
7/27/46	6	1	6 Blue Texas Moonlight *Thanks For The Heartaches*		$20		RCA Victor 20-1873

ELTON BRITT and The Skytoppers

| 8/24/46 | 4 | 1 | 7 Gotta Get Together With My Gal   *Rogue River Valley* | | $20 | | RCA Victor 20-1927 |
| 10/30/48 | 6 | 6 | 8 Chime Bells   S:6 / J:12 *Put My Little Shoes Away* | | $20 | | RCA Victor 20-3090 |

ELTON BRITT and The Skytoppers
45 rpm: 48-0143

| 3/19/49 | 4 | 12 | 9 Candy Kisses   S:4 / J:12 *You'll Be Sorry From Now On* | | $20 | | RCA Victor 21-0006 |

ELTON BRITT and The Skytoppers
45 rpm: 48-0218

| 2/4/50 | 7 | 4 | 10 Beyond The Sunset   A:7 *The Game Of Broken Hearts* | | $25 | | RCA Victor 47-3105 |

THE THREE SUNS with ROSALIE ALLEN and ELTON BRITT
78 rpm: 20-3599; #71 Pop hit for Pat Boone in 1959

| 2/25/50 | 3 | 10 | 11 Quicksilver   A:3 / J:6 / S:9 *The Yodel Blues* | | $25 | | RCA Victor 48-0168 |

ELTON BRITT and ROSALIE ALLEN with The Skytoppers
78 rpm: 21-0157

| 5/4/68 | 26 | 10 | 12 The Jimmie Rodgers Blues .... *Singin' In The Pines* | | $8 | | RCA Victor 9503 |
| 1/4/69 | 71 | 4 | 13 The Bitter Taste .... *My Carolina Sunshine Girl* | | $8 | | RCA Victor 9658 |

BROCK, Joe   '76
Born in Lake Placid, Florida.

| 5/29/76 | 98 | 3 | Everything You'd Never Want To Be .... *That's The Way My Woman Loves Me* | | $7 | | Ronnie 7601 |

★396★   **BRODY, Lane**   '84
Born Lynn Connie Voorlas in Oak Park, Illinois; raised in Racine, Wisconsin. Singer/actress.
1)*The Yellow Rose* 2)*Over You* 3)*He Burns Me Up*

4/24/82	60	6	1 He's Taken .... *My Side Of The Bed*		$4		Liberty 1457
7/17/82	61	7	2 More Nights .... *My Side Of The Bed*		$4		Liberty 1470
12/11/82	77	5	3 When It Comes To Love .... *Somebody Like You*		$4	▪	Liberty 1487

THOM BRESH & LANE BRODY

BRODY, Lane — Cont'd

DEBUT	PEAK	WKS	A-side / B-side	$	Pic	Label & Number
5/21/83	15	19	4 Over You........................*My Side Of The Bed*	$4	■	Liberty 1498
			from the movie *Tender Mercies* starring Robert Duvall			
11/19/83	60	7	5 It's Another Silent Night ....*It's A Bad Night For Good Girls*	$4		Liberty 1509
2/4/84	❶¹	22	6 The Yellow Rose *Say When*	$3		Warner 29375
			JOHNNY LEE with Lane Brody			
			same melody as "The Yellow Rose Of Texas" with new lyrics; from the TV series starring Cybill Shepherd			
5/12/84	59	7	7 Hanging On...........................*If I Were Loving You Now*	$4		Liberty 1519
8/25/84	81	5	8 Alibis ....*One Heart Away (From Being In Love)*	$4		EMI America 8218
5/18/85	29	14	9 He Burns Me Up........................S:29 / A:29 *Memory Now*	$4	■	EMI America 8266
9/7/85	51	10	10 Baby's Eyes ....*Anything But My Baby*	$4		EMI America 8283
4/5/86	50	8	11 I Could Get Used To This ....*It Ain't The Leaving*	$3		Warner 28747
			JOHNNY LEE & LANE BRODY			

BROKOP, Lisa   '95
Born on 6/6/73 in Surrey, British Columbia, Canada.

DEBUT	PEAK	WKS	A-side / B-side	$	Pic	Label & Number
8/20/94	52	10	1 Give Me A Ring Sometime....................*Let Me Live Another Day*	$4	▮	Patriot 18094
11/26/94+	52	20	2 Take That *Every Little Girl's Dream*	$4	▮	Patriot 58310
7/29/95	60	7	3 Who Needs You/			
4/15/95	64	5	4 One Of Those Nights	$3	▮	Capitol 58435
11/25/95+	55	12	5 She Can't Save Him ....*From The Heart*	$3	▮	Capitol 58502
3/23/96	63	7	6 Before He Kissed Me ....*Every Little Girl's Dream*	$3	▮	Capitol 58557

BROOKS, Garth ★48★   '93

Born Troyal Garth Brooks on 2/7/62 in Luba, Oklahoma; raised in Yukon, Oklahoma. Singer/songwriter/guitarist. His mother, Colleen Carroll, recorded with Capitol in 1954 and was a regular on **Red Foley**'s *Ozark Jubilee* TV show. Attended Oklahoma State University on a track scholarship. Played local clubs and worked as a bouncer. Joined the *Grand Ole Opry* in 1990. CMA Awards: 1990 Horizon Award; 1991, 1992, 1997 & 1998 Entertainer of the Year.

1)*Friends In Low Places* 2)*What She's Doing Now* 3)*The Dance* 4)*Longneck Bottle* 5)*Unanswered Prayers*

DEBUT	PEAK	WKS	A-side / B-side	$	Label & Number
3/25/89	8	26	1 Much Too Young (To Feel This Damn Old) *Alabama Clay*	$4	Capitol 44342
9/9/89	❶¹	26	2 If Tomorrow Never Comes *Much Too Young (To Feel This Damn Old)*	$3	Capitol 44430
1/20/90	2¹	25	3 Not Counting You *Cowboy Bill*	$3	Capitol 44492
5/5/90	❶³	21	4 The Dance *I Know One*	$3	Capitol 44629
8/18/90	❶⁴	20	5 Friends In Low Places *Nobody Gets Off In This Town*	$3	Capitol 44647
			CMA Award: Single of the Year		
11/3/90+	❶²	20	6 Unanswered Prayers *Alabama Clay*	$3	Capitol 44650
2/9/91	❶¹	20	7 Two Of A Kind, Workin' On A Full House *The Dance*	$3	Capitol 44701
5/18/91	❶²	20	8 The Thunder Rolls *Victim Of The Game*	$3	Capitol 44727
8/17/91	3	20	9 Rodeo *New Way To Fly*	$3	Capitol 44771
10/19/91	❶²	20	10 Shameless *Against The Grain*	$3	Capitol 44800
			first recorded by Billy Joel on his 1989 album *Storm Front*		
1/4/92	❶⁴	20	11 What She's Doing Now *Friends In Low Places*	$3	Liberty 57733
2/1/92	3	20	12 Papa Loved Mama *New Way To Fly*	$3	Liberty 57734
3/21/92	66	20	13 Against The Grain		album cut
			from the album *Ropin' The Wind* on Capitol 96330		
5/2/92	❶¹	20	14 The River *We Bury The Hatchet*	$3	Liberty 57765
9/12/92	12	20	15 We Shall Be Free ....*Night Rider's Lament*	$3	Liberty 57994
10/17/92+	❶¹	20	16 Somewhere Other Than The Night *Mr. Right*	$3	Liberty 56824
12/26/92	48	4	17 The Old Man's Back In Town..............*Santa Looked A Lot Like Daddy* [X]	$3	Liberty 57893
2/6/93	2¹	20	18 Learning To Live Again *Walking After Midnight*	$3	Liberty 56973
2/13/93	73	1	19 Dixie Chicken		album cut
			from the album *The Chase* on Liberty 98743		
5/8/93	❶¹	20	20 That Summer *Dixie Chicken*	$3	Liberty 17324
8/7/93	❶²	20	21 Ain't Going Down (Til The Sun Comes Up) *Kickin' And Screamin'*	$3	Liberty 17496
9/11/93	❶¹	20	22 American Honky-Tonk Bar Association *Everytime That It Rains*	$3	Liberty 17639
9/18/93+	3	20	23 Standing Outside The Fire *Cold Shoulder*	$3	Liberty 17802
9/18/93	70	5	24 Callin' Baton Rouge		album cut
9/18/93	74	1	25 One Night A Day		album cut
			above 2 from the album *In Pieces* on Liberty 80857		
5/14/94	7	19	26 One Night A Day *Mr. Blue* [R]	$3	Liberty 17972
7/16/94	67	11	27 Hard Luck Woman..		album cut
			#15 Pop hit for Kiss in 1977; from the album *Kiss My Ass: Classic Kiss Regrooved* on Mercury 522123		
8/13/94	2¹	15	28 Callin' Baton Rouge *Same Old Story* [R]	$3	Liberty 18136
11/26/94+	49	20	29 The Red Strokes *Burning Bridges*	$3	Liberty 18554
12/31/94	70	1	30 White Christmas ....[X]	$3	Liberty 57892
			#1 Pop hit for **Bing Crosby** in 1942		
9/9/95	❶¹	20	31 She's Every Woman *The Cowboy Song*	$3	Capitol 18842
11/25/95	23	14	32 The Fever...........................*The Night Will Only Know*	$3	Capitol 18948
			first recorded by Aerosmith on their 1993 album *Get A Grip*		
12/9/95+	❶¹	20	33 The Beaches Of Cheyenne *Ireland*	$3	Capitol 19022
12/9/95+	5	32	34 It's Midnight Cinderella		album cut
12/9/95+	19	20	35 The Change		album cut

DEBUT	PEAK	WKS	Gold	A-side (Chart Hit)..B-side	Pop	$	Pic	Label & Number
				BROOKS, Garth — Cont'd				
12/9/95	64	4	36	The Old Stuff				album cut
12/9/95	71	1	37	Rollin'				album cut
12/9/95	75	1	38	That Ol' Wind				album cut
10/5/96	4	19	39	That Ol' Wind [R]				album cut
				#34-39: from the album *Fresh Horses* on Capitol 32080				
8/23/97	2²	20	40	In Another's Eyes *I Want To Live Again*		$3		MCA 72021
				TRISHA YEARWOOD AND GARTH BROOKS				
11/22/97	❶³	20	41	Longneck Bottle *Rollin'*		$3		Capitol 19851
12/6/97+	❶¹	28	42	Two Piña Coladas				album cut
12/6/97+	2¹	20	43	She's Gonna Make It				album cut
12/6/97+	41	8	44	Belleau Wood				album cut
12/6/97	52	2	45	Cowboy Cadillac				album cut
12/6/97	57	2	46	Take The Keys To My Heart				album cut
12/6/97	59	2	47	How You Ever Gonna Know				album cut
12/6/97	62	2	48	Do What You Gotta Do				album cut
12/6/97	67	1	49	You Move Me				album cut
12/6/97	68	1	50	A Friend To Me				album cut
12/6/97	70	1	51	I Don't Have To Wonder				album cut
				#42-51: from the album *Sevens* on Capitol 56599				
12/27/97	56	2	52	Santa Looked A Lot Like Daddy/ [X]				
				first recorded by Buck Owens in 1965				
12/27/97	59	2	53	The Old Man's Back In Town [X-R]		$3		Liberty 57893
				BROOKS, Karen **'83**				
				Born on 4/29/54 in Dallas. Female singer.				
7/31/82	17	19	1	New Way Out *Country Girl*		$4		Warner 29958
11/20/82+	❶¹	20	2	Faking Love *Reno And Me*		$4		Warner/Curb 29854
				T.G. SHEPPARD AND KAREN BROOKS				
2/5/83	21	14	3	If That's What You're Thinking *Every Beat Of My Heart*		$4		Warner 29789
6/18/83	30	12	4	Walk On *Every Beat Of My Heart*		$4		Warner 29644
4/28/84	40	11	5	Born To Love You *A Little Common Kindness*		$4		Warner 29302
7/21/84	19	16	6	Tonight I'm Here With Someone Else *Give It Up*		$4		Warner 29225
1/5/85	63	8	7	A Simple I Love You *Give It Up*		$4		Warner 29154
7/13/85	45	9	8	I Will Dance With You *Too Bad For Love*		$4		Warner 28979
				KAREN BROOKS with Johnny Cash				
				BROOKS, Kix **'83**				
				Born Leon Eric Brooks III on 5/12/55 in Shreveport, Louisiana. Joined with **Ronnie Dunn** in 1991 in duo **Brooks & Dunn**.				
9/10/83	73	4	1	Baby, When Your Heart Breaks Down		$6		Avion 103
1/28/89	87	2	2	Sacred Ground *Story Of My Life*		$4		Capitol 44275

BROOKS & DUNN ★101★ **'92**

Duo of **Kix Brooks** (b: 5/12/55 in Shreveport, Louisiana) and **Ronnie Dunn** (b: 6/1/53 in Coleman, Texas). Both sing and play guitar. CMA Awards: 1992, 1993, 1994, 1995, 1996, 1997 & 1998 Vocal Duo of the Year; 1996 Entertainer of the Year.

1)Boot Scootin' Boogie 2)My Maria 3)My Next Broken Heart 4)Neon Moon
5)You're Gonna Miss Me When I'm Gone

DEBUT	PEAK	WKS		A-side	Pop	$	Pic	Label & Number
6/22/91	❶²	20	1	Brand New Man *I'm No Good*		$3		Arista 2232
10/12/91	❶²	20	2	My Next Broken Heart *Boot Scootin' Boogie*		$3		Arista 12337
2/1/92	❶²	20	3	Neon Moon *Cheating On The Blues*		$3		Arista 12388
5/23/92	❶⁴	20	4	Boot Scootin' Boogie *(album version)*	50	$3	▌	Arista 12440
9/19/92	6	20	5	Lost And Found *Cool Drink Of Water*		$3		Arista 12460
2/6/93	4	20	6	Hard Workin' Man *Texas Women (Don't Stay Lonely Long)*		$3		Arista 12513
5/15/93	2²	20	7	We'll Burn That Bridge *Heartbroke Out Of My Mind*		$3	▌	Arista 12563
9/4/93	❶¹	20	8	She Used To Be Mine *That Ain't No Way To Go*		$3		Arista 12602
12/11/93+	2²	20	9	Rock My World (Little Country Girl) *(club mix)*	97	$3	▌	Arista 12636
3/5/94	73	4	10	Ride 'em High, Ride 'em Low				album cut
				from the movie *8 Seconds* starring Luke Perry; from the soundtrack on MCA 10927				
3/19/94	73	1	11	Corine, Corina				album cut
				ASLEEP AT THE WHEEL Featuring Brooks & Dunn				
				#9 Pop hit for Ray Peterson in 1961; from the album *Tribute To Bob Wills* on Liberty 81470				
4/9/94	❶¹	20	12	That Ain't No Way To Go *I Can't Put Out This Fire*		$3		Arista 12669
8/27/94	❶²	20	13	She's Not The Cheatin' Kind *She's The Kind Of Trouble*		$3		Arista 12740
11/12/94+	6	20	14	I'll Never Forgive My Heart *A Few Good Rides Away*		$3		Arista 12779
2/18/95	❶¹	20	15	Little Miss Honky Tonk *Silver And Gold*		$3	▌	Arista 12790
6/10/95	❶²	20	16	You're Gonna Miss Me When I'm Gone *If That's The Way You Want It*		$3		Arista 12831
9/23/95	5	20	17	Whiskey Under The Bridge *My Kind Of Crazy*		$3		Arista 12993
4/6/96	❶³	20	18	My Maria S:❶⁸ *Mama Don't Get Dressed Up For Nothing*	79	$3	▌	Arista 12993
				#9 Pop hit for B.W. Stevenson in 1973				
4/27/96	2²	20	19	I Am That Man S:8 *More Than A Margarita*		$3	▌	Arista 13018
9/14/96	13	20	20	Mama Don't Get Dressed Up For Nothing S:15 *Tequila Town*		$3	▌	Arista 13043
12/7/96+	❶¹	20	21	A Man This Lonely S:12 *One Heartache At A Time*	124	$3	▌	Arista 13066

BROOKS & DUNN — Cont'd

DEBUT	PEAK	WKS		A-side	B-side	Pop	$	Pic	Label & Number
3/22/97	8	20	22	Why Would I Say Goodbye	White Line Casanova		$3		Arista 13073
10/18/97+	2²	24	23	He's Got You/					
8/30/97	3	20	24	Honky Tonk Truth			$3		Arista 13101

BROOKS BROTHERS BAND   '85
Group from Dallas. Led by brothers Bill and Randy Brooks.

1/12/85	81	6		Hurry On Home			$6		Buckboard 115

BROTHER PHELPS   '93
Duo of brothers Ricky Lee (b: 10/8/53) and Doug (b: 12/16/60) Phelps, formerly with The Kentucky Headhunters.

7/3/93	6	20	1	Let Go	Everything Will Work Out Fine		$3	▌	Asylum 64614
11/13/93+	28	18	2	Were You Really Livin'	Playin' House		$3	▌	Asylum 64598
3/26/94	53	9	3	Eagle Over Angel	Let Go		$3	▌	Asylum 64558
9/3/94	62	5	4	Ever-Changing Woman	Watch Your Step		$3	▌	Asylum 64517
2/18/95	54	11	5	Anyway The Wind Blows	Lookout Mountain		$3	▌	Asylum 64461
6/3/95	65	6	6	Not So Different After All	Johnny		$3	▌	Asylum 64436

BROWN, Billy   '79
Born in 1956 in Port Orange, Florida.

12/15/79	95	3		What It Means To Be An American	Star Spangled Banner [S]		$6		Bernes 101

BROWN, Cooter   '95

12/16/95	71	1		Pure Bred Redneck	My Apologies		$3	▌	Reprise 17711

BROWN, Floyd   '83
Born in Greenwell Springs, Louisiana.

6/18/77	100	1	1	Let's Get Acquainted Again	But I Do		$5		ABC/Dot 17702
7/9/83	79	6	2	Kiss Me Just One More Time	Fools Like Me		$6		Magnum 1002

BROWN, Jim Ed ★79★   '76
Born on 4/1/34 in Sparkman, Arkansas. Singer/songwriter/guitarist. Recorded in duo with older sister **Maxine Brown** in 1953, joined by younger sister Bonnie in 1955 (recorded as **The Browns**). Began solo recording in 1965. Hosted TNN's *You Can Be A Star* and *Going Our Way*. Joined the *Grand Ole Opry* in 1963. CMA Award: 1977 Vocal Duo of the Year (with **Helen Cornelius**).

1)I Don't Want To Have To Marry You 2)Lying In Love With You
3)Saying Hello, Saying I Love You, Saying Goodbye 4)Pop A Top 5)Fools

JIM EDWARD BROWN:

7/10/65	33	8	1	I Heard From A Memory Last Night	Just To Satisfy You		$8		RCA Victor 8566
10/16/65	37	5	2	I'm Just A Country Boy	To Be Or Not To Be		$8		RCA Victor 8644
4/9/66	41	4	3	Regular On My Mind	The Mounties		$8		RCA Victor 8766
7/30/66	23	10	4	A Taste Of Heaven	Paint Me The Color Of Your Wall		$8		RCA Victor 8867
11/19/66	57	7	5	The Last Laugh	Party Girl		$8		RCA Victor 8997
2/4/67	18	11	6	You Can Have Her	If You Were Mine, Mary		$8		RCA Victor 9077
				#12 Pop hit for Roy Hamilton in 1961.					

JIM ED BROWN:

5/20/67	3	20	7	Pop A Top	Too Good To Be True		$8		RCA Victor 9192
10/14/67	13	13	8	Bottle, Bottle	It Doesn't Know Any Better		$8		RCA Victor 9329
2/10/68	23	11	9	The Cajun Stripper	You'll Never Know (The Thrill of Loving You)		$8		RCA Victor 9434
5/25/68	13	12	10	The Enemy	I Just Came From There		$8		RCA Victor 9518
9/28/68	49	8	11	Jack And Jill	Honky Tonkin'		$8		RCA Victor 9616
12/14/68+	35	12	12	Longest Beer Of The Night	What's A Girl Like You (Doing In A Place Like This)		$8		RCA Victor 9677
3/22/69	17	11	13	Man And Wife Time	Healing Hands Of Time		$7		RCA Victor 0114
7/19/69	29	10	14	The Three Bells	Beyond The Shadow		$7		RCA Victor 0190
				new version of Jim's #1 hit with The Browns in 1959					
12/13/69+	35	9	15	Ginger Is Gentle And Waiting For Me/			$7		RCA Victor 0274
		7	16	Drink Boys, Drink					
4/4/70	71	4	17	Lift Ring, Pull Open	Going Up The Country		$7		RCA Victor 9810
7/11/70	31	9	18	Baby, I Tried	The City Cries At Night		$7		RCA Victor 9858
10/24/70	4	18	19	Morning	How To Lose A Good Woman	47	$6		RCA Victor 9909
3/27/71	13	15	20	Angel's Sunday	Every Mile Of The Way		$6		RCA Victor 9965
9/18/71	37	13	21	She's Leavin' (Bonnie, Please Don't Go)	Love Is Worth The Tryin'		$6		RCA Victor 0509
3/4/72	55	7	22	Evening	You Keep Right On Loving Me		$6		RCA Victor 0642
6/10/72	57	8	23	How I Love Them Old Songs	"Close"		$6		RCA Victor 0712
9/30/72	67	6	24	All I Had To Do	Triangle		$6		RCA Victor 0785
12/16/72+	29	12	25	Unbelievable Love	If Her Blue Eyes Don't Get You		$6		RCA Victor 0846
4/28/73	6	15	26	Southern Loving	How Long Does It Take A Memory To Drown		$6		RCA Victor 0928
9/1/73	15	14	27	Broad-Minded Man	Helpin' Her Get Over Him		$6		RCA Victor 0059
12/8/73+	10	15	28	Sometime Sunshine	Louisiana Woman		$6		RCA Victor 0180
5/4/74	10	17	29	It's That Time Of Night	If Wishes Were Horses		$6		RCA Victor 0267
9/21/74	47	8	30	Get Up I Think I Love You	A Nickel For The Fiddler		$6		RCA Victor 10047
1/11/75	63	7	31	Don Junior	Who's Gonna Love Me		$6		RCA Victor 10131
3/29/75	41	9	32	Barroom Pal, Goodtime Gals	Nearer My Love To You		$6		RCA Victor 10233
9/20/75	52	10	33	Fine Time To Get The Blues	Sweetsong		$6		RCA Victor 10370
1/3/76	24	12	34	Another Morning	An Old Flame Never Dies		$6		RCA Victor 10531
4/17/76	69	6	35	Let Me Love You Where It Hurts	I Love You All Over Again		$6		RCA Victor 10619

DEBUT	PEAK	WKS	Gold	A-side (Chart Hit) .... B-side	Pop	$	Pic	Label & Number
				JIM ED BROWN/HELEN CORNELIUS:				
7/4/76	**❶**²	16		36 I Don't Want To Have To Marry You *Have I Told You Lately That I Love You*		$5		RCA Victor 10711
10/16/76	65	7		37 I've Rode With The Best .... *Close The Door*		$5		RCA 10786
				JIM ED BROWN				
11/20/76+	**2**¹	17		38 Saying Hello, Saying I Love You, Saying Goodbye *My Heart Cries For You*		$5		RCA 10822
5/7/77	12	12		39 Born Believer .... *Here Today And Gone Tomorrow*		$5		RCA 10967
8/20/77	12	12		40 If It Ain't Love By Now .... *It Takes So Long*		$5		RCA 11044
11/12/77	66	8		41 When I Touch Her There .... *Mexican Joe*		$5		RCA 11134
				JIM ED BROWN				
12/24/77	91	3		42 Fall Softly Snow .... *Natividad (The Nativity)* [X]		$5		RCA 11162
3/11/78	11	13		43 I'll Never Be Free .... *Baby You Know How I Love You*		$5		RCA 11220
7/29/78	6	15		44 If The World Ran Out Of Love Tonight *Blue Ridge Mountains Turnin' Green*		$5		RCA 11304
11/25/78+	10	14		45 You Don't Bring Me Flowers *Dear Memory*		$5		RCA 11435
3/31/79	**2**²	13		46 Lying In Love With You *Let's Take The Long Way Around The World*		$5		RCA 11532
8/4/79	3	13		47 Fools *I Think About You*		$5		RCA 11672
10/27/79	38	11		48 You're The Part Of Me .... *Changes*		$5		RCA 11742
				JIM ED BROWN				
3/8/80	5	14		49 Morning Comes Too Early *Emotions*		$5		RCA 11927
7/19/80	24	12		50 The Bedroom .... *Everything Is Changing*		$5		RCA 12037
5/9/81	13	14		51 Don't Bother To Knock .... *Dear Memory*		$5		RCA 12220
				BROWN, Josie '73				
				Born Linda Brown in Corning, New York. Died of heart failure on 8/16/98 (age 55).				
9/15/73	44	13		1 Precious Memories Follow Me .... *After You've Had Me*		$5		RCA Victor 0042
2/2/74	58	8		2 Both Sides Of The Line .... *Pour A Little Water On The Flowers*		$5		RCA Victor 0209
5/18/74	83	7		3 Satisfy Me And I'll Satisfy You .... *Crackerbox Mansion*		$5		RCA Victor 0266
				BROWN, Junior '96				
				Born on 6/12/52 in Cottonwood, Arizona. Singer/songwriter/guitarist.				
8/26/95	73	2		1 Highway Patrol .... *Lovely Hula Hands*		$3	▌	MCG/Curb 76953
2/17/96	68	4		2 My Wife Thinks You're Dead .... *Sugarfoot Rag*		$3		MCG/Curb 76983
				BROWN, Marti '73				
				Female singer from Chattanooga, Tennessee.				
7/21/73	78	5		Let My Love Shine .... *Love Me Back To Sleep*		$5		Atlantic 4003
				BROWN, Marty '93				
				Born in 1965 in Maceo, Kentucky. Singer/songwriter/guitarist.				
5/22/93	74	3		It Must Be The Rain .... *Honky Tonk Special*		$3		MCA 54612
				BROWN, Max '79				
5/19/79	91	5		1 Take Time To Smell The Flowers .... *Love Away On Me*		$5		Door Knob 095
8/18/79	73	8		2 Take Good Care Of My Love .... *Call Me Silly*		$5		Door Knob 105
				BROWN, Maxine '69				
				Born Ella Maxine Brown on 4/27/32 in Samti, Louisiana. Eldest member of **The Browns**.				
12/14/68+	64	11		Sugar Cane County .... *My Biggest Mistake*		$7		Chart 1061
				BROWN, Roy '48				
				Born on 9/10/25 in New Orleans. Died of a heart attack on 5/25/81 (age 55). Black singer/pianist. Charted 16 R&B hits from 1948-57.				
12/25/48	12	1		'Fore Day In The Morning .... J:12 *Rainy Weather Blues*		$50		DeLuxe 3198
				ROY BROWN and his Orchestra				
	★202★			**BROWN, T. Graham** '86				
				Born Anthony Graham Brown on 10/30/54 in Arabi, Georgia. Singer/songwriter/actor. Former jingle singer. Acted in the movies *Greased Lightning*, *The Farm* and *Heartbreak Hotel*.				
				1)Don't Go To Strangers 2)Hell And High Water 3)Darlene				
7/27/85	39	10		1 Drowning In Memories .... *Stop, You're Killing Me*		$3		Capitol 5499
10/19/85+	7	27		2 I Tell It Like It Used To Be S:7 / A:7 *Quittin' Time*		$3		Capitol 5524
4/26/86	3	19		3 I Wish That I Could Hurt That Way Again S:2 / A:5 *You're Trying Too Hard*		$3		Capitol 5571
9/6/86	**❶**¹	23		4 Hell And High Water S:❶¹ / A:❶¹ *Don't Make A Liar Out Of Me*		$3	■	Capitol 5621
1/31/87	**❶**¹	21		5 Don't Go To Strangers S:❶² / A:❶¹ *Rock It, Billy*		$3	■	Capitol 5664
5/30/87	9	20		6 Brilliant Conversationalist S:3 *Talkin' To It*		$3	■	Capitol 44008
9/12/87	4	22		7 She Couldn't Love Me Anymore S:5 *R.F.D. 30529*		$3	■	Capitol 44061
1/23/88	4	20		8 The Last Resort S:13 *Sittin' On The Dock Of The Bay*		$3		Capitol 44125
7/30/88	**❶**¹	21		9 Darlene S:5 *Best Love I Never Had*		$3		Capitol 44205
12/10/88+	7	20		10 Come As You Were *The Time Machine*		$3		Capitol 44273
4/29/89	30	13		11 Never Say Never .... *I Read A Letter Today*		$3		Capitol 44349
4/7/90	6	21		12 If You Could Only See Me Now *We Tote The Note*		$3	▌	Capitol 44534
6/23/90	6	21		13 Don't Go Out		$3	▌	Capitol 44586
				TANYA TUCKER with T. Graham Brown				
9/15/90	18	20		14 Moonshadow Road				album cut
1/12/91	53	11		15 I'm Sending One Up For You				album cut
				above 2 from the album *Bumper To Bumper* on Capitol 91780				
4/20/91	31	12		16 With This Ring				album cut
				#14 Pop hit for The Platters in 1967; from the album *You Can't Take It With You* on Capitol 93547				

BROWNE, Jann   '90
Born on 3/14/54 in Anderson, Indiana; raised in Shelbyville, Indiana. Singer with **Asleep At The Wheel** from 1981-83. Married songwriter Roger Stebner in 1985.

7/1/89	**19**	21	1	You Ain't Down Home..*I'll Never Grow Tired Of You*		$3	Curb 10530
11/25/89+	**18**	26	2	Tell Me Why ....*There Ain't No Train*		$3	Curb 10568
9/15/90	**75**	1	3	Louisville ....*Lovebird*		$3	▮ Curb 76835

BROWNS, The ★195★   '59
Brother-and-sister trio from Sparkman, Arkansas: **Jim Ed Brown**, **Maxine Brown** and Bonnie Brown. Maxine and Jim Ed had worked as a duo from the late 1940s and Bonnie joined them in 1955. The trio worked **Red Foley**'s *Arkansas Jamboree* radio shows. Sister Norma subbed for Jim Ed while he was in the service. Joined the *Grand Ole Opry* in 1963. The trio disbanded in 1967, with Jim Ed and Maxine continuing as solo artists.

1)The Three Bells 2)I Take The Chance 3)I Heard The Bluebirds Sing 4)Scarlet Ribbons
5)Here Today And Gone Tomorrow

JIM EDWARD & MAXINE BROWN:

6/26/54	**8**	15	1	Looking Back To See A:8 *Rio De Janeiro*		$25	Fabor 107

JIM EDWARD, MAXINE & BONNIE BROWN:

11/12/55	**7**	7	2	Here Today And Gone Tomorrow A:7 *You Thought I Thought*		$25	Fabor 126
4/28/56	**2**[1]	24	3	I Take The Chance A:2 / S:6 / J:9 *Goo Goo Dada*		$20	RCA Victor 6480
9/22/56	**11**	2	4	Just As Long As You Love Me...............*Don't Tell Me Your Troubles*		$20	RCA Victor 6631
3/23/57	**15**	1	5	Money ....A:15 *It Takes A Long Long Train With A Red Caboose*		$20	RCA Victor 6823
9/2/57	**4**	17	6	I Heard The Bluebirds Sing A:4 / S:15 *The Last Thing I Want*		$20	RCA Victor 6995

THE BROWNS:

10/20/58	**13**	2	7	Would You Care..*The Trot*		$15	RCA Victor 7311
2/23/59	**11**	12	8	Beyond The Shadow ....*This Time I Would Know*		$15	RCA Victor 7427
8/3/59	**❶**[10]	19	● 9	The Three Bells *Heaven Fell Last Night*	❶[4]	$12	RCA Victor 7555
				#14 Pop hit for Les Compagnons De La Chanson in 1952			
11/9/59+	**7**	16	10	Scarlet Ribbons (For Her Hair) *Blue Bells Ring*	13	$12	RCA Victor 7614
				#14 Pop hit for Jo Stafford in 1950			

THE BROWNS Featuring Jim Edward Brown:

4/11/60	**20**	7	11	The Old Lamplighter ....*Teen-Ex (Pop #47)*	5	$12	▮ RCA Victor 7700
12/31/60	**23**	3	12	Send Me The Pillow You Dream On.........*You're So Much A Part Of Me*	56	$12	RCA Victor 7804
1/18/64	**42**	1	13	Oh No!..*Dear Teresa*		$10	RCA Victor 8242
5/16/64	**12**	26	14	Then I'll Stop Loving You ....*I Know My Place*		$10	RCA Victor 8348
11/7/64	**40**	6	15	Everybody's Darlin', Plus Mine ....*The Outskirts Of Town*	135	$10	RCA Victor 8423
2/5/66	**46**	4	16	Meadowgreen ....*One Take Away One*		$10	RCA Victor 8714

THE BROWNS:

7/2/66	**16**	13	17	I'd Just Be Fool Enough ....*Springtime*		$10	RCA Victor 8838
10/8/66	**19**	10	18	Coming Back To You ....*Gigawackem*		$10	RCA Victor 8942
5/6/67	**54**	7	19	I Hear It Now ....*He Will Set Your Fields On Fire*		$10	RCA Victor 9153
12/16/67+	**52**	7	20	Big Daddy/			
12/30/67+	**64**	4	21	I Will Bring You Water		$10	RCA Victor 9364

BRUCE, Ed ★133★   '82
Born William Edwin Bruce, Jr. on 12/29/40 in Keiser, Arkansas; raised in Memphis. Singer/songwriter/guitarist/actor. Recorded for Sun in 1957. Moved to Nashville in 1964 and worked with the Marijohn Wilkins Singers. Did TV commercials as "The Tennessean." Played "Tom Guthrie" on TV's *Bret Maverick*. Hosted TV's *American Sports Cavalcade* and *Truckin' U.S.A.*

1)You're The Best Break This Old Heart Ever Had 2)You Turn Me On 3)Ever, Never Lovin' You
4)After All 5)Nights

1/14/67	**57**	9	1	Walker's Woods...*Lonesome Is Me*		$8	RCA Victor 9044
4/15/67	**69**	5	2	Last Train To Clarksville..*I'm Getting Better*		$8	RCA Victor 9155
				#1 Pop hit for The Monkees in 1966			
7/13/68	**52**	5	3	Painted Girls And Wine................................*Ninety-Seven More To Go*		$8	RCA Victor 9553
1/4/69	**53**	10	4	Song For Jenny ....*Puzzles*		$6	Monument 1118
5/24/69	**52**	7	5	Everybody Wants To Get To Heaven............*When A Man Becomes A Man*		$6	Monument 1138
12/15/73+	**77**	8	6	July, You're A Woman ....*The Rain In Baby's Life*		$5	United Artists 353
				#100 Pop hit for Pat Boone in 1969			
11/15/75+	**15**	14	7	Mammas Don't Let Your Babies Grow Up To Be			
				Cowboys.........................*It's Not What She's Done (It's What You Didn't Do)*		$5	United Artists 732
3/20/76	**32**	10	8	The Littlest Cowboy Rides Again ....*The Feel Of Being Gone*		$5	United Artists 774
6/19/76	**57**	7	9	Sleep All Mornin' ....*Workingman's Prayer*		$5	United Artists 811
9/25/76	**36**	10	10	For Love's Own Sake ....*When Wide Open Spaces And Cowboys Are Gone*		$5	United Artists 862
8/13/77	**52**	10	11	When I Die, Just Let Me Go To Texas..............*I've Not Forgot Marie*		$5	Epic 50424
11/19/77	**54**	10	12	Star-Studded Nights ....*The Wedding Dress*		$5	Epic 50475
2/11/78	**57**	7	13	Love Somebody To Death ....*I Can't Seem To Get The Hang Of Telling Her Goodbye*		$5	Epic 50503
5/20/78	**94**	3	14	Man Made Of Glass ....*Never Take Candy From A Stranger*		$5	Epic 50544
10/7/78	**70**	6	15	The Man That Turned My Mama On.................*Give My Old Memory A Call*		$5	Epic 50613
12/16/78+	**60**	9	16	Angeline ....*Give My Old Memory A Call*		$5	Epic 50645

DEBUT	PEAK	WKS	Gold	A-side (Chart Hit)..B-side	Pop	$	Pic	Label & Number
				BRUCE, Ed — Cont'd				
3/8/80	21	15		17 Diane .... *Blue Umbrella*		$4		MCA 41201
7/5/80	12	15		18 The Last Cowboy Song .... *The Outlaw And The Stranger*		$4		MCA 41273
				Willie Nelson (guest vocal)				
11/8/80+	14	16		19 Girls, Women And Ladies .... *The Last Thing She Said*		$4		MCA 51018
3/28/81	24	14		20 Evil Angel .... *Easy Temptations*		$4		MCA 51076
7/25/81	14	15		21 (When You Fall In Love) Everything's A Waltz .... *Thirty-Nine And Holding*		$4		MCA 51139
11/28/81+	❶¹	21		22 You're The Best Break This Old Heart Ever Had *It Just Makes Me Want You More*		$4		MCA 51210
4/24/82	13	16		23 Love's Found You And Me .... *I Take The Chance*		$4		MCA 52036
8/28/82	4	19		24 Ever, Never Lovin' You .... *Theme From "Bret Maverick"*		$4		MCA 52109
1/22/83	6	18		25 My First Taste Of Texas *One More Shot Of "Old Back Home Again"*		$4		MCA 52156
5/14/83	21	15		26 You're Not Leavin' Here Tonight .... *I Think I'm In Love*		$4		MCA 52210
8/6/83	19	17		27 If It Was Easy .... *You've Got Her Eyes*		$4		MCA 52251
11/12/83+	4	21		28 After All *It Would Take A Fool*		$4		MCA 52295
8/18/84	45	12		29 Tell 'Em I've Gone Crazy .... *Birds Of Paradise*		$4		MCA 52433
11/3/84+	3	22		30 You Turn Me On (Like A Radio) *S:3 / A:3 If It Ain't Love*		$3		RCA 13937
3/23/85	17	16		31 When Givin' Up Was Easy .... *S:13 / A:18 Texas Girl I'm Closing In On You*		$3		RCA 14037
8/3/85	20	16		32 If It Ain't Love .... *A:18 / S:20 The Migrant*		$3		RCA 14150
4/12/86	4	19		33 Nights *S:4 / A:4 Fifteen To Forty-Three (Man In The Mirror)*		$3		RCA 14305
9/13/86	49	9		34 Fools For Each Other .... *S:28 Memphis Roots*		$3		RCA 5005
				ED BRUCE with Lynn Anderson				
12/6/86+	36	14		35 Quietly Crazy .... *Memphis Roots*		$3		RCA 5077
				BRUSH ARBOR '73				
				Group from San Diego: brothers Jim (guitar), Joe (mandolin) and Wayne (banjo) Rice, Kenny Munds (vocals, guitar), Dave Rose (bass) and Dale Cooper (drums).				
11/25/72+	56	10		1 Proud Mary .... *Denver Woman*		$5		Capitol 3468
				#2 Pop hit for Creedence Clearwater Revival in 1969				
3/10/73	41	7		2 Brush Arbor Meeting *Bear Creek Dam*		$5		Capitol 3538
8/4/73	72	4		3 Alone Again (Naturally) .... *Washington County*		$5		Capitol 3672
				#1 Pop hit for Gilbert O'Sullivan in 1972				
11/17/73	98	2		4 Now That It's Over .... *Song To Mary Anne*		$5		Capitol 3733
12/8/73+	73	8		5 Trucker And The U.F.O. .... *Song To Mary Anne*		$5		Capitol 3774
7/31/76	90	3		6 Emmylou .... *One Woman's Man*		$5		Monument 8702
11/12/77	56	11		7 Get Down Country Music .... *Don't Play That Song Again*		$5		Monument 230
				BRYANT, Jimmy — see ORVILLE & IVY				
				BRYANT, Ronnie '89				
11/4/89	81	2		Neither One Of Us		$5		Evergreen 1102
				#2 Pop hit for Gladys Knight & The Pips in 1973				
	★340★			**BRYCE, Sherry** '71				
				Born in Duncanville, Alabama. Married to Mack Sanders.				
				1)Take My Hand 2)Living And Learning 3)Don't Let Go				
6/5/71	8	15		1 Take My Hand *Life's Little Surprises*	110	$6		MGM 14255
				MEL TILLIS AND SHERRY BRYCE with The Statesiders				
10/30/71	9	14		2 Living And Learning *Tangled Vines*		$6		MGM 14303
				MEL TILLIS & SHERRY BRYCE				
4/8/72	38	10		3 Anything's Better Than Nothing .... *Then It Will Be All Over*		$6		MGM 14365
				MEL TILLIS & SHERRY BRYCE And The Statesiders				
8/11/73	64	10		4 Leaving's Heavy On My Mind .... *Coffee & Tears*		$6		MGM 14548
11/17/73+	26	13		5 Let's Go All The Way Tonight .... *In The Vine*		$6		MGM 14660
				MEL TILLIS & SHERRY BRYCE & The Statesiders				
2/9/74	45	11		6 Don't Stop Now .... *Saving What You're Spending It For*		$6		MGM 14695
4/13/74	11	14		7 Don't Let Go .... *Why Not Do The Things (They Think We've Done)*		$6		MGM 14714
				MEL TILLIS & SHERRY BRYCE And The Statesiders				
				#13 Pop hit for Roy Hamilton in 1958				
6/29/74	62	9		8 Treat Me Like A Lady .... *Where Love Has Died*		$5		MGM 14726
10/5/74	70	6		9 Oh, How Happy .... *Come On Down To Our House*		$5		MGM 14747
				#12 Pop hit for Shades Of Blue in 1966				
1/4/75	14	13		10 You Are The One .... *I See Heaven In You*		$5		MGM 14776
				MEL TILLIS & SHERRY BRYCE with The Statesiders				
4/26/75	96	3		11 Love Song .... *I Love Loving You*		$5		MGM 14793
5/17/75	32	13		12 Mr. Right And Mrs. Wrong .... *Just Two Strangers Passing In The Night*		$5		MGM 14803
				MEL TILLIS AND SHERRY BRYCE And The Statesiders				
2/28/76	97	2		13 Hang On Feelin' .... *This Song's For You*		$5		MGM 14842
11/13/76	93	3		14 Everything's Coming Up Love .... *Let Your Body Speak Your Mind*		$5		MCA 40630
10/1/77	79	5		15 The Lady Ain't For Sale .... *Gone, Baby Gone*		$5		Pilot 45100
				BUCHANAN, Wes '68				
				Born in Vallejo, California. Singer/actor. Own *Hollywood Jamboree* TV series in 1967. Appeared in the movie *From Nashville With Love*.				
12/7/68	72	3		Warm Red Wine .... *Letting Me Down*		$8		Columbia 44686
				BUCHANAN BROTHERS '46				
				Duo of brothers Chester and Lester Buchanan from Trenton, Georgia.				
6/29/46	6	3		Atomic Power *Singing An Old Hymn*		$20		RCA Victor 20-1850

BUCK, Gary '63
Born on 3/21/40 in Thessalon, Ontario, Canada. Singer/songwriter/guitarist. Not to be confused with Gary Buck of The Four Guys.

DEBUT	PEAK	WKS		A-side / B-side	Pop	$	Pic	Label & Number
6/29/63	11	17		1 Happy To Be Unhappy .... *Savin' All My Love For You*		$20		Petal 1011
4/11/64	37	3		2 The Wheel Song .... *Suit Of Sorrow*		$20		Petal 1500
2/13/82	93	2		3 Midnight Magic .... *Kentucky Lady*		$5		Dimension 1029

BUCKAROOS, The '68
Backing band for **Buck Owens**: Don Rich (vocals, guitar, fiddle), Tom Brumley (steel guitar), **Doyle Holly** (bass) and Jerry Wiggins (drums). Rich was killed in a motorcycle accident on 7/17/74 (age 32). Also see **Buddy Alan**.

DEBUT	PEAK	WKS		A-side / B-side	Pop	$	Pic	Label & Number
11/25/67	69	4		1 Chicken Pickin' .... *Apple Jack* [I]		$8	■	Capitol 2010
6/8/68	38	9		2 I'm Coming Back Home To Stay .... *I Can't Stop (My Loving You)*		$8	■	Capitol 2173
9/21/68	50	8		3 I'm Goin' Back Home Where I Belong .... *Too Many Chiefs (Not Enough Indians)*		$8		Capitol 2264
				BUCK OWENS' BUCKAROOS Featuring Don Rich (above 2)				
4/19/69	63	2		4 Anywhere U.S.A. .... *Gathering Dust*		$8		Capitol 2420
				THE BUCKAROOS Featuring Don Rich				
10/25/69	43	6		5 Nobody But You .... *Lay A Little Light On Me*		$8		Capitol 2629
4/4/70	71	3		6 The Night They Drove Old Dixie Down .... *One More Time*		$8		Capitol 2750
				DON RICH And The Buckaroos (above 2)				
				#3 Pop hit for Joan Baez in 1971				

BUDDE, Rusty '86
Male singer from Houston.

DEBUT	PEAK	WKS		A-side / B-side	Pop	$	Pic	Label & Number
12/27/86	77	4		Misty Mississippi		$6		BPC 1002

BUFF, Beverly '63
Born in Washington, Georgia.

DEBUT	PEAK	WKS		A-side / B-side	Pop	$	Pic	Label & Number
11/24/62+	22	3		1 I'll Sign .... *Used To Be Sweethearts*		$15		Bethlehem 3027
3/30/63	23	5		2 Forgive Me.. *No Part Time Love*		$15		Bethlehem 3065

BUFFALO CLUB, The '97
Trio formed by former **Restless Heart** drummer John Dittrich, with singer Ron Hemby and guitarist Charlie Kelley.

DEBUT	PEAK	WKS		A-side / B-side	Pop	$	Pic	Label & Number
1/18/97	9	20		1 If She Don't Love You *We Lose*		$3		Rising Tide 56043
6/7/97	26	20		2 Nothin' Less Than Love				album cut
				from the album *The Buffalo Club* on Rising Tide 53044				
10/11/97	53	8		3 Heart Hold On .... *We Lose*		$3		Rising Tide 56053

★377★ BUFFETT, Jimmy '77
Born on 12/25/46 in Pascagoula, Mississippi; raised in Mobile, Alabama. Singer/songwriter/guitarist. Earned a degree in journalism from the University of Southern Mississippi. Nashville correspondent for *Billboard* magazine from 1969-70. Settled in Key West in 1971. Owner of the Margaritaville record label and a line of tropical clothing. Authored the novels *Tales From Margaritaville* and *Where Is Joe Merchant*.
1)*Margaritaville* 2)*If The Phone Doesn't Ring, It's Me* 3)*Changes In Latitudes, Changes In Attitudes*

DEBUT	PEAK	WKS		A-side / B-side	Pop	$	Pic	Label & Number
5/12/73	58	10		1 The Great Filling Station Holdup .... *Why Don't We Get Drunk*		$6		Dunhill/ABC 4348
6/15/74	58	7		2 Come Monday .... *The Wino And I Know*	30	$6		Dunhill/ABC 4385
8/23/75	88	5		3 Door Number Three....................................... *Dallas*	102	$5		ABC 12113
4/30/77	13	17		4 Margaritaville .... *Miss You So Badly*	8	$5		ABC 12254
10/1/77	24	10		5 Changes In Latitudes, Changes In Attitudes .... *Landfall*	37	$5	■	ABC 12305
8/19/78	91	3		6 Livingston Saturday Night.............................. *Cowboy In The Jungle*	52	$5		ABC 12391
9/8/84	42	13		7 When The Wild Life Betrays Me .... *Ragtop Day*		$3	■	MCA 52438
12/8/84+	58	13		8 Bigger Than The Both Of Us .... *Come To The Moon*		$3		MCA 52499
3/23/85	37	15		9 Who's The Blonde Stranger? .... S:24 *She's Going Out Of My Mind*		$3		MCA 52550
6/29/85	56	9		10 Gypsies In The Palace .... *Jolly Mon Sing*		$3	■	MCA 52607
9/7/85	16	19		11 If The Phone Doesn't Ring, It's Me ......A:11 / S:16 *Frank And Lola*		$3	■	MCA 52664
2/8/86	50	9		12 Please Bypass This Heart............................ *Beyond The End*		$3		MCA 52752
8/28/93	74	1		13 Another Saturday Night.............................. *Souvenirs*		$3		MCA 54680
				#10 Pop hit for Sam Cooke in 1963 and #6 Pop hit for Cat Stevens in 1974				

BUNZOW, John '95
Singer/songwriter from Portland, Oregon.

DEBUT	PEAK	WKS		A-side / B-side	Pop	$	Pic	Label & Number
4/8/95	69	4		Easy As One, Two, Three				album cut
				from the album *Stories Of The Years* on Liberty 28246				

BURBANK, Gary '80
DJ at WHAS in Louisville, Kentucky, at the time of his hit.

DEBUT	PEAK	WKS		A-side / B-side	Pop	$	Pic	Label & Number
7/26/80	91	2		Who Shot J.R.? .... *Honkin'* [N]	67	$5		Ovation 1150
				GARY BURBANK with Band McNally				
				inspired by the shooting of "J.R. Ewing" (Larry Hagman) on TV's *Dallas*				

BURBANK STATION '88
Group from Fargo, North Dakota. Features female singer Bunny Davis.

DEBUT	PEAK	WKS		A-side / B-side	Pop	$	Pic	Label & Number
8/6/88	77	3		1 Divided.. *Over Women*		$5		Prairie Dust 8841
5/27/89	90	2		2 Get Out Of My Way		$5		Prairie Dust 112

BURCH SISTERS, The '88
Sisters Cathy (b: 12/28/60), Charlene (b: 9/19/62) and Cindy (b: 8/1/63) Burch. All were born in Jacksonville, Florida.

DEBUT	PEAK	WKS		A-side / B-side	Pop	$	Pic	Label & Number
5/21/88	23	18		1 Everytime You Go Outside I Hope It Rains .... S:28 *Open Arms*		$3		Mercury 870362
10/15/88	61	5		2 What Do Lonely People Do.......................... *Open Arms*		$3	■	Mercury 870687
12/17/88+	45	11		3 I Don't Want To Mention Any Names........... *The Only Love You Need*		$3		Mercury 872324
4/1/89	46	11		4 Old Flame, New Fire .... *What We Don't Know Won't Hurt Us*		$3		Mercury 872730
7/1/89	59	8		5 The Way I Want To Go .... *I Missed That Train Again*		$3		Mercury 874560

BURDICK, Kathy — see LEE, Dickey

BURGESS, Frank '89

| 11/26/88 | 88 | 3 | | 1 American Man .... | | $6 | True 94 |
| 5/13/89 | 81 | 3 | | 2 What It Boils Down To .... | | $6 | True 96 |

★306★ BURGESS, Wilma '66

Born on 6/11/39 in Orlando, Florida. Female singer.
1)Misty Blue 2)Baby 3)Don't Touch Me

12/11/65+	7	18		1 Baby	*Wait Till The Sun Comes Up*	$8	Decca 31862
5/7/66	12	17		2 Don't Touch Me	*Turn Around Teardrops*	$8	Decca 31941
10/29/66	4	18		3 Misty Blue	*Ain't Got No Man*	$8	Decca 32027

#3 Pop hit for Dorothy Moore in 1976

3/25/67	24	15		4 Fifteen Days..	*Two Little Rivers Of Tears*	$8	Decca 32105
8/26/67	16	15		5 Tear Time ....(How Can I Write On Paper)	*What I Feel In My Heart*	$8	Decca 32178
8/17/68	59	9		6 Look At The Laughter	*Sweet Promises*	$8	Decca 32359
3/22/69	68	3		7 Parting (Is Such Sweet Sorrow)	*Shine A Little Sun On Me*	$8	Decca 32437
8/9/69	48	10		8 The Woman In Your Life	*Happiness Is So Hard To Forget*	$8	Decca 32522
12/27/69+	48	9		9 The Sun's Gotta' Shine.............................	*Only Mama That'll Walk The Line*	$8	Decca 32593
7/11/70	63	6		10 Lonely For You	*I Don't See My In Your Arms Anymore*	$8	Decca 32684
9/22/73	61	11		11 I'll Be Your Bridge (Just Lay Me Down).............	*I'll Always Love The Days*	$6	Shannon 813
12/22/73+	14	17		12 Wake Me Into Love..............................	*Here Together*	$6	Shannon 816
				BUD LOGAN & WILMA BURGESS			
7/6/74	53	10		13 The Best Day Of The Rest Of Our Love	*It Ain't Nothing But Love*	$6	Shannon 820
				BUD LOGAN & WILMA BURGESS			
9/14/74	46	11		14 Love Is Here/			
2/8/75	86	6		15 Sweet Lovin' Baby		$6	Shannon 821

BURKE, Fiddlin' Frenchie '75

Born Leon Bourke in Kaplan, Louisiana. Singer/fiddler.

11/23/74+	39	15		1 Big Mamou..	*There'll Be Love Tonight In My House*	$5	20th Century 2152
				FIDDLIN' FRENCHIE BOURQUE and THE OUTLAWS			
4/19/75	30	9		2 Colinda	*Pride, You Wouldn't Listen*	$5	20th Century 2182
10/11/75	73	5		3 The Fiddlin' Of Jacques Pierre Bordeaux	*Frenchie's Cotton-Eyed Joe*	$5	20th Century 2225
				FIDDLIN' FRENCHIE BURKE & THE OUTLAWS (above 2)			
7/1/78	94	5		4 Knock Knock Knock...		$6	Cherry 644
				FRENCHIE BURKE			
3/28/81	93	3		5 (Frenchie Burke's) Fire On The Mountain...	*Let's Go Get Drunk And Be Somebody* [I]	$6	Delta 11332

BURNETTE, Billy '85

Born on 5/8/53 in Memphis. Singer/songwriter/guitarist. Son of **Dorsey Burnette**, nephew of Johnny Burnette and cousin of Rocky Burnette. Member of Fleetwood Mac from 1987-1993. Acted in the movie *Saturday Night Special*.

11/3/79	76	5		1 What's A Little Love Between Friends......................	*Precious Time*	$4	Polydor 2024
8/10/85	51	8		2 Ain't It Just Like Love	*Guitar Bug*	$3	Curb/MCA 52626
12/28/85+	68	9		3 Try Me	*It Ain't Over*	$3	Curb/MCA 52749
7/12/86	54	7		4 Soldier Of Love	*Guitar Bug*	$3	Curb/MCA 52852
3/7/92	64	6		5 Nothin' To Do (And All Night To Do It)...................	*Can't Get Over You*	$3	Warner 19042

BURNETTE, Billy Joe '90

| 1/6/90 | 90 | 1 | | Three Flags ....[S] | | $7 | Badger 1004 |

★372★ BURNETTE, Dorsey '72

Born on 12/28/32 in Memphis. Died of a heart attack on 8/19/79 (age 46). Singer/songwriter/guitarist. Older brother of Johnny Burnette and father of **Billy Burnette**.
1)In The Spring 2)Darlin' 3)Molly

5/13/72	21	12		1 In The Spring (The Roses Always Turn Red)	*The Same Old You, The Same Old Me*	$5	Capitol 3307
9/2/72	40	8		2 I Just Couldn't Let Her Walk Away....................	*Church Bells*	$5	Capitol 3404
2/17/73	42	9		3 I Let Another Good One Get Away	*Take Your Weapons, Lay 'Em Down*	$5	Capitol 3529
5/12/73	53	5		4 Keep Out Of My Dreams	*Mama, Mama*	$5	Capitol 3588
8/11/73	26	14		5 Darlin' (Don't Come Back)	*Sweet Lovin' Woman*	$5	Capitol 3678
1/12/74	85	7		6 It Happens Every Time	*Mr. Jukebox, Sing A Lullabye*	$5	Capitol 3796
3/9/74	69	8		7 Bob, All The Playboys And Me	*The Bootleggers*	$5	Capitol 3829
				DORSEY BURNETTE with Sound Company (above 3)			
6/15/74	62	8		8 Daddy Loves You Honey	*True Love Means Forgiving*	$5	Capitol 3887
11/23/74	71	5		9 What Ladies Can Do (When They Want To)	*Tangerine*	$5	Capitol 3963
5/31/75	28	12		10 Molly (I Ain't Gettin' Any Younger).....................	*She's Feelin' Low*	$5	Melodyland 6007
10/18/75	97	3		11 Lyin' In Her Arms Again	*Doggone The Dogs*	$5	Melodyland 6019
4/24/76	74	5		12 Ain't No Heartbreak	*I Dreamed I Saw*	$5	Melodyland 6031
6/11/77	31	15		13 Things I Treasure	*One Mornin'*	$6	Calliope 8004
11/5/77	53	7		14 Soon As I Touched Her	*Dear Hearted Children*	$6	Calliope 8012
9/1/79	77	4		15 Here I Go Again	*What Would It Profit Me*	$4	Elektra 46513

BURNIN' DAYLIGHT '97

Trio of **Marc Beeson** (vocals), Sonny Lemaire (bass; **Exile**) and Kurt Howell (keyboards; **Southern Pacific**).

2/15/97	37	20		1 Say Yes!/			
10/19/96	49	16		2 Love Worth Fighting For..		$3	▮ Curb 73005
6/21/97	58	6		3 Live To Love Again			album cut
				from the album *Burnin' Daylight* on Curb 77850			

BURNS, Brent '78

Writer/producer from Phoenix.

| 5/6/78 | 91 | 4 | | I Hear You Coming Back .... | *Come Away With Me* | $7 | Pantheon Desert 79 |

BURNS, George '80
Born Nathan Birnbaum on 1/20/1896 in New York City. Died on 3/9/96 (age 100). Radio, movie and TV comedian.

1/5/80	15	14		1 I Wish I Was Eighteen Again ....One Of The Mysteries Of Life	49	$4	■	Mercury 57011
5/24/80	85	4		2 The Arizona Whiz ....A Real Good Cigar		$4		Mercury 57021
2/14/81	66	5		3 Willie, Won't You Sing A Song With Me..............Just Send Me One		$4		Mercury 57045

BURNS, Hughie '80

| 3/8/80 | 95 | 2 | | The Family Inn ....Tell Me A Good One | | $6 | | C-S-I 002 |

BURNS, Jackie '69
Female singer from Long Beach, California.

10/11/69	60	5		1 Something's Missing (It's You) ....What's A Daddy		$10		Honor Brigade 5
10/21/72	71	2		2 (If Loving You Is Wrong) I Don't Want To Be Right ...... A World Of Lonely Men		$8		JMI 8
				#3 Pop hit for Luther Ingram in 1972				

BURRITO BROTHERS '81
Group formed in 1968 as the **Flying Burrito Brothers** by **Chris Hillman** and **Gram Parsons**, ex-members of folk-rock band The Byrds. By 1980, consisted of "Sneaky" Pete Kleinow (steel guitar), Floyd "Gib" Guilbeau (fiddle; father of Ronnie Guilbeau of **Palomino Road**), Skip Battin (bass), Greg Harris (guitar) and Ed Ponder (drums). In 1981, relocated to Nashville, dropped "Flying" from band name, Harris and Ponder left and John Beland (guitar) joined. By late 1981, reduced to a duo of Guilbeau and Beland.
1)She Belongs To Everyone But Me 2)Does She Wish She Was Single Again
3)If Something Should Come Between Us

3/1/80	95	2		1 White Line Fever		$6		Regency 45001
				FLYING BURRITO BROTHERS				
				recorded "live" in Tokyo; written by **Merle Haggard**				
1/24/81	67	5		2 She's A Friend Of A Friend ....Too Much Honky Tonkin'		$4		Curb 5402
4/18/81	20	13		3 Does She Wish She Was Single Again.......................Oh, Lonesome Me		$4		Curb 01011
8/8/81	16	14		4 She Belongs To Everyone But Me Why Must The Ending Always Be So Sad		$4		Curb 02243
12/26/81+	27	14		5 If Something Should Come Between Us (Let It Be Love) ....Damned If I'll Be Lonely Tonight		$4		Curb 02641
4/17/82	40	10		6 Closer To You ....Coast To Coast		$4		Curb 02835
7/24/82	39	10		7 I'm Drinkin' Canada Dry ....How'd We Ever Get This Way		$4		Curb 03023
11/13/82	48	10		8 Blue And Broken Hearted Me ....Our Roots Are Country Music		$4		Curb 03314
1/28/84	49	9		9 Almost Saturday Night ....Jukebox Kind Of Night		$4		Curb 52329
				#78 Pop hit for **John Fogerty** in 1975				
5/26/84	53	8		10 My Kind Of Lady ....Dream Chaser		$4		Curb 52379

★251★ BUSH, Johnny '69
Born John Bush Shin III on 2/17/35 in Houston. Singer/songwriter/guitarist/drummer. Worked with **Ray Price** and **Willie Nelson** in the 1960s. Known as "The Country Caruso."
1)You Gave Me A Mountain 2)Undo The Right 3)Whiskey River 4)Each Time 5)I'll Be There

11/25/67	69	3		1 You Oughta Hear Me Cry ....Jealously Insane		$8		Stop 126
3/16/68	29	13		2 What A Way To Live ....I Can Feel You In His Arms		$8		Stop 160
8/3/68	10	16		3 Undo The Right Conscience Turn Your Back		$8		Stop 193
				above 3 written by **Willie Nelson**				
12/28/68+	16	13		4 Each Time ....Tonight We Steal Heaven Again		$8		Stop 232
3/22/69	7	15		5 You Gave Me A Mountain Back From The Wine		$8		Stop 257
				#24 Pop hit for **Frankie Laine** in 1969				
8/16/69	26	10		6 My Cup Runneth Over ....Tonight, I'm Going Home To An Angel		$8		Stop 310
				#8 Pop hit for **Ed Ames** in 1967				
1/3/70	56	8		7 Jim, Jack, And Rose/		$8		Stop 354
			5	8 I'll Go To A Stranger		$8		Stop 354
5/16/70	25	11		9 Warmth Of The Wine ....Daddy Lived In Houston		$8		Stop 371
11/7/70	44	11		10 My Joy ....I'll Warm By The Flame		$8		Stop 380
4/10/71	53	6		11 City Lights ....The Joy Of Loving You		$8		Stop 392
4/22/72	17	12		12 I'll Be There ....I Can Feel You In His Arms		$8		Million 1
7/22/72	14	15		13 Whiskey River ....Right Back In Your Arms Again		$5		RCA Victor 0745
				also see #24 below				
12/30/72+	34	9		14 There Stands The Glass ....These Lips Don't Know How To Say Goodbye		$5		RCA Victor 0867
5/5/73	38	11		15 Here Comes The World Again ....That Rain Makin' Baby Of Mine		$5		RCA Victor 0931
9/1/73	53	8		16 Green Snakes On The Ceiling ....Drinkin' My Baby Right Out Of My Mind		$5		RCA Victor 0041
12/1/73+	37	10		17 We're Back In Love Again ....(Wine Friend Of Mine) Stand By Me		$5		RCA Victor 0164
3/23/74	48	10		18 Toy Telephone		$5		RCA Victor 0240
			4	19 From Tennessee To Texas		$5		RCA Victor 0240
10/15/77	78	7		20 You'll Never Leave Me Completely/		$5		Gusto 165
4/29/78	99	2		21 Put Me Out Of My Memory		$5		Gusto 165
9/2/78	89	3		22 She Just Made Me Love You More ....Hands Can Say A Lot		$5		Gusto 9006
5/19/79	83	5		23 When My Conscience Hurts The Most ....Drivin' Nails In My Coffin		$6		Whiskey River 791
2/28/81	92	2		24 Whiskey River ....When My Conscience Hurts The Most [R]		$6		Delta 10041
				new version of #13 above				

BUTLER, Bobby "Sofine" '79
Born in El Paso, Texas. Worked as a DJ in Tucson, El Paso and Phoenix.

| 12/4/76 | 98 | 2 | | 1 Teddy Toad ....Theme From Teddy Toad | | $6 | | Pantheon Desert 77 |
| 5/26/79 | 46 | 6 | | 2 Cheaper Crude Or No More Food ....Bobby's (Nervous) Breakdown [N] | | $6 | | IBC 0001 |

	★267★			**BUTLER, Carl, and Pearl** '62				
				Carl was born on 6/2/27 in Knoxville, Tennessee. Died on 9/4/92 (age 65). Wife Pearl was born Pearl Dee Jones on 9/20/27 in Nashville. Died on 3/1/88 (age 60). Both appeared in the movie *Second Fiddle To A Steel Guitar*.				
				1)*Don't Let Me Cross Over* 2)*Too Late To Try Again* 3)*I'm Hanging Up The Phone*				
8/7/61	25	2		1 Honky Tonkitis .... *You Were The Orchid (She Was The Rose)*		$15		Columbia 41997
				CARL BUTLER				
12/8/62	❶11	24		2 **Don't Let Me Cross Over** *Wonder Drug*	88	$12	☐	Columbia 42593
7/6/63	14	14		3 Loving Arms ....*Who'll Be Next*		$10		Columbia 42778
1/11/64	9	8		4 **Too Late To Try Again/**				
1/11/64	36	1		5 My Tears Don't Show		$10		Columbia 42892
6/6/64	14	16		6 I'm Hanging Up The Phone .... *Just A Message*		$8		Columbia 43030
9/26/64	23	10		7 Forbidden Street ....*When The Door Swings Shut (On Old Memories)*		$8		Columbia 43102
3/27/65	22	13		8 Just Thought I'd Let You Know/				
2/27/65	38	10		9 We'd Destroy Each Other		$8		Columbia 43210
12/11/65	42	2		10 Our Ship Of Love .... *It's Called Cheating*		$8		Columbia 43433
8/6/66	31	7		11 Little Pedro .... *Cell 29*		$8		Columbia 43685
8/17/68	28	12		12 Punish Me Tomorrow .... *Goodbye Tennessee*		$7		Columbia 44587
1/4/69	46	8		13 I Never Got Over You .... *I Started Loving You Again*		$7		Columbia 44694
7/5/69	63	6		14 We'll Sweep Out The Ashes In The Morning .... *Your Way Of Life*		$7		Columbia 44862
				BUZZI, Ruth '77				
				Born on 7/24/36 in Westerley, Rhode Island. Comedienne featured on TV's *Laugh-In*.				
4/2/77	90	4		You Oughta Hear The Song .... *'57 Chevrolet*		$5		United Artists 951
				BUZZIN' COUSINS '92				
				Group that appeared in the movie *Falling From Grace*: **John Cougar Mellencamp** (director/star of the movie), **Dwight Yoakam**, **Joe Ely**, **John Prine**, and **James McMurtry**.				
2/15/92	68	5		Sweet Suzanne				album cut
				from the movie *Falling From Grace* starring **John Cougar Mellencamp** (soundtrack on Mercury 512004)				
				BYERS, Brenda '68				
				Singer/banjo player from Canterbury, Connecticut.				
10/26/68	51	9		1 The Auctioneer .... *Rainbows And Roses*		$8		MTA 160
10/11/69	65	6		2 Thank You For Loving Me .... *Night Life*		$8		MTA 176
1/24/70	66	4		3 Homeward Bound .... *The Other Side Of Me*		$8		MTA 177
				#5 Pop hit for Simon & Garfunkel in 1966				
				BYRAM, Judy '87				
12/5/87	71	5		1 No More One More Time		$5		F&L 554
6/4/88	74	5		2 One Fire Between Us		$5		Regal 001
				BYRD, Jerry — see ALLEN, Rex / KIRK, Red				
	★221★			**BYRD, Tracy** '93				
				Born on 12/17/66 in Beaumont, Texas; raised in Vidor, Texas. Male singer.				
				1)*Holdin' Heaven* 2)*The Keeper Of The Stars* 3)*Big Love*				
8/22/92	71	3		1 That's The Thing About A Memory .... *Back In The Swing Of Things*		$3		MCA 54426
2/13/93	42	20		2 Someone To Give My Love To .... *Talk To Me Texas*		$3	▌	MCA 54497
6/19/93	❶1	20		3 **Holdin' Heaven** *Edge Of A Memory*		$3	▌	MCA 54659
10/30/93	39	15		4 Why Don't That Telephone Ring .... *An Out Of Control Raging Fire (w/Dawn Sears)*		$3	▌	MCA 54735
4/30/94	4	20		5 **Lifestyles Of The Not So Rich And**				
				Famous *You Never Know Just How Good You've Got It*	115	$3	▌	MCA 54778
8/13/94	4	20		6 **Watermelon Crawl** *You Never Know Just How Good You've Got It*	81	$3	▌	MCA 54845
11/19/94+	5	20		7 **The First Step** *No Ordinary Man*		$3	▌	MCA 54945
1/21/95	2²	20		8 **The Keeper Of The Stars** *Pink Flamingos*	68	$3	▌	MCA 54988
6/3/95	15	20		9 Walking To Jerusalem .... *S:3 Down On The Bottom*	92	$3	▌	MCA 55049
9/9/95	9	20		10 **Love Lessons** *S:6 Don't Need That Heartache*	119	$3	▌	MCA 55102
2/3/96	14	20		11 Heaven In My Woman's Eyes .... *Walkin' In*		$3		MCA 55155
5/25/96	21	20		12 4 To 1 In Atlanta .... *Have A Good One*		$3		MCA 55201
9/21/96+	3	20		13 **Big Love** *S:13 (club mix)*		$3	▌	MCA 55230
1/25/97	4	20		14 **Don't Take Her She's All I Got** *I Love You, That's All*		$3		MCA 55292
				#39 Pop hit for Freddie North in 1971				
5/17/97	17	20		15 Don't Love Make A Diamond Shine .... *Tucson Too Soon*		$3		MCA 72002
9/27/97	47	10		16 Good Ol' Fashioned Love .... *Driving Me Out Of Your Mind*		$3		MCA 72011

C

	★			**CAGLE, Buddy** '63				
				Born Walter Cagle on 2/8/36 in Concord, North Carolina; raised in Winston-Salem. Singer/guitarist.				
5/18/63	29	3		1 Your Mother's Prayer .... *Once Again*		$12		Capitol 4923
11/16/63	26	2		2 Sing A Sad Song .... *Love Inside My Door*		$12		Capitol 5043
9/25/65	37	8		3 Honky Tonkin' Again .... *We The People (The Great Society)*		$10		Mercury 72452
4/23/66	31	10		4 Tonight I'm Coming Home .... *Honky Tonk College*		$7		Imperial 66161
1/14/67	57	7		5 Apologize .... *Help's On The Way*		$7		Imperial 66218

DEBUT	PEAK	WKS	Gold	A-side (Chart Hit) .... B-side	Pop	$	Pic	Label & Number

CAGLE, Buddy — Cont'd

| 8/12/67 | 75 | 2 | | 6 Longtime Traveling .... *Camptown Girl* | | $7 | | Imperial 66245 |

CAIN, Hunter   '88

| 7/16/88 | 82 | 2 | | 1 Hollywood Heroes/ | | | | |
| 5/13/89 | 95 | 1 | | 2 **She's Too Good To Be Cheated This Way** .... | | $6 | | Discovery 4587 |

CALAMITY JANE   '82
Female group: Pam Rose (vocals), Mary Fielder (guitar), Linda Moore (bass) and Mary Ann Kennedy (drums).

10/17/81	61	7		1 Send Me Somebody To Love ....*Don't You Leave Love Alone Too Long*		$4		Columbia 02503
2/27/82	44	9		2 I've Just Seen A Face .... *Midnight Bandit*		$4		Columbia 02715
				first recorded by The Beatles on their 1966 album *Rubber Soul*				
6/19/82	60	7		3 Walkin' After Midnight .... *Lover To Lover*		$4		Columbia 02958
10/16/82	87	3		4 Love Wheel ....*Pick Me Up (And Let Me Love Again)*		$4		Columbia 03229

CALHOUN, Linda   '79

| 4/28/79 | 85 | 4 | | I Can Feel Love .... *Our Tune Of Yesterday* | | $7 | | Grape 2004 |

CAMERON, Bart   '86

| 11/1/86 | 76 | 4 | | 1 Dark Eyed Lady... | | $5 | | Revolver 013 |
| 5/30/87 | 77 | 3 | | 2 Do It For The Love Of It................................... | | $5 | | Revolver 015 |

CAMP, Colleen   '82
Born in 1952 in San Francisco. Singer/actress.

| 1/23/82 | 72 | 4 | | One Day Since Yesterday ....*I Would Like To See You Again* | | $7 | | Moon Pictures 0001 |

CAMP, Shawn   '93
Born in Perryville, Arkansas. Male singer/songwriter/guitarist/fiddler.

| 7/31/93 | 39 | 20 | | 1 Fallin' Never Felt So Good...........................*Turn Loose Of My Pride* | | $3 | ▌ | Reprise 18465 |
| 11/20/93+ | 39 | 20 | | 2 Confessin' My Love .... *K-I-S-S-I-N-G* | | $3 | ▌ | Reprise 18331 |

CAMPBELL, Archie   '66
Born on 11/7/14 in Bulls Gap, Tennessee. Died of heart failure on 8/29/87 (age 72). Singer/songwriter/comedian. Joined the *Grand Ole Opry* in 1968. Chief writer and cast member of the TV series *Hee Haw*. Hosted TNN's *Yesteryear In Nashville*.

3/14/60	24	4		1 Trouble In The Amen Corner..............*Black Is The Color Of My True Love's Hair* [S]		$12		RCA Victor 7660
1/22/66	16	8		2 The Men In My Little Girl's Life *Abe Lincoln Comes Home*		$10		RCA Victor 8741
				#6 Pop hit for Mike Douglas in 1960				
3/11/67	44	10		3 The Cockfight............................*Red Silk Stockings And Green Perfume* [S]		$10		RCA Victor 9081
				ARCHIE CAMPBELL and LORENE MANN:				
1/6/68	24	15		4 The Dark End Of The Street....................... *The Gettin' Place*		$8		RCA Victor 9401
6/29/68	31	10		5 Tell It Like It Is.................................*If That's The Only Way*		$8		RCA Victor 9549
				#2 Pop hit for **Aaron Neville** in 1967				
9/28/68	57	8		6 Warm And Tender Love ....*Pledging My Love*		$8		RCA Victor 9615
				#17 Pop hit for Percy Sledge in 1966				
1/4/69	36	9		7 My Special Prayer.........................*What Am I Living For*		$8		RCA Victor 9691
12/8/73	87	4		8 Freedom Ain't The Same As Bein' Free .... *The House*		$6		RCA Victor 0155
				ARCHIE CAMPBELL				

CAMPBELL, Cecil   '49
Born on 3/22/11 in Stokes County, North Carolina. Died on 6/18/89 (age 78). Singer/songwriter/steel guitarist. Appeared in the movies *My Darling Clementine* and *Swing Your Partner*.

5/21/49	9	1		Steel Guitar Ramble *J:9 Left All Alone With A Broken Heart*		$25		RCA Victor 21-0014
				CECIL CAMPBELL'S TENNESSEE RAMBLERS				
				45 rpm: 48-0014				

CAMPBELL, Glen ★37★   '75

Born on 4/22/36 in Delight, Arkansas. Singer/songwriter/guitarist. With his uncle Dick Bills's band, 1954-58. To Los Angeles; recorded with The Champs in 1960. Became prolific studio musician; with The Hondells in 1964, **The Beach Boys** in 1965 and Sagittarius in 1967. Own TV show *The Glen Campbell Goodtime Hour*, 1968-72. Acted in the movies *True Grit*, *Norwood* and *Strange Homecoming*; voice in the animated movie *Rock-A-Doodle*. CMA Awards: 1968 Male Vocalist of the Year; 1968 Entertainer of the Year.

1)I Wanna Live 2)Rhinestone Cowboy 3)Galveston 4)Wichita Lineman 5)Southern Nights

12/29/62	20	5		1 Kentucky Means Paradise ....*Truck Driving Man*	114	$15		Capitol 4867
				THE GREEN RIVER BOYS Featuring Glen Campbell				
12/10/66+	18	13		2 Burning Bridges .... *Only The Lonely*		$10		Capitol 5773
				#3 Pop hit for Jack Scott in 1960				
4/29/67	73	2		3 I Gotta Have My Baby Back ....*Just To Satisfy You*		$10		Capitol 5854
7/29/67	30	12		4 Gentle On My Mind.............................*Just Another Man*	62	$8		Capitol 5939
				also see #9 below				
10/28/67+	2²	18		5 By The Time I Get To Phoenix *You've Still Got A Place In My Heart*	26	$7		Capitol 2015
				also see #24 below				
2/3/68	13	12		6 Hey Little One .... *My Baby's Gone*	54	$7	■	Capitol 2076
4/13/68	❶³	16		7 I Wanna Live *That's All That Matters*	36	$7		Capitol 2146
7/6/68	3	15		8 Dreams Of The Everyday Housewife *Kelli Hoedown*	32	$7		Capitol 2224
10/19/68	44	3		9 Gentle On My Mind.............................*Just Another Man* [R]	39	$8		Capitol 5939
				reissue of #4 above				
11/2/68	❶²	19	●	10 Wichita Lineman *Fate Of Man*	3	$6		Capitol 2302
11/23/68	44	7		11 Less Of Me .... *Mornin' Glory* (Pop #74)		$6		Capitol 2314
				BOBBIE GENTRY & GLEN CAMPBELL				
2/8/69	14	14		12 Let It Be Me .... *Little Green Apples*	36	$6		Capitol 2387
				GLEN CAMPBELL and BOBBIE GENTRY				

DEBUT	PEAK	WKS	Gold	A-side (Chart Hit)..B-side	Pop	$	Pic	Label & Number
				CAMPBELL, Glen — Cont'd				
3/15/69	❶³	14	●	13 **Galveston** *How Come Every Time I Itch I Wind Up Scratchin' You*	4	$6		Capitol 2428
5/10/69	28	10		14 **Where's The Playground Susie** ....*Arkansas*	26	$6		Capitol 2494
7/26/69	9	12		15 **True Grit** *Hava Nagila*	35	$6		Capitol 2573
				from the movie starring John Wayne and Campbell				
10/25/69	2¹	13		16 **Try A Little Kindness** *Lonely My Lonely Friend*	23	$6		Capitol 2659
1/24/70	2³	13		17 **Honey Come Back** *Where Do You Go*	19	$6		Capitol 2718
2/21/70	6	13		18 **All I Have To Do Is Dream** *Less Of Me*	27	$6		Capitol 2745
				BOBBIE GENTRY & GLEN CAMPBELL				
4/25/70	25	9		19 **Oh Happy Day** *Someone Above*	40	$6		Capitol 2787
				#4 Pop hit for the Edwin Hawkins Singers in 1969				
7/18/70	5	12		20 **Everything A Man Could Ever Need** *Norwood (Me And My Guitar)*	52	$6		Capitol 2843
				from the movie *Norwood* starring Campbell				
9/19/70	3	15		21 **It's Only Make Believe** *Pave Your Way Into Tomorrow*	10	$6		Capitol 2905
				#1 Pop hit for **Conway Twitty** in 1958				
3/13/71	7	14		22 **Dream Baby (How Long Must I Dream)** *Here And Now*	31	$6		Capitol 3062
				#4 Pop hit for **Roy Orbison** in 1962				
7/3/71	21	14		23 **The Last Time I Saw Her**...*Bach Talk*	61	$6		Capitol 3123
10/30/71	40	8		24 **I Say A Little Prayer/By The Time I Get To Phoenix** .... *All Through The Night*	81	$6		Capitol 3200
				GLEN CAMPBELL/ANNE MURRAY				
				"I Say A Little Prayer" was a #4 Pop hit for Dionne Warwick in 1967				
1/8/72	15	12		25 **Oklahoma Sunday Morning** ....*Everybody's Got To Go There Sometime*	104	$6		Capitol 3254
4/1/72	6	13		26 **Manhattan Kansas** *Wayfarin' Stranger*	114	$6		Capitol 3305
8/26/72	45	10		27 **I Will Never Pass This Way Again** *We All Pull The Load*	61	$6		Capitol 3411
12/16/72+	33	10		28 **One Last Time** ....*All My Tomorrows*	78	$5		Capitol 3483
3/24/73	48	8		29 **I Knew Jesus (Before He Was A Star)** *On This Road*	45	$5		Capitol 3548
7/28/73	49	9		30 **Bring Back My Yesterday** *Beautiful Love Song*		$5		Capitol 3669
10/20/73	20	12		31 **Wherefore And Why**......................*Give Me Back That Old Familiar Feeling*	111	$5		Capitol 3735
2/2/74	20	10		32 **Houston (I'm Comin' To See You)**............................*Honestly Love*	68	$5		Capitol 3808
8/3/74	3	18		33 **Bonaparte's Retreat** *Too Many Mornings*		$5		Capitol 3926
12/14/74+	16	13		34 **It's A Sin When You Love Somebody** ....*If I Were Loving You*		$5		Capitol 3988
6/7/75	❶³	21	●	35 **Rhinestone Cowboy** *Lovelight*	❶²	$5		Capitol 4095
11/1/75	3	15		36 **Country Boy (You Got Your Feet In L.A.)** *Record Collector's Dream*	11	$5		Capitol 4155
4/10/76	4	12		37 **Don't Pull Your Love/Then You Can Tell Me Goodbye** *I Miss You Tonight*	27	$5		Capitol 4245
				"Don't Pull Your Love" was a #4 Pop hit for Hamilton, Joe Frank & Reynolds in 1971; "Then You Can Tell Me Goodbye" was a #6 Pop hit for The Casinos in 1967				
7/10/76	18	11		38 **See You On Sunday**...*Bloodline*		$5		Capitol 4288
1/29/77	❶²	17	●	39 **Southern Nights** *William Tell Overture*	❶¹	$5		Capitol 4376
7/2/77	4	15		40 **Sunflower** *How High Did We Go*	39	$5		Capitol 4445
				written by Neil Diamond				
12/3/77+	39	10		41 **God Must Have Blessed America**.............................*Amazing Grace*		$5		Capitol 4515
6/10/78	21	12		42 **Another Fine Mess**...*Can You Fool*		$5		Capitol 4584
				from the movie *The End* starring **Burt Reynolds**				
9/23/78	16	16		43 **Can You Fool** ....*Let's All Sing A Song About It*	38	$4		Capitol 4638
2/17/79	13	11		44 **I'm Gonna Love You** *Love Takes You Higher*		$4		Capitol 4682
5/26/79	45	7		45 **California** *Never Tell You No Lies*		$4		Capitol 4715
9/1/79	25	10		46 **Hound Dog Man** *Tennessee Home*		$4		Capitol 4769
				#58 Pop hit for **Lenny LeBlanc** in 1977				
11/24/79	66	6		47 **My Prayer** *Don't Lose Me In The Confusion*		$4		Capitol 4799
5/24/80	60	6		48 **Somethin' 'Bout You Baby I Like** ....*Late Night Confession*	42	$4		Capitol 4865
				GLEN CAMPBELL and RITA COOLIDGE				
8/30/80	80	4		49 **Hollywood Smiles** ....*Hooked On Love*		$4		Capitol 4909
9/27/80	59	6		50 **Dream Lover** *Bronco*		$4		MCA 41323
				TANYA TUCKER AND GLEN CAMPBELL				
				#2 Pop hit for **Bobby Darin** in 1959				
11/22/80+	10	17		51 **Any Which Way You Can** *Medley From "Any Which Way You Can"*		$4		Warner 49609
				from the movie starring **Clint Eastwood**				
2/7/81	54	7		52 **I Don't Want To Know Your Name**..........................*Daisy A Day*	65	$4		Capitol 4959
4/11/81	85	4		53 **Why Don't We Just Sleep On It Tonight** ....*It's Your World*		$4		Capitol 4986
				GLEN CAMPBELL and TANYA TUCKER				
8/8/81	15	12		54 **I Love My Truck** *Melody's Melody*	94	$4		Mirage 3845
				from the movie *The Night The Lights Went Out In Georgia* starring Kristy McNichol				
10/30/82	44	8		55 **Old Home Town** *Heartache #3*		$3	■	Atlantic Amer. 99967
1/15/83	17	17		56 **I Love How You Love Me**.....................*Hang On Baby (Ease My Mind)*		$3		Atlantic Amer. 99930
				#5 Pop hit for The Paris Sisters in 1961				
6/11/83	85	3		57 **On The Wings Of My Victory**..................................*A Few Good Men*		$3		Atlantic Amer. 99893
6/23/84	10	22		58 **Faithless Love** *Scene Of The Crime*		$3		Atlantic Amer. 99768
10/27/84	47	12		59 **Slow Nights** *Midnight Love*		$3		MCA 52474
				MEL TILLIS WITH GLEN CAMPBELL				
12/1/84+	4	20		60 **A Lady Like You** *A:4 / S:5 Tennessee*		$3		Atlantic Amer. 99691
5/18/85	14	21		61 **(Love Always) Letter To Home** ....*A:11 / S:18 An American Trilogy*		$3		Atlantic Amer. 99647
11/16/85+	7	21		62 **It's Just A Matter Of Time** *S:7 / A:7 Gene Autry, My Hero*		$3	■	Atlantic Amer. 99600
				#3 Pop hit for Brook Benton in 1959				
4/26/86	38	11		63 **Cowpoke** *A:37 Rag Doll*		$3		Atlantic Amer. 99559
7/26/86	52	8		64 **Call Home** *Sweet Sixteen*		$3		Atlantic Amer. 99525
5/30/87	6	28		65 **The Hand That Rocks The Cradle** *S:11 Arkansas*		$3		MCA 53108
				GLEN CAMPBELL with Steve Wariner				
10/3/87+	5	23		66 **Still Within The Sound Of My Voice** *S:20 In My Life*		$3		MCA 53172

CAMPBELL, Glen — Cont'd

DEBUT	PEAK	WKS		A-side / B-side	Pop	$	Pic	Label & Number
2/20/88	32	12		67 I Remember You .... *For Sure, For Certain, Forever, For Always* #5 Pop hit for **Frank Ifield** in 1962		$3		MCA 53245
5/28/88	7	23		68 I Have You .... S:28 *I'm A One Woman Man*		$3		MCA 53218
10/1/88	35	10		69 Light Years .... *Heart Of The Matter*		$3		MCA 53426
1/21/89	47	14		70 More Than Enough .... *Our Movie*		$3		MCA 53493
9/30/89	6	26		71 She's Gone, Gone, Gone .... *William Tell Overture*		$3		Universal 66024
3/17/90	61	8		72 Walkin' In The Sun .... from the album *Walkin' In The Sun* on Capitol 93884				album cut
1/26/91	27	16		73 Unconditional Love				album cut
6/1/91	70	5		74 Livin' In A House Full Of Love .... above 2 from the album *Unconditional Love* on Capitol 90992				album cut
1/23/93	66	9		75 Somebody Like That .... from the album *Somebody Like That* on Liberty 97962				album cut

CAMPBELL, Jo Ann '62

Born on 7/20/38 in Jacksonville, Florida. Acted in the movies *Johnny Melody*, *Go Johnny Go* and *Hey, Let's Twist*. Married **Troy Seals**; recorded together as Jo Ann & Troy in 1964.

DEBUT	PEAK	WKS		A-side / B-side	Pop	$	Pic	Label & Number
9/22/62	24	3		(I'm The Girl On) Wolverton Mountain .... *Sloppy Joe* 38	38	$25		Cameo 223
				answer to "Wolverton Mountain" by **Claude King**; some pressings titled "I'm The Girl From Wolverton Mountain"				

CAMPBELL, Mike '84

Born in Odessa, Texas.

DEBUT	PEAK	WKS		A-side / B-side	Pop	$	Pic	Label & Number
12/26/81+	65	6		1 Barroom Games .... *All My Cloudy Days Are Gone*		$4		Columbia 02622
10/2/82	57	8		2 No Room To Cry .... *Just The Way I Am*		$4		Columbia 03154
5/14/83	76	5		3 Don't Say You Love Me (Just Love Me Again) .... *Barroom Games*		$4		Columbia 03838
12/17/83+	57	9		4 Sweet And Easy To Love .... *Nothing Shines Brighter Than You*		$4		Columbia 04225
3/17/84	52	10		5 One Sided Love Affair .... *Sweet And Easy To Love*		$4		Columbia 04387
7/14/84	77	3		6 You're The Only Star (In My Blue Heaven).................. *Sweet And Easy To Love* written and recorded by **Gene Autry** in 1946		$4		Columbia 04488

CAMPBELL, Stacy Dean '92

Born on 7/27/67 in Carlsbad, New Mexico. Male singer.

DEBUT	PEAK	WKS		A-side / B-side	Pop	$	Pic	Label & Number
7/4/92	54	8		1 Rosalee .... *Would You Run*		$3		Columbia 74357
10/17/92	65	3		2 Baby Don't You Know .... *One Little Teardrop*		$3		Columbia 74491
12/26/92+	55	11		3 Poor Man's Rose .... *I Won't*		$3		Columbia 74803
8/12/95	61	6		4 Honey I Do .... *Midnight Angel*		$3	▪	Columbia 77942

CANADIAN SWEETHEARTS, The '64

Canadian husband-and-wife duo: **Bob Regan** and **Lucille Starr**. Regan was born on 3/13/31. Died on 3/5/90 (age 58). Starr was born Lucille Savoie in St. Boniface, Manitoba, Canada. Divorced in 1977.

DEBUT	PEAK	WKS		A-side / B-side	Pop	$	Pic	Label & Number
2/1/64	45	1		1 Hootenanny Express .... *Half-Breed*		$10		A&M 727
9/30/67	72	2		2 Too Far Gone .... *Looking Back To See* **LUCILLE STARR**		$8		Epic 10205
2/10/68	51	5		3 Let's Wait A Little Longer .... *More Than Money Can Buy*		$8		Epic 10258
6/8/68	63	5		4 Is It Love?.............................. *Too Lonely, Too Long* **LUCILLE STARR**		$8		Epic 10317
1/3/70	50	9		5 Dream Baby.............................. *South Bound Plane* **BOB REGAN and LUCILLE STARR** #4 Pop hit for **Roy Orbison** in 1962		$8		Dot 17327

CANNON, Ace '77

Born Hubert Cannon on 5/4/34 in Grenada, Mississippi. Male saxophonist. Worked with **Bill Black's Combo**. Charted 5 pop hits from 1961-64.

DEBUT	PEAK	WKS		A-side / B-side	Pop	$	Pic	Label & Number
2/19/77	73	4		Blue Eyes Crying In The Rain .... *I'll Fly Away* [I]		$8		Hi 2313

CANNON, Jimmi '81

Female singer from Sylacauga, Alabama. Member of **Dean Martin**'s Golddiggers from 1971-73.

DEBUT	PEAK	WKS		A-side / B-side	Pop	$	Pic	Label & Number
10/24/81	63	5		1 Whole Lot Of Cheatin' Goin' On.................. *He Just Said Goodbye*		$4		Warner 49806
3/20/82	78	5		2 Even If It's Wrong .... *Stealin' Feelin's*		$4		Warner 50024
8/28/82	81	4		3 Fool's Gold .... *Heartache By Heartache*		$4		Warner 29949

CANNONS, The '86

Family trio from Oklahoma: twins Karla (piano, trumpet, fiddle) and Darla (guitar, saxophone), with brother Larry (guitar, trumpet, banjo).

DEBUT	PEAK	WKS		A-side / B-side	Pop	$	Pic	Label & Number
12/3/83	90	2		1 One Step Closer.......................... *Strangers Again*		$5		Compleat 116
11/8/86	72	7		2 Do You Mind If I Step Into Your Dreams .... *How Can I Love Now*		$4	▪	Mercury 888048
8/1/87	73	4		3 Love'll Come Lookin' For You.................... *I'll Save My Love For You*		$4		Mercury 888648

CANYON '89

Group from Texas: Steve Cooper (vocals, guitar), Johnny Boatright (guitar), Jay Brown (keyboards), Randy Russell Rigney (bass) and Keech Rainwater (drums). Rainwater later joined **Lonestar**.

DEBUT	PEAK	WKS		A-side / B-side	Pop	$	Pic	Label & Number
2/6/88	59	6		1 Overdue .... *In The Middle Of The Night*		$4		16th Avenue 70410
5/28/88	54	9		2 In The Middle Of The Night.................... *Overdue*		$4		16th Avenue 70415
9/10/88	55	9		3 I Guess I Just Missed You .... *Love Wins*		$4		16th Avenue 70419
11/26/88+	47	10		4 Love Is On The Line .... *Love Wins*		$4		16th Avenue 70423
5/13/89	44	8		5 Right Track, Wrong Train .... *Oh, Help Me*		$4		16th Avenue 70426
8/12/89	40	10		6 Hot Nights .... *Oh, Help Me*		$4		16th Avenue 70433
11/25/89+	53	8		7 Radio Romance .... *Streamline*		$4		16th Avenue 70437
5/12/90	74	1		8 Carryin' On .... *Streamline*		$4		16th Avenue 70439
11/3/90	71	4		9 Dam These Tears .... *Carryin' On*		$3	▪	16th Avenue 70445

CAPITALS, The '80
Vocal group from Columbus, Ohio: Arti Portilla, Ronnie Cochran, Terry Kaufman and Jack Crum.

1/5/80	91	4		1 Me Touchin' You .... If I Was Still Sinning		$5	Ridgetop 00779
9/27/80	29	11		2 A Little Ground In Texas .... If I Was Still Sinnin'		$5	Ridgetop 01080
3/7/81	45	8		3 Bridge Over Broadway .... Love Him Out Of Your Mind		$5	Ridgetop 01281

CAPPS, Hank '72

9/16/72	33	13		Bowling Green ....Roll Mississippi Roll		$7	Capitol 3416
				#40 Pop hit for **The Everly Brothers** in 1967			

CAPTAIN & TENNILLE '78
Husband-and-wife duo: Daryl "The Captain" Dragon (b: 8/27/42 in Los Angeles) and Toni Tennille (b: 5/8/43 in Montgomery, Alabama). Own TV show on ABC from 1976-77. Dragon is the son of noted conductor Carmen Dragon. Duo charted 14 pop hits from 1975-80.

5/6/78	97	3		I'm On My Way ....We Never Really Say Goodbye	74	$5	■ A&M 2027

CAPTAIN STUBBY & THE BUCCANEERS '49
Band led by Tom C. "Captain Stubby" Fouts (b: 11/24/18 in Carroll County, Indiana). Fouts played novelty instruments, such as a toilet seat with guitar strings ("gitarlet"). Worked on WLW-Cincinnati, own band from 1937. On WLS *National Barn Dance* for 10 years; made appearances on Don McNeil's *Breakfast Club*. Own *Polka-Go-Round* TV series on ABC from 1965-68. Later worked as a DJ on WLS-Chicago. The Buccaneers: Tiny Stokes (vocals, bass), Jerald Richards (tin whistle), Sonny Fleming (guitar) and Peter Kunatz (accordian).

2/12/49	13	1		1 Lavender Blue (Dilly Dilly) ....S:13 *Billy Boy*	16	$20	Decca 24547
				BURL IVES with Captain Stubby & The Buccaneers			
				#4 Pop hit for **Sammy Kaye** in 1949; #3 Pop hit for **Sammy Turner** in 1959			
7/16/49	12	1		2 Money, Marbles And Chalk ....J:12 *Tennessee Tears*		$20	Decca 46149
				Windy Breeze (vocal)			
7/23/49	14	1		3 Come Wet Your Mustache With Me..................J:14 *Country Boy*		$20	Decca 46169
				STUBBY AND THE BUCCANEERS (above 2)			

CARDWELL, Jack '53
Born on 11/9/30 in Chapman, Alabama; raised in Mobile, Alabama. Singer/songwriter/guitarist.

2/14/53	3	9		1 The Death Of Hank Williams S:3 / A:4 / J:5 *Two Arms*		$25	King 1172
9/26/53	7	2		2 Dear Joan S:7 *You're Looking For Something*		$25	King 1269
				answer to "A Dear John Letter" by **Jean Shepard**			

★273★ CARGILL, Henson '68
Born on 2/5/41 in Oklahoma City. Studied animal husbandry at Colorado State; worked as a deputy sheriff in Oklahoma County. Appeared on the TV series *Country Hayride* in Cincinnati. Later operated a large cattle ranch in Stillwater, Oklahoma.

1)Skip A Rope 2)None Of My Business 3)Row Row Row

12/9/67+	❶⁵	19		1 Skip A Rope *A Very Well Traveled Man*	25	$7	Monument 1041
4/27/68	11	12		2 Row Row Row ....Six White Horses		$7	Monument 1065
8/10/68	39	8		3 She Thinks I'm On That Train ....It Just Don't Take Me Long To Say Goodbye		$7	Monument 1084
1/25/69	8	14		4 None Of My Business *So Many Ways Of Saying She's Gone*		$7	Monument 1122
5/31/69	40	8		5 This Generation Shall Not Pass...............Little Girls And Little Boys		$7	Monument 1142
9/20/69	32	9		6 Then The Baby Came ....Hemphill Kentucky Consolidated Coal Mine		$7	Monument 1158
5/16/70	18	11		7 The Most Uncomplicated Goodbye I've Ever Heard.......Four Shades Of Love		$7	Monument 1198
7/17/71	44	9		8 Pencil Marks On The Wall ....Momma's Waiting		$6	Mega 0030
				#107 Pop hit for **Herschel Bernardi** in 1971			
11/27/71	65	3		9 Naked And Crying ....Afraid To Rock The Boat		$6	Mega 0043
3/4/72	64	4		10 I Can't Face The Bed Alone..............Daddy Don't You Walk So Fast		$6	Mega 0060
10/14/72	62	7		11 Red Skies Over Georgia 1932		$6	Mega 0090
10/13/73	28	13		12 Some Old California Memory ......A Writer Of Verses And A Singer Of Songs		$5	Atlantic 4007
3/2/74	78	7		13 She Still Comes To Me (To Pour The Wine) .... But You Know I Love You		$5	Atlantic 4016
5/25/74	29	13		14 Stop And Smell The Roses.........................Strawberry Roan		$5	Atlantic 4021
12/22/79+	29	13		15 Silence On The Line......................................Forever In Blue Jeans		$6	Copper Mountain 201
5/3/80	67	5		16 Have A Good Day..		$6	Copper Mountain 589

CARLETTE '85
Full name: Carlette Ruff. Wife of Oak Records owner Ray Ruff.

2/9/85	60	5		1 Any Way That You Want Me ....Oh Boy		$6	Oak 1079
4/6/85	71	5		2 Showdown		$5	Luv 106
6/8/85	52	9		3 You Can't Measure My Love		$5	Luv 107
8/17/85	65	7		4 Tonight's The Night ....You Know What I Need (When I Need It)		$5	Luv 109
2/22/86	72	5		5 Two Steps From The Blues...		$5	Luv 116
4/12/86	61	6		6 Sugar Shack ....You Know What I Need When I Need It		$5	Luv 118
				#1 Pop hit for **Jimmy Gilmer & The Fireballs** in 1963			
10/18/86	52	7		7 We Belong Together ....Tennessee		$5	■ Luv 125
5/2/87	63	4		8 Waltzin' With Daddy......................................Tennessee		$5	Luv 137
5/30/87	57	4		9 You've Lost That Loving Feeling		$5	Luv 142
				#1 Pop hit for **The Righteous Brothers** in 1965			

CARLILE, Tom '82
Born in 1943 in Miami.

6/20/81	93	2		1 Gold Cadillac ....Lay Down Sally		$5	Door Knob 157
8/29/81	73	6		2 Get It While You Can...................................M.D. 20/20 High		$5	Door Knob 162
10/17/81	49	12		3 Catch Me If You Can ....Get It While You Can		$5	■ Door Knob 167
1/30/82	84	3		4 Feel.....................................Walk Around The Block, Deanna		$5	■ Door Knob 172
2/20/82	70	5		5 Lover (Right Where I Want You) ....Walk Around The Block, Deanna		$5	■ Door Knob 170
5/8/82	59	9		6 Hurtin' For Your Love ....The Man Who Loved To Drink		$5	■ Door Knob 176
7/17/82	39	11		7 Back In Debbie's Arms ....Twenty Years Ago		$5	■ Door Knob 180
10/23/82	37	12		8 Green Eyes *No One To Tell My Heartache To*		$5	■ Door Knob 187
1/8/83	55	7		9 Rainin' Down In Nashville ....(I Went To) Heaven With The Devil		$5	Door Knob 191

CARLISLE, Bob '97
Born on 9/29/56 in Santa Anna, California. Contemporary Christian singer/songwriter/guitarist.

DEBUT	PEAK	WKS		A-side / B-side	Pop	$	Pic	Label & Number
5/24/97	45	12		**Butterfly Kisses** .... *(remix)*		$5		DMG/Jive 42456

#1 Adult Contemporary hit for 7 weeks in 1997

CARLISLES, The ★290★ '53
Group formed by **Bill Carlisle** (b: 12/19/08 in Wakefield, Kentucky) in 1951. Joined the *Grand Ole Opry* in 1953. From 1930-47, Bill performed with his brother Cliff (b: 5/6/04 in Mount Eden, Kentucky) as the **Carlisle Brothers**.

1)No Help Wanted 2)Is Zat You, Myrtle 3)Knothole

DEBUT	PEAK	WKS		#	A-side / B-side	Pop	$	Pic	Label & Number
10/26/46	5	1		1	**Rainbow At Midnight** .... *Don't Tell Me Your Worries* [N]		$20		King 535
					CARLISLE BROTHERS				
6/19/48	14	2		2	**Tramp On The Street** ....S:14 / J:14 *Don't Be Ashamed Of Mother* [N]		$20		King 697
					BILL CARLISLE				
12/15/51+	6	8		3	**Too Old To Cut The Mustard** ..... A:6 *My Happiness Belongs To Someone Else*		$20		Mercury 6348 (78)
1/10/53	❶⁴	24		4	**No Help Wanted** ..... A:❶⁴ / J:❶⁴ / S:2 *This Heart Is Not For Sale*		$20		Mercury 70028
4/11/53	3	13		5	**Knothole** .... A:3 / S:8 *Leave That Liar Alone* [N]		$20		Mercury 70109
7/25/53	2¹	8		6	**Is Zat You, Myrtle** ...... A:2 / S:9 *Something Different* [N]		$20		Mercury 70174
11/7/53+	5	6		7	**Tain't Nice (To Talk Like That)** .... A:5 / J:6 *Unpucker*		$20		Mercury 70232
					BILL CARLISLE & THE CARLISLES				
7/3/54	15	1		8	**Shake-A-Leg** ....A:15 *Let Me Hold Your Little Hand*		$20		Mercury 70351
10/9/54	12	5		9	**Honey Love** ....A:12 *Female Hercules*		$20		Mercury 70435
					#1 R&B hit for The Drifters in 1954				
12/11/65+	4	17		10	**What Kinda Deal Is This** ....*Shot Gun* [N]		$8		Hickory 1348
					BILL CARLISLE				

CARLLILE, Kathy '80
Born Mary Katherine Carllile in 1963. Daughter of Kenneth Ray "Thumbs" Carllile (guitarist with **Jimmy Dickens** and **Roger Miller**).

DEBUT	PEAK	WKS		A-side / B-side	Pop	$	Pic	Label & Number
4/5/80	61	8		**Stay Until The Rain Stops**		$6	■	Frontline 705

CARLSON, Paulette '92
Born on 10/11/52 in Northfield, Minnesota. Singer/songwriter/guitarist. Lead singer of **Highway 101**.

DEBUT	PEAK	WKS		#	A-side / B-side	Pop	$	Pic	Label & Number
6/25/83	65	7		1	**You Gotta Get To My Heart (Before You Lay A Hand On Me)** .... *With A Friend Like You (Who Needs A Lover)*		$4		RCA 13546
12/3/83	67	8		2	**I'd Say Yes** .... *Sweeter The Love*		$4		RCA 13599
3/10/84	72	4		3	**Can You Fool** .... *I Go To Pieces*		$4		RCA 13745
12/7/91+	21	20		4	**I'll Start With You**				album cut
					from the album *Love Goes On* on Capitol 97711				
5/30/92	68	1		5	**Not With My Heart You Don't** .... *It's Too Bad*		$3		Liberty 57737

CARMEN, Eric — see MANDRELL, Louise

CARNES, Kim '80
Born on 7/20/45 in Los Angeles. Singer/songwriter/pianist. Member of The New Christy Minstrels with husband/co-writer Dave Ellington and Kenny Rogers in the late 1960s.

DEBUT	PEAK	WKS		#	A-side / B-side	Pop	$	Pic	Label & Number
7/29/78	99	2		1	**You're A Part Of Me** ....*Shine On*	36	$5		Ariola America 7704
					GENE COTTON with Kim Carnes				
4/5/80	3	14		2	**Don't Fall In Love With A Dreamer** *Goin' Home To The Rock/Gideon Tanner*	4	$5	■	United Artists 1345
					KENNY ROGERS with Kim Carnes				
11/10/84	70	10		3	**What About Me?** .... *The Rest Of Last Night* (Rogers)	15	$3	■	RCA 13899
					KENNY ROGERS with KIM CARNES and JAMES INGRAM				
8/20/88	70	7		4	**Speed Of The Sound Of Loneliness** ....*Blood From The Bandit*		$3		MCA 53387
					Lyle Lovett (backing vocal)				
10/29/88	68	5		5	**Crazy In Love** ....*Blood From The Bandit*		$3	■	MCA 53433

CARNES, Rick & Janis '84
Husband-and-wife duo: Rick (b: 6/30/50 in Fayetteville, Arkansas; guitar) and Janis (b: 5/21/47 in Shelbyville, Tennessee; keyboards). Married in 1973; moved to Nashville in 1978.

DEBUT	PEAK	WKS		#	A-side / B-side	Pop	$	Pic	Label & Number
12/18/82+	67	6		1	**Have You Heard** .... *Blue, Only Blue*		$4		Elektra 69928
7/30/83	51	8		2	**Poor Girl** .... *Am I Wastin' My Time*		$4		Warner 29656
11/26/83+	32	16		3	**Does He Ever Mention My Name** .... *Silver Eagle*		$4		Warner 29448
8/18/84	74	4		4	**Long Lost Causes** .... *Standing In The Need Of Love*		$4		MCA 52414

CARPENTER, Kris '81
Male singer/guitarist from Amarillo, Texas.

DEBUT	PEAK	WKS		A-side / B-side	Pop	$	Pic	Label & Number
2/21/81	76	4		**My Song Don't Sing The Same** .... *Cheap Wine And Watered Down Whiskey*		$5		Door Knob 146

CARPENTER, Mary-Chapin ★149★ '94
Born on 2/21/58 in Princeton, New Jersey. Singer/songwriter/guitarist. Graduated from Brown University with a degree in American civilization. CMA Awards: 1992 & 1993 Female Vocalist of the Year.

1)Shut Up And Kiss Me 2)He Thinks He'll Keep Her 3)I Take My Chances 4)Down At The Twist And Shout
5)I Feel Lucky

DEBUT	PEAK	WKS		#	A-side / B-side	Pop	$	Pic	Label & Number
4/15/89	19	22		1	**How Do** ....*It Don't Bring You*		$3		Columbia 68677
9/2/89	8	26		2	**Never Had It So Good** *Other Streets And Other Towns*		$3		Columbia 69050
1/6/90	7	26		3	**Quittin' Time** *Heroes And Heroines*		$3		Columbia 73202
6/16/90	14	21		4	**Something Of A Dreamer**.....................*Slow Country Dance*		$3	▌	Columbia 73361
10/20/90+	16	20		5	**You Win Again** ....*The Moon And St. Christopher*		$3	▌	Columbia 73567
2/16/91	15	20		6	**Right Now**.................*What You Didn't Say*		$3		Columbia 73699

DEBUT	PEAK	WKS	Gold	A-side (Chart Hit)...B-side	Pop	$	Pic	Label & Number
				CARPENTER, Mary-Chapin — Cont'd				
6/8/91	2[1]	20		7 Down At The Twist And Shout _Halley Came To Jackson_		$3		Columbia 73838
10/26/91+	14	20		8 Going Out Tonight ...._When She's Gone_		$3		Columbia 74038
5/30/92	4	20		9 I Feel Lucky _Middle Ground_		$3		Columbia 74345
9/12/92	15	20		10 Not Too Much To Ask ...._I Am A Town_		$3		Columbia 74485
				MARY-CHAPIN CARPENTER with Joe Diffie				
12/26/92+	4	20		11 Passionate Kisses _Middle Ground_	57	$3	■	Columbia 74795
4/17/93	11	20		12 The Hard Way ...._Goodbye Again_		$3		Columbia 74930
8/21/93	16	20		13 The Bug _Rhythm Of The Blues_		$3		Columbia 77134
				first recorded by Dire Straits on their 1991 album _On Every Street_				
12/18/93+	2[1]	20		14 He Thinks He'll Keep Her _Only A Dream_		$3		Columbia 77316
4/30/94	2[1]	20		15 I Take My Chances _Come On Come On_		$3		Columbia 77476
9/10/94	❶[1]	20		16 Shut Up And Kiss Me _End Of My Pirate Days_	90	$3	■	Columbia 77696
12/10/94+	6	20		17 Tender When I Want To Be _John Doe No. 24_		$3	■	Columbia 77780
3/25/95	21	13		18 House Of Cards ...._Jubilee_		$3	■	Columbia 77826
7/1/95	45	9		19 Why Walk When You Can Fly ...._Stones In The Road_		$3	■	Columbia 77955
10/5/96+	11	20		20 Let Me Into Your Heart _S:18 Downtown_		$3	■	Columbia 78453
2/1/97	35	12		21 I Want To Be Your Girlfriend _Quittin' Time_		$3	■	Columbia 78511
4/19/97	64	7		22 The Better To Dream Of You				album cut
7/19/97	58	5		23 Keeping The Faith				album cut
				above 2 from the album _A Place In The World_ on Columbia 67501				
				CARPENTERS **'78**				
				Brother-sister duo from New Haven, Connecticut: Richard (b: 10/15/46) and Karen (b: 3/2/50) Carpenter. Karen died of heart failure due to anorexia nervosa on 2/4/83 (age 32). Duo charted 29 pop hits from 1970-82. Won the 1970 Best New Artist Grammy Award.				
2/18/78	8	14		Sweet, Sweet Smile _I Have You_	44	$5	■	A&M 2008
				written by Juice Newton				
				CARR, Eddie Lee **'89**				
7/29/89	98	1		Big Bad Mama		$5		Evergreen 1092
				CARR, Joe "Fingers" — see FORD, Tennessee Ernie				
				CARR, Kenny **'89**				
9/10/88	96	1		1 The Writing On The Wall		$6		Kottage 0090
5/20/89	88	3		2 Tell Me		$6		Kottage 0091
				CARSON, Jeff **'95**				
				Born Jeff Herndon on 12/16/64 in Tulsa, Oklahoma; raised in Gravette, Arkansas. Singer/songwriter/guitarist.				
3/11/95	69	4		1 Yeah Buddy _Betty's Takin' Judo_		$3	■	MCG/Curb 76946
6/3/95	❶[1]	20		2 Not On Your Love _S:5 Betty's Takin' Judo_	97	$3	■	MCG/Curb 76954
10/7/95	3	20		3 The Car/ _S:6_	113			
3/2/96	6	20		4 Holdin' Onto Somethin'		$3	■	MCG/Curb 76970
12/30/95	70	1		5 Santa Got Lost In Texas ...._(no B-side)_ [X]		$10		Curb 1208 (CD)
				available only as a promotional CD single				
8/10/96	62	6		6 That Last Mile				album cut
				from the album _Jeff Carson_ on MCG/Curb 77744				
4/5/97	55	10		7 Do It Again ...._(remix)_		$3	■	Curb 73018
8/16/97	64	4		8 Here's The Deal/ _S:7_	101			
6/14/97	66	7		9 Butterfly Kisses _S:6_	103	$3	■	Curb 73023
				CARSON, Joe **'64**				
				Singer from Brownwood, Texas. Died in a car crash in February 1964.				
8/3/63	27	2		1 I Gotta Get Drunk (And I Shore Do Dread It) ...._Who Will Buy My Memories_		$10		Liberty 55578
				written by Willie Nelson				
11/9/63+	19	10		2 Helpless ...._The Last Song (I'm Ever Gonna Sing)_		$10		Liberty 55614
3/7/64	34	11		3 Double Life ...._Fort Worth Jail_		$10		Liberty 55664
				CARSON, Wayne **'83**				
				Born Wayne Carson Thompson in Denver. Singer/songwriter.				
9/29/73	77	7		1 You're Gonna Love Yourself In The Morning............_Laurel Canyon_		$6		Monument 8581
12/25/76+	82	5		2 Barstool Mountain ...._Keep On_		$5		Elektra 45358
6/25/77	99	2		3 Bugle Ann ...._Down To The River_		$5		Elektra 45407
4/2/83	61	7		4 1 Yr 2 Mo 11 Days ...._The Timing's All Wrong_		$5		EMH 0017
				CARTEE, Alan **'77**				
				Recorded with brother Wayne as the Cartee Brothers in 1968 on the Reprise label.				
10/8/77	98	1		Let My Fingers Do The Walking (I'm Your Telephone Man) ....._Twenty-Five Women_ [N]		$7		Groovy 101
				answer to "Telephone Man" by Meri Wilson				
				CARTER, Anita **'51**				
				Born Ina Anita Carter on 3/31/33 in Maces Springs, Virginia. Member of **The Carter Family**. Daughter of Maybelle and Ezra Carter; sister of Helen and **June Carter**.				
5/19/51	2[1]	14		1 Down The Trail Of Achin' Hearts/ _J:2 / A:7 / S:7_				
4/21/51	4	11		2 Bluebird Island _S:4 / J:7_		$25		RCA Victor 48-0441
				HANK SNOW (The Singing Ranger) with ANITA CARTER and the Rainbow Ranch Boys (above 2)				
9/3/66	44	3		3 I'm Gonna Leave You ...._You Couldn't Get My Love Back (If You Tried)_		$8		RCA Victor 8923
10/21/67	61	3		4 Love Me Now (While I Am Living) ...._It's My Life (And I'll Live It)_		$8		RCA Victor 9307
3/30/68	4	15		5 I Got You _No One's Gonna Miss Me_		$8		RCA Victor 9480
				WAYLON JENNINGS & ANITA CARTER				
11/9/68	65	5		6 To Be A Child Again ...._Too Many Rivers_		$6		United Artists 50444

CARTER, Anita — Cont'd

DEBUT	PEAK	WKS	A-side	B-side	Pop	$	Label & Number
4/12/69	50	7	7 The Coming Of The Roads	*The Other Side Of The Coin*		$6	United Artists 50503
			JOHNNY DARRELL & ANITA CARTER				
1/16/71	41	8	8 Tulsa County	*Where Is The Start Of Lonely*		$5	Capitol 2994
10/23/71	61	8	9 A Whole Lotta Lovin'	*Loving Him Was Easier*		$5	Capitol 3194

CARTER, Benny   '44

Born Bennett Lester Carter on 8/8/07 in New York City. Alto saxophonist/trumpeter/clarinetist/pianist. Played in several bands, including **Duke Ellington**, until 1935. Own band to 1946. Appeared in the movie *The Snows Of Kilimanjaro* in 1952. Won Grammy's Lifetime Achievement Award in 1987.

DEBUT	PEAK	WKS	A-side	B-side	Pop	$	Label & Number
2/19/44	2¹	5	Hurry, Hurry!	*Poinciana (Pop #12)*	23	$20	Capitol 144
			BENNY CARTER And His Orchestra Savannah Churchill (vocal)				

CARTER, Brenda — see JONES, George

★309★   **CARTER, Carlene**   '90

Born Rebecca Carlene Smith on 9/26/55 in Madison, Tennessee. Daughter of **June Carter** and **Carl Smith**. Worked with **The Carter Family** from the late '60s into the early '70s. Went solo thereafter. Appeared in the London production of *Pump Boys And Dinettes*. Married to singer Nick Lowe from 1979-90. Later married Howie Epstein of Tom Petty & The Heartbreakers.
    1)Every Little Thing 2)Come On Back 3)I Fell In Love

DEBUT	PEAK	WKS	A-side	B-side	Pop	$	Pic	Label & Number
10/27/79	42	8	1 Do It In A Heartbeat	*Swap-Meat Rag*	108	$4		Warner 49083
10/25/80	76	5	2 Baby Ride Easy	*Too Bad About Sandy*		$4		Warner 49572
			CARLENE CARTER with Dave Edmunds					
12/2/89+	26	18	3 Time's Up	*Memphis Queen*		$3		Warner 22714
			SOUTHERN PACIFIC and CARLENE CARTER					
7/14/90	3	21	4 I Fell In Love	*Guardian Angel*		$3	▌	Reprise 19915
10/27/90+	3	20	5 Come On Back	*The Leavin' Side*		$3	▌	Reprise 19564
3/16/91	25	17	6 The Sweetest Thing	*Goodnight Dallas*		$3		Reprise 19398
8/10/91	33	12	7 One Love	*Easy From Now On*		$3		Reprise 19255
5/29/93	3	20	8 Every Little Thing	*Long Hard Fall*		$3	▌	Giant 18527
10/9/93	51	8	9 Unbreakable Heart	*Wastin' Time With You*		$3	▌	Giant 18373
2/5/94	50	9	10 I Love You 'Cause I Want To	*Nowhere Train*		$3		Giant 18265
5/14/94	43	10	11 Something Already Gone	*Amazing Grace*		$3		Atlantic 82595
			from the movie Maverick starring Mel Gibson and Jodie Foster					
12/31/94	66	1	12 Rockin' Little Christmas	*The Working Elf Blues* [X]		$3		Giant 18006
7/22/95	70	3	13 Love Like This	*One Tender Night*		$3	▌	Giant 17853
8/26/95	75	1	14 Hurricane	*One Tender Night*		$3	▌	Giant 17962

★389★   **CARTER, Deana**   '96

Pronounced: Dee-na. Born on 1/4/66 in Nashville. Singer/songwriter. Daughter of **Fred Carter, Jr.**

DEBUT	PEAK	WKS	A-side	B-side	Pop	$	Pic	Label & Number
8/17/96	❶²	20	1 Strawberry Wine S:❶³	*Before We Ever Heard Goodbye*	65	$3	▌	Capitol 58585
			1997 CMA winner: Single of the Year					
12/14/96+	❶²	20	2 We Danced Anyway S:❶⁵	*Rita Valentine*	72	$3	▌	Capitol 58626
3/29/97	5	20	3 Count Me In	*Did I Shave My Legs For This?*		$3		Capitol 19510
8/2/97	❶¹	20	4 How Do I Get There	*Did I Shave My Legs For This?*		$3		Capitol 19646
11/1/97	25	17	5 Did I Shave My Legs For This? S:9	*(live version)*	85	$3	▌	Capitol 58672

CARTER, Fred Jr.   '67

Born on 12/31/33 in Winnsboro, Louisiana. Singer/guitarist. Father of **Deana Carter**.

DEBUT	PEAK	WKS	A-side	B-side	Pop	$	Label & Number
10/14/67	70	3	And You Wonder Why	*It's A Rough Old Road*		$8	Monument 1022

★330★   **CARTER, June**   '67

Born Valerie June Carter on 6/23/29 in Maces Springs, Virginia. Member of **The Carter Family**. Daughter of Maybelle and Ezra Carter, sister of Helen and **Anita** Carter. Married **Carl Smith** in 1952 (later divorced); their daughter is **Carlene Carter**. Worked with **Elvis Presley**, then joined the **Johnny Cash** road show in 1961. Married Cash in 1968. CMA Award: 1969 Vocal Group of the Year (with Johnny Cash).
    1)If I Were A Carpenter 2)Jackson 3)Long-Legged Guitar Pickin' Man

DEBUT	PEAK	WKS	A-side	B-side	Pop	$	Label & Number
8/27/49	9	1	1 Baby, It's Cold Outside S:9 *Country Girl* [N]		22	$20	RCA Victor 21-0078
			HOMER and JETHRO with June Carter 45 rpm: 48-0075; from the movie *Neptune's Daughter* starring Esther Williams				
			JOHNNY CASH & JUNE CARTER:				
3/4/67	2¹	17	2 Jackson	*Pack Up Your Sorrows*		$8	Columbia 44011
			#14 Pop hit for Nancy Sinatra & Lee Hazlewood in 1967				
6/24/67	6	17	3 Long-Legged Guitar Pickin' Man	*You'll Be All Right*		$8	Columbia 44158
1/24/70	2¹	15	4 If I Were A Carpenter	*'Cause I Love You*	36	$8	Columbia 45064
			#8 Pop hit for Bobby Darin in 1966				
4/3/71	27	11	5 A Good Man	*Straw Upon The Wind*		$8	Columbia 45338
			JUNE CARTER CASH				
9/11/71	15	13	6 No Need To Worry	*I'll Be Loving You*		$8	Columbia 45431
7/15/72	29	7	7 If I Had A Hammer	*I Gotta Boy (And His Name Is John)*		$8	Columbia 45631
			#10 Pop hit for Peter, Paul & Mary in 1962				
1/20/73	27	10	8 The Loving Gift	*Help Me Make It Through The Night*		$7	Columbia 45758
9/29/73	69	10	9 Allegheny	*We're For Love*		$7	Columbia 45929
11/20/76+	26	11	10 Old Time Feeling	*Far Side Banks Of Jordan*		$5	Columbia 10436

CARTER, Woody   '49

DEBUT	PEAK	WKS	A-side	B-side	Pop	$	Label & Number
9/17/49	14	1	Sittin' On The Doorstep J:14 *Slippin' Around*			$50	Macy's 100
			WOODY CARTER and his Hoedown Boys				

CARTER FAMILY, The '63

Founded by Alvin Pleasant "A.P." Carter (b: 12/15/1893 in Maces Springs, Virginia; d: 11/7/60, age 66); with wife Sara Dougherty (b: 7/21/1899 in Flatwoods, Virginia; d: 1/8/79, age 79) and sister-in-law Maybelle Addington (b: 5/10/09 in Nickelsville, Virginia; d: 10/23/78, age 69). Joined from 1936-39 by Maybelle's daughters Helen, **Anita Carter**, and **June Carter**, and A.P.'s children Janette and Joe. Helen died on 6/2/98 (age 70). This group disbanded in 1943 and was re-formed by Maybelle and her daughters as the Carter Sisters and Mother Maybelle. Joined the *Grand Ole Opry* in 1948. Joined **Johnny Cash**'s road show in 1961. Original group entered the Country Music Hall of Fame in 1970. Known as "The First Family of Country Music." Chart hits below feature Maybelle and her daughters.

| 4/6/63 | 13 | 3 | | 1 Busted *Send A Picture Of Mother* | $10 | ■ | Columbia 42665 |

JOHNNY CASH With The Carter Family
#4 Pop hit for **Ray Charles** in 1963

| 9/4/71 | 37 | 11 | | 2 A Song To Mama...*One More Summer In Virginia* | $7 | | Columbia 45428 |

Johnny Cash (narration and vocal backing)

| 4/29/72 | 42 | 7 | | 3 Travelin' Minstrel Band ....*2001 (Ballad To The Future)* | $7 | | Columbia 45581 |
| 9/30/72 | 35 | 8 | | 4 The World Needs A Melody ....*A Bird With Broken Wings Can't Fly* | $7 | | Columbia 45679 |

THE CARTER FAMILY WITH JOHNNY CASH

| 8/4/73 | 57 | 7 | | 5 Praise The Lord And Pass The Soup..........................*The Ballad Of Barbara* | $7 | | Columbia 45890 |

JOHNNY CASH (With The Carter Family And The Oak Ridge Boys)

| 11/17/73+ | 34 | 10 | | 6 Pick The Wildwood Flower.................................*Diamonds In The Rough* | $7 | | Columbia 45938 |

JOHNNY CASH with MOTHER MAYBELLE CARTER

CARTWRIGHT, Lionel ★288★ '91

Born on 2/10/59 in Gallipolis, Ohio; raised in Milton, West Virginia. Singer/songwriter/guitarist.
1)Leap Of Faith 2)Give Me His Last Chance 3)My Heart Is Set On You

11/19/88+	45	13		1 You're Gonna Make Her Mine ....*In My Eyes*	$3		MCA 53444
2/18/89	14	25		2 Like Father Like Son..*A Little Lesser Blue*	$3		MCA 53498
6/17/89	3	24		3 Give Me His Last Chance *Let The Hard Times Roll*	$3		MCA 53651
10/14/89+	12	21		4 In My Eyes....................................*That's Why They Call It Falling*	$3		MCA 53723
3/24/90	8	23		5 I Watched It All (On My Radio) *Hard Act To Follow*	$3	∎	MCA 53779
7/28/90	7	20		6 My Heart Is Set On You *True Believer*	$3	∎	MCA 53849
12/1/90+	31	15		7 Say It's Not True...*In The Long Run*	$3		MCA 53955
7/6/91	❶¹	20		8 Leap Of Faith *Smack Dab In The Middle Of Love*	$3		MCA 54078
11/16/91+	24	20		9 What Kind Of Fool ....*I'm Your Man*	$3		MCA 54237
4/4/92	62	4		10 Family Tree ....*30 Nothin'*	$3		MCA 54366
8/15/92	63	11		11 Be My Angel ....*Sleep Walking*	$3		MCA 54440
10/31/92	50	15		12 Standing On The Promises ....*She Will*	$3		MCA 54514

CARVER, Johnny ★200★ '73

Born on 11/24/40 in Jackson, Mississippi. Singer/songwriter/guitarist. Began singing in the family's Gospel group. Started his own band, the Capital Cowboys, while still a teenager. Moved to Los Angeles in 1965, became leader of the house band at the Palomino Club.

1)Yellow Ribbon 2)You Really Haven't Changed 3)Afternoon Delight 4)Don't Tell
5)Tonight Someone's Falling In Love

12/23/67+	21	13		1 Your Lily White Hands...*What If It Happened To You*	$8		Imperial 66268
6/1/68	48	8		2 I Still Didn't Have The Sense To Go ....*Feelin' Kinda Sunday In My Thinkin'*	$8		Imperial 66297
12/7/68+	32	11		3 Hold Me Tight ....*My Heart's Been Marching*	$8		Imperial 66341

#5 Pop hit for Johnny Nash in 1968

4/5/69	26	9		4 Sweet Wine ....*With Every Heartbeat*	$8		Imperial 66361
8/2/69	41	10		5 That's Your Hang Up ....*Mother-In-Law*	$8		Imperial 66389
12/13/69+	43	9		6 Willie And The Hand Jive ....*Take Sadie Out To The Country*	$8		Imperial 66423

#9 Pop hit for the Johnny Otis Show in 1958

6/20/70	68	4		7 Harvey Harrington IV ....*Sybil's Rights*	$8		Imperial 66442
12/12/70	73	2		8 If You See My Baby ....*Paint Your Pretty Pictures*	$7		United Artists 50713
8/14/71	34	15		9 If You Think That It's All Right...........................*This Town's Not Big Enough*	$6		Epic 10760
12/25/71+	27	11		10 I Start Thinking About You..*Preserving Wildlife*	$6		Epic 10813
6/24/72	35	9		11 I Want You ....*I'm Talking About You Baby*	$6		Epic 10872
4/7/73	5	17		12 Yellow Ribbon *Since My Baby Left Me*	$5		ABC 11357

#1 Pop hit for Tony Orlando & Dawn in 1973

7/28/73	6	13		13 You Really Haven't Changed *Treat A Lady Like A Tramp*	$5		ABC 11374
12/8/73+	12	16		14 Tonight Someone's Falling In Love.................*Frank And Don, Howard, Too, Broadway Joe And You And Me*	$5		ABC 11403
4/13/74	27	12		15 Country Lullabye..*Pass Me By*	$5		ABC 11425
8/24/74	10	16		16 Don't Tell (That Sweet Ole Lady Of Mine) *'Till We Find It All Again*	$5		ABC 12017
1/18/75	39	11		17 January Jones ....*Did We Even Try*	$5		ABC 12052
6/7/75	64	7		18 Strings...*Double Exposure*	$5		ABC 12097
10/4/75	74	7		19 Start All Over Again ....*Love Signs*	$5		ABC/Dot 17576
3/6/76	77	5		20 Snap, Crackle And Pop ....*I Can't Go Swimming In Muddy Water*	$5		ABC/Dot 17614
7/4/76	9	14		21 Afternoon Delight *Double Exposure*	$5		ABC/Dot 17640
11/6/76	47	9		22 Love Is Only Love (When Shared By Two)............*It Don't Hurt To Be A Dreamer*	$5		ABC/Dot 17661
2/12/77	48	6		23 Sweet City Woman ....*'Till We Find It All Again*	$5		ABC/Dot 17675

#8 Pop hit for The Stampeders in 1971

| 3/12/77 | 29 | 10 | | 24 Living Next Door To Alice ....*Treat A Lady Like A Tramp* | $5 | | ABC/Dot 17685 |

#25 Pop hit for Smokie in 1977

| 6/18/77 | 36 | 9 | | 25 Down At The Pool ....*Double Exposure* | $5 | | ABC/Dot 17707 |
| 11/26/77 | 72 | 6 | | 26 Apartment ....*Frank And Don, Howard, Too, Broadway Joe And You And Me* | $5 | | ABC/Dot 17729 |

CARVER, Johnny — Cont'd

DEBUT	PEAK	WKS		A-side / B-side	Pop	$	Pic	Label & Number
6/14/80	90	3		27 Fingertips .... *Caribbean Nights*		$6		Equity 1902
1/24/81	73	5		28 S.O.S. .... *Fingertips*		$6		Tanglewood 1905
				#15 Pop hit for Abba in 1975				

CASEY, Karen '80

DEBUT	PEAK	WKS		A-side / B-side	Pop	$	Pic	Label & Number
2/23/80	92	2		Leavin' On Your Mind .... *Are You Lonesome Tonight?*		$6		Western Pride 112

CASH, Johnny ★3★ '58

Born J.R. Cash on 2/26/32 in Kingsland, Arkansas; raised in Dyess, Arkansas. In U.S. Air Force, 1950-54, where he adopted the name John Ray. Backed by The Tennessee Two: Luther Perkins (guitar) and Marshall Grant (bass). First recorded for Sun in 1955. On *Louisiana Hayride* and *Grand Ole Opry* in 1957. Own TV show for ABC from 1969-71. Worked with **June Carter** from 1961, married her in March 1968. Father of **Rosanne Cash** and stepfather of **Carlene Carter**. Brother of **Tommy Cash**. Acted on numerous TV shows. Known as "The Man In Black." CMA Awards: 1969 Vocal Group of the Year (with June Carter); 1969 Male Vocalist of the Year; 1969 Entertainer of the Year. Elected to the Country Music Hall of Fame in 1980. Won Grammy's Living Legends Award in 1990. Inducted into the Rock and Roll Hall of Fame in 1992.

1)Ballad Of A Teenage Queen 2)Guess Things Happen That Way 3)Ring Of Fire 4)I Walk The Line 5)Understand Your Man

DEBUT	PEAK	WKS		A-side / B-side	Pop	$	Pic	Label & Number
11/26/55	14	1		1 Cry! Cry! Cry! .... S:14 *Hey, Porter!*		$40		Sun 221
2/4/56	4	23		2 So Doggone Lonesome/ J:4 / A:8 / S:6				
2/11/56	4	20		3 Folsom Prison Blues A:4 / S:5 / J:5		$40		Sun 232
				also see #62 below				
6/9/56	❶⁶	43		4 I Walk The Line/ J:❶⁶ / A:❶¹ / S:2	17			Sun 241
		9		5 Get Rhythm .... S:flip / J:flip		$30		
				also see #65 below				
12/22/56+	❶⁵	28		6 There You Go/ J:❶⁵ / A:2 / S:2				Sun 258
12/22/56+	7	24		7 Train Of Love A:7 / S:13		$30		
5/27/57	9	15		8 Next In Line/ S:9 / A:9				Sun 266
		9		9 Don't Make Me Go .... S:flip	99	$30		
9/16/57	3	23		10 Home Of The Blues/ A:3 / S:5	88			Sun 279
10/7/57	13	2		11 Give My Love To Rose A:13		$30		
1/20/58	❶¹⁰	23		12 Ballad Of A Teenage Queen/ A:❶¹⁰ / S:❶⁸	14			Sun 283
				also see #133 below				
2/10/58	4	14		13 Big River A:4	flip	$25		
				also see #72 below				
5/26/58	❶⁸	24		14 Guess Things Happen That Way/ S:❶⁸ / A:❶³	11			
6/2/58	6	13		15 Come In Stranger A:6	66	$25	■	Sun 295
8/25/58	2⁴	16		16 The Ways Of A Woman In Love/ S:2 / A:2	24			
9/1/58	5	16		17 You're The Nearest Thing To Heaven	flip	$25		Sun 302
10/13/58	4	19		18 All Over Again/	38			
10/13/58	7	15		19 What Do I Care	52	$20	■	Columbia 41251
1/19/59	❶⁶	20		20 Don't Take Your Guns To Town *I Still Miss Someone*	32	$20	■	Columbia 41313
1/19/59	30	1		21 It's Just About Time .... *I Just Thought You'd Like To Know*	47	$25		Sun 309
3/30/59	8	13		22 Luther Played The Boogie/				
3/30/59	12	9		23 Thanks A Lot		$25		Sun 316
5/4/59	9	11		24 Frankie's Man, Johnny/	57			
5/11/59	13	11		25 You Dreamer You		$15		Columbia 41371
7/20/59	11	11		26 Katy Too/ *I Forgot To Remember To Forget*	66	$20		Sun 321
8/10/59	4	20		27 I Got Stripes/	43			
8/24/59	14	9		28 Five Feet High And Rising	76	$15		Columbia 41427
11/9/59	22	5		29 Goodbye Little Darlin' *You Tell Me*		$20		Sun 331
12/28/59	24	1		30 The Little Drummer Boy .... *I'll Remember You* [X]	63	$15	■	Columbia 41481
				#13 Pop hit for the Harry Simeone Chorale in 1958				
2/15/60	16	10		31 Straight A's In Love	84			
3/7/60	20	2		32 I Love You Because		$20		Sun 334
				JOHNNY CASH With The Gene Lowery Singers				
4/25/60	10	15		33 Seasons Of My Heart/				
5/9/60	13	8		34 Smiling Bill McCall [N]	110	$15		Columbia 41618
8/22/60	15	7		35 Second Honeymoon *Honky-Tonk Girl*	79	$15		Columbia 41707
12/26/60	30	1		36 Mean Eyed Cat *Port Of Lonely Hearts*		$20		Sun 347
				JOHNNY CASH And The Tennessee Two (all of above Sun Records, except #32)				
2/6/61	13	9		37 Oh Lonesome Me *Life Goes On*	93	$20		Sun 355
				JOHNNY CASH With The Gene Lowery Singers				
				all Sun records recorded from 1955-58				
6/12/61	24	2		38 The Rebel - Johnny Yuma .... *Forty Shades Of Green*	108	$15	■	Columbia 41995
				from the TV series *The Rebel* starring Nick Adams				
12/18/61+	11	14		39 Tennessee Flat-Top Box .... *Tall Men*	84	$10	■	Columbia 42147
3/31/62	24	3		40 The Big Battle *When I've Learned*		$10	■	Columbia 42301
7/14/62	8	10		41 In The Jailhouse Now *A Little At A Time*		$10	■	Columbia 42425
				#14 Pop hit for Jimmie Rodgers in 1928				
4/6/63	13	3		42 Busted *Send A Picture Of Mother*		$10	■	Columbia 42665
				JOHNNY CASH With The Carter Family				
				#4 Pop hit for Ray Charles in 1963				
6/8/63	❶⁷	26		43 Ring Of Fire *I'd Still Be There*	17	$10	■	Columbia 42788
11/9/63	2³	16		44 The Matador *Still In Town*	44	$10	■	Columbia 42880
2/22/64	❶⁶	22		45 Understand Your Man/	35			
3/7/64	49	1		46 Dark As A Dungeon	119	$10	☐	Columbia 42964

CASH, Johnny — Cont'd

DEBUT	PEAK	WKS	A-side (Chart Hit) / B-side	Pop	$	Pic	Label & Number
7/11/64	3	20	47 The Ballad Of Ira Hayes/				
7/25/64	8	15	48 Bad News		$10		Columbia 43058
11/7/64+	4	22	49 It Ain't Me, Babe — Time And Time Again	58	$10	☐	Columbia 43145
			June Carter (harmony vocal); #8 Pop hit for The Turtles in 1965				
2/20/65	3	16	50 Orange Blossom Special — All Of God's Children Ain't Free	80	$10		Columbia 43206
7/10/65	15	13	51 Mister Garfield — The Streets Of Laredo		$10		Columbia 43313
9/4/65	10	9	52 The Sons Of Katie Elder — A Certain Kinda Hurtin'	119	$10		Columbia 43342
			from the movie starring John Wayne				
11/20/65+	9	14	53 Happy To Be With You — Pickin' Time		$10		Columbia 43420
2/12/66	2²	18	54 The One On The Right Is On The Left — Cotton Pickin' Hands [N]	46	$10		Columbia 43496
7/2/66	17	9	55 Everybody Loves A Nut — Austin Prison	96	$10		Columbia 43673
9/10/66	39	5	56 Boa Constrictor — Bottom Of A Mountain [N]	107	$10		Columbia 43763
12/24/66+	20	13	57 You Beat All I Ever Saw — Put The Sugar To Bed		$10		Columbia 43921
3/4/67	2¹	17	58 Jackson — Pack Up Your Sorrows		$8		Columbia 44011
			JOHNNY CASH AND JUNE CARTER				
			#14 Pop hit for Nancy Sinatra & Lee Hazlewood in 1967				
6/24/67	6	17	59 Long-Legged Guitar Pickin' Man — You'll Be All Right		$8		Columbia 44158
			JOHNNY CASH AND JUNE CARTER				
10/28/67	60	6	60 The Wind Changes — Red Velvet		$8		Columbia 44288
12/23/67+	2²	15	61 Rosanna's Going Wild — Roll Call	91	$8	■	Columbia 44373
6/1/68	❶⁴	18	62 Folsom Prison Blues — The Folk Singer	32	$8	■	Columbia 44513
			"live" version of #3 above; recorded at Folsom Prison				
12/7/68+	❶⁶	20	63 Daddy Sang Bass — He Turned The Water Into Wine	42	$8		Columbia 44689
7/26/69	❶⁵	14	● 64 A Boy Named Sue — San Quentin [N]	2³	$8		Columbia 44944
			recorded "live" at San Quentin prison; CMA Award: Single of the Year				
10/11/69	23	12	65 Get Rhythm — Hey Porter [R]	60	$8		Sun 1103
			same version as #5 above with "live" effects dubbed-in				
11/22/69	4	13	66 Blistered/	50			
		12	67 See Ruby Fall		$8		Columbia 45020
1/24/70	2¹	15	68 If I Were A Carpenter — 'Cause I Love You	36	$8		Columbia 45064
			JOHNNY CASH & JUNE CARTER				
			#8 Pop hit for Bobby Darin in 1966				
2/28/70	35	7	69 Rock Island Line — Next In Line	93	$8		Sun 1111
			#8 Pop hit for Lonnie Donegan in 1956				
4/18/70	3	14	70 What Is Truth — Sing A Traveling Song [S]	19	$8		Columbia 45134
9/5/70	❶²	15	71 Sunday Morning Coming Down — I'm Gonna Try To Be That Way	46	$8		Columbia 45211
			"live" recording				
12/5/70	41	8	72 Big River — Come In Stranger [R]		$8		Sun 1121
			same version as #13 above				
12/19/70+	❶¹	13	73 Flesh And Blood — This Side Of The Law	54	$8		Columbia 45269
			from the movie I Walk The Line starring Gregory Peck				
3/27/71	3	13	74 Man In Black — Little Bit Of Yesterday	58	$8		Columbia 45339
6/26/71	18	10	75 Singing In Viet Nam Talking Blues — You've Got A New Light Shining [S]	124	$8		Columbia 45393
9/11/71	15	13	76 No Need To Worry — I'll Be Loving You		$8		Columbia 45431
			JOHNNY CASH & JUNE CARTER				
10/16/71	16	11	77 Papa Was A Good Man — I Promise You	104	$8		Columbia 45460
1/29/72	2¹	16	78 A Thing Called Love — Daddy	103	$8		Columbia 45534
			JOHNNY CASH And The Evangel Temple Choir (above 2)				
5/6/72	2³	12	79 Kate — The Miracle Man	75	$8		Columbia 45590
7/15/72	29	7	80 If I Had A Hammer — I Gotta Boy (And His Name Is John)		$8		Columbia 45631
			JOHNNY CASH & JUNE CARTER CASH				
			#10 Pop hit for Peter, Paul & Mary in 1962				
8/26/72	2²	15	81 Oney — Country Trash	101	$7		Columbia 45660
9/30/72	35	8	82 The World Needs A Melody — A Bird With Broken Wings Can't Fly		$7		Columbia 45679
			THE CARTER FAMILY WITH JOHNNY CASH				
12/23/72+	3	15	83 Any Old Wind That Blows — Kentucky Straight		$7		Columbia 45740
1/20/73	27	10	84 The Loving Gift — Help Me Make It Through The Night		$7		Columbia 45758
			JOHNNY CASH & JUNE CARTER CASH				
4/21/73	30	9	85 Children — Last Supper		$7		Columbia 45786
			from the movie The Gospel Road starring Cash				
8/4/73	57	7	86 Praise The Lord And Pass The Soup — The Ballad Of Barbara		$7		Columbia 45890
			JOHNNY CASH (With The Carter Family And The Oak Ridge Boys)				
9/29/73	69	10	87 Allegheny — We're For Love		$7		Columbia 45929
			JOHNNY CASH & JUNE CARTER				
11/17/73+	34	10	88 Pick The Wildwood Flower — Diamonds In The Rough		$7		Columbia 45938
			JOHNNY CASH with MOTHER MAYBELLE CARTER				
2/23/74	52	8	89 Orleans Parish Prison — Jacob Green		$7		Columbia 45997
4/27/74	31	13	90 Ragged Old Flag — Don't Go Near The Water		$7		Columbia 46028
12/14/74+	14	12	91 Lady Came From Baltimore — Lonesome To The Bone		$6		Columbia 10066
4/12/75	42	9	92 My Old Kentucky Home (Turpentine And Dandelion Wine) — Hard Times Comin'		$6		Columbia 10116
7/26/75	17	12	93 Look At Them Beans — All Around Cowboy		$6		Columbia 10177
11/15/75+	35	12	94 Texas - 1947 — I Hardly Ever Sing Beer Drinking Songs		$6		Columbia 10237
2/7/76	54	7	95 Strawberry Cake — I Got Stripes		$6		Columbia 10279
4/10/76	❶²	15	96 One Piece At A Time — Go On Blues [N]	29	$6		Columbia 10321
7/24/76	29	8	97 Sold Out Of Flagpoles — Mountain Lady		$6		Columbia 10381
10/23/76	41	8	98 It's All Over — Ridin' On The Cotton Belt		$6		Columbia 10424
			JOHNNY CASH & The Tennessee Three (above 3)				

DEBUT	PEAK	WKS	Gold	A-side (Chart Hit)...B-side	Pop	$	Pic	Label & Number
				CASH, Johnny — Cont'd				
11/20/76+	26	11		99 Old Time Feeling .... _Far Side Banks Of Jordan_		$5		Columbia 10436
				JOHNNY CASH & JUNE CARTER CASH				
2/26/77	38	9		100 The Last Gunfighter Ballad .... _City Jail_		$5		Columbia 10483
8/6/77	46	9		101 Lady .... _Hit The Road And Go_		$5		Columbia 10587
10/22/77	32	12		102 After The Ball .... _Calilou_		$5		Columbia 10623
2/11/78	12	13		103 I Would Like To See You Again .... _Lately_		$5		Columbia 10681
5/20/78	2²	13		104 There Ain't No Good Chain Gang/				
11/17/79+	22	12		105 I Wish I Was Crazy Again		$5		Columbia 10742
				JOHNNY CASH & WAYLON JENNINGS (above 2)				
9/9/78	44	8		106 Gone Girl .... _I'm Alright Now_		$5		Columbia 10817
12/9/78	89	2		107 It'll Be Her .... _It Comes And Goes_		$5		Columbia 10855
1/13/79	21	13		108 I Will Rock And Roll With You .... _A Song For The Life_		$5		Columbia 10888
5/19/79	2¹	16		109 (Ghost) Riders In The Sky _I'm Gonna Sit On The Porch And Pick On My Old Guitar_		$5	■	Columbia 10961
10/20/79	42	7		110 I'll Say It's True .... _Cocaine Blues_		$5		Columbia 11103
				George Jones (guest vocal)				
4/19/80	66	5		111 Bull Rider .... _Lonesome To The Bone_		$5		Columbia 11237
6/7/80	54	8		112 Song Of The Patriot .... _She's A Go-er_		$5		Columbia 11283
				Marty Robbins (harmony vocal)				
8/23/80	53	8		113 Cold Lonesome Morning .... _The Cowboy Who Started The Fight_		$5		Columbia 11340
11/29/80	85	4		114 The Last Time .... _Rockabilly Blues (Texas 1955)_		$5		Columbia 11399
1/24/81	78	5		115 Without Love .... _It Ain't Nothing New Babe_		$5		Columbia 11424
3/21/81	10	15		116 The Baron _I Will Dance With You_		$4		Columbia 60516
7/25/81	60	5		117 Mobile Bay .... _The Hard Way_		$4		Columbia 02189
1/23/82	71	5		118 The Reverend Mr. Black/		$4		
				#8 Pop hit for The Kingston Trio in 1963				
		5		119 Chattanooga City Limit Sign		$4		Columbia 02669
4/17/82	26	12		120 The General Lee _Duelin' Dukes_		$4		Scotti Brothers 02803
				from the TV series _The Dukes Of Hazzard_ starring **John Schneider** and **Tom Wopat**				
8/7/82	55	8		121 Georgia On A Fast Train .... _Sing A Song_		$4		Columbia 03058
2/26/83	84	2		122 We Must Believe In Magic .... _I'll Cross Over Jordan Someday_		$4		Columbia 03524
9/24/83	75	4		123 I'm Ragged But I'm Right .... _Brand New Dance_ (w/June Carter)		$4		Columbia 04060
5/12/84	84	5		124 That's The Truth .... _Joshua Gone Barbados_		$4		Columbia 04428
7/14/84	45	11		125 The Chicken In Black .... _Battle Of Nashville_ [N]		$4		Columbia 04513
5/18/85	❶¹	20		126 Highwayman S:❶¹ / A:❶¹ _The Human Condition_		$4	■	Columbia 04881
				WAYLON JENNINGS/WILLIE NELSON/JOHNNY CASH/KRIS KRISTOFFERSON				
7/13/85	45	9		127 I Will Dance With You .... _Too Bad For Love_		$4		Warner 28979
				KAREN BROOKS with **Johnny Cash**				
9/14/85	15	18		128 Desperados Waiting For A Train..... S:15 / A:16 _The Twentieth Century Is Almost Over_		$4		Columbia 05594
				WAYLON JENNINGS/WILLIE NELSON/JOHNNY CASH/KRIS KRISTOFFERSON				
5/17/86	35	11		129 Even Cowgirls Get The Blues .... A:34 _American By Birth_		$4		Columbia 05896
				JOHNNY CASH & WAYLON JENNINGS				
3/28/87	43	11		130 The Night Hank Williams Came To Town .... _I'd Rather Have You_		$3		Mercury 888459
				Waylon Jennings (guest vocal)				
12/12/87	72	5		131 W. Lee O'Daniel (And The Light Crust Dough Boys) .... _Letters From Home_		$3		Mercury 870010
9/24/88	21	20		132 That Old Wheel .... S:17 _Tennessee Flat Top Box_		$3		Mercury 870688
				JOHNNY CASH with **Hank Williams, Jr.**				
2/25/89	45	9		133 Ballad Of A Teenage Queen .... _Get Rhythm_ (Cash) [R]		$3		Mercury 872420
				JOHNNY CASH with **Rosanne Cash & The Everly Brothers**				
				new version of #12 above				
3/3/90	25	14		134 Silver Stallion .... _American Remains_		$3		Columbia 73233
				WAYLON JENNINGS/WILLIE NELSON/JOHNNY CASH/KRIS KRISTOFFERSON				
9/22/90	69	4		135 Goin' By The Book .... _Beans For Breakfast_		$3		Mercury 878292

CASH, Rosanne ★116★   **'86**

Born on 5/24/56 in Memphis. Daughter of **Johnny Cash** and Vivian Liberto. Raised by her mother in California, then moved to Nashville after high school graduation. Worked in the Johnny Cash Road Show. Married to **Rodney Crowell** from 1979-92. Moved to New York. Married producer John Leventhal in 1995. Released short-story collection _Bodies Of Water_ in 1996.

1)_Never Be You_ 2)_The Way We Make A Broken Heart_ 3)_If You Change Your Mind_ 4)_It's Such A Small World_
5)_Seven Year Ache_

DEBUT	PEAK	WKS	Gold	A-side	Pop	$	Pic	Label & Number
9/8/79	17	12		1 No Memories Hangin' Round .... _This Has Happened Before_		$4		Columbia 11045
				ROSANNE CASH with **BOBBY BARE**				
2/2/80	15	13		2 Couldn't Do Nothin' Right .... _Seeing's Believing_		$4		Columbia 11188
5/31/80	25	12		3 Take Me, Take Me .... _Right Or Wrong_		$4		Columbia 11268
2/21/81	❶¹	19		4 Seven Year Ache _Blue Moon With Heartache_	22	$4	□	Columbia 11426
8/29/81	❶¹	16		5 My Baby Thinks He's A Train .... _I Can't Resist_		$4		Columbia 02463
12/19/81+	❶¹	18		6 Blue Moon With Heartache .... _Only Human_	104	$4		Columbia 02659
5/29/82	4	18		7 Ain't No Money .... _The Feelin'_		$4		Columbia 02937
10/9/82+	8	20		8 I Wonder .... _Oh Yes I Can_		$4		Columbia 03283
3/12/83	14	15		9 It Hasn't Happened Yet .... _Somewhere In The Stars_		$4		Columbia 03705
6/1/85	❶¹	24		10 I Don't Know Why You Don't Want Me S:❶¹ / A:❶¹ _What You Gonna Do About It_		$3	■	Columbia 04809
10/5/85+	❶¹	24		11 Never Be You S:❶¹ / A:❶¹ _Closing Time_		$3		Columbia 05621
2/15/86	5	22		12 Hold On S:5 / A:5 _Never Gonna Hurt_		$3		Columbia 05794
7/19/86	5	20		13 Second To No One A:4 / S:6 _Never Alone_		$3		Columbia 06159

DEBUT	PEAK	WKS	Gold	A-side ... B-side	Pop	$	Pic	Label & Number
				CASH, Rosanne — Cont'd				
6/27/87	❶¹	23		14 The Way We Make A Broken Heart　　　　S:❶¹ *707*		$3		Columbia 07200
11/14/87+	❶¹	22		15 Tennessee Flat Top Box　S:❶³ *Why Don't You Quit Leaving Me Alone*		$3		Columbia 07624
1/23/88	❶¹	23		16 It's Such A Small World　　　S:❶³ *Crazy Baby*		$3		Columbia 07693
				RODNEY CROWELL & ROSANNE CASH				
4/2/88	❶¹	22		17 If You Change Your Mind　　　S:❶² *Somewhere Sometime*		$3		Columbia 07746
8/13/88	❶¹	23		18 Runaway Train　　　　　S:❶¹ *Seven Year Ache*		$3	■	Columbia 07988
2/25/89	45	9		19 Ballad Of A Teenage Queen............... *Get Rhythm* (Cash)		$3		Mercury 872420
				JOHNNY CASH with Rosanne Cash & The Everly Brothers				
3/25/89	❶¹	21		20 I Don't Want To Spoil The Party　　*Look What Our Love Is Coming To*		$3	■	Columbia 68599
				#39 Pop hit for The Beatles in 1965				
11/4/89	37	11		21 Black And White　　　　　　*Never Be You*		$3		Columbia 73054
3/3/90	63	6		22 One Step Over The Line......................... *Riding Alone*		$3		MCA 53795
				THE NITTY GRITTY DIRT BAND Featuring Rosanne Cash and John Hiatt				
9/29/90	39	11		23 What We Really Want .... *Portrait*		$3	▮	Columbia 73517
2/23/91	69	1		24 On The Surface				album cut
				from the album *Interiors* on Columbia 46079				
	★258★			**CASH, Tommy**　　　　　　　　**'70**				
				Born on 4/5/40 in Dyess, Arkansas. Singer/songwriter/guitarist. Younger brother of **Johnny Cash**.				
				1)Six White Horses 2)Rise And Shine 3)One Song Away				
8/31/68	41	9		1 The Sounds Of Goodbye................................... *Easy Woman*		$10		United Artists 50337
6/21/69	43	11		2 Your Lovin' Takes The Leavin' Out Of Me .... *That Lucky Old Sun*		$8		Epic 10469
11/22/69+	4	16		3 Six White Horses　　　　　*I Owe The World To You*	79	$8		Epic 10540
3/28/70	9	14		4 Rise And Shine　　　　　　　*The Honest Truth*		$8		Epic 10590
7/18/70	9	13		5 One Song Away　　　　　　　*The Ramblin' Kind*		$8		Epic 10630
11/21/70	36	9		6 The Tears On Lincoln's Face .... *Only Place For Me*		$8		Epic 10673
3/13/71	20	11		7 So This Is Love .... *Love Is Gone*		$8		Epic 10700
7/10/71	28	10		8 I'm Gonna Write A Song .... *I'm Nowhere Without You*		$8		Epic 10756
12/4/71	67	2		9 Roll Truck Roll .... *The Song Belongs To You*		$8		Epic 10795
3/25/72	32	11		10 You're Everything .... *Someday When All My Dreams Come True*		$8		Epic 10838
7/15/72	22	11		11 That Certain One .... *A Free Man*		$8		Epic 10885
10/28/72	24	11		12 Listen .... *Fool Maker*		$8		Epic 10915
3/24/73	37	10		13 Workin' On A Feelin' .... *Tomorrow Will Be A New Day*		$8		Epic 10964
7/28/73	16	13		14 I Recall A Gypsy Woman .... *You'll Need The Love (I Have For You One Day)*		$8		Epic 11026
11/24/73+	21	13		15 She Met A Stranger, I Met A Train .... *The Only Place For Me*		$8		Epic 11057
3/22/75	58	9		16 The One I Sing My Love Songs To .... *Goodbye Ringin' In My Ear*		$5		Elektra 45241
1/10/76	94	4		17 Broken Bones .... *The Ballad Of Jack And Lucille*		$5		20th Century 2263
7/16/77	63	6		18 The Cowboy And The Lady .... *Lady I Love You*		$5		Monument 45222
2/11/78	98	3		19 Take My Love To Rita .... *We Finally Got It Right*		$5		Monument 45238
				CASHMAN & WEST　　　　　　　　**'73**				
				Duo of singer/songwriters Dennis "Terry Cashman" Minogue and Thomas "Tommy West" Picardo.				
2/10/73	69	2		Songman .... *If You Were A Rainbow*	59	$6		Dunhill/ABC 4333
				CASSADY, Linda　　　　　　　　**'78**				
				Female singer from California.				
5/22/76	83	8		1 C.B. Widow .... *Do You Still Want What's Left Of Me*		$5		Cin Kay 107
9/11/76	91	4		2 If It's Your Song You Sing It .... *This Isn't Just Another Love Song*		$5		Cin Kay 111
1/29/77	79	6		3 Little Things Mean A Lot .... *Sounds Of Love*		$5		Cin Kay 115
				#1 Pop hit for Kitty Kallen in 1954				
4/9/77	92	4		4 I Don't Hurt Anymore .... *Baby There's Nothing Wrong With Me*		$5		Cin Kay 116
2/4/78	91	3		5 Little Teardrops (Are Smarter Than You Think)		$5		Cin Kay 127
4/29/78	87	4		6 (There's Nothing Like The Love) Between A Woman And A Man .... *Finer Side Of Life*		$5		Cin Kay 129
				LINDA CASSADY/BOBBY SPEARS				
8/5/78	76	6		7 Lonely Side Of The Bed　　　　*That's The Way It Is*		$5		Cin Kay 047
				CATES SISTERS, The　　　　　　**'78**				
				Duo of sisters Margie and Marcy Cates from Independence, Missouri. Both are singers and multi-instrumentalists.				
				1)I've Been Loved 2)I'll Always Love You 3)Lovin' You Off My Mind				
9/11/76	82	5		1 Mr. Guitar .... *Love Is A Beautiful Thing*		$5		Caprice 2024
1/29/77	50	8		2 Out Of My Mind .... *Run Your Sweet Love By Me*		$5		Caprice 2030
				THE CATES				
5/21/77	74	6		3 Can't Help It		$5		Caprice 2032
8/13/77	87	5		4 Throw Out Your Loveline .... *West Virginia Smile*		$5		Caprice 2038
10/1/77	30	11		5 I'll Always Love You .... *Second Chance*		$5		Caprice 2036
12/24/77+	29	11		6 I've Been Loved .... *Faded Love*		$5		Caprice 2041
3/18/78	61	7		7 Long Gone Blues .... *San Antonio Rose*		$5		Caprice 2047
9/2/78	39	8		8 Lovin' You Off My Mind .... *Amazing Grace*		$5		Caprice 2051
				THE CATES:				
2/17/79	78	5		9 Going Down Slow .... *Can I See You Tonight*		$5		Ovation 1123
6/30/79	57	8		10 Make Love To Me .... *Day After Day*		$5	■	Ovation 1126
12/22/79+	68	7		11 Let's Go Through The Motions .... *Don't Say Love*		$5		Ovation 1134
5/24/80	72	5		12 Gonna Get Along Without You Now ...... *I've Been Lovin' You Too Long*		$5		Ovation 1144
				#11 Pop hit for Patience & Prudence in 1956				
10/25/80	75	4		13 Lightnin' Strikin' .... *Touch And Go*		$5		Ovation 1155

CATO, Connie '75
Born Connie Ann Cato on 3/30/55 in Carlinville, Illinois.
1)Hurt 2)Superskirt 3)You Better Hurry Home

DEBUT	PEAK	WKS		A-side	B-side	$	Label & Number
2/2/74	33	16	1	Superskirt	*Big Stick Of Dynamite*	$5	Capitol 3788
7/13/74	73	7	2	Super Kitten	*We'd Better Stop*	$5	Capitol 3908
10/19/74	92	6	3	Lincoln Autry	*After Midnight*	$5	Capitol 3958
3/8/75	14	14	4	Hurt	*He'll Be Lovin' Her*	$5	Capitol 4035

#4 Pop hit for Timi Yuro in 1961

7/26/75	83	6	5	Yes	*Good Hearted Woman*	$5	Capitol 4113
11/22/75+	53	10	6	Who Wants A Slightly Used Woman	*Somewhere South Of Macon*	$5	Capitol 4169
4/24/76	91	4	7	I Love A Beautiful Guy	*Plastic Saddle*	$5	Capitol 4243
8/7/76	80	5	8	Here Comes That Rainy Day Feeling Again	*I'll Be A Lady Tomorrow*	$5	Capitol 4303

#15 Pop hit for The Fortunes in 1971

| 11/6/76 | 76 | 6 | 9 | I'm Sorry | *Evil On Your Mind* | $5 | Capitol 4345 |

#1 Pop hit for Brenda Lee in 1960

| 2/19/77 | 92 | 3 | 10 | Don't You Ever Get Tired (Of Hurting Me) | *I've Been Loved By You Today* | $5 | Capitol 4379 |
| 8/16/80 | 49 | 7 | 11 | You Better Hurry Home (Somethin's Burnin') | *Hangin' On My Heart* | $4 | MCA 41287 |

CAUDELL, Lane '87
Born in Asheboro, North Carolina. Male singer/actor. Played "Woody King" on TV's *Days Of Our Lives*.

| 9/19/87 | 66 | 5 | 1 | Souvenirs | *The Honeymoon Is Over* | $4 | 16th Avenue 70403 |
| 4/16/88 | 77 | 5 | 2 | I Need A Good Woman Bad | *Souvenirs* | $4 | 16th Avenue 70411 |

C COMPANY '71
Group of studio musicians led by DJ/singer Terry Nelson from Russellville, Alabama.

| 5/1/71 | 49 | 3 | ● | Battle Hymn Of Lt. Calley | *Routine Patrol* [S] | 37 | $5 | Plantation 73 |

C COMPANY Featuring TERRY NELSON

CEDAR CREEK '82
Eight-man group: Dave Holcraft, Ken Harden, Don Edmunds and Ron Spearman (vocals), Sam Stricklan (guitar), Garland Craft (keyboards), Tony Perkins (bass) and Chris Golden (drums). Golden is the son of William Lee Golden and a member of The Goldens.

11/14/81	80	4	1	Looks Like A Set-Up To Me	*This Old Heart (Is Gonna Rise Again)*	$5	Moon Shine 3001
2/6/82	42	10	2	Took It Like A Man, Cried Like A Baby	*Dreamin' Thru Another Day*	$5	Moon Shine 3003
1/22/83	83	3	3	Take A Ride On A Riverboat		$5	Moon Shine 3008
8/6/83	81	3	4	Lonely Heart		$5	Moon Shine 3013

CERRITO '89
Male singer.

| 4/22/89 | 84 | 3 | 1 | Daydream | | $5 | Soundwaves 4818 |
| 9/23/89 | 79 | 3 | 2 | Bad Moon Rising | *Born To Hurt Me* | $5 | Soundwaves 4826 |

#2 Pop hit for Creedence Clearwater Revival in 1969

CHAMBERLAIN, David '88
Born in 1944 in Ft. Worth, Texas.

| 1/30/88 | 72 | 4 | | I Owe, I Owe (It's Off To Work I Go) | *Love Me Tonight* | $6 | Country Int'l. 214 |

CHAMBERS, Carl '81

| 2/28/81 | 91 | 2 | | Take Me Home With You | | $6 | Prairie Dust 8001 |

CHANCE '85
Group from Texas: brothers Jeff (vocals, steel guitar) and Mick (drums) Barosh, John Buckley (guitar), Jon Mulligan (keyboards) and Billy Hafer (bass). Jeff Barosh began solo career in 1988 as Jeff Chance.

4/20/85	35	13	1	To Be Lovers	*Call It What You Want To (It's Still Love)*	$3	Mercury 880555
7/27/85	45	11	2	You Could Be The One Woman	*Free Sailin'*	$3	Mercury 880959
10/26/85	30	15	3	She Told Me Yes	A:26 / S:30 *Two Hearts Are Better Than One*	$3	Mercury 884178
3/29/86	53	7	4	I Need Some Good News Bad	*She Needs A Man Like Me*	$3	Mercury 884545
8/30/86	60	10	5	What Did You Do With My Heart	*One Too Many Heartaches*	$3	Mercury 884918

CHANCE, Jeff '88
Born Jeff Barosh in El Campo, Texas. Singer/steel guitarist. Member of Chance.

6/18/88	52	7	1	Hopelessly Falling/			
3/19/88	64	7	2	So Far Not So Good		$3	Curb 10506
11/26/88+	57	9	3	Let It Burn	*She Loves Me*	$3	Curb 10516

CHANEY, Hank '86

| 8/16/86 | 98 | 1 | | Be-Bop-A-Lula "86" | | $7 | CMI 04 |

CHANTILLY '82
Female group: Kim Williams (lead vocals), Debbie Pierce and P.J. Allman. Pierce, daughter of Webb Pierce, was later replaced by Joci Stevens.

| 5/1/82 | 81 | 4 | 1 | Whatever Turns You On | *Storm Of Love* | $5 | Jaroco 31082 |
| 6/26/82 | 43 | 10 | 2 | Stumblin' In | *Better Off Blue* | $5 | Jaroco 51282 |

CHANTILLY (Featuring Kim Williams) (above 2)
#4 Pop hit for Suzi Quatro & Chris Norman in 1979

10/9/82	65	6	3	Right Back Loving You Again	*Better Off Blue*	$5	F&L 519
12/25/82+	75	6	4	Better Off Blue	*Right Back Loving You Again*	$5	F&L 520
2/12/83	60	7	5	Storm Of Love	*Right Back Loving You Again*	$5	F&L 523
9/17/83	60	7	6	Have I Got A Heart For You	*Reached*	$5	F&L 527
2/11/84	72	4	7	Baby's Walkin'	*Have I Got A Heart For You*	$5	F&L 534

CHAPARRAL BROTHERS '68
Duo of brothers John and Paul Chaparral.

| 5/11/68 | 65 | 4 | 1 | Standing In The Rain | *Just One More Time* | $8 | Capitol 2153 |
| 2/14/70 | 70 | 2 | 2 | Running From A Memory | *Curly Brown* | $8 | Capitol 2708 |

DEBUT	PEAK	WKS	Gold	A-side (Chart Hit) .... B-side	Pop	$	Pic	Label & Number
				CHAPARRO, Tammy '83				
				Born in 1967 in Billings, Montana.				
5/7/83	89	3		Stay With Me..		$6		Compass 60
				CHAPMAN, Cee Cee '89				
				Born Melissa Carol Chapman on 12/13/58 in Portsmouth, Virginia. Female singer/songwriter/guitarist. Santa Fe is her backing band.				
11/26/88	60	8		1 Gone But Not Forgotten .... *Love Is A Liar*		$3		Curb 10518
				CEE CEE CHAPMAN & SANTA FE				
4/8/89	51	10		2 Frontier Justice/				
11/4/89	64	4		3 Love Is A Liar		$3		Curb 10529
8/5/89	49	7		4 Twist Of Fate .... *Back To Santa Fe*		$3		Curb 10547
1/2/93	64	6		5 Two Ships That Passed In The Moonlight................				album cut
				from the album *Cee Cee Chapman* on Curb/Capitol 94373				
				CHAPMAN, Gary '88				
				Born on 8/19/57 in Oklahoma; raised in DeLeon, Texas. Singer/songwriter. Married singer Amy Grant in 1982. Host of TNN's *Prime Time Country* since 1996.				
1/9/88	60	6		1 When We're Together .... *Your Love Stays With Me*		$3		RCA 5285
4/16/88	76	4		2 Everyday Man .... *Cecil (Life Goes On)*		$3		RCA 7601
				CHAPMAN, Marshall '77				
				Born on 1/7/49 in Spartanburg, South Carolina.				
3/5/77	100	2		Somewhere South Of Macon .... *Sweet Carolina And Texas*		$5		Epic 50307
				CHARLENE '82				
				Born Charlene D'Angelo on 6/1/50 in Hollywood. Female singer.				
4/10/82	60	8		I've Never Been To Me.......................... *Somewhere In My Life*	3	$4		Motown 1611
				first released on Prodigal 0636 in 1977 (hit #97 on the *Hot 100*)				
				CHARLES, Kim '79				
				Male singer.				
2/10/79	35	9		Want To Thank You .... *By Any Chance*		$4		MCA 40987
	★313★			**CHARLES, Ray** '85				
				Born Ray Charles Robinson on 9/23/30 in Albany, Georgia. To Greenville, Florida, while still an infant. Partially blind at age five, completely blind at seven (glaucoma). Studied classical piano and clarinet at State School for Deaf and Blind Children, St. Augustine, Florida, 1937-45. Formed own band in 1954. Inducted into the Rock and Roll Hall of Fame in 1986. Won Grammy's Lifetime Achievement Award in 1987. Legendary performer, with many TV and movie appearances. Charted 76 pop hits from 1957-90.				
				1)Seven Spanish Angels 2)We Didn't See A Thing 3)It Ain't Gonna Worry My Mind				
11/22/80	55	10		1 Beers To You .... *Cotton-Eyed Clint*		$4		Warner 49608
				RAY CHARLES & CLINT EASTWOOD				
				from the movie *Any Which Way You Can* starring Eastwood				
12/18/82+	20	18		2 Born To Love Me .... *String Bean*		$3		Columbia 03429
4/23/83	37	11		3 3/4 Time .... *You Feel Good All Over*		$3		Columbia 03810
9/24/83	82	3		4 Ain't Your Memory Got No Pride At All *I Don't Want No Stranger Sleepin' In My Bed*		$3		Columbia 04083
12/17/83+	6	18		5 We Didn't See A Thing *I Wish You Were Here Tonight*		$3		Columbia 04297
				RAY CHARLES & GEORGE JONES (Featuring Chet Atkins)				
4/14/84	50	10		6 Do I Ever Cross Your Mind .... *They Call It Love*		$3		Columbia 04420
8/4/84	14	18		7 Rock And Roll Shoes .... S:14 / A:21 *Then I'll Be Over You*		$3		Columbia 04531
				RAY CHARLES (with B.J. THOMAS)				
12/15/84+	❶¹	27		8 Seven Spanish Angels S:❶¹ / A:❶¹ *Who Cares*		$3		Columbia 04715
				RAY CHARLES (with WILLIE NELSON)				
5/4/85	12	17		9 It Ain't Gonna Worry My Mind .... A:11 / S:12 *Crazy Old Soldier*		$3		Columbia 04860
				RAY CHARLES (with Mickey Gilley)				
8/31/85	14	17		10 Two Old Cats Like Us .... S:13 / A:17 *Little Hotel Room*		$3		Columbia 05575
				RAY CHARLES (with Hank Williams, Jr.)				
7/19/86	34	13		11 The Pages Of My Mind...................... *Slip Away*		$3		Columbia 06172
11/1/86	66	4		12 Dixie Moon/				
1/31/87	76	3		13 A Little Bit Of Heaven		$3		Columbia 06370
				CHARLESTON EXPRESS '85				
				Group from Charleston, South Carolina. Led by singer Jesse Wales.				
12/15/84+	69	7		1 Sweet Love, Don't Cry .... *We Start Our Lives Again Today*		$5		Soundwaves 4743
5/18/85	82	4		2 Leaving .... *Take Me By Surprise*		$5		Soundwaves 4749
				CHARLESTON EXPRESS with Jesse Wales (above 2)				
				CHARNISSA — see PAYCHECK, Johnny				
				CHASE, Becky '85				
1/12/85	77	6		Until The Music Is Gone		$6		Spirit Horse 102
				CHASE, Carol '80				
				Born Carol Schulte in Stanley, North Dakota. Singer/songwriter.				
11/10/79+	32	13		1 This Must Be My Ship................... *It Always Takes A Fool To Fool Around*		$5		Casablanca 4501
12/15/79	92	4		2 Can't Love On Lies		$6		Macho 003
				JIM WEST with Carol Chase				
2/23/80	48	7		3 Sexy Song .... *Disco Devil*		$5		Casablanca 4502
10/18/80	87	3		4 Regrets .... *So Sad*		$4		Casablanca 2301
				CHASTAIN, Dawn '79				
				Born in Springfield, Illinois. Female singer. Former fashion model.				
4/15/78	83	4		1 Never Knew (How Much I Loved You 'Til I Lost You) .... *Ain't No Doubt About It*		$6		Prairie Dust 7623
1/6/79	72	4		2 Me Plus You Equals Love		$6		Oak 1018
5/5/79	91	2		3 Love Talks		$5		SCR 164
9/8/79	74	4		4 That's You, That's Me		$5		SCR 178

CHER '79

Born Cherilyn Sarkisian on 5/20/46 in El Centro, California. Adopted by stepfather at age 15 and last name changed to La Pierre. Singer/actress. Charted 30 pop hits from 1965-96. Starred in several movies. In successful recording duo with husband Sonny Bono from 1963 until their divorce in 1975.

| 7/14/79 | 87 | 2 | | It's Too Late To Love Me Now .... *Wasn't It Good (Pop #49)* | | $4 | | Casablanca 987 |

CHERRY, Don '68

Born on 1/11/24 in Wichita Falls, Texas. Vocalist with Jan Garber's band in the late '40s. Charted 11 pop hits from 1950-56.

| 10/5/68 | 71 | 2 | | Take A Message To Mary .... *In My Youth* | | $8 | | Monument 1088 |
| | | | | #16 Pop hit for The Everly Brothers in 1959 | | | | |

★319★ CHESNEY, Kenny '97

Born on 3/26/68 in Knoxville; raised in Luttrell, Tennessee. Singer/songwriter/guitarist.
1)She's Got It All 2)When I Close My Eyes 3)Me And You

12/18/93+	59	8		1 Whatever It Takes ....*I'd Love To Change Your Name*		$3	∎	Capricorn 18323
5/14/94	70	6		2 The Tin Man .... *I Finally Found Somebody*		$3	∎	Capricorn 49223
4/1/95	6	20		3 Fall In Love S:14 *Something About You And A Dirt Road*		$3	∎	BNA 64278
7/29/95	8	20		4 All I Need To Know .... *Someone Else's Hog*		$3	∎	BNA 64347
11/11/95+	23	20		5 Grandpa Told Me So .... *Whatever It Takes*		$3	∎	BNA 64352
4/6/96	41	16		6 Back In Your Arms Again .... S:22 *Honey Would You Stand By Me*		$3	∎	BNA 64523
7/20/96	2¹	20		7 Me And You S:7 *I Finally Found Somebody*	112	$3	∎	BNA 64589
12/21/96+	2²	21		8 When I Close My Eyes .... *My Poor Old Heart*		$3		BNA 64726
5/31/97	❶³	20		9 She's Got It All S:8 *Lonely, Needin' Lovin'*	110	$3	∎	BNA 64894
10/11/97+	11	22		10 A Chance .... *When I Close My Eyes*		$3		BNA 64987

CHESNUT, Jim '79

Born on 12/1/44 in Midland, Texas. Singer/songwriter/pianist.
1)Let's Take The Time To Fall In Love Again 2)Bedtime Stories 3)Out Run The Sun

7/23/77	99	1		1 Let Me Love You Now .... *Loaf Of Bread (A Jug Of Wine)*		$5		ABC/Hickory 54013
12/10/77+	76	8		2 The Wrong Side Of The Rainbow .... *I'm So Lonely For Your Baby*		$5		ABC/Hickory 54021
4/15/78	76	6		3 The Ninth Of September .... *I Love You Babe (For All The Little Things)*		$5		ABC/Hickory 54027
8/5/78	56	9		4 Show Me A Sign .... *Whiskey Lady*		$5		ABC/Hickory 54033
11/18/78	57	7		5 Get Back To Loving Me ....*Kinder Than The Last One*		$5		ABC/Hickory 54038
6/2/79	80	3		6 Just Let Me Make Believe .... *Let Me Just Say I Love You*		$4		MCA 41015
9/15/79	27	11		7 Let's Take The Time To Fall In Love Again *A Loaf Of Bread (A Jug Of Wine)*		$4		MCA 41106
9/13/80	46	9		8 Out Run The Sun .... *Pick Up The Pieces*		$4		United Artists 1372
6/6/81	36	10		9 Bedtime Stories ....*Pick Up The Pieces*		$4		Liberty 1405
10/24/81	70	4		10 The Rose Is For Today ....*Dark Eyed Lady*		$4		Liberty 1434

CHESNUTT, Mark ★107★ '97

Born on 9/6/63 in Beaumont, Texas. Singer/guitarist. Son of regional Texas star Bob Chesnutt. CMA Award: 1993 Horizon Award.

1)Brother Jukebox 2)It's A Little Too Late 3)Almost Goodbye 4)It Sure Is Monday
5)I Just Wanted You To Know

8/4/90	3	20		1 Too Cold At Home *Life Of A Lucky Man*		$3	∎	MCA 53856
11/24/90+	❶²	20		2 Brother Jukebox *Life Of A Lucky Man*		$3		MCA 53965
3/30/91	5	20		3 Blame It On Texas *Danger At My Door*		$3		MCA 54053
7/13/91	3	20		4 Your Love Is A Miracle *Too Good A Memory*		$3		MCA 54136
10/26/91+	10	20		5 Broken Promise Land *Friends In Low Places*		$3		MCA 54256
2/29/92	5	20		6 Old Flames Have New Names *Postpone The Pain*		$3		MCA 54334
6/13/92	❶¹	20		7 I'll Think Of Something *Uptown Downtown (Misery's All The Same)*		$3		MCA 54395
6/20/92	4	25		8 Bubba Shot The Jukebox *Blame It On Texas*	121	$3	∎	MCA 54471
1/2/93	4	20		9 Old Country *Talking To Hank*		$3		MCA 54539
5/22/93	❶¹	20		10 It Sure Is Monday *I'm Not Getting Any Better At Goodbyes*	119	$3	∎	MCA 54630
9/4/93	❶¹	20		11 Almost Goodbye *Texas Is Bigger Than It Used To Be*		$3		MCA 54718
12/11/93+	❶¹	20		12 I Just Wanted You To Know *April's Fool*		$3	∎	MCA 54768
4/2/94	21	20		13 Woman, Sensuous Woman .... *Till A Better Memory Comes Along*		$3	∎	MCA 54822
7/23/94	6	20		14 She Dreams *What A Way To Live*		$3	∎	Decca 54887
10/29/94+	2²	20		15 Goin' Through The Big D *It's Almost Like You're Here*		$3	∎	Decca 54941
2/25/95	❶¹	20		16 Gonna Get A Life *Half Of Everything (And All Of My Heart)*		$3	∎	Decca 54978
6/17/95	23	17		17 Down In Tennessee .... *This Side Of The Door*		$3	∎	Decca 55050
9/23/95	18	20		18 Trouble .... *Strangers*		$3	∎	Decca 55103
12/30/95+	7	20		19 It Wouldn't Hurt To Have Wings *I May Be A Fool*		$3	∎	Decca 55164
5/4/96	37	20		20 Wrong Place, Wrong Time ....*As The Honky Tonk Turns*		$3		Decca 55198
10/5/96+	❶²	23		21 It's A Little Too Late *The King Of Broken Hearts*		$3	∎	Decca 55231
12/28/96	75	1		22 What Child Is This ....(no B-side) [X]		$10		Decca 3863 (CD)
				available only as a promotional CD single				
3/15/97	8	20		23 Let It Rain S:16 *Goin' Through The Big D*		$3	∎	Decca 55293
8/2/97	2¹	21		24 Thank God For Believers S:16 *Hello Honky Tonk*		$3	∎	Decca 72014
12/13/97+	34	13		25 It's Not Over .... *Useless*		$3		Decca 72032
				MARK CHESNUTT (Featuring Vince Gill and Alison Krauss)				

CHEVALIER, Jay — '79

3/17/79	90	2		Disco Blues .... Super Country USA **JAY CHEVALIER And SHELLEY FORD**		$6		Creole Gold 1114

CHICK AND HIS HOT RODS — see RENO & SMILEY

CHILDRESS, Lisa — '86
Born in Boliver, Missouri.

4/26/86	51	8		1 This Time It's You		$5		A.M.I. 1941
1/17/87	55	6		2 It's Goodbye And So-Long To You .... Touch My Heart		$5		A.M.I. 1947
5/7/88	63	6		3 (I Wanna Hear You) Say You Love Me Again .... It Don't Get Better Than This		$5		True 89
8/20/88	73	3		4 You Didn't Have To Jump The Fence .... I Never Will Outgrow My Love For You		$5		True 91
1/21/89	65	5		5 (Here Comes) That Old Familiar Feeling ...... I Should Have Known You'd Come Around		$5		True 95
7/15/89	83	3		6 Maybe There .... I Should Have Known You'd Come Around		$5		True 97

CHILDS, Andy — '94
Born in Memphis.

7/3/93	73	2		1 I Wouldn't Know.. Let The Good Times Roll		$3		RCA 62545
10/2/93	62	6		2 Broken .... Your Love Amazes Me		$3		RCA 62641
4/2/94	61	5		3 Simple Life .... Mine All Mine		$3		RCA 62763

CHINNOCK, Billy — '85
Singer/actor. Son-in-law of Dick Curless.

1/19/85	91	3		The Way She Makes Love .... Rock N' Roll Cowboy		$5		Paradise 630

CHIPMUNKS, The — '92
Characters created by Ross Bagdasarian ("David Seville") who named Alvin, Simon and Theodore after Liberty executives Alvin Bennett, Simon Waronker and Theodore Keep. The Chipmunks starred in own prime-time animated TV show in the early 1960s and a Saturday morning cartoon series in the mid-1980s. Bagdasarian died on 1/16/72 (age 52). His son, Ross Jr., resurrected the act in 1980.

10/31/92	71	1		Achy Breaky Heart.. I Ain't No Dang Cartoon [N] **ALVIN AND THE CHIPMUNKS** Billy Ray Cyrus (guest vocal)		$3		Epic 74776

CHOATES, Harry — '47
Born on 12/26/22 in Rayne, Louisiana; raised in Port Arthur, Texas. Died while in jail on 7/17/51 (age 28) in Austin, Texas. Cajun fiddler. Label misspelled last name as Coates.

1/4/47	4	2		Jole Blon .... Dragging The Bow **HARRY COATES** first released in 1946 on Gold Star 1314 ($50)		$40		Modern Mountain 511

CHRIS & LENNY — '89
Female/male vocal duo: Chris Thompson and Lenny Grasso.

8/5/89	93	2		When Daddy Did The Driving		$6	■	Happy Man 821

CHRISTINE, Anne — '71
Born Anne Christine Poux on 12/17/33 in Meadville, Pennsylvania.

7/17/71	69	5		Summer Man .... How Important Can It Be		$10		CME 4634

CLANTON, Darrell — '84
Born in Indianapolis. Singer/guitarist/banjo player.

10/15/83+	24	19		1 Lonesome 7-7203 .... Me-Oh-My		$6		Audiograph 474
3/31/84	75	6		2 I'll Take As Much Of You As I Can Get .... That's What Cheaters Do		$6		Audiograph 479
1/19/85	56	9		3 I Forgot That I Don't Live Here Anymore .... I Told You So		$4		Warner 29185

CLAPTON, Eric — '78
Born Eric Patrick Clapp on 3/30/45 in Ripley, England. Prolific rock-blues singer/guitarist. Charted 27 pop hits from 1970-96.

3/18/78	26	9	●	1 Lay Down Sally .... Next Time You See Her	3	$4		RSO 886
10/21/78	82	7		2 Promises .... Watch Out For Lucy (Pop #40) **ERIC CLAPTON AND HIS BAND**	9	$4		RSO 910

CLARK, Guy — '81
Born on 11/6/41 in Monahans, Texas; raised in Rockport, Texas. Singer/songwriter/guitarist.

1/6/79	96	2		1 Fools For Each Other .... Fool On The Roof		$4		Warner 8714
7/11/81	38	11		2 The Partner Nobody Chose .... Heartbroke		$4		Warner 49740
7/2/83	42	13		3 Homegrown Tomatoes .... Fool In A Mirror		$4		Warner 29595

CLARK, Jay — '85
Born in 1958 in Missouri; raised in Round Rock, Texas.

12/21/85	73	5		1 Love Gone Bad.. Modern Day Cowboy		$5		Concorde 301
4/12/86	75	4		2 Modern Day Cowboy .... Love Gone Bad		$5		Concorde 302

CLARK, Lucky — '77

6/4/77	99	1		Everytime Two Fools Collide .... Another Honky Tonk Tonight		$6		Polydor 14393

CLARK, Mickey — '87
Born Michael Clark on 5/2/40 in Louisville, Kentucky.

3/12/83	74	6		1 She's Gone To L.A. Again .... The Tequila Express		$5		Monument 03519
2/14/87	54	9		2 When I'm Over You (What You Gonna Do)		$5	■	Evergreen 1051
9/26/87	76	4		3 You Take The Leavin' Out Of Me .... She's Gone To L.A. Again		$5		Evergreen 1058

CLARK, Petula — '82
Born on 11/15/32 in Epsom, England. Singer/actress. Charted 22 pop hits from 1964-82.

2/6/82	20	14		Natural Love .... Because I Love Him	66	$4		Scotti Brothers 02676

CLARK, Roy ★98★   '73

Born on 4/15/33 in Meherrin, Virginia. Singer/songwriter/guitarist/banjo player. Acted on TV's *The Beverly Hillbillies*. Co-host of the TV series *Hee-Haw*. Joined the *Grand Ole Opry* in 1987. CMA Awards: 1973 Entertainer of the Year; 1977, 1978 & 1980 Musician of the Year.

1)Come Live With Me 2)If I Had It To Do All Over Again 3)Somewhere Between Love And Tomorrow
4)Honeymoon Feelin' 5)I Never Picked Cotton

DEBUT	PEAK	WKS		A-side / B-side	Pop	$	Pic	Label & Number
7/6/63	10	16	1	**Tips Of My Fingers** / Spooky Movies	45	$8		Capitol 4956
2/8/64	31	3	2	**Through The Eyes Of A Fool** / Sweet Violets	128	$8		Capitol 5099
				written by Bobby Bare				
3/20/65	37	10	3	**When The Wind Blows In Chicago** / Live Fast, Love Hard, Die Young		$8		Capitol 5350
				co-written by actor Audie Murphy				
8/3/68	53	8	4	Do You Believe This Town / It Just Happened That Way		$6		Dot 17117
1/18/69	57	6	5	Love Is Just A State Of Mind / Other People's Sunshine		$6		Dot 17187
6/7/69	9	16	6	**Yesterday, When I Was Young** / Just Another Man	19	$6		Dot 17246
9/27/69	40	7	7	September Song / For The Life Of Me	103	$6		Dot 17299
				#51 Pop hit for Jimmy Durante in 1963				
12/6/69+	21	9	8	Right Or Left At Oak Street / I Need To Be Needed	123	$6		Dot 17324
1/24/70	31	9	9	Then She's A Lover / Say Amen	94	$6		Dot 17335
6/6/70	5	15	10	**I Never Picked Cotton** / Lonesome Too Long	122	$6		Dot 17349
9/26/70	6	14	11	**Thank God And Greyhound** / Strangers	90	$6		Dot 17355
3/27/71	74	2	12	(Where Do I Begin) Love Story / Theme From Love Story		$6		Dot 17370
				from the movie starring Ali MacGraw and Ryan O'Neal				
4/24/71	45	9	13	A Simple Thing As Love / I'd Fight The World		$6		Dot 17368
8/14/71	63	4	14	She Cried / Back In The Race		$6		Dot 17386
10/30/71	39	9	15	Magnificent Sanctuary Band / Be Ready		$6		Dot 17395
8/19/72	9	14	16	**The Lawrence Welk - Hee Haw Counter-Revolution Polka** / When The Wind Blows (In Chicago) [N]		$5		Dot 17426
2/17/73	❶¹	16	17	**Come Live With Me** / Darby's Castle	89	$5		Dot 17449
7/7/73	27	11	18	**Riders In The Sky** / Roy's Guitar Boogie [I]		$5		Dot 17458
10/27/73+	2¹	16	19	**Somewhere Between Love And Tomorrow** / I'll Paint You A Song	81	$5		Dot 17480
3/16/74	4	16	20	**Honeymoon Feelin'** / I Really Don't Want To Know		$5		Dot 17498
8/17/74	12	17	21	The Great Divide / Chomp'n'		$5		Dot 17518
12/21/74+	64	6	22	Dear God / Take Good Care Of Her		$5		ABC/Dot 17530
3/29/75	35	10	23	You're Gonna Love Yourself In The Morning / Banjoy		$5		ABC/Dot 17545
8/9/75	16	14	24	Heart To Heart / Someone Cares For You		$5		ABC/Dot 17565
1/24/76	2²	16	25	**If I Had It To Do All Over Again** / It Sure Looks Good On You		$5		ABC/Dot 17605
6/5/76	21	11	26	Think Summer / Whatever Happened To Gauze?		$5		ABC/Dot 17626
12/25/76+	26	11	27	I Have A Dream, I Have A Dream/				
4/9/77	80	4	28	Half A Love		$5		ABC/Dot 17667
8/13/77	40	10	29	We Can't Build A Fire In The Rain / I'm So Lonesome I Could Cry		$5		ABC/Dot 17712
2/11/78	60	6	30	Must You Throw Dirt In My Face / Lazy River		$4		ABC 12328
6/3/78	65	6	31	Where Have You Been All Of My Life / Near You		$4		ABC 12365
2/17/79	34	10	32	Shoulder To Shoulder (Arm And Arm)/				
9/23/78	89	2	33	The Happy Days		$4		ABC 12402
12/15/79+	21	13	34	Chain Gang Of Love / Why Don't We Go Somewhere And Love		$4		MCA 41153
4/12/80	48	7	35	If There Were Only Time For Love / Then I'll Be Over You		$4		MCA 41208
8/16/80	73	5	36	For Love's Own Sake / They'll Never Take Her Love From Me		$4		MCA 41288
12/20/80+	60	8	37	I Ain't Got Nobody / Play Me A Little Traveling Music		$4		MCA 51031
4/4/81	86	2	38	She Can't Give It Away / Dig A Little Deeper In The Well		$4		MCA 51079
5/23/81	63	6	39	Love Takes Two / Come Sundown		$4		MCA 51111
9/26/81	73	4	40	The Last Word In Jesus Is Us / Shinin' Face		$5		Songbird 51167
5/15/82	54	9	41	Paradise Knife And Gun Club / I Don't Care		$5		Churchill 94002
9/11/82	85	3	42	Tennessee Saturday Night / Tumbling Tumbleweeds		$5	■	Churchill 94007
10/30/82	65	7	43	Here We Go Again / Early In The Morning		$5		Churchill 94011
				#15 Pop hit for Ray Charles in 1967				
2/19/83	74	5	44	I'm A Booger/				
		5	45	A Way Without Words		$5		Churchill 94017
8/27/83	55	9	46	Wildwood Flower / Southern Nights [I]		$5		Churchill 94025
10/27/84	48	11	47	Another Lonely Night With You / (instrumental)		$5		Churchill 52469
4/12/86	56	7	48	Tobacco Road / Black Sapphire		$5	■	Silver Dollar 0001
				#14 Pop hit for the Nashville Teens in 1964				
8/30/86	61	7	49	Juke Box Saturday Night/				
				#7 Pop hit for Glenn Miller in 1942				
		7	50	Night Life		$5		Silver Dollar 0004
3/11/89	73	4	51	What A Wonderful World / (instrumental)		$5		Hallmark 0001
				#32 Pop hit for Louis Armstrong in 1988				
10/14/89	68	5	52	But, She Loves Me		$5		Hallmark 0004

CLARK, Sanford   '56

Born in 1935 in Tulsa, Oklahoma. Singer/songwriter/guitarist.

DEBUT	PEAK	WKS		A-side / B-side	Pop	$	Pic	Label & Number
10/6/56	14	1		The Fool / A:14 Lonesome For A Letter	7	$40		Dot 15481
				first released in 1956 on MCI 1003 ($125)				

CLARK, Steve '84
Singer/songwriter from Big Hill, Kentucky.

3/10/84	68	5		That It's All Over Feeling (All Over Again).................. *Margarita, You're No Lady*		$3		Mercury 818058

CLARK, Terri ★378★ '96
Born on 8/5/68 in Montreal; raised in Medicine Hat, Alberta, Canada. Female singer/guitarist.

7/15/95	3	20		1 Better Things To Do S:11 *Tyin' A Heart To A Tumbleweed*		$3	■	Mercury 852046
10/28/95+	3	20		2 When Boy Meets Girl S:6 *Flowers After The Fact*	122	$3	■	Mercury 852388
3/9/96	8	20		3 If I Were You S:4 *Something You Should've Said*	113	$3	■	Mercury 852708
7/13/96	34	12		4 Suddenly Single.. *Catch 22*		$3		Mercury 578280
10/12/96	5	20		5 Poor, Poor Pitiful Me S:6 *Something You Should've Said*	109	$3	■	Mercury 578644
1/11/97	10	20		6 Emotional Girl S:6 *Something In The Water*	113	$3	■	Mercury 574016
5/17/97	49	10		7 Just The Same...S:23 *Hold Your Horses*		$3	■	Mercury 574456

CLAYPOOL, Philip '95
Singer/songwriter/guitarist from Memphis.

6/24/95	71	5		1 Swinging On My Baby's Chain .... *She Kicked My Dog*		$3	■	Curb 76952
9/2/95	60	8		2 Feel Like Makin' Love .... *Circus Leaving Town*		$3	■	Curb 76966
				#10 Pop hit for Bad Company in 1975				
2/3/96	73	2		3 The Strength Of A Woman .... *Honky Tonk Nights*		$3	■	Curb 76977
6/15/96	70	7		4 Circus Leaving Town				album cut
				from the album *A Circus Leaving Town* on Curb 77755				

CLEMENT, Jack '78
Born on 4/5/32 in Memphis. Singer/songwriter/guitarist/producer. Owner of the Fernwood and JMI record labels.

6/24/78	86	4		1 We Must Believe In Magic/				
		4		2 When I Dream		$4		Elektra 45474
9/16/78	84	4		3 All I Want To Do In Life.. *It'll Be Her*		$4		Elektra 45518

CLEMENTS, Boots '86
Born in Tiffin, Ohio; raised in San Diego. Male singer.

4/19/86	96	1		Sukiyaki "My First Lonely Night" .... *The Other Side Of Love*		$6		West 719
				#1 Pop hit for Kyu Sakamoto in 1963				

CLEMENTS, Vassar '80
Born on 4/25/28 in Kinard, Florida; raised in Kissimmee, Florida. Singer/songwriter/fiddler. Popular session musician.

7/12/80	70	5		1 There'll Be No Teardrops Tonight.............................. *Move*		$6		Flying Fish 4004
				written by Hank Williams				
4/9/88	83	2		2 I Hear The South		$6		Shikata 10102

CLIFFORD, Buzz '61
Born Reese Francis Clifford III on 10/8/42 in Berwyn, Illinois.

3/20/61	28	1		Baby Sittin' Boogie ....*Driftwood* [N]	6	$15	■	Columbia 41876

CLINE, Patsy ★198★ '62
Born Virginia Patterson Hensley on 9/8/32 in Gore, Virginia. Died in a plane crash on 3/5/63 (age 30) near Camden, Tennessee (with **Cowboy Copas** and **Hawkshaw Hawkins**). Joined the *Grand Ole Opry* in 1961. Elected to the Country Music Hall of Fame in 1973. Jessica Lange portrayed Cline in the 1985 movie biography *Sweet Dreams*. Won Grammy's Lifetime Achievement Award in 1995.

1)She's Got You 2)I Fall To Pieces 3)Crazy

3/2/57	2²	19		1 Walkin' After Midnight/ J:2 / A:3 / S:3	12			
6/10/57	14	1		2 A Poor Man's Roses (Or A Rich Man's Gold)........................ A:14		$20	■	Decca 30221
4/3/61	❶²	39		3 I Fall To Pieces *Lovin' In Vain*	12	$12		Decca 31205
				also see #17 and #19 below				
11/13/61+	2²	21		4 Crazy *Who Can I Count On* (Pop #99)	9	$12		Decca 31317
				written by Willie Nelson				
3/3/62	❶⁵	19		5 She's Got You *Strange* (Pop #97)	14	$12		Decca 31354
6/2/62	10	12		6 When I Get Thru With You (You'll Love Me Too)/	53			
6/30/62	21	3		7 Imagine That	90	$12	■	Decca 31377
8/25/62	14	10		8 So Wrong .... *You're Stronger Than Me* (Pop #107)	85	$12		Decca 31406
2/16/63	8	17		9 Leavin' On Your Mind *Tra Le La La La Triangle*	83	$12	■	Decca 31455
5/11/63	5	16		10 Sweet Dreams (Of You) *Back In Baby's Arms*	44	$12		Decca 31483
9/14/63	7	13		11 Faded Love *Blue Moon Of Kentucky*	96	$12		Decca 31522
1/11/64	47	3		12 When You Need A Laugh .... *I'll Sail My Ship Alone*		$10		Decca 31552
10/31/64	23	12		13 He Called Me Baby .... *Bill Bailey, Won't You Please Come Home*		$10		Decca 31671
1/25/69	73	2		14 Anytime .... *In Care Of The Blues*		$10		Decca 25744
4/8/78	98	1		15 Life's Railway To Heaven .... *If I Could See The World (Through The Eyes Of A Child)*		$8		4 Star 1033
8/30/80	18	12		16 Always .... *I'll Sail My Ship Alone*		$5		MCA 41303
				#19 Pop hit for Sammy Turner in 1959				
12/20/80+	61	7		17 I Fall To Pieces .... *True Love* [R]		$5		MCA 51038
				newly mixed version of #3 above (with orchestra and chorus added)				
11/7/81+	5	17		18 Have You Ever Been Lonely (Have You Ever Been Blue) *Welcome To My World*		$5		RCA 12346
				JIM REEVES AND PATSY CLINE				
6/5/82	54	8		19 I Fall To Pieces .... *So Wrong* [R]		$5		MCA 52052
				PATSY CLINE/JIM REEVES				
				new version of #3 above				

|---|---|---|---|---|---|---|---|---|

COCHRAN, Anita '97
Born on 2/6/67 in Pontiac, Michigan. Female singer/songwriter/guitarist.

DEBUT	PEAK	WKS	A-side	B-side	Pop	$	Pic	Label & Number
4/5/97	64	4	1 I Could Love A Man Like That .... *Wrong Side Of Town*			$3	▮	Warner 17486
8/9/97	69	1	2 Daddy Can You See Me					album cut
			from the album *Back To You* on Warner 46395					
11/8/97+	❶¹	23	3 What If I Said S:3 *Daddy Can You See Me*		59	$3	▮	Warner 17263
			ANITA COCHRAN with Steve Wariner					

COCHRAN, Cliff '79
Born in Pascagoula, Mississippi; raised in Greenville, Mississippi. Cousin of **Hank Cochran**.

8/10/74	54	10	1 The Way I'm Needing You .... *Hearts Are Like That, Yes They Are*			$6		Enterprise 9103
1/11/75	73	7	2 All The Love You'll Ever Need........................... *I'd Do As Much For You*			$6		Enterprise 9109
5/26/79	24	13	3 Love Me Like A Stranger .... *The Rose Is For Today*			$4		RCA 11562
9/22/79	29	9	4 First Thing Each Morning (Last Thing At Night) .... *100% Chance Of Love Tonight*			$4		RCA 11711

COCHRAN, Hank '62
Born Garland Perry Cochran on 8/2/35 in Greenville, Mississippi. Singer/songwriter/guitarist. Cousin of **Cliff Cochran**. Formerly married to Jeannie Seeley.

9/1/62	20	5	1 Sally Was A Good Old Girl *The Picture Behind The Picture*			$12		Liberty 55461
11/10/62	23	2	2 I'd Fight The World .... *Lucy, Let Your Lovelight Shine*			$12		Liberty 55498
10/5/63	25	1	3 A Good Country Song........................... *Same Old Hurt*			$10		Gaylord 6431
4/15/67	70	2	4 All Of Me Belongs To You .... *I Just Burned A Dream*			$8		Monument 994
7/8/78	91	4	5 Willie .... *Uphill All The Way*			$5		Capitol 4585
			Merle Haggard (guest vocal)					
10/14/78	77	5	6 Ain't Life Hell........................... *I'm Going With You This Time*			$5		Capitol 4635
			HANK COCHRAN & WILLIE NELSON					
11/8/80	57	9	7 A Little Bitty Tear .... *He's Got You*			$4		Elektra 47062
			Willie Nelson (harmony vocal)					

CODY, Betty '53
Born Rita Coté on 8/17/21 in Sherbrooke, Quebec, Canada; raised in Auburn, Maine.

12/26/53	10	1	I Found Out More Than You Ever Knew J:10 *Don't Believe Everything That You Read About Love*			$20		RCA Victor 5462
			answer to "I Forgot More Than You'll Ever Know" by The Davis Sisters					

★208★ COE, David Allan '84
Born on 9/6/39 in Akron, Ohio. Singer/songwriter/guitarist/actor. Billed as "The Mysterious Rhinestone Cowboy" until 1978. Acted in such movies as *Take This Job And Shove It*, *The Last Days Of Frank And Jesse James* and *Stagecoach*.
1)Mona Lisa Lost Her Smile 2)The Ride 3)You Never Even Called Me By My Name
4)She Used To Love Me A Lot 5)Longhaired Redneck

11/30/74	80	6	1 (If I Could Climb) The Walls Of The Bottle.................... *Another Pretty Country Song*			$5		Columbia 10024
5/10/75	91	4	2 Would You Be My Lady........................... *Rock & Roll Holiday*			$5		Columbia 10093
7/5/75	8	17	3 You Never Even Called Me By My Name *Would You Lay With Me*			$5		Columbia 10159
12/27/75+	17	11	4 Longhaired Redneck .... *Family Reunion*			$5		Columbia 10254
4/24/76	60	6	5 When She's Got Me (Where She Wants Me) ....*Living On The Run*			$5		Columbia 10323
9/25/76	25	11	6 Willie, Waylon And Me .... *Please Come To Boston* [N]			$5		Columbia 10395
2/26/77	49	8	7 Lately I've Been Thinking Too Much Lately ....*Under Rachel's Wings*			$5		Columbia 10475
8/6/77	82	5	8 Just To Prove My Love For You........................... *Play Me A Sad Song*			$5		Columbia 10583
10/29/77	92	3	9 Face To Face .... *Play Me A Sad Song*			$5		Columbia 10621
3/25/78	86	3	10 Divers Do It Deeper .... *Million Dollar Memories*			$5		Columbia 10701
7/22/78	85	4	11 You Can Count On Me .... *Bad Impressions*			$5		Columbia 10753
9/9/78	45	8	12 If This Is Just A Game .... *Tomorrow's Another Day*			$5		Columbia 10811
3/17/79	72	5	13 Jack Daniel's, If You Please .... *Human Emotions*			$5		Columbia 10911
6/21/80	46	7	14 Get A Little Dirt On Your Hands........................... *What Can I Do*			$5		Columbia 11277
			DAVID ALLAN COE AND BILL ANDERSON					
3/14/81	88	3	15 Stand By Your Man .... *Take This Job And Shove It*			$4		Columbia 60501
7/4/81	77	5	16 Tennessee Whiskey .... *This Bottle (In My Hand)*			$4		Columbia 02118
1/23/82	62	5	17 Now I Lay Me Down To Cheat .... *If I Knew*			$4		Columbia 02678
4/10/82	58	8	18 Take Time To Know Her .... *London Homesick Blues*			$4		Columbia 02815
			#11 Pop hit for Percy Sledge in 1968					
3/19/83	4	19	19 The Ride *Son Of A Rebel Son*			$4		Columbia 03778
7/23/83	45	10	20 Cheap Thrills........................... *You Never Even Called Me By My Name*			$4	▮	Columbia 03997
10/22/83	85	5	21 Crazy Old Soldier .... *Drinkin' Too Much*			$4		Columbia 04136
12/24/83+	48	13	22 Ride 'Em Cowboy .... *Yesterday's Wine*			$4		Kat Family 04258
3/17/84	2¹	22	23 Mona Lisa Lost Her Smile *Someone Special*			$4		Columbia 04396
8/25/84	44	11	24 It's Great To Be Single Again .... *Sweet Angeline*			$4		Columbia 04553
12/8/84+	11	19	25 She Used To Love Me A Lot ....S:9 / A:19 *For Lovers Only (Part IV)*			$4		Columbia 04688
4/13/85	29	12	26 Don't Cry Darlin' ....S:27 / A:30 *You're The Only Song I Sing Today*			$4		Columbia 04846
			George Jones (recitation)					
11/2/85	52	8	27 I'm Gonna Hurt Her On The Radio ....*He Has To Pay (For What I Get For Free)*			$4		Columbia 05631
5/10/86	44	10	28 A Country Boy (Who Rolled The Rock Away) .... *Take My Advice*			$4		Columbia 05876
8/2/86	56	8	29 I've Already Cheated On You .... S:29 *Take My Advice*			$4		Columbia 06227
			DAVID ALLAN COE and WILLIE NELSON					
2/14/87	34	16	30 Need A Little Time Off For Bad Behavior........S:22 *It's A Matter Of Life And Death*			$4		Columbia 06661
6/6/87	62	5	31 Tanya Montana .... *The Ten Commandments Of Love*			$4		Columbia 07129

COHN, Marc '91
Born on 7/5/59 in Cleveland. Pop singer. Won the 1991 Best New Artist Grammy Award.

8/3/91	74	1	Walking In Memphis .... *Dig Down Deep*		13	$3	▮	Atlantic 87747

DEBUT	PEAK	WKS	Gold	A-side (Chart Hit)..B-side	Pop	$	Pic	Label & Number
				COHRON, Phil **'90**				
1/6/90	86	2		Across The Room From You		$6		Air 182
				COIN, R.C. **'87**				
				Male singer from San Antonio, Texas.				
10/17/87	76	3		Bed Of Roses ....*Confidential*		$6		BGM 82087
				COLDER, Ben — see WOOLEY, Sheb				
				COLE, Brenda **'87**				
				Singer/actress.				
6/27/87	83	3		1 But I Never Do ....*Barefoot Lady*		$5	■	Melody Dawn 77701
12/19/87	86	3		2 Gone, Gone, Gone		$5	■	Melody Dawn 77702
4/16/88	84	2		3 Boots (These Boots Are Made For Walking) ....*Gone, Gone, Gone*		$5		Melody Dawn 77703
				#1 Pop hit for **Nancy Sinatra** in 1966				
				COLE, Nat "King" **'44**				
				Born Nathaniel Adams Coles on 3/17/17 in Montgomery, Alabama; raised in Chicago. Died of cancer on 2/15/65 (age 47). Father of singer Natalie Cole. Won Grammy's Lifetime Achievement Award in 1990. Formed **The King Cole Trio** in 1939: Cole (vocals, piano), Oscar Moore (guitar) and Wesley Prince (bass).				
5/13/44	❶[6]	15		1 Straighten Up And Fly Right/	9			
5/20/44	2[1]	5		2 I Can't See For Lookin'	24	$15		Capitol 154
				THE KING COLE TRIO (above 2)				
				COLE, Patsy **'89**				
				Born in Galesburg, Illinois; raised in Maquon, Illinois.				
4/22/89	89	2		1 I Never Had A Chance With You ....*Morning Train*		$5		Tra-Star 1225
7/15/89	80	3		2 Death and Taxes (And Me Lovin' You) ....*Lead Me On*		$5		Tra-Star 1226
11/4/89	91	2		3 You And The Horse (That You Rode In On) ....*Lot Of Getting Over You*		$5		Tra-Star 1227
				COLE, Sami Jo — see SAMI JO				
				COLEMAN('S), Albert, Atlanta Pops **'82**				
				Atlanta-based studio group conducted by Albert Coleman.				
5/29/82	42	15		1 Just Hooked On Country (Parts I & II)......................................[I]		$4		Epic 02938
9/25/82	77	4		2 Just Hooked On Country (Part III) ....*Rock Around The Country* [I]		$4		Epic 03215
				above 2 are medleys of many classic tunes				
				COLLIE, Biff — see BOWMAN, Billy Bob				
	★270★			**COLLIE, Mark** **'92**				
				Born George Mark Collie on 1/18/56 in Waynesboro, Tennessee. Singer/songwriter/guitarist.				
				1)Even The Man In The Moon Is Crying 2)Born To Love You 3)Hard Lovin' Woman				
2/10/90	54	11		1 Something With A Ring To It ....*Another Old Soldier*		$3		MCA 53778
6/9/90	35	21		2 Looks Aren't Everything ....*Something With A Ring To It*		$3		MCA 79023
10/6/90	59	5		3 Hardin County Line ....*Bound To Ramble*		$3		MCA 79078
2/9/91	18	20		4 Let Her Go ....*Where There's Smoke*		$3		MCA 53971
6/29/91	31	18		5 Calloused Hands ....*Johnny Was A Rebel*		$3		MCA 54079
10/26/91+	28	20		6 She's Never Comin' Back....................................*Lucky Dog*		$3		MCA 54244
3/7/92	70	4		7 It Don't Take A Lot ....*Ballad Of Thunder Road*		$3		MCA 54224
8/29/92	5	20		8 Even The Man In The Moon Is Crying *Trouble's Coming Like A Train*		$3		MCA 54448
1/30/93	6	20		9 Born To Love You *The Heart Of The Matter*		$3		MCA 54515
6/5/93	26	19		10 Shame Shame Shame Shame ....*Keep It Up*		$3		MCA 54668
9/18/93	24	20		11 Something's Gonna Change Her Mind ....*Linda Lou*		$3		MCA 54720
5/7/94	53	8		12 It Is No Secret ....*Rainy Day Woman*		$3	▮	MCA 54832
9/10/94+	13	20		13 Hard Lovin' Woman ....*Ring Of Fire*		$3	▮	MCA 54907
6/17/95	25	20		14 Three Words, Two Hearts, One Night ....*Tunica Motel*		$3	▮	Giant 17855
11/25/95	65	2		15 Steady As She Goes ....*Memories (Still Missing Her)*		$3	▮	Giant 17762
2/24/96	72	2		16 Love To Burn ....*Oh King Richard*		$3		Columbia 78236
				COLLIE, Shirley **'62**				
				Born Shirley Caddell on 3/16/31 in Chillicothe, Missouri. Formerly married to **Biff Collie** and **Willie Nelson**.				
6/12/61	25	5		1 Dime A Dozen ....*Oh Yes, Darling*		$15		Liberty 55324
9/11/61	23	3		2 Why, Baby, Why ....*Why I'm Walking*		$15		Liberty 55361
				WARREN SMITH and SHIRLEY COLLIE				
3/17/62	10	13		3 Willingly *Chain Of Love*		$20		Liberty 55403
				WILLIE NELSON & SHIRLEY COLLIE				
	★398★			**COLLINS, Brian** **'74**				
				Born on 10/19/50 in Baltimore; raised in Texas City, Texas. Singer/songwriter/guitarist.				
				1)Statue Of A Fool 2)That's The Way Love Should Be 3)I Wish				
10/16/71	67	3		1 All I Want To Do Is Say I Love You ....*Time To Try My Wings*		$6		Mega 0038
2/21/72	47	8		2 There's A Kind Of Hush (All Over The World)........*Ain't Gonna Be Your Fool No More*		$6		Mega 0058
				#4 Pop hit for **Herman's Hermits** in 1967				
7/1/72	61	6		3 Spread It Around ....*Let's Give It A Try*		$6		Mega 0078
7/14/73	24	14		4 I Wish (You Had Stayed) ....*Hand In Hand With Love*		$5		Dot 17466
12/8/73+	43	12		5 I Don't Plan On Losing You ....*Lonely Too Long*		$5		Dot 17483
5/18/74	10	15		6 Statue Of A Fool *How Can I Tell Her (About You)*		$5		Dot 17499
11/9/74+	23	14		7 That's The Way Love Should Be ....*Come A Little Bit Closer*		$5		ABC/Dot 17527
4/26/75	84	5		8 I'd Still Be In Love With You ....*Sweet Memories*		$5		ABC/Dot 17546
12/6/75	83	5		9 Queen Of Temptation ....*Before You Close The Door*		$5		ABC/Dot 17593
3/6/76	65	8		10 To Show You That I Love You ....*My Heart Would Know*		$5		ABC/Dot 17613
5/7/77	83	6		11 If You Love Me (Let Me Know) ....*Round And Round*		$5		ABC/Dot 17694

COLLINS, Brian — Cont'd

6/24/78	86	3		12 Old Flames (Can't Hold A Candle To You) .... *Falsely Accused*		$5		RCA 11277
3/10/79	94	3		13 Hello Texas ....*Barefoot Angels*		$5		RCA 11478
4/17/82	80	4		14 Before I Got To Know Her...*Something Very Special*		$5		Primero 1001
7/2/83	80	4		15 Nickel's Worth Of Heaven ....*Something Very Special*		$5		Primero 1018

COLLINS, Dugg '77
Born on 7/2/43 in Memphis, Texas. Singer/songwriter/DJ.

| 5/21/77 | 92 | 4 | | 1 I'm The Man .... | | $6 | | SCR 143 |
| 9/17/77 | 99 | 2 | | 2 How Do You Talk To A Baby .... | | $6 | | SCR 147 |

COLLINS, Gwen & Jerry '70
Husband-and-wife duo from Miami.

| 1/17/70 | 34 | 9 | | Get Together .... *We're Not Bad* | | $6 | | Capitol 2710 |
| | | | | #5 Pop hit for The Youngbloods in 1969 | | | | |

COLLINS, Jim '85
Born in 1959 in Nacogdoches, Texas. Moved to Houston in 1975. Worked as a session musician.

6/8/85	78	3		1 You Can Always Say Good-Bye In The Morning		$5		White Gold 22250
8/24/85	59	6		2 I Wanna Be A Cowboy 'Til I Die...		$5		White Gold 22252
12/14/85	75	6		3 What A Memory You'd Make		$5		White Gold 22251
6/21/86	65	5		4 The Things I've Done To Me		$5		TKM 111216
11/1/86	59	5		5 Romance		$5		TKM 111217
11/22/97+	55	8		6 The Next Step *Not Me*		$3	∎	Arista 13107

COLLINS, Judy '84
Born on 5/1/39 in Seattle; raised in Denver. Female singer/songwriter. Charted 11 pop hits from 1967-79.

| 9/29/84 | 57 | 9 | | Home Again .... *Dream On* | | $4 | | Elektra 69697 |
| | | | | JUDY COLLINS with T.G. Sheppard | | | | |

★310★ **COLLINS, Tommy** '54
Born Leonard Raymond Sipes on 9/28/30 in Bethany, Oklahoma. Singer/songwriter/guitarist. Regular on the *Town Hall Party* radio series in the early 1950s. Wrote several hits for **Merle Haggard**. The song "Leonard" by Haggard is about Collins.
    1)You Better Not Do That 2)Whatcha Gonna Do Now 3)It Tickles

2/20/54	2[7]	21		1 You Better Not Do That *S:2 / A:2 High On A Hilltop*		$25		Capitol 2701
9/4/54	4	15		2 Whatcha Gonna Do Now *A:4 / S:7 You're For Me*		$25		Capitol 2891
2/5/55	10	1		3 Untied *J:10 / S:15 Boob-I-Lak*		$25		Capitol 3017
4/30/55	5	9		4 It Tickles *J:5 / A:9 / S:10 Let Down*		$25		Capitol 3082
10/1/55	13	2		5 I Guess I'm Crazy/ *S:13*				
10/1/55	15	2		6 You Oughta See Pickles Now *S:15*		$25		Capitol 3190
1/11/64	47	1		7 I Can Do That ....*You'd Better Be Nice* (Tommy Collins)		$15		Capitol 5051
				TOMMY AND WANDA COLLINS				
2/5/66	7	13		8 If You Can't Bite, Don't Growl *Man Machine*	105	$10		Columbia 43489
7/16/66	47	2		9 Shindig In The Barn .... *Be Serious, Ann*		$10		Columbia 43628
3/4/67	60	5		10 Birmingham/		$10		
2/11/67	62	4		11 Don't Wipe The Tears That You Cry For Him (On My Good				
				White Shirt)		$10		Columbia 43972
9/23/67	52	6		12 Big Dummy ....*What-Cha Gonna Do Now?*		$10		Columbia 44260
1/13/68	64	6		13 I Made The Prison Band.................................... *No Love Have I*		$10		Columbia 44386

★294★ **COLTER, Jessi** '75
Born Mirriam Johnson on 5/25/47 in Phoenix. Female singer/songwriter/pianist. Married to **Duane Eddy** from 1962-68. Married **Waylon Jennings** in October 1969.
    1)I'm Not Lisa 2)Suspicious Minds 3)What's Happened To Blue Eyes

11/14/70	25	10		1 Suspicious Minds ....*I Ain't The One*		$7		RCA Victor 9920
				WAYLON JENNINGS AND JESSI COLTER				
				#1 Pop hit for Elvis Presley in 1969; also see #7 below				
6/19/71	39	8		2 Under Your Spell Again ....*Bridge Over Troubled Water*		$7		RCA Victor 9992
				WAYLON JENNINGS AND JESSI COLTER				
2/15/75	❶[1]	18		3 I'm Not Lisa *For The First Time*	4	$5		Capitol 4009
8/23/75	5	17		4 What's Happened To Blue Eyes *You Ain't Never Been Loved* (Pop #64)	57	$5		Capitol 4087
1/3/76	11	13		5 It's Morning (And I Still Love You) ....*Would You Walk With Me* (To The Lilies)		$5		Capitol 4200
4/17/76	50	7		6 Without You ....*All My Life, I've Been Your Lady*		$5		Capitol 4252
5/1/76	2[1]	14		7 Suspicious Minds *I Ain't The One* [R]		$6		RCA Victor 10653
				WAYLON & JESSI				
				same version as #1 above				
9/4/76	29	12		8 I Thought I Heard You Calling My Name .. *You Hung The Moon* (Didn't You Waylon?)		$5		Capitol 4325
11/4/78	45	10		9 Maybe You Should've Been Listening ....*My Cowboy's Last Ride*		$5		Capitol 4641
4/14/79	91	4		10 Love Me Back To Sleep ....*Don't You Think I Feel It Too*		$5		Capitol 4696
2/21/81	17	12		11 Storms Never Last..*I Ain't The One*		$4		RCA 12176
				WAYLON & JESSI				
6/6/81	10	13		12 Wild Side Of Life/It Wasn't God Who Made Honky Tonk				
				Angels *I'll Be Alright*		$4		RCA 12245
				WAYLON & JESSI				
2/13/82	70	4		13 Holdin' On ....*Somewhere Along The Way*		$4		Capitol 5073

COMEAUX, Amie '95
Pronounced: Como. Born on 12/4/76 in West Baton Rouge, Louisiana. Died in a car crash on 12/21/97 (age 21).

| 1/14/95 | 64 | 4 | | Who's She To You ....*Written In The Stars* | | $3 | ∎ | Polydor 851208 |

COMMANDER CODY '72

Commander Cody is George Frayne (vocals, piano). Formed His Lost Planet Airmen in San Francisco: John Tichy, Billy Farlow, Rick Higginbotham, Stan Davis, Bill Kirchen and Andy Stein.

5/6/72	51	9		1 Hot Rod Lincoln .... *My Home In My Hand* [N]	9	$5		Paramount 0146
7/28/73	97	2		2 Smoke! Smoke! Smoke! (That Cigarette) .... *Rock That Boogie* [N]	94	$5	■	Paramount 0216
				COMMANDER CODY And His Lost Planet Airmen (above 2)				

COMO, Perry '76

Born Pierino Como on 5/18/12 in Canonsburg, Pennsylvania. Legendary singer. Charted 132 pop hits from 1943-74.

| 1/17/76 | 100 | 1 | | Just Out Of Reach.. *Love Put A Song In My Heart* | | $5 | | RCA Victor 10402 |
| | | | | #24 Pop hit for Solomon Burke in 1961 | | | | |

COMPTON BROTHERS, The '69

Duo of brothers Bill (vocals, guitar) and Harry (vocals, guitar, drums) Compton from St. Louis. Won a Columbia Records talent contest in 1965. Operated their own publishing company, Wepedol Music.
   1)Haunted House 2)Charlie Brown 3)Claudette

12/31/66+	61	5		1 Pickin' Up The Mail .... *Feathers To Stone*		$6		Dot 16948
3/23/68	64	5		2 Honey .... *Poor Side Of Town*		$6		Dot 17070
8/3/68	75	2		3 Two Little Hearts ....*Money*		$6		Dot 17110
11/23/68	62	5		4 Everybody Needs Somebody .... *Loneliness Was Made By Man*		$6		Dot 17167
9/20/69	11	12		5 Haunted House .... *Sound Of An Angel's Wings*		$6		Dot 17294
				#11 Pop hit for Gene Simmons in 1964; "live" effects dubbed-in				
1/24/70	16	11		6 Charlie Brown.. *Just A Dream Away*		$6		Dot 17336
				#2 Pop hit for The Coasters in 1959				
8/22/70	61	3		7 That Ain't No Stuff .... *I Wanna Sing A Country Song*		$6		Dot 17352
6/12/71	65	6		8 Pine Grove .... *Old Memories*		$6		Dot 17378
9/4/71	62	6		9 May Old Acquaintance Be Forgot (Before I Lose My Mind).. *Learning The Hard Way*		$6		Dot 17391
2/26/72	49	10		10 Yellow River....................................... *Sometimes You Ain't No Fun To Love*		$6		Dot 17408
				#23 Pop hit for Christie in 1970				
8/26/72	41	9		11 Claudette... *It Happens All The Time*		$6		Dot 17427
				written by Roy Orbison				
10/6/73	65	12		12 California Blues (Blue Yodel No. 4) .... *Direct Distance Dialing*		$6		Dot 17477
				written and recorded in 1929 by Jimmie Rodgers				
3/15/75	97	2		13 Cat's In The Cradle .... *A Bird With Broken Wings Can't Fly*		$5		ABC/Dot 17538
				#1 Pop hit for Harry Chapin in 1974				

CONCRETE COWBOY BAND '81

Group of Nashville session musicians led by Buddy Skipper. Vocals by **Donna Hazard** and Nancy Walker.

| 7/11/81 | 87 | 2 | | Country Is The Closest Thing To Heaven (You Can Hear).. *San Antonio Rose* | | $5 | | Excelsior 1011 |

CONFEDERATE RAILROAD ★283★ '93

Country-rock group from Marietta, Georgia: **Danny Shirley** (vocals), Michael Lamb (guitar), Gates Nichols (steel guitar), Chris McDaniel (keyboards), Wayne Secrest (bass) and Mark DuFresne (drums). Jimmy Dormire replaced Lamb in 1995.
   1)Queen Of Memphis 2)Jesus And Mama 3)Daddy Never Was The Cadillac Kind

4/4/92	37	19		1 She Took It Like A Man...				album cut
				from the album *Confederate Railroad* on Atlantic 82335				
11/21/92+	2[1]	20		2 Queen Of Memphis/				
7/4/92	4	20		3 Jesus And Mama		$3	■	Atlantic 87404
7/24/93	10	20		4 Trashy Women/	113			
4/10/93	14	20		5 When You Leave That Way You Can Never Go Back		$3	■	Atlantic 87357
12/11/93+	27	20		6 She Never Cried				album cut
				from the album *Confederate Railroad* on Atlantic 82335				
3/12/94	9	20		7 Daddy Never Was The Cadillac Kind *Jesus And Mama*		$3	■	Atlantic 87273
7/9/94	20	20		8 Elvis And Andy.. *Three Verses*		$3	■	Atlantic 87229
11/5/94	55	7		9 Summer In Dixie				album cut
				from the album *Notorious* on Atlantic 82505				
5/13/95	24	20		10 When And Where/				
9/9/95	54	8		11 Bill's Laundromat, Bar And Grill..		$3	■	Atlantic 87104
11/4/95	66	5		12 When He Was My Age				album cut
5/25/96	51	9		13 See Ya				album cut
				above 2 from the album *When And Where* on Atlantic 882774				

CONLEE, John ★85★ '84

Born on 8/11/46 in Versailles, Kentucky. Singer/songwriter/guitarist. Former mortician and DJ. Joined the *Grand Ole Opry* in 1981.
   1)Lady Lay Down 2)In My Eyes 3)Backside Of Thirty 4)Got My Heart Set On You 5)Common Man

5/27/78	5	20		1 Rose Colored Glasses *I'll Be Easy*		$5		ABC 12356
11/4/78+	❶[1]	16		2 Lady Lay Down *Something Special*		$5		ABC 12420
3/3/79	❶[1]	15		3 Backside Of Thirty *Hold On*		$5		ABC 12455
8/11/79	2[2]	15		4 Before My Time *Forever*		$4		MCA 41072
12/15/79+	7	14		5 Baby, You're Something *The In Crowd*		$4		MCA 41163
5/3/80	2[2]	16		6 Friday Night Blues *When I'm Out Of You*		$4		MCA 41233

DEBUT	PEAK	WKS	Gold	A-side (Chart Hit)..B-side	Pop	$	Pic	Label & Number
				CONLEE, John — Cont'd				
9/13/80	2²	17		7 She Can't Say That Anymore _Always True_		$4		MCA 41321
1/24/81	12	14		8 What I Had With You .... _We Belong In Love Tonight_		$4		MCA 51044
5/30/81	26	12		9 Could You Love Me (One More Time)................................_When It Hurts You Most_		$4		MCA 51112
8/29/81	2²	20		10 Miss Emily's Picture _Love Is What You Need_		$4		MCA 51164
2/20/82	6	18		11 Busted _I'd Rather Have What We Had_		$4		MCA 52008
				#4 Pop hit for **Ray Charles** in 1963				
7/3/82	26	12		12 Nothing Behind You, Nothing In Sight..................................._Shame_		$4		MCA 52070
10/2/82+	10	22		13 I Don't Remember Loving You _Two Hearts_		$4		MCA 52116
3/5/83	❶¹	19		14 Common Man _Rose Colored Glasses_		$4		MCA 52178
6/25/83	❶¹	20		15 I'm Only In It For The Love _Lay Down Sally_		$4		MCA 52231
10/15/83+	❶¹	23		16 In My Eyes _Don't Count The Rainy Days_		$4		MCA 52282
3/10/84	❶¹	19		17 As Long As I'm Rockin' With You _An American Trilogy_		$4		MCA 52351
6/23/84	4	19		18 Way Back _Together Alone_		$4		MCA 52403
10/20/84+	2²	21		19 Years After You _S:❶¹ / A:2 But She Loves Me_		$4		MCA 52470
3/2/85	7	20		20 Working Man _S:7 / A:7 Radio Lover_		$4		MCA 52543
7/6/85	15	17		21 Blue Highway ...._A:14 / S:15 De Island_		$4		MCA 52625
10/26/85+	5	21		22 Old School _S:4 / A:5 She Loves My Troubles Away_		$4	■	MCA 52695
2/22/86	10	20		23 Harmony _S:9 / A:11 She Told Me So_		$3		Columbia 05778
6/14/86	❶¹	22		24 Got My Heart Set On You _S:❶¹ / A:3 You've Got A Right_		$3		Columbia 06104
10/25/86+	6	19		25 The Carpenter _S:❶¹ / A:6 I'll Be Seeing You_		$3		Columbia 06311
2/28/87	4	24		26 Domestic Life _S:3 / A:6 I Can Sail To China_		$3		Columbia 06707
7/18/87	11	21		27 Mama's Rockin' Chair _S:6 Faded Brown Eyes_		$3		Columbia 07203
11/28/87	55	7		28 Living Like There's No Tomorrow (Finally Got To Me Tonight) ...._Slow Passin' Time_		$3		Columbia 07643
1/21/89	43	10		29 Hit The Ground Runnin'.................................._Hopelessly Yours_		$3		16th Avenue 70424
4/8/89	48	9		30 Fellow Travelers ...._Knowin' You Were Leavin'_		$3		16th Avenue 70427
8/19/89	67	5		31 Hopelessly Yours ...._I Love You_		$3		16th Avenue 70432
12/15/90+	61	9		32 Doghouse ...._Love Stands Tall_		$3	▌	16th Avenue 70447

CONLEY, Earl Thomas ★63★   **'83**

Born on 10/17/41 in West Portsmouth, Ohio. Singer/songwriter/guitarist. Served in the U.S. Army from 1960-62. Worked in a steel mill in Huntsville, Alabama, in the early '70s. Also recorded as **The ETC Band**.

1)Fire & Smoke 2)Love Out Loud 3)What I'd Say 4)Chance Of Lovin' You 5)Once In A Blue Moon

DEBUT	PEAK	WKS		A-side	Pop	$	Pic	Label & Number
				EARL CONLEY:				
7/26/75	87	4		1 I Have Loved You Girl (But Not Like This Before) ...._Tryin' To Beat The Morning Home_ also see #15 below		$5		GRT 027
11/22/75	87	5		2 It's The Bible Against The Bottle (In The Battle For Daddy's Soul) ...._I Have Loved You Girl (But Not Like This Before)_		$5		GRT 032
3/27/76	67	6		3 High And Wild..................................._The Weeds Outlived The Roses_		$5		GRT 041
8/14/76	77	5		4 Queen Of New Orleans ...._I Have Loved You Girl (But Not Like This Before)_		$5		GRT 064
1/6/79	32	12		5 Dreamin's All I Do ...._My Love_		$5		Warner 8717
				EARL THOMAS CONLEY:				
6/23/79	41	8		6 Middle-Age Madness..................................._When You Were Blue And I Was Green_		$4		Warner 8798
10/6/79	26	11		7 Stranded On A Dead End Street ...._My Love_		$4		Warner 49072
				THE ETC BAND				
11/15/80+	7	20		8 Silent Treatment _This Time I've Hurt Her More (Than She Loves Me)_		$4		Sunbird 7556
4/4/81	❶¹	19		9 Fire & Smoke _I've Loved You Girl_		$4		Sunbird 7561
10/17/81+	10	18		10 Tell Me Why _Too Much Noise (Trucker's Waltz)_		$3		RCA 12344
2/6/82	16	13		11 After The Love Slips Away/				
		13		12 Smokey Mountain Memories		$3		RCA 13053
6/12/82	8	18		13 Heavenly Bodies _The Highway Home_		$3		RCA 13246
10/2/82	❶¹	18		14 Somewhere Between Right And Wrong _Fire And Smoke_		$3		RCA 13320
1/15/83	2²	21		15 I Have Loved You, Girl (But Not Like This Before) _Bottled Up Blues_ [R] new version of #1 above		$3		RCA 13414
5/14/83	❶¹	19		16 Your Love's On The Line _Under Control_		$3		RCA 13525
9/10/83	❶¹	25		17 Holding Her And Loving You _Home So Fine_		$3	■	RCA 13596
1/14/84	❶¹	18		18 Don't Make It Easy For Me _You Can't Go On (Like A Rolling Stone)_		$3		RCA 13702
5/5/84	❶¹	21		19 Angel In Disguise _Crowd Around The Corner_		$3	■	RCA 13758
9/8/84	❶¹	22		20 Chance Of Lovin' You _S:❶¹ / A:❶¹ Feels Like A Saturday Night_		$3		RCA 13877
11/10/84+	8	21		21 All Tangled Up In Love _S:5 / A:8 More Or Less (Hardin)_		$3		RCA 13938
				GUS HARDIN (with Earl Thomas Conley)				
1/5/85	❶¹	22		22 Honor Bound _S:❶¹ / A:❶¹ Too Hot To Handle_		$3	■	RCA 13960
5/4/85	❶¹	19		23 Love Don't Care (Whose Heart It Breaks) _S:❶¹ / A:❶¹ Turn This Bus Around (Bad Bob's)_		$3		RCA 14060
9/14/85	❶¹	22		24 Nobody Falls Like A Fool _S:❶¹ / A:❶¹ Silent Treatment_		$3		RCA 14172
2/1/86	❶¹	22		25 Once In A Blue Moon _A:❶² / S:❶¹ I Have Loved You, Girl (But Not Like This Before)_		$3		RCA 14282

CONLEY, Earl Thomas — Cont'd

8/2/86	2¹	20		**26 Too Many Times** S:❶¹ / A:2 *Changes Of Love (Conley)*		$3	■	RCA 14380
				EARL THOMAS CONLEY AND ANITA POINTER				
11/29/86+	❶¹	23		**27 I Can't Win For Losin' You** A:❶¹ / S:5 *Love's On The Move Again*		$3		RCA 5064
4/4/87	❶¹	21		**28 That Was A Close One** S:4 / A:18 *Right From The Start*		$3		RCA 5129
8/1/87	❶¹	23		**29 Right From The Start** S:9 *Attracted To Pain*		$3		RCA 5226
3/12/88	❶¹	23		**30 What She Is (Is A Woman In Love)** S:4 *Carol*		$3		RCA 6894
7/2/88	❶¹	21		**31 We Believe In Happy Endings** S:3 *No Chance, No Dance*		$3		RCA 8632
				EARL THOMAS CONLEY with Emmylou Harris				
11/12/88+	❶¹	24		**32 What I'd Say** S:13 *Carol*		$3		RCA 8717
3/18/89	❶¹	21		**33 Love Out Loud** *No Chance, No Dance*		$3		RCA 8824
10/7/89	26	15		**34 You Must Not Be Drinking Enough** .... *Too Far From The Heart Of It All*		$3		RCA 8973
2/24/90	11	22		**35 Bring Back Your Love To Me** .... *Chance Of Lovin' You*		$3		RCA 9121
7/14/90	61	6		**36 Who's Gonna Tell Her Goodbye** .... *Love Don't Care (Whose Heart)*		$3		RCA 2511
6/1/91	8	20		**37 Shadow Of A Doubt** *I Wanna Be Loved Back*		$3		RCA 2826
9/7/91	2¹	20		**38 Brotherly Love** *Backbone Job*		$3		RCA 62037
				KEITH WHITLEY & EARL THOMAS CONLEY				
1/11/92	36	13		**39 Hard Days And Honky Tonk Nights** .... *Borrowed Money*		$3		RCA 62167
5/23/92	74	3		**40 If Only Your Eyes Could Lie**... *One Of Those Days*		$3		RCA 62252

CONWAY, Dave   '77

8/6/77	68	6		If You're Gonna Love (You Gotta Hurt).................................*Too Late For Words*		$6		True 105

COOK, Steven Lee   '80

Born in Shelbyville, Kentucky.

12/22/79+	92	5		Please Play More Kenny Rogers .... [N]		$6		Grind. Switch 1709
				STEVEN LEE COOK with The Jordanaires				

★354★   COOLEY, Spade   '45

Born Donnell Clyde Cooley on 12/17/10 in Grand, Oklahoma. Died of a heart attack on 11/23/69 (age 58). Singer/fiddler/actor. Acted in numerous movies. Hosted own TV shows from the late '40s to 1958. Married Ella Mae Evans in 1945, murdered her on 4/3/61. Sentenced to life imprisonment at Vacaville, California. Died performing at the Oakland Deputy Sheriff's Show two months before he was to be paroled.

3/3/45	❶⁹	31		**1 Shame On You/**				
				Tex Williams and Oakie (vocals)				
4/28/45	8	1		**2 A Pair Of Broken Hearts**		$25		Okeh 6731
10/6/45	4	1		**3 I've Taken All I'm Gonna Take From You** *Forgive Me One More Time*		$25		Okeh 6746
3/16/46	2¹	11		**4 Detour/**				
				Oakie, Arkie and *Tex Williams* (vocals); #5 Pop hit for *Patti Page* in 1951				
4/20/46	3	11		**5 You Can't Break My Heart**		$20		Columbia 36935
3/8/47	4	1		**6 Crazy 'Cause I Love You** *Three Way Boogie*		$20		Columbia 37058
				Tex Williams (vocal: #2, 3, 5 & 6)				

COOLIDGE, Rita   '80

Born on 5/1/44 in Nashville. Singer/songwriter/pianist. Married to **Kris Kristofferson** from 1973-80. Known as "The Delta Lady." Acted in the 1983 movie *Club Med.*

    1)I'd Rather Leave While I'm In Love   2)Somethin' 'Bout You Baby I Like   3)The Jealous Kind

12/22/73+	92	5		**1 A Song I'd Like To Sing**............................... *From The Bottle To The Bottom*	49	$5	■	A&M 1475
				KRIS KRISTOFFERSON & RITA COOLIDGE				
3/23/74	98	2		**2 Loving Arms**...............................*I'm Down (But I Keep Falling)*	86	$5		A&M 1498
				KRIS KRISTOFFERSON & RITA COOLIDGE				
8/31/74	94	5		**3 Mama Lou** .... *Hold An Old Friend's Hand*		$5		A&M 1545
12/28/74+	87	4		**4 Rain** .... *What'cha Gonna Do*		$5		Monument 8630
				KRIS KRISTOFFERSON & RITA COOLIDGE				
10/15/77	82	8	●	**5 We're All Alone**..................................... *Southern Lady*	7	$4	■	A&M 1965
11/25/78	63	9		**6 The Jealous Kind/**		$4		
11/25/78	83	9		**7 Love Me Again**	68	$4		A&M 2090
12/22/79+	32	10		**8 I'd Rather Leave While I'm In Love** *Sweet Emotion*	38	$4		A&M 2199
5/24/80	60	6		**9 Somethin' 'Bout You Baby I Like** .... *Late Night Confession*	42	$4		Capitol 4865
				GLEN CAMPBELL and RITA COOLIDGE				
1/31/81	72	4		**10 Fool That I Am** .... *Can She Keep You Satisfied*	46	$4		A&M 2281

COOPER, Jerry   '88

Born in Arlington, Virginia.

10/3/87	88	2		**1 I'll Forget You**		$6		Bear 178
1/9/88	83	3		**2 As Long As There's Women Like You**		$6		Bear 187

★383★   COOPER, Wilma Lee & Stoney   '59

Husband-and-wife duo: Wilma Leigh Leary (b: 2/7/21 in Valley Head, West Virginia; vocals, guitar, banjo, piano) and Dale Troy "Stoney" Cooper (b: 10/16/18 in Harman, West Virginia; d: 3/22/77, age 58; vocals, fiddle). Joined the *Grand Ole Opry* in 1957. Own band, The Clinch Mountain Clan. Daughter Carolee Cooper is leader of The Carol Lee Singers.

				WILMA LEE & STONEY COOPER and The Clinch Mountain Clan:				
9/29/56	14	1		**1 Cheated Too** ....A:14 *This Crazy Crazy World*		$20		Hickory 1051
12/15/58+	4	26		**2 Come Walk With Me** *Is It Right*		$15		Hickory 1085
				WILMA LEE & STONEY COOPER With Carolee and The Clinch Mountain Clan				
5/25/59	4	23		**3 Big Midnight Special** *X Marks The Spot*		$15		Hickory 1098
				#16 Pop hit for *Paul Evans* in 1960				
10/19/59	3	24		**4 There's A Big Wheel** *Rachel's Guitar*		$15		Hickory 1107
				written by Don Gibson				
5/16/60	17	8		**5 Johnny, My Love (Grandma's Diary)** .... *More Love*		$15		Hickory 1118
9/12/60	16	14		**6 This Ole House** .... *Heartbreak Street*		$15		Hickory 1126
				#1 Pop hit for *Rosemary Clooney* in 1954				
6/12/61	8	7		**7 Wreck On The Highway** *Night After Night*		$15		Hickory 1147

COPAS, Cowboy '60

★218★

Born Lloyd Estel Copas on 7/15/13 in Adams County, Ohio. Died in a plane crash on 3/5/63 (age 49) near Camden, Tennessee (with **Patsy Cline** and **Hawkshaw Hawkins**). Singer/songwriter/guitarist. Replaced **Eddy Arnold** as lead singer with **Pee Wee King**'s Golden West Cowboys. Joined the *Grand Ole Opry* in 1946.

1)*Alabam* 2)*Signed Sealed And Delivered* 3)*Tennessee Waltz*

DEBUT	PEAK	WKS		A-side	B-side	Pop	$	Pic	Label & Number
8/31/46	4	1		1 Filipino Baby *I Don't Blame You*			$20		King 505
				COWBOY (PAPPY) COPAS					
1/3/48	2³	20		2 Signed Sealed And Delivered *Opportunity Is Knocking At Your Door*			$20		King 658
				also see #14 below					
5/1/48	3	17		3 Tennessee Waltz S:3 / J:4 *How Much Do I Owe You*			$20		King 696
7/3/48	7	9		4 Tennessee Moon S:7 / J:7 *The Hope Of A Broken Heart*			$20		King 714
9/18/48	12	1		5 Breeze J:12 *Dolly Dear*			$20		King 618
2/12/49	12	1		6 I'm Waltzing With Tears In My Eyes S:12 *Down In Nashville, Tennessee*			$20		King 775
2/19/49	5	13		7 Candy Kisses J:5 / S:7 *Forever*			$20		King 777
11/12/49	14	2		8 Hangman's Boogie S:14 / J:14 *Blue Pacific Waltz*			$20		King 811
				from the movie *Square Dance Jubilee*					
4/28/51	5	11		9 The Strange Little Girl A:5 / S:7 / J:10 *You'll Never Ever See Me Cry*			$30		King 45-951
1/19/52	8	3		10 'Tis Sweet To Be Remembered A:8 *Because Of You*			$30		King 45-1000
7/4/60	❶¹²	34		11 Alabam *I Can*	63	$15		Starday 501
4/24/61	9	8		12 Flat Top *True Love (Is The Greatest Thing)*			$15		Starday 542
7/31/61	12	10		13 Sunny Tennessee *Dreaming*			$15		Starday 552
9/11/61	10	8		14 Signed Sealed And Delivered *New Filipino Baby* [R]			$15		Starday 559
				new version of #2 above					
4/27/63	12	14		15 Goodbye Kisses *The Gypsy Girl*			$12		Starday 621

CORBIN, Ray '69

Born in Lubbock, Texas. Died of a gunshot wound on 10/26/71 (age 35). Also known as Slim Corbin.

DEBUT	PEAK	WKS		A-side	B-side	Pop	$	Pic	Label & Number
1/11/69	67	2		Passin' Through *Life Doesn't Move Me*			$7		Monument 1102

CORBIN/HANNER BAND, The '82

Duo of Bob Corbin (b: 4/9/51 in Butler, Pennsylvania) and Dave Hanner (b: 2/22/49 in Kittanning, Pennsylvania). Band included Al Snyder (keyboards), Kip Paxton (bass) and Dave Freeland (drums).

1)*Everyone Knows I'm Yours* 2)*Livin' The Good Life* 3)*I Will Stand By You*

DEBUT	PEAK	WKS		A-side	B-side	Pop	$	Pic	Label & Number
1/20/79	85	4		1 America's Sweetheart *Like I Used To*			$6		Lifesong 1783
				CORBIN & HANNER					
5/30/81	64	6		2 Time Has Treated You Well *On The Wings Of My Victory*			$5		Alfa 7001
8/8/81	46	9		3 Livin' The Good Life *Long Gone Blues*			$5		Alfa 7007
11/28/81+	49	10		4 Oklahoma Crude *Too Lazy For Love*			$5		Alfa 7010
4/10/82	46	9		5 Everyone Knows I'm Yours *Son Of America/Let Her Go/One Fine Morning*			$5		Alfa 7022
12/4/82	75	7		6 One Fine Morning *Lord, I Hope This Day Is Good*			$5		Lifesong 45120
				CORBIN/HANNER:					
8/11/90	55	8		7 Work Song *Wild Winds*			$3	∎	Mercury 875688
3/9/91	59	4		8 Concrete Cowboy *Wild Winds*			$3		Mercury 878746
9/12/92	73	2		9 Just Another Hill *Wild Winds*			$3	∎	Mercury 864146
12/12/92+	49	14		10 I Will Stand By You					album cut
4/24/93	71	3		11 Any Road					album cut
				above 2 from the album *Just Another Hill* on Mercury 512288					

CORNELIUS, Helen '76

★233★

Born Helen Johnson on 12/6/41 in Monroe City, Missouri. Singer/songwriter. Staff writer with Screen Gems in 1970. Teamed with **Jim Ed Brown** and appeared on the *Nashville On The Road* TV series from 1976-80. CMA Award: 1977 Vocal Duo of the Year (with Jim Ed Brown).

1)*I Don't Want To Have To Marry You* 2)*Lying In Love With You*
3)*Saying Hello, Saying I Love You, Saying Goodbye*

DEBUT	PEAK	WKS		A-side	B-side	Pop	$	Pic	Label & Number
				JIM ED BROWN/HELEN CORNELIUS:					
7/4/76	❶²	16		1 I Don't Want To Have To Marry You *Have I Told You Lately That I Love You*			$5		RCA Victor 10711
10/30/76	91	3		2 There's Always A Goodbye *Only Road Worth Taking*			$5		RCA 10795
				HELEN CORNELIUS:					
11/20/76+	2¹	17		3 Saying Hello, Saying I Love You, Saying Goodbye *My Heart Cries For You*			$5		RCA 10822
5/7/77	12	12		4 Born Believer *Here Today And Gone Tomorrow*			$5		RCA 10967
8/20/77	12	12		5 If It Ain't Love By Now *It Takes So Long*			$5		RCA 11044
12/24/77	91	3		6 Fall Softly Snow *Natividad (The Nativity)* [X]			$5		RCA 11162
3/11/78	11	13		7 I'll Never Be Free *Baby You Know How I Love You*			$5		RCA 11220
7/29/78	6	15		8 If The World Ran Out Of Love Tonight *Blue Ridge Mountains Turnin' Green*			$5		RCA 11304
9/30/78	30	8		9 What Cha Doin' After Midnight, Baby *Oh What A Night For Love*			$5		RCA 11375
				HELEN CORNELIUS:					
11/25/78+	10	14		10 You Don't Bring Me Flowers *Dear Memory*			$5		RCA 11435
3/31/79	2²	13		11 Lying In Love With You *Let's Take The Long Way Around The World*			$5		RCA 11532
8/4/79	3	13		12 Fools *I Think About You*			$5		RCA 11672
12/1/79	68	5		13 It Started With A Smile *I'm Changing*			$5		RCA 11753
				HELEN CORNELIUS:					
3/8/80	5	14		14 Morning Comes Too Early *Emotions*			$5		RCA 11927
7/19/80	24	12		15 The Bedroom *Everything Is Changing*			$5		RCA 12037
5/9/81	13	14		16 Don't Bother To Knock *Dear Memory*			$5		RCA 12220
				HELEN CORNELIUS:					
12/5/81+	42	10		17 Love Never Comes Easy *Losing You*			$5		Elektra 47237
11/26/83	70	6		18 If Your Heart's A Rollin' Stone			$6		Ameri-Can 1011

DEBUT	PEAK	WKS	Gold	A-side (Chart Hit)..B-side	Pop	$	Pic	Label & Number

CORNOR, Randy   **'76**
Born in 1954 in Houston. Singer/songwriter/guitarist.

11/1/75+	9	15		1 **Sometimes I Talk In My Sleep** *Used To Be*		$5		ABC/Dot 17592
5/15/76	33	11		2 Heart Don't Fail Me Now.............................. *Sugar Foot Rag*		$5		ABC/Dot 17625
10/2/76	72	6		3 I Guess You Never Loved Me Anyway .... *Rocky Top*		$5		ABC/Dot 17655
3/5/77	86	3		4 Love Doesn't Live Here Anymore .... *(Play That Song Again) About The Loser*		$5		ABC/Dot 17676
7/1/78	95	3		5 Ring Telephone Ring (Damn Telephone) .... *If You'd Love Me Like You Loved Me*		$6		Cherry 643
12/23/78	100	2		6 Hurt As Big As Texas .... *Maybe You Should've Been Listenin*		$6		Cherry 783

COTTON, Gene   **'82**
Born on 6/30/44 in Columbus, Ohio. Singer/songwriter/guitarist.

12/11/76+	92	7		1 You've Got Me Runnin'............................ *It's Over Goodbye*	33	$5		ABC 12227
7/29/78	99	2		2 You're A Part Of Me .... *Shine On*	36	$5		Ariola America 7704
				GENE COTTON with Kim Carnes				
5/22/82	78	4		3 If I Could Get You (Into My Life)....................... *Rained On Before*	76	$5		Knoll 5002

COUCH, Orville   **'63**
Born in Ferris, Texas.

11/24/62+	5	21		1 **Hello Trouble** *Anywhere There's A Crowd*		$20		Vee Jay 470
				first released on Custom 101 ($30)				
9/28/63	25	1		2 Did I Miss You? .... *The Lonesomes*		$20		Vee Jay 528

COULTERS, The   **'83**
Family trio from Durham, North Carolina.

2/26/83	70	5		Caroline's Still In Georgia .... *Free To Love You*		$7	■	Dolphin 45003

COUNTRY CAVALEERS, The   **'76**
Duo of **James Marvell** and Buddy Good. Both were members of the vocal group Mercy.

10/20/73	99	2		1 Humming Bird .... *Hang On To What*		$5		MGM 14606
8/28/76	97	2		2 Te' Quiero (I Love You In Many Ways) .... *I've Got My Mind Satisfied*		$6		Country Show. 171

COUNTRY GENTLEMEN, The   **'65**
Bluegrass group: Charlie Waller (vocals, guitar), John Duffey (mandolin; d: 12/10/96, age 62), Eddie Adcock (banjo) and Ed McGlothlin (string bass). Numerous personnel changes through the years. **Ricky Skaggs** played fiddle in the group in 1972.

10/30/65	43	4		Bringing Mary Home................................... *Northbound*		$15		Rebel 250

COX, Don   **'79**
Singer/songwriter/guitarist from Texas.

12/1/79	94	3		Smooth Southern Highway .... *The Prophet And The Saint*		$5		ARC 5902

COX, Don   **'94**
Born on 1/14/64 in Belhaven, North Carolina. Former member of the **Super Grit Cowboy Band**.

4/9/94	53	13		All Over Town .... *Chase The Moon*		$3		Step One 474

CRADDOCK, Billy "Crash" ★83★ **'74**
Born on 6/13/39 in Greensboro, North Carolina. Singer/songwriter/guitarist. Formed the Four Rebels in 1957. Charted the pop hit "Don't Destroy Me" in 1959. Known as "Mr. Country Rock."

     1)Rub It In 2)Broken Down In Tiny Pieces 3)Ruby, Baby 4)Easy As Pie 5)Knock Three Times

2/13/71	3	17		1 **Knock Three Times** *The Best I Ever Had*	113	$7		Cartwheel 193
				#1 Pop hit for Dawn in 1971				
6/19/71	5	14		2 **Dream Lover** *I Ran Out Of Time*		$7		Cartwheel 196
				#2 Pop hit for **Bobby Darin** in 1959				
11/6/71	10	14		3 **You Better Move On** *Confidence And Common Sense*		$7		Cartwheel 201
				#24 Pop hit for Arthur Alexander in 1962				
3/4/72	10	16		4 **Ain't Nothin' Shakin' (But The Leaves On The Trees)** *She's My Angel*		$7		Cartwheel 210
7/1/72	5	16		5 **I'm Gonna Knock On Your Door** *What He Don't Know Won't Hurt Him*		$7		Cartwheel 216
				#12 Pop hit for Eddie Hodges in 1961				
11/18/72+	22	12		6 Afraid I'll Want To Love Her One More Time........................... *Treat Her Right*		$6		ABC 11342
2/24/73	33	9		7 Don't Be Angry .... *White Boy*		$6		ABC 11349
5/26/73	14	11		8 Slippin' And Slidin' .... *A Living Example*		$6		ABC 11364
				#33 Pop hit for Little Richard in 1956				
9/1/73	8	15		9 **'Till The Water Stops Runnin'** *What Does A Loser Say*		$5		ABC 11379
1/5/74	3	16		10 **Sweet Magnolia Blossom** *Home Is Such A Lonely Place To Go*		$5		ABC 11412
6/1/74	❶²	16		11 **Rub It In** *It's Hard To Love A Hungry, Worried Man*	16	$5		ABC 12013
11/9/74+	❶¹	14		12 **Ruby, Baby** *Walk When Love Walks*	33	$5		ABC 12036
				#2 Pop hit for Dion in 1963				
2/22/75	4	14		13 **Still Thinkin' 'Bout You** *Stay A Little Longer In Your Bed*		$5		ABC 12068
6/21/75	10	14		14 **I Love The Blues And The Boogie Woogie** *No Deposit, No Return*		$5		ABC 12104
10/18/75	2³	17		15 **Easy As Pie** *She's Mine*	54	$5		ABC/Dot 17584
4/3/76	7	13		16 **Walk Softly** *She's About A Mover*		$5		ABC/Dot 17619
7/4/76	4	13		17 **You Rubbed It In All Wrong** *I Need Somebody To Love Me*		$5		ABC/Dot 17635
10/23/76+	❶¹	16		18 **Broken Down In Tiny Pieces** *Shake It Easy*		$5		ABC/Dot 17659
3/12/77	28	10		19 Just A Little Thing .... *The First Time*		$5		ABC/Dot 17682
6/4/77	7	15		20 **A Tear Fell** *Piece Of The Rock*		$5		ABC/Dot 17701
				#5 Pop hit for Teresa Brewer in 1956				

CRADDOCK, Billy "Crash" — Cont'd

DEBUT	PEAK	WKS		A-side / B-side	Pop	$	Label & Number
11/12/77+	10	15		21 The First Time .... *Walk When Love Walks*		$5	ABC/Dot 17725
2/4/78	4	15		22 I Cheated On A Good Woman's Love .... *Not A Day Goes By*		$4	Capitol 4545
2/18/78	92	2		23 Another Woman .... *The Words Still Rhyme*		$4	ABC 12335
5/6/78	50	9		24 Think I'll Go Somewhere (And Cry Myself To Sleep) .... *It All Came Back*		$4	ABC 12357
5/20/78	28	10		25 I've Been Too Long Lonely Baby .... *Jailhouse Rock*		$4	Capitol 4575
7/29/78	57	6		26 Don Juan .... *Things Are Mostly Fine*		$4	ABC 12384
9/16/78	14	12		27 Hubba Hubba .... *Let's Go Back To The Beginning*		$4	Capitol 4624
1/6/79	4	14		28 If I Could Write A Song As Beautiful As You .... *Never Ending*		$4	Capitol 4672
4/28/79	28	10		29 My Mama Never Heard Me Sing .... *As Long As I Live*		$4	Capitol 4707
8/4/79	16	13		30 Robinhood .... *We Never Made It To Chicago*		$4	Capitol 4753
11/10/79+	24	14		31 Till I Stop Shaking .... *Sneak Out Of Love With You*		$4	Capitol 4792
3/15/80	22	11		32 I Just Had You On My Mind .... *You Just Want To Be Mine*		$4	Capitol 4838
6/14/80	50	8		33 Sea Cruise .... *She's Got Legs*		$4	Capitol 4875
				#14 Pop hit for Frankie Ford in 1959			
10/18/80	20	13		34 A Real Cowboy (You Say You're) .... *One Dream Coming, One Dream Going*		$4	Capitol 4935
2/14/81	37	10		35 It Was You .... *Betty Ruth*		$4	Capitol 4972
6/20/81	11	16		36 I Just Need You For Tonight .... *Leave Your Love A 'Smokin'*		$4	Capitol 5011
10/17/81	38	10		37 Now That The Feeling's Gone .... *She's Good To Me*		$4	Capitol 5051
7/17/82	28	12		38 Love Busted .... *Darlin' Take Care Of Yourself*		$4	Capitol 5139
11/20/82	62	5		39 The New Will Never Wear Off Of You .... *Hold Me Tight*		$4	Capitol 5170
				CRASH CRADDOCK			
10/22/83	86	2		40 Tell Me When I'm Hot .... *When The Feeling Is Right*		$5	Cee Cee 5400
8/5/89	68	7		41 Just Another Miserable Day (Here In Paradise) ...... *Softly Diana*		$3 ■	Atlantic 88851

CRAFT, Paul '74
Born in Memphis; raised in Proctor, Arkansas. Singer/songwriter/publisher.

DEBUT	PEAK	WKS		A-side / B-side	Pop	$	Label & Number
10/12/74	55	10		1 It's Me Again, Margaret .... *For Linda (Child In The Cradle)* [N]		$6	Truth 3205
6/11/77	98	2		2 We Know Better .... *Dropkick Me, Jesus*		$5	RCA 10971
10/1/77	55	7		3 Lean On Jesus "Before He Leans On You" ...... *Daddy Please Don't Go To Vegas*		$5	RCA 11078
3/4/78	84	6		4 Teardrops In My Tequila .... *Rise Up*		$5	RCA 11211

CRAMER, Floyd '61
Born on 10/27/33 in Samti, Louisiana; raised in Huttig, Arkansas. Died of cancer on 12/31/97 (age 64). Top session pianist.

DEBUT	PEAK	WKS		A-side / B-side	Pop	$	Label & Number
11/7/60+	11	18	●	1 Last Date .... *Sweetie Baby* [I]	2⁴	$10	RCA Victor 7775
6/19/61	8	10		2 San Antonio Rose .... *I Can Just Imagine* [I]	8	$10	RCA Victor 7893
				written by Bob Wills			
2/18/67	53	7		3 Stood Up .... *Good Vibrations* [I]		$8	RCA Victor 9065
4/16/77	67	7		4 Rhythm Of The Rain .... *Prelude To Love* [I]		$4	RCA 10908
				FLOYD CRAMER AND THE KEYBOARD KICK BAND			
				#3 Pop hit for The Cascades in 1963; The Keyboard Kick Band is Floyd Cramer playing eight different keyboards			
3/15/80	32	10		5 Dallas .... *Lover's Minuet* [I]	104	$4 ■	RCA 11916
				from the TV series starring Larry Hagman			

CRAWFORD, Calvin — see HOUSTON, David

CRAWFORD/WEST '97
Duo of Rick Crawford (from Texas) and Kenny West (from Arkansas).

DEBUT	PEAK	WKS		A-side / B-side	Pop	$	Label & Number
6/14/97	75	1		Summertime Girls .... *Hard To Stop A Train*		$3 ▮	Warner 17358

CREECH, Alice '71
Singer from Panther Branch, North Carolina.

DEBUT	PEAK	WKS		A-side / B-side	Pop	$	Label & Number
5/29/71	73	2		1 The Hunter .... *Isn't It A Shame About Jeannie*		$7	Target 00313
11/13/71	33	11		2 The Night They Drove Old Dixie Down ...... *When I'm Not With You*		$7	Target 0138
				#3 Pop hit for Joan Baez in 1971			
2/12/72	34	11		3 We'll Sing In The Sunshine .... *I Used To Cry Over You*		$7	Target 0144

CREEDENCE CLEARWATER REVIVAL '82
Rock group from El Cerrito, California: **John Fogerty** (vocals, guitar), brother Tom Fogerty (guitar), Stu Cook (keyboards, bass) and Doug Clifford (drums). Group charted 20 pop hits from 1968-76; disbanded in 1972. Tom Fogerty died on 9/6/90 (age 48).

DEBUT	PEAK	WKS		A-side / B-side	Pop	$	Label & Number
12/5/81+	50	8		Cotton Fields .... *Lodi*		$5	Fantasy 920
				recorded in 1969; #13 Pop hit for The Highwaymen in 1962			

CREWS, Dwayne '90

DEBUT	PEAK	WKS		A-side / B-side	Pop	$	Label & Number
1/6/90	81	2		Selfish Man		$7	Killer 124

CROCE, Jim '74
Born on 1/10/43 in Philadelphia. Killed in a plane crash on 9/20/73 (age 30) in Natchitoches, Louisiana. Charted 10 pop hits from 1972-76.

DEBUT	PEAK	WKS		A-side / B-side	Pop	$	Label & Number
4/13/74	68	7		I'll Have To Say I Love You In A Song .... *Salon And Saloon*	9	$5	ABC 11424

CROCKETT, Howard '73
Born Howard Hausey in Minden, Louisiana. Died on 12/27/94 (age 69). Singer/songwriter.

DEBUT	PEAK	WKS		A-side / B-side	Pop	$	Label & Number
5/19/73	52	10		Last Will And Testimony (Of A Drinking Man) ...... *House Where Momma Lived*		$6	Dot 17457

CROFT, Sandy '83
Born in 1969 in Chattanooga, Tennessee. Female singer.

DEBUT	PEAK	WKS		A-side / B-side	Pop	$	Label & Number
1/22/83	61	8		1 Easier .... *If I Was As Pretty As You*		$6 ■	Angelsong 1821
8/4/84	91	2		2 Easier .... *If I Was As Pretty As You* [R]		$4	Capitol 5363
				above 2 are the same version			
6/15/85	68	6		3 Piece Of My Heart .... *Heart Stealer*		$4 ■	Capitol 5471
				#12 Pop hit for Big Brother and The Holding Company (Janis Joplin) in 1968			

CROSBY, Bing '44
Born Harry Lillis Crosby on 5/3/03 in Tacoma, Washington. Died of a heart attack on 10/14/77 (age 74). One of the most popular entertainers of all-time. Charted 156 pop hits from 1940-65.

1/8/44	❶⁵	11	●	1 Pistol Packin' Mama .... *Vict'ry Polka (Pop #6)*	2⁴	$20		Decca 23277
				BING CROSBY and ANDREWS SISTERS				
8/30/52	10	1		2 Till The End Of The World *J:10 Just A Little Lovin' (Will Go A Long Way)*	16	$20		Decca 9-28265
				BING CROSBY And GRADY MARTIN And His Slew Foot Five				

CROSBY, Eddie '49
12/10/49	7	2		Blues Stay Away From Me *A:7 / J:10 Foolish Notion*		$20		Decca 46180

CROSBY, Rob '91
Born Robert Crosby Hoar on 4/25/54 in Sumter, South Carolina. Singer/songwriter/guitarist.

11/10/90+	12	20		1 Love Will Bring Her Around *(Nobody's Gonna) Hurt My Heart*		$3	▌	Arista 2124
4/20/91	15	20		2 She's A Natural .... *Somewhere Down The Line*		$3		Arista 2180
9/28/91	20	20		3 Still Burnin' For You .... *Solid Ground*		$3		Arista 12336
2/1/92	28	14		4 Working Woman .... *The Woman In You*		$3		Arista 12397
7/4/92	53	9		5 She Wrote The Book .... *One Night Down*		$3		Arista 12443
12/26/92+	48	12		6 In The Blood .... *Cold Day In Tennessee*		$3		Arista 12481
9/30/95	64	8		7 The Trouble With Love .... *I've Got Just The Heart*		$3	▌	River North 3006
1/20/96	64	6		8 Lady's Man		$3		album cut
				from the album *Starting Now* on River North 1162				

CROSBY, STILLS & NASH '94
Folk-rock trio: David Crosby (guitar; from The Byrds); Stephen Stills (guitar, bass; from Buffalo Springfield) and Graham Nash (guitar; from The Hollies). Occasionally joined by **Neil Young** (guitar). Group charted 13 pop hits from 1969-89. Also see **The Red Hots**.

8/14/82	87	4		1 Wasted On The Way .... *Delta*	9	$4	■	Atlantic 4058
3/11/89	92	2		2 This Old House .... *Got It Made (Pop #69)*		$3	■	Atlantic 88966
				CROSBY, STILLS, NASH & YOUNG				

CROW, Alvin '77
Born on 9/29/50 in Oklahoma City. Leader of The Pleasant Valley Boys based in Austin, Texas.

6/11/77	83	4		1 Yes She Do, No She Don't (I'm Satisfied With My Gal) .... *Retirement Run*		$5		Polydor 14387
9/10/77	97	2		2 Crazy Little Mama (At My Front Door) .... *You're The One I Thought I'd Never Lose*		$5		Polydor 14410
				ALVIN CROW And The Pleasant Valley Boys (above 2)				
				#7 Pop hit for Pat Boone in 1955				
12/17/77	94	4		3 Nyquil Blues .... *Fiddler's Lady*		$5		Polydor 14437

CROWELL, Rodney ★180★ '89
Born on 8/7/50 in Houston. Singer/songwriter/guitarist. Moved to Nashville in 1972 and worked as staff writer for **Jerry Reed**. Worked with **Emmylou Harris** from 1975-77. Married to **Rosanne Cash** from 1979-92. Cousin of **Larry Willoughby**.

1)She's Crazy For Leavin' 2)I Couldn't Leave You If I Tried 3)Above And Beyond
4)It's Such A Small World 5)After All This Time

9/9/78	95	3		1 Elvira .... *Ashes By Now*		$4		Warner 8637
5/19/79	90	3		2 (Now And Then, There's) A Fool Such As I .... *Voila, An American Dream*		$4		Warner 8794
				#2 Pop hit for Elvis Presley in 1959				
5/31/80	78	6		3 Ashes By Now .... *Blues In The Daytime*	37	$4		Warner 49224
10/10/81	30	11		4 Stars On The Water .... *Don't Need No Other Now*	105	$4		Warner 49810
2/13/82	34	11		5 Victim Or A Fool .... *Only Two Hearts*		$4		Warner 50008
11/15/86+	38	12		6 When I'm Free Again .... *S:29 The Best I Can*		$3		Columbia 06415
3/21/87	71	7		7 She Loves The Jerk .... *Past Like A Mask*		$3		Columbia 06584
6/20/87	59	8		8 Looking For You .... *Stay (Don't Be Cruel)*		$3		Columbia 07137
1/23/88	❶¹	23		9 It's Such A Small World *S:❶³ Crazy Baby*		$3		Columbia 07693
				RODNEY CROWELL & ROSANNE CASH				
6/11/88	❶¹	21		10 I Couldn't Leave You If I Tried *S:❶⁴ When The Blue Hour Comes*		$3		Columbia 07918
10/15/88+	❶¹	19		11 She's Crazy For Leavin' *S:❶² Brand New Rag*		$3		Columbia 08080
2/25/89	❶¹	21		12 After All This Time *Oh King Richard*		$3		Columbia 68585
7/1/89	❶¹	20		13 Above And Beyond *She Loves The Jerk*		$3		Columbia 68948
10/14/89+	3	26		14 Many A Long & Lonesome Highway *I Know You're Married*		$3		Columbia 73042
3/3/90	6	26		15 If Looks Could Kill *I Didn't Know I Could Lose You*		$3	▌	Columbia 73254
7/14/90	22	15		16 My Past Is Present *You Been On My Mind*		$3	▌	Columbia 73423
10/20/90+	17	20		17 Now That We're Alone *I Guess We've Been Together For Too Long*		$3	▌	Columbia 73569
4/27/91	72	5		18 Things I Wish I'd Said .... *Soul Searchin'*		$3		Columbia 73760
3/7/92	10	20		19 Lovin' All Night *I Didn't Know I Could Lose You*		$3		Columbia 74250
6/27/92	11	20		20 What Kind Of Love .... *Nobody's Going To Tear My Playhouse Down*		$3	▌	Columbia 74360
4/2/94	60	7		21 Let The Picture Paint Itself .... *The Rose Of Memphis*		$3	▌	MCA 54821
9/17/94	75	1		22 Big Heart .... *The Best Years Of Our Lives*		$3	▌	MCA 54880
4/29/95	69	9		23 Please Remember Me .... *Give My Heart A Rest*		$3	▌	MCA 55024

CROWLEY, J.C. '89
Born John Crowley on 11/13/47 in Houston. Singer/songwriter/guitarist. Former member of the pop group Player ("Baby Come Back").

9/3/88	49	7		1 Boxcar 109 .... *Living For The Fire*		$3		RCA 8634
10/29/88+	13	19		2 Paint The Town And Hang The Moon Tonight .... *Serenade*		$3		RCA 8747
3/25/89	21	15		3 I Know What I've Got .... *Living For The Fire*		$3		RCA 8822
7/22/89	55	9		4 Beneath The Texas Moon .... *Living For The Fire*		$3		RCA 9012

CRUM, Simon — see HUSKY, Ferlin

CRYNER, Bobbie   '95
Born on 9/13/61 in Woodland, California. Female singer.

7/3/93	63	6		1 Daddy Laid The Blues On Me.................................... *I'm Through Waitin' On You*		$3	▌	Epic 77044
11/20/93	68	5		2 He Feels Guilty.................................... *This Heart Speaks For Itself*		$3	▌	Epic 77195
5/14/94	72	3		3 You Could Steal Me.................................... *Leavin' Houston Blues*		$3	▌	Epic 77487
10/14/95	63	8		4 I Just Can't Stand To Be Unhappy............................ *Nobody Leaves*		$3	▌	MCA 55099
3/2/96	56	7		5 You'd Think He'd Know Me Better *Oh To Be The One*		$3		MCA 55167

CUMMINGS, Barbara   '67

12/24/66+	69	8		She's The Woman .... *There's Something Funny Going On*		$10		London 104

CUMMINGS, Burton   '79
Born on 12/31/47 in Winnipeg, Canada. Lead singer of rock group The Guess Who.

3/3/79	33	12		Takes A Fool To Love A Fool .... *I Will Play A Rhapsody*		$5		Portrait 70024

CUMMINGS, Chris   '98
Born in 1975 in Norton, New Brunswick, Canada. Male singer.

12/20/97+	50	7		The Kind Of Heart That Breaks .... *Almost Always*		$3	▌	Warner 17267

CUNHA, Rick   '74
Session singer/guitarist from Los Angeles.

5/18/74	49	10		(I'm A) YoYo Man .... *Wild Side Of Life*	61	$5		GRC 2016

CUNNINGHAM, J.C.   '84
Born John Collins Cunningham on 11/13/50 in Brownsville, Texas.

7/5/80	85	2		1 The Pyramid Song .... *I'm A Lover Not A Fighter* [N]	104	$4		Scotti Brothers 601
4/21/84	70	6		2 Light Up...................... *The Greatest Love*		$4		Viva 29311

CURB, Mike   '70
Born on 12/24/44 in Savannah, Georgia. Pop music mogul and politician. President of MGM Records from 1969-73. Elected lieutenant governor of California in 1978; served as governor of California in 1980. Formed own company, Sidewalk Records in 1964, became Curb Records in 1974. Currently resides in Nashville.

8/1/70	❶²	15		1 All For The Love Of Sunshine *Ballad Of The Moonshine*		$7		MGM 14152
				HANK WILLIAMS, JR. With THE MIKE CURB CONGREGATION				
				from the movie *Kelly's Heroes* starring **Clint Eastwood**				
12/19/70+	3	15		2 Rainin' In My Heart *A-EEE*	108	$7		MGM 14194
				HANK WILLIAMS, JR. With THE MIKE CURB CONGREGATION				
				#34 Pop hit for Slim Harpo in 1961				
12/18/71+	7	14		3 Ain't That A Shame *The End Of A Bad Day*		$7		MGM 14317
				HANK WILLIAMS, JR. with The Mike Curb Congregation				
				#1 R&B hit for Fats Domino in 1955				
5/27/72	24	11		4 Gone (Our Endless Love) .... *All I Have To Offer You Is Me*		$6		MGM 14377
				BILLY WALKER with The Mike Curb Congregation				

CURLESS, Dick   ★253★   '65
Born on 3/17/32 in Fort Fairfield, Maine. Died on 5/25/95 (age 63). Singer/guitarist. Had own radio show as "The Tumbleweed Kid" in Ware, Massachusetts, in 1948. On Armed Forces Radio Network as "The Rice-Paddy Ranger" from 1951-54. Father-in-law of Billy Chinnock.
1)A Tombstone Every Mile 2)Six Times A Day 3)Big Wheel Cannonball 4)All Of Me Belongs To You 5)Drag 'Em Off The Interstate, Sock It To 'Em, J.P. Blues

3/13/65	5	17		1 A Tombstone Every Mile *Heart Talk*		$15		Tower 124
				first released in 1965 on Allagash 101 ($20)				
6/19/65	12	13		2 Six Times A Day (The Trains Came Down) .... *Down By The Old River*		$15		Tower 135
11/6/65	42	3		3 'Tater Raisin' Man.................................... *The Friend Who Makes It Four*		$15		Tower 161
1/15/66	44	3		4 Travelin' Man.................................... *Rocky Mountain Queen*		$15		Tower 193
10/15/66	63	3		5 The Baron.................................... *A Good Job-Huntin' And Fishin'*		$15	▌	Tower 255
2/4/67	28	11		6 All Of Me Belongs To You .... *My Side Of The Night*		$15		Tower 306
7/29/67	72	1		7 House Of Memories......................(Standing) On The Outside Looking In		$10		Tower 335
				above 2 written by Merle Haggard				
11/4/67	70	2		8 Big Foot.................................... *Tornado Tillie*		$15		Tower 362
3/23/68	55	7		9 Bury The Bottle With Me .... *Bummin' On Track "E"*		$15		Tower 399
6/15/68	34	9		10 I Ain't Got Nobody.................................... *Shoes*		$15		Tower 415
5/2/70	27	11		11 Big Wheel Cannonball .... *I Miss A Lot Of Trains*		$8		Capitol 2780
				new "trucker" version of "Wabash Cannonball"				
8/8/70	31	10		12 Hard, Hard Traveling Man .... *Winter's Comin' On Again*		$8		Capitol 2848
11/21/70	29	9		13 Drag 'Em Off The Interstate, Sock It To 'Em, J.P. Blues *Drop Some Silver In The Juke Box*		$8		Capitol 2949
2/20/71	41	9		14 Juke Box Man .... *Please Buy My Flowers*		$8		Capitol 3034
7/31/71	36	9		15 Loser's Cocktail.................................... *Hot Springs*		$8		Capitol 3105
10/2/71	40	10		16 Snap Your Fingers .... *Bully Of The Town*		$8		Capitol 3182
				#8 Pop hit for Joe Henderson in 1962				
2/26/72	34	11		17 January, April And Me .... *Lay Your Hands On Me (And Heal Me)*		$8		Capitol 3267
7/1/72	31	9		18 Stonin' Around .... *For The Life Of Me*		$8		Capitol 3354
11/25/72	55	7		19 She Called Me Baby .... *Wait A Little Longer*		$6		Capitol 3470
3/24/73	54	7		20 Chick Inspector (That's Where My Money Goes)............ *Travelin' Light*		$6		Capitol 3541
7/14/73	80	3		21 China Nights (Shina No Yoru) .... *Old Bob Burton*		$6		Capitol 3630
				#58 Pop hit for Kyu Sakamoto in 1963				
9/15/73	65	7		22 The Last Blues Song .... *Room Full Of Roses*		$6		Capitol 3698

CURREY, Diana Sicily   '89

10/21/89	91	2		Longneck Lone Star (And Two Step Dancin')		$6		Condor 13

DEBUT	PEAK	WKS	Gold	A-side (Chart Hit) .... B-side	Pop	$	Pic	Label & Number

CURTIS, Larry   '78
Male singer from Van Nuys, California.

DEBUT	PEAK	WKS		A-side		$		Label & Number
6/10/78	88	5		It Feels Like Love for the first time		$7		ScrimShaw 1315

CURTIS, Mac   '70
Born Wesley Erwin Curtis on 1/16/39 in Fort Worth, Texas; raised in Olney, Texas. Singer/songwriter.

DEBUT	PEAK	WKS		A-side	Pop	$		Label & Number
6/15/68	64	5		1 The Quiet Kind .... *Love's Been Good To Me*		$6		Epic 10324
10/19/68	54	7		2 The Sunshine Man .... *It's My Way*		$6		Epic 10385
5/24/69	63	7		3 Happiness Lives In This House .... *Little Old Wine Drinker*		$6		Epic 10468
11/8/69	60	5		4 Don't Make Love .... *Us*		$6		Epic 10530
2/28/70	43	9		5 Honey, Don't .... *Today's Teardrops*		$6		Epic 10574
				written by **Carl Perkins**; recorded by The Beatles on their 1965 album *Beatles '65*				
10/17/70	35	10		6 Early In The Morning .... *When The Hurt Moves In*		$5		GRT 26
				#24 Pop hit for **Bobby Darin** in 1958				

★392★ CURTIS, Sonny   '81
Born on 5/9/37 in Meadow, Texas. Singer/songwriter/guitarist/fiddler. Member of Buddy Holly & The Three Tunes.
1)Good Ol' Girls 2)Love Is All Around 3)Married Women

DEBUT	PEAK	WKS		A-side	Pop	$		Label & Number
10/8/66	49	2		1 My Way Of Life .... *Last Call*	134	$15		Viva 602
9/23/67	50	11		2 I Wanna Go Bummin' Around .... *I'm A Gypsy Man*		$15		Viva 617
2/24/68	36	11		3 Atlanta Georgia Stray .... *Day Drinker*	120	$15		Viva 626
7/20/68	45	9		4 The Straight Life .... *How Little Men Care*		$15		Viva 630
11/29/75	78	5		5 Lovesick Blues .... *It's Only A Question Of Time*		$6		Capitol 4158
9/15/79	77	6		6 The Cowboy Singer .... *Cheatin' Clouds*		$4		Elektra 46526
1/19/80	86	3		7 Do You Remember Roll Over Beethoven .... *Walk Right Back*		$4		Elektra 46568
3/29/80	38	9		8 The Real Buddy Holly Story .... *Ain't Nobody Honest*		$5		Elektra 46616
7/19/80	29	10		9 Love Is All Around .... *The Clone Song*		$4		Elektra 46663
				theme from TV's *The Mary Tyler Moore Show*				
11/8/80	70	3		10 Fifty Ways To Leave Your Lover .... *You Made My Life A Song*		$4		Elektra 47048
				#1 Pop hit for Paul Simon in 1976				
4/25/81	15	16		11 Good Ol' Girls .... *So Used To Loving You*		$4		Elektra 47129
8/22/81	33	10		12 Married Women .... *I Like Your Music*		$4		Elektra 47176
1/25/86	69	5		13 Now I've Got A Heart Of Gold		$6		'Steem 110185

★250★ CYRUS, Billy Ray   '92
Born on 8/25/61 in Flatwoods, Kentucky. Singer/songwriter/guitarist.
1)Achy Breaky Heart 2)Could've Been Me 3)In The Heart Of A Woman

DEBUT	PEAK	WKS		A-side	Pop	$	Pic	Label & Number
4/4/92	❶⁵	20	▲	1 Achy Breaky Heart *(album snippets)*	4	$3	▮	Mercury 866522
				CMA Award: Single of the Year				
6/13/92	72	1		2 Some Gave All				album cut
				from the album *Some Gave All* on Mercury 510635				
7/4/92	2¹	20		3 Could've Been Me *(album mix) / I'm So Miserable*	72	$3	▮	Mercury 866998
9/5/92+	6	20		4 She's Not Cryin' Anymore *Achy Breaky Heart (live)*	70	$3	▮	Mercury 864778
10/17/92	23	20		5 Wher'm I Gonna Live? .... *Some Gave All*		$3		Mercury 864502
4/24/93	52	11		6 Some Gave All .... *Star Spangled Banner* [R]		$3		Mercury 862094
7/3/93	3	20		7 In The Heart Of A Woman *Right Face Wrong Time*	76	$3	▮	Mercury 862448
10/23/93	9	20		8 Somebody New *Only Time Will Tell*	104	$3	▮	Mercury 862754
1/29/94	12	20		9 Words By Heart .... *Throwin' Stones*	119	$3	▮	Mercury 858132
6/4/94	63	2		10 Talk Some .... *Ain't Your Dog No More*		$3		Mercury 858746
10/22/94	33	18		11 Storm In The Heartland .... *I Ain't Even Left*	108	$3	▮	Mercury 856260
2/4/95	66	4		12 Deja Blue .... *A Heart With Your Name On It*		$3		Mercury 856482
8/19/95	75	1		13 The Fastest Horse In A One Horse Town .... *Cadillac Ranch* (**Rick Trevino**)		$3		Columbia 77971
8/31/96	69	5		14 Trail Of Tears .... *Harper Valley P.T.A.*		$3		Mercury 578304
2/8/97	65	6		15 Three Little Words		$3		album cut
				from the album *Trail Of Tears* on Mercury 532829				
5/31/97	19	20		16 It's All The Same To Me .... *Achy Breaky Heart*		$3		Mercury 574638

D

★323★ DAFFAN, Ted   '45
Born Theron Eugene Daffan on 9/21/12 in Beauregarde Parish, Louisiana; raised in Houston. Died of cancer on 10/6/96 (age 84). Singer/songwriter/guitarist.

TED DAFFAN'S TEXANS:

DEBUT	PEAK	WKS		A-side		$		Label & Number
1/8/44	2³	8		1 No Letter Today/				
				Chuck Keeshan and Leon Seago (vocals)				
1/15/44	3	21		2 Born To Lose		$25		Okeh 6706
				#41 Pop hit for **Ray Charles** in 1962				
6/3/44	4	2		3 Look Who's Talkin' *Bluest Blues*		$25		Okeh 6719
				Leon Seago (vocal, above 2)				
3/3/45	5	3		4 You're Breaking My Heart/				
2/24/45	6	2		5 Time Won't Heal My Broken Heart		$25		Okeh 6729
				Ted Daffan (vocal, above 2)				

DEBUT	PEAK	WKS	Gold	A-side (Chart Hit)...B-side	Pop	$	Pic	Label & Number

DAFFAN, Ted — Cont'd

DEBUT	PEAK	WKS		A-side / B-side	Pop	$	Pic	Label & Number
9/1/45	2³	13	6	Headin' Down The Wrong Highway/				
8/25/45	5	3	7	Shadow On My Heart		$25		Okeh 6744
				"Idaho" (vocal, above 2)				
10/26/46	5	3	8	Shut That Gate .... Broken Vows		$20		Columbia 37087
				TED DAFFAN and His Texans				
				George Strange (vocal)				

DAISY, Pat   '72
Born Patricia Key Deasy on 10/10/44 in Gallatin, Tennessee. Female singer.

DEBUT	PEAK	WKS		A-side / B-side	Pop	$	Pic	Label & Number
2/19/72	20	13	1	Everybody's Reaching Out For Someone................................. I'll Be There	112	$6		RCA Victor 0637
7/29/72	48	7	2	Beautiful People .... I Think I'm Falling		$6		RCA Victor 0743
				#38 Pop hit for Kenny O'Dell in 1967				
5/5/73	49	7	3	The Lonesomest Lonesome............ I Was Meant For You And You Were Meant For Me		$6		RCA Victor 0932
10/13/73	53	9	4	My Love Is Deep, My Love Is Wide .... You've Got Everything		$6		RCA Victor 0087

DALE, Kenny   ★298★   '79
Born Kenneth Dale Eoff on 10/3/51 in Artesia, New Mexico. Singer/songwriter/guitarist.
1)Only Love Can Break A Heart 2)Bluest Heartache Of The Year 3)Shame, Shame On Me

DEBUT	PEAK	WKS		A-side / B-side	Pop	$	Pic	Label & Number
3/5/77	11	17	1	Bluest Heartache Of The Year .... I'll Believe Every Word That You Lie		$5		Capitol 4389
7/30/77	11	14	2	Shame, Shame On Me (I Had Planned To Be Your Man) .... Love Walked In Again		$5		Capitol 4457
1/21/78	17	14	3	Red Hot Memory .... This Is A Sad Song		$5		Capitol 4528
5/6/78	28	11	4	The Loser .... For Love		$5		Capitol 4570
9/2/78	18	13	5	Two Hearts Tangled In Love .... Let's Make Love		$5		Capitol 4619
4/21/79	16	11	6	Down To Earth Woman .... Every Other Word Is You		$5		Capitol 4704
7/21/79	7	15	7	Only Love Can Break A Heart .... Child Of The Wind		$5		Capitol 4746
				#2 Pop hit for Gene Pitney in 1962				
11/3/79	15	13	8	Sharing .... Child Of The Wind		$5		Capitol 4788
2/23/80	23	10	9	Let Me In .... Rainbow Man		$5		Capitol 4829
6/28/80	33	11	10	Thank You, Ever-Lovin' .... There Are Women (Then There's My Woman)		$5		Capitol 4882
11/22/80+	31	13	11	When It's Just You And Me .... If The World Should Ever Run Out Of Love		$5		Capitol 4943
3/6/82	65	6	12	Moanin The Blues		$7		Funderburg 5001
1/28/84	85	6	13	Two Will Be One .... One Of A Kind		$6		Republic 8301
9/1/84	86	3	14	Take It Slow		$6		Republic 8403
4/13/85	83	3	15	Look What Love Did To Me .... I'm In Over My Heart		$6		Saba 9214
5/31/86	63	7	16	I'm Going Crazy .... Macon Georgia Love		$6		BGM 30186

DALE, Terry   '82
Male singer.

DEBUT	PEAK	WKS		A-side / B-side	Pop	$	Pic	Label & Number
1/9/82	93	2	1	Intimate Strangers		$6		Lanedale 1001
3/27/82	73	4	2	Loving You Is Always On My Mind		$6		Lanedale 711

DALICE   '90
Female singer.

DEBUT	PEAK	WKS		A-side / B-side	Pop	$	Pic	Label & Number
1/6/90	87	2		Crazy Driver		$6		Country Pride 0021

DALLAS, Johnny   '67
Singer from Plano, Texas.

DEBUT	PEAK	WKS		A-side / B-side	Pop	$	Pic	Label & Number
12/24/66+	62	7		Heart Full Of Love .... Gray Flannel World		$10		Little Darlin' 0013

DALTON, Bob   '70
Singer from Itman, West Virginia.

DEBUT	PEAK	WKS		A-side / B-side	Pop	$	Pic	Label & Number
10/17/70	73	3		Mama, Call Me Home .... Papa's Home		$6	■	Mega 0003

DALTON, Lacy J.   ★163★   '81
Born Jill Byrem on 10/13/46 in Bloomsburg, Pennsylvania. Singer/songwriter/guitarist. Formed the psychedelic rock band Office in 1968. Recorded as Jill Croston in 1978.

1)Takin' It Easy 2)Everybody Makes Mistakes 3)16th Avenue 4)Hard Times 5)Hillbilly Girl With The Blues

DEBUT	PEAK	WKS		A-side / B-side	Pop	$	Pic	Label & Number
10/6/79	17	13	1	Crazy Blue Eyes................................... Late Night Kind Of Lonesome		$4		Columbia 11107
2/2/80	18	12	2	Tennessee Waltz....................................... Beer Drinkin' Song		$4		Columbia 11190
4/26/80	14	14	3	Losing Kind Of Love .... Carolina Come-On		$4		Columbia 11253
8/30/80	7	14	4	Hard Times .... Old Soldier		$4		Columbia 11343
12/13/80+	8	15	5	Hillbilly Girl With The Blues .... Me 'N' You		$4		Columbia 11410
4/4/81	10	13	6	Whisper .... China Doll		$4		Columbia 01036
7/18/81	2²	18	7	Takin' It Easy .... Golden Memories		$4		Columbia 02188
12/5/81+	5	17	8	Everybody Makes Mistakes/		$4		Columbia 02637
		16	9	Wild Turkey				
5/1/82	13	15	10	Slow Down .... One Of The Unsatisfied	106	$4		Columbia 02847
9/11/82	7	19	11	16th Avenue .... You Can't Take The Texas Out Of Me		$4		Columbia 03184
3/12/83	30	14	12	It's A Dirty Job .... Caught In The Spotlight		$4		Columbia 03628
				BOBBY BARE & LACY J. DALTON				
6/11/83	9	20	13	Dream Baby (How Long Must I Dream) .... Hold Me Again		$4		Columbia 03926
				#4 Pop hit for Roy Orbison in 1962				
10/15/83	54	8	14	Windin' Down .... Dixie Devil		$4		Columbia 04133

DEBUT	PEAK	WKS	Gold	A-side (Chart Hit) / B-side	Pop	$	Pic	Label & Number
				DALTON, Lacy J. — Cont'd				
11/24/84+	15	20		15 If That Ain't Love ..... S:12 / A:16 _Too Many Miles_		$4		Columbia 04696
4/27/85	19	18		16 Size Seven Round (Made Of Gold) ..... S:17 / A:19 _All I Want To Do In Life_		$4		Epic 04876
				GEORGE JONES and LACY J. DALTON				
6/8/85	20	17		17 You Can't Run Away From Your Heart ..... S:19 / A:20 _The Night Has A Heart Of It's Own_		$3		Columbia 04884
10/19/85	58	8		18 The Night Has A Heart Of It's Own ..... _Adios And Run_		$3		Columbia 05644
1/18/86	43	16		19 Don't Fall In Love With Me ..... _Over You_		$3		Columbia 05759
6/14/86	16	19		20 Working Class Man ..... S:16 / A:16 _Can't See Me Without You_		$3		Columbia 06098
				#74 Pop hit for Jimmy Barnes in 1986				
12/6/86+	33	14		21 This Ol' Town ..... _Up With The Wind_		$3		Columbia 06360
1/28/89	13	16		22 The Heart ..... _Hard Luck Ace_		$3		Universal 53487
5/13/89	57	6		23 I'm A Survivor ..... _Walking Wounded_		$3		Universal 66007
7/22/89	38	10		24 Hard Luck Ace ..... _Turn To The One_		$3		Universal 66015
3/31/90	15	22		25 Black Coffee ..... _I'm Right Here_		$3		Capitol 44519
				DALTON, Larry '81				
				Born on 4/24/46 in Big Stone Gap, Virginia.				
9/5/81	82	3		Cowboy ..... _Too Many Nights_		$5		Soundwaves 4645
				LARRY DALTON and The Dalton Gang				
				DANDY '80				
4/14/79	57	6		1 Stay With Me ..... _Come And Love Me_		$4		Warner/Curb 8771
7/28/79	67	5		2 I Don't Want To Love You Anymore ..... _Early Morning Love_		$4		Warner/Curb 8880
12/1/79	71	6		3 I'm Just Your Yesterday ..... _Number One Fan_		$4		Warner/Curb 49111
10/18/80	54	7		4 Who Were You Thinkin' Of ..... _Arizona Highways_	49	$4		Columbia 11355
				THE DOOLITTLE BAND				
				early pressings credit artist as: DANDY & THE DOOLITTLE BAND				
				DANIEL '78				
				Born Daniel Willis on 11/23/53 in Washington, D.C.				
6/25/77	91	3		1 But Tonight I'm Gonna Love You ..... _Knight In Faded Blue Jeans_		$7		LS 122
12/3/77	100	1		2 Stolen Moments ..... _Knight In Faded Blue Jeans_		$7		LS 136
7/29/78	78	5		3 I Bow My Head (When They Say Grace) ..... _Where Does Love Go_		$7		LS 166
				DANIEL, Cooter '80				
				Born on 11/9/56 in Knoxville, Tennessee. Owner of the Connection record label.				
3/22/80	89	2		Where Are We Going From Here ..... _One More Time Southern Style_		$6		Connection 1
				DANIEL, Davis '91				
				Born Robert Andrykowski on 3/1/61 in Arlington Heights, Illinois; raised in Nebraska.				
5/11/91	28	20		1 Picture Me ..... _No Place To Go_		$3	▌	Mercury 878972
8/31/91	13	20		2 For Crying Out Loud ..... _No Place To Go_		$3	▌	Mercury 868544
1/4/92	27	20		3 Fighting Fire With Fire ..... _Across The Room To You_		$3		Mercury 866132
5/9/92	48	13		4 Still Got A Crush On You ..... _Down On My Knees_		$3		Mercury 866822
4/30/94	74	2		5 I Miss Her Missing Me ..... _Out Here Sits The King_		$3		Mercury 858568
9/3/94	64	6		6 William And Mary ..... _Out Here Sits The King_		$3	▌	Polydor 856032
1/28/95	58	9		7 Tyler ..... _Shame On Me_		$3	▌	Polydor 851398
				DANIEL, Pebble '80				
				Female singer.				
6/21/80	86	3		Goodbye Eyes ..... _Next To You_		$4		Elektra 46643
				DANIÉLLE, Tina '87				
				Singer from Jena, Louisiana.				
11/15/86	75	4		1 Standing Too Close To The Moon ..... _Treat Him Like A Dog_		$5		Charta 202
2/14/87	71	5		2 Burned Out ..... _Lady Blue_		$5		Charta 204
5/9/87	73	4		3 Warmed Over Romance ..... _Maybe Maybe_		$5		Charta 206
	★203★			**DANIELS, Charlie** '79				
				Born on 10/28/36 in Wilmington, North Carolina. Singer/songwriter/fiddler. His band included: Tom Crain (guitar), Joe "Taz" DiGregorio (keyboards), Charles Hayward (bass) and James W. Marshall & Fred Edwards (drums). Marshall and Edwards left in 1986; replaced by Jack Gavin. Group appeared in the movie _Urban Cowboy_.				
				1)The Devil Went Down To Georgia 2)Drinkin' My Baby Goodbye 3)Boogie Woogie Fiddle Country Blues 4)Simple Man 5)In America				
8/4/73	67	6		1 Uneasy Rider ..... _Funky Junky_	9	$6		Kama Sutra 576
				CHARLIE DANIELS BAND:				
1/31/76	36	11		2 Texas ..... _Everything Is Kinda Allright_	91	$5		Kama Sutra 607
6/26/76	22	11		3 Wichita Jail ..... _It's My Life_		$4		Epic 50243
1/22/77	75	4		4 Billy The Kid ..... _Slow Song_		$4		Epic 50322
10/22/77	85	5		5 Heaven Can Be Anywhere (Twin Pines Theme) ..... _Good Ole Boy_		$4		Epic 50456
6/30/79	❶¹	14	▲	6 The Devil Went Down To Georgia ..... _Rainbow Ride_	3	$4		Epic 50700
				CMA Award: Single of the Year; also see #29 below				
10/6/79	19	11		7 Mississippi ..... _Passing Lane_		$4		Epic 50768
1/12/80	87	4		8 Behind Your Eyes ..... _Blue Star_		$4		Epic 50806
2/23/80	27	10		9 Long Haired Country Boy ..... _Sweet Louisiana_		$4		Epic 50845
				same version was a #56 Pop hit in 1975 on Kama Sutra 601 ($5)				
6/7/80	13	11		10 In America ..... _Blue Star_	11	$4		Epic 50888
9/6/80	80	4		11 The Legend Of Wooley Swamp ..... _Money_	31	$4		Epic 50921
12/27/80+	44	10		12 Carolina (I Remember You) ..... _South Sea Song_		$4	☐	Epic 50955
7/25/81	94	2		13 Sweet Home Alabama ..... _Falling In Love For The Night_	110	$4		Epic 02185
				#8 Pop hit for Lynyrd Skynyrd in 1974				

DANIELS, Charlie, Band — Cont'd

DEBUT	PEAK	WKS		A-side / B-side	Pop	$	Pic	Label & Number
7/17/82	76	4		14 Ragin' Cajun .... *The Universal Hand*	109	$4		Epic 02995
10/16/82	69	5		15 We Had It All One Time .... *Makes You Want To Go Home*		$4		Epic 03251
8/13/83	65	6		16 Stroker's Theme .... *El Toreador*		$4		Epic 03918
				from the movie *Stroker Ace* starring **Burt Reynolds**				
10/5/85	54	10		17 American Farmer .... *Runnin' With That Crowd*		$4	■	Epic 05638
12/7/85+	33	17		18 Still Hurtin' Me ....S:29 *American Rock And Roll*		$4	■	Epic 05699
3/22/86	8	22		19 Drinkin' My Baby Goodbye S:7 / A:7 *Ever Changing Lady*		$4		Epic 05835
8/20/88	10	17		20 Boogie Woogie Fiddle Country Blues S:4 *Working Man You Got It All*		$4		Epic 08002
1/21/89	36	11		21 Cowboy Hat In Dallas .... *Uneasy Rider '88*		$3		Epic 68542
4/22/89	43	9		22 Midnight Train .... *Get Me Back To Dixie*		$3		Epic 68738
10/14/89+	12	26		23 Simple Man .... *Ill Wind*		$3		Epic 73030
2/24/90	34	18		24 Mister DJ .... *It's My Life*		$3		Epic 73236
8/25/90	56	5		25 (What This World Needs Is) A Few More Rednecks .... *It's My Life*		$3	▌	Epic 73426

CHARLIE DANIELS:

DEBUT	PEAK	WKS		A-side / B-side	Pop	$	Pic	Label & Number
4/27/91	65	7		26 Honky Tonk Life .... *Willie Jones*		$3	▌	Epic 73768
11/2/91	47	14		27 Little Folks.. *Let Freedom Ring*		$3		Epic 74061
3/20/93	73	2		28 America, I Believe In You				album cut
				from the album *America, I Believe In You* on Liberty 80477				
12/25/93+	54	10		29 The Devil Comes Back To Georgia .... *Diggy Liggy Lo*		$3		Warner 18342
				MARK O'CONNOR With Charlie Daniels				
				Johnny Cash, **Marty Stuart** and Travis Tritt (guest vocals); sequel to #6 above				

DARIN, Bobby   **'58**

Born Walden Robert Cassotto on 5/14/36 in New York City. Died of heart failure on 12/20/73 (age 37). Charted 41 pop hits from 1958-73.

DEBUT	PEAK	WKS		A-side / B-side	Pop	$	Pic	Label & Number
8/4/58	14	3	●	Splish Splash.. S:14 *Judy, Don't Be Moody*	3	$20		Atco 6117

DARLING, Helen   **'95**

Born in Baton Rouge, Louisiana; raised in Houston.

DEBUT	PEAK	WKS		A-side / B-side	Pop	$	Pic	Label & Number
8/5/95	69	3		Jenny Come Back .... *When The Butterflies Have Flown Away*		$3	▌	Decca 55060

| | ★279★ | | | **DARRELL, Johnny**   **'68** | | | | |

Born on 7/23/40 in Hopewell, Alabama. Died on 10/7/97 (age 57). Singer/songwriter/guitarist.

1)With Pen In Hand 2)Ruby, Don't Take Your Love To Town 3)Why You Been Gone So Long

DEBUT	PEAK	WKS		A-side / B-side	Pop	$	Pic	Label & Number
12/25/65+	30	7		1 As Long As The Wind Blows.............................. *Beggars Can't Be Choosers*		$8		United Artists 943
6/4/66	44	3		2 Johnny Lose It All .... *For Old Time Sake*		$6		United Artists 50008
11/12/66	72	4		3 She's Mighty Gone .... *The Baby Sitter*		$6		United Artists 50047
				written by **Johnny Cash** and **June Carter**				
4/1/67	9	15		4 Ruby, Don't Take Your Love To Town *The Little Things I Love*		$6		United Artists 50126
7/22/67	73	3		5 My Elusive Dreams .... *Pickin' White Gold*		$6		United Artists 50183
10/7/67	37	10		6 Come See What's Left Of Your Man .... *Passin' Through*		$6		United Artists 50207
12/23/67+	22	14		7 The Son Of Hickory Holler's Tramp .... *But That's Alright*		$6	■	United Artists 50235
				#40 Pop hit for **O.C. Smith** in 1968				
4/27/68	3	18		8 With Pen In Hand *Poetry Of Love*	126	$6		United Artists 50292
				#35 Pop hit for **Vikki Carr** in 1969				
9/21/68	27	10		9 I Ain't Buying .... *Little Things*		$6		United Artists 50442
11/30/68+	20	13		10 Woman Without Love .... *I Fought The Law*		$6		United Artists 50481
4/12/69	50	7		11 The Coming Of The Roads .... *The Other Side Of The Coin*		$6		United Artists 50503
				JOHNNY DARRELL & ANITA CARTER				
4/26/69	17	13		12 Why You Been Gone So Long .... *You're Always The One*		$6		United Artists 50518
9/13/69	23	10		13 River Bottom .... *Ain't That Livin'*		$6		United Artists 50572
2/14/70	68	7		14 Mama Come'n Get Your Baby Boy .... *These Days*		$6		United Artists 50629
7/11/70	75	2		15 Brother River.. *Bed Of Roses*		$6		United Artists 50675
11/14/70	74	2		16 They'll Never Take Her Love From Me *One Love, Two Hearts, Three Lives*		$6		United Artists 50716
7/28/73	66	10		17 Dakota The Dancing Bear .... *Just A Memory*		$5		Monument 8579
10/12/74	63	9		18 Orange Blossom Special .... *Glendale, Arizona*		$5		Capricorn 0207

DARREN, James   **'78**

Born James Ercolani on 10/3/36 in Philadelphia. Singer/actor. Acted in several movies. Played "Tony Newman" on TV's *The Time Tunnel* and "Jim Corrigan" on *T.J. Hooker*. Charted 10 pop hits from 1959-77.

DEBUT	PEAK	WKS		A-side / B-side	Pop	$	Pic	Label & Number
7/29/78	53	9		Let Me Take You In My Arms Again............................. *California*		$4		RCA 11316
				written by **Neil Diamond**				

DAVE & SUGAR   ★188★   **'79**

Trio consisting of **Dave Rowland** (b: 1/26/42 in Los Angeles), Vicki Hackeman and Jackie Frantz. Trio worked as backup singers for **Charley Pride**. Frantz was replaced by **Sue Powell** in 1977. Hackeman was replaced by Melissa Dean in 1979. Powell was replaced by Jamie Jaye in 1980. Rowland went solo in 1982.

1)Golden Tears 2)The Door Is Always Open 3)Tear Time

DEBUT	PEAK	WKS		A-side / B-side	Pop	$	Pic	Label & Number
11/15/75+	25	17		1 Queen Of The Silver Dollar.. *Fools*		$4		RCA Victor 10425
4/17/76	❶¹	19		2 The Door Is Always Open *Late Nite Country Lovin' Music*		$4		RCA Victor 10625
9/11/76	3	17		3 I'm Gonna Love You *I'm Leavin' The Leavin' To You*		$4		RCA 10768
2/12/77	5	13		4 Don't Throw It All Away *Queen Of My Heart*		$4		RCA 10876
7/16/77	7	14		5 That's The Way Love Should Be *It's A Beautiful Morning With You*		$4		RCA 11034
10/29/77	2⁴	16		6 I'm Knee Deep In Loving You *Livin' At The End Of The Rainbow*		$4		RCA 11141
4/8/78	4	14		7 Gotta' Quit Lookin' At You Baby *We Are The One*		$4		RCA 11251

DEBUT	PEAK	WKS	Gold	A-side (Chart Hit)..B-side	Pop	$	Pic	Label & Number
				DAVE & SUGAR — Cont'd				
8/12/78	❶¹	16		8 **Tear Time** *Easy To Love*		$4	■	RCA 11322
1/20/79	❶³	14		9 **Golden Tears** *Feel Like A Little Love*		$4		RCA 11427
6/30/79	6	13		10 **Stay With Me** *What I Feel Is You*		$4		RCA 11654
10/20/79	4	14		11 **My World Begins And Ends With You/**		$4		RCA 11749
		14		12 **Why Did You Have To Be So Good**		$4		
4/5/80	18	12		13 **New York Wine And Tennessee Shine** .... *Learnin' To Feel Love Again*		$4		RCA 11947
8/16/80	40	8		14 **A Love Song** ....*Things To Do (Without You)*		$4		RCA 12063
2/7/81	32	9		15 **It's A Heartache** ....*It Ain't Easy Lovin' Me*		$4		RCA 12168
				DAVE ROWLAND & SUGAR:				
5/9/81	6	15		16 **Fool By Your Side** *Don't Let Our Dreams Die Young*		$4		Elektra 47135
8/29/81	32	8		17 **The Pleasure's All Mine**.....................................*One Step At A Time*		$4		Elektra 47177
				DAVE ROWLAND:				
5/15/82	77	5		18 **Natalie/**				
		5		19 **Why Didn't I Think Of That**		$4		Elektra 47442
7/31/82	84	3		20 **Lovin' Our Lives Away** ....*Women & Wine*		$4		Elektra 69998

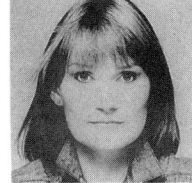

DAVIES, Gail ★194★   **'81**

Born Patricia Gail Dickerson on 6/5/48 in Broken Bow, Oklahoma. Singer/songwriter/guitarist. Did session work in Los Angeles and worked as a staff writer for Vogue Music. Moved to Nashville in the mid-1970s. Lead singer with the **Wild Choir** in 1986.

1)I'll Be There 2)It's A Lovely, Lovely World 3)Blue Heartache 4)'Round The Clock Lovin' 5)Grandma's Song

DEBUT	PEAK	WKS		A-side	Pop	$	Pic	Label & Number
7/8/78	26	12		1 **No Love Have I** ....*It's No Wonder I Feel Blue*		$5		Lifesong 1771
10/21/78	27	12		2 **Poison Love**...*Bucket To The South*		$5		Lifesong 1777
2/10/79	11	16		3 **Someone Is Looking For Someone Like You**......................*Soft Spoken Man*		$5		Lifesong 1784
11/17/79+	7	16		4 **Blue Heartache** *When I Had You In My Arms*		$4		Warner 49108
3/22/80	21	11		5 **Like Strangers** ....*Love Is Living Around Us*		$4		Warner 49199
				#22 Pop hit for **The Everly Brothers** in 1960				
6/28/80	21	12		6 **Good Lovin' Man** ....*Careless Love*		$4		Warner 49263
11/29/80+	4	16		7 **I'll Be There** *(If You Ever Want Me)* *Farewell Song*		$4		Warner 49592
4/4/81	5	18		8 **It's A Lovely, Lovely World** *I'm Hungry, I'm Tired*		$4		Warner 49694
8/15/81	9	15		9 **Grandma's Song** *Mama's Gonna Give You Sweet Things*		$4		Warner 49790
2/13/82	9	18		10 **'Round The Clock Lovin'** *It's Amazing What A Little Love Can Do*		$4		Warner 50004
6/26/82	17	15		11 **You Turn Me On I'm A Radio** ....*All The Fire Is Gone*		$4		Warner 29972
				#25 Pop hit for **Joni Mitchell** in 1973				
10/30/82+	24	15		12 **Hold On** ....*Dawn*		$4		Warner 29892
3/26/83	17	15		13 **Singing The Blues**.......................................*Movin' (I Might Decide To Stay)*		$4		Warner 29726
				#1 Pop hit for **Guy Mitchell** in 1956				
10/15/83	18	19		14 **You're A Hard Dog (To Keep Under The Porch)** .... *The Boy In You Is Showing*		$4		Warner 29472
2/25/84	19	17		15 **Boys Like You** ....*What Can I Say*		$4		Warner 29374
8/4/84	55	12		16 **It's You Alone** ....*Following You Around*		$4		Warner 29219
10/6/84	20	25		17 **Jagged Edge Of A Broken Heart** ....*A:18 / S:20 Lion In The Winter*		$3	■	RCA 13912
2/23/85	37	12		18 **Nothing Can Hurt Me Now** ....*Lovin' Me Too*		$3		RCA 14017
6/22/85	56	8		19 **Unwed Fathers** ....*Different Train Of Thought*		$3		RCA 14095
9/21/85	15	25		20 **Break Away** ....*S:12 / A:15 Not A Day Goes By*		$3		RCA 14184
3/11/89	50	10		21 **Waiting Here For You** ....*Meet Me Halfway*		$3		MCA 53505
6/24/89	69	4		22 **Hearts In The Wind** ....*I Will Rise And Shine Again*		$3		MCA 53442

DAVIS, Carrie   **'89**

| 3/4/89 | 84 | 3 | | **Another Heart To Break The Fall** ....*I'm Just Looking For The Real Thing* | | $6 | | Fountain Hills 130 |

DAVIS, Danny, and The Nashville Brass   **'80**

Born George Nowlan on 4/29/25 in Dorchester, Massachusetts. Trumpet player/bandleader educated at the New England Conservatory of Music. Played with many swing bands including Gene Krupa, Bob Crosby, Freddy Martin, Blue Barron, and Sammy Kaye. Producer for Joy and MGM Records in the late '50s. Production assistant to **Chet Atkins** in 1965. Owner of the Wartrace record label. Formed The Nashville Brass in 1968.

1/3/70	68	3		1 **Please Help Me, I'm Falling** ....*Anna*		$8		RCA Victor 0287
				HANK LOCKLIN AND DANNY DAVIS AND THE NASHVILLE BRASS				
2/14/70	63	3		2 **Wabash Cannon Ball** ....*Sweet Dreams* [I]	131	$8		RCA Victor 9785
6/27/70	56	6		3 **Flying South** ....*Rosalita*		$8		RCA Victor 9849
				HANK LOCKLIN AND DANNY DAVIS AND THE NASHVILLE BRASS				
7/4/70	70	2		4 **Columbus Stockade Blues**................................*Wings Of A Dove* [I]		$8		RCA Victor 9847
10/15/77	91	6		5 **How I Love Them Old Songs** ....*Tara Jeanne*		$5		RCA 11073
2/2/80	20	12		6 **Night Life** *December Day*		$4		RCA 11893
				DANNY DAVIS AND WILLIE NELSON With The Nashville Brass				
5/17/80	41	8		7 **Funny How Time Slips Away** ....*The Local Memory*		$4		RCA 11999
				DANNY DAVIS AND WILLIE NELSON with The Nashville Brass				
3/23/85	82	3		8 **I Dropped Your Name**		$5		Wartrace 730
				Arlene Baird (vocal)				
10/10/87	62	5		9 **Green Eyes (Cryin' Those Blue Tears)**.........................*Little Pink Cloud*		$5		Jaroco 8742
				DANNY DAVIS AND THE NASHVILLE BRASS AND DONA MASON				

DAVIS, Dianne '89
Born in Celina, Tennessee.

7/29/89	75	4		Baby Don't Go		$3		16th Avenue 70430

DAVIS, Gene '76

11/27/76	97	4		Oh Those Texas Women.. *She Says It With Love*		$6		Maverick 301

DAVIS, Jimmie '45
Born on 9/11/02 in Beech Grove, Louisiana. Singer/songwriter/guitarist. Acted in the movies *Strictly In The Groove*, *Frontier Fury*, *Louisiana* and *Square Dance Katy*. Governor of Louisiana from 1944-48 and 1960-64. Elected to the Country Music Hall of Fame in 1972.

9/2/44	3	2		1 Is It Too Late Now/				
9/30/44	4	2		2 There's A Chill On The Hill Tonight		$40		Decca 6100
2/17/45	❶¹	18		3 There's A New Moon Over My Shoulder *Love Please Don't Let Me Down*		$40		Decca 6105
3/2/46	4	1		4 Grievin' My Heart Out For You *I'm Sorry If That's The Way You Feel*		$40		Decca 18756
1/18/47	4	2		5 Bang Bang *I'm Gonna Write Myself A Letter*		$30		Decca 46016
6/16/62	15	9		6 Where The Old Red River Flows .... *Lonesome Whistle*		$20		Decca 31368

DAVIS, Joey '78
Male singer from Waynesboro, Virginia.

8/12/78	99	1		1 Why Don't You Leave Me Alone		$6		MRC 1017
12/16/78	94	3		2 Takin' It Easy................................... *Got My Throttle Wide Open*		$6		MRC 1023

DAVIS, Linda '93
Born on 11/26/62 in Dodson, Texas. Former jingle singer. In duo **Skip & Linda**. Married to **Lang Scott**.

10/29/88	50	10		1 All The Good One's Are Taken............................... *Cry Baby*		$3		Epic 08057
2/4/89	51	6		2 Back In The Swing Again................. *All The Good One's Are Taken*		$3		Epic 68544
6/10/89	67	5		3 Weak Nights.................................... *All The Good One's Are Taken*		$3		Epic 68919
1/12/91	61	7		4 In A Different Light/				
5/4/91	68	5		5 Some Kinda Woman		$3	▮	Capitol 44684
2/26/94	43	13		6 Company Time.............................. *How Can I Make You Love Me*		$3	▮	Arista 12664
6/18/94	58	8		7 Love Didn't Do It.. *He's In Dallas*		$3	▮	Arista 12701
12/2/95+	13	20		8 Some Things Are Meant To Be *S:12 There Isn't One*		$3	▮	Arista 12896
4/13/96	33	19		9 A Love Story In The Making .... *What Do I Know*		$3	▮	Arista 12991

DAVIS, Mac ★168★ '81
Born Scott Davis on 1/21/42 in Lubbock, Texas. Singer/songwriter/guitarist. Acted in several movies. Host of own musical variety TV series from 1974-76.

1)Hooked On Music 2)You're My Bestest Friend 3)Texas In My Rear View Mirror 4)Let's Keep It That Way
5)It's Hard To Be Humble

4/25/70	43	13		1 Whoever Finds This, I Love You .... *Half And Half (Song For Sarah)*	53	$6	■	Columbia 45117
8/29/70	68	4		2 I'll Paint You A Song .... *Closest I Ever Came*	110	$6		Columbia 45192
				from the movie *Norwood* starring **Glen Campbell**				
8/26/72	26	11	●	3 Baby Don't Get Hooked On Me .... *Poem For My Little Lady*	❶³	$5		Columbia 45618
2/24/73	47	8		4 Dream Me Home .... *Spread Your Love On Me*	73	$5		Columbia 45773
5/12/73	36	11		5 Your Side Of The Bed .... *(Hope You Didn't) Chop No Wood*	88	$5		Columbia 45839
9/1/73	29	15		6 Kiss It And Make It Better .... *Sunshine*	105	$5		Columbia 45911
9/7/74	40	12		7 Stop And Smell The Roses.................................. *Poor Boy Boogie*	9	$5		Columbia 10018
1/4/75	29	11		8 Rock N' Roll (I Gave You The Best Years Of My Life)............ *Emily Suzanne*	15	$5		Columbia 10070
4/12/75	69	6		9 (If You Add) All The Love In The World................................. *Smiley*	54	$5		Columbia 10111
6/7/75	31	12		10 Burnin' Thing .... *A Special Place In Heaven*	53	$5		Columbia 10148
9/27/75	81	5		11 I Still Love You (You Still Love Me) .... *The Hits Just Keep On Coming*		$5		Columbia 10187
3/27/76	17	13		12 Forever Lovers .... *The Love Lamp*	76	$5		Columbia 10304
10/9/76	34	10		13 Every Now And Then .... *I'm Just In Love*		$5		Columbia 10418
5/21/77	42	9		14 Picking Up The Pieces Of My Life.......... *Do It (With Someone You Love)*		$5		Columbia 10535
6/10/78	92	5		15 Music In My Life .... *You Are*		$5		Columbia 10745
3/22/80	10	12		16 It's Hard To Be Humble *The Greatest Gift Of All* [N]	43	$4		Casablanca 2244
7/12/80	10	15		17 Let's Keep It That Way *I Know You're Out There Somewhere*		$4		Casablanca 2286
10/11/80	9	17		18 Texas In My Rear View Mirror *Sad Songs*	51	$4		Casablanca 2305
2/21/81	2²	15		19 Hooked On Music *Me And Fat Boy*	102	$4		Casablanca 2327
7/18/81	47	10		20 Secrets................................... *Remember When (Beverly's Song)*	76	$4		Casablanca 2336
10/24/81+	5	18		21 You're My Bestest Friend *You Are So Lovely*	106	$4		Casablanca 2341
5/29/82	37	10		22 Rodeo Clown .... *Dammit Girl*		$4		Casablanca 2350
9/25/82	58	8		23 The Beer Drinkin' Song.................................. *You Are So Lovely*		$4		Casablanca 2355
12/18/82+	62	7		24 Lying Here Lying .... *The Quiet Times*		$4		Casablanca 2363
2/11/84	41	14		25 Most Of All.................................. *Springtime Down In Dixie*		$4		Casablanca 818168
5/19/84	76	5		26 Caroline's Still In Georgia.................................. *I've Got A Dream*		$4		Casablanca 818929
5/25/85	10	24		27 I Never Made Love (Till I Made Love With You) *S:9 / A:10 I Think I'm Gonna Rain*		$3		MCA 52573
10/5/85	34	16		28 I Feel The Country Callin' Me .... *Rainy Day Lovin'*		$3		MCA 52669
2/1/86	46	9		29 Sexy Young Girl.................................. *A Special Place In Heaven*		$3		MCA 52765
6/7/86	65	5		30 Somewhere In America .... *I Need A Hug*		$3		MCA 52826

DEBUT	PEAK	WKS	Gold	A-side (Chart Hit)	B-side	Pop	$	Pic	Label & Number
				DAVIS, Paul '60					
7/18/60	28	5		One Of Her Fools .... *When You Fall*			$25		Doke 107
				DAVIS, Paul '88					
				Born on 4/21/48 in Meridian, Mississippi. Singer/songwriter/producer. Charted 15 pop hits from 1970-82.					
1/11/75	47	8		1 Ride 'Em Cowboy..*I'm The Only Sinner (In Salt Lake City)*	23	$5		Bang 712
12/16/78+	85	4		2 Sweet Life .... *Bad Dream*	17	$5		Bang 738
				also see #5 below					
8/30/86	❶¹	21		3 You're Still New To Me .... *New Love*		$3	■	Capitol/Curb 5613
				MARIE OSMOND WITH PAUL DAVIS					
11/21/87+	❶¹	24		4 I Won't Take Less Than Your Love ...... S:2 *Heartbreaker*		$3		Capitol 44100
				TANYA TUCKER with PAUL DAVIS & PAUL OVERSTREET					
8/20/88	47	8		5 Sweet Life .... *Somebody Else's Moon* [R]		$3		Capitol/Curb 44215
				MARIE OSMOND (with Paul Davis)					
				new version of #2 above					
				DAVIS, Sammy Jr. '82					
				Born on 12/8/25 in New York City. Died of throat cancer on 5/16/90 (age 64). Singer/dancer/actor. Numerous appearances on TV, Broadway and in movies. Charted 17 pop hits from 1955-72.					
12/11/82	89	2		Smoke, Smoke, Smoke (That Cigarette) ... *We Could Have Been The Closest Of Friends*		$5		Applause 100

DEBUT	PEAK	WKS	Gold	A-side (Chart Hit)	B-side	Pop	$	Pic	Label & Number
				DAVIS, Skeeter ★104★ '63					
				Born Mary Frances Penick on 12/30/31 in Dry Ridge, Kentucky. Worked as **The Davis Sisters** with friend Betty Jack Davis, and later with Georgia Davis. Went solo in 1956. Joined the *Grand Ole Opry* in 1959. Married to **Ralph Emery** from 1960-64. Married to Joey Spampinato, the bassist of rock band NRBQ, from 1983-96.					
				1)The End Of The World 2)I'm Falling Too 3)What Does It Take 4)My Last Date 5)Set Him Free					
2/24/58	15	1		1 Lost To A Geisha Girl .... A:15 *I'm Going Steady With A Heartache*		$15		RCA Victor 7084
				answer to "Geisha Girl" by **Hank Locklin**					
3/30/59	5	17		2 Set Him Free .... *The Devil's Doll*		$15		RCA Victor 7471
				also see #24 below					
9/21/59	15	13		3 Homebreaker.. *Give Me Death*		$15		RCA Victor 7570
3/7/60	11	12		4 Am I That Easy To Forget? .... *Wishful Thinking*		$15		RCA Victor 7671
8/29/60	2³	16		5 (I Can't Help You) I'm Falling Too .... *No Never*	39	$12		RCA Victor 7767
				answer to "Please Help Me, I'm Falling" by **Hank Locklin**					
12/31/60+	5	13		6 My Last Date (With You) .... *Someone I'd Like To Forget*	26	$12		RCA Victor 7825
				answer to "Last Date" by **Floyd Cramer**					
4/24/61	11	11		7 The Hand You're Holding Now .... *Someday, Someday*		$12		RCA Victor 7863
10/16/61	10	11		8 Optimistic .... *Blueberry Hill*		$12		RCA Victor 7928
3/10/62	9	9		9 Where I Ought To Be/		$12		RCA Victor 7979
6/2/62	23	3		10 Something Precious..		$12		
9/8/62	22	1		11 The Little Music Box.. *The Final Step*		$12		RCA Victor 8055
12/15/62+	2³	24		12 The End Of The World .... *Somebody Loves You*	2¹	$12		RCA Victor 8098
5/25/63	9	14		13 I'm Saving My Love .... *Somebody Else On Your Mind*	41	$12		RCA Victor 8176
10/12/63	14	10		14 I Can't Stay Mad At You .... *It Was Only A Heart*	7	$12	■	RCA Victor 8219
1/25/64	17	15		15 He Says The Same Things To Me ....*How Much Can A Lonely Heart Stand* (Pop #92)	47	$12		RCA Victor 8288
5/16/64	8	14		16 Gonna Get Along Without You Now .... *Now You're Gone*	48	$12		RCA Victor 8347
				#11 Pop hit for Patience & Prudence in 1956					
9/26/64	45	4		17 Let Me Get Close To You .... *The Face Of A Clown*	106	$12		RCA Victor 8397
11/14/64	38	5		18 What Am I Gonna Do With You .... *Don't Let Me Stand In Your Way*	123	$12		RCA Victor 8450
3/13/65	11	12		19 A Dear John Letter................................ *Too Used To Being With You*	114	$10		RCA Victor 8496
				SKEETER DAVIS & BOBBY BARE					
				#44 Pop hit for Pat Boone in 1960					
9/11/65	30	7		20 Sun Glasses .... *He Loved Me Too Little*	120	$10		RCA Victor 8642
10/15/66	36	9		21 Goin' Down The Road (Feelin' Bad) .... *I Can't Stand The Sight Of You*		$10		RCA Victor 8932
1/28/67	11	16		22 Fuel To The Flame .... *You Call This Love*		$10		RCA Victor 9058
				co-written by **Dolly Parton**					
7/22/67	5	18		23 What Does It Take (To Keep A Man Like You Satisfied) .... *What I Go Thru*	121	$10		RCA Victor 9242
12/16/67+	52	7		24 Set Him Free .... *Is It Worth It To You* [R]		$10		RCA Victor 9371
				new version of #2 above					
2/24/68	72	2		25 For Loving You................................ *Baby It's Cold Outside* [N]		$8		RCA Victor 9415
				SKEETER DAVIS AND DON BOWMAN					
3/23/68	54	7		26 Instinct For Survival .... *How In The World*		$8		RCA Victor 9459
6/22/68	16	10		27 There's A Fool Born Every Minute .... *I Can't See Past My Tears*		$8		RCA Victor 9543
1/11/69	66	7		28 The Closest Thing To Love (I've Ever Seen) ..... *Mama Your Big Girl's 'Bout To Cry*		$8		RCA Victor 9695
12/13/69+	9	15		29 I'm A Lover (Not A Fighter) .... *I Didn't Cry Today*		$8		RCA Victor 0292
1/24/70	22	7		30 Your Husband, My Wife .... *Before The Sunrise*		$6		RCA Victor 9789
				BOBBY BARE AND SKEETER DAVIS					
5/9/70	65	5		31 It's Hard To Be A Woman .... *What A Little Girl Don't Know*		$7		RCA Victor 9818
8/8/70	69	3		32 We Need A Lot More Of Jesus ....*When You Gonna Bring Our Soldiers Home*		$7		RCA Victor 9871
9/26/70	65	2		33 Let's Get Together .... *Everything Is Beautiful*		$7		RCA Victor 9893
				SKEETER DAVIS AND GEORGE HAMILTON IV					
				#5 Pop hit for The Youngbloods in 1969					
3/6/71	21	13		34 Bus Fare To Kentucky .... *From Her Arms Into Mine*		$7		RCA Victor 9961
7/17/71	58	8		35 Love Takes A Lot Of My Time .... *Love, Love, Love*		$7		RCA Victor 9997

DAVIS, Skeeter — Cont'd

DEBUT	PEAK	WKS	A-side	B-side	Pop	$	Label & Number
1/8/72	54	7	36 One Tin Soldier	Rachel		$7	RCA Victor 0608
			#26 Pop hit for Coven in 1971; from the movie *Billy Jack* starring Tom Laughlin				
5/20/72	46	8	37 Sad Situation	All I Ever Wanted Was Love		$7	RCA Victor 0681
6/16/73	12	17	38 I Can't Believe That It's All Over	Try Jesus	101	$7	RCA Victor 0968
12/15/73+	44	10	39 Don't Forget To Remember	Baby, Get That Leavin' Off Your Mind		$7	RCA Victor 0188
			#73 Pop hit for the **Bee Gees** in 1969				
5/25/74	65	8	40 One More Time	Stay Awhile With Me		$7	RCA Victor 0277
9/18/76	60	7	41 I Love Us	It Feels So Good		$6	Mercury 73818

DAVIS, Stephanie   '93
Female singer/songwriter from San Francisco.

8/28/93	72	2	It's All In The Heart	Summer Nights In Dixie		$3	▮	Asylum 64616

DAVIS SISTERS, The   '53
Vocal duo from Lexington, Kentucky: **Skeeter Davis** and Betty Jack Davis. The two were not related. Betty Jack was killed and Skeeter was seriously injured in a car crash on 8/2/53. Betty Jack was replaced by her sister Georgia.

8/15/53	❶⁸	26	I Forgot More Than You'll Ever Know	A:❶⁸ / S:❶⁸ / J:❶² Rock-A-Bye Boogie	18	$25	RCA Victor 5345

DEAL, Don   '79

6/16/79	90	2	Second Best (Is Too Far Down The Line)	When		$7	Donjim 1008

★223★ DEAN, Billy   '91
Born on 4/1/62 in Quincy, Florida. Singer/songwriter/guitarist.
1)Somewhere In My Broken Heart 2)If There Hadn't Been You 3)Only Here For A Little While

DEBUT	PEAK	WKS	A-side	B-side	Pop	$	Pic	Label & Number
12/22/90+	3	22	1 Only Here For A Little While					album cut
			from the album *Young Man* on Capitol 94302					
5/4/91	3	20	2 Somewhere In My Broken Heart	Young Man		$3	▮	Capitol 44757
9/14/91	4	20	3 You Don't Count The Cost	She's Taken		$3		Capitol 44773
1/4/92	4	20	4 Only The Wind	Simple Things		$3		Capitol 44803
5/23/92	4	20	5 Billy The Kid	Simple Things		$3		Liberty 57745
8/29/92	3	20	6 If There Hadn't Been You	Small Favors		$3		Liberty 57884
12/12/92+	6	20	7 Tryin' To Hide A Fire In The Dark	Steam Roller		$3		Liberty 56804
4/10/93	22	20	8 I Wanna Take Care Of You/					
8/21/93	34	13	9 I'm Not Built That Way			$3		Liberty 56984
11/13/93+	9	20	10 We Just Disagree					album cut
			#12 Pop hit for Dave Mason in 1977; from the album *Fire In The Dark* on Liberty 98947					
3/5/94	53	8	11 Once In A While					album cut
			from the movie *8 Seconds* starring Luke Perry (soundtrack on MCA 10927)					
6/4/94	24	20	12 Cowboy Band	Billy The Kid		$3	▮	Liberty 58189
10/8/94	60	6	13 Men Will Be Boys					album cut
			from the album *Men'll Be Boys* on Liberty 27760					
2/3/96	5	20	14 It's What I Do	S:17 The Mountain Moved		$3	▮	Capitol 58526
6/15/96	4	20	15 That Girl's Been Spyin' On Me	S:13 Don't Threaten Me With A Good Time		$3	▮	Capitol 58563
11/2/96	45	14	16 I Wouldn't Be A Man					album cut
			from the album *It's What I Do* on Capitol 30525					

DEAN, Eddie   '55
Born Edgar Dean Glosup on 7/9/07 in Posey, Texas. Singer/songwriter/guitarist. Regular on the WLS *National Barn Dance* and Judy Canova's radio show. Acted in several movies from 1937-48.

9/25/48	11	1	1 One Has My Name (The Other Has My Heart)	S:11		$40	Crystal 132
			#13 Pop hit for Barry Young in 1966				
1/22/55	10	3	2 I Dreamed Of A Hill-Billy Heaven	A:10 / J:10 / S:15 Stealing		$30	Sage and Sand 180
			The Frontiersmen (instrumental backing, above 2)				

DEAN, Jimmy ★176★   '61
Born on 8/10/28 in Plainview, Texas. Singer/songwriter/guitarist. Hosted own CBS-TV series from 1957-58; ABC-TV series from 1963-66. Business interests include a line of pork sausage. Married **Donna Meade** on 10/27/91.

1)Big Bad John 2)The First Thing Ev'ry Morning 3)P.T. 109 4)Bumming Around 5)Dear Ivan

DEBUT	PEAK	WKS	A-side	B-side	Pop	$	Pic	Label & Number
3/7/53	5	7	1 Bumming Around JIMMIE DEAN	A:5 / S:9 / J:10 Picking Sweethearts		$25		4 Star 1613
10/16/61	❶²	22	● 2 Big Bad John	I Won't Go Huntin' With You Jake	❶⁵	$10	■	Columbia 42175
2/3/62	9	10	3 Dear Ivan	Smoke, Smoke, Smoke That Cigarette [S]	24	$10	■	Columbia 42259
3/10/62	15	6	4 To A Sleeping Beauty/	[S]	26	$10	■	Columbia 42282
			also see #24 below					
2/10/62	16	10	5 The Cajun Queen	[S]	22	$10	■	
4/21/62	3	13	6 P.T. 109	Walk On, Boy	8	$10	■	Columbia 42338
			based on the sinking of John F. Kennedy's torpedo boat in 1943					
9/29/62	10	11	7 Little Black Book	Please Pass The Biscuits	29	$10	■	Columbia 42529
2/1/64	35	6	8 Mind Your Own Business	I Really Don't Want To Know		$8	■	Columbia 42934
6/5/65	❶²	17	9 The First Thing Ev'ry Morning (And The Last Thing Ev'ry Night)	Awkward Situation	91	$8		Columbia 43263
10/30/65	35	6	10 Harvest Of Sunshine	Under The Sun		$8		Columbia 43382
10/22/66	10	18	11 Stand Beside Me	A Tiny Drop Of Sadness		$7		RCA Victor 8971
2/18/67	16	14	12 Sweet Misery	When Somebody Mentions Your Name		$7		RCA Victor 9091

DEBUT	PEAK	WKS	Gold	A-side (Chart Hit)..B-side	Pop	$	Pic	Label & Number
				DEAN, Jimmy — Cont'd				
7/22/67	41	9		13 Ninety Days .... *In The Same Old Way*		$7		RCA Victor 9241
11/18/67+	30	10		14 I'm A Swinger .... *Your Country Boy*		$7		RCA Victor 9350
3/9/68	21	14		15 A Thing Called Love .... *One Last Time*		$7		RCA Victor 9454
8/10/68	52	8		16 Born To Be By Your Side .... *Read 'Em And Weep*		$7		RCA Victor 9567
11/9/68	22	11		17 A Hammer And Nails ....*I Taught Her Everything She Knows*		$7		RCA Victor 9652
4/5/69	52	7		18 A Rose Is A Rose Is A Rose.. *She's Mine*		$7		RCA Victor 0122
1/30/71	29	11		19 Slowly .... *Sweet Thang*		$6		RCA Victor 9947
				JIMMY DEAN AND DOTTIE WEST				
4/17/71	54	7		20 Everybody Knows .... *Ain't Life Sweet*		$6		RCA Victor 9966
1/1/72	38	12		21 The One You Say Good Mornin' To .... *And I'm Still Missing You*		$6		RCA Victor 0600
10/6/73	90	6		22 Your Sweet Love (Keeps Me Homeward Bound)................ *I'm Gonna Be Gone*		$5		Columbia 45922
5/15/76	9	6	●	23 I.O.U. .... *Let's Pick Up The Pieces (And Start Over Again)* [S]	35	$5		Casino 052
				also see #25 & #26 below				
9/25/76	85	3		24 To A Sleeping Beauty ....*I Didn't Have Time* [R-S]		$5		Casino 074
				new version of #4 above				
5/14/77	90	2		25 I.O.U...................... *Let's Pick Up The Pieces (And Start Over Again)* [R-S]		$5		Casino 052
				same version as #23 above				
5/14/83	77	4		26 I.O.U. .... *To A Sleeping Beauty* [R-S]		$5	■	Churchill 94024
				new version of #23 above				
				DEAN, Larry **'89**				
10/7/89	91	2		Outside Chance...		$6	■	USA 620
				DEBONAIRES **'85**				
				Male vocal group from Tyler, Texas.				
4/13/85	79	6		I'm On Fire .... *Loving You Is Always On My Mind*		$6		MTM 72051
				#6 Pop hit for Bruce Springsteen in 1985				
				DEE, Duane **'71**				
				Born Duane DeRosia in Hartford, Wisconsin.				
11/11/67+	44	12		1 Before The Next Teardrop Falls............................. *You're Not Painting The Town*		$10		Capitol 5986
12/21/68+	58	7		2 True Love Travels On A Gravel Road .... *Have A Little Faith*		$8		Capitol 2332
2/6/71	71	2		3 I've Got To Sing .... *There Will Be An Answer*		$6		Cartwheel 192
10/16/71	36	13		4 How Can You Mend A Broken Heart *Georgeanna*		$6		Cartwheel 200
				#1 Pop hit for the **Bee Gees** in 1971				
3/4/72	64	6		5 Sweet Apple Wine ....*I Can't Get Over You*		$6		Cartwheel 207
4/20/74	88	3		6 Morning Girl .... *She's My Woman*		$5		ABC 11417
				#17 Pop hit for Neon Philharmonic in 1969				
				DEE, Gordon **'84**				
				Born Gordon Dillingham in New Bridge, North Carolina. Singer/songwriter/guitarist.				
12/15/84	87	5		(Nothing Left Between Us) But Alabama .... *Slowly Going Out Of My Mind*		$5		Southern Tracks 1029
				DEE, Kathy **'63**				
				Born Kathleen Dearth in Moundsville, West Virginia. Died on 11/3/68.				
9/21/63	18	3		1 Unkind Words.................................. *Only As Far As The Door*		$10		United Artists 627
2/15/64	44	4		2 Don't Leave Me Lonely Too Long .... *I Promise Not To Cry*		$10		United Artists 687
				DEER, John **'70**				
10/10/70	57	7		Waxahachie Woman .... *Big Train*		$7		Royal American 21
				THE JOHN DEER COMPANY				
	★373★			**DeHAVEN, Penny** **'70**				
				Born Charlotte DeHaven on 5/17/48 in Winchester, Virginia. Singer/actress. Acted in the movies *Valley Of Blood*, *Traveling Light* and *Country Music Story*. Also recorded as **Penny Starr**.				
				1)Land Mark Tavern 2)Mama Lou 3)Down In The Boondocks				
1/7/67	69	3		1 A Grain Of Salt .... *Thing Of Pleasure*		$15		Band Box 372
				PENNY STARR				
8/9/69	34	11		2 Mama Lou .... *That's Just The Way I Am*		$8		Imperial 66388
11/15/69	37	10		3 Down In The Boondocks .... *When The Sun Sets In Jackson*		$8		Imperial 66421
				#9 Pop hit for Billy Joe Royal in 1965				
3/21/70	59	5		4 I Feel Fine.. *Stop & Go*		$8		Imperial 66437
				#1 Pop hit for The Beatles in 1964				
5/30/70	20	12		5 Land Mark Tavern *So Sad*		$7		United Artists 50669
				DEL REEVES & PENNY DeHAVEN				
9/19/70	69	2		6 Awful Lotta Lovin' .... *Tomorrow Never Comes*		$7		United Artists 50703
1/30/71	46	9		7 The First Love .... *The Price I Had To Pay*		$7		United Artists 50742
6/19/71	42	9		8 Don't Change On Me............................. *That's Just The Way I Am*		$6		United Artists 50787
12/25/71+	61	9		9 Another Day Of Loving .... *Mama, Have All The Good Guys Gone?*		$6		United Artists 50854
6/24/72	54	6		10 Crying In The Rain .... *Time*		$6		United Artists 50829
				DEL REEVES & PENNY DeHAVEN				
				#6 Pop hit for The Everly Brothers in 1962				
7/14/73	96	2		11 The Lovin' Of Your Life .... *When You Get Home*		$6		Mercury 73384
12/1/73+	67	8		12 I'll Be Doggone...*Love Me To Sleep*		$6		Mercury 73434
				#8 Pop hit for Marvin Gaye in 1965				
5/4/74	93	5		13 Play With Me .... *Shine On Me*		$6		Mercury 73468
8/7/76	83	4		14 (The Great American) Classic Cowboy .... *Thank God I'm A Country Girl*		$6		Starcrest 066
7/10/82	77	5		15 We Made Memories.................... *To My Baby I'm A Big Star All The Time*		$5		Main Street 952
				BOXCAR WILLIE and PENNY DeHAVEN				
11/5/83	74	5		16 Only The Names Have Been Changed ....*Waltz Me Once Again*		$5		Main Street 93015
4/14/84	78	4		17 Friendly Game Of Hearts		$5		Main Street 93019

DEBUT	PEAK	WKS	Gold	A-side (Chart Hit) ....B-side	Pop	$	Pic	Label & Number

DEKLE, Mike   **'84**
Singer/songwriter from Athens, Georgia. Worked as a staff writer for **Kenny Rogers**.

| 6/30/84 | 93 | 2 | | 1 Hanky Panky ....*Lady Luck (Can Be A Bitch Sometimes)* | | $5 | | NSD 188 |
| 11/3/84 | 79 | 4 | | 2 The Minstrel ....*April's Fool* | | $5 | | NSD 195 |

DELICATO, Paul   **'75**
Singer from St. Louis.

| 9/13/75 | 91 | 5 | | Lean On Me ....*Ice Cream Sodas And Lollipops And A Red Hot Spinning Top* | | $5 | | Artists Of Am. 101 |

#1 Pop hit for Bill Withers in 1972; B-side was a #7 Adult Contemporary hit in 1975

DELMORE BROTHERS   **'50**
Duo from Elkmont, Alabama: brothers Alton (b: 12/25/08; d: 6/8/64, age 55) and Rabon (b: 12/3/16; d: 12/4/52, age 36) Delmore. Both were singers/songwriters/guitarists/fiddle players. Joined the *Grand Ole Opry* in 1933.

12/14/46	2[1]	4		1 Freight Train Boogie ....*Somebody Else's Darling*		$30		King 570
9/17/49+	❶[1]	23		2 Blues Stay Away From Me J:❶[1] / S:2 / A:3 *Goin' Back To The Blue Ridge Mountains*		$30		King 803 **(78)**
2/18/50	7	1		3 Pan American Boogie J:7 *Troubles Ain't Nothin' But The Blues*		$30		King 826 **(78)**

DELRAY, Martin   **'91**
Born Michael Ray Martin on 9/26/49 in Texarkana, Arkansas. Also recorded as **Mike Martin**.

3/23/85	76	3		1 Temptation ....*What My Mind's Been On All Day*		$5		Compleat 139
				MIKE MARTIN				
2/23/91	27	20		2 Get Rhythm *The Very Thought Of You*		$4	▌	Atlantic 87869
				Johnny Cash (guest vocal)				
7/20/91	58	9		3 Lillies White Lies ....*I Let Love Do My Talkin'*		$3		Atlantic 87680
2/1/92	51	12		4 Who, What, Where, When, Why, How..				album cut
				from the album *Get Rhythm* on Atlantic 82176				
12/19/92+	61	9		5 What Kind Of Man				album cut
				from the album *What Kind Of Man* on Atlantic 82439				

DENNIS, Wesley   **'95**
Born in Clanton, Alabama; raised in Montgomery, Alabama.

2/25/95	46	11		1 I Don't Know (But I've Been Told).............................*Borrowed Angel*		$3	▌	Mercury 856486
6/3/95	51	10		2 Don't Make Me Feel At Home ....*This Hat Ain't No Act*		$3	▌	Mercury 856834
9/2/95	58	8		3 Who's Counting ....*It Ain't Fair*		$3		Mercury 852286

DENNY, Burch   **'89**

| 3/4/89 | 86 | 2 | | Yesterday Is Too Far Away.. | | $5 | | Oak 1068 |

DENTON, Jack   **'89**

| 10/7/89 | 95 | 1 | | Anna ("Go With Him") ....*Something About You* | | $7 | | M.V.P. 10001 |

#68 Pop hit for Arthur Alexander in 1962

DENVER, John   ★179★   **'75**
Born Henry John Deutschendorf on 12/31/43 in Roswell, New Mexico. Died on 10/12/97 (age 53) at the controls of a light plane which crashed off the California coast. Singer/songwriter/guitarist. With the **Chad Mitchell Trio** from 1965-68. Starred in the 1977 movie *Oh, God*. CMA Award: 1975 Entertainer of the Year.

    1)*I'm Sorry* 2)*Thank God I'm A Country Boy* 3)*Back Home Again* 4)*Sweet Surrender* 5)*Dreamland Express*

6/26/71	50	12	●	1 Take Me Home, Country Roads ....*Poems, Prayers And Promises*	2[1]	$5		RCA Victor 0445
				Fat City (Bill Danoff & Taffy Nivert of **Starland Vocal Band**; backing vocals)				
12/15/73	69	7		2 Please, Daddy ....*Rocky Mountain Suite (Cold Nights In Canada)* [X]	69	$5		RCA Victor 0182
2/16/74	42	12	●	3 Sunshine On My Shoulders.................................*Around And Around*	❶[1]	$5		RCA Victor 0213
6/8/74	9	14	●	4 Annie's Song *Cool An' Green An' Shady*	❶[2]	$5		RCA Victor 0295
				written for his wife Annie Martell (married 1967-83)				
9/28/74	❶[1]	14	●	5 Back Home Again *It's Up To You*	5	$5		RCA Victor 10065
1/4/75	7	12	●	6 Sweet Surrender *Summer*	13	$5		RCA Victor 10148
3/29/75	❶[1]	14	●	7 Thank God I'm A Country Boy *My Sweet Lady*	❶[1]	$5		RCA Victor 10239
				above 2 recorded "live" at Universal City Amphitheater in California				
8/16/75	❶[1]	18	●	8 I'm Sorry *Calypso (Pop #2)*	❶[1]	$5		RCA Victor 10353
12/13/75+	12	11		9 Fly Away ....*Two Shots*	13	$5		RCA Victor 10517
				Olivia Newton-John (backing vocal)				
3/13/76	30	10		10 Looking For Space ....*Windsong*	29	$5		RCA Victor 10586
5/29/76	70	5		11 It Makes Me Giggle ....*Spirit*	60	$5		RCA Victor 10687
9/18/76	34	9		12 Like A Sad Song ....*Pegasus*	36	$4		RCA 10774
12/18/76+	22	11		13 Baby, You Look Good To Me Tonight ....*Wrangle Mountain Song*	65	$4		RCA 10854
3/12/77	62	7		14 My Sweet Lady ....*Welcome To My Morning (Farewell Andromeda)*	32	$4		RCA 10911
11/26/77+	22	13		15 How Can I Leave You Again ....*To The Wild Country*	44	$4		RCA 11036
2/25/78	72	6		16 It Amazes Me ....*Druthers*	59	$4		RCA 11214
2/17/79	64	5		17 Downhill Stuff ....*Life Is So Good*	106	$4		RCA 11479
4/7/79	47	7		18 What's On Your Mind/	107			
		7		19 Sweet Melinda		$4		RCA 11535
3/1/80	84	5		20 Autograph ....*The Mountain Song*	52	$4	■	RCA 11915
6/13/81	10	18		21 Some Days Are Diamonds (Some Days Are Stone) *Country Love*	36	$4		RCA 12246
11/14/81	50	9		22 The Cowboy And The Lady ....*Till You Opened My Eyes*	66	$4		RCA 12345
7/9/83	14	19		23 Wild Montana Skies...*I Remember Romance*		$4		RCA 13562
				JOHN DENVER AND EMMYLOU HARRIS				
12/14/85+	9	21		24 Dreamland Express A:7 / S:10 *African Sunrise*		$4	■	RCA 14227
8/30/86	57	9		25 Along For The Ride ('56 T-Bird) ....*Let Us Begin*		$4		RCA 14406

DEBUT	PEAK	WKS	Gold	A-side (Chart Hit)..B-side	Pop	$	Pic	Label & Number

DENVER, John — Cont'd

10/29/88	96	2		26 Country Girl In Paris .... *Bread And Roses*		$5	■	Windstar 75720
5/27/89	14	23		27 And So It Goes .... *Amazing Grace*		$3		Universal 66008

JOHN DENVER AND THE NITTY GRITTY DIRT BAND

★230★ **DESERT ROSE BAND, The**   **'88**
Nucleus of group: Southern California natives **Chris Hillman**, John Jorgenson and **Herb Pedersen**. Hillman was a founding member of The Byrds and the **Flying Burrito Brothers**. Jorgenson left in 1992. Disbanded in early 1994.
1)*I Still Believe In You* 2)*He's Back And I'm Blue* 3)*Summer Wind*

3/21/87	26	18		1 Ashes Of Love... *Leave This Town*		$3		Curb/MCA 53048
7/11/87	6	21		2 Love Reunited .... S:19 *Hard Times*		$3		Curb/MCA 53142
10/31/87+	2¹	25		3 One Step Forward .... S:6 *Glass Hearts*		$3		Curb/MCA 53201
3/26/88	❶¹	19		4 He's Back And I'm Blue .... S:7 *One That Got Away*		$3		Curb/MCA 53274
7/30/88	2¹	20		5 Summer Wind .... S:8 *Our Songs*		$3		Curb/MCA 53354
11/26/88+	❶¹	20		6 I Still Believe In You .... *Livin' In The House*		$3		Curb/MCA 53454
3/18/89	3	20		7 She Don't Love Nobody .... *Step On Out*		$3		Curb/MCA 53616
7/8/89	11	22		8 Hello Trouble .... *Homeless*		$3		Curb/MCA 53671
11/4/89+	6	26		9 Start All Over Again .... *Fooled Again*		$3		Curb/MCA 53746
3/24/90	13	23		10 In Another Lifetime .... *Just A Memory*		$3		Curb/MCA 53804
7/21/90	10	20		11 Story Of Love .... *Darkness On The Playground*		$3		Curb/MCA 79052
2/9/91	37	12		12 Will This Be The Day.................... *Our Baby's Gone*		$3		Curb/MCA 54002
5/25/91	65	6		13 Come A Little Closer................... *Everybody's Hero*		$3		Curb/MCA 54107
10/5/91	53	11		14 You Can Go Home .... *Glory And Power*		$3		Curb/MCA 54188
1/25/92	67	3		15 Twilight Is Gone .... *Shades Of Blue*		$3		Curb/MCA 54316
9/4/93	71	1		16 What About Love				album cut

from the album *Life Goes On* on Curb 77627

DESERT WIND BAND, The — see SHAW, Ron

DeVAL, Buddy — see LORRIE, Myrna

DeWITT, Lew   **'85**
Born on 3/12/38 in Roanoke, Virginia. Died on 8/15/90 (age 52). Member of **The Statler Brothers** from 1955-82.

11/30/85	77	7		You'll Never Know .... *Wanda Glen*		$6		Compleat 147

#1 Pop hit for Dick Haymes in 1943

DEXTER, Al ★129★   **'44**
Born Clarence Albert Poindexter on 5/4/02 in Jacksonville, Texas. Died on 1/28/84 (age 81). Singer/songwriter/guitarist/violinist.

1)*Guitar Polka* 2)*So Long Pal* 3)*I'm Losing My Mind Over You*

AL DEXTER and his Troopers:

1/8/44	❶³	10	●	1 Pistol Packin' Mama/	❶¹			
1/8/44	❶¹	25		2 Rosalita	22	$30		Okeh 6708
3/11/44	❶¹³	30		3 So Long Pal/				
3/11/44	❶²	30		4 Too Late To Worry	18	$30		Okeh 6718
1/20/45	❶⁷	21		5 I'm Losing My Mind Over You/				
1/27/45	2¹	10		6 I'll Wait For You Dear		$30		Okeh 6727
7/7/45	2⁵	11		7 Triflin' Gal/				
8/25/45	5	3		8 I'm Lost Without You		$30		Okeh 6740
2/2/46	❶¹⁶	29		9 Guitar Polka/ [I]	16			
2/9/46	2¹	8		10 Honey Do You Think It's Wrong		$25		Columbia 36898
8/31/46	❶⁵	13		11 Wine, Women And Song/				
9/14/46	3	5		12 It's Up To You		$25		Columbia 37062
1/25/47	4	1		13 Kokomo Island .... *I Learned About Love*		$25		Columbia 37200
5/10/47	4	7		14 Down At The Roadside Inn .... *My Love Goes With You*		$25		Columbia 37303
7/3/48	14	1		15 Rock And Rye Rag .... J:14 *I'm Leaving My Troubles Behind* [I]		$25		Columbia 20422
9/18/48	11	2		16 Calico Rag .... J:11 *Rose Of Mexico*		$25		Columbia 20438

DIAMOND, Neil   **'78**
Born on 1/24/41 in Brooklyn. Pop singer/songwriter/guitarist. Charted 56 pop hits from 1966-86.

11/25/78	70	8	●	1 You Don't Bring Me Flowers .... *(instrumental)*	❶²	$4		Columbia 10840
				BARBRA & NEIL				
2/17/79	73	7		2 Forever In Blue Jeans............................ *Remember Me*	20	$4		Columbia 10897

DIAMOND RIO ★153★ '97
Six-man band: Marty Roe (vocals), Jimmy Olander (guitar), Gene Johnson (mandolin), Dan Truman (piano), Dana Williams (bass) and Brian Prout (drums; married to Nancy Given, drummer for **Wild Rose**). Joined the *Grand Ole Opry* in 1998. CMA Awards: 1992, 1993, 1994 & 1997 Vocal Group of the Year. Also see **Jed Zeppelin**.

1)How Your Love Makes Me Feel 2)Meet In The Middle 3)Norma Jean Riley

3/23/91	❶²	20	1	**Meet In The Middle** — *The Ballad Of Conley And Billy (The Proof's In The Pickin')*		$3		Arista 2182
7/20/91	3	20	2	**Mirror Mirror** — *The Ballad Of Conley And Billy (The Proofs In The Pickin')*		$3		Arista 2262
11/16/91+	9	20	3	**Mama Don't Forget To Pray For Me** — *Norma Jean Riley*		$3		Arista 2258
3/28/92	2²	20	4	**Norma Jean Riley** — *Pick Me Up*		$3		Arista 12407
7/11/92	7	20	5	**Nowhere Bound** — *They Don't Make Hearts (Like They Used To)*		$3		Arista 12441
11/21/92+	2²	20	6	**In A Week Or Two** — *Close To The Edge*		$3		Arista 12457
4/3/93	5	20	7	**Oh Me, Oh My, Sweet Baby** — *Nothing In This World*		$3	■	Arista 12464
7/24/93	13	20	8	**This Romeo Ain't Got Julie Yet** ....*I Was Meant To Be With You*		$3		Arista 12580
11/27/93+	21	20	9	**Sawmill Road** ....*I Was Meant To Be With You*		$3		Arista 12610
5/28/94	2²	20	10	**Love A Little Stronger** — *It Does Get Better Than This*		$3	■	Arista 12696
10/22/94+	9	20	11	**Night Is Fallin' In My Heart** — *Down By The Riverside*	107	$3	■	Arista 12764
2/4/95	16	20	12	**Bubba Hyde** ....*S:11 (dance mix)*	102	$3	■	Arista 12787
5/20/95	19	20	13	**Finish What We Started** .... *Appalachian Dream*		$3		Arista 12739
12/16/95+	2¹	20	14	**Walkin' Away** — *S:20 It's All In Your Head*		$3	■	Arista 12934
5/4/96	4	20	15	**That's What I Get For Lovin' You** — *Big*		$3		Arista 12992
8/24/96	15	20	16	**It's All In Your Head** ....*Is That Asking Too Much*		$3		Arista 13019
12/14/96+	4	20	17	**Holdin'** — *She Sure Did Like To Run*		$3		Arista 13067
6/7/97	❶³	22	18	**How Your Love Makes Me Feel/**				
11/1/97+	4	21	19	**Imagine That**		$3		Arista 13091

DIAMONDS, The '87
Vocal group from Canada: Bob Duncan, Gary Cech, Gary Owens and Steve Smith. The original group consisting of Dave Somerville, Ted Kowalski, Phil Leavitt and Bill Reed charted 16 pop hits from 1956-61. Duncan joined in 1978 and recruited the other three members in 1982.

2/14/87	63	8	1	**Just A Little Bit**		$6		Churchill 94101
7/11/87	83	3	2	**Two Kinds Of Woman**		$6		Churchill 94102

DIANA '81
Born Diana Murrell on 5/26/55 in Cincinnati.

6/23/79	40	8	1	**Just When I Needed You Most** ....*Tie Me Down*		$5		Elektra 46061
10/6/79	41	9	2	**Lonely Together** .... *This Is The Way A Woman Wants To Feel*		$5		Elektra 46539
8/1/81	29	12	3	**He's The Fire** ....*What A Fool I Was (To Fall In Love With You)*		$5		Sunbird 7564
12/18/82	88	3	4	**Who's Been Sleeping In My Bed**		$6	■	Adamas 103

DICKENS, "Little" Jimmy ★241★ '65
Born James Cecil Dickens on 12/19/20 in Bolt, West Virginia. Singer/songwriter/guitarist. Joined the *Grand Ole Opry* in 1948. Nicknamed "Tater." Elected to the Country Music Hall of Fame in 1982.

1)May The Bird Of Paradise Fly Up Your Nose 2)Hillbilly Fever 3)A-Sleeping At The Foot Of The Bed

4/16/49	7	7	1	**Take An Old Cold 'Tater (And Wait)/** — *S:7 / J:11* [N]				
9/3/49	12	1	2	**Pennies For Papa** *S:12*		$20		Columbia 20548
				JIMMIE DICKENS (above 2)				
6/25/49	7	10	3	**Country Boy** — *S:7 / J:8 I'm Fading Fast With The Time*		$20		Columbia 20585
9/24/49	10	1	4	**My Heart's Bouquet** — *J:10 I'll Be Back A-Sunday*		$20		Columbia 20598
1/14/50	6	3	5	**A-Sleeping At The Foot Of The Bed** — *S:6 / A:7 I'm In Love Up To My Ears*		$20		Columbia 20644 (78)
4/22/50	3	10	6	**Hillbilly Fever** — *A:3 / S:5 / J:9 Then I Had To Turn Around And Get Married*		$20		Columbia 20677 (78)
8/7/54	9	7	7	**Out Behind The Barn** — *A:9 Closing Time*		$25		Columbia 21247
11/3/62	10	8	8	**The Violet And A Rose** — *Honky Tonk Troubles*		$10		Columbia 42485
12/14/63	28	2	9	**Another Bridge To Burn** ....*I Ain't Comin' Home Tonight*		$10		Columbia 42845
4/10/65	21	18	10	**He Stands Real Tall** ....*Life Turned Her That Way*		$8		Columbia 43243
10/9/65	❶²	19	11	**May The Bird Of Paradise Fly Up Your Nose** — *My Eyes Are Jealous* [N]	15	$8		Columbia 43388
2/26/66	27	8	12	**When The Ship Hit The Sand** .... *Truck Load Of Starvin' Kangaroos* [N]	103	$8		Columbia 43514
7/9/66	41	5	13	**Who Licked The Red Off Your Candy** ....*You Don't Have Time For Me* [N]		$8		Columbia 43701
3/11/67	23	14	14	**Country Music Lover** ....*You've Destroyed Me* [N]		$8		Columbia 44025
				JIMMY DICKENS:				
7/6/68	69	5	15	**How To Catch An African Skeeter Alive** .... *Can You Build Your House* [N]		$7		Decca 32326
1/25/69	55	8	16	**When You're Seventeen** .... *She Never Likes Nothing For Long*		$7		Decca 32426
5/9/70	75	2	17	**(You've Been Quite A Doll) Raggedy Ann** ....*I'd Rather Sleep In Peace*		$7		Decca 32644
2/13/71	70	3	18	**Everyday Family Man** ....*One More Time*		$6		United Artists 50730
4/15/72	61	6	19	**Try It, You'll Like It** ....*Helpless*		$6		United Artists 50889

DICKEY, Dan '79
Born on 6/22/49 in Houston.

6/9/79	96	2	1	**Hot Mama** ....*Close The Door*		$6		Chartwheel 123
10/6/79	96	2	2	**Bye, Bye, Baby**		$6		Chartwheel 126

DICKINSON, Hal '66

10/29/66	73	2		**You're Cheatin' On Me Again** ....*Cowboy Blues*		$12		Grass 3301

106

DIFFIE, Joe ★112★   '94

Born on 12/28/58 in Tulsa; raised in Duncan, Oklahoma. Singer/songwriter/guitarist. Joined the *Grand Ole Opry* in 1993.

1)Pickup Man 2)Bigger Than The Beatles 3)Third Rock From The Sun 4)If The Devil Danced 5)Home

DEBUT	PEAK	WKS		A-side / B-side	Pop	$	Pic	Label & Number
8/25/90	❶¹	20	1	**Home** — *Liquid Heartache*		$3	∎	Epic 73447
12/15/90+	2²	20	2	**If You Want Me To** — *Home*		$3	∎	Epic 73637
4/6/91	❶¹	20	3	**If The Devil Danced (In Empty Pockets)** — *I Ain't Leavin' 'Til She's Gone*		$3	∎	Epic 73747
8/3/91	2²	20	4	**New Way (To Light Up An Old Flame)** — *Coolest Fool In Town*		$3		Epic 73935
12/7/91+	5	20	5	**Is It Cold In Here** — *Back To Heratache*		$3		Epic 74123
4/18/92	5	20	6	**Ships That Don't Come In** — *Startin' Over Blues*		$3		Epic 74285
8/15/92	16	20	7	**Next Thing Smokin'** .... *I Just Don't Know*		$3		Epic 74415
9/12/92	15	20	8	**Not Too Much To Ask** ....*I Am A Town*		$3		Columbia 74485
				MARY-CHAPIN CARPENTER with Joe Diffie				
12/19/92+	41	13	9	**Startin' Over Blues** — *Just A Regular Joe*		$3		Epic 74796
3/20/93	5	20	10	**Honky Tonk Attitude** — *Just A Regular Joe*		$3		Epic 74911
7/24/93	3	20	11	**Prop Me Up Beside The Jukebox (If I Die)** — *I Can Walk The Line*	122	$3	∎	Epic 77071
11/13/93+	5	20	12	**John Deere Green** — *Somewhere Under The Rainbow*	69	$3	∎	Epic 77235
3/12/94	19	20	13	**In My Own Backyard** ....*Here Comes That Train*		$3		Epic 77380
7/16/94	❶²	20	14	**Third Rock From The Sun** — *(dance mix)*	84	$3	∎	Epic 77577
10/22/94	❶⁴	20	15	**Pickup Man** — *From Here On Out*	60	$3	∎	Epic 77715
2/4/95	2²	20	16	**So Help Me Girl** — S:8 *The Cows Came Home*	84	$3	∎	Epic 77808
5/27/95	21	12	17	**I'm In Love With A Capital "U"** .... S:22 *Wild Blue Yonder*		$3	∎	Epic 77902
8/12/95	40	11	18	**That Road Not Taken** — *The Cows Came Home*		$3		Epic 77978
12/2/95+	❶²	20	19	**Bigger Than The Beatles** — S:11 *Whole Lotta Gone*		$3	∎	Epic 78202
12/16/95	33	5	20	**Leroy The Redneck Reindeer** .... *Wrap Me In Your Love* [X-N]		$3		Epic 78201
3/2/96	23	20	21	**C-O-U-N-T-R-Y** .... *Third Rock From The Sun*		$3		Epic 78246
6/22/96	23	20	22	**Whole Lotta Gone** .... *Back To The Cave*		$3		Epic 78333
12/21/96	46	4	23	**Leroy The Redneck Reindeer** .... *Wrap Me In Your Love* [X-N-R]		$3		Epic 78201
3/8/97	25	17	24	**This Is Your Brain** ....S:23 *I Got A Feelin'*		$3	∎	Epic 78521
7/5/97	40	11	25	**Somethin' Like This** .... *This Is Your Brain*		$3	∎	Epic 78638
10/25/97	61	4	26	**The Promised Land**				album cut
				from the album *Twice Upon A Time* on Epic 67693				
12/20/97	54	4	27	**Leroy The Redneck Reindeer** .... *Wrap Me In Your Love* [X-N-R]		$3		Epic 78201

DILLINGHAM, Craig   '84

Born in 1958 in Brownwood, Texas. Singer/songwriter/guitarist.

DEBUT	PEAK	WKS		A-side / B-side		$		Label & Number
12/3/83+	32	14	1	**Have You Loved Your Woman Today** — *Every Man Should Have One*		$4		MCA/Curb 52301
3/31/84	47	9	2	**Honky Tonk Women Make Honky Tonk Men** .... *Slow Dancin' With Fast Women*		$4		MCA/Curb 52352
7/21/84	58	6	3	**1984** .... *Neon Light Idea*		$4		MCA/Curb 52406
8/31/85	78	5	4	**Next To You** ....*Brand New Blues*		$4		MCA/Curb 52647
6/14/86	80	3	5	**I'll Pull You Through** ......*Too Soon To Say It's Too Late*		$4		MCA/Curb 52823
				TISH HINOJOSA/CRAIG DILLINGHAM				

DILLON, Dean   ★301★   '81

Born on 3/26/55 in Lake City, Tennessee. Singer/songwriter/guitarist.
1)Nobody In His Right Mind 2)What Good Is A Heart 3)I'm Into The Bottle 4)Friday Night's Woman
5)I Go To Pieces

DEBUT	PEAK	WKS		A-side / B-side		$		Label & Number
12/15/79+	30	12	1	**I'm Into The Bottle (To Get You Out Of My Mind)** .... *Tonight*		$4		RCA 11881
5/31/80	28	12	2	**What Good Is A Heart** .... *He's Number One*		$4		RCA 12003
11/1/80+	25	15	3	**Nobody In His Right Mind (Would've Left Her)** — *Smelling Like A Rose*		$4		RCA 12109
5/30/81	57	6	4	**They'll Never Take Me Alive** ....*Tonight One Of Us Is Going Out Of My Mind*		$4		RCA 12234
10/17/81	77	5	5	**Jesus Let Me Slide** .... *If You're Going Crazy*		$4		RCA 12319
4/10/82	41	11	6	**Brotherly Love** ....*Firewater Friends*		$4	∎	RCA 13049
				GARY STEWART/DEAN DILLON				
6/19/82	74	4	7	**Play This Old Working Day Away** .... *You To Come Home To*		$4		RCA 13208
9/18/82	65	6	8	**You To Come Home To** .... *I'm Into The Bottle (To Get You Off My Mind)*		$4		RCA 13295
1/8/83	47	12	9	**Those Were The Days** ....*Drinkin' Thing*		$4		RCA 13401
				GARY STEWART AND DEAN DILLON				
4/16/83	71	4	10	**Smokin' In The Rockies** ....*Hard Time For Lovers*		$4		RCA 13472
				GARY STEWART & DEAN DILLON				
11/12/83	67	6	11	**Famous Last Words Of A Fool** ....*Ten Years And Two Babies Later*		$4		RCA 13628
7/2/88	51	9	12	**The New Never Wore Off My Sweet Baby** ....*Appalachia Got To Have You Feelin' In My Bones*		$3		Capitol 44179
9/17/88	39	12	13	**I Go To Pieces** .... *Hard Time For Lovers*		$3		Capitol 44239
				#9 Pop hit for Peter & Gordon in 1965				
12/24/88+	58	9	14	**Hey Heart** ....*Appalachia Got To Have You Feelin' In My Bones*		$3		Capitol 44294
8/26/89	61	6	15	**It's Love That Makes You Sexy** ....*Appalachia Got To Have You Feelin' In My Bones*		$3		Capitol 44400
11/18/89	66	5	16	**Back In The Swing Of Things**		$3		Capitol 79827
2/23/91	69	6	17	**Holed Up In Some Honky Tonk** ....*All Out Of Love*		$3	∎	Atlantic 87774
6/22/91	39	12	18	**Friday Night's Woman** ....*Her Thinkin' I'm Doing Her Wrong (Ain't Doin' Me Right)*		$3		Atlantic 87794

DEBUT	PEAK	WKS	Gold	A-side (Chart Hit)..B-side	Pop	$	Pic	Label & Number
				DILLON, Dean — Cont'd				
9/21/91	62	12		19 Don't You Even (Think About Leavin') .... *She Knows What She Wants*		$3		Atlantic 87606
5/22/93	62	5		20 Hot, Country And Single... *Holding My Own*		$3	▮	Atlantic 87356
				DILLON, Lola Jean — see WHITE, L.E.				
				DIRKSEN, Senator Everett McKinley **'67**				
				Born on 1/4/1896 in Pekin, Illinois. Died on 9/7/69 (age 73). Served as a United States senator from 1950-69.				
1/7/67	58	7		Gallant Men .... *The New Colossus (Statue Of Liberty)* [S]	29	$7	■	Capitol 5805
				DIRT BAND, The — see NITTY GRITTY DIRT BAND				
				DIXIANA **'92**				
				Group from Greenville, South Carolina: Cindy Murphy (vocals), brothers Mark and Phil Lister, Randall Griffith and Colonel Shuford.				
2/22/92	39	20		1 Waitin' For The Deal To Go Down................................... *It Comes And It Goes*		$3		Epic 74221
6/27/92	40	13		2 That's What I'm Working On Tonight .... *If I Can't Have You*		$3		Epic 74361
4/24/93	66	3		3 Now You're Talkin' .... *Love Gone Good*		$3		Epic 74936
				DIXIE CHICKS **'97**				
				Female trio from Lubbock, Texas: sisters Emily Erwin (guitar, banjo) and Martie Seidel (fiddle, mandolin), with Natalie Maines (lead vocals). CMA Awards: 1998 Vocal Group of the Year; 1998 Horizon Award.				
10/25/97+	7	26		I Can Love You Better S:5 *Give It Up Or Let Me Go*	77	$3	▮	Monument 78746
				DR. HOOK **'77**				
				Pop-rock group from New Jersey: Ray Sawyer (vocals), Dennis Locorriere (vocals, guitar), George Cummings and Rik Elswit (guitars), William Francis (keyboards), Bob Henke (bass) and John Wolters (drums). Wolters died of cancer on 6/16/97 (age 52). Group charted 21 pop hits from 1972-82.				
				1)If Not You 2)Daddy's Little Girl 3)Sharing The Night Together				
3/6/76	55	8	●	1 Only Sixteen.. *Let Me Be Your Lover*	6	$5		Capitol 4171
				#28 Pop hit for Sam Cooke in 1959				
6/19/76	51	12		2 A Couple More Years .... *A Little Bit More (Pop #11)*		$5		Capitol 4280
11/6/76	28	12		3 (One More Year Of) Daddy's Little Girl................................. *I Need The High*	81	$5		Capitol 4344
				RAY SAWYER				
12/4/76+	26	13		4 If Not You *Bad Eye Bill*	55	$5		Capitol 4364
6/25/77	92	3		5 Walk Right In.. *Sexy Energy*	46	$5		Capitol 4423
10/7/78	50	11	●	6 Sharing The Night Together .... *You Make My Pants Want To Get Up And Dance*	6	$4		Capitol 4621
2/10/79	82	4		7 All The Time In The World .... *Dooley Jones*	54	$4		Capitol 4677
5/19/79	68	9	●	8 When You're In Love With A Beautiful Woman ....*Knowing She's There*	6	$4		Capitol 4705
11/3/79	91	4		9 Better Love Next Time... *Mountain Mary*	12	$4		Capitol 4785
2/16/80	80	4		10 I Don't Feel Much Like Smilin'.......................................*Drinking Wine Alone*		$4		Capitol 4820
				RAY SAWYER				
				DODD, Deryl **'97**				
				Born on 4/12/64 in Comanche, Texas; raised in Dallas. Singer/songwriter/guitarist.				
10/5/96	68	3		1 Friends Don't Drive Friends.. *That's Just Me*		$3	▮	Columbia 78437
11/9/96+	36	20		2 That's How I Got To Memphis .... *(album snippets)*		$3	▮	Columbia 78478
5/17/97	61	8		3 Movin' Out To The Country ....*Friends Don't Drive Friends...*		$3	▮	Columbia 78571
				DODSON, Darrell **'77**				
4/16/77	99	2		Love Song Sing Along		$7		SCR 139
				DOLAN, Madonna **'88**				
				Born in McLeansboro, Illinois. Female singer/multi-instrumentalist.				
9/24/88	82	3		The Home Team...		$6		True 92
				DOLAN, Ramblin' Jimmie **'51**				
				Born in Missouri in 1924. Died on 7/31/94 (age 70). Singer/guitarist. Known as "America's Country Troubador."				
2/3/51	7	4		Hot Rod Race S:7 *Walkin' With The Blues* [N]		$30		Capitol F1322
				DOLLAR, Johnny **'66**				
				Born on 3/8/33 in Kilgore, Texas. Died on 4/13/86 (age 53). Singer/songwriter/guitarist.				
2/12/66	49	2		1 Tear-Talk .... *Big Red (The Hound)*		$10		Columbia 43343
3/19/66	15	15		2 Stop The Start (Of Tears In My Heart) *You Ain't Wrong*		$10		Columbia 43537
2/25/67	65	5		3 Your Hands .... *Don't Take My Future From Me*		$8		Dot 16990
9/16/67	47	12		4 The Wheels Fell Off The Wagon Again....................... *Watching Me Losing You*		$7		Date 1566
1/13/68	42	12		5 Everybody's Got To Be Somewhere....................... *Did You Talk To Him Today*		$7		Date 1585
11/16/68	48	7		6 Big Rig Rollin' Man .... *I've Gotta Stay High*		$7		Chart 1057
3/15/69	65	4		7 Big Wheels Sing For Me .... *Wild Cherry*		$7		Chart 1070
2/14/70	71	3		8 Truck Driver's Lament ....*Changing Her Thinking*		$7		Chart 5049
				DOMINO, Fats **'81**				
				Born Antoine Domino on 2/26/28 in New Orleans. R&B singer/pianist. Charted 66 pop hits from 1955-68.				
12/20/80+	51	9		Whiskey Heaven..................................... *Beers To You (Texas Opera Company)*		$4		Warner 49610
				from the movie *Any Which Way You Can* starring **Clint Eastwood**				
				DONALDSON, Craig **'76**				
9/25/76	99	2		I Believe He's Gonna Drive That Rig To Glory....................... *(long version)*		$7		Great American 281
				DON JUAN **'88**				
				Vocal trio from Rock Island, Illinois: Stu Stuart, Ed Allen and Toby Strause.				
3/12/88	75	4		1 We're Gonna Love Tonight..		$7		Maxx 821
8/20/88	78	2		2 Let It Go		$7		Maxx 827
				DOOLITTLE BAND, The — see DANDY				

DEBUT	PEAK	WKS	Gold	A-side (Chart Hit)..B-side	Pop	$	Pic	Label & Number
	★321★			**DOTTSY** '77				
				Born Dottsy Brodt on 4/6/54 in Seguin, Texas. Female singer.				
				1)Play Born To Lose Again 2)Tryin' To Satisfy You 3)I'll Be Your San Antone Rose				
5/31/75	17	17		1 Storms Never Last .... *Follow Me*		$5		RCA Victor 10280
11/22/75+	12	14		2 I'll Be Your San Antone Rose .... *If You Say It's So*		$5		RCA Victor 10423
5/29/76	86	4		3 The Sweetest Thing (I've Ever Known) ......*We Still Sing Love Songs Here In Texas*		$5		RCA Victor 10666
9/25/76	68	6		4 Love Is A Two-Way Street ....*Lying In My Arms*		$5		RCA 10766
6/4/77	10	16		5 (After Sweet Memories) Play Born To Lose Again *Send Me The Pillow You Dream On*		$5		RCA 10982
10/29/77	22	13		6 It Should Have Been Easy ....*Everybody's Reaching Out For Someone*		$5		RCA 11138
2/11/78	20	12		7 Here In Love ....*A Good Love Is Like A Good Song*		$5		RCA 11203
7/8/78	21	11		8 I Just Had You On My Mind ....*Just Remember Who Your Friends Are*		$5		RCA 11293
1/20/79	12	14		9 Tryin' To Satisfy You ....*If I Only Had The Words (To Tell You)*		$5		RCA 11448
				Waylon Jennings (backing vocal)				
6/16/79	22	10		10 Slip Away ....*Love Is A Two-Way Street*		$5		RCA 11610
11/10/79	34	10		11 When I'm Gone ....*Storms Never Last*		$5		RCA 11743
6/27/81	32	12		12 Somebody's Darling, Somebody's Wife ....*Sing Me A Love Song*		$6		Tanglewood 1908
9/19/81	58	8		13 Let The Little Bird Fly ....*Love In My Baby's Eyes*		$6		Tanglewood 1910
				DOUGLAS — see BLOCK, Doug				
				DOUGLAS, Joe '81				
				Singer/songwriter from New Orleans.				
1/20/79	84	5		1 You're Still On My Mind ....*Wine Flow Free*		$7		D 1315
1/26/80	88	2		2 Back Street Affair ....*Bollweevil*		$7		Foxy Cajun 1001
6/20/81	75	4		3 Leavin You Is Easier (Than Wishing You Were Gone)/				
		4		4 Louisiana Joe		$7		Foxy Cajun 1005
				DOUGLAS, Steve '80				
				Born on 2/17/51 in Greenville, Mississippi.				
6/7/80	67	7		1 This Is True ....*Saying I'm Sorry*		$7		Demon 1954
8/5/89	91	2		2 To A San Antone Rose ....*Texas, I'm In Love With You*		$7		Dorman 98915
1/13/90	80	1		3 Funny Ways Of Loving Me ....*Little Daughters*		$7		Dorman 981101
				DOUGLAS, Tony '63				
				Born on 4/12/29 in Martins Mill, Texas.				
3/30/63	23	1		1 His And Hers *Gabby Abby*		$20		Vee Jay 481
				also see #5 below				
12/30/72+	35	15		2 Thank You For Touching My Life ....*Walkin' Over Yonder*		$6		Dot 17443
6/30/73	37	9		3 My Last Day ....*I'll Fight Every Step Of The Way*		$6		Dot 17464
12/13/75+	72	7		4 If I Can Make It (Through The Mornin') ....*Honky-Tonk Man*		$5		20th Century 2257
2/20/82	87	3		5 His 'N Hers ....*Shrimpin'* [R]		$6		Cochise 118
				new version of #1 above				
				DOVE, Ronnie '75				
				Born on 9/9/40 in Herndon, Virginia; raised in Baltimore. Charted 20 pop hits from 1964-69.				
1/29/72	61	8		1 Kiss The Hurt Away ....*He Cries Like A Baby*		$6		Decca 32919
2/3/73	69	5		2 Lilacs In Winter ....*Is It Wrong*		$6		Decca 33038
4/12/75	75	7		3 Please Come To Nashville ....*Pictures On Paper*		$5		Melodyland 6004
6/14/75	25	12		4 Things *Here We Go Again*		$5		Melodyland 6011
				#3 Pop hit for **Bobby Darin** in 1962				
4/25/87	77	4		5 Heart		$5	■	Diamond 378
11/7/87	73	7		6 Rise And Shine		$5		Diamond 379
				DOWNEY, Sean Morton '81				
				Born on 12/9/33 in New York City. TV/radio talkshow host better known as Morton Downey, Jr.				
3/14/81	95	2		Green Eyed Girl		$7		ESO 932
	★357★			**DOWNING, Big Al** '79				
				Born on 1/9/40 in Lenapah, Oklahoma. Black singer/songwriter/pianist.				
				1)Touch Me 2)Mr. Jones 3)Bring It On Home				
12/2/78+	20	13		1 Mr. Jones ....*I Don't Cry (The Onion Song)*		$5		Warner 8716
4/21/79	18	13		2 Touch Me (I'll Be Your Fool Once More) *I Ain't No Fool*		$5		Warner 8787
9/8/79	59	5		3 Midnight Lace ....*Counting Highway Signs*		$5		Warner 49034
11/17/79	73	4		4 I Ain't No Fool ....*Mr. Jones*		$5		Warner 49141
2/9/80	33	8		5 The Story Behind The Story ....*Daddy Played The Banjo*		$5		Warner 49161
7/12/80	20	11		6 Bring It On Home ....*Beer Drinking People*		$5		Warner 49270
7/3/82	48	9		7 I'll Be Loving You ....*Don't Mess With An Angel*		$5		Team 1001
10/23/82	67	7		8 Darlene		$5		Team 1002
2/12/83	38	11		9 It Takes Love ....*If You're Leaving*		$5		Team 1004
10/1/83	64	5		10 Let's Sing About Love ....*We Can Only Say Goodbye*		$5		Team 1003
1/7/84	45	11		11 The Best Of Families ....*Fool Of The Year*		$5		Team 1007
4/28/84	76	4		12 There'll Never Be A Better Night For Bein' Wrong		$5		Team 1008
1/17/87	69	5		13 How Beautiful You Are (To Me) ....*The Only Thing Missing Is You*		$6		Vine St. 103
9/12/87	67	5		14 Just One Night Won't Do ....*How Beautiful You Are (To Me)*		$6		Vine St. 105
8/5/89	82	3		15 I Guess By Now		$5		Door Knob 328
				DOWNS, Laverne '60				
7/4/60	16	7		But You Use To ....*What Have I Done*		$20		Peach 735

DRAKE, Guy — '70
Born in Weir, Kentucky. Singer/comedian.

DEBUT	PEAK	WKS	Gold	A-side	B-side	Pop	$	Pic	Label & Number
1/10/70	6	14		Welfare Cadilac	Keep Off My Grass [N-S]	63	$7		Royal American 1

DRAPER, Rusty — '53
Born Farrell Draper in Kirksville, Missouri. Male singer/songwriter/guitarist. Known as "Ol' Redhead."

DEBUT	PEAK	WKS	Gold	A-side	B-side	Pop	$	Pic	Label & Number
8/29/53	6	5	● 1	Gambler's Guitar	S:6 / J:6 Free Home Demonstration	6	$20		Mercury 70167
7/8/67	70	3	2	My Elusive Dreams	Memory Lane		$8		Monument 1019
3/2/68	70	4	3	California Sunshine	The Gypsy		$8		Monument 1044
8/3/68	58	3	4	Buffalo Nickel	Make Believe I'm Him		$8		Monument 1074
4/25/70	73	2	5	Two Little Boys	It Don't Mean A Thing To Me		$8		Monument 1188
				written in 1903; #119 Pop hit for Rolf Harris in 1970					
1/19/80	87	3	6	Harbor Lights	Ramblin' Man		$10		KL 001
				#8 Pop hit for The Platters in 1960					

DRESSER, Lee — '83
Born on 5/22/41 in Washington, D.C.; raised in Moberly, Missouri. Male singer/guitarist.

DEBUT	PEAK	WKS	Gold	A-side	B-side	Pop	$	Pic	Label & Number
2/11/78	78	5	1	You're All The Woman I'll Ever Need	Fallin'		$5		Capitol 4529
12/2/78	86	5	2	A Beautiful Song (For A Beautiful Lady)	The Man Up In The Mansion		$5		Capitol 4613
4/2/83	77	4	3	The Hero	All I Have To Do		$5		Air Int'l. 10021
9/3/83	96	1	4	Feelings Feelin Right			$5		Air Int'l. 10022

DRIFTING COWBOYS, The — '78
Former backing band for **Hank Williams**. The 1978 lineup consisted of original members Bob McNett (guitar), Don Helms (steel guitar) and Jerry Rivers (fiddle), with new members Bobby Andrews (bass) and Jimmy Heap, Jr. (drums). Rivers died of cancer on 10/4/96 (age 68).

DEBUT	PEAK	WKS	Gold	A-side	B-side	Pop	$	Pic	Label & Number
1/28/78	97	2	1	Lovesick Blues	A Gift In The Name Of Love		$6		Epic 50498
				JIM OWEN***THE DRIFTING COWBOYS					
5/6/78	90	4	2	Rag Mop	Mud Hut		$6		Epic 50543
				#1 Pop hit for the Ames Brothers in 1950					

DRIFTWOOD, Jimmie — '59
Born James Corbett Morris on 6/21/07 in Mountain View, Arkansas. Died of heart failure on 7/12/98 (age 91). Singer/songwriter/guitarist.

DEBUT	PEAK	WKS	Gold	A-side	B-side	Pop	$	Pic	Label & Number
6/8/59	24	3		The Battle Of New Orleans	Damyankee Lad		$15		RCA Victor 7534

DRUMM, Don — '78
Singer/guitarist/pianist from Springfield, Massachusetts.

DEBUT	PEAK	WKS	Gold	A-side	B-side	Pop	$	Pic	Label & Number
11/30/74+	86	7	1	In At Eight And Out At Ten	Baby's Gone		$6		Chart 5223
1/7/78	18	14	2	Bedroom Eyes	Stoney		$5		Churchill 7704
5/27/78	35	8	3	Just Another Rhinestone	If Her Love Was A Window		$5		Churchill 7710
10/7/78	81	3	4	Something To Believe In	Sad Songs		$5		Churchill 7717

DRUSKY, Roy ★89★ — '65
Born on 6/22/30 in Atlanta. Singer/songwriter/guitarist. Joined the *Grand Ole Opry* in 1958. Acted in the movies *The Golden Guitar* and *Forty-Acre Feud*.

1)Yes, Mr. Peters 2)Three Hearts In A Tangle 3)Another 4)Second Hand Rose 5)Anymore

DEBUT	PEAK	WKS	Gold	A-side	B-side	Pop	$	Pic	Label & Number
1/18/60	2³	24	1	Another	The Same Corner		$15		Decca 31024
7/11/60	3	20	2	Anymore	I'm So Helpless		$15		Decca 31109
12/19/60	26	3	3	I Can't Tell My Heart That	When Do You Love Me		$15		Decca 31164
				KITTY WELLS And ROY DRUSKY					
3/13/61	2⁴	27	4	Three Hearts In A Tangle/		35			
2/20/61	10	12	5	I'd Rather Loan You Out			$12		Decca 31193
9/11/61	9	20	6	I Went Out Of My Way (To Make You Happy)	I've Got Some		$12		Decca 31297
4/21/62	17	2	7	There's Always One (Who Loves A Lot)	Marking Time		$12		Decca 31366
12/22/62+	3	21	8	Second Hand Rose	It Worries Me		$12		Decca 31443
12/7/63+	8	19	9	Peel Me A Nanner	The Room Across The Hall		$10	■	Mercury 72204
5/9/64	13	16	10	Pick Of The Week	Yesterday		$10		Mercury 72265
12/26/64+	41	3	11	Summer, Winter, Spring And Fall	Almost Can't		$10		Decca 31717
1/16/65	6	21	12	(From Now On All My Friends Are Gonna Be) Strangers	Birmingham Jail		$8		Mercury 72376
5/29/65	❶²	23	13	Yes, Mr. Peters	More Than We Deserve		$8		Mercury 72416
				ROY DRUSKY & PRISCILLA MITCHELL					
10/23/65	21	15	14	White Lightnin' Express	Lonely Thing Called Me		$8		Mercury 72471
12/4/65	45	2	15	Slippin' Around	Trouble On Our Line		$8		Mercury 72497
				ROY DRUSKY & PRISCILLA MITCHELL					
2/26/66	20	14	16	Rainbows And Roses	A Thing Called Sadness		$8		Mercury 72532
6/25/66	10	16	17	The World Is Round	Unless You Make Him Set You Free		$8		Mercury 72586
11/19/66+	12	14	18	If The Whole World Stopped Lovin'	Too Many Footprints		$8		Mercury 72627
3/25/67	61	5	19	I'll Never Tell On You	Bed Of Roses		$8		Mercury 72650
				ROY DRUSKY & PRISCILLA MITCHELL					
6/24/67	25	11	20	New Lips	Now		$8		Mercury 72689
11/11/67+	18	16	21	Weakness In A Man	I've Got A Right To The Blues		$8		Mercury 72742
3/30/68	28	10	22	You Better Sit Down Kids	Let's Put Our World Back Together		$8		Mercury 72784
				#9 Pop hit for Cher in 1967					
7/20/68	24	11	23	Jody And The Kid	Your Little Deeds Of Kindness (And Your Little Words Of Love)		$8		Mercury 72823
1/25/69	10	15	24	Where The Blue And Lonely Go	I'm Gonna Get You Off My Mind		$7		Mercury 72886

DRUSKY, Roy — Cont'd

DEBUT	PEAK	WKS	A-side / B-side	Pop	$	Label & Number
6/7/69	14	11	25 My Grass Is Green ....*Alone With You*		$7	Mercury 72928
10/4/69	7	11	26 Such A Fool / *All Over My Mind*		$7	Mercury 72964
1/17/70	11	11	27 I'll Make Amends..*Our Everlasting Love Has Died*		$7	Mercury 73007
5/9/70	5	16	28 Long Long Texas Road / *Emotion - Devotion*		$7	Mercury 73056
9/19/70	9	12	29 All My Hard Times / *At Times Everybody's Blind*		$7	Mercury 73111
3/6/71	15	12	30 I Love The Way That You've Been Lovin' Me....................*On And On And On*		$7	Mercury 73178
7/3/71	37	10	31 I Can't Go On Loving You ....*You're Shaking The Hand*		$7	Mercury 73212
12/11/71+	17	13	32 Red Red Wine ....*Without You Baby*		$7	Mercury 73252
			written by **Neil Diamond**; #1 Pop hit for UB40 in 1988			
5/20/72	58	9	33 Sunshine And Rainbows/		$7	Mercury 73293
		2	34 The Night's Not Over Yet			
8/12/72	25	12	35 The Last Time I Called Somebody Darlin' ....*Long Way Back To Love*		$7	Mercury 73314
1/13/73	32	10	36 I Must Be Doin' Something Right ....*Always You, Always Me*		$7	Mercury 73356
5/12/73	50	7	37 That Rain Makin' Baby Of Mine ....*This Time Of The Year*		$7	Mercury 73376
8/4/73	25	11	38 Satisfied Mind ....*I'll Take Care Of You*		$7	Mercury 73405
4/20/74	81	6	39 Close To Home ....*One Day At A Time*		$6	Capitol 3859
9/21/74	45	11	40 Dixie Lily ....*If I Could Paint The World*		$6	Capitol 3942
			first recorded by **Elton John** on his 1974 *Caribou* album			
1/15/77	81	5	41 Night Flying ....*Lifetime In A Week*		$5	Scorpion 0521
8/13/77	91	4	42 Betty's Song ....*Naked Truth*		$5	Scorpion 0540

DUCAS, George   '95
Born on 8/1/66 in Texas City, Texas; raised in San Diego and Houston. Singer/songwriter/guitarist.

DEBUT	PEAK	WKS	A-side / B-side	Pop	$	Pic	Label & Number
9/10/94	38	12	1 Teardrops ....*Waiting And Wishing*		$3		Liberty 18093
12/10/94+	9	20	2 Lipstick Promises / *In No Time At All*		$3		Liberty 18306
5/13/95	52	10	3 Hello Cruel World ....*Waiting And Wishing*		$3		Liberty 18731
9/23/95	72	3	4 Kisses Don't Lie ....*In No Time At All*		$3	▌	Capitol 58464
6/8/96	57	12	5 Every Time She Passes By ....S:22 *Lipstick Promises*		$3	▌	Capitol 58565
2/8/97	55	9	6 Long Trail Of Tears ....*The Invisible Man*		$3		Capitol 19512

DUDLEY, Dave   ★93★   '70
Born David Pedruska on 5/3/28 in Spencer, Wisconsin. Singer/songwriter/guitarist. Worked as a DJ at stations in Iowa, Idaho and Minnesota.

1)The Pool Shark 2)Six Days On The Road 3)Truck Drivin' Son-Of-A-Gun 4)Cowboy Boots
5)What We're Fighting For

DEBUT	PEAK	WKS	A-side / B-side	Pop	$	Label & Number
10/16/61	28	2	1 Maybe I Do ....*Your Only One*		$30	Vee 7003
9/15/62	18	9	2 Under Cover Of The Night............................*Please Let Me Prove (My Love For You)*		$20	Jubilee 5436
6/1/63	2²	21	3 Six Days On The Road / *I Feel A Cry Coming On*	32	$12	Golden Wing 3020
10/5/63	3	20	4 Cowboy Boots / *I Think I'll Cheat (A Little Tonight)*	95	$12	Golden Ring 3030
12/14/63+	7	16	5 Last Day In The Mines / *Last Year's Heartaches*	125	$10	Mercury 72212
10/10/64	6	17	6 Mad / *Don't Be Surprised*		$10	Mercury 72308
3/13/65	15	17	7 Two Six Packs Away ....*Hiding Behind The Curtain*		$10	Mercury 72384
7/10/65	3	21	8 Truck Drivin' Son-Of-A-Gun / *I Got Lost*	125	$8	Mercury 72442
11/20/65+	4	16	9 What We're Fighting For / *Coffee, Coffee, Coffee*		$8	Mercury 72500
3/12/66	12	12	10 Viet Nam Blues ....*Then I'll Come Home Again* [S]	127	$8	Mercury 72550
7/2/66	13	14	11 Lonelyville ....*Time And Place*		$8	Mercury 72585
10/8/66	15	12	12 Long Time Gone..*I Feel A Cry Comin' On*		$8	Mercury 72618
2/25/67	12	15	13 My Kind Of Love ....*Subject To Change*		$8	Mercury 72655
7/15/67	23	14	14 Trucker's Prayer ....*Don't Come Cryin' To Me*		$8	Mercury 72697
11/4/67+	12	16	15 Anything Leaving Town Today ....*I'd Rather Be Forgotten*		$7	Mercury 72741
3/2/68	10	13	16 There Ain't No Easy Run / *Why I Can't Be With You (Is A Shame)*		$7	Mercury 72779
7/13/68	14	11	17 I Keep Coming Back For More ....*Where Does A Little Boy Go*		$7	Mercury 72818
11/16/68+	10	16	18 Please Let Me Prove (My Love For You) / *I'll Be Moving Along*		$7	Mercury 72856
3/29/69	12	15	19 One More Mile ....*Angel*		$7	Mercury 72902
8/30/69	10	13	20 George (And The North Woods) / *It's Not A Very Pleasant Day Today*		$7	Mercury 72952
3/14/70	❶¹	16	21 The Pool Shark / *The Bigger They Come, The Harder They Fall*		$7	Mercury 73029
8/1/70	20	12	22 This Night (Ain't Fit For Nothing But Drinking) ....*I'm Not So Easy Anymore*		$7	Mercury 73089
11/14/70	23	13	23 Day Drinkin' ....*Let's Get On With The Show*		$7	Mercury 73139
			DAVE DUDLEY & TOM T. HALL			
12/26/70+	15	13	24 Listen Betty (I'm Singing Your Song) ....*I Hope My Kind Of Love*		$7	Mercury 73138
4/17/71	8	14	25 Comin' Down / *Six-O-One*		$7	Mercury 73193
8/21/71	8	15	26 Fly Away Again / *There You Are Again*		$7	Mercury 73225
3/18/72	14	14	27 If It Feels Good Do It ....*Sometime In The Future*		$7	Mercury 73274
7/22/72	12	16	28 You've Gotta Cry Girl.................................*The Arms Of A Satisfied Woman*		$7	Mercury 73309
12/9/72+	40	10	29 We Know It's Over ....*Gettin' Back Together*		$7	Mercury 73345
			DAVE DUDLEY & KAREN O'DONNAL			
3/3/73	19	12	30 Keep On Truckin' ....*It Won't Hurt As Much Tomorrow*		$7	Mercury 73367
8/4/73	37	9	31 It Takes Time ....*I Almost Didn't Make It Through The Door*		$7	Mercury 73404
11/3/73	47	12	32 Rollin' Rig ....*Six Days On The Road*		$8	Rice 5064

DUDLEY, Dave — Cont'd

DEBUT	PEAK	WKS		A-side / B-side	Pop	$	Label & Number
4/6/74	67	7		33 Have It Your Way .... Blue Bedroom Eyes		$8	Rice 5067
8/31/74	61	9		34 Counterfeit Cowboy .... That's How Cold		$8	Rice 5069
2/8/75	74	10		35 How Come It Took So Long (To Say Goodbye) .... I've Lived Like A Piece Of Grass		$6	United Artists 585
5/3/75	21	12		36 Fireball Rolled A Seven .... Blue Bedroom Eyes		$6	United Artists 630
10/25/75+	12	15		37 Me And Ole C.B. ....I Can't Remember You		$6	United Artists 722
2/28/76	47	8		38 Sentimental Journey ....The Night You Broke The News		$6	United Artists 766
				#1 Pop hit for Les Brown in 1945			
8/21/76	83	5		39 38 And Lonely .... Texas Ruby		$6	United Artists 836
3/4/78	95	3		40 One A.M. Alone		$6	Rice 5077
9/6/80	77	5		41 Rolaids, Doan's Pills And Preparation H .... Maybe I Can		$6	Sun 1154

DUFF, Arlie '54
Born Arleigh Duff on 3/28/24 in Jack's Branch, Texas. Male singer. Worked as a DJ in Colorado and Texas.

| 12/5/53+ | 7 | 10 | | You All Come S:7 / A:7 / J:8 Poor Ole Teacher | | $25 | Starday 104 |

DUGAN, Jeff '88

| 8/15/87 | 68 | 12 | | 1 Once A Fool, Always A Fool.................... Somebody Kill The Jukebox | | $3 | Warner 28376 |
| 5/28/88 | 52 | 8 | | 2 I Wish It Was That Easy Going Home .... That Won't Ever Stop Me Loving You | | $3 | Warner 27995 |

DUNCAN, Johnny ★110★ '76
Born on 10/5/38 in Dublin, Texas. Singer/songwriter/guitarist. Worked as a DJ on WAGG in Franklin, Tennessee. Related to **Brady Seals**, **Dan Seals** and **Troy Seals**.

1)Thinkin' Of A Rendezvous 2)She Can Put Her Shoes Under My Bed 3)It Couldn't Have Been Any Better
4)Hello Mexico 5)Come A Little Bit Closer

DEBUT	PEAK	WKS		A-side / B-side	Pop	$	Label & Number
8/12/67	54	7		1 Hard Luck Joe................................Gotta Get Back (On The Right Track)		$7	Columbia 44196
1/13/68	67	3		2 Baby Me Baby .... Mystery		$7	Columbia 44383
8/17/68	47	9		3 To My Sorrow ....I'm In This Town For Good		$7	Columbia 44580
10/19/68	21	8		4 Jackson Ain't A Very Big Town .... The True And Lasting Kind		$7	Columbia 44656
				JOHNNY DUNCAN AND JUNE STEARNS			
2/8/69	70	4		5 I Live To Love You.................... Louisville Nashville Southbound Train		$7	Columbia 44693
3/15/69	74	3		6 Back To Back (We're Strangers) .... If That's The Only Way		$7	Columbia 44752
				JOHNNY DUNCAN AND JUNE STEARNS			
6/21/69	30	12		7 When She Touches Me .... Shreveport To L.A.		$7	Columbia 44864
12/13/69+	65	6		8 Window Number Five .... Day Drinker		$7	Columbia 45006
5/9/70	39	10		9 You're Gonna Need A Man .... Long Tall Drawn Out Day		$7	Columbia 45124
9/19/70	68	3		10 My Woman's Love .... (There's Still) Someone I Can't Forget		$7	Columbia 45201
10/31/70	27	13		11 Let Me Go (Set Me Free) ....What I Don't Know		$7	Columbia 45227
3/13/71	19	13		12 There's Something About A Lady..................I Don't Know Why I Keep Loving You		$7	Columbia 45319
7/24/71	39	9		13 One Night Of Love .... (A Whole Lot Of) Peaches In Georgia		$7	Columbia 45418
11/27/71+	12	13		14 Baby's Smile, Woman's Kiss .... I'd Rather Love You		$7	Columbia 45479
3/18/72	19	12		15 Fools .... Tiny Fingers		$7	Columbia 45556
9/30/72	66	5		16 Here We Go Again .... (I'll Always Love) When We Loved		$7	Columbia 45674
3/31/73	6	16		17 Sweet Country Woman The Look In Baby's Eyes		$6	Columbia 45818
9/8/73	18	14		18 Talkin' With My Lady .... You're My Woman		$6	Columbia 45917
4/6/74	47	9		19 The Pillow ....Ain't No Way That I Can Forget You		$6	Columbia 46018
9/21/74	66	9		20 Scarlet Water .... We're Not Fooling Our Hearts		$5	Columbia 10007
3/8/75	57	8		21 Charley Is My Name .... Gentle Fire		$5	Columbia 10085
8/23/75	26	14		22 Jo And The Cowboy .... Taking A Chance On You		$5	Columbia 10182
12/20/75+	86	7		23 Gentle Fire .... Good Morning Love		$5	Columbia 10262
3/27/76	4	20		24 Stranger Flashing, Screaming, Silent Neon Sign		$5	Columbia 10302
10/2/76	1²	17		25 Thinkin' Of A Rendezvous Love Should Be Easy		$5	Columbia 10417
2/5/77	1¹	15		26 It Couldn't Have Been Any Better Denver Woman		$5	Columbia 10474
6/4/77	5	16		27 A Song In The Night Use My Love	105	$5	Columbia 10554
10/29/77+	4	16		28 Come A Little Bit Closer Loneliness (Can Break A Good Man Down)		$5	Columbia 10634
				JOHNNY DUNCAN (with Janie Fricke)			
				#3 Pop hit for Jay & The Americans in 1964			
3/11/78	1¹	18		29 She Can Put Her Shoes Under My Bed			
				(Anytime) Maybe I Just Crossed Your Mind		$5	Columbia 10694
7/15/78	4	14		30 Hello Mexico (And Adios Baby To You) I Watched An Angel (Going Through Hell)		$5	Columbia 10783
2/24/79	6	14		31 Slow Dancing One Night Of Love		$5	Columbia 10915
				#10 Pop hit for Johnny Rivers in 1977			
9/29/79	9	12		32 The Lady In The Blue Mercedes Too Far Gone		$5	Columbia 11097
1/5/80	17	14		33 Play Another Slow Song .... My Woman's Good To Me		$4	Columbia 11185
6/7/80	17	14		34 I'm Gonna Love You Tonight (In My Dreams) .... Wine Oh Wine		$4	Columbia 11280
7/12/80	17	14		35 He's Out Of My Life ....Loving Arms		$4	Columbia 11312
				JOHNNY DUNCAN and JANIE FRICKE			
				#10 Pop hit for Michael Jackson in 1980			
11/8/80+	16	14		36 Acapulco ....Am I That Easy To Forget		$4	Columbia 11385
11/7/81	40	10		37 All Night Long .... My Heart's Not In It		$4	Columbia 02570
4/12/86	69	6		38 The Look Of A Lady In Love		$5	Pharoah 2502
8/16/86	81	2		39 Texas Moon		$5	Pharoah 2503

DEBUT	PEAK	WKS	Gold	A-side (Chart Hit)..B-side	Pop	$	Pic	Label & Number

DUNCAN, Tommy   **'49**
Born on 1/11/11 in Hillsboro, Texas. Died of a heart attack on 7/25/67 (age 56). Featured vocalist with **Bob Wills**.

| 8/13/49 | 8 | 3 | | Gamblin' Polka Dot Blues _____ S:8 / J:8 _September_ | | $25 | | Capitol 40178 |
| | | | | TOMMY DUNCAN And His Western All Stars | | | | |

DUNN, Holly ★186★   **'89**
Born on 8/22/57 in San Antonio, Texas. Singer/songwriter/guitarist. Sister of **Chris Waters**. Former staff writer at CBS and MTM Records. Joined the *Grand Ole Opry* in 1989. Worked as a DJ at WWWW in Detroit. CMA Award: 1987 Horizon Award.

    1)*You Really Had Me Going* 2)*Are You Ever Gonna Love Me* 3)*Love Someone Like Me* 4)*Only When I Love*
      5)*There Goes My Heart Again*

6/8/85	62	6		1 Playing For Keeps _____ _I'm Not Through Loving You Yet_		$3		MTM 72052
10/5/85	64	8		2 My Heart Holds On _____ _Shot In The Dark_		$3		MTM 72057
5/17/86	39	12		3 Two Too Many _____ S:39 / A:39 _You_		$3		MTM 72064
8/23/86	7	25		4 Daddy's Hands _____ S:4 / A:7 _Hideaway Heart_		$3		MTM 72075
2/7/87	4	21		5 A Face In The Crowd _____ A:4 / S:15 _You're History_		$3		Warner 28471
				MICHAEL MARTIN MURPHEY AND HOLLY DUNN				
5/2/87	2²	25		6 Love Someone Like Me _____ S:❶¹ _Burnin' Wheel_		$3		MTM 72082
8/29/87	4	25		7 Only When I Love _____ S:❶¹ _Little Frame House_		$3		MTM 72091
1/16/88	7	24		8 Strangers Again _____ S:2 _Wrap Me Up_		$3		MTM 72093
6/25/88	5	20		9 That's What Your Love Does To Me ____ S:3 _Lonesome Highway_		$3		MTM 72108
11/5/88+	11	19		10 (It's Always Gonna Be) Someday _____ _On The Wings Of An Angel_		$3		MTM 72116
5/27/89	❶¹	23		11 Are You Ever Gonna Love Me _____ _If I'd Never Loved You_		$3		Warner 22957
9/23/89	4	26		12 There Goes My Heart Again _____ _The Blue Rose Of Texas_		$3		Warner 22796
2/17/90	25	13		13 Maybe _____ _If I Knew Then What I Know Now_		$3	▌	Reprise 19972
				KENNY ROGERS (with Holly Dunn)				
6/2/90	63	4		14 My Anniversary For Being A Fool ____ _The Light In The Window Went Out_		$3		Warner 19847
9/1/90	❶¹	20		15 You Really Had Me Going _____ _When No Place Is Home_		$3	▌	Warner 19756
1/5/91	19	20		16 Heart Full Of Love _____ _Temporary Loss Of Memory_		$3		Warner 19472
7/13/91	48	9		17 Maybe I Mean Yes _____ _Daddy's Hands_		$3		Warner 19266
4/25/92	67	4		18 No Love Have I _____ _Love Someone Like Me_		$3		Warner 18956
8/1/92	68	7		19 As Long As You Belong To Me _____ _You Can Have Him_		$3		Warner 18831
12/26/92+	51	10		20 Golden Years _____		$3		album cut
				from the album *Getting It Dunn* on Warner 26949				
4/8/95	56	11		21 I Am Who I Am _____ _Love Across The Line_		$3	▌	River North 3003

DUNN, Ronnie   **'84**
Born on 6/1/53 in Coleman, Texas. Joined with **Kix Brooks** in duo **Brooks & Dunn**.

| 3/5/83 | 59 | 7 | | 1 It's Written All Over Your Face _____ _You Never Crossed My Mind_ | | $6 | ■ | Churchill 94018 |
| 6/23/84 | 59 | 8 | | 2 She Put The Sad In All His Songs _____ _Change Of Attitude_ | | $6 | | Churchill 52383 |

DURHAM, Bobby   **'88**
Singer from Bakersfield, California.

| 5/21/88 | 92 | 2 | | Let's Start A Rumor Today _____ | | $6 | | Hightone 502 |

DURRENCE, Sam   **'73**
Worked as a DJ at WHOO in Orlando, Florida.

| 9/15/73 | 98 | 3 | | Last Days Of Childhood _____ _She Almost Believed Me_ | | $7 | | River 3875 |

DYCKE, Jerry   **'80**
Born in Topeka, Kansas.

| 5/3/80 | 93 | 3 | | 1 Daddy Played Harmonica _____ _I Never Said Goodbye_ | | $6 | | Churchill 7757 |
| 2/28/81 | 94 | 2 | | 2 Beethoven Was Before My Time _____ _My Shoes Keep Walking Back To You_ | | $6 | | Churchill 7766 |

E

EAGLES   **'75**
Rock-country group fromed in Los Angeles: Glenn Frey (vocals, guitar), Randy Meisner (bass), **Don Henley** (drums) and Bernie Leadon (guitar). Meisner founded **Poco**. Leadon had been in the **Flying Burrito Brothers**. Frey and Henley were with **Linda Ronstadt**. Don Felder (guitar) added in 1975. Leadon replaced by Joe Walsh in 1975. Meisner replaced by Timothy B. Schmit in 1977. Disbanded in 1982. Henley, Frey, Felder, Walsh and Schmit reunited in 1994. Group inducted into the Rock and Roll Hall of Fame in 1998.

10/11/75	8	13		1 Lyin' Eyes _____ _Too Many Hands_	2²	$5		Asylum 45279
1/8/77	43	12	●	2 New Kid In Town _____ _Victim Of Love_	❶¹	$5		Asylum 45373
1/24/81	55	7		3 Seven Bridges Road _____ _The Long Run (live version)_	21	$5		Asylum 47100
				recorded "live" on 7/28/80 at the Santa Monica Civic Auditorium				
11/12/94	58	6		4 The Girl From Yesterday _____				album cut
				from the album *Hell Freezes Over* on Geffen 24725				

EARL, Kenny   **'81**
Singer/songwriter. Member of **The Wolfpack**.

| 5/9/81 | 84 | 3 | | 1 We Have To Start Meeting Like This _____ _Raindrops_ | | $6 | | Kik 904 |
| 9/19/81 | 73 | 4 | | 2 Wasn't It Supposed To Be Me _____ _Raindrops_ | | $6 | | Kari 124 |

EARLE, Steve '86
Born on 1/17/55 in Fort Monroe, Virginia; raised in Schertz, Texas. Singer/songwriter/guitarist.

DEBUT	PEAK	WKS		A-side / B-side		$		Label & Number
10/1/83	70	4		1 Nothin' But You .... Continental Trailways Blues		$4		Epic 04070
				STEVE EARLE & The Dukes				
12/8/84	76	6		2 What'll You Do About Me? .... Cry Myself To Sleep		$4	■	Epic 04666
3/22/86	37	13		3 Hillbilly Highway .... Down The Road		$3		MCA 52785
6/21/86	7	22		4 Guitar Town S:6 / A:8 Little Rock 'N' Roller		$3		MCA 52856
10/25/86	28	15		5 Someday .... A:28 / S:30 Hillbilly Highway		$3		MCA 52920
2/14/87	8	19		6 Goodbyes All We've Got Left A:8 / S:15 Good Ol' Boy (Gettin Tough)		$3		MCA 53011
6/13/87	20	16		7 Nowhere Road .... I Ain't Ever Satisfied		$3		MCA 53103
10/17/87	37	13		8 Sweet Little '66 .... Angry Young Man		$3		MCA 53182
1/9/88	29	13		9 Six Days On The Road .... The Week Of Living Dangerously		$3		Hughes/MCA 53249
				STEVE EARLE & THE DUKES (above 2)				
				from the movie Planes, Trains & Automobiles starring Steve Martin and John Candy				

★261★ EARWOOD, Mundo '78
Pronounced: moon-doe. Born Raymond Earwood on 10/13/52 in Del Rio, Texas. Singer/songwriter/guitarist.
1)Things I'd Do For You 2)Fooled Around And Fell In Love 3)Can't Keep My Mind Off Of Her
4)You're In Love With The Wrong Man 5)Behind Blue Eyes

DEBUT	PEAK	WKS		A-side / B-side		$		Label & Number
10/21/72	57	10		1 Behind Blue Eyes .... Breaking Up Is Hard To Do		$7		Royal American 65
				also see #7 below				
6/29/74	59	10		2 Let's Hear It For Loneliness .... Angeline		$6		GRT 003
10/25/75	91	4		3 She Brings Her Lovin' Home To Me .... Life Has It's Little Ups And Downs		$5		Epic 50141
				MUNDO RAY				
2/7/76	86	7		4 I Can't Quit Cheatin' On You .... That's My Desire		$5		Epic 50185
6/26/76	70	7		5 Lonesome Is A Cowboy .... (Don't Give Your Love To Any Man) Who Buys The Wine		$5		Epic 50232
3/19/77	86	4		6 I Can Give You Love .... Let's Get Naked		$5		True 101
7/9/77	32	11		7 Behind Blue Eyes .... Let's Get Naked [R]		$5		True 104
				same version as #1 above				
12/17/77+	69	8		8 Angelene .... Just Another One Of Those Days		$5		True 111
5/20/78	36	11		9 When I Get You Alone .... Let Me Down Easy		$5		GMC 102
9/2/78	18	13		10 Things I'd Do For You Breaking Up Is Hard To Do		$5		GMC 104
12/2/78+	25	13		11 Fooled Around And Fell In Love .... Love Me Now		$5		GMC 105
4/28/79	38	10		12 My Heart Is Not My Own .... My Weakness Is Stronger Than I Am		$5		GMC 106
8/4/79	34	9		13 We Got Love .... It's Magic		$5		GMC 107
11/24/79	67	6		14 Sometimes Love/				
10/13/79	73	3		15 Philodendron		$5		GMC 108
4/5/80	27	13		16 You're In Love With The Wrong Man .... Before We Call It Love		$5	■	GMC 109
				Mel Tillis (harmony vocal)				
9/27/80	26	12		17 Can't Keep My Mind Off Of Her .... Just Another One Of Those Days		$5		GMC 111
2/14/81	40	9		18 Blue Collar Blues .... Softer Place To Fall		$5		Excelsior 1005
5/16/81	32	12		19 Angela .... Pyramid Of Cans		$5		Excelsior 1010
10/17/81	45	8		20 I'll Still Be Loving You .... Pyramid Of Cans		$5		Excelsior 1019
4/17/82	58	8		21 All My Lovin .... Breaking Up Is Hard To Do		$6		Primero 1002
				#45 Pop hit for The Beatles in 1964				
9/4/82	68	5		22 Pyramid Of Cans .... Breaking Up Is Hard To Do		$6		Primero 1009
4/15/89	80	3		23 A Woman's Way .... Love Me Now		$5		Pegasus 110

EAST, Lyndel '78
Singer from Oklahoma City.

DEBUT	PEAK	WKS		A-side / B-side		$		Label & Number
7/29/78	97	2		Why Do You Come Around .... All She Ever Wanted		$6		NSD 2

EASTON, Sheena '83
Born on 4/27/59 in Glasgow, Scotland. Pop singer/actress. Charted 20 pop hits from 1981-91.

DEBUT	PEAK	WKS		A-side / B-side	Pop	$	Pic	Label & Number
1/29/83	❶¹	17		1 We've Got Tonight You Are So Beautiful (Rogers)	6	$4	■	Liberty 1492
				KENNY ROGERS and SHEENA EASTON				
				#13 Pop hit for Bob Seger in 1979				
3/24/84	86	7		2 Almost Over You .... I Don't Need Your Word	25	$3		EMI America 8186

EASTWOOD, Clint — see CHARLES, Ray / HAGGARD, Merle

EATON, Connie '75
Born on 3/1/50 in Nashville. Daughter of singer Bob Eaton.

DEBUT	PEAK	WKS		A-side / B-side		$		Label & Number
2/7/70	34	7		1 Angel Of The Morning .... One Time Too Many		$6		Chart 5048
				#7 Pop hit for Merrilee Rush in 1968				
5/23/70	44	9		2 Hit The Road Jack .... The Question		$6		Chart 5066
				CONNIE EATON & DAVE PEEL				
				#1 Pop hit for Ray Charles in 1961				
11/7/70	56	7		3 It Takes Two .... No Rest For The Wicked		$6		Chart 5099
				CONNIE EATON & DAVE PEEL				
				#14 Pop hit for Marvin Gaye & Kim Weston in 1967				
2/6/71	74	2		4 Sing A Happy Song .... Glad To Be Your Woman		$6		Chart 5110
9/11/71	56	10		5 Don't Hang No Halos On Me .... These Hills		$6		Chart 5138
1/25/75	23	13		6 Lonely Men, Lonely Women Midnight Train To Georgia		$5		Dunhill/ABC 15022
6/14/75	93	4		7 If I Knew Enough To Come Out Of The Rain .... Magic Mystery		$5		ABC 12098

EATON, Skip — see SKIP & LINDA

EBERLY, Bob '49
Born Robert Eberle on 7/24/16 in Mechanicsville, New York. Died on 11/17/81 (age 65). Vocalist with Jimmy Dorsey from 1935-43.

| 1/1/49 | 8 | 1 | | One Has My Name The Other Has My Heart   J:8 / S:15   *Just A Little Lovin' (Will Go A Long Way)* | | $15 | | Decca 24492 |

BOB EBERLY with The Sunshine Serenaders
#13 Pop hit for Barry Young in 1966

EDDY, Duane '58
Born on 4/26/38 in Corning, New York. Originator of the "twangy" guitar sound. Married to **Jessi Colter** from 1962-68. Charted 28 pop hits from 1958-86. Inducted into the Rock and Roll Hall of Fame in 1994.

| 8/4/58 | 17 | 5 | | 1 Rebel-'Rouser... S:17   *Stalkin'* [I] | 6 | $25 | | Jamie 1104 |

The Sharps (later known as The Rivingtons, rebel yells)

| 5/7/77 | 69 | 6 | | 2 You Are My Sunshine .... *From 8 To 7* | | $6 | | Elektra 45359 |

Waylon Jennings, Willie Nelson, Kin Vassy and Duane's wife, **Deed Eddy** (vocals); #7 Pop hit for **Ray Charles** in 1962; instrumental version recorded by Eddy on his 1960 album *The Twangs The Thang*

EDGE, Kathy '87
Born in Huntsville, Alabama; raised in Memphis.

| 3/21/87 | 89 | 5 | | I Take The Chance .... *You Always Come Back To Hurting Me* | | $5 | | NSD 228 |

EDMUNDS, Dave — see CARTER, Carlene

EDWARDS, Bobby '61
Born Robert Moncrief in Anniston, Alabama.

| 9/4/61 | 4 | 24 | | 1 You're The Reason   *I'm A Fool For Loving You* | 11 | $12 | | Crest 1075 |

The Four Young Men (backing vocals)

| 9/14/63 | 23 | 2 | | 2 Don't Pretend .... *Help Me* | | $10 | | Capitol 5006 |

EDWARDS, Jimmy '58
Born James Bullington on 2/9/33 in Senath, Missouri.

| 11/11/57+ | 12 | 6 | | Love Bug Crawl .... A:12   *Honey Lovin'* | 78 | $25 | | Mercury 71209 |

EDWARDS, Jonathan '89
Born on 7/28/46 in Aitkin, Minnesota; raised in Virginia. Singer/songwriter/guitarist.

9/17/88	64	6		1 We Need To Be Locked Away .... *Back Up Grinnin'*		$3		MCA/Curb 53390
12/10/88+	56	14		2 Look What We Made (When We Made Love)............*Fewer Threads Than These*		$3		MCA/Curb 53467
3/18/89	59	7		3 It's A Natural Thing ....*My Baby's A Country Song*		$3		MCA/Curb 53613

EDWARDS, Stoney '73
| | ★382★ | | | | | | | |

Born Frenchy Edwards on 12/24/29 in Seminole, Oklahoma. Died in April 1997 (age 67). Black singer/songwriter/guitarist.
1)She's My Rock 2)Mississippi You're On My Mind 3)Hank And Lefty Raised My Country Soul

1/23/71	68	3		1 A Two Dollar Toy................................ *An Old Mule's Hip*		$6		Capitol 3005
4/3/71	61	7		2 Poor Folks Stick Together .... *Mama's Love*		$6		Capitol 3061
8/28/71	73	2		3 The Cute Little Waitress .... *Please Bring A Bottle*		$6		Capitol 3131
11/11/72+	20	14		4 She's My Rock *I Won't Make It Through The Day*		$5		Capitol 3462
3/17/73	54	6		5 You're A Believer .... *She's Helping Me Get Over You*		$5		Capitol 3550
8/11/73	39	10		6 Hank And Lefty Raised My Country Soul ....*A Few Of The Reasons*		$5		Capitol 3671
12/22/73+	85	7		7 Daddy Bluegrass ....*It's Rainin' On My Sunny Day*		$5		Capitol 3766
2/8/75	77	8		8 Clean Your Own Tables .... *Do You Know The Man*		$5		Capitol 4015
4/19/75	20	12		9 Mississippi You're On My Mind .... *A Two Dollar Toy*		$5		Capitol 4051
11/29/75+	41	11		10 Blackbird (Hold Your Head High) ....*Pickin' Wildflowers*		$5		Capitol 4188
4/10/76	51	8		11 Love Still Makes The World Go 'Round .... *(I Want) The Real Thing*		$5		Capitol 4246
10/23/76	90	4		12 Don't Give Up On Me .... *July 12, 1939*		$5		Capitol 4337
11/4/78	60	7		13 If I Had It To Do All Over Again .... *I Feel Chained*		$5		JMI 47
5/24/80	53	10		14 No Way To Drown A Memory .... *Reverend Leroy*		$5		Music America 107
9/20/80	85	3		15 One Bar At A Time .... *Stranger In My Arms*		$5		Music America 109

ELLEDGE, Jimmy '75
Born on 1/8/43 in Nashville. Singer/songwriter/pianist.

| 5/17/75 | 95 | 4 | | One By One .... *After You* | | $5 | | 4 Star 1003 |

ELLIS, Darryl & Don '92
Brothers Darryl (b: 12/1/64) and Don (b: 7/2/67) Ellis Gatlin. Both born in Norfolk, Virginia; raised in Beaver Falls, Pennsylvania.

6/27/92	70	2		1 Goodbye Highway................................*I Knew You'd Come Around*		$3		Epic 74325
9/5/92	58	8		2 No Sir ....*I Knew You'd Come Around*		$3	▮	Epic 74454
11/21/92	73	4		3 Something Moving In Me .... *You Know Why*		$3		Epic 74758

ELLIS, Mike '78
| 7/29/78 | 89 | 3 | | I Never Meant To Harm You .... *West Virginian* | | $5 | | Cin Kay 130 |

ELLWANGER, Sandy '89
Born in Fremont, California. Female singer/songwriter/pianist.

| 7/29/89 | 96 | 2 | | 1 I Just Came In Here (To Let A Little Hurt Out)................................ | | $5 | | Door Knob 326 |
| 11/11/89 | 79 | 2 | | 2 What Kind Of Girl Do You Think I Am .... | | $5 | | Door Knob 334 |

ELMO & PATSY '83
Husband-and-wife team of Elmo Shropshire and Patsy Trigg. Divorced in 1985.

| 12/31/83 | 92 | 2 | | 1 Grandma Got Run Over By A Reindeer .... *Christmas* [X-N] | | $4 | | Soundwaves 4658 |

ELMO 'N PATSY
originally released on Oink 2984 in 1979 ($6); first issued on Soundwaves in 1982

| 12/27/97 | 64 | 2 | | 2 Grandma Got Run Over By A Reindeer .... *Percy, The Puny Poinsettia* [X-N-R] | | $3 | ▮ | Epic 05479 |

above 2 are different versions

ELY, Joe '77
Born on 9/2/47 in Amarillo, Texas; raised in Lubbock, Texas. Singer/songwriter/guitarist. Member of the **Buzzin' Cousins**.

| 2/12/77 | 89 | 3 | | All My Love .... *Mardi Gras Waltz* | | $5 | | MCA 40666 |

DEBUT	PEAK	WKS	Gold	A-side (Chart Hit)..B-side	Pop	$	Pic	Label & Number
				EME '81				
2/21/81	86	2		Every Breath I Take ....*Goodbye To Love*		$7		EPI 1541
				EMERY, Ralph '61				
				Born Walter Ralph Emery on 3/10/33 in McEwen, Tennessee. Former host of TNN's *Nashville Now*. Married to **Skeeter Davis** from 1960-64.				
8/28/61	4	15		Hello Fool *It's Not A Lot (But It's All I've Got)* [S]		$15		Liberty 55352
				answer to "Hello Walls" by **Faron Young**				
				EMILIO '95				
				Born Emilio Navaira on 8/23/62 in San Antonio, Texas.				
8/19/95	27	20		1 It's Not The End Of The World S:20 *Life Is Good*		$3	▮	Capitol 58432
1/20/96	41	15		2 Even If I Tried .... S:10 *There'll Be No More Crying*		$3	▮	Capitol 58507
5/11/96	56	7		3 I Think We're On To Something				album cut
10/12/96	62	1		4 Have I Told You Lately				album cut
				#5 Pop hit for Rod Stewart in 1993; above 2 from the album *Life Is Good* on Capitol 32392				
2/15/97	56	9		5 I'd Love You To Love Me .... S:22 *Any Little Lie*		$3	▮	Capitol 58632
6/7/97	64	3		6 She Gives .... *Any Little Lie*		$3		Capitol 19603
				ENGLAND, Ty '95				
				Born on 12/5/63 in Oklahoma City. Singer/songwriter/guitarist.				
6/10/95	3	20		1 Should've Asked Her Faster S:11 *A Swing Like That*	121	$3	▮	RCA 64280
10/28/95+	44	16		2 Smoke In Her Eyes .... S:25 *Redneck Son*		$3	▮	RCA 64405
2/24/96	55	7		3 Redneck Son ....*It's Lonesome Everywhere*		$3		RCA 64496
8/10/96	22	20		4 Irresistible You.....................................S:17 *You'll Find Somebody New*		$3	▮	RCA 64598
12/28/96+	46	9		5 All Of The Above ....*Sure*		$3		RCA 64676
				ENGVALL, Bill '97				
				Born on 7/27/57 in Galveston, Texas. Comedian/actor. Cast member of TV's *The Jeff Foxworthy Show*.				
1/25/97	29	20	●	1 Here's Your Sign (Get The Picture)............. S:**1**8 *Things Have Changed* (Engvall) [C]	43	$3	▮	Warner 17491
				BILL ENGVALL with Travis Tritt				
8/16/97	56	5		2 Warning Signs .... S:21 *Baby Barf And The Turkey Hunt* (Engvall) [C]		$3	▮	Warner 43934
				BILL ENGVALL with John Michael Montgomery				
				ESMERELDY '48				
				Married to opera singer Harry Boersma. Mother of pop singer Amy Holland.				
3/20/48	10	1		Slap Her Down Again Paw *Red Wing* [N]		$20		Musicraft 524
				ESMERELDY And Her Novelty Band				
				#7 Pop hit for Arthur Godfrey in 1948				
				ETC BAND, The — see CONLEY, Earl Thomas				
				ETHEL & THE SHAMELESS HUSSIES '88				
				Female trio from Huntsville, Alabama: "Ethel Beaverton" (Gayle Zeiler), "Blanche Hickey" (Valerie Hunt) and "Bunny O'Hare" (Beki Fogle). Name taken from a line in "The Streak" by Ray Stevens.				
5/21/88	71	5		1 One Nite Stan ....*Smokin' In Bed* [N]		$3		MCA 53323
1/21/89	86	2		2 It's Just The Whiskey Talkin' .... *Mr. Cadillac*		$3		MCA 53472
				EVANGELINE '94				
				Female group from Louisiana: Kathleen Stieffel (vocals, guitar), Rhonda Lohmeyer (guitar), Sharon Leger (bass) and Beth McKee (keyboards).				
1/22/94	70	4		Let's Go Spend Your Money Honey ....*On The Levee*		$3	▮	MCA 54787
				EVANS, Ashley '90				
				Female singer.				
1/6/90	76	2		I'm So Afraid Of Losing You Again...		$5		Door Knob 338
				EVANS, Paul '78				
				Born on 3/5/38 in New York City. Singer/songwriter. Charted 4 pop hits from 1959-60.				
5/20/78	57	10		1 Hello, This Is Joannie (The Telephone Answering Machine Song) ....*Lullabye Tissue Paper Co.*		$5		Spring 183
5/5/79	81	4		2 Disneyland Daddy ....*Build An Ark*		$5		Spring 193
8/16/80	80	4		3 One Night Led To Two ....*Hangin' Out And Hangin' In*		$5		Cinnamon 604
				EVANS, Paula Kay '77				
				Female singer from Garland, Texas.				
4/23/77	100	2		Runnin' Out Again ....*Hangin' Out Again*		$6		Autumn 368
				EVANS, Sara '97				
				Born on 2/5/71 in Boonesboro, Missouri. Female singer.				
3/29/97	59	6		1 True Lies... *The Week The River Raged*		$3	▮	RCA 64784
7/12/97	44	11		2 Three Chords And The Truth ....*The Week The River Raged*		$3		RCA 64876
12/27/97+	48	8		3 Shame About That..*(remix)*		$3	▮	RCA 65324

EVERETTE, Leon ★189★ '81
Born Leon Everette Baughman on 6/21/48 in Aiken, South Carolina; raised in New York City. Singer/songwriter/guitarist.

1)Hurricane 2)Giving Up Easy 3)I Could'a Had You 4)Just Give Me What You Think Is Fair 5)Midnight Rodeo

12/3/77	84	5		1 I Love That Woman (Like The Devil Loves Sin)...........................Still Loving You		$6		True 110
				also see #6 below				
1/20/79	89	3		2 We Let Love Fade Away ....Never Ending Crowded Circle		$5		Orlando 100
4/7/79	81	4		3 Giving Up Easy.................................. Mama Rocked Us To Sleep (With Country Music)		$5		Orlando 102
				also see #9 below				
6/9/79	33	10		4 Don't Feel Like The Lone Ranger .... We Let Love Fade Away		$5	■	Orlando 103
9/15/79	42	7		5 The Sun Went Down In My World Tonight ....Cheater's Trap		$5		Orlando 104
12/8/79+	28	12		6 I Love That Woman (Like The Devil Loves Sin)...... Never Ending Crowded Circle [R]		$5		Orlando 105
				new version of #1 above				
3/1/80	30	12		7 I Don't Want To Lose ....Mama Rocked Us To Sleep		$5		Orlando 106
5/31/80	10	17		8 Over ....Let Me Apologize		$5		Orlando 107
10/25/80+	5	18		9 Giving Up Easy ....Setting Me Up [R]		$4		RCA 12111
				same version as #3 above				
3/7/81	11	13		10 If I Keep On Going Crazy...........................The Sun Went Down In My World Tonight		$4		RCA 12177
7/18/81	4	16		11 Hurricane ....Make Me Stop Loving Her		$4		RCA 12270
11/14/81+	9	17		12 Midnight Rodeo ....Don't Be Angry		$4		RCA 12355
3/27/82	7	18		13 Just Give Me What You Think Is Fair ....Over		$4		RCA 13079
8/7/82	10	17		14 Soul Searchin' ....Misery		$4		RCA 13282
11/27/82+	15	18		15 Shadows Of My Mind...If I Keep On Going Crazy		$4		RCA 13391
3/19/83	9	18		16 My Lady Loves Me (Just As I Am) ....Somebody Killed Dewey Jones' Daughter		$4		RCA 13466
8/13/83	31	13		17 The Lady, She's Right ....Knocking On Her Door		$4		RCA 13584
				Rex Gosdin (harmony vocal)				
2/4/84	6	20		18 I Could'a Had You ....I Wanna Know Your Name		$4		RCA 13717
7/7/84	30	14		19 Shot In The Dark ....I Want To Be In Pictures		$4		RCA 13834
3/30/85	47	10		20 Too Good To Say No To ....It Never Felt Like This Before		$4		Mercury 880611
6/15/85	53	9		21 A Good Love Died Tonight .... (You're Never Guilty) When Love Is Your Alibi		$4		Mercury 880829
10/5/85	44	9		22 'Til A Tear Becomes A Rose ....It Never Felt Like This Before		$4		Mercury 884040
5/24/86	46	9		23 Danger List (Give Me Someone I Can Love) ....Over		$5		Orlando 112
				first recorded by John Cougar Mellencamp on his 1982 album American Fool				
8/2/86	59	5		24 Sad State Of Affairs .... Danger List (Give Me Someone I Can Love)		$5		Orlando 114
11/15/86	56	6		25 Still In The Picture........................ Danger List (Give Me Someone I Can Love)		$5		Orlando 115

EVERLY, Don '76
Born Isaac Donald Everly on 2/1/37 in Brownie, Kentucky. One-half of The Everly Brothers.

4/10/76	50	8		1 Yesterday Just Passed My Way Again ....Never Like This		$7		Hickory/MGM 368
2/5/77	84	4		2 Since You Broke My Heart ....Deep Water		$5		ABC/Hickory 54005
5/7/77	96	4		3 Brother Juke-Box ....Oh, What A Feeling		$5		ABC/Hickory 54012

EVERLY, Phil '83
Born on 1/19/39 in Chicago. One-half of The Everly Brothers.

12/27/80+	63	7		1 Dare To Dream Again .... Lonely Days, Lonely Nights		$5		Curb 5401
6/13/81	52	8		2 Sweet Southern Love ....In Your Eyes		$5		Curb 02116
2/19/83	37	12		3 Who's Gonna Keep Me Warm .... One Way Love		$5		Capitol 5197

EVERLY BROTHERS, The ★187★ '57
Duo of vocalists/guitarists/songwriters Don Everly and Phil Everly. Charted 38 pop hits from 1957-84. Duo split up in July 1973 and reunited in September 1983. Inducted into the Rock and Roll Hall of Fame in 1986.

1)Wake Up Little Susie 2)Bye Bye Love 3)Bird Dog

5/13/57	❶[7]	26	●	1 Bye Bye Love ....S:❶[7] / A:❶[7] I Wonder If I Care As Much (Pop flip)	2[4]	$25		Cadence 1315
9/30/57	❶[8]	22	●	2 Wake Up Little Susie ....A:❶[8] / S:❶[7] Maybe Tomorrow	❶[4]	$25	■	Cadence 1337
2/10/58	4	13		3 This Little Girl Of Mine/ ....S:4 / A:5	26			
				#9 R&B hit for Ray Charles in 1955				
3/24/58	10	1		4 Should We Tell Him A:10	flip	$25		Cadence 1342
4/28/58	❶[3]	20	●	5 All I Have To Do Is Dream/ ....S:❶[3] / A:❶[1]	❶[5]			
6/16/58	15	1		6 Claudette A:15	30	$20		Cadence 1348
				written by Roy Orbison				
8/18/58	❶[6]	13	●	7 Bird Dog/ ....S:❶[6] / A:3	❶[1]			
9/1/58	7	5		8 Devoted To You A:7	10	$20		Cadence 1350
12/1/58+	17	7		9 Problems...Love Of My Life (Pop #40)	2[1]	$20	■	Cadence 1355
8/31/59	8	12		10 ('Til) I Kissed You ....Oh, What A Feeling	4	$20	■	Cadence 1369

EVERLY BROTHERS, The — Cont'd

3/6/61	25	3	11 Ebony Eyes .... *Walk Right Back (Pop-#7)*	8	$15	■ Warner 5199
9/29/84	49	12	12 On The Wings Of A Nightingale .... *Asleep*	50	$4	■ Mercury 880213
			written by Paul McCartney			
1/5/85	44	11	13 The First In Line .... *The Story Of Me*		$4	Mercury 880423
3/1/86	17	18	14 Born Yesterday .... S:12 / A:18 *Don't Say Goodnight*		$4	Mercury 884428
7/5/86	56	6	15 I Know Love/			
9/13/86	57	8	16 These Shoes		$4	■ Mercury 884694
2/25/89	45	9	17 Ballad Of A Teenage Queen .... *Get Rhythm (Cash)*		$3	Mercury 872420
			JOHNNY CASH with Rosanne Cash & The Everly Brothers			

E.W.B.   **'81**
Vocal trio: Jerrel Elliott, Richard Wesley, Gerald Bennett.

9/12/81	96	2	We Could Go On Forever..	$5	Paid 142

★312★   **EWING, Skip**   **'89**
Born Donald Ralph Ewing on 3/6/64 in Redlands, California. Singer/songwriter/guitarist.
1)Burnin' A Hole In My Heart 2)It's You Again 3)I Don't Have Far To Fall

3/5/88	17	18	1 Your Memory Wins Again .... *Burnin' A Hold In My Heart*	$3	■ MCA 53271
6/25/88	8	24	2 I Don't Have Far To Fall .... S:17 *Still Under The Weather*	$3	MCA 53353
10/29/88+	3	22	3 Burnin' A Hole In My Heart .... S:21 *Autumn's Not That Cold*	$3	MCA 53435
3/4/89	10	20	4 The Gospel According To Luke .... *Dad*	$3	MCA 53481
6/24/89	15	24	5 The Coast Of Colorado .... *Dad*	$3	MCA 53663
10/7/89+	5	26	6 It's You Again .... *Ain't That The Way It Always Ends*	$3	MCA 53732
3/3/90	70	5	7 If A Man Could Live On Love Alone .... *She's Makin' Plans*	$3	MCA 53777
8/18/90	69	4	8 I'm Your Man .... *The Will To Love*	$3	▌ MCA 53853
5/25/91	73	1	9 I Get The Picture		album cut
3/28/92	71	1	10 Naturally		album cut
			above 2 from the album *Naturally* on Capitol 96097		
12/30/95	68	1	11 Christmas Carol ....[X]		album cut
			from the album *Following Yonder Star* on MCA 10068		
4/19/97	58	12	12 Mary Go Round		album cut
8/23/97	66	7	13 Answer To My Prayer		album cut
			above 2 from the album *Until I Found You* on Word 471202		
12/27/97	60	3	14 Christmas Carol ....[X-R]		album cut
			from the album *Following Yonder Star* on MCA 10068		

EXILE ★135★   **'84**
Group from Lexington, Kentucky: **J.P. Pennington** (vocals, guitar), **Les Taylor** (guitar), Marlon Hargis (keyboards), Sonny Lemaire (bass) and Steve Goetzman (drums). **Mark Gray** was a member from 1979-82. Member Bernie Faulkner formed **Hazard**. Hargis was replaced by Lee Carroll in 1985. Pennington was replaced by Paul Martin in 1989. Taylor was replaced by Mark Jones in 1989.
1)Give Me One More Chance 2)Hang On To Your Heart 3)It'll Be Me 4)I Don't Want To Be A Memory
5)I Can't Get Close Enough

8/20/83	27	16	1 High Cost Of Leaving .... *Like A Fool's Supposed To Do*	$3	Epic 04041
12/3/83+	❶¹	22	2 Woke Up In Love	*First Things First*	$3	Epic 04247
4/7/84	❶¹	24	3 I Don't Want To Be A Memory	*After All These Years (I'm Still Chasing You)*	$3	Epic 04421
8/11/84	❶¹	26	4 Give Me One More Chance	A:❶² / S:❶¹ *Ain't That A Pity*	$3	■ Epic 04567
12/8/84+	❶¹	23	5 Crazy For Your Love	S:❶¹ / A:❶¹ *Just In Case*	$3	Epic 04722
3/30/85	86	4	6 Stay With Me .... *Kiss You All Over*	$3	Curb/MCA 52551
			recorded in 1978		
4/6/85	❶¹	22	7 She's A Miracle	S:❶¹ / A:❶¹ *I've Never Seen Anything*	$3	Epic 04864
8/17/85	❶¹	24	8 Hang On To Your Heart	S:❶¹ / A:❶¹ *She Likes Her Lovin'*	$3	Epic 05580
12/7/85+	❶¹	22	9 I Could Get Used To You	S:❶¹ / A:❶¹ *Practice Makes Perfect*	$3	Epic 05723
4/5/86	14	16	10 Super Love .... A:13 / S:14 *Proud To Be Her Man*	$3	Epic 05860
7/26/86	❶¹	22	11 It'll Be Me	A:❶¹ / S:3 *Music*	$3	Epic 06229
6/6/87	❶¹	23	12 She's Too Good To Be True	S:2 *Promises, Promises*	$3	Epic 07135
10/10/87+	❶¹	22	13 I Can't Get Close Enough	S:❶² *As Long As I Have Your Memory*	$3	Epic 07597
2/20/88	60	4	14 Feel Like Foolin' Around .... *Showdown*	$3	Epic 07710
4/23/88	9	18	15 Just One Kiss	S:5 *As Long As I Have Your Memory*	$3	Epic 07775
9/3/88	21	18	16 It's You Again.................................... S:23 *The Girl Can't Help It*	$3	Epic 08020
12/16/89+	17	25	17 Keep It In The Middle Of The Road .... *Yet*	$3	Arista 9911
4/14/90	2¹	21	18 Nobody's Talking	*Don't Hang Up (Girl)*	$3	Arista 2009
9/1/90	7	20	19 Yet	*Show Me*	$3	▌ Arista 2075
12/15/90+	32	20	20 There You Go .... *I'm Still Standing*	$3	Arista 2139
6/22/91	16	20	21 Even Now .... *One Too Many Times*	$3	Arista 2228

F

DEBUT	PEAK	WKS	Gold	A-side (Chart Hit)..B-side	Pop	$	Pic	Label & Number

FAIRCHILD, Barbara ★192★   '73
Born on 11/12/50 in Knobel, Arkansas; raised in St. Louis. Singer/songwriter/guitarist.

1)Teddy Bear Song 2)Kid Stuff 3)Baby Doll 4)Cheatin' Is 5)Standing In Your Line

DEBUT	PEAK	WKS	A-side / B-side	Pop	$	Label & Number
5/31/69	69	5	1 Love Is A Gentle Thing .... *You Can't Stop My Heart From Breaking*		$6	Columbia 44797
8/9/69	66	6	2 A Woman's Hand .... *Got A Chance And I Took It*		$6	Columbia 44925
2/14/70	26	11	3 A Girl Who'll Satisfy Her Man .... *Chains Of Love (Around My Neck)*		$6	Columbia 45063
8/1/70	52	6	4 Find Out What's Happenin' .... *(When You Close Your Eyes) I'll Make You See*		$6	Columbia 45173
1/2/71	33	10	5 (Loving You Is) Sunshine .... *What Ever Happened To Happiness*		$6	Columbia 45272
4/10/71	62	8	6 What Do You Do .... *Break Away*		$6	Columbia 45344
8/7/71	28	11	7 Love's Old Song .... *Back Then*		$6	Columbia 45422
1/15/72	38	8	8 Color My World .... *Tell Me Again*		$6	Columbia 45522
			#16 Pop hit for **Petula Clark** in 1967			
5/27/72	29	10	9 Thanks For The Mem'ries .... *Let Me Be Your Queen*		$5	Columbia 45589
10/14/72	53	9	10 A Sweeter Love (I'll Never Know) .... *That's Loving You*		$5	Columbia 45690
12/30/72+	❶²	19	11 Teddy Bear Song *(You Make Me Feel Like) Singing A Song*	32	$5	Columbia 45743
7/28/73	2²	16	12 Kid Stuff *Make No Mistakes*	95	$5	Columbia 45903
1/26/74	6	14	13 Baby Doll *Color Them With Love*		$5	Columbia 45988
6/29/74	17	13	14 Standing In Your Line .... *You're The One I'm Living For*		$5	Columbia 46053
11/2/74	31	10	15 Little Girl Feeling .... *His Green Eyes*		$5	Columbia 10047
5/10/75	52	10	16 Let's Love While We Can .... *Tara*		$5	Columbia 10128
9/6/75	41	11	17 You've Lost That Lovin' Feelin' .... *Singing Your Way Out Of My Life*		$5	Columbia 10195
			#1 Pop hit for The Righteous Brothers in 1965			
12/20/75+	63	8	18 I Just Love Being A Woman .... *Your Good Girl's Gonna Go Bad*		$5	Columbia 10261
4/10/76	65	7	19 Under Your Spell Again .... *Too Far Gone*		$5	Columbia 10314
7/24/76	31	11	20 Mississippi .... *Over The Rainbow*		$5	Columbia 10378
10/30/76	15	13	21 Cheatin' Is .... *Touch My Heart*		$5	Columbia 10423
3/12/77	22	14	22 Let Me Love You Once Before You Go .... *You Are Always There*		$5	Columbia 10485
			#48 Pop hit for **Greg Lake** in 1981			
10/1/77	49	8	23 For All The Right Reasons/			
5/27/77	72	6	24 The Other Side Of The Morning		$5	Columbia 10607
3/4/78	96	3	25 She Can't Give It Away .... *Painted Faces*		$5	Columbia 10686
10/14/78	91	5	26 It's Sad To Go To The Funeral (Of A Good Love That Has			
			Died) .... *Good Time Days*		$5	Columbia 10825
7/12/80	74	5	27 Let Me Be The One .... *If We Take Our Time*		$5	Paid 102
			BILLY WALKER & BARBARA FAIRCHILD			
12/20/80+	70	7	28 Bye Bye Love/			
10/11/80	79	3	29 Love's Slipping Through Our Fingers (Leaving Time On Our Hands)		$5	Paid 107
			BILLY WALKER & BARBARA FAIRCHILD (above 2)			
5/17/86	84	4	30 Just Out Riding Around .... *You Burned Me So Bad*		$4	Capitol 5582

FAIRGROUND ATTRACTION   '89
British pop group: Eddi Reader (female vocals), Mark Nevin (guitar), Simon Edwards (bass) and Roy Dodds (drums).

DEBUT	PEAK	WKS	A-side / B-side	Pop	$	Pic	Label & Number
1/28/89	85	2	Perfect .... *Mythology*	80	$3	■	RCA 8789

FALLS, Ruby   '77
Born Bertha Dorsey in 1946 in Jackson, Tennessee; raised in Milwaukee. Died on 6/15/86 (age 40). Black singer/songwriter.

DEBUT	PEAK	WKS	A-side / B-side	$	Label & Number
3/15/75	86	7	1 Sweet Country Music .... *Love Away The Wrong I'm About To Do*	$5	50 States 31
7/12/75	77	8	2 He Loves Me All To Pieces .... *Let's Spend Summer In The Country*	$5	50 States 33
2/7/76	81	9	3 Show Me Where .... *Somewhere There's A Rainbow Over Texas*	$5	50 States 39
7/17/76	81	7	4 Beware Of The Woman (Before She Gets To Your Man) ... *Jump In A River Of Tears*	$5	50 States 43
3/12/77	88	4	5 Do The Buck Dance .... *Too Many Hurts, Too Many Heartaches*	$5	50 States 50
9/24/77	40	8	6 You've Got To Mend This Heartache *Loves Sweeter Than Sugar*	$5	50 States 56
4/15/78	81	5	7 Three Nights A Week .... *Give Me Some Lovin'*	$5	50 States 60
			#15 Pop hit for **Fats Domino** in 1960		
9/30/78	86	3	8 If That's Not Loving You (You Can't Say I Didn't Try) .... *Nobody's Baby But Mine*	$5	50 States 63
6/9/79	56	7	9 I'm Gettin' Into Your Love .... *Midnight Rendezvous*	$5	50 States 70

FAMILY BROWN   '82
Canadian group featuring Tracey and Barry Brown.

DEBUT	PEAK	WKS	A-side / B-side	$	Label & Number
7/18/81	57	8	1 It's Really Love This Time .... *Nothing Really Changes*	$5	Ovation 1174
1/23/82	30	11	2 But It's Cheating *No One's Gonna Love Me (Like You Do)*	$4	RCA 13015
8/21/82	61	7	3 Some Never Stand A Chance .... *Arkansas Traveler*	$4	RCA 13285
10/22/83	67	5	4 We Really Got A Hold On Love .... *Mister And Misbehavin'*	$4	RCA 13565
3/3/84	56	10	5 Repeat After Me .... *Everyday People*	$4	RCA 13734

DEBUT	PEAK	WKS	Gold	A-side (Chart Hit)..B-side	Pop	$	Pic	Label & Number
				FAMILY BROWN — Cont'd				
11/30/85	66	7		6 Feel The Fire .... Comin' From A Blue Place		$4		RCA 50837
4/5/86	80	3		7 What If It's Right .... Guess Who		$4		RCA 50851

FARGO, Donna ★95★   '72
Born Yvonne Vaughan on 11/10/45 in Mount Airy, North Carolina. Singer/songwriter.

1)The Happiest Girl In The Whole U.S.A. 2)Funny Face 3)Superman 4)You Can't Be A Beacon 5)That Was Yesterday

DEBUT	PEAK	WKS	Gold	A-side ....B-side	Pop	$	Pic	Label & Number
3/25/72	$\mathbf{0}^3$	23	●	1 The Happiest Girl In The Whole U.S.A. The Awareness Of Nothing	11	$5	■	Dot 17409
				CMA Award: Single of the Year				
9/2/72	$\mathbf{0}^3$	16	●	2 Funny Face How Close You Came (To Being Gone)	5	$5		Dot 17429
2/17/73	$\mathbf{0}^1$	14		3 Superman Forever Is As Far As I Could Go	41	$5		Dot 17444
5/26/73	$\mathbf{0}^1$	14		4 You Were Always There He Can Have All He Wants	93	$5		Dot 17460
9/29/73	2^1	14		5 Little Girl Gone Just Call Me	57	$5	■	Dot 17476
2/23/74	6	12		6 I'll Try A Little Bit Harder All About A Feeling		$5		Dot 17491
6/8/74	$\mathbf{0}^1$	15		7 You Can't Be A Beacon (If Your Light Don't Shine) Just A Friend Of Mine	57	$5		Dot 17506
10/12/74+	9	15		8 U.S. Of A A Woman's Prayer	86	$5	■	ABC/Dot 17523
2/15/75	7	11		9 It Do Feel Good Only The Strong	98	$5		ABC/Dot 17541
6/7/75	14	14		10 Hello Little Bluebird .... 2 Sweet 2 Be 4 Gotten		$5		ABC/Dot 17557
10/4/75	38	11		11 Whatever I Say .... Rain Song		$5		ABC/Dot 17579
12/20/75+	58	7		12 What Will The New Year Bring? .... A Woman's Prayer		$5		ABC/Dot 17586
2/28/76	60	6		13 You're Not Charlie Brown (And I'm Not Raggedy Ann) .... Sing, Sing, Sing		$5		ABC/Dot 17609
4/3/76	20	10		14 Mr. Doodles If You Can't Love All Of Me		$5	■	Warner 8186
7/17/76	15	13		15 I've Loved You All Of The Way .... One Of God's Children		$5		Warner 8227
10/23/76+	3	19		16 Don't Be Angry You Don't Mess Around With Jim		$5		ABC/Dot 17660
2/12/77	9	13		17 Mockingbird Hill Second Choice		$5		Warner 8305
				#2 Pop hit for Patti Page in 1951				
4/30/77	$\mathbf{0}^1$	14		18 That Was Yesterday The Cricket Song		$5		Warner 8375
9/10/77	8	15		19 Shame On Me Hey, Mister Music Man		$5		Warner 8431
1/7/78	2^2	15		20 Do I Love You (Yes In Every Way) Dee Dee		$5		Warner 8509
5/27/78	19	11		21 Ragamuffin Man .... Everybody's Girl		$5		Warner 8578
8/26/78	10	13		22 Another Goodbye Changes In My Life		$4		Warner 8643
1/13/79	6	15		23 Somebody Special Changes In My Life		$4		Warner 8722
7/21/79	14	13		24 Daddy .... For The Rest Of My Life		$4		Warner 8867
11/17/79	45	7		25 Preacher Berry I Don't Know What I'd Do		$4		Warner 49093
3/8/80	43	7		26 Walk On By .... I Wrote This Song Just For You		$4		Warner 49183
8/9/80	63	7		27 Land Of Cotton I Still Believe In You		$4		Warner 49514
11/1/80	55	6		28 Seeing Is Believing .... Look What You've Done		$4		Warner 49575
8/1/81	73	6		29 Lonestar Cowboy Utah Song		$4	■	Warner 49757
11/21/81	72	4		30 Jacamo .... Song To Celebrate Life		$4		Warner 49852
7/10/82	40	9		31 It's Hard To Be The Dreamer (When I Used To Be The				
				Dream) .... I Just Saw My Reflection In You		$4		RCA 13264
10/9/82	80	3		32 Did We Have To Go This Far (To Say Goodbye) .... All I Need To Know		$4		RCA 13329
10/1/83	72	4		33 The Sign Of The Times .... Reasons To Be		$4		Columbia 04097
7/7/84	80	4		34 My Heart Will Always Belong To You .... Reasons To Be		$4		Cleveland Int'l 1
7/19/86	58	8		35 Woman Of The 80's S:33 She Never Knew Me		$3		Mercury 884712
11/8/86+	29	17		36 Me And You S:20 I've Laid Too Many Eggs		$3		Mercury 888093
6/27/87	23	15		37 Members Only .... S:21 Funny Face		$3		Mercury 888680
				DONNA FARGO AND BILLY JOE ROYAL				
2/16/91	71	2		38 Soldier Boy Stand Tall		$4		Cleveland Int'l 10
				#1 Pop hit for The Shirelles in 1962				
				FAUCETT, Dawnett '89				
				Female singer from Abilene, Texas.				
9/30/89	74	3		Money Don't Make A Man A Lover .... Cross My Broken Heart		$5		Step One 407
				FAUTHEREE, Jimmy Lee — see JIMMY & JOHNNY				
				FELICIANO, Jose '83				
				Born on 9/8/45 in Puerto Rico; raised in New York City. Blind since birth. Singer/guitarist. Won the 1968 Best New Artist Grammy Award.				
9/3/83	64	7		Let's Find Each Other Tonight .... Cuidado		$4		Motown 1674
				FELL, Terry '54				
				Born on 5/13/21 in Dora, Alabama. Male singer/songwriter/guitarist.				
8/7/54	4	11		Don't Drop It J:4 / S:11 / A:12 Truck Driving Man		$30		"X" 0010
				TERRY FELL & The Fellers				
				FELLER, Dick '74				
				Born on 1/2/43 in Bronaugh, Missouri. Singer/songwriter/guitarist.				
11/17/73+	22	11		1 Biff, The Friendly Purple Bear .... Goodbye California [S]	101	$5		United Artists 316
6/8/74	11	14		2 Makin' The Best Of A Bad Situation .... She's Taken A Gentle Lover [N]	85	$5		Asylum 11037
9/21/74	10	15		3 The Credit Card Song Just Short Of The Line [N]	105	$5		United Artists 535

FELLER, Dick — Cont'd

| 12/6/75+ | 49 | 9 | | 4 Uncle Hiram And The Homemade Beer ....*Let It Ride* [N] | | $5 | | Asylum 45290 |

FELTS, Narvel ★136★   '75

Born Albert Narvel Felts on 11/11/38 near Keiser, Arkansas. Singer/songwriter/guitarist. Known as "Narvel The Marvel." Member of **The Wolfpack.**

1)Reconsider Me 2)Lonely Teardrops 3)Drift Away 4)Somebody Hold Me 5)Funny How Time Slips Away

6/16/73	8	16		1 **Drift Away** *Foggy Misty Morning*		$6		Cinnamon 763
				#5 Pop hit for **Dobie Gray** in 1973				
10/13/73	13	13		2 All In The Name Of Love .... *Before You Have To Go*		$6		Cinnamon 771
1/19/74	14	14		3 When Your Good Love Was Mine .... *Fraulein*		$6		Cinnamon 779
4/27/74	39	11		4 Until The End Of Time ....*Someone To Give My Love To*		$6		Cinnamon 793
				NARVEL FELTS and SHARON VAUGHN				
5/11/74	26	13		5 I Want To Stay .... *Wrap My Arms Around The World*		$6		Cinnamon 798
9/14/74	33	13		6 Raindrops .... *Tilted Cup Of Love*		$6		Cinnamon 809
				#2 Pop hit for **Dee Clark** in 1961				
4/5/75	2[1]	21		7 **Reconsider Me** *Foggy Misty Morning*	67	$5		ABC/Dot 17549
8/23/75	12	15		8 Funny How Time Slips Away .... *No One Knows*		$5		ABC/Dot 17569
				written by **Willie Nelson;** #13 Pop hit for **Joe Hinton** in 1964				
12/6/75+	10	16		9 **Somebody Hold Me (Until She Passes By)** *Away*		$5		ABC/Dot 17598
4/3/76	5	16		10 **Lonely Teardrops** *I Remember You*	62	$5		ABC/Dot 17620
				#7 Pop hit for **Jackie Wilson** in 1959				
8/7/76	14	11		11 My Prayer .... *If Ever Two Were One (Then Surely We Are)*		$5		ABC/Dot 17643
				#1 Pop hit for **The Platters** in 1956				
11/13/76+	20	12		12 My Good Thing's Gone ....*I'm Afraid To Be Alone*		$5		ABC/Dot 17664
2/26/77	19	11		13 The Feeling's Right ....*Another Crazy Dream*		$5		ABC/Dot 17680
5/28/77	37	10		14 I Don't Hurt Anymore................................. *When We Were Together*		$5		ABC/Dot 17700
8/20/77	22	11		15 To Love Somebody...*Remember*		$5		ABC/Dot 17715
				#17 Pop hit for the **Bee Gees** in 1967				
12/3/77+	34	11		16 Please/				
		6		17 Blue Darlin'		$5		ABC/Dot 17731
3/18/78	30	10		18 Runaway .... *Free*		$5		ABC 12338
				#1 Pop hit for **Del Shannon** in 1961				
7/1/78	31	9		19 Just Keep It Up ....*Lonely Lady*		$5		ABC 12374
				#18 Pop hit for **Dee Clark** in 1959				
10/21/78	26	10		20 One Run For The Roses .... *(Darling) Lie To Me*		$5		ABC 12414
1/6/79	14	11		21 Everlasting Love .... *Small Enough To Crawl*		$5		ABC 12441
				#6 Pop hit for **Carl Carlton** in 1974				
4/21/79	43	8		22 Moment By Moment... *Never Again*		$5		MCA 41011
7/7/79	33	9		23 Tower Of Strength .... *You're A Heartbreaker*		$5		MCA 41055
				#5 Pop hit for **Gene McDaniels** in 1961				
10/20/79	73	4		24 Because Of Losing You..*After You*		$6		Collage 101
8/22/81	67	5		25 Louisiana Lonely................................*Look What Love Has Done*		$5		GMC 114
12/12/81	84	4		26 Fire In The Night................................*Look What Love Has Done*		$5		GMC 115
2/13/82	58	8		27 I'd Love You To Want Me .... *The First Time We Made Love*		$6		Lobo 3
				Lobo (backing vocal); #2 Pop hit for **Lobo** in 1972				
6/5/82	84	3		28 Sweet Southern Moonlight................................ *The First Time We Made Love*		$6		Lobo 8
7/17/82	64	6		29 Roll Over Beethoven .... *I'd Love You To Want Me*		$6		Lobo 11
				#29 Pop hit for **Chuck Berry** in 1956				
12/11/82	82	4		30 You're The Reason/				
11/13/82	84	3		31 Smoke Gets In Your Eyes...		$5		Compleat 101
				#1 Pop hit for **The Platters** in 1959				
4/2/83	52	9		32 Cry Baby .... *Now I Don't Have You To Lose*		$5		Compleat 104
9/17/83	79	4		33 Anytime You're Ready .... *Nobody's Fool*		$5		Evergreen 1011
12/10/83+	52	10		34 Fool .... *Anytime You're Ready*		$5		Evergreen 1014
3/10/84	70	6		35 You Lay So Easy On My Mind .... *Nobodys Fool*		$5		Evergreen 1017
6/30/84	53	8		36 Let's Live This Dream Together .... *Nobody's Fool*		$5		Evergreen 1022
10/6/84	63	5		37 I'm Glad You Couldn't Sleep Last Night .... *It Amazes Me*		$5		Evergreen 1025
1/5/85	51	10		38 Hey Lady .... *Anytime You're Ready*		$5		Evergreen 1027
6/1/85	68	4		39 If It Was Any Better (I Couldn't Stand It)................................ *Nobody's Fool*		$5		Evergreen 1030
9/7/85	71	5		40 Out Of Sight Out Of Mind .... *It Amazes Me*		$5		Evergreen 1034
				#23 Pop hit for **The Five Keys** in 1956				
6/7/86	70	5		41 Rockin' My Angel .... *Anytime You're Ready*		$5		Evergreen 1041
5/16/87	60	7		42 When A Man Loves A Woman .... *Hey Lady*		$5		Evergreen 1054
				#1 Pop hit for **Percy Sledge** in 1966				

FENDER, Freddy ★190★   **'75**
Born Baldemar Huerta on 6/4/37 in San Benito, Texas. Singer/songwriter/guitarist. Acted in the movie *The Milagro Beanfield War*. Joined the Texas Tornados in 1990.

1)Wasted Days And Wasted Nights 2)Before The Next Teardrop Falls 3)Secret Love
4)You'll Lose A Good Thing 5)Living It Down

1/11/75	❶²	17	●	1 Before The Next Teardrop Falls *Waiting For Your Love*	❶¹	$5		ABC/Dot 17540
				CMA Award: Single of the Year				
6/21/75	❶²	16	●	2 Wasted Days And Wasted Nights *I Love My Rancho Grande*	8	$5		ABC/Dot 17558
10/4/75	10	14		3 Since I Met You Baby *Little Mama*	45	$6		GRT 031
				#12 Pop hit for Ivory Joe Hunter in 1956				
10/11/75	❶¹	16		4 Secret Love *Loving Cajun Style*	20	$5		ABC/Dot 17585
				#1 Pop hit for Doris Day in 1954				
1/10/76	13	12		5 Wild Side Of Life .... Go On Baby (I Can Do Without You)		$6		GRT 039
2/7/76	❶¹	15		6 You'll Lose A Good Thing *I'm To Blame*	32	$5		ABC/Dot 17607
				#8 Pop hit for Barbara Lynn in 1962				
5/22/76	7	13		7 Vaya Con Dios *My Happiness*	59	$5		ABC/Dot 17627
				#1 Pop hit for Les Paul & Mary Ford in 1953				
9/18/76	2²	14		8 Living It Down *Take Her A Message! I'm Lonely*	72	$5		ABC/Dot 17652
3/19/77	4	15		9 The Rains Came/				
				#31 Pop hit for Sir Douglas Quintet in 1966				
		15		10 Sugar Coated Love		$5		ABC/Dot 17686
7/30/77	11	12		11 If You Don't Love Me (Why Don't You Just Leave Me				
				Alone) .... *Thank You! My Love*		$5		ABC/Dot 17713
11/26/77+	18	11		12 Think About Me .... If That's The Way You Want It (That's The Way It's Gonna Be)		$5		ABC/Dot 17730
3/11/78	34	9		13 If You're Looking For A Fool .... *Louisiana Woman*		$5		ABC 12339
6/17/78	13	12		14 Talk To Me .... *Please Mr. Sandman*	103	$5		ABC 12370
				#20 Pop hit for Little Willie John in 1958				
10/14/78	26	9		15 I'm Leaving It All Up To You .... When It Rains It Really Pours		$5		ABC 12415
				#1 Pop hit for Dale & Grace in 1963				
2/17/79	22	12		16 Walking Piece Of Heaven .... *Sweet Summer Day*		$5		ABC 12453
6/23/79	22	11		17 Yours .... *Rock Down In My Shoe*		$5		Starflite 4900
10/13/79	61	5		18 Squeeze Box .... *Turn Around*		$5		Starflite 4904
				#16 Pop hit for The Who in 1976				
1/12/80	83	3		19 My Special Prayer .... *Turn Around*		$5		Starflite 4906
4/5/80	82	3		20 Please Talk To My Heart .... *Walk Under A Snake*		$5		Starflite 4908
2/19/83	87	3		21 Chokin' Kind .... *I Might As Well Forget You*		$4		Warner 29794
				#13 Pop hit for Joe Simon in 1969				

FENDERMEN, The   **'60**
Duo of Jim Sundquist (from Niagara, Wisconsin) and Phil Humphrey (from Stoughton, Wisconsin). Both guitarists were born on 11/26/37.

7/11/60	16	8	Mule Skinner Blues .... *Torture*	5	$25		Soma 1137
			written in 1931 by **Jimmie Rodgers**; first released on Cuca 1003 in 1959 ($150)				

FENSTER, Zoot — see BARLOW, Jack

FERRARI, CW   **'88**
CW Ferrari is actually pianist Bill Ferreira.

3/19/88	76	4	Country Highways .... [I]		$5		Southern Snd. 1001

FINNEY, Maury   **'77**
Born in Humboldt, Minnesota. Saxophonist.

1)Coconut Grove 2)Lonely Wine 3)Rollin' In My Sweet Baby's Arms

1/3/76	84	9	1 Maiden's Prayer/ [F]				
			vocals by a female chorus				
		9	2 San Antonio Stroll [I]		$5		Soundwaves 4525
4/24/76	76	7	3 Rollin' In My Sweet Baby's Arms/ [I]				
4/24/76	78	7	4 Wild Side Of Life .... [I]		$5		Soundwaves 4531
9/4/76	81	7	5 Waltz Across Texas/ [I]				
		7	6 Off And Running .... [I]		$5		Soundwaves 4536
1/29/77	85	6	7 Everybody's Had The Blues .... Too Pretty For Words [I]		$5		Soundwaves 4541
6/25/77	72	10	8 Coconut Grove *It's Such A Pretty World Today*		$5		Soundwaves 4548
			vocals by a female chorus				
11/19/77	85	5	9 Poor People of Paris/ [I]				
			#1 Pop hit for Les Baxter in 1956				
		5	10 Almost Persuaded .... [I]		$5		Soundwaves 4557
4/15/78	88	6	11 I Don't Wanna Cry .... *Happy Sax* [I]		$5		Soundwaves 4566
8/12/78	84	7	12 Whispering .... Send Me The Pillow [I]		$5		Soundwaves 4572
			#1 Pop hit for Paul Whiteman in 1920				
2/3/79	92	2	13 Happy Sax .... *Faded Love* [I]		$5		Soundwaves 4578
6/16/79	93	2	14 Your Love Takes Me So High/ [I]				
		2	15 I Want To Play My Horn On The Grand Ole' Opry..............		$5		Soundwaves 4585
			vocals by Finney and a female chorus				
9/20/80	75	5	16 Lonely Wine *Misery And Gin* [I]		$5		Soundwaves 4613

FIRST EDITION, The — see ROGERS, Kenny

				FISCHOFF, George **'79**				
				Born on 8/3/38 in South Bend, Indiana. Pianist/songwriter.				
3/31/79	74	7		The Piano Picker .... *Love Dust* [I]		$5		Drive 6273
				FITZGERALD, Ella **'44**				
				Born on 4/25/18 in Newport News, Virginia. Died of diabetes on 6/15/96 (age 78). Legendary jazz singer. Won Grammy's Lifetime Achievement Award in 1967				
3/18/44	2[1]	1		When My Sugar Walks Down The Street *Cow-Cow Boogie (Pop #10)*	22	$20		Decca 18587
				ELLA FITZGERALD And Her Famous Orchestra				
				#2 Pop hit for Aileen Stanley & Gene Austin in 1925				
				5 RED CAPS **'44**				
				R&B vocal group from Los Angeles: Steve Gibson, Emmett Matthews, Dave Patillo, Jimmy Springs and Romaine Brown.				
4/29/44	2[1]	8		I Learned A Lesson, I'll Never Forget *Words Can't Explain*	14	$40		Beacon 7120
	★229★			**FLATT & SCRUGGS** **'63**				
				Bluegrass duo of Lester Flatt (guitar) and Earl Scruggs (banjo). Flatt was born on 6/19/14 in Overton County, Tennessee. Died on 5/11/79 (age 64). Scruggs was born on 1/6/24 in Flintville, North Carolina. Both were members of **Bill Monroe**'s band from 1944-48. Left Monroe to form the Foggy Mountain Boys. Joined the *Grand Ole Opry* in 1955. Elected to the Country Music Hall of Fame in 1985.				
				1)The Ballad Of Jed Clampett 2)Pearl Pearl Pearl 3)Cabin In The Hills 4)'Tis Sweet To Be Remembered 5)Go Home				
				LESTER FLATT, EARL SCRUGGS & The Foggy Mountain Boys:				
2/2/52	9	1		1 'Tis Sweet To Be Remembered *A:9 Earl's Breakdown*		$20		Columbia 4-20886
6/8/59	9	30		2 Cabin In The Hills *Someone You Have Forgotten*		$15		Columbia 41389
2/1/60	21	6		3 Crying My Heart Out Over You .... *Foggy Mountain Rock*		$15		Columbia 41518
12/5/60+	12	14		4 Polka On A Banjo .... *Shuckin' The Corn*		$15		Columbia 41786
10/9/61	10	16		5 Go Home *Where Will I Shelter My Sheep*		$15		Columbia 42141
4/7/62	16	8		6 Just Ain't .... *Cold, Cold Loving*		$15		Columbia 42280
6/23/62	27	1		7 The Legend Of The Johnson Boys ....*Hear The Whistle Blow A Hundred Miles*		$15		Columbia 42413
12/8/62+	❶[3]	20		8 The Ballad Of Jed Clampett *Coal Loadin' Johnny*	44	$15	■	Columbia 42606
				theme from the TV series *The Beverly Hillbillies* starring Buddy Ebsen (as "Jed Clampett")				
5/11/63	8	11		9 Pearl Pearl Pearl *Hard Travelin'*	113	$15	■	Columbia 42755
				"Cousin Pearl" (Bea Benaderet) was a featured character on TV's *The Beverly Hillbillies*				
9/28/63	26	3		10 New York Town ....*Mama Don't Allow It*		$15		Columbia 42840
2/15/64	12	18		11 You Are My Flower/		$15		
2/22/64	40	2		12 My Saro Jane		$15		Columbia 42954
				LESTER FLATT & EARL SCRUGGS:				
3/14/64	14	11		13 Petticoat Junction .... *Have You Seen My Dear Companion*		$15		Columbia 42982
				theme from the TV series starring Edgar Buchanan				
8/15/64	21	15		14 Workin' It Out .... *Fireball*		$12		Columbia 43080
3/13/65	43	10		15 I Still Miss Someone .... *Father's Table Grace*		$12		Columbia 43204
4/15/67	54	5		16 Nashville Cats .... *Roust-A-Bout*		$12		Columbia 44040
				#8 Pop hit for The Lovin' Spoonful in 1967				
7/29/67	20	14		17 California Up Tight Band .... *Last Train To Clarksville*		$12	■	Columbia 44194
				FLATT & SCRUGGS:				
1/13/68	45	8		18 Down In The Flood/		$12		
4/6/68	58	6		19 Foggy Mountain Breakdown ....[I]	55	$12		Columbia 44380
				from the movie *Bonnie & Clyde* starring Warren Beatty and Faye Dunaway; also charted on Mercury 72739 as "Theme From Bonnie & Clyde (Foggy Mountain Breakdown)"				
9/14/68	58	8		20 Like A Rolling Stone .... *I'd Like To Say A Word For Texas*	125	$12		Columbia 44623
				#2 Pop hit for Bob Dylan in 1965				
				FLETCHER, Vicky **'74**				
7/20/74	92	3		1 Touching Me, Touching You.................... *That's The Way We Fall In Love*		$5		Columbia 46043
6/12/76	97	2		2 Ain't It Good To Be In Love Again................... *Countin' Charlie's Ribs*		$6		Music Row 213
				FLORES, Rosie **'87**				
				Born in San Antonio, Texas; raised in San Diego. Joined **Asleep At The Wheel** in 1997.				
9/12/87	51	10		1 Crying Over You .... *Midnight To Moonlight*		$3	■	Reprise 28250
12/26/87+	67	6		2 Somebody Loses, Somebody Wins .... *Heart Beats To A Different Drum*		$3		Reprise 28134
7/9/88	74	3		3 He Cares .... *One-Track Mem'ry*		$3		Reprise 27980
				FLOYD, Charlie **'94**				
				Born in Aynor, South Carolina. Singer/songwriter/guitarist.				
10/23/93	75	1		1 I've Fallen In Love (And I Can't Get Up)		$3	▌	Liberty 58051
1/1/94	58	7		2 Good Girls Go To Heaven		$3	▌	album cut
				from the album *Charlie's Nite Life* on Liberty 80475				
				FLYING BURRITO BROTHERS — see BURRITO BROTHERS				
				FOGELBERG, Dan **'85**				
				Born on 8/13/51 in Peoria, Illinois. Singer/songwriter/guitarist. Charted 14 pop hits from 1975-87.				
2/16/80	85	8		1 Longer.. *Along The Road*	2[2]	$4		Full Moon 50824
4/20/85	56	16		2 Go Down Easy .... *High Country Snows*	85	$3		Full Moon 04835
8/24/85	33	13		3 Down The Road Mountain Pass .... *High Country Snows*		$3		Full Moon 05446
				written by Flatt & Scruggs				
				FOGERTY, John **'85**				
				Born on 5/28/45 in Berkeley, California. Leader of **Creedence Clearwater Revival**.				
2/10/73	66	6		1 Jambalaya (On The Bayou)................... *Workin' On A Building*	16	$5		Fantasy 689
				THE BLUE RIDGE RANGERS				
2/2/85	38	11		2 Big Train (From Memphis) .... *The Old Man Down The Road (Pop #10)*		$4	■	Warner 29100
8/16/97	67	2		3 Southern Streamline				album cut
				from the album *Blue Moon Swamp* on Warner 45426				

DEBUT	PEAK	WKS	Gold	A-side (Chart Hit)..B-side	Pop	$	Pic	Label & Number

FOLEY, Betty '55
Born on 2/3/33 in Chicago; raised in Berea, Kentucky. Daughter of **Red Foley**.

DEBUT	PEAK	WKS	A-side / B-side	Pop	$	Label & Number
3/6/54	8	10	1 As Far As I'm Concerned *A:8 / J:8 / S:11 Tennessee Whistling Man* RED FOLEY and BETTY FOLEY		$20	Decca 29000
6/25/55	3	23	2 Satisfied Mind *J:3 / S:4 / A:6 How About Me* RED FOLEY And BETTY FOLEY		$20	Decca 29526
8/31/59	7	12	3 Old Moon *Magic Love*		$25	Bandera 1304

FOLEY, Red ★29★ '50
Born Clyde Foley on 6/17/10 in Blue Lick, Kentucky. Died of a heart attack on 9/19/68 (age 58). On the WLS *National Barn Dance* from 1930-37 and the *Renfro Valley Show* from 1937-39. Member of the *Grand Ole Opry* from 1946-54. Hosted the *Ozark Jubilee* series on ABC-TV from 1954-60. Regular on TV's *Mr. Smith Goes To Washington*. **Pat Boone** married his daughter Shirley in 1953. Elected to the Country Music Hall of Fame in 1967.

1)Smoke On The Water 2)Chattanoogie Shoe Shine Boy 3)Birmingham Bounce 4)Goodnight Irene 5)New Jolie Blonde

DEBUT	PEAK	WKS	A-side / B-side	Pop	$	Label & Number
8/26/44	❶¹³	27	1 Smoke On The Water/	7		
9/30/44	5	1	2 There's A Blue Star Shining Bright (In A Window Tonight)		$20	Decca 6102
6/23/45	4	2	3 Hang Your Head In Shame/			
6/23/45	5	1	4 I'll Never Let You Worry My Mind		$20	Decca 6108
9/8/45	❶¹	14	5 Shame On You/	13		
11/10/45	3	2	6 At Mail Call Today		$20	Decca 18698
			LAWRENCE WELK AND HIS ORCHESTRA with RED FOLEY (above 2)			
5/4/46	4	1	7 Harriet *My Poor Little Heart Is Broken*		$20	Decca 9003
11/30/46	5	1	8 Have I Told You Lately That I Love You *Atomic Power*		$20	Decca 46014
			RED FOLEY with Roy Ross & His Ramblers (above 2) from the movie *Over The Trail*; also see #65 below			
			RED FOLEY and The Cumberland Valley Boys:			
3/15/47	4	1	9 That's How Much I Love You *Rye Whiskey*		$20	Decca 46028
4/5/47	❶²	16	10 New Jolie Blonde (New Pretty Blonde) *A Pillow Of Sighs And Tears*		$20	Decca 46034
6/21/47	5	1	11 Freight Train Boogie *Rockin' Chair Money*		$20	Decca 46035
11/22/47	2¹	13	12 Never Trust A Woman *A Smile Will Chase Away A Tear*		$20	Decca 46074
10/2/48+	❶¹	40	13 Tennessee Saturday Night/ *A:❶¹ / S:3*		$20	Decca 46136
5/14/49	15	1	14 Blues In My Heart...S:15			
			RED FOLEY:			
4/2/49	3	21	15 Tennessee Border/ *J:3 / S:4*			
3/26/49	4	15	16 Candy Kisses *J:4 / S:6*		$20	Decca 46151
6/25/49	4	13	17 Tennessee Polka/ *J:4 / S:6*			
7/23/49	11	2	18 I'm Throwing Rice (At The Girl I Love) ....S:11 / J:14		$20	Decca 46170
8/6/49	8	4	19 Two Cents, Three Eggs And A Postcard *J:8 I Wish I Had A Nickel*		$20	Decca 46165
12/17/49+	3	6	20 Sunday Down In Tennessee *A:3 / J:3 / S:10 Every Step Of The Way*		$20	Decca 46197
12/31/49+	2²	10	21 Tennessee Border No. 2/ *S:2 / J:2* RED FOLEY and ERNEST TUBB		$20	Decca 46200
1/21/50	7	2	22 Don't Be Ashamed Of Your Age *J:7 / A:9* ERNEST TUBB and RED FOLEY			
1/14/50	8	1	23 Careless Kisses/ *J:8 / S:14*			
1/7/50	10	1	24 I Gotta Have My Baby Back *J:10 / S:13*		$20	Decca 46201
1/21/50	❶¹³	20	● 25 Chattanoogie Shoe Shine Boy/ *A:❶¹³ / J:❶¹³ / S:❶¹²* ❶⁸		$20	Decca 46205
2/18/50	4	11	26 Sugarfoot Rag *J:4 / A:8* 24			
			Hank "Sugarfoot" Garland (guitar solo)			
5/6/50	9	1	27 Steal Away/ *S:9*			
7/22/50	9	5	28 Just A Closer Walk With Thee *S:9* RED FOLEY With The Jordanaires		$25	Decca Faith 9-14505
5/13/50	❶⁴	15	29 Birmingham Bounce/ *S:❶⁴ / J:❶³ / A:4* 14			
6/3/50	5	4	30 Choc'late Ice Cream Cone *A:5 / J:8 / S:10*		$25	Decca 9-46234
6/3/50	❶¹	14	31 Mississippi *J:❶¹ / S:2 / A:3 Old Kentucky Fox Chase*		$25	Decca 9-46241
			RED FOLEY with The Dixie Dons (above 2)			
8/12/50	❶³	15	32 Goodnight Irene/ *J:❶³ / S:❶² / A:2* 10			
			RED FOLEY-ERNEST TUBB with The Sunshine Trio #1 Pop hit for Gordon Jenkins & The Weavers in 1950			
9/2/50	9	2	33 Hillbilly Fever No. 2 *J:9* ERNEST TUBB-RED FOLEY		$25	Decca 9-46255
9/9/50	2¹	12	34 Cincinnati Dancing Pig *S:2 / J:3 / A:6 Somebody's Crying* 7		$25	Decca 9-46261
11/4/50	8	4	35 Our Lady Of Fatima *S:8 The Rosary* 16		$25	Decca Faith 9-14526
2/17/51	6	1	36 My Heart Cries For You *A:6 Tater Pie* 28		$25	Decca 9-27378
			EVELYN KNIGHT and RED FOLEY			
2/17/51	7	3	37 Hot Rod Race *S:7 / J:8 / A:10 Smoke On The Water No. 2*		$25	Decca 9-46286
5/12/51	8	3	38 Hobo Boogie *J:8 Heska-Holka (Pretty Girl)*		$25	Decca 9-46304
5/19/51	9	1	39 The Strange Little Girl *J:9 Kentucky Waltz*		$25	Decca 9-46311
			RED FOLEY and ERNEST TUBB with Anita Kerr Singers			
7/7/51	5	11	● 40 There'll Be Peace In The Valley For Me *A:5 / J:5 / S:7 Old Soldiers Never Die* RED FOLEY With The Sunshine Boys Quartet		$25	Decca 9-46319

DEBUT	PEAK	WKS	Gold	A-side (Chart Hit)..B-side	Pop	$	Pic	Label & Number
				FOLEY, Red — Cont'd				
11/24/51	3	16		41 **Alabama Jubilee** J:3 / S:5 / A:6 *Dixie*	28	$25		Decca 9-27810
				RED FOLEY with The Nashville Dixielanders				
2/2/52	5	9		42 **Too Old To Cut The Mustard** S:5 / J:8 / A:10 *I'm In Love With Molly*		$25		Decca 9-46387
				ERNEST TUBB And RED FOLEY				
3/8/52	8	3		43 **Milk Bucket Boogie/** J:8				
3/29/52	8	2		44 **Salty Dog Rag** J:8		$25		Decca 9-27981
11/15/52+	❶¹	11		45 **Midnight** S:❶¹ / J:2 / A:5 *Deep Blues*		$20		Decca 28420
1/10/53	8	2		46 **Don't Let The Stars Get In Your Eyes** S:8 *Sally*		$20		Decca 28460
				#1 Pop hit for Perry Como in 1953				
3/21/53	6	4		47 **Hot Toddy** J:6 / S:10 *Playin' Dominoes And Shootin' Dice*		$20		Decca 28587
4/18/53	7	2		48 **No Help Wanted #2** S:7 / J:9 *You're A Real Good Friend*		$20		Decca 28634
				ERNEST TUBB - RED FOLEY				
5/9/53	8	1		49 **Slaves Of A Hopeless Love Affair** J:8 *Blue Letter*		$20		Decca 28567
10/10/53	6	4		50 **Shake A Hand** S:6 / J:7 / A:10 *Stranded In Deep Water*		$20		Decca 28839
				RED FOLEY with Anita Kerr Singers				
				#1 R&B hit for Faye Adams in 1953				
3/6/54	8	10		51 **As Far As I'm Concerned** A:8 / J:8 / S:11 *Tennessee Whistling Man*		$20		Decca 29000
				RED FOLEY and BETTY FOLEY				
5/8/54	7	4		52 **Jilted** J:7 / S:9 *Pin Ball Boogie*		$20		Decca 29100
				KITTY WELLS AND RED FOLEY:				
5/22/54	❶¹	41		53 **One By One/** J:❶¹ / A:2 / S:2				
7/10/54	12	1		54 **I'm A Stranger In My Home** A:12 / S:15		$20		Decca 29065
1/8/55	4	15		55 **Hearts Of Stone** A:4 / J:4 / S:6 *Never*		$20		Decca 29375
				RED FOLEY with Anita Kerr Singers				
				#1 Pop hit for The Fontane Sisters in 1955				
2/26/55	3	16		56 **As Long As I Live/** J:3 / S:7 / A:8				
2/26/55	6	17		57 **Make Believe ('Til We Can Make It Come True)** J:6 / S:7 / A:14		$20		Decca 29390
6/25/55	3	23		58 **Satisfied Mind** J:3 / S:4 / A:6 *How About Me*		$20		Decca 29526
				RED FOLEY And BETTY FOLEY				
1/28/56	3	31		59 **You And Me/** S:3 / A:3 / J:8		$20		Decca 29740
			6	60 **No One But You** S:flip / J:flip				
6/29/59	29	1		61 **Travelin' Man** *Just This Side Of Memphis*		$20		Decca 30882
				RED FOLEY				
5/6/67	43	11		62 **Happiness Means You/**				
6/3/67	60	5		63 **Hello Number One**		$8		Decca 32126
12/30/67+	63	4		64 **Living As Strangers** *Loved And Wanted*		$8		Decca 32223
1/18/69	74	2		65 **Have I Told You Lately That I Love You?** *We Need One More Chance* [R]		$8		Decca 32427
				new version of #8 above				

FORD, Joy '79

Born on 3/10/46 in Brilliant, Alabama; raised in Chicago and Poplar Bluff, Missouri.

DEBUT	PEAK	WKS		A-side .... B-side		$		Label & Number
12/16/78+	87	4		1 **Love Isn't Love (Til You Give It Away)** *Another Favour*		$5		Country Int'l. 134
10/13/79	97	4		2 **Take My Love** *I Love The Way You Love On Me*		$5		Country Int'l. 142
3/26/83	97	1		3 **You Are The Music In Time With My Heart** *Carousel*		$5		Country Int'l. 190
8/10/85	96	2		4 **Melted Down Memories** *Big City Turn Me Loose*		$5		Country Int'l. 206
8/20/88	99	1		5 **Yesterday's Rain**		$5		Country Int'l. 216

FORD, Shelley — see CHEVALIER, Jay

FORD, Tennessee Ernie ★117★ '51

Born on 2/13/19 in Fordtown, Tennessee. Died of liver failure on 10/17/91 (age 72). Worked as a DJ. Hosted own TV series from 1955-65. Known as "The Old Pea Picker." Elected to the Country Music Hall of Fame in 1990.

1)The Shot Gun Boogie 2)Sixteen Tons 3)Mule Train 4)The Cry Of The Wild Goose 5)I'll Never Be Free

DEBUT	PEAK	WKS		**TENNESSEE ERNIE:** A-side .... B-side	Pop	$		Label & Number
4/30/49	8	1		1 **Tennessee Border** J:8 / S:15 *I Got The Milk 'Em In The Morning Blues*		$20		Capitol 15400
5/28/49	14	1		2 **Country Junction** J:14 *Philadelphia Lawyer*		$20		Capitol 15430
9/10/49	8	4		3 **Smokey Mountain Boogie** S:8 / J:13 *You'll Find Her Name Written There*		$20		Capitol 40212
11/26/49	❶⁴	10		4 **Mule Train/** A:❶⁴ / J:3 / S:4	9			
				#1 Pop hit for Frankie Laine in 1949				
12/10/49	3	11		5 **Anticipation Blues** A:3 / S:5 / J:8		$20		Capitol 40258
2/11/50	2²	10		6 **The Cry Of The Wild Goose** S:2 / A:3 / J:5 *The Donkey Serenade*	15	$25		Capitol F40280
				#1 Pop hit for Frankie Laine in 1950				
9/16/50	2¹	16		7 **I'll Never Be Free/** A:2 / J:2 / S:4	3			
8/26/50	5	6		8 **Ain't Nobody's Business But My Own** A:5 / J:10	22	$25		Capitol F1124
				KAY STARR and TENNESSEE ERNIE (above 2)				
12/16/50+	❶¹⁴	25		9 **The Shot Gun Boogie** J:❶¹⁴ / S:❶³ / A:❶¹ *I Ain't Gonna Let It Happen No More*	14	$25		Capitol F1295
3/3/51	8	2		10 **Tailor Made Woman** J:8 *Stack-O-Lee*		$25		Capitol F1349
				TENNESSEE ERNIE and JOE "FINGERS" CARR				
6/16/51	2¹	7		11 **Mr. And Mississippi** A:2 / S:4 / J:6 *She's My Baby*	18	$25		Capitol F1521
6/16/51	9	1		12 **The Strange Little Girl** S:9 *Kentucky Waltz*		$25		Capitol F1470
9/20/52	6	7		13 **Blackberry Boogie** J:6 / A:9 / S:9 *Tennessee Local*		$25		Capitol F2170
6/6/53	8	3		14 **Hey, Mr. Cotton Picker** J:8 *Three Things (A Man Must Do)*		$20		Capitol 2443

DEBUT	PEAK	WKS	Gold	A-side (Chart Hit)..B-side	Pop	$	Pic	Label & Number
				TENNESSEE ERNIE FORD:				
8/14/54	9	9	15	River Of No Return S:9 *Give Me Your Word*		$20		Capitol 2810
				from the movie starring **Robert Mitchum** and Marilyn Monroe				
3/26/55	4	16	16	Ballad Of Davy Crockett S:4 / J:5 / A:6 *Farewell*	5	$20		Capitol 3058
				from the ABC-TV *Disneyland* series starring Fess Parker as "Davy Crockett"				
7/9/55	13	2	17	His Hands .... S:13 *I Am A Pilgrim*		$20		Capitol 3135
11/12/55	❶[10]	21	● 18	Sixteen Tons S:❶[10] / J:❶[7] / A:❶[3]	❶[8]	$20		Capitol 3262
3/17/56	12	5	19	That's All .... S:12 *Bright Lights And Blonde-Haired Women*	17	$20		Capitol 3343
6/26/65	9	16	20	Hicktown *Sixteen Tons*		$15		Capitol 5425
7/26/69	54	3	21	Honey-Eyed Girl (That's You That's You) ....*Good Morning, Dear*		$10		Capitol 2522
4/24/71	58	9	22	Happy Songs Of Love .... *Don't Let The Good Life Pass You By*		$8		Capitol 3079
3/31/73	66	4	23	Printers Alley Stars ....*Baby*		$8		Capitol 3556
7/14/73	73	5	24	Farther Down The River (Where The Fishin's Good) ....*You've Still Got Love All Over You*		$8		Capitol 3631
9/22/73	70	7	25	Colorado Country Morning ....*Daddy Usta Say*		$8		Capitol 3704
1/4/75	52	8	26	Come On Down ....*Bits And Pieces Of Life*		$8		Capitol 3916
4/19/75	63	9	27	Baby ....*I'd Like To Be*		$6		Capitol 4044
				TENNESSEE ERNIE FORD & ANDRA WILLIS				
11/22/75	96	4	28	The Devil Ain't A Lonely Woman's Friend ....*Smokey Taverns, Bar Room Girls*		$6		Capitol 4160
7/31/76	95	3	29	I Been To Georgia On A Fast Train ....*Baby's Home*		$6		Capitol 4285

FORESTER SISTERS, The ★157★ '86

Family vocal group from Lookout Mountain, Georgia: Kathy (b: 1/4/55), Kim (b: 11/4/60), June (b: 9/22/56), and Christy (b: 12/21/62) Forester.

1)Just In Case 2)Too Much Is Not Enough 3)You Again 4)Mama's Never Seen Those Eyes
5)I Fell In Love Again Last Night

DEBUT	PEAK	WKS		A-side		$	Pic	Label & Number
1/26/85	10	22	1	(That's What You Do) When You're In Love S:9 / A:12 *Yankee Don't Go Home*		$3		Warner 29114
6/29/85	❶[1]	22	2	I Fell In Love Again Last Night S:❶[1] / A:❶[1] *Dixie Man*		$3		Warner 28988
11/2/85+	❶[1]	20	3	Just In Case S:❶[1] / A:❶[1] *Reckless Night*		$3		Warner 28875
3/15/86	❶[1]	22	4	Mama's Never Seen Those Eyes S:❶[1] / A:❶[1] *Something Tells Me*		$3		Warner 28795
7/5/86	2[2]	24	5	Lonely Alone A:❶[1] / S:2 *Heartless Night*		$3		Warner 28687
9/27/86	❶[1]	20	6	Too Much Is Not Enough S:❶[1] / A:❶[1] *Restless*		$3		Curb/MCA 52917
				THE BELLAMY BROTHERS with The Forester Sisters				
3/7/87	5	23	7	Too Many Rivers S:8 / A:8 *If I'm Gonna Fall (I'm Gonna Fall In Love)*		$3		Warner 28442
				#13 Pop hit for **Brenda Lee** in 1965				
6/27/87	❶[1]	24	8	You Again S:6 *Whatever You Do, Don't*		$3		Warner 28368
10/31/87+	5	25	9	Lyin' In His Arms Again S:11 *Wrap Me Up*		$3		Warner 28208
6/25/88	9	24	10	Letter Home S:23 *These Lips Don't Know How To Say Goodbye*		$3		Warner 27839
11/5/88+	8	22	11	Sincerely S:30 *On The Other Side Of The Gate*		$3		Warner 27686
				#1 Pop hit for **The McGuire Sisters** in 1955				
2/18/89	7	20	12	Love Will *You Love Me*		$3		Warner 27575
6/24/89	9	18	13	Don't You *All I Need*		$3	■	Warner 22943
11/25/89+	7	26	14	Leave It Alone *I Fell In Love Again Last Night*		$3		Warner 22773
4/14/90	63	7	15	Drive South ....*You Can't Have A Good Time Without Me*		$3		Warner 19874
				THE FORESTER SISTERS with The Bellamy Brothers				
8/25/90	63	3	16	Nothing's Gonna Bother Me Tonight ....*Born To Give My Love To You*		$3	▌	Warner 19744
1/26/91	8	20	17	Men *Just In Case*		$3		Warner 19450
6/29/91	62	5	18	Too Much Fun.................................*The Blues Don't Stand A Chance*		$3		Warner 19291
3/14/92	74	3	19	What'll You Do About Me...*Men*		$3		Warner 19047
7/18/92	58	6	20	I Got A Date *Show Me A Woman*		$3		Warner 18906

FORMAN, Peggy '81

Born in Centerville, Louisiana. Singer/songwriter.

DEBUT	PEAK	WKS		A-side		$	Pic	Label & Number
8/20/77	98	4	1	The Danger Zone ....*Yours To Hurt Tomorrow*		$5		MCA 40757
5/24/80	89	4	2	There Ain't Nothing Like A Rainy Night ....*Sugar On Your Lies*		$5		Dimension 1006
8/2/80	78	5	3	Burning Up Your Memory ....*Sugar On Your Lies*		$5		Dimension 1008
7/4/81	70	6	4	You're More To Me (Than He's Ever Been) ....*Steppin' Aside Ain't My Style*		$5		Dimension 1020
10/24/81	54	6	5	I Wish You Could Have Turned My Head (And Left My Heart Alone) *Falling Out Of Love*		$5		Dimension 1023
2/27/82	71	6	6	That's What Your Lovin' Does To Me ....*Foolish Talkin'*		$5		Dimension 1027

FORREST, Sylvia '89

| 9/23/89 | 84 | 2 | | The Nights Are Never Long Enough With You .... | | $5 | | Door Knob 319 |

FOSTER, Jerry '74

Born on 11/19/35 in Tallapoosa, Missouri. Singer/songwriter/guitarist.

8/18/73	98	3	1	Copperhead ....*Ain't It Sad*		$6		Cinnamon 764
12/8/73+	51	13	2	Looking Back ....*Hard To Handle*		$6		Cinnamon 774
				#5 Pop hit for **Nat King Cole** in 1958				
11/27/76	86	6	3	I Knew You When ....*One*		$5		Hitsville 6043
7/15/78	84	3	4	I Want To Love You ....*My Baby Left Me*		$5		Monument 256
				JERRY FOSTER and TENNESSEE TORNADO				

FOSTER, Lloyd David   '83
Born in 1952 in Wills Point, Texas. Singer/songwriter/guitarist.

6/19/82	32	13		1 Blue Rendezvous *Love At First Sight*		$4		MCA 52061
10/23/82	65	7		2 Honky Tonk Magic .... *The First Time I Saw Her (Was The Last Time)*		$4		MCA 52123
2/26/83	32	12		3 Unfinished Business .... *It Takes One To Know One*		$4		MCA 52173
9/3/83	60	6		4 You've Got That Touch.. *Just Once*		$4		MCA 52248
11/24/84+	44	15		5 I'm Gonna Love You Right Out Of The Blues .... *Wishful Drinkin'*		$3		Columbia 04670
4/13/85	55	9		6 I Can Feel The Fire Goin' Out.............................. *Anywhere You Want To Go*		$3		Columbia 04836
10/12/85	68	6		7 I'm As Over You As I'm Ever Gonna Get .... *Anywhere You Want To Go*		$3		Columbia 05601

FOSTER, Radney   '93
Born on 7/20/59 in Del Rio, Texas. Half of **Foster & Lloyd** duo.

8/15/92	10	20		1 Just Call Me Lonesome *Louisiana Blue*		$3		Arista 12448
1/23/93	2[2]	20		2 Nobody Wins *Don't Say Goodbye*		$3		Arista 12512
6/12/93	20	20		3 Easier Said Than Done .... *Don't Say Goodbye*		$3		Arista 12564
10/9/93	34	11		4 Hammer And Nails .... *A Fine Line*		$3		Arista 12608
2/26/94	59	6		5 Closing Time .... *Old Silver*		$3		Arista 12652
7/9/94	58	7		6 Labor Of Love.. *Jesse's Soul*		$3	▮	Arista 12716
10/29/94	64	5		7 The Running Kind .... *Silver Wings (Pam Tillis)*		$3		Arista 12758
				written by **Merle Haggard**				
4/1/95	54	8		8 Willin' To Walk .... *Last Chance For Love*		$3	▮	Arista 12752
9/2/95	59	5		9 If It Were Me .... *Walkin' Talkin' Woman*		$3	▮	Arista 12861

FOSTER, Sally — see HOOSIER HOT SHOTS

★359★   FOSTER & LLOYD   '88
Duo of singers/songwriters/guitarists **Radney Foster** and Bill Lloyd. Foster was born on 7/20/59 in Del Rio, Texas. Lloyd was born on 12/6/55 in Bowling Green, Kentucky.

7/4/87	4	21		1 Crazy Over You S:7 *The Part I Know By Heart*		$3	☐	RCA 5210
11/7/87+	8	21		2 Sure Thing S:15 *Hart To Say No*		$3	▮	RCA 5281
4/9/88	18	17		3 Texas In 1880 S:29 *Token Of Love*		$3		RCA 6900
8/6/88	6	23		4 What Do You Want From Me This Time S:17 *Don't Go Out With Him*		$3		RCA 8633
1/28/89	5	17		5 Fair Shake *After I'm Gone*		$3		RCA 8795
6/3/89	43	11		6 Before The Heartache Rolls In................................... *Happy For A While*		$3		RCA 8942
8/19/89	48	8		7 Suzette .... *I'll Always Be Here Loving You*		$3		RCA 9028
4/7/90	43	14		8 Is It Love .... *Workin' On Me*		$3		RCA 2502
11/24/90+	38	12		9 Can't Have Nothin' .... *Workin' On Me*		$3	▮	RCA 2635

FOUR GUYS, The   '82
Vocal group from Steubenville, Ohio: Brent Burkett, Sam Wellington, Gary Chadwick and Gary Buck (not to be confused with the solo singer). Buck was formerly married to **Louise Mandrell**. Buck was replaced by Laddie Cain in 1980. Chadwick was replaced by John Frost in 1981. Group joined the *Grand Ole Opry* in 1967.

10/19/74	88	3		1 Too Late To Turn Back Now .... *Gatherin' Dust*		$5		RCA Victor 10055
12/8/79	93	4		2 Mama Rocked Us To Sleep (With Country Music) .... *Forever In Blue Jeans*		$6		Collage 102
3/13/82	85	4		3 Made In The U.S.A... *Pretty Lady*		$6		J&B 1001

4 RUNNER   '95
Vocal group: Craig Morris, Billy Crittenden, Lee Hilliard and Jim Chapman.

3/18/95	26	20		1 Cain's Blood S:6 *Ten Pound Hammer*	118	$3	▮	Polydor 851622
7/1/95	51	10		2 A Heart With 4 Wheel Drive... *Southern Wind*		$3	▮	Polydor 579450
10/14/95	65	4		3 Home Alone .... *You Make The Moonlight*		$3		Polydor 577040
1/20/96	57	9		4 Ripples .... *Oh No*		$3	▮	Polydor 577730
7/6/96	54	12		5 That Was Him (This Is Now)........................... *Let The Good Times Roll*		$3	▮	A&M 581650

FOWLER, Ken   '86

2/8/86	96	2		You're A Heartache To Follow .... *The Way That I Remember You*		$6	▮	Deja Vu 111

FOWLER, Wally — see TENNESSEE VALLEY BOYS

FOX, Dolly   '78

12/9/78	93	2		I've Got A Reason For Living.................. *Who's Gonna Love Me (When You're Gone)*		$6		Artic 1025

FOX, Kent   '73
Born Walter Kent Fox on 10/16/47 in Lexington, Kentucky.

6/2/73	73	4		New York Callin' Miami.............................. *Have Patience ('Til I Learn To Love You)*		$5		MCA 40038

FOXFIRE   '79
Vocal trio: Dave Hall, Russ Allison and Don Miller.

6/9/79	30	10		1 Fell Into Love .... *Head Over Heels In Love With You*		$5		NSD 24
4/26/80	38	9		2 I Can See Forever Loving You .... *Dreaming Won't Take Me That Far*		$4		Elektra 46625
11/15/80	55	8		3 Whatever Happened To Those Drinking Songs.............. *Do That To Me Again*		$4		Elektra 47070

FOXTON, Kelly — see SNOW, Hank

FOXWORTHY, Jeff   '95
Born on 9/6/58 in Atlanta; raised in Hapeville, Georgia. Comedian/actor. Starred in own TV sitcom, 1995-97.

9/10/94	67	8		1 Redneck Stomp... S:8 *Words In The South* [C]	75	$3	▮	Warner 18116
7/8/95	53	17		2 Party All Night .... S:5 *Southern Accent* [C]	101	$3	▮	Warner 17806
				JEFF FOXWORTHY with Little Texas				
12/16/95	18	5		3 Redneck 12 Days Of Christmas *'Twas The Night After Christmas* [X-N]		$3		Warner 17526
6/8/96	42	12		4 Redneck Games .... S:2 *NASA & Alabama & Fishing Shows* [N]	66	$3	▮	Warner 17648
				JEFF FOXWORTHY with Alan Jackson				

FOXWORTHY, Jeff — Cont'd

DEBUT	PEAK	WKS		A-side / B-side	Pop	$	Pic	Label & Number
12/14/96	39	5		5 Redneck 12 Days Of Christmas/ [X-N-R]				
12/28/96	67	2		6 'Twas The Night After Christmas ....[X-C]		$3		Warner 17526
12/27/97	39	3		7 Redneck 12 Days Of Christmas .... 'Twas The Night After Christmas [X-N-R]		$3		Warner 17526

FRADY, Garland '73
Born in Lexington, North Carolina. Band leader for **Bob Luman** and **Dorsey Burnette**.

DEBUT	PEAK	WKS		A-side / B-side	Pop	$	Pic	Label & Number
8/18/73	89	7		The Barrooms Have Found You............................... Silver Moon		$7		Countryside 45104

FRANCIS, Cleve '92
Born Cleveland Francis on 4/22/45 in Jennings, Louisiana. Black male singer. Worked as a cardiologist in Alexandria, Virginia.

DEBUT	PEAK	WKS		A-side / B-side	Pop	$	Pic	Label & Number
1/18/92	52	11		1 Love Light ....Happy		$3		Liberty 57728
5/2/92	47	14		2 You Do My Heart Good				album cut
9/19/92	74	2		3 How Can I Hold You				album cut
				above 2 from the album Tourist In Paradise on Liberty 96498				
5/8/93	63	8		4 Walkin'				album cut
				from the album Walkin' on Liberty 80033				

FRANCIS, Connie '60
Born Concetta Rosa Maria Franconero on 12/12/38 in Newark, New Jersey. Charted 56 pop hits from 1957-69.

DEBUT	PEAK	WKS		A-side / B-side	Pop	$	Pic	Label & Number
7/25/60	24	3	●	1 Everybody's Somebody's Fool ....Jealous Of You (Pop #19)	❶²	$15	■	MGM 12899
3/1/69	33	10		2 The Wedding Cake .... Over Hill Underground	91	$8		MGM 14034
3/12/83	84	3		3 There's Still A Few Good Love Songs Left In Me....... Let's Make It Love Tonight		$4		Polydor 810087

FRANKS, Tillman '64
Born on 9/29/20 in Stamps, Arkansas. Singer/guitarist. In the car crash which killed **Johnny Horton** in 1960.

DEBUT	PEAK	WKS		A-side / B-side	Pop	$	Pic	Label & Number
12/21/63	30	4		1 Tadpole......................................Pretty Little Girls [I]		$15		Starday 651
				TILLMAN FRANKS and the Cedar Grove Three				
5/2/64	30	11		2 When The World's On Fire .... Uncle Eph		$15		Starday 670
				TILLMAN FRANKS SINGERS				

FRAZIER, Brenda '80

DEBUT	PEAK	WKS		A-side / B-side	Pop	$	Pic	Label & Number
12/6/80	92	2		I've Given Up Giving In To The Blues................Steppin' Out Tonight		$7		Tyro 1004

FRAZIER, Dallas '68
Born on 10/27/39 in Spiro, Oklahoma; raised in Bakersfield, California. Singer/songwriter/guitarist.

DEBUT	PEAK	WKS		A-side / B-side	Pop	$	Pic	Label & Number
11/11/67+	28	11		1 Everybody Oughta Sing A Song Only A Fool		$10		Capitol 2011
4/13/68	43	8		2 The Sunshine Of My World....................Lonelier And More In Love		$10		Capitol 2133
9/21/68	59	5		3 I Hope I Like Mexico Blues ....I Just Thought That I Loved Her (Till I Lost You)		$10		Capitol 2257
3/8/69	63	9		4 The Conspiracy Of Homer Jones................ Sundown Of My Mind [N]	120	$10		Capitol 2402
				parody of "Ode To Billy Joe" by Bobbie Gentry and "Harper Valley P.T.A." by Jeannie C. Riley				
11/8/69	45	10		5 California Cotton Fields.................Sweetheart Don't Throw Yourself Away		$8		RCA Victor 0259
8/29/70	45	7		6 The Birthmark Henry Thompson Talks About........If My Heart Had Windows		$8		RCA Victor 9881
2/27/71	43	8		7 Big Mable Murphy ....White Fences And Evergreen Trees		$8		RCA Victor 9950
7/29/72	42	11		8 North Carolina ....The Last Time I Called Somebody Darlin'		$8		RCA Victor 0748

FRAZIER RIVER '96
Group from Cincinnati: Danny Frazier, Chuck Adair, Jim Morris, Bob Wilson, Brian Braverman and Greg Amburgy.

DEBUT	PEAK	WKS		A-side / B-side	Pop	$	Pic	Label & Number
2/10/96	57	9		1 She Got What She Deserves ....Heaven Is Smiling		$3		Decca 55173
6/22/96	67	8		2 Tangled Up In Texas .... Last Request		$3		Decca 55101

FREE, Johnny '79

DEBUT	PEAK	WKS		A-side / B-side	Pop	$	Pic	Label & Number
4/28/79	100	1		Borrowed Time		$7		Sabre 4509
				first recorded by Olivia Newton-John on her 1979 album Totally Hot				

FREEMAN, Ernie '58
Born on 8/16/22 in Cleveland. Died of a heart attack on 5/16/81 (age 58). Pianist/composer/conductor.

DEBUT	PEAK	WKS		A-side / B-side	Pop	$	Pic	Label & Number
1/13/58	11	2		Raunchy ....S:11 Puddin' [I]	4	$20		Imperial 5474

FRICKE, Janie ★77★ '83
Born on 12/19/47 in South Whitney, Indiana. Former backing singer for RCA. Sang numerous commercial jingles. Later a regular on TNN's *The Statler Brothers Show*. Occasionally spells her name "Frickie." CMA Awards: 1982 & 1983 Female Vocalist of the Year.

1)He's A Heartache 2)Tell Me A Lie 3)A Place To Fall Apart 4)Always Have Always Will 5)Your Heart's Not In It

DEBUT	PEAK	WKS		A-side / B-side	Pop	$	Pic	Label & Number
9/17/77	21	13		1 What're You Doing Tonight ....We're A Love Song		$5		Columbia 10605
10/29/77+	4	16		2 Come A Little Bit Closer Loneliness (Can Break A Good Man Down)		$5		Columbia 10634
				JOHNNY DUNCAN (with Janie Fricke)				
				#3 Pop hit for Jay & The Americans in 1964				
3/4/78	21	12		3 Baby It's You....................I Loved You All The Way		$4		Columbia 10695
5/27/78	12	13		4 Please Help Me, I'm Falling (In Love With You)..........Get Ready For My World		$4		Columbia 10743
10/7/78	❶¹	14		5 On My Knees Mellow Melody		$4		Epic 50616
				CHARLIE RICH (with Janie Fricke)				
11/11/78+	22	12		6 Playin' Hard To Get ....Let Me Love You Goodbye		$4		Columbia 10849
3/3/79	14	12		7 I'll Love Away Your Troubles For Awhile....................River Blue		$4		Columbia 10910
7/7/79	28	10		8 Let's Try Again....................Love Is Worth It All		$4		Columbia 11029
11/17/79+	26	13		9 But Love Me ....One Piece At A Time		$4		Columbia 11139
3/22/80	22	12		10 Pass Me By (If You're Only Passing Through)....................This Ain't Tennessee And He Ain't You		$4		Columbia 11224

FRICKE, Janie — Cont'd

DEBUT	PEAK	WKS		A-side / B-side	Pop	$	Pic	Label & Number
7/12/80	17	14		11 He's Out Of My Life .... *Loving Arms*		$4		Columbia 11312
				JOHNNY DUNCAN and JANIE FRICKE				
				#10 Pop hit for Michael Jackson in 1980				
11/1/80+	2¹	18		12 **Down To My Last Broken Heart** *Every Time A Teardrop Falls*		$4		Columbia 11384
3/14/81	12	14		13 **Pride** .... *Going Through The Motions*		$4		Columbia 60509
7/25/81	4	18		14 **I'll Need Someone To Hold Me (When I Cry)** *It's Raining Too*		$3		Columbia 02197
12/12/81+	4	19		15 **Do Me With Love** *If You Could See Me Now*		$3		Columbia 02644
5/8/82	❶¹	18		16 **Don't Worry 'Bout Me Baby** *Always*		$3		Columbia 02859
9/18/82	❶¹	19		17 **It Ain't Easy Bein' Easy** *A Little More Love*		$3		Columbia 03214
1/15/83	4	19		18 **You Don't Know Love** *Heart To Heart Talk*		$3		Columbia 03498
5/21/83	❶¹	20		19 **He's A Heartache (Looking For A Place To Happen)** *Tryin' To Fool A Fool*		$3		Columbia 03899
9/17/83	❶¹	20		20 **Tell Me A Lie** *Love Have Mercy*		$3		Columbia 04091
1/14/84	❶¹	18		21 **Let's Stop Talkin' About It** *I've Had All The Love I Can Stand*		$3		Columbia 04317
5/12/84	8	17		22 **If The Fall Don't Get You** *Where's The Fire*		$3		Columbia 04454
9/1/84	❶¹	23		23 **Your Heart's Not In It** S:❶¹ / A:❶¹ *Take It From The Top*		$3		Columbia 04578
10/27/84+	❶¹	22		24 **A Place To Fall Apart** S:❶¹ / A:❶¹ *All I Want To Do Is Sing My Song*		$3		Epic 04663
				MERLE HAGGARD (with Janie Fricke)				
1/5/85	7	19		25 **The First Word In Memory Is Me** S:6 / A:7 *One Way Ticket*		$3		Columbia 04731
5/18/85	2¹	22		26 **She's Single Again** S:2 / A:2 *The Only Thing You Took Away*		$3		Columbia 04896
9/21/85	4	23		27 **Somebody Else's Fire** S:4 / A:4 *My Heart's Hearin' Footsteps*		$3		Columbia 05617
2/1/86	5	22		28 **Easy To Please** A:4 / S:5 *Party Shoes*		$3		Columbia 05781
				JANIE FRICKIE:				
6/28/86	❶¹	22		29 **Always Have Always Will** S:❶¹ / A:2 *Don't Put It Past My Heart*		$3	■	Columbia 06144
11/8/86+	20	16		30 **When A Woman Cries** .... S:7 / A:20 *Nothing Left To Say*		$3		Columbia 06417
3/14/87	32	11		31 **Are You Satisfied** .... S:24 *Till I Can't Take It Anymore*		$3		Columbia 06985
				#11 Pop hit for Rusty Draper in 1956				
5/9/87	21	12		32 **From Time To Time (It Feels Like Love Again)** .... S:18 *Texas*		$3		Columbia 07088
				LARRY GATLIN & JANIE FRICKIE (with The Gatlin Brothers)				
8/29/87	63	4		33 **Baby You're Gone** *I Don't Like Being Lonely*		$3		Columbia 07353
4/16/88	54	8		34 **Where Does Love Go (When It's Gone)** .... *The Last Thing*		$3		Columbia 07770
6/25/88	50	8		35 **I'll Walk Before I'll Crawl** ....*The Healing Hands Of Time*		$3		Columbia 07927
9/24/88	64	4		36 **Heart** ....*The Healing Hands Of Time*		$3		Columbia 08031
5/20/89	56	7		37 **Love Is One Of Those Words** ....*No Ordinary Memory*		$3		Columbia 68758
9/16/89	43	9		38 **Give 'Em My Number** ....*Walking On The Moon*		$3		Columbia 69057

FRIEDMAN, Kinky '73

Born Richard Friedman on 10/31/44 in Palestine, Texas. Formed band, The Texas Jewboys, in 1971.

DEBUT	PEAK	WKS		A-side / B-side	Pop	$	Pic	Label & Number
7/14/73	69	8		**Sold American** .... *Western Union Wire*		$7		Vanguard 35173

FRIZZELL, Allen '85

Singer/songwriter/guitarist. Younger brother of **Lefty Frizzell** and **David Frizzell**. Formerly married to **Shelly West**.

DEBUT	PEAK	WKS		A-side / B-side	Pop	$	Pic	Label & Number
5/16/81	86	4		1 **Beer Joint Fever** ....*Look What Thoughts Will Do*		$5		Sound Factory 429
8/29/81	81	3		2 **She's Livin' It Up (And I'm Drinkin' 'Em Down)** ..... *Every Night I Take Her Memory To Bed*		$5		Sound Factory 447
6/8/85	73	3		3 **It'll Be Love By Morning** ....*Mystery*		$4		Epic 04870

FRIZZELL, David ★178★ '81

Born on 9/26/41 in El Dorado, Arkansas. Singer/songwriter/guitarist. Younger brother of **Lefty Frizzell** and older brother of **Allen Frizzell**. Formed a duo with sister-in-law **Shelly West**. CMA Awards: 1981 & 1982 Vocal Duo of the Year (with Shelly West).

1)You're The Reason God Made Oklahoma 2)I'm Gonna Hire A Wino To Decorate Our Home
3)I Just Came Here To Dance 4)Lost My Baby Blues 5)Another Honky-Tonk Night On Broadway

DEBUT	PEAK	WKS		A-side / B-side	Pop	$	Pic	Label & Number
6/20/70	67	3		1 **L.A. International Airport** ....*Just Passing Through*		$8		Columbia 45139
10/31/70	36	10		2 **I Just Can't Help Believing** ....*Carmen Jones*		$8		Columbia 45238
				#9 Pop hit for **B.J. Thomas** in 1970				
12/18/71	73	2		3 **Goodbye** .... *500 Times*		$7		Cartwheel 202
5/19/73	63	5		4 **Words Don't Come Easy** ....*It's Too Late To Keep From Losing You*		$5		Capitol 3589
8/25/73	94	4		5 **Take Me One More Ride** .... *The Bottle, Me, And Joann*		$5		Capitol 3684
10/2/76	100	1		6 **A Case Of You** ....*Forever (And Always)*		$5		RSO 856
				#67 Pop hit for Frank Stallone in 1980				
1/17/81	❶¹	17		7 **You're The Reason God Made Oklahoma** *That's Where Lovers Go Wrong*		$4		Warner 49650
				DAVID FRIZZELL & SHELLY WEST				
				from the movie *Any Which Way You Can* starring **Clint Eastwood**				
6/20/81	9	15		8 **A Texas State Of Mind** *Let's Duet*		$4		Warner 49745
				DAVID FRIZZELL & SHELLY WEST				
9/5/81	45	9		9 **Lefty** ....*Three Blind Hearts (w/Shelly West)*		$4		Warner 49778
				Merle Haggard (guest vocal)				
10/10/81	16	16		10 **Husbands And Wives** ....*Yours For The Asking*		$4		Warner 49825
				DAVID FRIZZELL & SHELLY WEST				

DEBUT	PEAK	WKS	Gold	A-side (Chart Hit)..B-side	Pop	$	Pic	Label & Number
				FRIZZELL, David — Cont'd				
2/6/82	**8**	18		11 **Another Honky-Tonk Night On Broadway** _Three Act Play_		$4		Warner 50007
				DAVID FRIZZELL & SHELLY WEST				
5/29/82	**❶**[1]	23		12 **I'm Gonna Hire A Wino To Decorate Our**				
				Home _She's Up To All Her Old Tricks Again_		$4		Warner 50063
7/17/82	**4**	18		13 **I Just Came Here To Dance** _Our Day Will Come_		$4		Warner 29980
				DAVID FRIZZELL & SHELLY WEST				
10/9/82+	**5**	20		14 **Lost My Baby Blues** _Single And Alone_		$4		Warner 29901
12/4/82+	**43**	11		15 **Please Surrender** _Being A Man, Being A Woman_		$4		Warner 29850
				DAVID FRIZZELL & SHELLY WEST				
				from the movie _Honkytonk Man_ starring **Clint Eastwood**				
3/26/83	**52**	10		16 **Cajun Invitation**..._Yesterday's Lovers_		$4		Warner 29756
				FRIZZELL & WEST				
5/28/83	**10**	16		17 **Where Are You Spending Your Nights These Days** _We're Back In Love Again_		$3		Viva 29617
9/3/83	**71**	4		18 **Pleasure Island**....................................._Betcha Can't Cry Just One_		$3		Viva 29544
				FRIZZELL & WEST				
10/8/83	**39**	13		19 **A Million Light Beers Ago**........................._Sweet Sweet Sin_		$3		Viva 29498
1/14/84	**64**	6		20 **Black And White**....................................._All The King's Memories_		$3		Viva 29388
2/4/84	**20**	17		21 **Silent Partners**..._Confidential_		$3		Viva 29404
				FRIZZELL & WEST				
4/28/84	**60**	6		22 **Who Dat**..._Honest Man_		$3		Viva 29332
7/28/84	**49**	9		23 **When We Get Back To The Farm (That's When We Really Go To**				
				Town)..._Settin' The Night On Fire_		$3		Viva 29232
9/15/84	**13**	20		24 **It's A Be Together Night** ....S:8 / A:16 _Straight From The Heart_		$3		Viva 29187
				FRIZZELL & WEST				
12/1/84+	**49**	13		25 **No Way José**....................._Who Dat (Messin' With That Woman Of Mine)_		$3		Viva 29158
3/2/85	**63**	7		26 **Country Music Love Affair**.............._Maybe There's Love After You, After All_		$3		Viva 29066
4/13/85	**60**	8		27 **Do Me Right**....................................._Easy, Soft And Slow_		$3		Viva 29048
				FRIZZELL & WEST				
3/29/86	**71**	5		28 **Celebrity**..		$6		Nashville Amer. 1002
5/9/87	**74**	7		29 **Beautiful Body**.............................._All That I Am_		$4		Compleat 168

FRIZZELL, Lefty ★78★   '51

Born William Orville Frizzell on 3/31/28 in Corsicana, Texas; raised in El Dorado, Arkansas. Died of a stroke on 7/19/75 (age 47). Singer/songwriter/guitarist. Older brother of **Allen Frizzell** and **David Frizzell**. Elected to the Country Music Hall of Fame in 1982.

1)_Always Late_ 2)_I Want To Be With You Always_ 3)_Saginaw, Michigan_ 4)_I Love You A Thousand Ways_
5)_If You've Got The Money I've Got The Time_

DEBUT	PEAK	WKS		A-side	B-side	Pop	$	Pic	Label & Number
10/28/50	**❶**[3]	22		1 **If You've Got The Money I've Got The Time/** _J:_**❶**[3] _/ A:2 / S:2_					
11/4/50+	**❶**[3]	32		2 **I Love You A Thousand Ways** _A:_**❶**[3] _/ J:3 / S:5_			$25		Columbia 4-20739
3/3/51	**4**	12		3 **Look What Thoughts Will Do/** _A:4 / S:9 / J:9_					
3/10/51	**7**	2		4 **Shine, Shave, Shower (It's Saturday)** _J:7_			$25		Columbia 4-20772
4/14/51	**❶**[11]	27		5 **I Want To Be With You Always** _A:_**❶**[11] _/ S:_**❶**[8] _/ J:_**❶**[5] _My Baby's Just Like Money_	29	$25		Columbia 4-20799
8/4/51	**❶**[12]	28		6 **Always Late (With Your Kisses)/** _S:_**❶**[12] _/ A:_**❶**[6] _/ J:_**❶**[6]					
8/18/51	**2**[8]	29		7 **Mom And Dad's Waltz** _S:2 / A:2 / J:3_			$25		Columbia 4-20837
10/13/51	**6**	9		8 **Travellin' Blues** _S:6 / J:7 / A:8 Blue Yodel No. 6_			$25		Columbia 4-20842
12/22/51+	**❶**[3]	21		9 **Give Me More, More, More (Of Your Kisses)/** _A:_**❶**[3] _/ J:_**❶**[3] _/ S:3_					
1/12/52	**7**	5		10 **How Long Will It Take (To Stop Loving You)** _A:7_			$25		Columbia 4-20885
4/12/52	**2**[1]	12		11 **Don't Stay Away (Till Love Grows**					
				Cold) _S:2 / J:2 / A:4 You're Here, So Everything's All Right_			$25		Columbia 4-20911
9/27/52	**6**	5		12 **Forver (And Always)** _S:6 I Know You're Lonesome While Waiting For Me_			$25		Columbia 4-20997
12/6/52+	**3**	9		13 **I'm An Old, Old Man (Tryin' To Live While I**					
				Can) _S:3 / J:4 You're Just Mine (Only In My Dreams)_			$25		Columbia 21034
5/23/53	**8**	1		14 **(Honey, Baby, Hurry!) Bring Your Sweet Self Back**					
				To Me _A:8 Time Changes Things_			$25		Columbia 21084
2/20/54	**8**	2		15 **Run 'Em Off** _J:8 The Darkest Moment_			$25		Columbia 21194
1/15/55	**11**	4		16 **I Love You Mostly**....................................._S:11 / A:13 Mama!_			$25		Columbia 21328
11/24/58+	**13**	11		17 **Cigarettes And Coffee Blues**.............................._You're Humbuggin' Me_			$20		Columbia 41268
				written by **Marty Robbins**					
6/8/59	**6**	15		18 **The Long Black Veil** _Knock Again, True Love_			$15		Columbia 41384
4/27/63	**23**	2		19 **Forbidden Lovers**....................................._A Few Steps Away_			$12		Columbia 42676
11/9/63	**30**	1		20 **Don't Let Her See Me Cry**....................................._James River_			$12		Columbia 42839
1/11/64	**❶**[4]	26		21 **Saginaw, Michigan** _When It Rains The Blues_	85	$12		Columbia 42924
8/8/64	**28**	11		22 **The Nester**..._The Rider_			$10		Columbia 43051
1/16/65	**50**	2		23 **'Gator Hollow**.............._Make That One For The Road A Cup Of Coffee_			$10		Columbia 43169
5/1/65	**12**	15		24 **She's Gone Gone Gone**....................................._Confused_			$10		Columbia 43256
10/16/65	**36**	5		25 **A Little Unfair/**					
11/13/65	**41**	4		26 **Love Looks Good On You**.................................			$10		Columbia 43364
10/15/66	**51**	6		27 **I Just Couldn't See The Forest (For The**					
				Trees) ...._Everything Keeps Coming Back (But You)_			$10		Columbia 43747

DEBUT	PEAK	WKS	Gold	A-side (Chart Hit)...B-side	Pop	$	Pic	Label & Number

FRIZZELL, Lefty — Cont'd

DEBUT	PEAK	WKS		A-side ...... B-side	Pop	$	Label & Number
3/25/67	49	10		28 You Gotta Be Puttin' Me On .... A Song From A Lonely Heart		$10	Columbia 44023
9/2/67	63	4		29 Get This Stranger Out Of Me.. Hobo's Pride		$10	Columbia 44205
8/10/68	59	3		30 The Marriage Bit .... When The Grass Grows Green Again		$10	Columbia 44563
3/22/69	64	4		31 An Article From Life .... Only Way To Fly		$10	Columbia 44738
8/22/70	49	10		32 Watermelon Time In Georgia .... Out Of You		$10	Columbia 45197
8/12/72	59	10		33 You, Babe .... When It Rains The Blues		$10	Columbia 45652
9/22/73	43	13		34 I Can't Get Over You To Save My Life............................... Somebody's Words		$6	ABC 11387
2/16/74	25	12		35 I Never Go Around Mirrors.................................... That's The Way Love Goes		$6	ABC 11416
6/15/74	52	9		36 Railroad Lady .... If I Had Half The Sense (A Fool Was Born With)		$6	ABC 11442
9/21/74	21	14		37 Lucky Arms .... If She Just Helps Me Get Over You		$6	ABC 12023
2/22/75	67	7		38 Life's Like Poetry .... Sittin' And Thinkin'		$6	ABC 12061
7/5/75	50	11		39 Falling .... I Love You A Thousand Ways		$6	ABC 12103

FRUSHAY, Ray   **'80**
Born Raymond Frusha on 3/1/44 in San Diego; raised in Austin, Texas.

DEBUT	PEAK	WKS		A-side ...... B-side	Pop	$	Label & Number
9/8/79	93	2		1 I Got Western Pride........................ Woman, Quit Walking Around In My Mind		$7	Western Pride 105
3/22/80	90	2		2 Pickin' Up Love .... Dreamer's Room		$7	Western Pride 113

FUHRMAN, Micki   **'84**
Female singer/songwriter from Coushatta, Louisiana.

DEBUT	PEAK	WKS		A-side ...... B-side	Pop	$	Label & Number
11/11/78	93	4		1 Leave While I'm Sleeping .... Big Bright Rainbow		$7	Louisiana Hay. 785
7/28/79	86	3		2 Blue River Of Tears .... I Need You		$4	MCA 41057
11/22/80	60	7		3 Hold Me, Thrill Me, Kiss Me .... Holding Me		$4	MCA 51005
				#8 Pop hit for Mel Carter in 1965			
2/18/84	48	10		4 I Bet You Never Thought I'd Go This Far................ I Don't Want To Go Too Far		$4	MCA 52321

FULLER, Jerry   **'79**
Born Jerrell Lee Fuller on 11/19/38 in Fort Worth, Texas. Singer/songwriter/producer.

DEBUT	PEAK	WKS		A-side ...... B-side	Pop	$	Label & Number
1/13/79	98	1		1 Salt On The Wound .... No Time		$5	ABC 12436
6/2/79	90	4		2 Lines.. Over You		$5	MCA 41022

G

GABRIEL   **'81**
Born Gabriel Ernest Miklos Farago in Hungary; at four months old, fled with family to Innsbruck, Austria. Emmigrated to Buffalo, New York, at age four.

DEBUT	PEAK	WKS		A-side ...... B-side	Pop	$	Label & Number
1/24/81	85	3		1 I Think I Could Love You (Better Than He Did) .... Til I Stop Falling In		$6	NSD 70
4/18/81	93	2		2 Friends Before Lovers		$6	Ridgetop 01381

GALLIMORE, Byron   **'80**
Born in Puryear, Tennessee. Singer/songwriter.

DEBUT	PEAK	WKS		A-side ...... B-side	Pop	$	Label & Number
6/14/80	93	2		No Ordinary Woman .... Simple Ways		$7	Little Giant 025

GALLION, Bob   **'62**
Born on 4/22/31 in Ashland, Kentucky. Singer/songwriter/guitarist.

DEBUT	PEAK	WKS		A-side ...... B-side	Pop	$	Label & Number
11/3/58	28	1		1 That's What I Tell My Heart .... Run Boy		$15	MGM 12700
5/18/59	18	9		2 You Take The Table And I'll Take The Chairs .... Out Of A Honky Tonk		$15	MGM 12777
11/28/60+	7	22		3 Loving You (Was Worth This Broken Heart) Start All Over		$12	Hickory 1130
6/19/61	20	4		4 One Way Street .... Six Pallbearers		$12	Hickory 1145
12/4/61	20	2		5 Sweethearts Again .... You Don't Know (Or You Don't Care)		$12	Hickory 1154
11/10/62	5	15		6 Wall To Wall Love Happy Birthday, My Darlin'		$10	Hickory 1181
8/31/63	23	2		7 Ain't Got Time For Nothin' .... The Wrong Side Of Town		$10	Hickory 1220
7/20/68	71	2		8 Pick A Little Happy Song .... Happy Anniversary		$8	United Artists 50309
9/8/73	99	2		9 Love By Appointment................. If You Could Do Any Better (You'd Done Been Gone)		$7	Metromedia 0037
				PATI POWELL & BOB GALLION			

GALWAY, James   **'83**
Born on 12/8/39 in Belfast, Ireland. Classical flutist.

DEBUT	PEAK	WKS		A-side ...... B-side	Pop	$	Label & Number
2/19/83	57	11		The Wayward Wind .... Shenandoah		$3	RCA 13441
				JAMES GALWAY WITH SYLVIA			
				#1 Pop hit for Gogi Grant in 1956			

GARNETT, Gale   **'64**
Born on 7/17/42 in Auckland, New Zealand. Came to the U.S. in 1951. Worked as an actress from age 15. Appeared on many TV shows.

DEBUT	PEAK	WKS		A-side ...... B-side	Pop	$	Label & Number
12/5/64	43	3		We'll Sing In The Sunshine .... Prism Song	4	$8	RCA Victor 8388

GARRETT, Pat   **'81**
Born in Lebanon, Pennsylvania. Male singer/bassist.

DEBUT	PEAK	WKS		A-side ...... B-side	Pop	$	Label & Number
11/12/77	98	1		1 A Little Something On The Side		$7	Kansa 3000
8/2/80	80	5		2 Sexy Ole Lady .... Humpty Dumpty		$6	Gold Dust 101
10/18/80	89	3		3 Your Magic Touch.................................... How Can I Please You		$6	Gold Dust 102
11/7/81	73	5		4 Everlovin' Woman		$6	Gold Dust 104
9/13/86	74	6		5 Rockin' My Country Heart .... Daddy What Did I Do Wrong		$5	Compleat 157
10/3/87	82	3		6 Suck It In		$5	MDJ 73087

GARRISON, Al   **'87**

DEBUT	PEAK	WKS		A-side ...... B-side	Pop	$	Label & Number
9/26/87	87	2		Where Do I Go From Here		$6	Motion 1032

DEBUG	PEAK	WKS	Gold	A-side (Chart Hit)..B-side	Pop	$	Pic	Label & Number

GARRISON, Glen   '68
Born on 6/13/41 in Slarcy, Arkansas.

11/4/67	72	2		1 Goodbye Swingers .... Hello Mama		$10		Imperial 66257
6/22/68	48	6		2 I'll Be Your Baby Tonight................................... You Know I Love You		$10		Imperial 66300

first recorded by Bob Dylan on his 1968 album *John Wesley Harding*

GARRON, Jess   '79

3/31/79	30	11		1 Lo Que Sea (What Ever May The Future Be) .... Those Good Times Are Over		$6		Charta 131
8/4/79	65	6		2 It's Summer Time................... You Can't Love A Woman (Who Doesn't Want To Be Loved)		$6		Charta 136

GATLIN, Larry, & The Gatlin Brothers ★75★ '83
Trio of brothers: Larry (b: 5/2/48 in Seminole, Texas), Steve (b: 4/4/51 in Olney, Texas) and Rudy (b: 8/20/52 in Olney, Texas) Gatlin. Larry is the chief singer/songwriter with Steve (guitar) and Rudy (bass) providing the harmony vocals. Worked as a gospel trio and had their own TV series in Abilene, Texas. Joined the *Grand Ole Opry* in 1976.

1)Houston 2)All The Gold In California 3)I Just Wish You Were Someone I Love 4)Night Time Magic
5)She Used To Be Somebody's Baby

LARRY GATLIN:

10/20/73	40	13		1 Sweet Becky Walker.............................. You've Been Handed Down To Me		$6		Monument 8584
3/16/74	45	12		2 Bitter They Are Harder They Fall .... To Make Me Wanna Stay Home		$6		Monument 8602
9/7/74	14	15		3 Delta Dirt.. Those Also Love	84	$6		Monument 8622
8/23/75	71	7		4 Let's Turn The Lights On .... Takin' A Chance On You		$6		Monument 8657

LARRY GATLIN with Family & Friends:

12/27/75+	5	19		5 Broken Lady .... The Heart		$6		Monument 8680
6/12/76	43	9		6 Warm And Tender .... The Heart Is Quicker Than The Eye		$6		Monument 8696
10/30/76+	5	16		7 Statues Without Hearts .... What Will I Do Now		$5		Monument 201
2/26/77	12	11		8 Anything But Leavin' .... Take Back 'It's Over'		$5		Monument 212
5/28/77	3	16		9 I Don't Wanna Cry .... Mercy River		$5		Monument 221
9/10/77	3	14		10 Love Is Just A Game .... Everytime A Plane Flies Over Our House		$5		Monument 226
12/10/77+	❶[1]	16		11 I Just Wish You Were Someone I Love .... Kiss It All Goodbye		$5	■	Monument 234

LARRY GATLIN with Brothers and Friends

LARRY GATLIN:

4/15/78	2[2]	14		12 Night Time Magic .... It's Love At Last		$5		Monument 249
8/12/78	13	11		13 Do It Again Tonight .... Cold Day In Hell		$5		Monument 259
11/11/78+	7	14		14 I've Done Enough Dyin' Today .... Nothin' You Do		$5		Monument 270

LARRY GATLIN & THE GATLIN BROTHERS BAND:

8/25/79	❶[2]	15		15 All The Gold In California .... How Much Is A Man Supposed To Take		$4		Columbia 11066
1/5/80	43	8		16 The Midnight Choir .... Hold Me Closer		$4		Columbia 11169
3/8/80	12	12		17 Taking Somebody With Me When I Fall .... Piece By Piece	108	$4		Columbia 11219
6/14/80	18	13		18 We're Number One .... Can't Cry Anymore		$4		Columbia 11282
10/4/80	5	17		19 Take Me To Your Lovin' Place .... Straight To My Heart		$4		Columbia 11369
2/21/81	25	11		20 It Don't Get No Better Than This .... Straight To My Heart		$4		Columbia 11438
6/6/81	20	12		21 Wind Is Bound To Change .... Help Yourself To Me		$4		Columbia 02123
10/3/81	4	17		22 What Are We Doin' Lonesome .... You Wouldn't Know Love		$4		Columbia 02522
2/6/82	15	13		23 In Like With Each Other .... Hard Workin' Hands		$4		Columbia 02698
5/29/82	19	12		24 She Used To Sing On Sunday .... Can't Take It With You		$4		Columbia 02910
9/11/82	5	19		25 Sure Feels Like Love .... Home Is Where The Healin' Is		$4		Columbia 03159
1/29/83	20	15		26 Almost Called Her Baby By Mistake .... Somethin' Like Each Other's Arms		$4		Columbia 03517
5/21/83	32	11		27 Easy On The Eye .... Anything But Leavin'		$4		Columbia 03885
9/24/83	❶[2]	22		28 Houston (Means I'm One Day Closer To You) .... The Whole Wide World Stood Still		$4		Columbia 04105
3/24/84	7	18		29 Denver .... A Dream That Got A Little Out Of Hand		$4		Columbia 04395

LARRY GATLIN & THE GATLIN BROTHERS:

7/21/84	3	24		30 The Lady Takes The Cowboy Everytime .... S:3 / A:3 It's Me		$3		Columbia 04533
10/12/85	43	13		31 Runaway Go Home .... Nothing But Your Love Matters		$3		Columbia 05632
1/18/86	12	21		32 Nothing But Your Love Matters .... S:12 / A:13 When The Night Closes In		$3		Columbia 05764

LARRY, STEVE, RUDY: THE GATLIN BROTHERS:

8/23/86	2[1]	22		33 She Used To Be Somebody's Baby .... S:2 / A:2 Being Alone		$3		Columbia 06252
12/27/86+	4	21		34 Talkin' To The Moon .... S:3 / A:4 Give Me A Chance		$3		Columbia 06592
5/9/87	21	12		35 From Time To Time (It Feels Like Love Again) .... S:18 Texas		$3		Columbia 07088

LARRY GATLIN & JANIE FRICKIE (with The Gatlin Brothers)

8/15/87	16	15		36 Changin' Partners .... S:15 Got A Lot Of Woman On His Hands		$3		Columbia 07320
3/26/88	4	21		37 Love Of A Lifetime .... S:8 Don't Blame Me For Colorado		$3		Columbia 07747

THE GATLIN BROS.

8/13/88	34	13		38 Alive And Well .... S:24 One On One		$3		Columbia 07998

LARRY GATLIN AND THE GATLIN BROTHERS:

2/25/89	54	7		39 When She Holds Me .... Go Or Stay		$3		Universal 53501
5/6/89	37	10		40 I Might Be What You're Lookin' For............................. Rain		$3		Universal 66005
9/2/89	51	8		41 #1 Heartache Place .... Your Door		$3		Universal 66021
8/4/90	65	6		42 Boogie And Beethoven .... (remix)		$3	▌	Capitol 44563

THE GATLIN BROTHERS

DEBUG	PEAK	WKS	Gold	A-side (Chart Hit)..B-side	Pop	$	Pic	Label & Number
				GATTIS, Keith '96				
				Born on 5/26/71 in Georgetown, Texas. Singer/songwriter/guitarist.				
3/30/96	53	9		Little Drops Of My Heart.. Only Lonely Fool		$3	▌	RCA 64488
				GAULT, Lenny '79				
9/30/78	87	3		1 Turn On The Bright Lights .... When A Woman Cries		$6		MRC 1020
1/6/79	78	4		2 I Just Need A Coke (To Get The Whiskey Down)................................. Steppin' Aside Just Ain't My Style		$6		MRC 1024
4/7/79	89	3		3 The Honky-Tonks Are Calling Me Again..............................I'm Gonna Leave		$6		King Coal 03

GAYLE, Crystal ★40★ '77

Born Brenda Gail Webb on 1/9/51 in Paintsville, Kentucky; raised in Wabash, Indiana. Singer/songwriter. Sister of **Loretta Lynn**, **Peggy Sue** and **Jay Lee Webb**; distant cousin of **Patty Loveless**. Known for her trademark ankle-length hair. CMA Awards: 1977 & 1978 Female Vocalist of the Year.

1)Don't It Make My Brown Eyes Blue 2)Talking In Your Sleep 3)Why Have You Left The One You Left Me For
4)I'll Get Over You 5)Cry

DEBUG	PEAK	WKS	Gold	A-side	Pop	$	Pic	Label & Number
9/19/70	23	13		1 I've Cried (The Blues Right Out Of My Eyes).........................Sparklin' Look Of Love		$8		Decca 32721
				written by **Loretta Lynn**; also see #14 below				
3/11/72	70	2		2 Everybody Oughta Cry .... M.R.S. Degree		$8		Decca 32925
7/1/72	49	5		3 I Hope You're Havin' Better Luck Than Me ....Too Far		$8		Decca 32969
5/25/74	39	12		4 Restless .... Lay Back Lover		$5		United Artists 428
10/26/74+	6	21		5 Wrong Road Again They Come Out At Night		$5		United Artists 555
3/29/75	27	11		6 Beyond You Loving You So Long Now		$5		United Artists 600
7/26/75	21	15		7 This Is My Year For Mexico......................................When I Dream		$5		United Artists 680
11/29/75+	8	16		8 Somebody Loves You Coming Closer		$5		United Artists 740
4/3/76	❶¹	18		9 I'll Get Over You High Time	71	$5		United Artists 781
8/21/76	31	9		10 One More Time (Karneval) .... Oh My Soul		$5		United Artists 838
11/6/76+	❶¹	16		11 You Never Miss A Real Good Thing (Till He Says Goodbye) Forgettin' 'Bout You		$5		United Artists 883
3/26/77	2²	15		12 I'll Do It All Over Again I'm Not So Far Away		$5		United Artists 948
7/9/77	❶⁴	18	●	13 Don't It Make My Brown Eyes Blue It's All Right With Me	2³	$4		United Artists 1016
12/10/77+	40	11		14 I've Cried (The Blues Right Out Of My Eyes)....................Sparklin' Look Of Love [R]		$4		MCA 40837
				same version as #1 above				
2/11/78	❶¹	14		15 Ready For The Times To Get Better Beyond You	52	$4		United Artists 1136
6/17/78	❶²	16		16 Talking In Your Sleep Paintin' This Old Town Blue	18	$4		United Artists 1214
12/2/78+	❶²	14		17 Why Have You Left The One You Left Me For Cry Me A River		$4		United Artists 1259
4/14/79	3	13		18 When I Dream Hello I Love You	84	$4		United Artists 1288
7/21/79	7	13		19 Your Kisses Will Time Will Prove That I'm Right		$4		United Artists 1306
9/1/79	2³	15		20 Half The Way Room For One More	15	$4		Columbia 11087
12/8/79+	5	14		21 Your Old Cold Shoulder We Should Be Together		$4		United Artists 1329
2/9/80	❶¹	14		22 It's Like We Never Said Goodbye Don't Go My Love	63	$4		Columbia 11198
5/3/80	64	6		23 River Road Come Home Daddy		$4		United Artists 1347
5/10/80	8	15		24 The Blue Side Danger Zone	81	$4		Columbia 11270
7/26/80	58	7		25 Heart Mender This Is My Year For Mexico		$4		United Artists 1362
9/13/80	❶¹	18		26 If You Ever Change Your Mind I Just Can't Leave Your Love Alone		$4		Columbia 11359
2/7/81	17	14		27 Take It Easy .... Ain't No Love In The Heart Of The City		$4		Columbia 11436
5/23/81	❶¹	17		28 Too Many Lovers Help Yourselves To Each Other		$4		Columbia 02078
10/10/81	3	18		29 The Woman In Me Crying In The Rain	76	$4		Columbia 02523
2/20/82	5	19		30 You Never Gave Up On Me Tennessee		$4		Columbia 02718
8/7/82	9	15		31 Livin' In These Troubled Times Ain't No Sunshine		$4		Columbia 03048
10/9/82	❶¹	19		32 You And I All My Life, All My Love	7	$4		Elektra 69936
				EDDIE RABBITT with **CRYSTAL GAYLE**				
11/20/82+	❶¹	22		33 'Til I Gain Control Again Easier Said Than Done		$4	▌	Elektra 69893
4/2/83	❶¹	16		34 Our Love Is On The Faultline Deeper In The Fire		$4		Warner 29719
7/16/83	❶¹	19		35 Baby, What About You He Is Beautiful To Me	83	$4		Warner 29582
9/24/83	49	9		36 Keepin' Power Half The Way		$4		Columbia 04093
10/29/83+	❶¹	21		37 The Sound Of Goodbye Take Me Home	84	$4		Warner 29452
2/25/84	2²	19		38 I Don't Wanna Lose Your Love Victim Or A Fool		$3		Warner 29356
7/7/84	❶¹	20		39 Turning Away S:30 On Our Way To Love		$3		Warner 29254
10/27/84+	4	23		40 Me Against The Night A:2 / S:4 You Made A Fool Of Me		$3		Warner 29151
3/23/85	3	21		41 Nobody Wants To Be Alone A:3 / S:4 Coming To The Dance		$3		Warner 29050
8/10/85	5	18		42 A Long And Lasting Love A:4 / S:5 Someone Like You		$3		Warner 28963
11/23/85+	❶¹	19		43 Makin' Up For Lost Time (The Dallas Lovers' Song) S:❶¹ / A:❶¹ A Few Good Men		$3	▌	Warner 28856
				CRYSTAL GAYLE AND GARY MORRIS				
				from the TV series *Dallas* starring Larry Hagman				
7/26/86	❶¹	19		44 Cry S:❶¹ / A:❶¹ Crazy In The Heart		$3		Warner 28689
				#1 Pop hit for Johnnie Ray in 1951				
11/22/86+	❶¹	22		45 Straight To The Heart A:❶¹ / S:10 Do I Have To Say Goodbye		$3		Warner 28518
4/25/87	4	18		46 Another World S:5 / A:29 Makin' Up For Lost Time		$3		Warner 28373
				CRYSTAL GAYLE & GARY MORRIS				
				theme from the TV serial				

GAYLE, Crystal — Cont'd

DEBUT	PEAK	WKS		A-side	B-side	Pop	$	Pic	Label & Number
7/18/87	26	15		47 Nobody Should Have To Love This Way .... *A Little Bit Closer*			$3		Warner 28409
10/24/87+	11	18		48 Only Love Can Save Me Now .... *Til I Gain Control Again*			$3		Warner 28209
2/13/88	26	15		49 All Of This & More .... *Makin' Up For Lost Time*			$3		Warner 28106
				CRYSTAL GAYLE/GARY MORRIS					
8/27/88	22	15		50 Nobody's Angel .... *When Love Is New*			$3		Warner 27811
1/7/89	44	9		51 Tennessee Nights .... *When Love Is New*			$3		Warner 27682
9/15/90	72	2		52 Never Ending Song Of Love					album cut
				#13 Pop hit for Delany & Bonnie in 1971; from the album *Ain't Gonna Worry* on Capitol 94301					

GEEZINSLAW BROTHERS, The   **'67**
Novelty duo from Austin, Texas: Sam Allred (b: 5/5/38) and DeWayne "Son" Smith (b: 9/17/46).

DEBUT	PEAK	WKS		A-side	B-side	Pop	$	Pic	Label & Number
10/15/66	66	3		1 You Wouldn't Put The Shuck On Me .... *Snook Is The Only Town For Me* [N]			$10		Capitol 5722
7/15/67	57	6		2 Change Of Wife .... *Brooklyn Bridge* [N]			$10		Capitol 5918
10/21/67	48	8		3 Chubby (Please Take Your Love To Town)......................... *Tender-Hearted Me* [N]			$10		Capitol 2002
				parody of "Ruby, Don't Take Your Love To Town" by Kenny Rogers					
8/22/92	56	13		4 Help, I'm White And I Can't Get Down .... *You Belong To Me* [N]			$5	▌	Step One 442
				THE GEEZINSLAWS					

GENTRY, Bobbie   **'70**
Born Roberta Streeter on 7/27/44 in Chickasaw County, Mississippi; raised in Greenwood, Mississippi. Singer/songwriter/guitarist. Formerly married to Jim Stafford. Won the 1967 Best New Artist Grammy Award.

DEBUT	PEAK	WKS		A-side	B-side	Pop	$	Pic	Label & Number
9/9/67	17	8	●	1 Ode To Billie Joe .... *Mississippi Delta*	❶⁴	$6		Capitol 5950
6/1/68	72	4		2 Louisiana Man .... *Courtyard*	100	$6		Capitol 2147
11/23/68	44	7		3 Less Of Me .... *Mornin' Glory* (Pop #74)		$6		Capitol 2314
				BOBBIE GENTRY & GLEN CAMPBELL					
2/8/69	14	14		4 Let It Be Me .... *Little Green Apples*	36	$6		Capitol 2387
				GLEN CAMPBELL and BOBBIE GENTRY					
12/13/69+	26	12		5 Fancy .... *Courtyard*	31	$6		Capitol 2675
2/21/70	6	13		6 All I Have To Do Is Dream *Less Of Me*	27	$6		Capitol 2745
				BOBBIE GENTRY & GLEN CAMPBELL					

GENTRY, Gary   **'81**
Singer/songwriter from Athens, Texas.

DEBUT	PEAK	WKS		A-side	B-side	Pop	$	Pic	Label & Number
4/25/81	84	2		1 I Sold All Of Tom T's Songs Last Night........................... *Because Of You* [N]		$4		Elektra 47122
12/19/81	83	4		2 (s.o.b.) Same Old Boy .... *The Devil Offered More*		$4		Elektra 47238

GHOST TRAIN — see TAYLOR, Chip

★341★				**GIBBS, Terri** **'81**					

Born on 6/15/54 in Augusta, Georgia. Female singer/songwriter/pianist. Blind since birth. CMA Award: 1981 Horizon Award.
1)Somebody's Knockin' 2)Mis'ry River 3)Anybody Else's Heart But Mine

DEBUT	PEAK	WKS		A-side	B-side	Pop	$	Pic	Label & Number
10/11/80+	8	20		1 Somebody's Knockin' *Some Days It Rains All Night Long*	13	$4		MCA 41309
6/6/81	19	12		2 Rich Man... *I Won't Cry In Dallas Anymore*	89	$4		MCA 51119
9/26/81	38	10		3 I Wanna Be Around .... *Rocky Top*		$4		MCA 51180
				#14 Pop hit for Tony Bennett in 1963					
12/26/81+	12	17		4 Mis'ry River .... *Too Long*		$4		MCA 51225
5/1/82	19	13		5 Ashes To Ashes .... *Plans*		$4		MCA 52040
8/14/82	45	8		6 Some Days It Rains All Night Long .... *All I Wanna Do In Life*		$4		MCA 52088
11/13/82+	33	14		7 Baby I'm Gone ....*I Don't Need You (But I Want You)*		$4		MCA 52134
8/13/83	17	17		8 Anybody Else's Heart But Mine .... *What A Night*		$4		MCA 52252
12/3/83	65	8		9 Tell Mama .... *Bells*		$4		MCA 52308
				#23 Pop hit for Etta James in 1968					
3/30/85	43	12		10 A Few Good Men .... *Ain't Nobody*		$3		Warner 29056
				Kathy Mattea (guest vocal)					
7/6/85	70	5		11 Rockin' In A Brand New Cradle..................... *You Can't Run Away From Your Heart*		$3		Warner 28993
11/2/85	70	5		12 Someone Must Be Missing You Tonight.................................*Here I Go Again*		$3		Warner 28895
10/24/87	87	3		13 Turn Around..		$3		Horizon 2963

GIBSON, Don   ★36★   **'58**
Born on 4/3/28 in Shelby, North Carolina. Singer/songwriter/guitarist. Joined the *Grand Ole Opry* in 1958.

1)Oh Lonesome Me 2)Blue Blue Day 3)Woman 4)Just One Time 5)Sea Of Heartbreak

DEBUT	PEAK	WKS		A-side	B-side	Pop	$	Pic	Label & Number
8/11/56	9	1		1 Sweet Dreams *A:9 The Road Of Life Alone*		$30		MGM 12194
				also see #15 below					
2/17/58	❶⁸	34		2 Oh Lonesome Me/ *S:❶⁸ / A:❶⁸*	7				
3/17/58	7	14		3 I Can't Stop Lovin' You *A:7*	81	$15		RCA Victor 7133
6/9/58	❶²	24		4 Blue Blue Day *S:❶² / A:2 Too Soon To Know*	20	$15		RCA Victor 7010
9/29/58	5	19		5 Give Myself A Party/	46				
10/6/58	8	9		6 Look Who's Blue *A:8*	58	$15		RCA Victor 7330
2/2/59	3	16		7 Who Cares/	43				
2/23/59	27	2		8 A Stranger To Me		$15		RCA Victor 7437
5/11/59	11	13		9 Lonesome Old House .... *I Couldn't Care Less*	71	$15		RCA Victor 7505

DEBUT	PEAK	WKS	Gold	A-side (Chart Hit)..B-side	Pop	$	Pic	Label & Number
				GIBSON, Don — Cont'd				
8/17/59	5	16		10 **Don't Tell Me Your Troubles** *Heartbreak Avenue*	85	$15		RCA Victor 7566
12/7/59+	14	9		11 **I'm Movin' On/**				RCA Victor 7629
1/4/60	29	1		12 **Big Hearted Me**		$15		RCA Victor 7629
3/7/60	2[1]	21		13 **Just One Time** *I May Never Get To Heaven*	29	$15		RCA Victor 7690
8/8/60	11	11		14 **Far, Far Away** ....*A Legend In My Time*	72	$15		RCA Victor 7762
				also see #48 below				
11/28/60+	6	16		15 **Sweet Dreams** *The Same Street* [R]	93	$15		RCA Victor 7805
				new version of #1 above				
3/13/61	22	6		16 **What About Me** .... *The World Is Waiting For The Sunrise* (Pop #108)	100	$15		RCA Victor 7841
6/19/61	2[1]	26		17 **Sea Of Heartbreak** *I Think It's Best (To Forget Me)*	21	$15		RCA Victor 7890
12/18/61+	2[1]	21		18 **Lonesome Number One** *The Same Old Trouble*	59	$15		RCA Victor 7959
5/19/62	5	14		19 **I Can Mend Your Broken Heart** *I Let Her Get Lonely*	105	$12		RCA Victor 8017
11/17/62	22	4		20 **So How Come (No One Loves Me)**................................ *Baby We're Really In Love*		$12	■	RCA Victor 8085
4/6/63	12	10		21 **Head Over Heels In Love With You** .... *It Was Worth It All*		$12	■	RCA Victor 8144
8/31/63	22	5		22 **Anything New Gets Old (Except My Love For You)** .... *After The Heartache*		$12	■	RCA Victor 8192
11/28/64+	23	16		23 **Cause I Believe In You**................................. *A Love That Can't Be*		$12		RCA Victor 8456
7/3/65	19	13		24 **Again** .... *You're Going Away*		$10		RCA Victor 8589
10/9/65	10	13		25 **Watch Where You're Going** *There's A Big Wheel*		$10		RCA Victor 8678
1/22/66	12	12		26 **A Born Loser** *All The World Is Lonely Now*		$10		RCA Victor 8732
5/7/66	6	17		27 **(Yes) I'm Hurting** *My Whole World Is Hurt*		$10		RCA Victor 8812
11/5/66+	8	17		28 **Funny, Familiar, Forgotten, Feelings** *Forget Me*		$10		RCA Victor 8975
6/3/67	51	4		29 **Lost Highway** .... *Around The Town*		$10		RCA Victor 9177
8/26/67	23	12		30 **All My Love** .... *No Doubt About It*		$10		RCA Victor 9266
3/23/68	37	7		31 **Ashes Of Love/**				
6/1/68	71	3		32 **Good Morning, Dear**		$10		RCA Victor 9460
7/13/68	12	14		33 **It's A Long, Long Way To Georgia** .... *Low And Lonely*		$10		RCA Victor 9563
11/23/68+	30	9		34 **Ever Changing Mind** .... *Thoughts*		$10		RCA Victor 9663
2/22/69	2[1]	17		35 **Rings Of Gold** *Final Examination*		$8		RCA Victor 9715
				DOTTIE WEST & DON GIBSON				
5/3/69	28	9		36 **Solitary** .... *I Just Said Goodbye To My Dreams*		$8		RCA Victor 0143
7/12/69	32	10		37 **Sweet Memories** *How's The World Treating You*		$8		RCA Victor 0178
				DOTTIE WEST And DON GIBSON				
9/6/69	21	8		38 **I Will Always** .... *Half As Much*		$8		RCA Victor 0219
12/13/69+	7	13		39 **There's A Story (Goin' 'Round)** *Lock, Stock, And Teardrops*		$8		RCA Victor 0291
				DOTTIE WEST AND DON GIBSON				
3/14/70	17	12		40 **Don't Take All Your Loving** ....*Pretending Everyday*		$8		Hickory 1559
6/27/70	16	13		41 **A Perfect Mountain** *Would You Believe Me*		$8		Hickory 1571
7/18/70	46	10		42 **Til I Can't Take It Anymore** *I Love You Because*		$8		RCA Victor 9867
				DOTTIE WEST & DON GIBSON				
10/10/70	37	12		43 **Someway** *Comfort For Your Mind*		$8		Hickory 1579
1/23/71	19	13		44 **Guess Away The Blues** *I Wanna Live*		$8		Hickory 1588
5/22/71	29	11		45 **(I Heard That) Lonesome Whistle** ....*Window Shopping*		$8		Hickory 1598
				written by Hank Williams and Jimmie Davis				
8/28/71	50	8		46 **The Two Of Us Together** *Oh Yes, I Love You*		$8		Hickory 1607
				DON GIBSON & SUE THOMPSON				
10/23/71	5	17		47 **Country Green** *Move It On Over*		$8		Hickory 1614
2/19/72	12	13		48 **Far, Far Away** .... *What's Happened To Me* [R]		$8		Hickory 1623
				new version of #14 above				
4/22/72	71	3		49 **Did You Ever Think** ....*Love's Garden*		$8		Hickory 1629
				DON GIBSON & SUE THOMPSON				
6/10/72	❶[1]	18		50 **Woman (Sensuous Woman)** *If You Want Me To I'll Go*		$8		Hickory 1638
8/12/72	37	11		51 **I Think They Call It Love** *Over There's The Door*		$8		Hickory 1646
				DON GIBSON AND SUE THOMPSON				
10/21/72	11	13		52 **Is This The Best I'm Gonna Feel**................*Watching It Go*		$8		Hickory 1651
12/23/72	64	5		53 **Cause I Love You** *My Tears Don't Show*		$8		Hickory 1654
				DON GIBSON & SUE THOMPSON				
2/17/73	26	11		54 **If You're Goin' Girl** *Lonesome Number One*		$8		Hickory 1661
3/17/73	52	6		55 **Go With Me** *The Two Of Us Together*		$8		Hickory 1665
				DON GIBSON & SUE THOMPSON				
5/26/73	6	14		56 **Touch The Morning** *Too Soon To Know*		$8		Hickory 1671
9/15/73	53	9		57 **Warm Love** *Fly The Friendly Skies With Jesus*		$6		Hickory/MGM 303
				DON GIBSON & SUE THOMPSON				
10/6/73	30	11		58 **That's What I'll Do**...............................*Sweet Dreams*		$6		Hickory/MGM 306
12/29/73+	12	13		59 **Snap Your Fingers** *Love Is A Lonesome Thing*		$6		Hickory/MGM 312
				#8 Pop hit for Joe Henderson in 1962				
5/4/74	8	15		60 **One Day At A Time** *Rainbow Love*		$6		Hickory/MGM 318
8/10/74	31	12		61 **Good Old Fashioned Country Love** ....*Ages And Ages Ago*		$6		Hickory/MGM 324
				DON GIBSON & SUE THOMPSON				
8/31/74	9	17		62 **Bring Back Your Love To Me** *Drinking Champagne*		$6		Hickory/MGM 327
1/18/75	27	12		63 **I'll Sing For You**...................................*Pocatello*		$6		Hickory/MGM 338
4/19/75	24	11		64 **(There She Goes) I Wish Her Well**................*Funny, Familiar, Forgotten Feelings*		$6		Hickory/MGM 345
7/19/75	36	11		65 **Oh, How Love Changes** *Sweet And Tender Times*		$6		Hickory/MGM 350
				DON GIBSON AND SUE THOMPSON				
8/16/75	43	11		66 **Don't Stop Loving Me** *Somebody's Words*		$6		Hickory/MGM 353
12/6/75+	76	8		67 **I Don't Think I'll Ever (Get Over You)** ....*It Can't Last Always*		$6		Hickory/MGM 361
3/13/76	79	5		68 **You've Got To Stop Hurting Me Darling** ....*Blues In My Mind*		$6		Hickory/MGM 365

DEBUT	PEAK	WKS	A-side	B-side	Pop	$	Pic	Label & Number
			GIBSON, Don — Cont'd					
4/3/76	98	2	69 Get Ready-Here I Come .... *Once More*			$6		Hickory/MGM 367
			DON GIBSON AND SUE THOMPSON					
5/29/76	39	10	70 Doing My Time .... *The World Is Waiting For The Sunrise*			$6		Hickory/MGM 372
11/6/76	23	12	71 I'm All Wrapped Up In You .... *We Live In Two Different Worlds*			$5		ABC/Hickory 54001
3/12/77	30	10	72 Fan The Flame, Feed The Fire .... *Bringin' In The Georgia Mail*			$5		ABC/Hickory 54010
7/2/77	16	13	73 If You Ever Get To Houston (Look Me Down) .... *It's All Over*			$5		ABC/Hickory 54014
10/22/77	67	5	74 When Do We Stop Starting Over .... *Love Is Not The Way (You Told Me)*			$5		ABC/Hickory 54019
2/11/78	16	14	75 Starting All Over Again .... *I'd Rather Die Young (Than Grow Old Without You)*			$5		ABC/Hickory 54024
			#19 Pop hit for Mel & Tim in 1972					
6/3/78	22	10	76 The Fool .... *Every Song I Sang Would Be Blue*			$5		ABC/Hickory 54029
			#7 Pop hit for Sanford Clark in 1956					
10/7/78	61	7	77 Oh, Such A Stranger/					
		7	78 I Love You Because			$5		ABC/Hickory 54036
			#3 Pop hit for Al Martino in 1963					
12/23/78+	26	12	79 Any Day Now .... *Baby's Not Home*			$5		ABC/Hickory 54039
			#23 Pop hit for Chuck Jackson in 1962					
6/9/79	37	10	80 Forever One Day At A Time .... *Look Who's Blue*			$5		MCA 41031
3/29/80	42	7	81 Sweet Sensuous Sensations .... *Stranger To Me*			$4		Warner/Curb 49193
12/13/80+	80	6	82 Love Fires .... *Come Back And Love Me*			$4		Warner/Curb 49602
			GIBSON, Hal **'89**					
12/16/89	87	3	The Love She Found In Me			$7		Sundial 163
			GIBSON/MILLER BAND **'93**					
			Five-man band led by singer/songwriter Dave Gibson (from Arkansas) and guitarist Bill "Blue" Miller (from Detroit). Includes Mike Daly (steel guitar), Bryan Grassmeyer (bass) and Steve Grossman (drums).					
11/14/92+	37	20	1 Big Heart .... *(remix)*			$3	▮	Epic 74739
2/13/93	20	20	2 High Rollin' .... *Stone Cold Country*			$3		Epic 74856
6/12/93	22	20	3 Texas Tattoo .... *Southern Man*			$3	▮	Epic 74991
9/25/93	46	11	4 Small Price .... *Where There's Smoke*			$3		Epic 77169
1/22/94	40	13	5 Stone Cold Country .... *Thank Virginia*			$3		Epic 77355
5/28/94	49	10	6 Mammas Don't Let Your Babies Grow Up To Be Cowboys .... *Right Off The Top Of My Heart*			$3	▮	Epic 77488
			from the movie *The Cowboy Way* starring Woody Harrelson					
9/24/94	59	7	7 Red, White And Blue Collar .... *Johnny Get Your Gun*			$3	▮	Epic 77651

GILKYSON, Terry — see WEAVERS, The

GILL, Vince ★60★ **'92**

Born on 4/12/57 in Norman, Oklahoma. Singer/songwriter/guitarist. Member of *Pure Prairie League* from 1979-83. Married to Janis Oliver of **Sweethearts Of The Rodeo** from 1980-97. Joined the *Grand Ole Opry* in 1991. CMA Awards: 1991, 1992, 1993, 1994 & 1995 Male Vocalist of the Year; 1993 & 1994 Entertainer of the Year.

1)Don't Let Our Love Start Slippin' Away 2)I Still Believe In You 3)The Heart Won't Lie 4)One More Last Chance 5)Tryin' To Get Over You

DEBUT	PEAK	WKS	A-side	B-side	Pop	$	Pic	Label & Number
2/11/84	40	13	1 Victim Of Life's Circumstances .... *Don't Say That You Love Me*			$4		RCA 13731
5/19/84	38	11	2 Oh Carolina .... *Half A Chance*			$4		RCA 13809
9/22/84	39	15	3 Turn Me Loose .... *'Til The Best Comes Along*			$4		RCA 13860
3/16/85	32	17	4 True Love .... S:26 *Livin' The Way I Do*			$4		RCA 14020
7/13/85	10	18	5 If It Weren't For Him A:6 / S:10 *Savannah (Do You Ever Think of Me)*			$4		RCA 14140
			Rosanne Cash (guest vocal)					
11/23/85+	9	25	6 Oklahoma Borderline S:9 / A:9 *She Don't Know*			$4		RCA 14216
6/7/86	33	15	7 With You A:32 *Colder Than Winter*			$4		RCA 14371
5/2/87	5	21	8 Cinderella S:11 *Something's Missing*			$4	☐	RCA 5131
9/19/87	16	16	9 Let's Do Something S:25 *It Doesn't Matter Anymore*			$4		RCA 5257
1/30/88	11	17	10 Everybody's Sweetheart S:20 *The Way Back Home*			$4		RCA 5331
6/4/88	39	10	11 The Radio .... *The Way Back Home*			$4		RCA 8301
9/16/89	22	20	12 Never Alone .... *Oh Girl (You Know Where To Find Me)*			$3		MCA 53717
1/20/90	13	26	13 Oklahoma Swing .... *We Could Have Been*			$3		MCA 53780
			Reba McEntire (guest vocal)					
5/26/90	2²	21	14 When I Call Your Name *Rita Ballou*			$3		MCA 79011
			Patty Loveless (backing vocal); CMA Award: Single of the Year.					
9/29/90	3	20	15 Never Knew Lonely *Riding The Rodeo*			$3		MCA 53892
2/16/91	7	20	16 Pocket Full Of Gold *A Little Left Over*			$3		MCA 54026
6/15/91	7	20	17 Liza Jane *What's A Man To Do*			$3		MCA 54123
9/21/91+	4	20	18 Look At Us *I Quit*			$3		MCA 54179
2/1/92	2²	20	19 Take Your Memory With You *Sparkle*			$3		MCA 54282
7/4/92	❶²	20	20 I Still Believe In You *One More Last Chance*			$3		MCA 54406
10/17/92	❶³	20	21 Don't Let Our Love Start Slippin' Away *Love Never Broke Anyone's Heart*			$3		MCA 54489
2/20/93	❶²	20	22 The Heart Won't Lie *Will He Ever Go Away*			$3		MCA 54599
			REBA McENTIRE AND VINCE GILL					
4/10/93	3	20	23 No Future In The Past *Pretty Words*			$3		MCA 54540
7/31/93	❶¹	20	24 One More Last Chance *Under These Conditions*			$3		MCA 54715

DEBUT	PEAK	WKS	Gold	A-side (Chart Hit)..B-side	Pop	$	Pic	Label & Number
				GILL, Vince — Cont'd				
10/30/93	**42**	20		25 I Can't Tell You Why				album cut
				#8 Pop hit for the **Eagles** in 1980; from the album *Common Thread* on Giant 24531				
12/18/93	**52**	4		26 Have Yourself A Merry Little Christmas .... [X]				album cut
				from the album *Let There Be Peace On Earth* on MCA 10877				
1/8/94	**❶**¹	20		27 **Tryin' To Get Over You** *Nothing Like A Woman*	88	$3	▌	MCA 54706
4/16/94	**2**³	20		28 **Whenever You Come Around** *South Side Of Dixie*	72	$3	▌	MCA 54833
7/9/94	**2**²	20		29 **What The Cowgirls Do** *Go Rest High On That Mountain*		$3	▌	MCA 54879
10/15/94	**3**	20		30 **When Love Finds You** *If I Had My Way*	109	$3	▌	MCA 54937
12/24/94	**54**	3		31 Have Yourself A Merry Little Christmas .... [X-R]				album cut
12/31/94	**74**	1		32 It Won't Be The Same This Year .... [X]				album cut
				above 2 from the album *Let There Be Peace On Earth* on MCA 10877				
2/4/95	**4**	20		33 **Which Bridge To Cross (Which Bridge To Burn)** *If There's Anything I Can Do*		$3	▌	MCA 54976
5/13/95	**2**¹	20		34 **You Better Think Twice** *A Real Lady's Man*		$3		MCA 55035
9/2/95	**14**	20		35 **Go Rest High On That Mountain** *Maybe Tonight*		$3		MCA 55098
9/16/95	**15**	20		36 **I Will Always Love You** *Speakin' Of The Devil*		$3		Columbia 78079
				DOLLY PARTON WITH VINCE GILL				
				#1 Pop hit for Whitney Houston in 1992				
4/13/96	**12**	20		37 **High Lonesome Sound** *(bluegrass version)*		$3		MCA 55188
7/20/96	**5**	20		38 **Worlds Apart** *Down To New Orleans*		$3		MCA 55213
11/9/96+	**2**¹	20		39 **Pretty Little Adriana** *Tell Me Lover*		$3		MCA 55251
3/29/97	**2**¹	20		40 **A Little More Love** S:21 *Jenny Dreamed Of Trains*		$3	▌	MCA 55307
7/19/97	**8**	20		41 **You And You Alone** *Given More Time*		$3		MCA 72010
12/13/97+	**34**	13		42 **It's Not Over** *Useless*		$3		Decca 72032
				MARK CHESNUTT (Featuring Vince Gill and Alison Krauss)				
12/27/97	**64**	2		43 Have Yourself A Merry Little Christmas .... [X-R]				album cut
				from the album *Let There Be Peace On Earth* on MCA 10877				
				GILLETTE, Steve **'80**				
				Born in California. Singer/songwriter.				
2/23/80	**76**	5		Lost The Good Thing *Three Lines*		$5		Regency 45002
				STEVE GILLETTE (with Jennifer Warnes)				

				GILLEY, Mickey ★47★ **'83**				
				Born on 3/9/36 in Natchez, Mississippi; raised in Ferriday, Lousiana. Singer/songwriter/pianist. Co-owner with Sherwood Cryer of Gilleys nightclub in Pasadena, Texas, from 1971-89. Gilley and the club were featured in the movie *Urban Cowboy*. Cousin of **Jerry Lee Lewis** and Reverend Jimmy Swaggart.				
				1)She's Pulling Me Back Again 2)Window Up Above 3)I Overlooked An Orchid 4)Lonely Nights 5)Paradise Tonight				
10/19/68	**68**	6		1 Now I Can Live Again *Without You*		$12		Paula 1200
4/20/74	**❶**¹	16		2 **Room Full Of Roses** *She Called Me Baby*	50	$5		Playboy 50056
				#2 Pop hit for Sammy Kaye in 1949				
8/10/74	**❶**¹	18		3 **I Overlooked An Orchid** *Swinging Doors*		$5		Playboy 6004
12/7/74+	**❶**¹	12		4 **City Lights** *Fraulein*		$5		Playboy 6015
3/15/75	**❶**¹	15		5 **Window Up Above** *I'm Moving On*		$5		Playboy 6031
7/5/75	**11**	13		6 Bouquet Of Roses *If You Were Mine To Lose*		$5		Playboy 6041
10/18/75	**32**	9		7 **Roll You Like A Wheel** *Let's Sing A Song Together*		$5	■	Playboy 6045
				MICKEY GILLEY & BARBI BENTON				
11/22/75+	**7**	13		8 **Overnight Sensation** *I'll Sail My Ship Alone*		$5		Playboy 6055
2/21/76	**❶**¹	16		9 **Don't The Girls All Get Prettier At Closing Time** *Where Do You Go To Lose A Heartache*		$5		Playboy 6063
6/26/76	**❶**¹	14		10 **Bring It On Home To Me** *How's My Ex Treating You*	101	$5		Playboy 6075
				#13 Pop hit for Sam Cooke in 1962				
10/16/76	**3**	14		11 **Lawdy Miss Clawdy** *What Is It*		$5		Playboy 6089
				#1 R&B hit for Lloyd Price in 1952				
2/19/77	**❶**¹	17		12 **She's Pulling Me Back Again** *Sweet Mama Goodtimes*		$5		Playboy 6100
6/11/77	**4**	14		13 **Honky Tonk Memories** *Five Foot Two Eyes Of Blue (Has Anybody Seen My Girl)*		$5		Playboy 5807
11/5/77	**9**	14		14 **Chains Of Love** *#1 Rock'n Roll C&W Boogie Blues Man*		$5		Playboy 5818
				#1 R&B hit for Joe Turner in 1951				
3/18/78	**8**	13		15 **The Power Of Positive Drinkin'** *Playing My Old Piano*		$5		Playboy 5826
7/29/78	**9**	14		16 **Here Comes The Hurt Again** *I Hate It, But I Drink It Anyway*		$4		Epic 50580
11/18/78+	**13**	15		17 **The Song We Made Love To** *Memphis Memories*		$4		Epic 50631
3/17/79	**10**	14		18 **Just Long Enough To Say Goodbye** *Tying One On (To Take One Off My Mind)*		$4		Epic 50672
7/21/79	**8**	14		19 **My Silver Lining** *Picture Of Our Love*		$4		Epic 50740
11/17/79+	**17**	14		20 **A Little Getting Used To** *Can't Nobody Love You*		$4		Epic 50801
5/10/80	**❶**¹	16		21 **True Love Ways** *The More I Turn The Bottle Up*	66	$4		Epic 50876
				co-written by Buddy Holly; #14 Pop hit for Peter & Gordon in 1965				
5/31/80	**❶**¹	17		22 **Stand By Me** *Cotton Eyed Joe*	22	$4	■	Full Moon 46640
				#4 Pop hit for Ben E. King in 1961; from the movie *Urban Cowboy* starring John Travolta				
10/18/80	**❶**¹	16		23 **That's All That Matters** *The Blues Don't Care Who's Got 'Em*	101	$3		Epic 50940
2/14/81	**❶**¹	15		24 **A Headache Tomorrow (Or A Heartache Tonight)** *Million Dollar Memories*		$3		Epic 50973
7/4/81	**❶**¹	16		25 **You Don't Know Me** *Jukebox Argument*	55	$3		Epic 02172
				#2 Pop hit for **Ray Charles** in 1962				

GILLEY, Mickey — Cont'd

DEBUT	PEAK	WKS	A-side	B-side	Pop	$	Pic	Label & Number
11/7/81+	❶¹	18	26 Lonely Nights	We've Watched Another Evening Waste Away		$3		Epic 02578
3/20/82	3	18	27 Tears Of The Lonely	Ladies Night		$3		Epic 02774
7/31/82	❶¹	16	28 Put Your Dreams Away	If I Can't Hold Her On The Outside		$3		Epic 03055
11/13/82+	❶¹	18	29 Talk To Me	Honky Tonkin' (I Guess I Done Me Some)	106	$3		Epic 03326
			#20 Pop hit for Little Willie John in 1958					
4/2/83	❶¹	18	30 Fool For Your Love	Shakin' A Heartache		$3		Epic 03783
7/16/83	❶¹	22	31 Paradise Tonight	The Four Seasons Of Love		$3		Epic 04007
			CHARLY McCLAIN and MICKEY GILLEY					
9/3/83	5	21	32 Your Love Shines Through	Wish You Were Mine Again		$3		Epic 04018
1/7/84	2¹	20	33 You've Really Got A Hold On Me	Giving Up Getting Over You		$3		Epic 04269
			#8 Pop hit for The Miracles in 1963					
2/18/84	5	18	34 Candy Man	The Phone Call		$3		Epic 04368
			MICKEY GILLEY and CHARLY McCLAIN					
			#25 Pop hit for Roy Orbison in 1961					
6/16/84	14	17	35 The Right Stuff	We Got A Love Thing		$3		Epic 04489
			CHARLY McCLAIN and MICKEY GILLEY					
9/1/84	4	22	36 Too Good To Stop Now	S:4 / A:4 Shoulder To Cry On		$3		Epic 04563
2/2/85	10	17	37 I'm The One Mama Warned You About	A:9 / S:10 You Can Lie To Me Tonight		$3		Epic 04746
5/4/85	12	17	38 It Ain't Gonna Worry My Mind	A:11 / S:12 Crazy Old Soldier		$3		Columbia 04860
			RAY CHARLES (with Mickey Gilley)					
8/24/85	10	22	39 You've Got Something On Your Mind	A:9 / S:10 I Feel Good About Lovin' You		$3		Epic 05460
12/21/85+	5	21	40 Your Memory Ain't What It Used To Be	S:2 / A:6 Lonely Nights, Lonely Heartache		$3		Epic 05744
7/26/86	6	19	41 Doo-Wah Days	S:6 / A:6 After She's Gone		$3		Epic 06184
4/4/87	16	14	42 Full Grown Fool	S:15 / A:28 To My One And Only		$3		Epic 07009
7/16/88	49	8	43 I'm Your Puppet	Don't Show Me Your Memories (And I Won't Show You Mine)		$4		Airborne 10002
			#6 Pop hit for James & Bobby Purify in 1966					
10/29/88+	23	19	44 She Reminded Me Of You	S:28 Easy Climb		$4		Airborne 10008
4/15/89	62	5	45 You Still Got A Way With My Heart	It's Killing Me To Watch Love Die		$4		Airborne 10016
7/15/89	53	8	46 There! I've Said It Again	It's Killing Me To Watch Love Die		$4		Airborne 75740
			#1 Pop hit for Bobby Vinton in 1964					

GILMORE, Jimmie Dale   '88
Born on 5/6/45 in Tulia, Texas. Singer/songwriter/guitarist.

DEBUT	PEAK	WKS	A-side	B-side	Pop	$	Pic	Label & Number
8/27/88	72	5	1 White Freight Liner Blues	Trying To Get To You		$5		Hightone 504
6/10/89	85	2	2 Honky Tonk Song			$5		Hightone 510

GIMBLE, Johnny — see PRICE, Ray

GINO THE NEW GUY   '95
Born Gino Ruberto on 10/14/63 in Wabasha, Minnesota. Morning show producer at Minneapolis radio station KEEY-FM.

DEBUT	PEAK	WKS	A-side	B-side	Pop	$	Pic	Label & Number
8/12/95	56	11	Any Gal Of Mine	(no B-side) [N]		$10		no label
			parody of "Any Man Of Mine" by Shania Twain; not commercially available; created on tape and sent to radio stations					

GIRLS NEXT DOOR   '86
Female vocal group: Doris King, Diane Williams, Cindy Nixon and Tammy Stephens. Disbanded in 1991.

DEBUT	PEAK	WKS	A-side	B-side	Pop	$	Pic	Label & Number
2/1/86	14	21	1 Love Will Get You Through Times With No Money	S:11 / A:16 Ruins Of Love		$4		MTM 72059
6/14/86	8	21	2 Slow Boat To China	S:6 / A:8 Pretty Boy's Cadillac		$4		MTM 72068
11/1/86	26	14	3 Baby I Want It	A:26 (sing-along version)		$4		MTM 72078
2/7/87	28	13	4 Walk Me In The Rain	A:28 The Fool In Me		$4		MTM 72084
7/4/87	43	9	5 What A Girl Next Door Could Do	I Think I'm Gonna Fall (In Love With You)		$4		MTM 72088
10/17/87	57	6	6 Easy To Find	Message From My Heart		$4		MTM 72095
9/10/88	73	4	7 Love And Other Fairy Tales	I Can Hear My Heart Begin To Cry		$4		MTM 72106
12/2/89+	54	7	8 He's Gotta Have Me	Wasn't It You		$3		Atlantic 88791
9/1/90	71	1	9 How 'Bout Us	Last Goodbye		$3	▌	Atlantic 87868
			#12 Pop hit for Champaign in 1981					

GLASER, Chuck   '74
Born on 2/27/36 in Spalding, Nebraska. Member of The Glaser Brothers.

DEBUT	PEAK	WKS	A-side	B-side	Pop	$	Pic	Label & Number
1/5/74	81	7	Gypsy Queen	That's When I Love You The Most		$5		MGM 14663

GLASER, Jim   ★239★   '84
Born on 12/16/37 in Spalding, Nebraska. Singer/songwriter/guitarist. Member of The Glaser Brothers.
1)You're Gettin' To Me Again 2)If I Could Only Dance With You 3)Let Me Down Easy
4)When You're Not A Lady 5)The Man In The Mirror

DEBUT	PEAK	WKS	A-side	B-side	Pop	$	Pic	Label & Number
8/31/68	32	8	1 God Help You Woman	She Was Too Good To Me		$6		RCA Victor 9587
1/4/69	40	10	2 Please Take Me Back	Kiss Her Once For Me		$6		RCA Victor 9696
5/10/69	52	7	3 I'm Not Through Loving You	Can't Keep My Mind On The Game		$6		RCA Victor 0142
10/11/69	53	5	4 Molly	Permanent Kind Of Lovin' (From A Temporary Man)		$6		RCA Victor 0231
9/1/73	67	12	5 I See His Love All Over You	It's Still A Long Way		$5		MGM 14590
6/15/74	68	8	6 Fool Passin' Through	If It Pleases You		$5		MGM 14758
12/21/74+	51	12	7 Forgettin' 'Bout You	If It Pleases You		$5		MGM 14758
5/31/75	88	5	8 One, Two, Three (Never Gonna Fall In Love Again)	One Night Man		$5		MGM 14798
11/15/75	43	10	9 Woman, Woman	Turn To Me		$5		MGM 14834
			#4 Pop hit for Gary Puckett and The Union Gap in 1968					
11/6/76	66	10	10 She's Free But She's Not Easy	Lonely Bein' Free		$4		MCA 40636
7/23/77	88	4	11 Chasin' My Tail	Sleeping Beauty		$4		MCA 40742
11/26/77	86	4	12 Don't Let My Love Stand In Your Way	Honky Tonk Lady		$4		MCA 40813
11/20/82+	16	22	13 When You're Not A Lady	I Don't Wanna Make Love		$4		Noble Vision 101
4/2/83	28	13	14 You Got Me Running			$4		Noble Vision 102
8/27/83	17	21	15 The Man In The Mirror	Pretend		$4		Noble Vision 103

GLASER, Jim — Cont'd

DEBUT	PEAK	WKS		A-side / B-side	Pop	$	Label & Number
1/28/84	10	24		16 If I Could Only Dance With You — *Woman, Woman*		$4	Noble Vision 104
6/9/84	❶[1]	24		17 You're Gettin' To Me Again — *Stand By The Road*		$4	Noble Vision 105
11/17/84+	16	19		18 Let Me Down Easy .... S:15 / A:18 *I'd Love To See You Again*		$4	Noble Vision 107
6/29/85	54	8		19 I'll Be Your Fool Tonight .... *Tough Act To Follow*		$4	MCA 52619
9/14/85	27	18		20 In Another Minute .... A:25 / S:28 *Merry-Go-Round*		$4	MCA 52672
12/28/85+	53	9		21 If I Don't Love You .... *It's Not Easy*		$4	MCA 52748
4/26/86	40	11		22 The Lights Of Albuquerque .... A:37 *Waltzing Through A Rock And Roll Life*		$4	MCA 52808

GLASER, Tompall '75

Born Thomas Paul Glaser on 9/3/33 in Spalding, Nebraska. Singer/songwriter/guitarist. Lead singer of **The Glaser Brothers**.

DEBUT	PEAK	WKS		A-side / B-side	Pop	$	Label & Number
10/6/73	77	7		1 Bad, Bad, Bad Cowboy — *Let It Be Pretty*		$6	MGM 14622
				TOMPALL GLASER Of The Glaser Brothers			
3/23/74	96	5		2 Texas Law Sez.......... *Pass Me On By*		$6	MGM 14701
9/14/74	63	8		3 Musical Chairs.......... *Grab A Hold*		$6	MGM 14740
5/24/75	21	19		4 Put Another Log On The Fire (Male Chauvinist National Anthem) — *Mendocino* [N]	103	$6	MGM 14800
				TOMPALL			
4/24/76	36	9		5 T For Texas.......... *Broken Down Momma*		$5	Polydor 14314
				TOMPALL And His Outlaw Band #2 Pop hit for Jimmie Rodgers in 1928 as "Blue Yodel"			
4/9/77	45	9		6 It'll Be Her .... *Sweethearts Or Strangers/I Will Always Love You*		$4	ABC 12261
				also see #20 under **Tompall & The Glaser Brothers**			
12/3/77	91	3		7 It Never Crossed My Mind .... *Easy On My Mind*		$4	ABC 12309
2/25/78	79	6		8 Drinking Them Beers.......... *Duncan And Brady*		$4	ABC 12329

GLASER BROTHERS, Tompall & The ★217★ '81

Family trio from Spalding, Nebraska: brothers **Tompall Glaser**, **Chuck Glaser** and **Jim Glaser**. Opened own recording studio in Nashville in 1969 which was a hangout for the budding "outlaw" music movement. Trio split up in 1973. Reunited in 1979 and then split up once again in 1982. CMA Award: 1970 Vocal Group of the Year.

1)Lovin' Her Was Easier 2)Rings 3)California Girl 4)Ain't It All Worth Living For 5)Just One Time

DEBUT	PEAK	WKS		A-side / B-side	Pop	$	Label & Number
12/31/66+	24	15		1 Gone, On The Other Hand.......... *Streets Of Baltimore*		$7	MGM 13611
7/22/67	27	16		2 Through The Eyes Of Love .... *She Loved The Wrong Man*		$7	MGM 13754
2/24/68	42	9		3 The Moods Of Mary .... *No End Of Love*		$7	MGM 13880
7/27/68	36	10		4 One Of These Days .... *Where Has All The Love Gone*		$7	MGM 13954
3/22/69	11	16		5 California Girl (And The Tennessee Square).......... *All That Keeps Ya Goin'*	92	$7	MGM 14036
7/19/69	24	11		6 Wicked California .... *This Eve Of Parting*		$7	MGM 14064
12/27/69+	30	9		7 Walk Unashamed .... *Gonna Miss Me*		$7	MGM 14096
4/11/70	33	11		8 All That Keeps Ya Goin' .... *Theme From "...tick...tick..."*		$6	MGM 14113
				from the movie *...tick...tick...tick...* starring George Kennedy			
10/24/70	23	11		9 Gone Girl.......... *I'll Say My Words*		$6	MGM 14169
6/12/71	22	9		10 Faded Love .... *Pretty Eyes*		$6	MGM 14249
				TOMPALL AND THE GLASER BROTHERS WITH LEON McAULIFFE AND THE CIMARRON BOYS			
8/28/71	7	15		11 Rings — *That's When I Love You The Most*		$6	MGM 14291
				#17 Pop hit for Cymarron in 1971			
1/15/72	23	13		12 Sweet, Love Me Good Woman .... *Stand Beside Me*		$6	MGM 14339
6/17/72	15	15		13 Ain't It All Worth Living For .... *Blue Ridge Mountains*		$6	MGM 14390
				TOMPALL & THE GLASER BROTHERS And The Nashville Studio Band			
1/20/73	46	9		14 A Girl Like You .... *Delta Lost*		$6	MGM 14462
5/12/73	47	8		15 Charlie .... *Lovin' You Again*		$6	MGM 14516
4/19/80	43	8		16 Weight Of My Chains .... *The Ballad Of Lucy Jordon*		$4	Elektra 46595
11/8/80	34	11		17 Sweet City Woman .... *Tryin' To Outrun The Wind*		$4	Elektra 47056
				#8 Pop hit for the Stampeders in 1971			
5/2/81	2[2]	16		18 Lovin' Her Was Easier (Than Anything I'll Ever Do Again) — *United We Fall*		$4	Elektra 47134
				#26 Pop hit for Kris Kristofferson in 1971			
9/19/81	17	14		19 Just One Time .... *Feelin' The Weight Of My Chains*		$4	Elektra 47193
2/13/82	19	13		20 It'll Be Her .... *A Mansion On The Hill* [R]		$4	Elektra 47405
				new version of #6 under **Tompall Glaser**			
6/12/82	28	10		21 I Still Love You (After All These Years).......... *Feelin' The Weight Of My Chains*		$4	Elektra 47461
11/6/82	88	3		22 Maria Consuela .... *I Could Never Live Alone Again*		$4	Elektra 69947

GLENN, Darrell '53

Born on 12/7/35 in Waco, Texas. Died of cancer on 4/9/90 (age 54). Son of Artie Glenn who wrote "Crying In The Chapel."

DEBUT	PEAK	WKS		A-side / B-side	Pop	$	Label & Number
7/25/53	4	13		Crying In The Chapel — A:4 / J:4 / S:7 *Hang Up That Telephone*	6	$40	Valley 105
				#3 Pop hit for Elvis Presley in 1965			

GLENN, Howdy '77

Black male singer.

DEBUT	PEAK	WKS		A-side / B-side	Pop	$	Label & Number
9/17/77	62	6		1 Touch Me .... *White Line Fever*		$4	Warner 8447
				written by Willie Nelson			
7/29/78	72	5		2 You Mean The World To Me .... *That Lucky Old Sun*		$4	Warner 8616

GODFREY, Ray '60

Born Arnold Godfrey in Copperville, Tennessee.

DEBUT	PEAK	WKS		A-side / B-side	Pop	$	Label & Number
6/27/60	8	15		1 The Picture — *The Overall Song*		$25	Savoy 3021
				first released on J&J 001 ($30)			
12/29/62+	20	6		2 Better Times A Comin' .... *Ten Silver Dollars*		$20	Sims 130

DEBUT	PEAK	WKS		A-side	B-side	Pop	$	Pic	Label & Number
				GOLDEN, Jeff '89					
				Singer/songwriter from Atlanta.					
9/10/88	91	2		1 Southern And Proud Of It			$5		MGA 30274
11/26/88	91	2		2 This Old World Ain't The Same			$5		MGA 30275
3/18/89	80	3		3 That Newsong (They're Playin)			$5		Soundwaves 4816
6/24/89	87	3		4 Singing The Blues			$5		MGA 104
				#1 Pop hit for **Guy Mitchell** in 1956					
				GOLDEN, William Lee '86					
				Born on 1/12/35 in Brewton, Alabama. Member of the **Oak Ridge Boys**.					
6/21/86	53	7		1 Love Is The Only Way Out	Music For My Soul		$4		MCA 52819
11/1/86	72	4		2 You Can't Take It With You	Somebody Gotta Pay		$4		MCA 52944
				GOLDENS, The '88					
				Duo of brothers from Brewton, Alabama: Rusty (b: 1/3/59) and Chris (b: 10/17/62) Golden. Sons of **William Lee Golden**. Chris a member of **Cedar Creek**. Rusty was a member of The Boys Band.					
3/5/88	55	6		1 Put Us Together Again	Country Comfort		$3		Epic 07716
7/2/88	63	6		2 Sorry Girls	Best Friend's Baby		$3		Epic 07928
5/4/91	67	3		3 Keep The Faith					album cut
				from the album *Rush For Gold* on Capitol/SBK 94395					
	★234★			**GOLDSBORO, Bobby** '68					
				Born on 1/18/41 in Marianna, Florida. Singer/songwriter/guitarist. Hosted own syndicated TV show from 1972-75.					
				1)*Honey* 2)*Watching Scotty Grow* 3)*Autumn Of My Life* 4)*Muddy Mississippi Line* 5)*Goodbye Marie*					
3/9/68	56	5		1 I Just Wasted The Rest	Our Way Of Life		$8		United Artists 50243
				DEL REEVES & BOBBY GOLDSBORO					
3/30/68	❶³	15	●	2 Honey	Danny	❶⁵	$7		United Artists 50283
7/13/68	15	11		3 Autumn Of My Life	She Chased Me	19	$7	■	United Artists 50318
10/26/68	37	10		4 The Straight Life	Tomorrow Is Forgotten	36	$7		United Artists 50461
3/15/69	49	5		5 Glad She's A Woman	Letter To Emily	61	$7		United Artists 50497
5/3/69	22	11		6 I'm A Drifter	Hoboes And Kings	46	$7		United Artists 50525
8/30/69	15	10		7 Muddy Mississippi Line	Richer Man Than I	53	$7		United Artists 50565
11/1/69	31	10		8 Take A Little Good Will Home	She Thinks I Still Care		$7		United Artists 50591
				BOBBY GOLDSBORO & DEL REEVES					
12/20/69+	56	7		9 Mornin Mornin	Requiem	78	$7		United Artists 50614
5/16/70	71	2		10 Can You Feel It	Time Good, Time Bad	75	$7		United Artists 50650
1/2/71	7	15		11 Watching Scotty Grow	Water Color Days	11	$7		United Artists 50727
5/29/71	48	7		12 And I Love You So	The Gentle Of A Man	83	$7		United Artists 50776
8/4/73	100	2		13 Summer (The First Time)	Childhood -- 1949	21	$6	■	United Artists 251
1/19/74	52	10		14 Marlena	Sing Me A Smile		$6		United Artists 371
5/11/74	62	6		15 I Believe The South Is Gonna Rise Again	She		$6		United Artists 422
				BOBBY GOLDSBORO with The TSU Chorus					
9/7/74	79	5		16 Hello Summertime	And Then There Was Gina		$6		United Artists 529
5/15/76	22	14		17 A Butterfly For Bucky	Another Night Alone	101	$6		United Artists 793
3/19/77	82	5		18 Me And The Elephants	I Love Music	104	$5		Epic 50342
7/9/77	85	4		19 The Cowboy And The Lady	Me And Millie		$5		Epic 50413
10/25/80+	17	15		20 Goodbye Marie	Love Has Made A Woman Out Of You		$4		Curb 5400
3/7/81	20	12		21 Alice Doesn't Love Here Anymore	Green Eyed Woman, Nashville, Blues		$4		Curb 70052
7/4/81	19	14		22 Love Ain't Never Hurt Nobody	Wings Of An Eagle		$4		Curb 02117
11/14/81	31	11		23 The Round-Up Saloon	Green Eyed Woman, Nashville, Blues		$4		Curb 02583
2/20/82	49	9		24 Lucy And The Stranger	Out Run The Sun		$4		Curb 02726
				GOODNIGHT, Gary '82					
				Born in 1954 in Immokalee, Florida.					
11/8/80	90	3		1 I Have To Break The Chains That Bind Me			$5		Door Knob 138
1/24/81	91	2		2 Make Me Believe	Back Door Slam		$5		Door Knob 141
3/21/81	90	3		3 Get Me High, Off This Low			$5		Door Knob 149
5/16/81	75	5		4 Tell Me So	There'll Be A Blue Moon Tonight		$5		Door Knob 155
8/8/81	72	5		5 Let Me Fill For You A Fantasy			$5		Door Knob 159
11/28/81	90	3		6 Losin' Myself In You	Vagabond Cowboy		$5		Door Knob 166
1/16/82	67	7		7 Lady, Lay Down (Lay Down On My Pillow)			$5		Door Knob 169
7/17/82	64	7		8 Bringing Out The Fool In Me	Texas Let Me In		$5		Soundwaves 4675
				GOODSON, C.L. '75					
9/13/75	93	4		18 Yellow Roses	The More She Thinks About Him		$7		Island 030
				#10 Pop hit for **Bobby Darin** in 1963					
				GOODSON, Lloyd '76					
12/11/76	80	6		Jesus Is The Same In California	Wearin' Out The Patches On My Knees		$6		United Artists 891
				GOODSON, Mitch '80					
				Born in Dothan, Alabama.					
2/9/80	95	3		1 Draggin' Leather	She Loves It (As Much As Me)		$6		Partridge 002
4/12/80	70	6		2 Do You Wanna Spend The Night			$6		Partridge 011
				GOODWIN, Bill '63					
				Born on 6/2/30 in Cumberland City, Tennessee.					
5/11/63	17	8		Shoes Of A Fool	It Keeps Right On A-Hurtin'		$15		Vee Jay 501
				GORDON, Luke '59					
				Born on 4/15/32 in Quincy, Kentucky.					
12/22/58+	13	7		Dark Hollow	You May Be Someone (Where You Come From)		$20		Island 0640

GORDON, Noah   **'95**
Born on 9/19/71 in Sparta, Illinois. Singer/guitarist/drummer.

| 1/14/95 | 68 | 3 | | **The Blue Pages** .... | | | | album cut |

         from the album *I Need A Break* on Patriot 81221

GORDON, Robert   **'79**
Born in 1947 in Washington, D.C. Rockabilly singer.

| 3/31/79 | 99 | 1 | | 1 **It's Only Make Believe** .... *Rock Billy Boogie* | | $5 | | RCA 11471 |

         #1 Pop hit for **Conway Twitty** in 1958

| 6/23/79 | 98 | 1 | | 2 **Walk On By** .... *Black Slacks* | | $5 | | RCA 11608 |

GORME, Eydie   **'73**
Born on 8/16/31 in New York City. Former big band singer. Married Steve Lawrence on 12/29/57. Charted 17 pop hits from 1956-72.

| 8/11/73 | 94 | 5 | | **Take One Step** .... *The Garden* | | $5 | | MGM 14563 |

GOSDIN, Rex   **'80**
Born Equen Manual Gosdin in Woodland, Alabama. Died on 5/23/83 (age 45). Brother of **Vern Gosdin**. Member of **The Gosdin Bros.**

| 7/14/79 | 94 | 3 | | 1 **We're Making Up For Lost Time** .... | | $7 | | MRC 10589 |
| 5/31/80 | 51 | 10 | | 2 **Just Give Me What You Think Is Fair** .... *Things I Remember* | | $7 | | Sabre 4520 |

         REX GOSDIN with Tommy Jennings

| 11/8/80 | 92 | 2 | | 3 **Lovin' You Is Music To My Mind** .... *How Can Anything That Sounds So Good* | | $7 | | Grape Vine 12046 |
| 6/11/83 | 90 | 3 | | 4 **That Old Time Feelin'** .... *Morning Noon And Night* | | $7 | | Sun 1178 |

GOSDIN, Vern ★**82**★   **'84**
Born on 8/5/34 in Woodland, Alabama. Singer/songwriter/guitarist. Brother of **Rex Gosdin**. Member of **The Gosdin Bros.**

    1)*I Can Tell By The Way You Dance* 2)*Set 'Em Up Joe* 3)*I'm Still Crazy* 4)*Who You Gonna Blame It On This Time*
    5)*That Just About Does It*

| 3/5/77 | 9 | 15 | | 1 **Yesterday's Gone/** | | | | |
| 10/30/76+ | 16 | 15 | | 2   **Hangin' On** .... | | $5 | | Elektra 45353 |

         also see The Gosdin Bros.; Emmylou Harris (harmony vocal, above 2)

6/25/77	7	15		3 **Till The End/**				
1/21/78	23	11		4 **It Started All Over Again**		$5		Elektra 45411
10/22/77	17	13		5 **Mother Country Music** .... *We Make Beautiful Music Together*		$5		Elektra 45436
5/20/78	9	12		6 **Never My Love** .... *I Sure Can Love You*		$5		Elektra 45483

         #2 Pop hit for The Association in 1967; **Janie Fricke** (harmony vocal, above 2)

10/7/78	13	11		7 **Break My Mind** .... *Without You There's A Sadness In My Song*		$5		Elektra 45532
3/17/79	16	13		8 **You've Got Somebody, I've Got Somebody** .... *Till I'm Over Gettin' Over You*		$5		Elektra 46021
7/7/79	21	14		9 **All I Want And Need Forever** .... *Fifteen Hundred Times A Day*		$5		Elektra 46052
11/3/79	57	6		10 **Sarah's Eyes** .... *She's Gone*		$5		Elektra 46550
1/24/81	28	11		11 **Too Long Gone** .... *She's Just A Place To Fall*		$5		Ovation 1163
5/16/81	7	17		12 **Dream Of Me** .... *Ain't It Been Love*		$5		Ovation 1171
1/16/82	28	15		13 **Don't Ever Leave Me Again** .... *Love Is All We Had To Share*		$5		AMI 1302
7/10/82	22	13		14 **Your Bedroom Eyes** .... *Love Is All We Had To Share*		$5		AMI 1307
10/23/82+	10	19		15 **Today My World Slipped Away** .... *Ain't It Been Love*		$5		AMI 1310
2/12/83	5	21		16 **If You're Gonna Do Me Wrong (Do It Right)** .... *Favorite Fool Of All*		$5		Compleat 102
2/12/83	49	7		17 **Friday Night Feelin'** .... *Lovin' You Is Music To My Mind*		$5		AMI 1312
6/4/83	5	22		18 **Way Down Deep** .... *Today My World Slipped Away*		$5		Compleat 108
10/1/83	10	21		19 **I Wonder Where We'd Be Tonight** .... *I Feel Love Closin' In*		$5		Compleat 115
3/31/84	❶[1]	25		20 **I Can Tell By The Way You Dance (You're Gonna Love Me Tonight)** .... *My Heart Is In Good Hands*		$5		Compleat 122
7/21/84	10	20		21 **What Would Your Memories Do** *S:26 Love Me Right To The End*		$5		Compleat 126
12/1/84+	10	20		22 **Slow Burning Memory** *A:9 / S:10 I've Got A Heart Full Of You*		$5		Compleat 135
5/4/85	20	17		23 **Dim Lights, Thick Smoke (And Loud, Loud Music)** .... *S:19 / A:22 For A Minute There*		$5		Compleat 142
8/31/85	35	13		24 **I Know The Way To You By Heart** .... *Rainbows And Roses*		$5		Compleat 145
3/22/86	68	8		25 **It's Only Love Again** .... *Today My World Slipped Away*		$5		Compleat 153
6/7/86	61	10		26 **Was It Just The Wine** .... *Way Down Deep*		$5		Compleat 155
9/13/86	51	8		27 **Time Stood Still** .... *Slow Burning Memory*		$5		Compleat 158
11/7/87+	4	23		28 **Do You Believe Me Now** *S:2 Nobody Calls From Vegas Just To Say Hello*		$3		Columbia 07627
4/9/88	❶[1]	22		29 **Set 'Em Up Joe** *S:❶[2] There Ain't Nothing Wrong (Just Ain't Nothing Right)*		$3		Columbia 07762

         tribute to Ernest Tubb

8/27/88	6	23		30 **Chiseled In Stone** *S:2 Tight As Twin Fiddles*		$3		Columbia 08003
1/7/89	2[1]	22		31 **Who You Gonna Blame It On This Time** *It's Not Over Yet*		$3		Columbia 08528
5/27/89	❶[1]	22		32 **I'm Still Crazy** *Paradise '83*		$3		Columbia 68888
9/30/89+	4	26		33 **That Just About Does It** *Set 'Em Up Joe*		$3		Columbia 69084
2/3/90	10	26		34 **Right In The Wrong Direction** *Tanqueray*		$3	▌	Columbia 73221
6/23/90	75	1		35 **Tanqueray** .... *You're Not By Yourself*		$3	▌	Columbia 73350
9/1/90	14	20		36 **This Ain't My First Rodeo** .... *If You're Gonna Do Me Wrong (Do It Right)*		$3	▌	Columbia 73491
12/8/90+	10	20		37 **Is It Raining At Your House** *Today My World Slipped Away*		$3		Columbia 73632
5/25/91	64	8		38 **I Knew My Day Would Come** .... *Love Will Keep Your Hand On The Wheel*		$3		Columbia 73814
8/24/91	51	12		39 **The Garden** .... *I'd Better Write It Down*		$3		Columbia 73946
11/30/91+	54	13		40 **A Month Of Sundays** .... *The Bridge I'm Still Building On*		$3		Columbia 74103

DEBUT	PEAK	WKS		A-side (Chart Hit) ... B-side	Pop	$	Pic	Label & Number
				GOSDIN, Vern — Cont'd				
4/10/93	67	5		41 Back When .... *What Are We Gonna Do About Me*		$3		Columbia 74905
				GOSDIN BROS., The '67				
				Duo from Woodland, Alabama: **Vern Gosdin** and **Rex Gosdin**. Rex died on 5/23/83 (age 45).				
10/7/67	37	11		Hangin' On .... *Multiple Heartaches*		$15		Bakersfield I. 1002
				GRAHAM, Tammy '97				
				Born on 2/7/68 in Little Rock, Arkansas. Singer/pianist.				
5/11/96	63	8		1 Tell Me Again .... *Cool Water*		$3		Career 12953
3/22/97	37	15		2 A Dozen Red Roses .... S:4 *Tell Me Again*	108	$3	■	Career 13075
8/2/97	59	4		3 Cool Water............................... *More About Love*		$3		Career 13089
				GRAMMER, Billy '59				
				Born on 8/28/25 in Benton, Illinois. Singer/songwriter/guitarist. Joined the *Grand Ole Opry* in 1959.				
1/5/59	5	13		1 **Gotta Travel On** *Chasing A Dream*	4	$15		Monument 400
				based on 19th-century tune that originated in the British Isles				
1/19/63	18	5		2 I Wanna Go Home............................... *The Bottom Of The Glass*		$10		Decca 31449
				song also known as "Detroit City"				
1/11/64	43	2		3 I'll Leave The Porch Light A-Burning .... *Old Foolish Me*		$10		Decca 31562
8/27/66	35	3		4 Bottles .... *Temporarily*		$10		Epic 10052
12/31/66+	30	12		5 The Real Thing .... *Heaven Help This Heart Of Mine*		$10		Epic 10103
9/23/67	48	11		6 Mabel (You Have Been A Friend To Me)............................... *Papa And Mama*		$10		Rice 5025
8/31/68	70	4		7 The Ballad Of John Dillinger .... *Do You Still Believe*		$8		Mercury 72836
10/18/69	66	5		8 Jesus Is A Soul Man .... *Peace On Earth Begins Today*		$8		Stop 321
				#28 Pop hit for Lawrence Reynolds in 1969				
				GRANT, Barry '81				
				Singer/DJ from West Palm Beach, Florida. Also recorded as **Amarillo** and **Breakfast Barry**.				
9/29/79	95	2		1 We're In For Hard Times .... *Most Wanted Outlaw*		$6		Countrystock 1602
				BREAKFAST BARRY				
4/26/80	89	3		2 Pretty Poison/				
12/15/79	91	5		3 Out With The Boys...............................		$6		CSI 001
				AMARILLO:				
12/27/80+	82	4		4 That's The Way My Woman Loves............................... *Pretty Poison*		$5		NSD 72
6/13/81	70	5		5 Somehow, Someway And Someday/				
3/21/81	87	3		6 How Long Has This Been Going On		$5		NSD 81
10/10/81	86	4		7 A Little Bit Crazy .... *Out With The Boys*		$5		NSD 104
				GRANT, Tom '79				
				Born on 8/28/50 in Milwaukee. Singer/songwriter. Member of **Trinity Lane**.				
1/27/79	40	8		1 If You Could See You Through My Eyes .... *You're Easy To Love*		$6		Republic 036
6/30/79	63	5		2 We've Gotta Get Away From It All .... *Catching Up On Love*		$6		Republic 043
9/8/79	16	11		3 Sail On .... *I'll Meet You In Paradise*		$6		Republic 045
				#4 Pop hit for the Commodores in 1979				
10/16/82	76	4		4 I'm Gonna Love You Right Out Of This World .... *Sundown Lady*		$5		Elektra 69961
8/10/85	63	8		5 Everyday People...............................		$5		Bermuda Dunes 110
				MARGO SMITH AND TOM GRANT				
				GRAY, Billy — see JACKSON, Wanda				
	★213★			**GRAY, Claude** '61				
				Born on 1/26/32 in Henderson, Texas. Singer/songwriter/guitarist. Nicknamed "The Tall Texan."				
				1)My Ears Should Burn 2)I'll Just Have A Cup Of Coffee 3)I Never Had The One I Wanted 4)Family Bible 5)How Fast Them Trucks Can Go				
3/21/60	10	13		1 Family Bible *Crying In The Night*		$25		D 1118
				written by **Willie Nelson**				
1/9/61	4	23		2 I'll Just Have A Cup Of Coffee (Then I'll Go) *I Just Want To Be Alone*	84	$12		Mercury 71732
6/26/61	3	19		3 My Ears Should Burn (When Fools Are Talked About) *Crying In The Night*		$12		Mercury 71826
1/13/62	26	1		4 Let's End It Before It Begins .... *Talk To Me Old Lonesome Heart*		$12		Mercury 71898
10/20/62	20	5		5 Daddy Stopped In .... *Three Times*		$12		Mercury 72001
2/9/63	18	6		6 Knock Again, True Love .... *Call Of The Wild*		$12		Mercury 72063
3/21/64	43	12		7 Eight Years (And Two Children Later)............................... *Lonesome*		$12		Mercury 72236
7/30/66	22	10		8 Mean Old Woman .... *Then Cry You Away*		$10		Columbia 43614
11/26/66+	9	18		9 I Never Had The One I Wanted *Effects Your Leaving Had On Me*		$6		Decca 32039
				also see #25 below				
6/3/67	45	9		10 Because Of Him/				
6/24/67	67	3		11 If I Ever Need A Lady (I'll Call You)...............................		$6		Decca 32122
				also see #24 below				
9/23/67	12	14		12 How Fast Them Trucks Can Go .... *Next Time You See Me*		$6		Decca 32180
5/18/68	31	12		13 Night Life .... *Just Between Us Tears*		$6		Decca 32312
11/9/68	68	2		14 The Love Of A Woman .... *The Kind You Find Tonight Forget Tomorrow*		$6		Decca 32393
5/3/69	41	11		15 Don't Give Me A Chance .... *Once In Every Lifetime*		$6		Decca 32456
10/25/69	34	10		16 Take Off Time .... *Sherry Ann*		$6		Decca 32566
4/11/70	54	6		17 The Cleanest Man In Cincinnati .... *Crazy Arms*		$6		Decca 32648
7/18/70	40	8		18 Everything Will Be Alright .... *Apartment #9*		$6		Decca 32697
3/27/71	41	9		19 Angel............................... *Save My Mind*		$6		Decca 32786
9/2/72	66	7		20 What Every Woman Wants To Hear............................... *There's You*		$8		Million 18
1/20/73	58	8		21 Woman Ease My Mind .... *Don't Fight The Feeling*		$8		Million 31
10/16/76	88	5		22 Rockin' My Memories (To Sleep)............................... *But That's All Right*		$7		Granny White 10001
1/22/77	92	4		23 We Fell In Love That Way .... *That's My Baby*		$7		Granny White 10002

GRAY, Claude — Cont'd

DEBUT	PEAK	WKS	A-side / B-side	$	Label & Number
6/3/78	68	7	24 If I Ever Need A Lady .... *The Bar* [R]	$7	Granny White 10006
			new version of #11 above		
1/13/79	78	6	25 I Never Had The One I Wanted................................ *Late Cup Of Coffee* [R]	$7	Granny White 10007
			new version of #9 above		
2/6/82	68	6	26 Let's Go All The Way .... *We Climbed A Mountain Last Night*	$7	Granny White 10009
			CLAUDE GRAY and NORMA JEAN		
2/22/86	77	4	27 Sweet Caroline .... *Half A Mind*	$6	Country Int'l. 208
			#4 Pop hit for Neil Diamond in 1969		

GRAY, Dobie   '86
Born Lawrence Darrow Brown on 7/26/40 in Brookshire/Simonton, Texas. Charted 8 pop hits from 1963-79.

DEBUT	PEAK	WKS	A-side / B-side	$	Label & Number
3/22/86	35	13	1 That's One To Grow On............................... *Gonna Be A Long Night*	$3	Capitol 5562
7/12/86	42	9	2 The Dark Side Of Town........................ *A Night In The Life Of A Country Boy*	$3	Capitol 5596
11/15/86	67	9	3 From Where I Stand... *So Far So Good*	$3	Capitol 5647
11/21/87	82	2	4 Take It Real Easy............................ *You Must Have Been Reading My Heart*	$3	Capitol 44087

GRAY, Jan   '83
Born in Oneida, Kentucky.

DEBUT	PEAK	WKS	A-side / B-side	$	Label & Number
11/15/80	80	3	1 No Love At All .... *There's No Way We Can Go Wrong*	$5	Paid 106
			#16 Pop hit for B.J. Thomas in 1971		
8/21/82	85	3	2 There I Go Dreamin' Again	$5	Jamex 006
11/6/82	89	3	3 Closer To Crazy .... *It's About Time*	$5	Jamex 008
6/18/83	49	11	4 No Fair Fallin' In Love *Win Some, Lose Some, Lonesome*	$5	Jamex 010
10/15/83	55	7	5 Before We Knew It .... *The Heart*	$5	Jamex 011
1/21/84	51	9	6 Bad Night For Good Girls ....*Dear Me*	$5	Jamex 012
5/10/86	64	6	7 Cross My Heart..	$7	Cypress 8510

GRAY, Mark   ★317★   '84
Born on 10/24/53 in Vicksburg, Mississippi. Singer/songwriter/pianist. Member of Exile from 1979-82.
1)Sometimes When We Touch 2)Please Be Love 3)Diamond In The Dust

DEBUT	PEAK	WKS	A-side / B-side	$	Label & Number
5/28/83	25	20	1 It Ain't Real (If It Ain't You)..................... *Whatever Happened To Old Fashioned Love*	$4	Columbia 03893
10/15/83+	18	18	2 Wounded Hearts .... *Til You And Your Lover Are Lovers Again*	$4	Columbia 04137
1/28/84	10	22	3 Left Side Of The Bed *Fire From A Friend*	$3	Columbia 04324
5/26/84	9	23	4 If All The Magic Is Gone *Til Her Heartache Is Over*	$3	Columbia 04464
9/29/84	9	21	5 Diamond In The Dust A:8 / S:9 *I Guess You Must Have Touched Me Just Right*	$3	■ Columbia 04610
2/23/85	6	22	6 Sometimes When We Touch A:5 / S:6 *You're Gonna Be The Last Love*	$3	Columbia 04782
			MARK GRAY and TAMMY WYNETTE		
			#3 Pop hit for Dan Hill in 1978		
7/27/85	43	13	7 Smooth Sailing (Rock In The Road)........................... *Dixie Girl*	$3	Columbia 05403
11/23/85+	7	21	8 Please Be Love S:7 / A:7 *I Need You Again*	$3	Columbia 05695
4/12/86	14	17	9 Back When Love Was Enough .... S:13 / A:15 *Dance With Me*	$3	Columbia 05857
5/28/88	69	5	10 Song In My Heart	$6	615 1014
			MARK GRAY and BOBBI LACE		
12/17/88+	70	5	11 It's Gonna Be Love	$6	615 1016
			MARK GRAY and BOBBI LACE		

GRAYGHOST   '87
Group from Arkansas led by Bill White. Formerly known as Razorback.

RAZORBACK:

DEBUT	PEAK	WKS	A-side / B-side	$	Label & Number
4/11/87	70	3	1 As Long As I've Been Loving You .... *Out Of Control*	$5	Compleat 166
6/13/87	61	7	2 Make A Living Out Of Loving You	$5	Compleat 174
11/28/87	66	7	3 This Ole House..	$6	ICR 184
9/17/88	70	4	4 Where Were You When I Was Blue .... *Something So Hot*	$3	Mercury 870633
			GRAYGHOST:		
6/10/89	70	5	5 Let's Sleep On It	$3	Mercury 874194
9/23/89	69	4	6 If This Ain't Love (There Ain't No Such Thing) .... *Take A Little Time*	$3	Mercury 874770

GRAYSON, Jack   '82
Born Jack Lebsock. Legally changed his name to Jack Grayson. Staff writer for ABC/Dot records in the 1970s.
1)When A Man Loves A Woman 2)A Loser's Night Out 3)Tonight I'm Feeling You

JACK LEBSOCK:

DEBUT	PEAK	WKS	A-side / B-side	$	Label & Number
8/11/73	94	3	1 For Lovers Only .... *World That Cannot See*	$6	Capitol 3665
1/5/74	76	6	2 Lovin' Comes Easy .... *I'll Be Damned If I Do (Damned If I Don't)*	$6	Capitol 3751
			"BLACKJACK" JACK GRAYSON:		
4/14/79	92	3	3 I Ain't Never Been To Heaven (But I've Spent The Night With You)... *Tonight I'm Feeling You (All Over Again)*	$5	Churchill 7729
12/22/79+	65	8	4 Tonight I'm Feelin' You (All Over Again) .... *Free To Love*	$5	Hitbound 4501
			also see #11 below		
6/14/80	70	6	5 The Stores Are Full Of Roses	$5	Hitbound 4503
8/30/80	59	7	6 The Devil Stands Only Five Foot Five .... *Free To Love*	$5	Hitbound 4504
			JACK GRAYSON and Blackjack:		
12/13/80+	37	14	7 A Loser's Night Out .... *Devil Stands Only 5 Foot 5*	$5	■ Koala 328
4/4/81	56	6	8 Magic Eyes .... *The Stores Are Full Of Roses*	$5	Koala 331
7/25/81	45	9	9 My Beginning Was You .... *Hanging On By A Heartstring*	$5	Koala 334
12/19/81+	18	17	10 When A Man Loves A Woman .... *A Little Tear*	$5	Koala 340
			#1 Pop hit for Percy Sledge in 1966		

JACK GRAYSON:

DEBUT	PEAK	WKS		A-side / B-side	Pop	$	Pic	Label & Number
5/22/82	38	11		11 Tonight I'm Feeling You (All Over Again) .... *Let's Hold Hands* [R]		$5		Joe-Wes 81000
				new version of #4 above				
8/14/82	68	6		12 I Ain't Giving Up On Her Yet................................ *Mama's Secret*		$5		Joe-Wes 81006
1/14/84	77	4		13 Lean On Me		$5		AMI 1318
				#1 Pop hit for Bill Withers in 1972				

GRAYSON, Kim '87
Born in Dallas; raised in Plano, Texas. Singer/actress. Acted in the movie *Target* and on TV's *Dallas*.

DEBUT	PEAK	WKS		A-side / B-side	Pop	$	Pic	Label & Number
8/1/87	74	3		1 Love's Slippin' Up On Me		$5	■	Soundwaves 4787
12/5/87	62	7		2 If You Only Knew .... *Love's Slippin' Up On Me*		$5	■	Soundwaves 4795
4/16/88	65	6		3 Missin' Texas		$5	■	Soundwaves 4800

GREAT PLAINS '92
Group of Nashville session musicians: Jack Sundrud (vocals, guitar), Russ Pahl (guitar), Denny Dadmun-Bixby (bass) and Michael Young (drums). Pahl and Young left in 1993. Lex Browning (guitar) joined in 1996.

DEBUT	PEAK	WKS		A-side / B-side	Pop	$	Pic	Label & Number
10/5/91	63	7		1 A Picture Of You .... *Give It Some Time*		$3		Columbia 73961
1/11/92	41	15		2 Faster Gun.................................... *Oh Sweetness*		$3		Columbia 74137
5/23/92	63	6		3 Iola .... *Take Me To Topeka*		$3		Columbia 74310
5/25/96	58	9		4 Dancin' With The Wind .... *Homeland*		$3	▌	Magnatone 1105

GREEN, Bill '76
Born in Athens, Alabama.

DEBUT	PEAK	WKS		A-side / B-side	Pop	$	Pic	Label & Number
9/18/76	94	3		1 Texas On A Saturday Night .... *Let's Cheat Again*		$8		Phono 2629
12/9/78	98	1		2 Fool Such As I .... *Let's Cheat Again*		$5		NSD 11
				#2 Pop hit for Elvis Presley in 1959				

GREEN, Jerry '77
Worked as a DJ at KVET-Austin, Texas.

DEBUT	PEAK	WKS		A-side / B-side	Pop	$	Pic	Label & Number
10/15/77	96	1		1 I Know The Feeling .... *How Sweet It Is*		$6		Concorde 152
12/10/77	96	4		2 Genuine Texas Good Guy		$6		Concorde 154

GREEN, Lloyd '73
Born on 10/4/37 in Mobile, Alabama. Leading session steel guitarist.

DEBUT	PEAK	WKS		A-side / B-side	Pop	$	Pic	Label & Number
2/10/73	36	10		1 I Can See Clearly Now .... *Steelin' Away* [I]		$6		Monument 8562
				#1 Pop hit for Johnny Nash in 1972				
6/30/73	73	3		2 Here Comes The Sun .... *Peace* [I]		$6		Monument 8574
				#16 Pop hit for Richie Havens in 1971				
12/25/76+	92	6		3 You And Me .... *Edgewater Beach* [I]		$6		October 1002

GREENE, Jack ★106★ '67
Born on 1/7/30 in Maryville, Tennessee. Singer/songwriter/guitarist. Drummer with Ernest Tubb's group from 1962-64. Joined the *Grand Ole Opry* in 1967. Nicknamed the "Jolly Green Giant." CMA Award: 1967 Male Vocalist of the Year.

1)There Goes My Everything 2)All The Time 3)Statue Of A Fool 4)Until My Dreams Come True 5)You Are My Treasure

DEBUT	PEAK	WKS		A-side / B-side	Pop	$	Pic	Label & Number
12/25/65+	37	7		1 Ever Since My Baby Went Away .... *Room For One More Heartache*		$8		Decca 31856
				written by Marty Robbins				
10/22/66	❶7	23		2 There Goes My Everything .... *The Hardest Easy Thing*	65	$7		Decca 32023
				CMA Award: Single of the Year				
4/22/67	❶5	20		3 All The Time/	103			
5/13/67	63	5		4 Wanting You But Never Having You		$7		Decca 32123
9/30/67	2⁴	20		5 What Locks The Door .... *Left Over Feelings*		$7		Decca 32190
2/17/68	❶1	15		6 You Are My Treasure .... *If God Can Forgive You, So Can I*		$7		Decca 32261
7/20/68	4	16		7 Love Takes Care Of Me .... *Your Favorite Fool*		$7		Decca 32352
12/14/68+	❶2	17		8 Until My Dreams Come True .... *We'll Try A Little Bit Harder*		$7		Decca 32423
5/10/69	❶2	18		9 Statue Of A Fool .... *There's More To Love*		$7		Decca 32490
10/4/69	4	14		10 Back In The Arms Of Love/				
10/25/69	66	2		11 The Key That Fits Her Door		$7		Decca 32558
11/15/69+	2²	16		12 Wish I Didn't Have To Miss You .... *My Tears Don't Show*		$7		Decca 32580
				JACK GREENE And JEANNIE SEELY				
3/14/70	16	11		13 Lord Is That Me .... *Just A Little While Ago*		$7		Decca 32631
7/18/70	14	14		14 The Whole World Comes To Me/				
		14		15 If This Is Love		$7		Decca 32699
11/14/70	15	12		16 Something Unseen/				
11/14/70	45	12		17 What's The Use		$7		Decca 32755
4/10/71	13	14		18 There's A Whole Lot About A Woman (A Man Don't Know)/				
		13		19 Makin' Up His Mind		$7		Decca 32823
9/4/71	26	12		20 Hanging Over Me .... *Birth Of Our Love*		$7		Decca 32863
12/11/71+	15	13		21 Much Oblige .... *First Day*		$7		Decca 32898
				JACK GREENE/JEANNIE SEELY				
3/25/72	31	11		22 If You Ever Need My Love .... *Ask Me To Stay*		$7		Decca 32939
8/12/72	19	12		23 What In The World Has Gone Wrong With Our Love .... *Willingly*		$6		Decca 32991
				JACK GREENE/JEANNIE SEELY				
12/9/72+	17	12		24 Satisfaction .... *From Here On Out*		$7		Decca 33008
4/14/73	40	12		25 The Fool I've Been Today .... *You Left Me*		$5		MCA 40035
8/18/73	11	16		26 I Need Somebody Bad .... *Joyride*		$5		MCA 40108

DEBUT	PEAK	WKS	Gold	A-side (Chart Hit)..B-side	Pop	$	Pic	Label & Number
				GREENE, Jack — Cont'd				
2/9/74	13	13		27 It's Time To Cross That Bridge.. Half That Much		$5		MCA 40179
7/27/74	66	9		28 Sing For The Good Times .... Something Seems To Fall Apart Inside		$5		MCA 40263
11/22/75	88	5		29 He Little Thing'd Her Out Of My Arms .... Let Me Love You Back Together Again		$5		MCA 40481
1/5/80	28	11		30 Yours For The Taking .... Sixty Days		$5		Frontline 704
5/17/80	48	7		31 The Rock I'm Leaning On ....I'll Do It Better The Next Time		$5		Frontline 706
11/1/80	63	6		32 Devil's Den .... It's Not The End Of The World		$5		Firstline 709
3/5/83	98	2		33 The Jukebox Never Plays Home Sweet Home ... I Don't Want To Be Alone Tonight		$5		EMH 0016
6/11/83	92	3		34 From Cotton To Satin ....I'd Be Home On Christmas Day		$5		EMH 0019
7/14/84	93	3		35 Dying To Believe .... There Goes My Everything		$5		EMH 0031
11/17/84	81	5		36 If It's Love (Then Bet It All) .... Statue Of A Fool		$5		EMH 0035

GREENE, Lorne '64

Born on 2/12/14 in Ottawa, Canada. Died of heart failure on 9/11/87 (age 73). Acted in several movies. Played "Ben Cartwright" on TV's *Bonanza* and "Adama" on *Battlestar Galactica*.

DEBUT	PEAK	WKS		A-side	Pop	$	Pic	Label & Number
12/5/64	21	10		1 Ringo .... Bonanza [S]	**❶**[1]	$8		RCA Victor 8444
8/13/66	50	2		2 Waco .... All But The Remembering [S]		$8		RCA Victor 8901
				from the movie starring Howard Keel				

GREEN RIVER BOYS, The — see CAMPBELL, Glen

GREENWOOD, Lee ★86★ '85

Born Melvin Lee Greenwood on 10/27/42 in Los Angeles; raised in Sacramento. Singer/songwriter. Worked as a blackjack dealer in Las Vegas casinos from 1973-77. Married former Miss Tennessee, Kimberly Payne, on 4/11/92. CMA Awards: 1983 & 1984 Male Vocalist of the Year.

1)Dixie Road 2)Hearts Aren't Made To Break 3)Going, Going, Gone 4)Mornin' Ride 5)I Don't Mind The Thorns

DEBUT	PEAK	WKS		A-side	Pop	$	Pic	Label & Number
9/19/81+	17	22		1 It Turns Me Inside Out .... Thank You For Changing My Life		$4		MCA 51159
3/27/82	5	18		2 Ring On Her Finger, Time On Her Hands .... Doncha Hear Me Callin'		$4		MCA 52026
8/7/82	7	17		3 She's Lying .... Home Away From Home		$4		MCA 52087
12/11/82+	7	21		4 Ain't No Trick (It Takes Magic) .... Broken Pieces Of My Heart		$4		MCA 52150
4/9/83	6	20		5 I.O.U. .... Another You	53	$4	■	MCA 52199
8/20/83	**❶**[1]	22		6 Somebody's Gonna Love You .... You're The Woman I Love	96	$4		MCA 52257
12/17/83+	**❶**[1]	19		7 Going, Going, Gone .... Come On Back And Love Me Some More		$4		MCA 52322
5/26/84	7	17		8 God Bless The USA .... This Old Bed		$4	■	MCA 52386
7/21/84	3	20		9 To Me .... A:15 We Were Meant For Each Other		$4	■	MCA 52415
				BARBARA MANDRELL/LEE GREENWOOD				
8/18/84	3	25		10 Fool's Gold .... S:2 / A:3 Worth It For The Ride		$4		MCA 52426
12/22/84+	9	19		11 You've Got A Good Love Comin' .... A:7 / S:10 Even Love Can't Save Us Now		$4		MCA 52509
2/2/85	19	15		12 It Should Have Been Love By Now . A:18 / S:20 Can't Get Too Much Of A Good Thing		$4		MCA 52525
				BARBARA MANDRELL/LEE GREENWOOD				
4/20/85	**❶**[1]	20		13 Dixie Road .... S:**❶**[1] / A:**❶**[1] (I Found) Love In Time		$3	■	MCA 52564
8/31/85	**❶**[1]	23		14 I Don't Mind The Thorns (If You're The Rose) .. S:**❶**[1] / A:**❶**[1] Same Old Song		$3		MCA 52656
12/28/85+	**❶**[1]	20		15 Don't Underestimate My Love For You .... S:**❶**[1] / A:**❶**[1] Leave My Heart The Way You Found It		$3	■	MCA 52741
4/19/86	**❶**[1]	22		16 Hearts Aren't Made To Break (They're Made To Love) .. S:**❶**[1] / A:**❶**[1] The Will To Love		$3		MCA 52807
8/9/86	10	18		17 Didn't We .... S:8 / A:10 Heartbreak Radio		$3		MCA 52896
11/29/86+	**❶**[1]	24		18 Mornin' Ride .... A:**❶**[1] / S:8 Little Red Caboose		$3		MCA 52984
5/9/87	5	17		19 Someone .... S:7 Let's Make The Most Of Love		$3		MCA 53096
8/29/87	9	19		20 If There's Any Justice .... S:21 We Could Have Been		$3		MCA 53156
12/26/87+	5	22		21 Touch And Go Crazy .... S:11 Silver Dollar		$3		MCA 53234
4/30/88	12	18		22 I Still Believe .... S:22 I'll Be Lovin' You		$3		MCA 53312
8/20/88	20	17		23 You Can't Fall In Love When You're Cryin' .... S:24 I'll Still Be Lovin' You		$3		MCA 53386
1/28/89	16	17		24 I'll Be Lovin' You .... Do That To Me One More Time		$3		MCA 53475
6/3/89	43	11		25 I Love The Way He Left You .... Home To Alaska		$3		MCA 53655
9/16/89	55	5		26 I Go Crazy .... Any Way The Law Allows		$3		MCA 53716
				#7 Pop hit for **Paul Davis** in 1978				
7/7/90	2[1]	21		27 Holdin' A Good Hand/				
10/27/90+	14	20		28 We've Got It Made		$3	▌	Capitol 44576
3/2/91	52	8		29 Just Like Me				album cut
				from the album *Holdin' A Good Hand* on Capitol 94153				
5/11/91	12	20		30 Hopelessly Yours..				album cut
				LEE GREENWOOD with Suzy Bogguss				
				from the album *A Perfect 10* on Capitol 95541				
10/5/91	46	11		31 Between A Rock And A Heartache..				album cut
2/8/92	58	6		32 If You'll Let This Fool Back In				album cut
				above 2 from the album *When You're In Love* on Capitol 95527				
8/22/92	73	2		33 Before I'm Ever Over You..				album cut
				from the album *Love's On The Way* on Liberty 98834				

GREGG, Ricky Lynn '93
Born on 8/22/62 in Longview, Texas. Singer/songwriter/guitarist.

DEBUG	PEAK	WKS		A-side / B-side	Pop	$	Pic	Label & Number
3/13/93	36	20	1	If I Had A Cheatin' Heart .... (club mix) / Can You Feel It (2 versions)	109	$3	■	Liberty 44948
7/24/93	58	9	2	Can You Feel It.. Bring On The Neon		$3		Liberty 17399
8/13/94	73	2	3	Get A Little Closer .... If I Had A Cheatin' Heart		$3	■	Liberty 18092

GREGORY, Clinton '92
Born on 3/1/66 in Martinsville, Virginia. Singer/fiddle player.
1)Play, Ruby, Play 2)I'd Go Crazy 3)Who Needs It

DEBUG	PEAK	WKS		A-side / B-side	Pop	$	Pic	Label & Number
1/5/91	64	7	1	Couldn't Love Have Picked A Better Place To Die.... You Can't Take It With You		$3		Step One 422
4/6/91	26	20	2	(If It Weren't For Country Music) I'd Go Crazy.............................. Darlin' Does He		$3	■	Step One 427
7/13/91	51	11	3	One Shot At A Time .... There's Never Been A Honky Tonk		$3	■	Step One 430
11/2/91	53	15	4	Satisfy Me And I'll Satisfy You .... Your Uncharted Mind		$3	■	Step One 434
2/15/92	25	20	5	Play, Ruby, Play She Can't Believe My Eyes		$3	■	Step One 437
7/4/92	50	13	6	She Takes The Sad Out Of Saturday Night............. Blue Country Frame Of Mind		$3		Step One 439
9/26/92	29	20	7	Who Needs It .... The Jukebox Has A 45		$3		Step One 444
3/6/93	65	5	8	Look Who's Needing Who .... I'll Never Always Love You		$3		Step One 457
6/12/93	52	7	9	Standing On The Edge Of Love .... Till This Ring Turns Green		$3	■	Step One 461
9/25/93	59	5	10	Master Of Illusion .... Watermelon Time In Georgia		$3		Step One 466
3/4/95	68	4	11	You Didn't Miss A Thing ....Hacksaw		$3	■	Polydor 851566

GREGORY, Terry '81
Born Teresa Ann Gregory Burdine on 4/30/56 in Takoma Park, Maryland. Female singer.

DEBUG	PEAK	WKS		A-side / B-side	Pop	$	Pic	Label & Number
5/2/81	16	15	1	Just Like Me Love Left Over		$4		Handshake 70071
9/5/81	59	6	2	Cinderella .... We'd Better Talk It Over		$4		Handshake 02442
11/14/81+	30	13	3	I Can't Say Goodbye To You ..... We Had All It Takes To Fall In Love		$4		Handshake 02563
3/13/82	44	11	4	I Never Knew The Devil's Eyes Were Blue...................... I Need Another Lover		$4		Handshake 02736
6/26/82	48	7	5	I'm Takin' A Heart Break .... After You've Shopped Around		$4		Handshake 02959
4/21/84	75	5	6	Cowgirl In A Coupe DeVille .... The Old Songs		$3		Scotti Brothers 04410
2/2/85	66	7	7	Pardon Me, But This Heart's Taken .... Fallin'		$3		Scotti Brothers 04735

★260★ GRIFF, Ray '76
Born John Raymond David Griff on 4/22/40 in Vancouver; raised in Winfield, Alberta, Canada. Singer/songwriter/guitarist.
1)If I Let Her Come In 2)The Mornin' After Baby Let Me Down 3)You Ring My Bell 4)That's What I Get 5)Patches

DEBUG	PEAK	WKS		A-side / B-side	Pop	$	Pic	Label & Number
12/23/67+	49	9	1	Your Lily White Hands .... One Of The Chosen Few		$8		MGM 13855
4/27/68	50	7	2	The Sugar From My Candy................................. Till The Right One Comes Along		$7		Dot 17082
10/3/70	26	9	3	Patches .... Dixie		$7		Royal American 19
				#4 Pop hit for Clarence Carter in 1970				
11/20/71+	14	15	4	The Mornin' After Baby Let Me Down............. I'll Love You Enough For Both Of Us		$7		Royal American 46
12/2/72	62	6	5	It Rains Just The Same In Missouri .... Somewhere Between Atlanta And Mobile		$6		Dot 17440
4/28/73	66	3	6	A Song For Everyone .... Another Sad Affair		$6		Dot 17456
11/24/73+	42	11	7	Darlin'/		$6		
8/25/73	46	10	8	What Got To You (Before It Got To Me)		$6		Dot 17471
5/11/74	65	7	9	That Doesn't Mean (I Don't Love My God) .... Lost Love Of Mine		$6		Dot 17501
10/12/74	91	2	10	The Hill..All Loved Out		$6		Dot 17519
3/8/75	65	9	11	If That's What It Takes .... Adam's Child		$6		ABC/Dot 17542
9/6/75	16	16	12	You Ring My Bell .... Dear Jesus		$5		Capitol 4126
1/24/76	11	15	13	If I Let Her Come In Runnin'		$5		Capitol 4208
5/22/76	40	10	14	I Love The Way That You Love Me .... Wrapped Around Your Finger		$5		Capitol 4266
8/28/76	24	12	15	That's What I Get (For Doin' My Own Thinkin') .... Falling		$5		Capitol 4320
12/18/76+	27	11	16	The Last Of The Winfield Amateurs/		$5		
		6	17	You Put The Bounce Back Into My Step.......................................		$5		Capitol 4368
4/23/77	28	10	18	A Passing Thing ....Piano Man		$5		Capitol 4415
7/30/77	69	5	19	A Cold Day In July .... Rusty		$5		Capitol 4446
10/22/77	52	9	20	Raymond's Place .... Goodbye Baby		$5		Capitol 4492
11/7/81	87	3	21	Draw Me A Line .... Heaven		$5		Vision 440
7/3/82	95	2	22	Things That Songs Are Made Of................................Light As A Feather		$5	■	Vision 442
5/7/83	86	3	23	If Tomorrow Never Comes ....Draw Me A Line		$4		RCA 50722
4/19/86	71	5	24	What My Woman Does To Me		$4		RCA 50846

GRIFFITH, Glenda '78
Born in California; raised in Wichita, Kansas.

DEBUG	PEAK	WKS		A-side / B-side	Pop	$	Pic	Label & Number
1/7/78	96	4		Don't Worry ('Bout Me) .... Heavenly Island		$4		Ariola America 7680

GRIFFITH, Nanci '87
Born on 7/16/54 in Seguin, Texas; raised in Austin, Texas. Singer/songwriter/guitarist.

DEBUG	PEAK	WKS		A-side / B-side	Pop	$	Pic	Label & Number
6/21/86	85	3	1	Once In A Very Blue Moon		$5		Philo 1096
1/17/87	36	14	2	Lone Star State Of Mind There's A Light Beyond These Woods (Mary Margaret)		$3		MCA 53008
4/25/87	57	7	3	Trouble In The Fields .... Love In A Memory		$3		MCA 53082
8/1/87	64	6	4	Cold Hearts/Closed Minds ....Ford Econoline		$3		MCA 53147
12/5/87	58	7	5	Never Mind .... From A Distance		$3		MCA 53184
4/9/88	37	13	6	I Knew Love .... So Long Ago		$3		MCA 53306
7/23/88	64	5	7	Anyone Can Be Somebody's Fool............ Love Wore A Halo (Back Before The War)		$3		MCA 53374

GROCE, Larry '76
Born on 4/22/48 in Dallas. Singer/songwriter.

DEBUG	PEAK	WKS		A-side / B-side	Pop	$	Pic	Label & Number
1/31/76	61	8		Junk Food Junkie .... Muddy Boggy Banjo Man [N]	9	$5		Warner/Curb 8165
				recorded "live" at McCabe's guitar shop in Santa Monica				

GROOMS, Sherry '78
Born in Caruthersville, Missouri; raised in West Memphis.

10/15/77	97	1		1 The King Of Country Music Meets The Queen Of Rock & Roll .... I'm From Outer Space		$5		Elektra 45430
				EVEN STEVENS & SHERRY GROOMS				
9/9/78	87	4		2 Me .... Mama's Boys		$5		Parachute 514

GROOVEGRASS BOYZ, The '96
Studio group assembled by producers Scott Rouse and Ronnie McCoury. Vocalists include Doc Watson and Mac Wiseman.

| 11/23/96 | 70 | 5 | | Macarena (Country version) .... S:6 (2 versions) | 107 | $4 | ▮ | Imprint 18007 |
| | | | | #1 Pop hit (14 weeks) for Los Del Rio in 1996 | | | | |

GROVES, Edgel '81
| 5/9/81 | 42 | 9 | | Footprints In The Sand .... (instrumental) [S] | | $6 | | Silver Star 20 |

GUITAR, Bonnie ★278★ '67
Born Bonnie Buckingham on 3/25/23 in Seattle. Singer/songwriter/guitarist. Owner of Dolphin/Dolton record labels.
1)A Woman In Love 2)I'm Living In Two Worlds 3)I Believe In Love

6/10/57	14	1		1 Dark Moon .... A:14 Big Mike	6	$15		Dot 15550
11/11/57	15	1		2 Mister Fire Eyes .... A:15 There's A New Moon Over My Shoulder	71	$15		Dot 15612
3/5/66	9	16		3 I'm Living In Two Worlds .... Goodtime Charlie	99	$8		Dot 16811
7/23/66	14	9		4 Get Your Lie The Way You Want It .... Would You Believe		$8		Dot 16872
10/15/66	24	10		5 The Tallest Tree .... Are You Sincere		$8		Dot 16919
2/25/67	64	5		6 The Kickin' Tree .... Only I		$8		Dot 16987
4/29/67	33	11		7 You Can Steal Me .... Ramblin' Man		$8		Dot 17007
8/12/67	4	16		8 A Woman In Love .... I Want My Baby		$8		Dot 17029
12/23/67+	13	16		9 Stop The Sun .... Wings Of A Dove		$8		Dot 17057
6/8/68	10	14		10 I Believe In Love .... Faded Love		$8		Dot 17097
9/28/68	41	10		11 Leaves Are The Tears Of Autumn .... Almost Like Being With You		$7		Dot 17150
7/5/69	55	5		12 A Truer Love You'll Never Find (Than Mine) ..... That's When (Our Love Will Be Over)		$7		Paramount 0004
				BONNIE & BUDDY (Buddy Killen)				
8/23/69	36	7		13 That See Me Later Look .... I'll Pick Up My Heart (And Go Home)		$7		Dot 17276
10/24/70	70	3		14 Allegheny .... Red Checkered Blazer		$7		Paramount 0045
8/5/72	54	7		15 Happy Everything .... Just As Soon As I Get Over Loving You		$5		Columbia 45643
12/14/74+	95	6		16 From This Moment On .... Shine (And We've Got To Have It)		$5		MCA 40306
4/19/80	92	3		17 Honey On The Moon .... Lonely Eyes		$5		4 Star 1041
12/2/89	79	3		18 Still The Same .... If You Were Here		$5		Playback 75714
				#4 Pop hit for Bob Seger in 1978				

GUNN, J.W. '82
| 11/27/82 | 87 | 3 | | Love Me Today, Love Me Forever .... Bessie, Jane & I | | $6 | | Primero 1013 |

GURLEY, Randy '78
Born Eleanor Rand Gurley on 11/29/53 in Salem, Massachusetts; raised in Burbank, California. Female singer.

9/2/78	77	5		1 True Love Ways .... I'll Never Get Over Loving You		$4		ABC 12392
				co-written by Buddy Holly; #14 Pop hit for Peter & Gordon in 1965				
7/14/79	97	2		2 Don't Treat Me Like A Stranger .... Every Night		$4		RCA 11611
10/27/79	92	3		3 If I Ever .... How Long		$4		RCA 11726

GUTHRIE, Jack '45
Born Leon Guthrie on 11/13/15 in Olive, Oklahoma. Died of tuberculosis on 1/15/48. Singer/songwriter/guitarist. Cousin of Woody Guthrie.

JACK GUTHRIE and his Oklahomans:
7/7/45	❶[6]	19		1 Oklahoma Hills/				
7/21/45	5	2		2 I'm A Brandin' My Darlin' With My Heart		$25		Capitol 201
3/1/47	3	3		3 Oakie Boogie The Clouds Rained Trouble Down		$25		Capitol 341

GUY & RALNA '75
Husband-and-wife vocal duo of Guy Hovis (born in Tupelo, Mississippi) and Ralna English (born in Lubbock, Texas). Regulars on TV's The Lawrence Welk Show from 1970-82.

| 7/26/75 | 95 | 3 | | We've Got It All Together Now .... Red River Valley | | $5 | | Ranwood 1029 |

H

HADDOCK, Durwood '75
Born on 8/16/34 in Lamasco, Texas. Singer/songwriter/fiddler.

11/23/74+	67	8		1 Angel In An Apron		$6		Caprice 2004
3/12/77	98	1		2 Low Down Time .... She Gave Me Good Love		$5		Eagle Int'l. 1137
				also see #5 below				
6/17/78	75	9		3 The Perfect Love Song .... You Loved Me So Good (That's Why I Miss You So Bad)		$5		Country Int'l. 132
11/4/78	87	4		4 Everynight Sensation .... Low Down Time		$5		Eagle Int'l. 1148
5/12/79	96	2		5 Low Down Time .... Everynight Sensation [R]		$5		Country Int'l. 140
				same version as #2 above				
10/25/80	89	3		6 It Sure Looks Good On You		$5		Eagle Int'l. 1161

HAGER, Charley '89
| 1/14/89 | 88 | 2 | | Men With Broken Hearts .... | | $6 | | Killer 114 |

147

HAGERS, The   '69

Identical twin brothers Jim and John Hager. Born on 8/30/46 in Chicago. Regulars on TV's *Hee Haw*.

DEBUT	PEAK	WKS		A-side / B-side	Pop	$	Pic	Label & Number
11/8/69	41	8		1 **Gotta Get To Oklahoma ('Cause California's Gettin' To Me)** *Your Tender Loving Care*		$6		Capitol 2647
4/4/70	74	2		2 **Loneliness Without You** .... *Give It Time*		$6		Capitol 2740
5/23/70	50	6		3 **Goin' Home To Your Mother**.................. *I'm Not Going Back To Jackson*		$6		Capitol 2803
9/12/70	59	8		4 **Silver Wings**.................................. *Flowers Need Sun, Too*		$6		Capitol 2887
				written by **Merle Haggard**				
1/23/71	47	6		5 **I'm Miles Away** .... *Loony Caboose*		$6		Capitol 3012

HAGGARD, Marty   '88

Born on 6/18/58 in Bakersfield, California. Singer/songwriter/guitarist. Son of **Merle Haggard**.

DEBUT	PEAK	WKS		A-side / B-side	Pop	$	Pic	Label & Number
3/7/81	85	3		1 **Charleston Cotton Mill** .... *Rain*		$5		Dimension 1016
9/13/86	62	7		2 **Talkin' Blue Eyes**..................................... *I Broke The Rules Today*		$4		MTM 72073
3/21/87	75	6		3 **Weekend Cowboys** .... *Forget He's Your Husband*		$4		MTM 72085
3/26/88	57	8		4 **Trains Make Me Lonesome** *By The Dawn's Early Light*		$4		MTM 72103
6/25/88	70	5		5 **Now You See 'Em, Now You Don't** .... *Missing California Blues*		$4		MTM 72107

HAGGARD, Merle ★5★   '69

Born on 4/6/37 in Bakersfield, California. Singer/songwriter/guitarist. Served nearly three years in San Quentin prison for burglary, from 1957-60. Granted full pardon by Governor Ronald Reagan on 3/14/72. Formed his backing band, The Strangers, in 1965. Acted in the movies *Bronco Billy*, *Huckleberry Finn*, *Killers Three* and *Doc Elliot*, and TV's *The Waltons* and *Centennial*. Formerly married to singers **Bonnie Owens** and **Leona Williams**. Father of **Marty Haggard** and **Noel Haggard**. Elected to the Country Music Hall of Fame in 1994. CMA Awards: 1970 Male Vocalist of the Year; 1970 Entertainer of the Year; 1983 Vocal Duo of the Year (with **Willie Nelson**).

1)*Okie From Muskogee* 2)*Mama Tried* 3)*If We Make It Through December* 4)*Carolyn* 5)*The Fightin' Side Of Me*

DEBUT	PEAK	WKS		A-side / B-side	Pop	$	Pic	Label & Number
12/28/63+	19	3		1 Sing A Sad Song .... *You Don't Even Try*		$25		Tally 155
6/6/64	45	5		2 Sam Hill .... *You Don't Have Far To Go*		$25		Tally 178
9/12/64	28	26		3 Just Between The Two Of Us .... *Slowly But Surely*		$25		Tally 181
				MERLE HAGGARD And BONNIE OWENS				
1/2/65	10	22		4 **(My Friends Are Gonna Be) Strangers** *Please Mr. D.J.*		$25		Tally 179
9/18/65	42	4		5 I'm Gonna Break Every Heart I Can .... *Falling For You*		$12		Capitol 5460
				MERLE HAGGARD And The Strangers:				
4/9/66	5	27		6 Swinging Doors *The Girl Turned Ripe*		$10		Capitol 5600
8/27/66	3	20		7 The Bottle Let Me Down *The Longer You Wait*		$10		Capitol 5704
12/17/66+	❶¹	18		8 The Fugitive/		$10		
12/31/66+	32	11		9 Someone Told My Story .... *Loneliness Is Eating Me Alive*		$10		Capitol 5803
3/18/67	2²	18		10 I Threw Away The Rose *Loneliness Is Eating Me Alive*		$10	■	Capitol 5844
7/8/67	❶¹	16		11 Branded Man *You Don't Have Very Far To Go*		$10		Capitol 5931
11/18/67+	❶²	20		12 Sing Me Back Home *Good Times*		$10	■	Capitol 2017
3/9/68	❶²	15		13 The Legend Of Bonnie And Clyde *I Started Loving You Again*		$10		Capitol 2123
7/27/68	❶⁴	15		14 Mama Tried *You'll Never Love Me Now*		$8		Capitol 2219
				from the movie *Killers Three* starring Haggard				
11/9/68+	3	16		15 I Take A Lot Of Pride In What I Am *Keep Me From Cryin' Today*		$8	■	Capitol 2289
2/22/69	❶¹	17		16 Hungry Eyes *California Blues*		$8		Capitol 2383
7/5/69	❶¹	15		17 Workin' Man Blues *Silver Wings*		$8	■	Capitol 2503
10/11/69	❶⁴	16		18 Okie From Muskogee *If I Had Left It Up To You*	41	$8	■	Capitol 2626
				CMA Award: Single of the Year				
2/7/70	❶³	14		19 The Fightin' Side Of Me *Every Fool Has A Rainbow*	92	$8	■	Capitol 2719
4/18/70	9	13		20 Street Singer *Mexican Rose* [I]	124	$8		Capitol 2778
6/13/70	3	14		21 Jesus, Take A Hold *No Reason To Quit*	107	$8		Capitol 2838
10/10/70	3	17		22 I Can't Be Myself/	106			
		16		23 Sidewalks Of Chicago	flip	$8	■	Capitol 2891
2/20/71	3	13		24 Soldier's Last Letter *The Farmer's Daughter*	90	$8	■	Capitol 3024
7/3/71	2²	15		25 Someday We'll Look Back *It's Great To Be Alive*	119	$8		Capitol 3112
10/16/71	❶²	14		26 Daddy Frank (The Guitar Man) *My Heart Would Know*		$8	■	Capitol 3198
12/4/71+	❶³	16		27 Carolyn *When The Feelin' Goes Away*	58	$8		Capitol 3222
3/25/72	❶²	15		28 Grandma Harp/				
		10		29 Turnin' Off A Memory		$8		Capitol 3294
9/2/72	❶¹	14		30 It's Not Love (But It's Not Bad) *My Woman Keeps Lovin' Her Man*		$8		Capitol 3419
12/9/72+	❶¹	14		31 I Wonder If They Ever Think Of Me *I Forget You Every Day*		$7		Capitol 3488
3/10/73	3	14		32 The Emptiest Arms In The World *Radiator Man From Wasco*		$7		Capitol 3552
6/30/73	❶²	16		33 Everybody's Had The Blues *Nobody Knows I'm Hurtin'*	62	$7		Capitol 3641
10/27/73	❶⁴	17		34 If We Make It Through December *Bobby Wants A Puppy Dog For Christmas* [X]	28	$7		Capitol 3746
				MERLE HAGGARD				
3/2/74	❶¹	15		35 Things Aren't Funny Anymore *Honky Tonk Night Time Man*		$7		Capitol 3830
6/29/74	❶¹	14		36 Old Man From The Mountain *Holding Things Together*		$7		Capitol 3900
11/9/74+	❶¹	15		37 Kentucky Gambler *I've Got A Darlin' (For A Wife)*		$7		Capitol 3974
				written by **Dolly Parton**				
2/15/75	❶²	14		38 Always Wanting You *I've Got A Yearning*		$7		Capitol 4027
5/24/75	❶¹	15		39 Movin' On *Here In Frisco*		$7		Capitol 4085
				theme from the TV series starring Claude Akins				
10/4/75	❶¹	15		40 It's All In The Movies *Living With The Shades Pulled Down*		$7		Capitol 4141

DEBUT	PEAK	WKS	Gold	A-side (Chart Hit)..B-side	Pop	$	Pic	Label & Number
				HAGGARD, Merle — Cont'd				
1/17/76	❶¹	14		41 **The Roots Of My Raising** *The Way It Was In '51*		$7		Capitol 4204
5/22/76	10	11		42 **Here Comes The Freedom Train** *I Won't Give Up My Train*		$7		Capitol 4267
9/11/76	❶¹	13		43 **Cherokee Maiden/**				
				written and recorded by **Bob Wills** in 1941				
		13		44 **What Have You Got Planned Tonight Diana**		$7		Capitol 4326
				MERLE HAGGARD:				
4/2/77	2²	14		45 **If We're Not Back In Love By Monday** *I Think It's Gone Forever*		$5		MCA 40700
7/2/77	2²	14		46 **Ramblin' Fever/**				
		12		47 **When My Blue Moon Turns To Gold Again**		$5		MCA 40743
				#19 Pop hit for **Elvis Presley** in 1956				
9/3/77	16	13		48 **A Working Man Can't Get Nowhere Today** .... *Blues Stay Away From Me*		$5		Capitol 4477
10/8/77	4	15		49 **From Graceland To The Promised Land** *Are You Lonesome Tonight*	58	$5		MCA 40804
				tribute to **Elvis Presley**; The Jordanaires (backing vocals)				
1/14/78	12	12		50 **Running Kind/**				
		9		51 **Making Believe**		$5		Capitol 4525
3/18/78	2²	16		52 **I'm Always On A Mountain When I Fall** *Life Of A Rodeo Cowboy*		$5		MCA 40869
8/12/78	2³	13		53 **It's Been A Great Afternoon/**				
		7		54 **Love Me When You Can**		$5		MCA 40936
10/28/78	8	12		55 **The Bull And The Beaver** *I'm Gettin' High*		$5		MCA 40962
				MERLE HAGGARD/LEONA WILLIAMS				
10/28/78	82	4		56 **The Way It Was In '51** .... *Moanin' The Blues*		$5		Capitol 4636
				MERLE HAGGARD And The Strangers				
				recorded in 1975				
4/14/79	4	13		57 **Red Bandana/**				
		13		58 **I Must Have Done Something Bad**		$4		MCA 41007
9/15/79	4	13		59 **My Own Kind Of Hat/**				
		13		60 **Heaven Was A Drink Of Wine**		$4		MCA 41112
3/15/80	2²	14		61 **The Way I Am** *Wake Up*		$4		MCA 41200
5/17/80	❶¹	16		62 **Bar Room Buddies** *The Not So Great Train Robbery*		$4	■	Elektra 46634
				MERLE HAGGARD AND CLINT EASTWOOD				
7/5/80	3	15		63 **Misery And Gin** *No One To Sing For (But The Band)*		$4	■	MCA 41255
				above 2 from the movie *Bronco Billy* starring **Clint Eastwood**				
10/25/80+	❶¹	17		64 **I Think I'll Just Stay Here And Drink** *Back To The Barrooms Again*		$4		MCA 51014
2/14/81	9	14		65 **Leonard** *Our Paths May Never Cross*		$4		MCA 51048
				tribute to **Tommy Collins** (real name: Leonard Sipes)				
3/28/81	41	8		66 **I Can't Hold Myself In Line** .... *Carolyn*		$4		Epic 51012
				JOHNNY PAYCHECK AND MERLE HAGGARD				
6/6/81	4	16		67 **Rainbow Stew** *Blue Yodel #9 (Standin' On The Corner)*		$4		MCA 51120
9/19/81	❶¹	17		68 **My Favorite Memory** *Texas Fiddle Song*		$4		Epic 02504
1/16/82	❶¹	19		69 **Big City** *I Think I'm Gonna Live Forever*		$4		Epic 02686
				Leona Williams (harmony vocal)				
4/17/82	49	10		70 **Dealing With The Devil** .... *Fiddle Breakdown*		$4		MCA 52020
5/15/82	2²	18		71 **Are The Good Times Really Over (I Wish A Buck Was Still**				
				Silver) *I Always Get Lucky With You*		$4		Epic 02894
8/7/82	❶¹	15		72 **Yesterday's Wine** *I Haven't Found Her Yet*		$5		Epic 03072
				MERLE HAGGARD/GEORGE JONES				
10/23/82+	❶¹	21		73 **Going Where The Lonely Go** *Someday You're Gonna Need Your Friends Again*		$4		Epic 03315
12/4/82+	10	19		74 **C.C. Waterback** *After I Sing All My Songs*		$5		Epic 03405
				GEORGE JONES/MERLE HAGGARD				
1/15/83	6	18		75 **Reasons To Quit** *Half A Man*		$4		Epic 03494
				MERLE HAGGARD AND WILLIE NELSON				
3/12/83	❶¹	18		76 **You Take Me For Granted** *I Won't Give Up My Train*		$4		Epic 03723
4/30/83	❶¹	21		77 **Pancho And Lefty** *Opportunity To Cry*		$4		Epic 03842
				WILLIE NELSON AND MERLE HAGGARD				
5/28/83	42	14		78 **We're Strangers Again** .... *Sally Let Your Bangs Hang Down*		$4		Mercury 812214
				MERLE HAGGARD & LEONA WILLIAMS				
7/16/83	3	20		79 **What Am I Gonna Do (With The Rest Of My Life)** *I Think I'll Stay*		$4		Epic 04006
10/8/83	54	10		80 **It's All In The Game** .... *The New Cocaine Blues*		$4		MCA 52276
				#1 Pop hit for **Tommy Edwards** in 1958				
11/19/83+	❶¹	21		81 **That's The Way Love Goes** *Don't Seem Like We've Been Together All Our Lives*		$3		Epic 04226
3/24/84	❶¹	21		82 **Someday When Things Are Good** *If You Hated Me*		$3		Epic 04402
7/14/84	❶¹	18		83 **Let's Chase Each Other Around The Room** *You Nearly Lose Your Mind*		$3		Epic 04512
10/27/84+	❶¹	22		84 **A Place To Fall Apart** S:❶¹/A:❶¹ *All I Want To Do Is Sing My Song*		$3		Epic 04663
				MERLE HAGGARD (with Janie Fricke)				
3/16/85	❶¹	19		85 **Natural High** S:❶¹/A:❶¹ *I Never Go Home Anymore*		$3		Epic 04830
				Janie Frickie (guest vocal)				
6/15/85	55	10		86 **Make-Up And Faded Blue Jeans** .... *Love Me When You Can*		$3		MCA 52595
				recorded in 1980				
7/6/85	10	17		87 **Kern River** S:10/A:10 *The Old Watermill*		$3		Epic 05426
10/5/85	36	15		88 **Amber Waves Of Grain** .... *I Wish Things Were Simple Again*		$3		Epic 05659
12/14/85	60	11		89 **American Waltz** .... *Farmer's Daughter*		$3		Epic 05734
1/25/86	5	20		90 **I Had A Beautiful Time** S:4/A:5 *This Time I Really Do*		$3		Epic 05782
5/31/86	9	23		91 **A Friend In California** S:6/A:7 *Mama's Prayers*		$3		Epic 06097
10/18/86	21	15		92 **Out Among The Stars** .... S:18/A:22 *Susie*		$3		Epic 06344
4/18/87	58	8		93 **Almost Persuaded** .... *Love Don't Hurt Everytime*		$3		Epic 07036

HAGGARD, Merle — Cont'd

DEBUT	PEAK	WKS	A-side / B-side	Pop	$	Pic	Label & Number
9/19/87	58	5	94 If I Could Only Fly .... *Without You On My Side*		$3		Epic 07400

MERLE HAGGARD & WILLIE NELSON

DEBUT	PEAK	WKS	A-side / B-side	Pop	$	Pic	Label & Number
11/21/87+	❶¹	22	95 Twinkle, Twinkle Lucky Star S:❶³ *I Don't Have Any Love Around*		$3		Epic 07631
3/19/88	9	19	96 Chill Factor S:6 *Thanking The Good Lord*		$3		Epic 07754
7/9/88	22	18	97 We Never Touch At All ....S:14 *Man From Another Time*		$3		Epic 07944
11/19/88+	23	17	98 You Babe ....S:19 *Thirty Again*		$3		Epic 08111
4/8/89	18	18	99 5:01 Blues .... *Man From Another Time*		$3		Epic 68598
7/22/89	4	26	100 A Better Love Next Time *Losin' In Las Vegas*		$3		Epic 68979
12/2/89+	23	16	101 If You Want To Be My Woman................. *Someday We'll Know*		$3		Epic 73076
9/1/90	60	6	102 When It Rains It Pours .... *Me And Crippled Soldiers*		$3	∎	Curb 76832
1/29/94	58	12	103 In My Next Life				album cut

from the album *Merle Haggard 1994* on Curb 77636

HAGGARD, Noel   '97

Born on 4/4/63 in Bakersfield, California. Singer/songwriter/guitarist. Son of **Merle Haggard**.

DEBUT	PEAK	WKS	A-side / B-side	Pop	$	Pic	Label & Number
2/1/97	75	1	1 Once You Learn				album cut
8/9/97	75	1	2 Tell Me Something Bad About Tulsa				album cut

above 2 from the album *One Lifetime* on Atlantic 82877

HALL, Buck   '89

Singer/songwriter from Arlington, Texas.

DEBUT	PEAK	WKS	A-side / B-side	Pop	$	Pic	Label & Number
9/23/89	87	2	Swinging Doors .... *I Like My Whiskey Chased With Women*		$6		Track 206

HALL, Connie   '60

Born on 6/24/29 in Walden, Kentucky; raised in Cincinnati.

DEBUT	PEAK	WKS	A-side / B-side	Pop	$	Pic	Label & Number
2/15/60	21	4	1 The Bottle Or Me............................ *After Date Rendezvous*		$12		Mercury 71540
10/17/60	17	2	2 It's Not Wrong/				
			answer to "Is It Wrong (For Loving You)" by **Warner Mack**				
10/10/60	25	2	3 The Poison In Your Hand		$10		Decca 31130
4/24/61	20	5	4 Sleep, Baby, Sleep .... *Sittin' Out The Last Dance*		$8		Decca 31208
1/20/62	23	5	5 What A Pleasure .... *The Key To Your World*		$8		Decca 31310
1/5/63	14	3	6 Fool Me Once *We Don't Have Much In Common (Anymore)*		$8		Decca 31438

HALL, Rebecca   '85

Born in Rustburg, Virginia.

DEBUT	PEAK	WKS	A-side / B-side	Pop	$	Pic	Label & Number
8/3/85	83	3	Heartbeat .... *Melted Down Memories*		$3		Capitol 5486

HALL, Sammy   '84

Gospel singer from North Carolina.

DEBUT	PEAK	WKS	A-side / B-side	Pop	$	Pic	Label & Number
4/28/84	88	3	Anything For Your Love		$6		Dream 300

HALL, Tom T.   ★59★   '74

Born Thomas Hall on 5/25/36 in Olive Hill, Kentucky. Singer/songwriter/guitarist. Worked as a DJ on WMOR-Morehead, Kentucky. Added "T." to his name when he began singing career. Hosted *Pop Goes The Country* TV series. Joined the *Grand Ole Opry* in 1980. Known as "The Storyteller".

1)*The Year That Clayton Delaney Died* 2)*I Love* 3)*A Week In A Country Jail* 4)*Faster Horses* 5)*Watermelon Wine*

DEBUT	PEAK	WKS	A-side / B-side	Pop	$	Pic	Label & Number
8/5/67	30	10	1 I Washed My Face In The Morning Dew .... *A Picture Of Your Mother*		$10		Mercury 72700
5/11/68	66	3	2 The World The Way I Want It .... *Shame On The Rain*		$10		Mercury 72786
9/14/68	68	4	3 Ain't Got The Time .... *Hope*		$10		Mercury 72835
11/16/68+	4	18	4 Ballad Of Forty Dollars *Highways*		$8		Mercury 72863
5/10/69	40	8	5 Strawberry Farms *3*		$8		Mercury 72913
8/23/69	5	15	6 Homecoming *Myra*		$8		Mercury 72951
12/20/69+	❶²	15	7 A Week In A Country Jail *Flat-Footin' It*		$8		Mercury 72998
4/4/70	8	14	8 Shoeshine Man *Kentucky In The Morning*		$7		Mercury 73039
7/11/70	8	13	9 Salute To A Switchblade *That'll Be All Right With Me*		$7		Mercury 73078
11/14/70	23	13	10 Day Drinkin' *Let's Get On With The Show*		$7		Mercury 73139

DAVE DUDLEY & TOM T. HALL

DEBUT	PEAK	WKS	A-side / B-side	Pop	$	Pic	Label & Number
12/26/70+	14	12	11 One Hundred Children *I Took A Memory To Lunch*		$7		Mercury 73140
4/3/71	21	11	12 Ode To A Half A Pound Of Ground Round .... *Pinto The Wonder Horse Is Dead*		$7		Mercury 73189
7/10/71	❶²	20	13 The Year That Clayton Delaney Died *Second Handed Flowers*	42	$7		Mercury 73221
3/18/72	8	15	14 Me And Jesus *Coot Marseilles Blues*	98	$7		Mercury 73278
			The Mt. Pisgah United Methodist Church Choir (backing vocals)				
7/8/72	11	12	15 The Monkey That Became President...................... *She Gave Her Heart To Jethro*		$7		Mercury 73297
10/7/72	26	9	16 More About John Henry................................ *Windy City Anne*		$7		Mercury 73327
12/2/72+	❶¹	15	17 (Old Dogs-Children And) Watermelon Wine *Grandma Whistled*		$7		Mercury 73346
12/16/72+	14	12	18 Hello We're Lonely .... *We're Not Getting Old*		$7		Mercury 73347

PATTI PAGE & TOM T. HALL

DEBUT	PEAK	WKS	A-side / B-side	Pop	$	Pic	Label & Number
5/5/73	3	13	19 Ravishing Ruby *I Flew Over Our House Last Night*		$7		Mercury 73377
6/30/73	16	11	20 Watergate Blues/	101			
		11	21 Spokane Motel Blues		$6		Mercury 73394
11/10/73+	❶²	18	22 I Love *Back When We Were Young*	12	$6		Mercury 73436
6/1/74	2²	15	23 That Song Is Driving Me Crazy *Forget It*	63	$6		Mercury 73488
9/14/74	❶¹	16	24 Country Is *God Came Through Bellville, Georgia*		$6		Mercury 73617

HALL, Tom T. — Cont'd

DEBUT	PEAK	WKS		A-side / B-side	Pop	$	Label & Number
12/28/74+	❶¹	15	25	I Care/			
12/21/74	69	16	26	Sneaky Snake	55	$6	Mercury 73641
5/31/75	8	15	27	Deal *It Rained In Every Town Except Paducah*		$6	Mercury 73686
9/6/75	4	15	28	I Like Beer *From A Mansion To A Honky Tonk*		$6	Mercury 73704
1/10/76	❶¹	16	29	Faster Horses (The Cowboy And The Poet) *No New Friends Please*		$6	Mercury 73755
5/15/76	24	12	30	Negatory Romance ....*It's Got To Be Kentucky For Me*		$6	Mercury 73795
10/16/76	9	14	31	Fox On The Run *Bluegrass Festival In The Sky*		$6	Mercury 73850
4/9/77	4	16	32	Your Man Loves You, Honey *One Of The Mysteries Of Life*		$6	Mercury 73899
8/6/77	12	12	33	It's All In The Game...........................*The Little Green Flower With The Yellow On Top*		$6	Mercury 55001
				#1 Pop hit for Tommy Edwards in 1958			
12/3/77+	13	14	34	May The Force Be With You Always ....*No One Feels My Hurt*		$5	RCA 11158
				inspired by the movie *Star Wars*			
4/8/78	13	13	35	I Wish I Loved Somebody Else...*Whiskey*		$5	RCA 11253
				Bonnie and Maxine Brown (backing vocals, above 2)			
9/16/78	9	13	36	What Have You Got To Lose *The Three Sofa Story*		$5	RCA 11376
1/20/79	14	12	37	Son Of Clayton Delaney .... *The Great East Broadway Onion Championship Of 1978*		$5	RCA 11453
5/12/79	20	10	38	There Is A Miracle In You ....*The Saturday Morning Song*		$5	RCA 11568
9/29/79	11	14	39	Show Me Your Heart (And I'll Show You Mine) ....*Old Habits Die Hard*		$5	RCA 11713
1/5/80	9	13	40	The Old Side Of Town/			
		13	41	Jesus On The Radio (Daddy On The Phone)		$5	RCA 11888
5/24/80	51	7	42	Soldier Of Fortune ....*The World According To Raymond*		$5	RCA 12005
8/16/80	36	10	43	Back When Gas Was Thirty Cents A Gallon ...... *Texas Never Fell In Love With Me*		$5	RCA 12066
5/2/81	41	8	44	The All New Me ....*Poor Me (Pour Me Another Drink)*		$5	RCA 12219
5/22/82	77	4	45	There Ain't No Country Music On This Jukebox ....*Don't This Road Look Rough And Rocky*		$4	Columbia 02858
				TOM T. HALL & EARL SCRUGGS			
7/31/82	72	5	46	Song Of The South ....*Shackles And Chains*		$4	Columbia 03033
				TOM T. HALL AND EARL SCRUGGS			
7/30/83	42	10	47	Everything From Jesus To Jack Daniels ..... *Old Dogs, Children & Watermelon Wine*		$3	Mercury 812835
7/14/84	81	3	48	Famous In Missouri *I Only Think About You When I'm Drunk*		$3	Mercury 880030
9/8/84	8	21	49	P.S. I Love You *S:8 / A:8 My Heroes Have Always Been Highways*		$3	Mercury 880216
				#12 Pop hit for Rudy Vallee in 1934			
5/25/85	40	9	50	A Bar With No Beer ....*Red Sails In The Sunset*		$3	Mercury 880690
8/31/85	42	11	51	Down In The Florida Keys ....*A Song In A Seashell*		$3	Mercury 884017
7/19/86	52	8	52	Susie's Beauty Shop/			
10/4/86	79	3	53	Love Letters In The Sand..		$3	Mercury 884850
				#1 Pop hit for Pat Boone in 1957			
12/6/86	65	7	54	Down At The Mall ....*We're All Through Dancing*		$3	Mercury 888155

HALLMAN, Victoria '87

Singer/actress. Regular on TV's *Hee Haw* from 1980-90.

DEBUT	PEAK	WKS		A-side / B-side	Pop	$	Label & Number
8/22/87	92	2		Next Time I Marry ....*Don't You Think It's Time*		$5	Evergreen 1055
				Those Hallman Girls (backing vocals)			

HALLMARK, Roger — see THRASHER BROTHERS

HAMBLEN, Stuart '50

Born Carl Stuart Hamblen on 10/20/08 in Kellerville, Texas. Died of a brain tumor on 3/8/89 (age 80). Singer/songwriter/actor. Moved to Hollywood in the early 1930s and appeared in many western movies and on radio with own band. Ran for president on Prohibition Party ticket in 1952.

DEBUT	PEAK	WKS		A-side / B-side	Pop	$	Label & Number
11/12/49+	3	7	1	(I Won't Go Huntin', Jake) But I'll Go Chasin' Women *J:3 / S:9 Let's See You Fix It*		$20	Columbia 20625
8/5/50	2⁹	26	2	(Remember Me) I'm The One Who Loves You *A:2 / S:3 / J:4 I'll Find You*		$25	Columbia 4-20714
				#32 Pop hit for Dean Martin in 1965			
1/6/51	8	2	3	It's No Secret *A:8 Blood On Your Hands*		$25	Columbia 4-20724
8/21/54	2¹	30	4	This Ole House *A:2 / S:3 / J:5 When My Lord Picks Up The 'Phone*	26	$20	RCA Victor 5739
				#1 Pop hit for Rosemary Clooney in 1954			

HAMILTON, George IV ★103★ '63

Born on 7/19/37 in Winston-Salem, North Carolina. Singer/guitarist. Joined the *Grand Ole Opry* in 1960. Own TV series on ABC in 1959, and in Canada in the late 1970s. Father of George Hamilton V.

1)Abilene 2)She's A Little Bit Country 3)Before This Day Ends 4)If You Don't Know I Ain't Gonna Tell You 5)Break My Mind

DEBUT	PEAK	WKS		A-side / B-side	Pop	$	Label & Number
10/10/60	4	17	1	Before This Day Ends *Loneliness All Around Me*		$15	ABC-Para. 10125
6/12/61	9	13	2	Three Steps To The Phone (Millions of Miles) *The Ballad Of Widder Jones*		$10	RCA Victor 7881
11/13/61	13	8	3	To You And Yours (From Me and Mine) ....*I Want A Girl*		$10	RCA Victor 7934
6/16/62	22	2	4	China Doll ....*Commerce Street And Sixth Avenue North*		$10	RCA Victor 8001
				#38 Pop hit for The Ames Brothers in 1960			
8/25/62	6	14	5	If You Don't Know I Ain't Gonna Tell You *Where Nobody Knows Me*		$10	RCA Victor 8062
1/19/63	21	5	6	In This Very Same Room *If You Want Me To*		$10	RCA Victor 8118
6/15/63	❶⁴	24	7	Abilene *Oh So Many Years*	15	$10	RCA Victor 8181
1/18/64	21	8	8	There's More Pretty Girls Than One.................... *If You Don't Somebody Else Will*	116	$10	RCA Victor 8250

DEBUT	PEAK	WKS	Gold	A-side (Chart Hit)..B-side	Pop	$	Pic	Label & Number
				HAMILTON, George IV — Cont'd				
3/28/64	25	8		9 Linda With The Lonely Eyes/				
4/18/64	28	6		10 Fair And Tender Ladies		$10		RCA Victor 8304
8/29/64	9	14		11 **Fort Worth, Dallas Or Houston** _Life's Railway To Heaven_		$10		RCA Victor 8392
12/5/64+	11	18		12 **Truck Driving Man** _The Little Grave_		$10		RCA Victor 8462
7/10/65	18	16		13 **Walking The Floor Over You** ...._Driftwood On The River_		$8		RCA Victor 8608
				written and recorded by **Ernest Tubb** in 1941				
12/4/65+	16	12		14 **Write Me A Picture**.._Twist Of The Wrist_		$8		RCA Victor 8690
4/23/66	15	17		15 **Steel Rail Blues** _Tobacco_		$8		RCA Victor 8797
9/3/66	9	16		16 **Early Morning Rain** _Slightly Used_		$8		RCA Victor 8924
				above 2 written by **Gordon Lightfoot**				
1/21/67	7	21		17 **Urge For Going** _Changes_		$8		RCA Victor 9059
				written by **Joni Mitchell**				
7/1/67	6	17		18 **Break My Mind** _Something Special To Me_		$8		RCA Victor 9239
12/23/67+	18	13		19 **Little World Girl**....................................._Song For A Winter's Night_		$8		RCA Victor 9385
6/1/68	50	8		20 **It's My Time** ...._The Canadian Railroad Trilogy_		$8		RCA Victor 9519
10/19/68	38	10		21 **Take My Hand For Awhile** ...._Wonderful World Of My Dreams_		$8		RCA Victor 9637
3/15/69	26	10		22 **Back To Denver** ...._The Little Folks_		$7		RCA Victor 0100
6/21/69	25	13		23 **Canadian Pacific** ...._Sisters Of Mercy_		$7		RCA Victor 0171
11/8/69	29	9		24 **Carolina In My Mind**...................._I'm Gonna Be A Country Boy Again_		$7		RCA Victor 0256
				#67 Pop hit for **James Taylor** in 1970				
5/2/70	3	16		25 **She's A Little Bit Country** _My Nova Scotia Home_		$7		RCA Victor 9829
8/29/70	16	12		26 **Back Where It's At** ...._Then I Miss You_		$7		RCA Victor 9886
9/26/70	65	2		27 **Let's Get Together** ...._Everything Is Beautiful_		$7		RCA Victor 9893
				SKEETER DAVIS AND GEORGE HAMILTON IV				
				#5 Pop hit for The **Youngbloods** in 1969				
1/30/71	13	12		28 **Anyway** ...._The Best That I Can Do_		$7		RCA Victor 9945
5/22/71	35	11		29 **Countryfied** ...._My North Country Home_		$7		RCA Victor 0469
9/18/71	23	12		30 **West Texas Highway** ...._There's No Room In This Rat Race (For A Slowpoke Like Me)_		$7		RCA Victor 0531
2/5/72	33	10		31 **10 Degrees & Getting Colder** ...._Tumbleweed_		$7		RCA Victor 0622
5/13/72	63	8		32 **Country Music In My Soul** ...._The Child's Song_		$7		RCA Victor 0697
9/9/72	52	9		33 **Travelin' Light** ...._Alberta Bound_		$7		RCA Victor 0776
12/23/72+	22	13		34 **Blue Train (Of The Heartbreak Line)** ...._Maritime Farewell_		$7		RCA Victor 0854
5/19/73	38	10		35 **Dirty Old Man** ...._Abilene_		$7		RCA Victor 0948
9/22/73	50	7		36 **Second Cup Of Coffee** ...._The Farmers Song_		$7		RCA Victor 0084
1/26/74	59	9		37 **Claim On Me** ...._Early Morning Rain_		$7		RCA Victor 0203
4/9/77	81	5		38 **I Wonder Who's Kissing Her Now** ...._In The Palm Of Your Hand_		$6		ABC/Dot 17687
				#1 Pop hit for Henry Burr in 1909				
10/15/77	93	2		39 **Everlasting (Everlasting Love)** ...._In The Palm Of Your Hand_		$6		ABC/Dot 17723
4/1/78	81	4		40 **Only The Best** ...._My Ship Will Sail_		$6		ABC 12342
				HAMILTON, George V '88				
				Singer/songwriter/guitarist. Son of **George Hamilton IV**. Member of his father's touring band.				
2/20/88	75	3		**She Says** ...._Grass Grows Greener_		$4		MTM 72101
				HAMILTON, Penny '79				
8/4/79	94	4		**You Lit The Fire, Now Fan The Flame**		$5		Door Knob 096
				HANDY, Cheryl '87				
				Born in 1969 in Virginia; raised in Goodlettsville, Tennessee.				
4/14/84	83	4		1 **Here I Go Again**		$6		Audiograph 475
1/24/87	67	5		2 **One Of The Boys**		$6		RCM 00105
8/8/87	56	6		3 **Will You Still Love Me Tomorrow?** ...._Don't Take My Heart Away_		$6		Compleat 176
				#1 Pop hit for The **Shirelles** in 1961				
				HANKS, Kamryn '89				
10/21/89	85	2		**Eyes Never Lie**		$6		Country Pride 0025
				HANSON, Connie '83				
				Born in Houston. Acted in the movies _Urban Cowboy_ and _Hot Wire_.				
12/25/82+	64	9		**There's Still A Lot Of Love In San Antone** ...._Muffy's Going Crazy_		$6	■	Soundwaves 4692
				CONNIE HANSON And FRIEND				
				Darrell McCall (guest vocal)				
★296★				**HARDEN, Arlene** '70				
				Born Ava Harden on 3/1/45 in England, Arkansas. Member of **The Harden Trio**.				
				1)Lovin' Man 2)Would You Walk With Me Jimmy 3)True Love Is Greater Than Friendship				
7/15/67	48	9		1 **Fair Weather Love** ...._Don't Ask For Tomorrow_		$6		Columbia 44133
12/9/67+	49	7		2 **You're Easy To Love** ...._What Has The World Done To My Baby_		$6		Columbia 44310
4/6/68	32	11		3 **He's A Good Ole Boy** ...._When_		$6		Columbia 44461
8/17/68	41	9		4 **What Can I Say** ...._Like You Love Me Now_		$6		Columbia 44581
5/3/69	45	9		5 **Too Much Of A Man (To Be Tied Down)** ...._When True Love Walks In_		$6		Columbia 44783
12/20/69+	63	4		6 **My Friend**..._Baby_		$6		Columbia 45016
4/25/70	13	14		7 **Lovin' Man (Oh Pretty Woman)** _My World Walked Away With A Blond_		$6		Columbia 45120
				female version of the #1 Pop hit for **Roy Orbison** in 1964				
8/29/70	28	11		8 **Crying** ...._It's Over_		$6	■	Columbia 45203
				#2 Pop hit for **Roy Orbison** in 1961				
1/9/71	22	11		9 **True Love Is Greater Than Friendship** ...._Funny Familiar Forgotten Feeling_		$6		Columbia 45287
				from the movie _Little Fauss And Big Halsy_ starring Robert Redford				
5/1/71	25	11		10 **Married To A Memory**......................................._Coming Home Soldier_		$6		Columbia 45365
7/31/71	49	9		11 **Congratulations (You Sure Made A Man Out Of Him)** ...._Sing Me Some Sunshine_		$6		Columbia 45420
12/18/71+	46	9		12 **Ruby Gentry's Daughter** ...._With Pen In Hand_		$6		Columbia 45489

DEBUT	PEAK	WKS		A-side (Chart Hit)...B-side	Pop	$	Pic	Label & Number
				HARDEN, Arlene — Cont'd				
4/15/72	29	12		13 A Special Day .... *What A Woman In Love Won't Do*		$6		Columbia 45577
11/4/72	45	8		14 It Takes A Lot Of Tenderness .... *It's Over*		$5		Columbia 45708
6/30/73	21	13		15 Would You Walk With Me Jimmy .... *You Can Always Have Me*		$5		Columbia 45845
				ARLEEN HARDEN:				
7/20/74	72	8		16 Leave Me Alone (Ruby Red Dress) .... *It's So Good With You*		$5		Capitol 3911
				#3 Pop hit for **Helen Reddy** in 1973				
10/29/77	100	2		17 A Place Where Love Has Been .... *Lady In Waiting*		$4		Elektra 45434
4/1/78	74	4		18 You're Not Free And I'm Not Easy .... *Do You Ever Dream*		$4		Elektra 45463
				HARDEN, Bobby **'75**				
				Born in England, Arkansas. Member of **The Harden Trio.**				
3/15/75	48	8		One Step .... *Holding On*		$5		United Artists 597
				HARDEN TRIO, The **'66**				
				Family trio from England, Arkansas: **Bobby Harden** and sisters **Robbie** and **Arlene Harden**.				
2/12/66	2¹	21		1 Tippy Toeing *Don't Remind Me*	44	$6		Columbia 43463
11/5/66	28	11		2 Seven Days Of Crying (Makes One Weak) .... *Husbands And Wives*		$6		Columbia 43844
4/22/67	16	14		3 Sneaking 'Cross The Border .... *Childhood Place*		$6		Columbia 44059
2/10/68	56	4		4 He Looks A Lot Like You........................... *My Friend Mister Echo*		$6		Columbia 44420
6/29/68	47	7		5 Everybody Wants To Be Somebody Else .... *Diddle Diddle Dumplin'*		$6		Columbia 44552
12/7/68+	64	6		6 Who Loves You .... *This Is Where You Get Off*		$6		Columbia 44675
				THE HARDENS ARLENE & ROBBIE				
				HARDIN, Gus **'85**				
				Born Carolyn Ann Blankenship on 4/9/45 in Tulsa, Oklahoma. Died in a car crash on 2/18/96 (age 50). Female singer.				
				1)*All Tangled Up In Love* 2)*After The Last Goodbye* 3)*If I Didn't Love You*				
2/19/83	10	16		1 After The Last Goodbye *I've Been Loving You Too Long*		$4		RCA 13445
5/28/83	26	14		2 If I Didn't Love You .... *You Can Call Me Blue*		$4		RCA 13532
9/24/83	32	12		3 Loving You Hurts .... *Since I Don't Have You*		$4		RCA 13597
12/24/83+	41	12		4 Fallen Angel (Flyin' High Tonight) .... *Not Tonight, I've Got A Heartache*		$4		RCA 13704
3/24/84	43	11		5 I Pass .... *Night Lights*		$4	■	RCA 13751
6/23/84	52	8		6 How Are You Spending My Nights .... *Night Lights*		$4		RCA 13814
11/10/84+	8	21		7 All Tangled Up In Love *S:5 / A:8 More Or Less (Hardin)*		$4		RCA 13938
				GUS HARDIN (with Earl Thomas Conley)				
4/20/85	79	4		8 My Mind Is On You .... *What About When It Rains*		$4		RCA 14040
8/17/85	72	7		9 Just As Long As I Have You .... *More Or Less*		$4		RCA 14159
				GUS HARDIN and DAVE LOGGINS				
1/11/86	73	7		10 What We Gonna Do .... *What About When It Rains*		$4		RCA 14255
				HARDING, Gayle **'79**				
11/11/78	92	2		1 Sexy Eyes		$6		Robchris 1008
1/27/79	84	3		2 I'm Lovin' The Lovin' Out Of You .... *I Fooled Around Behind You*		$6		Robchris 1009
				HARDY, Johnny **'61**				
				Born in Rockmont, Georgia.				
2/13/61	17	10		In Memory Of Johnny Horton .... *Wasting My Time*		$20		J&J 003
				HARGROVE, Danny **'78**				
				Born in Detroit. Singer/songwriter/guitarist.				
5/13/78	73	7		1 Sweet Mary .... *Four Strong Winds*		$6		50 States 61
				#7 Pop hit for **Wadsworth Mansion** in 1971				
9/23/78	98	2		2 I Wanna Be Her #1 .... *She Belongs To The Man At The Bar*		$6		50 States 64
				HARGROVE, Linda **'76**				
				Born on 2/3/49 in Jacksonville, Florida. Singer/songwriter/pianist.				
10/19/74	98	2		1 Blue Jean Country Queen .... *Where Do I Begin*		$6		Elektra 45204
12/28/74+	82	4		2 I've Never Loved Anyone More .... *Grandma Was The Motor*		$6		Elektra 45215
11/8/75+	39	13		3 Love Was (Once Around The Dance Floor) *Half My Heart's In Texas*		$5		Capitol 4153
3/6/76	86	5		4 Love, You're The Teacher .... *Save The Children*		$5		Capitol 4228
7/24/76	86	4		5 Fire At First Sight.. *20/20 Hindsight*		$5		Capitol 4283
4/2/77	91	3		6 Down To My Pride .... *Old Fashioned Love*		$5		Capitol 4330
9/24/77	61	9		7 Mexican Love Songs .... *Not Even For Love*		$5		Capitol 4447
10/14/78	93	4		8 You Are Still The One .... *I Forgave (But I Forgot To Forget)*		$5		RCA 11378
				HARLESS, Ogden **'88**				
				Born William Harless in 1949 in Hattiesburg, Mississippi.				
9/19/87	84	2		1 Somebody Ought To Tell Him That She's Gone		$5		Door Knob 283
11/28/87	74	3		2 Walk On Boy		$5		Door Knob 287
1/16/88	64	5		3 I Wish We Were Strangers		$5		Door Knob 293
4/23/88	82	3		4 Down On The Bayou..		$5		Door Knob 297
8/27/88	92	2		5 Together Alone		$6		MSC 188
				HARMS, Joni **'89**				
				Born on 11/5/59 in Canby, Oregon.				
3/11/89	34	11		1 I Need A Wife .... *The Only Thing Bluer Than His Eyes*		$3		Universal 53492
6/24/89	54	8		2 The Only Thing Bluer Than His Eyes .... *A Woman Knows*		$3		Universal 66012
				HARRELL & SCOTT **'90**				
9/23/89	96	2		1 Weak Men Break		$6		Associated Art. 503
12/16/89+	75	5		2 Darkness Of The Light..		$6		Associated Art. 505

DEBUT	PEAK	WKS	Gold	A-side (Chart Hit)..B-side	Pop	$	Pic	Label & Number
				HARRINGTON, Carly '88				
8/6/88	64	6		Badland Preacher..		$6		Oak 1055
				HARRIS, Donna '66				
10/1/66	45	8		He Was Almost Persuaded................................. *I'm Sending Him Back Home To You*		$7		ABC 10839
				answer to "Almost Persuaded" by **David Houston**				

HARRIS, Emmylou ★55★ '76

Born on 4/2/47 in Birmingham, Alabama. Singer/songwriter/guitarist. Joined the *Grand Ole Opry* in 1992. CMA Award: 1980 Female Vocalist of the Year.

1)*Sweet Dreams* 2)*Beneath Still Waters* 3)*Together Again* 4)*We Believe In Happy Endings* 5)*On Our Last Date*

DEBUT	PEAK	WKS		A-side ...B-side	Pop	$	Pic	Label & Number
4/19/75	73	8	1	Too Far Gone .... *Boulder To Birmingham*		$6		Reprise 1326
				also see #13 below				
7/5/75	4	17	2	If I Could Only Win Your Love *Boulder To Birmingham*	58	$6		Reprise 1332
				Herb Pedersen (harmony vocal)				
12/27/75	99	1	3	Light Of The Stable... *Bluebird Wine* [X]		$6	■	Reprise 1341
				Dolly Parton, Linda Ronstadt and **Neil Young** (backing vocals)				
1/3/76	12	12	4	The Sweetest Gift .... *Tracks Of My Tears*		$6		Asylum 45295
				LINDA RONSTADT AND EMMYLOU HARRIS				
3/6/76	❶¹	14	5	Together Again *Here, There And Everywhere* (Pop #65)		$5		Reprise 1346
6/5/76	3	16	6	One Of These Days *Till I Gain Control Again*		$5		Reprise 1353
10/23/76	❶²	14	7	Sweet Dreams *Amarillo*		$5		Reprise 1371
2/26/77	6	13	8	(You Never Can Tell) C'est La Vie *You're Supposed To Be Feeling Good*		$5		Warner 8329
				#14 Pop hit for **Chuck Berry** in 1964				
5/28/77	8	14	9	Making Believe *I'll Be Your San Antone Rose*		$5		Warner 8388
				Herb Pedersen (harmony vocal)				
12/3/77+	3	15	10	To Daddy *Tulsa Queen*	102	$5		Warner 8498
				written by **Dolly Parton**				
4/15/78	❶¹	14	11	Two More Bottles Of Wine *I Ain't Living Long Like This*		$5		Warner 8553
8/5/78	12	11	12	Easy From Now On .... *You're Supposed To Be Feeling Good*		$4		Warner 8623
2/3/79	13	13	13	Too Far Gone *Tulsa Queen* [R]		$4		Warner 8732
				same version as #1 above				
5/12/79	11	13	14	Play Together Again Again.................... *He Don't Deserve You Anymore*		$4		Warner 8830
				BUCK OWENS With Emmylou Harris				
6/2/79	4	14	15	Save The Last Dance For Me *Even Cowgirls Get The Blues*		$4		Warner 8815
				#1 Pop hit for **The Drifters** in 1960				
9/8/79	91	6	16	Love Don't Care .... *Who's Gonna Love Me Now* (Louvin)		$5		Little Darlin' 7922
				CHARLIE LOUVIN with Emmylou Harris				
9/22/79	6	12	17	Blue Kentucky Girl *Leaving Louisiana In The Broad Daylight*		$4		Warner 49056
3/1/80	❶¹	14	18	Beneath Still Waters *Till I Gain Control Again*		$4		Warner 49164
5/31/80	7	15	19	Wayfaring Stranger *Green Pastures*		$4	■	Warner 49239
6/28/80	6	15	20	That Lovin' You Feelin' Again *Lola*	55	$4		Warner 49262
				ROY ORBISON & EMMYLOU HARRIS				
				from the movie *Roadie* starring **Meat Loaf**				
9/13/80	13	11	21	The Boxer.. *Precious Love*		$4		Warner 49551
				#7 Pop hit for **Simon & Garfunkel** in 1969				
3/7/81	10	12	22	Mister Sandman *Fools Thin Air*	37	$4		Warner 49684
				#1 Pop hit for **The Chordettes** in 1954				
6/13/81	44	8	23	I Don't Have To Crawl .... *Colors Of Your Heart*	106	$4		Warner 49739
9/19/81	3	17	24	If I Needed You *Ashes By Now*		$4		Warner 49809
				EMMYLOU HARRIS & DON WILLIAMS				
1/16/82	9	16	25	Tennessee Rose *Mama Help*		$4		Warner 49892
5/29/82	3	17	26	Born To Run *Colors Of Your Heart*		$4		Warner 29993
10/10/82+	❶¹	20	27	(Lost His Love) On Our Last Date *Another Pot O' Tea*		$4		Warner 29898
3/19/83	5	17	28	I'm Movin' On *Maybe Tonight*		$4		Warner 29729
7/2/83	28	13	29	So Sad (To Watch Good Love Go Bad) .... *Amarillo*		$4		Warner 29583
				#7 Pop hit for **The Everly Brothers** in 1960				
7/9/83	14	19	30	Wild Montana Skies .... *I Remember Romance*		$4		RCA 13562
				JOHN DENVER AND EMMYLOU HARRIS				
11/19/83+	26	13	31	Drivin' Wheel.. *Good News*		$3		Warner 29443
3/24/84	9	21	32	In My Dreams *Like An Old Fashioned Waltz*		$3		Warner 29329
8/11/84	9	22	33	Pledging My Love *S:9 / A:9 Baby, Better Start Turnin' 'Em Down*		$3		Warner 29218
				#17 Pop hit for **Johnny Ace** in 1955				
11/24/84+	26	18	34	Someone Like You .... *S:23 Light Of The Stable*		$3		Warner 29138
3/30/85	14	17	35	White Line .... *S:12 / A:14 Long Tall Sally Rose*		$3		Warner 29041
7/20/85	44	11	36	Rhythm Guitar.. *Diamond In My Crown*		$3		Warner 28952
11/30/85	55	9	37	Timberline .... *Sweet Chariot*		$3		Warner 28852
3/1/86	60	6	38	I Had My Heart Set On You .... *Your Long Journey*		$3		Warner 28770
5/3/86	43	13	39	Today I Started Loving You Again............................... *When I Was Yours*		$3		Warner 28714
				written by **Merle Haggard** and **Bonnie Owens**				
2/21/87	❶¹	19	40	To Know Him Is To Love Him *S:❶¹ / A:❶¹ Farther Along*		$3	■	Warner 28492
				DOLLY PARTON, LINDA RONSTADT, EMMYLOU HARRIS				
				#1 Pop hit for **The Teddy Bears** in 1958				

HARRIS, Emmylou — Cont'd

DEBUT	PEAK	WKS	A-side	B-side	Pop	$	Pic	Label & Number
5/30/87	3	18	41 Telling Me Lies	S:10 *Rosewood Casket*		$3		Warner 28371
			DOLLY PARTON, LINDA RONSTADT, EMMYLOU HARRIS					
7/11/87	60	7	42 Someday My Ship Will Sail	*When He Calls*		$3		Warner 28302
9/26/87	5	22	43 Those Memories Of You	S:10 *My Dear Companion*		$3	■	Warner 28248
			DOLLY PARTON, LINDA RONSTADT, EMMYLOU HARRIS					
12/12/87+	53	13	44 Back In Baby's Arms	*I Still Dream Of You*		$3		Hughes/MCA 53236
			from the movie *Planes, Trains & Automobiles* starring Steve Martin and John Candy					
3/26/88	6	18	45 Wildflowers	S:13 *Hobo's Meditation*		$3		Warner 27970
			DOLLY PARTON, LINDA RONSTADT, EMMYLOU HARRIS					
7/2/88	❶[1]	21	46 We Believe In Happy Endings	S:3 *No Chance, No Dance*		$3		RCA 8632
			EARL THOMAS CONLEY with Emmylou Harris					
12/17/88+	8	22	47 Heartbreak Hill	*Icy Blue Heart*		$3		Reprise 27635
4/29/89	16	21	48 Heaven Only Knows	*A River For Him*		$3		Reprise 22999
8/26/89	51	6	49 I Still Miss Someone	*No Regrets*		$3		Reprise 22850
1/19/91	71	3	50 Wheels Of Love	*Better Off Without You*		$3		Reprise 19510
10/16/93	63	8	51 High Powered Love...	*Ballad Of A Runaway Horse*		$3	▌	Asylum 64610
1/29/94	65	5	52 Thanks To You	*Lovin' You Again*		$3		Asylum 64570

HARRISON, B.J.   '80

DEBUT	PEAK	WKS	A-side	B-side	Pop	$	Pic	Label & Number
5/24/80	93	2	I Need A Little More Time			$7		TeleSonic 801

HARRISON, Dixie   '82

Born on 8/17/53 in Faulkner County, Arkansas.

DEBUT	PEAK	WKS	A-side	B-side	Pop	$	Pic	Label & Number
10/23/82	98	2	Yes Mam (He Found Me In A Honky Tonk)...........................	*Careless Kinda Heart*		$6		Air Int'l. 10078

HART, Clay   '69

Born Henry Clay Hart III in Providence, Rhode Island. Regular on TV's *The Lawrence Welk* Show from 1969-75. Married to Sally Flynn, another regular on the Welk show.

DEBUT	PEAK	WKS	A-side	B-side	Pop	$	Pic	Label & Number
5/31/69	30	11	1 Spring...	*Child Of The Wind*		$5		Metromedia 119
9/20/69	25	9	2 Another Day, Another Mile, Another Highway	*Penny*		$5		Metromedia 140
1/31/70	73	3	3 Face Of A Dear Friend	*Gotta Be Free*		$5		Metromedia 158
5/2/70	62	7	4 If I'd Only Come And Gone .... *Take Your Precious Love From Me*			$5		Metromedia 172

HART, Freddie ★69★   '72

Born Frederick Segrest on 12/21/26 in Loachapoka, Alabama. Singer/songwriter/guitarist.

1)My Hang-Up Is You 2)Easy Loving 3)Got The All Overs For You 4)Bless Your Heart 5)Super Kind Of Woman

DEBUT	PEAK	WKS	A-side	B-side	Pop	$	Pic	Label & Number
4/20/59	24	4	1 The Wall	*Davy Jones*		$12		Columbia 41345
11/16/59	17	4	2 Chain Gang	*Rock Bottom*		$12		Columbia 41456
5/2/60	18	11	3 The Key's In The Mailbox	*Starvation Days*		$12		Columbia 41597
1/9/61	27	2	4 Lying Again	*Do My Heart A Favor*		$12		Columbia 41805
11/6/61	23	2	5 What A Laugh!...	*Heart Attack*		$12		Columbia 42146
10/30/65	23	12	6 Hank Williams' Guitar	*I Created A Monster*		$10		Kapp 694
5/7/66	45	4	7 Why Should I Cry Over You	*The Key's In The Mailbox*		$10		Kapp 743
			FREDDIE HART And The Heartbeats (above 2)					
7/8/67	63	5	8 I'll Hold You In My Heart................................	*Too Much Of You (Left In Me)*		$10		Kapp 820
12/30/67+	24	15	9 Togetherness	*Portrait Of A Lonely Man*		$10	■	Kapp 879
6/8/68	21	15	10 Born A Fool	*The Hands Of A Man*		$10		Kapp 910
			also see #21 below					
11/23/68	70	2	11 Don't Cry Baby	*Here Lies A Heart*		$10		Kapp 944
1/3/70	27	10	12 The Whole World Holding Hands	*Without You*		$7		Capitol 2692
4/11/70	48	9	13 One More Mountain To Climb..................................	*Just Another Girl*		$7		Capitol 2768
7/4/70	41	11	14 Fingerprints	*I Can't Keep My Hands Off Of You*		$7		Capitol 2839
11/21/70	68	4	15 California Grapevine .... *What's Wrong With Your Head, Fred*			$7		Capitol 2933
7/10/71	❶[3]	24	● 16 Easy Loving	*Brother Bluebird*	17	$6		Capitol 3115
1/29/72	❶[6]	19	17 My Hang-Up Is You	*Big Bad Wolf*		$6		Capitol 3261
			FREDDIE HART And The Heartbeats:					
6/24/72	❶[2]	14	18 Bless Your Heart	*Conscience Makes Cowards (Of Us All)*		$6		Capitol 3353
10/14/72	❶[3]	17	19 Got The All Overs For You (All Over Me)	*Just Another Girl*		$6		Capitol 3453
2/3/73	❶[1]	14	20 Super Kind Of Woman	*Mother Nature Made A Believer Out Of Me*		$6		Capitol 3524
5/19/73	41	10	21 Born A Fool	*My Anna Maria* [R]		$6		MCA 40011
			FREDDIE HART					
			same version as #10 above					
6/2/73	❶[1]	16	22 Trip To Heaven	*Look-A Here*		$6		Capitol 3612
10/6/73	3	16	23 If You Can't Feel It (It Ain't There)	*Skid Row Street*		$6		Capitol 3730
2/23/74	2[1]	12	24 Hang In There Girl	*You Belong To Me*		$6		Capitol 3827
			FREDDIE HART					
6/22/74	3	14	25 The Want-To's	*Phoenix City*		$6		Capitol 3898
11/2/74+	3	16	26 My Woman's Man	*Let's Clean Up The Country*		$6		Capitol 3970
3/1/75	5	15	27 I'd Like To Sleep Til I Get Over You	*Nothing's Better Than That*		$6		Capitol 4031
6/28/75	2[2]	16	28 The First Time	*Sexy*		$6		Capitol 4099
10/18/75	6	15	29 Warm Side Of You	*I Love You, I Just Don't Like You*		$6		Capitol 4152

DEBUT	PEAK	WKS	Gold	A-side (Chart Hit) ... B-side	Pop	$	Pic	Label & Number
				HART, Freddie — Cont'd				
1/31/76	11	11		30 You Are The Song (Inside Of Me) .... *I Can Almost See Houston From Here*		$6		Capitol 4210
4/10/76	12	14		31 She'll Throw Stones At You .... *Love Makes It All Alright*		$6		Capitol 4251
8/21/76	11	14		32 That Look In Her Eyes................................. *Try My Love For Size*		$6		Capitol 4313
12/4/76+	8	14		33 Why Lovers Turn To Strangers *Paper Sack Full Of Memories*		$6		Capitol 4363
				FREDDIE HART:				
4/16/77	11	11		34 Thank God She's Mine.............................. *Falling All Over Me*		$5		Capitol 4409
7/16/77	13	12		35 The Pleasure's Been All Mine/				Capitol 4448
		10		36 It's Heaven Loving You		$5		
11/5/77	43	10		37 The Search .... *Honky Tonk Toys*		$5		Capitol 4498
				FREDDIE HART And The Heartbeats				
1/21/78	27	11		38 So Good, So Rare, So Fine............... *There's An Angel Living There*		$5		Capitol 4530
4/22/78	34	10		39 Only You..............................*I Love You, I Just Don't Like You*		$5		Capitol 4561
				#1 Pop hit for The Platters in 1955				
8/19/78	21	12		40 Toe To Toe .... *And Then Some*		$5		Capitol 4609
2/24/79	40	8		41 My Lady .... *Guilty*		$5		Capitol 4684
5/26/79	28	12		42 Wasn't It Easy Baby .... *My Lady Loves*		$5		Capitol 4720
6/7/80	15	12		43 Sure Thing .... *Makin' Love To A Memory*		$5	■	Sunbird 7550
9/13/80	33	10		44 Rose's Are Red .... *Battle of the Sexes*		$5		Sunbird 7553
4/18/81	31	10		45 You're Crazy Man .... *Playboy's Centerfold*		$5		Sunbird 7560
9/12/81	38	9		46 You Were There .... *The Weaker Sex*		$5		Sunbird 7565
6/29/85	81	4		47 I Don't Want To Lose You .... *My Favorite Entertainer*		$7		El Dorado 101
9/5/87	77	4		48 Best Love I Never Had .... *I'm Not Going Hungry*		$6		Fifth Street 1091
				HART, J.D. '89				
				Male singer from Albemarle, North Carolina.				
11/4/89	79	3		Come Back Brenda .... *Love Still Lives*		$3		Universal 66017
				HART, Rod '77				
				Born in Beulah, Michigan. Acted in the movie *Junior Bonner*.				
11/27/76+	23	11		C.B. Savage...........................*Better Off Gone* [N]	67	$5		Plantation 144
				"gay" answer to "Convoy" by C.W. McCall				
				HART, Sally June '75				
9/20/75	91	3		Takin' What I Can Get .... *Beautiful Love Song Melodies*		$5		Buddah 479
				HARTFORD, Chapin '78				
				Born Paula Hartford Foster on 5/15/44 in Boston. Female singer.				
8/26/78	91	3		I Knew The Mason .... *Rio Grande*		$6		LS 165
				HARTFORD, John '67				
				Born on 12/30/37 in New York City; raised in St. Louis. Singer/songwriter/banjo player. Regular on TV's *The Smothers Brothers Comedy Hour*.				
5/27/67	60	7		1 Gentle On My Mind ....*(Good Old Electric) Washing Machine (Circa. 1943)*		$10		RCA Victor 9175
8/18/84	81	3		2 Piece Of My Heart .... *No Expectations*		$6		Flying Fish 4013
				#12 Pop hit for Big Brother & The Holding Company (Janis Joplin) in 1968				
				HARTSOOK, Jimmy '74				
				Born on 8/10/59 in Lenoir City, Tennessee.				
1/26/74	94	5		Anything To Prove My Love To You .... *Dreamin' Again*		$6	■	RCA Victor 0202
				HARTT, Dolly '88				
2/13/88	85	3		Here Comes The Night....................................		$6		Kass 1015
				HARVELL, Nate '78				
				Singer/songwriter from Alabama.				
7/15/78	23	13		1 Three Times A Lady .... *Happy Ending*		$5		Republic 025
				#1 Pop hit for the Commodores in 1978				
12/2/78	73	5		2 One In A Million .... *Silver Rails*		$5		Republic 033
				HATFIELD, Vince and Dianne '82				
8/1/81	83	4		1 I Won't Last A Day Without You...................*Divided Love*		$5		Soundwaves 4638
				#11 Pop hit for the Carpenters in 1974				
5/1/82	81	3		2 Back In My Baby's Arms ....*Travelin' Man*		$5		Soundwaves 4668
7/2/83	90	2		3 Love Has Made A Woman Out Of You.............*Texas, I Dream Of You*		$5		Soundwaves 4704
				HAUSER, Bruce '85				
				Singer/songwriter from Kansas.				
10/24/81	90	3		1 Barely Gettin' By...................................... *Friends*		$6		Cowboy 1045
				SAWMILL CREEK				
12/21/85	77	6		2 I Just Came Back (To Break My Heart Again)......................		$6		Cowboy 200
				BRUCE HAUSER AND THE SAWMILL CREEK BAND				
7/19/86	81	3		3 Bidding America Goodbye (The Auction)		$6		Cowboy 202
				BRUCE HAUSER and Sawmill Creek				
				HAVENS, Bobby '78				
				Born on 3/13/48 in Baird, Texas. Singer/songwriter/guitarist.				
12/9/78	100	2		Hey You .... *Typical Saturday Night*		$6		Cin Kay 043
				BOBBY HAVENS and Country Company				
				HAWKINS, Debi '77				
				Born Deborah Kaye Hawkins in Paso Robles, California.				
3/22/75	61	9		1 Making Believe .... *The Man In My Life*		$5		Warner 8076
7/26/75	80	5		2 What I Keep Sayin', Is A Lie .... *A Beautiful Memory Tonight*		$5		Warner 8104
11/8/75	88	3		3 When I Stop Dreaming ....*I Want To Hold You In My Arms*		$5		Warner 8140

| --- | --- | --- | --- | --- | --- | --- | --- | --- |
				HAWKINS, Debi — Cont'd				
3/27/76	97	2		4 Walnut Street Wrangler .... *Magic Cloud Of Love*		$5		Warner 8188
6/18/77	57	8		5 Love Letters		$5		Warner 8394
				Hey Mister Train				
				#5 Pop hit for Ketty Lester in 1962				
				HAWKINS, Erskine **'44**				
				Born on 7/26/14 in Birmingham, Alabama. Died on 11/11/93 (age 79). Trumpeter/bandleader/composer.				
2/5/44	6	1		Don't Cry, Baby	15	$25		Bluebird 30-0813
				Bear-Mash Blues				
				ERSKINE HAWKINS and his Orchestra				
				Jimmy Mitchelle (vocal)				
	★362★			**HAWKINS, Hawkshaw** **'63**				
				Born Harold Franklin Hawkins on 12/22/21 in Huntington, West Virginia. Died in a plane crash on 3/5/63 (age 41) near Camden, Tennessee (with **Patsy Cline** and **Cowboy Copas**). Singer/songwriter/guitarist. Joined the *Grand Ole Opry* in 1955. Married to **Jean Shepard** at the time of his death.				
				1)Lonesome 7-7203 2)Dog House Boogie 3)Slow Poke				
5/1/48	9	4		1 Pan American		$25		King 689
				J:9 / I Suppose				
8/21/48	6	15		2 Dog House Boogie		$25		King 720
				J:6 / S:12 I Can't Tell My Broken Heart A Lie				
12/24/49	15	1		3 I Wasted A Nickel .... *S:15 I'm Kissing Your Picture Counting Tears*		$25		King 821
3/17/51	8	1		4 I Love You A Thousand Ways		$25		King 918 (**78**)
				A:8 Teardrops From My Eyes				
10/13/51	8	2		5 I'm Waiting Just For You		$30		King 45-969
				A:8 A Heartache To Recall				
12/8/51+	7	4		6 Slow Poke		$30		King 45-998
				J:7 / S:8 Two Roads	26			
8/10/59	15	7		7 Soldier's Joy	87	$20		Columbia 41419
				Big Red Benson				
3/2/63	❶⁴	25		8 Lonesome 7-7203	108	$15		King 5712
				Everything Has Changed				
				HAWKS, Mickey **'89**				
				Male singer from High Point, North Carolina.				
9/23/89	94	2		Me And My Harley-Davidson .... *The Good Old Days*		$10		C-Horse 589
	★345★			**HAYES, Wade** **'95**				
				Born on 4/20/69 in Bethel Acres, Oklahoma. Singer/songwriter.				
11/19/94+	❶²	20		1 Old Enough To Know Better		$3	▌	Columbia 77739
				Family Reunion				
3/18/95	4	20		2 I'm Still Dancin' With You	113	$3		Columbia 77842
				S:3 It's Gonna Take A Miracle				
7/15/95	10	20		3 Don't Stop		$3		Columbia 77954
				S:16 Someone Had To Teach You				
10/28/95+	5	20		4 What I Meant To Say	116	$3		Columbia 78087
				S:6 Kentucky Bluebird				
5/11/96	2²	20		5 On A Good Night		$3		Columbia 78312
				S:11 Steady As She Goes				
10/5/96	42	9		6 Where Do I Go To Start All Over .... *My Side Of Town*		$3		Columbia 78369
12/21/96+	46	11		7 It's Over My Head		$3		Columbia 78486
				Hurts Don't It				
8/9/97	55	8		8 Wichita Lineman		$3	▌	Columbia 78674
				S:18 On A Good Night				
11/1/97+	5	25		9 The Day That She Left Tulsa (In A Chevy)	86	$3	▌	Columbia 78745
				S:8 Wichita Lineman				
				HAZARD **'83**				
				Vocal trio from Hazard, Kentucky: Wayne Davis, Bernie Faulkner and Bruce Dees. Faulkner was a member of **Exile**.				
4/2/83	69	5		Love Letters .... *Island*		$4		Warner 29755
				#5 Pop hit for Ketty Lester in 1962				
				HAZARD, Donna **'81**				
				Session vocalist with **The Concrete Cowboy Band**.				
1/17/81	45	9		1 My Turn .... *I Don't Want To Dance With You (No More)*		$5		Excelsior 1004
5/2/81	55	7		2 Go Home And Go To Pieces		$5		Excelsior 1009
7/11/81	54	8		3 Love Never Hurt So Good .... *I'm Your Lady*		$5		Excelsior 1016
12/26/81+	76	5		4 Slow Texas Dancing .... *Tailwinds*		$5		Excelsior 1020
	★268★			**HEAD, Roy** **'78**				
				Born on 6/30/36 in Perkins, Oklahoma. Singer/songwriter/guitarist. Charted seven pop hits from 1965-71.				
				1)Come To Me 2)The Most Wanted Woman In Town 3)Now You See 'Em, Now You Don't 4)The Door I Used To Close 5)Tonight's The Night				
10/19/74	66	9		1 Baby's Not Home .... *Do What You Can Do*		$6		Mega 1219
4/5/75	19	14		2 The Most Wanted Woman In Town .... *Gingers Breade Man*		$5		Shannon 829
8/16/75	47	10		3 Help Yourself To Me .... *To Make A Big Man Cry*		$5		Shannon 833
11/22/75+	55	8		4 I'll Take It .... *The One That Got Away*		$5		Shannon 838
2/7/76	28	11		5 The Door I Used To Close .... *Lady Luck And Mother Nature*		$5		ABC/Dot 17608
6/5/76	50	8		6 Bridge For Crawling Back .... *Ain't It Funny (How Times Haven't Changed)*		$5		ABC/Dot 17629
9/4/76	51	8		7 One Night .... *Deep Elem Blues*		$5		ABC/Dot 17650
				#11 R&B hit for Smiley Lewis in 1956				
12/25/76+	57	8		8 Angel With A Broken Wing .... *Just Because*		$5		ABC/Dot 17669
7/2/77	79	6		9 Julianne .... *Velvet Strings*		$5		ABC/Dot 17706
10/8/77+	16	20		10 Come To Me .... *Georgia On My Mind*		$5		ABC/Dot 17722
4/1/78	19	13		11 Now You See 'Em, Now You Don't .... *Smooth Whiskey*		$5		ABC 12346
7/22/78	28	10		12 Tonight's The Night (It's Gonna Be Alright) .... *The Lady In My Room*		$5		ABC 12383
				#1 Pop hit for Rod Stewart in 1976				
11/4/78	45	7		13 Love Survived .... *Dixie*		$5		ABC 12418
3/24/79	74	5		14 Kiss You And Make It Better .... *Do It Again*		$5		ABC 12462
				written by **Mac Davis**				
11/10/79	79	4		15 In Our Room .... *Things I Never Could Leave Behind*		$4		Elektra 46549
2/2/80	65	4		16 The Fire Of Two Old Flames .... *Under Suspicion*		$4		Elektra 46582
7/5/80	59	6		17 Long Drop .... *Gonna Save It For My Baby*		$4		Elektra 46653
9/27/80	70	5		18 Drinkin' Them Long Necks .... *Baby's Found Another Way To Love Me*		$4		Elektra 47029
10/24/81	75	5		19 After Texas .... *California Day*		$5		Churchill 7778
5/29/82	89	3		20 Play Another Gettin' Drunk And Take Somebody Home Song		$5		NSD 129
				Your Next One And Only				

DEBUT	PEAK	WKS	Gold	A-side (Chart Hit)...B-side	Pop	$	Pic	Label & Number
				HEAD, Roy — Cont'd				
9/11/82	64	7		21 The Trouble With Hearts .... *Naughty Smile*		$5		NSD 146
1/8/83	85	4		22 Your Mama Don't Dance .... *Party Time*		$5		NSD 156
				#4 Pop hit for **Loggins & Messina** in 1973				
12/10/83	79	5		23 Where Did He Go Right		$7		Avion 105
9/7/85	93	2		24 Break Out The Good Stuff .... *She Needs Time*		$7		Texas Crude 614

HEAP, Jimmy '54
Born on 3/3/22 in Taylor, Texas. Drowned in a boating accident on 12/4/77 (age 55). Singer/songwriter/guitarist. Leader of swing band, The Melody Masters, which featured lead singer Houston "Perk" Williams.

1/9/54	5	13		Release Me S:5 / J:8 / A:10 *Just To Be With You*		$25		Capitol 2518
				JIMMY HEAP and The Melody Masters with PERK WILLIAMS				
				#4 Pop hit for **Engelbert Humperdinck** in 1967				

HEARTLAND '89

9/24/88	79	3		1 New River .... *Way Down*		$5		Tra-Star 1221
12/17/88	82	3		2 Making Love To Dixie		$5		Tra-Star 1222
3/18/89	61	5		3 Keep The Faith		$5		Tra-Star 1223

HEART OF NASHVILLE '85
The Heart of Nashville Foundation was founded to benefit the nation's hungry and homeless. Some of the singers participating in this recording include Roy Acuff, Lynn Anderson, Eddy Arnold, Bobby Bare, Sonny James, George Jones, Webb Pierce, Jerry Reed, Tanya Tucker, Porter Wagoner and Faron Young.

6/8/85	61	9		One Big Family .... *(instrumental)*		$5	■	Compleat 679001
				written and produced by **Ronnie McDowell**				

HEATH, Boyd '45
Emcee of the NBC-TV show *Saturday Night Jamboree* in 1949.

5/5/45	7	1		Smoke On The Water *Dreamy Rio Grande*		$30		Bluebird 33-0522

HEAVENER, David '82
Born on 12/22/53 in Louisville, Kentucky.

11/28/81	73	4		1 Cheat On Him Tonight .... *Please Help Me Lord*		$5		Brent 1017
2/20/82	70	4		2 Honky Tonk Tonight .... *Jesus Is Coming To Town*		$5		Brent 1019
7/31/82	86	3		3 I Am The Fire		$5		Brent 1020

HECKEL, Beverly '78
Born in Elkins, West Virginia. Member of The Heckels. Formerly married to **Johnny Russell**.

6/11/77	88	5		1 Don't Hand Me No Hand Me Down Love .... *Halfway To Paradise*		$4		RCA 10981
9/16/78	56	7		2 Bluer Than Blue .... *Living Without*		$4		RCA 11360
				Wayland Holyfield (guest vocal); #12 Pop hit for **Michael Johnson** in 1978				

HECKELS, The '76
Family vocal trio from Elkins, West Virginia: sisters Susie and **Beverly Heckel**, with Susie's husband Denny Franks.

6/26/76	91	5		A Cowboy Like You .... *The Devil's Way Of Tempting Me*		$4		RCA Victor 10685

★271★ **HELMS, Bobby** '57
Born on 8/15/35 in Bloomington, Indiana. Died of emphysema on 6/19/97 (age 61). Singer/songwriter/guitarist.
1)Fraulein 2)My Special Angel 3)Jacqueline

3/30/57	❶⁴	52		1 Fraulein A:❶⁴ / S:❶³ / J:9 *(Got A) Heartsick Feeling*	36	$20	■	Decca 30194
10/14/57	❶⁴	26	●	2 My Special Angel S:❶⁴ / A:❶¹ *Standing At The End Of My World*	7	$15		Decca 30423
12/23/57	13	1	●	3 Jingle Bell Rock .... A:13 *Captain Santa Claus (And His Reindeer Space Patrol)* [X]	6	$15	■	Decca 30513
				also see #13 below				
3/3/58	10	9		4 Just A Little Lonesome S:10 / A:12 *Love My Lady*		$15		Decca 30557
5/12/58	5	12		5 Jacqueline S:5 *Living In The Shadow Of The Past*	63	$15		Decca 30619
				from the movie *The Case Against Brooklyn* starring Darren McGavin				
3/30/59	26	3		6 New River Train .... *Miss Memory*		$15		Decca 30831
10/24/59	16	4		7 Lonely River Rhine .... *Guess We Thought The World Would End*		$15		Decca 31148
6/24/67	46	7		8 He Thought He'd Die Laughing .... *You'd Better Make Up Your Mind*		$10		Little Darlin' 0030
12/30/67+	60	6		9 The Day You Stop Loving Me .... *You Can Tell The World*		$10		Little Darlin' 0034
4/20/68	53	9		10 I Feel You, I Love You .... *All I Need Is You*		$10		Little Darlin' 0041
8/2/69	43	9		11 So Long .... *Just Do The Best You Can*		$10		Little Darlin' 0062
6/27/70	41	9		12 Mary Goes 'Round .... *Cold Winds Blow On Me*		$10		Certron 10022
12/28/96	60	2		13 Jingle Bell Rock .... [X-R]				album cut
				same version as #3 above; from the movie *Jingle All The Way* starring Arnold Schwarzenegger (soundtrack on TVT 8070)				

HENDERSON, Brice '83
Born on 1/4/54 in Frederick, Maryland.

1/22/83	61	7		1 Lonely Eyes .... *She Still Has That Hold On Me*		$6		Union Station 1000
4/30/83	55	8		2 Lovers Again .... *She Still Has That Hold On Me*		$6		Union Station 1001
9/17/83	64	5		3 Flames .... *Crossing The Love Line*		$6		Union Station 1003

HENDERSON, Mike '94
Born on 7/14/53 in Independence, Missouri. Singer/songwriter.

2/5/94	69	4		Hillbilly Jitters		$3	▌	RCA 62730

HENHOUSE FIVE PLUS TOO — see STEVENS, Ray

HENLEY, Don — see YEARWOOD, Trisha

HENRY, Audie '85
Born in Brazil; raised in Canada. Female singer.

1/19/85	97	3		1 You'll Never Find A Good Man (Playing In A Country Band)		$5		Canyon Creek 2025
4/27/85	91	2		2 Being A Fool Again		$5		Canyon Creek 2008
7/27/85	73	5		3 Heaven Knows .... *I Knew The First Time I Saw You*		$5		Canyon Creek 5020
10/19/85	71	5		4 Sweet Salvation .... *A Step In The Right Direction*		$5		Canyon Creek 8019

DEBUT	PEAK	WKS	Gold	A-side (Chart Hit)..B-side	Pop	$	Pic	Label & Number
				HENSLEY, Tari '86				
				Born Tari Dean Hodges on 3/6/53 in Independence, Missouri. Female singer.				
4/9/83	86	3		1 Falling In Love... *Down To My Last Time*		$3		Mercury 76197
9/8/84	69	4		2 Love Isn't Love ('Til You Give It Away) .... *Sweet Nights*		$3		Mercury 880054
2/9/85	61	6		3 I'm The One Who's Breaking Up .... *It's The Nights That Drive Me Crazy*		$3		Mercury 880424
7/27/85	64	6		4 Hard Baby To Rock .... *Down To My Last Time*		$3		Mercury 880801
4/5/86	57	7		5 Oh Yes I Can .... *Sweet Nights*		$3		Mercury 884484
7/26/86	52	10		6 I've Cried A Mile *We Can't Communicate*		$3		Mercury 884852
				HERMAN, Woody — see WISEMAN, Mac				
	★333★			**HERNDON, Ty** '96				
				Born Boyd Tyrone Herndon on 5/2/62 in Meridian, Mississippi; raised in Butler, Alabama. Singer/songwriter/guitarist.				
2/25/95	❶[1]	20		1 What Mattered Most *S:4 You Don't Mess Around With Jim*		$3	▌	Epic 77843
6/10/95	7	20		2 I Want My Goodbye Back *S:22 Heart Half Empty*		$3	▌	Epic 77946
10/14/95+	21	20		3 Heart Half Empty ....*S:10 Love At 90 Miles An Hour*		$3	▌	Epic 78073
				TY HERNDON Featuring Stephanie Bentley				
3/30/96	63	2		4 In Your Face .... *What Mattered Most*		$3		Epic 78247
6/29/96	❶[1]	20		5 Living In A Moment *S:8 Returning The Faith*		$3	▌	Epic 78364
11/2/96+	21	20		6 She Wants To Be Wanted Again ....*S:20 Before There Was You*		$3	▌	Epic 78482
3/22/97	2[2]	20		7 Loved Too Much				album cut
9/20/97	17	20		8 I Have To Surrender				album cut
				above 2 from the album *Living In A Moment* on Epic 67564				
				HERRING, Red '60				
7/4/60	27	2		Wasted Love		$25		Country Jubilee 533
				HESTER, Hoot '79				
				Born Hubert Hester on 8/13/51 in Louisville, Kentucky.				
4/21/79	95	3		I Still Love Her Memory .... *Forever Ended Yesterday*		$7		Little Darlin' 7911
				HEWITT, Dolph '49				
				Born Dolph Edward Hewitt on 7/15/14 in West Finley, Pennsylvania. Regular on the WLS *National Barn Dance* from 1946-60.				
12/17/49	8	1		I Wish I Knew *A:8 I Would Send You Roses*		$20		RCA Victor 21-0107
				45 rpm: 48-0107				
				HIATT, John — see NITTY GRITTY DIRT BAND				
				HICKEY, Sara "Honeybear" '83				
6/25/83	82	2		This Ain't Tennessee And He Ain't You		$7		PCM 203
				HICKS, Jeanette — see JONES, George				
				HICKS, Laney — see SMALLWOOD, Laney				
				HIGGINS, Bertie '82				
				Born Elbert Higgins on 12/8/44 in Tarpon Springs, Florida. Singer/songwriter.				
3/13/82	50	10	●	1 Key Largo .... *White Line Fever*	8	$5		Kat Family 02524
				inspired by the movie starring Humphrey Bogart and Lauren Bacall				
6/19/82	90	3		2 Just Another Day In Paradise .... *She's Gone To Live On The Mountain*	46	$5		Kat Family 02839
9/3/88	72	5		3 You Blossom Me .... *Florida*		$5		Southern Tracks 2000
1/21/89	75	5		4 Homeless People .... *Cannonball*		$5		Southern Tracks 2005
				HIGHFILL, George '87				
				Born in Fort Smith, Arkansas; raised in Stigler, Oklahoma. Singer/songwriter.				
7/18/87	69	4		1 Waitin' Up .... *West Texas*		$3		Warner 28312
10/31/87	72	4		2 Mad Money .... *Nickels And Dimes*		$3		Warner 28177
				 **HIGHWAY 101** ★183★ '87				
				Group formed in Los Angeles: **Paulette Carlson** (vocals, guitar), Jack Daniels (guitar), Curtis Stone (bass) and Scott "Cactus" Moser (drums). Stone is the son of **Cliffie Stone**. Carlson left in late 1990; replaced by Nikki Nelson. CMA Awards: 1988 & 1989 Vocal Group of the Year.				
				1)Somewhere Tonight 2)Who's Lonely Now 3)Cry, Cry, Cry				
1/10/87	4	24		1 The Bed You Made For Me *S:4 / A:4 I'm Gonna Run Through The Wind*		$3		Warner 28483
5/23/87	2[1]	23		2 Whiskey, If You Were A Woman *S:❶[1] I'll Take You (Heartache And All)*		$3		Warner 28372
9/26/87	❶[2]	23		3 Somewhere Tonight *S:3 Are You Still Mine*		$3	■	Warner 28223
2/13/88	❶[1]	19		4 Cry, Cry, Cry *S:2 One Step Closer*		$3	■	Warner 28105
6/18/88	❶[1]	20		5 (Do You Love Me) Just Say Yes *S:2 I'll Be Missing You*		$3	■	Warner 27867
10/22/88+	5	19		6 All The Reasons Why *S:6 Higher Ground*		$3		Warner 27735
2/11/89	7	18		7 Setting Me Up *Long Way Down*		$3		Warner 27581
				first recorded by Dire Straits on their 1979 album *Dire Straits*				
6/17/89	6	21		8 Honky Tonk Heart *Desperate Road*		$3		Warner 22955
10/7/89+	❶[1]	26		9 Who's Lonely Now *Don't It Make Your Mama Cry*		$3		Warner 22779
2/10/90	4	26		10 Walkin', Talkin', Cryin', Barely Beatin' Broken Heart *Sweet Baby James*		$3	▌	Warner 19968
5/26/90	11	21		11 This Side Of Goodbye .... *If Love Had A Heart*		$3	▌	Warner 19829

HIGHWAY 101 — Cont'd

DEBUT	PEAK	WKS	A-side	B-side	Pop	$	Pic	Label & Number
9/22/90	14	20	12 Someone Else's Trouble Now	The Bed You Made For Me		$3	▌	Warner 19593
4/13/91	14	20	13 Bing Bang Boom	Baby, I'm Missing You		$3	▌	Warner 19346
9/14/91	31	20	14 The Blame	River Of Tears		$3		Warner 19203
1/11/92	22	20	15 Baby, I'm Missing You	Desperate		$3		Warner 19043
5/23/92	54	7	16 Honky Tonk Baby	Storm Of Love		$3		Warner 18878
10/2/93	67	2	17 You Baby You	You Are What You Do		$3		Liberty 17497

HILKA '79
Born Hilka Maria Cornelius in Germany; raised in Salt Lake City.

DEBUT	PEAK	WKS	A-side	B-side	Pop	$	Pic	Label & Number
10/13/79	89	3	1 I Just Wonder Where He Could Be Tonight	(And) Robin Danced		$5		IBC 0004
			HILKA & JEBRY (Jebry Lee Briley)					
2/9/80	96	2	2 (I'm Just The) Cuddle Up Kind	Here Comes The Dawn		$5		IBC 0006

HILL, Billy — see BILLY

★238★ HILL, Faith '94
Born on 9/21/67 in Jackson, Mississippi. Adopted at less than a week and raised as Audrey Faith Perry in Star, Mississippi. Married **Tim McGraw** on 10/6/96.

1)It's Your Love 2)Wild One 3)It Matters To Me

DEBUT	PEAK	WKS	A-side	B-side	Pop	$	Pic	Label & Number
10/16/93+	❶[4]	20	1 Wild One	Go The Distance		$3	▌	Warner 18411
2/12/94	❶[1]	20	2 Piece Of My Heart	I Would Be Stronger Than That	115	$3	▌	Warner 18261
			#12 Pop hit for Big Brother & The Holding Company (Janis Joplin) in 1968					
6/4/94	35	12	3 But I Will	Life's Too Short To Love Like That		$3	▌	Warner 18179
9/24/94	2[2]	20	4 Take Me As I Am					album cut
			from the album *Take Me As I Am* on Warner 45389					
8/5/95	5	20	5 Let's Go To Vegas	S:8 You Will Be Mine	122	$3	▌	Warner 17817
11/11/95+	❶[3]	20	6 It Matters To Me	S:❶[10] Keep Walkin' On	74	$3	▌	Warner 17718
2/24/96	3	20	7 Someone Else's Dream					album cut
7/13/96	6	20	8 You Can't Lose Me					album cut
			above 2 from the album *It Matters To Me* on Warner 45872					
10/19/96+	8	20	9 I Can't Do That Anymore	Take Me As I Am		$3		Warner 17531
5/10/97	❶[6]	20	▲ 10 It's Your Love	S:❶[12] She Never Lets It Go To Her Heart	7	$3	▌	Curb 73019
			TIM McGRAW with Faith Hill					

HILL, Goldie '53
Born Argolda Voncile Hill on 1/11/33 in Karnes County, Texas. Married **Carl Smith** in 1957. Known as "The Golden Hillbilly."

DEBUT	PEAK	WKS	A-side	B-side	Pop	$	Pic	Label & Number
1/10/53	❶[3]	9	1 I Let The Stars Get In My Eyes	J:❶[3] / S:4 Waiting For A Letter		$25		Decca 28473
			GOLDIE HILL (The Golden Hillbilly)					
			answer to "Don't Let The Stars Get In Your Eyes" by **Slim Willet**					
7/3/54	4	21	2 Looking Back To See	J:4 / A:5 / S:5 I Miss You So		$20		Decca 29145
			GOLDIE HILL - JUSTIN TUBB					
1/8/55	11	2	3 Sure Fire Kisses	A:11 / S:13 Fickle Heart		$20		Decca 29349
			JUSTIN TUBB - GOLDIE HILL					
3/26/55	14	2	4 Are You Mine	S:14 Ko Ko Mo (I Love You So)		$20		Decca 29411
			RED SOVINE - GOLDIE HILL					
2/23/59	17	4	5 Yankee, Go Home	What's Happened To Us		$15		Decca 30826
			Red Sovine (narration)					
4/6/68	73	2	6 Lovable Fool	Making Plans		$10		Epic 10296
			GOLDIE HILL SMITH					

HILL, Kim '94
Born on 12/30/63 in Starkville, Mississippi.

DEBUT	PEAK	WKS	A-side	B-side	Pop	$	Pic	Label & Number
4/2/94	68	6	Janie's Gone Fishin'	Natural Thing		$4	▌	BNA 62768

HILL, Tiny '46
Born Harry Hill on 7/19/06 in Sullivan Township, Illinois. Died in 1972. Nicknamed "Tiny" because of his weight (350 pounds).

DEBUT	PEAK	WKS	A-side	B-side	Pop	$	Pic	Label & Number
1/26/46	3	4	1 Sioux City Sue	I'll Keep On Lovin' You [N]		$20		Mercury 2024
1/10/48	5	1	2 Never Trust A Woman	Behind The Eight Ball [N]		$20		Mercury 6062
			TINY HILL And the Cactus Cutups					
2/3/51	7	2	3 Hot Rod Race	S:7 Lovebug Itch [N]	29	$20		Mercury 5547 **(78)**
			original version of **Charlie Ryan**'s 1960 hit "Hot Rod Lincoln"					
3/24/51	10	1	4 I'll Sail My Ship Alone	J:10 Back In Your Own Backyard		$25		Mercury 5508-X45

HILL CITY '85
Group from Fort Worth, Texas.

DEBUT	PEAK	WKS	A-side	B-side	Pop	$	Pic	Label & Number
8/10/85	86	3	I'd Do It In A Heartbeat	The Ghost Of Brandy Jones		$5		Moon Shine 3040

HILLMAN, Chris '89
Born on 12/4/44 in Los Angeles. Member of The Byrds from 1964-68 and the **Flying Burrito Brothers** from 1968-72. Formed **The Desert Rose Band** in 1986.

DEBUT	PEAK	WKS	A-side	B-side	Pop	$	Pic	Label & Number
9/29/84	81	6	1 Somebody's Back In Town	Desert Rose		$5		Sugar Hill 4105
4/27/85	77	5	2 Running The Roadblocks	Turn Your Radio On		$5		Sugar Hill 4106
4/29/89	6	21	3 You Ain't Going Nowhere	Don't You Hear Jerusalem Moan		$3		Universal 66006
			CHRIS HILLMAN & ROGER McGUINN					
			written by Bob Dylan; #74 Pop hit for The Byrds in 1968					

HILTON, Denny '81

DEBUT	PEAK	WKS	A-side	B-side	Pop	$	Pic	Label & Number
3/28/81	84	2	1 Layin' Low	Delores		$6		Oak 1027
2/13/82	92	2	2 How'd You Get So Good			$6		Rosebridge 0014
2/5/83	88	2	3 Sharing The Night Together			$6		Rosebridge 010

HINOJOSA, Tish '90
Pronounced: ee-no-hoe-sah. Born Leticia Hinojosa on 12/6/55 in San Antonio, Texas. Singer/songwriter.

DEBUT	PEAK	WKS		A-side / B-side	Pop	$	Pic	Label & Number
6/14/86	80	3		1 I'll Pull You Through ....Too Soon To Say It's Too Late		$4		MCA/Curb 52823
				TISH HINOJOSA/CRAIG DILLINGHAM				
12/23/89+	75	4		2 Til U Love Me Again		$3		A&M 1468

HITCHCOCK, Stan '69
Born on 3/21/36 in Kansas City, Missouri. Singer/songwriter. Worked as a DJ on KWTO and KTTS in Springfield, Missouri. Moved to Nashville in 1962. Own TV series in the mid-1960s. Former program director for Country Music Television.
1)Honey, I'm Home 2)Call Me Gone 3)Dixie Belle

DEBUT	PEAK	WKS		A-side / B-side	Pop	$	Pic	Label & Number
9/16/67	54	6		1 She's Looking Good ....Have I Stayed Away Too Long		$8		Epic 10182
12/9/67	66	2		2 Rings ....Such A Little Teardrop		$8		Epic 10246
5/18/68	57	8		3 I'm Easy To Love.................Don't Do Like I've Done (Do Like I Say)		$8		Epic 10307
10/19/68	60	4		4 The Phoenix Flash ....My Memory		$8		Epic 10388
10/11/69	17	11		5 Honey, I'm Home Slip-Up And She'll Slip Away		$8		Epic 10525
4/18/70	46	6		6 Call Me Gone ....Your Kind Of Man		$8		Epic 10586
10/17/70	54	7		7 Dixie Belle ....I Did It All For You		$6		GRT 23
3/13/71	59	7		8 At Least Part Of The Way ....The Shadow Of Your Smile		$6		GRT 39
7/14/73	65	7		9 The Same Old Way ....Lonely Wine		$6		Cinnamon 759
12/8/73	91	4		10 Half-Empty Bed ....When Love Was At Its Best		$6		Cinnamon 770
3/9/74	80	7		11 I'm Free ....Oklahoma Wind		$6		Cinnamon 782
6/3/78	100	2		12 Falling ....Only One		$6		MMI 1024
				#13 Pop hit for LeBlanc & Carr in 1978				
3/10/79	85	3		13 Finders Keepers Losers Weepers		$6		MMI 1028
				STAN HITCHCOCK with Sue Richards				
4/11/81	81	4		14 She Sings Amazing Grace ....Janet		$5		Ramblin' 1711

★363★ HOBBS, Becky '83
Born Rebecca Ann Hobbs on 1/24/50 in Bartlesville, Oklahoma. Singer/songwriter/guitarist.
1)Let's Get Over Them Together 2)Jones On The Jukebox 3)Hottest "Ex" In Texas

DEBUT	PEAK	WKS		A-side / B-side	Pop	$	Pic	Label & Number
12/23/78+	95	5		1 The More I Get The More I Want ....I Feel Like Breakin' Somebody's Heart Tonight		$4		Mercury 55049
6/30/79	44	11		2 I Can't Say Goodbye To You...............What Love Is All About		$4		Mercury 55062
12/8/79+	52	9		3 Just What The Doctor Ordered.........You Can't Tie A Ramblin' Man Down		$4		Mercury 57010
5/3/80	79	6		4 I'm Gonna Love You Tonight (Like There's No Tomorrow) ....Good-For-Nothin' Guitar Pickin' Man		$4		Mercury 57020
10/11/80	87	2		5 I Learned All About Cheatin' From You ....Stay Away From Married Men		$4		Mercury 57033
2/7/81	84	4		6 Honky-Tonk Saturday Night ....Old Memories		$4		Mercury 57041
6/25/83	10	18		7 Let's Get Over Them Together In Love		$4		Columbia 03970
				MOE BANDY (Featuring Becky Hobbs)				
6/2/84	46	10		8 Oklahoma Heart ....Fool Me Once, Fool Me Twice		$4		Liberty 1520
9/8/84	64	6		9 Pardon Me (Haven't We Loved Somewhere Before) ....Anyway		$3		EMI America 8224
12/8/84	77	6		10 Wheels In Emotion ....Slow Dancin' Lies		$3		EMI America 8247
6/22/85	37	12		11 Hottest "Ex" In Texas ....The Lover Of You		$3	■	EMI America 8273
3/5/88	31	19		12 Jones On The Jukebox.................S:13 I'm-A-Gonna Get You Baby		$3		MTM 72104
7/9/88	43	10		13 They Always Look Better When They're Leavin'.................S:18 Mama Was A Working Man		$3		MTM 72109
10/8/88	53	9		14 Are There Any More Like You (Where You Came From)...........Cowgirl's Heart		$3		MTM 72114
8/5/89	39	11		15 Do You Feel The Same Way Too?..............Jones On The Jukebox		$3		RCA 8974

HOBBS, Bud '49
Singer/songwriter/guitarist from San Francisco.
BUD HOBBS with His Trail Herders:

DEBUT	PEAK	WKS		A-side / B-side	Pop	$	Pic	Label & Number
9/25/48	13	1		1 Lazy Mary................J:13 You're Mine Tonight (But Will You Be Mine Tomorrow)		$20		MGM 10206
1/29/49	12	4		2 I Heard About You........................J:12 / S:13 Oklahoma Sweetheart		$20		MGM 10305
5/21/49	12	1		3 Candy Kisses ....J:12 / S:13 Tennessee Border		$20		MGM 10366

HOBBS, Lou '81
Born in Cape Girardeau, Missouri.

DEBUT	PEAK	WKS		A-side / B-side	Pop	$	Pic	Label & Number
3/7/81	79	3		1 Loving You Was All I Ever Needed ....It's All Your Fault		$6		Kik 902
9/5/81	93	2		2 We're Building Our Love On A Rock ....Run Right Back		$6		Kik 911

HOBBS, Pam '81

DEBUT	PEAK	WKS		A-side / B-side	Pop	$	Pic	Label & Number
2/7/81	85	4		1 Have You Ever Seen The Rain		$5		50 States 79
				#8 Pop hit for Creedence Clearwater Revival in 1971				
5/2/81	88	2		2 I Thought I Heard You Calling My Name...............Love Is Not A Game		$5		50 States 81
9/26/81	93	2		3 You're The Only Dancer		$5		50 States 84

HOGSED, Roy '48
Born on 12/24/19 in Flippin, Arkansas.

DEBUT	PEAK	WKS		A-side / B-side	Pop	$	Pic	Label & Number
8/21/48	15	1		Cocaine Blues ....J:15 Fishtail Boogie		$25		Capitol 40120

HOKUM, Suzi Jane '67

DEBUT	PEAK	WKS		A-side / B-side	Pop	$	Pic	Label & Number
9/9/67	51	7		1 Here We Go Again...Hangin' On		$7		LHI 17018
				VIRGIL WARNER & SUZI JANE HOKUM				
2/24/68	65	4		2 Storybook Children...................................Lady Bird		$7		LHI 1204
				VIRGIL WARNER & SUZI JANE HOKUM				
				#54 Pop hit for Billy Vera & Judy Clay in 1968				
8/30/69	75	2		3 Reason To Believe ....I'll Never Fall In Love Again		$7		LHI 14
				#19 Pop hit for Rod Stewart in 1993				

DEBUT	PEAK	WKS	A-side / B-side	Pop	$	Pic	Label & Number
			HOLDEN, Rebecca '89				
			Born on 6/12/53 in Austin, Texas. Singer/actress. Played "April Curtis" on TV's *Knight Rider*.				
11/25/89	82	2	1 The Truth Doesn't Always Rhyme ....*If You Ever Wanna Try Again*		$6		Tra-Star 1229
12/16/89	78	4	2 License To Steal		$6		Tra-Star 1234
			HOLLADAY, Dave '86				
12/13/86	83	4	Now She's In Paris ....*I. O. Blues*		$5		Step One 365
			HOLLAND, Greg '94				
			Born on 2/22/67 in Douglas, Georgia.				
8/6/94	63	5	1 Let Me Drive ....*Up To Feelin' Down*		$3	▌	Warner 18152
11/12/94	66	5	2 When I Come Back (I Wanna Be My Dog) ....*Oh To Be The One*		$3	▌	Warner 18033
			HOLLIER, Jill '86				
			Singer/songwriter from Port Arthur, Texas.				
11/15/86	79	2	1 Sweet Time...*Magic Of The Moment*		$3		Warner 28559
8/12/89	83	3	2 If It Wasn't For The Heartache ....*Empty Arms*		$3		Warner 22966
			from the movie *Pink Cadillac* starring **Clint Eastwood**				
12/23/89+	81	4	3 Mama's Daily Bread ....*Cry So Easy*		$3		Warner 22700
			HOLLOWELL, Terri '79				
			Born on 7/2/56 in Jeffersonville, Indiana. Female singer.				
6/17/78	81	4	1 Happy Go Lucky Morning ....*Say What I Feel Tonight*		$6		Con Brio 134
9/23/78	76	4	2 Strawberry Fields Forever ....*If You Wanna Love Me, It's Okay*		$6		Con Brio 139
			#8 Pop hit for The Beatles in 1967				
12/23/78+	76	6	3 Just Stay With Me...................................*Sweet Virginia Morning*		$6		Con Brio 144
3/24/79	35	11	4 May I ....*I Wasn't There*		$6		Con Brio 150
7/21/79	56	8	5 It's Too Soon To Say Goodbye ....*Holding It Back, Letting You Go*		$6		Con Brio 156
			HOLLY, Doyle '73				
			Born Doyle Floyd Hendricks on 6/30/36 in Perkins, Oklahoma. Singer/songwriter/bassist. Member of **The Buckaroos** from 1963-70.				
11/18/72	63	6	1 My Heart Cries For You....................*All The Way From Alabama*		$5		Barnaby 5004
			#2 Pop hit for **Guy Mitchell** in 1951				
6/16/73	29	14	2 Queen Of The Silver Dollar...................*Take A Walk In The Country*		$5		Barnaby 5018
10/6/73	17	13	3 Lila ....*Darling, Are You Ever Coming Home*		$5		Barnaby 5027
3/2/74	58	9	4 Lord How Long Has This Been Going On................*January Bittersweet Jones*		$5		Barnaby 5030
			DOYLE HOLLY And The Vanishing Breed				
6/15/74	75	8	5 A Rainbow In My Hand ....*Free Love*		$5		Barnaby 602
9/7/74	69	6	6 Just Another Cowboy Song ....*January Bittersweet Jones*		$5		Barnaby 605
11/16/74+	53	11	7 Richard And The Cadillac Kings ....*She Can't Make The Hurt Go Away*		$5		Barnaby 608
			HOLM, Johnny '77				
			Born in Fargo, North Dakota. Singer/songwriter/guitarist.				
10/1/77	100	2	Lightnin' Bar Blues ....*Ain't It A Beauty*		$6		ASI 1012
			HOLMES, Monty '89				
1/21/89	82	3	A Way To Survive		$6		Ashley 1001
			HOLT, Darrell '88				
			Former singer with the group **Sweetwater**.				
12/12/87+	57	10	1 Catch 22..		$6		Anoka 222
3/26/88	58	9	2 I Can't Take Her Anywhere		$6		Anoka 221
10/1/88	66	6	3 I'd Throw It All Away		$6		Anoka 224
2/11/89	71	5	4 Only The Strong Survive		$6		Anoka 225
			#4 Pop hit for Jerry Butler in 1969				
			HOMER AND JETHRO '53				
			Comedy duo from Knoxville, Tennessee: Henry "Homer" Haynes (guitar) and Kenneth "Jethro" Burns (mandolin). Homer was born on 7/27/20; died of a heart attack on 8/7/71 (age 51). Jethro was born on 3/10/20; died of cancer on 2/4/89 (age 68). Regulars on the WLS National Barn Dance from 1950-58.				
3/26/49	14	1	1 I Feel That Old Age Creeping On ....J:14 *Goodbye Ole Booze* [N]		$25		King 749
8/27/49	9	1	2 Baby, It's Cold Outside S:9 *Country Girl* [N]	22	$20		RCA Victor 21-0078
			HOMER and JETHRO with June Carter				
			45 rpm: 48-0075; from the movie *Neptune's Daughter* starring Esther Williams				
11/5/49	14	1	3 Tennessee Border--No. 2.................J:14 *I'm Gettin' Older Every Day* [N]		$20		RCA Victor 21-0110
			45 rpm: 48-0113; parody of "Tennessee Border" by Red Foley				
5/23/53	2²	9	4 (How Much Is) That Hound Dog In The Window S:2 / J:3 / A:10 *Pore Ol' Koo-Liger* [N]	17	$20		RCA Victor 5280
			parody of "The Doggie In The Window" by Patti Page				
8/14/54	14	1	5 Hernando's Hideaway ....S:14 *Wanted* [N]		$20		RCA Victor 5788
			parody of the #2 Pop hit for Archie Bleyer in 1954				
10/19/59	26	3	6 The Battle Of Kookamonga ....*Waterloo* [N]	14	$15		RCA Victor 7585
			parody of "The Battle Of New Orleans" by Johnny Horton				
4/18/64	49	1	7 I Want To Hold Your Hand ....*She Loves You* [N]		$15	■	RCA Victor 8345
			parody of the #1 Pop hit for The Beatles in 1964				
			HOMESTEADERS, The '66				
			Vocal trio led by Jerry Rivers.				
10/15/66	44	7	1 Show Me The Way To The Circus ....*Country Joined The Country Club*		$10		Little Darlin' 0010
8/3/68	67	2	2 Gonna Miss Me ....*Homewrecker*		$10		Little Darlin' 0045

HOOD, Bobby '79

Gospel singer from Alabama.

1)Easy 2)I've Got An Angel 3)It Takes One To Know One

4/1/78	91	3		1 Come On In ....*Southern Ladies Kind Of Man*		$5		Plantation 169
8/5/78	60	7		2 I've Got An Angel (That Loves Me Like The Devil) ....*Tennessee Frost*		$5		Chute 101
10/14/78	87	3		3 Come To Me		$5		Chute 102
2/24/79	85	3		4 Slow Tunes And Promises ....*You Gotta Go Down*		$5		Chute 004
8/11/79	45	8		5 Easy ....*No Love Lost*		$5		Chute 008
12/8/79	72	5		6 It Takes One To Know One ....*After The Rain*		$5		Chute 009
3/22/80	75	4		7 When She Falls		$5		Chute 010
9/13/80	85	3		8 Mexico Winter		$5		Chute 015
11/29/80	89	3		9 Pick Up The Pieces Joanne		$5		Chute 016
9/26/81	74	4		10 Woman In My Heart		$5		Chute 018

HOOD, Ray '96

5/4/96	73	3		Freedom				album cut

from the album *Back To Back Heartaches* on Caption/Curb 5561

HOOSIER HOT SHOTS '46

Novelty group from Fort Wayne, Indiana: brothers Paul "Hezzie" (song whistle, washboard, drums, alto horn) and Kenneth "Rudy" Triesch (banjo, guitar, bass horn), with Charles Otto "Gabe" Ward (clarinet, saxophone, fife) and Frank Kettering (banjo, guitar, flute, piano, bass fiddle). Regulars on the WLS *National Barn Dance* from 1933-42. Also appeared in several western movies.

6/17/44	3	2		1 She Broke My Heart In Three Places *Don't Change Horses* [N]	21	$20		Decca 4442
1/26/46	3	10		2 Someday (You'll Want Me To Want You) *You Two-Timed Me One Time Too Often* [N]	12	$20		Decca 18738
				HOOSIER HOT SHOTS and SALLY FOSTER				
				#1 Pop hit for Vaughn Monroe in 1949				
2/9/46	2[1]	16		3 Sioux City Sue *There's A Tear In My Beer Tonight* [N]		$20		Decca 18745
				HOOSIER HOT SHOTS And TWO TON BAKER				
				#3 Pop hit for Bing Crosby & The Jesters in 1946				

HOPE '96

All-star collaboration for the T.J. Martell Foundation (cancer research): **John Berry, Terri Clark, Vince Gill, Faith Hill, Tracy Lawrence, Little Texas, Neal McCoy, Tim McGraw, Lorrie Morgan, Marty Stuart, Travis Tritt** and **Trisha Yearwood.**

5/4/96	57	4		Hope ....*S:17 (different version)*		$3	▌	Giant 17669

HORN, DeAnne '78

2/18/78	97	2		1 I Just Want To Love You ....*I'm A Country Girl (Livin' In A City World)*		$6		Chartwheel 102
7/8/78	100	1		2 I Know		$6		Chartwheel 108

HORN, James T. '97

11/8/97	72	1		Texas Diary ....*Geronimo*		$3	▌	Curb/Universal 56096

HORNSBY, Bruce '87

Born on 11/23/54 in Williamsburg, Virginia. Singer/songwriter/pianist. Won the 1986 Best New Artist Grammy Award. Charted 10 pop hits from 1986-95.

3/14/87	38	10		Mandolin Rain ....*The Red Plains*	4	$3	■	RCA 5087
				BRUCE HORNSBY AND THE RANGE				

HORTON, Billie Jean '61

Born Billie Jean Jones Eshlimar in Bossier City, Louisiana. Married to **Hank Williams** from 10/18/52 until his death on 1/1/53. Married to **Johnny Horton** from September 1953 until his death on 11/5/60.

8/28/61	29	3		Ocean Of Tears ....*Don't Take His Love*		$15		20th Fox 266

★227★ HORTON, Johnny '59

Born on 4/30/25 in Los Angeles; raised in Tyler, Texas. Died in a car crash on 11/5/60 (age 35). Singer/songwriter/guitarist. Known as "The Singing Fisherman." Joined the *Louisiana Hayride* in 1951. Married to **Billie Jean Horton**, widow of **Hank Williams**, from September 1953 until his death.

1)The Battle Of New Orleans 2)North To Alaska 3)When It's Springtime In Alaska

5/5/56	9	12		1 Honky-Tonk Man *A:9 / S:14 I'm Ready If You're Willing*		$30		Columbia 21504
				also see #13 below				
9/8/56	7	13		2 I'm A One-Woman Man *A:7 / S:9 / J:9 I Don't Like I Did*		$25		Columbia 21538
2/23/57	11	5		3 I'm Coming Home ....*A:11 / S:15 I Got A Hole In My Pirogue*		$25		Columbia 40813
5/27/57	9	1		4 The Woman I Need *J:9 She Knows Why*		$25		Columbia 40919
9/29/58	8	8		5 All Grown Up *A:8 Counterfeit Love*		$20		Columbia 41210
				also see #14 below				
1/12/59	❶[1]	23	●	6 When It's Springtime In Alaska (It's Forty Below) *Whispering Pines*		$15	□	Columbia 41308
4/27/59	❶[10]	21	●	7 The Battle Of New Orleans *All For The Love Of A Girl*	❶[6]	$15	■	Columbia 41339
				original melody written in celebration of the final battle of the War of 1812; a promotional 4-page fold-out picture sleeve was also issued				
9/7/59	10	9		8 Johnny Reb/	54			
9/7/59	19	7		9 Sal's Got A Sugar Lip	81	$15		Columbia 41437
3/28/60	6	15		10 Sink The Bismarck *The Same Old Tale The Crow Told Me*	3	$12	■	Columbia 41568
				inspired by the movie starring Kenneth Moore, which is based on the sinking of the German battleship in World War II				
11/14/60+	❶[5]	22		11 North To Alaska *The Mansion You Stole*	4	$12	■	Columbia 41782
				from the movie starring John Wayne				
4/24/61	9	8		12 Sleepy-Eyed John *They'll Never Take Her Love From Me*	54	$12	■	Columbia 41963
4/14/62	11	12		13 Honky-Tonk Man *Words* [R]	96	$12	■	Columbia 42302
				new version of #1 above				
2/9/63	26	5		14 All Grown Up *I'm A One-Woman Man* [R]		$12	■	Columbia 42653
				same version as #5 above				

HORTON, Steven Wayne '89

Singer/guitarist from Memphis.

8/19/89	68	5		Roll Over ....*I've Been Stung*		$3		Capitol 44350

HOSFORD, Larry '75
Born in 1943 in Alisal, California. Singer/songwriter/guitarist.

12/7/74+	62	8		1 Long Distance Kisses...Long Line To Chicago		$5		Shelter 40312
4/26/75	78	6		2 Everything's Broken Down.....................................Long Line To Chicago		$5		Shelter 40381

HOUSE, David '82
Singer/songwriter from Lubbock, Texas.

6/26/82	96	2		1 Everything's All Right ....Should've Been Chasin' My Dreams		$5		Door Knob 177
10/9/82	88	2		2 Little White Lies ....Maybe Now We Can Be Friends		$5		Door Knob 183

HOUSE, James '95
Born on 3/21/55 in Sacramento, California. Singer/songwriter/guitarist.

3/25/89	25	14		1 Don't Quit Me Now ....Call It In The Air		$3		MCA 53510
7/15/89	52	6		2 That'll Be The Last Thing ....Lucinda		$3		MCA 53669
10/21/89	48	11		3 Hard Times For An Honest Man ....Born Ready		$3		MCA 53731
12/8/90	60	9		4 You Just Get Better All The Time .... I Ain't Like That Anymore		$3		MCA 53934
8/27/94	52	8		5 A Real Good Way To Wind Up Lonesome .... That's Something		$3	▮	Epic 77610
11/26/94+	25	20		6 Little By Little ....Take Me Away		$3	▮	Epic 77752
4/29/95	6	20		7 This Is Me Missing You S:16 Take Me Away		$3	▮	Epic 77870
9/16/95	49	11		8 Anything For Love......................Silence Makes A Lonesome Sound		$3	▮	Epic 77982
8/24/96	69	1		9 Little Deuce Coupe..(no B-side)		$5	▮	River North 3014

THE BEACH BOYS Featuring James House
#15 Pop hit for The Beach Boys in 1963

HOUSTON, David ★43★ '67
Born on 12/9/38 in Shreveport, Louisiana. Died of a brain aneurysm 11/30/93 (age 54). Singer/songwriter/guitarist. Acted in the movies *Cottonpickin' Chicken-Pluckers* and *Horse Soldiers*. Joined the *Grand Ole Opry* in 1972.

1)Almost Persuaded 2)Baby, Baby 3)You Mean The World To Me 4)My Elusive Dreams 5)With One Exception

10/19/63	2[1]	18		1 Mountain Of Love Angeline	132	$10		Epic 9625
3/28/64	17	15		2 Chickashay/		$10		Epic 9658
3/7/64	37	6		3 Passing Through..		$10		
7/11/64	11	17		4 One If For Him, Two If For Me ....Your Memories		$10		Epic 9690
10/10/64	17	14		5 Love Looks Good On You ....My Little Lady		$10		Epic 9720
1/30/65	18	17		6 Sweet, Sweet Judy ....Too Many Times (Away From You)		$8		Epic 9746
9/11/65	3	18		7 Livin' In A House Full Of Love Cowpoke	117	$8		Epic 9831
3/5/66	47	2		8 Sammy ....I'll Take You Home Again, Kathleen		$8	▮	Epic 9884
6/25/66	❶[9]	25		9 Almost Persuaded We Got Love	24	$8	▢	Epic 10025
12/24/66+	3	16		10 A Loser's Cathedral/	135			
12/10/66	14	12		11 Where Could I Go? (But To Her)................................	133	$8	▮	Epic 10102
4/29/67	❶[1]	18		12 With One Exception Sweet, Sweet Judy		$8	▮	Epic 10154
7/15/67	❶[2]	18		13 My Elusive Dreams Marriage On The Rocks	89	$10		Epic 10194
				DAVID HOUSTON and TAMMY WYNETTE				
9/23/67	❶[2]	17		14 You Mean The World To Me Don't Mention Tomorrow	75	$8	▮	Epic 10224
1/20/68	11	14		15 It's All Over ....Together We Stand (Divided We Fall)		$10		Epic 10274
				DAVID HOUSTON & TAMMY WYNETTE				
3/9/68	❶[1]	14		16 Have A Little Faith Too Far Gone	98	$8	▮	Epic 10291
6/15/68	❶[1]	14		17 Already It's Heaven Lighter Shade Of Blue		$8	▮	Epic 10338
10/19/68	2[2]	14		18 Where Love Used To Live I Love A Rainbow		$8		Epic 10394
1/18/69	4	17		19 My Woman's Good To Me Lullaby To A Little Girl		$8		Epic 10430
6/28/69	3	16		20 I'm Down To My Last "I Love You" Watching My World Walk Away		$8		Epic 10488
11/8/69+	❶[4]	17		21 Baby, Baby (I Know You're A Lady) True Love's A Lasting Thing		$8		Epic 10539
4/4/70	3	17		22 I Do My Swinging At Home Then I'll Know You Care		$8		Epic 10596
8/8/70	6	15		23 Wonders Of The Wine If God Can Forgive Me (Why Can't You?)		$8		Epic 10643
10/3/70	6	14		24 After Closing Time My Song Of Love		$8		Epic 10656
				DAVID HOUSTON AND BARBARA MANDRELL				
1/9/71	2[4]	16		25 A Woman Always Knows The Rest Of My Life		$8		Epic 10696
6/12/71	9	13		26 Nashville That's Why I Cry		$8		Epic 10748
10/9/71	10	14		27 Maiden's Prayer/		$8		Epic 10778
9/25/71	32	16		28 Home Sweet Home..		$8		Epic 10778
10/2/71	20	12		29 We've Got Everything But Love ....Try A Little Harder		$8		Epic 10779
				DAVID HOUSTON AND BARBARA MANDRELL				
2/19/72	18	13		30 The Day That Love Walked In.....................Sweet Lovin'		$8		Epic 10830
6/10/72	8	12		31 Soft, Sweet And Warm Rest Of My Life		$8		Epic 10870
9/16/72	24	13		32 A Perfect Match ....Almost Persuaded		$8		Epic 10908
				DAVID HOUSTON AND BARBARA MANDRELL				
10/14/72	41	9		33 I Wonder How John Felt (When He Baptized Jesus) ....Will The Circle Be Unbroken?		$8		Epic 10911
12/30/72+	2[2]	16		34 Good Things The Love She Gives		$8		Epic 10939
6/2/73	3	14		35 She's All Woman Sweet Lovin'		$7		Epic 10995
11/3/73	22	11		36 The Lady Of The Night ....Thank You Teardrop		$7		Epic 11048

DEBUT	PEAK	WKS	Gold	A-side (Chart Hit)..B-side	Pop	$	Pic	Label & Number
				HOUSTON, David — Cont'd				
12/22/73+	6	16		37 I Love You, I Love You *Let's Go Down Together*		$7		Epic 11068
				DAVID HOUSTON and BARBARA MANDRELL				
3/30/74	33	12		38 That Same Ol' Look Of Love .... *Clinging Vine*		$7		Epic 11096
5/25/74	40	12		39 Lovin' You Is Worth It............................*How Can It Be Wrong (When It Feels So Right)*		$7		Epic 11120
				DAVID HOUSTON and BARBARA MANDRELL				
8/10/74	14	16		40 Ten Commandments Of Love .... *Try A Little Harder*		$7		Epic 20005
				DAVID HOUSTON and BARBARA MANDRELL				
				#22 Pop hit for Harvey & The Moonglows in 1958				
9/14/74	9	15		41 Can't You Feel It *I Walk And I Walk And I Walk*		$7		Epic 50009
3/1/75	36	10		42 A Man Needs Love .... *Flower Of Love*		$7		Epic 50066
6/14/75	40	10		43 I'll Be Your Steppin' Stone .... *Then I'll Know You Care*		$7		Epic 50113
9/27/75	69	6		44 Sweet Molly .... *The Old Blind Fiddler* (Houston)		$7		Epic 50134
				DAVID HOUSTON AND CALVIN CRAWFORD				
11/1/75	35	10		45 The Woman On My Mind .... *I Can't Sit Still*		$7		Epic 50156
2/7/76	51	9		46 What A Night .... *From The Bottom Of My Heart*		$7		Epic 50186
9/25/76	24	12		47 Come On Down (To Our Favorite Forget-About-Her				
				Place).. *Me And Susan Wright*		$7		Epic 50275
4/30/77	33	9		48 So Many Ways .... *Touch My World*		$6		Gusto 156
				#6 Pop hit for Brook Benton in 1959				
8/6/77	68	6		49 Ain't That Lovin' You Baby .... *Love Is A Miracle*		$6		Gusto 162
				#3 R&B hit for Jimmy Reed in 1956				
11/19/77	98	1		50 The Twelfth Of Never .... *Barroom Champagne*		$6		Gusto 168
				#9 Pop hit for Johnny Mathis in 1957				
12/24/77+	56	9		51 It Started All Over Again........................... *Touch My World*		$6		Gusto 172
4/8/78	72	5		52 No Tell Motel ....*I Hate To Tell Baby A Lie*		$6		Gusto 184
6/24/78	51	9		53 Waltz Of The Angels		$8		Colonial 101
12/9/78+	46	10		54 Best Friends Make The Worst Enemies.................... *There Won't Be A Wedding*		$5		Elektra 45552
4/21/79	33	10		55 Faded Love And Winter Roses................... *Beyond The Blue Horizon*		$5		Elektra 46028
8/18/79	57	8		56 Let Your Love Fall Back On Me .... *Take Me To Your Heart*		$6		Derrick 126
11/10/79	60	8		57 Here's To All The Too Hard Working Husbands (In The				
				World)................................. *Next Sunday I'm Gonna Be Saved*		$6		Derrick 127
5/31/80	64	7		58 You're The Perfect Reason .... *We Couldn't Make It Love*		$6		Country Int'l. 145
9/13/80	78	4		59 Sad Love Song Lady.................. *Thanks For Being You And Loving Me*		$6		Country Int'l. 148
5/9/81	69	6		60 Texas Ida Red		$6		Excelsior 1012
4/22/89	85	2		61 A Penny For Your Thoughts Tonight Virginia............................		$6		Country Int'l. 220
				HOWARD, Chuck **'80**				
				Born in Flat Fork, Kentucky. Died on 8/15/83 (age 45). Singer/songwriter/producer.				
8/23/80	66	7		I've Come Back (To Say I Love You One More Time).................... *Everyone But Me*		$4		Warner/Curb 49509
				HOWARD, Eddy **'47**				
				Born on 9/12/14 in Woodland, California. Died on 5/23/63 (age 48). Charted 42 pop hits from 1946-55.				
8/9/47	5	1		Ragtime Cowboy Joe *On The Old Spanish Trail*	16	$12		Majestic 1155
				from the movie *Hello Frisco, Hello* starring Alice Faye; #16 Pop hit for **The Chipmunks** in 1959				
				HOWARD, Harlan **'71**				
				Born on 9/8/27 in Lexington, Kentucky; raised in Detroit. Legendary songwriter. Formerly married to **Jan Howard**. Inducted into the Country Music Hall of Fame in 1997.				
4/10/71	38	15		Sunday Morning Christian .... *That Little Boy Who Follows Me*		$10		Nugget 1058

				HOWARD, Jan ★158★ **'67**				
				Born Lula Grace Johnson on 3/13/30 in West Plains, Missouri. Singer/songwriter. Formerly married to **Harlan Howard**. Joined the *Grand Ole Opry* in 1971.				
				1)For Loving You 2)If It's All The Same To You 3)Someday We'll Be Together 4)Dis-Satisfied 5)Evil On Your Mind				
1/11/60	13	12		1 The One You Slip Around With .... *I Wish I Could Fall In Love Again*		$15		Challenge 59059
5/30/60	26	2		2 Wrong Company ....*We'll Never Love Again*		$15		Challenge 9071
				WYNN STEWART AND JAN HOWARD				
11/16/63	27	3		3 I Wish I Was A Single Girl Again .... *The Saddest Part Of All*		$12		Capitol 5035
1/16/65	25	13		4 What Makes A Man Wander? .... *Slipping Back To You*		$10		Decca 31701
2/19/66	29	8		5 I Know You're Married (But I Love You Still)/				
3/12/66	44	1		6 Time Out...		$10		Decca 31884
				BILL ANDERSON AND JAN HOWARD (above 2)				
4/23/66	5	20		7 Evil On Your Mind *Crying For Love*		$10		Decca 31933
10/8/66	10	13		8 Bad Seed *You Go Your Way (I'll Go Crazy)*		$10		Decca 32016
3/11/67	32	11		9 Any Old Way You Do .... *Your Ole Handy Man*		$10		Decca 32096
7/22/67	26	10		10 Roll Over And Play Dead .... *You And Me And Tears And Roses*		$10		Decca 32154
10/28/67	❶⁴	20		11 For Loving You *The Untouchables*		$8		Decca 32197
				BILL ANDERSON And JAN HOWARD				
3/9/68	16	13		12 Count Your Blessings, Woman ....*But Not For Love My Dear*		$8		Decca 32269
8/10/68	27	11		13 I Still Believe In Love .... *Life's That Way*		$8		Decca 32357
11/23/68+	15	14		14 My Son .... *The Tip Of My Fingers*		$8		Decca 32407
3/8/69	24	11		15 When We Tried .... *I Hurt All Over*		$8		Decca 32447

DEBUT	PEAK	WKS		A-side	B-side	Pop	$	Pic	Label & Number
				HOWARD, Jan — Cont'd					
9/20/69	20	9		16 We Had All The Good Things Going .... *I'll Go Where You Go*			$8		Decca 32543
11/15/69+	2[1]	15		17 If It's All The Same To You .... *I Thank God For You*			$8		Decca 32511
				BILL ANDERSON And JAN HOWARD					
3/21/70	26	10		18 Rock Me Back To Little Rock ....*Hello Stranger*			$8		Decca 32636
6/20/70	4	15		19 Someday We'll Be Together .... *Who Is The Biggest Fool*			$8		Decca 32689
				BILL ANDERSON AND JAN HOWARD #1 Pop hit for Diana Ross & The Supremes in 1969					
11/14/70	64	5		20 The Soul You Never Had................................. *I Have Your Love*			$8		Decca 32743
2/13/71	56	10		21 Baby Without You/					
		2		22 Marriage Has Ruined More Good Love Affairs			$8		Decca 32778
10/9/71	4	15		23 Dis-Satisfied .... *Knowing You're Mine*			$8		Decca 32877
				BILL ANDERSON AND JAN HOWARD					
12/25/71+	36	14		24 Love Is Like A Spinning Wheel .... *I Never Once Stopped Loving You*			$8		Decca 32905
5/6/72	43	10		25 Let Him Have It .... *Remember The Good*			$8		Decca 32955
3/31/73	74	2		26 Too Many Ties That Bind .... *Everybody Knows I Love You*			$6		MCA 40020
11/9/74	96	4		27 Seein' Is Believin' ....*My Kind Of People*			$6		GRT 010
4/30/77	70	6		28 I'll Hold You In My Heart (Till I Can Hold You In My Arms).. *I Thought I Had Him*			$6		Con Brio 118
10/1/77	65	7		29 Better Off Alone ....*My Coloring Book*			$6		Con Brio 125
4/22/78	93	3		30 To Love A Rolling Stone .... *Thought I Had Him*			$6		Con Brio 132
				HOWARD, Jim **'64**					
7/18/64	38	9		Meet Me Tonight Outside Of Town ....*Too Much Taking-Not Enough Giving*			$15		Del-Mar 1013
				HOWARD, Randy **'88** Born on 5/9/50 in Macon, Georgia. Singer/songwriter/guitarist.					
4/9/83	84	4		1 All-American Redneck .... *(dirty version)* "live" recording			$4	■	Warner 29781
1/9/88	66	5		2 Ring Of Fire			$3		Atlantic Amer. 99387
				HUBBLE, Hal **'78** Born in 1940 in Indianapolis.					
11/25/78	76	6		My Pulse Pumps Passions .... *Before I Leave This Land*			$5		50 States 66
				HUDSON, Helen **'79** Born on 1/19/53 in Sydney, Australia. Singer/model.					
5/26/79	91	5		Nothing But Time .... *One More Guitar*			$6		Cyclone 102
				HUDSON, Larry G. **'79** Born on 12/19/49 in Hawkinsville, Georgia; raised in Unadilla, Georgia. Singer/songwriter/guitarist.					
6/12/76	89	4		1 Singing A Happy Song .... *Legend In My Time*			$6		Aquarian 605
10/14/78	37	10		2 Just Out Of Reach Of My Two Open Arms .... *Warm And Tender Love* #24 Pop hit for Solomon Burke in 1961			$5		Lone Star 702
1/27/79	31	10		3 Loving You Is A Natural High *You Don't Know Me*			$5		Lone Star 706
3/15/80	34	10		4 I Can't Cheat.. *Just For The Heaven Of It*			$4		Mercury 57015
8/16/80	39	9		5 I'm Still In Love With You .... *Easy Come, Easy Go*			$4		Mercury 57029
				HUGHES, Hollie **'87** Born in Carrollton, Texas. Daughter of Luv Records owner Kent Hughes.					
2/14/87	75	3		67 Miles To Cow Town .... *I'm In Love*			$7		Luv 130
				HUGHES, Joel **'82** Born on 10/2/55 in Jenkins, Kentucky.					
3/13/82	75	4		Handy Man .... #2 Pop hit for Jimmy Jones in 1960			$6		Sunbird 7569
				HUMMERS, The **'73**					
7/21/73	38	7		1 Old Betsy Goes Boing, Boing, Boing .... *One Good Thing About Being Down* [N] adapted from a Mazda jingle	104	$6		Capitol 3646
6/1/74	91	4		2 Julianna .... *Big Toy Train*			$6		Capitol 3870
				HUMMON, Marcus **'96** Singer/songwriter from Fort Wayne, Indiana.					
3/16/96	73	6		God's Country .... *Somebody's Leaving*			$3	▌	Columbia 78251
				HUMPERDINCK, Engelbert **'83** Born Arnold George Dorsey on 5/2/36 in Madras, India; raised in Leicester, England. Starred in his own musical variety TV series in 1970. Charted 23 pop hits from 1967-83.					
1/8/77	40	12	●	1 After The Lovin' .... *Let's Remember The Good Times*	8	$5		Epic/MAM 50270
7/2/77	93	3		2 Goodbye My Friend.. *I Believe In Miracles*	97	$5		Epic/MAM 50365
1/27/79	93	4		3 This Moment In Time.. *And The Day Begins*	58	$5		Epic/MAM 50632
5/14/83	39	14		4 Til You And Your Lover Are Lovers Again .... *What Will I Write*	77	$4		Epic 03817
	★225★			**HUNLEY, Con** **'81** Born Conrad Hunley on 4/9/45 in Fountain City, Tennessee. Singer/songwriter/pianist. *1)What's New With You 2)Oh Girl 3)Week-End Friend 4)I've Been Waiting For You All Of My Life 5)You've Still Got A Place In My Heart*					
1/29/77	96	4		1 Pick Up The Pieces................................ *(It Looks Like) A Good Night For Drinking*			$5		Prairie Dust 7608
4/16/77	75	6		2 I'll Always Remember That Song .... *Never Felt More Like Dying (Than I Do Now)*			$5		Prairie Dust 7614
7/23/77	67	7		3 Breaking Up Is Hard To Do................................ *Woman To Man, Man To Woman*			$5		Prairie Dust 7618
2/4/78	34	10		4 Cry Cry Darling .... *Just Hangin' On*			$4		Warner 8520
5/13/78	13	12		5 Week-End Friend .... *Only The Strong Survive*			$4		Warner 8572
10/7/78	14	13		6 You've Still Got A Place In My Heart .... *Honky Tonk Heart*			$4		Warner 8671

HUNLEY, Con — Cont'd

DEBUT	PEAK	WKS	A-side (Chart Hit) .... B-side	$	Label & Number
1/27/79	14	14	7 I've Been Waiting For You All Of My Life .... *Just Hangin' On*	$4	Warner 8723
			#48 Pop hit for Paul Anka in 1981		
5/26/79	20	12	8 Since I Fell For You.................... *Cry Cry Darling*	$4	Warner 8812
			#4 Pop hit for Lenny Welch in 1963		
11/3/79+	20	14	9 I Don't Want To Lose You .... *That's All That Matters*	$4	Warner 49090
3/8/80	19	12	10 You Lay A Whole Lot Of Love On Me .... *When It Hurts You Most*	$4	Warner 49187
8/16/80	19	13	11 They Never Lost You .... *Lover's Lullaby*	$4	Warner 49528
12/20/80+	11	16	12 What's New With You *This Ol' Cowboy's Going Home*	$4	Warner 49613
8/29/81	17	15	13 She's Steppin' Out................ *Ask Any Woman*	$4	Warner 49800
1/9/82	20	14	14 No Relief In Sight .... *Table For One*	$4	Warner 49887
5/22/82	12	15	15 Oh Girl................. *Tonight I Took Your Memory Off The Wall*	$4	Warner 50058
			Oak Ridge Boys (backing vocals); #1 Pop hit for The Chi-Lites in 1972		
10/9/82	43	9	16 Confidential .... *I Still Have Dreamin'*	$4	Warner 29902
4/30/83	42	10	17 Once You Get The Feel Of It .... *It's Tearin' Me Up, To Lay Your Memory Down*	$4	MCA 52208
9/3/83	84	4	18 Satisfied Mind.............. *Let Me Love You Once Before You Go*	$4	MCA 52259
			Porter Wagoner (guest vocal)		
3/17/84	75	7	19 Deep In The Arms Of Texas .... *Never Felt More Like Dying*	$4	Prairie Dust 84110
12/15/84+	57	11	20 All American Country Boy .... *Sad But True*	$3	Capitol 5428
3/16/85	54	8	21 I'd Rather Be Crazy .... *Sad But True*	$3	Capitol 5457
7/13/85	49	9	22 Nobody Ever Gets Enough Love .... *Sad But True*	$3	Capitol 5485
11/30/85+	48	15	23 What Am I Gonna Do About You .... *Lord, She Sure Looks Good Tonight*	$3	Capitol 5525
5/31/86	49	13	24 Blue Suede Blues .... *Sad But True*	$3	Capitol 5586
9/27/86	55	9	25 Quittin' Time .... *Late At Night*	$3	Capitol 5631

HUNNICUTT, Ed   '84
Born on 7/29/51 in Troy, New York; raised in Columbia, South Carolina.

DEBUT	PEAK	WKS	A-side .... B-side	$	Label & Number
5/21/83	69	6	1 Fade To Blue .... *Gettin' It Right With You*	$4	MCA 52207
10/8/83	59	7	2 My Angel's Got The Devil In Her Eyes .... *Home Is Where The Heart Is*	$4	MCA 52262
3/17/84	41	9	3 In Real Life................. *There Oughta Be A Law*	$4	MCA 52353

HUNT, John — see BACKTRACK

HUNTER, Jesse   '94
Born on 1/14/59 in Shelby County, Tennessee. Male singer.

DEBUT	PEAK	WKS	Pic	A-side .... B-side	$	Label & Number
3/5/94	56	9	▌	1 Born Ready .... *L. A. Freeway*	$3	BNA 62735
6/18/94	65	8		2 By The Way She's Lookin' .... *Long Steady Rain*	$3	BNA 62857
10/22/94	42	15		3 Long Legged Hannah (From Butte Montana) .... *(remix)*	$3	BNA 62976

HUNTER, Tommy   '67
Born on 3/20/37 in London, Ontario, Canada. Singer/songwriter/guitarist. Regular on CBC-TV series *Country Hoedown* from 1956-65. Hosted own CBC-TV series from 1965-89. Known as "Canada's Country Gentleman."

DEBUT	PEAK	WKS	A-side .... B-side	$	Label & Number
9/9/67	66	3	Mary In The Morning.............. *The Battle Of The Little Big Horn*	$6	Columbia 44234
			#27 Pop hit for Al Martino in 1967		

HURLEY, Libby   '88
Female singer from Clarksville, Arkansas.

DEBUT	PEAK	WKS	A-side .... B-side	$	Label & Number
10/3/87	60	6	1 Don't Get Me Started .... *The Last One To Know*	$3	Epic 07366
1/16/88	43	10	2 You Just Watch Me .... *The Last One To Know*	$3	Epic 07650
4/23/88	59	8	3 Don't Talk To Me .... *I'm Turning Blue*	$3	Epic 07771

HURT, Charlotte   '78

DEBUT	PEAK	WKS	A-side .... B-side	$	Label & Number
9/16/78	85	5	The Price Of Borrowed Love Is Just To High .... *Wheel Of Fortune*	$7	Compass 0020

HURT, Cindy   '82
Born in 1956 in Mundelein, Illinois. Singer/actress. Toured with the musical *Sophisticated Ladies* in 1980.

DEBUT	PEAK	WKS	Pic	A-side .... B-side	$	Label & Number
3/21/81	74	5		1 Single Girl .... *Dark Moon*	$5	Churchill 7767
				#12 Pop hit for Sandy Posey in 1966		
6/6/81	56	8		2 Headin' For A Heartache	$5	Churchill 7772
9/5/81	46	10		3 Dreams Can Come In Handy................ *Headin' For A Heartache*	$5	Churchill 7777
1/30/82	28	13		4 Don't Come Knockin'............... *Love Me Up*	$5	Churchill 94000
6/12/82	35	10		5 Talk To Me Loneliness............. *Dreams Can Come In Handy*	$5	Churchill 94004
11/20/82	67	8		6 What's Good About Goodbye............... *You Make It Feel Like Love*	$5	Churchill 94010
7/2/83	65	6	■	7 I'm In Love All Over Again .... *Dark Moon*	$5	Churchill 94013

HUSKEY, Kenni   '71
Born Nora Carolyn Huskey on 12/2/54 in Newport, Arkansas. Female singer.

DEBUT	PEAK	WKS	A-side .... B-side	$	Label & Number
10/23/71	71	6	1 A Living Tornado .... *Only You Can Break My Heart*	$6	Capitol 3184
1/29/72	74	2	2 Within My Loving Arms .... *(Bring Back My) Peace Of Mind*	$6	Capitol 3229
			written by Buck Owens		

HUSKY, Ferlin ★66★   '57

Born on 12/3/25 in Flat River, Missouri. Singer/songwriter/guitarist. Acted in several movies. Also recorded as **Simon Crum**. Also see **Jean Shepard**.

1)Wings Of A Dove 2)Gone 3)A Dear John Letter 4)Country Music Is Here To Stay 5)Just For You

DEBUT	PEAK	WKS	A-side	B-side	Pop	$	Pic	Label & Number
7/25/53	❶⁶	23	1 A Dear John Letter S:❶⁶ / J:❶⁴ / A:2 I'd Rather Die Young (Shepard)		4	$25		Capitol 2502
			JEAN SHEPARD with FERLIN HUSKEY					
			#44 Pop hit for Pat Boone in 1960					
10/10/53	4	7	2 Forgive Me John S:4 / J:6 / A:8 My Wedding Ring (Shepard)			$25		Capitol 2586
			JEAN SHEPARD with FERLIN HUSKEY					
1/15/55	6	10	3 I Feel Better All Over (More Than Anywhere's Else)/ A:6 / S:15					
1/15/55	7	8	4 Little Tom A:7			$25		Capitol 3001
			FERLIN HUSKEY (above 2)					
4/16/55	5	15	5 Cuzz Yore So Sweet A:5 My Gallina [N]			$25		Capitol 3063
			SIMON CRUM					
5/28/55	14	1	6 I'll Baby Sit With You S:14 She's Always There (When I Come Home)			$25		Capitol 3097
			FERLIN HUSKEY and His Hush Puppies					
2/23/57	❶¹⁰	27	7 Gone S:❶¹⁰ / A:❶⁹ / J:❶⁵ Missing Persons		4	$20		Capitol 3628
			originally recorded by Husky in 1952 as by Terry Preston on Capitol 2298 ($30)					
7/1/57	8	13	8 A Fallen Star/ S:8 / A:8		47			
7/15/57	12	1	9 Prize Possession A:12			$20		Capitol 3742
10/27/58	23	1	10 I Will All Of The Time			$20		Capitol 4046
11/3/58+	2³	24	11 Country Music Is Here To Stay Stand Up, Sit Down, Shut Your Mouth [N]			$20		Capitol 4073
			SIMON CRUM					
2/16/59	14	12	12 My Reason For Living Wrong			$20		Capitol 4123
6/1/59	11	10	13 Draggin' The River Sea Sand			$20		Capitol 4186
11/16/59	21	8	14 Black Sheep I'll Always Return			$20		Capitol 4278
9/5/60	❶¹⁰	36	15 Wings Of A Dove Next To Jimmy		12	$15		Capitol 4406
10/9/61	23	1	16 Willow Tree Take A Look			$15		Capitol 4594
1/27/62	13	10	17 The Waltz You Saved For Me Out Of A Clear Blue Sky		94	$12	■	Capitol 4650
			#4 Pop hit for Wayne King in 1931					
5/26/62	16	11	18 Somebody Save Me Just Another Lonely Night			$12		Capitol 4721
9/22/62	28	1	19 Stand Up It Scares Me			$12		Capitol 4779
12/1/62	21	2	20 It Was You Near You			$12		Capitol 4853
2/22/64	13	21	21 Timber I'm Falling Don't Count The Diamonds			$12		Capitol 5111
4/10/65	46	7	22 True True Lovin' Love Built The House			$12		Capitol 5355
			also see #40 below					
12/11/65	48	2	23 Money Greases The Wheels Lasting Love			$12		Capitol 5522
6/4/66	27	5	24 I Could Sing All Night What Does Your Conscience Say To You			$12		Capitol 5615
7/9/66	17	12	25 I Hear Little Rock Calling Stand Beside Me			$12		Capitol 5679
12/3/66+	4	17	26 Once Why Do I Put Up With You			$12		Capitol 5775
			FERLIN HUSKY And The Hushpuppies:					
4/1/67	37	11	27 What Am I Gonna Do Now General "G"			$12		Capitol 5852
7/15/67	14	15	28 You Pushed Me Too Far The Bridge I Have Never Crossed			$12		Capitol 5938
12/23/67+	4	18	29 Just For You Don't Hurt Me Anymore			$12	■	Capitol 2048
			FERLIN HUSKY					
5/25/68	26	10	30 I Promised You The World You Should Live My Life			$12	■	Capitol 2154
10/19/68	25	10	31 White Fences And Evergreen Trees Love's Been Good To Me			$10		Capitol 2288
3/15/69	33	10	32 Flat River, MO. One Life To Live			$10		Capitol 2411
6/21/69	16	14	33 That's Why I Love You So Much Forever Yours			$10		Capitol 2512
			FERLIN HUSKY:					
11/22/69	21	10	34 Every Step Of The Way That's What I'd Do			$10		Capitol 2666
5/16/70	11	13	35 Heavenly Sunshine All Her Little Loving Ways			$10		Capitol 2793
9/12/70	45	9	36 Your Sweet Love Lifted Me You're The Happy Song I Sing			$10		Capitol 2882
12/26/70+	14	11	37 Sweet Misery Because You're Mine			$10		Capitol 2999
3/27/71	28	11	38 One More Time Don't Let The Good Life Pass You By			$10		Capitol 3069
9/11/71	45	9	39 Open Up The Book (And Take A Look) Even If It's True			$10		Capitol 3165
4/22/72	39	10	40 Just Plain Lonely Always In All Ways			$10		Capitol 3308
9/9/72	53	8	41 How Could You Be Anything But Love I'd Walk A Mile For A Smile			$10		Capitol 3415
1/13/73	35	10	42 True True Lovin' Legend In My Time [R]			$7		ABC 11345
			new version of #20 above					
4/28/73	46	9	43 Between Me And Blue My Special Angel			$7		ABC 11360
8/11/73	75	4	44 Baby's Blue One			$7		ABC 11381
11/3/73+	17	13	45 Rosie Cries A Lot Shoes			$7		ABC 11395
5/4/74	26	15	46 Freckles And Polliwog Days Everything Is Nothing Without You			$7		ABC 11432
9/21/74	60	7	47 A Room For A Boy...Never Used Ring Of String			$7		ABC 12021
12/28/74+	34	11	48 Champagne Ladies And Blue Ribbon Babies I Feel Better All Over			$7		ABC 12048
4/19/75	37	11	49 Burning A Touch Of Yesterday			$7		ABC 12085
10/4/75	74	5	50 She's Not Yours Anymore/			$7		
9/27/75	90	6	51 An Old Memory (Got In My Eye)			$7		ABC/Dot 17574

HUTCHENS, The   **'95**
Trio of brothers from Sandy Rudge, North Carolina: Barry, Bill and Bryan Hutchens.

| 10/7/95 | 56 | 7 | Knock, Knock ....*She Just Wants To Dance* | | $3 | | Atlantic 87092 |

HUTCHINS, Loney   **'87**
Born on 11/7/46 in Sullivan County, Tennessee.

| 7/4/87 | 92 | 2 | Still Dancing .... | | $5 | ■ | ARC 0005 |

I

IFIELD, Frank   **'66**
Born on 11/30/37 in Coventry, England; raised in New South Wales, Australia. Singer/songwriter/actor.

8/27/66	42	6	1 No One Will Ever Know ....*I'm Saving All My Love (For You)*		$8		Hickory 1397
10/22/66	28	14	2 Call Her Your Sweetheart ....*Give Myself A Party*		$8		Hickory 1411
12/23/67+	68	4	3 Oh, Such A Stranger ....*Then You Can Tell Me Goodbye*		$8		Hickory 1486
			written by Don Gibson				
10/5/68	67	3	4 Good Morning, Dear ....*Innocent Years*		$8		Hickory 1514

IGLESIAS, Julio   **'84**
Born on 9/23/43 in Madrid. Spanish singer. CMA Award: Vocal Duo of the Year (with **Willie Nelson**).

3/10/84	❶²	20	●	1 To All The Girls I've Loved Before ....*I Don't Want To Wake You*	5	$4	■	Columbia 04217
				JULIO IGLESIAS & WILLIE NELSON				
9/17/88	8	19		2 Spanish Eyes ....*S:2 Ole Buttermilk Sky*		$3		Columbia 08066
				WILLIE NELSON (with Julio Iglesias)				
				#15 Pop hit for **Al Martino** in 1966				

INDIANA   **'87**

| 4/18/87 | 85 | 2 | Midnite Rock.. | | $6 | | Killer 1005 |

INGLE, Red   **'47**
Born Ernest Ingle on 11/7/06 in Toledo, Ohio. Died in August 1965 (age 58). Comic singer/violinist/clarinetist/saxophonist. Formed group The Natural Seven: Luke "Red" Roundtree (guitar), Noel Boggs (steel guitar), Herman "The Hermit" Snyder (banjo), Art Wenzel (accordion), Joseph "Country" Washbourne (suitcase), Rull Hall (bass) and Ray Hagan (drums).

6/21/47	2¹¹	18	Temptation (Tim-Tayshun) ....*(I Love You) For Seventy Mental Reasons* [N]	❶¹	$15		Capitol 412
			RED INGLE & THE NATURAL SEVEN				
			Cinderella G. Stump (**Jo Stafford**) and Red Ingle (vocals); hillbilly version of song that was a #3 Pop hit for **Bing Crosby** in 1934 and a #27 Pop hit for **The Everly Brothers** in 1961				

INGLES, David   **'69**
Gospel singer from Tulsa, Oklahoma.

| 11/29/69 | 72 | 2 | Johnny Let The Sunshine In ....*You're A Part Of This Man* | | $8 | | Capitol 2648 |

INGRAM, Jack   **'97**
Born on 11/15/70 in Houston. Singer/songwriter/guitarist.

| 7/19/97 | 51 | 10 | Flutter .... | | | | album cut |
| | | | from the album *Livin' Or Dyin'* on Rising Tide 53046 | | | | |

INGRAM, James — see ROGERS, Kenny

INMAN, Autry   **'53**
Born Robert Autry Inman on 1/6/29 in Florence, Alabama. Died on 9/6/88 (age 59). Singer/songwriter/guitarist.

7/11/53	4	4	1 That's All Right ....*J:4 Uh-Huh Honey*		$25		Decca 28629
4/13/63	22	3	2 The Volunteer ....*Unlucky Am I*		$10		Sims 131
11/2/68	14	15	3 Ballad Of Two Brothers ....*Don't Call Me (I'll Call You)*	48	$8		Epic 10389
			patriotic-styled narrative, featuring strains of "Battle Hymn Of The Republic"				

INMAN, Jerry   **'79**

12/28/74+	95	2	1 You're The One ....*Leah*		$5		Chelsea 3006
8/26/78	95	2	2 Why, Baby, Why ....*Gonna Save It For My Baby*		$4		Elektra 45508
2/17/79	94	2	3 Why Don't We Lie Down And Talk It Over ....*Gonna Save It For My Baby*		$4		Elektra 46006

IRBY, Jerry   **'48**
Born in 1917 in Pineland, Texas. Singer/songwriter/guitarist.

6/19/48	11	2	1 Cryin' In My Beer ....*J:11 Answer To Drivin' Nails In My Coffin*		$20		MGM 10151
7/3/48	10	1	2 Great Long Pistol ....*J:10 49 Women*		$20		MGM 10188
			JERRY IRBY And His Texas Ranchers (above 2)				

IRVING, Lonnie   **'60**
Born on 6/11/32 in Stoneville, North Carolina. Died of leukemia on 12/2/60 (age 28).

| 3/14/60 | 13 | 15 | Pinball Machine ....*I Got Blues On My Mind* | | $20 | | Starday 486 |
| | | | first released on the Lonnie Irving label in 1959 ($25) | | | | |

ISAACSON, Peter   **'84**
Singer/songwriter from Vermont.

7/23/83	76	5	1 Froze In Her Line Of Fire ....*Baby Your Love*		$7		Union Station 1002
11/26/83	61	6	2 Don't Take Much		$7		Union Station 1004
3/24/84	93	2	3 No Survivors		$7		Union Station 1005
5/12/84	71	5	4 It's A Cover Up		$7		Union Station 1006

DEBUT	PEAK	WKS	Gold	A-side (Chart Hit)..B-side	Pop	$	Pic	Label & Number

★367★ IVES, Burl   **'62**

Born on 6/14/09 in Huntington Township, Illinois. Died of cancer on 4/14/95 (age 85). Actor/singer. Acted in several movies and TV shows.

1)A Little Bitty Tear 2)Call Me Mr. In-Between 3)Wild Side Of Life

2/12/49	13	1		1 Lavender Blue (Dilly Dilly)..S:13 Billy Boy	16	$20		Decca 24547
				BURL IVES with Captain Stubby & The Buccaneers				
				#4 Pop hit for Sammy Kaye in 1949; #3 Pop hit for Sammy Turner in 1959				
5/21/49	8	5		2 Riders In The Sky (Cowboy				Columbia 38445
				Legend) J:8 / S:15 Wayfaring Stranger / Woolie Boogie Bee	21	$15		
				#30 Pop hit for The Ramrods in 1961				
7/26/52	6	4		3 Wild Side Of Life J:8 / S:10 It's So-Long And Good-Bye To You	30	$20		Decca 9-28055
				BURL IVES and GRADY MARTIN And His Slew Foot Five				
2/3/62	2²	17		4 A Little Bitty Tear Shanghied	9	$10		Decca 31330
4/28/62	9	13		5 Funny Way Of Laughin' Mother Wouldn't Do That	10	$10		Decca 31371
8/11/62	3	11		6 Call Me Mr. In-Between What You Gonna Do, Leroy?	19	$10		Decca 31405
12/1/62+	12	7		7 Mary Ann Regrets...How Do You Fall Out Of Love	39	$10		Decca 31433
9/17/66	47	6		8 Evil Off My Mind.. A Taste Of Heaven		$8		Decca 31997
2/4/67	72	2		9 Lonesome 7-7203 ....Hollow Words (Empty Phrases)		$8		Decca 32078

IVIE, Roger — see SILVER CREEK

IVORY JACK   **'80**

2/9/80	78	4		1 Made In The USA ....Borrowed Angel		$6		NSD 36
5/9/81	81	4		2 Love Signs ....I Came So Close To Calling You Last Night		$6		Country Int'l. 154

J

JACK AND TRINK   **'78**

Husband-and-wife duo of Jack and Trink Ruthven.

9/9/78	93	4		I'm Tired Of Being Me .... Ain't No Way Of Gettin...		$6		NSD 4

JACKSON, Alan ★61★   **'92**

Born on 10/17/58 in Newnan, Georgia. Singer/songwriter/guitarist. Joined the Grand Ole Opry in 1991. CMA Award: 1995 Entertainer of the Year.

1)Chattahoochee 2)Little Bitty 3)Don't Rock The Jukebox 4)Livin' On Love 5)Summertime Blues

10/21/89	45	12		1 Blue Blooded Woman ....Home		$5		Arista 9892
1/13/90	3	26		2 Here In The Real World Blue Blooded Woman		$3		Arista 9922
6/23/90	3	21		3 Wanted (album snippets)		$3	▌	Arista 2032
10/6/90	2²	20		4 Chasin' That Neon Rainbow Short Sweet Ride		$3		Arista 2095
1/19/91	❶²	20		5 I'd Love You All Over Again Home		$3		Arista 2166
5/18/91	❶³	20		6 Don't Rock The Jukebox Home		$3	▌	Arista 2220
8/31/91	❶¹	20		7 Someday From A Distance		$3		Arista 12335
12/14/91	41	6		8 I Only Want You For Christmas .... Merry Christmas To Me [X]		$3	▌	Arista 12372
1/11/92	❶¹	20		9 Dallas Just Playin' Possum		$3		Arista 12385
4/25/92	3	20		10 Midnight In Montgomery Working Class Hero		$3		Arista 12418
7/25/92	❶²	20		11 Love's Got A Hold On You That's All I Need To Know		$3		Arista 12447
10/24/92	❶¹	20		12 She's Got The Rhythm (And I Got The Blues) She Likes It Too		$3		Arista 12463
2/6/93	4	20		13 Tonight I Climbed The Wall Up To My Ears In Tears		$3		Arista 12514
5/15/93	❶⁴	20	●	14 Chattahoochee (club mix)	46	$3	▌	Arista 12573
				CMA Award: Single of the Year				
8/28/93	75	1		15 Tropical Depression				album cut
				from the album A Lot About Livin' on Arista 18711				
9/18/93	2¹	20		16 Mercury Blues Chattahoochee		$3		Arista 12607
				tune later used for a Ford truck commercial				
10/30/93	64	17		17 Tequila Sunrise				album cut
				#64 Pop hit for the Eagles in 1973; from the album Common Thread on Giant 24531				
12/18/93	53	4		18 Honky Tonk Christmas .... The Angels Cried [X]		$3		Arista 12611
1/29/94	4	20		19 (Who Says) You Can't Have It All If It Ain't One Thing (It's You)		$3		Arista 12649
6/18/94	❶³	20		20 Summertime Blues Hole In The Wall	104	$3	▌	Arista 12697
				#8 Pop hit for Eddie Cochran in 1958				
8/27/94+	❶¹	26		21 Gone Country All American Country Boy		$3		Arista 12778
9/3/94	❶³	20		22 Livin' On Love Let's Get Back To Me And You	101	$3	▌	Arista 12745
11/12/94	56	7		23 A Good Year For The Roses................I've Still Got Some Hurtin' Left To Do		$3	▌	MCA 54969
				GEORGE JONES with Alan Jackson				
12/31/94	59	1		24 Honky Tonk Christmas .... The Angels Cried [X-R]		$3		Arista 12611
2/11/95	6	20		25 Song For The Life You Can't Give Up On Love		$3		Arista 12792
5/13/95	❶¹	20		26 I Don't Even Know Your Name If I Had You		$3		Arista 12830

JACKSON, Alan — Cont'd

DEBUT	PEAK	WKS	A-side (Chart Hit) ... B-side	Pop	$	Pic	Label & Number
10/21/95	❶²	20	27 **Tall, Tall Trees** .... *Home*		$3		Arista 12879
12/23/95	48	4	28 **I Only Want You For Christmas** .... *Merry Christmas To Me* [X-R]		$3	■	Arista 12372
12/30/95+	❶¹	20	29 **I'll Try**		$3		album cut
			from the album *The Greatest Hits Collection* on Arista 18801				
4/20/96	3	20	30 **Home** .... *I'll Try*		$3		Arista 12942
			recorded in 1989				
6/8/96	42	12	31 **Redneck Games** .... S:2 *NASA & Alabama & Fishing Shows* [N]	66	$3	■	Warner 17648
			JEFF FOXWORTHY with Alan Jackson				
10/26/96	❶³	20	32 **Little Bitty** .... S:❶⁷ *Must've Had A Ball*	58	$3	■	Arista 13048
12/28/96	56	3	33 **Rudolph The Red-Nosed Reindeer** .... *We Three Kings (Star Of Wonder)* [X]		$3		Arista 13060
1/18/97	9	20	34 **Everything I Love** .... *It's Time You Learned About Good-Bye*		$3		Arista 13068
4/12/97	2²	20	35 **Who's Cheatin' Who** .... S:15 *Bucks To The Moon*		$3	■	Arista 13069
7/12/97	❶¹	20	36 **There Goes** .... *A House With No Curtains*		$3		Arista 13070
10/11/97+	2¹	20	37 **Between The Devil And Me** .... *Walk On The Rocks*		$3		Arista 13106
12/27/97	48	2	38 **I Only Want You For Christmas** .... *Merry Christmas To Me* [X-R]		$3	■	Arista 12372
12/27/97	51	3	39 **A Holly Jolly Christmas** .... *I Only Want You For Christmas* [X]		$3		Arista 10001
			introduced by **Burl Ives** in the 1964 animated TV special *Rudolph The Red-Nosed Reindeer*				

JACKSON, Carl ★'84★

Born on 9/18/53 in Louisville, Mississippi. Bluegrass singer/songwriter/banjo player.

DEBUT	PEAK	WKS	A-side (Chart Hit) ... B-side	Pop	$	Pic	Label & Number
11/3/84	44	15	1 **She's Gone, Gone, Gone** .... *You Made A Memory Of Me*		$3		Columbia 04647
3/2/85	70	7	2 **All That's Left For Me** .... *I'm Beside Myself*		$3		Columbia 04786
6/1/85	45	9	3 **Dixie Train** .... *I'm Beside Myself*		$3		Columbia 04926
1/25/86	85	7	4 **You Are The Rock (And I'm A Rolling Stone)** .... *Tennessee Girl*		$3		Columbia 05645

JACKSON, Lolita '89

DEBUT	PEAK	WKS	A-side (Chart Hit) ... B-side	Pop	$	Pic	Label & Number
3/18/89	89	2	**Every Time You Walk In The Room**		$5		Oak 1069

JACKSON, Nisha '87

Female singer.

DEBUT	PEAK	WKS	A-side (Chart Hit) ... B-side	Pop	$	Pic	Label & Number
10/24/87	81	3	**Alive And Well** .... *Going Down Slow*		$3		Capitol 44064

JACKSON, Stonewall ★87★ '59

Born on 11/6/32 in Emerson, North Carolina. Singer/songwriter/guitarist. Joined the *Grand Ole Opry* in 1956. Descended from General Thomas Jonathan "Stonewall" Jackson.

1)Waterloo 2)B.J. The D.J. 3)Life To Go 4)A Wound Time Can't Erase 5)Don't Be Angry

DEBUT	PEAK	WKS	A-side (Chart Hit) ... B-side	Pop	$	Pic	Label & Number
11/3/58+	2¹	23	1 **Life To Go** .... *Misery Known As Heartache*		$20		Columbia 41257
			written by **George Jones**				
6/8/59	❶⁵	19	2 **Waterloo/**	4			
6/29/59	24	5	3 **Smoke Along The Track**		$15		Columbia 41393
11/23/59	29	1	4 **Igmoo (The Pride Of South Central High)** .... *Uncle Sam And Big John Bull*	95	$15		Columbia 41488
1/18/60	12	12	5 **Mary Don't You Weep** .... *Run*	41	$15		Columbia 41533
4/4/60	6	17	6 **Why I'm Walkin'/**	83			
4/25/60	15	5	7 **Life Of A Poor Boy**		$15		Columbia 41591
11/7/60	13	15	8 **A Little Guy Called Joe** .... *I'm Gonna Find You*		$15		Columbia 41785
3/13/61	26	6	9 **Greener Pastures** .... *Wedding Bells For You And Him*		$15		Columbia 41932
8/7/61	27	2	10 **Hungry For Love** .... *For The Last Time*		$15		Columbia 42028
1/20/62	3	22	11 **A Wound Time Can't Erase/**				
2/3/62	18	3	12 **Second Choice**		$15		Columbia 42229
7/21/62	9	7	13 **Leona/**				
6/30/62	11	10	14 **One Look At Heaven**		$15		Columbia 42426
1/26/63	11	10	15 **Can't Hang Up The Phone** .... *Slowly*		$12		Columbia 42628
5/18/63	8	14	16 **Old Showboat** .... *A Toast To The Bride*		$12		Columbia 42765
11/9/63	15	8	17 **Wild Wild Wind** .... *The Water's So Cold*		$12		Columbia 42846
12/7/63+	❶¹	22	18 **B.J. The D.J.** .... *Big House On The Corner*		$12		Columbia 42889
4/25/64	24	13	19 **Not My Kind Of People** .... *Give It Back To The Indians*		$12		Columbia 43011
8/22/64	4	25	20 **Don't Be Angry** .... *It's Not Me*		$10		Columbia 43076
2/27/65	8	19	21 **I Washed My Hands In Muddy Water** .... *I've Got To Change*		$10		Columbia 43197
			#19 Pop hit for **Johnny Rivers** in 1966				
8/14/65	22	7	22 **Lost In The Shuffle/**				
7/17/65	30	9	23 **Trouble And Me**		$10		Columbia 43304
11/27/65+	24	12	24 **If This House Could Talk/**				
11/6/65	44	3	25 **Poor Red Georgia Dirt**		$10		Columbia 43411
4/30/66	24	8	26 **The Minute Men (Are Turning In Their Graves)** .... *I Wish I Had A Girl*		$10	■	Columbia 43552
8/6/66	12	15	27 **Blues Plus Booze (Means I Lose)** .... *Still Awake*		$10		Columbia 43718
2/4/67	5	17	28 **Stamp Out Loneliness** .... *Road To Recovery*		$10		Columbia 43966
6/10/67	15	15	29 **Promises And Hearts (Were Made To Break)** .... *While The Daisies Grow Free*		$10		Columbia 44121
10/7/67	27	12	30 **This World Holds Nothing (Since You're Gone)** .... *Almost Hear The Blues*		$10		Columbia 44283
2/17/68	39	10	31 **Nothing Takes The Place Of Loving You** .... *If Heartaches Were Wine*		$10		Columbia 44416
6/8/68	31	9	32 **I Believe In Love** .... *Drinking And Driving*		$10	■	Columbia 44501

JACKSON, Stonewall — Cont'd

DEBUT	PEAK	WKS	A-side / B-side	Pop	$	Label & Number
9/28/68	16	15	33 Angry Words .... *Red Roses Blooming Back Home*		$10	Columbia 44625
3/1/69	52	7	34 Somebody's Always Leaving .... *Recess Time*		$10	Columbia 44726
6/14/69	25	9	35 "Never More" Quote The Raven .... *How Many Lies Can I Tell*		$10	Columbia 44863
10/4/69	19	10	36 Ship In The Bottle .... *Thoughts Of A Lonely Man*		$10	Columbia 44976
3/7/70	72	2	37 Better Days For Mama .... *The Harm You've Done*		$10	Columbia 45075
7/4/70	72	2	38 Born That Way .... *Blue Field*		$8	Columbia 45151
10/10/70	63	4	39 Oh, Lonesome Me .... *When He Was Nine*		$8	Columbia 45217
5/22/71	7	13	40 Me And You And A Dog Named Boo *Here's To Hank*		$8	Columbia 45381
			#5 Pop hit for **Lobo** in 1971			
3/11/72	51	9	41 That's All This Old World Needs .... *Big Busy World*		$8	Columbia 45546
			STONEWALL JACKSON And The Brentwood Children's Choir			
7/29/72	71	5	42 Torn From The Pages Of Life .... *Waterloo*		$8	Columbia 45632
1/27/73	70	3	43 I'm Not Strong Enough (To Build Another Dream)........... *I've Run Out Of Reasons*		$8	Columbia 45738
7/28/73	41	9	44 Herman Schwartz .... *Lovin' The Fool Out Of Me*		$7	MGM 14569

JACKSON, Wanda ★177★   **'62**
Born on 10/20/37 in Maud, Oklahoma; raised in Bakersfield, California and Oklahoma City. Singer/songwriter/guitarist/pianist.

1)In The Middle Of A Heartache 2)You Can't Have My Love 3)Right Or Wrong
4)Tears Will Be The Chaser For Your Wine 5)Fancy Satin Pillows

DEBUT	PEAK	WKS	A-side / B-side	Pop	$	Pic	Label & Number
7/24/54	8	8	1 You Can't Have My Love S:8 / A:8 / J:10 *Lovin', Country Style*		$40		Decca 29140
			WANDA JACKSON and BILLY GRAY				
10/20/56	15	1	2 I Gotta Know .... A:15 *Half As Good A Girl*		$30		Capitol 3485
7/31/61	9	14	3 Right Or Wrong *Funnel Of Love*	29	$25		Capitol 4553
11/20/61+	6	15	4 In The Middle Of A Heartache *I'd Be Ashamed*	27	$25		Capitol 4635
6/9/62	28	1	5 If I Cried Every Time You Hurt Me........................... *Let My Love Walk In*	58	$25	■	Capitol 4723
1/25/64	46	1	6 Slippin'........................... *Just For You*		$15		Capitol 5072
3/28/64	36	11	7 The Violet And A Rose .... *To Tell You The Truth*		$15		Capitol 5142
2/26/66	18	11	8 The Box It Came In........................... *Look Out Heart*		$15		Capitol 5559
6/25/66	28	7	9 Because It's You .... *Long As I Have You*		$15		Capitol 5645
9/3/66	46	10	10 This Gun Don't Care........................... *I Wonder If She Knows*		$15		Capitol 5712
12/17/66+	11	18	11 Tears Will Be The Chaser For Your Wine .... *Reckless Love Affair*		$15		Capitol 5789
			WANDA JACKSON And The Party Timers:				
4/22/67	21	12	12 Both Sides Of The Line .... *Famous Last Words*		$15		Capitol 5863
8/19/67	51	7	13 My Heart Gets All The Breaks/				
8/19/67	64	2	14 You'll Always Have My Love		$15		Capitol 5960
11/25/67+	22	12	15 A Girl Don't Have To Drink To Have Fun ...... *My Days Are Darker Than Your Nights*		$15		Capitol 2021
1/27/68	46	6	16 By The Time You Get To Phoenix .... *Wishing Well*		$15		Capitol 2085
			answer to "By The Time I Get To Phoenix" by **Glen Campbell**				
5/4/68	34	10	17 My Baby Walked Right Out On Me........................... *No Place To Go But Home*		$15		Capitol 2151
9/7/68	46	6	18 Little Boy Soldier .... *I Talk A Pretty Story*		$12		Capitol 2245
11/16/68+	51	9	19 I Wish I Was Your Friend .... *Poor Ole Me*		$12		Capitol 2315
			WANDA JACKSON:				
2/8/69	41	10	20 If I Had A Hammer .... *The Pain Of It All*		$10		Capitol 2379
			#10 Pop hit for **Peter, Paul & Mary** in 1962				
7/12/69	48	7	21 Everything's Leaving .... *You Created Me*		$10		Capitol 2524
9/27/69	20	11	22 My Big Iron Skillet .... *The Hunter*		$10		Capitol 2614
1/3/70	35	10	23 Two Separate Bar Stools .... *Two Wrongs Don't Make A Right*		$10		Capitol 2693
4/4/70	17	11	24 A Woman Lives For Love........................... *What Have We Done*		$10		Capitol 2761
9/12/70	50	7	25 Who Shot John .... *Stop The World*		$10		Capitol 2872
12/12/70+	13	11	26 Fancy Satin Pillows .... *Why Don't We Love Like That Anymore*		$10		Capitol 2986
8/7/71	25	12	27 Back Then .... *I'm Gonna Walk Out Of Your Life*		$10		Capitol 3143
11/27/71+	35	11	28 I Already Know (What I'm Getting For My Birthday) ....*The Man You Could Have Been*		$10		Capitol 3218
4/8/72	57	7	29 I'll Be Whatever You Say .... *The More You See Me Less*		$10		Capitol 3293
1/26/74	98	4	30 Come On Home (To This Lonely Heart) .... *It's A Long, Long Time To Cry*		$7		Myrrh 125

JACOBS, Lori   **'80**
Singer/songwriter from Ann Arbor, Michigan.

| 3/15/80 | 94 | 2 | Tugboat Annie .... *Blue Eyes* | | $6 | | Neostat 102 |

JACQUES, Rick   **'78**
Born in Nashville. Singer/songwriter.

| 5/6/78 | 89 | 2 | Song Man .... *Time Is A Slow Moving Train* | | $6 | | Caprice 2046 |

JAMES, Atlanta — see VICKERY, Mack

JAMES, Brett   **'95**
Singer/songwriter from Oklahoma.

7/15/95	60	6	1 Female Bonding .... *Dark Side Of The Moon*		$3	▮	Career 12838
10/21/95	68	5	2 If I Could See Love .... *Many Tears Ago*		$3	▮	Career 12869
1/20/96	73	2	3 Worth The Fall .... *Wake Up And Smell The Whiskey*		$3	▮	Career 12935

JAMES, Dusty '79

Male singer.

| 7/14/79 | 76 | 4 | | You're All The Woman I'll Ever Need .... *Old Flame New Fire* | | $6 | | SCR 172 |

JAMES, George '79

Born in 1958 in Rockford, Illinois.

| 5/12/79 | 94 | 3 | | 1 It's Gonna Be Magic..*I'm Takin' A Heartbreak* | | $7 | | Janc 10417 |
| 10/20/79 | 95 | 2 | | 2 When Our Love Began (Cowboys And Indians) .... *Break My Mind* | | $7 | | Janc 103 |

JAMES, Jesseca '85

Born Kathy Twitty in 1960. Daughter of **Conway Twitty**.

10/2/76	87	4		1 Johnny One Time ....*Lying In My Arms*		$6		MCA 40613
4/30/77	93	3		2 My First Country Song ....*Let It Ring*		$6		MCA 40703
1/12/85	82	5		3 Green Eyes .... *That's What Your Lovin' Does To Me*		$5		Permian 82009
				KATHY TWITTY				

JAMES, Mary Kay '74

Born Mary Kay Mulkey in Atlanta. Singer/guitarist.

5/4/74	78	6		1 Please Help Me Say No...*Before The Curtain Falls*		$6		JMI 38
9/14/74	48	13		2 It Amazes Me (Sweet Lovin' Time) .... *Before I'm Fool Enough*		$6		JMI 46
1/25/75	57	8		3 The Crossroad...*Before The Curtain Falls*		$5		Avco 605
5/3/75	76	7		4 I Think I'll Say Goodbye ....*Which Way Do We Go*		$5		Avco 610

JAMES, Sonny ★19★ '70

Born James Hugh Loden on 5/1/29 in Hackleburg, Alabama. Singer/songwriter/guitarist. Sang with his four sisters as The Loden Family. Served in the U.S. Army from 1950-52. Acted in the movies *Second Fiddle To A Steel Guitar*, *Nashville Rebel*, *Las Vegas Hillbillies* and *Hillbillys In A Haunted House*. Known as "The Southern Gentleman."

1)Young Love 2)It's The Little Things 3)You're The Only World I Know 4)I'll Never Find Another You 5)Empty Arms

2/7/53	9	1		1 That's Me Without You	*A:9 Cool, Cold, And Colder*		$25		Capitol 2259
11/20/54	14	1		2 She Done Give Her Heart To Me .... *A:14 Oceans Of Tears (I've Shed For You)*		$25		Capitol 2906
3/24/56	7	11		3 For Rent (One Empty Heart)	*A:7 / J:8 / S:12 My Stolen Love*		$20		Capitol 3357
6/30/56	11	6		4 Twenty Feet Of Muddy Water.......................................*A:11 All Mixed Up*		$20		Capitol 3441
11/10/56	12	1		5 The Cat Came Back ....*A:12 Hello Old Broken Heart*		$20		Capitol 3542
12/22/56+	❶⁹	24	●	6 Young Love/	*A:❶⁹ / S:❶⁷ / J:❶³*	❶¹			
				#1 Pop hit for Tab Hunter in 1957					
1/26/57	6	12		7 You're The Reason I'm In Love	*A:6*		$20		Capitol 3602
4/13/57	9	9		8 First Date, First Kiss, First Love	*S:9 / A:9 Speak To Me*	25	$20		Capitol 3674
8/12/57	15	1		9 Lovesick Blues	*A:15 Dear Love*		$20		Capitol 3734
1/6/58	8	5		10 Uh-Huh--mm	*A:8 / S:14 Why Can't They Remember?*	92	$20		Capitol 3840
5/9/60	22	6		11 Jenny Lou ....*Passin' Through*	67	$25	■	NRC 050
7/20/63	9	15		12 The Minute You're Gone	*Gold And Silver*	95	$12	▢	Capitol 4969
12/21/63	17	9		13 Going Through The Motions (Of Living) .... *Bad Times A Comin'*		$12		Capitol 5057
3/28/64	6	17		14 Baltimore	*Least Of All You*	134	$12		Capitol 5129
8/8/64	19	13		15 Ask Marie/			$12		Capitol 5197
7/18/64	27	6		16 Sugar Lump ....*Tying The Pieces Together*		$12		
11/14/64+	❶⁴	25		17 You're The Only World I Know	*Tying The Pieces Together*	91	$12	■	Capitol 5280
4/3/65	2¹	20		18 I'll Keep Holding On (Just To Your Love)	*I'm Getting Gray From Being Blue*	116	$12	■	Capitol 5375
8/14/65	❶³	22		19 Behind The Tear	*Runnin'*	113	$12	■	Capitol 5454
12/11/65+	3	18		20 True Love's A Blessing	*Just Ask Your Heart*		$12	■	Capitol 5536
4/9/66	❶²	20		21 Take Good Care Of Her	*On The Fingers Of One Hand*		$12	■	Capitol 5612
				#7 Pop hit for Adam Wade in 1961					
8/13/66	2²	20		22 Room In Your Heart	*How Many Times Can A Man Be A Fool*		$12	■	Capitol 5690
2/25/67	❶²	18		23 Need You	*On And On*		$12	■	Capitol 5833
				#7 Pop hit for Jo Stafford & Gordon MacRae in 1949					
6/10/67	❶⁴	17		24 I'll Never Find Another You	*Goodbye, Maggie, Goodbye*	97	$12	■	Capitol 5914
				#4 Pop hit for The Seekers in 1965					
9/23/67	❶⁵	18		25 It's The Little Things	*Don't Cut Timber On A Windy Day*		$12	■	Capitol 5987
1/20/68	❶³	17		26 A World Of Our Own	*An Old Sweetheart Of Mine*	118	$12	■	Capitol 2067
				#19 Pop hit for The Seekers in 1965					
6/1/68	❶¹	17		27 Heaven Says Hello	*Fairy Tales*		$12	■	Capitol 2155
10/12/68	❶¹	16		28 Born To Be With You	*In Waikiki*	81	$10	■	Capitol 2271
				#5 Pop hit for The Chordettes in 1956					
1/18/69	❶³	16		29 Only The Lonely	*The Journey*	92	$10	■	Capitol 2370
				#2 Pop hit for Roy Orbison in 1960					
5/10/69	❶³	15		30 Running Bear	*A Midnight Mood*	94	$10	■	Capitol 2486
				#1 Pop hit for Johnny Preston in 1960					
9/6/69	❶³	15		31 Since I Met You, Baby	*Clinging To A Hope*	65	$10	■	Capitol 2595
				#12 Pop hit for Ivory Joe Hunter in 1956					
1/17/70	❶⁴	14		32 It's Just A Matter Of Time	*This World Of Ours*	87	$8	■	Capitol 2700
				#3 Pop hit for Brook Benton in 1959					
4/11/70	❶³	15		33 My Love	*Blue For You*	125	$8	■	Capitol 2782
				#1 Pop hit for Petula Clark in 1966					
7/4/70	❶⁴	15		34 Don't Keep Me Hangin' On	*Woodbine Valley*		$8	■	Capitol 2834

DEBUT	PEAK	WKS	Gold	A-side .... B-side	Pop	$	Pic	Label & Number
				JAMES, Sonny — Cont'd				
10/17/70	❶³	16		35 **Endlessly** — *Happy Memories*	108	$8	■	Capitol 2914
				#12 Pop hit for Brook Benton in 1959				
2/27/71	❶⁴	16		36 **Empty Arms** — *Everything Begins And Ends With You*	93	$8	■	Capitol 3015
				#13 Pop hit for Teresa Brewer in 1957				
6/19/71	❶¹	13		37 **Bright Lights, Big City** — *True Love Lasts Forever*	91	$8	■	Capitol 3114
				#58 Pop hit for Jimmy Reed in 1961				
10/2/71	❶¹	15		38 **Here Comes Honey Again** — *The Only Ones We Truly Hurt (Are The Ones We Truly Love)*		$8	■	Capitol 3174
1/15/72	2²	16		39 **Only Love Can Break A Heart** — *He Has Walked This Way Before*		$8	■	Capitol 3232
				#2 Pop hit for Gene Pitney in 1962				
5/13/72	❶¹	11		40 **That's Why I Love You Like I Do** — *Still Water Runs Deep*		$8		Capitol 3322
7/22/72	❶¹	15		41 **When The Snow Is On The Roses** — *Love Is A Rainbow*	103	$7	■	Columbia 45644
9/2/72	30	9		42 Traces .... *I'm In Love With You*		$7		Capitol 3398
				#2 Pop hit for the Classics IV in 1969				
10/21/72	5	14		43 **White Silver Sands** — *Why Is It I'm The Last To Know*		$7		Columbia 45706
				#7 Pop hit for Don Rondo in 1957				
12/2/72+	32	10		44 Downfall Of Me .... *I'll Follow You*		$7		Capitol 3475
2/10/73	4	14		45 **I Love You More And More Everyday** — *I'll Think About That Tomorrow*		$7	■	Columbia 45770
				#9 Pop hit for Al Martino in 1964				
4/14/73	61	4		46 Reach Out Your Hand And Touch Me .... *Just Keep Thinking Of Me*		$7		Capitol 3564
6/9/73	15	11		47 If She Just Helps Me Get Over You .... *I Won't Think About It Now*		$6		Columbia 45871
7/21/73	66	5		48 Heaven On Earth .... *She Believes In Me*		$6		Capitol 3653
12/15/73+	49	9		49 Surprise, Surprise .... *What Am I Living For*		$6		Capitol 3779
3/2/74	❶¹	15		50 **Is It Wrong (For Loving You)** — *Suddenly There's A Valley*		$6		Columbia 46003
7/27/74	4	17		51 **A Mi Esposa Con Amor (To My Wife With Love)** — *Just Don't Stop Lovin' Me*		$5	■	Columbia 10001
1/25/75	6	12		52 **A Little Bit South Of Saskatoon** — *Home Style Lovin'*		$5	■	Columbia 10072
4/26/75	5	15		53 **Little Band Of Gold** — *Pop And Me*		$5	■	Columbia 10121
				#21 Pop hit for James Gilreath in 1963				
8/9/75	10	15		54 **What In The World's Come Over You** — *Walking The Railroad Trestle*		$5	■	Columbia 10184
				#5 Pop hit for Jack Scott in 1960				
12/13/75+	67	8		55 Eres Tu (Touch The Wind) .... *Apache* [I]		$5		Columbia 10249
				#9 Pop hit for Mocedades in 1974				
1/31/76	14	13		56 The Prisoner's Song/				
				#1 Pop hit for Vernon Dalhart in 1925				
		12		57 Back In The Saddle Again		$5	■	Columbia 10276
				co-written and first recorded by Gene Autry in 1939				
5/15/76	6	15		58 **When Something Is Wrong With My Baby** — *Big Silver Bird*		$5		Columbia 10335
				#42 Pop hit for Sam & Dave in 1967				
8/28/76	8	14		59 **Come On In** — *Baby's Eyes*		$5		Columbia 10392
1/29/77	9	13		60 **You're Free To Go** — *Puttin' On The Dog Tonight*		$5		Columbia 10466
6/18/77	15	11		61 In The Jailhouse Now .... *Amazing Grace*		$5	■	Columbia 10551
				#14 Pop hit for Jimmie Rodgers in 1928				
10/22/77	24	13		62 Abilene .... *Pistol Packin' Mama*		$5		Columbia 10628
				SONNY JAMES with his Tennessee State Prison Band (above 2)				
				above 2 recorded "live" at the Tennessee State Prison				
3/18/78	16	12		63 This Is The Love .... *It'll Still Be Worth It All*		$5	■	Columbia 10703
7/22/78	18	12		64 Caribbean .... *Each Time I Look At You*		$5		Columbia 10764
12/2/78+	30	12		65 Building Memories .... *Little Band Of Gold*		$5		Columbia 10852
3/31/79	36	9		66 Hold What You've Got .... *Hanging On To Yesterday*		$5	■	Monument 280
				#5 Pop hit for Joe Tex in 1965				
7/21/79	62	6		67 Lorelei .... *If I Ever Wanted You*		$5		Monument 288
				SONNY JAMES and His Southern Gentlemen:				
12/26/81+	19	16		68 Innocent Lies .... *Don't Let The Stars Get In Your Eyes*		$5	■	Dimension 1026
5/15/82	60	7		69 A Place In The Sun .... *Lean On Me Girl*		$5	■	Dimension 1033
				SONNY JAMES and SILVER:				
10/9/82	66	7		70 I'm Looking Over The Rainbow .... *Something's Got A Hold On Me*		$5	■	Dimension 1036
12/25/82+	33	13		71 The Fool In Me .... *Little Rainbow*		$5		Dimension 1040
8/13/83	58	9		72 A Free Roamin' Mind .... *Don't Let The Stars Get In Your Eyes*		$5		Dimension 1045
				JAMES, Tommy **'80**				
				Born Thomas Jackson on 4/29/47 in Dayton, Ohio; raised in Niles, Michigan. Leader of The Shondells. Charted 32 pop hits from 1966-81.				
3/15/80	93	2		Three Times In Love .... *I Just Wanna Play The Music*	19	$4		Millennium 11785
				JAMESON, Cody **'77**				
				Female singer from New York City.				
4/16/77	64	7		Brooklyn .... *That Little Bit Of Us*	74	$5		Atco 7073
				JAN & MALCOLM **'77**				
				Male/female duo from Dallas.				
3/12/77	99	2		Rainbow In Your Eyes (Love's Got A Hold On Me) .... *You Are What I Am*		$7		Paula 421
				JANO **'79**				
				Male singer Jano Bourland.				
10/20/79	94	2		Sundown Sideshow		$6		SCR 180
				JANSKY, Clifton **'85**				
				Born in 1956 in Pleasanton, Texas.				
4/13/85	97	2		Will You Love Me In The Morning .... *Just Can't Help Believing*		$7		Axbar 6033

DEBUT	PEAK	WKS	Gold	A-side (Chart Hit)..B-side	Pop	$	PIC	Label & Number

JAYE, Jerry   '76

Born Gerald Jaye Hatley on 10/19/37 in Manila, Arkansas.

8/9/75	53	8		1 It's All In The Game................................Love Me 'Til The Morning Comes		$5		Columbia 10170
				#1 Pop hit for Tommy Edwards in 1958				
6/12/76	32	13		2 Honky Tonk Women Love Red Neck Men ....What's Left Never Will Be Right		$5		Hi 2310
11/20/76	78	9		3 Hot And Still Heatin' ....Crazy		$5		Hi 2318

JEAN — see NORMA JEAN

JED ZEPPELIN   '95

All-star group: Diamond Rio, Lee Roy Parnell and Steve Wariner. Group name is a pun on Led Zeppelin.

12/10/94+	48	15		Workin' Man Blues...........................Tonight The Bottle Let Me Down (Brooks & Dunn)		$3		Arista 12755 ·
				written by Merle Haggard				

JEFFERSON, Paul   '96

Born in Woodside, California. Singer/songwriter/guitarist.

5/18/96	50	10		1 Check Please......................................That's As Close As I'll Get To Loving You		$3	▌	Almo Sounds 89003
8/17/96	73	1		2 Fear Of A Broken Heart ....Missouri		$3	▌	Almo Sounds 89005
10/19/96	73	1		3 I Might Just Make It...Common Ground		$3		Almo Sounds 89006

JENKINS, Bob   '82

2/6/82	76	3		1 The Cube...Sometimes I Wish [N]		$4		Liberty 1448
				BOB JENKINS (& 3 Year Old Daughter Mandy)				
				song about Rubick's Cube				
2/19/83	86	3		2 Workin' In A Coalmine ....Muscle And Blood		$6		Picap 009

JENKINS, Bobby   '84

Born in 1942 in Corpus Christi, Texas.

6/16/84	69	5		1 Blackjack Whiskey		$5		Zone 7 40984
8/25/84	82	3		2 Louisiana Heatwave..		$5		Zone 7 61884
5/11/85	85	3		3 Me And Margarita		$5		Zone 7 30185

JENKINS, Larry   '82

Singer/songwriter from West Helena, Arkansas. Nephew of Conway Twitty.

10/30/82	76	6		1 I'm So Tired Of Going Home Drunk ....I Laughed 'Till I Cried		$4		Capitol 5167
7/28/84	87	3		2 You're The Best I Never Had ....When It Comes To Makin' Love		$4		MCA 52396

JENNINGS, Bob   '64

Born on 9/26/24 in Liberty, Tennessee. Died of a self-inflicted gunshot on 4/19/84 (age 59).

5/9/64	32	13		1 The First Step Down (Is The Longest) ....It Takes A Lot Of Money		$10		Sims 161
11/14/64	34	8		2 Leave A Little Play (In The Chain Of Love) ....I'm Barely Hangin' On To Me		$10		Sims 202

JENNINGS, Tommy   '80

Born on 8/8/38 in Littlefield, Texas. Brother of Waylon Jennings.

8/2/75	96	4		1 Make It Easy On Yourself...................................I Almost Did		$6		Paragon 102
4/15/78	71	7		2 Don't You Think It's Time ....That's The Way It Was		$5		Monument 248
5/31/80	51	10		3 Just Give Me What You Think Is Fair ....Things I Remember		$7		Sabre 4520
				REX GOSDIN with Tommy Jennings				

JENNINGS, Waylon   ★11★   '77

Born on 6/15/37 in Littlefield, Texas. Singer/songwriter/guitarist. Played bass for Buddy Holly on the ill-fated "Winter Dance Party" tour in 1959. Gave up his seat to the Big Bopper on the plane, which crashed on 2/3/59, killing Holly, Ritchie Valens and the Big Bopper. Established himself in the mid-1970s as a leader of the "outlaw" music movement. Married to Jessi Colter since 1969. Acted in the movies *Nashville Rebel* and *MacKintosh And T.J.* Narrator for TV's *The Dukes Of Hazzard.* CMA Awards: 1975 Male Vocalist of the Year; 1976 Vocal Duo of the Year (with Willie Nelson).

1)Luckenbach, Texas 2)Mammas Don't Let Your Babies Grow Up To Be Cowboys 3)Amanda 4)Good Hearted Woman 5)I've Always Been Crazy

8/21/65	49	2		1 That's The Chance I'll Have To Take................I Wonder Just Where I Went Wrong		$10		RCA Victor 8572
9/25/65	16	13		2 Stop The World (And Let Me Off) ....The Dark Side Of Fame		$8		RCA Victor 8652
1/15/66	17	15		3 Anita, You're Dreaming ....Look Into My Teardrops		$8		RCA Victor 8729
6/4/66	17	13		4 Time To Bum Again ....Norwegian Wood		$8		RCA Victor 8822
9/3/66	9	18		5 (That's What You Get) For Lovin' Me Time Will Tell The Story		$8		RCA Victor 8917
				#30 Pop hit for Peter, Paul & Mary in 1965				
12/17/66+	11	15		6 Green River..Silver Ribbons		$8		RCA Victor 9025
				from the movie *Nashville Rebel* starring Jennings				
4/1/67	12	16		7 Mental Revenge...Born To Love You		$8		RCA Victor 9146
8/19/67	8	17		8 The Chokin' Kind/		$8		
				#13 Pop hit for Joe Simon in 1969				
9/9/67	67	5		9 Love Of The Common People		$8		RCA Victor 9259
				WAYLON JENNINGS AND THE WAYLORS (above 2)				
				#45 Pop hit for Paul Young in 1984				
1/27/68	5	16		10 Walk On Out Of My Mind Julie		$8		RCA Victor 9414
3/30/68	4	15		11 I Got You No One's Gonna Miss Me		$8		RCA Victor 9480
				WAYLON JENNINGS & ANITA CARTER				
7/13/68	2⁵	18		12 Only Daddy That'll Walk The Line Right Before My Eyes		$8		RCA Victor 9561
11/16/68+	5	17		13 Yours Love Six Strings Away		$7		RCA Victor 9642
3/8/69	19	12		14 Something's Wrong In California ....Farewell Party		$7		RCA Victor 0105
5/24/69	20	12		15 The Days Of Sand And Shovels/		$7		RCA Victor 0157
				#34 Pop hit for Bobby Vinton in 1969				
5/31/69	37	6		16 Delia's Gone	124	$7		
				#66 Pop hit for Pat Boone in 1960				

JENNINGS, Waylon — Cont'd

DEBUT	PEAK	WKS		A-side / B-side	Pop	$	Pic	Label & Number
8/23/69	23	11	17	MacArthur Park .... But You Know I Love You **WAYLON JENNINGS AND THE KIMBERLYS** #2 Pop hit for Richard Harris in 1968	93	$7		RCA Victor 0210
11/29/69+	3	15	18	Brown Eyed Handsome Man *Sorrow (Breaks A Good Man Down)* written and first recorded by Chuck Berry in 1956		$7		RCA Victor 0281
4/18/70	12	14	19	Singer Of Sad Songs .... *Lila*		$7		RCA Victor 9819
8/29/70	5	15	20	The Taker *Shadow Of The Gallows*	94	$7		RCA Victor 9885
11/14/70	25	10	21	Suspicious Minds .... *I Ain't The One* **WAYLON JENNINGS AND JESSI COLTER** also see #40 below		$7		RCA Victor 9920
12/5/70+	16	12	22	(Don't Let The Sun Set On You) Tulsa .... *You'll Look For Me*		$7		RCA Victor 9925
4/3/71	14	14	23	Mississippi Woman *Life Goes On*		$7		RCA Victor 9967
6/19/71	39	8	24	Under Your Spell Again .... *Bridge Over Troubled Water* **WAYLON JENNINGS AND JESSI COLTER**		$7		RCA Victor 9992
8/7/71	12	15	25	Cedartown, Georgia .... *I Think It's Time She Learned*		$7		RCA Victor 1003
1/8/72	3	18	26	Good Hearted Woman *It's All Over Now* also see #39 below		$7		RCA Victor 0615
6/10/72	7	13	27	Sweet Dream Woman *Sure Didn't Take Him Long*		$6		RCA Victor 0716
10/21/72	6	15	28	Pretend I Never Happened *Nothin' Worth Takin' Or Leavin'*		$6		RCA Victor 0808
2/17/73	7	14	29	You Can Have Her *Gone To Denver* #12 Pop hit for Roy Hamilton in 1961	114	$6		RCA Victor 0886
5/26/73	28	10	30	We Had It All .... *Do No Good Woman*		$6		RCA Victor 0961
10/6/73	❶[8]	15	31	You Ask Me To *Willy The Wandering Gypsy And Me*		$6		RCA Victor 0086
4/27/74	❶[1]	13	32	This Time *Mona*		$6		RCA Victor 0251
8/10/74	❶[1]	13	33	I'm A Ramblin' Man *Got A Lot Going For Me*	75	$6		RCA Victor 10020
12/21/74+	2[1]	15	34	Rainy Day Woman/		$6		RCA Victor 10142
		12	35	Let's All Help The Cowboys (Sing The Blues)				
5/3/75	10	15	36	Dreaming My Dreams With You *Waymore's Blues (Pop #110)*		$6		RCA Victor 10270
9/6/75	❶[1]	16	37	Are You Sure Hank Done It This Way/	60			
		15	38	Bob Wills Is Still The King		$6		RCA Victor 10379
12/27/75+	❶[3]	17	39	Good Hearted Woman *Heaven Or Hell* [R] **WAYLON & WILLIE** new "live" duet version of #26 above; CMA Award: Single of the Year	25	$6		RCA Victor 10529
5/1/76	2[1]	14	40	Suspicious Minds *I Ain't The One* [R] **WAYLON & JESSI** #1 Pop hit for Elvis Presley in 1969; same version as #21 above		$6		RCA Victor 10653
7/31/76	4	14	41	Can't You See/	97			
		8	42	I'll Go Back To Her		$6		RCA Victor 10721
11/20/76+	7	14	43	Are You Ready For The Country/				
		13	44	So Good Woman		$5		RCA 10842
4/16/77	❶[6]	18	45	Luckenbach, Texas (Back To The Basics Of Love) *Belle Of The Ball* Willie Nelson (ending vocal)	25	$5		RCA 10924
10/8/77	❶[2]	16	46	The Wurlitzer Prize (I Don't Want To Get Over You)/				
		16	47	Lookin' For A Feeling		$5		RCA 11118
1/21/78	❶[4]	16	48	Mammas Don't Let Your Babies Grow Up To Be Cowboys/	42			
		15	49	I Can Get Off On You .... *(above 2)* **WAYLON & WILLIE**		$5		RCA 11198
5/20/78	2[2]	13	50	There Ain't No Good Chain Gang/				
11/17/79+	22	12	51	I Wish I Was Crazy Again .... *(above 2)* **JOHNNY CASH & WAYLON JENNINGS**		$5		Columbia 10742
7/29/78	❶[3]	13	52	I've Always Been Crazy *I Never Said It Would Be Easy*		$5		RCA 11344
				WAYLON:				
10/28/78	5	13	53	Don't You Think This Outlaw Bit's Done Got Out Of Hand/				
		11	54	Girl I Can Tell (You're Trying To Work It Out)		$4		RCA 11390
5/19/79	❶[3]	14	55	Amanda *Lonesome, On'ry And Mean*	54	$4	■	RCA 11596
9/22/79	❶[2]	13	56	Come With Me *Mes'kin*		$4		RCA 11723
1/5/80	❶[1]	15	57	I Ain't Living Long Like This *It's The World's Gone Crazy*		$4		RCA 11898
5/31/80	7	13	58	Clyde *I Came Here To Party*	103	$4		RCA 12007
8/23/80	❶[1]	17	59	● Theme From The Dukes Of Hazzard (Good Ol' Boys) *It's Alright* from the TV series starring John Schneider and Tom Wopat	21	$4	■	RCA 12067
2/21/81	17	12	60	Storms Never Last .... *I Ain't The One* **WAYLON & JESSI**		$4		RCA 12176
6/6/81	10	13	61	Wild Side Of Life/It Wasn't God Who Made Honky Tonk Angels *I'll Be Alright* **WAYLON & JESSI**		$4		RCA 12245
11/21/81+	5	19	62	Shine *White Water* from the movie The Pursuit Of D.B. Cooper starring Robert Duvall		$4		RCA 12367
3/13/82	❶[2]	18	63	Just To Satisfy You *Get Naked With Me* **WAYLON & WILLIE**	52	$4		RCA 13073
6/26/82	4	16	64	Women Do Know How To Carry On *Honky Tonk Blues*		$4		RCA 13257
10/23/82	13	15	65	(Sittin' On) The Dock Of The Bay .... *Luckenbach, Texas* **WAYLON & WILLIE** #1 Pop hit for Otis Redding in 1968		$4		RCA 13319
3/19/83	❶[1]	16	66	Lucille (You Won't Do Your Daddy's Will) *Medley Of Hits* #21 Pop hit for Little Richard in 1957		$4		RCA 13465
				WAYLON JENNINGS:				
7/2/83	10	18	67	Breakin' Down *Living Legends (A Dyin' Breed)*		$4		RCA 13543

JENNINGS, Waylon — Cont'd

DEBUT	PEAK	WKS	A-side / B-side	Pop	$	Pic	Label & Number
8/6/83	**20**	14	68 Hold On, I'm Comin'..*Waiting On Down The Line*		$4		RCA 13580
			WAYLON JENNINGS & JERRY REED #21 Pop hit for Sam & Dave in 1966				
10/8/83	**8**	19	69 Take It To The Limit *Till I Gain Control Again*	102	$4	■	Columbia 04131
			WILLIE NELSON & WAYLON JENNINGS #4 Pop hit for the Eagles in 1976				
10/22/83	**15**	16	70 The Conversation...*Fancy Free*		$4		RCA 13631
			WAYLON JENNINGS with Hank Williams, Jr.				
3/3/84	**4**	20	71 I May Be Used (But Baby I Ain't Used Up) *So You Want To Be A Cowboy Singer*		$4		RCA 13729
6/16/84	**6**	18	72 Never Could Toe The Mark *Talk Good Boogie*		$4		RCA 13827
9/29/84	**6**	21	73 America S:5 / A:6 *People Up In Texas*		$4		RCA 13908
1/19/85	**10**	19	74 Waltz Me To Heaven S:9 / A:9 *Dream On*		$4		RCA 13984
			written by Dolly Parton				
5/18/85	**❶**[1]	20	75 Highwayman S:❶[1] / A:❶[1] *The Human Condition*		$4	■	Columbia 04881
			WAYLON JENNINGS/WILLIE NELSON/JOHNNY CASH/KRIS KRISTOFFERSON				
6/22/85	**2**[2]	21	76 Drinkin' And Dreamin' S:❶[1] / A:2 *Prophets Show Up In Strange Places*		$4		RCA 14094
9/14/85	**15**	18	77 Desperados Waiting For A Train ..... S:15 / A:16 *The Twentieth Century Is Almost Over*		$4		Columbia 05594
			WAYLON JENNINGS/WILLIE NELSON/JOHNNY CASH/KRIS KRISTOFFERSON				
11/16/85+	**13**	18	78 The Devil's On The Loose S:11 / A:13 *Good Morning John*		$4		RCA 14215
2/15/86	**7**	19	79 Working Without A Net S:6 / A:8 *They Ain't Got 'Em All*		$4		MCA 52776
5/17/86	**5**	19	80 Will The Wolf Survive S:6 / A:6 *I've Got Me A Woman*		$4		MCA 52830
			#78 Pop hit for Los Lobos in 1985				
5/17/86	**35**	11	81 Even Cowgirls Get The Blues............................ A:34 *American By Birth*		$4		Columbia 05896
			JOHNNY CASH & WAYLON JENNINGS				
9/20/86	**8**	21	82 What You'll Do When I'm Gone S:8 / A:8 *That Dog Won't Hunt*		$3		MCA 52915
1/31/87	**❶**[1]	19	83 Rose In Paradise A:❶[1] / S:12 *Crying Don't Even Come Close*		$3		MCA 53009
5/16/87	**8**	19	84 Fallin' Out S:16 *Deep In The West*		$3		MCA 53088
9/12/87	**6**	22	85 My Rough And Rowdy Days S:14 *A Love Song (I Can't Sing Anymore)*		$3		MCA 53158
1/23/88	**16**	16	86 If Ole Hank Could Only See Us Now (Chapter Five...Nashville)........................... S:29 *You Went Out With Rock 'N' Roll*		$3		MCA 53243
9/24/88	**38**	9	87 How Much Is It Worth To Live In L.A.................................. *G.I. Joe*		$3		MCA 53314
1/7/89	**28**	16	88 Which Way Do I Go (Now That I'm Gone)................... *Hey Willie*		$3		MCA 53476
5/20/89	**61**	5	89 Trouble Man.................. *Yoyos, Bozos, Bimbos, And Heroes*		$3		MCA 53634
9/2/89	**59**	6	90 You Put The Soul In The Song .... *Woman I Hate It*		$3		MCA 53710
3/3/90	**25**	14	91 Silver Stallion............................... *American Remains*		$3		Columbia 73233
			WAYLON JENNINGS/WILLIE NELSON/JOHNNY CASH/KRIS KRISTOFFERSON				
5/26/90	**5**	21	92 Wrong *Waking Up With You*		$3	▌	Epic 73352
10/13/90	**67**	6	93 Where Corn Don't Grow .... *Waking Up With You*		$3	▌	Epic 73519
1/12/91	**66**	4	94 What Bothers Me Most *Wrong*		$3		Epic 73647
2/9/91	**22**	12	95 The Eagle *What Bothers Me Most*		$3		Epic 73718
6/15/91	**51**	10	96 If I Can Find A Clean Shirt................. *Put Me On A Train Back To Texas*		$3		Epic 73832
			WAYLON & WILLIE				

JEREMIAH '88

DEBUT	PEAK	WKS	A-side / B-side	Pop	$	Pic	Label & Number
10/8/88	96	1	To Be Loved		$7		Chariot 1921
			#22 Pop hit for Jackie Wilson in 1958				

JERRICO, Sherri '77

DEBUT	PEAK	WKS	A-side / B-side	Pop	$	Pic	Label & Number
10/8/77	95	2	Thanks For Leaving, Lucille........................... *All Over Me*		$6		Gusto 164
			answer to "Lucille" by Kenny Rogers				

JIM & JESSE '67

Duo of brothers from Coeburn, Virginia: Jim (b: 2/13/27, guitar) and Jesse (b: 7/9/29, mandolin) McReynolds. Joined the *Grand Ole Opry* in 1964.

1)Diesel On My Tail 2)The Golden Rocket 3)Better Times A-Coming

DEBUT	PEAK	WKS	A-side / B-side	Pop	$	Pic	Label & Number
7/18/64	43	2	1 Cotton Mill Man .... *(It's A Long, Long Way) To The Top Of The World*		$7		Epic 9676
12/19/64+	39	6	2 Better Times A-Coming .... *Wild Georgia Boys*		$7		Epic 9729
4/1/67	18	16	3 Diesel On My Tail *All For The Love Of A Girl*		$7		Epic 10138
			JIM & JESSE And The Virginia Boys (above 2)				
9/23/67	44	4	4 Ballad Of Thunder Road................. *Tijuana Taxi*		$7		Epic 10213
			#62 Pop hit for Robert Mitchum in 1958				
1/27/68	49	6	5 Greenwich Village Folk Song Salesman................... *Truck Drivin' Man*		$7		Epic 10263
9/7/68	56	6	6 Yonder Comes A Freight Train .... *Banderilla*		$7		Epic 10370
1/10/70	38	9	7 The Golden Rocket .... *A Freight Train In My Mind*		$7		Epic 10563
2/13/71	41	9	8 Freight Train .... *Just Wondering Why*		$6		Capitol 3026
			#6 Pop hit for Rusty Draper in 1957				
6/5/82	56	9	9 North Wind................. *Sweeter Than The Flowers*		$5		Soundwaves 4671
			JIM & JESSE and CHARLIE LOUVIN				
9/27/86	78	3	10 Oh Louisiana		$6		MSR 198310

JIMMY & JOHNNY '54

Duo of Jimmy Lee Fautheree (b: 1934 in El Dorado, Arkansas) and Country Johnny Mathis (b: 9/28/33 in Maud, Texas).

DEBUT	PEAK	WKS	A-side / B-side	Pop	$	Pic	Label & Number
9/25/54	3	18	If You Don't Somebody Else Will J:3 / A:5 / S:6 *I'm Beginning To Remember*		$30		Chess 4859

JJ WHITE '92

Duo of sisters Janice and Jayne White from California.

DEBUT	PEAK	WKS	A-side / B-side	Pop	$	Pic	Label & Number
7/20/91	69	4	1 The Crush................... *Everyday*		$3	▌	Curb 76852
1/4/92	73	1	2 Heart Break Train .... *Less Than Zero*		$3		Curb 76896
4/25/92	63	4	3 Jezebel Kane				album cut
9/12/92	64	3	4 One Like That				album cut
			above 2 from the album *Janice & Jayne* on Curb 77492				

DEBUT	PEAK	WKS	Gold	A-side (Chart Hit)..B-side	Pop	$	Pic	Label & Number

JOE BOB'S NASHVILLE SOUND COMPANY '75
Studio group led by Joe Bob Barnhill (b: 10/14/33 in Turkey, Texas). Father of **Joe Barnhill**.

| 5/17/75 | 84 | 6 | | In The Mood ....A String Of Pearls [I] | | $6 | | Capitol 4059 |

#1 Pop hit for Glenn Miller in 1940

JOHN DEER — see DEER, John

★245★ **JOHNNIE & JACK** '54
Duo of **Johnnie Wright** and **Jack Anglin**. Wright was born on 5/13/14 in Mount Juliet, Tennessee. Anglin was born on 5/13/16 in Franklin, Tennessee. Anglin died in a car crash on 3/7/63 (age 46) enroute to the memorial service for **Patsy Cline**. Duo were regulars on the *Louisiana Hayride* from 1948-52. Joined the *Grand Ole Opry* in 1952.
1)I Get So Lonely 2)Goodnight, Sweetheart, Goodnight 3)Poison Love

JOHNNIE and JACK and Their Tennessee Mountain Boys:

1/20/51	4	17		1 Poison Love	A:4 / S:5 / J:9 *Lonesome*		$25		RCA Victor 48-0377
8/4/51	5	11		2 Cryin' Heart Blues	J:5 / A:6 / S:10 *How Can I Believe You*		$25		RCA Victor 48-0478
5/10/52	7	5		3 Three Ways Of Knowing	J:7 *When You Want A Little Lovin'*		$25		RCA Victor 47-4555

JOHNNIE and JACK (The Tennessee Mountain Boys):

| 4/10/54 | ❶² | 18 | | 4 (Oh Baby Mine) I Get So Lonely | A:❶² / S:5 *You're Just What The Doctor Ordered* | | $20 | | RCA Victor 5681 |

#2 Pop hit for The Four Knights in 1954

7/17/54	3	17		5 Goodnight, Sweetheart, Goodnight/	A:3 / S:4 / J:4				
8/7/54	15	1		6 Honey, I Need You	A:15		$20		RCA Victor 5775
11/27/54+	7	4		7 Kiss-Crazy Baby/	J:7 / S:13				
11/13/54	9	10		8 Beware Of "It"	S:9 / J:9 / A:10		$20		RCA Victor 5880
5/21/55	14	3		9 No One Dear But You	A:14 *We Live In Two Different Worlds*		$20		RCA Victor 6094
12/17/55	15	1		10 S.O.S.	A:15 *Weary Moments*		$20		RCA Victor 6295
3/3/56	13	3		11 I Want To Be Loved	A:13 *Feet Of Clay*		$20		RCA Victor 6395

JOHNNIE & JACK with Ruby Wells

JOHNNIE AND JACK:

2/24/58	7	18		12 Stop The World (And Let Me Off)	S:7 / A:9 *Camel Walk Stroll*		$15		RCA Victor 7137
10/20/58	18	3		13 Lonely Island Pearl	*Leave Our Moon Alone*		$15		RCA Victor 7324
8/10/59	16	12		14 Sailor Man	*Wild And Wicked World*		$15		RCA Victor 7545
8/11/62	17	4		15 Slow Poison	*You'll Never Get A Better Chance Than This*		$12		Decca 31397

JOHNNY AND JACK

JOHNS, Sammy '81
Born on 2/7/46 in Charlotte, North Carolina. Singer/songwriter/guitarist.

11/30/74+	79	7		1 Early Morning Love	*Holy Mother, Aging Father*	68	$6		GRC 2021
9/19/81	50	7		2 Common Man	*Easy To Be With You*		$4		Elektra 47189
9/3/88	80	6		3 Chevy Van	*Love Me Off The Road*		$3		MCA 53398

new version of his #5 Pop hit from 1975

JOHNS, Sarah '75

| 8/30/75 | 75 | 3 | | 1 I'm Ready To Love You Now | *Love Me Back Together Again* | | $5 | | RCA Victor 10333 |
| 1/10/76 | 97 | 4 | | 2 Feelings | *I'm Making Love To A Memory* | | $5 | | RCA Victor 10465 |

#6 Pop hit for Morris Albert in 1975

| 3/27/76 | 86 | 3 | | 3 Let The Big Wheels Roll | *Glory, Tennessee* | | $5 | | RCA Victor 10590 |

JOHNS, Tricia '81
Born in Austin, Texas.

5/14/77	100	1		1 The Heat Is On	*You Lift Me Up*		$5		Warner 8357
12/27/80+	90	3		2 Did We Fall Out Of Love	*Night Romancing*		$4		Elektra 47057
8/8/81	57	8		3 Cathy's Clown	*Out Among The Stars*		$4		Elektra 47172

#1 Pop hit for The Everly Brothers in 1960

JOHNSON, Buddy '44
Born Woodrow Wilson Johnson on 1/10/15 in Darlington, South Carolina. Died of a brain tumor on 2/9/77 (age 62). Black orchestra leader/pianist. Charted 14 R&B hits from 1943-57.

| 3/11/44 | 2² | 7 | | When My Man Comes Home | *I'll Be With You* | 18 | $20 | | Decca 8655 |

BUDDY JOHNSON And His Orchestra
Ella Johnson (vocal)

★291★ **JOHNSON, Lois** '75
Born in Knoxville, Tennessee.
1)Loving You Will Never Grow Old 2)So Sad 3)Send Me Some Lovin' 4)Come On In And Let Me Love You
5)Your Pretty Roses Came Too Late

| 1/25/69 | 74 | 3 | | 1 Softly And Tenderly | *Goin' Down (For The Third Time)* | | $8 | | Columbia 44725 |
| 7/4/70 | 23 | 12 | | 2 Removing The Shadow | *Party People* | | $7 | | MGM 14136 |

HANK WILLIAMS, JR. and LOIS JOHNSON

| 10/3/70 | 12 | 13 | | 3 So Sad (To Watch Good Love Go Bad) | *Let's Talk It Over Again* | | $7 | | MGM 14164 |

HANK WILLIAMS, JR. & LOIS JOHNSON
#7 Pop hit for The Everly Brothers in 1960

12/5/70+	48	9		4 When He Touches Me (Nothing Else Matters)	*When A Woman Stands Alone*		$7		MGM 14186
2/27/71	65	2		5 From Warm To Cool To Cold	*You Didn't Stop To Say Hello*		$7		MGM 14217
4/1/72	14	14		6 Send Me Some Lovin'	*What We Used To Hang On To (Is Gone)*		$7		MGM 14356

HANK WILLIAMS, JR. & LOIS JOHNSON

| 7/15/72 | 63 | 8 | | 7 Rain-Rain | *My Heart Has A Mind Of Its Own* | | $7 | | MGM 14401 |
| 11/18/72+ | 22 | 11 | | 8 Whole Lotta Loving | *Why Should We Try Anymore* | | $7 | | MGM 14443 |

HANK WILLIAMS, JR. & LOIS JOHNSON
#6 Pop hit for Fats Domino in 1959

11/17/73	97	2		9 Love Will Stand	*Don't Be Cruel*		$7		MGM 14638
7/20/74	19	19		10 Come On In And Let Me Love You	*If I Throw Away My Pride*		$6		20th Century 2106
12/28/74+	6	15		11 Loving You Will Never Grow Old	*Lonesome Number One*		$6		20th Century 2151

JOHNSON, Lois — Cont'd

DEBUT	PEAK	WKS		A-side / B-side	Pop	$	Pic	Label & Number
5/17/75	48	8		12 You Know Just What I'd Do .... *You're The Rock Of Ages*		$6		20th Century 2187
9/13/75	95	4		13 Hope For The Flowers .... *Merrily We Love Along*		$6		20th Century 2223
10/11/75	70	8		14 The Door's Always Open .... *Bring It On Home*		$6		20th Century 2242
7/24/76	87	2		15 Weep No More My Baby .... *Birthday Wish*		$5		Polydor 14328
1/15/77	20	13		16 Your Pretty Roses Came Too Late .... *Birthday Wish*		$5		Polydor 14371
5/14/77	40	8		17 I Hate Goodbyes .... *I'm Your Friend*		$5		Polydor 14392
11/19/77	97	3		18 All The Love We Threw Away .... *We Can't Make It Anymore*		$5		Polydor 14435
				LOIS JOHNSON & BILL RICE				
5/20/78	63	7		19 When I Need You .... *A Dreamer Of Dreams*		$5		Polydor 14476
				#1 Pop hit for Leo Sayer in 1977				
6/2/84	89	3		20 It Won't Be Easy .... *You Are The Melody*		$5		EMH 0030

★308★ **JOHNSON, Michael** **'87**

Born on 8/8/44 in Alamosa, Colorado; raised in Denver. Singer/songwriter/guitarist. Best known for his 1978 pop hit "Bluer Than Blue."

1)Give Me Wings 2)The Moon Is Still Over Her Shoulder 3)Crying Shame

DEBUT	PEAK	WKS		A-side / B-side	Pop	$	Pic	Label & Number
11/16/85+	9	25		1 I Love You By Heart — A:9 / S:10 *Eyes Like Mine*		$3		RCA 14217
				SYLVIA & MICHAEL JOHNSON				
4/26/86	12	20		2 Gotta Learn To Love Without You .... S:8 / A:13 *River Colorado*		$3		RCA 14294
9/27/86+	❶[1]	23		3 Give Me Wings — S:❶[1] / A:2 *Magic Time*		$3	□	RCA 14412
1/31/87	❶[1]	26		4 The Moon Is Still Over Her Shoulder A:❶[1] / S:7 *That's What Your Love Does To Me*		$3		RCA 5091
6/13/87	26	13		5 Ponies .... *Cool Me In The River Of Love*		$3		RCA 5171
10/17/87+	4	20		6 Crying Shame — S:17 *True Love*		$3		RCA 5279
4/2/88	7	22		7 I Will Whisper Your Name — S:17 *Too Soon To Tell*		$3		RCA 6833
8/27/88	9	20		8 That's That — S:23 *Some People's Lives*		$3		RCA 8650
12/17/88+	52	8		9 Roller Coaster Run (Up Too Slow, Down Too Fast) .... *Diamond Dreams*		$3		RCA 8748

JOHNSON, Roland **'59**

DEBUT	PEAK	WKS		A-side / B-side	Pop	$	Pic	Label & Number
3/2/59	25	3		I Traded Her Love (For Deep Purple Wine) .... *I'll Be With You*		$20		Brunswick 55110

JOHNSON, Tim **'87**

Singer from Pennsylvania.

DEBUT	PEAK	WKS		A-side / B-side	Pop	$	Pic	Label & Number
9/19/87	78	3		Hard Headed Heart		$6		Sundial 135

JOHNSTON, Day **'88**

Female singer/songwriter from New Mexico.

DEBUT	PEAK	WKS		A-side / B-side	Pop	$	Pic	Label & Number
9/3/88	82	3		What Cha' Doin' To Me .... *Little Red Heart*		$6		Roadrunner 4639

JOHNSTONS, The **'87**

DEBUT	PEAK	WKS		A-side / B-side	Pop	$	Pic	Label & Number
2/28/87	82	5		Two-Name Girl .... *This Time*		$6		Hidden Valley 1286

JON AND LYNN **'82**

Husband-and-wife duo Jon and Lynn Hargis. Both were born in Cincinnati. Married in 1975.

DEBUT	PEAK	WKS		A-side / B-side	Pop	$	Pic	Label & Number
12/19/81+	59	7		1 Let The Good Times Roll .... *I Want To (Do Everything For You)*		$5		Soundwaves 4656
				#20 Pop hit for Shirley & Lee in 1956				
8/21/82	86	3		2 (What A Day For A) Day Dream .... *I Never Do Get Tired Of Telling You*		$5		Soundwaves 4677
				#2 Pop hit for The Lovin' Spoonful in 1966				

JONES, Ann **'49**

Born Ann Matthews in Hutchison, Kansas; raised in Enid, Oklahoma. Singer/songwriter.

DEBUT	PEAK	WKS		A-side / B-side	Pop	$	Pic	Label & Number
10/15/49	15	1		Give Me A Hundred Reasons .... J:15 *I Believe You, Baby*		$20		Capitol 15414

JONES, Anthony Armstrong **'70**

Born Ronnie Jones on 6/2/49 in Ada, Oklahoma. Singer/guitarist. Took stage name from the British photographer who married Princess Margaret.

1)Take A Letter Maria 2)Proud Mary 3)New Orleans

DEBUT	PEAK	WKS		A-side / B-side	Pop	$	Pic	Label & Number
6/28/69	22	13		1 Proud Mary .... *The Only Girl I Can't Forget*		$7		Chart 5017
				#2 Pop hit for Creedence Clearwater Revival in 1969				
10/18/69	28	8		2 New Orleans .... *And Say Goodbye*		$7		Chart 5033
				#6 Pop hit for U.S. Bonds in 1960				
1/10/70	8	11		3 Take A Letter Maria — *I Still Love You*		$7		Chart 5045
				#2 Pop hit for R.B. Greaves in 1969				
5/23/70	56	5		4 Lead Me Not Into Temptation .... *One For The Road*		$7		Chart 5064
7/25/70	38	11		5 Sugar In The Flowers .... *If You Gotta Go, Go Now*		$7		Chart 5083
11/21/70	40	9		6 Sweet Caroline .... *Too Much Of You*		$7		Chart 5100
				#4 Pop hit for Neil Diamond in 1969				
4/14/73	70	3		7 I'm Right Where I Belong .... *I Can Take On The World*		$6		Epic 10970
7/7/73	33	10		8 Bad, Bad Leroy Brown .... *There's Never Been Anyone Like You*		$6		Epic 11002
				#1 Pop hit for Jim Croce in 1973				
11/17/73	69	8		9 I've Got Mine .... *Quietly Doin' My Thing*		$6		Epic 11042
5/3/86	74	5		10 Those Eyes .... *One Night At A Time*		$5		AIR 103

JONES, David Lynn **'87**

Born on 1/15/50 in Bexar, Arkansas. Singer/songwriter/bassist.

DEBUT	PEAK	WKS		A-side / B-side	Pop	$	Pic	Label & Number
8/22/87	10	20		1 Bonnie Jean (Little Sister) — S:15 *Valley Of A Thousand Years*		$3	■	Mercury 888733
3/26/88	14	19		2 High Ridin' Heroes .... S:27 *Living In The Promiseland*		$3	■	Mercury 870128
				Waylon Jennings (guest vocal)				
7/30/88	36	10		3 The Rogue .... *Home Of My Heart*		$3		Mercury 870525
11/12/88	66	6		4 Tonight In America .... *Valley Of A Thousand Years*		$3		Mercury 872054

JONES, George ★2★   '61

Born on 9/12/31 in Saratoga, Texas. Singer/songwriter/guitarist. Started singing on radio stations KTXJ in Jasper, Texas, and KRIC in Beaumont, Texas. Served in the U.S. Marines from 1950-52. Recorded rockabilly as Thumper Jones and Hank Smith. Married to **Tammy Wynette** from 1969-75. Joined the *Grand Ole Opry* in 1969. Known as "No Show Jones" (due to several missed shows in the late 1970s) and "Possum." CMA Awards: 1980 & 1981 Male Vocalist of the Year. Elected to the Country Music Hall of Fame in 1992.

1)*Tender Years* 2)*She Thinks I Still Care* 3)*White Lightning* 4)*Walk Through This World With Me* 5)*We're Gonna Hold On*

DEBUT	PEAK	WKS		A-side / B-side	Pop	$	Pic	Label & Number
10/29/55	4	18	1	Why Baby Why — S:4 / A:4 / J:4 *Seasons Of My Heart*		$30		Starday 202
1/28/56	7	7	2	What Am I Worth — J:7 / A:10 / S:14 *Still Hurtin'*		$30		Starday 216
7/14/56	7	8	3	You Gotta Be My Baby — J:7 / A:10 *It's OK*		$30		Starday 247
10/20/56	3	11	4	Just One More/ — J:3		$30		Starday 264
		5	5	Gonna Come Get You ....J:flip		$30		
1/26/57	10	1	6	Yearning — J:10 *So Near*		$30		Starday 279
				GEORGE JONES and JEANETTE HICKS				
3/9/57	10	2	7	Don't Stop The Music/ — J:10 / A:15 / S:15		$20		Mercury 71029
		1	8	Uh, Uh, No ....J:flip		$20		
6/10/57	13	6	9	Too Much Water — S:13 *All I Want To Do*		$20		Mercury 71096
				co-written by **Sonny James**				
4/14/58	7	10	10	Color Of The Blues — A:7 / S:18 *Eskimo Pie*		$20		Mercury 71257
11/17/58	6	16	11	Treasure Of Love/		$20		
12/8/58	29	1	12	If I Don't Love You (Grits Ain't Groceries)		$20		Mercury 71373
3/9/59	❶⁵	22	13	White Lightning — *Long Time To Forget*	73	$20		Mercury 71406
				written by the Big Bopper (J.P. Richardson)				
7/20/59	7	13	14	Who Shot Sam — *Into My Arms Again*	93	$20		Mercury 71464
11/23/59+	15	12	15	Money To Burn/		$20		
11/23/59	19	12	16	Big Harlan Taylor		$20		Mercury 71514
4/4/60	16	12	17	Accidently On Purpose/		$20		
4/25/60	30	1	18	Sparkling Brown Eyes		$20		Mercury 71583
8/22/60	25	2	19	Out Of Control — *Just Little Boy Blue*		$20		Mercury 71641
11/7/60+	2¹	34	20	The Window Up Above — *Candy Hearts*		$15		Mercury 71700
5/29/61	16	2	21	Family Bible — *Taggin' Along*		$15		Mercury 71721
6/19/61	❶⁷	32	22	Tender Years — *Battle Of Love*	76	$15	■	Mercury 71804
9/18/61	15	3	23	Did I Ever Tell You .... *Not Even Friends*		$15		Mercury 71856
				GEORGE JONES & MARGIE SINGLETON				
2/24/62	5	12	24	Aching, Breaking Heart — *When My Heart Hurts No More*		$15	■	Mercury 71910
4/14/62	❶⁶	23	25	She Thinks I Still Care/		$15		
				#57 Pop hit for **Connie Francis** in 1962 as "He Thinks I Still Care"				
4/28/62	17	5	26	Sometimes You Just Can't Win		$15	■	United Artists 424
				also see #77 below				
6/16/62	11	10	27	Waltz Of The Angels — *Talk About Lovin'*		$15		Mercury 71955
				GEORGE JONES & MARGIE SINGLETON				
7/21/62	13	11	28	Open Pit Mine — *Geronimo*		$15		United Artists 462
8/25/62	28	1	29	You're Still On My Mind .... *Cold Cold Heart*		$15	■	Mercury 72010
10/6/62	3	18	30	A Girl I Used To Know/		$15		
10/13/62	13	9	31	Big Fool Of The Year		$15		United Artists 500
2/9/63	7	18	32	Not What I Had In Mind/		$15		
4/6/63	29	1	33	I Saw Me		$15		United Artists 528
				GEORGE JONES & The Jones Boys (above 4)				
5/4/63	3	28	34	We Must Have Been Out Of Our Minds — *Until Then*		$15		United Artists 575
				GEORGE JONES & MELBA MONTGOMERY				
7/13/63	5	22	35	You Comb Her Hair — *Ain't It Funny What Love Will Do* (Pop #124)		$12	■	United Artists 578
12/7/63	17	7	36	Let's Invite Them Over/		$12		
11/30/63	20	5	37	What's In Our Heart		$12		United Artists 635
				GEORGE JONES AND MELBA MONTGOMERY (above 2)				
2/1/64	5	18	38	Your Heart Turned Left (And I Was On The Right)/		$12		
2/8/64	15	9	39	My Tears Are Overdue		$12		United Artists 683
3/28/64	39	3	40	The Last Town I Painted — *Tarnished Angel*		$12	■	Mercury 72233
6/20/64	10	16	41	Where Does A Little Tear Come From/		$12		
6/6/64	31	7	42	Something I Dreamed		$12		United Artists 724
9/5/64	31	5	43	Please Be My Love .... *Will There Ever Be Another*		$12		United Artists 732
				GEORGE JONES AND MELBA MONTGOMERY				
9/26/64	3	28	44	The Race Is On — *She's Lonesome Again*	96	$12		United Artists 751
12/12/64+	25	15	45	Multiply The Heartaches — *Once More*		$12		United Artists 784
				GEORGE JONES AND MELBA MONTGOMERY				
1/30/65	15	15	46	Least Of All — *Brown To Blue*		$12		United Artists 804
3/13/65	9	21	47	Things Have Gone To Pieces — *Wearing My Heart Away*		$12	■	Musicor 1067
4/24/65	16	10	48	I've Got Five Dollars And It's Saturday Night .... *Wreck On The Highway*	99	$12		Musicor 1066
				GEORGE & GENE George Jones & Gene Pitney				
6/5/65	14	12	49	Wrong Number — *The Old, Old House*		$12		United Artists 858
7/3/65	25	7	50	Louisiana Man .... *I'm A Fool To Care* (Pop #115)		$12	■	Musicor 1097
				GEORGE & GENE George Jones & Gene Pitney				
8/28/65	6	18	51	Love Bug — *I Can't Get Used To Being Lonely*		$12		Musicor 1098
10/9/65	40	3	52	What's Money .... *I Get Lonely In A Hurry*		$12		United Artists 901

JONES, George — Cont'd

DEBUT	PEAK	WKS	Gold	A-side / B-side	Pop	$	Pic	Label & Number
11/6/65+	8	18		53 Take Me / *Ship Of Fools* — also see #80 below		$12		Musicor 1117
11/20/65	50	2		54 Big Job .... *Your Old Standby*		$12	■	Musicor 1115
				GEORGE & GENE George Jones & Gene Pitney				
3/12/66	6	17		55 I'm A People / *I Woke Up From Dreaming*		$12		Musicor 1143
3/12/66	46	3		56 World's Worse Loser .... *I Can't Change Over Night*		$12		United Artists 965
6/4/66	47	3		57 That's All It Took / *Y'All Come*		$12		Musicor 1165
				GEORGE & GENE George Jones & Gene Pitney				
6/25/66	30	7		58 Old Brush Arbors .... *Flowers For Mama*		$12		Musicor 1174
7/30/66	5	16		59 Four-O-Thirty Three / *Don't Think I Don't*		$12		Musicor 1181
11/19/66	70	3		60 Close Together (As You And Me) .... *Long As We're Dreaming*		$12		Musicor 1204
				GEORGE JONES & MELBA MONTGOMERY				
1/21/67	❶²	22		61 Walk Through This World With Me / *Developing My Pictures*		$12		Musicor 1226
5/20/67	5	17		62 I Can't Get There From Here / *Poor Man's Riches*		$12		Musicor 1243
9/9/67	24	10		63 Party Pickin' .... *Simply Divine*		$12		Musicor 1238
				GEORGE JONES & MELBA MONTGOMERY				
10/7/67	7	18		64 If My Heart Had Windows / *The Honky Tonk Downstairs*		$12		Musicor 1267
2/3/68	8	14		65 Say It's Not You / *The Poor Chinee*		$12		Musicor 1289
4/13/68	35	11		66 Small Time Laboring Man .... *Well It's Alright*		$12		Musicor 1297
7/6/68	3	13		67 As Long As I Live / *Your Angel Steps Out Of Heaven*		$12		Musicor 1298
9/28/68	12	12		68 Milwaukee, Here I Come .... *Great Big Spirit Of Love*		$12		Musicor 1325
				GEORGE JONES & BRENDA CARTER				
11/23/68+	2²	17		69 When The Grass Grows Over Me / *Heartaches And Hangovers*		$12	■	Musicor 1333
3/29/69	2²	18		70 I'll Share My World With You / *I'll See You While Ago*	124	$12		Musicor 1351
7/19/69	6	14		71 If Not For You / *When The Wife Runs Off*		$12		Musicor 1366
11/15/69+	6	14		72 She's Mine /		$12		
11/22/69	72	13		73 No Blues Is Good News		$12		Musicor 1381
3/14/70	28	10		74 Where Grass Won't Grow .... *Shoulder To Shoulder*		$12		Musicor 1392
7/4/70	13	14		75 Tell Me My Lying Eyes Are Wrong .... *You've Become My Everything*		$12		Musicor 1408
				GEORGE JONES And The Jones Boys				
11/21/70+	2¹	15		76 A Good Year For The Roses / *Let A Little Loving Come In* — also see #156 below	112	$12		Musicor 1425
3/20/71	10	13		77 Sometimes You Just Can't Win / *Brothers Of A Bottle* [R] — new version of #26 above		$12		Musicor 1432
6/12/71	7	14		78 Right Won't Touch A Hand / *Someone Sweet To Love*		$12		Musicor 1440
10/2/71	13	12		79 I'll Follow You (Up To Our Cloud) .... *Getting Over The Storm*		$12		Musicor 1446
12/25/71+	9	13		80 Take Me / *We Go Together* [R]		$10		Epic 10815
				TAMMY WYNETTE & GEORGE JONES — new version of #53 above				
2/12/72	6	14		81 We Can Make It / *One Of These Days*		$10		Epic 10831
2/12/72	30	8		82 A Day In The Life Of A Fool .... *The Old Old House*		$10		RCA Victor 0625
5/20/72	2¹	14		83 Loving You Could Never Be Better / *Try It, You'll Like It*		$10		Epic 10858
7/8/72	6	15		84 The Ceremony / *The Great Divide*		$10		Epic 10881
				TAMMY WYNETTE & GEORGE JONES				
10/14/72	46	7		85 Wrapped Around Her Finger .... *With Half A Heart*		$10		RCA Victor 0792
10/28/72	5	16		86 A Picture Of Me (Without You) / *The Man Worth Lovin' You*		$10		Epic 10917
11/25/72+	38	9		87 Old Fashioned Singing .... *We Love To Sing About Jesus*		$10		Epic 10923
				GEORGE JONES & TAMMY WYNETTE				
3/3/73	6	14		88 What My Woman Can't Do / *My Loving Wife*		$10		Epic 10959
4/7/73	32	9		89 Let's Build A World Together .... *Touching Shoulders*		$10		Epic 10963
				GEORGE JONES AND TAMMY WYNETTE				
6/23/73	7	13		90 Nothing Ever Hurt Me (Half As Bad As Losing You) / *Wine*		$8		Epic 11006
9/1/73	❶²	17		91 We're Gonna Hold On / *My Elusive Dreams*		$8		Epic 11031
				GEORGE JONES & TAMMY WYNETTE				
11/24/73+	3	16		92 Once You've Had The Best / *Mary Don't Go 'Round*		$8		Epic 11053
2/9/74	15	13		93 (We're Not) The Jet Set .... *Crawdad Song*		$8		Epic 11083
				GEORGE JONES and TAMMY WYNETTE				
4/6/74	25	12		94 The Telephone Call .... *No Charge*		$8		Epic 11099
				TINA & DADDY (Jones & his stepdaughter)				
6/8/74	❶¹	17		95 The Grand Tour / *Our Private Life*		$8		Epic 11122
7/27/74	8	12		96 We Loved It Away / *Ain't Love Been Good*		$8		Epic 11151
				GEORGE JONES & TAMMY WYNETTE				
10/26/74+	❶¹	13		97 The Door / *Wean Me*		$7		Epic 50038
3/22/75	10	14		98 These Days (I Barely Get By) / *Baby, There's Nothing Like You*		$7		Epic 50088
5/17/75	25	13		99 God's Gonna Get'cha (For That) .... *Those Were The Good Times*		$7		Epic 50099
				GEORGE JONES AND TAMMY WYNETTE				
7/26/75	21	11		100 Memories Of Us /		$7		
11/1/75	92	4		101 I Just Don't Give A Damn		$7		Epic 50127
2/7/76	16	12		102 The Battle .... *I'll Come Back*		$7		Epic 50187
5/22/76	37	9		103 You Always Look Your Best (Here In My Arms) ...... *Have You Seen My Chicken*		$7		Epic 50227
6/5/76	❶¹	15		104 Golden Ring / *We're Putting It Back Together*		$7		Epic 50235
				GEORGE JONES and TAMMY WYNETTE				
9/4/76	3	16		105 Her Name Is... / *Diary Of My Mind*		$7		Epic 50271
12/11/76+	❶²	16		106 Near You / *Tattletale Eyes*		$7		Epic 50314
				GEORGE JONES and TAMMY WYNETTE — #1 Pop hit for Francis Craig in 1947				
5/21/77	34	8		107 Old King Kong .... *It's A 10-33 (Let's Get Jesus On The Line)*		$7		Epic 50385

DEBUT	PEAK	WKS	Gold	A-side (Chart Hit) ....B-side	Pop	$	Pic	Label & Number
				JONES, George — Cont'd				
7/1/95	69	4		157 One .... *Golden Ring*		$3		MCA 55048
				GEORGE JONES AND TAMMY WYNETTE				
9/14/96	66	6		158 Honky Tonk Song .... *The Lone Ranger*		$3		MCA 55228
9/20/97	14	20		159 You Don't Seem To Miss Me ....S:9 *Where Are You Boy*	109	$3	▮	Epic 78704
				PATTY LOVELESS With George Jones				

JONES, Grandpa   '63

Born Louis Marshall Jones on 10/20/13 in Niagra, Kentucky; raised in Akron, Ohio. Died of a stroke on 2/19/98 (age 84). Singer/banjo player. Began appearing as "Grandpa" in 1935. Joined the *Grand Ole Opry* in 1947. Regular on TV's *Hee-Haw*. Elected to the Country Music Hall of Fame in 1978.

DEBUT	PEAK	WKS	Gold	A-side	Pop	$	Pic	Label & Number
2/23/59	21	2		1 The All-American Boy .... *Pickin' Time*		$20		Decca 30823
				#2 Pop hit for **Bobby Bare** (Bill Parsons) in 1959				
12/15/62+	5	16		2 T For Texas .... *Tritzem Yodel*		$15		Monument 801
				#2 Pop hit for **Jimmie Rodgers** in 1928				

JONES, Harrison   '74

Born on 2/13/47 in Corbin, Kentucky.

| 6/22/74 | 72 | 7 | | But Tonight I'm Gonna Love You ....*It's That Time Again* | | $6 | | GRT 004 |

JONES, Mickey   '89

Born in Denham Springs, Louisiana. Member of **Kenny Rogers & The First Edition**.

3/3/79	94	5		1 She Loves My Troubles Away .... *Forever*		$6		Bayshore 100
9/2/89	85	3		2 A Song A Day Keeps The Blues Away ....*Here's A Rose*		$6		Stop Hunger 1102
11/25/89	80	3		3 Bigger Man Than Me!..............*Play Another Good Old Country Song!*		$6		Stop Hunger 1103

| ★272★ | | | | **JONES, Tom**   '77 | | | | |

Born Thomas Jones Woodward on 6/7/40 in Pontypridd, South Wales. Charted 30 pop hits from 1965-89. Won the 1965 Best New Artist Grammy Award. Hosted own TV variety series from 1969-71.

   1)Say You'll Stay Until Tomorrow 2)Touch Me 3)I've Been Rained On Too

12/25/76+	❶¹	17		1 Say You'll Stay Until Tomorrow	15	$5		Epic/MAM 50308
6/4/77	87	3		2 Take Me Tonight ....*I Hope You'll Understand*	101	$5		Epic/MAM 50382
				adapted from Tchaikovsky's *Pathetique Symphony*				
11/19/77	71	8		3 What A Night .... *That's Where I Belong*		$5		Epic/MAM 50468
4/18/81	19	14		4 Darlin' .... *I Don't Want To Know You That Well*	103	$4		Mercury 76100
				#103 Pop hit for **Frankie Miller** in 1979				
8/8/81	25	11		5 What In The World's Come Over You .... *The Things That Matter Most To Me*	109	$4		Mercury 76115
				#5 Pop hit for **Jack Scott** in 1960				
11/28/81+	26	14		6 Lady Lay Down ....*A Daughter's Question*		$4		Mercury 76125
9/18/82	16	18		7 A Woman's Touch...............................*I'll Never Get Over You*		$4		Mercury 76172
2/26/83	4	18		8 Touch Me (I'll Be Your Fool Once More) *We're Wasting Our Time*		$4		Mercury 810445
7/2/83	34	12		9 It'll Be Me ....*If I Ever Had To Say Goodbye To You*		$3		Mercury 812631
12/10/83+	13	22		10 I've Been Rained On Too ....*That Old Piano*		$3		Mercury 814820
4/28/84	30	14		11 This Time .... *Memphis, Tennessee*		$3		Mercury 818801
9/1/84	53	9		12 All The Love Is On The Radio ....*You Are No Angel*		$3		Mercury 880173
12/8/84+	67	9		13 I'm An Old Rock And Roller (Dancin' To A Different Beat)...........*My Kind Of Girl*		$3		Mercury 880402
3/2/85	48	9		14 Give Her All The Roses (Don't Wait Until Tomorrow) ....*Picture Of You*		$3		Mercury 880569
9/14/85	76	6		15 Not Another Heart Song ....*Only My Heart Knows*		$3		Mercury 884039
11/23/85+	36	13		16 It's Four In The Morning ....*I'll Never Get Over You*		$3		Mercury 884252

JORDAN, Jill   '88

Born Jill Galehouse in Wooster, Ohio. Grandfather was pro baseball pitcher Denny Galehouse.

| 2/20/88 | 68 | 5 | | 1 Calendar Blues .... | | $6 | | Maxx 822 |
| 6/11/88 | 72 | 4 | | 2 I Did It For Love... | | $6 | | Maxx 823 |

JORDAN, Louis   '44

Born on 7/8/08 in Brinkley, Arkansas. Died of a heart attack on 2/4/75 (age 66). Black singer/saxophonist. Charted 57 R&B hits from 1942-51. Inducted into the Rock and Roll Hall of Fame in 1987.

     LOUIS JORDAN And His Tympany Five:

1/15/44	❶³	13		1 Ration Blues/	16			
1/29/44	7	1		2 Deacon Jones		$20		Decca 8654
7/1/44	❶⁵	9		3 Is You Is Or Is You Ain't (Ma' Baby) *G.I. Jive (Pop #1)*	2³	$20		Decca 8659
				from the movie *Follow The Boys* starring Marlene Dietrich; #81 Pop hit for Buster Brown in 1960				

JOY, Homer   '74

Singer/songwriter from Arkansas.

| 3/23/74 | 80 | 5 | | John Law ....*Ain't No Sunshine All The Time* | | $5 | | Capitol 3834 |

JOYCE, Brenda   '79

Born in 1955 in Indianapolis.

| 9/15/79 | 96 | 1 | | Don't Touch Me ....*I've Been Burned* | | $7 | | Western Pacific 107 |

JUAN, Don — see DON JUAN

JUDD, Wynonna — see WYNONNA

JUDDS, The ★96★   '85

Family duo from Ashland, Kentucky: Naomi (born Diana Ellen Judd on 1/11/46) and daughter **Wynonna** (born Christina Ciminella on 5/30/64) Judd. Moved to Hollywood in 1968. Moved to Nashville in 1979. Naomi's chronic hepatitis forced duo to split at the end of 1991. Naomi's daughter and Wynonna's sister is actress Ashley Judd. CMA Awards: 1984 Horizon Award; 1985, 1986 & 1987 Vocal Group of the Year; 1988, 1989, 1990 & 1991 Vocal Duo of the Year.

1)Have Mercy 2)Why Not Me 3)Cry Myself To Sleep 4)Change Of Heart 5)Grandpa

THE JUDDS (Wynonna & Naomi):

DEBUT	PEAK	WKS		A-side / B-side	Pop	$	Pic	Label & Number
12/17/83+	17	18	1	Had A Dream (For The Heart) ....*Don't You Hear Jerusalem Moan*		$4		RCA/Curb 13673
4/28/84	**❶**¹	23	2	Mama He's Crazy *Down Home*		$3	■	RCA/Curb 13772
10/6/84	**❶**²	22	3	Why Not Me A:**❶**² / S:2 *Lazy Country Evening*		$3		RCA/Curb 13923
				CMA Award: Single of the Year				
2/2/85	**❶**¹	22	4	Girls Night Out S:**❶**¹ / A:**❶**¹ *Sleeping Heart*		$3		RCA/Curb 13991
6/8/85	**❶**¹	21	5	Love Is Alive S:**❶**¹ / A:**❶**¹ *Mr. Pain*		$3		RCA/Curb 14093
10/5/85	**❶**²	22	6	Have Mercy A:**❶**² / S:2 *Bye Bye Baby Blues*		$3		RCA/Curb 14193
2/15/86	**❶**¹	20	7	Grandpa (Tell Me 'Bout The Good Old Days) S:**❶**¹ / A:**❶**¹ *Drops Of Water*		$3		RCA/Curb 14290
5/24/86	**❶**¹	18	8	Rockin' With The Rhythm Of The Rain S:**❶**¹ / A:**❶**¹ *River Roll On*		$3		RCA/Curb 14362
10/18/86+	**❶**¹	20	9	Cry Myself To Sleep A:**❶**¹ / S:2 *Dream Chaser*		$3		RCA/Curb 5000
2/14/87	10	13	10	Don't Be Cruel S:6 / A:10 *The Sweetest Gift*		$3	■	RCA/Curb 5094
5/9/87	**❶**¹	19	11	I Know Where I'm Going S:**❶**² *If I Were You*		$3		RCA/Curb 5164
8/22/87	**❶**¹	22	12	Maybe Your Baby's Got The Blues S:3 *My Baby's Gone*		$3		RCA/Curb 5255
1/16/88	**❶**¹	17	13	Turn It Loose S:3 *Cow Cow Boogie*		$3		RCA/Curb 5329
6/11/88	2²	17	14	Give A Little Love S:4 *Why Don't You Believe Me*		$3		RCA/Curb 8300
				THE JUDDS:				
10/22/88+	**❶**¹	20	15	Change Of Heart S:2 *I Wish She Wouldn't Treat You That Way*		$3		RCA/Curb 8715
2/25/89	**❶**¹	21	16	Young Love *Cow Cow Boogie*		$3		Curb/RCA 8820
7/8/89	**❶**¹	21	17	Let Me Tell You About Love *Water Of Love*		$3		Curb/RCA 8947
11/25/89+	8	26	18	One Man Woman *Sleepless Nights*		$3		Curb/RCA 9077
3/31/90	16	21	19	Guardian Angels ....*Cadillac Red*		$3		Curb/RCA 2524
8/11/90	5	21	20	Born To Be Blue *Rompin' Stompin' Blues*		$3	▮	Curb/RCA 2597
12/8/90+	5	20	21	Love Can Build A Bridge *This Country's Rockin'*		$3		Curb/RCA 2708
4/13/91	6	20	22	One Hundred And Two *Are The Roses Not Blooming*		$3		Curb/RCA 2782
9/14/91	29	16	23	John Deere Tractor ....*Calling In The Wind*		$3		Curb/RCA 62038
12/27/97	68	1	24	Silver Bells ....[X]				album cut

#78 Pop hit for **Bing Crosby** & Carol Richards in 1957; from the album *Christmas Time With The Judds* on Curb/RCA 6422

JURGENS, Dick   '47
Born on 1/9/10 in Sacramento, California. Died of cancer on 10/5/95 (age 85). Orchestra leader/songwriter.

DEBUT	PEAK	WKS		A-side / B-side	Pop	$	Pic	Label & Number
3/8/47	4	2		(Oh Why, Oh Why, Did I Ever Leave) Wyoming *Bless You*	14	$12		Columbia 37210

DICK JURGENS and his Orchestra
Jimmy Castle, Al Galante and Band (vocals)

JUSTIS, Bill   '58
Born on 10/14/26 in Birmingham, Alabama. Died on 7/15/82 (age 55). Session saxophonist/arranger/producer.

DEBUT	PEAK	WKS	Gold	A-side / B-side	Pop	$	Pic	Label & Number
11/25/57+	6	16	●	Raunchy S:6 / A:14 *The Midnite Man* [I]	2¹	$30		Phillips 3519

BILL JUSTIS and his Orchestra
Sid Manker (guitar); Bill Justis (sax)

K

KALIN TWINS   '58
Duo of twins Herbert and Harold Kalin. Born on 2/16/34 in Port Jervis, New York.

DEBUT	PEAK	WKS	Gold	A-side / B-side	Pop	$	Pic	Label & Number
8/4/58	13	7	●	When..S:13 *Three O'Clock Thrill*	5	$25		Decca 30642

KANDY, Jim   '65

DEBUT	PEAK	WKS		A-side / B-side	Pop	$	Pic	Label & Number
9/4/65	29	6		I'm The Man..*Angelville - Sky*		$15		K-Ark 647

KANE, Kieran   '81
Born on 10/7/49 in Queens, New York. Singer/songwriter. Member of **The O'Kanes**.

DEBUT	PEAK	WKS		A-side / B-side	Pop	$	Pic	Label & Number
3/21/81	80	4	1	The Baby ....*I Don't Drink From The River*		$4		Elektra 47111
6/20/81	14	16	2	You're The Best *Finishing Touches*		$4		Elektra 47148
11/7/81+	16	18	3	It's Who You Love ....*Doctor's Orders*		$4		Elektra 47228
3/6/82	26	14	4	I Feel It With You..............................*She's Looking For Something New*		$4		Elektra 47415
7/10/82	26	12	5	I'll Be Your Man Around The House ....*Blue All Over You*		$4		Elektra 47478
10/30/82	45	8	6	Gonna Have A Party ....*As Long As I'm Rockin' With You*		$4		Elektra 69943
4/30/83	30	12	7	It's You..*Makin' It Up*		$3		Warner 29711
3/17/84	28	14	8	Dedicate ....*Surrender To Your Heart*		$3		Warner 29336

KANTER, Hillary '85
Born in Cincinnati. Singer/songwriter/pianist.

DEBUT	PEAK	WKS		A-side / B-side	Pop	$	Pic	Label & Number
8/18/84	51	9	1	Good Night For Falling In Love .... *I Couldn't Help Myself*		$3		RCA 13835
12/1/84+	54	18	2	Hey .... *My Heart's Saying Yes*		$3		RCA 13935
5/4/85	50	9	3	We Work .... *Harbor Of Your Heart*		$3		RCA 14053

KAY, Melissa '88
Singer from Winter Garden, Florida.

2/6/88	75	3	1	Don't Forget Your Way Home		$6		Reed 1115
8/6/88	79	3	2	After Lovin' You		$6		Reed 1119
5/6/89	87	3	3	Poison Sugar		$6		Reed 1123

KAYE, Angela '81
Born in 1966.

10/10/81	81	5		Catching Fire		$6		Yatahey 804

KAYE, Barry '78
Born on 4/24/46 in Los Angeles.

3/11/78	89	5		Easy .... *Life*		$5		MCA 40868
				#4 Pop hit for the Commodores in 1977				

KAYE, Debbie Lori '68
Born on 5/6/50 in New York.

6/22/68	68	3		Come On Home .... *Help Me Love You*		$7		Columbia 44538

KAYE, Lois '79
Born Lois Kaye Edmiston on 12/8/50 in Knox, Indiana; raised in Beecher, Indiana.

11/3/79	96	2		Drown In The Flood .... *Why'd You Have To Be So Good*		$6		Ovation 1130

KAYE, Sandra '78
Born Sandra Kaye Van Auken in Longview, Washington.

7/29/78	52	7	1	This Magic Moment *Baby Doesn't Live Here Anymore*		$5		Door Knob 068
				#6 Pop hit for Jay & The Americans in 1969				
10/21/78	80	5	2	One More Time .... *My Dolly And I*		$5		Door Knob 075
12/23/78+	84	5	3	I'll Still Love You In My Dreams .... *Kiss And Run*		$5		Door Knob 088
3/3/79	83	5	4	I've Seen It All .... *I'll Still Love You In My Dreams*		$5		Door Knob 093
8/18/79	95	4	5	You Broke My Heart So Gently (It Almost Didn't Break).......... *Where Would I Be*		$5		Door Knob 097

KEARNEY, Ramsey '85
Born William Ramsey Kearney on 10/30/33 in Bolivar, Tennessee.

8/24/85	96	1	1	King Of Oak Street .... *Je T'aime Beaucoup (I Love You Very Much)*		$8		Safari 114
9/10/88	97	1	2	One Time Thing		$8		Safari 117

★207★ KEITH, Toby '93
Born Toby Keith Covel on 7/8/61 in Clinton, Oklahoma. Singer/songwriter/guitarist.
1)Should've Been A Cowboy 2)Who's That Man 3)Me Too

3/6/93	❶²	20	1	Should've Been A Cowboy *(3 album snippets)*	93	$3	▌	Mercury 864990
7/3/93	5	20	2	He Ain't Worth Missing *A Little Less Talk And A Lot More Action*	107	$3	▌	Mercury 862262
11/13/93+	2¹	20	3	A Little Less Talk And A Lot More Action *Mama Come Quick*		$3	▌	Mercury 862844
3/19/94	2¹	20	4	Wish I Didn't Know Now *Under The Fall*		$3		Mercury 858290
7/30/94	❶¹	20	5	Who's That Man *(album snippets)*	102	$3	▌	Polydor 853358
12/3/94+	10	20	6	Upstairs Downtown *Woman Behind The Man*		$3	▌	Polydor 851136
3/25/95	2³	20	7	You Ain't Much Fun S:9 *Life Was A Play (The World A Stage)*		$3	▌	Polydor 851728
7/15/95	15	20	8	Big Ol' Truck .... *In Other Words*		$3		Polydor 579574
12/16/95	50	5	9	Santa I'm Right Here .... *Blame It On The Mistletoe* [X]		$3		Polydor 577416
3/9/96	2²	20	10	Does That Blue Moon Ever Shine On You S:3 *(album snippets)*	112	$3	▌	Polydor 576140
7/13/96	6	20	11	A Woman's Touch *She's Perfect*		$3		A&M 581714
11/23/96+	❶¹	20	12	Me Too *The Lonely*		$3		Mercury 578810
6/14/97	2²	20	13	We Were In Love S:11 *Tired*	116	$3	▌	Mercury 574636
10/11/97+	2¹	20	14	I'm So Happy I Can't Stop Crying S:7 *Jacky Don Tucker*	84	$3	▌	Mercury 568114
				TOBY KEITH with Sting				
				#94 Pop hit for Sting in 1996				

KELLEY, John '82
Born in Little Rock, Arkansas; raised in Indiana.

7/24/82	81	4		This Morning I Woke Up In New York City		$7		ComStar 8201

KELLUM, Murry '71
Born in Jackson, Tennessee; raised in Plain, Texas. Died in a plane crash on 9/30/90 (age 47).

6/19/71	26	10	1	Joy To The World .... *In A Phone Booth On My Knees*		$6		Epic 10741
				#1 Pop hit for Three Dog Night in 1971				
11/20/71	74	2	2	Train Train (Carry Me Away) .... *What's Made Milwaukee Famous*		$6		Epic 10784
2/2/74	55	9	3	Lovely Lady .... *Alive And Doing Well*		$5		Cinnamon 777
5/25/74	98	2	4	Girl Of My Life .... *Since You've Been Gone*		$5		Cinnamon 794

KELLY, Irene '89
Singer from Latrobe, Pennsylvania.

12/2/89	67	7		Love Is A Hard Road .... *Too Late (To Turn Back Now)*		$3		MCA 53756

KELLY, Jerri '82

Born on 10/11/47 in Phoenix; raised in Stephenville, Texas. Female singer.

DEBUT	PEAK	WKS		A-side / B-side		$		Label & Number
1/18/75	65	10		1 I Can't Help Myself (Sugar Pie, Honey Bunch) ....*Got You On My Mind*		$7		GRT 016
				PRICE MITCHELL & JERRI KELLY				
				#1 Pop hit for the Four Tops in 1965				
1/26/80	90	2		2 For A Slow Dance With You ....*Stop Startin' Over*		$6		Little Giant 021
8/2/80	66	9		3 Fallin' For You ....*Guess I'd Better Be Strong (And Move Along)*		$6	■	Little Giant 026
11/8/80	85	3		4 Forsaking All The Rest ....*I'm As Much Of A Woman (As You Care To Make Me)*		$6	■	Little Giant 030
1/31/81	85	3		5 Be My Lover, Be My Friend ....*Drifter's Lullaby*		$6		Little Giant 040
				MICK LLOYD & JERRI KELLY				
8/8/81	85	4		6 Sweet Natural Love ....*Forsaking All The Rest*		$6		Little Giant 046
				MICK LLOYD & JERRI KELLY				
8/14/82	56	8		7 Walk Me 'Cross The River *All That Shines Is Gold*		$5		Carrere 03017

KELLY, Karen '70

9/19/70	75	2		Let Me Go, Lover ....*Susie's Toys*		$7		Capitol 2883
				#1 Pop hit for Joan Weber in 1955				

KEMP, Dave '83

5/28/83	75	4		Ain't That The Way It Goes ....*Prisoner Of Honky Tonk Hell*		$5		Soundwaves 4702

★287★ KEMP, Wayne '73

Born on 6/1/41 in Greenwood, Arkansas. Singer/prolific songwriter.
1)Honky Tonk Wine 2)Listen 3)Your Wife Is Cheatin' On Us Again 4)Just Got Back From No Man's Land
5)I'll Leave This World Loving You

2/1/69	61	6		1 Won't You Come Home (And Talk To A Stranger) ....*I Turn My Mind On You*		$6		Decca 32422
9/27/69	73	2		2 Bar Room Habits ....*Here We Go Again*		$6		Decca 32534
1/9/71	57	8		3 Who'll Turn Out The Lights ....*Burn Another Honky Tonk Down*		$6		Decca 32767
5/29/71	52	9		4 Award To An Angel ....*Darling Who's The Stranger*		$6		Decca 32824
12/18/71	72	2		5 Did We Have To Come This Far (To Say Goodbye).........*Play Me A Cheatin' Song*		$6		Decca 32891
6/3/72	53	5		6 Darlin' ....*Just To Know She'd Let Me Leave Her (Is Enough To Make Me Stay)*		$6		Decca 32946
3/17/73	17	14		7 Honky Tonk Wine *Pretty Mansions*		$5		MCA 40019
9/1/73	53	10		8 Kentucky Sunshine ....*I'll Leave This World Loving You*		$5		MCA 40112
2/2/74	32	11		9 Listen ....*She Knows When You're On My Mind Again*		$5		MCA 40176
7/6/74	57	11		10 Harlan County......................................*I'll Leave This World Loving You*		$5		MCA 40249
6/12/76	72	7		11 Waiting For The Tables To Turn ....*I Can't Wait To Dream That Dream Again*		$5		United Artists 805
8/28/76	71	5		12 I Should Have Watched That First Step ....*Tell Ole I Ain't Here To Get On Home*		$5		United Artists 850
5/21/77	91	3		13 Leona Don't Live Here Anymore ....*Baby This And Baby That*		$5		United Artists 980
8/27/77	76	6		14 I Love It (When You Love All Over Me)....................*Love's Already Been Here And Gone*		$5		United Artists 1031
7/12/80	62	6		15 Love Goes To Hell When It Dies ....*She Won't Close The Book On Me*		$4		Mercury 57023
11/15/80	47	10		16 I'll Leave This World Loving You ....*Who Left The Door To Heaven Open*		$4		Mercury 57035
4/4/81	35	12		17 Your Wife Is Cheatin' On Us Again ....*God Made Her Special*		$4		Mercury 57047
7/25/81	46	7		18 Just Got Back From No Man's Land.............................*Turn Me Loose*		$4		Mercury 57053
11/14/81	75	5		19 Why Am I Doing Without ....*Wrecked Up Frame Of Mind*		$4		Mercury 57060
4/10/82	78	4		20 Sloe Gin And Fast Women ....*I'm The Man*		$4		Mercury 76139
9/4/82	64	6		21 She Only Meant To Use Him.....................*I Know Just How She Feels*		$4		Mercury 76165
7/16/83	55	10		22 Don't Send Me No Angels.......................................*Living Off The Memories*		$5		Door Knob 200
6/30/84	75	4		23 I've Always Wanted To		$5		Door Knob 211
3/8/86	70	4		24 Red Neck And Over Thirty ....*State Of The Union*		$5		Door Knob 243
				WAYNE KEMP & BOBBY G. RICE				

KENDALLS, The ★111★ '77

Father-and-daughter duo. Royce was born on 9/25/34 in St. Louis. Died of a heart attack on 5/22/98 (age 63). Jeannie was born on 11/30/54 in St. Louis.

1)Heaven's Just A Sin Away 2)Sweet Desire 3)Thank God For The Radio
4)It Don't Feel Like Sinnin' To Me 5)I Had A Lovely Time

7/25/70	52	6		1 Leaving On A Jet Plane ....*She Thinks I Still Care*		$10		Stop 373
				#1 Pop hit for Peter, Paul & Mary in 1969				
2/12/72	53	9		2 Two Divided By Love ....*Easy To Love*		$8		Dot 17405
				#16 Pop hit for The Grass Roots in 1971				
7/1/72	66	4		3 Everything I Own ....*Big Silver Jet*		$8		Dot 17422
				THE KENDALLS Featuring Jeannie Kendall				
				#5 Pop hit for Bread in 1972				
4/2/77	80	7		4 Makin' Believe ....*Let The Music Play*		$7		Ovation 1101
8/6/77	❶⁴	20		5 Heaven's Just A Sin Away *Live And Let Live*	69	$5		Ovation 1103
				CMA Award: Single of the Year				
2/11/78	2²	15		6 It Don't Feel Like Sinnin' To Me *Try Me Again*		$5		Ovation 1106
5/27/78	6	14		7 Pittsburgh Stealers *When Can We Do This Again*		$5		Ovation 1109
9/23/78	❶¹	15		8 Sweet Desire/		$5		Ovation 1112
		15		9 Old Fashioned Love..		$5		
1/13/79	5	14		10 I Had A Lovely Time *Love Is A Hurting Thing*		$5		Ovation 1119
5/5/79	11	11		11 Just Like Real People..*Another Dream Just Came True*		$5		Ovation 1125

KENDALLS, The — Cont'd

DEBUT	PEAK	WKS	A-side / B-side	Pop	$	Pic	Label & Number
8/18/79	16	11	12 I Don't Do Like That No More/		$5		Ovation 1129
		11	13 Never My Love		$5		
11/17/79+	5	15	14 You'd Make An Angel Wanna Cheat — *I Take The Chance*		$5		Ovation 1136
4/5/80	5	13	15 I'm Already Blue — *I Don't Drink From The River*		$5		Ovation 1143
8/2/80	9	15	16 Put It Off Until Tomorrow — *Gone Away*		$5		Ovation 1154
			co-written by Dolly Parton				
3/28/81	26	11	17 Heart Of The Matter.................. *Mandolin Man*		$5		Ovation 1169
8/22/81	7	16	18 Teach Me To Cheat — *Summer Melodies*		$4		Mercury 57055
12/12/81+	10	19	19 If You're Waiting On Me (You're Backing Up) — *I'm Lettin' You In (On A Feelin')*		$4		Mercury 76131
6/5/82	30	12	20 Cheater's Prayer — *Borrowing Lovin'*		$4		Mercury 76155
9/18/82	35	10	21 That's What I Get For Thinking........... *Honey Dew*		$4		Mercury 76178
5/28/83	19	14	22 Precious Love .... *Take Me To Heaven (Before You Take Me Home)*		$3		Mercury 812300
			Emmylou Harris (harmony vocal)				
8/27/83	20	19	23 Movin' Train........... *Say The Word*		$3		Mercury 814195
1/14/84	❶[1]	23	24 Thank God For The Radio — *Flaming Eyes*		$3		Mercury 818056
6/2/84	15	17	25 My Baby's Gone............. *I'll Be Faithful To You*		$3		Mercury 822203
10/27/84+	20	17	26 I'd Dance Every Dance With You............. S:16 / A:21 *The Dark End Of The Street*		$3		Mercury 880306
3/2/85	27	14	27 Four Wheel Drive .... S:21 / A:26 *This Ain't The First Time I've Fallen*		$3		Mercury 880588
6/1/85	26	14	28 If You Break My Heart............. S:21 / A:25 *One Good-Bye From Gone*		$3		Mercury 880828
10/12/85	45	8	29 Two Heart Harmony............. *I Don't Know Any Better*		$3		Mercury 884140
6/28/86	42	9	30 Too Late .... *Party Line*		$3		MCA/Curb 52850
9/27/86	60	7	31 Fire At First Sight............. *You Can't Fool Love*		$3		MCA/Curb 52933
12/6/86+	46	9	32 Little Doll............. *He Can't Make Your Kind Of Love*		$3		MCA/Curb 52983
5/2/87	54	8	33 Routine............. *A Far Cry*		$3		Step One 371
7/11/87	51	8	34 Dancin' With Myself Tonight............. *A Whole Lot To Lose*		$3		Step One 374
12/12/87+	62	7	35 Still Pickin' Up After You............. *Country Music Station*		$3		Step One 379
4/16/88	57	7	36 The Rhythm Of Romance............. *They Can't Stop Me*		$3		Step One 384
6/24/89	69	6	37 Blue Blue Day............. *Temporarily Out Of Order*		$3		Epic 68933

KENNARD AND JOHN   '89
Duo of Phillip Kennard and Ron John.

DEBUT	PEAK	WKS	A-side / B-side	Pop	$	Pic	Label & Number
11/18/89	73	4	Thrill Of Love............. *Maria*		$3		Curb/MCA 10563

KENNEDY, Gene, & Karen Jeglum   '82
Husband-and-wife duo. Gene was born Kenneth Kennedy on 10/3/33 in Florence, South Carolina. Karen was born in Blanchardville, Wisconsin. Co-owners of the Door Knob record label.

DEBUT	PEAK	WKS	A-side / B-side	Pop	$	Pic	Label & Number
2/28/81	80	4	1 I Want To See Me In Your Eyes............. *Nothing Left To Lose*		$5		Door Knob 145
4/25/81	84	4	2 I'd Rather Be The Stranger In Your Eyes.............		$5		Door Knob 151
3/20/82	49	9	3 A Thing Or Two On My Mind/				
7/18/81	87	2	4 Easier To Go		$5		Door Knob 173
7/24/82	80	4	5 What About Tonight (We Might Find Something Beautiful Tonight)............. *Your Still The One (Who Makes My Life Complete)*		$5		Door Knob 179
4/23/83	86	3	6 Be Happy For Me............. *What About Tonight*		$5		Door Knob 192
8/2/86	78	4	7 My Wife's House		$5		Society 110
			GENE KENNEDY				

KENNEDY, Larry Wayne   '85

DEBUT	PEAK	WKS	A-side / B-side	Pop	$	Pic	Label & Number
11/30/85	83	3	She Almost Makes Me Forget About You.............		$5		Jere 1001

KENNEDY, Ray   '91
Born on 5/13/54 in Buffalo, New York. Singer/songwriter/guitarist.

DEBUT	PEAK	WKS	A-side / B-side	Pop	$	Pic	Label & Number
11/17/90+	10	20	1 What A Way To Go — *The Storm*		$3	▌	Atlantic 87960
4/13/91	58	10	2 Scars............. *I'm Sending One Up For You*		$3	▌	Atlantic 87743
8/10/91	74	1	3 I Like The Way It Feels............. *I'm Sending One Up For You*		$3		Atlantic 87651
11/7/92	70	5	4 No Way Jose.............				album cut
			from the album *Guitar Man* on Atlantic 82422				

KENNY O.   '81
Full name: Kenny O. Smith.

DEBUT	PEAK	WKS	A-side / B-side	Pop	$	Pic	Label & Number
8/22/81	83	3	Old Fangled Country Songs .... *Walking By My Side*		$6		Rhinestone 1002

KENT, George   '70
Born on 6/12/35 in Dallas.

DEBUT	PEAK	WKS	A-side / B-side	Pop	$	Pic	Label & Number
12/13/69+	26	15	1 Hello, I'm A Jukebox .... *I Always Did Like Leavenworth* [S]		$6		Mercury 72985
			Diana Duke (female vocal)				
7/4/70	70	3	2 Doogie Ray .... *The Great South State Truck Stop Disaster*		$6		Mercury 73066
12/5/70+	62	7	3 Mama Bake A Pie (Daddy Kill A Chicken) .... *Let's Just Pretend*		$6		Mercury 73127
5/18/74	48	9	4 Take My Life And Shape It With Your Love .... *Sunshine Light*		$5		Shannon 818
12/28/74+	65	6	5 Whole Lotta Difference In Love .... *Coming Back On My Mind*		$5		Shannon 824
11/22/75	97	3	6 She'll Wear It Out Leaving Town .... *Don't Tell It To Me*		$5		Shannon 834
3/13/76	75	6	7 Shake 'Em Up and Let 'Em Roll............. *Singin' Lonesome Cowboy Songs*		$5		Shannon 840
2/26/77	89	5	8 Low Class Reunion............. *(How Can I Write On Paper) What I Feel In My Heart*		$5		Soundwaves 4542

KENTUCKY HEADHUNTERS, The ★390★ '90

Group from Edmonton, Kentucky: brothers Ricky Lee (vocals) and Doug (bass) Phelps, brothers Richard (guitar) and Fred (drums) Young, and their cousin Greg Martin (guitar). The Phelps brothers left in 1992 to form **Brother Phelps**; replaced by Mark Orr (vocals) and Anthony Kenney (bass). CMA Awards: 1990 & 1991 Vocal Group of the Year.

1)Oh Lonesome Me 2)Dumas Walker 3)Rock 'N' Roll Angel

DEBUT	PEAK	WKS		A-side / B-side	Pop	$	Pic	Label & Number
9/30/89	25	21	1	Walk Softly On This Heart Of Mine .... *Skip A Rope*		$3		Mercury 874744
2/24/90	15	26	2	Dumas Walker .... *High Steppin' Daddy*		$3	■	Mercury 876536
6/2/90	8	21	3	Oh Lonesome Me .... *My Daddy Was A Milkman*		$3	■	Mercury 875450
10/13/90	23	20	4	Rock 'N' Roll Angel .... *Rag Top*		$3		Mercury 878214
3/30/91	49	11	5	The Ballad Of Davy Crockett .... *Smooth*		$3	■	Mercury 868122
				#1 Pop hit for Bill Hayes in 1955				
6/22/91	56	9	6	With Body And Soul... *Some Folks Like To Steal*		$3		Mercury 868418
9/21/91	63	6	7	It's Chitlin' Time .... *Dumas Walker*		$3	■	Mercury 868760
11/23/91	60	7	8	Only Daddy That'll Walk The Line .... *Walk Softly On This Heart Of Mine*		$3		Mercury 866134
2/20/93	54	6	9	Honky Tonk Walkin' .... *Redneck Girl*		$3	■	Mercury 864808
5/22/93	71	4	10	Dixie Fried .... *Celina Tennessee*		$3		Mercury 862150
3/22/97	70	3	11	Singin' The Blues .... *Kentucky Wildcat*		$3	■	BNA 64782
				#1 Pop hit for **Guy Mitchell** in 1956				

KENYON, Joe '87

Pseudonym for producer/guitarist Jerry Kennedy and pianist David Briggs.

DEBUT	PEAK	WKS		A-side / B-side	Pop	$	Pic	Label & Number
6/27/87	33	15		Hymne .... *My Only Love* [I]		$3		Mercury 888642
				tune featured in Gallo Wine commercials; written by Greek composer, Vangelis				

KERSH, David '97

Born on 12/9/70 in Humble, Texas. Singer/songwriter.

DEBUT	PEAK	WKS		A-side / B-side	Pop	$	Pic	Label & Number
8/3/96	6	22	1	Goodnight Sweetheart/ *S:7*	113			
5/4/96	65	5	2	Breaking Hearts And Taking Names		$3	■	Curb 76990
1/18/97	3	20	3	Another You				album cut
5/31/97	11	20	4	Day In, Day Out				album cut
				above 2 from the album *Goodnight Sweetheart* on Curb 77848				
12/6/97+	3	25	5	If I Never Stop Loving You *S:4 The Need*	67	$3	■	Curb 73045

KERSHAW, Doug ★400★ '81

Born on 1/24/36 in Tiel Ridge, Louisiana. Cajun fiddler/singer/songwriter. Teamed with brother Russell "Rusty" Kershaw in duo **Rusty & Doug**. Acted in the movies *Zachariah*, *Medicine Ball Caravan* and *Days Of Heaven*. Third cousin of **Sammy Kershaw**.

1)Louisiana Man 2)Diggy Liggy Lo 3)So Lovely, Baby

RUSTY & DOUG:

DEBUT	PEAK	WKS		A-side / B-side	Pop	$	Pic	Label & Number
8/13/55	14	2	1	So Lovely, Baby... *A:14 Why Cry For You*		$20		Hickory 1027
9/23/57	14	1	2	Love Me To Pieces .... *A:14 I Never Had The Blues*		$20		Hickory 1068
				#11 Pop hit for Jill Corey in 1957				
10/20/58	22	2	3	Hey Sheriff... *Sweet Thing*		$20		Hickory 1083
2/6/61	10	15	4	Louisiana Man .... *Make Me Realize*	104	$20		Hickory 1137
8/21/61	14	10	5	Diggy Liggy Lo .... *Hey Mae*		$20		Hickory 1151
				also see #6 below				

DOUG KERSHAW:

DEBUT	PEAK	WKS		A-side / B-side	Pop	$	Pic	Label & Number
10/11/69	70	3	6	Diggy Liggy Lo .... *Papa And Mama Had Love* [R]		$6		Warner 7329
				new version of #5 above				
2/2/74	77	9	7	Mama's Got The Know How .... *Hippy Ti Yo*		$5		Warner 7763
5/1/76	76	6	8	It Takes All Day To Get Over Night .... *Mon Chapeau*		$5		Warner 8195
5/21/77	96	3	9	I'm Walkin'... *Kershaw's Two Step*		$5		Warner 8374
				#4 Pop hit for **Fats Domino** in 1957				
6/27/81	29	13	10	Hello Woman .... *Sing Along*		$4		Scotti Brothers 02137
8/27/88	52	7	11	Cajun Baby .... *I Wanna Hold You*		$4		BGM 81588
				DOUG KERSHAW with HANK WILLIAMS, JR.				
3/11/89	66	6	12	Boogie Queen .... *Jamabalaya*		$4		BGM 12989

KERSHAW, Sammy ★174★ '93

Born Samuel Cashat on 2/24/58 in Abbeville, Louisiana; raised in Kaplan, Louisiana. Singer/songwriter/guitarist. Third cousin of **Doug Kershaw**. Acted in the 1995 movie *Fall Time*.

1)She Don't Know She's Beautiful 2)Love Of My Life 3)Third Rate Romance 4)National Working Woman's Holiday 5)Cadillac Style

DEBUT	PEAK	WKS		A-side / B-side	Pop	$	Pic	Label & Number
10/12/91+	3	20	1	Cadillac Style *Harbor For A Lonely Heart*		$3	■	Mercury 868812
2/8/92	12	20	2	Don't Go Near The Water .... *Every Third Monday*		$3		Mercury 866324
6/13/92	17	20	3	Yard Sale .... *What Am I Worth*		$3		Mercury 866754
10/3/92+	10	20	4	Anywhere But Here *Real Old-Fashioned Broken Heart*		$3		Mercury 864316
2/13/93	❶[1]	20	5	She Don't Know She's Beautiful *I Buy Her Roses*	119	$3	■	Mercury 864854
5/8/93	9	20	6	Haunted Heart *Cry, Cry Darlin'*		$3	■	Mercury 862096
9/4/93	7	20	7	Queen Of My Double Wide Trailer *A Memory That Just Won't Quit*		$3	■	Mercury 862600
1/15/94	3	20	8	I Can't Reach Her Anymore *What Might Have Been*		$3	■	Mercury 858102
3/12/94	52	10	9	Never Bit A Bullet Like This				album cut
				GEORGE JONES with Sammy Kershaw from the album *High-Tech Redneck* on MCA 10910				

DEBUT	PEAK	WKS	Gold	A-side (Chart Hit)..B-side	Pop	$	Pic	Label & Number
				KERSHAW, Sammy — Cont'd				
5/21/94	2[1]	20		10 National Working Woman's Holiday .... *The Heart That Time Forgot*		$3	▌	Mercury 858722
8/27/94	2[2]	20		11 Third Rate Romance .... *Paradise From Nine To One*	105	$3	▌	Mercury 858922
12/3/94+	27	16		12 Southbound .... *Better Call A Preacher*		$3	▌	Mercury 856410
12/24/94	50	3		13 Christmas Time's A Comin' .... *Up On The Housetop* [X]		$3		Mercury 856408
3/18/95	18	20		14 If You're Gonna Walk, I'm Gonna Crawl .... *If You Ever Come This Way Again*		$3		Mercury 856686
8/26/95	47	8		15 Your Tattoo .... *Still Lovin' You*		$3		Mercury 852208
3/23/96	5	20		16 Meant To Be/	S:14			
7/27/96	10	20		17 Vidalia		$3	▌	Mercury 852874
11/9/96+	28	20		18 Politics, Religion And Her .... *Here She Comes*		$3		Mercury 578612
4/12/97	29	20		19 Fit To Be Tied Down .... *For Years*		$3		Mercury 574182
10/25/97+	2[2]	26		20 Love Of My Life .... *S:8 Roamin' Love*	85	$3	▌	Mercury 568140
12/27/97	53	2		21 Christmas Time's A Comin' .... *Up On The Housetop* [X-R]		$3		Mercury 856408
	★248★			**KETCHUM, Hal** **'93**				
				Born on 4/9/53 in Greenwich, New York. Singer/songwriter/guitarist. Joined the *Grand Ole Opry* in 1994.				
				1)*Past The Point Of Rescue* 2)*Small Town Saturday Night* 3)*Hearts Are Gonna Roll*				
5/11/91	2[1]	21		1 Small Town Saturday Night .... *Don't Strike A Match (To The Book Of Love)*		$3	▌	Curb 76865
10/26/91+	13	20		2 I Know Where Love Lives.............................. *Long Day Comin'*		$3		Curb 76892
2/15/92	2[1]	20		3 Past The Point Of Rescue				album cut
5/30/92	16	20		4 Five O'Clock World				album cut
				#4 Pop hit for The Vogues in 1966; above 2 from the album *Past The Point Of Rescue* on Curb 77450				
9/26/92+	3	20		5 Sure Love/				
6/19/93	8	20		6 Mama Knows The Highway		$3	▌	Curb 76915
2/20/93	2[1]	20		7 Hearts Are Gonna Roll				album cut
10/9/93	24	20		8 Someplace Far Away (Careful What You're Dreamin')...................				album cut
				above 2 from the album *Sure Love* on Curb 77581				
4/23/94	20	20		9 (Tonight We Just Might) Fall In Love Again .... *Drive On*		$3	▌	Curb 76922
9/24/94	22	19		10 That's What I Get (For Losin' You)				album cut
				from the album *Every Little Word* on MCG/Curb 77660				
2/11/95	8	20		11 Stay Forever .... *S:15 Every Little Word*	124	$3	▌	MCG/Curb 76929
8/26/95	49	8		12 Every Little Word/				
11/18/95	56	7		13 Veil Of Tears		$3	▌	MCG/Curb 76965
				KILGORE, Merle **'60**				
				Born Wyatt Merle Kilgore on 9/8/34 in Chickasha, Oklahoma; raised in Shreveport, Louisiana. Singer/prolific songwriter.				
2/1/60	12	13		1 Dear Mama.. *Jimmie Brings Sunshine*		$20		Starday 469
7/4/60	10	11		2 Love Has Made You Beautiful/				
7/18/60	29	1		3 Getting Old Before My Time		$20		Starday 497
				recitation by Jimmy Jay				
10/21/67	71	3		4 Fast Talking Louisiana Man .... *Avenue Of Tears*		$20		Columbia 44279
8/24/74	95	4		5 Montgomery Mable .... *Old Home Filler-Up An' Keep-On-A-Truckin Cafe*		$5		Warner 7831
1/16/82	54	7		6 Mister Garfield .... *I'm A One Woman Man*		$4		Elektra 47252
				MERLE KILGORE AND FRIENDS				
				Johnny Cash and **Hank Williams, Jr.** (backing vocals)				
7/14/84	74	4		7 Just Out Of Reach .... *Road Women*		$4		Warner 29267
				#24 Pop hit for Solomon Burke in 1961				
5/11/85	92	4		8 Guilty .... *When You Leave That Way You Can Never Go Back*		$4		Warner 29062
				KILLEN, Buddy — see GUITAR, Bonnie				
				KIMBERLYS, The — see JENNINGS, Waylon				
				KIMBERLY SPRINGS **'84**				
				Four sisters and brothers, and a cousin (children of **The Kimberlys**).				
6/23/84	49	10		1 Slow Dancin'.. *Temptation*		$4		Capitol 5366
10/20/84	74	5		2 Old Memories Are Hard To Lose .... *That's One To Grow On*		$4		Capitol 5404

				KING, Claude ★150★ **'62**				
				Born on 2/5/33 in Shreveport, Louisiana. Singer/songwriter/guitarist. Acted in the movies *Swamp Girl* and *Year Of The Wahoo*, and in the TV miniseries *The Blue And The Gray*.				
				1)*Wolverton Mountain* 2)*Tiger Woman* 3)*Big River, Big Man* 4)*The Comancheros* 5)*All For The Love Of A Girl*				
7/3/61	7	16		1 Big River, Big Man .... *Sweet Lovin'*	82	$12		Columbia 42043
11/13/61+	7	15		2 The Comancheros .... *I Can't Get Over The Way You Got Over Me*	71	$12	■	Columbia 42196
				inspired by the movie starring John Wayne				
5/5/62	❶[9]	26	●	3 Wolverton Mountain .... *Little Bitty Heart*	6	$12	■	Columbia 42352
				title is an actual place in Arkansas where Clifton Clowers lived (d: 8/15/94, age 102)				
10/20/62	10	7		4 The Burning Of Atlanta .... *Don't That Moon Look Lonesome*	53	$10	■	Columbia 42581
12/22/62+	11	9		5 I've Got The World By The Tail .... *Shopping Center*	111	$10	■	Columbia 42630
3/9/63	12	9		6 Sheepskin Valley .... *I Backed Out*		$10	■	Columbia 42688
6/29/63	12	5		7 Building A Bridge.. *What Will I Do*		$10	■	Columbia 42782
8/17/63	13	5		8 Hey Lucille!... *Scarlet O'Hara*		$10	■	Columbia 42833
2/29/64	33	7		9 That's What Makes The World Go Around ...... *A Lace Mantilla And A Rose Of Red*		$8		Columbia 42959

KING, Claude — Cont'd

DEBUT	PEAK	WKS	A-side	B-side	Pop	$	Pic	Label & Number
8/15/64	11	18	10 Sam Hill .... Big Ole Shoulder			$8		Columbia 43083
12/26/64+	47	3	11 Whirlpool (Of Your Love) .... This Land Of Yours And Mine			$8		Columbia 43157
6/26/65	6	18	12 Tiger Woman .... When You Gotta Go (You Gotta Go)	110		$8		Columbia 43298
11/27/65+	17	11	13 Little Buddy .... Come On Home			$8		Columbia 43416
3/12/66	13	15	14 Catch A Little Raindrop .... Hold That Tiger (Tiger Rag)			$8		Columbia 43510
11/26/66+	50	12	15 Little Things That Every Girl Should Know .... The Right Place			$8		Columbia 43867
4/29/67	32	10	16 The Watchman .... That's The Way The Wind Blows			$7		Columbia 44035
8/26/67	50	10	17 Laura (What's He Got That I Ain't Got)....................... Good-By My Love			$7		Columbia 44237
12/9/67	59	2	18 Yellow Haired Woman .... Ninety-Nine Years			$7		Columbia 44340
6/8/68	67	3	19 Parchman Farm Blues .... Birmingham Bus Station			$7		Columbia 44504
10/19/68	48	6	20 The Power Of Your Sweet Love .... Beertops And Teardrops			$7		Columbia 44642
3/1/69	52	7	21 Sweet Love On My Mind .... Four Roses			$7		Columbia 44749
5/17/69	9	15	22 All For The Love Of A Girl .... I Remember Johnny			$7	■	Columbia 44833
11/8/69	18	10	23 Friend, Lover, Woman, Wife .... The House Of The Rising Sun			$7		Columbia 45015
5/30/70	33	10	24 I'll Be Your Baby Tonight.............. It's Good To Have My Baby Home			$7		Columbia 45142
			first recorded by Bob Dylan on his 1968 album John Wesley Harding					
11/7/70+	17	15	25 Mary's Vineyard .... Johnny Valentine			$7		Columbia 45248
4/10/71	23	13	26 Chip 'N' Dale's Place .... Highway Lonely			$7		Columbia 45340
9/18/71	54	5	27 When You're Twenty-One .... Heart			$7		Columbia 45441
2/5/72	57	6	28 Darlin' Raise The Shade (Let The Sun Shine In)...................... Sweet Mary Ann			$7		Columbia 45515
11/4/72	48	8	29 He Ain't Country .... This Time I'm Through			$7		Columbia 45704
5/28/77	94	3	30 Cotton Dan .... I'll Spend My Lifetime Loving You			$6		True 103

★274★ KING, Don '77

Born on 5/1/54 in Freemont, Nebraska. Singer/songwriter/guitarist.
1)I've Got You 2)She's The Girl Of My Dreams 3)The Feelings So Right Tonight

DEBUT	PEAK	WKS	A-side	B-side	Pop	$	Pic	Label & Number
9/11/76	78	5	1 Cabin High (In The Blue Ridge Mountains) .... Leavin' Talk			$5		Con Brio 112
2/19/77	16	13	2 I've Got You (To Come Home To) .... Diamond Reo Cowboy (Truck Stop Romeo)			$5		Con Brio 116
6/4/77	17	13	3 She's The Girl Of My Dreams .... Dancing Across My Memory			$5		Con Brio 120
10/8/77	41	9	4 I Must Be Dreaming .... Truck Drivin' Lash Larue			$5		Con Brio 126
1/28/78	29	9	5 Music Is My Woman .... Drinkin' In Texas			$5		Con Brio 129
5/13/78	29	10	6 Don't Make No Promises (You Can't Keep) .... Cabin High			$5		Con Brio 133
8/5/78	26	11	7 The Feelings So Right Tonight .... Where Were You On My Saturday Nights			$5		Con Brio 137
11/25/78+	28	13	8 You Were Worth Waiting For........................ Don't Get Around Much			$5		Con Brio 142
3/10/79	39	8	9 Live Entertainment .... I Must Be Dreaming			$5		Con Brio 149
6/23/79	73	3	10 I've Got Country Music In My Soul .... She's The Girl Of My Dreams			$5		Con Brio 153
2/16/80	40	9	11 Lonely Hotel .... Same Old Feeling			$4		Epic 50840
5/24/80	32	12	12 Here Comes That Feeling Again .... My Happiness Is You			$4		Epic 50877
9/27/80	44	8	13 Take This Heart... Saddle The Stallion			$4		Epic 50928
5/9/81	38	11	14 I Still Miss Someone .... More Than A Memory			$4		Epic 02046
			written by Johnny Cash					
9/19/81	27	12	15 The Closer You Get .... The Time Of Our Lives			$4		Epic 02468
1/16/82	40	9	16 Running On Love .... Lean On Jesus			$4		Epic 02674
10/2/82	64	6	17 Maximum Security (To Minimum Wage) .... The Shadow Of My Love			$4		Epic 03155
3/15/86	71	6	18 All We Had Was One Another			$5		Bench Mark 8601
10/15/88	86	2	19 Can't Stop The Music			$5		615 1015

KING, Donny '75

Born Joseph Mier in Crowley, Louisiana. Singer/guitarist.

DEBUT	PEAK	WKS	A-side	B-side	Pop	$	Pic	Label & Number
3/1/75	20	11	1 Mathilda .... I Played That Song For You			$4		Warner 8074
			#47 Pop hit for Cookie & His Cupcakes in 1959					
11/8/75	72	6	2 I'm A Fool To Care .... Hello Mary Lou, Goodbye Heart			$4		Warner 8145
			#24 Pop hit for Joe Barry in 1961					
7/31/76	91	4	3 Stop The World (And Let Me Off) .... Wake Me Gently			$4		Warner 8229

KING, Matt '97

Singer/songwriter/guitarist from Asheville, North Carolina.

DEBUT	PEAK	WKS	A-side	B-side	Pop	$	Pic	Label & Number
8/23/97	54	11	1 A Woman Like You					album cut
11/8/97	70	4	2 I Wrote The Book					album cut
			above 2 from the album Five O'Clock Hero on Atlantic 82981					

★252★ KING, Pee Wee '51

Born Julius Frank Kuczynski on 2/18/14 in Abrams, Wisconsin; raised in Milwaukee. Singer/songwriter/accordionist/fiddle player. Led own band, the Golden West Cowboys, from 1936. On the Grand Ole Opry from 1937-47. Own radio and TV series on WAVE-Louisville from 1947-57. Elected to the Country Music Hall of Fame in 1974.
1)Slow Poke 2)Tennessee Waltz 3)Tennessee Polka

PEE WEE KING and his Golden West Cowboys:

DEBUT	PEAK	WKS	A-side	B-side	Pop	$	Pic	Label & Number
4/3/48	3	35	1 Tennessee Waltz .... S:3 / J:4 Rootie Tootie			$20		RCA Victor 20-2680
			45 rpm: 48-0003; see also #5 below					
6/18/49	12	2	2 Tennessee Tears .... S:12 Alabama Moon			$20		RCA Victor 21-0037
			Dave Denney (vocal)					
9/10/49	3	3	3 Tennessee Polka .... J:3 The Nashville Waltz			$20		RCA Victor 21-0086
			45 rpm: 48-0085					
1/21/50	10	1	4 Bonaparte's Retreat .... A:10 The Waltz Of Regret			$25		RCA Victor 48-0114
			78 rpm: 21-0111					
2/17/51	6	4	5 Tennessee Waltz .... A:6 / J:7 Helegged Hilegged [R]			$25		RCA Victor 48-0407
			same version as #1 above					
9/15/51	❶15	31	6 Slow Poke .... J:❶15 / S:❶14 / A:❶9 Whisper Waltz	❶3		$25		RCA Victor 48-0489

DEBUT	PEAK	WKS	Gold	A-side (Chart Hit)..B-side	Pop	$	Pic	Label & Number
				PEE WEE KING and his Band featuring Redd Stewart:				
2/16/52	5	14		7 **Silver And Gold** S:5 / J:5 / A:7 *Ragtime Annie Lee*	18	$20		RCA Victor 47-4458
5/17/52	8	3		8 **Busybody** J:8 / A:9 *I Don't Mind*	27	$20		RCA Victor 47-4655
1/2/54	4	10		9 **Changing Partners/** A:4		$20		
				#3 Pop hit for **Patti Page** in 1954				
1/23/54	9	2		10 **Bimbo** J:9 / A:10 / S:10		$20		RCA Victor 5537
7/10/54	15	1		11 **Backward, Turn Backward** .... A:15 *Indian Giver*		$20		RCA Victor 5694
				Redd Stewart (vocal, all of above - except #2)				
				KING, Sherri '76				
				Born in Knoxville, Tennessee.				
10/2/76	95	2		**Almost Persuaded** .... *A Good Woman Waits On Her Man*		$4		United Artists 855
				KING COLE TRIO — see COLE, Nat "King"				
				KING EDWARD IV AND THE KNIGHTS '81				
				Born Edward Smith on 7/13/31 in Cincinnati. Died on 3/24/81 (age 49). The Knights featured male singer Cary Len and female singer Gigi.				
9/3/77	90	5		1 **Greenback Shuffle** .... *New Corena*		$5		Soundwaves 4550
3/11/78	87	5		2 **Wipe You From My Eyes (Gettin' Over You)** .... *No News Is Good News*		$5		Soundwaves 4563
7/22/78	68	8		3 **Baby Blue** .... *Rabbit Run*		$5		Soundwaves 4573
5/26/79	89	3		4 **A Couple More Years** .... *The Old Spinning Wheel*		$5		Soundwaves 4583
4/26/80	91	2		5 **A Song For Noel** .... *Desperado*		$5		Soundwaves 4597
1/31/81	48	9		6 **Dixie Road** *Joyful Noise*		$5		Soundwaves 4626
5/30/81	49	8		7 **Keep On Movin'** .... *Kentucky Flower*		$5		Soundwaves 4635
				KING SISTERS, The '46				
				Family vocal group from Salt Lake City: sisters Alyce, Yvonne, Donna and Louise Driggs. Group hosted own TV series. Louise married orchestra leader Alvino Rey. Alyce died on 8/21/96 (age 80). Louise died on 8/4/97 (age 83).				
12/28/46	5	1		**Divorce Me C.O.D.** *It's A Pity To Say Goodnight*		$12		Victor 20-2018
				Buddy Cole (orch.)				
				KINGSTON, Larry '74				
				Singer/songwriter.				
4/6/74	61	10		1 **Good Morning Loving** .... *Make A Dream Come True*		$6		JMI 37
12/13/75	91	4		2 **Good Morning Lovin'** .... *Make A Dream Come True* [R]		$5		Warner 8139
				above 2 are the same version				
				KINLEYS, The '97				
				Vocal duo of identical twin sisters Heather and Jennifer Kinley (b: 11/5/70 in Philadelphia).				
8/2/97	7	22		1 **Please** S:4 *(album snippets)*	67	$3	▮	Epic 78656
12/20/97+	12	20		2 **Just Between You And Me** .... S:20 *(album snippets)*	122	$3	▮	Epic 78766
				KIRBY, Dave '81				
				Singer/prolific songwriter. Married **Leona Williams** in 1985.				
11/8/69	67	4		1 **Her And The Car And The Mobile Home** .... *Don't It Make You Want To Go Home*		$6		Monument 1168
5/16/81	37	11		2 **North Alabama** .... *How Can I Tell You Goodbye*		$5		Dimension 1019
9/12/81	64	5		3 **Moccasin Man** .... *When Will Forgetting Begin*		$5		Dimension 1022
				KIRK, Eddie '48				
				Born on 3/21/19 in Greeley, Colorado. Singer/songwriter. National Yodeling Champion in 1935 and 1936. On the **Gene Autry** radio shows and **Town Hall Party** in Compton, California during the late '40s. Appeared in several western movies.				
10/2/48	9	6		1 **The Gods Were Angry With Me** J:9 / S:10 *You Little Sweet Little You*		$20		Capitol 15176
				Tex Ritter (recitation)				
3/12/49	9	3		2 **Candy Kisses** S:9 / J:10 *Save The Next Waltz For Me*		$15		Capitol 15391
				KIRK, Red '50				
				Worked on WNOX-Knoxville and WIMA-Lima, Ohio. Known as "The Voice Of The Country."				
6/25/49	14	1		1 **Lovesick Blues** .... J:14 *A Package Tied In Blue*		$15		Mercury 6189
7/22/50	7	7		2 **Lose Your Blues** A:7 *Over An Ocean Of Golden Dreams*		$15		Mercury 6257
				Jerry Byrd (lead vocal)				
				KNIGHT, Evelyn '51				
				Born in 1920 in Reedsville, Virginia. Known as "The Lass With The Delicate Air."				
2/17/51	6	1		**My Heart Cries For You** A:6 *Tater Pie*	28	$25		Decca 9-27378
				EVELYN KNIGHT and RED FOLEY				
				KNOBLOCK, Fred '81				
				Born in Jackson, Mississippi. Member of **Schuyler, Knobloch & Overstreet.**				
8/2/80	30	11		1 **Why Not Me** .... *Can I Get A Wish*	18	$4		Scotti Brothers 518
10/18/80	53	6		2 **Let Me Love You** *It's Over*		$4		Scotti Brothers 607
11/29/80+	10	18		3 **Killin' Time** *Love Is No Friend To A Fool*	28	$4		Scotti Brothers 609
				FRED KNOBLOCK AND SUSAN ANTON				
8/22/81	10	14		4 **Memphis** *Love Isn't Easy*	102	$4		Scotti Brothers 02434
				written by Chuck Berry; #2 Pop hit for **Johnny Rivers** in 1964				
3/20/82	33	10		5 **I Had It All** *Love, Love, Love*		$4		Scotti Brothers 02752
				KNOX, Buddy '68				
				Born on 7/20/33 in Happy, Texas. Singer/songwriter/guitarist. Charted 10 pop hits from 1957-61.				
6/22/68	64	6		**Gypsy Man** .... *This Time Tomorrow*		$12		United Artists 50301
				KOLANDER, Steve '94				
				Singer/guitarist from Austin, Texas.				
11/26/94	63	5		1 **Listen To Your Woman** .... *(remix)*		$4	▮	River North 4514
3/11/95	70	5		2 **Black Dresses** .... *(remix)*		$4	▮	River North 3002

DEBUT	PEAK	WKS	Gold	A-side (Chart Hit) ... B-side	Pop	$	Pic	Label & Number
				KRAMER, Rex '76				
				Born in Smackover, Arkansas; raised in Baytown, Texas. Had own surf-rock band, The Coastliners, in the mid-1960s. Played banjo with The New Christy Minstrels in the late '60s.				
3/6/76	100	2		You Oughta Be Against The Law .... *Our Love Is Blooming*		$5		Columbia 10286
				KRAUSS, Alison '95				
				Born on 7/23/71 in Champaign, Illinois. Singer/bluegrass fiddler. Union Station is her backing band: Dan Tyminski (guitar), Ron Block (banjo), Adam Steffey (mandolin) and Barry Bales (bass). Joined the *Grand Ole Opry* in 1993. CMA Awards: 1995 Horizon Award; 1995 Female Vocalist of the Year. Also see **The Red Hots**.				
				ALISON KRAUSS & UNION STATION:				
9/21/91	73	1		1 Steel Rails				album cut
				from the album *I've Got That Old Feeling* on Rounder 0275				
12/3/94+	7	20		2 Somewhere In The Vicinity Of The Heart *Damed If I Don't*		$3		Liberty 18484
				SHENANDOAH With Alison Krauss				
2/25/95	3	20		3 When You Say Nothing At All S:2 *Charlotte's In North Carolina*		$3	■	BNA 64277
				CMA Award: Single of the Year				
7/15/95	49	13		4 Baby, Now That I've Found You ....S:15 *(same version)*		$3	■	Rounder 4601
				#11 Pop hit for The Foundations in 1968				
5/24/97	73	2		5 Find My Way Back To My Heart				album cut
				from the album *So Long So Wrong* on Rounder 0365				
12/13/97+	34	13		6 It's Not Over *Useless*		$3		Decca 72032
				MARK CHESNUTT (Featuring Vince Gill and Alison Krauss)				
	★374★			**KRISTOFFERSON, Kris** '73				
				Born on 6/22/36 in Brownsville, Texas. Singer/songwriter/guitarist. Married to **Rita Coolidge** from 1973-80. Starred in many movies. 1)Why Me 2)Highwayman 3)Desperados Waiting For A Train				
4/22/72	70	2		1 Josie *Border Lord*	63	$6		Monument 8536
4/7/73	❶¹	20	●	2 Why Me *Help Me*	16	$6		Monument 8571
				Rita Coolidge and Larry Gatlin (backing vocals)				
12/22/73+	92	5		3 A Song I'd Like To Sing ....*From The Bottle To The Bottom*	49	$5	■	A&M 1475
				KRIS KRISTOFFERSON & RITA COOLIDGE				
3/23/74	98	2		4 Loving Arms *I'm Down (But I Keep Falling)*	86	$5		A&M 1498
				KRIS KRISTOFFERSON & RITA COOLIDGE				
12/28/74+	87	4		5 Rain *What'cha Gonna Do*		$5		Monument 8630
				KRIS KRISTOFFERSON & RITA COOLIDGE				
1/5/80	91	5		6 Prove It To You One More Time Again ....*Fallen Angel*		$4		Columbia 11160
4/18/81	68	7		7 Nobody Loves Anybody Anymore *Maybe You Heard*		$4		Columbia 60507
11/3/84	46	11		8 How Do You Feel About Foolin' Around *Eye Of The Storm*		$4		Columbia 04652
				WILLIE NELSON & KRIS KRISTOFFERSON				
5/18/85	❶¹	20		9 Highwayman S:❶¹ / A:❶¹ *The Human Condition*		$4	■	Columbia 04881
				WAYLON JENNINGS/WILLIE NELSON/JOHNNY CASH/KRIS KRSITOFFERSON				
9/14/85	15	18		10 Desperados Waiting For A Train..... S:15 / A:16 *The Twentieth Century Is Almost Over*		$4		Columbia 05594
				WAYLON JENNINGS/WILLIE NELSON/JOHNNY CASH/KRIS KRISTOFFERSON				
2/28/87	67	6		11 They Killed Him ....*Anthem '84*		$3		Mercury 888345
3/3/90	25	14		12 Silver Stallion ....*American Remains*		$3		Columbia 73233
				WAYLON JENNINGS/WILLIE NELSON/JOHNNY CASH/KRIS KRISTOFFERSON				
				KUNKEL, Leah — see TAYLOR, Livingston				
				# L				
				LaBEEF, Sleepy '71				
				Born Thomas LaBeff on 7/20/35 in Smackover, Arkansas. Singer/songwriter/guitarist.				
4/13/68	73	3		1 Every Day ....*If I Go Right I'm Wrong*		$10		Columbia 44455
6/19/71	67	5		2 Blackland Farmer ....*Got You On My Mind*		$10		Plantation 74
				LACE, Bobbi '89				
				Born Laura Smith in Florida. Model/actress/singer. Acted in the movie *Scarface*.				
3/29/86	94	2		1 You've Been My Rock For Ages		$5		GBS 730
6/13/87	79	4		2 Skin Deep		$5	■	615 1008
12/19/87	88	3		3 There's A Real Woman In Me		$5	■	615 1010
3/5/88	89	2		4 Another Woman's Man		$5		615 1011
5/28/88	69	5		5 Song In My Heart		$6		615 1014
				MARK GRAY and BOBBI LACE				
8/20/88	77	3		6 If Hearts Could Talk		$5		615 1012
12/17/88+	70	5		7 It's Gonna Be Love		$6		615 1016
				MARK GRAY and BOBBI LACE				
6/24/89	95	2		8 Son Of A Preacher Man		$5		615 1017
				#10 Pop hit for Dusty Springfield in 1969				
	★328★			**LA COSTA** '74				
				Born LaCosta Tucker on 4/6/51 in Seminole, Texas. Sister of **Tanya Tucker**. 1)Get On My Love Train 2)He Took Me For A Ride 3)Western Man				
4/20/74	25	15		1 I Wanta Get To You ....*That's What Your Love Has Done*		$5		Capitol 3856
9/14/74	3	17		2 Get On My Love Train *I Can Feel Love Growing*		$5		Capitol 3945
2/15/75	10	13		3 He Took Me For A Ride *Sugarman*		$5		Capitol 4022

DEBUT	PEAK	WKS	Gold	A-side (Chart Hit)..B-side	Pop	$	Pic	Label & Number
				LA COSTA — Cont'd				
6/7/75	19	12		4 **This House Runs On Sunshine** ....*Ain't It Good*		$5		Capitol 4082
9/27/75	11	14		5 **Western Man** ....*Rescue Me*		$5		Capitol 4139
1/31/76	28	9		6 **I Just Got A Feeling** ....*Let's Talk It Over*		$5		Capitol 4209
5/15/76	23	12		7 **Lovin' Somebody On A Rainy Night** ....*The Best Of My Love*		$5		Capitol 4264
9/11/76	37	10		8 **What'll I Do** ....*Your Love*		$5		Capitol 4327
5/7/77	75	7		9 **We're All Alone** ....*I Second That Emotion*		$5		Capitol 4414
11/26/77	100	1		10 **Jessie And The Light**.....................................*I Still Love You*		$5		Capitol 4495
2/25/78	79	7		11 **Even Cowgirls Get The Blues** ....*Alice, Texas*		$5		Capitol 4541
6/3/78	94	3		12 **#1 With A Heartache** ....*Take Your Love Away*		$4		Capitol 4577
				written and first recorded by Neil Sedaka on his 1976 album *Steppin' Out*				
5/17/80	68	6		13 **Changing All The Time** ....*Had To Fall In Love*		$4		Capitol 4830
2/27/82	48	9		14 **Love Take It Easy On Me**.....................*The Best Is Yet To Come*		$4		Elektra 47414
				LaCOSTA TUCKER				
				LaFLEUR, Don **'88**				
10/8/88	97	2		**Beggars Can't Be Choosers**		$6		Worth 102
				LaMASTER, Don **'89**				
3/11/89	94	1		**My Rose Is Blue** ....*Key's In The Mailbox*		$6		K-Ark 1046
				LANA RAE — see RAE				
				LANCE, Lynda K. **'71**				
				Born in 1949 in Smithfield, Pennsylvania.				
11/1/69	59	5		1 **A Woman's Side Of Love** ....*That's All I Want From You*		$6		Royal American 290
1/30/71	46	6		2 **My Guy** *Weakness Of A Woman*		$6		Royal American 24
				#1 Pop hit for Mary Wells in 1964				
8/21/71	74	2		3 **Will You Love Me Tomorrow**.....................................*Bad Water*		$6		Royal American 35
				#1 Pop hit for The Shirelles in 1961				
8/11/73	77	5		4 **You, You, You**.....................*I've Just Gotta Feel Like A Woman Tonight*		$6		Triune 7207
				#1 Pop hit for The Ames Brothers in 1953				
10/23/76	93	5		5 **Say You Love Me**		$6		Gar-Pax 081
				#11 Pop hit for Fleetwood Mac in 1976				
1/13/79	78	4		6 **I Hate The Way Our Love Is**.....................................		$6		Vista 101
				JIMMY PETERS and LYNDA K. LANCE				
4/28/79	98	3		7 **First Class Fool**		$6		Vista 106
				JIMMIE PETERS/LYNDA K. LANCE				
				LANDERS, Dave **'49**				
				Singer/songwriter/guitarist. Uncle of **Rich Landers**.				
7/9/49	10	7		**Before You Call** *S:10 / J:12 Is There Any Need To Worry*		$15		MGM 10427
				LANDERS, Rich **'81**				
				Born in St. Louis. Singer/songwriter/guitarist/pianist. Nephew of **Dave Landers**.				
3/28/81	41	10		1 **Friday Night Feelin'** ....*The Lady Waiting At Home*		$5		Ovation 1166
7/11/81	40	9		2 **Hold On** ....*Honky Tonkin' Lover*		$5		Ovation 1173
12/19/81+	52	9		3 **Lay Back Down And Love Me** ....*Your Bedroom Eyes*		$5		AMI 1301
6/12/82	74	5		4 **Pull My String** ....*Friday Night Feeling*		$5		AMI 1305
1/29/83	40	10		5 **Take It All** *What Will I Do Without You*		$5		AMI 1311
9/10/83	68	5		6 **Every Breath You Take**		$5		AMI 1316
				#1 Pop hit for the Police in 1983				
	★228★			**LANE, Cristy** **'80**				
				Born Eleanor Johnston on 1/8/40 in Peoria, Illinois. Singer/songwriter. Married Lee Stoller in 1960. Stoller started the LS record label in 1976.				
				1)One Day At A Time 2)I Just Can't Stay Married To You 3)Let Me Down Easy 4)Penny Arcade 5)Sweet Sexy Eyes				
2/12/77	52	10		1 **Tryin' To Forget About You** ....*By The Way*		$5		LS 110
6/4/77	53	7		2 **Sweet Deceiver**.....................................*Walk On Baby*		$5		LS 121
8/20/77	7	16		3 **Let Me Down Easy** *This Is The First Time (I've Seen The Last Time On Your Face)*		$5		LS 131
12/17/77+	16	13		4 **Shake Me I Rattle** ....*Pretty Paper*		$5		LS 148
4/1/78	10	14		5 **I'm Gonna Love You Anyway** *I Can't Tell You*		$5		LS 156
7/22/78	7	14		6 **Penny Arcade** *Somebody's Baby*		$5		LS 167
12/2/78+	5	16		7 **I Just Can't Stay Married To You** *Rainsong*		$5		LS 169
5/5/79	10	14		8 **Simple Little Words** *He Believes In Me*		$4		United Artists 1304
				first released on LS 172 in 1979 ($5)				
8/25/79	17	11		9 **Slippin' Up, Slippin' Around** ....*He's Back In Town*		$4		United Artists 1314
12/15/79+	16	13		10 **Come To My Love** ....*Love Lies*		$4		United Artists 1328
3/29/80	❶¹	18		11 **One Day At A Time** *I Knew The Mason*		$4		United Artists 1342
8/16/80	8	14		12 **Sweet Sexy Eyes** *Maybe I'm Thinkin'*		$4		United Artists 1369
1/17/81	17	14		13 **I Have A Dream**.....................................*Rio Grande*		$3	■	Liberty 1396
				first recorded by Abba on their 1979 *Voulez-Vous* album				
5/2/81	21	13		14 **Love To Love You** ....*Everything I Own*		$3		Liberty 1406
10/10/81	38	10		15 **Cheatin' Is Still On My Mind** ....*Just A Mile From Nowhere*		$3		Liberty 1432
1/9/82	22	14		16 **Lies On Your Lips** ....*I've Really Got The Blues*		$3		Liberty 1443
5/8/82	52	8		17 **Fragile--Handle With Care** ....*Tangerine*		$3		Liberty 1461
11/13/82	81	3		18 **The Good Old Days** ....*Do I Dare*		$3		Liberty 1483
7/23/83	63	7		19 **I've Come Back (To Say I Love You One More Time)**.....................*Now The Day Is Over*		$3		Liberty 1501
10/29/83	80	4		20 **Footprints In The Sand** ....*Miracle Maker* [S]		$3		Liberty 1508

LANE, Cristy — Cont'd

DEBUT	PEAK	WKS	A-side	B-side	$	Label & Number
5/9/87	88	2	21 I Wanna Wake Up With You/			
		2	22 He's Got The Whole World In His Hands		$4	LS 1987

#1 Pop hit for Laurie London in 1958

LANE, Jerry "Max" '67
Singer/songwriter/guitarist from Fort Worth, Texas.

DEBUT	PEAK	WKS	A-side	B-side	$	Label & Number
7/1/67	49	6	1 Keeping Up Appearances	You've Gotta Be The Greatest	$8	Chart 1425

LYNN ANDERSON & JERRY LANE

DEBUT	PEAK	WKS	A-side	B-side	$	Label & Number
11/16/74	63	8	2 Right Out Of This World	Fine As Wine	$5	ABC 12031
6/14/75	81	5	3 I've Got A Lotta Missin' You To Do............................	Back On My Feeet Again	$5	ABC 12091
4/23/83	87	2	4 When The Music Stops		$6	Stockyard 1000
12/17/83	96	3	5 I've Got A Lot Of Missin' You To Do..............................	[R]	$6	Stockyard 1003

also see #5 below
new version of #3 above

LANE, Red '71
Born Hollis DeLaughter on 2/9/39 in Bogalusa, Louisiana. Singer/songwriter/guitarist.

DEBUT	PEAK	WKS	A-side	B-side	$	Label & Number
4/24/71	32	11	1 The World Needs A Melody	The Barker Store	$6	RCA Victor 9970
10/30/71	68	2	2 Set The World On Fire (With Love)..............	They Don't Make Love Like They Used To	$6	RCA Victor 0534
1/22/72	66	5	3 Throw A Rope Around The Wind	Singeree	$6	RCA Victor 0616
7/8/72	65	3	4 It Was Love While It Lasted	Lovin', Likin' Kind	$6	RCA Victor 0721

from the movie Going Home starring Robert Mitchum

LANE, Terri '73
Born in Joelton, Tennessee. Female jingle singer.

DEBUT	PEAK	WKS	A-side	B-side	$	Label & Number
3/24/73	37	11	1 Daisy May (And Daisy May Not)......................................	Gonna Be Alright Now	$6	Monument 8565
10/20/73	98	2	2 Be Certain...	Brand New Woman	$6	Monument 8582
5/25/74	94	3	3 Mockingbird..	Let It Be Me	$6	Monument 8610

TERRI LANE & JIMMY NALL
#5 Pop hit for Carly Simon & James Taylor in 1974

LANE, Trinity — see TRINITY

LANE BROTHERS, The '81
Vocal trio from New York City: brothers Pete, Frank and Art Loconto.

DEBUT	PEAK	WKS	A-side	B-side	$	Label & Number
3/28/81	83	4	Marianne	(You've Gotta) Believe In America	$7	FXL 0026

new version of their #64 Pop hit from 1957

lang, k.d. '88
Born Kathryn Dawn Lang on 11/2/61 in Consort, Alberta, Canada. Singer/songwriter.

DEBUT	PEAK	WKS	A-side	B-side	$	Label & Number
12/5/87+	42	13	1 Crying	Falling	$3	■ Virgin 99388

ROY ORBISON/k.d. lang
new version of his #2 Pop hit from 1961; from the movie Hiding Out starring Jon Cryer

DEBUT	PEAK	WKS	A-side	B-side	$	Label & Number
5/14/88	21	17	2 I'm Down To My Last Cigarette	S:16 Western Stars	$3	■ Sire 27919
9/17/88	53	8	3 Lock, Stock And Teardrops............................	Don't Let The Stars Get In Your Eyes	$3	■ Sire 27813

k.d. lang and the reclines:

DEBUT	PEAK	WKS	A-side	B-side	$	Label & Number
7/1/89	22	16	4 Full Moon Full Of Love	Wallflower Waltz	$3	■ Sire 22932
11/11/89	55	5	5 Three Days	Trail Of Broken Hearts	$3	■ Sire 22734

written by Willie Nelson

LANG, Kelly '82
Born on 1/10/67 in Oklahoma City; raised in Hendersonville, Tennessee.

DEBUT	PEAK	WKS	A-side	B-side	$	Label & Number
9/25/82	88	2	Lady, Lady	Doctor's Orders	$5	■ Soundwaves 4681

LANSDOWNE, Jerry '89
Singer/songwriter from California.

DEBUT	PEAK	WKS	A-side	B-side	$	Label & Number
4/29/89	98	2	She Had Every Right To Do You Wrong	I Will Carry You	$3	Step One 400

LaPOINTE, Perry '86
Born in Orange, Texas. Singer/songwriter/guitarist.

DEBUT	PEAK	WKS	A-side	B-side	$	Label & Number
6/21/86	64	5	1 New Shade Of Blue		$5	Door Knob 249
10/18/86	92	2	2 You're A Better Man Than I	New Shade Of Blue	$5	Door Knob 252
12/27/86+	73	5	3 Chosen	You're A Better Man Than I	$5	Door Knob 260
4/11/87	73	4	4 Walk On By...		$5	Door Knob 270
8/1/87	72	4	5 The Power Of A Woman		$5	Door Knob 281
9/17/88	76	4	6 Clean Livin' Folk		$5	Door Knob 307

BOBBY G. RICE and PERRY LaPOINTE

DEBUT	PEAK	WKS	A-side	B-side	$	Label & Number
3/25/89	68	4	7 Open For Suggestions		$5	Door Knob 303
10/14/89	79	3	8 Sweet Memories Of You		$5	Door Knob 333

LARGE, Billy '66

DEBUT	PEAK	WKS	A-side	B-side	$	Label & Number
10/15/66	62	6	The Goodie Wagon...	Big Yellow Peaches	$8	■ Columbia 43741

LARKIN, Billy '75
Born in Huntland, Tennessee. Singer/songwriter/guitarist.
1)Leave It Up To Me 2)The Devil In Mrs. Jones 3)Longing For The High

DEBUT	PEAK	WKS	A-side	B-side	$	Label & Number
1/11/75	22	13	1 Leave It Up To Me	When You Left	$6	Bryan 1010
5/3/75	23	12	2 The Devil In Mrs. Jones	No Reason Why	$6	Bryan 1018
9/6/75	34	10	3 Indian Giver..	Dig A Little Deeper	$6	Bryan 1026
6/5/76	66	7	4 #1 With A Heartache	If Misery Loves Company	$5	Casino 053
8/28/76	36	9	5 Kiss And Say Goodbye	There's A Soul Brother In A Country Band	$5	Casino 076
12/18/76+	88	4	6 Here's To The Next Time	Lonely Woman	$5	Casino 097
10/7/78	67	4	7 My Side Of Town	Ring In My Pocket	$4	Mercury 55040

#1 Pop hit for the Manhattans in 1976

LARKIN, Billy — Cont'd

4/19/80	72	4		8 I Can't Stop Now .... *Lovin' A Lie*		$4		Sunbird 107
1/10/81	35	13		9 20/20 Hindsight ....*Lonely Woman (Love A Lonely Man)*		$4		Sunbird 7557
5/30/81	24	13		10 Longing For The High ....*Is There Nothing Left To Say*		$4		Sunbird 7562

LARRATT, Iris   **'79**
Born in Lloydminster, Saskatchewan; raised in Prince George, British Columbia.

| 7/21/79 | 100 | 1 | | You Can't Make Love To A Memory ....*Country Love Song* | | $5 | | Infinity 50,015 |

LARSON, Nicolette   **'86**
Born on 7/17/52 in Helena, Montana; raised in Kansas City. Died of a cerebral edema on 12/16/97 (age 45). Singer/songwriter/guitarist. Best known for her 1979 pop hit "Lotta Love." Married session drummer Russ Kunkel.

2/9/85	42	12		1 Only Love Will Make It Right.......................................*Blow On Chilly Wind*		$4		MCA 52528
5/4/85	46	11		2 When You Get A Little Lonely.....................................*I Just Keep Falling In Love*		$4		MCA 52571
9/21/85	72	8		3 Building Bridges .... *You Were The One*		$4		MCA 52653
3/22/86	63	5		4 Let Me Be The First..*If I Didn't Love You*		$4		MCA 52797
6/7/86	9	23		5 That's How You Know When Love's Right A:9 / S:11 *As An Eagle Stirreth Her Nest*		$4		MCA 52839
				Steve Wariner (guest vocal)				
10/11/86	49	8		6 That's More About Love (Than I Wanted To Know)............*Captured By Love*		$4		MCA 52937

LATHAM, Buddy   **'88**
Born in Cookville, Tennessee. Singer/songwriter/drummer.

| 9/3/88 | 97 | 2 | | (She Likes) Warm Summer Days...*Higher Roller* | | $6 | | Prairie Dust 8853 |

LAUDERDALE, Jim   **'88**
Born on 4/11/57 in Statesville, North Carolina.

| 12/17/88 | 86 | 3 | | Stay Out Of My Arms ....*Highways Through My Home* | | $3 | | Epic 08113 |

LAWRENCE, Tracy ★115★   **'93**
Born on 1/27/68 in Atlanta, Texas; raised in Foreman, Arkansas. Singer/songwriter/guitarist.

    1)Time Marches On 2)Alibis 3)If The Good Die Young 4)Sticks And Stones 5)Can't Break It To My Heart

11/9/91+	**❶**[1]	20		1 Sticks And Stones	*Paris, TN*	$3		Atlantic 87588
2/8/92	3	20		2 Today's Lonely Fool				album cut
6/20/92	4	20		3 Runnin' Behind				album cut
10/10/92+	8	20		4 Somebody Paints The Wall				album cut
				above 3 from the album *Sticks And Stones* on Atlantic 82326				
2/20/93	**❶**[2]	20		5 Alibis	*(album snippets)*	72	$3	▪	Atlantic 87372
6/5/93	**❶**[1]	20		6 Can't Break It To My Heart	*(album snippets)*		$3	▪	Atlantic 87330
9/4/93	**❶**[1]	20		7 My Second Home	*(album snippets)*		$3	▪	Atlantic 87312
2/5/94	**❶**[2]	20		8 If The Good Die Young					album cut
				from the album *Alibis* on Atlantic 82483				
5/28/94	7	20		9 Renegades, Rebels And Rogues					album cut
				from the movie *Maverick* starring Mel Gibson and Jodie Foster (soundtrack on Atlantic 82595)				
9/10/94	2[1]	20		10 I See It Now	*(album snippets)*	84	$3	▪	Atlantic 87199
12/31/94+	2[2]	20		11 As Any Fool Can See	*(album snippets)*		$3	▪	Atlantic 87180
4/15/95	**❶**[1]	20		12 Texas Tornado/					
7/29/95	2[1]	20		13 If The World Had A Front Porch	*S:25*		$3	▪	Atlantic 87119
12/16/95+	4	20		14 If You Loved Me					album cut
3/23/96	**❶**[3]	20		15 Time Marches On					album cut
				above 2 from the album *Time Marches On* on Atlantic 82866				
7/27/96	2[1]	20		16 Stars Over Texas	*S:13 (album snippets)*		$3	▪	Atlantic 87052
11/2/96+	2[2]	20		17 Is That A Tear	*S:7 (album snippets)*	104	$3	▪	Atlantic 87020
2/22/97	2[1]	20		18 Better Man, Better Off	*S:4 (album snippets)*	108	$3	▪	Atlantic 83004
5/31/97	4	20		19 How A Cowgirl Says Goodbye					album cut
9/20/97	26	13		20 The Coast Is Clear..					album cut
				above 2 from the album *The Coast Is Clear* on Atlantic 82985				

LAWRENCE, Vicki   **'73**
Born on 5/26/49 in Inglewood, California. Regular on Carol Burnett's CBS-TV series from 1967-78. Also starred in TV's *Mama's Family*, 1982-87. Married songwriter/singer **Bobby Russell** in 1972.

| 4/28/73 | 36 | 8 | ● | The Night The Lights Went Out In Georgia ....*Dime A Dance* | **❶**[2] | $5 | | Bell 45,303 |

LAWSON, Janet   **'70**

| 7/25/70 | 74 | 2 | | Two Little Rooms ....*Dindi* | 124 | $6 | | United Artists 50671 |

LAY, Rodney, and The Wild West   **'82**
Born on 2/13/40 in Coffeyville, Kansas. Singer/bassist. Regular on TV's *Hee Haw* from 1980-87. Musical director for **Roy Clark** from 1980-87. The Wild West consisted of Vernon Sandusky (guitar), Troy Klontz (steel guitar), Shelby Eicher and Kenny Putnam (fiddles), John French (keyboards) and Terrell Glaze (drums).

5/30/81	85	4		1 Seven Days Come Sunday...*Close*		$5		Sun 1164
				RODNEY LAY				
4/24/82	72	5		2 Happy Country Birthday Darling ....*Her Memories Faster Than Me*		$5		Churchill 94001
8/14/82	45	11		3 I Wish I Had A Job To Shove	*The Way I Feel Tonight*		$5	■	Churchill 94005
1/8/83	53	8		4 You Could've Heard A Heart Break ....*Hollywood & Wine*		$5		Churchill 94012

LAY, Rodney, and The Wild West — Cont'd

DEBUT	PEAK	WKS	A-side	B-side	Pop	$	PIC	Label & Number
5/14/83	64	5	5 Marylee	Blue With Envy		$5	■	Churchill 94020
11/29/86	79	3	6 Walk Softly On The Bridges	Ten Toes Up, Ten Toes Down		$5		Evergreen 1046

RODNEY LAY

LEAPY LEE '68
Born Lee Graham on 7/2/42 in Eastbourne, England. Male singer/actor.

10/19/68	11	15	1 Little Arrows	Time Will Tell	16	$7		Decca 32380
3/21/70	55	4	2 Good Morning	Teresa		$7		Decca 32625
11/8/75	82	5	3 Every Road Leads Back To You	Honey Go Drift Away		$5		MCA 40470

LEATHERWOOD, Bill '60

7/11/60	11	13	The Long Walk			$15		Country Jubilee 539

LEATHERWOOD, Patti '77
Born Patti DiAngelo in 1950 in Cleveland. Singer/songwriter.

12/18/76+	79	7	1 It Should Have Been Easy	Super Love		$5		Epic 50303
7/30/77	98	1	2 Feels So Much Better	Burning Love		$5		Epic 50409

LeBEAU, Tim '88

10/22/88	98	1	Playing With Matches			$7		Rose Hill 001

LEBSOCK, Jack — see GRAYSON, Jack

LEDFORD, Susan '89
Female singer from Fort Payne, Alabama.

8/5/89	81	4	Ancient History			$6		Project One 6189

LeDOUX, Chris ★370★ '92
Born on 10/2/48 in Biloxi, Mississippi; raised in Austin, Texas. Singer/songwriter/guitarist. Also a successful rodeo performer.
1)Whatcha Gonna Do With A Cowboy 2)Cadillac Ranch 3)For Your Love

4/14/79	99	1	1 Lean, Mean And Hungry			$5		Lucky Man 10270
11/17/79	98	3	2 Cabello Diablo (Devil Horse)	Point Me Back Home		$5		Lucky Man 6520
8/23/80	96	2	3 Ten Seconds In The Saddle	Dirt & Sweat Cowboy		$5		Lucky Man 6834
7/6/91	63	10	4 This Cowboy's Hat					album cut
1/4/92	69	5	5 Workin' Man's Dollar					album cut
			above 2 from the album Western Underground on Capitol 96499					
5/23/92	72	2	6 Riding For A Fall	Cadillac Cowboy		$3		Liberty 57736
7/25/92	7	20	7 Whatcha Gonna Do With A Cowboy	Western Skies		$3		Liberty 57885
			Garth Brooks (backing vocal)					
11/7/92+	18	20	8 Cadillac Ranch	Call Of The Wild		$3		Liberty 56787
2/20/93	52	10	9 Look At You Girl	Little Long-Haired Outlaw		$3		Liberty 56952
6/26/93	54	6	10 Under This Old Hat	Cowboys Like A Little Rock And Roll		$3		Liberty 17443
9/11/93	61	6	11 Every Time I Roll The Dice	Wild And Wooly		$3		Liberty 17638
12/25/93+	50	13	12 For Your Love	Get Back On That Pony		$3		Liberty 17714
8/27/94	71	3	13 Honky Tonk World	Sons Of The Pioneers		$3	▌	Liberty 18090
1/21/95	67	8	14 Tougher Than The Rest					album cut
			written and first recorded by Bruce Springsteen on his 1987 Tunnel of Love album; from the album Haywire on Liberty 28770					
7/1/95	68	3	15 Dallas Days And Fort Worth Nights	Big Love		$3		Liberty 18555
4/20/96	71	9	16 Gravitational Pull	Five Dollar Fine		$3		Capitol 19039
2/8/97	65	1	17 When I Say Forever	Stampede		$3		Capitol 19513

LEE, Billy — see NUNN, Earl

LEE, Brenda ★145★ '74
Born Brenda Mae Tarpley on 12/11/44 in Lithonia, Georgia. Known as "Little Miss Dynamite." Charted 55 pop hits from 1957-73. Inducted into the Country Music Hall of Fame in 1997.

1)Big Four Poster Bed 2)Nobody Wins 3)Sunday Sunrise 4)Wrong Ideas 5)Rock On Baby

4/6/57	15	1	1 One Step At A Time	S:15 Fairyland	43	$25		Decca 30198
2/15/69	50	11	2 Johnny One Time	I Must Have Been Out Of My Mind	41	$7	■	Decca 32428
8/7/71	30	13	3 If This Is Our Last Time	Everybody's Reaching Out For Someone		$6		Decca 32848
1/29/72	37	12	4 Misty Memories	I'm A Memory		$6		Decca 32918
7/8/72	45	10	5 Always On My Mind	That Ain't Right		$6		Decca 32975
2/17/73	5	15	6 Nobody Wins	We Had A Good Thing Going	70	$5		MCA 40003
8/18/73	6	15	7 Sunday Sunrise	Must I Believe		$5		MCA 40107
1/12/74	6	15	8 Wrong Ideas	Something For A Rainy Day		$5		MCA 40171
7/13/74	4	14	9 Big Four Poster Bed	Castles In The Sand		$5		MCA 40262
11/2/74+	6	14	10 Rock On Baby	More Than A Memory		$5		MCA 40318
4/12/75	8	13	11 He's My Rock	Feel Free		$5		MCA 40385
8/9/75	23	12	12 Bringing It Back	Papa's Knee		$5		MCA 40442
2/7/76	38	9	13 Find Yourself Another Puppet	What I Had With You		$5		MCA 40511
7/17/76	77	5	14 Brother Shelton	Now He's Coming Home		$5		MCA 40584
11/13/76	41	9	15 Takin' What I Can Get	Your Favorite Wornout Nightmare's Coming Home		$5		MCA 40640
3/19/77	78	5	16 Ruby's Lounge	Oklahoma Superstar		$5		MCA 40683

DEBUT	PEAK	WKS	Gold	A-side (Chart Hit)..B-side	Pop	$	Pic	Label & Number
				LEE, Brenda — Cont'd				
6/17/78	62	6		17 Left-Over Love................................*Could It Be Love I Found Tonight*		$4		Elektra 45492
10/20/79	8	15		18 Tell Me What It's Like *Let Your Love Fall Back On Me*		$4		MCA 41130
2/16/80	10	12		19 The Cowgirl And The Dandy *Do You Wanna Spend The Night*		$4		MCA 41187
7/12/80	49	7		20 Don't Promise Me Anything (Do It) ....*You Only Broke My Heart*		$4		MCA 41270
9/20/80	9	14		21 Broken Trust *Right Behind The Rain*		$4		MCA 41322
				The Oak Ridge Boys (guest vocals)				
1/31/81	26	10		22 Every Now And Then ....*He'll Play The Music (But You Can't Make Him Dance)*		$4		MCA 51047
6/6/81	67	5		23 Fool, Fool...*Right Behind The Rain*		$4		MCA 51113
8/15/81	75	5		24 Enough For You ....*What Am I Gonna Do*		$4		MCA 51154
10/24/81	32	13		25 Only When I Laugh ....*Too Many Nights Alone*		$4		MCA 51195
				from the movie starring Marsha Mason				
1/30/82	33	11		26 From Levis To Calvin Klein Jeans ....*I Know A Lot About Love*		$4		MCA 51230
6/19/82	70	6		27 Keeping Me Warm For You ....*There's More To Me Than What You Can See*		$4		MCA 52060
11/6/82	78	4		28 Just For The Moment..........................*Love Letters*		$4		MCA 52124
				The Oak Ridge Boys (guest vocals)				
4/9/83	43	9		29 You're Gonna Love Yourself (In The Morning) ... *What Do You Think About Lovin'*		$4		Monument 03781
				WILLIE NELSON/BRENDA LEE				
9/24/83	75	4		30 Didn't We Do It Good ....*We're So Close*		$4		MCA 52268
8/11/84	22	16		31 A Sweeter Love (I'll Never Know).........................*A Woman's Mind*		$4		MCA 52394
12/22/84+	15	16		32 Hallelujah, I Love You So ....*A:13 / S:15 The Second Time Around*		$4		Epic 04723
				GEORGE JONES with BRENDA LEE				
				#5 R&B hit for Ray Charles in 1956				
8/24/85	54	9		33 I'm Takin' My Time ....*That Was The Way It Was Then*		$4		MCA 52654
12/21/85+	50	12		34 Why You Been Gone So Long ....*He Can't Make Your Kind Of Love*		$4	■	MCA 52720
12/27/97	62	2		35 Rockin' Around The Christmas Tree ....*Papa Noël* [X]		$3		MCA 54292
				#14 Pop hit in 1960 (recorded in 1958)				
				LEE, Chandy **'79**				
				Female singer.				
7/7/79	100	2		She's Still Around ....*Three Riddles*		$6		ODC 548

				LEE, Dickey ★171★ **'75**				
				Born Royden Dickey Lipscombe on 9/21/36 in Memphis. Singer/songwriter/guitarist. Charted five pop hits from 1962-65.				
				1)Rocky 2)9,999,999 Tears 3)Never Ending Song Of Love 4)Angels, Roses, And Rain 5)Ashes Of Love				
6/19/71	55	8		1 The Mahogany Pulpit................................*Everybody's Reaching Out For Someone*		$6		RCA Victor 9988
9/18/71	8	14		2 Never Ending Song Of Love *On The Southbound*		$6		RCA Victor 1013
				#13 Pop hit for Delaney & Bonnie in 1971				
1/22/72	25	13		3 I Saw My Lady ....*What We Used To Hang On To (Is Gone)*		$6		RCA Victor 0623
6/17/72	15	13		4 Ashes Of Love ....*A Kingdom I Call Home*		$6		RCA Victor 0710
10/7/72	31	11		5 Baby, Bye Bye ....*She Thinks I Still Care*		$6		RCA Victor 0798
3/10/73	43	11		6 Crying Over You ....*My World Around You*		$6		RCA Victor 0892
6/30/73	30	7		7 Put Me Down Softly ....*If She Turns Up In Atlanta*		$6		RCA Victor 0980
9/22/73	49	9		8 Sparklin' Brown Eyes ....*A Country Song*		$6		RCA Victor 0082
2/23/74	46	11		9 I Use The Soap ....*Strawberry Women*		$6		RCA Victor 0227
8/17/74	90	4		10 Give Me One Good Reason..........................*Sweet Fever*		$5		RCA Victor 10014
11/30/74+	22	13		11 The Busiest Memory In Town ....*A Way To Go On*		$5		RCA Victor 10091
8/23/75	❶¹	18		12 Rocky *The Closest Thing To You*		$5		RCA Victor 10361
				#9 Pop hit for Austin Roberts in 1975				
1/31/76	9	14		13 Angels, Roses, And Rain *Danna*		$5		RCA Victor 10543
6/5/76	35	10		14 Makin' Love Don't Always Make Love Grow ....*I Never Will Get Over You*		$5		RCA Victor 10684
9/11/76	3	18		15 9,999,999 Tears *I Never Will Get Over You*	52	$5		RCA 10764
3/19/77	20	13		16 If You Gotta Make A Fool Of Somebody ....*My Love Shows Thru*		$5		RCA 10914
				#22 Pop hit for James Ray in 1962				
7/2/77	22	11		17 Virginia, How Far Will You Go ....*My Love Shows Thru*		$5		RCA 11009
10/15/77	21	14		18 Peanut Butter ....*Breezy Was Her Name*		$5		RCA 11125
2/4/78	27	11		19 Love Is A Word ....*I'll Be Leaving Alone*		$5		RCA 11191
7/15/78	49	6		20 My Heart Won't Cry Anymore ....*Danna*		$5		RCA 11294
10/21/78	58	6		21 It's Not Easy ....*I've Been Honky Tonkin' Too Long*		$5		RCA 11389
7/28/79	58	9		22 I'm Just A Heartache Away ....*Midnight Flyer*		$4		Mercury 55068
11/10/79	94	3		23 He's An Old Rock 'N' Roller ....*It Hurts To Be In Love*		$4		Mercury 57005
3/29/80	61	5		24 Don't Look Back..............................*I'm Trustin' A Feelin'*		$4		Mercury 57017
7/26/80	30	12		25 Workin' My Way To Your Heart ....*If You Want Me*		$4		Mercury 57027
11/8/80+	30	12		26 Lost In Love ....*Again*		$4		Mercury 57036
				DICKEY LEE with Kathy Burdick				
				#3 Pop hit for Air Supply in 1980				
6/27/81	37	10		27 Honky Tonk Hearts ....*It's Best I Hit The Road*		$4		Mercury 57052
10/3/81	53	7		28 I Wonder If I Care As Much ....*Further Than A Country Mile*		$4		Mercury 57056
				made the Pop charts as a flip side by The Everly Brothers in 1957				
1/30/82	56	6		29 Everybody Loves A Winner ....*You Won't Be Here Tonight*		$4		Mercury 76129

LEE, Don '82
Singer/songwriter/guitarist.

9/11/82	86	3		**16 Lovin' Ounces To The Pound**............. *All I Ever Wanted Was You (Here Lovin' Me)*		$6		Crescent 103

LEE, Harold '68

4/6/68	56	6		1 **The Two Sides Of Me** ....*Bringing Daddy Home*		$8		Columbia 44458
9/25/71	74	3		2 **Mountain Woman** ....*If I Never Hear Goodbye*		$6		Cartwheel 198

LEE, Johnny ★121★ '80
Born John Lee Ham on 7/3/46 in Texas City, Texas; raised in Alta Loma, Texas. Singer/songwriter/guitarist. Married to actress Charlene Tilton from 1982-84.

> 1)Lookin' For Love 2)One In A Million 3)Bet Your Heart On Me 4)The Yellow Rose
> 5)You Could've Heard A Heart Break

12/27/75+	59	9		1 **Sometimes** ....*Get Off My Back*		$5		ABC/Dot 17603
7/31/76	22	12		2 **Red Sails In The Sunset**......................................*In My Own Way*		$5		GRT 065
				#1 Pop hit for both **Bing Crosby** and **Guy Lombardo** in 1935; #36 Pop hit for The Platters in 1960				
12/4/76+	37	10		3 **Ramblin' Rose** ....*Congratulations*		$5		GRT 096
				#2 Pop hit for **Nat King Cole** in 1962				
5/21/77	15	13		4 **Country Party** ....*This Should Go On Forever*		$5		GRT 125
				same tune as "Garden Party" by **Rick Nelson** with new lyrics				
10/29/77	58	7		5 **Dear Alice** ....*It's Gonna' Be Me*		$5		GRT 137
3/4/78	43	8		6 **This Time** ....*Frisco*		$5		GRT 144
				#6 Pop hit for **Troy Shondell** in 1961				
7/19/80	❶³	14	●	7 **Lookin' For Love** — *Lyin' Eyes*	5	$4	■	Full Moon 47004
				from the movie *Urban Cowboy* starring John Travolta				
10/25/80	❶²	16		8 **One In A Million** — *Anni*	102	$4		Full Moon 47076
2/14/81	3	14		9 **Pickin' Up Strangers** — *Never Lay My Lovin' Down*		$4		Full Moon 47105
4/25/81	52	6		10 **Rode Hard And Put Up Wet** ....*Honky Tonk Wine*		$4		Full Moon 02012
				from the movie *Urban Cowboy* starring John Travolta				
5/30/81	3	16		11 **Prisoner Of Hope** — *Fool For Love*		$4		Full Moon 47138
10/3/81	❶¹	15		12 **Bet Your Heart On Me** — *Highways Run On Forever*	54	$4		Full Moon 47215
1/23/82	10	15		13 **Be There For Me Baby** — *Finally Fallin'*		$4		Full Moon 47301
5/15/82	14	13		14 **When You Fall In Love** ....*Crossfire*		$4		Full Moon 47444
10/9/82	10	18		15 **Cherokee Fiddle** — *You Know Me*		$4		Full Moon 69945
				JOHNNY LEE AND FRIENDS				
				Charlie Daniels and **Michael Martin Murphey** (backing vocals)				
2/5/83	6	18		16 **Sounds Like Love** — *The Deeper We Fall*		$4		Full Moon 69848
6/11/83	2²	22		17 **Hey Bartender** — *Blue Monday*		$4		Full Moon 29605
10/8/83	23	16		18 **My Baby Don't Slow Dance** ....*You've Really Got A Hold On Me*		$3		Warner 29486
2/4/84	❶¹	22		19 **The Yellow Rose/**		$3		Warner 29375
				JOHNNY LEE with Lane Brody				
				same melody as "The Yellow Rose Of Texas" with new lyrics; from the TV series starring Cybill Shepherd				
		3		20 **Say When**		$3		
5/26/84	42	12		21 **One More Shot** ....*The Eyes Of Love*		$3		Warner 29270
8/25/84	❶¹	24		22 **You Could've Heard A Heart Break** — S:❶¹ / A:❶¹ *Waitin' On Ice*		$3		Warner 29206
1/5/85	9	20		23 **Rollin' Lonely** — S:8 / A:9 *Rock It, Billy*		$3		Warner 29110
5/11/85	12	18		24 **Save The Last Chance** — A:11 / S:12 *It Ain't The Leaving*		$3		Warner 29021
10/5/85	19	18		25 **They Never Had To Get Over You** ....A:17 / S:19 *Rock 'N' Roll Money*		$3		Warner 28901
1/25/86	56	9		26 **The Loneliness In Lucy's Eyes (The Life Sue Ellen Is**				
				Living) ....*If I Knew Then What I Know Now*		$3		Warner 28839
				from the TV series *Dallas* starring Larry Hagman				
4/5/86	50	8		27 **I Could Get Used To This** ....*It Ain't The Leaving*		$3		Warner 28747
				JOHNNY LEE & LANE BRODY				
6/3/89	59	6		28 **Maybe I Won't Love You Anymore** ....*Annie*		$3		Curb/MCA 10536
8/19/89	69	5		29 **I'm Not Over You** ....*Anniversary Song*		$3		Curb/MCA 10552
10/14/89	53	8		30 **I Can Be A Heartbreaker, Too**..............................*Anniversary Song*		$3		Curb/MCA 10564
12/23/89+	66	4		31 **You Can't Fly Like An Eagle** ....*By-Pass Row*		$3		Curb 10573

LEE, Joni '76
Born Joni Lee Jenkins in 1957 in Arkansas; raised in Oklahoma City. Daughter of **Conway Twitty**.

12/13/75+	16	12		1 **I'm Sorry Charlie** — *A Little Girl Cried*		$5		MCA 40501
5/15/76	42	9		2 **Angel On My Shoulder**.....................................*Just Lead The Way*		$5		MCA 40553
				#22 Pop hit for **Shelby Flint** in 1961				
7/31/76	62	6		3 **Baby Love** ....*It Really Doesn't Matter Anymore*		$5		MCA 40592
				#1 Pop hit for The Supremes in 1964				
4/23/77	97	2		4 **The Reason Why I'm Here** ....*We Loved*		$5		MCA 40687
1/7/78	94	4		5 **I Love How You Love Me** ....*I Think Of You*		$5		MCA 40826
				#5 Pop hit for The Paris Sisters in 1961				

LEE, Leapy — see LEAPY

DEBUT	PEAK	WKS	Gold	A-side (Chart Hit) ... B-side	Pop	$	Pic	Label & Number
	★338★			**LEE, Robin** '90				
				Born Robin Lee Irwin on 11/7/53 in Nashville. Female singer/songwriter/pianist.				
				1)Black Velvet 2)I'll Take Your Love Anytime 3)Safe In The Arms Of Love				
2/26/83	87	3		1 Turning Back The Covers (Don't Turn Back The Time) .... *Angel In Your Arms*		$5	■	Evergreen 1003
6/11/83	81	3		2 Heart For A Heart		$5		Evergreen 1006
1/7/84	54	10		3 Angel In Your Arms .... *Turning Back The Covers (Don't Turn Back The Time)*		$5		Evergreen 1016
				#6 Pop hit for Hot in 1977				
4/28/84	63	7		4 Want Ads .... *Breaking The Chains*		$5		Evergreen 1018
				#1 Pop hit for Honey Cone in 1971				
8/11/84	62	5		5 Cold In July .... *Breaking The Chains*		$5		Evergreen 1023
12/1/84	71	7		6 I Heard It On The Radio .... *Angel In Your Arms*		$5	■	Evergreen 1026
6/29/85	49	7		7 Paint The Town Blue.. *Angel In Your Arms*		$5		Evergreen 1033
				ROBIN LEE AND LOBO				
11/16/85	44	10		8 Safe In The Arms Of Love		$5		Evergreen 1037
3/29/86	37	12		9 I'll Take Your Love Anytime .... *Between The Lies*		$5		Evergreen 1039
8/2/86	48	8		10 If You're Anything Like Your Eyes		$5		Evergreen 1043
4/23/88	52	8		11 This Old Flame .... *Maybe I Will, Maybe I Won't*		$4	■	Atlantic Amer. 99353
8/20/88	56	7		12 Shine A Light On A Lie .... *I'm Gettin' Good At Bein' Bad*		$4	■	Atlantic Amer. 99307
11/26/88	51	8		13 Before You Cheat On Me Once (You Better Think Twice) .... *Serious Affection*		$4	■	Atlantic Amer. 99264
3/10/90	12	25		14 Black Velvet *Stay With Me*		$3	▮	Atlantic 87979
				#1 Pop hit for Alannah Myles in 1990				
9/1/90	70	2		15 How About Goodbye .... *Younger Love*		$3	▮	Atlantic 87890
11/10/90	67	3		16 Love Letter .... *Every Little Bit Hurts*		$3	▮	Atlantic 87835
7/6/91	51	9		17 Nothin' But You .... *Betrayed*		$3		Atlantic 87681
2/5/94	71	1		18 When Love Comes Callin' .... *Fallin' In Love*		$3	▮	Atlantic 87196
				LEE, T.L. '87				
				Male singer/songwriter/guitarist.				
2/21/87	78	4		A Silent Understanding .... *Hers And Mine*		$4	■	Compleat 164
				T.L. LEE (with Kathy Walker)				
				LEE, Vicki '86				
				Born in Pensacola, Florida.				
11/1/86	93	2		Bluemonia		$6		Sunshine 1400
				LEE, Wilma — see COOPER, Stoney				
				LEE, Woody '95				
				Born on 4/1/68 in Garland, Texas. Singer/songwriter/guitarist.				
3/25/95	46	18		1 Get Over It/				
7/15/95	58	7		2 I Like The Sound Of That		$3	▮	Atlantic 87123
				LeGARDES, The '79				
				Duo of twin brothers Ted and Tom LeGarde. Born on 3/15/31 in MacKay, Australia. Moved to the U.S. in 1957. Worked on **Doye O'Dell**'s *Western Varieties* TV shows in Hollywood. Hosted own TV series on KTLA in Los Angeles.				
6/3/78	88	3		1 True Love .... *25 Years and 15 Days*		$7		Raindrop 012
				#3 Pop hit for **Bing Crosby** & Grace Kelly in 1956				
3/24/79	82	4		2 I Can Almost Touch The Feelin' .... *True Love*		$5		4 Star 1037
10/18/80	92	3		3 Daddy's Makin' Records In Nashville .... *Grady Family Band*		$6		Invitation 101
8/27/88	92	1		4 Crocodile Man (From Walk-About-Creek)...		$6		Bear 194
				LeGARDE TWINS (above 2)				
	★322★			**LEHR, Zella** '78				
				Born on 3/14/51 in Burbank, California. Accomplished juggler/unicyclist. Regular on TV's *Hee-Haw*.				
				1)Two Doors Down 2)Feedin' The Fire 3)Danger, Heartbreak Ahead				
12/17/77+	7	18		1 Two Doors Down *Two Sides To Every Woman*		$4		RCA 11174
5/27/78	31	10		2 When The Fire Gets Hot .... *Can't Help But Wonder*		$4		RCA 11265
8/26/78	20	12		3 Danger, Heartbreak Ahead..............*I Can't Imagine Laying Down (With Anyone But You)*		$4		RCA 11359
1/6/79	24	10		4 Play Me A Memory .... *Expert At Everything*		$4		RCA 11433
5/5/79	59	5		5 Only Diamonds Are Forever .... *Music Maker*		$4		RCA 11543
7/14/79	34	10		6 Once In A Blue Moon ....*All He Did Was Tell Me Lies (To Try To Woo Me)*		$4		RCA 11648
12/15/79+	26	12		7 Love Has Taken Its' Time .... *If You Only Knew*		$4		RCA 11754
4/12/80	25	12		8 Rodeo Eyes .... *You Look So Good On Me*		$4		RCA 11953
10/11/80	34	10		9 Love Crazy Love .... *It Feels Good Enough To Call It Love*		$4		RCA 12073
8/15/81	16	15		10 Feedin' The Fire .... *What A Man, My Man Is*		$4		Columbia 02431
1/23/82	56	6		11 Blue Eyes Don't Make An Angel.....................*Doin' A Lot (Of Not Gettin' Over You)*		$4		Columbia 02677
9/25/82	85	2		12 What A Way To Spend The Night .... *Ain't It Funny*		$4		Columbia 03164
3/19/83	86	4		13 Haven't We Loved Somewhere Before .... *Get Out Of My Heart*		$4		Columbia 03593
9/29/84	72	5		14 All Heaven Is About To Break Loose .... *I'll Get You Back*		$4		Compleat 129
2/9/85	66	6		15 You Bring Out The Lover In Me .... *I'll Get You Back*		$4		Compleat 136
				LEIGH, Bonnie '86				
				Born in Ashland, Maine.				
12/6/86	76	3		1 Runaway		$6		R.C.P. 010
				#1 Pop hit for Del Shannon in 1961				
7/25/87	80	3		2 That's When (You Can Call Me Your Own)		$6		R.C.P. 016
12/19/87	77	3		3 Moon Walking		$6		R.C.P. 020
				LEIGH, Richard '83				
				Born on 5/26/51 in McLean, Virginia. Singer/prolific songwriter.				
8/13/83	65	5		Ain't Gonna Worry My Mind................................... *Whole New World*		$4		Capitol 5247

DEBUT	PEAK	WKS	Gold	A-side (Chart Hit) / B-side	Pop	$	Pic	Label & Number
				LEIGH, Shannon '82				
				Female singer.				
10/2/82	90	2		Rock N' Roll Stories		$6		AMI 1308
				LEMMON, Dave '83				
				Born in Preston, Idaho.				
1/29/83	89	2		Too Good To Be Through ....Maggie		$7		SCP 9781
				LESTER, Chester '79				
				Born in Charleston, West Virginia.				
2/10/79	86	4		Mama, Make Up My Room ....High On Love		$6		Con Brio 148
	★236★			**LEWIS, Bobby** '66				
				Born on 5/9/42 in Hodgenville, Kentucky. Singer/songwriter/lute player.				
				1)How Long Has It Been 2)From Heaven To Heartache 3)Love Me And Make It All Better 4)Hello Mary Lou 5)Too Many Memories				
10/15/66	6	18		1 How Long Has It Been Easy To Say Hard To Do		$8		United Artists 50067
3/25/67	49	7		2 Two Of The Usual ....Your B.A.B.Y. Baby Don't Love You		$8		United Artists 50133
6/17/67	12	14		3 Love Me And Make It All Better...........My Tears Don't Care (They'll Fall Anywhere)		$8		United Artists 50161
10/21/67	26	12		4 I Doubt It...........Laughing Girl She Not Happy		$8		United Artists 50208
3/23/68	29	10		5 Ordinary Miracle ....These Are Things I Miss		$8	■	United Artists 50263
7/27/68	10	16		6 From Heaven To Heartache Only For Me		$8		United Artists 50327
12/28/68+	27	13		7 Each And Every Part Of Me ....My (Is Such A Lonely Word)		$8		United Artists 50476
5/31/69	41	8		8 Til Something Better Comes Along ....I'm Only A Man		$8		United Artists 50528
9/13/69	25	10		9 Things For You And I ....Somebody Lied To Me		$8		United Artists 50573
1/17/70	41	10		10 I'm Going Home ....I May Never Be Free		$8		United Artists 50620
5/30/70	14	16		11 Hello Mary Lou...........Love, Wonderful Love		$8		United Artists 50668
				#9 Pop hit for Rick Nelson in 1961				
11/14/70	67	3		12 Simple Days And Simple Ways ....Love's Garden		$7		United Artists 50719
7/31/71	51	7		13 If I Had You...........Doggone This Heartache (And That Neon Sign)		$7		United Artists 50791
11/27/71	45	9		14 Today's Teardrops...........Love's Satisfaction		$7		United Artists 50850
				written by Gene Pitney; #54 Pop hit for Rick Nelson in 1964				
7/14/73	95	4		15 Here With You...........Where Happiness Is		$6		Ace of Hearts 0466
10/6/73	21	15		16 Too Many Memories ....With Meaning		$6		Ace of Hearts 0472
2/16/74	32	10		17 I Never Get Through Missing You...........Lady Lover		$6		Ace of Hearts 0480
4/27/74	47	12		18 Lady Lover ....Never Get Through Missing You		$6		GRT 007
10/12/74	78	8		19 I See Love ....Your Love		$6		GRT 008
6/21/75	71	8		20 Let Me Take Care Of You ....Where Happiness Is		$6		Ace of Hearts 0502
11/22/75	79	5		21 It's So Nice To Be With You		$6		Ace of Hearts 7503
				#4 Pop hit for Gallery in 1972				
9/11/76	52	7		22 For Your Love		$6		RPA 7603
				#13 Pop hit for Ed Townsend in 1958				
1/8/77	74	5		23 I'm Getting High Remembering...........With Meaning		$6		RPA 7613
5/7/77	81	6		24 What A Diff'rence A Day Made...........I Can Feel It		$6		RPA 7622
				#8 Pop hit for Dinah Washington in 1959				
4/21/79	39	10		25 She's Been Keepin' Me Up Nights ....I Keep Falling In Love With You		$5		Capricorn 0318
7/6/85	91	3		26 Love Is An Overload		$5		HME 04853
	★381★			**LEWIS, Hugh X.** '65				
				Born Hubert Brad Lewis on 12/7/32 in Yeaddiss, Kentucky. Singer/songwriter/guitarist. Acted in the movies 40-Acre Feud, Gold Guitar and Cottonpickin' Chicken-Pluckers.				
				1)What I Need Most 2)I'd Better Call The Law On Me 3)Out Where The Ocean Meets The Sky				
12/26/64+	21	16		1 What I Need Most Too Late		$7		Kapp 622
9/4/65	32	6		2 Out Where The Ocean Meets The Sky ....Talking To A Bottle		$7		Kapp 673
12/18/65+	30	10		3 I'd Better Call The Law On Me ....Talk Me Out Of It		$7		Kapp 717
6/25/66	45	2		4 I'm Losing You (I Can Tell) ....Just Before Dawn		$7		Kapp 757
10/15/66	61	2		5 Wish Me A Rainbow ....You Belong To My Heart		$7		Kapp 771
				from the movie This Property Is Condemned starring Robert Redford				
7/1/67	38	11		6 You're So Cold (I'm Turning Blue) ....No Chance For Happiness		$7		Kapp 830
12/9/67+	49	9		7 Wrong Side Of The World...........Your Steppin' Stone		$7		Kapp 868
3/23/68	36	10		8 Evolution And The Bible ....Gone, Gone, Gone		$7		Kapp 895
1/4/69	69	5		9 Tonight We're Calling It A Day ....Sittin' And Thinkin'		$7		Kapp 955
3/29/69	72	6		10 All Heaven Broke Loose ....Some Other Time		$7		Kapp 978
7/26/69	74	2		11 Restless Melissa...........Our Angels Just Aren't Singing Anymore		$7		Kapp 2020
1/17/70	56	6		12 Everything I Love...........Mr. Policeman		$6		Columbia 45047
11/28/70	68	4		13 Blues Sells A Lot Of Booze ....Help Yourself To Me		$6		GRT 28
7/22/78	93	4		14 Love Don't Hide From Me ....I'm Thinking Of You Thinking Of Him		$6		Little Darlin' 7803
4/21/79	92	5		15 What Can I Do (To Make You Love Me)...........Once Before I Die		$6		Little Darlin' 7913
				LEWIS, J.D. '89				
				Singer/songwriter James D. Lewis.				
12/9/89	82	2		My Heart's On Hold		$6	■	Sing Me 43

LEWIS, Jerry Lee ★42★ '72
Born on 9/29/35 in Ferriday, Louisiana. Singer/songwriter/pianist. Married to Myra Gale Brown, his 13-year-old cousin, from 1958-71. Known as "The Killer." Survived several personal setbacks and serious illnesses. Cousin of singer **Mickey Gilley** and TV evangelist Jimmy Swaggart. Brother of **Linda Gail Lewis**. Inducted into the Rock and Roll Hall of Fame in 1986. Early career was documented in the 1989 movie *Great Balls Of Fire* starring Dennis Quaid as Lewis.

1)*Chantilly Lace* 2)*Whole Lot Of Shakin' Going On* 3)*Great Balls Of Fire*
4)*There Must Be More To Love Than This* 5)*Would You Take Another Chance On Me*

DEBUT	PEAK	WKS	Gold		A-side / B-side	Pop	$	Pic	Label & Number
6/17/57	**❶**²	23	●	1	Whole Lot Of Shakin' Going On S:❶²/A:6 *It'll Be Me*	3	$30		Sun 267
12/2/57+	**❶**²	19	●	2	Great Balls Of Fire/ S:❶²/A:4	2⁴	$30		Sun 281
12/23/57+	**4**	10		3	You Win Again A:4 / S:flip	95	$30	■	Sun 281
					written by **Hank Williams**; #13 Pop hit for Tommy Edwards in 1952				
3/17/58	**4**	13		4	Breathless S:4 / A:12 *Down The Line*	7	$30		Sun 288
6/9/58	**9**	10		5	High School Confidential S:9 *Fools Like Me*	21	$30	■	Sun 296
					title song from the movie starring Russ Tamblyn (song introduced by Lewis in the movie)				
10/13/58	**19**	1		6	I'll Make It All Up To You S:19 *Break-Up*	85	$30		Sun 303
5/8/61	**27**	1		7	What'd I Say *Livin' Lovin' Wreck*	30	$25		Sun 356
8/7/61	**22**	5		8	Cold Cold Heart *It Won't Happen With Me*		$25		Sun 364
					also see #51 below				
2/1/64	**36**	2		9	Pen And Paper *Hit The Road Jack* (Pop #103)		$15		Smash 1857
3/9/68	**4**	17		10	Another Place Another Time *Walking The Floor Over You*	97	$10		Smash 2146
6/8/68	**2**²	16		11	What's Made Milwaukee Famous (Has Made A Loser Out Of Me) *All The Good Is Gone*	94	$10		Smash 2164
9/28/68	**2**²	12		12	She Still Comes Around (To Love What's Left Of Me) *Slipping Around*		$10		Smash 2186
12/28/68+	**❶**¹	15		13	To Make Love Sweeter For You *Let's Talk About Us*		$10		Smash 2202
5/24/69	**9**	11		14	Don't Let Me Cross Over *We Live In Two Different Worlds*		$10	■	Smash 2220
					JERRY LEE LEWIS & LINDA GAIL LEWIS				
5/31/69	**3**	15		15	One Has My Name (The Other Has My Heart) *I Can't Stop Loving You*		$10		Smash 2224
8/16/69	**6**	12		16	Invitation To Your Party *I Could Never Be Ashamed Of You*		$10		Sun 1101
					recorded on 8/28/63				
10/4/69	**2**²	13		17	She Even Woke Me Up To Say Goodbye *Echoes*		$10		Smash 2244
11/29/69+	**2**²	16		18	One Minute Past Eternity *Frankie & Johnny*		$10		Sun 1107
					recorded on 8/28/63				
1/10/70	**71**	2		19	Roll Over Beethoven *Secret Places*		$10		Smash 2254
					LINDA GAIL LEWIS & JERRY LEE LEWIS				
					#29 Pop hit for Chuck Berry in 1956				
2/21/70	**2**²	14		20	Once More With Feeling *You Went Out Of Your Way (To Walk On Me)*		$10		Smash 2257
4/25/70	**7**	15		21	I Can't Seem To Say Goodbye *Good Night Irene*		$10		Sun 1115
					recorded on 8/28/63				
8/22/70	**❶**²	15		22	There Must Be More To Love Than This *Home Away From Home*		$8		Mercury 73099
11/21/70+	**11**	12		23	Waiting For A Train (All Around The Watertank) *Big Legged Woman*		$10		Sun 1119
					recorded on 6/5/62; #14 Pop hit for **Jimmie Rodgers** in 1929				
1/30/71	**48**	8		24	In Loving Memories *I Can't Have A Merry Christmas, Mary, (Without You)*		$8		Mercury 73155
3/27/71	**3**	16		25	Touching Home *Woman, Woman (Get Out Of Our Way)*	110	$8		Mercury 73192
6/26/71	**31**	9		26	Love On Broadway *Matchbox*		$10		Sun 1125
					recorded on 8/27/63				
7/24/71	**11**	13		27	When He Walks On You (Like You Have Walked On Me) *Foolish Kind Of Man*		$8		Mercury 73227
11/6/71+	**❶**¹	17		28	Would You Take Another Chance On Me/		$8		Mercury 73248
			15	29	Me And Bobby McGee	40	$8		
					#1 Pop hit for Janis Joplin in 1971				
3/11/72	**❶**³	15		30	Chantilly Lace/	43			
					#6 Pop hit for the Big Bopper in 1958				
			15	31	Think About It Darlin'		$8		Mercury 73273
6/17/72	**11**	11		32	Lonely Weekends *Turn On Your Love Light* (Pop #95)		$8		Mercury 73296
					#22 Pop hit for **Charlie Rich** in 1960				
10/7/72	**14**	13		33	Who's Gonna Play This Old Piano *No Honky Tonks In Heaven*		$8		Mercury 73328
2/17/73	**19**	10		34	No More Hanging On *The Mercy Of A Letter*		$8		Mercury 73361
4/21/73	**20**	11		35	Drinking Wine Spo-Dee O'Dee *Rock & Roll Medley*	41	$8		Mercury 73374
					#2 R&B hit for Stick McGhee in 1949				
8/4/73	**60**	6		36	No Headstone On My Grave *Jack Daniels (Old No. 7)*	104	$8		Mercury 73402
					written by **Charlie Rich**				
9/29/73	**6**	14		37	Sometimes A Memory Ain't Enough *I Think I Need To Pray*		$8		Mercury 73423
2/9/74	**21**	12		38	I'm Left, You're Right, She's Gone *I've Fallen To The Bottom*		$8		Mercury 73452
6/22/74	**18**	12		39	Tell Tale Signs *Cold, Cold Morning Light*		$8		Mercury 73491
10/19/74	**8**	12		40	He Can't Fill My Shoes *Tomorrow Taking Baby Away*		$7		Mercury 73618
2/22/75	**13**	12		41	I Can Still Hear The Music In The Restroom *(Remember Me) I'm The One Who Loves You*		$7		Mercury 73661
6/28/75	**24**	13		42	Boogie Woogie Country Man *I'm Still Jealous Of You*		$7		Mercury 73685
12/6/75	**68**	5		43	A Damn Good Country Song *When I Take My Vacation In Heaven*		$7		Mercury 73729
2/14/76	**58**	6		44	Don't Boogie Woogie *That Kind Of Fool*		$7		Mercury 73763
8/7/76	**6**	15		45	Let's Put It Back Together Again *Jerry Lee's Rock & Roll Revival Show*		$7		Mercury 73822
12/18/76+	**27**	11		46	The Closest Thing To You *You Belong To Me*		$7		Mercury 73872
10/29/77+	**4**	18		47	Middle Age Crazy *Georgia On My Mind*		$7		Mercury 55011
3/11/78	**10**	12		48	Come On In *Who's Sorry Now*		$7		Mercury 55021

DEBUT	PEAK	WKS	Gold	A-side (Chart Hit)..B-side	Pop	$	Pic	Label & Number

LEWIS, Jerry Lee — Cont'd

DEBUT	PEAK	WKS	A-side / B-side	Pop	$	Label & Number
6/24/78	10	12	49 I'll Find It Where I Can *Don't Let The Stars Get In Your Eyes*		$7	Mercury 55028
12/16/78+	26	13	50 Save The Last Dance For Me.................... *Am I To Be The One*		$7	Sun 1139
			recorded on 6/12/61; #1 Pop hit for The Drifters in 1960			
4/7/79	84	3	51 Cold, Cold Heart.................................*Hello Josephine* [R]		$7	Sun 1141
			JERRY LEE LEWIS And Friends			
			same recording as #8 above; Orion (dubbed-in vocals, above 2)			
4/7/79	18	11	52 Rockin' My Life Away/	101		
		11	53 I Wish I Was Eighteen Again...............................		$6	Elektra 46030
7/21/79	20	11	54 Who Will The Next Fool Be .... *Rita May*		$6	Elektra 46067
2/9/80	11	12	55 When Two Worlds Collide .... *Good News Travels Fast*		$5	Elektra 46591
5/24/80	28	12	56 Honky Tonk Stuff...................... *Rockin' Jerry Lee*		$5	Elektra 46642
9/6/80	10	12	57 Over The Rainbow *Folsom Prison Blues*		$5	Elektra 47026
			first heard in the 1939 movie *The Wizard Of Oz* starring Judy Garland			
1/17/81	4	15	58 Thirty Nine And Holding *Change Places With Me*		$5	Elektra 47095
4/24/82	43	11	59 I'm So Lonesome I Could Cry .... *Pick Me Up On Your Way Down*		$5	Mercury 76148
9/25/82	52	7	60 I'd Do It All Again .... *Who Will Buy The Wine*		$5	Elektra 69962
12/18/82+	44	10	61 My Fingers Do The Talkin'................... *Forever Forgiving*		$4	MCA 52151
3/19/83	66	6	62 Come As You Were .... *Circumstantial Evidence*		$4	MCA 52188
7/9/83	69	5	63 Why You Been Gone So Long................ *She Sings Amazing Grace*		$4	MCA 52233
8/23/86	61	6	64 Sixteen Candles .... *Rock And Roll (Fais-Do-Do)*		$4	America/Sm. 884934
			#2 Pop hit for The Crests in 1959			
1/14/89	50	7	65 Never Too Old To Rock 'N' Roll .... *Rock And Roll Kiss*		$3	Curb 10521
			RONNIE McDOWELL WITH JERRY LEE LEWIS			

LEWIS, Linda Gail   '69
Born on 7/18/47 in Ferriday, Louisiana. Singer/songwriter. Sister of **Jerry Lee Lewis.**

DEBUT	PEAK	WKS	A-side / B-side	$	Pic	Label & Number
5/24/69	9	11	1 Don't Let Me Cross Over *We Live In Two Different Worlds*	$10	■	Smash 2220
			JERRY LEE LEWIS & LINDA GAIL LEWIS			
1/10/70	71	2	2 Roll Over Beethoven .... *Secret Places*	$10		Smash 2254
			LINDA GAIL LEWIS & JERRY LEE LEWIS			
			#29 Pop hit for Chuck Berry in 1956			
8/19/72	39	8	3 Smile, Somebody Loves You .... *Louisiana*	$7		Mercury 73316

LEWIS, Margaret   '68

| 6/29/68 | 74 | 3 | Honey (I Miss You Too)................... *Milk And Honey* | $7 | | SSS Int'l. 741 |
| | | | answer to "Honey" by Bobby Goldsboro | | | |

LEWIS, Melissa   '80
Born on 10/16/64 in Exeter, New Hampshire; raised in New Hope, North Carolina.

| 3/1/80 | 75 | 5 | 1 The First Time.................. *When Love Finds A Place In Your Heart* | $5 | | Door Knob 122 |
| 5/17/80 | 71 | 6 | 2 One Good Reason .... *You'll Never Know (How Close He Came To Hurting You)* | $5 | | Door Knob 129 |

LEWIS, Ross   '89

12/17/88	89	4	1 Hold Your Fire........................	$6	■	Wolf Dog 4
1/28/89	70	5	2 Love In Motion	$6	■	Wolf Dog 5
4/1/89	67	5	3 The Chance You Take	$6	■	Wolf Dog 6
9/23/89	91	2	4 Of All The Foolish Things To Do	$6		Wolf Dog 7

LEWIS, Texas Jim   '44
Born on 10/15/09 in Meigs, Georgia. Died on 1/23/90 (age 80). Singer/guitarist/actor. Appeared in several western movies.

| 9/2/44 | 3 | 6 | Too Late To Worry Too Blue To Cry   *'Leven Miles From Leavenworth* | $20 | | Decca 6099 |
| | | | **TEXAS JIM LEWIS And His Lone Star Cowboys** | | | |

LIBBY, Brenda   '83

| 11/26/83 | 97 | 1 | Give It Back .... *We Don't Make Sense Anymore* | $7 | | Comstock 1726 |

LIGHTFOOT, Gordon   '74
Born on 11/17/38 in Orilla, Ontario, Canada. Folk-pop singer/songwriter/guitarist. Charted 11 pop hits from 1970-82.

DEBUT	PEAK	WKS	A-side / B-side	Pop	$	Pic	Label & Number
6/1/74	13	15	● 1 Sundown *Too Late For Prayin'*	❶[1]	$5		Reprise 1194
10/19/74	81	6	2 Carefree Highway .... *Seven Island Suite*	10	$5		Reprise 1309
4/5/75	47	7	3 Rainy Day People .... *Cherokee Bend*	26	$5		Reprise 1328
10/9/76	50	11	4 The Wreck Of The Edmund Fitzgerald .... *The House You Live In*	2[2]	$5		Reprise 1369
			true story of the shipwreck in Lake Superior on 11/10/75				
2/25/78	92	4	5 The Circle Is Small (I Can See It In Your Eyes) .... *Sweet Guinevere*	33	$4		Warner 8518
9/2/78	100	2	6 Dreamland .... *Songs The Minstrel Sang*		$4		Warner 8644
5/24/80	80	5	7 Dream Street Rose .... *Make Way For The Lady*		$4		Warner 49230
8/30/86	71	9	8 Anything For Love .... *Let It Ride*		$4	■	Warner 28655

LINCOLN COUNTY   '81
Vocal trio from Lincoln County, Mississippi.

| 4/11/81 | 84 | 4 | Making The Night The Best Part Of My Day.............. *I'm Gonna' Be Strong* | $5 | | Soundwaves 4629 |

LINDSEY, Bennie   '76

| 11/13/76 | 100 | 2 | Save The Last Dance............................ | $7 | | Phono 2633 |

LINDSEY, Judy   '89
Female singer from Arlington, Texas.

| 1/28/89 | 83 | 3 | Wrong Train .... *From My Heart's Point Of View* | $6 | | Gypsy 83881 |

DEBUT	PEAK	WKS	Gold	A-side (Chart Hit) ....B-side	Pop	$	Pic	Label & Number

LINDSEY, LaWanda ★387★ '70
Born on 1/12/53 in Tampa, Florida; raised in Savannah, Georgia. Singer/songwriter.
1)Pickin' Wild Mountain Berries 2)Hello Out There
3)Today Will Be The First Day Of The Rest Of My Life

DEBUT	PEAK	WKS		A-side / B-side	Pop	$	Pic	Label & Number
1/4/69	58	9		1 Eye To Eye .... Looking Over Our Shoulders		$7		Chart 1063
				LaWANDA LINDSEY & KENNY VERNON				
12/20/69	48	10		2 Partly Bill .... Making Waves		$6		Chart 5042
3/21/70	27	14		3 Pickin' Wild Mountain Berries _We Don't Deserve Each Other_		$6		Chart 5055
				LaWANDA LINDSEY & KENNY VERNON				
				#27 Pop hit for Peggy Scott & Jo Jo Benson in 1968				
7/25/70	63	6		4 We'll Sing In The Sunshine .... I'll Just Take Your Word For It, Baby		$6		Chart 5076
9/19/70	51	9		5 Let's Think About Where We're Going .... Puzzles Of My Mind		$6		Chart 5090
				LaWANDA LINDSEY & KENNY VERNON				
2/27/71	42	9		6 The Crawdad Song .... Wrong Number		$6		Chart 5114
				LaWANDA LINDSEY & KENNY VERNON				
2/26/72	60	7		7 Wish I Was A Little Boy Again .... Time Heals All Wounds		$6		Chart 5153
7/14/73	38	10		8 Today Will Be The First Day Of My Life .... Paint Me A Picture Of Our Love		$5		Capitol 3652
11/17/73	87	5		9 Sunshine Feeling .... Love Makes The World Go Around		$5		Capitol 3739
2/23/74	62	8		10 Hello Trouble .... Your Tender Loving Care		$5		Capitol 3819
6/1/74	28	14		11 Hello Out There .... Top Of The Morning To You		$5		Capitol 3875
9/28/74	67	7		12 I Ain't Hangin' 'Round .... Your Monkey Won't Be Home Tonight		$5		Capitol 3950
4/2/77	76	5		13 Walk Right Back .... (Try To Love Him) A Little Bit More		$4		Mercury 73889
				#7 Pop hit for The Everly Brothers in 1961				
10/7/78	85	4		14 I'm A Woman In Love .... Let Your Body Speak Your Mind		$4		Mercury 55041

LINTON, Sherwin '77
Born in Volga, South Dakota. Singer/songwriter/pianist.

10/22/77	88	3		Jesse I Wanted That Award .... Men Talk		$6		Soundwaves 4556

LIPTON, Holly '89

10/21/89	89	2		At This Moment		$5		Evergreen 1096

LITTLE, Peggy '70
Born in Marlin, Texas; raised in Waco, Texas. Regular on TV's The Mike Douglas Show.

3/15/69	40	10		1 Son Of A Preacher Man .... One More Nightly Cry		$6		Dot 17199
				#10 Pop hit for Dusty Springfield in 1969				
6/21/69	43	10		2 Sweet Baby Girl .... My Heart's Not In It Anymore		$6		Dot 17259
10/18/69	44	9		3 Put Your Lovin' Where Your Mouth Is .... Softly And Tenderly		$6		Dot 17308
2/21/70	37	11		4 Mama, I Won't Be Wearing A Ring _Love's Biggest Fool_		$6		Dot 17338
8/8/70	59	3		5 I Knew You'd Be Leaving .... Gentle Man		$6		Dot 17353
5/1/71	75	2		6 I've Got To Have You .... I've Got A Lot Of Love (Left In Me)		$6		Dot 17371
4/14/73	70	2		7 Listen, Spot .... Everything's All Right		$5		Epic 10968
8/18/73	37	10		8 Sugarman .... If Lovin' You Starts Hurtin' Me		$5		Epic 11028

LITTLE TEXAS ★193★ '94
Group from Arlington, Texas: Tim Rushlow (vocals), Porter Howell and Dwayne O'Brien (guitars), **Brady Seals** (keyboards), Duane Propes (bass) and Del Gray (drums). Jeff Huskins replaced Seals in 1995.

1)My Love 2)What Might Have Been 3)Amy's Back In Austin 4)God Blessed Texas 5)Kick A Little

DEBUT	PEAK	WKS		A-side / B-side	Pop	$	Pic	Label & Number
9/14/91	8	20		1 Some Guys Have All The Love/				
2/8/92	13	20		2 First Time For Everything		$3		Warner 19024
6/20/92	5	20		3 You And Forever And Me _Dance_		$3		Warner 18867
10/10/92+	17	20		4 What Were You Thinkin' .... Just One More Night		$3		Warner 18741
1/30/93	16	20		5 I'd Rather Miss You .... Cry On		$3		Warner 18668
5/29/93	2[1]	20		6 What Might Have Been _Stop On A Dime_	79	$3	▌	Warner 18516
7/17/93	4	24		7 God Blessed Texas _Cutoff Jeans_	55	$3	▌	Warner 18385
12/11/93	73	4		8 Peaceful Easy Feeling				album cut
				#22 Pop hit for the Eagles in 1973; from the album Common Thread on Giant 24531				
1/15/94	❶[2]	20		9 My Love _Only Thing I'm Sure Of_	83	$3	▌	Warner 18295
5/21/94	14	20		10 Stop On A Dime		$3		album cut
				from the album Big Time on Warner 45276				
8/27/94	5	20		11 Kick A Little _Hit Country Song_	108	$3	▌	Warner 18103
12/24/94+	4	20		12 Amy's Back In Austin _Excerpts From Country World Premiere Radio Show_		$3	▌	Warner 18001
4/29/95	27	16		13 Southern Grace				album cut
				from the album Kick A Little on Warner 45739				
7/8/95	53	17		14 Party All Night _S:5 Southern Accent_ [C]	101	$3	▌	Warner 17806
				JEFF FOXWORTHY with Little Texas				
9/2/95	5	20		15 Life Goes On/				
12/30/95+	44	13		16 Country Crazy		$3		Warner 17770
10/19/96+	52	20		17 Kiss The Girl				album cut
				from the 1989 animated movie The Little Mermaid; from the album The Best Of Country Sing The Best Of Disney on Disney 60902				
3/1/97	45	10		18 Bad For Us .... Long Way Down		$3		Warner 17391

LITTLE TEXAS — Cont'd

DEBUT	PEAK	WKS	A-side	B-side	Pop	$	Label & Number
5/17/97	64	5	19 Your Mama Won't Let Me				album cut
9/20/97	71	2	20 The Call				album cut

above 2 from the album Little Texas on Warner 46501

LLOYD, Mick '81
Vice President of Giant Records during the early 1980s.

DEBUT	PEAK	WKS	A-side	B-side	$	Label & Number
1/31/81	85	3	1 Be My Lover, Be My Friend	Drifter's Lullaby	$6	Little Giant 040
			MICK LLOYD & JERRI KELLY			
8/8/81	85	4	2 Sweet Natural Love	Forsaking All The Rest	$6	Little Giant 046
			MICK LLOYD & JERRI KELLY			

LOBO '82
Born Roland Kent Lavoie on 7/31/43 in Tallahassee, Florida. Singer/songwriter/guitarist. Started own Lobo record label in 1981. Member of The Wolfpack. Charted 16 pop hits from 1971-80.

DEBUT	PEAK	WKS	A-side	B-side	$	Label & Number
12/5/81+	40	12	1 I Don't Want To Want You	No One Will Ever Know	$5	Lobo 1
3/27/82	63	7	2 Come Looking For Me	I Don't Want To Want You	$5	Lobo 4
9/4/82	88	3	3 Living My Life Without You	A Simple Man	$5	Lobo 10
3/9/85	57	5	4 Am I Going Crazy (Or Just Out Of My Mind)	I Don't Want To Want You	$5	Evergreen 1028
6/29/85	49	7	5 Paint The Town Blue	Angel In Your Arms	$5	Evergreen 1033
			ROBIN LEE AND LOBO			

LOCKLIN, Hank ★123★ '60
Born Lawrence Hankins Locklin on 2/15/18 in McLellan, Florida. Singer/songwriter/guitarist. Once known as "The Rocky Mountain Boy." Joined the Grand Ole Opry in 1960.

1)Please Help Me, I'm Falling 2)Let Me Be The One 3)It's A Little More Like Heaven 4)Geisha Girl
5)Send Me The Pillow You Dream On

DEBUT	PEAK	WKS	A-side	B-side	Pop	$	Label & Number
6/25/49	8	5	1 The Same Sweet Girl	J:8 / S:15 The Last Look At Mother		$25	4 Star 1313
9/5/53	❶³	32	2 Let Me Be The One	A:❶³ / J:❶² / S:2 I'm Tired Of Bummin' Around		$30	4 Star 1641
3/24/56	9	1	3 Why Baby Why	A:9 Love Or Spite		$20	RCA Victor 6347
8/19/57	4	39	4 Geisha Girl/	S:4 / A:6	66		RCA Victor 6984
		6	5 Livin' Alone			$20	RCA Victor 6984
3/31/58	5	35	6 Send Me The Pillow You Dream On	S:5 / A:5 Why Don't You Haul Off And Love Me	77	$15	RCA Victor 7127
4/28/58	3	23	7 It's A Little More Like Heaven/	A:3 / S:8		$15	RCA Victor 7203
		7	8 Blue Glass Skirt			$15	RCA Victor 7203
3/7/60	❶¹⁴	36	9 Please Help Me, I'm Falling	My Old Home Town	8	$15	RCA Victor 7692
			also see #30 below				
12/31/60+	14	12	10 One Step Ahead Of My Past	Toujours Moi		$12	RCA Victor 7813
6/5/61	12	7	11 From Here To There To You	This Song Is Just For You		$12	RCA Victor 7871
10/2/61	7	14	12 Happy Birthday To Me/			$12	RCA Victor 7921
9/11/61	14	12	13 You're The Reason		107	$12	RCA Victor 7921
1/13/62	10	14	14 Happy Journey	I Need You Now		$12	RCA Victor 7965
6/23/62	14	11	15 We're Gonna Go Fishin'	Welcome Home, Mister Blues		$12	RCA Victor 8034
4/20/63	23	4	16 Flyin' South	Behind The Footlights		$12	RCA Victor 8156
			also see #31 below				
1/18/64	41	4	17 Wooden Soldier	Kiss On The Door		$12	RCA Victor 8248
3/21/64	15	17	18 Followed Closely By My Teardrops	You Never Want To Love Me		$12	RCA Victor 8318
5/15/65	32	9	19 Forty Nine, Fifty One	Faith And Truth		$10	RCA Victor 8560
12/25/65+	35	9	20 The Girls Get Prettier (Every Day)	To Him		$10	RCA Victor 8695
4/9/66	48	2	21 Insurance	I Feel A Cry Coming On		$10	RCA Victor 8783
10/15/66	69	2	22 The Best Part Of Loving You	The Last Thing On My Mind		$10	RCA Victor 8928
3/4/67	41	10	23 Hasta Luego (See You Later)	Wishing On A Star		$10	RCA Victor 9092
7/1/67	73	4	24 Nashville Women	Behind My Back		$10	RCA Victor 9218
10/21/67+	8	20	25 The Country Hall Of Fame	Evergreen		$10	RCA Victor 9323
3/30/68	40	8	26 Love Song For You	Little Geisha Girl		$10	RCA Victor 9476
8/24/68	57	5	27 Everlasting Love	I'm Slowly Going Out Of Your Mind		$10	RCA Victor 9582
11/2/68	62	6	28 Lovin' You (The Way I Do)	Hot Pepper Doll		$10	RCA Victor 9646
2/1/69	34	10	29 Where The Blue Of The Night Meets The Gold Of The Day	The Girls Who Wait		$8	RCA Victor 9710
			#4 Pop hit for Bing Crosby in 1932				
1/3/70	68	3	30 Please Help Me, I'm Falling	Anna [R]		$8	RCA Victor 0287
			HANK LOCKLIN AND DANNY DAVIS AND THE NASHVILLE BRASS				
			new version of #9 above				
6/27/70	56	6	31 Flying South	Rosalita [R]		$8	RCA Victor 9849
			HANK LOCKLIN AND DANNY DAVIS AND THE NASHVILLE BRASS				
			new version of #16 above				
10/10/70	68	4	32 Bless Her Heart...I Love Her	Morning		$8	RCA Victor 9894
3/13/71	61	4	33 She's As Close As I Can Get To Loving You	I Like A Woman		$8	RCA Victor 9955

LOFTIS, Bobby Wayne '77
Singer/pianist from Battle Creek, Michigan.

8/14/76	85	6	1 See The Big Man Cry .... *Number One Lady In Town*	$5	Charta 100
12/25/76+	54	11	2 Poor Side Of Town *Don't Wake Up The Children*	$5	Charta 104

#1 Pop hit for **Johnny Rivers** in 1966

6/11/77	75	6	3 You're So Good For Me (And That's Bad) .... *We're Back Together Once Again*	$5	Charta 108
3/4/78	87	5	4 Can't Shake You Off My Mind .... *Let's Pretend We Just Got Married*	$5	Charta 118
4/21/79	89	2	5 Small Time Picker .... *I'll Remember*	$5	Charta 132

LOGAN, Bud '74
Singer/bassist. Former member of **The Blue Boys** (backing group for **Jim Reeves**).

12/22/73+	14	17	1 Wake Me Into Love.................................... *Here Together*	$6	Shannon 816
			BUD LOGAN & WILMA BURGESS		
7/6/74	53	10	2 The Best Day Of The Rest Of Our Love .... *It Ain't Nothing But Love*	$6	Shannon 820
			BUD LOGAN & WILMA BURGESS		

LOGAN, Josh '89
Born in Richmond, Kentucky.

12/10/88+	58	9	1 Everytime I Get To Dreamin' .... *Easy Lovin' Kind*	$3	Curb 10519
6/3/89	62	7	2 Somebody Paints The Wall .... *The Light Of My Life*	$3	Curb/MCA 10528
9/2/89	75	4	3 I Was Born With A Broken Heart........................... *I've Learned To Lie*	$3	Curb/MCA 10553

LOGGINS, Dave — see HARDIN, Gus / MURRAY, Anne

LOGGINS & MESSINA '76
Duo of Kenny Loggins and Jim Messina. Loggins was born on 1/7/47 in Everett, Washington; raised in Alhambra, California. Charted 21 pop hits from 1977-91. Messina was born on 12/5/47 in Maywood, California; raised in Harlingen, Texas. Former member of **Poco**. Loggins & Messina charted 10 pop hits from 1972-75.

12/20/75+	92	6	Oh, Lonesome Me .... *A Lover's Question (Pop #89)*	$5	Columbia 10222

LONDON, Eddie '91
Born Kenneth Edward London on 7/31/56 to an American military family in Dreux, France. Singer/bassist.

7/6/91	41	19	If We Can't Do It Right .... *Business As Usual*	$3	∎ RCA 2821

LONESOME STRANGERS, The '89
Vocal group from Los Angeles: Jeff Rymes, Randy Weeks, Lorne Rall and Mike McLean.

2/11/89	32	13	1 Goodbye Lonesome, Hello Baby Doll .... *We Used To Fuss*	$6	Hightone 508
6/24/89	66	5	2 Just Can't Cry No More	$6	Hightone 511

LONESTAR ★369★ '96
Group from Nashville: **Richie McDonald** (vocals, guitar), John Rich (vocals, bass), Michael Britt (guitar), Dean Sams (keyboards) and Keech Rainwater (drums). Also see **Mindy McCready**.

1/13/96	❶³	20	1 No News/ S:5	122		
8/19/95	8	20	2 Tequila Talkin'	flip	$3	∎ BNA 64386
5/25/96	8	20	3 Runnin' Away With My Heart *I Love The Way You Do That*		$3	BNA 64549
9/28/96	45	15	4 When Cowboys Didn't Dance .... *Ragtop Cadillac*		$3	BNA 64638
12/7/96+	18	20	5 Heartbroke Every Day...		$3	album cut
			from the album *Lonestar* on BNA 66642			
12/28/96	75	1	6 I'll Be Home For Christmas .... *White Christmas* [X]		$3	BNA 64687
			#3 Pop hit for **Bing Crosby** in 1943			
5/3/97	❶²	20	7 Come Cryin' To Me S:18 *What Would It Take*		$3	∎ BNA 64841
8/30/97+	12	22	8 You Walked In S:8 *Keys To My Heart*	93	$3	∎ BNA 64942

LONG, Shorty '48
Born Emidio Vagnoni on 10/11/23 in Reading, Pennsylvania. Not to be confused with the R&B singer of the same name.

10/30/48	12	1	Sweeter Than The Flowers....................S:12 *I Love You So Much It Hurts*	$25	Decca 46139
			SHORTY LONG And The Santa Fe Rangers		

LONZO & OSCAR '48
Comedy duo: Ken "Lonzo" Marvin (real name: Lloyd George) and Rollin "Oscar" Sullivan (b: 7/7/17 in Edmonton, Kentucky). Marvin was replaced in 1944 by Rollin's brother, John "Lonzo" Sullivan (b: 1/19/19 in Edmonton, Kentucky). It was this brother team that became the most popular Lonzo & Oscar duo. Joined the *Grand Ole Opry* in 1947. They were often joined on-stage by Clell "Cousin Jody" Summey. John Sullivan died on 6/5/67 (age 48). Rollin continued the duo with David "Lonzo" Hooten.

1/31/48	5	7	1 I'm My Own Grandpa J:5 *You Blacked My Blue Eyes Once Too Often* [N]	$25	Victor 20-2563
			LONZO and OSCAR with the Winston County Pea Pickers		
			#10 Pop hit for **Guy Lombardo** in 1948		
6/5/61	26	1	2 Country Music Time................................... *Can't Pitch Woo (In An Igloo)* [N]	$20	Starday 543
1/12/74	29	12	3 Traces Of Life .... *Lubbock*	$7	GRC 1006

LORD, Bobby '56
Born on 1/6/34 in Sanford, Florida. Singer/songwriter/guitarist. Hosted own syndicated TV show in 1966.

9/8/56	10	2	1 Without Your Love J:10 / A:15 *Everybody's Rockin' But Me*	$75	Columbia 21539
1/11/64	21	10	2 Life Can Have Meaning .... *Pickin' White Gold*	$10	Hickory 1232
4/6/68	44	11	3 Live Your Life Out Loud .... *Charlotte, North Carolina*	$6	Decca 32277
9/14/68	49	5	4 The True And Lasting Kind .... *It's My Life*	$6	Decca 32373
2/15/69	40	9	5 Yesterday's Letters .... *Don't Forget To Smell The Flowers Along The Way*	$6	Decca 32431
11/22/69+	28	11	6 Rainbow Girl .... *Do You Ever Think Of Me*	$6	Decca 32578
5/2/70	15	13	7 You And Me Against The World .... *Something Real*	$6	Decca 32657
8/22/70	21	14	8 Wake Me Up Early In The Morning .... *Violets Are Red*	$6	Decca 32718
3/27/71	75	2	9 Goodbye Jukebox .... *Do It To Someone You Love*	$6	Decca 32797

LORD, Mike '87
Singer/drummer from San Antonio, Texas.

6/27/87	94	2	Just Try Texas .... *Lying Here Lonely*	$5	NSD 230

LORIE ANN   '89

9/3/88	81	3		1 **Down On Market Street**...		$6	■	Sing Me 34
1/14/89	78	3		2 **Say The Part About I Love You**..................................		$6	■	Sing Me 37
6/24/89	98	1		3 **Just Because You're Leavin'**............................*Reasons A Plenty*		$6	■	Sing Me 41

LORRIE, Myrna & Buddy DeVal   '55
Lorrie was born Myrna Petrunke on 8/6/40 in Fort William, Ontario, Canada. Singer/songwriter. DeVal was born on 4/15/15 in Port Arthur, Ontario, Canada.

| 1/1/55 | 6 | 14 | | **Are You Mine**   A:6 / J:7 / S:12   *You Bet I Kissed Him* (Lorrie) | | $25 | | Abbott 172 |

LOS LOBOS   '87
Rock group from Los Angeles: David Hildago (vocals), Cesar Rosas (guitar), Steve Berlin (saxophone), Conrad Lozano (bass) and Louie Perez (drums).

8/22/87	57	8		1 **La Bamba**..*Charlena* [F]	**❶**³	$3	■	Slash 28336
				from the movie starring Lou Diamond Phillips				
3/19/88	55	10		2 **One Time One Night**........................*All I Wanted To Do Was Dance*		$3	■	Slash 28464

LOU, Bonnie — see BONNIE

LOUDERMILK, John D.   '65
Born on 3/31/34 in Durham, North Carolina. Singer/prolific songwriter. Cousin of **The Louvin Brothers**.

6/29/63	23	4		1 **Bad News**..*The Guitar Player*		$12		RCA Victor 8154
3/7/64	44	7		2 **Blue Train (Of The Heartbreak Line)**.....................*Rhythm And Blues*	132	$12		RCA Victor 8308
9/26/64	45	5		3 **Th' Wife**..*Nothing To Gain* [N]		$12		RCA Victor 8389
7/3/65	20	11		4 **That Ain't All**............................*Then You Can Tell Me Goodbye*		$12		RCA Victor 8579
6/17/67	51	5		5 **It's My Time**..*Bahama Mama*		$10		RCA Victor 9189

LOUVIN, Charlie ★181★   '64
Born Charlie Elzer Loudermilk on 7/7/27 in Section, Alabama. Singer/songwriter/guitarist. Half of **The Louvin Brothers**.

1)*I Don't Love You Anymore* 2)*See The Big Man Cry* 3)*You Finally Said Something Good* 4)*Hey Daddy*
5)*Something To Brag About*

6/20/64	4	27		1 **I Don't Love You Anymore** *My Book Of Memories*		$10		Capitol 5173
12/12/64+	27	15		2 **Less And Less**..*I Don't Want It*		$10		Capitol 5296
3/27/65	7	17		3 **See The Big Man Cry** *I Just Don't Understand*		$10		Capitol 5369
10/23/65	26	8		4 **Think I'll Go Somewhere And Cry Myself To Sleep**..........*Life Begins At Love*		$8		Capitol 5475
				#30 Pop hit for **Al Martino** in 1966				
12/18/65+	15	12		5 **You Finally Said Something Good (When You Said Goodbye)**....................*Something To Think About*		$10		Capitol 5550
10/15/66	58	5		6 **The Proof Is In The Kissing**....................*Scared Of The Blues*		$10		Capitol 5729
12/24/66+	38	11		7 **Off And On**..*Still Loving You*		$10		Capitol 5791
4/22/67	44	10		8 **On The Other Hand**....................*Someone's Heartache*		$10		Capitol 5872
8/5/67	46	9		9 **I Forgot To Cry**....................*Drive Me Out Of My Mind*		$10		Capitol 5948
11/4/67+	36	12		10 **The Only Way Out (Is To Walk Over Me)**....................*Too Little And Too Late*		$10		Capitol 2007
3/9/68	20	14		11 **Will You Visit Me On Sundays?**....................*Tears, Wine, And Flowers*		$10		Capitol 2106
8/17/68	15	12		12 **Hey Daddy**....................*She Will Get Lonesome*		$8		Capitol 2231
12/21/68+	19	13		13 **What Are Those Things (With Big Black Wings)**....................*What Then*		$8		Capitol 2350
4/19/69	27	11		14 **Let's Put Our World Back Together**....................*Heart Of Clay*		$8		Capitol 2448
9/27/69	29	9		15 **Little Reasons**....................*After Awhile*		$8		Capitol 2612
1/17/70	42	9		16 **Here's A Toast To Mama**....................*Show Me The Way Back To Your Heart*		$8		Capitol 2703
7/4/70	47	8		17 **Come And Get It Mama**....................*Is Home Sweet Home*		$8		Capitol 2824
10/24/70	18	14		18 **Something To Brag About**....................*Let's Help Each Other To Forget*		$8		Capitol 2915
				CHARLIE LOUVIN & MELBA MONTGOMERY				
11/28/70+	54	7		19 **Sittin' Bull**....................*It Ain't No Big Thing (But It's Growing)*		$8		Capitol 2972
2/13/71	26	12		20 **Did You Ever**....................*Don't Believe Me*		$8		Capitol 3029
				CHARLIE LOUVIN & MELBA MONTGOMERY				
6/12/71	30	10		21 **Baby, You've Got What It Takes**....................*If We Don't Make It*		$8		Capitol 3111
				CHARLIE LOUVIN & MELBA MONTGOMERY				
				#5 Pop hit for **Dinah Washington & Brook Benton** in 1960				
11/27/71	60	5		22 **I'm Gonna Leave You**....................*When I Stop Dreaming*		$8		Capitol 3208
				CHARLIE LOUVIN & MELBA MONTGOMERY				
5/20/72	70	2		23 **Just In Time (To Watch Love Die)**....................*She Just Wants To Be Needed*		$8		Capitol 3319
8/19/72	66	4		24 **Baby, What's Wrong With Us**....................*Unmatched Wedding Bands*		$8		Capitol 3388
				CHARLIE LOUVIN & MELBA MONTGOMERY				
1/20/73	59	6		25 **A Man Likes Things Like That**....................*That Don't Mean I Don't Love You*		$8		Capitol 3508
				CHARLIE LOUVIN & MELBA MONTGOMERY				
1/5/74	36	13		26 **You're My Wife, She's My Woman**..........*If I Had To Build A Bridge (I'll Get Over You)*		$6		United Artists 368
6/15/74	76	8		27 **It Almost Felt Like Love**....................*Until I'm Out Of Sight*		$6		United Artists 430
9/8/79	91	6		28 **Love Don't Care**....................*Who's Gonna Love Me Now* (Louvin)		$5		Little Darlin' 7922
				CHARLIE LOUVIN with Emmylou Harris				
6/5/82	56	9		29 **North Wind**....................*Sweeter Than The Flowers*		$5		Soundwaves 4671
				JIM & JESSE and CHARLIE LOUVIN				
6/17/89	87	2		30 **The Precious Jewel**....................*Buried Alive*		$7		Hal Kat 63058
				CHARLIE LOUVIN - ROY ACUFF				

LOUVIN, Ira '65

Born Ira Lonnie Loudermilk on 4/21/24 in Section, Alabama. Died in a car crash on 6/20/65 (age 41). Singer/songwriter/mandolin player. Half of **The Louvin Brothers**.

8/14/65	**44**	4	Yodel, Sweet Molly..*You're Looking For An Angel*	$10	Capitol 5428

★285★

LOUVIN BROTHERS, The '56

Duo of brothers from Section, Alabama: **Charlie Louvin** (vocals, guitar) and **Ira Louvin** (vocals, mandolin). Joined the *Grand Ole Opry* in 1955. Ira died in a car crash on 6/20/65 (age 41). Charlie remained a member of the *Grand Ole Opry* as a solo artist.

1)I Don't Believe You've Met My Baby 2)You're Running Wild 3)Hoping That You're Hoping

9/10/55	**8**	13	1	When I Stop Dreaming	A:8 / S:13 *Pitfall*	$20	Capitol 3177
1/14/56	**❶²**	24	2	I Don't Believe You've Met My Baby	A:❶² / S:5 / J:5 *In The Middle Of Nowhere*	$20	Capitol 3300
5/26/56	**7**	10	3	Hoping That You're Hoping	A:7 / S:8 *Childish Love*	$20	Capitol 3413
10/6/56	**7**	12	4	You're Running Wild/	S:7 / A:11		
10/6/56	**7**	11	5	Cash On The Barrel Head	S:7 / A:11	$20	Capitol 3523
3/9/57	**11**	4	6	Don't Laugh	A:11 *The New Partner Waltz*	$20	Capitol 3630
7/15/57	**14**	1	7	Plenty Of Everything But You	A:14 *The First One To Love You*	$20	Capitol 3715

IRA and CHARLEY LOUVIN

10/20/58+	**9**	22	8	My Baby's Gone	*Lorene*	$15	Capitol 4055
2/16/59	**19**	7	9	Knoxville Girl	*I Wish It Had Been A Dream*	$15	Capitol 4117
3/13/61	**12**	14	10	I Love You Best Of All	*Scared Of The Blues*	$15	Capitol 4506
9/25/61	**26**	1	11	How's The World Treating You	*It Hurt Me More*	$15	Capitol 4628
11/17/62	**21**	6	12	Must You Throw Dirt In My Face	*The First Time In Life*	$15	Capitol 4822

LOVELESS, Patty ★81★ '96

Born Patricia Ramey on 1/4/57 in Pikeville, Kentucky. Singer/songwriter/guitarist. Joined the *Grand Ole Opry* in 1988. Married to record producer Emory Gordy, Jr. Distant cousin of **Loretta Lynn**, **Crystal Gayle**, **Peggy Sue** and Jay Lee Webb. CMA Award: 1996 Female Vocalist of the Year.

1)You Can Feel Bad 2)Blame It On Your Heart 3)Chains 4)Lonely Too Long
5)Timber, I'm Falling In Love

12/7/85+	**46**	10	1	Lonely Days, Lonely Nights	*Country I'm Coming Home To You*		$3	■	MCA 52694
11/29/86+	**49**	10	2	Wicked Ways	*Half Over You*		$3		MCA 52969
3/14/87	**56**	8	3	I Did	*You Are Everything*		$3		MCA 53040
6/20/87	**43**	10	4	After All	*I Did*		$3		MCA 53097
10/31/87	**43**	11	5	You Saved Me	*Fly Away*		$3		MCA 53179
2/6/88	**10**	20	6	If My Heart Had Windows	S:14 *So Good To Be In Love*		$3		MCA 53270
6/4/88	**2¹**	20	7	A Little Bit In Love	S:11 *I Can't Get You Off Of My Mind*		$3		MCA 53333
10/8/88+	**4**	20	8	Blue Side Of Town	S:5 *I'll Never Grow Tired Of You*		$3		MCA 53418
2/4/89	**5**	20	9	Don't Toss Us Away	*After All*		$3		MCA 53477
5/27/89	**❶¹**	20	10	Timber, I'm Falling In Love	*Go On*		$3		MCA 53641
9/9/89	**6**	26	11	The Lonely Side Of Love	*I'll Never Grow Tired Of You*		$3		MCA 53702
1/6/90	**❶¹**	26	12	Chains	*I'm On Your Side*		$3		MCA 53764
5/19/90	**5**	21	13	On Down The Line	*Feeling Of Love*		$3	■	MCA 53811
9/22/90	**20**	20	14	The Night's Too Long	*Overtime*		$3		MCA 53895
1/12/91	**5**	20	15	I'm That Kind Of Girl	*Some Morning Soon*		$3		MCA 53977
5/11/91	**22**	20	16	Blue Memories	*You Can't Run Away From Your Heart*		$3		MCA 54075
9/7/91	**3**	20	17	Hurt Me Bad (In A Real Good Way)	*God Will*		$3		MCA 54178
1/4/92	**13**	20	18	Jealous Bone	*I Came Straight To You*		$3		MCA 54271
4/25/92	**30**	20	19	Can't Stop Myself From Loving You	*If You Don't Want Me*		$3		MCA 54371
8/8/92	**47**	10	20	Send A Message To My Heart	*Takes A Lot To Rock You*		$3		Reprise 18846

DWIGHT YOAKAM & PATTY LOVELESS

4/3/93	**❶²**	20	21	Blame It On Your Heart	*What's A Broken Heart*	112	$3	■	Epic 74906
7/17/93	**20**	20	22	Nothin' But The Wheel	*Love Builds The Bridges (Pride Builds The Walls)*		$3		Epic 77076
11/20/93+	**6**	20	23	You Will	*You Don't Know How Lucky You Are*		$3	■	Epic 77271
3/19/94	**3**	20	24	How Can I Help You Say Goodbye	*How About You*		$3		Epic 77416
7/30/94	**3**	20	25	I Try To Think About Elvis	*Ships*	115	$3	■	Epic 77609
11/12/94+	**4**	20	26	Here I Am	*When The Fallen Angels Fly*		$3	■	Epic 77734
3/18/95	**5**	20	27	You Don't Even Know Who I Am	S:4 *Over My Shoulder*	117	$3	■	Epic 77856
7/8/95	**6**	20	28	Halfway Down	*Feelin' Good About Feelin' Bad*		$3	■	Epic 77956
12/30/95+	**❶²**	20	29	You Can Feel Bad	S:12 *Feelin' Good About Feelin' Bad*		$3	■	Epic 78209
4/13/96	**13**	20	30	A Thousand Times A Day	*Feelin' Good About Feelin' Bad*		$3		Epic 78309
8/24/96	**❶¹**	20	31	Lonely Too Long	*Feelin' Good About Feelin' Bad*		$3		Epic 78371
12/21/96+	**4**	20	32	She Drew A Broken Heart					album cut
4/26/97	**15**	20	33	The Trouble With The Truth					album cut

above 2 from the album The Trouble With The Truth on Epic 67269

9/20/97	**14**	20	34	You Don't Seem To Miss Me	S:9 *Where Are You Boy*	109	$3	■	Epic 78704

PATTY LOVELESS With George Jones

LOVETT, Lyle ★332★ '87

Born on 11/1/56 in Klein, Texas. Singer/songwriter/guitarist. Acted in the movies *The Player* and *Short Cuts*. Married to actress Julia Roberts from 1993-95. No relation to Ruby Lovett.

1)Cowboy Man 2)Give Back My Heart 3)Why I Don't Know

DEBUT	PEAK	WKS		A-side		B-side	$	Label & Number
7/12/86	21	19	1	Farther Down The Line	S:14 / A:24 *Why I Don't Know*		$3	Curb/MCA 52818
11/1/86+	10	19	2	Cowboy Man	S:7 / A:10 *The Waltzing Fool*		$3	Curb/MCA 52951
2/21/87	18	14	3	God Will	A:19 *An Acceptable Level Of Ecstasy (The Wedding Song)*		$3	Curb/MCA 53030
6/6/87	15	14	4	Why I Don't Know	*If I Were The Man You Wanted*		$3	Curb/MCA 53102
10/3/87	13	18	5	Give Back My Heart	S:19 *Simple Song*		$3	Curb/MCA 53157
1/30/88	17	16	6	She's No Lady	S:14 *Pontiac*		$3	Curb/MCA 53246
5/21/88	24	14	7	I Loved You Yesterday	S:27 *L.A. County*		$3	Curb/MCA 53316
9/17/88	66	4	8	If I Had A Boat	*Black And Blue*		$3	Curb/MCA 53401
12/10/88+	45	9	9	I Married Her Just Because She Looks Like You	*If I Had A Boat*		$3	Curb/MCA 53471
3/4/89	82	3	10	Stand By Your Man	*Wallisville Road*		$3	Curb/MCA 53611
6/17/89	84	2	11	Nobody Knows Me	*Here I Am*		$3	Curb/MCA 53650
9/23/89	49	7	12	If I Were The Man You Wanted	*Cryin' Shame*		$3	Curb/MCA 53703
9/28/96	68	2	13	Don't Touch My Hat				album cut
1/18/97	72	1	14	Private Conversation				album cut

above 2 from the album *The Road To Ensenada* on Curb/MCA 11409

LOVETT, Ruby '97

Born on 2/16/67 in Laurel, Mississippi. No relation to Lyle Lovett.

| 10/4/97 | 73 | 1 | | Look What Love Can Do | | | | album cut |

from the album *Ruby Lovett* on Curb 77857

LOWE, Jim '57

Born on 5/7/27 in Springfield, Missouri. Singer/pianist. Working as a DJ in New York City when he recorded the #1 pop hit "The Green Door" in 1956.

5/20/57	8	3	1	Talkin' To The Blues/	S:8	15		
		1		from the TV series *Modern Romances*				
			2	Four Walls		15	$15	Dot 15569

LOWES, The '86

7/19/86	61	5	1	Good And Lonesome	*He's Got A Heartache On His Mind*		$5	Soundwaves 4775
11/8/86	84	4	2	Cry Baby			$6	API 1001
1/17/87	70	5	3	I Ain't Never			$6	API 1002

LOWRY, Ron '70

| 2/28/70 | 39 | 11 | 1 | Marry Me | *World Champion Fool* | | $10 | Republic 1409 |
| 8/22/70 | 65 | 6 | 2 | Oh How I Waited | *Look At Me* | | $10 | Republic 1415 |

LUCAS, Tammy '89

| 2/11/89 | 75 | 4 | | 9,999,999 Tears | *Don't Go To Sleep* | | $7 | SOA 005 |

LUKE THE DRIFTER, JR. — see WILLIAMS, Hank Jr.

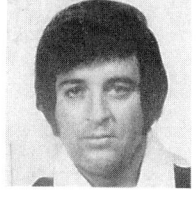

LUMAN, Bob ★141★ '72

Born on 4/15/37 in Nacogdoches, Texas. Died of pneumonia on 12/27/78 (age 51). Singer/songwriter/guitarist. Joined the *Grand Ole Opry* in 1965.

1)Lonely Women Make Good Lovers 2)When You Say Love 3)Neither One Of Us 4)Still Loving You
5)Let's Think About Living

10/10/60	9	10	1	Let's Think About Living	*You've Got Everything*	7	$20	■ Warner 5172
2/22/64	24	14	2	The File	*Bigger Men Than I (Have Cried)*		$10	Hickory 1238
1/29/66	39	5	3	Five Miles From Home (Soon I'll See Mary)	*(I Get So) Sentimental*		$10	Hickory 1355
6/4/66	39	5	4	Poor Boy Blues	*(Can't Get You) Off My Mind*		$10	Hickory 1382
				written by Carl Perkins				
9/24/66	42	11	5	Come On And Sing	*It's A Sin*		$10	Hickory 1410
2/18/67	59	6	6	Hardly Anymore	*Freedom Of Living*		$10	Hickory 1430
7/22/67	61	2	7	If You Don't Love Me (Then Why Don't You Leave Me Alone)	*Throwin' Kisses*		$10	Hickory 1460
5/11/68	19	14	8	Ain't Got Time To Be Unhappy	*I Can't Remember To Forget*		$7	Epic 10312
9/28/68	50	7	9	I Like Trains	*World Of Unhappiness*		$7	Epic 10381
2/22/69	24	12	10	Come On Home And Sing The Blues To Daddy	*Big, Big World*		$7	Epic 10439
6/7/69	65	5	11	It's All Over (But The Shouting)	*Bad, Bad Day*		$8	Hickory 1536
6/28/69	23	13	12	Every Day I Have To Cry Some	*Livin' In A House Full Of Love*		$7	Epic 10480
				#45 Pop hit for Arthur Alexander in 1975				
11/29/69+	60	9	13	The Gun	*Cleanin' Up The Streets Of Memphis*		$7	Epic 10535
3/28/70	56	5	14	Gettin' Back To Norma	*Maybellene*		$7	Epic 10581
5/9/70	56	8	15	Still Loving You	*Meet Mr. Mud*		$8	Hickory 1564
				also see #26 below				
7/11/70	22	14	16	Honky Tonk Man	*I Ain't Built That Way*		$7	Epic 10631
11/28/70+	44	10	17	What About The Hurt	*A Time To Remember*		$7	Epic 10667
3/27/71	60	5	18	Is It Any Wonder That I Love You	*Give Us One More Chance*		$7	Epic 10699
7/17/71	40	9	19	I Got A Woman	*One Hundred Songs On The Jukebox*		$7	Epic 10755
				#1 R&B hit for Ray Charles in 1955				
11/6/71	30	10	20	A Chain Don't Take To Me	*Don't Let Love Pass By*		$7	Epic 10786

LUMAN, Bob — Cont'd

DEBUT	PEAK	WKS	A-side (Chart Hit) / B-side	Pop	$	Label & Number
1/29/72	6	17	21 When You Say Love — *Have A Little Faith*		$7	Epic 10823
			#32 Pop hit for Sonny & Cher in 1972 (adapted from a Budweiser jingle)			
6/3/72	21	10	22 It Takes You — *Let's Think About Livin'*		$7	Epic 10869
9/2/72	4	19	23 Lonely Women Make Good Lovers — *Love Ought To Be A Happy Thing*		$7	Epic 10905
1/27/73	7	14	24 Neither One Of Us — *Anything But Lonesome*		$7	Epic 10943
			#2 Pop hit for Gladys Knight & The Pips in 1973			
6/9/73	23	11	25 A Good Love Is Like A Good Song .... *Have I Ever Said "I Love You" To A Lady*		$7	Epic 10994
10/20/73+	7	15	26 Still Loving You — *I'm Gonna Write A Song* [R]		$6	Epic 11039
			new version of #15 above			
3/9/74	23	11	27 Just Enough To Make Me Stay .... *Baby Made It Good*		$6	Epic 11087
7/13/74	25	11	28 Let Me Make The Bright Lights Shine For You ...... *The Closest Thing To Heaven*		$6	Epic 11138
2/8/75	22	13	29 Proud Of You Baby .... *Tonight My Baby's Coming Home*		$6	Epic 50065
9/13/75	48	12	30 Shame On Me .... *How Do You Start Over*		$6	Epic 50136
2/7/76	41	9	31 A Satisfied Mind .... *Cleanin' Up The Streets Of Memphis*		$6	Epic 50183
5/8/76	82	4	32 The Man From Bowling Green .... *It's Only Make Believe*		$6	Epic 50216
8/7/76	89	4	33 How Do You Start Over .... *Red Cadillac And Black Mustache*		$6	Epic 50247
11/27/76	94	4	34 Labor Of Love .... *Blond Haired Woman*		$6	Epic 50297
1/22/77	63	8	35 He's Got A Way With Women .... *Here We Are Making Love Again*		$6	Epic 50323
8/6/77	33	9	36 I'm A Honky-Tonk Woman's Man .... *Lonely Women (Don't Need To Be Lonely)*		$5	Polydor 14408
10/8/77	13	16	37 The Pay Phone .... *He'll Be The One*		$5	Polydor 14431
12/24/77	92	3	38 A Christmas Tribute .... *Give Someone You Love* [X]		$5	Polydor 14444
2/11/78	47	8	39 Proud Lady .... *Let Me Love Him Out Of You*		$5	Polydor 14454

LUNSFORD, Mike '76
Born on 6/30/50 in Guyman, Oklahoma. Singer/songwriter/guitarist.
1)Honey Hungry 2)Stealin' Feelin' 3)While The Feelings Good

DEBUT	PEAK	WKS	A-side / B-side	Pop	$	Label & Number
3/1/75	56	12	1 While The Feelings Good .... *Blanket Of The Blues*		$7	Gusto 124
11/8/75	87	5	2 Sugar Sugar .... *Mumbled Round, Fumbled Round*		$6	Starday 133
			#1 Pop hit for The Archies in 1969			
7/31/76	16	12	3 Honey Hungry — *Tonight My Lady Learns To Love*		$6	Starday 143
11/20/76+	28	11	4 Stealin' Feelin' .... *Part Time Lovers, Full Time Fools*		$6	Starday 146
2/26/77	61	7	5 If There Ever Comes A Day .... *Think About It One More Time*		$6	Starday 149
7/16/77	71	5	6 I Can't Stop Now .... *I Haven't Seen Mama In Years*		$6	Starday 160
5/27/78	85	4	7 The Reason Why I'm Here .... *I Feel Love*		$6	Starday 187
11/18/78	91	5	8 I Wish I'd Never Borrowed Anybody's Angel........ *Honky Tonk Super Star*		$5	Gusto 9013
5/26/79	82	4	9 I Still Believe In You .... *It's My Life*		$5	Gusto 9018
2/23/80	93	3	10 Is It Wrong .... *Lost Letter*		$5	Gusto 9024
4/23/88	89	2	11 Tonight She Went Crazy Without Me		$5	Evergreen 1068

LYERLY, Bill '81

DEBUT	PEAK	WKS	A-side / B-side	Pop	$	Label & Number
6/20/81	53	7	My Baby's Coming Home Again Today .... *Tryin' To Drink You Off My Mind*		$4	RCA 12255

LYNDELL, Liz '81
Born Elizabeth Jones Tidwell in Fairview, Tennessee. Singer/songwriter. Acted in the movie *That's Country*.

DEBUT	PEAK	WKS	A-side / B-side	Pop	$	Label & Number
10/11/80	88	2	1 Undercover Man .... *How I'd Love To Be With You Tonight*		$5	Koala 326
3/7/81	78	4	2 I'm Gonna Let Go (And Love Somebody) .... *Leavin' Your Tracks On My Mind*		$5	Koala 330
7/11/81	85	3	3 Right In The Wrong Direction .... *Goin' Back To The Country*		$5	Koala 332

LYNDEN, Tracy '85

DEBUT	PEAK	WKS	A-side / B-side	Pop	$	Label & Number
5/25/85	80	5	Straight Laced Lady		$4	RCA 14059

LYNN, Jenny '78

DEBUT	PEAK	WKS	A-side / B-side	Pop	$	Label & Number
9/23/78	86	3	Taste Of Love		$8	Colonial 102

LYNN, Judy '62
Born Judy Lynn Voiten on 4/12/36 in Boise, Idaho. Singer/songwriter. Retired in 1980 to become an ordained minister.

DEBUT	PEAK	WKS	A-side / B-side	Pop	$	Label & Number
8/18/62	7	16	1 Footsteps Of A Fool — *This Lonely Pillow*		$12	United Artists 472
1/26/63	29	1	2 My Secret .... *I Just Want To See You Once More*		$12	United Artists 519
4/6/63	16	15	3 My Father's Voice .... *When You Thanked Me For The Roses*		$12	United Artists 571
5/15/71	74	2	4 Married To A Memory .... *So Natural Is My Love*	104	$8	Amaret 131
1/18/75	92	5	5 Padre .... *Burden Of Freedom*		$6	Warner 8059
			#13 Pop hit for Toni Arden in 1958			

LYNN, Loretta ★18★ '72
Born Loretta Webb on 4/14/34 in Butcher Holler, Kentucky. Singer/songwriter/guitarist. Married to Oliver "Mooney" Lynn from 1/10/48 until his death on 8/22/96 (age 69). Joined the *Grand Ole Opry* in 1962. Her autobiography and movie called *Coal Miner's Daughter* (which starred **Sissy Spacek** as Lynn). Elected to the Country Music Hall of Fame in 1988. Sister of **Crystal Gayle**, **Peggy Sue** and **Jay Lee Webb**; distant cousin of **Patty Loveless**. Her son **Ernest Ray** and daughters Patsy and Peggy (as **The Lynns**) also recorded. CMA Awards: 1967, 1972 & 1973 Female Vocalist of the Year; 1972 Entertainer of the Year; 1972, 1973, 1974 & 1975 Vocal Duo of the Year (with **Conway Twitty**).

1)One's On The Way 2)Love Is The Foundation 3)Somebody Somewhere 4)After The Fire Is Gone
5)Out Of My Head And Back In My Bed

DEBUT	PEAK	WKS	A-side / B-side	Pop	$	Label & Number
6/13/60	14	9	1 I'm A Honky Tonk Girl .... *Whispering Sea*		$500	Zero 107
7/7/62	6	16	2 Success — *A Hundred Proof Heartache*		$15	Decca 31384
6/8/63	13	11	3 The Other Woman .... *Who'll Help Me Get Over You*		$10	Decca 31471
11/16/63+	4	25	4 Before I'm Over You — *Where Were You*		$10	Decca 31541
5/2/64	3	24	5 Wine Women And Song — *This Haunted House*		$10	Decca 31608

DEBUT	PEAK	WKS	Gold	A-side *(Chart Hit)* .... B-side	Pop	$	Pic	Label & Number
				LYNN, Loretta — Cont'd				
7/25/64	11	23		6 **Mr. And Mrs. Used To Be** .... *Love Was Right Here All The Time*		$10		Decca 31643
				ERNEST TUBB AND LORETTA LYNN				
12/5/64+	3	23		7 **Happy Birthday** *When Lonely Hits Your Heart*		$10		Decca 31707
5/22/65	7	18		8 **Blue Kentucky Girl** *Two Steps Forward*		$10		Decca 31769
7/24/65	24	11		9 **Our Hearts Are Holding Hands** .... *We're Not Kids Anymore*		$10		Decca 31793
				ERNEST TUBB AND LORETTA LYNN				
9/18/65	10	16		10 **The Home You're Tearin' Down** *Farther To Go*		$10		Decca 31836
2/5/66	4	14		11 **Dear Uncle Sam** *Hurtin' For Certain*		$10		Decca 31893
6/4/66	2²	23		12 **You Ain't Woman Enough** *God Gave Me A Heart To Forgive*		$10		Decca 31966
11/12/66+	❶¹	19		13 **Don't Come Home A'Drinkin' (With Lovin' On Your Mind)** *Saint To A Sinner*		$10		Decca 32045
2/25/67	45	9		14 **Sweet Thang** ....*Beautiful, Unhappy Home*		$10		Decca 32091
				ERNEST TUBB AND LORETTA LYNN				
5/13/67	7	17		15 **If You're Not Gone Too Long/**		$8		Decca 32127
6/10/67	72	2		16 **A Man I Hardly Know**		$8		Decca 32127
9/23/67	5	17		17 **What Kind Of Girl (Do You Think I Am?)** *Bargain Basement Dress*		$8		Decca 32184
2/24/68	❶¹	17		18 **Fist City** *Slowly Killing Me*		$8		Decca 32264
6/15/68	2¹	16		19 **You've Just Stepped In (From Stepping Out On Me)** *Taking The Place Of My Man*		$8		Decca 32332
10/26/68	3	16		20 **Your Squaw Is On The Warpath** *Let Me Go, You're Hurtin' Me*		$8		Decca 32392
2/22/69	❶¹	16		21 **Woman Of The World (Leave My World Alone)** *Sneakin' In*		$8		Decca 32439
6/14/69	18	10		22 **Who's Gonna Take The Garbage Out** .... *Somewhere Between*		$8		Decca 32496
				ERNEST TUBB And LORETTA LYNN				
7/19/69	3	15		23 **To Make A Man (Feel Like A Man)** *One Little Reason*		$8		Decca 32513
11/29/69+	11	16		24 **Wings Upon Your Horns** ....*Let's Get Back Down To Earth*		$8		Decca 32586
3/7/70	4	14		25 **I Know How** *Journey To The End Of My World*		$8		Decca 32637
6/27/70	6	15		26 **You Wanna Give Me A Lift** *What's The Bottle Done To My Baby*		$8		Decca 32693
10/31/70	❶¹	15		27 **Coal Miner's Daughter** *The Man Of The House*	83	$8	■	Decca 32749
2/6/71	❶²	14		28 **After The Fire Is Gone** *The One I Can't Live Without*	56	$7		Decca 32776
				CONWAY TWITTY/LORETTA LYNN				
3/27/71	3	15		29 **I Wanna Be Free** *If I Never Love Again (It'll Be Too Soon)*	94	$7		Decca 32796
7/31/71	5	16		30 **You're Lookin' At Country** *When You're Poor*		$7		Decca 32851
10/2/71	❶¹	17		31 **Lead Me On** *Four Glass Walls*		$7		Decca 32873
				LORETTA LYNN AND CONWAY TWITTY				
12/11/71+	❶²	16		32 **One's On The Way** *Kinfolks Holler*		$7		Decca 32900
				first released on Decca 32900 as "Here In Topeka" ($15)				
7/8/72	3	15		33 **Here I Am Again** *My Kind Of Man*		$7		Decca 32974
12/9/72+	❶¹	16		34 **Rated "X"** *'Til The Pain Outwears The Shame*		$7		Decca 33039
5/19/73	❶²	15		35 **Love Is The Foundation** *What Sundown Does To You*	102	$6		MCA 40058
6/23/73	❶¹	14		36 **Louisiana Woman, Mississippi Man** *Living Together Alone*		$6		MCA 40079
				LORETTA LYNN/CONWAY TWITTY				
11/17/73+	3	16		37 **Hey Loretta** *Turn Me Anyway But Loose*		$6		MCA 40150
4/27/74	4	15		38 **They Don't Make 'Em Like My Daddy** *Nothin'*		$6		MCA 40223
6/15/74	❶¹	15		39 **As Soon As I Hang Up The Phone** *A Lifetime Before*		$6		MCA 40251
				LORETTA LYNN/CONWAY TWITTY				
9/7/74	❶¹	17		40 **Trouble In Paradise** *We've Already Tasted Love*		$6		MCA 40283
2/15/75	5	12		41 **The Pill** *Will You Be There*	70	$6		MCA 40358
6/21/75	❶¹	16		42 **Feelins'** *You Done Lost Your Baby*		$6		MCA 40420
				LORETTA LYNN/CONWAY TWITTY				
8/2/75	10	14		43 **Home** *You Take Me To Heaven Every Night*		$6		MCA 40438
11/15/75+	2¹	14		44 **When The Tingle Becomes A Chill** *All I Want From You (Is Away)*		$6		MCA 40484
4/10/76	20	10		45 **Red, White And Blue** .... *Sounds Of A New Love (Being Born)*		$6		MCA 40541
6/19/76	3	12		46 **The Letter** *God Bless America Again*		$6		MCA 40572
				LORETTA LYNN/CONWAY TWITTY				
9/11/76	❶²	17		47 **Somebody Somewhere (Don't Know What He's Missin' Tonight)** *Sundown Tavern*		$6		MCA 40607
2/26/77	❶¹	17		48 **She's Got You** *The Lady That Lived Here Before*		$6		MCA 40679
6/4/77	2³	14		49 **I Can't Love You Enough** *The Bed I'm Dreaming On*		$6		MCA 40728
				LORETTA LYNN/CONWAY TWITTY				
8/6/77	7	13		50 **Why Can't He Be You** *I Keep On Putting On*		$6		MCA 40747
12/3/77+	❶²	15		51 **Out Of My Head And Back In My Bed** *Old Rooster*		$6		MCA 40832
5/27/78	12	11		52 **Spring Fever** ....*God Bless The Children*		$6		MCA 40910
6/24/78	6	11		53 **From Seven Till Ten/**		$6		MCA 40920
		9		54 **You're The Reason Our Kids Are Ugly**		$6		MCA 40920
				LORETTA LYNN/CONWAY TWITTY (above 2)				
11/4/78	10	13		55 **We've Come A Long Way, Baby** *I Can't Feel You Anymore*		$5	■	MCA 40954
5/5/79	3	14		56 **I Can't Feel You Anymore** *True Love Needs To Keep In Touch*		$5		MCA 41021
10/13/79	5	14		57 **I've Got A Picture Of Us On My Mind** *I Don't Feel Like A Movie Tonight*		$5		MCA 41129
11/10/79+	9	14		58 **You Know Just What I'd Do/**		$5		MCA 41141
		14		59 **The Sadness Of It All**		$5		MCA 41141
				CONWAY TWITTY/LORETTA LYNN (above 2)				
3/1/80	35	8		60 **Pregnant Again** .... *You're A Cross I Can't Bear*		$4		MCA 41185
5/10/80	5	15		61 **It's True Love** *Hit The Road Jack*		$4		MCA 41232
				CONWAY TWITTY & LORETTA LYNN				
6/7/80	30	11		62 **Naked In The Rain** .... *I Should Be Over You By Now*		$4		MCA 41250
10/25/80	20	13		63 **Cheatin' On A Cheater** .... *Until I Met You*		$4		MCA 51015
1/31/81	7	15		64 **Lovin' What Your Lovin' Does To Me** *Silent Partner*		$4		MCA 51050
				CONWAY TWITTY & LORETTA LYNN				

210

LYNN, Loretta — Cont'd

DEBUT	PEAK	WKS	A-side / B-side	$	Pic	Label & Number
2/28/81	20	12	65 Somebody Led Me Away .... *Everybody's Lookin' For Somebody New*	$4		MCA 51058
5/30/81	2²	18	66 I Still Believe In Waltzes *Oh Honey - Oh Babe*	$4		MCA 51114
			CONWAY TWITTY & LORETTA LYNN			
1/23/82	9	19	67 I Lie *If I Ain't Got It (You Don't Need It)*	$4		MCA 52005
8/14/82	19	16	68 Making Love From Memory .... *Don't It Feel Good*	$4		MCA 52092
1/22/83	39	12	69 Breakin' It/	$4		MCA 52158
		12	70 There's All Kinds Of Smoke (In The Barroom)			
5/28/83	53	10	71 Lyin', Cheatin', Woman Chasin', Honky Tonkin', Whiskey Drinkin' You.............. *Starlight, Starbright*	$4		MCA 52219
11/26/83	59	9	72 Walking With My Memories .... *It's Gone*	$4		MCA 52289
7/20/85	19	18	73 Heart Don't Do This To Me .... S:19 / A:22 *Adam's Rib*	$4	■	MCA 52621
11/9/85	72	5	74 Wouldn't It Be Great .... *One Man Band*	$4	■	MCA 52706
2/8/86	81	5	75 Just A Woman .... *Take Me In Your Arms (And Hold Me)*	$4		MCA 52766
4/16/88	57	12	76 Who Was That Stranger .... *Elzie Banks*	$4		MCA 53320
12/25/93+	68	2	77 Silver Threads And Golden Needles .... *Let Her Fly*	$3	▌	Columbia 77294
			PARTON/WYNETTE/LYNN			

LYNN, Marcia **'88**
Born Marcia Lynne Dickinson on 11/19/63 in North Adams, Massachusetts.

DEBUT	PEAK	WKS	A-side / B-side	$	Pic	Label & Number
3/14/87	77	5	1 You've Got That Leaving Look In Your Eye .... *Lie Left On His Finger*	$5		Soundwaves 4784
12/26/87+	62	8	2 Don't Start The Fire	$5		Evergreen 1063

LYNN, Michelle **'89**

DEBUT	PEAK	WKS	A-side / B-side	$	Pic	Label & Number
1/14/89	92	2	1 The Letter................	$6		Master 07
6/3/89	88	2	2 Brand New Week .... *The Letter*	$6		Master 11

LYNN, Rebecca **'78**

DEBUT	PEAK	WKS	A-side / B-side	$	Pic	Label & Number
7/8/78	39	8	1 Music, Music, Music *No More Tears*	$6		Scorpion 0550
			#1 Pop hit for Teresa Brewer in 1950			
10/14/78	69	5	2 Minstrel Man .... *He Loves Me All To Pieces*	$6		Scorpion 0559
2/24/79	83	5	3 Goody Goody .... *My Happiness*	$6		Scorpion 0573
			#1 Pop hit for Benny Goodman's Orchestra in 1936; #20 Pop hit for Frankie Lymon & The Teenagers in 1957			
7/21/79	69	6	4 Make Believe You Love Me/	$6		Scorpion 0581
6/2/79	82	3	5 Disco Girl Go Away			
3/1/80	87	3	6 Fairytale	$6		Sunbird 106

LYNN, Trisha **'89**

DEBUT	PEAK	WKS	A-side / B-side	$	Pic	Label & Number
7/2/88	76	2	1 I Go To Pieces	$6		Oak 1053
			#9 Pop hit for Peter & Gordon in 1965			
5/13/89	82	3	2 Kiss Me Darling	$6		Oak 1072
7/29/89	69	5	3 Not Fade Away	$6		Oak 1062
			TRISH LYNN			
			#48 Pop hit for The Rolling Stones in 1964			
10/28/89	65	4	4 I Can't Help Myself	$6		Oak 1083
			#1 Pop hit for the Four Tops in 1965			

LYNNE, Shelby **'91**
Born Shelby Lynn Moorer on 10/22/68 in Quantico, Virginia; raised in Jackson, Alabama. Female singer.
1)Things Are Tough All Over 2)I'll Lie Myself To Sleep 3)The Hurtin' Side

DEBUT	PEAK	WKS	A-side / B-side	$	Pic	Label & Number
9/3/88	43	10	1 If I Could Bottle This Up .... S:22 *I Always Get It Right With You*	$3		Epic 08011
			GEORGE JONES & SHELBY LYNNE			
3/18/89	93	1	2 Under Your Spell Again .... *Blue To The Bone*	$3		Epic 68584
6/24/89	38	11	3 The Hurtin' Side .... *If I Could Bottle This Up*	$3		Epic 68942
10/21/89	62	7	4 Little Bits And Pieces .... *Your Love Stays With Me*	$3		Epic 73032
6/30/90	26	17	5 I'll Lie Myself To Sleep .... *What About This Girl*	$3	▌	Epic 73319
10/27/90+	23	20	6 Things Are Tough All Over *I Walk The Line*	$3	▌	Epic 73521
3/23/91	45	16	7 What About The Love We Made .... *I'll Lie Myself To Sleep*	$3		Epic 73716
7/27/91	50	9	8 The Very First Lasting Love .... *Lonely Weekends*	$3		Epic 73904
			SHELBY LYNNE WITH LES TAYLOR			
11/9/91	54	13	9 Don't Cross Your Heart .... *Stop Me*	$3		Epic 74062
7/17/93	69	6	10 Feelin' Kind Of Lonely Tonight .... *Don't Cry For Me*	$4	▌	Morgan Creek 23018
6/24/95	59	8	11 Slow Me Down		▌	album cut
			from the album *Restless* on Magnatone 102			

LYNNS, The **'97**
Identical twin daughters of **Loretta Lynn**: Peggy and Patsy Lynn (b: 8/6/64).

DEBUT	PEAK	WKS	A-side / B-side	$	Pic	Label & Number
10/25/97	48	10	Nights Like These .... *Oh My Goodness*	$3	▌	*Reprise 17276*

M

MAC, Jimmy **'84**

DEBUT	PEAK	WKS	A-side / B-side	$	Pic	Label & Number
6/23/84	93	1	You Really Know How To Break A Heart................	$7		AV 924

MacGREGOR, Byron '74

Born Gary Mack in 1948 in Calgary, Alberta, Canada. Died on 1/3/95 (age 46). News director at radio station CKLW in Detroit when he did the narration for "Americans."

DEBUT	PEAK	WKS	Gold	A-side	B-side	Pop	$	Pic	Label & Number
1/26/74	59	5	●	Americans .... *America The Beautiful* [S]		4	$5		Westbound 222
				background music: "America The Beautiful"					

MacGREGOR, Mary '77

Born on 5/6/48 in St. Paul, Minnesota. Pop singer.

1/8/77	3	16	●	1 Torn Between Two Lovers	*I Just Want To Love You*	❶²	$5		Ariola America 7638
4/23/77	36	10		2 This Girl (Has Turned Into A Woman)	*Good Together*	46	$5		Ariola America 7662
8/6/77	86	3		3 For A While	*The Lady I Am*	90	$5		Ariola America 7667

MACK, Bobby '73

| 8/18/73 | 79 | 6 | | Love Will Come Again (Just Like The Roses) .... *A Love Nobody Knows* | | | $6 | | Ace of Hearts 0467 |

MACK, Gary '83

Born in Odessa, Texas.

3/20/76	94	2		1 To Be With You Again .... *No Easy Way*			$6		Soundwaves 4528
6/26/76	95	2		2 One Love Down .... *Mister And Mississippi*			$6		Soundwaves 4532
4/2/83	90	2		3 I've Been Out Of Love Too Long .... *My Most Requested Song*			$6		Grand Prize 5205

MACK, Warner ★169★ '65

Born Warner MacPherson on 4/2/38 in Nashville; raised in Vicksburg, Mississippi. Singer/songwriter/guitarist.

1)The Bridge Washed Out 2)Sittin' On A Rock 3)Talkin' To The Wall 4)How Long Will It Take 5)Sittin' In An All Nite Cafe

8/12/57+	9	36		1 Is It Wrong (For Loving You)	S:9 / A:11 *Baby Squeeze Me*	61	$15		Decca 30301
1/11/64	34	7		2 Surely	*This Little Hurt*		$15		Decca 31559
11/28/64+	4	24		3 Sittin' In An All Nite Cafe	*Blue Mood*		$15		Decca 31684
5/29/65	❶¹	23		4 The Bridge Washed Out	*The Biggest Part Of Me*		$8		Decca 31774
11/6/65+	3	19		5 Sittin' On A Rock (Crying In A Creek)	*The Way It Feels To Die*		$8		Decca 31853
3/26/66	3	20		6 Talkin' To The Wall	*One Mile More*		$8		Decca 31911
9/3/66	4	17		7 It Takes A Lot Of Money	*A Million Thoughts From My Mind*		$8		Decca 32004
2/11/67	8	17		8 Drifting Apart	*When We're Alone At Night*		$8		Decca 32082
6/24/67	4	17		9 How Long Will It Take	*As Long As I Keep Wantin' (I'll Keep Wanting You)*		$8		Decca 32142
11/11/67+	11	16		10 I'd Give The World (To Be Back Loving You) .... *It's Been A Good Life Loving You*			$8		Decca 32211
5/18/68	7	16		11 I'm Gonna Move On	*Tell Me To Go (Tell Me To Stay)*		$8		Decca 32308
11/23/68+	23	19		12 Don't Wake Me I'm Dreaming .... *When The Walls Come Tumbling Down*			$8		Decca 32394
5/3/69	6	13		13 Leave My Dream Alone	*You're Always Turnin' Up Again (And I'm Always Fallin' Down)*		$8		Decca 32473
9/27/69	8	13		14 I'll Still Be Missing You	*Sunshine Bring Back My Sunshine*		$8		Decca 32547
4/4/70	19	12		15 Love Hungry .... *Love Is Where The Heart Is*			$8		Decca 32646
9/12/70	16	13		16 Live For The Good Times .... *Another Mountain To Climb*			$8		Decca 32725
2/20/71	34	11		17 You Make Me Feel Like A Man .... *Changin' Your Style*			$8		Decca 32781
8/28/71	53	9		18 I Wanna Be Loved Completely .... *Sweetie*			$7		Decca 32858
2/26/72	45	9		19 Draggin' The River .... *These Arms*			$7		Decca 32926
8/5/72	59	6		20 You're Burnin' My House Down................... *Your Warm Love*			$7		Decca 32982
1/27/73	54	7		21 Some Roads Have No Ending .... *I've Got A Feeling (About You)*			$7		Decca 33045
11/10/73+	91	7		22 Goodbyes Don't Come Easy .... *Christie, Christie*			$5		MCA 40137
11/19/77	87	5		23 These Crazy Thoughts (Run Through My Mind) .... *I Wanna Go Back*			$5		Pageboy 31

MACKEY, Bobby '82

Born on 3/25/48 in Concord, Kentucky. Singer/songwriter/guitarist.

| 6/12/82 | 57 | 8 | | Pepsi Man .... *What A Difference* | | | $6 | | Moon Shine 3007 |

★275★ MADDOX, Rose '63

Born Roselea Arbana Brogdon on 8/15/25 in Boaz, Alabama; raised in Bakersfield, California. Died of kidney failure on 4/15/98 (age 72). Singer/songwriter/fiddle player.

1)Sing A Little Song Of Heartache 2)Loose Talk 3)Mental Cruelty

5/18/59	22	3		1 Gambler's Love.. *What Makes Me Hang Around*			$20		Capitol 4177
1/30/61	14	13		2 Kissing My Pillow/			$15		Capitol 4487
2/13/61	15	7		3 I Want To Live Again....................................			$15		Capitol 4487
5/22/61	4	14		4 Loose Talk/			$15		Capitol 4550
5/15/61	8	12		5 Mental Cruelty			$15		Capitol 4550
				BUCK OWENS And ROSE MADDOX (above 2)					
8/14/61	14	6		6 Conscience, I'm Guilty .... *Lonely Street*			$15		Capitol 4598
11/10/62+	3	18		7 Sing A Little Song Of Heartache	*Tie A Ribbon In The Apple Tree*		$15		Capitol 4845
3/16/63	18	8		8 Lonely Teardrops .... *George Carter*			$15		Capitol 4905
6/15/63	18	13		9 Down To The River...................................... *I Don't Hear You*			$15		Capitol 4975
8/3/63	15	6		10 We're The Talk Of The Town/			$15		Capitol 4992
8/10/63	19	6		11 Sweethearts In Heaven			$15		Capitol 4992
				BUCK OWENS AND ROSE MADDOX (above 2)					
11/23/63	18	6		12 Somebody Told Somebody .... *Let Me Kiss You For Old Times*			$12		Capitol 5038
3/7/64	44	6		13 Alone With You .... *When The Sun Goes Down*			$12		Capitol 5110
8/1/64	30	8		14 Blue Bird Let Me Tag Along .... *Stand Up Fool*			$12		Capitol 5186

MAGGARD, Cledus   '76
Born Jay Huguely in Quick Sand, Kentucky. Recorded "The White Knight" while working at Leslie Advertising in Greenville, South Carolina.

CLEDUS MAGGARD And The Citizen's Band:

DEBUT	PEAK	WKS	# A-side	B-side	Pop	$	Label & Number
12/20/75+	❶¹	14	1 The White Knight	(long version) [N]	19	$4	Mercury 73751
4/17/76	42	7	2 Kentucky Moonrunner	Dad I Gotta Go [N]	85	$4	Mercury 73789

CLEDUS MAGGARD:

8/14/76	73	4	3 Virgil And The $300 Vacation	The Banana Bowl [N]		$4	Mercury 73823
7/15/78	82	4	4 The Farmer	Lovin' May Be Dangerous To Your Health [N]		$4	Mercury 55033

MAINES BROTHERS BAND, The   '85
Family group from Texas: Kenny (guitar, harmonica), Steve (guitar), Lloyd (steel guitar) and Donnie (drums) Maines. With Richard Bowden (fiddle), Cary Banks (keyboards) and Jerry Brownlow (bass).f

12/3/83	72	6	1 Louisiana Anna	They Call It Love		$4	Mercury 814561
3/24/84	85	3	2 You Are A Miracle	Dixieland Rock		$4	Mercury 818346
2/9/85	24	16	3 Everybody Needs Love On Saturday Night S:21 / A:23 Little Broken Pieces			$3	Mercury 880536
8/10/85	84	4	4 When My Blue Moon Turns To Gold Again Have You Heard The Latest Blues			$3	Mercury 880995
			#19 Pop hit for Elvis Presley in 1956				
11/23/85	72	8	5 Some Of Shelly's Blues	Roll Truck Roll		$3	Mercury 884228
			written by Mike Nesmith of The Monkees				
3/15/86	59	7	6 Danger Zone	Gonna Get Well Tonite		$3	Mercury 884483

MALCHAK, Tim   '88
Born on 6/25/57 in Binghamton, New York. Singer/songwriter/guitarist. Half of **Malchak & Rucker** duo.

11/22/86	68	7	1 Easy Does It	Let Me Down Easy		$5	Alpine 004
3/7/87	37	13	2 Colorado Moon	Let Me Down Easy		$5	Alpine 006
8/1/87	39	11	3 Restless Angel	I Owe It All To You		$5	Alpine 007
1/30/88	35	14	4 It Goes Without Saying	I Owe It All To You		$5	Alpine 008
10/1/88	43	11	5 Not A Night Goes By	I Owe It All To You		$5	Alpine 009
4/15/89	70	4	6 Not Like This	I Owe It All To You		$3	Universal 66004
8/5/89	54	6	7 If You Had A Heart	Sweet Virginia		$3	Universal 66013

MALCHAK & RUCKER   '86
Duo of **Tim Malchak** and Dwight Rucker. White singer Malchak was born on 6/25/57 in Binghamton, New York. Black singer Rucker was born on 3/21/52 in Oxford, New York.

11/10/84	92	2	1 Just Like That			$5	Revolver 004
3/23/85	67	5	2 Why Didn't I Think Of That			$5	Revolver 007
11/2/85	69	6	3 I Could Love You In A Heartbeat			$5	Alpine 001
5/3/86	67	5	4 Let Me Down Easy	I Could Love You In A Heartbeat		$5	Alpine 002
8/2/86	64	6	5 Slow Motion			$5	Alpine 003

MALENA, Don   '87
Born in Bakersfield, California. Singer/songwriter/guitarist.

1/10/87	72	4	1 Ready Or Not	Lodi		$6	Maxima 1256
6/27/87	76	4	2 Moonwalkin'			$6	Maxima 1277
1/23/88	75	4	3 Dance For Me			$6	Maxima 1311

MALLORY, Doug — see MURRAY, Anne

MANCINI, Henry — see PRIDE, Charley

MANDRELL, Barbara ★46★   '78
Born on 12/25/48 in Houston; raised in Oceanside, California. Singer/multi-instrumentalist. Sister of **Louise Mandrell**. Hosted own TV series from 1980-82; acted on TV's *Sunset Beach* in 1997. Joined the *Grand Ole Opry* in 1972. CMA Awards: 1979 & 1981 Female Vocalist of the Year; 1980 & 1981 Entertainer of the Year.

1)Sleeping Single In A Double Bed 2)I Don't Want To Be Right 3)Years 4)One Of A Kind Pair Of Fools 5)'Till You're Gone

9/13/69	55	7	1 I've Been Loving You Too Long (To Stop Now)	Baby, Come Home		$10	Columbia 44955
			#21 Pop hit for Otis Redding in 1965				
5/23/70	18	12	2 Playin' Around With Love	I Almost Lost My Mind		$8	Columbia 45143
10/3/70	6	14	3 After Closing Time	My Song Of Love		$8	Epic 10656
			DAVID HOUSTON AND BARBARA MANDRELL				
1/30/71	17	12	4 Do Right Woman - Do Right Man	The Letter	128	$8	Columbia 45307
6/26/71	12	12	5 Treat Him Right	Break My Mind		$8	Columbia 45391
			#2 Pop hit for Roy Head in 1965				
10/2/71	20	12	6 We've Got Everything But Love	Try A Little Harder		$8	Epic 10779
			DAVID HOUSTON AND BARBARA MANDRELL				
12/11/71+	10	13	7 Tonight My Baby's Coming Home	He'll Never Take The Place Of You		$8	Columbia 45505
4/15/72	11	13	8 Show Me	Satisfied		$8	Columbia 45580
			#35 Pop hit for Joe Tex in 1967				
9/16/72	24	13	9 A Perfect Match	Almost Persuaded		$8	Epic 10908
			DAVID HOUSTON AND BARBARA MANDRELL				
11/4/72	27	12	10 Holdin' On (To The Love I Got)	Smile Somebody Loves You		$8	Columbia 45702
4/21/73	24	11	11 Give A Little, Take A Little	Ain't It Good		$7	Columbia 45819
8/18/73	7	17	12 The Midnight Oil	In The Name Of Love		$7	Columbia 45904
12/22/73+	6	16	13 I Love You, I Love You	Let's Go Down Together		$7	Epic 11068
			DAVID HOUSTON and BARBARA MANDRELL				

DEBUT	PEAK	WKS	Gold	A-side (Chart Hit)..B-side	Pop	$	Pic	Label & Number
				MANDRELL, Barbara — Cont'd				
5/25/74	40	12		14 Lovin' You Is Worth It .... *How Can It Be Wrong (When It Feels So Right)*		$7		Epic 11120
				DAVID HOUSTON and BARBARA MANDRELL				
6/15/74	12	16		15 This Time I Almost Made It ....*Son-Of-A-Gun*		$7		Columbia 46054
8/10/74	14	16		16 Ten Commandments Of Love..*Try A Little Harder*		$7		Epic 20005
				DAVID HOUSTON and BARBARA MANDRELL				
				#22 Pop hit for Harvey & The Moonglows in 1958				
2/22/75	39	9		17 Wonder When My Baby's Comin' Home ....*Kiss The Hurt Away*		$7		Columbia 10082
12/20/75+	5	17		18 Standing Room Only *Can't Help But Wonder*		$6		ABC/Dot 17601
5/8/76	16	13		19 That's What Friends Are For ....*The Beginning Of The End*		$6		ABC/Dot 17623
8/14/76	24	12		20 Love Is Thin Ice..*Will We Ever Make Love In Love Again*		$6		ABC/Dot 17644
12/18/76+	16	12		21 Midnight Angel ....*I Count You*		$6		ABC/Dot 17668
4/2/77	3	17		22 Married But Not To Each Other *Fool's Gold*		$6		ABC/Dot 17688
				#16 R&B hit for Denise LaSalle in 1976				
9/3/77	12	14		23 Hold Me ....*This Is Not Another Cheatin' Song*		$6		ABC/Dot 17716
12/24/77+	4	16		24 Woman To Woman *Let The Rain Out*	92	$6		ABC/Dot 17736
				#22 Pop hit for Shirley Brown in 1974				
5/20/78	5	13		25 Tonight *If I Were A River*	103	$5		ABC 12362
9/9/78	❶³	15		26 Sleeping Single In A Double Bed *Just One More Of Your Goodbyes*	102	$5		ABC 12403
2/17/79	❶¹	14		27 (If Loving You Is Wrong) I Don't Want To Be Right *I Feel The Hurt Coming On*	31	$5		ABC 12451
				#3 Pop hit for Luther Ingram in 1972				
8/11/79	4	14		28 Fooled By A Feeling *Love Takes A Long Time To Die*	89	$4		MCA 41077
12/15/79+	❶¹	15		29 Years *Darlin'*	102	$4	■	MCA 41162
				#35 Pop hit for Wayne Newton in 1980				
6/21/80	3	16		30 Crackers *Using Him To Get To You*	105	$4		MCA 41263
10/11/80	6	17		31 The Best Of Strangers *Sometime, Somewhere, Somehow*		$4		MCA 51001
2/7/81	13	13		32 Love Is Fair/		$4		MCA 51062
		13		33 Sometime, Somewhere, Somehow		$4		MCA 51062
5/9/81	❶¹	13		34 I Was Country When Country Wasn't Cool *A Woman's Got A Right*		$4		MCA 51107
				George Jones (guest vocal)				
9/5/81	2¹	16		35 Wish You Were Here *She's Out There Dancin' Alone*		$4		MCA 51171
				above 2 are "live" recordings				
5/1/82	❶¹	19		36 'Till You're Gone *You're Not Supposed To Be Here*		$4		MCA 52038
9/4/82	9	15		37 Operator, Long Distance Please *Black And White*		$4		MCA 52111
4/23/83	4	19		38 In Times Like These *Loveless*		$4		MCA 52206
8/27/83	❶¹	21		39 One Of A Kind Pair Of Fools *As Well As Can Be Expected*		$4		MCA 52258
2/18/84	3	21		40 Happy Birthday Dear Heartache *A Man's Not A Man ('Til He's Loved By A Woman)*		$4		MCA 52340
6/9/84	2¹	21		41 Only A Lonely Heart Knows *I Wonder What The Rich Folk Are Doin' Tonight*		$4		MCA 52397
7/21/84	3	20		42 To Me S:15 / A:23 *We Were Meant For Each Other*		$4	■	MCA 52415
				BARBARA MANDRELL/LEE GREENWOOD				
10/6/84	11	20		43 Crossword Puzzle ....A:9 / S:12 *If It's Not One Thing It's Another*		$4		MCA 52465
2/2/85	19	15		44 It Should Have Been Love By Now ..A:18 / S:20 *Can't Get Too Much Of A Good Thing*		$4		MCA 52525
				BARBARA MANDRELL/LEE GREENWOOD				
3/9/85	7	20		45 There's No Love In Tennessee S:5 / A:8 *Sincerely I'm Yours*		$4	■	MCA 52537
8/24/85	8	18		46 Angel In Your Arms S:8 / A:8 *Don't Look In My Eyes*		$4		MCA 52645
				#6 Pop hit for Hot in 1977				
12/7/85+	4	19		47 Fast Lanes And Country Roads S:3 / A:4 *You Only You*		$4	■	MCA 52737
3/29/86	20	14		48 When You Get To The Heart ....A:20 / S:21 *Survivors*		$4		MCA 52802
				BARBARA MANDRELL with the Oak Ridge Boys				
8/16/86	6	22		49 No One Mends A Broken Heart Like You S:8 *Love Is Adventure In The Great Unknown*		$4		MCA 52900
7/4/87	13	17		50 Child Support..S:7 *I'm Glad I Married You*		$3		EMI America 43032
12/5/87	48	11		51 Sure Feels Good..*Sunshine Street*		$3		EMI America 50102
3/12/88	49	11		52 Angels Love Bad Men ....*Sunshine Street*		$3		EMI America 43042
				Waylon Jennings (guest vocal)				
8/20/88	5	22		53 I Wish That I Could Fall In Love Today S:9 *I'll Be Your Jukebox Tonight*		$3		Capitol 44220
2/4/89	19	16		54 My Train Of Thought...*Blanket Of Love*		$3		Capitol 44276
7/1/89	49	8		55 Mirror Mirror...*Blanket Of Love*		$3		Capitol 44383

MANDRELL, Louise ★185★   '85

Born on 7/13/54 in Corpus Christi, Texas. Singer/multi-instrumentalist. Sister of **Barbara Mandrell**. Formerly married to **R.C. Bannon** and Gary Buck (of **The Four Guys**).

1)I Wanna Say Yes 2)Save Me 3)I'm Not Through Loving You Yet 4)Maybe My Baby 5)Too Hot To Sleep

DEBUT	PEAK	WKS		A-side	B-side	$	Label & Number
8/26/78	77	5		1 Put It On Me..*Yes, I Do*		$5	Epic 50565
1/6/79	69	5		2 Everlasting Love ....*You Never Cross My Mind*		$5	Epic 50651
				#6 Pop hit for Carl Carlton in 1974			
3/10/79	46	8		3 I Thought You'd Never Ask ....*Yes, I Do*		$4	Epic 50668
				LOUISE MANDRELL & R.C. BANNON			
6/2/79	13	12		4 Reunited ....*Hello There Stranger*		$4	Epic 50717
				LOUISE MANDRELL & R.C. BANNON			
				#1 Pop hit for Peaches & Herb in 1979			

DEBUT	PEAK	WKS	Gold	A-side (Chart Hit) ... B-side	Pop	$	Pic	Label & Number
				MANDRELL, Louise — Cont'd				
9/1/79	72	5		5 I Never Loved Anyone Like I Love You .... *Surrender To My Heart*		$4		Epic 50752
11/17/79	48	8		6 We Love Each Other .... *I Want To (Do Everything For You)*		$4		Epic 50789
				LOUISE MANDRELL & R.C. BANNON				
3/29/80	63	5		7 Wake Me Up .... *That Song Called Forever*		$4		Epic 50856
7/19/80	82	4		8 Beggin' For Mercy .... *Come Here*		$4		Epic 50896
9/27/80	61	6		9 Love Insurance .... *When It Hurts You Most*		$4		Epic 50935
11/28/81+	35	11		10 Where There's Smoke There's Fire .... *Before You*		$4		RCA 12359
				LOUISE MANDRELL AND R.C. BANNON				
2/13/82	35	12		11 (You Sure Know Your Way) Around My Heart .... *Dance Me Around Cowboy*		$4	■	RCA 13039
6/5/82	56	7		12 Our Wedding Band/		$4		RCA 13095
		7		13 Just Married				
				LOUISE MANDRELL AND R.C. BANNON (above 2)				
7/24/82	20	15		14 Some Of My Best Friends Are Old Songs *689-Double 2-0-3*		$4		RCA 13278
11/6/82+	22	16		15 Romance .... *Better Things To Do*		$4		RCA 13373
12/11/82	35	7		16 Christmas Is Just A Song For Us This Year .... *Christmas In Dixie* [X]		$4		RCA 13358
				LOUISE MANDRELL/R.C. BANNON				
2/26/83	6	17		17 Save Me .... *Trust Me*		$3		RCA 13450
7/16/83	10	19		18 Too Hot To Sleep .... *We Put On Quite A Show*		$3	■	RCA 13567
11/5/83+	13	17		19 Runaway Heart .... *There's More To Love*		$3		RCA 13649
3/24/84	7	20		20 I'm Not Through Loving You Yet .... *A New Girl In Town*		$3		RCA 13752
8/18/84	24	15		21 Goodbye Heartache .... S:19 / A:25 *You're A Hard Act To Follow*		$3		RCA 13850
12/8/84+	52	12		22 This Bed's Not Big Enough .... *Paying Through The Heart*		$3	■	RCA 13954
3/30/85	8	19		23 Maybe My Baby .... S:8 / A:10 *Are You Just Playing With Me*		$3		RCA 14039
8/17/85	5	21		24 I Wanna Say Yes .... S:4 / A:5 *There'll Never Be Another For Me*		$3		RCA 14151
12/14/85+	22	17		25 Some Girls Have All The Luck .... S:20 / A:23 *How Did It Get So Late, So Early*		$3		RCA 14251
				#10 Pop hit for Rod Stewart in 1984				
6/28/86	35	11		26 I Wanna Hear It From Your Lips .... A:39 *Summer Nights*		$3		RCA 14364
				#35 Pop hit for Eric Carmen in 1985				
2/28/87	28	13		27 Do I Have To Say Goodbye ....A:28 *Keep What We Had Going*		$3		RCA 5115
11/21/87	74	3		28 Tender Time .... *Take Me Back*		$3		RCA 5208
4/9/88	51	9		29 As Long As We Got Each Other .... *Weak Moment*		$3		RCA 20288
				LOUISE MANDRELL (with Eric Carmen)				
				MANN, Carl '76				
				Born on 8/24/42 in Huntingdon, Tennessee. Rockabilly singer/pianist. Member of the **Carl Perkins** band from 1962-64.				
5/15/76	100	1		Twilight Time .... *Belly-Rubbin' Country Soul*		$5		ABC/Dot 17621
				#1 Pop hit for The Platters in 1958				
				MANN, Lorene '65				
				Born on 1/4/37 in Huntland, Tennessee. Female singer/songwriter.				
10/2/65	23	9		1 Hurry, Mr. Peters .... *We've Got A Lot In Common*		$8		RCA Victor 8659
				JUSTIN TUBB & LORENE MANN				
				answer to "Yes, Mr. Peters" by Roy Drusky & Priscilla Mitchell				
7/30/66	44	2		2 We've Gone Too Far, Again .... *Together But Still Alone*		$8		RCA Victor 8834
				JUSTIN TUBB & LORENE MANN				
1/7/67	47	11		3 Don't Put Your Hands On Me .... *Stay Out Of My Dreams*		$8		RCA Victor 9045
5/20/67	50	8		4 Have You Ever Wanted To? .... *It Tears Me Up*		$8		RCA Victor 9183
9/23/67	63	6		5 You Love Me Too Little .... *I Couldn't Hardly*		$8		RCA Victor 9288
				ARCHIE CAMPBELL and LORENE MANN:				
1/6/68	24	15		6 The Dark End Of The Street .... *The Gettin' Place*		$8		RCA Victor 9401
6/29/68	31	10		7 Tell It Like It Is .... *If That's The Only Way*		$8		RCA Victor 9549
				#2 Pop hit for Aaron Neville in 1967				
9/28/68	57	8		8 Warm And Tender Love .... *Pledging My Love*		$8		RCA Victor 9615
				#17 Pop hit for Percy Sledge in 1966				
1/4/69	36	9		9 My Special Prayer .... *What Am I Living For*		$8		RCA Victor 9691
				MANNERS, Zeke '46				
				Born Leo Manness on 10/10/11 in San Francisco. Pianist/accordionist.				
2/16/46	2⁹	19		1 Sioux City Sue .... *Don't Dog Me 'Round* [N]		$20		Victor 20-1797
				Curly Gribbs (vocal); #3 Pop hit for **Bing Crosby** & The Jesters in 1946				
12/14/46	5	2		2 Inflation .... *Missouri* [N]		$20		Victor 20-2013
				ZEKE MANNERS and his Band (above 2)				
				MANNING, Linda '69				
				Born in Cullman, Arkansas.				
12/28/68+	54	8		Since They Fired The Band Director (At Murphy High) .... *Talk Of The Town*		$8		Mercury 72875
				MANNING, Rhonda '88				
				Born in Nashville. Daughter of DJ Ron Manning.				
12/19/87	87	3		1 Out With The Boys		$5		Soundwaves 4792
6/11/88	73	3		2 You Really Know How To Break A Heart .... *Out With The Boys*		$5		Soundwaves 4799
				MANTELLI, Steve '83				
10/9/82	94	2		1 I'll Baby You		$7		Picap 008
1/8/83	84	4		2 You're A Keep Me Wondering Kind Of Woman		$7		Picap 005
				MARCY BROS., The '89				
				Vocal trio of brothers from Hay Springs, Nebraska: Kevin, Kris and Kendal Marcy.				
5/7/88	68	5		1 The Things I Didn't Say .... *Nobody Knows/Everybody's Guessin'*		$3	■	Warner 27938
2/11/89	52	9		2 Threads Of Gold .... *Boys You Gotta Learn To Dance*		$3		Warner 27573
5/20/89	34	10		3 Cotton Pickin' Time .... *If Only Your Eyes Could Lie*		$3		Warner 22956

DEBUT	PEAK	WKS	Gold	A-side (Chart Hit) .... B-side	Pop	$	Pic	Label & Number
				MARCY BROS., The — Cont'd				
11/4/89	70	4		4 You're Not Even Crying .... *The Things I Didn't Say*		$3		Warner 22753
1/13/90	79	1		5 Missing You .... *Walkin' Shoes*		$3		Warner 22659
8/24/91	71	2		6 She Can .... *One Less Lonely Heart*		$3	▮	Atlantic 87741
				THE MARCY BROTHERS				
				MARGO & NORRO — see SMITH, Margo / WILSON, Norro				
				MARIPAT **'89**				
				Female singer Maripat Davis.				
6/24/89	97	1		No One To Talk To But The Blues		$6		Oak 1073
				MARLIN SISTERS, The — see YANKOVIC, Frankie				
				MARNEY, Ben **'81**				
				Born in Jackson, Mississippi. Singer/songwriter/guitarist.				
7/18/81	92	2		Where Cheaters Go .... *Until The Day We Die*		$7		Southern Bis. 107
				MARR, Leah **'90**				
10/1/88	83	3		1 Sealed With A Kiss		$6		Oak 1060
				#3 Pop hit for Brian Hyland in 1962				
9/23/89	80	3		2 Half Heaven Half Heartache		$6		Oak 1071
12/16/89+	76	4		3 I've Been A Fool		$6		Oak 1084
				MARRIOTT, John **'89**				
12/9/89	92	4		Modern Day Cowboy		$7		Phoenix 152
				MARSHALL, Roger **'88**				
7/16/88	73	4		1 Hocus Pocus		$6		AVM 17
11/19/88	99	1		2 Take A Letter Maria		$6		Master 05
				#2 Pop hit for R.B. Greaves in 1969				
				MARSHALL TUCKER BAND, The **'87**				
				Southern-rock band from Spartanburg, South Carolina: Doug Gray (vocals), brothers Toy (guitar) and Tommy Caldwell (bass), George McCorkle (guitar), Jerry Eubanks (sax, flute) and Paul Riddle (drums). Tommy Caldwell died in a car crash on 4/28/80 (age 30); replaced by Franklin Wilkie. Toy Caldwell left in 1985; died of respiratory failure on 2/25/93 (age 45). Marshall Tucker was the owner of the band's rehearsal hall.				
3/13/76	82	3		1 Searchin' For A Rainbow .... *Walkin' And Talkin'*	104	$5		Capricorn 0251
9/4/76	63	7		2 Long Hard Ride .... *Windy City Blues*		$5		Capricorn 0258
4/16/77	51	10		3 Heard It In A Love Song .... *Life In A Song*	14	$5		Capricorn 0270
6/25/83	62	7		4 A Place I've Never Been *8:05*		$4		Warner 29619
9/5/87	44	11		5 Hangin' Out In Smokey Places .... *He Don't Know*		$3		Mercury 888775
1/16/88	79	3		6 Once You Get The Feel Of It .... *Slow Down*		$3		Mercury 870050
12/19/92+	68	6		7 Driving You Out Of My Mind				album cut
				from the album *Still Smokin* on Cabin Fever 913				
6/26/93	71	1		8 Walk Outside The Lines				album cut
				from the album *Walk Outside The Lines* on Cabin Fever 929				
				MARTEL, Marty **'79**				
				Born Don Robert Martel on 3/9/39 in Ogdensburg, New York.				
11/17/79	96	2		First Step		$6		Ridgetop 00679
				MARTELL, Linda **'69**				
				Born in Leesville, South Carolina. Black singer.				
8/2/69	22	10		1 Color Him Father .... *I Almost Called Your Name*		$6		Plantation 24
				#7 Pop hit for The Winstons in 1969				
12/13/69+	33	8		2 Before The Next Teardrop Falls .... *Tender Leaves Of Love*		$6		Plantation 35
3/28/70	58	6		3 Bad Case Of The Blues .... *Old Letter Song*		$6		Plantation 46
				MARTIN, Benny **'63**				
				Born on 5/8/28 in Sparta, Tennessee. Bluegrass singer/fiddle player.				
5/25/63	28	1		1 Rosebuds And You .... *Sinful Cinderella*		$15		Starday 623
1/8/66	46	3		2 Soldier's Prayer In Viet Nam .... *Five By Eight* [S]		$12		Monument 912
				DON RENO & BENNY MARTIN and The Tennessee Cut Ups				
				MARTIN, Betty **'78**				
				Singer/songwriter from Powhatan, Virginia.				
10/7/78	77	4		Don't You Feel It Now .... *I Love Being Lied To*		$5		Door Knob 071
				MARTIN, Bobbi **'66**				
				Born Barbara Anne Martin on 11/29/43 in Brooklyn; raised in Baltimore. Pop singer.				
10/15/66	64	3		Oh, Lonesome Me .... *It's A Sin To Tell A Lie*	134	$7		Coral 62488
				MARTIN, Dean **'83**				
				Born Dino Crocetti on 6/7/17 in Steubenville, Ohio. Died of respiratory failure on 12/25/95 (age 78). Singer/actor. Charted 37 pop hits from 1948-69. Teamed with comedian Jerry Lewis from 1946-56. Martin starred in several movies with and without Lewis. Hosted own TV variety show from 1965-74.				
7/9/83	35	12		My First Country Song .... *Hangin' Around*		$4		Warner 29584
				Conway Twitty (guest vocal; writer)				
				MARTIN, Grady — see CROSBY, Bing / IVES, Burl				
				MARTIN, Gypsy **'81**				
				Female singer.				
10/10/81	93	2		This Ain't Tennessee And He Ain't You		$7		Omni 61581

MARTIN, J.D.   '86
Born Jerald Derstine Martin in Harrisonburg, Virginia. Singer/songwriter.

5/10/86	72	6		1 Running Out Of Reasons To Run.............................*Wrap Me Up In Your Love*		$3		Capitol 5573
9/6/86	77	5		2 Wrap Me Up In Your Love ....*Hold On*		$3		Capitol 5606

MARTIN, Jerry   '91

3/16/91	71	1		Letter To Saddam Hussein..[S]		$5	▮	Desert Storm 116179

MARTIN, Jimmy   '58
Born on 8/10/27 in Sneedville, Tennessee. Bluegrass singer/guitarist/mandolin player. Member of **Bill Monroe**'s Bluegrass Boys from 1949-53.

12/8/58	14	6		1 Rock Hearts *I'll Never Take No For An Answer*		$15		Decca 30703
5/25/59	26	3		2 Night *It's Not Like Home*		$12		Decca 30877
2/8/64	19	15		3 Widow Maker *Red River Valley*		$8		Decca 31558
5/7/66	49	2		4 I Can't Quit Cigarettes *Run Boy Run* [N]		$8		Decca 31921
5/18/68	72	2		5 Tennessee *Steal Away Some Where And Die*		$8		Decca 32300
8/4/73	97	2		6 Grand Ole Opry Song *Orange Blossom Special*		$7		United Artists 247

NITTY GRITTY DIRT BAND Featuring Jimmy Martin

MARTIN, Joey   '78
Born in Georgia. Singer/actor.

10/14/78	92	1		I've Been A Long Time Leaving (But I'll Be A Long Time Gone) ....*Dance Hall Girl*		$7		Nickolodean 1002

MARTIN, Mike — see DELRAY, Martin

MARTINDALE, Wink   '59
Born Winston Martindale on 12/4/33 in Jackson, Tennessee. Worked as a DJ and hosted several TV game shows.

10/19/59	11	10	●	Deck Of Cards ....*Love's Old Sweet Song* [S]	7	$12	▮	Dot 15968

MARTINE, Layng Jr.   '76
Male singer/songwriter from Greenwich, Connecticut.

8/28/76	93	2		Summertime Lovin'..*Piece By Piece*		$6		Playboy 6081

MARTINO, Al   '70
Born Alfred Cini on 10/7/27 in Philadelphia. Charted 37 pop hits from 1952-78. Played "Johnny Fontaine" in movie *The Godfather*.

12/20/69+	69	3		I Started Loving You Again ....*Let Me Stay Awhile With You*	86	$6		Capitol 2674

MARVELL, James   '81
Born in Tampa, Florida. Singer/songwriter/guitarist. Member of the groups Mercy and **The Country Cavaleers**.

5/30/81	90	3		1 Love (Can Make You Happy)/				
				#2 Pop hit for Mercy in 1969				
3/14/81	94	2		2 Urban Cowboys, Outlaws, Cavaleers		$7		Cavaleer 117

MASON, Dona — see DAVIS, Danny, & The Nashville Brass

MASON, Mila   '96
Born on 8/22/63 in Dawson Springs, Kentucky.

8/17/96	18	20		1 That's Enough Of That ....*Heart Without A Past*		$3	▮	Atlantic 87047
2/8/97	21	20		2 Dark Horse...S:15 *I Do*		$3	▮	Atlantic 84866
6/28/97	59	8		3 That's The Kinda Love (That I'm Talkin' About)				album cut
11/29/97+	31	20		4 Closer To Heaven				album cut

above 2 from the album *That's Enough Of That* on Atlantic 82923

MASON, Sandy   '67
Born Sandy Theoret in Birdville, Pennsylvania.

5/13/67	64	5		There You Go ....*Give Me A Sweetheart*		$8		Hickory 1442

MASON DIXON   ★391★   '89
Trio formed in Beaumont, Texas: Frank Gilligan (vocals, bass), Jerry Dengler (guitar, banjo) and Rick Henderson (guitar).
1)*Exception To The Rule* 2)*3935 West End Avenue* 3)*Only A Dream Away*

10/22/83	69	7		1 Every Breath You Take..............................*Armadillo Country*		$6		Texas 5502
				#1 Pop hit for the Police in 1983				
4/21/84	51	11		2 I Never Had A Chance With You ....*Circle*		$6		Texas 5556
9/22/84	49	15		3 Gettin' Over You...		$5		Texas 5557
2/23/85	47	10		4 Only A Dream Away.......................S:27 *Buried Treasure*		$5		Texas 5558
8/31/85	76	9		5 Houston Heartache ....*Mason Dixon Lines*		$5		Texas 5508
1/11/86	72	10		6 Got My Heart Set On You ....*Armadillo Country*		$5		Texas 5510
8/2/86	53	10		7 Home Grown ....*Savin' The Best For Last*		$5		Premier One 101
4/18/87	39	14		8 3935 West End Avenue ....*Baby's Song*		$5		Premier One 112
10/10/87	51	8		9 Don't Say No Tonight ....*Natchez Queen*		$5		Premier One 115
8/6/88	62	5		10 Dangerous Road ....*Where Does Love Go*		$3		Capitol 44189
11/5/88	49	13		11 When Karen Comes Around ....*Where Does Love Go*		$3		Capitol 44249
2/11/89	35	13		12 Exception To The Rule *A Woman Like You*		$3		Capitol 44331
6/17/89	52	7		13 A Mountain Ago ....*When It Hurts You Most*		$3		Capitol 44381

MASSEY, Wayne   '85
Born in Glendale, California. Singer/actor. Played "Johnny Drummond" on TV's daytime soap opera *One Life To Live*. Married **Charly McClain** in July 1984.

1/17/81	82	3		1 Diamonds And Teardrops ....*The Best Of The Rest Of Our Lives*		$4		Polydor 2147
5/21/83	71	6		2 Lover In Disguise ....*Born To Love You*		$4		MCA 52211
8/6/83	57	7		3 Say You'll Stay ....*Born To Love You*		$4		MCA 52246

CHARLY McCLAIN & WAYNE MASSEY:

7/6/85	5	22		4 With Just One Look In Your Eyes S:5 / A:6 *Tangled In A Tightrope*		$3	▮	Epic 05398

DEBUT	PEAK	WKS	Gold	A-side (Chart Hit)..B-side	Pop	$	Plc	Label & Number
				CHARLY McCLAIN & WAYNE MASSEY — Cont'd				
11/16/85+	10	20		5 You Are My Music, You Are My Song S:9 / A:10 We Got Love		$3		Epic 05693
3/29/86	17	15		6 When It's Down To Me And You ..... S:16 / A:17 I'll Always Try Forever One More Time		$3		Epic 05842
12/6/86	74	6		7 When Love Is Right .... Someone Like You		$3		Epic 06433
2/11/89	81	3		8 Shoot The Moon .... What A Perfect Way		$3		Mercury 870994
				WAYNE MASSEY				
				MASTERS, A.J. '86				
				Born Arthur John Masters in Walden, New York. Singer/songwriter/bassist.				
11/16/85	98	1		1 Lonely Together		$5		Bermuda Dunes 111
3/8/86	48	9		2 Back Home Lonely Together		$5		Bermuda Dunes 112
7/26/86	54	9		3 Love Keep Your Distance .... Get Outta My House Blues		$5		Bermuda Dunes 114
11/8/86	65	5		4 I Don't Mean Maybe		$5		Bermuda Dunes 115
1/17/87	58	6		5 Take A Little Bit Of It Home		$5		Bermuda Dunes 104
4/18/87	70	4		6 In It Again .... On A Night Like This		$5		Bermuda Dunes 116
8/15/87	67	7		7 255 Harbor Drive/				
11/21/87	77	3		8 Our Love Is Like The South		$5		Bermuda Dunes 117
				MATA, Billy '88				
				Singer/songwriter from San Antonio, Texas.				
1/30/88	82	3		1 Macon Georgia Love .... She Ain't Got Nothin On You		$6		BGM 92087
1/7/89	89	2		2 Photographic Memory		$6		BGM 70188
				MATHIS, Country Johnny '63				
				Born on 9/28/33 in Maud, Texas. Recorded with Jimmy Lee Fautheree as **Jimmy & Johnny**.				
3/9/63	14	13		Please Talk To My Heart ....Let's Go Home		$12		United Artists 536
				MATHIS, Joel '74				
				Singer from Valdosta, Georgia.				
6/8/74	89	3		1 Ann.. Glasses Of Beer		$6		Chart 5217
1/28/78	89	2		2 The Farmer's Song (We Ain't Gonna Work For Peanuts)/		$6		Soundwaves 4562
		2		3 Dirt Farming Man				

MATTEA, Kathy ★90★   '88

Born on 6/21/59 in Cross Lane, West Virginia. Singer/songwriter/guitarist. CMA Awards: 1989 & 1990 Female Vocalist of the Year. Also see The Red Hots.

1)Eighteen Wheels And A Dozen Roses 2)Goin' Gone 3)Come From The Heart 4)Burnin' Old Memories
5)She Came From Fort Worth

DEBUT	PEAK	WKS		A-side		$	Plc	Label & Number
10/8/83	25	18		1 Street Talk ....Heartbeat		$3		Mercury 814375
2/25/84	26	16		2 Someone Is Falling In Love .... That's Easy For You To Say		$3		Mercury 818289
6/16/84	44	10		3 You've Got A Soft Place To Fall................Back To The Heartbreak Kid		$3		Mercury 822218
9/15/84	50	11		4 That's Easy For You To Say .... Somewhere Down The Road		$3		Mercury 880192
3/16/85	34	14		5 It's Your Reputation Talkin' .... Never Look Back		$3		Mercury 880595
7/6/85	22	19		6 He Won't Give In .... S:19 / A:22 I Believe I Could Fall In Love (With Loving You)		$3		Mercury 880867
11/2/85	46	11		7 Heart Of The Country .... Talkin' To Myself		$3		Mercury 884177
4/12/86	3	22		8 Love At The Five & Dime A:3 / S:4 You Can't Run Away From Your Heart		$3		Mercury 884573
9/13/86	10	24		9 Walk The Way The Wind Blows S:7 / A:12 Come Home To West Virginia		$3		Mercury 884978
2/7/87	5	25		10 You're The Power S:❶¹ / A:5 Song For The Life		$3		Mercury 888319
5/23/87	6	20		11 Train Of Memories S:4 Evenin'		$3		Mercury 888574
10/17/87+	❶¹	24		12 Goin' Gone S:3 Every Love		$3	■	Mercury 888874
3/12/88	❶²	20		13 Eighteen Wheels And A Dozen Roses S:❶² Like A Hurricane		$3	■	Mercury 870148
				CMA Award: Single of the Year				
7/9/88	4	19		14 Untold Stories S:8 Late In The Day		$3		Mercury 870476
11/12/88+	4	22		15 Life As We Knew It S:17 As Long As I Have A Heart		$3		Mercury 872082
4/15/89	❶¹	20		16 Come From The Heart True North		$3		Mercury 872766
8/19/89	❶¹	21		17 Burnin' Old Memories Hills Of Alabam		$3		Mercury 874672
11/25/89+	10	26		18 Where've You Been I'll Take Care Of You		$3		Mercury 876262
4/7/90	2¹	21		19 She Came From Fort Worth Here's Hopin'		$3	▌	Mercury 876746
7/21/90	9	20		20 The Battle Hymn Of Love Leaving West Virginia		$3	▌	Mercury 875692
				KATHY MATTEA & TIM O'BRIEN				
11/10/90+	9	20		21 A Few Good Things Remain Evenin'		$3		Mercury 878246
3/9/91	7	20		22 Time Passes By What Could Have Been		$3	▌	Mercury 878934
7/6/91	18	20		23 Whole Lotta Holes .... Quarter Moon		$3		Mercury 868394
10/19/91+	27	20		24 Asking Us To Dance .... Where've You Been		$3		Mercury 868866
9/26/92	11	20		25 Lonesome Standard Time ....Asking Us To Dance		$3		Mercury 864318
1/23/93	19	20		26 Standing Knee Deep In A River (Dying Of Thirst) .... Listen To The Radio		$3		Mercury 864810
5/29/93	50	9		27 Seeds .... Lonely At The Bottom		$3		Mercury 862064
8/21/93	64	4		28 Listen To The Radio .... Slow Boat		$3		Mercury 862650
3/26/94	3	20		29 Walking Away A Winner The Cape		$3	▌	Mercury 858464
7/23/94	13	20		30 Nobody's Gonna Rain On Our Parade .... Grand Canyon		$3	▌	Mercury 858800
11/12/94+	34	15		31 Maybe She's Human .... Who Turned Out The Light		$3	▌	Mercury 856262
4/1/95	20	15		32 Clown In Your Rodeo .... Who's Gonna Know		$3		Mercury 856484
1/18/97	21	20		33 455 Rocket... All Roads To The River		$3		Mercury 578950

MATTEA, Kathy — Cont'd

DEBUT	PEAK	WKS	A-side / B-side	$	Pic	Label & Number
8/16/97	39	16	34 Love Travels .... *I'm On Your Side*	$3		Mercury 578550

MATTHEWS, WRIGHT & KING '92

Vocal trio: Raymond Matthews (b: 10/13/56 in Alabama), Woody Wright (b: 10/10/57 in Tennessee) and Tony King (b: 6/27/57 in North Carolina). Wright was a member of **Memphis**. King was a member of **The Tennesseans**.

4/4/92	41	19	1 The Power Of Love *Everytime She Says Yes*	$3		Columbia 74275
8/22/92	55	7	2 Mother's Eyes.................................. *When The River Runs High*	$3		Columbia 74400
11/28/92	68	4	3 House Huntin'.. *Leavin' Reasons*	$3		Columbia 74749
6/19/93	45	19	4 I Got A Love .... *The Truth Is Killin' Me*	$3		Columbia 77020
10/16/93	74	2	5 One Of These Days .... *Big Money*	$3	▌	Columbia 77180

★384★ MAVERICKS, The '96

Group from Miami: Raul Malo (vocals, guitar), David Lee Holt (guitar), Robert Reynolds (bass) and Paul Deakin (drums). Holt was replaced by Nick Kane in 1995. Reynolds married **Trisha Yearwood** on 5/21/94. CMA Award: 1995 & 1996 Vocal Group of the Year.

1)All You Ever Do Is Bring Me Down 2)O What A Thrill 3)There Goes My Heart

6/20/92	74	1	1 Hey Good Lookin'			album cut
			from the album *From Hell To Paradise* on MCA 10544			
1/1/94	25	20	2 What A Crying Shame .... *The Things You Said To Me*	$3	▌	MCA 54748
5/14/94	18	20	3 O What A Thrill .... *Ain't Found Nobody*	$3	▌	MCA 54780
10/1/94	20	20	4 There Goes My Heart .... *Just A Memory*	$3	▌	MCA 54909
1/28/95	30	16	5 I Should Have Been True .... *The Losing Side Of Me*	$3	▌	MCA 54975
5/13/95	49	12	6 All That Heaven Will Allow .... *Pretend*	$3		MCA 55026
			written and first recorded by Bruce Springsteen on his 1987 *Tunnel of Love* album			
8/19/95	22	20	7 Here Comes The Rain............................... *I'm Not Gonna Cry For You*	$3	▌	MCA 55080
1/20/96	13	20	8 All You Ever Do Is Bring Me Down *Volver, Volver*	$3		MCA 55154
6/22/96	54	10	9 Missing You .... *Foolish Heart*	$3	▌	MCA 55021
11/16/96	65	5	10 I Don't Care (If You Love Me Anymore) .... *Something Stupid*	$3		MCA 55247

MAY, Ralph '83

5/2/81	93	2	1 Cajun Lady.. *Together We're Falling Apart*	$6		Soundwaves 4630
2/20/82	83	3	2 In A Stranger's Eyes	$6		AMI 1901
			RALPH MAY and The Ohio River Band			
8/28/82	88	3	3 Here Comes That Feelin' Again	$6		Primero 1006
2/19/83	57	8	4 Angels Get Lonely Too *Keep Me From Blowin Away*	$6		Primero 1021
1/17/87	73	4	5 Memory Attack	$5		Evergreen 1048
			RALPH MAY & The Ohio River Band			

McANALLY, Mac '90

Born Lyman McAnally, Jr. on 7/15/57 in Red Bay, Alabama. Singer/songwriter/guitarist.

2/3/90	14	21	1 Back Where I Come From *Company Time*	$3		Warner 22662
7/7/90	70	5	2 Down The Road .... *She's Going Out Of My Mind*	$3	▌	Warner 19800
5/9/92	62	6	3 Live And Learn .... *All These Years*	$3		MCA 54372
9/19/92	72	3	4 The Trouble With Diamonds .... *Socrates*	$3		MCA 54450
1/9/93	72	2	5 Junk Cars.. *Somewhere Nice Forever*	$3		MCA 54537

McAULIFFE, Leon '49

Born William Leon McAuliffe on 1/3/17 in Houston. Died on 8/20/88 (age 71). Singer/steel guitarist. Member of **Bob Wills & His Texas Playboys** from 1935-42. Appeared in several western movies.

6/4/49	6	5	1 Panhandle Rag *S:6 / J:10 Careless Hands* [I]	$20		Columbia 20546
			LEON McAULIFFE and his Western Swing Band			
8/21/61	16	15	2 Cozy Inn .... *Ain't Gonna Hurt No More*	$15		Cimarron 4050
12/22/62+	22	11	3 Faded Love .... *My Little Red Wagon* [I]	$15		Cimarron 4057
			also see #6 below			
1/11/64	35	1	4 Shape Up Or Ship Out/			
2/8/64	47	1	5 I Don't Love Nobody	$10		Capitol 5066
6/12/71	22	9	6 Faded Love .... *Pretty Eyes* [R]	$6		MGM 14249
			TOMPALL AND THE GLASER BROTHERS WITH LEON McAULIFFE AND THE CIMARRON BOYS			
			new version of #3 above			

McBEE, Jerry '80

Member of Bluestone.

4/12/80	86	4	That's The Chance We'll Have To Take	$5		Dimension 1004

McBRIDE, Dale '77

Born on 12/18/36 in Bell County, Texas; raised in Lampasas, Texas. Died of a brain tumor on 11/30/92 (age 55). Singer/songwriter/guitarist. Son Terry formed **McBride & The Ride**.

1)Ordinary Man 2)Always Lovin Her Man 3)I Don't Like Cheatin' Songs

3/27/71	70	2	1 Corpus Christi Wind .... *Anybody Going To San Antone*	$7		Thunderbird 539
5/22/76	90	6	2 Getting Over You Again .... *You Have Missed Nothing*	$5		Con Brio 109
			also see #12 below			
11/20/76+	26	13	3 Ordinary Man .... *Mexicalli Rose*	$5		Con Brio 114
3/12/77	60	8	4 I'm Savin' Up Sunshine .... *It's Hell To Know She's Heaven*	$5		Con Brio 117
7/9/77	53	7	5 Love I Need You .... *A Love For All Seasons*	$5		Con Brio 121
9/24/77	73	6	6 My Girl .... *She Makes Love Feel Good*	$5		Con Brio 124
12/10/77+	37	10	7 Always Lovin Her Man .... *I Know The Feeling*	$5		Con Brio 127
3/18/78	56	8	8 A Sweet Love Song The World Can Sing .... *I'm Savin' Up Sunshine*	$5		Con Brio 131
7/15/78	45	7	9 I Don't Like Cheatin' Songs .... *My Girl*	$5		Con Brio 135
10/21/78	72	5	10 Let's Be Lonely Together .... *She Makes Love Feel Good*	$5		Con Brio 140
2/3/79	66	5	11 It's Hell To Know She's Heaven .... *You Have Missed Nothing*	$5		Con Brio 145
5/12/79	67	7	12 Getting Over You Again .... *She Makes Love Feel Good* [R]	$5		Con Brio 151
			same version as #2 above			

DEBUT	PEAK	WKS	Gold	A-side (Chart Hit)..B-side	Pop	$	Pic	Label & Number
				McBRIDE, Dale — Cont'd				
9/22/79	61	7		13 Get Your Hands On Me Baby ....*I Know The Feeling*		$5		Con Brio 158
	★242★			**McBRIDE, Martina** '97				
				Born Martina Schiff on 7/29/66 in Medicine Lodge, Kansas; raised in Sharon, Kansas. Joined the *Grand Ole Opry* in 1995.				
				1)A Broken Wing 2)Wild Angels 3)My Baby Loves Me				
5/2/92	23	20		1 The Time Has Come ....*The Rope*		$3		RCA 62215
8/22/92	43	15		2 That's Me ....*Losing You Feels Good*		$3		RCA 62291
12/5/92+	44	15		3 Cheap Whiskey ....*I Can't Sleep*		$3		RCA 62398
7/31/93	2¹	21		4 My Baby Loves Me *A Woman Knows*		$3		RCA 62599
1/8/94	6	20		5 Life #9 *Ashes*		$3	∎	RCA 62697
5/7/94	12	20		6 Independence Day...*True Blue Fool*		$3	∎	RCA 62828
10/22/94+	21	20		7 Heart Trouble ....*That Wasn't Me*		$3	∎	RCA 62961
3/11/95	49	9		8 Where I Used To Have A Heart ....*Heart Trouble*		$3	∎	RCA 62948
7/29/95	4	20		9 Safe In The Arms Of Love S:20 *Life #9*		$3	∎	RCA 64345
12/2/95+	❶¹	20		10 Wild Angels S:15 *Two More Bottles Of Wine*		$3	∎	RCA 64437
4/6/96	28	19		11 Phones Are Ringin' All Over Town ....*Beyond The Blue*		$3	∎	RCA 64487
8/31/96	38	15		12 Swingin' Doors ....*Phones Are Ringin' All Over Town*		$3	∎	RCA 64610
12/28/96	74	1		13 O Holy Night ....*Silver Bells* [X]		$3		RCA 64688
1/25/97	26	16		14 Cry On The Shoulder Of The Road ....*A Great Disguise*		$3	∎	RCA 64728
9/13/97+	❶¹	25		15 A Broken Wing/ S:4	61			
2/22/97	53	4		16 Valentine..	50	$3	∎	RCA 64963
				MARTINA McBRIDE with Jim Brickman				
6/14/97	11	20		17 Still Holding On ....*(long version)*		$3		RCA 64850
				CLINT BLACK & MARTINA McBRIDE				
12/27/97	67	1		18 O Holy Night ....*Silver Bells* [X-R]		$3		RCA 64688
	★302★			**McBRIDE & THE RIDE** '92				
				Group of Nashville session musicians: Terry McBride (vocals, bass; b: 9/16/58 in Lampasas, Texas), Ray Herndon (guitar) and Billy Thomas (drums). Herndon and Thomas left in 1993; Kenny Vaughn (guitar), Randy Frazier (bass) and Keith Edwards (drums) joined. Gary Morse and Jeff Roach also joined by 1994. McBride is the son of **Dale McBride**.				
				1)Sacred Ground 2)Love On The Loose, Heart On The Run 3)Going Out Of My Mind				
3/16/91	15	20		1 Can I Count On You ....*Turn To Blue*		$3		MCA 54022
8/3/91	28	20		2 Same Old Star ....*Stone Country*		$3		MCA 54125
3/14/92	2²	20		3 Sacred Ground *Your One And Only*		$3		MCA 54356
7/18/92	5	20		4 Going Out Of My Mind *Trick Rider*		$3		MCA 54413
11/14/92+	5	20		5 Just One Night *All I Have To Offer You Is Me*		$3	∎	MCA 54494
3/27/93	3	20		6 Love On The Loose, Heart On The Run *Hangin' In And Hangin' On*		$3		MCA 54601
7/31/93	17	20		7 Hurry Sundown.............................*Just The Thought Of Losing You*		$3		MCA 54688
11/27/93+	26	20		8 No More Cryin' ....*Don't Be Mean To Me*		$3		MCA 54761
				from the movie *8 Seconds* starring Luke Perry				
				TERRY McBRIDE & THE RIDE:				
7/2/94	45	12		9 Been There ....*He's Living My Dreams*		$3	∎	MCA 54853
11/5/94	72	3		10 High Hopes And Empty Pockets ....*Teardrops*		$3	∎	MCA 54936
2/18/95	57	7		11 Somebody Will ....*I'll See You Again Someday*		$3	∎	MCA 54986
	★307★			**McCALL, C.W.** '75				
				Born William Fries on 11/15/28 in Audubon, Iowa. Singer/songwriter. Was working for the Bozell and Jacobs advertising agency when he created the "C.W. McCall" character. Elected mayor of Ouray, Colorado, in the early '80s.				
				1)Convoy 2)Roses For Mama 3)Wolf Creek Pass				
7/13/74	19	11		1 Old Home Filler-Up An' Keep On-A-Truckin' Cafe ....*Old 30* [N]	54	$6		MGM 14738
12/7/74+	12	16		2 Wolf Creek Pass ....*Sloan* [N]	40	$6		MGM 14764
5/10/75	13	12		3 Classified.......................................*I've Trucked All Over This Land* [N]	101	$6		MGM 14801
9/20/75	24	11		4 Black Bear Road ....*Four Wheel Drive* [N]		$6		MGM 14825
11/29/75	❶⁶	15	●	5 Convoy *Long Lonesome Road* [N]	❶¹	$5		MGM 14839
				also see #9 below				
3/27/76	19	10		6 There Won't Be No Country Music (There Won't Be No Rock 'N' Roll) ....*Green River* [S]	73	$4		Polydor 14310
7/4/76	32	9		7 Crispy Critters ....*Jackson Hole* [N]		$4		Polydor 14331
10/16/76	88	4		8 Four Wheel Cowboy ....*Aurora Borealis* [N]		$4		Polydor 14352
12/18/76+	40	8		9 'Round The World With The Rubber Duck...................*Night Rider* [N]	101	$4		Polydor 14365
				sequel to #5 above				
2/26/77	56	7		10 Audubon ....*Ratchetjaw* [N]		$4		Polydor 14377
9/17/77	2²	16		11 Roses For Mama *Columbine* [S]		$4		Polydor 14420
1/20/79	81	4		12 Outlaws And Lone Star Beer ....*Silver Cloud Breakdown*		$4		Polydor 14527
	★394★			**McCALL, Darrell** '63				
				Born on 4/30/40 in New Jasper, Ohio. Singer/songwriter/guitarist. Lead tenor with the Little Dippers (hit #9 on the pop charts with "Forever" in 1960). Acted in the movies *Nahville Rebel, Road To Nashville* and *What Am I Bid.*				
				1)A Stranger Was Here 2)Lily Dale 3)Dreams Of A Dreamer				
1/12/63	17	8		1 A Stranger Was Here *I'm A Little Bit Lonely*		$10		Philips 40079
				DARRELL McCALL with The Milestones				
4/27/68	67	5		2 I'd Love To Live With You Again....................*I Love You Baby*		$7		Wayside 1011
8/17/68	60	8		3 Wall Of Pictures ....*I'd Die To See You Smile*		$7		Wayside 1021
7/12/69	53	9		4 Hurry Up ....*Wedding Band*		$6		Wayside 003
2/7/70	62	4		5 The Arms Of My Weakness ....*Big Oak Tree*		$6		Wayside 008
4/27/74	48	9		6 There's Still A Lot Of Love In San Antone ....*A Texas Honky Tonk*		$5		Atlantic 4019
3/20/76	52	8		7 Pins And Needles (In My Heart) ....*Every Girl I See*		$5		Columbia 10296

McCALL, Darrell — Cont'd

DEBUT	PEAK	WKS	A-side	B-side	Pop	$	Pic	Label & Number
3/12/77	32	13	8 Lily Dale	Please Don't Leave Me		$5		Columbia 10480
			DARRELL McCALL & WILLIE NELSON					
7/16/77	35	10	9 Dreams Of A Dreamer..................................	Sad Songs And Waltzes		$5		Columbia 10576
1/7/78	59	9	10 Down The Roads Of Daddy's Dreams	An Old Memory's Arms		$5		Columbia 10653
5/13/78	91	5	11 The Weeds Outlived The Roses	Love Didn't Drive My Good Woman Wild		$5		Columbia 10723
3/1/80	89	5	12 San Antonio Medley	Thank God For Country Music		$6		Hillside 01
			CURTIS POTTER/DARRELL McCALL					
8/9/80	43	9	13 Long Line Of Empties..................................	I Wonder Which One Of Us Is To Blame		$4		RCA 12033
6/9/84	79	4	14 Memphis In May			$5		Indigo 304

McCANN, Lila '98
Born in 12/4/81 in Steilacoom, Washington. Female singer.

DEBUT	PEAK	WKS	A-side	B-side	Pop	$	Pic	Label & Number
5/17/97	28	20	1 Down Came A Blackbird					album cut
9/27/97+	3	29	2 I Wanna Fall In Love					album cut

above 2 from the album *Lila* on Asylum 62042

McCARTERS, The '88
Vocal trio of sisters from Sevierville, Tennessee: Jennifer (b: 3/1/64) and twins Lisa and Teresa (b: 11/21/66) McCarter.

DEBUT	PEAK	WKS	A-side	B-side	Pop	$	Pic	Label & Number
1/16/88	5	20	1 Timeless And True Love	S:12 *My Songbird*		$3	■	Warner 28125
6/11/88	4	20	2 The Gift	S:14 *Loving You*		$3	■	Warner 27868
10/8/88	28	15	3 I Give You Music	The Memories Remain		$3		Warner 27721
4/15/89	9	20	4 Up And Gone	Letter From Home		$3		Warner 22991
			JENNIFER McCARTER and THE McCARTERS:					
10/28/89+	26	15	5 Quit While I'm Behind.................................	Oh Lonesome You		$3		Warner 22763
3/31/90	73	2	6 Better Be Home Soon	Moving On		$3		Warner 19964
			#42 Pop hit for Crowded House in 1988					
6/9/90	73	2	7 Shot Full Of Love	Mountain Memories		$3	▌	Warner 19836

McCARTNEY, Paul '75
Born on 6/18/42 in Allerton, Liverpool, England. Singer/songwriter/bassist. Founding member of The Beatles. Formed group Wings with wife Linda (keyboards, backing vocals). They married on 3/12/69; Linda died of cancer on 4/17/98 (age 55). Paul charted 45 pop hits from 1971-97. Won Grammy's Lifetime Achievement Award in 1990.

DEBUT	PEAK	WKS	A-side	B-side	Pop	$	Pic	Label & Number
12/21/74+	51	10	Sally G..	Junior's Farm (Pop #3)	17	$8		Apple 1875
			PAUL McCARTNEY & WINGS					

McCLAIN, Charly ★94★ '85
Born Charlotte Denise McClain on 3/26/56 in Jackson, Tennessee. Female singer/songwriter. Acted in several TV shows. Married **Wayne Massey** in July 1984.

1)Radio Heart 2)Paradise Tonight 3)Who's Cheatin' Who 4)Sentimental Ol' You
5)Dancing Your Memory Away

DEBUT	PEAK	WKS	A-side	B-side	Pop	$	Pic	Label & Number
10/23/76	67	11	1 Lay Down	Pride And Sorrow		$4		Epic 50285
3/5/77	82	5	2 Lay Something On My Bed Besides A Blanket...	Love Me 'Til The Morning Comes		$4		Epic 50338
5/14/77	87	4	3 It's Too Late To Love Me Now	You Can Love It Away		$4		Epic 50378
10/1/77	73	5	4 Make The World Go Away	Leanin' On The Bottle (And Slowly Falling Down)		$4		Epic 50436
4/8/78	13	16	5 Let Me Be Your Baby	Your Eyes		$4		Epic 50525
9/16/78	8	14	6 That's What You Do To Me	1 + 1 = Love		$4		Epic 50598
1/27/79	24	11	7 Take Me Back	Bedtime Comes Earlier At Our House		$4		Epic 50653
5/19/79	11	14	8 When A Love Ain't Right	You Can't Make Love By Yourself		$4		Epic 50706
9/15/79	20	12	9 You're A Part Of Me	I've Never Loved Nobody Like I Love You		$4		Epic 50759
10/20/79	16	14	10 I Hate The Way I Love It.............................	Almost Persuaded		$4		Epic 50791
			JOHNNY RODRIGUEZ and CHARLY McCLAIN					
1/12/80	7	15	11 Men	Come Take Care Of Me		$4		Epic 50825
5/3/80	23	13	12 Let's Put Our Love In Motion	I'm Puttin' My Love Inside You		$4		Epic 50873
8/9/80	18	13	13 Women Get Lonely	I'd Rather Fall In Love With You		$4		Epic 50916
11/29/80+	❶¹	17	14 Who's Cheatin' Who	Love Scenes		$3		Epic 50948
4/11/81	5	18	15 Surround Me With Love	He's Back		$3		Epic 01045
8/22/81	4	16	16 Sleepin' With The Radio On	That's All A Woman Lives For		$3		Epic 02421
12/26/81+	5	18	17 The Very Best Is You	Love Left Over		$3		Epic 02656
6/26/82	3	20	18 Dancing Your Memory Away	Love This Time		$3		Epic 02975
10/23/82+	7	21	19 With You	Crazy Hearts		$3		Epic 03308
4/9/83	20	15	20 Fly Into Love	The Best That Never Was		$3		Epic 03808
7/16/83	❶¹	22	21 Paradise Tonight	The Four Seasons Of Love		$3		Epic 04007
			CHARLY McCLAIN and MICKEY GILLEY					
11/5/83+	3	21	22 Sentimental Ol' You	I'll Get You Back		$3		Epic 04172
2/18/84	5	18	23 Candy Man	The Phone Call		$3		Epic 04368
			MICKEY GILLEY and CHARLY McCLAIN #25 Pop hit for Roy Orbison in 1961					
4/7/84	22	15	24 Band Of Gold..	His Love Is Out Of My Hands		$3		Epic 04423
			#3 Pop hit for Freda Payne in 1970					
6/16/84	14	17	25 The Right Stuff	We Got A Love Thing		$3		Epic 04489
			CHARLY McCLAIN and MICKEY GILLEY					
9/22/84	25	18	26 Some Hearts Get All The Breaks	A:22 / S:30 *Someone Just Like You*		$3		Epic 04586
2/16/85	❶¹	23	27 Radio Heart	S:❶¹ / A:❶¹ *You Make Me Feel So Good*		$3		Epic 04777

McCLAIN, Charly — Cont'd

7/6/85	5	22		28 With Just One Look In Your Eyes S:5 / A:6 *Tangled In A Tightrope*		$3	■	Epic 05398
				CHARLY McCLAIN With Wayne Massey				
11/16/85+	10	20		29 You Are My Music, You Are My Song S:9 / A:10 *We Got Love*		$3		Epic 05693
				CHARLY McCLAIN (With Wayne Massey)				
3/29/86	17	15		30 When It's Down To Me And You ..... S:16 / A:17 *I'll Always Try Forever One More Time*		$3		Epic 05842
				CHARLY McCLAIN & WAYNE MASSEY				
8/16/86	41	11		31 So This Is Love .... *Too Many Tears Too Late*		$3		Epic 06167
12/6/86	74	6		32 When Love Is Right .... *Someone Like You*		$3		Epic 06433
				CHARLY McCLAIN & WAYNE MASSEY				
3/7/87	20	24		33 Don't Touch Me There................................... S:18 / A:22 *I Know The Way By Heart*		$3		Epic 06980
8/22/87	51	9		34 And Then Some .... *What Makes Love Go Round N' Round*		$3		Epic 07244
2/6/88	60	5		35 Still I Stay .... *If You Didn't Need Me*		$3		Epic 07670
8/20/88	55	7		36 Sometimes She Feels Like A Man .... *You Can Be You (And Be Mine Too)*		$3		Mercury 870508
11/12/88	58	6		37 Down The Road .... *You Can Be You (And Be Mine Too)*		$3		Mercury 872036
2/4/89	50	6		38 One In Your Heart One On Your Mind .... *You Got The Job*		$3		Mercury 872506
7/29/89	65	5		39 You Got The Job .... *You Can Be You (And Be Mine Too)*		$3		Mercury 872998

McCLINTON, Delbert   **'93**
Born on 11/4/40 in Lubbock, Texas. Singer/songwriter/harmonica player.

4/17/93	4	20		1 Tell Me About It *What Do They Know*		$3		Liberty 56985
				TANYA TUCKER with Delbert McClinton				
11/29/97+	65	9		2 Sending Me Angels .... *Better Off With The Blues*		$4		Rising Tide 56050

McCLINTON, O.B.   **'73**
Born Obie Burnett McClinton on 4/25/40 in Senatobia, Mississippi. Died of cancer on 9/23/87 (age 47). Black singer/songwriter/guitarist.
Known as "The Chocolate Cowboy."
    1)My Whole World Is Falling Down 2)Don't Let The Green Grass Fool You 3)Soap

7/1/72	70	6		1 Six Pack Of Trouble.................................... *You Don't Love Me*		$6		Enterprise 9051
11/4/72+	37	13		2 Don't Let The Green Grass Fool You .... *Lay A Little Lovin' On Her*		$6		Enterprise 9059
				#17 Pop hit for Wilson Pickett in 1971				
3/10/73	36	8		3 My Whole World Is Falling Down *Music City, Tennesee*		$6		Enterprise 9062
6/30/73	67	6		4 I Wish It Would Rain.................................... *Obie From Senatobie*		$6		Enterprise 9070
				#4 Pop hit for the Temptations in 1968				
3/16/74	62	9		5 Something Better .... *I'd Rather Be A Stranger*		$6		Enterprise 9091
6/29/74	86	6		6 If You Loved Her That Way ....*Mr. Miller's Granddaughter*		$6		Enterprise 9100
1/4/75	77	6		7 Yours And Mine .... *Lean On Me*		$6		Enterprise 9108
5/1/76	100	1		8 It's So Good Lovin' You .... *She'll Never Be That Easy Again*		$5		Mercury 73777
7/8/78	90	4		9 Hello, This Is Anna .... *Let's Get It On*		$5		Epic 50563
				O.B. McCLINTON Featuring Peggy Jo Adams				
12/2/78	82	5		10 Natural Love .... *I Can't Get Over Last Night*		$5		Epic 50620
5/19/79	79	5		11 The Real Thing .... *The Crack Of Dawn*		$4		Epic 50698
8/25/79	58	8		12 Soap .... *Miss Sara Lee*		$4		Epic 50749
10/4/80	62	5		13 Not Exactly Free ....*Walking After Kim*		$5		Sunbird 7554
6/9/84	69	5		14 Honky Tonk Tan		$5		Moon Shine 3024
3/14/87	61	6		15 Turn The Music On ....*(Country Music Is) American Soul*		$3		Epic 6682

McCORD, Cali   **'88**
Female singer from Springfield, Ohio.

| 12/12/87+ | 46 | 10 | | 1 Bad Day For A Break Up................................ *Slow Healing* | | $6 | | Gazelle 011 |
| 4/16/88 | 60 | 6 | | 2 All In My Mind .... | | $6 | | Gazelle 012 |

McCORISON, Dan   **'77**
Born in Denver; raised in Detroit. Singer/songwriter/guitarist.

| 6/25/77 | 96 | 3 | | That's The Way My Woman Loves Me.............................. *Don't Forget The Man* | | $5 | | MCA 40729 |

| ★364★ | | | | **McCOY, Charlie**   **'72** | | | | |

Born on 3/28/41 in Oak Hill, West Virginia. Top Nashville harmonica player and session musician.
    1)I Started Loving You Again 2)I Really Don't Want To Know 3)Boogie Woogie

2/5/72	16	15		1 I Started Loving You Again *The Real McCoy* [I]		$6		Monument 8529
7/8/72	23	12		2 I'm So Lonesome I Could Cry .... *Grade A* [I]		$6		Monument 8546
11/4/72	19	11		3 I Really Don't Want To Know............................. *Minor, Miner* [I]		$6		Monument 8554
3/10/73	26	10		4 Orange Blossom Special ....*Hangin' On* [I]	101	$6		Monument 8566
7/14/73	33	9		5 Shenandoah ....*John Henry* [I]		$6		Monument 8576
10/20/73	33	13		6 Release Me .... *The Fastest Harp In The South* [I]		$6		Monument 8589
3/2/74	68	6		7 Silver Threads And Golden Needles .... *I Just Can't Stand To See You Cry* [I]		$6		Monument 8600
6/1/74	22	13		8 Boogie Woogie (a/k/a T.D.'s Boogie Woogie)...................*Keep On Harpin'* [I]		$6		Monument 8611
				CHARLIE McCOY & BAREFOOT JERRY				
				#4 Pop hit for Tommy Dorsey in 1945				
8/14/76	97	2		9 Wabash Cannonball .... *Ode To Billie Joe* [I]		$6		Monument 8703
2/5/77	98	3		10 Summit Ridge Drive .... [I]		$5		Monument 210
				CHARLIE McCOY (featuring Barefoot Jerry)				
				#10 Pop hit for Artie Shaw in 1941				
8/12/78	30	10		11 Fair And Tender Ladies .... *18th Century Rosewood Clock*		$5		Monument 258
12/16/78	96	3		12 Drifting Lovers		$5		Monument 272
4/28/79	94	3		13 Midnight Flyer..*Cripple Creek*		$5		Monument 282
9/8/79	94	2		14 Ramblin' Music Man ....*Red Haired Boy*		$5		Monument 289
12/19/81	92	3		15 Until The Nights .... *I Love The Way You Love Me*		$5		Monument 21001
				CHARLIE McCOY & LANEY SMALLWOOD				
				written and first recorded by Billy Joel on his 1978 *52nd Street* album				
4/16/83	74	4		16 The State Of Our Union...................... *Just Doin' Nothin' With You (Is Really Somethin')*		$5		Monument 03518
				CHARLIE McCOY & LANEY HICKS				

DEBUT	PEAK	WKS	Gold	A-side / B-side	Pop	$	Pic	Label & Number
	★204★			**McCOY, Neal** '94				
				Born Hubert Neal McGauhey on 7/30/58 in Jacksonville, Texas. Also recorded as **Neal McGoy**.				
				1)Wink 2)No Doubt About It 3)They're Playin' Our Song				
8/27/88	85	2		1 That's How Much I Love You .... *Memphis Might As Well Be On The Moon* **NEAL McGOY**		$4		16th Avenue 70417
1/5/91	48	10		2 If I Built You A Fire .... *The Big Heat*		$3	▌	Atlantic 87833
9/7/91	50	10		3 This Time I Hurt Her More (Than She Loves Me) .... *Down On The River*		$3		Atlantic 87636
5/9/92	40	14		4 Where Forever Begins				album cut
9/5/92	57	8		5 There Ain't Nothin' I Don't Like About You				album cut
2/13/93	26	16		6 Now I Pray For Rain				album cut
				above 3 from the album *Where Forever Begins* on Atlantic 82396				
12/18/93+	❶²	20		7 No Doubt About It *(album snippets)*	75	$3	▌	Atlantic 87287
4/23/94	❶⁴	20		8 Wink *(album snippets)*	91	$3	▌	Atlantic 87247
8/6/94	5	20		9 The City Put The Country Back In Me *Why Not Tonight*		$3	▌	Atlantic 87213
12/17/94+	3	20		10 For A Change *S:24 (album snippets)*	108	$3	▌	Atlantic 87176
4/29/95	3	20		11 They're Playin' Our Song				album cut
				from the album *You Gotta Love That!* on Atlantic 82727				
1/6/96	3	20		12 You Gotta Love That/				
8/12/95	16	20		13 If I Was A Drinkin' Man *S:15*		$3	▌	Atlantic 87120
5/18/96	4	20		14 Then You Can Tell Me Goodbye *S:3 (album snippets)*	107	$3	▌	Atlantic 87053
				#6 Pop hit for The Casinos in 1967				
7/20/96	71	3		15 Hillbilly Rap				album cut
				from the album *Neal McCoy* on Atlantic 82907				
9/28/96	35	11		16 Going, Going, Gone *(album snippets)*		$3	▌	Atlantic 87045
12/14/96+	35	17		17 That Woman Of Mine				album cut
				from the album *Neal McCoy* on Atlantic 82907				
5/24/97	5	21		18 The Shake				album cut
				from the album *Greatest Hits* on Atlantic 83011				
10/18/97+	22	20		19 If You Can't Be Good (Be Good At It)				album cut
				from the album *Be Good At It* on Atlantic 83057				
				McCREADY, Mindy '96				
				Born on 11/30/75 in Fort Myers, Florida. No relation to Rich McCready.				
2/3/96	6	23		1 Ten Thousand Angels *S:4 Not Somebody's Fool*	124	$3	▌	BNA 64470
6/8/96	❶¹	20		2 Guys Do It All The Time *S:2 (dance mix)*	72	$3	▌	BNA 64575
3/1/97	4	20		3 A Girl's Gotta Do (What A Girl's Gotta Do)/ *S:5*	105			
10/12/96+	18	20		4 Maybe He'll Notice Her Now **MINDY McCREADY (Featuring Richie McDonald)**	102	$3	▌	BNA 64757
9/20/97	26	18		5 What If I Do *S:8 If I Don't Stay The Night*	102	$3	▌	BNA 64990
				McCREADY, Rich '96				
				Born on 2/9/70 in Seneca, Missouri. Singer/songwriter/guitarist. No relation to Mindy McCready.				
1/27/96	58	10		1 Hangin' On *Back In The Swing Of Things*		$3	▌	Magnatone 1104
4/27/96	53	6		2 Thinkin' Strait *Just Like Me*		$3	▌	Magnatone 2104
5/10/97	74	1		3 That Just About Covers It				album cut
				from the album *That Just About Covers It* on Magnatone 1115				
				McCULLA, Paula '88				
2/6/88	69	5		Thanks For Leavin' Him (For Me) .... *Heart Over Mind*		$6		Rivermark 1001
				McCULLOUGH, Gary '87				
5/23/87	80	2		I'd Know A Lie .... *Easy Way Out*		$5		Soundwaves 4786

DEBUT	PEAK	WKS	Gold	A-side / B-side	Pop	$	Pic	Label & Number
				McDANIEL, Mel ★105★ '85				
				Born on 9/6/42 in Checotah, Oklahoma. Singer/songwriter/guitarist. Joined the *Grand Ole Opry* in 1986.				
				1)Baby's Got Her Blue Jeans On 2)Big Ole Brew 3)Stand Up 4)Let It Roll 5)Louisiana Saturday Night				
5/8/76	51	10		1 Have A Dream On Me .... *Gotta Lotta Love*		$5		Capitol 4249
9/18/76	70	7		2 I Thank God She Isn't Mine .... *Or I'll Keep On Lovin' You*		$5		Capitol 4324
1/22/77	39	11		3 All The Sweet .... *A Little More Country*		$5		Capitol 4373
6/4/77	18	14		4 Gentle To Your Senses .... *Honky Tonk Lady*		$5		Capitol 4430
9/17/77	27	11		5 Soul Of A Honky Tonk Woman .... *Roll Your Own*		$5		Capitol 4481
12/17/77+	11	16		6 God Made Love .... *I'll Just Take It Out In Love*		$5		Capitol 4520
5/20/78	80	5		7 The Farm .... *Every Square Has An Angle*		$5		Capitol 4569
8/19/78	26	11		8 Bordertown Woman .... *The Grandest Lady Of Them All*		$5		Capitol 4597
3/17/79	33	10		9 Love Lies .... *Oklahoma Wind*		$5		Capitol 4691
6/30/79	24	13		10 Play Her Back To Yesterday .... *T.J.'s Last Ride*		$5		Capitol 4740
10/20/79	27	11		11 Lovin' Starts Where Friendship Ends .... *I Tried*		$5		Capitol 4784
7/5/80	39	9		12 Hello Daddy, Good Morning Darling .... *Cold Hard Facts Of Love*		$5		Capitol 4886
11/29/80+	23	14		13 Countryfied .... *Manhattan Affair*		$5		Capitol 4949
3/28/81	7	14		14 Louisiana Saturday Night *My Ship's Comin' In*		$4		Capitol 4983
7/18/81	10	16		15 Right In The Palm Of Your Hand *Who's Been Sleeping In My Bed*		$4		Capitol 5022
11/14/81+	19	16		16 Preaching Up A Storm .... *In The Heat Of The Night*		$4		Capitol 5059

McDANIEL, Mel — Cont'd

DEBUT	PEAK	WKS		A-side / B-side	Pop	$	Pic	Label & Number
3/20/82	10	16		17 Take Me To The Country · *10 Years, 3 Kids And 2 Loves Too Late*		$4		Capitol 5095
				MEL McDANIELS				
7/3/82	4	18		18 Big Ole Brew · *Lay Down*		$4		Capitol 5138
11/6/82+	20	16		19 I Wish I Was In Nashville · *Stars*		$4		Capitol 5169
4/9/83	22	15		20 Old Man River (I've Come To Talk Again) · *The Big Time*		$4		Capitol 5218
7/30/83	39	12		21 Hot Time In Old Town Tonight · *Some Folks Are Dying To Live Like This*		$3		Capitol 5259
11/5/83+	9	20		22 I Call It Love · *Goodbye Marie*		$3		Capitol 5298
3/10/84	49	9		23 Where'd That Woman Go · *You've Got Another Think Comin'*		$3		Capitol 5333
5/19/84	59	8		24 Most Of All I Remember You · *The Gunfighter's Song*		$3		Capitol 5349
7/28/84	64	6		25 All Around The Water Tank · *Cheatin's Only Cheatin'*		$3		Capitol 5371
				MEL McDANIEL with Oklahoma Wind (above 3)				
11/10/84+	❶[1]	28		26 Baby's Got Her Blue Jeans On · S:❶[1] / A:❶[1] *The Gunfighter's Song*		$3		Capitol 5418
3/16/85	6	21		27 Let It Roll (Let It Rock) · S:6 / A:6 *Dreamin' With You*		$3		Capitol 5458
				#64 Pop hit for Chuck Berry in 1960				
9/14/85	5	21		28 Stand Up · S:4 / A:5 *I Feel A Storm Coming*		$3	■	Capitol 5513
1/25/86	22	16		29 Shoe String · A:19 / S:21 *Worn Out Shoe*		$3	■	Capitol 5544
5/31/86	53	9		30 Doctor's Orders · S:37 *Thank You Nadine*		$3		Capitol 5587
9/27/86	12	19		31 Stand On It · A:11 / S:12 *In Oklahoma*		$3	■	Capitol 5620
				written by Bruce Springsteen (B-side of his 1985 "Glory Days" single)				
2/7/87	56	7		32 Oh What A Night · *Chain Smokin'*		$3		Capitol 5682
5/16/87	49	17		33 Anger & Tears · *Sunday Mornin' Preachers*		$3		Capitol 5705
8/15/87	60	8		34 Love Is Everywhere · *Do You Want To Say Goodbye*		$3		Capitol 44052
11/21/87	64	8		35 Now You're Talkin' · *Sunday Mornin' Preachers*		$3		Capitol 44106
2/13/88	58	7		36 Ride This Train · *Jump Into Love*		$3		Capitol 44127
5/14/88	9	21		37 Real Good Feel Good Song · S:18 *Chain Smokin'*		$3		Capitol 44158
10/22/88	62	6		38 Henrietta · *Under My Skin*		$3		Capitol 44244
2/4/89	54	7		39 Walk That Way · *The Tractor*		$3		Capitol 44303
4/29/89	70	4		40 Blue Suede Blues · *Oklahoma Shines*		$3		Capitol 44358
10/21/89	80	3		41 You Can't Play The Blues (In An Air-Conditioned Room)				album cut
				from the album *Rock-A-Billy Boy* on Capitol 93882				

McDONALD, Richie — see McCREADY, Mindy

McDONALD, Skeets '52
Born Enos William McDonald on 10/1/15 in Greenway, Arkansas. Died of a heart attack on 3/31/68 (age 52). Singer/songwriter/guitarist.

DEBUT	PEAK	WKS		A-side / B-side	Pop	$	Pic	Label & Number
10/25/52	❶[3]	18		1 Don't Let The Stars Get In Your Eyes · J:❶[3] / S:2 / A:3 *Big Family Trouble*		$20		Capitol F2216
				#1 Pop hit for Perry Como in 1953				
10/24/60	21	6		2 This Old Heart · *Make Room For The Blues*		$12		Columbia 41773
9/28/63	9	18		3 Call Me Mr. Brown · *This Old Broken Heart*		$10		Columbia 42807
12/25/65+	29	5		4 Big Chief Buffalo Nickel (Desert Blues) · *Day Sleeper*		$10		Columbia 43425
				written and first recorded by Jimmie Rodgers in 1929				
1/7/67	28	11		5 Mabel · *Too Much Of Me (Walked Away With You)*		$10		Columbia 43946

McDOWELL, Ronnie ★100★ '83
Born on 3/26/50 in Fountain Head, Tennessee; raised in Portland, Tennessee. Singer/songwriter/guitarist.

1) You're Gonna Ruin My Bad Reputation 2) Older Women 3) Wandering Eyes 4) You Made A Wanted Man Of Me 5) Watchin' Girls Go By

DEBUT	PEAK	WKS		A-side / B-side	Pop	$	Pic	Label & Number
9/10/77	13	9	●	1 The King Is Gone · *Walking Through Georgia In The Rain*	13	$7		Scorpion 135
				tribute to Elvis Presley				
12/24/77+	5	17		2 I Love You, I Love You, I Love You · *Fallin'*	81	$7		Scorpion 149
4/29/78	15	12		3 Here Comes The Reason I Live · *Travelin' Wanderin' Man*		$7		Scorpion 159
7/29/78	59	5		4 I Just Wanted You To Know/				
7/29/78	68	5		5 Animal		$7		Scorpion 0553
				RONNIE McDOWELL with the Jordanaires (above 2)				
10/7/78	39	8		6 This Is A Holdup · *The Bridge Washed Out*		$7		Scorpion 0560
1/13/79	68	4		7 He's A Cowboy From Texas · *When It Comes To You*		$7		Scorpion 0569
4/28/79	18	14		8 World's Most Perfect Woman · *Rockin' You Easy, Lovin' You Slow*		$4		Epic 50696
8/25/79	26	11		9 Love Me Now/				
1/5/80	29	10		10 Never Seen A Mountain So High		$4		Epic 50753
3/29/80	37	8		11 Lovin' A Livin' Dream · *When The Right Time Comes*		$4		Epic 50857
7/5/80	80	4		12 How Far Do You Want To Go · *You've Already Gone To My Heart*		$4		Epic 50895
8/23/80	36	11		13 Gone · *24 Hours Of Love*		$4		Epic 50925
12/27/80+	2[1]	17		14 Wandering Eyes · *What Would Heaven Say*		$4		Epic 50962
6/27/81	❶[1]	16		15 Older Women · *No Body's Perfect*		$4		Epic 02129
11/14/81+	4	18		16 Watchin' Girls Go By · *Good Time Lovin' Man*		$4		Epic 02614
5/8/82	11	19		17 I Just Cut Myself · *World's Greatest Lover*		$4		Epic 02884
9/11/82	7	17		18 Step Back · *I Never Felt So Much Love (In One Bed)*		$4		Epic 03203
1/29/83	10	19		19 Personally · *You Make My Day Pay Off (All Night Long)*		$4		Epic 03526
				#19 Pop hit for Karla Bonoff in 1982				
6/11/83	❶[1]	22		20 You're Gonna Ruin My Bad Reputation · *I Should've Lied*		$4		Epic 03946

224

DEBUT	PEAK	WKS	Gold	A-side (Chart Hit)...B-side	Pop	$	Pic	Label & Number
				McDOWELL, Ronnie — Cont'd				
10/15/83+	3	23		21 **You Made A Wanted Man Of Me** *This Could Take Forever*		$4		Epic 04167
2/25/84	7	19		22 **I Dream Of Women Like You** *Your Baby's Not My Baby*		$4		Epic 04367
6/23/84	8	21		23 **I Got A Million Of 'Em** *My Baby Don't Wear No Pajamas*		$4		Epic 04499
2/23/85	5	23		24 **In A New York Minute** A:4 / S:5 *Something Special*		$4		Epic 04816
7/20/85	9	20		25 **Love Talks** S:7 / A:9 *She Lays Me Down*		$4		Epic 05404
5/3/86	6	18		26 **All Tied Up** S:4 / A:7 *Strings Of Silver Satin*		$3		Curb/MCA 52816
9/6/86	37	14		27 **When You Hurt, I Hurt**..........................*Whoopah*		$3		Curb/MCA 52907
12/13/86+	30	14		28 **Lovin' That Crazy Feelin'**.........A:30 *I Don't Want To Set The World On Fire*		$3		Curb/MCA 52994
6/20/87	55	8		29 **Make Me Late For Work Today** ....*Hold Me Tight*		$3		MCA 53126
12/26/87+	8	23		30 **It's Only Make Believe** S:6 *Baby Me Baby*		$3		Curb 10501
				Conway Twitty (guest vocal)				
7/16/88	27	14		31 **Suspicion/**				
				#3 Pop hit for Terry Stafford in 1964				
5/28/88	36	12		32 **I'm Still Missing You**		$3		Curb 10508
1/14/89	50	7		33 **Never Too Old To Rock 'N' Roll**..................*Rock And Roll Kiss*		$3		Curb 10521
				RONNIE McDOWELL WITH JERRY LEE LEWIS				
4/1/89	39	12		34 **Sea Of Heartbreak** ....*Ain't Love Wonderful*		$3		Curb 10525
7/8/89	69	6		35 **Who'll Turn Out The Lights** ....*Hey Hey Miss Lucy*		$3		Curb 10544
12/2/89+	50	15		36 **She's A Little Past Forty**.........................*Under These Conditions*		$3		Curb 10558
12/8/90+	26	20		37 **Unchained Melody** ....*Sheet Music*		$3	▌	Curb 76850
				#4 Pop hit for The Righteous Brothers in 1965				
				McENTIRE, Pake **'86**				
				Born Dale Stanley McEntire in 6/23/53 in Chockie, Oklahoma. Singer/guitarist. Brother of **Reba McEntire**.				
1/18/86	20	16		1 **Every Night** ....S:14 / A:21 *Too Old To Grow Up Now*		$3	■	RCA 14220
5/10/86	3	22		2 **Savin' My Love For You** S:3 / A:3 *I'm Having Fun*		$3		RCA 14336
10/11/86	12	19		3 **Bad Love** ....S:10 / A:11 *Every Night*		$3	□	RCA 5004
2/21/87	25	12		4 **Heart Vs. Heart** ....A:25 *(What I Got Is) Good For You*		$3		RCA 5092
				Reba McEntire (harmony vocal)				
6/6/87	46	11		5 **Too Old To Grow Up Now** ....*Caroline's Still In Georgia*		$3		RCA 5207
9/26/87	29	21		6 **Good God, I Had It Good** ....*Every Night*		$3	■	RCA 5256
2/27/88	62	6		7 **Life In The City** ....*Another Place, Another Time*		$3		RCA 5332

McENTIRE, Reba ★24★   **'87**

Born on 3/28/54 on in Chockie, Oklahoma. Singer/songwriter. Sister of **Pake McEntire**. Competed in rodeos as a horseback barrel rider. Married to rodeo champion Charlie Battles from 1976-87. Married her manager, Narvel Blackstock, in 1989. Joined the *Grand Ole Opry* in 1985. Acted in the movies *Tremors* and *North* as well as several TV movies. Seven members of her band plus her tour manager were killed in a plane crash on 3/16/91. CMA Awards: 1984, 1985, 1986 & 1987 Female Vocalist of the Year; 1986 Entertainer of the Year.

1)Is There Life Out There 2)For My Broken Heart 3)The Heart Won't Lie 4)You Lie
5)What Am I Gonna Do About You

DEBUT	PEAK	WKS		A-side / B-side	Pop	$	Pic	Label & Number
5/8/76	88	5		1 **I Don't Want To Be A One Night Stand** ....*I'm Not Your Kind Of Girl*		$10		Mercury 73788
2/12/77	86	4		2 **(There's Nothing Like The Love) Between A Woman And A Man** ....*I Was Glad To Give My Everything To You*		$10		Mercury 73879
8/6/77	88	4		3 **Glad I Waited Just For You** ....*Invitation To The Blues*		$10		Mercury 73929
5/20/78	20	12		4 **Three Sheets In The Wind/**				
		11		5 **I'd Really Love To See You Tonight** ....*I'd Really Love To See You Tonight*		$6		Mercury 55026
				JACKY WARD & REBA McENTIRE (above 2)				
				#2 Pop hit for England Dan & John Ford Coley in 1976				
9/2/78	28	12		6 **Last Night, Ev'ry Night** ....*Angel In Your Arms*		$8		Mercury 55036
4/21/79	36	10		7 **Runaway Heart** ....*Make Me Feel Like A Woman Wants To Feel*		$8		Mercury 55058
7/7/79	26	11		8 **That Makes Two Of Us**......................................*Good Friends*		$8		Mercury 55054
				JACKY WARD/REBA McENTIRE				
9/22/79	19	12		9 **Sweet Dreams** ....*I'm A Woman*		$7		Mercury 57003
1/5/80	40	8		10 **(I Still Long To Hold You) Now And Then**................*It's Gotta Be Love*		$7		Mercury 57014
6/14/80	8	15		11 **(You Lift Me) Up To Heaven** *Rain Fallin'*		$7		Mercury 57025
10/18/80	18	14		12 **I Can See Forever In Your Eyes**...........*A Poor Man's Rosess (Or A Rich Man's Gold)*		$7		Mercury 57034
3/14/81	13	16		13 **I Don't Think Love Ought To Be That Way** ....*Tears On My Pillow*		$7		Mercury 57046
7/4/81	5	19		14 **Today All Over Again** *Look At The One (Who's Been Lookin' At You)*		$7		Mercury 57054
11/21/81+	13	18		15 **Only You (And You Alone)** ....*Love By Love*		$7	■	Mercury 57062
				#5 Pop hit for the Platters in 1955				
6/5/82	3	19		16 **I'm Not That Lonely Yet** *Over, Under And Around*		$6		Mercury 76157
10/2/82+	❶[1]	22		17 **Can't Even Get The Blues** *Sweet Dreams*		$6		Mercury 76180
2/5/83	❶[1]	21		18 **You're The First Time I've Thought About Leaving** *Up To Heaven*		$5		Mercury 810338
7/30/83	7	18		19 **Why Do We Want (What We Know We Can't Have)** *I Can See Forever In Your Eyes*		$5		Mercury 812632
12/3/83+	12	22		20 **There Ain't No Future In This** ....*Reasons*		$5		Mercury 814629
3/17/84	5	19		21 **Just A Little Love** *Your Heart's Not In It (What's In It For Me)*		$3	■	MCA 52349
6/23/84	15	20		22 **He Broke Your Mem'ry Last Night**..............................*If Only*		$3		MCA 52404
10/13/84+	❶[1]	23		23 **How Blue** S:❶[1] / A:❶[1] *That's What He Said*		$3		MCA 52468
2/16/85	❶[1]	22		24 **Somebody Should Leave** S:❶[1] / A:❶[1] *Don't You Believe Him*		$3	■	MCA 52527
6/15/85	6	19		25 **Have I Got A Deal For You** S:5 / A:7 *Whose Heartache Is This Anyway*		$3	■	MCA 52604
10/5/85	5	24		26 **Only In My Mind** S:5 / A:5 *She's The One Loving You Now*		$3		MCA 52691
2/22/86	❶[1]	23		27 **Whoever's In New England** S:❶[1] / A:❶[1] *Can't Stop Now*		$3		MCA 52767

225

McENTIRE, Reba — Cont'd

DEBUT	PEAK	WKS	Gold	A-side (Chart Hit) / B-side	Pop	$	Pic	Label & Number
6/28/86	❶¹	19		28 Little Rock — A:❶¹ / S:2 *If You Only Knew*		$3		MCA 52848
10/11/86+	❶¹	22		29 What Am I Gonna Do About You — A:❶² / S:❶¹ *I Heard Her Crying*		$3		MCA 52922
2/7/87	4	17		30 Let The Music Lift You Up — A:4 / S:8 *Lookin' For A New Love Story*		$3		MCA 52990
5/23/87	❶¹	21		31 One Promise Too Late — S:❶¹ *Why Not Tonight*		$3		MCA 53092
9/19/87	❶¹	22		32 The Last One To Know — S:❶¹ *I Don't Want To Be Alone*		$3		MCA 53159
1/23/88	❶¹	20		33 Love Will Find Its Way To You — S:4 *Someone Else*		$3		MCA 53244
5/14/88	5	16		34 Sunday Kind Of Love — S:3 *So, So, So Long* #15 Pop hit for **Jo Stafford** in 1947		$3		MCA 53315
9/10/88	❶¹	22		35 I Know How He Feels — S:3 *So, So, So Long*		$3		MCA 53402
12/24/88+	❶¹	21		36 New Fool At An Old Game — *You're The One I Dream About*		$3		MCA 53473
5/13/89	❶¹	19		37 Cathy's Clown — *Walk On* #1 Pop hit for **The Everly Brothers** in 1960		$3		MCA 53638
9/2/89	4	26		38 'Til Love Comes Again — *You Must Really Love Me*		$3		MCA 53694
12/23/89+	7	26		39 Little Girl — *Am I The Only One Who Cares*		$3		MCA 53763
4/14/90	2²	21		40 Walk On — *It Always Rains On Saturday*		$3		MCA 79009
8/25/90	❶¹	20		41 You Lie — *That's All She Wrote*		$3		MCA 79071
12/1/90+	3	20		42 Rumor Has It — *You Remember Me*		$3		MCA 53970
3/2/91	8	20		43 Fancy — *This Picture*		$3		MCA 54042
5/25/91	2¹	20		44 Fallin' Out Of Love — *Now You Tell Me*		$3		MCA 54108
10/12/91	❶²	20		45 For My Broken Heart — *Bobby*		$3		MCA 54223
1/25/92	❶²	20		46 Is There Life Out There — *Buying Her Roses*		$3		MCA 54319
4/25/92	12	20		47 The Night The Lights Went Out In Georgia..............*All Dressed Up*		$3		MCA 54386
8/15/92	3	20		48 The Greatest Man I Never Knew — *If I Had Only Known*		$3		MCA 54441
11/21/92+	5	20		49 Take It Back — *Baby's Gone Blues*		$3		MCA 54544
2/20/93	❶²	20		50 The Heart Won't Lie — *Will He Ever Go Away* **REBA McENTIRE AND VINCE GILL**		$3		MCA 54599
5/15/93	5	20		51 It's Your Call — *For Herself*	110	$3	∎	MCA 54496
8/28/93	❶¹	20		52 Does He Love You — *Straight From You* **Linda Davis** (guest vocal)		$3		MCA 54719
12/18/93+	7	20		53 They Asked About You — *For Herself*		$3		MCA 54769
2/26/94	72	6		54 If I Had Only Known .... from the movie *8 Seconds* starring Luke Perry (soundtrack on MCA 10927)				album cut
4/9/94	5	20		55 Why Haven't I Heard From You — *If I Had Only Known*	101	$3	∎	MCA 54823
7/30/94	15	20		56 She Thinks His Name Was John..............*I Wish That I Could Tell You*	101	$3	∎	MCA 54899
11/5/94+	2¹	20		57 Till You Love Me — *I Wouldn't Wanna Be You*	78	$3	∎	MCA 54888
2/18/95	❶¹	20		58 The Heart Is A Lonely Hunter — *Read My Mind*		$3		MCA 54987
5/27/95	2¹	20		59 And Still — *I Won't Stand In Line*		$3		MCA 55047
9/16/95	20	12		60 On My Own ....*Read My Mind* **Linda Davis, Martina McBride** and **Trisha Yearwood** (backing vocals); #1 Pop hit for **Patti LaBelle** & **Michael McDonald** in 1986		$3	∎	MCA 55100
11/11/95+	9	20		61 Ring On Her Finger, Time On Her Hands — *You Keep Me Hangin' On*		$3		MCA 55161
3/30/96	19	20		62 Starting Over Again ....*I Won't Mention It Again*		$3		MCA 55183
10/5/96	2³	20		63 The Fear Of Being Alone — *Never Had A Reason To*		$3		MCA 55249
12/28/96+	❶¹	20		64 How Was I To Know — *Just Looking For Him*		$3		MCA 55290
12/28/96	63	2		65 The Christmas Song (Chestnuts Roasting On An Open Fire) ....[X] #3 Pop hit for **Nat "King" Cole** in 1946; from the album *Merry Christmas To You* on MCA 42031				album cut
4/12/97	2¹	20		66 I'd Rather Ride Around With You — *State Of Grace*		$3		MCA 72006
9/6/97	15	20		67 What If It's You..............*Close To Crazy*		$3		MCA 72001
12/20/97+	23	15		68 What If — S:3 *(same version)*	50	$3	∎	MCA 72026

McEUEN, John — '85
Born on 12/19/45 in Long Beach, California. Singer/songwriter/banjo player. Founding member of the **Nitty Gritty Dirt Band**.

DEBUT	PEAK	WKS	Gold	A-side / B-side	Pop	$	Pic	Label & Number
4/6/85	81	4		Blue Days Black Nights ....*John Hardy*		$4		Warner 29047

McGILL, Tony — '87
Born in Pearl, Mississippi.

DEBUT	PEAK	WKS	Gold	A-side / B-side	Pop	$	Pic	Label & Number
1/17/87	76	4		1 Like An Oklahoma Morning		$6		Killer 1004
6/27/87	82	3		2 Taming My Mind		$6		Killer 1006
1/9/88	78	4		3 For Your Love .... #13 Pop hit for **Ed Townsend** in 1958		$6		Killer 1008

McGOVERN, Maureen — '79
Born on 7/27/49 in Youngstown, Ohio. Singer/actress. Charted six pop hits from 1973-79. Acted in the movies *The Towering Inferno* and *Airplane*. Starred in Broadway's *Pirates Of Penzance*.

DEBUT	PEAK	WKS	Gold	A-side / B-side	Pop	$	Pic	Label & Number
3/3/79	93	3		Can You Read My Mind..............*You Love Me Too Late* love theme from the movie *Superman* starring Christopher Reeves	52	$4		Warner/Curb 8750

McGRAW, Tim ★167★   '98
Born Samuel Timothy McGraw on 5/1/67 in Delhi, Louisiana; raised in Start, Louisiana. Singer/songwriter/guitarist. Son of former professional baseball pitcher Tug McGraw. Married **Faith Hill** on 10/6/96.

1)Just To See You Smile 2)It's Your Love 3)I Like It, I Love It

DEBUT	PEAK	WKS	Gold	A-side	B-side	Pop	$	Pic	Label & Number
10/10/92	47	15		1 Welcome To The Club					album cut
4/10/93	60	7		2 Memory Lane					album cut
7/24/93	71	2		3 Two Steppin' Mind					album cut
				above 3 from the album Tim McGraw on Curb 77603					
1/22/94	8	20	●	4 Indian Outlaw	*(dance mix)*	15	$3	▌	Curb 76920
4/2/94	❶²	20	●	5 Don't Take The Girl	S:16 *Welcome To The Club*	17	$3	▌	Curb 76925
7/16/94	2³	20		6 Down On The Farm					album cut
				from the album Not A Moment Too Soon on Curb 77659					
10/29/94+	❶²	20		7 Not A Moment Too Soon/	S:11				
2/25/95	5	20		8 Refried Dreams		106	$3	▌	Curb 76931
8/12/95	❶⁵	20		9 I Like It, I Love It	S:❶¹⁹ *(dance mix)*	25	$3	▌	Curb 76961
10/7/95	2²	20		10 Can't Be Really Gone	S:4 *That's Just Me*	87	$3	▌	Curb 76971
11/4/95+	5	21		11 All I Want Is A Life					album cut
6/22/96	❶²	20		12 She Never Lets It Go To Her Heart					album cut
10/12/96+	4	20		13 Maybe We Should Just Sleep On It					album cut
				above 3 from the album All I Want on Curb 77800					
5/10/97	❶⁶	20	▲	14 It's Your Love	S:❶¹² *She Never Lets It Go To Her Heart*	7	$3	▌	Curb 73019
				TIM McGRAW with Faith Hill					
7/5/97	❶²	26		15 Everywhere					album cut
8/9/97+	❶⁶	42		16 Just To See You Smile					album cut
				above 2 from the album Everywhere on Curb 77886					

McGUFFEY LANE   '83
Country-rock group from Columbus, Ohio: Bob McNelley (vocals), John Schwab (guitar), Terry Efaw (steel guitar), Stephen Douglass (keyboards), Stephen Reis (bass) and Dave Rangeler (drums). Group name taken from a street in Athens, Ohio. Douglass died in a car crash on 1/12/84 (age 33). McNelley died of a self-inflicted gunshot wound on 1/7/87 (age 36).

DEBUT	PEAK	WKS	A-side	B-side	$	Label & Number
11/20/82+	44	13	1 Making A Living's Been Killing Me	*You Wouldn't Give Up On Me*	$4	Atco 99959
3/26/83	62	6	2 Doing It Right	*Too Many Days*	$4	Atco 99908
5/12/84	44	12	3 Day By Day	*Jamaica In My Mind*	$4	Atlantic Amer. 99778
9/1/84	63	8	4 The First Time	*You've Got A Right*	$4	Atlantic Amer. 99717

McGUINN, Roger — see HILLMAN, Chris

McGUIRE, Doug   '80

DEBUT	PEAK	WKS	A-side	B-side	$	Label & Number
7/26/80	64	6	Stranger, I'm Married	*Oh What A Moment*	$6	Multi-Media 7

McKUHEN, Lanier   '87
Singer from Macon, Georgia.

DEBUT	PEAK	WKS	A-side	B-side	$	Label & Number
4/25/87	75	4	Searching (For Someone Like You)	*Face To Face*	$5	Soundwaves 4785

McLEAN, Don   '81
Born on 10/2/45 in New Rochelle, New York. Singer/songwriter/guitarist. Charted 10 pop hits from 1971-81.

DEBUT	PEAK	WKS	A-side	B-side	Pop	$	Label & Number
1/31/81	6	14	1 Crying	*Genesis (In The Beginning)*	5	$4	Millennium 11799
5/9/81	68	6	2 Since I Don't Have You	*Your Cheating Heart*	23	$4	Millennium 11804
			#12 Pop hit for The Skyliners in 1959				
4/18/87	73	4	3 He's Got You	*To Have And To Hold*		$3	EMI America 8375
			male version of "She's Got You" by Patsy Cline				
11/14/87	49	8	4 You Can't Blame The Train	*Perfect Love*		$3	Capitol 44098
7/30/88	65	4	5 Love In The Heart	*Every Day's A Miracle*		$3	Capitol 44186

McMILLAN, Jimmy   '80
Singer from Fort Worth, Texas.

DEBUT	PEAK	WKS	A-side	B-side	$	Label & Number
12/20/80	92	3	1 Footsteps	*I Can't Look Into Your Eyes*	$6	Blum 001
			written by Sheb Wooley			
3/14/81	96	2	2 Her Empty Pillow (Lying Next To Mine)	*It Feels So Good*	$6	Blum 767

McMILLAN, Terry   '82
Born on 10/12/53 in Lexington, North Carolina. Nashville studio harmonica player.

DEBUT	PEAK	WKS	A-side	B-side	$	Label & Number
12/11/82	85	4	Love Is A Full Time Thing	*You're Bringing Out The Fool In Me*	$4	RCA 13360

McPHERSON, Wyley   '82
Real name: Paul Richey. Brother George Richey married **Tammy Wynette**.

DEBUT	PEAK	WKS	A-side	B-side	$	Pic	Label & Number
8/7/82	89	2	1 Jedediah Jones	*Longneck Lonestar*	$6	■	i.e. 007
10/9/82	81	3	2 The Devil Inside	*Love Is What You Make It*	$6	■	i.e. 009

McQUAIG, Scott   '89
Born on 1/27/60 in Meridian, Mississippi.

DEBUT	PEAK	WKS	A-side	B-side	$	Label & Number
8/12/89	56	8	1 Honky Tonk Amnesia	*My Friend The Bottle*	$3	Universal 66001
11/4/89	54	7	2 Johnny And The Dreamers	*High Friends In The Places (All Over Town)*	$3	Universal 66028

McVICKER, Dana '87
Born in Baltimore; raised in Phillipe, West Virginia. Married Michael Thomas, **Reba McEntire**'s guitarist, who died in a plane crash on 3/16/91 (age 34).

DEBUT	PEAK	WKS		A-side / B-side		$		Label & Number
3/14/87	64	6		1 I'd Rather Be Crazy .... *Love Spent The Night*		$3		EMI America 8371
6/27/87	64	5		2 Call Me A Fool .... *Love Spent The Night*		$3		EMI America 43017
5/28/88	65	5		3 Rock-A-Bye Heart .... *It's All So New To Me*		$3		Capitol 44155
10/22/88	88	2		4 I'm Loving The Wrong Man Again .... *I'm Lonely For Only You*		$3		Capitol 44223

MEADE, Donna '88
Born in 1953 in Chase City, Virginia. Married **Jimmy Dean** on 10/27/91.

DEBUT	PEAK	WKS		A-side / B-side		$		Label & Number
1/9/88	63	8		1 Be Serious... *I'm Out Of The Blue*		$3		Mercury 888993
5/7/88	50	9		2 Love's Last Stand *I'm Out Of The Blue*		$3		Mercury 870283
7/30/88	69	4		3 Congratulations .... *Slow Fire*		$3		Mercury 870527
10/29/88	78	3		4 Leavin' On Your Mind .... *From A Distance*		$3		Mercury 872010
6/3/89	57	7		5 When He Leaves You		$3		Mercury 874280
10/7/89	61	4		6 Cry Baby... *The Chokin' Kind*		$3		Mercury 874806

MEDLEY, Bill '84
Born on 9/19/40 in Santa Ana, California. Baritone of The Righteous Brothers.

DEBUT	PEAK	WKS		A-side / B-side		$		Label & Number
1/6/79	91	3		1 Statue Of A Fool .... *Wasn't That You Last Night*		$5		United Artists 1270
12/10/83+	28	18		2 Till Your Memory's Gone .... *I've Got Dreams To Remember*		$4		RCA 13692
4/14/84	17	18		3 I Still Do *I've Got Dreams To Remember*		$4		RCA 13753
8/4/84	26	14		4 I've Always Got The Heart To Sing The Blues .... *Turn It Loose*		$4		RCA 13851
3/2/85	47	9		5 Is There Anything I Can Do .... *Old Friend*		$4		RCA 14021
5/11/85	55	7		6 Women In Love .... *Stand Up*		$4		RCA 14081

MELLENCAMP, John Cougar '89
Born on 10/7/51 in Seymour, Indiana. Rock singer/songwriter/producer. Director/star of the movie *Falling from Grace*; leader of the **Buzzin' Cousins** who appeared in the movie. Married model Elaine Irwin on 9/5/92. Charted 28 pop hits from 1979-97.

DEBUT	PEAK	WKS		A-side / B-side	Pop	$	Pic	Label & Number
8/12/89	82	5		Jackie Brown .... *(acoustic version)*	48	$3	■	Mercury 874644

MELLONS, Ken '94
Born on 6/10/65 in Kingsport, Tennessee; raised in Nashville. Singer/songwriter/guitarist.

DEBUT	PEAK	WKS		A-side / B-side		$	Pic	Label & Number
4/2/94	55	9		1 Lookin' In The Same Direction .... *Seven Lonely Days (Make One Weak)*		$3	▮	Epic 77390
7/30/94	8	20		2 Jukebox Junkie *The Pleasure's All Mine*		$3	▮	Epic 77579
12/17/94+	42	14		3 I Can Bring Her Back .... *Honky Tonk Teachers*		$3		Epic 77764
3/25/95	40	12		4 Workin' For The Weekend .... *Keepin' It Country*		$3	▮	Epic 77861
9/30/95	39	20		5 Rub-A-Dubbin' .... *Jukebox Junkie*		$3	▮	Epic 78066
4/27/96	55	8		6 Stranger In Your Eyes .... *Memory Remover*		$3		Epic 78240

MELTON, Terri — see MUNDY, Jim

MEMPHIS '84
Group from Memphis led by Woody Wright (later a member of **Matthews, Wright & King**).

DEBUT	PEAK	WKS		A-side / B-side		$		Label & Number
8/25/84	85	4		We've Got to Start Meeting Like This .... *Gone But Not Forgotten*		$6		MPI 1691

MENSY, Tim '92
Born Timothy Ray Menzies on 8/25/59 in Mechanicsville, Virginia. Singer/songwriter/guitarist. Member of **Bandana**.

DEBUT	PEAK	WKS		A-side / B-side		$		Label & Number
4/15/89	67	5		1 Hometown Advantage..................................... *I've Got To Hand It To You*		$3		Columbia 68676
8/19/89	60	7		2 Stone By Stone *I've Got To Hand It To You*		$3		Columbia 69007
1/13/90	82	1		3 You Still Love Me In My Dreams .... *Stone By Stone*		$3		Columbia 73204
7/11/92	53	9		4 This Ol' Heart .... *The Grandpa That I Know*		$3		Giant 18864
10/31/92	52	14		5 That's Good *The Grandpa That I Know*		$3		Giant 18742
2/27/93	74	2		6 She Dreams				album cut

from the album *This Ol' Heart* on Giant 24463

MEREDITH, Buddy '62
Born William Meredith on 4/13/26 in Beaver Falls, Pennsylvania.

DEBUT	PEAK	WKS		A-side / B-side		$		Label & Number
5/12/62	27	2		I May Fall Again .... *Haunted House*		$20		Nashville 5042

MERRILL AND JESSICA '87
Merrill was born Merrill Osmond on 4/30/53 in Ogden, Utah. Member of the **Osmond Brothers**. Jessica Boucher is married to record producer Paul Worley.

DEBUT	PEAK	WKS		A-side / B-side		$		Label & Number
5/9/87	62	6		You're Here To Remember (I'm Here To Forget) .... *The Price You Pay*		$3		EMI America 8388

MESSINA, Jo Dee '96
Born on 8/25/70 in Holliston, Massachusetts. Female singer.

DEBUT	PEAK	WKS		A-side / B-side	Pop	$	Pic	Label & Number
1/27/96	2[1]	20		1 Heads Carolina, Tails California *S:3 Walk To The Light*	111	$3	▮	Curb 76982
7/6/96	7	20		2 You're Not In Kansas Anymore				album cut
11/16/96	53	13		3 Do You Wanna Make Something Of It				album cut
5/3/97	64	5		4 He'd Never Seen Julie Cry				album cut

above 3 from the album *Jo Dee Messina* on Curb 77820

MESSNER, Bud '50
Born Norman Messner on 10/9/17 in Luray, Virginia. The Sky Line Boys included Buddy Allen, Jack Throckmorton, Jimmy Throckmorton and Ray Ingram.

DEBUT	PEAK	WKS		A-side / B-side		$		Label & Number
6/3/50	7	6		Slippin' Around With Jole Blon *J:7 / S:9 I Died All Over You*		$30		Abbey 15004

BUD MESSNER & His Sky Line Boys
Bill Franklin (vocal); same melody as the 1949 hit "Slippin' Around."

MEYERS, Augie '88
Born on 5/31/40 in San Antonio, Texas. Singer/keyboardist/accordionist. Co-founded the San Francisco "Tex-Mex" rock group, the Sir Douglas Quintet, in the mid-1960's. Joined the Texas Tornados in 1990.

DEBUT	PEAK	WKS		A-side / B-side		$		Label & Number
2/20/88	86	3		Kep Pa So .... *To Nothing At All*		$3		Atlantic Amer. 99382

DEBUT	PEAK	WKS	Gold	A-side (Chart Hit)..B-side	Pop	$	Pic	Label & Number
				MEYERS, Michael '82				
1/16/82	94	2		I'm Just The Leavin' Kind..		$7		MBP 1980
				MICHAELS, Jill — see SCHNEIDER, John				
				MIDDLETON, Eddie '77				
				Born in Albany, Georgia.				
6/11/77	87	6		1 Midnight Train To Georgia .... *I've Been Hurt*		$4		Epic 50388
				#1 Pop hit for Gladys Knight & The Pips in 1973				
9/10/77	38	10		2 Endlessly .... *After The Lovin'*		$4		Epic 50431
				#12 Pop hit for Brook Benton in 1959				
12/10/77+	44	10		3 What Kind Of Fool (Do You Think I Am) .... *Don't Say Let's Wait*		$4		Epic 50481
				#9 Pop hit for The Tams in 1964				
				MILES, Dick '68				
3/16/68	17	10		The Last Goodbye.............................. *Candle-Lighted World* [S]	114	$10		Capitol 2113
				MILLER, Carl '83				
				Singer from Broadway, Virginia.				
6/18/83	84	3		Life Of The Party .... *Memories*		$7		Country Bach 0004
				MILLER, Dean '97				
				Born on 10/15/65 in Santa Fe, New Mexico. Singer/songwriter/guitarist. Son of **Roger Miller**.				
7/26/97	54	7		1 Nowhere, USA .... *If I Was Your Man*		$3	▌	Capitol 58665
11/8/97	67	1		2 My Heart's Broke Down (But My Mind's Made Up)...... *The Running Side Of Me*		$3	▌	Capitol 58682
				MILLER, Ellen Lee '89				
2/11/89	92	2		You Only Love Me When I'm Leavin'		$6		Golden Trumpet 103
				MILLER, Frankie '59				
				Born on 12/17/30 in Victoria, Texas. Singer/songwriter/guitarist.				
4/13/59	5	19		1 Black Land Farmer *True Blue*		$15		Starday 424
				also see #4 below				
10/5/59	7	21		2 Family Man *Poppin' Johnny*		$15		Starday 457
5/23/60	15	14		3 Baby Rocked Her Dolly .... *Rain Rain*		$15		Starday 496
7/17/61	16	5		4 Black Land Farmer.. *True Blue* [R]	82	$15		Starday 424
				same version as #1 above				
2/15/64	34	6		5 A Little South Of Memphis .... *Too Hot To Handle*		$15		Starday 655

				MILLER, Jody ★199★ '72				
				Born Myrna Joy Miller on 11/29/41 in Phoenix; raised in Blanchard, Oklahoma. Singer/songwriter/guitarist.				
				1)There's A Party Goin' On 2)He's So Fine 3)Baby I'm Yours 4)Queen Of The House				
				5)Darling, You Can Always Come Back Home				
5/29/65	5	11		1 Queen Of The House *The Greatest Actor*	12	$10		Capitol 5402
				answer to "King Of The Road" by **Roger Miller**				
11/9/68	73	2		2 Long Black Limousine................................... *Back In The Race*		$10		Capitol 2290
8/15/70	21	13		3 Look At Mine...................................... *Safe In These Lovin' Arms Of Mine*		$8		Epic 10641
1/2/71	19	13		4 If You Think I Love You Now (I've Just Started)........... *Looking Out My Back Door*		$8		Epic 10692
6/12/71	5	15		5 He's So Fine *You Number Two*	53	$8		Epic 10734
10/9/71	5	14		6 Baby, I'm Yours *Good Lovin' (Makes It Right)*	91	$8		Epic 10785
3/25/72	15	13		7 Be My Baby .... *Your Love's Been A Long Time Coming*		$7		Epic 10835
				#2 Pop hit for The Ronettes in 1963				
5/27/72	13	11		8 Let's All Go Down To The River .... *In The Garden*		$7		Epic 10863
				JODY MILLER AND JOHNNY PAYCHECK				
6/17/72	4	14		9 There's A Party Goin' On *Love's The Answer*	115	$7		Epic 10878
11/4/72	18	11		10 To Know Him Is To Love Him .... *Make Me Your Kind Of Woman*		$7		Epic 10916
				#1 Pop hit for The Teddy Bears in 1958				
3/17/73	9	12		11 Good News *Soul Song*		$7		Epic 10960
7/14/73	5	13		12 Darling, You Can Always Come Back Home *We'll Sing Our Song Together*		$6		Epic 11016
11/24/73+	29	13		13 The House Of The Rising Sun .... *In The Name Of Love*		$6		Epic 11056
				#1 Pop hit for The Animals in 1964				
3/16/74	55	9		14 Reflections .... *One More Chance*		$6		Epic 11094
6/22/74	46	11		15 Natural Woman.. *Jimmy's Roses*		$6		Epic 11134
				#8 Pop hit for Aretha Franklin in 1967				
11/16/74+	41	10		16 Country Girl.................................... *Safe In These Lovin' Arms Of Mine*		$6		Epic 50042
3/15/75	78	9		17 The Best In Me.............................*I'm Alright 'Til I See You (Then I Fall Apart)*		$6		Epic 50079
7/12/75	67	9		18 Don't Take It Away .... *Long, Long Time*		$6		Epic 50117
11/8/75	69	8		19 Will You Love Me Tomorrow? .... *Love, You Never Had It So Good*		$6		Epic 50158
				#1 Pop hit for The Shirelles in 1961				
3/27/76	48	9		20 Ashes Of Love .... *She Calls Me "Baby"*		$6		Epic 50203
12/4/76+	25	12		21 When The New Wears Off Our Love .... *Silver And Gold*		$6		Epic 50304
4/9/77	71	7		22 Spread A Little Love Around .... *Montana Cowboy*		$6		Epic 50360
9/17/77	76	5		23 Another Lonely Night .... *All Night Long*		$6		Epic 50432
4/15/78	97	2		24 Soft Lights And Slow Sexy Music ....*Home*		$6		Epic 50512

MILLER, Jody — Cont'd

DEBUT	PEAK	WKS	A-side	B-side	$	Label & Number
7/15/78	67	6	25 (I Wanna) Love My Life Away	I'm Gonna Write A Song	$6	Epic 50568
			#39 Pop hit for Gene Pitney in 1961			
10/7/78	65	4	26 Kiss Away	Hold Me, Thrill Me, Kiss Me	$6	Epic 50612
			#25 Pop hit for Ronnie Dove in 1965			
7/7/79	97	2	27 Lay A Little Lovin' On Me	Crazy On You	$6	Epic 50734
			#11 Pop hit for Robin McNamara in 1970			

MILLER, Mary K.   '79

Born in 1957 in Houston.

1)Next Best Feeling 2)Handcuffed To A Heartache 3)I Can't Stop Loving You

DEBUT	PEAK	WKS	A-side	B-side	$	Label & Number
7/30/77	89	5	1 I Fall To Pieces	Just Can't Believe You're Gone	$5	Inergi 300
			MARY MILLER			
10/8/77	54	8	2 You Just Don't Know	Lovesick Blues	$5	Inergi 302
			written by Bobby Darin			
12/24/77+	33	10	3 The Longest Walk	Love Is	$5	Inergi 304
			#6 Pop hit for Jaye P. Morgan in 1955			
3/4/78	41	9	4 Right Or Wrong	Smile Me A Song	$5	Inergi 306
6/3/78	28	8	5 I Can't Stop Loving You	Let Me Go Lover	$5	Inergi 307
			#1 Pop hit for Ray Charles in 1962			
9/16/78	19	11	6 Handcuffed To A Heartache	Over And Over (I Fall In Love Again)	$5	Inergi 310
12/9/78+	45	9	7 Going, Going, Gone	Woman, Woman	$5	Inergi 311
3/10/79	17	14	8 Next Best Feeling	One Woman's Heaven	$5	Inergi 312
7/28/79	47	7	9 Guess Who Loves You	Georgia On My Mind	$4	RCA 11665
4/5/80	85	3	10 Say A Long Goodbye	You Asked Me To	$5	Inergi 315

★347★   MILLER, Ned   '63

Born Henry Ned Miller on 4/12/25 in Raines, Utah. Singer/songwriter/guitarist.

1)From A Jack To A King 2)Do What You Do Do Well 3)Invisible Tears

DEBUT	PEAK	WKS	A-side	B-side	Pop	$	Label & Number
12/15/62+	2[4]	19	1 From A Jack To A King	Parade Of Broken Hearts	6	$15	Fabor 114
5/25/63	27	3	2 One Among The Many	The Man Behind The Gun		$12	Fabor 116
9/14/63	28	1	3 Another Fool Like Me	Magic Moon		$12	Fabor 121
4/25/64	13	22	4 Invisible Tears	Old Restless Ocean	131	$12	Fabor 128
1/16/65	7	20	5 Do What You Do Do Well	Dusty Guitar	52	$12	Fabor 137
8/14/65	28	8	6 Whistle Walkin'	Two Voices, Two Shadows, Two Faces		$10	Capitol 5431
6/18/66	39	8	7 Summer Roses	Right Behind These Lips		$10	Capitol 5661
10/15/66	44	9	8 Teardrop Lane	Lorraine		$10	Capitol 5742
5/13/67	53	6	9 Hobo	Echo Of The Pines		$10	Capitol 5868
2/17/68	61	5	10 Only A Fool	Endless		$10	Capitol 2074
4/25/70	39	9	11 The Lover's Song	Cold Grey Bars		$8	Republic 1411

MILLER, Roger ★92★   '65

Born on 1/2/36 in Fort Worth, Texas; raised in Erick, Oklahoma. Died of cancer on 10/25/92 (age 56). Singer/songwriter/guitarist. With Faron Young as writer/drummer in 1962. Hosted own TV show in 1966. Wrote the Broadway musical Big River. Elected to the Country Music Hall of Fame in 1995.

1)Dang Me 2)King Of The Road 3)Engine Engine #9 4)Chug-A-Lug 5)England Swings

DEBUT	PEAK	WKS	A-side	B-side	Pop	$	Pic	Label & Number
10/31/60+	14	16	1 You Don't Want My Love	Footprints In The Snow		$15		RCA Victor 7776
6/5/61	6	18	2 When Two Worlds Collide	Every Which-A-Way		$15		RCA Victor 7878
6/1/63	26	1	3 Lock, Stock And Teardrops	I Know Who It Is		$15		RCA Victor 8175
6/6/64	❶[6]	25	4 Dang Me	Got 2 Again [N]	7	$10	■	Smash 1881
9/19/64	3	17	5 Chug-A-Lug	Reincarnation [N]	9	$10		Smash 1926
12/12/64+	15	11	6 Do-Wacka-Do	Love Is Not For Me [N]	31	$10	■	Smash 1947
2/13/65	❶[5]	20	● 7 King Of The Road	Atta Boy Girl	4	$10		Smash 1965
5/22/65	2[2]	18	8 Engine Engine #9	The Last Word In Lonesome Is Me	7	$10		Smash 1983
7/24/65	10	12	9 One Dyin' And A Buryin'	It Happened Just That Way (Pop #105)	34	$10	■	Smash 1994
10/2/65	7	13	10 Kansas City Star	Guess I'll Pick Up My Heart (And Go Home)	31	$10		Smash 1998
11/20/65+	3	16	11 England Swings	Good Old Days	8	$10		Smash 2010
2/26/66	5	14	12 Husbands And Wives/		26			
2/26/66	13	10	13 I've Been A Long Time Leavin' (But I'll Be A Long Time Gone)		103			Smash 2024
7/9/66	35	5	14 You Can't Roller Skate In A Buffalo Herd	Train Of Life [N]	40	$8		Smash 2043
9/24/66	39	9	15 My Uncle Used To Love Me But She Died	You're My Kingdom [N]	58	$8		Smash 2055
11/19/66	55	3	16 Heartbreak Hotel	Less And Less	84	$8		Smash 2066
4/1/67	7	17	17 Walkin' In The Sunshine	Home	37	$8		Smash 2081
10/28/67	27	11	18 The Ballad Of Waterhole #3 (Code Of The West)	Rainbow Valley	102	$8	■	Smash 2121
			from the movie Waterhole #3 starring James Coburn					
3/9/68	6	13	19 Little Green Apples	Our Little Love	39	$8	■	Smash 2148
12/14/68+	15	12	20 Vance	Little Children Run And Play	80	$8		Smash 2197
7/5/69	12	16	21 Me And Bobby McGee	I'm Gonna Teach My Heart To Bend (Instead of Break)	122	$8		Smash 2230
			#1 Pop hit for Janis Joplin in 1971					
10/18/69	14	10	22 Where Have All The Average People Gone	Boeing Boeing 707		$8		Smash 2246
3/14/70	36	7	23 The Tom Green County Fair	I Know Who It Is		$8		Smash 2258

MILLER, Roger — Cont'd

DEBUT	PEAK	WKS	A-side / B-side	Pop	$	Pic	Label & Number
8/29/70	15	12	24 South/				
		12	25 Don't We All Have The Right		$7		Mercury 73102
4/17/71	11	14	26 Tomorrow Night In Baltimore .... *A Million Years Or So*		$7		Mercury 73190
8/7/71	28	11	27 Loving Her Was Easier (Than Anything I'll Ever Do Again) .... *Qua La Linta*		$7		Mercury 73230
3/25/72	34	11	28 We Found It In Each Other's Arms/				
3/25/72	63	11	29 Sunny Side Of My Life		$7		Mercury 73268
9/9/72	41	11	30 Rings For Sale .... *Conversation*		$7		Mercury 73321
12/30/72+	42	8	31 Hoppy's Gone............ *The Day I Jumped From Uncle Harvey's Plane*		$7		Mercury 73354
7/14/73	14	14	32 Open Up Your Heart.................................... *Qua La Linta*	105	$6		Columbia 45873
11/17/73+	24	11	33 I Believe In The Sunshine .... *Shannon's Song*		$6		Columbia 45948
3/9/74	86	3	34 Whistle Stop .... *The 4th Of July* from the animated movie *Robin Hood*		$6		Columbia 46000
12/7/74+	44	10	35 Our Love .... *The Yester Waltz*		$6		Columbia 10052
4/12/75	57	10	36 I Love A Rodeo .... *Lovin' You Is Always On My Mind*		$6		Columbia 10107
9/10/77	68	6	37 Baby Me Baby .... *Dark Side Of The Moon*		$5		Windsong 11072
10/27/79	98	2	38 The Hat .... *Pleasing The Crowd*		$4		20th Century 2421
10/10/81	36	10	39 Everyone Gets Crazy Now And Then .... *Aladambama*		$4		Elektra 47192
6/5/82	19	16	40 Old Friends............................. *When A House Is Not A Home*		$4		Columbia 02681
			ROGER MILLER & WILLIE NELSON (with Ray Price)				
10/5/85	36	12	41 River In The Rain.............................. *Hand For The Hog* from the Broadway musical *Big River* starring Daniel H. Jenkins		$4		MCA 52663
8/2/86	81	8	42 Some Hearts Get All The Breaks.......................... *Arkansas*		$4		MCA 52855

MILLINDER, Lucky, And His Orchestra   '44
Born Lucius Millinder on 8/8/1900 in Anniston, Alabama. Died on 9/28/66 (age 66). Black bandleader.

DEBUT	PEAK	WKS	A-side / B-side	Pop	$	Pic	Label & Number
1/15/44	4	5	1 Sweet Slumber *Don't Cry Baby* Trevor Bacon (vocal)	15	$20		Decca 18569
7/29/44	4	2	2 Hurry, Hurry *I Can't See For Lookin'* Wynonie "Mr. Blues" Harris (vocal)	20	$20		Decca 18609

MILLS, Frank   '79
Born in 1943 in Toronto. Pianist/composer/producer/arranger.

DEBUT	PEAK	WKS	A-side / B-side	Pop	$	Pic	Label & Number
2/24/79	44	14	● Music Box Dancer................................... *The Poet And I* [I]	3	$4		Polydor 14517

MILLS BROTHERS, The   '70
R&B family vocal trio from Piqua, Ohio: Herbert (b: 4/2/12; d: 4/12/89), Harry (b: 8/19/13; d: 6/28/82) and Donald (b: 4/29/15) Mills.

DEBUT	PEAK	WKS	A-side / B-side	Pop	$	Pic	Label & Number
3/21/70	64	3	It Ain't No Big Thing .... *Help Yourself To Some Tomorrow*		$7		Dot 17321

MILSAP, Ronnie ★23★   '80
Born on 1/16/46 in Robbinsville, North Carolina. Singer/songwriter/pianist. Blind since birth. Formed the Apparitions while in high school. Joined J.J. Cale's band. Played session keyboards for **Elvis Presley** in 1969. Joined the *Grand Ole Opry* in 1976. CMA Awards: 1974, 1976 & 1977 Male Vocalist of the Year; 1977 Entertainer of the Year.

1)My Heart 2)Only One Love In My Life 3)It Was Almost Like A Song 4)Lost In The Fifties Tonight
5)A Woman In Love

DEBUT	PEAK	WKS	A-side / B-side	Pop	$	Pic	Label & Number
6/30/73	10	14	1 I Hate You/				
		14	2 (All Together Now) Let's Fall Apart		$7		RCA Victor 0969
11/3/73+	11	18	3 That Girl Who Waits On Tables .... *You're Drivin' Me Out Of Your Mind*		$7		RCA Victor 0097
3/30/74	❶[1]	15	4 Pure Love *Love The Second Time Around*		$6		RCA Victor 0237
7/20/74	❶[2]	14	5 Please Don't Tell Me How The Story Ends *Streets Of Gold*	95	$6		RCA Victor 0313
11/30/74+	❶[1]	13	6 (I'd Be) A Legend In My Time *The Biggest Lie*		$6	■	RCA Victor 10112
3/15/75	6	14	7 Too Late To Worry, Too Blue To Cry *Country Cookin'*	101	$6		RCA Victor 10228
7/19/75	❶[2]	16	8 Daydreams About Night Things *(After Sweet Memories) Play Born To Lose Again*		$6		RCA Victor 10335
9/20/75	15	13	9 She Even Woke Me Up To Say Goodbye .... *Loving You's A Natural Thing* recorded in 1970		$6		Warner 8127
10/25/75+	4	16	10 Just In Case *Remember To Remind Me (I'm Leaving)*		$6		RCA Victor 10420
12/27/75+	77	6	11 A Rose By Any Other Name..................... *Please Don't Tell Me How The Story Ends* #125 Pop hit in 1970 (on Chips 2987)		$6		Warner 8160
3/20/76	❶[1]	14	12 What Goes On When The Sun Goes Down *Love Takes A Long Time To Die*		$6		RCA Victor 10593
6/19/76	79	5	13 Crying... *Why* recorded in 1970; #2 Pop hit for **Roy Orbison** in 1961		$6		Warner 8218
7/10/76	❶[2]	14	14 (I'm A) Stand By My Woman Man *Lovers, Friends And Strangers*		$6		RCA Victor 10724
11/27/76+	❶[1]	15	15 Let My Love Be Your Pillow *Busy Makin' Plans*		$5		RCA 10843
5/28/77	❶[3]	18	16 It Was Almost Like A Song *It Don't Hurt To Dream*	16	$5		RCA 10976
11/19/77+	❶[1]	16	17 What A Difference You've Made In My Life *Selfish*	80	$5		RCA 11146
6/3/78	❶[3]	13	18 Only One Love In My Life *Back On My Mind Again*	63	$5		RCA 11270
9/2/78	❶[1]	12	19 Let's Take The Long Way Around The World *I'm Not Trying To Forget*		$5		RCA 11369
12/16/78+	2[3]	15	20 Back On My Mind Again/				
		15	21 Santa Barbara		$5		RCA 11421
4/28/79	❶[1]	15	22 Nobody Likes Sad Songs *Just Because It Feels Good*		$5		RCA 11553
8/18/79	6	13	23 In No Time At All/				
		13	24 Get It Up..	43	$5		RCA 11695
1/12/80	❶[1]	15	25 Why Don't You Spend The Night *Heads I Go, Hearts I Stay*		$4		RCA 11909

DEBUT	PEAK	WKS	Gold	A-side (Chart Hit) ....B-side	Pop	$	Pic	Label & Number
				MILSAP, Ronnie — Cont'd				
4/12/80	❶³	15	26	My Heart/				
		15	27	Silent Night (After The Fight)		$4		RCA 11952
6/21/80	❶¹	16	28	Cowboys And Clowns/	103			
				from the movie *Bronco Billy* starring **Clint Eastwood**				
		16	29	Misery Loves Company		$4		RCA 12006
10/11/80	❶¹	14	30	Smoky Mountain Rain _Crystal Fallin' Rain_	24	$4		RCA 12084
3/21/81	❶¹	14	31	Am I Losing You _He'll Have To Go_		$3		RCA 12194
7/4/81	❶²	15	32	(There's) No Gettin' Over Me _I Live My Whole Life At Night_	5	$3		RCA 12264
10/31/81+	❶¹	16	33	I Wouldn't Have Missed It For The World _It Happens Every Time_	20	$3		RCA 12342
5/1/82	❶¹	17	34	Any Day Now _It's Just A Room_	14	$3		RCA 13216
8/7/82	❶¹	18	35	He Got You _I Love New Orleans Music_	59	$3		RCA 13286
11/20/82+	❶¹	19	36	Inside/				
		18	37	Carolina Dreams		$3		RCA 13362
4/2/83	5	18	38	Stranger In My House _Is It Over_	23	$3		RCA 13470
7/23/83	❶¹	19	39	Don't You Know How Much I Love You _Feelings Change_	58	$3		RCA 13564
11/12/83+	❶¹	19	40	Show Her _Watch Out For The Other Guy_	103	$3		RCA 13658
5/19/84	❶¹	19	41	Still Losing You _I'll Take Care Of You_		$3		RCA 13805
9/1/84	6	19	42	Prisoner Of The Highway _S:6 / A:7 She Loves My Car (Pop #84)_		$3		RCA 13847
4/6/85	❶¹	20	43	She Keeps The Home Fires Burning _S:❶¹ / A:❶¹ Is It Over_		$3		RCA 14034
7/13/85	❶²	23	44	Lost In The Fifties Tonight (In The Still Of The Night) _A:❶² / S:❶¹ I Might Have Said_		$3	■	RCA 14135
				"In The Still Of The Night" was a #3 R&B hit for **The Five Satins** in 1956				
3/8/86	❶¹	20	45	Happy, Happy Birthday Baby _S:❶¹ / A:❶¹ I'll Take Care Of You_		$3		RCA 14286
				#5 Pop hit for **The Tune Weavers** in 1957				
7/5/86	❶¹	20	46	In Love _A:❶² / S:❶¹ Old Fashioned Girl Like You_		$3		RCA 14365
11/22/86+	❶¹	21	47	How Do I Turn You On _S:❶¹ / A:❶¹ Don't Take It Tonight_		$3		RCA 5033
5/23/87	❶¹	19	48	Snap Your Fingers _S:❶¹ This Time Last Year_		$3		RCA 5169
				#8 Pop hit for **Joe Henderson** in 1962				
6/27/87	❶¹	17	49	Make No Mistake, She's Mine _S:3 You're My Love_		$3	■	RCA 5209
				RONNIE MILSAP & KENNY ROGERS				
				#51 Pop hit for **Barbra Streisand & Kim Carnes** in 1985				
10/24/87+	❶¹	20	50	Where Do The Nights Go _S:2 If You Don't Want Me To_		$3		RCA 5259
3/5/88	2¹	21	51	Old Folks _S:5 Earthquake_		$3	■	RCA 6896
				RONNIE MILSAP & MIKE REID				
7/23/88	4	18	52	Button Off My Shirt _S:4 One Night_		$3		RCA 8389
				#91 Pop hit for **Paul Carrack** in 1988				
12/24/88+	❶¹	20	53	Don't You Ever Get Tired (Of Hurting Me) _I Never Expected To See You_		$3		RCA 8746
4/29/89	4	21	54	Houston Solution _If You Don't Want Me To_		$3		RCA 8868
9/23/89	❶²	26	55	A Woman In Love _Starting Today_		$3		RCA 9027
2/10/90	2²	26	56	Stranger Things Have Happened _Southern Roots_		$3		RCA 9120
3/9/91	3	20	57	Are You Lovin' Me Like I'm Lovin' You _Back To The Grindstone_		$3		RCA 2509
7/13/91	6	20	58	Since I Don't Have You _I Ain't Gonna Cry No More_		$3		RCA 2848
				#12 Pop hit for **The Skyliners** in 1959				
12/7/91+	4	20	59	Turn That Radio On _Old Habits Are Hard To Break_		$3		RCA 62104
3/28/92	11	20	60	All Is Fair In Love And War .... Back To The Grindstone		$3		RCA 62217
9/12/92	45	9	61	L.A. To The Moon .... When The Hurt Comes Down		$3		RCA 62332
7/10/93	30	15	62	True Believer .... These Foolish Things (Remind Me Of You)		$3		Liberty 17595
				MINNIE PEARL **'66**				
				Born Sarah Ophelia Colley on 10/25/12 in Centerville, Tennessee. Died of a stroke on 3/4/96 (age 83). Comedienne/actress. Joined the *Grand Ole Opry* in 1940. Elected to the Country Music Hall of Fame in 1975. Trademark was her straw hat with its $1.98 price tag still attached.				
3/5/66	10	12		Giddyup Go - Answer _Road Runner_ [S]		$10		Starday 754
				answer to "Giddyup Go" by **Red Sovine**				
				MINTER, Pat **'89**				
12/9/89	84	2		Whiskey River You Win		$6		Killer 121
				MITCHELL, Charles **'44**				
				Steel guitarist for **Jimmie Davis**.				
4/29/44	4	1		If It's Wrong To Love You _Mean Mama Blues_		$20		Bluebird 33-0508
				CHARLES MITCHELL and his Orchestra				
				MITCHELL, Charlie **'88**				
11/12/88	81	4		I'm Goin' Nowhere		$5		Soundwaves 4810
				MITCHELL, Guy **'67**				
				Born Al Cernik on 2/27/27 in Detroit. Charted 26 pop hits from 1950-60. Acted in the movies *Those Redheads From Seattle* and *Red Garters*.				
11/4/67	51	8	1	Traveling Shoes .... Every Night Is A Lifetime		$8		Starday 819
2/24/68	61	5	2	Alabam _Irene Good-By_		$8		Starday 828
12/14/68	71	3	3	Frisco Line .... It's A New World Every Day		$8		Starday 846
				MITCHELL, Marty **'78**				
				Singer from Birmingham, Alabama.				
6/15/74	64	7	1	Midnight Man _I'd Be Your Fool Again_		$5		Atlantic 4023
12/11/76	87	4	2	My Eyes Adored You .... Devil Woman		$5		Hitsville 6044
				#1 Pop hit for **Frankie Valli** in 1975				
2/18/78	34	10	3	You Are The Sunshine Of My Life .... Yester-Me, Yester-You, Yesterday		$5		MC/Curb 5005
				#1 Pop hit for **Stevie Wonder** in 1973				

DEBUT	PEAK	WKS	A-side (Chart Hit) ... B-side	Pop	$	Pic	Label & Number
			MITCHELL, Price '75				
			Male singer.				
1/18/75	65	10	1 I Can't Help Myself (Sugar Pie, Honey Bunch) ...... *Got You On My Mind*		$7		GRT 016
			PRICE MITCHELL & JERRI KELLY				
			#1 Pop hit for the Four Tops in 1965				
4/19/75	29	11	2 Personality .... *Daddy's Going Bye-Bye*		$6		GRT 020
			#2 Pop hit for Lloyd Price in 1959				
2/7/76	83	5	3 Seems Like I Can't Live With You, But I Can't Live Without You .... *(I Wanna Be) The Man Who Takes You Home*		$6		GRT 037
5/29/76	75	5	4 Tra-La-La-La Suzy .... *Sweet Molly Brown*		$6		GRT 050
9/4/76	75	4	5 You're The Reason I'm Living .... *Take Me Back*		$6		GRT 067
			#3 Pop hit for Bobby Darin in 1963				
1/5/80	45	9	6 Mr. & Mrs. Untrue .... *Savin' It All For You*		$5		Sunbird 101
			PRICE MITCHELL/RENE SLOANE				
			MITCHELL, Priscilla '65				
			Born on 9/18/41 in Marietta, Georgia. Formerly married to **Jerry Reed**.				
			ROY DRUSKY & PRISCILLA MITCHELL:				
5/29/65	❶²	23	1 Yes, Mr. Peters *More Than We Deserve*		$8		Mercury 72416
12/4/65	45	2	2 Slippin' Around .... *Trouble On Our Line*		$8		Mercury 72497
3/25/67	61	5	3 I'll Never Tell On You .... *Bed Of Roses*		$8		Mercury 72650
			PRISCILLA MITCHELL:				
6/17/67	53	4	4 He's Not For Real .... *Take Me Home To Your Mama*		$8		Mercury 72681
2/3/68	73	3	5 Your Old Handy Man .... *Who's Cheating Who*		$8		Mercury 72757
			written by **Dolly Parton**				
			MITCHUM, Robert '67				
			Born on 8/6/17 in Bridgeport, Connecticut. Died of cancer on 7/1/97 (age 79). Starred in several movies.				
5/13/67	9	17	1 Little Old Wine Drinker Me *Walker's Woods*	96	$8		Monument 1006
10/21/67	55	7	2 You Deserve Each Other .... *That Man Right There*		$8		Monument 1025
			MIZE, Billy '76				
			Born on 4/29/29 in Kansas City, Kansas; raised in California. Singer/songwriter/steel guitarist.				
			1)It Hurts To Know The Feeling's Gone 2)Make It Rain 3)While I'm Thinkin' About It				
10/15/66	57	5	1 You Can't Stop Me .... *The Bigger The Fool (The Harder The Fall)*		$10		Columbia 43770
			BILLY MIZE with The Jordanaires				
9/28/68	58	7	2 Walking Through The Memories Of My Mind .... *Wind (I'll Catch Up To You)*		$10		Columbia 44621
4/26/69	40	9	3 Make It Rain .... *You Done Me Wrong*		$8		Imperial 66365
9/13/69	43	9	4 While I'm Thinkin' About It .... *The Absence Of You*		$8		Imperial 66403
6/20/70	71	2	5 If This Was The Last Song .... *I Learned To Walk*		$8		Imperial 66447
11/14/70	49	7	6 Beer Drinking, Honky Tonkin' Blues .... *Someday When It Gets To Be Tomorrow*		$6		United Artists 50717
9/2/72	66	5	7 Take It Easy .... *Susan's Floor*		$6		United Artists 50945
			#12 Pop hit for the **Eagles** in 1972				
7/28/73	99	2	8 California Is Just Mississippi .... *Just The Other Side Of Nowhere*		$6		United Artists 265
2/16/74	79	5	9 Thank You For The Feeling .... *Detroit City*		$6		United Artists 372
9/25/76	31	13	10 It Hurts To Know The Feeling's Gone *Living Her Life In A Song*		$5		Zodiac 1011
2/12/77	68	5	11 Livin' Her Life In A Song .... *Linda's Love Stop*		$5		Zodiac 1014
			MOEBAKKEN, Dick '78				
9/30/78	98	3	Heaven Is Being Good To Me .... *The Lord's Prayer*		$6		ASI 1016
			an impression of **Walter Brennan** to the tune of "Old Rivers"				
			MOFFATT, Hugh '78				
			Born on 11/10/48 in Fort Worth, Texas. Singer/songwriter/guitarist. Brother of **Katy Moffatt**.				
5/6/78	95	2	The Gambler .... *That Light In Your Eyes*		$4		Mercury 55024
			MOFFATT, Katy '84				
			Born in 1950 in Fort Worth, Texas. Singer/guitarist. Sister of **Hugh Moffatt**.				
1/17/76	83	5	1 I Can Almost See Houston From Here .... *Take Me Back To Texas*		$5		Columbia 10271
7/4/81	83	3	2 Take It As It Comes .... *Hard Country*		$4		Epic 02075
			MICHAEL MURPHEY with KATY MOFFATT				
11/5/83	66	6	3 Under Loved And Over Lonely .... *Let's Make Something Of It*		$5		Permian 82002
2/11/84	82	4	4 Reynosa .... *Lonely But Only For You*		$5		Permian 82004
5/5/84	66	6	5 This Ain't Tennessee And He Ain't You *Midnight Harbour*		$5		Permian 82005
			MOLLY & THE HEYMAKERS '91				
			Group from Hayward, Wisconsin: Martha "Molly" Scheer (vocals, fiddle, rhythm guitar), Andy Dee (lead guitar), Jeff Nelson (bass) and Joe Lindzius (drums).				
12/22/90+	50	15	1 Chasin' Something Called Love .... *Gulf Of Mexico*		$3	▌	Reprise 19517
5/18/91	59	6	2 He Comes Around .... *This Time*		$3		Reprise 19332
5/16/92	69	5	3 Jimmy McCarthy's Truck .... *Milkhouse*		$3		Reprise 18944
			MONDAY, Carla '87				
10/24/87	79	3	No One Can Touch Me		$6	☐	MCM 001

★393★

MONROE, Bill, and His Blue Grass Boys '46
Born on 9/13/11 in Rosine, Kentucky. Died of a stroke on 9/9/96 (age 84). Singer/songwriter/mandolin player. Known as "The Father Of Bluegrass." Formed the Blue Grass Boys which included **Flatt & Scruggs**. Joined the *Grand Ole Opry* in 1939. Elected to the Country Music Hall of Fame in 1970. Won Grammy's Lifetime Achievement Award in 1993. Inducted into the Rock and Roll Hall of Fame in 1997 as an early influence of rock and roll.

DEBUT	PEAK	WKS		A-side	B-side	Pop	$		Label & Number
3/23/46	3	6		1 Kentucky Waltz	*Rocky Road Blues*		$20		Columbia 36907
12/7/46	5	4		2 Footprints In The Snow	*True Life Blues*		$20		Columbia 37151
6/19/48	11	1		3 Sweetheart, You Done Me Wrong	J:11 *My Rose Of Old Kentucky*		$20		Columbia 38172
11/6/48	13	1		4 Wicked Path Of Sin	S:13 *Summertime Is Past And Gone*		$20		Columbia 20503
11/27/48	11	5		5 Little Community Church	S:11 / J:12 *That Home Above*		$20		Columbia 20488

BILL MONROE and his BLUE GRASS QUARTET

DEBUT	PEAK	WKS		A-side	B-side	Pop	$		Label & Number
4/16/49	12	2		6 Toy Heart	S:12 *Blue Grass Breakdown*		$20		Columbia 20552
8/6/49	12	1		7 When You Are Lonely	J:12 *It's Mighty Dark To Travel*		$20		Columbia 20526

BILL MONROE

DEBUT	PEAK	WKS		A-side	B-side	Pop	$		Label & Number
11/3/58	27	1		8 Scotland	*Panhandle Country* [I]		$15		Decca 30739
3/2/59	15	6		9 Gotta Travel On	*No One But My Darlin'*		$15		Decca 30809

MONROE, Vaughn '49
Born on 10/7/11 in Akron, Ohio. Died on 5/21/73 (age 61). Singer/bandleader/trumpeter.

DEBUT	PEAK	WKS		A-side	B-side	Pop	$		Label & Number
5/14/49	2¹	5	●	Riders In The Sky (A Cowboy Legend) S:2 / J:10 *Single Saddle*		❶¹²	$15		RCA Victor 20-3411

45 rpm: 47-2902; #30 Pop hit for The Ramrods in 1961

MONTANA '81
Group from Reno, Nevada. Entire group killed in a plane crash on 7/4/87 near Flathead Lake, Montana.

DEBUT	PEAK	WKS		A-side	B-side	Pop	$		Label & Number
11/14/81	83	3		The Shoe's On The Other Foot Tonight			$7		Waterhouse 15005

MONTANA, Billy '87
Singer/bassist Billy Montana was born William Schlappi in Voorheesville, New York. The Long Shots: Bobby Kendall and Kyle Montana (guitars), Dave Flint (fiddle) and Doug Bernhard (drums). Billy Montana later recorded solo.

BILLY MONTANA & THE LONG SHOTS:

DEBUT	PEAK	WKS		A-side	B-side	Pop	$		Label & Number
3/21/87	46	9		1 Crazy Blue	*That's The Bottom Line*		$3		Warner 28426
8/22/87	40	11		2 Baby I Was Leaving Anyhow	*And So It Goes (With Everything But Love)*		$3		Warner 28256
8/20/88	48	9		3 Oh Jenny	*All I Need*		$3		Warner 27809

BILLY MONTANA:

DEBUT	PEAK	WKS		A-side	B-side	Pop	$		Label & Number
4/8/95	55	11		4 Didn't Have You					album cut
8/19/95	58	7		5 Rain Through The Roof					album cut
11/11/95	70	1		6 No Yesterday					album cut

above 3 from the album *No Yesterday* on Magnatone 101

MONTANA SKYLINE '82
Group from Missoula, Montana.

DEBUT	PEAK	WKS		A-side	B-side	Pop	$		Label & Number
12/26/81+	87	4		Full Moon - Empty Pockets	*The Circle Of Love*		$7		Snow 2022

MONTGOMERY, John Michael ★146★ '94
Born on 1/20/65 in Danville, Kentucky. Singer/songwriter/guitarist. CMA Award: 1994 Horizon Award.

1) I Swear 2) Sold 3) I Can Love You Like That

DEBUT	PEAK	WKS		A-side	B-side	Pop	$		Label & Number
10/3/92+	4	20		1 Life's A Dance					album cut
				from the album *Life's A Dance* on Atlantic 82420					
3/13/93	❶³	20		2 I Love The Way You Love Me	*(album snippets)*	60	$3	▌	Atlantic 87371
7/10/93	21	20		3 Beer And Bones	*(album snippets)*	123	$3	▌	Atlantic 87326
12/18/93+	❶⁴	20	●	4 I Swear	*(album snippets)*	42	$3	▌	Atlantic 87288
				CMA Award: Single of the Year; #1 Pop hit for All-4-One in 1994					
3/19/94	4	20		5 Rope The Moon	*(album snippets)*	115	$3	▌	Atlantic 87248
4/9/94	72	2		6 Kick It Up					album cut
				from the album *Kickin' It Up* on Atlantic 82559					
5/7/94	❶²	20		7 Be My Baby Tonight	*(album snippets)*	73	$3	▌	Atlantic 87236
9/24/94	❶¹	20		8 If You've Got Love	*Kick It Up*		$3	▌	Atlantic 87198
3/4/95	❶³	20		9 I Can Love You Like That					album cut
				#5 Pop hit for All-4-One in 1995					
5/6/95	❶³	20		10 Sold (The Grundy County Auction Incident)					album cut
				above 2 from the album *John Michael Montgomery* on Atlantic 82728					
8/26/95	3	20		11 No Man's Land	S:5 *(album snippets)*	112	$3	▌	Atlantic 87105
11/18/95+	4	20		12 Cowboy Love					album cut
3/2/96	4	20		13 Long As I Live					album cut
				above 2 from the album *John Michael Montgomery* on Atlantic 82728					
9/14/96	15	19		14 Ain't Got Nothin' On Us	S:9 *(album snippets)*	115	$3	▌	Atlantic 87044
10/19/96+	2³	20		15 Friends	S:❶³ *(album snippets)*	69	$3	▌	Atlantic 87019
3/1/97	6	20		16 I Miss You A Little	S:4 *(album snippets)*	109	$3	▌	Atlantic 84865
6/14/97	2¹	20		17 How Was I To Know					album cut
				from the album *What I Do Best* on Atlantic 82947					
8/16/97	56	5		18 Warning Signs	S:21 *Baby Barf And The Turkey Hunt* (Engvall) [C]		$3	▌	Warner 43934

BILL ENGVALL with John Michael Montgomery

MONTGOMERY, John Michael — Cont'd

DEBUT	PEAK	WKS		A-side / B-side	Pop	$	Pic	Label & Number
10/4/97+	4	21		19 Angel In My Eyes from the album *Greatest Hits* on Atlantic 83060			album cut	

MONTGOMERY, Melba ★184★   '74
Born on 10/14/38 in Iron City, Tennessee; raised in Florence, Alabama. Singer/guitarist/fiddle player.

1)No Charge 2)We Must Have Been Out Of Our Minds 3)Baby, Ain't That Fine
4)Don't Let The Good Times Fool You 5)Let's Invite Them Over

DEBUT	PEAK	WKS		A-side / B-side	Pop	$	Label & Number
5/4/63	3	28		1 We Must Have Been Out Of Our Minds *Until Then* GEORGE JONES & MELBA MONTGOMERY		$15	United Artists 575
8/24/63	26	6		2 Hall Of Shame .... *What's Bad For You Is Good For Me*		$12	United Artists 576
12/7/63	17	7		3 Let's Invite Them Over/		$12	United Artists 635
11/30/63	20	5		4 What's In Our Heart.............................. GEORGE JONES AND MELBA MONTGOMERY (above 2)		$12	United Artists 635
12/7/63+	22	9		5 The Greatest One Of All .... *Lies Can't Hide What's On My Mind*		$12	United Artists 652
9/5/64	31	5		6 Please Be My Love.............. *Will There Ever Be Another* GEORGE JONES AND MELBA MONTGOMERY		$12	United Artists 732
12/12/64+	25	15		7 Multiply The Heartaches............... *Once More* GEORGE JONES AND MELBA MONTGOMERY		$12	United Artists 784
1/15/66	15	12		8 Baby Ain't That Fine ...... *Everybody Knows But You And Me* GENE PITNEY and MELBA MONTGOMERY		$12	Musicor 1135
11/19/66	70	3		9 Close Together (As You And Me) .... *Long As We're Dreaming* GEORGE JONES & MELBA MONTGOMERY		$12	Musicor 1204
7/8/67	61	3		10 What Can I Tell The Folks Back Home .... *The Right Time To Lose My Mind*		$12	Musicor 1241
9/9/67	24	10		11 Party Pickin' .... *Simply Divine* GEORGE JONES & MELBA MONTGOMERY		$12	Musicor 1238
10/24/70	18	14		12 Something To Brag About .... *Let's Help Each Other To Forget* CHARLIE LOUVIN & MELBA MONTGOMERY		$8	Capitol 2915
2/13/71	26	12		13 Did You Ever.................. *Don't Believe Me* CHARLIE LOUVIN & MELBA MONTGOMERY		$8	Capitol 3029
6/12/71	30	10		14 Baby, You've Got What It Takes .... *If We Don't Make It* #5 Pop hit for Dinah Washington & Brook Benton in 1960		$8	Capitol 3111
6/19/71	61	4		15 He's My Man .... *We Don't Live Here Anymore*		$8	Capitol 3091
11/27/71	60	5		16 I'm Gonna Leave You .... *When I Stop Dreaming* CHARLIE LOUVIN & MELBA MONTGOMERY		$8	Capitol 3208
8/19/72	66	4		17 Baby, What's Wrong With Us .... *Unmatched Wedding Bands* CHARLIE LOUVIN & MELBA MONTGOMERY		$8	Capitol 3388
1/20/73	59	6		18 A Man Likes Things Like That .... *That Don't Mean I Don't Love You* CHARLIE LOUVIN & MELBA MONTGOMERY		$8	Capitol 3508
10/6/73	38	11		19 Wrap Your Love Around Me .... *Let Me Show You How I Can*		$6	Elektra 45866
1/12/74	58	9		20 He'll Come Home .... *Country Written Up And Down Her Face*		$6	Elektra 45875
3/16/74	❶[1]	16		21 No Charge *I Love Him Because He's That Way*	39	$6	Elektra 45883
7/20/74	67	8		22 Your Pretty Roses Came Too Late .... *My Feel Good Sure Feels Fine*		$6	Elektra 45894
10/19/74	59	10		23 If You Want The Rainbow.............. *Love, I Need You*		$6	Elektra 45211
2/1/75	15	12		24 Don't Let The Good Times Fool You.............. *It Sure Gets Lonely*		$6	Elektra 45229
5/24/75	45	9		25 Searchin' (For Someone Like You) .... *Hiding In The Darkness Of My Mind*		$5	Elektra 45247
1/10/76	67	7		26 Love Was The Wind .... *I Never Dreamed That Love Could Be This Good*		$5	Elektra 45296
7/16/77	83	4		27 Never Ending Love Affair .... *You*		$5	United Artists 1008
12/10/77+	22	14		28 Angel Of The Morning .... *The Pinkerton's Flowers* #7 Pop hit for Merrilee Rush in 1968		$5	United Artists 1115
10/25/80	92	2		29 The Star.................. *Carolina In My Mind*		$6	Kari 111
8/30/86	79	4		30 Straight Talkin		$6	Compass 45-7

MONTGOMERY, Nancy   '81

DEBUT	PEAK	WKS		A-side / B-side		$	Label & Number
7/4/81	85	2		All I Have To Do Is Dream		$4	Ovation 1172

MOODY, Clyde   '50
Born on 9/19/14 in Cherokee, North Carolina; raised in Marion, North Carolina. Died on 4/7/89 (age 74). Singer/songwriter/guitarist. Known as "The Hillbilly Waltz King."

DEBUT	PEAK	WKS		A-side / B-side		$	Label & Number
8/14/48	8	1		1 Red Roses Tied In Blue/ *S:8*			King 706
6/19/48	15	1		2 Carolina Waltz.............. *S:15*		$20	King 706
3/11/50	8	2		3 I Love You Because *A:8 Afraid*		$20	King 837

MOORE, Beth   '71
Born on 11/27/44 in Michigan.

DEBUT	PEAK	WKS		A-side / B-side		$	Label & Number
1/23/71	61	8		Put Your Hand In The Hand .... *I'm Losin' My Man* #2 Pop hit for Ocean in 1971		$6	Capitol 3013

MOORE, Jim   '88

DEBUT	PEAK	WKS		A-side / B-side		$	Label & Number
9/3/88	88	2		Ain't She Shinin' Tonight .... JIM MOORE & SIDEWINDER		$6	Willow Wind 0511

MOORE, Lattie   '61
Born on 10/17/24 in Scotsville, Kentucky. Male rockabilly singer/songwriter/guitarist.

DEBUT	PEAK	WKS		A-side / B-side		$	Label & Number
1/30/61	25	3		Drunk Again.............. *Driving Nails*		$25	King 5413

DEBUT	PEAK	WKS	Gold	A-side (Chart Hit)..B-side	Pop	$	Pic	Label & Number

MORGAN, Al '49
Pianist from Chicago. Own TV series from 1949-51. Known as "Mr. Flying Fingers."

| 9/17/49 | 8 | 1 | | Jealous Heart   S:8 *Turnabout* | 4 | $12 | | London 500 |

first released on Universal 148 in 1949 ($15); 45 rpm: 3001; #47 Pop hit for **Connie Francis** in 1965

MORGAN, Billie '59
Born on 12/13/22 in Nashville. Female singer.

| 3/23/59 | 22 | 3 | | Life To Live...*Thinking All Night* | | $12 | | Starday 420 |

MORGAN, David '97

| 11/1/97 | 72 | 1 | | Those Who Couldn't Wait... | | | | album cut |

from the album *The Well* on Stage Coach 0326

MORGAN, George ★125★ '49
Born on 6/28/24 in Waverly, Tennessee. Died of a heart attack on 7/7/75 (age 51). Singer/songwriter/guitarist. Joined the *Grand Ole Opry* in 1948. Father of **Lorrie Morgan**. Elected to the Country Music Hall of Fame in 1998.

1)Candy Kisses 2)Almost 3)I'm In Love Again 4)You're The Only Good Thing
5)Please Don't Let Me Love You

2/26/49	❶³	23		1 Candy Kisses/ S:❶³ / J:2				
3/19/49	4	14		2 Please Don't Let Me Love You S:4 / J:4		$20		Columbia 20547
4/30/49	8	6		3 Rainbow In My Heart/ S:8 / J:10				
5/7/49	11	1		4 All I Need Is Some More Lovin'..S:11		$20		Columbia 20563
7/23/49	4	12		5 Room Full Of Roses S:4 / J:10 *Put All Your Love In A Cookie Jar*	25	$20		Columbia 20594
12/10/49	4	4		6 I Love Everything About You/ A:4 / S:14				
10/29/49	5	9		7 Cry-Baby Heart S:5 / J:6 / A:7		$20		Columbia 20627
4/19/52	2⁶	23		8 Almost S:2 / A:2 / J:2 *You're A Little Doll*		$25		Columbia 4-20906
3/7/53	10	1		9 (I Just Had A Date) A Lover's Quarrel J:10 *Most Of All*		$25		Columbia 21070
1/26/57	15	1		10 There Goes My Love ....A:15 *Can I Be Dreaming*		$20		Columbia 40792
2/16/59	3	23		11 I'm In Love Again *It Was All In Your Mind*		$15		Columbia 41318
8/17/59	20	9		12 Little Dutch Girl/		$15		
8/24/59	26	1		13 The Last Thing I Want To Know		$15		Columbia 41420
1/11/60	4	20		14 You're The Only Good Thing (That's Happened To Me) *Come Away From His Arms*		$15		Columbia 41523
1/18/64	23	7		15 One Dozen Roses (And Our Love)/				
3/7/64	45	2		16 All Right (I'll Sign The Papers)...		$15		Columbia 42882
5/9/64	23	17		17 Slipping Around ....*I Love You So Much It Hurts*		$15		Columbia 43020

MARION WORTH AND GEORGE MORGAN

9/26/64	37	9		18 Tears And Roses ....*You're Not Home Yet*		$15		Columbia 43098
12/11/65+	27	10		19 A Picture That's New...*Roses*		$15		Columbia 43393
4/15/67	40	12		20 I Couldn't See.....................................*Look At The Lonely*		$10		Starday 804
8/19/67	58	5		21 Shiny Red Automobile ....*Have Some Of Mine*		$10		Starday 814
1/13/68	55	6		22 Barbara ....*Sad Bird*		$10		Starday 825
4/27/68	56	7		23 Living ....*Rosebuds And You*		$10		Starday 834
8/31/68	31	10		24 Sounds Of Goodbye ....*The Ballad Of The Grand Ole Opry*		$10		Starday 850
4/19/69	30	9		25 Like A Bird ....*Left Over Feelings*		$8		Stop 252
4/18/70	17	13		26 Lilacs And Fire...................................*Hardest Easy Thing*		$8		Stop 365
12/11/71	68	3		27 Gentle Rains Of Home ....*Walking Shadow, Talking Mem'ry*		$6		Decca 32886

GEORGE MORGAN Featuring "Little" Roy Wiggins:

1/20/73	62	7		28 Makin' Heartaches ....*Sing My Blues A Birthday Song*		$6		Decca 33037
6/30/73	56	9		29 Mr. Ting-A-Ling (Steel Guitar Man) ....*Our Wedding Song*		$5		MCA 40069
12/15/73+	21	14		30 Red Rose From The Blue Side Of Town ....*You Turn Me On*		$5		MCA 40159

GEORGE MORGAN

6/1/74	66	6		31 Somewhere Around Midnight ....*I Never Knew Love (Until I Met You)*		$5		MCA 40227
11/2/74	82	6		32 A Candy Mountain Melody ....*You're That Much Woman To Me*		$5		MCA 40298
2/22/75	65	9		33 In The Misty Moonlight ....*Welcome Back To My World*		$5		4 Star 1001

#19 Pop hit for **Jerry Wallace** in 1964

| 7/5/75 | 62 | 11 | | 34 From This Moment On ....*One Wife Five Kids Later* | | $5 | | 4 Star 1009 |
| 11/24/79 | 93 | 3 | | 35 I'm Completely Satisfied With You ....*From This Moment On* | | $5 | | 4 Star 1040 |

LORRIE & GEORGE MORGAN

MORGAN, Jane '70
Born Jane Currier in Boston in 1920; raised in Florida. Died in 1974 (age 54). Best known for her 1957 pop hit "Fascination."

| 5/30/70 | 61 | 5 | | 1 A Girl Named Johnny Cash ....*Charley* [N] | | $8 | | RCA Victor 9839 |

answer to "A Boy Named Sue" by **Johnny Cash**

| 11/7/70 | 70 | 2 | | 2 The First Day..*I'm Only A Woman* | | $6 | | RCA Victor 9901 |

MORGAN, Lorrie ★108★ '93

Born Loretta Lynn Morgan on 6/27/59 in Nashville. Singer/songwriter/guitarist. Daughter of **George Morgan**. Joined the *Grand Ole Opry* in 1984. Married to **Keith Whitley** from 1986-89. Married **Jon Randall** on 11/16/96.

1)*What Part Of No* 2)*Five Minutes* 3)*I Didn't Know My Own Strength* 4)*Out Of Your Shoes* 5)*Watch Me*

DEBUT	PEAK	WKS		A-side	B-side	Pop	$	Pic	Label & Number
3/10/79	75	5		1 Two People In Love .... *I Don't Care*			$5		ABC/Hickory 54041
7/28/79	88	3		2 Tell Me I'm Only Dreaming .... *In For Rain*			$5		MCA 41052
11/24/79	93	3		3 I'm Completely Satisfied With You .... *From This Moment On*			$5		4 Star 1040
				LORRIE & GEORGE MORGAN					
3/17/84	69	5		4 Don't Go Changing .... *Everything You Say*			$4		MCA 52331
12/10/88+	20	19		5 Trainwreck Of Emotion .... *One More Last Time*			$3		RCA 8638
4/15/89	9	22		6 Dear Me	*Eight Days A Week*		$3		RCA 8866
9/9/89	2³	26		7 Out Of Your Shoes	*One More Last Time*		$3		RCA 9016
2/3/90	❶¹	26		8 Five Minutes	*I'll Take This Memories*		$3		RCA 9118
5/26/90	4	21		9 He Talks To Me	*If I Didn't Love You*		$3		RCA 2508
7/28/90	13	20		10 'Til A Tear Becomes A Rose .... *Lady's Choice*			$3		RCA 2619
				KEITH WHITLEY AND LORRIE MORGAN					
3/30/91	3	20		11 We Both Walk	*Faithfully*		$3	▪	RCA 2748
8/3/91	9	20		12 A Picture Of Me (Without You)	*Tears On My Pillow*		$3		RCA 62014
12/14/91+	4	20		13 Except For Monday	*Hand Over Your Heart*		$3		RCA 62105
5/9/92	14	20		14 Something In Red .... *It's Too Late (To Love Me Now)*			$3		RCA 62219
9/5/92	2²	20		15 Watch Me	*She's Takin' Him Back Again*		$3		BNA 62333
12/19/92+	❶³	20		16 What Part Of No	*You Leave Me Like This*		$3		BNA 62414
4/3/93	14	20		17 I Guess You Had To Be There .... *Someone To Call Me Darling*			$3		BNA 62415
7/31/93	8	20		18 Half Enough	*It's A Heartache*		$3		BNA 62576
11/27/93	59	6		19 Crying Time .... *I'm So Lonesome I Could Cry*			$3		BNA 62707
				from the movie *The Beverly Hillbillies* starring Jim Varney					
12/25/93	64	1		20 My Favorite Things .... [X]					album cut
				from the musical *The Sound of Music*; #45 Pop hit for Herb Alpert in 1969; from the album *Merry Christmas From London* on BNA 66282					
3/19/94	31	12		21 My Night To Howl .... *Evening Up The Odds*			$3		BNA 62767
5/21/94	51	11		22 If You Came Back From Heaven .... *Exit 99*			$3		BNA 62864
8/13/94	39	13		23 Heart Over Mind .... *The Hard Part Was Easy*			$3		BNA 62946
5/6/95	❶¹	20		24 I Didn't Know My Own Strength	*S:12 War Paint*		$3	▪	BNA 64287
9/2/95	4	20		25 Back In Your Arms Again	*S:15 My Favorite Things*		$3	▪	BNA 64353
12/23/95+	32	17		26 Standing Tall					album cut
				from the album *Greatest Hits* on BNA 66508					
12/30/95	67	1		27 Sleigh Ride .... [X]					album cut
				#24 Pop hit for the Boston Pops Orchestra in 1949; from the album *Merry Christmas From London* on BNA 66282					
4/6/96	18	20		28 By My Side .... *S:4 Candy Kisses*	110	$3	▪	BNA 64512
				LORRIE MORGAN & JON RANDALL					
8/10/96	45	12		29 I Just Might Be .... *Steppin' Stones*			$3	▪	BNA 64608
9/7/96	73	1		30 Don't Worry Baby..					album cut
				THE BEACH BOYS Featuring Lorrie Morgan					
				#24 Pop hit for The Beach Boys in 1964; from the album *Stars And Stripes Vol. 1* on River North 1205					
12/28/96	64	3		31 Sleigh Ride .... [X-R]					album cut
				from the album *Merry Christmas From London* on BNA 66282					
1/25/97	4	20		32 Good As I Was To You	*She Walked Beside The Wagon*		$3		BNA 64681
7/5/97	3	20		33 Go Away	*S:6 I've Enjoyed As Much Of This As I Can Stand*	85	$3	▪	BNA 64914
11/8/97+	14	20		34 One Of Those Nights Tonight .... *By My Side*			$3		BNA 65333

MORGAN, Misty — see BLANCHARD, Jack

MORI, Miki '80

Female singer from Nephi, Utah.

6/30/79	91	1		1 Tell All Your Troubles To Me .... *Driftin' Away*			$8		Red Feather 2280
				MICKIE MORI					
10/20/79	79	4		2 The Part Of Me That Needs You Most .... *Baby You Are The Answer*			$6		Oak 1002
2/2/80	48	7		3 Driftin Away	*Tell All Your Trouble*		$6		Oak 1010
7/19/80	51	8		4 The Last Farewell .... *You Are The Answer*			$5		NSD 49
1/10/81	59	6		5 Rainin' In My Eyes .... *Reunion*			$5		Starcom 1001

MORRIS, Bob '67

Born on 2/3/30 in Hasty, Arkansas. Died of cancer on 12/3/81 (age 51).

2/25/67	62	5		Fishin' On The Mississippi.. *A Little Bit Of You*			$10		Tower 307

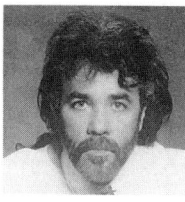

MORRIS, Gary ★120★   '85

Born on 12/7/48 in Fort Worth, Texas. Singer/songwriter/guitarist/actor. Acted in Broadway's *Les Miserables* and *La Boheme*. Portrayed "Wayne Masterson" on TV's *The Colbys*.

1)I'll Never Stop Loving You   2)Leave Me Lonely   3)Makin' Up For Lost Time   4)100% Chance Of Rain
5)Baby Bye Bye

DEBUT	PEAK	WKS		A-side / B-side		$	Plc	Label & Number
10/18/80	40	13	1	Sweet Red Wine...May I Borrow Some Sugar From You		$4		Warner 49564
3/7/81	40	10	2	Fire In Your Eyes ....Heartaches By The Number		$4		Warner 49668
10/17/81	8	17	3	Headed For A Heartache	I'm So Tired Of Losing	$3		Warner 49829
2/27/82	12	17	4	Don't Look Back	She Gave Me Till Friday	$3		Warner 50017
7/10/82	15	15	5	Dreams Die Hard	Eyes Of The World	$3		Warner 29967
11/27/82+	9	19	6	Velvet Chains	When I Close My Eyes	$3		Warner 29853
4/16/83	5	20	7	The Love She Found In Me	That's The Way It Is	$3		Warner 29683
8/6/83	4	25	8	The Wind Beneath My Wings	The Way I Love You Tonight	$3		Warner 29532
				#1 Pop hit for Bette Midler in 1989				
11/26/83+	4	19	9	Why Lady Why	The Way I Love You Tonight	$3		Warner 29450
12/17/83+	9	23	10	You're Welcome To Tonight	Your Kisses Lied	$4		Permian 82003
				LYNN ANDERSON & GARY MORRIS				
4/7/84	7	18	11	Between Two Fires	All She Said Was No	$3		Warner 29321
7/28/84	7	19	12	Second Hand Heart	A:19 / S:21 Whoever's Watchin'	$3		Warner 29230
11/24/84+	❶¹	20	13	Baby Bye Bye	S:❶¹ / A:❶¹ West Texas Highway And Me	$3		Warner 29131
5/4/85	9	20	14	Lasso The Moon	A:8 / S:9 When I Close My Eyes	$3		Warner 29028
				from the movie *Rustler's Rhapsody* starring Tom Berenger				
8/24/85	❶¹	23	15	I'll Never Stop Loving You	A:❶¹ / S:2 Heaven's Hell Without You	$3		Warner 28947
11/23/85+	❶¹	19	16	Makin' Up For Lost Time (The Dallas Lovers' Song)	A:❶¹ A Few Good Men	$3	■	Warner 28856
				CRYSTAL GAYLE AND GARY MORRIS				
				from the TV series *Dallas* starring Larry Hagman				
1/11/86	❶¹	20	17	100% Chance Of Rain	S:❶¹ / A:2 Back In Her Arms Again	$3		Warner 28823
5/17/86	28	12	18	Anything Goes	A:27 / S:32 Draggin' The Lake For The Moon	$3		Warner 28713
7/12/86	27	13	19	Honeycomb	S:21 / A:28 Whoever's Watchin'	$3		Warner 28654
11/1/86+	❶¹	21	20	Leave Me Lonely	A:❶¹ / S:4 Eleventh Hour	$3		Warner 28542
2/28/87	9	20	21	Plain Brown Wrapper	A:9 / S:24 Moonshine	$3		Warner 28468
4/25/87	4	18	22	Another World	A:5 Makin' Up For Lost Time	$3		Warner 28373
				CRYSTAL GAYLE & GARY MORRIS				
				theme from the TV serial				
10/10/87	64	5	23	Finishing Touches.....................................Mama You Can't Give Me No Whippin'		$3		Warner 28218
2/13/88	26	15	24	All Of This & More ....Makin' Up For Lost Time		$3		Warner 28106
				CRYSTAL GAYLE/GARY MORRIS				
5/27/89	48	12	25	Never Had A Love Song...Bread And Water		$3		Universal 66011
10/21/89	60	5	26	The Jaws Of Modern Romance ....Stand My Ground		$3		Universal 66026
2/9/91	47	19	27	Miles Across The Bedroom				album cut
				from the album *These Days* on Capitol 94103				

MORRIS, Lamar   '71

Born in Andalusia, Alabama. Member of **The Bama Band**.

DEBUT	PEAK	WKS		A-side / B-side		$		Label & Number
11/12/66	69	2	1	Send Me A Box Of Kleenex ....Both Of You		$7		MGM 13586
1/13/68	46	10	2	The Great Pretender.......................................The World's Perfect Couple		$7		MGM 13866
				#1 Pop hit for The Platters in 1956				
6/13/70	74	3	3	She Came To Me	Only With Teardrops	$6		MGM 14114
1/2/71	59	6	4	You're The Reason I'm Living ....Things		$6		MGM 14187
				#3 Pop hit for Bobby Darin in 1963				
4/17/71	27	12	5	If You Love Me (Really Love Me)	Pour The Wine	$6		MGM 14236
				#4 Pop hit for Kay Starr in 1954				
11/27/71	74	3	6	Near You	She Came To Me	$6		MGM 14289
				#1 Pop hit for Francis Craig in 1947				
2/17/73	71	3	7	You Call Everybody Darling ....I Need You		$6		MGM 14448
				#1 Pop hit for Al Trace in 1948				

MORRISON, Kathy — see WILBOURN, Bill

MORTON, Ann J.   '79

Born Anna Jane White on 4/4/43 in Muldrow, Oklahoma. Sister of **Jim Mundy** and **Bill White**.
1)My Empty Arms   2)I'm Not In The Mood   3)You Don't Have To Be A Baby To Cry

DEBUT	PEAK	WKS		A-side / B-side		$		Label & Number
11/6/76	82	7	1	Poor Wilted Rose ....Molly Jones (Is A Happy Hooker)		$5		Prairie Dust 7606
3/26/77	63	10	2	You Don't Have To Be A Baby To Cry ....Good Looking Cowboy		$5		Prairie Dust 7613
				#3 Pop hit for The Caravelles in 1963				
7/16/77	86	4	3	Don't Want To Take A Chance (On Loving You) ....Tainted Rose		$5		Prairie Dust 7617
10/1/77	72	6	4	Blueberry Hill ....Onions And Love Affairs		$5		Prairie Dust 7619
				#2 Pop hit for Fats Domino in 1957				
2/18/78	83	3	5	Black And Blue Heart ....Me And My Horse Named Daddy		$5		Prairie Dust 7621
9/30/78	83	4	6	Share Your Love Tonight...Willie I Will		$5		Prairie Dust 7627
1/27/79	59	6	7	I'm Not In The Mood (For Love)...Willie I Will		$5		Prairie Dust 7629
6/16/79	86	3	8	Don't Stay On Your Side Of The Bed Tonight .... It's Written All Over Your Face		$5		Prairie Dust 7631
8/18/79	42	10	9	My Empty Arms	Don't Stay On Your Side Of The Bed Tonight	$5		Prairie Dust 7632

MORTON, Ann J. — Cont'd

1/26/80	63	5		10 (We Used To Kiss Each Other On The Lips But It's) **All Over Now/**				
		5		11 **I Like Being Lonely**...		$5		Prairie Dust 7633
2/14/81	89	3		12 **You've Got The Devil In Your Eyes** ....*No Strings Attached*		$5		Prairie Dust 8004

★282★ **MOSBY, Johnny and Jonie** '69
Husband-and-wife team of Johnny (b: 4/26/33 in Fort Smith, Arkansas) and Jonie (b: Janice Irene Shields on 8/10/40 in Van Nuys, California) Mosby. Married from 1958-73.
1)Just Hold My Hand 2)Trouble In My Arms 3)Don't Call Me From A Honky Tonk

5/18/63	13	9		1 **Don't Call Me From A Honky Tonk** ....*The Wrong Side Of Town*		$10		Columbia 42668
10/12/63+	12	16		2 **Trouble In My Arms/**		$10		Columbia 42841
11/2/63	27	1		3 **Who's Been Cheatin' Who**				
4/18/64	16	13		4 **Keep Those Cards And Letters Coming In** ....*Take Me Home*		$8		Columbia 43005
10/10/64	21	11		5 **How The Other Half Lives** ....*Stolen Paradise*		$8		Columbia 43100
10/7/67	36	12		6 **Make A Left And Then A Right** ....*Take Back The World*		$7		Capitol 5980
2/17/68	53	6		7 **Mr. & Mrs. John Smith** ....*Hello There Stranger*		$7		Capitol 2087
6/22/68	58	5		8 **Our Golden Wedding Day** ....*Two Dollar Honeymoon Room*		$7		Capitol 2179
2/15/69	12	15		9 **Just Hold My Hand**	*Walkin' Papers*	$6		Capitol 2384
6/21/69	38	12		10 **Hold Me, Thrill Me, Kiss Me** ....*Comparing Him With You*		$6		Capitol 2505
				#8 Pop hit for Mel Carter in 1965				
10/25/69	26	9		11 **I'll Never Be Free** ....*The Pattern Of Our Lives*		$6		Capitol 2608
2/28/70	34	8		12 **Third World** ....*You Go Back To Your World (And I'll Go Back To Mine)*		$6		Capitol 2730
5/9/70	18	13		13 **I'm Leavin' It Up To You** ....*If It's Left Up To Me*		$6		Capitol 2796
				#1 Pop hit for Dale & Grace in 1963				
9/5/70	47	7		14 **My Happiness** ....*Let Your Sun Shine On Me*		$6	■	Capitol 2865
				#2 Pop hit for Connie Francis in 1959				
3/6/71	40	9		15 **Oh, Love Of Mine** ....*Closing Time Till Dawn*		$6		Capitol 3039
12/18/71+	70	3		16 **Just One More Time** ....*Meet Me Tonight*		$6		Capitol 3219
1/6/73	72	2		17 **I've Been There** ....*I'll Be Leaving You Again*		$5		Capitol 3454
				JONIE MOSBY				

MOWREY, Dude '93
Born Daniel Richard Mowrey on 2/10/72 in Ft. Lauderdale; raised in Ocala, Florida. Singer/songwriter/guitarist.

8/24/91	65	3		1 **Cowboys Don't Cry**				album cut
				from the album *Honky Tonk* on Capitol 95085				
4/17/93	57	8		2 **Maybe You Were The One** ....*View From The Bottom*		$3	▌	Arista 12515
8/14/93	69	4		3 **Hold On, Elroy** ....*Turn For The Worse*		$3	▌	Arista 12579
2/12/94	57	7		4 **Somewhere In Between** ....*I'll Never Listen To That Fool Again*		$3	▌	Arista 12643

MULLEN, Bruce '74

| 5/25/74 | 88 | 3 | | **Auctioneer Love** ....*The Love In The Touch Of Her Hand* | | $6 | | Chart 5215 |

★316★ **MULLICAN, Moon** '50
Born Aubrey Mullican on 3/27/09 in Corrigan, Texas. Died of a heart attack on 1/1/67 (age 57). Singer/pianist. Member of the *Grand Ole Opry* from 1949-55. Known as the "King Of The Hillbilly Piano Players."
1)I'll Sail My Ship Alone 2)New Pretty Blonde (New Jole Blon) 3)Sweeter Than The Flowers

2/8/47	2[1]	15		1 **New Pretty Blonde (Jole Blon)** *When A Soldier Knocks And Finds Nobody Home*		$25		King 578
				MOON MULLICAN and the Showboys				
7/26/47	4	1		2 **Jole Blon's Sister** *Showboy Special*		$25		King 632
5/15/48	3	26		3 **Sweeter Than The Flowers** *S:3 / J:3 I Left My Heart In Texas*		$25		King 673
3/18/50	❶[4]	36		4 **I'll Sail My Ship Alone** *J:❶[4] / S:❶[1] / A:2 Moon's Tune*	17	$25		King 830
8/26/50	4	11		5 **Mona Lisa/** *J:4 / A:7 / S:8*				
				#1 Pop hit for Nat "King" Cole in 1950; from the movie *Captain Carey, U.S.A.* starring Alan Ladd				
8/26/50	5	7		6 **Goodnight Irene** *J:5 / A:10 / S:10*		$25		King 886
				#1 Pop hit for Gordon Jenkins & The Weavers in 1950				
8/4/51	7	2		7 **Cherokee Boogie (Eh-Oh-Aleena)** *S:7 / J:10 Love Is The Light That Leads Me Home*		$25		King 965
5/29/61	15	4		8 **Ragged But Right** ....*Bottom Of The Glass*		$20		Starday 545
				written by George Jones				

MULLINS, Dee '68
Born on 4/7/37 in Gafford, Texas. Died on 3/13/91 (age 53). Male singer.

2/10/68	64	3		1 **I Am The Grass** ....*The World I'm Livin In*		$7		SSS Int'l. 728
7/13/68	51	7		2 **Texas Tea** *Parking For Cheaters*		$7		SSS Int'l. 745
4/26/69	53	6		3 **The Big Man** ....*Run Willie Run*		$6		Plantation 17
12/26/70	71	2		4 **Remember Bethlehem** ....*California, The Promise Land* [X]		$6		Plantation 68
4/14/73	61	9		5 **Circle Me** ....*Friday's Wine*		$6		Triune 7205

MUNDY, Jim '74
Born James White on 2/8/34 in Muldrow, Oklahoma. Brother of Ann J. Morton and Bill White.
1)The River's Too Wide 2)She's Already Gone 3)Come Home

12/1/73+	13	15		1 **The River's Too Wide**	*Run Away*	$6		ABC 11400
4/13/74	49	11		2 **Come Home** ....*Nobody Loves You*		$6		ABC 11428
9/7/74	71	5		3 **She's No Ordinary Woman (Ordinarily)** ....*Rosalie's Good-Eats Cafe*		$5		ABC 12001
4/19/75	37	9		4 **She's Already Gone** ....*While The Feeling's Good*		$5		ABC 12074
8/30/75	81	8		5 **Blue Eyes And Waltzes** ....*Holdin' On*		$5		ABC 12120
4/17/76	86	4		6 **I'm Knee Deep In Loving You** ....*Monroe, Louisiana*		$5		ABC/Dot 17617
8/7/76	94	4		7 **I Never Met A Girl I Didn't Like** ....*Lucy Ain't Your Loser Lookin' Good*		$5		ABC/Dot 17638
7/30/77	70	6		8 **Summertime Blues** ....*Gilpen County Sidewalks*		$7		Hill Country 778
				#8 Pop hit for Eddie Cochran in 1958				

JIM MUNDY and TERRI MELTON:

DEBUT	PEAK	WKS		A-side / B-side	Pop	$	Pic	Label & Number
9/9/78	76	4		9 If You Think I Love You Now		$6		MCM 100
1/6/79	87	2		10 Kiss You All Over		$6		MCM 101

#1 Pop hit for Exile in 1978

MUNDY, Marilyn '89
Born in Bokoshe, Oklahoma; raised in Flower Hill, Oklahoma.

| 6/17/89 | 85 | 2 | | 1 I Still Love You Babe .... | | $5 | | Door Knob 322 |
| 1/6/90 | 85 | 2 | | 2 Feelings For Each Other .... | | $5 | | Door Knob 336 |

MURPHEY, Mark '89

| 5/6/89 | 96 | 1 | | California Wine .... *Falling Into The Night* | | $7 | | Traveler Ent. 106 |

MURPHEY, Michael Martin ★139★ '82
Born on 5/5/38 in Dallas. Singer/songwriter/guitarist. Acted in the movies *Take This Job And Shove It* and *Hard Country*.

1)What's Forever For 2)A Long Line Of Love 3)I'm Gonna Miss You, Girl 4)From The Word Go
5)Still Taking Chances

MICHAEL MURPHEY:

2/21/76	36	10		1 A Mansion On The Hill .... *Renegade* (Pop #39)		$5		Epic 50184
1/22/77	58	8		2 Cherokee Fiddle .... *Running Wide Open*		$5		Epic 50319
4/28/79	93	3		3 Chain Gang .... *Lightning*		$4		Epic 50686

#2 Pop hit for Sam Cooke in 1960

| 8/18/79 | 92 | 3 | | 4 Backslider's Wine .... *South Coast* | | $4 | | Epic 50739 |
| 7/4/81 | 83 | 3 | | 5 Take It As It Comes .... *Hard Country* | | $4 | | Epic 02075 |

MICHAEL MURPHEY with KATY MOFFATT

3/27/82	44	10		6 The Two-Step Is Easy .... *Lost River*		$4		Liberty 1455
6/19/82	❶¹	24		7 What's Forever For *Crystal*	19	$4		Liberty 1466
11/13/82+	3	20		8 Still Taking Chances *Lost River*	76	$4		Liberty 1486
3/26/83	11	17		9 Love Affairs .... *Crystal*		$4		Liberty 1494
9/10/83	9	21		10 Don't Count The Rainy Days *The Heart Never Lies*		$4	■	Liberty 1505
1/28/84	7	18		11 Will It Be Love By Morning *Goodbye Money Mountain*		$4	■	Liberty 1514

MICHAEL MARTIN MURPHEY:

5/12/84	12	17		12 Disenchanted .... *Sacred Heart*		$4	■	Liberty 1517
8/25/84	19	16		13 Radio Land .... A:17 / S:21 *The Heart Never Lies*		$4		Liberty 1523
12/1/84+	8	23		14 What She Wants S:7 / A:8 *Still Taking Chances*		$3	■	EMI America 8243
5/25/85	9	20		15 Carolina In The Pines A:9 / S:10 *Cherokee Fiddle*		$3	■	EMI America 8265

new version of his #21 Pop hit from 1975

2/8/86	26	14		16 Tonight We Ride S:24 / A:27 *Santa Fe Cantina*		$3		Warner 28797
5/24/86	15	16		17 Rollin' Nowhere S:14 / A:15 *Face-To-Face With The Night*		$3		Warner 28694
8/30/86	40	14		18 Fiddlin' Man *Ghost Town (Messages From The Ghost Ranch)*		$3		Warner 28598
2/7/87	4	21		19 A Face In The Crowd A:4 / S:15 *You're History*		$3		Warner 28471

MICHAEL MARTIN MURPHEY AND HOLLY DUNN

5/23/87	❶¹	23		20 A Long Line Of Love S:9 *Worlds Apart*		$3		Warner 28370
11/21/87+	3	27		21 I'm Gonna Miss You, Girl S:7 *Running Blood*		$3	■	Warner 28168
4/16/88	4	20		22 Talkin' To The Wrong Man S:5 *What Am I Doin' Hangin' 'Round?*		$3	■	Warner 27947

MICHAEL MARTIN MURPHEY with Ryan Murphey

9/10/88	29	13		23 Pilgrims On The Way (Matthew's Song) .... *Still Got The Fire*		$3		Warner 27810
12/17/88+	3	27		24 From The Word Go *Vanishing Breed*		$3		Warner 27668
5/20/89	9	22		25 Never Givin' Up On Love *Desperation Road*		$3	■	Warner 22970

from the movie *Pink Cadillac* starring **Clint Eastwood**

| 10/7/89 | 48 | 11 | | 26 Family Tree .... *Woodsmoke In The Wind* | | $3 | | Warner 22765 |
| 1/6/90 | 67 | 3 | | 27 Route 66 .... *Jukebox* | | $3 | | Warner 22666 |

#11 Pop hit for Nat "King" Cole in 1946

| 9/8/90 | 52 | 11 | | 28 Cowboy Logic *Spanish Is The Lovin' Tongue* | | $3 | ▮ | Warner 19724 |
| 3/16/91 | 74 | 1 | | 29 Let The Cowboy Dance *Red River Valley* | | $3 | | Warner 19412 |

MURPHY, David Lee ★318★ '95
Born on 1/7/59 in Herrin, Illinois. Singer/songwriter/guitarist.

1)Dust On The Bottle 2)Every Time I Get Around You 3)The Road You Leave Behind

| 3/5/94 | 36 | 20 | | 1 Just Once *High Weeds And Rust* | | $3 | ▮ | MCA 54794 |

from the movie *8 Seconds* starring **Luke Perry**

8/20/94	52	7		2 Fish Ain't Bitin' *Why Can't People Just Get Along*		$3	▮	MCA 54877
3/18/95	6	22		3 Party Crowd S:5 *Can't Turn It Off*		$3	▮	MCA 54977
8/12/95	❶²	20		4 Dust On The Bottle S:13 *Mama 'N Them*		$3	▮	MCA 54944
11/25/95+	13	20		5 Out With A Bang *Greatest Show On Earth*		$3		MCA 55153
3/23/96	2¹	20		6 Every Time I Get Around You *Pirates Cove*		$3		MCA 55186
8/3/96	5	20		7 The Road You Leave Behind *Gettin' Out The Good Stuff*		$3		MCA 55205
1/25/97	53	5		8 Genuine Rednecks *(long version)*		$3		MCA 55269
3/15/97	51	7		9 Breakfast In Birmingham .... *100 Years Too Late*		$3		MCA 72000
7/5/97	25	20		10 All Lit Up In Love *She's Really Something To See*		$3		MCA 72008
11/15/97+	37	20		11 Just Don't Wait Around Til She's Leavin' .... *Kentucky Girl*		$3		MCA 72024

MURPHY, Jimmy   '87

| 10/25/86 | 74 | 4 | | 1 Two Sides .... *What Would The World Be Without Music?* | | $5 | | Encore 10033 |
| 1/31/87 | 51 | 9 | | 2 Keep The Faith .... *What Would The World Be Without Music?* | | $5 | | Encore 10036 |

MURPHY, Vern   '73

| 7/28/73 | 96 | 2 | | Blue And Lonely.. *Don't Cheat On Me* | | $7 | | Sunset 0021 |

MURRAY, Anne ★51★   '79

Born Morna Anne Murray on 6/20/45 in Springhill, Nova Scotia, Canada. Regular on **Glen Campbell**'s TV series. CMA Award: 1985 Vocal Duo of the Year (with **Dave Loggins**).

1)I Just Fall In Love Again 2)He Thinks I Still Care 3)Nobody Loves Me Like You Do
4)Blessed Are The Believers 5)Just Another Woman In Love

7/25/70	10	19	●	1 Snowbird *Just Bidin' My Time*	8	$6		Capitol 2738
1/16/71	53	5		2 Sing High - Sing Low .... *Days Of The Looking Glass*	83	$6		Capitol 2988
3/20/71	27	12		3 A Stranger In My Place .... *Sycamore Slick*	122	$6		Capitol 3059
				written by **Kenny Rogers**; also see #14 below				
5/22/71	67	2		4 Put Your Hand In The Hand .... *It Takes Time*		$6		Capitol 3082
				#2 Pop hit for Ocean in 1971				
10/30/71	40	8		5 I Say A Little Prayer/By The Time I Get To Phoenix .... *All Through The Night*	81	$6		Capitol 3200
				GLEN CAMPBELL/ANNE MURRAY				
				"I Say A Little Prayer" was a #4 Pop hit for Dionne Warwick in 1967				
1/22/72	11	15		6 Cotton Jenny *Destiny*	71	$6		Capitol 3260
12/23/72+	10	17		7 Danny's Song *Drown Me*	7	$5		Capitol 3481
				first recorded by **Loggins & Messina** on their 1972 album *Sittin' In*				
6/2/73	20	10		8 What About Me .... *Let Sunshine Have Its Day*	64	$5		Capitol 3600
8/25/73	79	7		9 Send A Little Love My Way .... *Head Above The Water*	72	$5		Capitol 3648
				from the movie *Oklahoma Crude* starring George C. Scott				
12/22/73+	5	15		10 Love Song *You Can't Go Back*	12	$5		Capitol 3776
				first recorded by **Loggins & Messina** on their 1973 album *Full Sail*				
4/27/74	❶²	17		11 He Thinks I Still Care *You Won't See Me* (Pop #8)		$5		Capitol 3867
9/28/74	5	16		12 Son Of A Rotten Gambler *Just One Look* (Pop #86)		$5		Capitol 3955
2/15/75	28	10		13 Uproar *Lift Your Hearts To The Sun*		$5		Capitol 4025
6/7/75	79	6		14 A Stranger In My Place .... *Dream Lover* [R]		$5		Capitol 4072
				same version as #3 above				
10/25/75	49	9		15 Sunday Sunrise *Out On The Road Again*	98	$5		Capitol 4142
2/7/76	19	14		16 The Call *Lady Bug*	91	$5		Capitol 4207
5/29/76	41	8		17 Golden Oldie *Together*		$5		Capitol 4265
9/11/76	22	12		18 Things *Caress Me Pretty Music*	89	$5		Capitol 4329
				#3 Pop hit for Bobby Darin in 1962				
2/5/77	57	8		19 Sunday School To Broadway .... *Dancin' All Night Long*		$5		Capitol 4375
1/21/78	4	16		20 Walk Right Back *A Million More*	103	$5		Capitol 4527
				#7 Pop hit for The Everly Brothers in 1961				
5/13/78	4	18	●	21 You Needed Me *I Still Wish The Very Best For You*	❶¹	$4		Capitol 4574
1/27/79	❶³	15		22 I Just Fall In Love Again *Just To Feel This Love From You*	12	$4	■	Capitol 4675
5/19/79	❶¹	15		23 Shadows In The Moonlight *Yucatan Cafe*	25	$4		Capitol 4716
9/29/79	❶¹	14		24 Broken Hearted Me *Why Don't You Stick Around*	12	$4		Capitol 4773
1/5/80	3	14		25 Daydream Believer *Do You Think Of Me*	12	$4		Capitol 4813
				#1 Pop hit for The Monkees in 1967				
4/5/80	9	14		26 Lucky Me *Somebody's Waiting*	42	$4		Capitol 4848
6/28/80	23	11		27 I'm Happy Just To Dance With You .... *What's Forever For*	64	$4		Capitol 4878
				#95 Pop hit for The Beatles in 1964				
9/6/80	❶¹	16		28 Could I Have This Dance *Somebody's Waiting*	33	$4	■	Capitol 4920
				from the movie *Urban Cowboy* starring John Travolta				
4/4/81	❶¹	14		29 Blessed Are The Believers *Only Love*	34	$4	■	Capitol 4987
7/4/81	16	13		30 We Don't Have To Hold Out .... *Call Me With The News*		$4	■	Capitol 5013
9/12/81	9	15		31 It's All I Can Do *If A Heart Must Be Broken*	53	$4		Capitol 5023
1/16/82	4	18		32 Another Sleepless Night *It Should Have Been Easy*	44	$4		Capitol 5083
7/31/82	7	16		33 Hey! Baby! *Song For The Mira*		$4		Capitol 5145
				#1 Pop hit for Bruce Channel in 1962				
11/20/82+	7	19		34 Somebody's Always Saying Goodbye *That'll Keep Me Dreamin'*		$4	■	Capitol 5183
9/17/83	❶¹	20		35 A Little Good News *I'm Not Afraid Anymore*	74	$4	■	Capitol 5264
				CMA Award: Single of the Year				
2/4/84	46	12		36 That's Not The Way (It's S'posed To Be)................... *The More We Try*	106	$4		Capitol 5305
4/28/84	❶¹	20		37 Just Another Woman In Love *Heart Stealer*		$4	■	Capitol 5344
9/8/84	❶¹	22		38 Nobody Loves Me Like You Do S:❶¹ / A:❶¹ *Love You Out Of Your Mind*	103	$4	■	Capitol 5401
				ANNE MURRAY (WITH DAVE LOGGINS)				
1/19/85	2¹	22		39 Time Don't Run Out On Me S:2 / A:3 *Let Your Heart Do The Talking*		$3	■	Capitol 5436
5/18/85	7	20		40 I Don't Think I'm Ready For You A:6 / S:7 *Take Good Care Of My Heart*		$3	■	Capitol 5472
				from the movie *Stick* starring Burt Reynolds				
1/25/86	❶¹	19		41 Now And Forever (You And Me) S:❶¹ / A:2 *I Don't Wanna Spend Another Night Without You*	92	$3	■	Capitol 5547
5/24/86	62	9		42 Who's Leaving Who .... *Reach For Me*		$3	■	Capitol 5576

MURRAY, Anne — Cont'd

DEBUT	PEAK	WKS	A-side / B-side	Pop	$	Pic	Label & Number
8/23/86	26	15	43 My Life's A Dance ....A:24 *Call Us Fools*		$3	■	Capitol 5610
12/27/86+	23	14	44 On And On ....A:23 *Gotcha*		$3		Capitol 5655
5/9/87	20	23	45 Are You Still In Love With Me ....S:12 *Give Me Your Love*		$3	■	Capitol 44005
8/29/87	27	13	46 Anyone Can Do The Heartbreak ....*Without You*		$3	■	Capitol 44053
2/20/88	52	8	47 Perfect Strangers ....*It Happens All The Time*		$3		Capitol 44134
			ANNE MURRAY (With Doug Mallory)				
9/3/88	52	7	48 Flying On Your Own ....*Slow All Night*		$3	■	Capitol 44219
11/26/88+	36	12	49 Slow Passin' Time ....*Flying On Your Own*		$3		Capitol 44272
3/25/89	55	9	50 Who But You ....*You Make Me Curious*		$3		Capitol 44341
9/30/89	28	15	51 If I Ever Fall In Love Again ....*Just Another Woman In Love*		$3		Capitol 44432
			ANNE MURRAY with Kenny Rogers				
8/25/90	5	20	52 Feed This Fire				album cut
12/8/90+	39	19	53 Bluebird				album cut
			above 2 from the album *You Will* on Capitol 94102				
10/5/91	56	11	54 Everyday..........				album cut
			from the album *Yes I Do* on Capitol 96310				

MUSIC ROW   **'81**
Duo of Glen Gill and Bill Pippin.

DEBUT	PEAK	WKS	A-side / B-side	Pop	$	Pic	Label & Number
3/7/81	86	4	1 There Ain't A Song		$6		Debut 8013
5/16/81	92	2	2 Lady's Man		$6		Debut 8115
6/27/81	88	3	3 It's Not The Rain		$6		Debut 8116

MYERS, Frank   **'74**
Born in Snowdoun, Alabama; raised in Montgomery, Alabama. Singer/songwriter.

DEBUT	PEAK	WKS	A-side / B-side	Pop	$	Pic	Label & Number
8/3/74	82	7	Hangin' On To What I've Got ....*She'll Have Sunshine Where She Goes*		$6		Caprice 1999

N

NAIL, Linda   **'79**
Born Linda Naile on 1/19/54 in Wabash, Arkansas.

DEBUT	PEAK	WKS	A-side / B-side	Pop	$	Pic	Label & Number
12/9/78+	58	9	1 Me Touchin' You ....*A Woman And A Man*		$5		Ridgetop 00178
3/10/79	67	5	2 There Hangs His Hat ....*The Love Line's Slippin'*		$5		Ridgetop 00279
2/5/83	85	2	3 You're A Part Of Me ....*Let It Be Me*		$6		Grand Prix 2
			DANNY WHITE & LINDA NAIL				
5/14/83	80	4	4 Reminiscing ....*I Go To Pieces*		$6		Grand Prix 3

NAILL, Jerry   **'80**

DEBUT	PEAK	WKS	A-side / B-side	Pop	$	Pic	Label & Number
2/2/80	92	4	Her Cheatin Heart (Made A Drunken Fool Of Me)		$7		El Dorado 156

NALL, Jimmy — see LANE, Terri

NASH, Bill   **'81**
Born in Pharr, Texas.

DEBUT	PEAK	WKS	A-side / B-side	Pop	$	Pic	Label & Number
7/4/81	79	4	1 Burning Bridges ....*Saturday Night Live*		$4		Liberty 1410
			#3 Pop hit for Jack Scott in 1960				
10/17/81	61	6	2 Slippin' Out, Slippin' In ....*Take Me As I Am*		$4		Liberty 1433
5/22/82	65	6	3 Survivor ....*I Don't Want To Hear A Heartache Song Again*		$4		Liberty 1463

NASH, Linda   **'73**

DEBUT	PEAK	WKS	A-side / B-side	Pop	$	Pic	Label & Number
10/27/73	83	10	Country Boogie Woogie ....*Good Things Just Don't Last*		$6		Ace of Hearts 0473

NASHVILLE BRASS — see DAVIS, Danny

NASHVILLE NIGHTSHIFT   **'85**

DEBUT	PEAK	WKS	A-side / B-side	Pop	$	Pic	Label & Number
8/31/85	89	2	Nightshift..........		$6		NCA 133737
			tribute to Marty Robbins; #3 Pop hit for the Commodores in 1985				

NASHVILLE SUPERPICKERS   **'81**
Group of top Nashville session musicians: **Phil Baugh** (guitar), **Buddy Emmons** (steel guitar), **Charlie McCoy** (harmonica), Johnny Gimble (fiddle), **Hargus "Pig" Robbins** (piano), Russ Hicks (guitar), Henry Strzelecki (bass) and Buddy Harman (drums).

DEBUT	PEAK	WKS	A-side / B-side	Pop	$	Pic	Label & Number
2/7/81	83	2	New York Cowboy ....*Sexy Southern Lady*		$6		Sound Factory 426

NAYLOR, Jerry   **'75**
Born on 3/6/39 in Stephenville, Texas. Singer/songwriter/bassist.
1)Is This All There Is To A Honky Tonk? 2)If You Don't Want To Love Her 3)The Last Time You Love Me

DEBUT	PEAK	WKS	A-side / B-side	Pop	$	Pic	Label & Number
1/25/75	27	12	1 Is This All There Is To A Honky Tonk? ....*You're The One*		$5		Melodyland 6003
10/2/76	94	2	2 The Bad Part Of Me ....*I Hate To Drink Alone*		$5		Hitsville 6041
12/4/76+	50	9	3 The Last Time You Love Me ....*Born To Fool Around*		$5		Hitsville 6046
2/4/78	37	9	4 If You Don't Want To Love Her ....*Love Away Her Memory Tonight*		$5		MC/Curb 5004
5/27/78	80	4	5 Rave On/				
			#37 Pop hit for Buddy Holly in 1958				
		2	6 Lady, Would You Like To Dance		$5		MC/Curb 5010
3/24/79	54	5	7 But For Love ....*Part Time Lover, Part Time Fool*		$5		Warner/Curb 8767
			new version of his #69 Pop hit from 1970				
7/7/79	72	4	8 She Wears It Well ....*Part Time Lover, Full Time Heartache*		$5		Warner/Curb 8881
11/17/79	69	4	9 Don't Touch Me ....*Never Been To Spain*		$6		Jeremiah 1002
			JERRY NAYLOR/KELLI WARREN				

NAYLOR, Jerry — Cont'd

| 3/8/80 | 61 | 5 | | 10 Cheating Eyes .... *America, I'm Coming Home To You* | | $6 | | Oak 1014 |
| 11/29/86 | 75 | 4 | | 11 For Old Time Sake .... *I Want To Be Loved* | | $6 | | West 723 |

NEEDMORE CREEK SINGERS — see ARNOLD, Eddy

NEEL, Jo Anna   '72
Female singer from Buckeye, Arizona.

| 11/13/71 | 68 | 5 | | 1 Daddy Was A Preacher But Mama Was A Go-Go Girl....... *A Perfect Stranger* | | $7 | | Decca 32865 |
| 4/22/72 | 44 | 10 | | 2 One More Time .... *The Sparrow And Me* | | $7 | | Decca 32950 |

NEELY, Sam   '74
Born on 8/22/48 in Cuero, Texas. Singer/songwriter/guitarist.

9/14/74	49	12		1 You Can Have Her	*It's A Fine Morning*	34	$6		A&M 1612
2/1/75	61	8		2 I Fought The Law .... *Guitar Man*	54	$6		A&M 1651
				#9 Pop hit for the Bobby Fuller Four in 1966				
9/10/77	98	3		3 Sail Away .... *My Lover And My Friend*	84	$4		Elektra 45419
3/12/83	78	4		4 The Party's Over (Everybody's Gone) .... *What Do I Tell My Heart*		$4		MCA 52194
				tribute to the final episode of TV's *M*A*S*H* which aired on 2/28/83				
6/18/83	77	5		5 When You Leave That Way You Can Never Go Back. *The Music Made Me Do It*		$4		MCA 52226
1/21/84	81	3		6 Old Photographs .... *Somebody's Leavin'*		$4		MCA 52323

NELSON, Bonnie   '86
Born in 1949 in Denver.

| 12/6/86 | 83 | 3 | | 1 Don't Let It Go To Your Heart .... *Willie, Where Are You* | | $5 | | Door Knob 257 |
| 5/23/87 | 84 | 2 | | 2 More Than Friendly Persuasion .... *If You Want To Be Loved* | | $5 | | Door Knob 264 |

NELSON, Nikki   '97
Born in San Diego; raised in Topaz City, Nevada. Female singer. Former lead singer of **Highway 101**.

| 3/15/97 | 62 | 5 | | Too Little Too Much .... | | $3 | ▌ | Columbia 78519 |

★395★   NELSON, Ricky   '58
Born Eric Hilliard Nelson on 5/8/40 in Teaneck, New Jersey. Died on 12/31/85 (age 45) in a plane crash in DeKalb, Texas. Son of bandleader Ozzie Nelson and vocalist Harriet Hilliard. Rick and brother David appeared on Nelson's radio show from March 1949; later on TV from 1952-66. Formed own Stone Canyon Band in 1969. In movies *Rio Bravo*, *The Wackiest Ship In The Army* and *Love And Kisses*. Married Kristin Harmon (sister of actor Mark Harmon) in 1963; divorced in 1982. Their daughter Tracy is an actress. Their twin sons, Matthew and Gunnar, began recording as Nelson in 1990. Charted 54 pop hits from 1957-73. Inducted into the Rock and Roll Hall of Fame in 1987.

1)*Poor Little Fool* 2)*Stood Up* 3)*My Bucket's Got A Hole In It*

1/20/58	8	12	●	1 Stood Up/	S:8	2³			
1/20/58	12	6		2 Waitin' In School	S:12	18	$25	■	Imperial 5483
4/14/58	10	11	●	3 My Bucket's Got A Hole In It/	S:10	12			
4/14/58	10	10		4 Believe What You Say	S:10	4	$25	■	Imperial 5503
7/7/58	3	15	●	5 Poor Little Fool	S:3 / A:8 *Don't Leave Me This Way*	❶²	$25		Imperial 5528

RICK NELSON:

6/10/67	58	5		6 Take A City Bride .... *I'm Called Lonely*		$15	■	Decca 32120
9/16/72	44	9	●	7 Garden Party .... *So Long Mama*	6	$10		Decca 32980
5/11/74	89	2		8 One Night Stand	*Lifestream*		$8		MCA 40214
				RICK NELSON & THE STONE CANYON BAND (above 2)				
4/21/79	59	9		9 Dream Lover .... *That Ain't The Way Love's Supposed To Be*		$6		Epic 50674
				#2 Pop hit for **Bobby Darin** in 1959				
7/12/86	88	7		10 Dream Lover .... *Rave On* [R]		$5	■	Epic 06066
				above 2 are the same version				

NELSON, Terry — see C COMPANY

NELSON, Willie ★9★   '78
Born on 4/30/33 in Fort Worth, Texas; raised in Abbott, Texas. Singer/songwriter/guitarist/actor. Played bass for **Ray Price**'s band. Acted in the several movies. Formerly married to **Shirley Collie**. CMA Awards: 1976 Vocal Duo of the Year (with **Waylon Jennings**); 1979 Entertainer of the Year; 1983 Vocal Duo of the Year (with **Merle Haggard**); 1984 Vocal Duo of the Year (with **Julio Iglesias**). Won Grammy's Living Legends Award in 1989. Elected to the Country Music Hall of Fame in 1993.

1)*Mammas Don't Let Your Babies Grow Up To Be Cowboys* 2)*Good Hearted Woman* 3)*To All The Girls I've Loved Before*
4)*Blue Eyes Crying In The Rain* 5)*My Heroes Have Always Been Cowboys*

3/17/62	10	13		1 Willingly	*Chain Of Love*		$20		Liberty 55403
				WILLIE NELSON & SHIRLEY COLLIE				
5/26/62	7	13		2 Touch Me	*Where My House Lives*	109	$20		Liberty 55439
4/6/63	25	5		3 Half A Man .... *The Last Letter*	129	$20		Liberty 55532
1/18/64	33	3		4 You Took My Happy Away .... *How Long Is Forever*		$20		Liberty 55638
5/8/65	43	5		5 She's Not For You .... *Permanently Lonely*		$15		RCA Victor 8519
10/16/65	48	2		6 I Just Can't Let You Say Goodbye .... *And So Will You Half*		$15		RCA Victor 8682
10/1/66	19	13		7 One In A Row .... *San Antonio Rose*		$15		RCA Victor 8933
3/4/67	24	16		8 The Party's Over .... *Make Way For A Better Man*		$15		RCA Victor 9100
6/24/67	21	11		9 Blackjack County Chain .... *Some Other World*		$12		RCA Victor 9202
10/21/67	50	9		10 San Antonio .... *To Make A Long Story Short (She's Gone)*		$12		RCA Victor 9324
2/10/68	22	11		11 Little Things .... *I'll Stay Around*		$12		RCA Victor 9427
6/15/68	44	8		12 Good Times .... *Don't You Ever Get Tired (Of Hurting Me)*		$12		RCA Victor 9536
				also see #68 below				
9/7/68	36	7		13 Johnny One Time .... *She's Still Gone*		$10		RCA Victor 9605
12/21/68+	13	14		14 Bring Me Sunshine .... *Don't Say Love Or Nothing*		$10		RCA Victor 9684

DEBUT	PEAK	WKS	Gold	A-side (Chart Hit)..B-side	Pop	$	Pic	Label & Number
				NELSON, Willie — Cont'd				
12/13/69+	36	9		15 I Hope So .... *Right Or Wrong*		$10		Liberty 56143
				recorded in 1963				
3/14/70	42	9		16 Once More With Feeling .... *Who Do I Know In Dallas*		$10		RCA Victor 9798
11/28/70	68	2		17 Laying My Burdens Down ....*Truth Number One*		$10		RCA Victor 9903
2/6/71	28	11		18 I'm A Memory.. *I'm So Lonesome I Could Cry*		$10		RCA Victor 9951
				also see #38 below				
10/23/71	62	7		19 Yesterday's Wine/		$10		
			4	20 Me And Paul				RCA Victor 0542
				also see #94 below				
2/19/72	73	2		21 The Words Don't Fit The Picture................................. *A Moment Isn't Very Long*		$10		RCA Victor 0635
7/14/73	60	5		22 Shotgun Willie .... *Sad Songs And Waltzes*		$8		Atlantic 2968
9/29/73	22	13		23 Stay All Night (Stay A Little Longer)................. *Devil In A Sleepin' Bag*		$8		Atlantic 2979
2/16/74	51	5		24 I Still Can't Believe You're Gone ....*Heaven And Hell*		$8		Atlantic 3008
4/6/74	17	13		25 Bloody Mary Morning........*Phases And Stages / Washing The Dishes / Phases And Stages*		$8		Atlantic 3020
8/17/74	17	11		26 After The Fire Is Gone ....*Whiskey River*		$8		Atlantic 4028
				WILLIE NELSON & TRACY NELSON				
12/7/74	93	3		27 Sister's Coming Home ....*Pick Up The Tempo*		$8		Atlantic 3228
7/19/75	❶²	18		28 Blue Eyes Crying In The Rain *Bandera*	21	$6		Columbia 10176
11/15/75+	29	11		29 Fire And Rain ....*I'm A Memory*		$6		RCA Victor 10429
				#3 Pop hit for **James Taylor** in 1970				
12/27/75+	❶³	17		30 Good Hearted Woman *Heaven Or Hell*	25	$6		RCA Victor 10529
				WAYLON & WILLIE				
				CMA Award: Single of the Year				
1/3/76	2¹	15		31 Remember Me *Time Of The Preacher*	67	$6		Columbia 10275
3/27/76	46	7		32 The Last Letter ....*There Goes A Man*		$6		United Artists 771
4/17/76	55	6		33 I Gotta Get Drunk ....*Summer Of Roses*	101	$6		RCA Victor 10591
				"live" recording				
5/1/76	11	13		34 I'd Have To Be Crazy ....*Amazing Grace*		$5		Columbia 10327
7/24/76	❶¹	15		35 If You've Got The Money I've Got The Time *The Sound In Your Mind*		$5		Columbia 10383
12/18/76+	4	14		36 Uncloudy Day *Precious Memories*		$5		Columbia 10453
3/12/77	32	13		37 Lily Dale ....*Please Don't Leave Me*		$5		Columbia 10480
				DARRELL McCALL & WILLIE NELSON				
5/14/77	22	11		38 I'm A Memory ....*It Should Be Easier Now* [R]		$5		RCA 10969
				same version as #18 above				
7/30/77	9	12		39 I Love You A Thousand Ways *Mom And Dad's Waltz*		$5		Columbia 10588
9/10/77	16	13		40 You Ought To Hear Me Cry....................................*One In A Row*		$5		RCA 11061
11/19/77+	9	16		41 Something To Brag About *Anybody's Darlin'*		$5		Columbia 10644
				MARY KAY PLACE with Willie Nelson				
1/21/78	❶⁴	16		42 Mammas Don't Let Your Babies Grow Up To Be Cowboys/	42			
			15	43 I Can Get Off On You		$5		RCA 11198
				WAYLON & WILLIE (above 2)				
3/18/78	5	15		44 If You Can Touch Her At All *Rainy Day Blues*	104	$5		RCA 11235
3/25/78	❶¹	16		45 Georgia On My Mind *On The Sunny Side Of The Street*	84	$5		Columbia 10704
				#1 Pop hit for **Ray Charles** in 1960				
7/15/78	❶¹	13		46 Blue Skies *Moonlight In Vermont*		$5		Columbia 10784
				#1 Pop hit for Ben Selvin in 1927				
10/14/78	77	5		47 Ain't Life Hell..*I'm Going With You This Time*		$5		Capitol 4635
				HANK COCHRAN & WILLIE NELSON				
10/21/78	3	14		48 All Of Me *Unchained Melody*		$5		Columbia 10834
				#1 Pop hit Louis Armstrong in 1932				
10/28/78	67	5		49 Will You Remember Mine ....*The End Of Understanding*		$5		Lone Star 703
11/25/78	86	3		50 There'll Be No Teardrops Tonight ....*Blue Must Be The Color Of The Blues*		$5		United Artists 1254
12/23/78+	12	12		51 Whiskey River ....*Under The Double Eagle*		$5		Columbia 10877
				"live" recording				
2/10/79	4	14		52 Sweet Memories *Little Things*		$5		RCA 11465
4/14/79	15	12		53 September Song ....*Don't Get Around Much Anymore*		$5		Columbia 10929
7/7/79	❶¹	13		54 Heartbreak Hotel *Sioux City Sue*		$5		Columbia 11023
				WILLIE NELSON AND LEON RUSSELL				
8/18/79	16	13		55 Crazy Arms ....*Hurricane Shirley* **(Bobby Bare)**		$5		RCA 11673
11/10/79+	4	14		56 Help Me Make It Through The Night *The Pilgrim: Chapter 33*		$4		Columbia 11126
1/12/80	❶²	14		57 My Heroes Have Always Been Cowboys *Rising Star (Love Theme)*	44	$4		Columbia 11186
				from the movie *The Electric Horseman* starring Robert Redford				
2/2/80	20	12		58 Night Life ....*December Day*		$4		RCA 11893
				DANNY DAVIS AND WILLIE NELSON With The Nashville Brass				
5/3/80	6	15		59 Midnight Rider *So You Think You're A Cowboy*		$4		Columbia 11257
				#19 Pop hit for Gregg Allman in 1974				
5/17/80	41	8		60 Funny How Time Slips Away....................................*The Local Memory*		$4		RCA 11999
				DANNY DAVIS AND WILLIE NELSON with The Nashville Brass				
8/9/80	3	15		61 Faded Love *This Cold War With You*		$4		Columbia 11329
				WILLIE NELSON AND RAY PRICE				
8/30/80	❶¹	16		62 On The Road Again *Jumpin' Cotton Eyed Joe*	20	$4		Columbia 11351
				from the movie *Honeysuckle Rose* starring Nelson				
10/4/80	92	2		63 Family Bible ....*In God's Eyes*		$4		Songbird 41313
12/6/80+	11	14		64 Don't You Ever Get Tired (Of Hurting Me)................*Funny How Time Slips Away*		$4		Columbia 11405
				WILLIE NELSON AND RAY PRICE				
1/10/81	❶¹	14		65 Angel Flying Too Close To The Ground *I Guess I've Come To Live Here*		$4		Columbia 11418
				from the movie *Honeysuckle Rose* starring Nelson				
2/28/81	65	6		66 There's A Crazy Man		$4		Kari 117
				JODY PAYNE & The Willie Nelson Family Band				

DEBUG	PEAK	WKS	Gold	A-side (Chart Hit)..B-side	Pop	$	Pic	Label & Number
				NELSON, Willie — Cont'd				
4/18/81	11	12		67 **Mona Lisa** .... *Twinkle, Twinkle Little Star*		$4		Columbia 02000
				#1 Pop hit for Nat King Cole in 1950				
6/27/81	25	12		68 **Good Times** .... *Where Do You Stand?* [R]		$4	■	RCA 12254
				same version as #12 above				
7/25/81	26	11		69 **I'm Gonna Sit Right Down And Write Myself A Letter** .... *Over The Rainbow*		$4		Columbia 02187
				#3 Pop hit for Billy Williams in 1957				
10/3/81	23	12		70 **Mountain Dew** .... *Laying My Burdens Down*		$4		RCA 12328
11/14/81	39	10		71 **Heartaches Of A Fool** .... *Uncloudy Day*		$4		Columbia 02558
3/6/82	❶²	21	▲	72 **Always On My Mind** *The Party's Over*	5	$4		Columbia 02741
				CMA Award: Single of the Year				
3/13/82	❶²	18		73 **Just To Satisfy You** *Get Naked With Me*	52	$4		RCA 13073
				WAYLON & WILLIE				
6/5/82	19	16		74 **Old Friends** .... *When A House Is Not A Home*		$4		Columbia 02681
				ROGER MILLER & WILLIE NELSON (with Ray Price)				
8/14/82	2²	17		75 **Let It Be Me** *Permanently Lonely*	40	$4		Columbia 03073
				#7 Pop hit for The Everly Brothers in 1960				
10/9/82	72	5		76 **In The Jailhouse Now** .... *Back Street Affair*		$4		Columbia 03231
				WILLIE NELSON & WEBB PIERCE				
10/23/82	13	15		77 **(Sittin' On) The Dock Of The Bay** .... *Luckenbach, Texas*		$4		RCA 13319
				WAYLON & WILLIE				
				#1 Pop hit for Otis Redding in 1968				
12/4/82+	2²	20		78 **Last Thing I Needed First Thing This Morning** *Old Fords And A Natural Stone*		$4		Columbia 03385
12/11/82+	7	20		79 **Everything's Beautiful (In It's Own Way)** *Put It Off Until Tomorrow*	102	$4		Monument 03408
				DOLLY PARTON/WILLIE NELSON				
1/15/83	6	18		80 **Reasons To Quit** *Half A Man*		$4		Epic 03494
				MERLE HAGGARD AND WILLIE NELSON				
3/12/83	10	16		81 **Little Old Fashioned Karma** *Beer Barrel Polka*		$4		Columbia 03674
4/9/83	43	9		82 **You're Gonna Love Yourself (In The Morning)** ... *What Do You Think About Lovin'*		$4		Monument 03781
				WILLIE NELSON/BRENDA LEE				
4/30/83	❶¹	21		83 **Pancho And Lefty** *Opportunity To Cry*		$4		Epic 03842
				WILLIE NELSON AND MERLE HAGGARD				
6/18/83	3	21		84 **Why Do I Have To Choose** *Would You Lay With Me (In A Field Of Stone)*		$4		Columbia 03965
10/8/83	8	19		85 **Take It To The Limit** *Till I Gain Control Again*	102	$4	■	Columbia 04131
				WILLIE NELSON & WAYLON JENNINGS				
				#4 Pop hit for the Eagles in 1976				
12/24/83+	11	16		86 **Without A Song** .... *I Can't Begin To Tell You*		$4		Columbia 04263
				#6 Pop hit for Paul Whiteman in 1930				
3/10/84	❶²	20	●	87 **To All The Girls I've Loved Before** *I Don't Want To Wake You*	5	$4	■	Columbia 04217
				JULIO IGLESIAS & WILLIE NELSON				
8/18/84	❶¹	25		88 **City Of New Orleans** A:❶²/S:❶¹ *Why Are You Pickin' On Me*		$4	■	Columbia 04568
				#18 Pop hit for Arlo Guthrie in 1972				
10/27/84	91	2		89 **Wabash Cannonball** .... *Tennessee Waltz*		$4		Paradise 629
				WILLIE NELSON & HANK WILSON				
11/3/84	46	11		90 **How Do You Feel About Foolin' Around** .... *Eye Of The Storm*		$4		Columbia 04652
				WILLIE NELSON & KRIS KRISTOFFERSON				
12/15/84+	❶¹	27		91 **Seven Spanish Angels** S:❶¹/A:❶¹ *Who Cares*		$3		Columbia 04715
				RAY CHARLES (with WILLIE NELSON)				
4/13/85	❶¹	22		92 **Forgiving You Was Easy** S:❶¹/A:❶¹ *You Wouldn't Cross The Street*		$4		Columbia 04847
5/18/85	❶¹	20		93 **Highwayman** S:❶¹/A:❶¹ *The Human Condition*		$4	■	Columbia 04881
				WAYLON JENNINGS/WILLIE NELSON/JOHNNY CASH/KRIS KRISTOFFERSON				
9/14/85	14	19		94 **Me And Paul** .... A:11/S:14 *I Let My Mind Wander* [R]		$4		Columbia 05597
				new version of #20 above				
9/14/85	15	18		95 **Desperados Waiting For A Train** ..... S:15/A:16 *The Twentieth Century Is Almost Over*		$4		Columbia 05594
				WAYLON JENNINGS/WILLIE NELSON/JOHNNY CASH/KRIS KRISTOFFERSON				
3/29/86	❶¹	20		96 **Living In The Promiseland** A:❶¹/S:2 *Bach Minuet In G*		$4		Columbia 05834
8/2/86	56	8		97 **I've Already Cheated On You** ....S:29 *Take My Advice*		$4		Columbia 06227
				DAVID ALLAN COE and WILLIE NELSON				
8/9/86	21	17		98 **I'm Not Trying To Forget You** .... A:21/S:28 *I've Got The Craziest Feeling*		$3		Columbia 06246
12/6/86+	24	13		99 **Partners After All** S:17/A:24 *Home Away From Home*		$3		Columbia 06530
3/21/87	44	11		100 **Heart Of Gold**...................................... *So Much Like My Dad*		$3		Columbia 07007
				#1 Pop hit for Neil Young in 1972				
7/11/87	27	12		101 **Island In The Sea**...................S:20 *There Is No Easy Way (But There Is A Way)*		$3		Columbia 07202
9/19/87	58	5		102 **If I Could Only Fly** .... *Without You On My Side*		$3		Epic 07400
				MERLE HAGGARD & WILLIE NELSON				
1/9/88	82	3		103 **Nobody There But Me**........................ *Wake Me When It's Over*		$3		Columbia 07636
9/17/88	8	19		104 **Spanish Eyes** S:2 *Ole Buttermilk Sky*		$3		Columbia 08066
				WILLIE NELSON (with Julio Iglesias)				
				#15 Pop hit for Al Martino in 1966				
1/21/89	41	8		105 **Twilight Time**...................................... *Ac-Cent-Tchu-Ate The Positive*		$3		Columbia 08541
				#1 Pop hit for The Platters in 1958				
6/10/89	❶¹	21		106 **Nothing I Can Do About It Now** *If I Were A Painting*		$3		Columbia 68923
10/7/89+	8	26		107 **There You Are** *Spirit*		$3		Columbia 73015
2/24/90	52	13		108 **The Highway**.................................... *Spirit*		$3		Columbia 73249
3/3/90	25	14		109 **Silver Stallion**.................................... *American Remains*		$3		Columbia 73233
				WAYLON JENNINGS/WILLIE NELSON/JOHNNY CASH/KRIS KRISTOFFERSON				
9/29/90	17	20		110 **Ain't Necessarily So** .... *I Never Cared For You*		$3	❙	Columbia 73518
1/19/91	70	3		111 **The Piper Came Today** .... *(I Don't Have A Reason) To Go To California Anymore*		$3		Columbia 73655
3/16/91	45	12		112 **Ten With A Two** .... *You Decide*		$3		Columbia 73749
6/15/91	51	10		113 **If I Can Find A Clean Shirt**.................................. *Put Me On A Train Back To Texas*		$3		Epic 73832
				WAYLON & WILLIE				

NELSON, Willie — Cont'd

| 6/26/93 | 70 | 1 | | 114 Graceland .... | | | | album cut |

#81 Pop hit for Paul Simon in 1987; from the album *Across The Borderline* on Columbia 52752

★336★ **NESBITT, Jim** '64

Born on 12/1/31 in Bishopville, South Carolina. Singer/comedian. Known as "The 'Lasses Sopper."

1)Looking For More In '64 2)Please Mr. Kennedy 3)A Tiger In My Tank

| 4/3/61 | 11 | 7 | | 1 Please Mr. Kennedy .... *The Horse Race* [N] | | $12 | | Dot 16197 |

melody is the same as "The Ballad Of Davy Crockett"

2/2/63	28	1		2 Livin' Offa Credit .... *I'm A Married Man* [N]		$12		Dot 16424
3/21/64	7	24		3 Looking For More In '64 *(Go On And) Cry Me A River* [N]		$8		Chart 1065
9/26/64	20	13		4 Mother-In-Law .... *If You Don't Love Me (Tell Me Now)* [N]		$8		Chart 1100
1/30/65	15	13		5 A Tiger In My Tank .... *I Can't Stand This Living Alone* [N]		$8		Chart 1165
6/26/65	34	6		6 Still Alive In '65 .... *I Laughed When You Said You Were Leaving* [N]		$8		Chart 1200
8/14/65	21	11		7 The Friendly Undertaker .... *Crying And Waiting For You* [N]		$8		Chart 1240
1/1/66	49	2		8 You Better Watch Your Friends .... *You're No Good* [N]		$8		Chart 1290
8/27/66	38	9		9 Heck Of A Fix In 66 .... *I'm From The Country* [N]		$8		Chart 1350
12/17/66+	60	8		10 Stranded .... *These Modern Things* [N]		$8		Chart 1410
6/10/67	74	2		11 Husbands-In-Law .... *I Want To Have My Operation On T-V* [N]		$8		Chart 1445
3/16/68	63	7		12 Truck Drivin' Cat With Nine Wives .... *Social Security* [N]		$8		Chart 1018
2/28/70	20	12		13 Runnin' Bare .... *A Good Woman Is Hard To Find* [N]		$8		Chart 5052

novelty version of Johnny Preston's #1 Pop hit "Running Bear"

NETTLES, Bill '49

Born on 3/13/07 in Natchitoches, Louisiana. Died of a heart attack on 4/5/67 (age 60).

| 6/25/49 | 9 | 6 | | Hadacol Boogie *J:9 I'm Footloose Now* | | $20 | | Mercury 6190 |

BILL NETTLES and His Dixie Blue Boys

NEVILLE, Aaron '93

Born on 1/24/41 in New Orleans. Black singer. Member of The Neville Brothers. Charted 9 pop hits from 1966-95.

| 7/31/93 | 38 | 20 | | 1 The Grand Tour .... *The Roadie Song* | 90 | $3 | ■ | A&M 0312 |
| 6/4/94 | 72 | 2 | | 2 I Fall To Pieces .... *(album version)* | | $3 | ■ | MCA 54836 |

AARON NEVILLE AND TRISHA YEARWOOD

NEWBURY, Mickey '73

Born Milton Newbury on 5/19/40 in Houston. Singer/prolific songwriter.

6/23/73	53	8		1 Sunshine *Song For Susan*	87	$5		Elektra 45853
2/5/77	94	3		2 Hand Me Another Of Those .... *Leavin' Kentucky*		$5		ABC/Hickory 54006
4/8/78	94	3		3 Gone To Alabama .... *Westphalia Texas Waltz*		$5		ABC/Hickory 54025
3/24/79	82	4		4 Looking For The Sunshine .... *A Weed Is A Weed*		$5		ABC/Hickory 54042
6/16/79	81	4		5 Blue Sky Shinin' .... *Darlin' Take Care Of Yourself*		$5		MCA/Hickory 41032
2/9/80	82	3		6 America The Beautiful .... *Freedom*		$5		Hickory 1673

written by poet Katherine Lee Bates at Pikes Peak in 1893

| 10/15/88 | 93 | 2 | | 7 An American Trilogy .... *San Francisco Mabel Joy* | | $5 | | Airborne 10005 |

new version of his #26 Pop hit from 1971

NEW GRASS REVIVAL '89

Group of session musicians: John Cowan (vocals, bass), Sam Bush (fiddle, mandolin), Pat Flynn (guitar) and Béla Fleck (banjo).

| 7/5/86 | 78 | 5 | | 1 What You Do To Me .... *Sweet Release* | | $4 | | EMI America 8329 |

#72 Pop hit for Carl Wilson in 1983

| 9/20/86 | 53 | 8 | | 2 Ain't That Peculiar .... *Seven By Seven* | | $4 | | EMI America 8347 |

#8 Pop hit for Marvin Gaye in 1965

10/3/87	44	9		3 Unconditional Love .... *I Can Talk To You*		$3		Capitol 44078
3/5/88	45	11		4 Can't Stop Now .... *I Can Talk To You*		$3		Capitol 44128
5/27/89	37	13		5 Callin' Baton Rouge *Let Me Be Your Man*		$3		Capitol 44357
10/7/89	58	9		6 You Plant Your Fields .... *Friday Night In America*		$3		Capitol 44453

NEWMAN, Jack '59

| 8/24/59 | 24 | 1 | | House Of Blue Lovers .... *I Didn't Think This Could Happen To Me* | | $25 | | TNT 170 |

NEWMAN, Jimmy ★124★ '57

Born Jimmy Yves Newman on 8/27/27 in High Point, Louisiana. Singer/songwriter/guitarist. Joined the *Grand Ole Opry* in 1956. The "C" in his stage name stands for Cajun.

1)A Fallen Star 2)Cry, Cry, Darling 3)A Lovely Work Of Art 4)Daydreamin' 5)Blue Darlin'

| 5/22/54 | 4 | 11 | | 1 Cry, Cry, Darling *A:4 / J:8 / S:9 You Didn't Have To Go* | | $20 | | Dot 1195 |

first released on Khoury's 530 in 1954 ($25)

3/26/55	7	7		2 Daydreamin' *J:7 / A:9 / S:13 Crying For A Pastime*		$20		Dot 1237
7/9/55	7	10		3 Blue Darlin' *A:7 / J:8 / S:13 Let Me Stay In Your Arms*		$20		Dot 1260
12/17/55+	9	2		4 God Was So Good *A:9 I Thought I'd Never Fall In Love Again*		$20		Dot 1270
4/7/56	9	6		5 Seasons Of My Heart *J:9 / A:10 Let's Stay Together*		$20		Dot 1278
7/7/56	13	4		6 Come Back To Me *A:13 I Wanta Tell All The World*		$20		Dot 1283
5/20/57	2[2]	21		7 A Fallen Star *A:2 / S:4 / J:9 I Can't Go On This Way*	23	$15		Dot 1289
11/3/58+	7	16		8 You're Makin' A Fool Out Of Me *Outside Your Door*		$12		MGM 12707
4/13/59	19	4		9 So Soon .... *What'cha Gonna Do*		$12		MGM 12749

DEBUT	PEAK	WKS	Gold	A-side (Chart Hit)..B-side	Pop	$	Pic	Label & Number
				NEWMAN, Jimmy — Cont'd				
6/22/59	30	1		10 Lonely Girl ....*I'd Be Fool Enough*		$12		MGM 12790
7/27/59	9	13		11 Grin And Bear It ....*The Ballad Of Baby Doe*		$12		MGM 12812
11/2/59	29	1		12 Walkin' Down The Road ....*Angels Cryin'*		$10		MGM 12830
3/7/60	21	7		13 I Miss You Already ....*The End Of The Line*		$10		MGM 12864
6/20/60	6	14		14 A Lovely Work Of Art ....*What About Me*		$10		MGM 12894
11/7/60	11	18		15 Wanting You With Me Tonight...............................*Now That You're Gone*		$10		MGM 12945
4/17/61	14	8		16 Everybody's Dying For Love ....*Just One More Night (With You)*		$8		Decca 31217
12/25/61+	22	2		17 Alligator Man ....*Give Me Heaven*		$8		Decca 31324
12/22/62+	12	9		18 Bayou Talk ....*I May Fall Again*		$8		Decca 31440
12/14/63+	9	19		19 D.J. For A Day ....*The Mover*		$8		Decca 31553
5/16/64	34	3		20 Angel On Leave/				
5/30/64	34	3		21 Summer Skies And Golden Sands		$8		Decca 31609
				JIMMY "C" NEWMAN (above 4)				
4/24/65	13	16		22 Back In Circulation/				
4/10/65	37	7		23 City Of The Angels		$6		Decca 31745
9/25/65	8	21		24 Artificial Rose ....*My Love For You*		$6		Decca 31841
3/26/66	10	16		25 Back Pocket Money ....*For Better Or For Worse (But Not For Long)*		$6		Decca 31916
10/8/66	25	8		26 Bring Your Heart Home ....*Unwanted Feeling*		$6		Decca 31994
1/14/67	32	11		27 Dropping Out Of Sight ....*We Lose A Little Ground*		$6		Decca 32067
5/27/67	24	12		28 Louisiana Saturday Night ....*Gentleman Loafer*		$6		Decca 32130
10/28/67+	11	17		29 Blue Lonely Winter ....*The Devil Was Laughing At Me*		$6		Decca 32202
4/13/68	47	8		30 Sunshine And Bluebirds ....*I'm Sorry Letters*		$6		Decca 32285
8/31/68	20	13		31 Born To Love You ....*Carmelita*		$6		Decca 32366
5/31/69	31	8		32 Boo Dan ....*Surrounded By Your Love*		$6		Decca 32484
11/28/70	65	6		33 I'm Holding Your Memory (But He's Holding You)..............*It'll Take A Lot Of You*		$6		Decca 32740
				NEWMAN, Randy '78				
				Born on 11/28/43 in New Orleans. Singer/songwriter/pianist. Nephew of composers Alfred, Emil and Lionel Newman.				
8/19/78	78	4		Rider In The Rain .... *Sigmund Freud's Impersonation Of Albert Einstein In America*		$4		Warner 8630
				NEWMAN, Terri Sue '79				
				Born in 1954 in Levelland, Texas. Singer/pianist/guitarist.				
1/13/79	43	10		Gypsy Eyes ....*Time For One More Song*		$7		Texas Soul 71378

NEWTON, Juice ★152★ '82
Born Judy Kay Newton on 2/18/52 in New Jersey; raised in Virginia Beach. Singer/songwriter/guitarist.

1)The Sweetest Thing 2)Both To Each Other 3)Hurt 4)You Make Me Want To Make You Mine
5)Break It To Me Gently

DEBUT	PEAK	WKS	Gold	A-side	B-side	Pop	$	Pic	Label & Number
2/21/76	88	6		1 Love Is A Word.............................*The Sweetest Thing (I've Ever Known)*			$5		RCA Victor 10538
				JUICE NEWTON & SILVER SPUR					
2/10/79	37	9		2 Let's Keep It That Way ....*Tell My Baby Goodbye*			$4		Capitol 4679
5/26/79	80	4		3 Lay Back In The Arms Of Someone ....*It's Not Impossible*			$4		Capitol 4714
9/15/79	81	4		4 Any Way That You Want Me ....*The Dream Never Dies*			$4		Capitol 4768
				#53 Pop hit for Evie Sands in 1969					
11/10/79	42	8		5 Until Tonight ....*Lay Back In The Arms Of Someone*			$4		Capitol 4793
2/2/80	35	10		6 Sunshine ....*Go Easy On Me*			$4		Capitol 4818
				#4 Pop hit for Jonathan Edwards in 1972					
4/26/80	41	10		7 You Fill My Life ....*Tear It Up*			$4		Capitol 4856
3/7/81	22	11	●	8 Angel Of The Morning ....*Headin' For A Heartache*	4	$4	■	Capitol 4976
6/13/81	14	16	●	9 Queen Of Hearts ....*River Of Love*	2²	$4	■	Capitol 4997
10/24/81+	❶¹	19		10 The Sweetest Thing (I've Ever Known)...........*Ride 'Em Cowboy*	7	$4	■	Capitol 5046
5/22/82	30	10		11 Love's Been A Little Bit Hard On Me ....*Ever True*	7	$4	■	Capitol 5120
8/28/82	2²	19		12 Break It To Me Gently ....*Adios Mi Corazon*	11	$4	■	Capitol 5148
12/11/82+	53	11		13 Heart Of The Night ....*Love Sail Away*	25	$4	■	Capitol 5192
9/3/83	45	13		14 Stranger At My Door ....*Tell Her No (Pop #27)*		$4	■	Capitol 5265
6/23/84	64	9		15 A Little Love ....*Waiting For The Sun*	44	$4		RCA 13823
8/18/84	32	13		16 Ride 'Em Cowboy...*Love Sail Away*		$4		Capitol 5379
10/20/84	57	7		17 Restless Heart ....*Eye Of A Hurricane*		$3		RCA 13907
7/20/85	❶¹	22		18 You Make Me Want To Make You Mine *S:❶¹ / A:❶¹ Waiting For The Sun*		$3	■	RCA 14139
11/9/85+	❶¹	24		19 Hurt *S:❶¹ / A:❶¹ Eye Of A Hurricane*		$3	■	RCA 14199
				#4 Pop hit for Timi Yuro in 1961					
4/5/86	5	21		20 Old Flame *A:3 / S:5 One Touch*		$3		RCA 14295
7/12/86	❶¹	20		21 Both To Each Other (Friends & Lovers) *S:❶¹ / A:❶¹ A World Without Love*		$3	■	RCA 14377
				EDDIE RABBITT AND JUICE NEWTON					
				#2 Pop hit for Gloria Loring & Carl Anderson in 1986					
8/23/86	9	18		22 Cheap Love *S:8 / A:9 Old Flame*		$3		RCA 14417
12/13/86+	9	20		23 What Can I Do With My Heart *A:9 / S:19 Let Your Woman Take Care Of You*		$3		RCA 5068
7/18/87	24	15		24 First Time Caller ....*'Til You Cry*		$3	☐	RCA 5170
11/14/87+	8	22		25 Tell Me True *S:19 If I Didn't Love You*		$3		RCA 5283
5/6/89	40	12		26 When Love Comes Around The Bend		$3		RCA 8815

NEWTON, Wayne '72
Born on 4/3/42 in Roanoke, Virginia. Singer/multi-instrumentalist. Charted 17 pop hits from 1963-80.

| 7/15/72 | 55 | 8 | ● | 1 Daddy Don't You Walk So Fast...Echo Valley 2-6809 | 4 | $5 | | Chelsea 0100 |
| 10/7/89 | 63 | 5 | | 2 While The Feeling's Good ....Our Wedding Band | | $3 | | Curb 10559 |

WAYNE NEWTON (with Tammy Wynette)

NEWTON, Wood '79
Born in Hampton, Arkansas; raised in Louisiana. Singer/prolific songwriter.

10/28/78	52	7		1 Last Exit For Love ....Too Good To Be True		$4		Elektra 45528
3/3/79	44	8		2 Lock, Stock, & Barrel ....Dreams Of Desireé		$4		Elektra 46013
7/7/79	81	4		3 Julie (Do I Ever Cross Your Mind?) ....Cotton Pickin' Time		$4		Elektra 46059

★249★ NEWTON-JOHN, Olivia '74
Born on 9/26/48 in Cambridge, England; raised in Australia. Singer/actress. Charted 39 pop hits from 1971-96. Acted in the movies *Grease*, *Xanadu* and *Two Of A Kind*. CMA Award: 1974 Female Vocalist of the Year.

1)If You Love Me 2)Have You Never Been Mellow 3)Let It Shine

8/25/73	7	22	●	1 Let Me Be There	Maybe Then I'll Think Of You	6	$6		MCA 40101
4/13/74	2²	18	●	2 If You Love Me (Let Me Know)	Brotherly Love	5	$6		MCA 40209
8/24/74	6	17	●	3 I Honestly Love You	Home Ain't Home Anymore	❶²	$5		MCA 40280
2/1/75	3	14	●	4 Have You Never Been Mellow	Water Under The Bridge	❶¹	$5		MCA 40349
6/14/75	5	15	●	5 Please Mr. Please	And In The Morning	3	$5	■	MCA 40418
9/27/75	19	12		6 Something Better To Do	He's My Rock	13	$5	■	MCA 40459
12/6/75+	5	12		7 Let It Shine	He Ain't Heavy...He's My Brother (Pop flip)	30	$5		MCA 40495
3/13/76	5	13		8 Come On Over	Small Talk And Pride	23	$5		MCA 40525
8/14/76	14	10		9 Don't Stop Believin'	Greensleeves	33	$5	■	MCA 40600
10/30/76	21	11		10 Every Face Tells A Story	Love You Hold The Key	55	$5		MCA 40642
1/29/77	40	10		11 Sam	I'll Bet You A Kangaroo	20	$5		MCA 40670
7/22/78	20	13	●	12 Hopelessly Devoted To You	Love Is A Many Splendored Thing	3	$5		RSO 903

from the movie *Grease* starring Newton-John and John Travolta

1/6/79	94	3	●	13 A Little More Love	Borrowed Time	3	$4	■	MCA 40975
5/5/79	87	5		14 Deeper Than The Night	Please Don't Keep Me Waiting	11	$4	■	MCA 41009
8/4/79	29	11		15 Dancin' 'Round And 'Round	Totally Hot (Pop #52)	82	$4	■	MCA 41074

NEYMAN, June '78

| 11/11/78 | 93 | 2 | | 1 He Ain't Heavy, He's My Brother | Release Me | | $7 | | Starship 101 |

#7 Pop hit for The Hollies in 1970

| 2/17/79 | 97 | 3 | | 2 You're Gonna Miss Me | Kansas City | | $7 | | Starship 110 |

NICKS, Stevie '82
Born Stephanie Nicks on 5/26/48 in Phoenix; raised in California. Member of Fleetwood Mac. Charted 14 pop hits from 1981-94.

| 6/19/82 | 70 | 5 | | After The Glitter Fades | Think About It | 32 | $4 | ■ | Modern 7405 |

NIELSEN, Shaun '80
Born Sherrill Nielsen. Male singer.

| 3/15/80 | 88 | 3 | | Lights Of L.A. | I've Never Loved Anyone More | | $6 | | Adonda 79022 |

NIELSEN WHITE BAND, The '87
Group of former rock musicians: Gary Nielsen (of The Trashmen), Jack White (of McKendree Spring), Tom Eckhoff (of the Dillman Band) and Lonnie Knight.

| 12/20/86+ | 67 | 6 | | 1 Somethin' You Got | | | $4 | | Vision 122574 |
| 5/2/87 | 56 | 7 | | 2 I Got The One I Wanted | | | $4 | | Vision 122575 |

NIGHTSTREETS '80
Vocal trio: Rick Taylor, Jerry Taylor and Joyce Hawthorne. Also recorded as **Streets**.

| 1/26/80 | 32 | 10 | | 1 Love In The Meantime | Cheatin' Like This | | $4 | | Epic 50827 |

STREETS

6/14/80	74	5		2 Falling Together	You Never Knew		$4		Epic 50886
11/15/80	81	5		3 If I Had It My Way	A Little Gettin' Used To		$4		Epic 50944
3/21/81	72	4		4 (Lookin' At Things) In A Different Light	Out Of The Spotlight		$4		Epic 51004

NILLES, Lynn '77

| 2/12/77 | 93 | 4 | | You're Gonna Make Love To Me | Got A Feeling | | $5 | | GRT 100 |

NITTY GRITTY DIRT BAND ★119★ '87
Country-folk-rock group from Long Beach, California. Led by Jeff Hanna (vocals, guitar) and **John McEuen** (banjo, mandolin). Various members included Jimmie Fadden (harmonica), Jim Ibbotson (guitar), Al Garth (violin) and Bernie Leadon (guitar; **Eagles**), who replaced McEuen briefly in early 1987. In the movies *For Singles Only* and *Paint Your Wagon*. Hanna married **Matraca Berg**.

1)Fishin' In The Dark 2)Modern Day Romance 3)Long Hard Road 4)High Horse 5)I've Been Lookin'

| 11/27/71 | 56 | 6 | | 1 I Saw The Light | The Precious Jewel | | $8 | | United Artists 50849 |

NITTY GRITTY DIRT BAND with ROY ACUFF

| 8/4/73 | 97 | 2 | | 2 Grand Ole Opry Song | Orange Blossom Special | | $7 | | United Artists 247 |

NITTY GRITTY DIRT BAND Featuring Jimmy Martin

| 7/12/75 | 79 | 7 | | 3 (All I Have To Do Is) Dream | Raleigh-Durham Reel | 66 | $5 | | United Artists 655 |
| 2/9/80 | 58 | 9 | | 4 An American Dream | Take Me Back | 13 | $4 | | United Artists 1330 |

Linda Ronstadt (harmony vocal)

DEBUT	PEAK	WKS	Gold	A-side (Chart Hit)..B-side	Pop	$	Pic	Label & Number
				NITTY GRITTY DIRT BAND — Cont'd				
8/2/80	77	4		5 Make A Little Magic..Jas' Moon	25	$4		United Artists 1356
				THE DIRT BAND (above 2)				
				Nicolette Larson (backing vocal)				
6/11/83	19	18		6 Shot Full Of Love ....Let's Go		$4		Liberty 1499
10/1/83	9	23		7 Dance Little Jean Maryann		$4		Liberty 1507
12/31/83	93	2		8 Colorado Christmas ....Mr. Bojangles [X]		$4		Liberty 1513
5/26/84	❶¹	20		9 Long Hard Road (The Sharecropper's Dream)		$3		Warner 29282
				Video Tape				
9/22/84	3	24		10 I Love Only You S:3 / A:3 Face On The Cutting Room Floor		$3		Warner 29203
1/12/85	2²	20		11 High Horse S:2 / A:2 Must Be Love		$3		Warner 29099
6/8/85	❶¹	21		12 Modern Day Romance S:❶¹ / A:❶¹ Queen Of The Road		$3		Warner 29027
10/12/85+	3	21		13 Home Again In My Heart S:3 / A:3 Telluride		$3		Warner 28897
3/1/86	6	19		14 Partners, Brothers And Friends A:6 / S:7 Redneck Riviera		$3		Warner 28780
6/21/86	5	21		15 Stand A Little Rain A:5 / S:7 Miner's Night Out		$3		Warner 28690
11/15/86+	7	20		16 Fire In The Sky A:7 / S:14 Cadillac Ranch		$3		Warner 28547
				new version of their #76 Pop hit from 1981				
3/28/87	2¹	17		17 Baby's Got A Hold On Me S:4 / A:11 Oleanna		$3		Warner 28443
7/11/87	❶¹	23		18 Fishin' In The Dark S:2 Keepin' The Road Hot		$3		Warner 28311
11/14/87+	5	22		19 Oh What A Love S:12 America, My Sweetheart		$3	■	Warner 28173
4/16/88	4	18		20 Workin' Man (Nowhere To Go) S:9 Brass Sky		$3		Warner 27940
9/3/88	2¹	22		21 I've Been Lookin' S:6 Must Be Love		$3		Warner 27750
12/24/88+	6	20		22 Down That Road Tonight A Lot Like Me		$3		Warner 27679
5/13/89	27	15		23 Turn Of The Century ....Blues Berry Hill		$3		Universal 66009
5/27/89	14	23		24 And So It Goes ....Amazing Grace		$3		Universal 66008
				JOHN DENVER AND THE NITTY GRITTY DIRT BAND				
10/7/89+	10	26		25 When It's Gone I'm Sittin' On Top Of The World		$3		Universal 66023
3/3/90	63	6		26 One Step Over The Line ....Riding Alone		$3		MCA 53795
				THE NITTY GRITTY DIRT BAND Featuring Rosanne Cash and John Hiatt				
5/26/90	65	9		27 From Small Things (Big Things One Day Come)...........Blues Berry Hill		$3		MCA 79013
				written by Bruce Springsteen				
9/1/90	60	19		28 You Made Life Good Again ....Snowballs		$3		MCA 79075
7/25/92	66	3		29 I Fought The Law ....Mr. Bojangles		$3		Liberty 57766
				#9 Pop hit for the Bobby Fuller Four in 1966				
12/12/92	74	2		30 One Good Love				album cut
				from the album Not Fade Away on Liberty 98564				
				NIX, Tom **'81**				
				Born in Denver.				
1/10/81	79	4		Home Along The Highway		$7		RMA 6009
				NIXON, Nick **'76**				
				Born Hershel Paul Nixon on 3/20/41 in Poplar Bluff, Missouri. Singer/songwriter.				
				1)Rocking In Rosalee's Boat 2)I'll Get Over You 3)I'm Too Use To Loving You				
8/10/74	90	3		1 I'm Turning You Loose ....An Old Memory (Got In My Eye)		$5		Mercury 73467
10/5/74	63	7		2 A Habit I Can't Break ....Walk On By		$5		Mercury 73506
3/8/75	55	9		3 It's Only A Barroom ....You Stood By Me Through It All		$5		Mercury 73654
7/12/75	38	12		4 I'm Too Use To Loving You ....I Just Love Here		$5		Mercury 73691
11/29/75	64	10		5 She's Just An Old Love Turned Memory..................It's Much Too Rainy		$5		Mercury 73726
3/13/76	28	13		6 Rocking In Rosalee's Boat I'll Get Over You		$5		Mercury 73772
1/8/77	83	5		7 Neon Lights ....Everyday		$5		Mercury 73866
7/2/77	51	10		8 Love Songs And Romance Magazines ....It's A Cryin' Shame (But People Change)		$5		Mercury 73930
11/5/77+	34	13		9 I'll Get Over You ....Long Stemmed Rosie		$5		Mercury 55010
8/12/78	87	4		10 She's Lying Next To Me.........................You Really Know My Song		$5		Mercury 55035
6/2/79	79	4		11 What're We Doing, Doing This Again ....Have A Heart		$5		MCA 41030
9/29/79	86	4		12 San Francisco Is A Lonely Town ....Suspicion		$5		MCA 41100
				NOACK, Eddie **'58**				
				Born Armona Noack on 4/29/30 in Houston. Died on 2/5/78 (age 47).				
12/15/58	14	2		Have Blues--Will Travel ....The Price Of Love		$30		D 1019
				NOBLE, Nick **'80**				
				Born Nicholas Valkan on 6/21/36 in Chicago. Charted 4 pop hits from 1955-57.				
8/26/78	40	10		1 Stay With Me ....My Country Kind Of Girl		$6		Churchill 7713
4/14/79	36	10		2 The Girl On The Other Side.................Why Don't You Believe Me		$6		TMS 601
9/22/79	72	5		3 I Wanna Go Back...		$6		TMS 612
2/9/80	35	10		4 Big Man's Cafe ....My Country Kind Of Girl		$6		Churchill 7755
				NOEL **'85**				
				Born Noel Haughey in Salina, California. Female singer.				
12/25/82	90	3		1 One Tear (At A Time) ....Lonely For Too Long		$6		Deep South 706
10/5/85	86	3		2 P.S. ....How Sweet It Is		$6		Madd Cash 1045

DEBUT	PEAK	WKS	Gold	A-side (Chart Hit)..B-side	Pop	$	Pic	Label & Number

★235★

NORMA JEAN '66
Born Norma Jean Beasler on 1/30/38 in Wellston, Oklahoma. Singer/guitarist. Regular on **Porter Wagoner**'s TV series from 1960-67.
1)The Game Of Triangles 2)Go Cat Go 3)I Wouldn't Buy A Used Car From Him 4)Let's Go All The Way
5)Heaven Help The Working Girl

DEBUT	PEAK	WKS		A-side	Pop	$		Label & Number
1/4/64	11	19		1 Let's Go All The Way.. *Private Little World*		$12		RCA Victor 8261
				also see #22 below				
6/20/64	25	16		2 Put Your Arms Around Her/				
5/30/64	32	11		3 I'm A Walkin' Advertisement (For The Blues)............................		$12		RCA Victor 8328
10/10/64	8	22		4 Go Cat Go *Lonesome Number One*	134	$12		RCA Victor 8433
4/10/65	21	8		5 I Cried All The Way To The Bank .... *You Have To Be Out Of Your Mind*		$12		RCA Victor 8518
7/31/65	8	14		6 I Wouldn't Buy A Used Car From Him *I'm No Longer In Your Heart*		$12		RCA Victor 8623
2/19/66	41	3		7 You're Driving Me Out Of My Mind/				
3/5/66	48	1		8 Then Go Home To Her..		$12		RCA Victor 8720
4/16/66	28	8		9 The Shirt .... *Please Don't Hurt Me*		$12		RCA Victor 8790
8/13/66	28	11		10 Pursuing Happiness............................. *It Wasn't God Who Made Honky Tonk Angels*		$12		RCA Victor 8887
10/15/66	5	17		11 The Game Of Triangles *Bye Bye, Love*		$10		RCA Victor 8963
				BOBBY BARE, NORMA JEAN, LIZ ANDERSON				
11/19/66+	24	13		12 Don't Let That Doorknob Hit You................... *Company's Comin'*		$10		RCA Victor 8989
4/1/67	48	10		13 Conscience Keep An Eye On Me .... *Still*		$10		RCA Victor 9147
8/19/67	38	10		14 Jackson Ain't A Very Big Town .... *Now It's Every Night*		$10		RCA Victor 9258
11/18/67+	18	14		15 Heaven Help The Working Girl............................. *Your Alibi Called Today*		$10		RCA Victor 9362
3/30/68	53	6		16 Truck Driving Woman .... *Supper Time*		$10		RCA Victor 9466
7/20/68	35	10		17 You Changed Everything About Me But My Name *A-11*		$10		RCA Victor 9558
11/30/68	61	5		18 One Man Band .... *I Can't Leave Him*		$10		RCA Victor 9645
4/12/69	44	8		19 Dusty Road... *Love's A Woman's Job*		$8		RCA Victor 0115
10/10/70	48	9		20 Whiskey-Six Years Old................................... *I'm Givin' Up*		$8		RCA Victor 9900
1/30/71	42	9		21 The Kind Of Needin' I Need ....*A Little Unfair*		$8		RCA Victor 9946
2/6/82	68	6		22 Let's Go All The Way ....*We Climbed A Mountain Last Night* [R]		$7		Granny White 10009
				CLAUDE GRAY and NORMA JEAN				
				new version of #1 above				

NORMAN, Jim '78

11/18/78	98	2		The Love In Me .... *Love Makes The World Go Square*		$5		Republic 030

NORWOOD, Daron '94
Born on 9/30/65 in Lubbock, Texas; raised in Tahoka, Texas. Singer/pianist.

11/27/93+	26	20		1 If It Wasn't For Her I Wouldn't Have You........ *A Little Bigger Piece Of American Pie*		$3	▌	Giant 18386
4/16/94	24	19		2 Cowboys Don't Cry .... *J.T. Miller's Farm*		$3	▌	Giant 18216
8/6/94	48	9		3 If I Ever Love Again				album cut
				from the album *Daron Norwood* on Giant 24527				
12/31/94	75	1		4 The Working Elf Blues .... *Rockin' Little Christmas* [X]		$3		Giant 18006
2/4/95	50	9		5 Bad Dog, No Biscuit.............................. *There'll Always Be A Honky Tonk Somewhere*		$3	▌	Giant 17958
6/3/95	58	9		6 My Girl Friday...*Break The Radio*		$3	▌	Giant 17881

NUNLEY, Bill '88

4/2/88	74	3		1 I'll Know The Good Times .... *That's How Long I'll Wait For You*		$6		Cannery 0402
				COUNTRY BILL NUNLEY				
8/27/88	98	2		2 The Way You Got Over Me		$6		Cannery 0525

NUNN, Earl '49

4/9/49	13	1		Double Talkin' Woman .... *J:13 I've Loved You Too Long To Forget You*		$30		Specialty 701
				EARL NUNN and His Alabama Ramblers Featuring Billy Lee				

NUTTER, Mayf '71
Born Mayfred Nutter Adamson on 10/19/41 in Jane Lew, West Virginia. Male singer/guitarist/actor.

2/14/70	65	5		1 Hey There Johnny .... *My Kind Of Music*		$6		Reprise 0882
				MAYF NUTTER with the Hugh Jarrett Singers				
10/16/71	57	6		2 Never Ending Song Of Love *Okla.*		$6		Capitol 3181
				#13 Pop hit for Delaney & Bonnie & Friends in 1971				
12/18/71+	58	7		3 Never Had A Doubt.............................. *The Litterbug Song*		$6		Capitol 3226
4/15/72	59	7		4 The Sing-Along Song .... *I Better Let You Be*		$6		Capitol 3296
10/27/73	78	10		5 Green Door .... *One More Lie*		$6		Capitol 3734
				#1 Pop hit for Jim Lowe in 1956				
5/8/76	87	5		6 Sweet Southern Lovin' ....*Hitch Hike Nightmare*		$5		GNP Crescendo 805
1/15/77	99	2		7 Goin' Skinny Dippin' ....*(Take Me Home) Country Roads* [N]		$5		GNP Crescendo 809

O

OAK RIDGE BOYS ★44★   '85
Vocal group formed in 1972: Duane Allen (lead), Joe Bonsall (tenor), **William Lee Golden** (baritone) and Richard Sterban (bass). All had previously sung in gospel groups. Steve Sanders replaced Golden from 1987 until Golden returned in 1996. Sanders died of a self-inflicted gunshot wound on 6/10/98 (age 45). CMA Award: 1978 Vocal Group of the Year.

    1)No Matter How High   2)Bobbie Sue   3)Leaving Louisiana In The Broad Daylight   4)It Takes A Little Rain
    5)Make My Life With You

DEBUT	PEAK	WKS		A-side / B-side	Pop	$	Pic	Label & Number
8/4/73	57	7	1	**Praise The Lord And Pass The Soup** .... *The Ballad Of Barbara*		$7		Columbia 45890
				JOHNNY CASH (With The Carter Family And The Oak Ridge Boys)				
6/26/76	83	5	2	**Family Reunion** .... *Don't Be Late*		$6		Columbia 10349
7/16/77	3	18	3	**Y'All Come Back Saloon** .... *Emmylou*		$5		ABC/Dot 17710
12/3/77+	2²	16	4	**You're The One** .... *Morning Glory Do*		$5		ABC/Dot 17732
4/15/78	❶¹	15	5	**I'll Be True To You** .... *An Old Time Family Bluegrass Band*	102	$5		ABC 12350
9/2/78	3	13	6	**Cryin' Again** .... *I Can Love You*	107	$5		ABC 12397
12/9/78+	3	15	7	**Come On In** .... *Morning Glory Do*		$5		ABC 12434
4/7/79	2²	13	8	**Sail Away** .... *The Only One*		$5		MCA 12463
6/23/79	94	1	9	**Rhythm Guitar** .... *All Our Favorite Songs*		$5		Columbia 11009
				recorded in 1975				
8/18/79	7	13	10	**Dream On** .... *Sometimes The Rain Won't Let Me Sleep*		$4		MCA 41078
				#32 Pop hit for The Righteous Brothers in 1974				
12/1/79+	❶¹	15	11	**Leaving Louisiana In The Broad Daylight** .... *I Gotta Get Over This*		$4		MCA 41154
4/19/80	❶¹	15	12	**Trying To Love Two Women** .... *Hold On Til Sunday*		$4	■	MCA 41217
7/19/80	3	16	13	**Heart Of Mine** .... *Love Takes Two*	105	$4		MCA 41280
11/15/80+	3	17	14	**Beautiful You** .... *Ready To Take My Chances*		$4		MCA 51022
4/4/81	❶¹	14	▲ 15	**Elvira** .... *A Woman Like You*	5	$4		MCA 51084
				#72 Pop hit for **Dallas Frazier** in 1966; CMA Award: Single of the Year				
9/5/81	❶¹	15	16	**Fancy Free** .... *How Long Has It Been*	104	$4		MCA 51169
1/23/82	❶¹	15	17	**Bobbie Sue** .... *Live In Love*	12	$4		MCA 51231
6/5/82	22	10	18	**So Fine** .... *I Wish You Were Here (Oh My Darlin')*	76	$4		MCA 52065
7/31/82	2²	19	19	**I Wish You Could Have Turned My Head (And Left My Heart**				
				Alone) .... *Back In Your Arms Again*		$4		MCA 52095
11/20/82+	3	16	20	**Thank God For Kids** .... *Christmas Is Paintin' The Town*		$4		MCA 52145
2/26/83	❶¹	16	21	**American Made** .... *The Cure For My Broken Heart*	72	$4		MCA 52179
6/4/83	❶¹	18	22	**Love Song** .... *Heart On The Line (Operator, Operator)*		$4		MCA 52224
10/22/83+	5	19	23	**Ozark Mountain Jubilee** .... *Down Deep Inside*		$4		MCA 52288
2/25/84	❶¹	22	24	**I Guess It Never Hurts To Hurt Sometimes** .... *Through My Eyes*		$4		MCA 52342
7/14/84	❶¹	21	25	**Everyday** .... S:27 *Ain't No Cure For The Rock And Roll*		$4	❑	MCA 52419
11/10/84+	❶¹	21	26	**Make My Life With You** .... S:❶¹ / A:❶¹ *Break My Mind*		$4	■	MCA 52488
3/30/85	❶¹	20	27	**Little Things** .... S:❶¹ / A:❶¹ *The Secret Of Love*		$4	■	MCA 52556
8/3/85	❶¹	21	28	**Touch A Hand, Make A Friend** .... S:❶¹ / A:❶¹ *Only One I Love*		$4		MCA 52646
				#23 Pop hit for The Staple Singers in 1974				
11/23/85+	3	19	29	**Come On In (You Did The Best You Could Do)** S:3 / A:3 *Roll Tennessee River*		$4	■	MCA 52722
3/22/86	15	15	30	**Juliet** .... S:14 / A:15 *Everybody Wins*		$4		MCA 52801
3/29/86	20	14	31	**When You Get To The Heart** .... A:20 / S:21 *Survivors*		$4		MCA 52802
				BARBARA MANDRELL with the Oak Ridge Boys				
7/12/86	24	15	32	**You Made A Rock Of A Rolling Stone** .... A:24 *Hidin' Place*		$4		MCA 52873
2/21/87	❶¹	24	33	**It Takes A Little Rain (To Make Love Grow)** A:3 / S:6 *Looking For Love*		$3		MCA 53010
6/13/87	❶¹	23	34	**This Crazy Love** .... S:11 *Where The Fast Lane Ends*		$3		MCA 53023
10/10/87	17	15	35	**Time In** .... *A Little More Coal On The Fire*		$3		MCA 53175
2/27/88	5	22	36	**True Heart** .... S:20 *Love Without Mercy*		$3		MCA 53272
7/30/88	❶¹	21	37	**Gonna Take A Lot Of River** .... S:❶¹ *Private Lives*		$3		MCA 53381
12/3/88+	10	20	38	**Bridges And Walls** .... *Never Together (But Close Sometimes)*		$3		MCA 53460
4/1/89	7	22	39	**Beyond Those Years** .... *Too Many Heartaches*		$3		MCA 53625
8/19/89	4	25	40	**An American Family** .... *Too Many Heartaches*		$3		MCA 53705
12/16/89+	❶¹	26	41	**No Matter How High** .... *Bed Of Roses*		$3		MCA 53757
5/19/90	71	3	42	**Baby, You'll Be My Baby** .... *Cajun Girl*		$3		MCA 79006
12/1/90+	31	15	43	**(You're My) Soul And Inspiration** .... *(same version)*		$3		MCA 79103
				#1 Pop hit for The Righteous Brothers in 1966; from the movie *My Heroes Have Always Been Cowboys* starring Scott Glenn				
3/23/91	6	20	44	**Lucky Moon** .... *Walkin' After Midnight*		$3		RCA 2779
8/10/91	70	5	45	**Change My Mind** .... *Our Love Is Here To Stay*		$3		RCA 62013
10/5/91	44	13	46	**Baby On Board** .... *When It Comes To You*		$3		RCA 62099
6/27/92	69	4	47	**Fall** .... *Until You're Back In My Arms Again*		$3		RCA 62228

O'BRIEN, Tim — see MATTEA, Kathy

O'CONNOR, Mark   '91
Born on 8/5/61 in Seattle. Fiddle player. Member of rock group The Dregs in early '80s. CMA Awards: 1991, 1992, 1993, 1994, 1995 & 1996 Musician of the Year.

3/30/91	25	20		1 **Restless** .... *Dance Of The Ol' Swamp Rat*		$3		Warner 19354
				Vince Gill, Ricky Skaggs and Steve Wariner (guest vocals)				
8/3/91	71	3		2 **Now It Belongs To You**				album cut
				Steve Wariner (guest vocal); from the album *New Nashville Cats* on Warner 26509				
12/25/93+	54	10		3 **The Devil Comes Back To Georgia** .... *Diggy Liggy Lo*		$3		Warner 18342
				MARK O'CONNOR With Charlie Daniels				
				Johnny Cash, Marty Stuart and Travis Tritt (guest vocals)				

O'DAY, Tommy   '78
Born in Fresno, California.

1/28/78	96	3		1 **Mr. Sandman** .... *Winter Winds Of Love*		$6		Nu-Trayl 916
				#1 Pop hit for The Chordettes in 1954				
4/8/78	82	4		2 **Memories Are Made Of This** *Up & Over Your Love*		$6		Nu-Trayl 919
				#1 Pop hit for Dean Martin in 1956				
8/12/78	97	2		3 **When A Woman Cries** .... *Round And Round*		$6		Nu-Trayl 923
12/23/78+	93	4		4 **I Heard A Song Today** .... *Today's Woman*		$6		Nu-Trayl 926
5/5/79	89	2		5 **Accentuate The Positive** .... *Blue River*		$6		Nu-Trayl 929
				#1 Pop hit for Johnny Mercer in 1945				
7/14/79	99	2		6 **Your Other Love** .... *Painted Tainted Rose*		$6		Nu-Trayl 930
				#54 Pop hit for The Flamingos in 1961				

O'DELL, Doye   '48
Born Allen Doye O'Dell on 11/22/12 in Plainview, Texas.

7/24/48	12	3		**Dear Oakie** ....*J:12 / S:13 Lookin' Poor, But Feelin' Rich*		$20		Exclusive 33

O'DELL, Kenny   '78
Born Kenneth Gist in 1942 in Oklahoma. Singer/songwriter/guitarist.

3/9/74	58	10		1 **You Bet Your Sweet, Sweet Love** .... *Let's Go Find Some Country Music*		$5		Capricorn 0038
1/18/75	18	13		2 **Soulful Woman** .... *Let's Get On The Road*		$5		Capricorn 0219
5/31/75	37	10		3 **My Honky Tonk Ways** .... *Behind Closed Doors*	105	$5		Capricorn 0233
7/8/78	9	14		4 **Let's Shake Hands And Come Out Lovin'** *We Might Be All Nite*		$5		Capricorn 0301
11/4/78+	12	15		5 **As Long As I Can Wake Up In Your Arms** ....*Soulful Woman*		$5		Capricorn 0309
3/10/79	32	10		6 **Medicine Woman** .... *Who Do I Know In Denver*		$5		Capricorn 0317

ODESSA   '89

4/8/89	89	2		**Hooked On You**		$6		Sing Me 40

ODOM, Donna   '68
Born on 8/14/44 in Ebbwvale, South Wales.

1/20/68	65	5		**She Gets The Roses (I Get The Tears)** ....*I'm A Woman*		$7		Decca 32214

O'DONNAL, Karen — see DUDLEY, Dave

O'DOSKI, Gail   '88
Born in Bartow, Florida. Male singer.

12/26/87+	73	4		1 **First Came The Feelin'**		$5		Door Knob 288
5/28/88	77	4		2 **(Just An) Old Wives' Tale**		$5		Door Knob 300

O'GWYNN, James   '62
Born on 1/26/28 in Winchester, Mississippi; raised in Hattiesburg, Mississippi. Singer/songwriter. Known as "The Smilin' Irishman."

10/20/58	16	3		1 **Talk To Me Lonesome Heart** ....*Changeable*		$30		D 1006
12/29/58	28	3		2 **Blue Memories** ....*You Don't Want To Hold Me*		$30		D 1022
4/27/59	13	4		3 **How Can I Think Of Tomorrow** ....*Were You Ever A Stranger*		$15		Mercury 71419
12/21/59+	26	4		4 **Easy Money** ....*Tears Of Tomorrow*		$15		Mercury 71513
2/20/61	21	6		5 **House Of Blue Lovers** ....*Another Falling Tear*		$15		Mercury 71731
4/21/62	7	10		6 **My Name Is Mud** *You're Getting All Over Me*		$15		Mercury 71935

★368★ O'KANES, The   '87
Duo of Jamie O'Hara (b: 8/8/50 in Toledo, Ohio) and Kieran Kane (b: 10/7/49 in Queens, New York).

9/20/86	10	25		1 **Oh Darlin'** *S:6 / A:11 When I Found You*		$3	■	Columbia 06242
2/7/87	❶¹	22		2 **Can't Stop My Heart From Loving You** *S:2 / A:2 Bluegrass Blues*		$3	■	Columbia 06606
6/27/87	9	18		3 **Daddies Need To Grow Up Too** *S:7 Oh Darlin'*		$3		Columbia 07187
10/17/87+	5	25		4 **Just Lovin' You** *S:2 When We're Gone, Long Gone*		$3		Columbia 07611
3/5/88	4	20		5 **One True Love** *S:3 If I Could Be There*		$3		Columbia 07736
7/9/88	10	20		6 **Blue Love** *S:2 Highway 55*		$3		Columbia 07943
11/12/88	71	5		7 **Rocky Road** ....*All Because Of You*		$3		Columbia 08099

O'KEEFE, Danny   '72
Born in Spokane, Washington. Singer/songwriter.

10/28/72	63	6		**Good Time Charlie's Got The Blues** ....*The Valentine Pieces*	9	$6		Signpost 70006

O'NEAL, Austin   '83

8/27/83	93	2		**Nights Like Tonight**		$7		Project One 002

O'NEAL, Coleman   '63
Singer/songwriter from Philadelphia.

1/5/63	8	16		**Mr. Heartache, Move On** *Make Him Know*		$12		Chancellor 108

DEBUT	PEAK	WKS	Gold	A-side (Chart Hit)..B-side	Pop	$	Pic	Label & Number

ORBISON, Roy '89
Born on 4/23/36 in Vernon, Texas. Died of a heart attack on 12/6/88 (age 52). Singer/songwriter/guitarist. Charted 32 pop hits from 1956-92. Inducted into the Rock and Roll Hall of Fame in 1987.

DEBUT	PEAK	WKS	A-side	Pop	$	Pic	Label & Number
6/28/80	6	15	1 That Lovin' You Feelin' Again............................Lola	55	$4		Warner 49262

ROY ORBISON & EMMYLOU HARRIS
from the movie *Roadie* starring Meat Loaf

10/10/87	75	4	2 In Dreams..Leah		$4	■	Virgin 99434

new version of his #7 Pop hit from 1963; from the movie *Blue Velvet* starring Kyle McLachlan

12/5/87+	42	13	3 Crying..Falling		$3	■	Virgin 99388

ROY ORBISON/k.d. lang
new version of his #2 Pop hit from 1961; from the movie *Hiding Out* starring Jon Cryer

2/4/89	7	20	4 You Got It..Crying	9	$3	■	Virgin 99245
6/24/89	51	13	5 California Blue..In Dreams		$3	■	Virgin 99202
12/23/89	89	4	6 Oh Pretty Woman..Claudette		$3	■	Virgin 99159

recorded "live" in September 1987 at the Coconut Grove in Los Angeles; new version of his #1 Pop hit from 1964

ORDGE, Jimmy Arthur '81
Born in Donalda, Alberta, Canada.

7/11/81	89	3	Stay Away From Jim..Hard Times		$6		Dore 969

ORENDER, DeWayne '78

11/27/76	53	9	1 If You Want To Make Me Feel At Home.........Don't Let Any Of Her Love Get On You		$5		RCA 10813
4/23/77	87	3	2 To Make A Good Love Die............................I Can't Keep My Eyes Off Her		$5		RCA 10936
8/27/77	97	2	3 Love Me Into Heaven Again............................If You're Gonna Love		$5		RCA 11039
5/6/78	51	7	4 Brother..Standing In The Rain		$6		Nu-Trayl 920
12/23/78+	92	4	5 Better Than Now..		$6		Volunteer 102

ORIGINAL TEXAS PLAYBOYS '77
Veterans of Bob Wills's longtime band: **Leon Rausch** (vocals), Bob Kizer (guitar), **Leon McAuliffe** (steel guitar), Rudy Martin (clarinet), Jack Stidham and Bob Boatwright (fiddles), Al Stricklin (piano), Joe Ferguson (bass) and Smokey Dacus (drums).

4/2/77	94	3	Gambling Polka Dot Blues............................Osage Stomp		$5		Capitol 4401

written by **Jimmie Rodgers**

ORION '81
Born Jimmy Ellis in 1945 in Orrville, Alabama. Based his masked character on the novel *Orion* by Gail Brewer-Giorgio. Many people speculated that it was actually **Elvis Presley** under the mask. Also see **Jerry Lee Lewis**.
1)Rockabilly Rebel 2)Am I That Easy To Forget 3)Texas Tea

6/23/79	89	6	1 Ebony Eyes/				
		6	2 Honey		$5		Sun 1142
4/26/80	69	5	3 A Stranger In My Place............................It Ain't No Mystery		$5		Sun 1152
7/19/80	68	6	4 Texas Tea..Faded Love		$5		Sun 1153
10/11/80	65	9	5 Am I That Easy To Forget............................Crazy Arms		$5		Sun 1156

#18 Pop hit for **Engelbert Humperdinck** in 1968

1/10/81	63	6	6 Rockabilly Rebel..Memphis Sun		$5		Sun 1159
3/21/81	79	4	7 Crazy Little Thing Called Love............................Matchbox		$5		Sun 1162

#1 Pop hit for Queen in 1980

6/27/81	76	5	8 Born..If I Can't Have You		$5		Sun 1165
12/12/81	83	4	9 Some You Win, Some You Lose............................Ain't No Good		$5		Sun 1170
7/10/82	69	6	10 Morning, Noon And Night/				
7/10/82	70	4	11 Honky Tonk Heaven..		$5		Sun 1175

ORLEANS '86
Pop-rock group from New York City: brothers Lawrence (vocals, guitar) and Lance (bass) Hoppen, Bob Leinback (keyboards), R.A. Martin (horns) and Wells Kelly (drums). Charted 5 pop hits from 1975-79.

11/15/86	59	6	You're Mine..Language Of Love		$3		MCA 52963

ORRALL, Robert Ellis '93
Born on 5/4/55 in Winthrop, Massachusetts. Singer/songwriter.

11/14/92+	19	20	1 Boom! It Was Over..Flying Colors		$3		RCA 62335
3/20/93	31	20	2 A Little Bit Of Her Love............................'Til The Tears Fell		$3		RCA 62475
7/24/93	64	5	3 Every Day When I Get Home............................True Believer		$3		RCA 62547

ORRALL & WRIGHT '94
Duo of Robert Ellis Orrall and Curtis Wright.

7/2/94	47	11	1 She Loves Me Like She Means It............................You Saved Me		$3	▮	Giant 18162
10/15/94	70	2	2 If You Could Say What I'm Thinking............................Pound, Pound, Pound		$3	▮	Giant 18049

ORTEGA, Gilbert '78
Born in Gallup, New Mexico.

1/28/78	91	3	1 Is It Wrong..Is This All There Is To A Honky Tonk		$7		LRJ 1050
5/20/78	93	4	2 I Don't Believe I'll Fall In Love Today............................Send Me The Pillow		$7		Ortega 1051

ORVILLE AND IVY '67
Duo of prolific session guitarists Wesley Webb "Speedy" West (b: 1/25/24 in Springfield, Missouri) and Ivy "Jimmy" Bryant (b: 3/5/25 in Moultrie, Georgia; d: 9/22/80).

4/1/67	73	2	Shinbone..Tabasco Road [I]		$8		Imperial 66219

OSBORNE, Jimmie '49
Born on 4/8/23 in Winchester, Kentucky. Committed suicide on 12/26/57 (age 34). Singer/songwriter/guitarist.

7/10/48	10	2	1 My Heart Echoes............................J:10 Your Lies Have Broken My Heart		$20		King 715
6/25/49	7	6	2 The Death Of Little Kathy Fiscus............................S:7 A Bundle Of Kisses		$20		King 788
10/7/50	9	3	3 God Please Protect America............................A:9 The Moon Is Weeping Over You		$20		King 893

OSBORNE BROTHERS '58

Bluegrass duo of brothers from Hyden, Kentucky: Bobby (b: 12/7/31; mandolin) and Sonny (b: 10/29/37; banjo) Osborne. Joined the *Grand Ole Opry* in 1964. CMA Award: 1971 Vocal Group of the Year.
1)Once More 2)Tennessee Hound Dog 3)Rocky Top

★346★

DEBUT	PEAK	WKS	Gold	A-side / B-side	Pop	$	Pic	Label & Number
3/24/58	13	2		1 Once More .... A:13 *She's No Angel*		$15		MGM 12583

THE OSBORNE BROTHERS And RED ALLEN

DEBUT	PEAK	WKS	Gold	A-side / B-side	Pop	$	Pic	Label & Number
3/12/66	41	4		2 Up This Hill And Down .... *Memories*		$8		Decca 31886
12/17/66+	33	10		3 The Kind Of Woman I Got .... *One Tear*		$8		Decca 32052
7/22/67	66	3		4 Roll Muddy River .... *Making Plans*		$8		Decca 32137
2/3/68	33	10		5 Rocky Top .... *My Favorite Memory*		$8		Decca 32242
6/15/68	60	7		6 Cut The Cornbread, Mama .... *If I Could Count On You*		$8		Decca 32325
10/19/68	58	6		7 Son Of A Sawmill Man .... *That Was Yesterday*		$8		Decca 32382
8/9/69	28	11		8 Tennessee Hound Dog .... *Thanks For All The Yesterdays*		$8		Decca 32516
1/17/70	58	6		9 Ruby, Are You Mad .... *Sempre*		$8		Decca 32598
12/5/70	69	2		10 My Old Kentucky Home (Turpentine And Dandelion Wine) . *No Good Son Of A Gun*		$8		Decca 32746
3/13/71	37	10		11 Georgia Pineywoods .... *Searching For Yesterday*		$8		Decca 32794
9/11/71	62	7		12 Muddy Bottom .... *Beneath Still Waters*		$8		Decca 32864
1/6/73	74	2		13 Midnight Flyer .... *Teardrops Will Kiss The Morning Dew*		$8		Decca 33028
4/28/73	66	2		14 Lizzie Lou .... *Tears*		$6		MCA 40028
9/1/73	64	6		15 Blue Heartache .... *You're Heavy On My Mind*		$6		MCA 40113
1/31/76	86	4		16 Don't Let Smokey Mountain Smoke Get In Your Eyes ....*A Born Ramblin' Man*		$6		MCA 40509
10/13/79	95	3		17 Shackles And Chains .... *Midnight Flyer*		$6		CMH 1522

OSBORNE BROS. & MAC WISEMAN

DEBUT	PEAK	WKS	Gold	A-side / B-side	Pop	$	Pic	Label & Number
4/26/80	75	5		18 I Can Hear Kentucky Calling Me .... *Shawnee*		$6		CMH 1524

O'SHEA, Cathy '78

Born Catherine Herbsleb on 7/20/41 in Kansas City, Missouri.

DEBUT	PEAK	WKS	Gold	A-side / B-side	Pop	$	Pic	Label & Number
8/26/78	94	4		Roses Ain't Red .... *Love Is Just A Bar Stool Away*		$4		MCA 40934

O'SHEA, Shad '76

Former president of Fraternity Records.

DEBUT	PEAK	WKS	Gold	A-side / B-side	Pop	$	Pic	Label & Number
3/27/76	85	3		Colorado Call .... *Bub-Bub-Bub-Boo* [N]	110	$5		Private Stock 45,071

SHAD O'SHEA & THE 18 WHEELERS

OSLIN, K.T. '90

★232★

Born Kay Toinette Oslin on 5/15/41 in Crossett, Arkansas; raised in Mobile, Alabama. Singer/songwriter/pianist/actress. Acted in the touring musicals *Hello Dolly*, *West Side Story* and *Promises Promises*. CMA Award: 1988 Female Vocalist of the Year. Also see **Alabama**.
1)Come Next Monday 2)Do Ya' 3)Hold Me

DEBUT	PEAK	WKS	Gold	A-side / B-side	Pop	$	Pic	Label & Number
5/16/81	72	4		1 Clean Your Own Tables .... *Nelda Jean Prudy*		$4		Elektra 47132

KAY T. OSLIN

DEBUT	PEAK	WKS	Gold	A-side / B-side	Pop	$	Pic	Label & Number
1/10/87	40	15		2 Wall Of Tears .... *Two Hearts Are Better Than One*		$3	■	RCA 5066
4/25/87	7	21		3 80's Ladies .... S:13 *Old Pictures*		$3	■	RCA 5154
9/12/87	❶¹	25		4 Do Ya' .... S:❶¹ *Lonely But Only For You*		$3		RCA 5239
1/30/88	❶¹	21		5 I'll Always Come Back .... S:3 *Old Pictures*		$3		RCA 5330
7/9/88	13	15		6 Money .... S:12 *Dr., Dr.*		$3		RCA 8388
10/15/88+	❶¹	20		7 Hold Me .... S:❶² *She Don't Talk Like Us No More*		$3		RCA 8725
2/11/89	2¹	19		8 Hey Bobby .... *Where Is A Woman To Go*		$3		RCA 8865
6/10/89	5	18		9 This Woman .... *Younger Men*		$3		RCA 8943
10/21/89	23	13		10 Didn't Expect It To Go Down This Way .... *Round The Clock Lovin'*		$3		RCA 9029
7/7/90	73	3		11 Two Hearts .... *Jealous*		$3		RCA 2567
9/29/90	❶²	20		12 Come Next Monday .... *Truly Blue*		$3		RCA 2667
2/16/91	28	13		13 Mary And Willie .... *Love Is Strange*		$3		RCA 2746
7/6/91	69	2		14 You Call Everybody Darling .... *Still On My Mind*		$3		RCA 2829
9/14/91	63	3		15 Cornell Crawford .... *Two Hearts*		$3		RCA 62053
5/1/93	64	3		16 New Way Home .... *You Gave Me A Heart Attack*		$3	■	RCA 62499
8/31/96	64	5		17 Silver Tongue And Goldplated Lies .... *Miss The Mississippi And You*		$3	■	BNA 64600

OSMOND, Donny And Marie '74

Brother-and-sister vocal duo from Ogden, Utah: Donny (b: 12/9/57) and **Marie Osmond**. Co-hosted of own musical/variety TV series from 1976-78. Starred in the movie *Goin' Coconuts*.

DEBUT	PEAK	WKS	Gold	A-side / B-side	Pop	$	Pic	Label & Number
7/27/74	17	13	●	1 I'm Leaving It (All) Up To You .... *The Umbrella Song*	4	$5		MGM/Kolob 14735

#1 Pop hit for Dale & Grace in 1963

DEBUT	PEAK	WKS	Gold	A-side / B-side	Pop	$	Pic	Label & Number
6/21/75	71	6		2 Make The World Go Away .... *Living On My Suspicion*	44	$5		MGM/Kolob 14807

OSMOND, Marie '86

★219★

Born Olive Marie Osmond on 10/13/59 in Ogden, Utah. Sister of **The Osmond Brothers**. Co-hosted TV series *Donny & Marie* from 1976-78. Hosted own TV series from 1980-81. Co-hosted TV's *Ripley's Believe It Or Not* from 1985-86. Starred in the 1995 TV series *Maybe This Time*. CMA Award: 1986 Vocal Duo of the Year (with **Dan Seals**).
1)Paper Roses 2)There's No Stopping Your Heart 3)Meet Me In Montana 4)You're Still New To Me 5)Read My Lips

DEBUT	PEAK	WKS	Gold	A-side / B-side	Pop	$	Pic	Label & Number
9/8/73	❶²	16	●	1 Paper Roses .... *Least Of All You*	5	$5		MGM/Kolob 14609

#5 Pop hit for Anita Bryant in 1960

DEBUT	PEAK	WKS	Gold	A-side / B-side	Pop	$	Pic	Label & Number
8/10/74	33	11		2 In My Little Corner Of The World .... *It's Just The Other Way Around*	102	$5		MGM/Kolob 14694

#10 Pop hit for Anita Bryant in 1960

DEBUT	PEAK	WKS	Gold	A-side / B-side	Pop	$	Pic	Label & Number
3/1/75	29	10		3 Who's Sorry Now .... *This I Promise You*	40	$5		MGM/Kolob 14786

#4 Pop hit for Connie Francis in 1958

DEBUT	PEAK	WKS	Gold	A-side / B-side	Pop	$	Pic	Label & Number
8/7/76	85	4		4 "A" My Name Is Alice .... *Weeping Willow*		$5		Polydor 14333
3/20/82	74	6		5 I've Got A Bad Case Of You .... *You Still Get The Best Of Me*		$4		Elektra/Curb 47430
8/14/82	58	7		6 Back To Believing Again .... *Look Who's Gettin' Over Who*		$4		Elektra/Curb 69995
3/24/84	82	4		7 Who's Counting .... *'Til The Best Comes Along*		$4		RCA/Curb 13680

OSMOND, Marie — Cont'd

DEBUT	PEAK	WKS	A-side	B-side	$	Pic	Label & Number
2/9/85	54	8	8 Until I Fall In Love Again	I Don't Want To Go Too Far	$3		Curb/Capitol 5445
7/6/85	❶¹	23	9 Meet Me In Montana S:❶¹/A:❶¹	What Do Lonely People Do	$3	■	Curb/Capitol 5478

MARIE OSMOND (With Dan Seals)

DEBUT	PEAK	WKS	A-side	B-side	$	Pic	Label & Number
11/9/85+	❶¹	21	10 There's No Stopping Your Heart S:❶¹/A:❶¹	Blue Sky Shinin'	$3	■	Curb/Capitol 5521
3/29/86	4	21	11 Read My Lips S:4/A:4	That Old Devil Moon	$3	■	Curb/Capitol 5563
8/30/86	❶¹	21	12 You're Still New To Me S:❶¹/A:❶¹	New Love	$3	■	Curb/Capitol 5613

MARIE OSMOND WITH PAUL DAVIS

DEBUT	PEAK	WKS	A-side	B-side	$	Pic	Label & Number
12/27/86+	14	18	13 I Only Wanted You S:3/A:14	We're Gonna Need A Love Song	$3	■	Curb/Capitol 5663
4/11/87	24	13	14 Everybody's Crazy 'Bout My Baby S:29	Making Magic	$3		Curb/Capitol 5703
7/25/87	50	12	15 Cry Just A Little	More Than Dancing	$3		Curb/Capitol 44044
5/28/88	50	10	16 Without A Trace	Baby's Blue Eyes	$3	■	Curb/Capitol 44176
8/20/88	47	8	17 Sweet Life	Somebody Else's Moon	$3		Curb/Capitol 44215

MARIE OSMOND (with Paul Davis)

DEBUT	PEAK	WKS	A-side	B-side	$	Pic	Label & Number
12/17/88+	59	8	18 I'm In Love And He's In Dallas	My Hometown Boy	$3		Curb/Capitol 44269
8/26/89	70	5	19 Steppin' Stone	What Would You Do About Me If You Were Me	$3		Curb/Capitol 44412
11/18/89	75	4	20 Slowly But Surely	What Would You Do About You	$3		Curb/Capitol 44468
10/13/90	57	10	21 Like A Hurricane	I'll Be Faithful To You	$3		Curb 76840
2/11/95	75	1	22 What Kind Of Man (Walks On A Woman)	(album snippets)	$3	▌	Curb 76943

OSMOND BROTHERS, The   '82

Family vocal group from Ogden, Utah: Alan, Wayne, Merrill and Jay Osmond. Brothers of **Donny And Marie Osmond**. Charted 13 pop hits from 1971-76. Also see **Merrill And Jessica**.

1)I Think About Your Lovin' 2)It's Like Falling In Love 3)If Every Man Had A Woman Like You

THE OSMONDS:

DEBUT	PEAK	WKS	A-side	B-side	$	Pic	Label & Number
5/1/82	17	15	1 I Think About Your Lovin'	Working Man's Blues	$4		Elektra/Curb 47438

THE OSMOND BROTHERS:

DEBUT	PEAK	WKS	A-side	B-side	$	Pic	Label & Number
9/4/82	28	12	2 It's Like Falling In Love (Over And Over)	Your Leaving Was The Last Thing On My Mind	$4		Elektra/Curb 69969
12/25/82+	43	10	3 Never Ending Song Of Love	You'll Be Seeing Me	$4		Elektra/Curb 69883
			#13 Pop hit for Delaney & Bonnie in 1971				
6/11/83	67	8	4 She's Ready For Someone To Love Her	You Make The Long Road Shorter	$4		Warner/Curb 29594
1/21/84	43	11	5 Where Does An Angel Go When She Cries	One More For Lovers	$4		Warner/Curb 29387
5/5/84	39	12	6 If Every Man Had A Woman Like You	Come Back To Me	$4		Warner/Curb 29312
6/8/85	54	9	7 Any Time	Desperately	$4		Warner/Curb 28982

THE OSMOND BROS.:

DEBUT	PEAK	WKS	A-side	B-side	$	Pic	Label & Number
12/14/85+	56	11	8 Baby When Your Heart Breaks Down	Love Burning Down	$3		Curb/EMI Amer. 8298
3/15/86	45	13	9 Baby Wants	Lovin' Proof	$3		EMI America 8313
6/21/86	69	5	10 You Look Like The One I Love	It's Only A Heartache	$3		EMI America 8325
11/1/86	70	7	11 Looking For Suzanne	Back In Your Arms	$3		EMI America 8360

OTT, Paul   '79

Born Paul Ott Carruth on 9/25/34 in McComb, Mississippi. Cousin of baseball player Mel Ott.

DEBUT	PEAK	WKS	A-side	B-side	$	Pic	Label & Number
6/30/79	87	2	A Salute To The Duke	Listen To The Eagle [S]	$5		Elektra 46066
			tribute to John Wayne				

★226★ OVERSTREET, Paul   '91

Born on 3/17/55 in Newton, Mississippi. Singer/songwriter/guitarist. Member of **Schuyler, Knobloch & Overstreet**. Formerly married to Freida Parton (sister of **Dolly Parton**). No relation to Tommy Overstreet.

1)Daddy's Come Around 2)I Won't Take Less Than Your Love 3)Seein' My Father In Me

DEBUT	PEAK	WKS	A-side	B-side	$	Pic	Label & Number
5/8/82	76	5	1 Beautiful Baby	Feels Good	$4		RCA 13042
11/21/87+	❶¹	24	2 I Won't Take Less Than Your Love S:2	Heartbreaker	$3		Capitol 44100
			TANYA TUCKER with PAUL DAVIS & PAUL OVERSTREET				
9/24/88	3	21	3 Love Helps Those S:7	What God Has Joined Together	$3		MTM 72113
4/8/89	9	21	4 Sowin' Love	Love Helps Those	$3		RCA 8919
8/26/89	5	26	5 All The Fun	Homemaker	$3		RCA 9015
1/6/90	2¹	26	6 Seein' My Father In Me	Love Never Sleeps	$3		RCA 9116
5/19/90	3	21	7 Richest Man On Earth	Neath The Light Of Your Love	$3		RCA 2505
11/24/90+	❶¹	20	8 Daddy's Come Around	The Calm At The Center Of My Storm	$3		RCA 2707
3/16/91	4	20	9 Heroes	Straight And Narrow	$3		RCA 2780
7/20/91	5	20	10 Ball And Chain	Love Lives On	$3		RCA 62012
11/23/91+	30	18	11 If I Could Bottle This Up	'Til The Mountains Disappear	$3		RCA 62106
3/14/92	57	9	12 Billy Can't Read	She Supports Her Man	$3		RCA 62193
7/11/92	22	19	13 Me And My Baby	Lord She Sure Is Good At Loving Me	$3		RCA 62254
11/7/92	57	11	14 Still Out There Swinging	Till The Answer Comes (Gotta Keep Praying)	$3		RCA 62361
4/3/93	60	7	15 Take Another Run	Take Some Action	$3		RCA 62473
1/20/96	73	2	16 We've Got To Keep On Meeting Like This		$3		album cut
			from the album *Time* on Scarlet Moon 873				

OVERSTREET, Tommy ★132★   '72
Born on 9/10/37 in Oklahoma City. Singer/songwriter/guitarist. Uncle of **Susan St. Marie**. No relation to Paul Overstreet.

1)Ann 2)Heaven Is My Woman's Love 3)You Were A Lady 4)Gwen 5)I Don't Know You

DEBUT	PEAK	WKS	#	A-side / B-side	Pop	$	Pic Label & Number
10/11/69	73	2	1	Rocking A Memory (That Won't Go To Sleep) .... *He's Already Been There*		$6	Dot 17281
12/12/70+	56	7	2	If You're Looking For A Fool .... *The Smartest Fool*		$6	Dot 17357
4/24/71	5	16	3	Gwen (Congratulations) .... *One Love, Two Hearts, Three Lives*	123	$6	Dot 17375
8/14/71	5	16	4	I Don't Know You (Anymore) ..... *I Still Love You Enough (To Love You All Over Again)*		$6	Dot 17387
1/1/72	2[1]	16	5	Ann (Don't Go Runnin') .... *Within This World Of Mine*		$6	Dot 17402
5/20/72	16	14	6	A Seed Before The Rose .... *How'd We Ever Get This Way*		$6	Dot 17418
9/23/72	3	18	7	Heaven Is My Woman's Love .... *Baby's Gone*	102	$6	■ Dot 17428
4/21/73	7	15	8	Send Me No Roses .... *Your Love Controls My Life*		$6	Dot 17455
9/15/73	7	17	9	I'll Never Break These Chains .... *Woman, Your Name Is My Song*		$6	Dot 17474
2/16/74	3	16	10	(Jeannie Marie) You Were A Lady .... *Smile At Me Sweet Nancy*		$6	Dot 17493
7/27/74	8	16	11	If I Miss You Again Tonight .... *I'm Not Ready Yet*		$6	Dot 17515
12/14/74+	9	14	12	I'm A Believer .... *This Land Is A Big Land*		$5	ABC/Dot 17533
5/10/75	6	16	13	That's When My Woman Begins .... *A Small Quiet Table (In The Corner)*		$5	ABC/Dot 17552
10/11/75	16	12	14	From Woman To Woman .... *Grass Don't Grow In Heaven*		$5	ABC/Dot 17580
6/12/76	15	13	15	Here Comes That Girl Again .... *I'll Give Up (When You Give Up On Me)*		$5	ABC/Dot 17630
10/2/76	29	11	16	Young Girl .... *90 Proof Lies*		$5	ABC/Dot 17657
				#2 Pop hit for Gary Puckett & The Union Gap in 1968			
12/25/76+	11	15	17	If Love Was A Bottle Of Wine .... *I Never Really Missed You ('Til You Were Gone)*		$5	ABC/Dot 17672
5/7/77	5	14	18	Don't Go City Girl On Me .... *I'll Give Up (When You Give Up On Me)*		$5	ABC/Dot 17697
9/17/77	20	12	19	This Time I'm In It For The Love .... *(Don't Make Me) A Memory Before My Time*		$5	ABC/Dot 17721
1/21/78	12	12	20	Yes Ma'am .... *It's All Coming Home*		$5	ABC/Dot 17737
6/10/78	20	12	21	Better Me .... *Tell My Woman I Miss Her*		$5	ABC 12367
9/30/78	11	12	22	Fadin' In, Fadin' Out .... *If This Is Freedom (Then I Want Out)*		$5	ABC 12408
1/27/79	91	3	23	Tears (There's Nowhere Else To Hide) .... *Lord, If I Make It To Heaven*		$6	Tina 523
				TOMMY OVERSTREET And The NASHVILLE EXPRESS			
3/3/79	45	7	24	Cheater's Kit .... *Stolen Wine*		$5	ABC 12456
5/5/79	27	11	25	I'll Never Let You Down .... *You Needed Me*		$4	Elektra 46023
8/25/79	23	10	26	What More Could A Man Need .... *Only A Fool*		$4	Elektra 46516
11/17/79+	36	11	27	Fadin' Renegade .... *Smokey Mountain Lullabye*		$4	Elektra 46564
3/22/80	41	9	28	Down In The Quarter .... *Forever In Blue Jeans*		$4	Elektra 46600
6/28/80	47	7	29	Sue .... *Her Heart Still Belongs To Me*		$4	Elektra 46658
10/4/80	72	5	30	Me And The Boys In The Band .... *You*		$4	Elektra 47041
7/30/83	69	7	31	Dream Maker .... *More Than You Can Stand*		$5	AMI 1314
12/3/83	84	3	32	Heart Of Dixie		$5	AMI 1317
5/19/84	87	3	33	I Still Love Your Body		$5	Gervasi 665
6/28/86	74	5	34	Next To You .... *Letting Go Was Easier*		$6	Silver Dollar 0002

OWEN, Jim   '80
Born on 4/21/41 in Robards, Kentucky. Singer/songwriter/guitarist/actor. Starred as **Hank Williams** in a one-man show.

DEBUT	PEAK	WKS	#	A-side / B-side	$	Label & Number
1/28/78	97	2	1	Lovesick Blues .... *A Gift In The Name Of Love*	$6	Epic 50498
				JIM OWEN*THE DRIFTING COWBOYS**		
11/29/80	82	4	2	Ten Anniversary Presents .... *Please Don't Go Home Till Morning* [S]	$5	Sun 1157
1/30/82	82	3	3	Hell Yes, I Cheated .... *Dragging These Chains*	$5	Sun 1171

OWEN BROTHERS   '83

DEBUT	PEAK	WKS	#	A-side / B-side	$	Label & Number
12/25/82	95	3	1	Nights Out At The Days End .... *Love In Tonight*	$6	Audiograph 445
9/17/83	86	3	2	Southern Women	$6	Audiograph 470

OWENS, A.L. "Doodle"   '78
Born Arthur Leo Owens. Singer/prolific songwriter.

DEBUT	PEAK	WKS	#	A-side / B-side	$	Pic Label & Number
1/14/78	78	4		Honky Tonk Toys .... *California Rose*	$7	■ Raindrop 010

OWENS, Bonnie   '63
Born Bonnie Campbell on 10/1/32 in Blanchard, Oklahoma. Singer/songwriter/guitarist. Married to **Buck Owens** from 1948-53. Married to Merle Haggard from 1965-78. Mother of **Buddy Alan**.

DEBUT	PEAK	WKS	#	A-side / B-side	$	Label & Number
6/22/63	25	1	1	Why Don't Daddy Live Here Anymore .... *Waggin' Tongues*	$25	Tally 149
4/4/64	27	6	2	Don't Take Advantage Of Me .... *Stop The World*	$25	Tally 156
9/12/64	28	26	3	Just Between The Two Of Us .... *Slowly But Surely*	$25	Tally 181
				MERLE HAGGARD And BONNIE OWENS		
9/18/65	41	4	4	Number One Heel .... *The Longer You Wait*	$10	Capitol 5459
11/19/66	69	4	5	Consider The Children .... *I Know He Loves Me*	$10	Capitol 5755
2/15/69	68	4	6	Lead Me On .... *I'll Always Be Glad To Take You Back*	$10	Capitol 2340
				BONNIE OWENS And The Strangers (above 2)		

OWERS, Buck ★10★ '65

Born Alvis Edgar Owens on 8/12/29 in Sherman, Texas; raised in Mesa, Arizona. Singer/songwriter/guitarist. Married to **Bonnie Owens** from 1948-53. Moved to Bakersfield, California, in 1951. Played lead guitar for **Tommy Collins** in the mid-1950s. Co-host of TV's *Hee-Haw* from 1969-86. Father of **Buddy Alan**. Backing group: **The Buckaroos**. Elected to the Country Music Hall of Fame in 1996.

1)*Love's Gonna Live Here* 2)*My Heart Skips A Beat* 3)*Waitin' In Your Welfare Line* 4)*I Don't Care* 5)*Before You Go*

DEBUT	PEAK	WKS		A-side	B-side	Pop	$	Pic	Label & Number
5/11/59	24	2		1 Second Fiddle .... *Everlasting Love*			$20		Capitol 4172
10/5/59	4	22		2 Under Your Spell Again .... *Tired Of Livin'*			$20		Capitol 4245
3/7/60	3	30		3 Above And Beyond .... *Til These Dreams Come True*			$15		Capitol 4337
9/19/60	2³	24		4 Excuse Me (I Think I've Got A Heartache)/					
10/24/60	25	3		5 I've Got A Right To Know			$15		Capitol 4412
1/30/61	2⁸	26		6 Foolin' Around/		113			
3/27/61	27	1		7 High As The Mountains			$15		Capitol 4496
5/22/61	4	14		8 Loose Talk/					
5/15/61	8	12		9 Mental Cruelty			$15		Capitol 4550
				BUCK OWENS And ROSE MADDOX (above 2)					
8/7/61	2¹	24		10 Under The Influence Of Love .... *Bad Bad Dream*			$15		Capitol 4602
2/24/62	11	16		11 Nobody's Fool But Yours .... *Mirror, Mirror On The Wall*			$15		Capitol 4679
7/28/62	11	11		12 Save The Last Dance For Me .... *King Of Fools*			$15		Capitol 4765
10/27/62	8	8		13 Kickin' Our Hearts Around/					
10/27/62	17	5		14 I Can't Stop (My Lovin' You)			$15		Capitol 4826
12/29/62+	10	14		15 You're For Me/					
1/5/63	24	3		16 House Down The Block			$15		Capitol 4872
4/13/63	❶⁴	28		17 Act Naturally .... *Over And Over Again*			$15		Capitol 4937
				#47 Pop hit for The Beatles in 1965; also see #89 below					
8/3/63	15	6		18 We're The Talk Of The Town/					
8/10/63	19	6		19 Sweethearts In Heaven			$15		Capitol 4992
				BUCK OWENS AND ROSE MADDOX (above 2)					
9/21/63	❶¹⁶	30		20 Love's Gonna Live Here .... *Getting Used To Losing You*			$12		Capitol 5025
3/28/64	❶⁷	26		21 My Heart Skips A Beat/		94			
4/4/64	❶²	27		22 Together Again			$12		Capitol 5136
8/29/64	❶⁶	27		23 I Don't Care (Just As Long As You Love Me)/		92			
10/10/64	33	9		24 Don't Let Her Know		130	$12		Capitol 5240
1/23/65	❶⁵	20		25 I've Got A Tiger By The Tail .... *Cryin' Time*		25	$12	■	Capitol 5336
5/15/65	❶⁶	20		26 Before You Go .... *(I Want) No One But You*		83	$12	■	Capitol 5410
7/31/65	❶¹	19		27 Only You (Can Break My Heart)/		120			
7/31/65	10	14		28 Gonna Have Love			$12		Capitol 5465
				also see #90 below					
				BUCK OWENS & THE BUCKAROOS:					
10/30/65	❶²	17		29 Buckaroo/ [I]		60			
12/11/65+	24	9		30 If You Want A Love			$10		Capitol 5517
1/22/66	❶⁷	19		31 Waitin' In Your Welfare Line/		57			
2/26/66	43	2		32 In The Palm Of Your Hand			$10		Capitol 5566
				also see #60 below					
5/21/66	❶⁶	21		33 Think Of Me .... *Heart Of Glass*		74	$10	■	Capitol 5647
9/3/66	❶⁴	20		34 Open Up Your Heart .... *No More Me And You*			$10	■	Capitol 5705
1/14/67	❶⁴	16		35 Where Does The Good Times Go ... *The Way That I Love You*		114	$10	■	Capitol 5811
4/1/67	❶³	16		36 Sam's Place .... *Don't Ever Tell Me Goodbye*		92	$10	■	Capitol 5865
7/15/67	❶¹	16		37 Your Tender Loving Care .... *What A Liar I Am*			$10	■	Capitol 5942
10/14/67+	2¹	18		38 It Takes People Like You (To Make People Like Me) .... *You Left Her Lonely Too Long*		114	$10	■	Capitol 2001
1/27/68	❶¹	15		39 How Long Will My Baby Be Gone ... *Everybody Needs Somebody*			$10	■	Capitol 2080
4/20/68	2¹	15		40 Sweet Rosie Jones .... *Happy Times Are Here Again*			$10	■	Capitol 2142
7/27/68	7	15		41 Let The World Keep On A Turnin' ... *I'll Love You Forever And Ever*			$10	■	Capitol 2237
				BUCK OWENS AND BUDDY ALAN AND THE BUCKAROOS					
10/26/68	5	15		42 I've Got You On My Mind Again *That's All Right With Me (If It's All Right With You)*			$8	■	Capitol 2300
2/1/69	❶²	15		43 Who's Gonna Mow Your Grass *There's Gotta Be Some Changes Made*		106	$8	■	Capitol 2377
5/24/69	❶²	15		44 Johnny B. Goode *Maybe If I Close My Eyes (It'll Go Away)*		114	$8	■	Capitol 2485
				#8 Pop hit for Chuck Berry in 1958					
8/9/69	❶¹	15		45 Tall Dark Stranger .... *Sing That Kind Of Song*			$8	■	Capitol 2570
11/15/69	5	13		46 Big In Vegas .... *White Satin Bed*		100	$8	■	Capitol 2646
2/21/70	13	11		47 We're Gonna Get Together .... *Everybody Needs Somebody*			$8	■	Capitol 2731
				BUCK OWENS & SUSAN RAYE					
5/9/70	12	12		48 Togetherness .... *Fallin' For You*			$8	■	Capitol 2791
				BUCK OWENS & SUSAN RAYE					
6/6/70	2²	15		49 The Kansas City Song .... *I'd Love To Be Your Man*			$8	■	Capitol 2783
8/29/70	8	13		50 The Great White Horse .... *Your Tender Loving Care*			$8	■	Capitol 2871
				BUCK OWENS & SUSAN RAYE					
11/7/70	9	13		51 I Wouldn't Live In New York City (If They Gave Me The Whole Dang Town) *No Milk And Honey In Baltimore*		110	$7	■	Capitol 2947

OWENS, Buck — Cont'd

DEBUT	PEAK	WKS		A-side / B-side	Pop	$	Pic	Label & Number
2/6/71	9	13	52	Bridge Over Troubled Water *(I'm Goin') Home*	119	$7	■	Capitol 3023
				#1 Pop hit for Simon & Garfunkel in 1970				
5/1/71	3	17	53	Ruby (Are You Mad) *Heartbreak Mountain*	106	$7		Capitol 3096
9/4/71	2²	14	54	Rollin' In My Sweet Baby's Arms *Corn Likker*		$7	■	Capitol 3164
12/4/71+	29	10	55	Too Old To Cut The Mustard ....*Wham Bam*		$7	■	Capitol 3215
				BUCK & BUDDY				
2/12/72	8	12	56	I'll Still Be Waiting For You *Full Time Daddy*		$7		Capitol 3262
4/29/72	❶¹	15	57	Made In Japan *Black Texas Dirt*		$7	■	Capitol 3314
7/15/72	13	14	58	Looking Back To See ....*Cryin' Time*		$7	■	Capitol 3368
				BUCK OWENS & SUSAN RAYE				
9/16/72	13	14	59	You Ain't Gonna Have Ol' Buck To Kick Around No More *I Love You So Much It Hurts*		$7		Capitol 3429
				"live" recording				
12/30/72+	23	10	60	In The Palm Of Your Hand ....*Get Out Of Town Before Sundown* [R]		$6		Capitol 3504
				new version of #32 above				
3/31/73	14	11	61	Ain't It Amazing, Gracie .... *The Good Old Days (Are Here Again)*		$6		Capitol 3563
6/16/73	35	8	62	The Good Old Days (Are Here Again).........*When You Get To Heaven (I'll Be There)*		$6		Capitol 3601
				BUCK OWENS & SUSAN RAYE				

BUCK OWENS:

DEBUT	PEAK	WKS		A-side / B-side	Pop	$	Pic	Label & Number
8/18/73	27	11	63	Arms Full Of Empty ....*Songwriter's Lament*		$6		Capitol 3688
12/1/73+	8	12	64	Big Game Hunter *That Loving Feeling*		$6		Capitol 3769
3/23/74	9	13	65	On The Cover Of The Music City News *Stony Mountain West Virginia* [N]		$6		Capitol 3841
				#6 Pop hit for Dr. Hook in 1973 (with different lyrics)				
7/20/74	6	13	66	(It's A) Monsters' Holiday *Great Expectations* [N]		$6		Capitol 3907
11/30/74+	8	15	67	Great Expectations *Let The Fun Begin*		$6		Capitol 3976
3/29/75	19	11	68	41st Street Lonely Hearts' Club/				
		7	69	Weekend Daddy		$6		Capitol 4043
7/5/75	20	13	70	Love Is Strange ....*Sweethearts In Heaven*		$6		Capitol 4100
				BUCK OWENS & SUSAN RAYE				
				#11 Pop hit for Mickey & Sylvia in 1957				
10/4/75	51	7	71	The Battle Of New Orleans .... *Run Him To The Round House Nellie*		$6		Capitol 4138
6/26/76	44	9	72	Hollywood Waltz ....*Rain On Your Parade*		$5		Warner 8223
9/25/76	43	8	73	California Okie *Child Support*		$5		Warner 8255
2/26/77	90	4	74	World Famous Holiday Inn ....*He Don't Deserve You Anymore*		$5		Warner 8316
7/16/77	100	1	75	It's Been A Long, Long Time *Rain On Your Parade*		$5		Warner 8395
9/10/77	91	3	76	Our Old Mansion *How Come My Dog Don't Bark*		$5		Warner 8433
8/19/78	27	12	77	Nights Are Forever Without You ....*When I Need You*		$4		Warner 8614
				#10 Pop hit for England Dan & John Ford Coley in 1976				
12/23/78+	80	5	78	Do You Wanna Make Love *Seasons Of My Heart*		$4		Warner 8701
				#5 Pop hit for Peter McCann in 1977				
5/12/79	11	13	79	Play Together Again Again .... *He Don't Deserve You Anymore*		$4		Warner 8830
				BUCK OWENS With Emmylou Harris				
9/8/79	30	10	80	Hangin' In And Hangin' On...................*Sweet Molly Brown's*		$4		Warner 49046
12/15/79+	22	13	81	Let Jesse Rob The Train ....*Victim Of Life's Circumstances*		$4		Warner 49118
4/5/80	42	9	82	Love Is A Warm Cowboy .... *I Don't Want To Live In San Francisco*		$4		Warner 49200
7/26/80	72	4	83	Moonlight And Magnolia *Nickels And Dimes*		$4		Warner 49278
5/30/81	92	2	84	Without You .... *Love Don't Make The Bars*		$4		Warner 49651
7/16/88	❶¹	18	85	Streets Of Bakersfield *S:❶³ One More Time*		$3	■	Reprise 27964
				DWIGHT YOAKAM & BUCK OWENS				
10/22/88	46	9	86	Hot Dog ....*Second Fiddle*		$3	■	Capitol 44248
				first recorded by Owens (as Corky Jones) in 1956 on Pep 107 ($250)				
1/28/89	54	6	87	A-11 *Sweethearts In Heaven*		$3		Capitol 44295
4/8/89	60	7	88	Put A Quarter In The Jukebox ....*Don't Let Her Know*		$3		Capitol 44356
7/15/89	27	11	89	Act Naturally .... *The Key's In The Mailbox* [R]		$3		Capitol 44409
				BUCK OWENS AND RINGO STARR				
				new version of #17 above				
10/14/89	76	7	90	Gonna Have Love .... [R]				album cut
				new version of #28 above; from the album *Act Naturally* on Capitol 92893				

OWENS, Marie   **'74**
Born in 1956 in Virginia.

DEBUT	PEAK	WKS		A-side / B-side	Pop	$	Pic	Label & Number
2/23/74	44	9	1	J. John Jones *Take It From Me*		$6		MCA 40184
6/8/74	71	8	2	Release Me *Just Out Of Reach*		$6		MCA 40241
				#4 Pop hit for Engelbert Humperdinck in 1967				
11/16/74	71	7	3	I Want To Lay Down Beside You *Broken Wings*		$6		MCA 40308
10/25/75	84	4	4	Someone Loves You Honey *The Devil's Song*		$6		4 Star 1019
2/12/77	92	4	5	When Your Good Love Was Mine *I'll Be In His Arms Tonight*		$7		MMI 1012
5/7/77	88	4	6	Burning *Wish You Were Here*		$7		MMI 1015
8/13/77	80	5	7	Ease My Mind On You *Sweet Love*		$7		Sing Me 12

OXFORD, Vernon   **'76**
Born on 6/8/41 in Larue, Arkansas; raised in Wichita, Kansas. Singer/songwriter/fiddle player.

DEBUT	PEAK	WKS		A-side / B-side	Pop	$	Pic	Label & Number
12/6/75+	54	12	1	Shadows Of My Mind *She's Always There*		$5		RCA Victor 10442
4/3/76	83	6	2	Your Wanting Me Is Gone *Don't Be Late*		$5		RCA Victor 10595
6/12/76	17	12	3	Redneck! (The Redneck National Anthem) *Leave Me Alone With The Blues*		$5		RCA Victor 10693
10/16/76	60	7	4	Clean Your Own Tables *Baby Sister*		$4		RCA 10787
1/29/77	55	6	5	A Good Old Fashioned Saturday Night Honky Tonk Barroom Brawl *One More Night To Spare*		$4		RCA 10872

DEBUT	PEAK	WKS	Gold	A-side (Chart Hit)..B-side	Pop	$	Pic	Label & Number
				OXFORD, Vernon — Cont'd				
5/7/77	87	3		6 Only The Shadows Know .... *We Sure Danced Us Some Goodn's*		$4		RCA 10952
7/23/77	95	2		7 Redneck Roots .... *Images*		$4		RCA 11020
				OZARK MOUNTAIN DAREDEVILS '76				
				Country-rock group from Springfield, Missouri: Larry Lee (vocals, drums), John Dillon (guitar), Steve Cash (harmonica) and Michael "Supe" Granda (bass). Best known for their 1975 pop hit "Jackie Blue."				
5/8/76	84	4		You Made It Right.. *Dreams*		$5		A&M 1809

P

				PACIFIC STEEL CO. '80				
				Steel guitar instrumental duo: Jay Dee Maness and Junior "Red" Rhodes.				
12/6/80	88	5		Fat 'N Sassy .... *Rio* [I]		$6		Pacific Arts 111
				PACIFIC STEEL CO. Featuring Jay Dee Maness				
				PACK, Bob '88				
7/23/88	74	4		The Request		$6		Oak 1051
				PACK, Ray '89				
2/11/89	91	2		Where Was I		$6		Happy Man 818
★263★				**PAGE, Patti** '51				
				Born Clara Ann Fowler on 11/8/27 in Muskogee, Oklahoma; raised in Tulsa. Own TV series *The Patti Page Show* from 1955-58 and *The Big Record* from 1957-58. Acted in the 1960 movie *Elmer Gantry*. Charted 81 pop hits from 1948-68.				
				1)The Tennessee Waltz 2)Go On Home 3)Hello We're Lonely 4)Money, Marbles And Chalk 5)Mom And Dad's Waltz				
5/7/49	15	1		1 Money, Marbles And Chalk .... J:15 *Where Is The One*	27	$15		Mercury 5251
1/6/51	2³	12	●	2 The Tennessee Waltz J:2 / A:5 / S:5 *Long, Long Ago*	❶¹³	$20		Mercury 5534-X45
7/17/61	21	3		3 Mom And Dad's Waltz .... *You'll Answer To Me* (Pop #46)	58	$10	■	Mercury 71823
2/17/62	13	15		4 Go On Home .... *Too Late To Cry*	42	$10	■	Mercury 71906
5/30/70	22	10		5 I Wish I Had A Mommy Like You .... *He'll Never Take The Place Of You*	114	$7		Columbia 45159
1/16/71	24	10		6 Give Him Love .... *I Wish I Could Take That Little Boy Home*		$7		Mercury 73162
5/8/71	37	8		7 Make Me Your Kind Of Woman............................ *I Wish I Was A Little Boy Again*		$7		Mercury 73199
8/14/71	63	4		8 I'd Rather Be Sorry .... *Words*		$7		Mercury 73222
11/20/71	38	9		9 Think Again/		$7		
		3		10 A Woman Left Lonely		$7		Mercury 73249
12/16/72+	14	12		11 Hello We're Lonely .... *We're Not Getting Old*		$7		Mercury 73347
				PATTI PAGE & TOM T. HALL				
9/8/73	42	11		12 I Can't Sit Still .... *Love Lives Again*		$6		Epic 11032
12/29/73+	29	11		13 You're Gonna Hurt Me (One More Time)........................ *Mama, Take Me Home*		$6		Epic 11072
5/18/74	59	7		14 Someone Came To See Me (In The Middle Of The Night)............ *One Final Stand*		$6		Epic 11109
11/30/74+	70	7		15 I May Not Be Lovin' You ....*Whoever Finds This I Love You*		$5		Avco 603
7/26/75	67	7		16 Less Than The Song .... *Did He Ask About Me*		$5		Avco 613
3/21/81	39	8		17 No Aces...*Everytime You Touch Me*		$4		Plantation 197
8/1/81	66	4		18 A Poor Man's Roses/		$4		
				new version of her #14 Pop hit from 1957				
7/18/81	76	2		19 On The Inside		$4		Plantation 201
				from the TV series *Prisoner: Cell Block H* starring Patsy King				
5/8/82	80	4		20 My Man Friday .... *Tennessee Waltz*		$4		Plantation 208
				PALMER, Keith '91				
				Born in Hayatt, Missouri; raised in Corning, Arkansas. Singer/songwriter.				
9/28/91	54	17		1 Don't Throw Me In The Briarpatch .... *My Arms Tonight*		$3		Epic 73988
1/25/92	60	8		2 Forgotten But Not Gone .... *Memory Lane*		$3		Epic 74174
				PALOMINO ROAD '93				
				Group of Nashville session musicians: Ronnie Guilbeau (vocals), Randy Frazier, J.T. Corenflos and Chip Lewis. Guilbeau is the son of Gib Guilbeau (of the **Burrito Brothers**).				
1/16/93	46	15		Why Baby Why ....*White Lightnin'*		$3		Liberty 56974
				PAPA JOE'S MUSIC BOX — see SMITH, Jerry				
				PARIS, Jack '78				
				Singer from Ottumwa, Iowa.				
2/14/76	94	3		1 It Sets Me Free .... *A Woman Ought To Be*		$7		2-J 201
3/19/77	98	2		2 Gypsy River .... *Mountain Of Love*		$5		50 States 49
12/10/77+	75	7		3 Mississippi *Heaven's Here Tonight*		$5		50 States 57
3/4/78	86	4		4 Lay Down Sally .... *I Wonder Where You Are Tonight*		$5		50 States 58
8/19/78	98	3		5 (It's Gonna Be A) Happy Day		$5		50 States 62

★349★ PARKER, Billy '82

Born on 7/19/37 in Okemah, Oklahoma; raised in Tulsa. Singer/songwriter/guitarist. DJ on KVOO-Tulsa. Member of **Ernest Tubb**'s band from 1968-70.

1)The Last Country Song 2)Until The Next Time 3)I See An Angel Every Day 4)If I Ever Need A Lady
5)I'll Drink To That

DEBUT	PEAK	WKS	A-side / B-side	Pop	$	Pic	Label & Number
9/18/76	79	8	1 It's Bad When You're Caught (With The Goods) ....*I Guess I Owe That Much To You*		$6		SCR 133
1/22/77	71	8	2 Lord, If I Make It To Heaven Can I Bring My Own Angel Along ....*Jerri Again*		$6		SCR 136
6/4/77	75	6	3 What Did I Promise Her Last Night ....*Let A Fool Take A Bow*		$6		SCR 144
10/1/77	94	3	4 If You Got To Have It Your Way (I'll Go Mine).........*Line Between Love And Hate*		$6		SCR 148
1/7/78	62	9	5 You Read Between The Lines .... *Trophy Of Gold*		$6		SCR 153
4/29/78	81	4	6 If There's One Angel Missing (She's Here In My Arms Tonight)..*Tough Act To Follow*		$5	■	SCR 157
8/26/78	50	7	7 Until The Next Time .... *Tough Act To Follow*		$5		SCR 160
12/23/78+	73	6	8 Pleasin' My Woman/		$5		SCR 162
3/10/79	98	1	9 Thanks E.T. Thanks A Lot		$5		SCR 162
			tribute to Ernest Tubb				
8/11/79	80	4	10 Thanks A Lot .... *Until The Next Time*		$5		SCR 177
12/22/79+	82	6	11 Tough Act To Follow..		$5		SCR 181
2/14/81	74	3	12 Better Side Of Thirty .... *Lord If I Make It*		$5		Oak 47565
8/22/81	53	7	13 I'll Drink To That ....*One More Last Time*		$5		Soundwaves 4643
1/9/82	51	10	14 I See An Angel Every Day ....*Hello Out There*		$5		Soundwaves 4659
5/1/82	41	11	15 (Who's Gonna Sing) The Last Country Song *What's A Nice Girl Like You*		$5		Soundwaves 4670
			BILLY PARKER and Friend				
7/31/82	53	8	16 If I Ever Need A Lady.......................... *Can I Have What's Left*		$5		Soundwaves 4678
			BILLY PARKER & Friend				
			Darrell McCall (harmony vocal, above 2)				
10/30/82	68	6	17 Too Many Irons In The Fire........................*Honky Tonk Girl*		$5		Soundwaves 4686
			BILLY PARKER and CAL SMITH				
3/26/83	68	6	18 Who Said Love Was Fair.................... *Take Me Back To Tulsa*		$5		Soundwaves 4699
			BILLY PARKER And FRIENDS				
7/9/83	59	8	19 Love Don't Know A Lady (From A Honky Tonk Girl) ....*It's Not Me*		$5		Soundwaves 4708
			BILLY PARKER and FRIENDS				
2/13/88	72	5	20 You Are My Angel...		$5		Canyon Creek 1208
10/22/88	81	4	21 She's Sittin' Pretty		$5		Canyon Creek 0801
5/27/89	87	4	22 It's Time For Your Dreams To Come True .... *You Are My Angel*		$5		Canyon Creek 0315

PARKER, Caryl Mack '97

Female singer from Abilene, Texas.

DEBUT	PEAK	WKS	A-side / B-side	Pop	$	Pic	Label & Number
10/26/96	67	5	1 Better Love Next Time				album cut
3/22/97	66	4	2 One Night Stand				album cut
			above 2 from the album *Caryl Mack Parker* on Magnatone 112				

PARKER, Gary Dale '90

Born on 7/6/58 in Nashville.

DEBUT	PEAK	WKS	A-side / B-side	Pop	$	Pic	Label & Number
1/13/90	87	1	Once And For Always		$5		615 1022

PARKER, Lori '77

DEBUT	PEAK	WKS	A-side / B-side	Pop	$	Pic	Label & Number
11/13/76	92	3	1 Steppin' Out Tonight..*Empty Arms*		$5		Con Brio 113
9/3/77	89	4	2 I Like Everything About Loving You...........................*Out Of Luck, Out Of Love*		$5		Con Brio 122

PARKS, Michael '70

Born on 4/4/38 in Corona, California. Singer/actor. Played "Jim Bronson" on TV's *Then Came Bronson*.

DEBUT	PEAK	WKS	A-side / B-side	Pop	$	Pic	Label & Number
3/21/70	41	9	Long Lonesome Highway..............................*Mountain High*	20	$6		MGM 14104
			from the TV series *Then Came Bronson* starring Parks				

PARKS, P.J. '81

Male singer.

DEBUT	PEAK	WKS	A-side / B-side	Pop	$	Pic	Label & Number
1/10/81	86	4	1 The Way You Are .... *Saint Of New Orleans*		$6		Kik 901
4/4/81	85	3	2 Falling In .... *Saint Of New Orleans*		$6		Kik 903

★211★ PARNELL, Lee Roy '93

Born on 12/21/56 in Stephenville, Texas. Singer/songwriter/guitarist. Also see **Jed Zeppelin**.

1)What Kind Of Fool Do You Think I Am 2)Tender Moment 3)A Little Bit Of You

DEBUT	PEAK	WKS	A-side / B-side	Pop	$	Pic	Label & Number
3/17/90	59	8	1 Crocodile Tears .... *Let's Have Some Fun*		$3		Arista 9912
6/30/90	54	13	2 Oughta Be A Law...................................*Crocodile Tears*		$3	▌	Arista 2028
10/27/90	73	1	3 Family Tree..*Red Hot*		$3		Arista 2093
2/22/92	50	20	4 The Rock ....*Road Scholar*		$3		Arista 12400
5/16/92	2²	20	5 What Kind Of Fool Do You Think I Am *Roller Coaster*		$3		Arista 12431
10/3/92+	8	20	6 Love Without Mercy *Done Deal*		$3		Arista 12462
3/6/93	2¹	20	7 Tender Moment *The Rock*		$3		Arista 12523
8/21/93	6	20	8 On The Road *Back In My Arms Again*		$3	▌	Arista 12588
1/8/94	3	20	9 I'm Holding My Own *Fresh Coat Of Paint*		$3	▌	Arista 12642
5/21/94	17	20	10 Take These Chains From My Heart ....*Straight Shooter*		$3	▌	Arista 12695
			#8 Pop hit for **Ray Charles** in 1963				
10/1/94	51	9	11 The Power Of Love ....*Straight And Narrow*		$3	▌	Arista 12747
5/20/95	2¹	20	12 A Little Bit Of You *Givin' Water To A Drowning Man*		$3		Career 12823
9/9/95+	12	20	13 When A Woman Loves A Man................*If The House Is Rockin'*		$3		Career 12862
1/20/96	3	20	14 Heart's Desire *Knock Yourself Out*		$3		Career 12952
5/18/96	12	20	15 Givin' Water To A Drowning Man...........................*Squeeze Me In*		$3		Career 10503

DEBUT	PEAK	WKS	Gold	A-side (Chart Hit)...B-side	Pop	$	Pic	Label & Number
				PARNELL, Lee Roy — Cont'd				
9/21/96	46	15		16 **We All Get Lucky Sometimes** .... _I Had To Let It Go_		$3		Career 13044
12/28/96	71	1		17 **Please Come Home For Christmas** .... [X]				album cut
				from the album _Star Of Wonder_ on Arista 18822				
4/19/97	35	18		18 **Lucky Me, Lucky You** .... _Every Night's A Saturday Night_		$3	▌	Career 13078
8/16/97	39	13		19 **You Can't Get There From Here** ...._Mama Screw Your Wig On Tight_		$3		Career 13079
				PARSONS, Rob **'82**				
				Singer/songwriter from Traverse City, Michigan.				
1/9/82	74	4		**Shadow Of Love**... _Today May Be The Day_		$4		MCA 51202

PARTON, Dolly ★7★   **'77**

Born on 1/19/46 in Sevier County, Tennessee. Singer/songwriter/guitarist/actress. Regular on **Porter Wagoner's** TV show from 1967-74. Joined the _Grand Ole Opry_ in 1969. Starred in the movies _9 To 5, The Best Little Whorehouse In Texas, Steel Magnolias_ and _Straight Talk_. In 1986, opened Dollywood theme park in the Smoky Mountains. Hosted own TV variety show in 1987. Sister of **Randy Parton** and **Stella Parton**. CMA Awards: 1968 Vocal Group of the Year (with Porter Wagoner); 1970 & 1971 Vocal Duo of the Year (with Porter Wagoner); 1975 & 1976 Female Vocalist of the Year; 1978 Entertainer of the Year.

1)Here You Come Again 2)Heartbreaker 3)Islands In The Stream 4)You're The Only One
5)It's All Wrong, But It's All Right

DEBUT	PEAK	WKS	Gold	A-side / B-side	Pop	$	Pic	Label & Number
1/21/67	24	14		1 Dumb Blonde... _The Giving And The Taking_		$15		Monument 982
6/10/67	17	12		2 Something Fishy.._I've Lived My Life_		$15		Monument 1007
12/2/67+	7	17		3 The Last Thing On My Mind _Love Is Worth Living_		$10		RCA Victor 9369
				PORTER WAGONER/DOLLY PARTON				
4/13/68	7	16		4 Holding On To Nothin' _Just Between You And Me_		$10		RCA Victor 9490
				PORTER WAGONER and DOLLY PARTON				
6/29/68	17	14		5 Just Because I'm A Woman ...._I Wish I Felt This Way At Home_		$10		RCA Victor 9548
7/27/68	5	13		6 We'll Get Ahead Someday/				
10/5/68	51	6		7 Jeannie's Afraid Of The Dark .... (above 2)		$10		RCA Victor 9577
				PORTER WAGONER & DOLLY PARTON				
11/16/68	25	11		8 In The Good Old Days (When Times Were Bad) .... _Try Being Lonely_		$10		RCA Victor 9657
3/8/69	9	14		9 Yours Love _Malena_		$8		RCA Victor 0104
				DOLLY PARTON/PORTER WAGONER				
4/12/69	40	10		10 Daddy .... _He's A Go Getter_		$8		RCA Victor 0132
6/21/69	16	11		11 Always, Always .... _No Reason To Hurry Home_		$8		RCA Victor 0172
				PORTER WAGONER AND DOLLY PARTON				
7/26/69	50	8		12 In The Ghetto .... _The Bridge_		$8		RCA Victor 0192
10/18/69	45	8		13 My Blue Ridge Mountain Boy .... _'Til Death Do Us Part_		$8		RCA Victor 0243
10/25/69	5	16		14 Just Someone I Used To Know _My Hands Are Tied_		$8		RCA Victor 0247
				PORTER WAGONER and DOLLY PARTON				
1/31/70	40	8		15 Daddy Come And Get Me .... _Chas_		$8		RCA Victor 9784
2/14/70	9	15		16 Tomorrow Is Forever _Mendy Never Sleeps_		$8		RCA Victor 9799
				PORTER WAGONER AND DOLLY PARTON				
7/4/70	3	16		17 Mule Skinner Blues (Blue Yodel No. 8) _More Than Their Share_		$8		RCA Victor 9863
				#5 Pop hit for The Fendermen in 1960				
8/1/70	7	15		18 Daddy Was An Old Time Preacher Man _A Good Understanding_		$8		RCA Victor 9875
				PORTER WAGONER AND DOLLY PARTON				
12/12/70+	❶[1]	15		19 Joshua _I'm Doing This For Your Sake_	108	$8		RCA Victor 9928
2/27/71	7	13		20 Better Move It On Home _Two Of A Kind_		$8		RCA Victor 9958
				PORTER WAGONER AND DOLLY PARTON				
4/10/71	23	12		21 Comin' For To Carry Me Home .... _Golden Streets Of Glory_		$8		RCA Victor 9971
				based on the American spiritual "Swing Low, Sweet Chariot"				
6/26/71	14	12		22 The Right Combination .... _The Pain Of Loving You_	106	$8		RCA Victor 9994
				PORTER WAGONER AND DOLLY PARTON				
7/17/71	17	12		23 My Blue Tears.. _The Mystery Of The Mystery_		$8		RCA Victor 9999
10/30/71	4	16		24 Coat Of Many Colors _Here I Am_		$7	▉	RCA Victor 0538
11/13/71+	11	13		25 Burning The Midnight Oil.............................._More Than Words Can Tell_		$7		RCA Victor 0565
				PORTER WAGONER AND DOLLY PARTON				
3/11/72	6	14		26 Touch Your Woman _Mission Chapel Memories_		$7		RCA Victor 0662
4/8/72	9	14		27 Lost Forever In Your Kiss _The Fog Has Lifted_		$7		RCA Victor 0675
				PORTER WAGONER AND DOLLY PARTON				
8/12/72	20	9		28 Washday Blues .... _Just As Good As Gone_		$7		RCA Victor 0757
9/2/72	14	13		29 Together Always .... _Love's All Over_		$7		RCA Victor 0773
				PORTER WAGONER AND DOLLY PARTON				
1/6/73	15	13		30 My Tennessee Mountain Home ...._The Better Part Of Life_		$7		RCA Victor 0868
3/3/73	30	9		31 We Found It .... _Love Have Mercy On Us_		$7		RCA Victor 0893
				PORTER WAGONER AND DOLLY PARTON				
5/19/73	20	11		32 Traveling Man.. _I Remember_		$7		RCA Victor 0950
6/23/73	3	17		33 If Teardrops Were Pennies _Come To Me_		$7		RCA Victor 0981
				PORTER WAGONER AND DOLLY PARTON				
11/3/73+	❶[1]	19		34 Jolene _Love, You're So Beautiful Tonight_	60	$7		RCA Victor 0145
4/6/74	❶[1]	15		35 I Will Always Love You _Lonely Comin' Down_		$7		RCA Victor 0234
				#1 Pop hit for Whitney Houston in 1992; also see #65 and #101 below				
8/3/74	❶[1]	17		36 Please Don't Stop Loving Me _Sounds Of Nature_		$7		RCA Victor 10010
				PORTER WAGONER & DOLLY PARTON				
8/31/74	❶[1]	17		37 Love Is Like A Butterfly _Sacred Memories_	105	$7		RCA Victor 10031
1/25/75	❶[1]	13		38 The Bargain Store _I'll Never Forget_		$7		RCA Victor 10164
6/7/75	2[1]	16		39 The Seeker _Love With A Feeling_	105	$6		RCA Victor 10310

DEBUT	PEAK	WKS	Gold	A-side (Chart Hit) .... B-side	Pop	$	Plc	Label & Number
				PARTON, Dolly — Cont'd				
7/12/75	5	17		40 Say Forever You'll Be Mine *How Can I (Help You Forgive Me)*		$6		RCA Victor 10328
				PORTER WAGONER & DOLLY PARTON				
9/27/75	9	14		41 We Used To *My Heart Started Breaking*		$6		RCA Victor 10396
2/28/76	19	11		42 Hey, Lucky Lady *Most Of All, Why*		$6		RCA Victor 10564
5/15/76	8	14		43 Is Forever Longer Than Always *If You Say I Can*		$6		RCA Victor 10652
				PORTER WAGONER AND DOLLY PARTON				
7/31/76	3	15		44 All I Can Do *Falling Out Of Love With Me*		$6		RCA Victor 10730
4/9/77	11	13		45 Light Of A Clear Blue Morning .... *There*	87	$6		RCA 10935
10/15/77	❶5	19	●	46 Here You Come Again *Me And Little Andy*	3	$5		RCA 11123
3/18/78	❶2	14		47 It's All Wrong, But It's All Right/		$5		RCA 11240
		12		48 Two Doors Down	19	$5		RCA 11240
8/19/78	❶3	13		49 Heartbreaker *Sure Thing*	37	$5		RCA 11296
11/25/78+	❶1	14		50 I Really Got The Feeling/		$5		RCA 11420
11/25/78	48	14		51 Baby I'm Burnin'	25	$5		RCA 11420
6/9/79	❶2	14		52 You're The Only One *Down*	59	$5		RCA 11577
9/1/79	7	13		53 Sweet Summer Lovin'/	77			RCA 11705
		13		54 Great Balls Of Fire		$5		RCA 11705
3/22/80	❶1	14		55 Starting Over Again *Sweet Agony*	36	$5		RCA 11926
6/21/80	2²	17		56 Making Plans *Beneath The Sweet Magnolia Tree*		$5		RCA 11983
				PORTER WAGONER AND DOLLY PARTON				
7/19/80	❶1	16		57 Old Flames Can't Hold A Candle To You *I Knew You When*		$5		RCA 12040
11/8/80+	12	14		58 If You Go, I'll Follow You .... *Hide Me Away*		$5		RCA 12119
				PORTER WAGONER & DOLLY PARTON				
11/29/80+	❶1	14	●	59 9 To 5 *Sing For The Common Man*	❶2	$4	■	RCA 12133
				from the movie starring Parton				
4/11/81	❶1	17		60 But You Know I Love You *Poor Folks Town*	41	$4		RCA 12200
8/29/81	14	13		61 The House Of The Rising Sun/	77			
				#1 Pop hit for The Animals in 1964				
		1		62 Working Girl		$4		RCA 12282
2/27/82	8	17		63 Single Women *Barbara On Your Mind*		$4		RCA 13057
5/29/82	7	15		64 Heartbreak Express *Act Like A Fool*		$4		RCA 13234
7/31/82	❶1	19		65 I Will Always Love You/ [R]	53			
				new version of #35 above; from the movie *The Best Little Whorehouse In Texas* starring Parton				
		19		66 Do I Ever Cross Your Mind		$4		RCA 13260
11/6/82	8	17		67 Hard Candy Christmas *Me And Little Andy* [X]		$4		RCA 13361
				also see #103 below; from the movie *The Best Little Whorehouse In Texas* starring Parton				
12/11/82+	7	20		68 Everything's Beautiful (In It's Own Way) *Put It Off Until Tomorrow*	102	$4		Monument 03408
				DOLLY PARTON/WILLIE NELSON				
4/30/83	20	16		69 Potential New Boyfriend .... *One Of Those Days*		$4		RCA 13514
9/3/83	❶2	23	▲	70 Islands In The Stream *I Will Always Love You*	❶2	$4	■	RCA 13615
				KENNY ROGERS with Dolly Parton				
12/24/83+	3	19		71 Save The Last Dance For Me *Elusive Butterfly*	45	$3		RCA 13703
				#1 Pop hit for The Drifters in 1960				
4/7/84	36	10		72 Downtown .... *The Great Pretender*	80	$3	■	RCA 13756
				#1 Pop hit for Petula Clark in 1965				
6/9/84	❶1	20		73 Tennessee Homesick Blues *Butterflies*		$3		RCA 13819
9/15/84	10	20		74 God Won't Get You *S:10 / A:11 Sweet Lovin' Friends*		$3		RCA 13883
				above 2 from the movie *Rhinestone* starring Parton				
12/15/84	53	7		75 The Greatest Gift Of All .... *White Christmas* [X]	81	$3		RCA 13945
				KENNY ROGERS & DOLLY PARTON				
1/26/85	3	22		76 Don't Call It Love *A:3 / S:4 We Got Too Much*		$3		RCA 13987
5/25/85	❶1	20		77 Real Love *S:❶1 / A:❶1 I Can't Be True*	91	$3	■	RCA 14058
				DOLLY PARTON (with Kenny Rogers)				
11/30/85+	❶1	22		78 Think About Love *S:❶1 / A:❶1 Come Back To Me*		$3		RCA 14218
5/3/86	17	15		79 Tie Our Love (In A Double Knot) *A:15 / S:17 I Hope You're Never Happy*		$3		RCA 14297
9/6/86	31	13		80 We Had It All *S:28 / A:29 Do I Ever Cross Your Mind*		$3		RCA 5001
2/21/87	❶1	19		81 To Know Him Is To Love Him *S:❶1 / A:❶1 Farther Along*		$3	■	Warner 28492
				DOLLY PARTON, LINDA RONSTADT, EMMYLOU HARRIS #1 Pop hit for The Teddy Bears in 1958				
5/30/87	3	18		82 Telling Me Lies *S:10 Rosewood Casket*		$3		Warner 28371
				DOLLY PARTON, LINDA RONSTADT, EMMYLOU HARRIS				
9/26/87	5	22		83 Those Memories Of You *S:10 My Dear Companion*		$3	■	Warner 28248
				DOLLY PARTON, LINDA RONSTADT, EMMYLOU HARRIS				
12/19/87+	63	8		84 The River Unbroken .... *More Than I Can Say*		$3	■	Columbia 07665
3/26/88	6	18		85 Wildflowers *S:13 Hobo's Meditation*		$3		Warner 27970
				DOLLY PARTON, LINDA RONSTADT, EMMYLOU HARRIS				
5/6/89	❶1	20		86 Why'd You Come In Here Lookin' Like That *Wait 'Till I Get You Home*		$3		Columbia 68760
8/26/89	❶1	26		87 Yellow Roses *Wait 'Till I Get You Home*		$3		Columbia 69040
12/9/89+	39	8		88 He's Alive *What Is It My Love*		$3		Columbia 73200
2/3/90	39	11		89 Time For Me To Fly *The Moon, The Stars And Me*		$3		Columbia 73226
				#56 Pop hit for REO Speedwagon in 1978				
5/12/90	29	12		90 White Limozeen *The Moon, The Stars And Me*		$3	▌	Columbia 73341
8/18/90	21	20		91 Love Is Strange .... *Walk Away*		$3	▌	Reprise 19760
				KENNY ROGERS and DOLLY PARTON #11 Pop hit for Mickey & Sylvia in 1957				
3/2/91	❶1	20		92 Rockin' Years *What A Heartache*		$3		Columbia 73711
				DOLLY PARTON WITH RICKY VAN SHELTON				

DEBUT	PEAK	WKS	Gold	A-side (Chart Hit)..B-side	Pop	$	Pic	Label & Number
				PARTON, Dolly — Cont'd				
6/8/91	15	20		93 Silver And Gold ....*Runaway Feelin'*		$3		Columbia 73826
10/19/91	33	20		94 Eagle When She Flies ....*Wildest Dreams*		$3		Columbia 74011
1/25/92	46	10		95 Country Road ....*Best Woman Wins*		$3		Columbia 74183
4/11/92	64	5		96 Straight Talk ....*Dirty Job*		$3	■	Hollywood 64776
				from the movie starring Parton				
2/13/93	27	20		97 Romeo ....*High And Mighty*	50	$3	■	Columbia 74876
				DOLLY PARTON AND FRIENDS				
				Mary Chapin-Carpenter, Billy Ray Cyrus, Kathy Mattea, Pam Tillis and Tanya Tucker (guest vocals)				
5/1/93	58	9		98 More Where That Came From ....*I'll Make Your Bed*		$3	■	Columbia 74954
12/25/93+	68	2		99 Silver Threads And Golden Needles ....*Let Her Fly*		$3	■	Columbia 77294
				PARTON/WYNETTE/LYNN				
10/15/94	70	4		100 PMS Blues ....*To Daddy*		$3		Columbia 77723
9/16/95	15	20		101 I Will Always Love You ....*Speakin' Of The Devil* [R]		$3		Columbia 78079
				DOLLY PARTON WITH VINCE GILL				
				new version of #35 and #65 above				
10/5/96	62	10		102 Just When I Needed You Most ....*For The Good Times*		$3		Rising Tide 56041
12/27/97	73	2		103 Hard Candy Christmas ....*Me And Little Andy* [X-R]		$4		RCA 13361
				same version as #67 above				
				PARTON, Randy **'81**				
				Born on 12/15/55 in Sevier County, Tennessee. Brother of **Dolly Parton**.				
3/7/81	30	12		1 Hold Me Like You Never Had Me *My Blue Tears*		$4		RCA 12137
8/1/81	30	10		2 Shot Full Of Love ....*Please Don't Lie*		$4		RCA 12271
12/19/81	80	4		3 Don't Cry Baby ....*Again And Again*		$4		RCA 12351
5/1/82	76	4		4 Oh, No ....*Hold Me Like You Never Had Me*		$4	◻	RCA 13087
				#4 Pop hit for the Commodores in 1981				
10/22/83	92	2		5 A Stranger In Her Bed.....................................*Waltz Across Texas*		$4		RCA 13608
★327★				**PARTON, Stella** **'75**				
				Born on 5/4/49 in Sevier County, Tennessee. Sister of **Dolly Parton**.				
				1)I Want To Hold You In My Dreams Tonight 2)Standard Lie Number One 3)The Danger Of A Stranger				
5/24/75	9	18		1 I Want To Hold You In My Dreams Tonight *Ode To Olivia*		$6		Country Soul 039
9/27/75	56	10		2 It's Not Funny Anymore ....*(I've Got To Get Back On) The Right Side Of God*		$6		Soul Country 088
1/8/77	87	5		3 Neon Women ....*Crying Steel Guitar*		$5		Elektra 45367
				CARMOL TAYLOR & STELLA PARTON				
3/19/77	60	9		4 I'm Not That Good At Goodbye ....*Love Me To Sleep*		$5		Elektra 45383
7/30/77	15	13		5 The Danger Of A Stranger ....*The More The Change*		$5		Elektra 45410
11/12/77+	14	15		6 Standard Lie Number One........................*The More The Change*		$5		Elektra 45437
3/25/78	20	10		7 Four Little Letters ....*Fade My Blues Away*		$5		Elektra 45463
7/1/78	28	9		8 Undercover Lovers................*There's A Rumor Going 'Round*		$5		Elektra 45490
10/14/78	21	10		9 Stormy Weather ....*Lie To Linda*		$5		Elektra 45533
4/21/79	26	11		10 Steady As The Rain ....*A Little Inconvenient*		$5		Elektra 46029
7/28/79	36	9		11 The Room At The Top Of The Stairs ....*Honey Come Home*		$5		Elektra 46502
3/6/82	65	7		12 I'll Miss You ....*I Hate The Night*		$5	■	Town House 1056
7/24/82	75	5		13 Young Love....................................*Something To Go By*		$5	■	Town House 1058
				#1 Pop hit for Tab Hunter in 1957				
3/21/87	86	3		14 Cross My Heart ....*Heart Don't Fail Me Now*		$5	■	Luv 132
4/1/89	74	3		15 I Don't Miss You Like I Used To		$5		Airborne 10015
				PASTELL, James **'77**				
				Born James Robert Futch in 1940 in El Dorado, Arkansas.				
9/10/77	95	5		Hell Yes I Cheated................................*Woman Of The World*		$5		Paula 425
				PAUL, Buddy **'60**				
				Worked as a DJ at KCIJ in Shreveport, Louisiana.				
8/1/60	22	4		This Old Town ....*Foolish Me*		$25		Murco 1018
				PAUL, Joyce **'68**				
6/22/68	36	10		Phone Call To Mama....................*Don't Keep Me Hanging On*		$7		United Artists 50315
				PAUL, Les, and Mary Ford **'51**				
				Husband-and-wife team. Les Paul was born Lester Polsfuss on 6/9/16 in Waukesha, Wisconsin. Innovator in electric guitar and multi-track recordings. Mary Ford was born Colleen Summer on 7/7/28 in Pasadena, California. Died on 9/30/77 (age 49). They were married from 1949-63. Charted 42 pop hits from 1945-61.				
3/10/51	7	1	●	Mockin' Bird Hill *A:7 Chicken Reel*	2⁵	$20		Capitol F1373
				#2 Pop hit for **Patti Page** in 1951				
				PAXTON, Gary S. **'76**				
				Born in Mesa, Arizona. Recorded with Clyde "Skip" Battin as "Gary & Clyde" and "Skip & Flip."				
2/7/76	85	5		Too Far Gone (To Care What You Do To Me) ....*Freedom Lives In A Country Song*		$5		RCA Victor 10449

PAYCHECK, Johnny ★67★   '78

Born Donald Eugene Lytle on 5/31/37 in Greenfield, Ohio. Singer/songwriter/guitarist. Played in the backing bands for **Porter Wagoner**, **Faron Young**, **Ray Price** and **George Jones**. Joined the *Grand Ole Opry* in 1997.

1)Take This Job And Shove It 2)Mr. Lovemaker 3)She's All I Got 4)Someone To Give My Love To
5)Slide Off Of Your Satin Sheets

DEBUT	PEAK	WKS		A-side	B-side	Pop	$		Label & Number
10/16/65	26	12	1	A-11 .... *Where (In The World)*			$15		Hilltop 3007
2/26/66	40	2	2	Heartbreak Tennessee .... *Help Me Hank I'm Fallin'*			$15		Hilltop 3009
6/4/66	8	19	3	The Lovin' Machine	*Pride Covered Ears*		$10		Little Darlin' 008
11/5/66+	13	15	4	Motel Time Again..*If You Should Come Back Today*			$10		Little Darlin' 0016
4/8/67	15	15	5	Jukebox Charlie ....*Something In Your World*			$10		Little Darlin' 0020
9/2/67	32	10	6	The Cave .... *Then Love Dies*			$10		Little Darlin' 0032
12/23/67+	41	11	7	Don't Monkey With Another Monkey's Monkey .... *You'll Recover In Time*			$10		Little Darlin' 0035
4/27/68	59	7	8	(It Won't Be Long) And I'll Be Hating You .... *Fool's Hall Of Fame*			$10		Little Darlin' 0042
8/17/68	66	4	9	My Heart Keeps Running To You .... *Yesterday, Today And Tomorrow*			$10		Little Darlin' 0046
12/14/68	73	4	10	If I'm Gonna Sink .... *The Loser*			$10		Little Darlin' 0052
6/28/69	31	13	11	Wherever You Are ....*I Can't Promise You Won't Get Lonely*			$10		Little Darlin' 0060
10/9/71	2[1]	19	12	She's All I Got	*You Touched My Life*	91	$7		Epic 10783
				#39 Pop hit for Freddie North in 1971					
3/11/72	4	14	13	Someone To Give My Love To	*Love Sure Is Beautiful*		$7		Epic 10836
5/27/72	13	11	14	Let's All Go Down To The River....................................... *In The Garden*			$7		Epic 10863
				JODY MILLER AND JOHNNY PAYCHECK					
6/24/72	12	11	15	Love Is A Good Thing .... *High On The Thought Of You*			$7		Epic 10876
10/7/72	21	12	16	Somebody Loves Me.............................*Without You (There's No Such Thing As Love)*			$7		Epic 10912
2/24/73	10	12	17	Something About You I Love	*Your Love Is The Key To It All*		$6		Epic 10947
6/9/73	2[3]	15	18	Mr. Lovemaker	*Once You've Had The Best*		$6		Epic 10999
11/3/73+	8	15	19	Song And Dance Man	*Love Is A Strange And Wonderful Thing*		$6		Epic 11046
3/16/74	19	12	20	My Part Of Forever .... *If Love Gets Any Better*			$6		Epic 11090
7/6/74	23	11	21	Keep On Lovin' Me .... *Ballad Of Thunder Road*			$6		Epic 11142
11/2/74+	12	15	22	For A Minute There.. *She's All I Live For*			$6		Epic 50040
3/1/75	26	11	23	Loving You Beats All I've Ever Seen .... *The Touch Of The Master's Hand*			$6		Epic 50073
5/31/75	38	12	24	I Don't Love Her Anymore .... *Loving You Is All I Thought It Would Be*			$6		Epic 50111
9/27/75	23	12	25	All-American Man .... *The Fool Strikes Again*			$6		Epic 50146
2/21/76	56	8	26	The Feminine Touch .... *Rhythm Guitar*			$6		Epic 50193
5/8/76	49	8	27	Gone At Last ....*Live With Me ('Til I Can Learn To Live Again)*			$6		Epic 50215
				JOHNNY PAYCHECK (With CHARNISSA)					
				#23 Pop hit for Paul Simon & Phoebe Snow in 1975					
7/24/76	34	10	28	11 Months And 29 Days....................*Live With Me ('Til I Can Learn To Live Again)*			$6		Epic 50249
10/23/76	44	8	29	I Can See Me Lovin' You Again .... *I Sleep With Her Memory Every Night*			$6		Epic 50291
2/12/77	7	16	30	Slide Off Of Your Satin Sheets	*That's What The Outlaws In Texas Want To Hear*		$6		Epic 50334
6/11/77	8	16	31	I'm The Only Hell (Mama Ever Raised)	*(To Be So Bad) She's Still Lookin' Good*		$6		Epic 50391
11/5/77+	❶[2]	18	32	Take This Job And Shove It/					
1/28/78	50	10	33	Colorado Kool-Aid ....[S]			$6		Epic 50469
4/15/78	17	10	34	Georgia In A Jug/					
4/15/78	33	10	35	Me And The I.R.S..			$6		Epic 50539
10/21/78	7	12	36	Friend, Lover, Wife	*Leave It To Me*		$6		Epic 50621
12/9/78+	7	13	37	Mabellene	*I Don't Want No Stranger Sleepin' In My Bed*		$7		Epic 50647
				GEORGE JONES AND JOHNNY PAYCHECK					
				#5 Pop hit for Chuck Berry in 1955					
1/27/79	27	11	38	The Outlaw's Prayer ....*Armed And Crazy*			$6		Epic 50655
1/27/79	94	4	39	Down On The Corner At A Bar Called Kelly's ...... *Something He'll Have To Learn*			$6		Little Darlin' 7808
				recorded in 1967					
5/26/79	14	11	40	You Can Have Her .... *Along Came Jones*			$6		Epic 50708
				GEORGE JONES AND JOHNNY PAYCHECK					
				#12 Pop hit for Roy Hamilton in 1961					
10/13/79	49	6	41	(Stay Away From) The Cocaine Train .... *Billy Bardo*			$5		Epic 50777
12/22/79+	17	13	42	Drinkin' And Drivin'.............................*Just Makin' Love Don't Make It Love*			$5		Epic 50818
4/5/80	40	9	43	Fifteen Beers................................... *Who Was That Man That Beat Me So*			$5		Epic 50863
6/21/80	31	9	44	When You're Ugly Like Us (You Just Naturally Got To Be Cool) .. *Kansas City*			$6		Epic 50891
				GEORGE JONES and JOHNNY PAYCHECK					
9/6/80	22	11	45	In Memory Of A Memory .... *New York Town*			$5		Epic 50923
12/13/80+	18	12	46	You Better Move On .... *Smack Dab In The Middle*			$6		Epic 50949
				GEORGE JONES and JOHNNY PAYCHECK					
				#24 Pop hit for Arthur Alexander in 1962					
3/28/81	41	8	47	I Can't Hold Myself In Line... *Carolyn*			$4		Epic 51012
				JOHNNY PAYCHECK AND MERLE HAGGARD					
7/4/81	57	7	48	Yesterday's News (Just Hit Home Today)................... *Someone Told My Story*			$4		Epic 02144
1/23/82	75	4	49	The Highlight Of '81 .... *Sharon Rae*			$4		Epic 02684
4/24/82	69	5	50	No Way Out .... *We've All Gone Crazy*			$4		Epic 02817
8/14/82	88	4	51	D.O.A. (Drunk On Arrival) .... *Gonna Get Right (And Do Somethin' Wrong)*			$4		Epic 03052
12/1/84+	30	18	52	I Never Got Over You .... S:27 / A:30 *Ole Pay Ain't Checked Out Yet*			$5		A.M.I. 1322
4/6/85	47	10	53	You're Every Step I Take.. *I Can't Quit Drinking*			$5		A.M.I. 1323

PAYCHECK, Johnny — Cont'd

DEBUT	PEAK	WKS	A-side	B-side	$	Label & Number
12/7/85	63	8	54 Everything Is Changing.. *Palimony*		$5	A.M.I. 1327
5/17/86	21	22	55 Old Violin .... S:12 / A:25 *Come To Me*		$4	Mercury 884720
11/8/86	49	10	56 Don't Bury Me 'Til I'm Ready .... *Ex-Wives And Lovers*		$4	Mercury 888088
2/28/87	56	7	57 Come To Me .... *Ragtime Redneck Boy*		$4	Mercury 888341
7/11/87	72	5	58 I Grow Old Too Fast (And Smart Too Slow) .. *Caught Between A Rock And A Soft Place*		$4	Mercury 888651
4/9/88	81	2	59 Out Of Beer .... *Oklahoma Lady*		$6	Desperado 1001
2/18/89	90	2	60 Scars		$6	Damascus 2001

PAYNE, Dennis   '88
Born in Bakersfield, California. Singer/songwriter.

DEBUT	PEAK	WKS	A-side	B-side	$	Label & Number
2/20/88	66	5	1 I Can't Hang On Anymore		$5	True 88
10/29/88	94	2	2 That's Why You Haven't Seen Me .... *Crazy Woman*		$5	True 93

PAYNE, Jimmy   '69
Born on 4/12/36 in Leachville, Arkansas. Singer/songwriter/guitarist.

DEBUT	PEAK	WKS	A-side	B-side	$	Label & Number
4/19/69	60	6	1 L.A. Angels .... *A Rose Is A Rose*		$6	Epic 10444
11/3/73	79	5	2 Ramblin' Man .... *One Man's Woman At A Time*		$6	Cinnamon 772
			#2 Pop hit for The Allman Brothers Band in 1973			
8/1/81	80	4	3 Turnin' My Love On .... *She's Free But She's Not Easy*		$6	Kik 907

PAYNE, Jody   '81
Male singer/harmonica player. Member of **Willie Nelson**'s band.

DEBUT	PEAK	WKS	A-side	B-side	$	Label & Number
2/28/81	65	6	There's A Crazy Man		$4	Kari 117
			JODY PAYNE & The Willie Nelson Family Band			

PAYNE, Leon   '50
Born on 6/15/17 in Alba, Texas. Died of a heart attack on 9/11/69 (age 52). Blind since early childhood.
Singer/songwriter/guitarist/pianist/drummer.

DEBUT	PEAK	WKS	A-side	B-side	$	Label & Number
11/5/49+	❶²	32	I Love You Because .... A:❶² / S:4 / J:10 *A Link In The Chain Of Broken Hearts*		$15	Capitol 40238

PEARCE, Kevin   '88
Born in 1960 in Lake Alfred, Florida.

DEBUT	PEAK	WKS	A-side	B-side	$	Label & Number
1/14/84	91	2	1 It's Gonna Be A Heartache		$5	Orlando 108
1/18/86	92	2	2 Pink Cadillac		$5	Orlando 111
			written by Bruce Springsteen (B-side of his 1984 Pop hit "Dancing In The Dark"); #5 Pop hit for Natalie Cole in 1988			
10/31/87	90	2	3 The Bigger The Love		$5	Evergreen 1057
2/27/88	66	6	4 Love Ain't Made For Fools		$5	Evergreen 1067
6/25/88	68	6	5 Took It Like A Man, Cried Like A Baby		$5	Evergreen 1074

PEARL, Minnie — see MINNIE

PEARL RIVER   '93
Group from Mississippi: Jeff Stewart (vocals), Chuck Ethredge, Ken Fleming, Bryan Culpepper, Joe Morgan and Derek George.

DEBUT	PEAK	WKS	A-side	B-side	$	Label & Number
5/1/93	62	8	Fool To Fall			album cut
			from the album *Find Out What's Happening* on Liberty 80478			

PEDERSEN, Herb   '77
Born on 4/27/44 in Berkeley, California. Singer/songwriter/banjo player. Member of **The Desert Rose Band**.

DEBUT	PEAK	WKS	A-side	B-side	$	Label & Number
1/15/77	56	7	Our Baby's Gone.. *Jesus Once Again*		$5	Epic 50309

PEEK, Everett   '77

DEBUT	PEAK	WKS	A-side	B-side	$	Label & Number
5/7/77	94	3	Sea Cruise		$7	Commercial 00016
			#14 Pop hit for Frankie Ford in 1959			

PEEL, Dave   '70
Singer/actor from Nashville. Acted in the movie *Nashville*.

DEBUT	PEAK	WKS	A-side	B-side	$	Label & Number
11/15/69	66	4	1 I'm Walkin' .... *My Baby*		$6	Chart 5037
			#4 Pop hit for Fats Domino in 1957			
3/14/70	62	7	2 Wax Museum .... *If You've Been Better Than I've Been (You've Been Bored)*		$6	Chart 5054
5/23/70	44	9	3 Hit The Road Jack .... *The Question*		$6	Chart 5066
			CONNIE EATON & DAVE PEEL #1 Pop hit for Ray Charles in 1961			
11/7/70	56	7	4 It Takes Two .... *No Rest For The Wicked*		$6	Chart 5099
			CONNIE EATON & DAVE PEEL #14 Pop hit for Marvin Gaye & Kim Weston in 1967			
1/23/71	56	4	5 (You've Got To) Move Two Mountains............. *Willard Crabtree's Running For Trustee*		$6	Chart 5109
			#20 Pop hit for Marv Johnson in 1960			

★343★ PEGGY SUE   '69
Born Peggy Sue Webb on 3/24/47 in Butcher Holler, Kentucky. Singer/songwriter. Sister of **Loretta Lynn**, **Crystal Gayle** and **Jay Lee Webb**; distant cousin of **Patty Loveless**. Married to **Sonny Wright**.
1)*I'm Dynamite* 2)*I'm Gettin' Tired Of Babyin' You* 3)*I Want To See Me In Your Eyes*

DEBUT	PEAK	WKS	A-side	B-side	$	Label & Number
6/7/69	28	11	1 I'm Dynamite .... *Love Whatcha Got At Home*		$6	Decca 32485
11/1/69	30	10	2 I'm Gettin' Tired Of Babyin' You .... *No Woman Can Hold Him Too Long*		$6	Decca 32571
4/18/70	65	3	3 After The Preacher's Gone........................... *You Can't Pull The Wool Over My Eyes*		$6	Decca 32640
7/11/70	37	11	4 All American Husband........................... *I'm Leaving The Bottle And You*		$6	Decca 32698
12/12/70	58	4	5 Apron Strings .... *You're Leavin' Me For Her Again*		$6	Decca 32754
5/15/71	68	5	6 I Say, "Yes, Sir" .... *Do It Girl Before It's Too Late*		$6	Decca 32812
1/15/77	34	10	7 Every Beat Of My Heart .... *This Time It's Love*		$5	Door Knob 021
			#6 Pop hit for Gladys Knight & The Pips in 1961			
4/9/77	51	9	8 I Just Came In Here (To Let A Little Hurt Out)........................... *Jody Come Home*		$5	Door Knob 029
7/2/77	81	4	9 Good Evening Henry .... *Fire In Texas*		$5	Door Knob 036
10/22/77	100	1	10 If This Is What Love's All About .... *Someone I Can't Say No To*		$5	Door Knob 038
			PEGGY SUE & SONNY WRIGHT			

DEBUT	PEAK	WKS	Gold	A-side (Chart Hit) ... B-side	Pop	$	Pic	Label & Number
				PEGGY SUE — Cont'd				
2/4/78	85	5		11 To Be Loved .... *I've Been Close To Love (Too Many Times)*		$5		Door Knob 045
				#22 Pop hit for Jackie Wilson in 1958				
6/10/78	87	2		12 Let Me Down Easy .... *Come And Lay Down With Me*		$5		Door Knob 052
9/2/78	80	5		13 All Night Long .... *Good Evening Henry*		$5		Door Knob 069
11/18/78+	37	12		14 How I Love You In The Morning .... *Where Your Memories Play*		$5		Door Knob 079
3/24/79	30	10		15 I Want To See Me In Your Eyes .... *Let Me Down Easy*		$5		Door Knob 094
6/30/79	51	6		16 The Love Song And The Dream Belong To Me .... *Rainy Day Lovin*		$5		Door Knob 102
11/10/79	86	5		17 Gently Hold Me .... *If This Is What Love's All About*		$5		Door Knob 113
				PEGGY SUE and SONNY WRIGHT				
3/29/80	80	4		18 For As Long As You Want Me .... *Only One Thing Left To Do*		$5		Door Knob 121
7/12/80	93	3		19 Why Don't You Go To Dallas .... *Only One Thing Left To Do*		$5		Door Knob 131
				PENN, Bobby '71				
				Born in Houston.				
7/3/71	51	11		1 You Were On My Mind .... *Pretty Girl From Kingston Town*		$6		50 States 1
				#3 Pop hit for We Five in 1965				
9/7/74	88	5		2 Watch Out For Lucy .... *The Worst I Ever Had Was Good*		$5		50 States 29
7/4/76	100	1		3 Little Weekend Warriors .... *You're All That Really Matters To Me*		$5		50 States 42
				PENNINGTON, J.P. '91				
				Born James Preston Pennington in Berea, Kentucky. Former member of **Exile**.				
3/23/91	45	19		1 Whatever It Takes .... *If I Were You*		$3		MCA 54047
8/3/91	72	1		2 You Gotta Get Serious .... *Blue Highway*		$3		MCA 54126
				PENNINGTON, Ray '67				
				Born Ramon Daniel Pennington 1933 in Clay County, Kentucky. Singer/songwriter/guitarist. Member of **Bluestone** and **The Swing Shift Band**.				
11/5/66	43	9		1 Who's Been Mowing The Lawn (While I Was Gone) .... *I Don't Feel At Home*		$8		Capitol 5751
5/6/67	29	8		2 Ramblin' Man .... *Let Go*		$8		Capitol 5855
11/18/67	65	3		3 Who's Gonna Walk The Dog (And Put Out The Cat) .... *You Turned The Lights On*		$8		Capitol 2006
7/5/69	70	6		4 What Eva Doesn't Have .... *Denver*		$6		Monument 1145
12/6/69	69	5		5 This Song Don't Care Who Sings It .... *I Wouldn't Treat A Doggone Dog*		$6		Monument 1170
5/2/70	61	7		6 You Don't Know Me .... *Country Blues*		$6		Monument 1194
				#2 Pop hit for **Ray Charles** in 1962				
8/8/70	74	2		7 The Other Woman .... *I Know Love*		$6		Monument 1208
1/2/71	68	5		8 Bubbles In My Beer .... *Don't Build No Fences For Me*		$6		Monument 1231
11/18/78	79	4		9 She Wanted A Little Bit More		$5		MRC 1022
				PENNY, Hank '46				
				Born Herbert Clayton Penny on 8/18/18 in Birmingham, Alabama. Died of heart failure on 4/17/92 (age 73). Singer/songwriter/banjo player. Worked as a comedian on **Spade Cooley**'s TV series in Los Angeles. Married to **Sue Thompson** from 1953-63.				
6/15/46	4	6		1 Steel Guitar Stomp .... *I'm Counting The Days* [I]		$25		King 528
9/14/46	4	4		2 Get Yourself A Red Head .... *Missouri*		$25		King 540
2/25/50	4	12		3 Bloodshot Eyes .... J:4 *I Was Satisfied*		$25		King 828
				PENNY, Joe '64				
7/18/64	41	7		Frosty Window Pane .... *Hatty Fatty*		$20		Sims 173
				PEPPER, Brenda '75				
				Female singer from Chicago.				
6/21/75	97	4		You Bring Out The Best In Me .... *Goodbye Ain't As Far Away As Gone*		$5		Playboy 6038
				PEREZ, Tony '89				
3/4/89	79	3		1 Oh How I Love You (Como Te Quiero) .... *Bridge To Burn*		$3		Reprise 27591
10/14/89	78	4		2 Take Another Run .... *Texarkana*		$3		Reprise 22838
				PERFECT STRANGER '95				
				Group from Texas: Steve Murray (vocals), Richard Raines (guitar), Shayne Morrison (bass) and Andy Ginn (drums).				
4/15/95	4	22		1 You Have The Right To Remain Silent .... S:2 *It's Up To You*	61	$3	∎	Curb 76956
9/30/95	52	10		2 I'm A Stranger Here Myself .... *I Ain't Never*		$3	∎	Curb 76969
2/17/96	56	10		3 Remember The Ride .... *Cut Me Off*		$3	∎	Curb 76978
3/29/97	62	7		4 Fire When Ready .... *(remix)*		$3	∎	Curb 73014
	★303★			**PERKINS, Carl** '56				
				Born on 4/9/32 near Tiptonville, Tennessee. Died of a stroke on 1/19/98 (age 65). Rockabilly singer/guitarist/songwriter. Member of **Johnny Cash**'s touring band from 1965-75. Inducted into the Rock and Roll Hall of Fame in 1987.				
				1)Blue Suede Shoes 2)Boppin' The Blues 3)Dixie Fried				
2/18/56	❶³	24		1 Blue Suede Shoes .... J:❶³ / A:2 / S:2 *Honey, Don't!*	2⁴	$50		Sun 234
6/30/56	7	6		2 Boppin' The Blues .... J:7 / S:9 *All Mama's Children*	70	$50		Sun 243
10/6/56	10	2		3 Dixie Fried/ S:10		$50		Sun 243
				also see #13 below				
		2		4 I'm Sorry, I'm Not Sorry		$60		Sun 249
3/9/57	13	8		5 Your True Love .... S:13 *Matchbox*	67	$50		Sun 261
3/31/58	17	9		6 Pink Pedal Pushers .... S:17 *Jive After Five*	91	$40	∎	Columbia 41131
12/17/66+	22	15		7 Country Boy's Dream .... *If I Could Come Back*		$30		Dollie 505
5/20/67	40	8		8 Shine, Shine, Shine .... *Almost Love*		$30		Dollie 508
1/4/69	20	15		9 Restless *11:43*		$15		Columbia 44723
5/29/71	65	5		10 Me Without You .... *Red Headed Woman*		$10		Columbia 45347
12/11/71+	53	7		11 Cotton Top .... *About All I Can Give Is My Love*		$10		Columbia 45466
5/6/72	60	5		12 High On Love .... *Take Me Back To Memphis*		$10		Columbia 45582
10/13/73	61	7		13 (Let's Get) Dixiefried .... *One More Loser Goin' Home* [R]		$8		Mercury 73425
				new version of #3 above				

DEBUT	PEAK	WKS	Gold	A-side (Chart Hit)..B-side	Pop	$	Pic	Label & Number
				PERKINS, Carl — Cont'd				
6/7/86	31	14		14 Birth Of Rock And Roll.................................S:26 / A:29 *Rock And Roll (Fais Do Do)*		$5	■	America Sm. 884760
3/28/87	83	3		15 Class Of '55..*We Remember The King*		$5		America Sm. 888142
				PERKINS, Dal '68				
				Born in Abilene, Texas. Male singer.				
1/13/68	73	3		Helpless...*Woman In The Darkness*		$10		Columbia 44343
				PERRY, Brenda Kaye '78				
				Female singer from Waynesboro, Virginia.				
10/22/77	64	9		1 Ringgold Georgia............................*Have I Told You Lately That I Loved You*		$5		MRC 1005
				BILLY WALKER AND BRENDA KAYE PERRY				
1/21/78	35	11		2 Deeper Water *Home Sweet Home*		$5		MRC 1010
4/22/78	37	9		3 I Can't Get Up By Myself ....*Free*		$5		MRC 1013
10/14/78	78	5		4 My Daddy Was A Travelin' Man ....*I Am A Woman*		$5		MRC 1021
2/17/79	90	3		5 Make Me Your Woman ....*(What A) Wonderful World*		$5		MRC 1026
				PETERS, Ben '69				
				Born on 6/20/37 in Hattiesburg, Mississippi. Singer/prolific songwriter. Father of **Debbie Peters**.				
7/19/69	46	9		1 San Francisco Is A Lonely Town ....*You're The Happy Song I Sing*		$7		Liberty 56114
9/1/73	92	4		2 Would You Still Love Me ....*This Has Got To Last*		$6		Capitol 3687
				PETERS, Debbie '80				
				Born in 1959. Daughter of **Ben Peters**.				
3/15/80	84	2		It Can't Wait ....*I Can't Get Enough Of You*		$6		Oak 1012
				PETERS, Doug '88				
				Born Doug Volchko on 8/4/59 in Chicago.				
8/6/88	85	2		My Heart's Way Behind		$6		Comstock 1895
				PETERS, Gretchen '96				
				Born in New York City; raised in Boulder, Colorado.				
4/20/96	68	3		When You Are Old ....*I Was Looking For You*		$3	▌	Imprint 18001
				PETERS, Jimmie '77				
				Born on 10/12/38 in Whiteface, Texas. Singer/songwriter/bassist.				
5/28/77	59	7		1 Somebody Took Her Love (And Never Gave It Back) .... *I'm What I Am*		$5		Mercury 73911
10/8/77	73	6		2 Lipstick Traces ....*Even If It's Wrong*		$5		Mercury 55005
				#48 Pop hit for The O'Jays in 1965				
2/18/78	75	4		3 634-5789 ....*Just Because It Feels Good*		$5		Mercury 55016
				#13 Pop hit for Wilson Pickett in 1966				
6/3/78	84	4		4 I Will Always Love You ....*Just Because It Feels Good*		$5		Mercury 55025
1/13/79	78	4		5 I Hate The Way Our Love Is....................................		$6		Vista 101
				JIMMY PETERS and LYNDA K. LANCE				
4/28/79	98	3		6 First Class Fool		$6		Vista 106
				JIMMIE PETERS/LINDA K. LANCE				
3/1/80	75	4		7 Hearts ....*Let's Write A Love Song*		$5	■	Sunbird 105
				PETERS & LEE '74				
				British duo: Lennie Peters (who was blind) and Dianne Lee. Duo split in 1980. Peters died of cancer on 10/10/92 (age 59).				
3/16/74	79	8		Welcome Home ....*Can't Keep My Mind On The Game*	119	$6		Philips 40729
				PETERSON, Colleen '76				
				Born on 11/14/50 in Peterboro, Canada. Died of cancer on 10/9/96 (age 45).				
11/27/76	100	2		Souvenirs ....*Six Days On The Road*		$5		Capitol 4349
				PETERSON, Michael '97				
				Born on 8/7/59 in Tucson, Arizona. Singer/songwriter/guitarist.				
5/17/97	3	20		1 Drink, Swear, Steal & Lie S:4 *For A Song*	86	$3	▌	Reprise 17379
9/13/97	❶¹	22		2 From Here To Eternity				album cut
				from the album *Michael Peterson* on Reprise 46618				
				PFEIFER, Diane '82				
				Born on 11/4/50 in St. Louis.				
3/1/80	85	3		1 Free To Be Lonely Again................................*Oh No, Not Love Again*		$4		Capitol 4823
5/17/80	59	7		2 Roses Ain't Red ....*Do You Mind (If I Fall In Love With You)*		$4		Capitol 4858
10/4/80	83	3		3 Wishful Drinkin' ....*Just When I Needed A Love Song*		$4		Capitol 4916
11/28/81+	35	10		4 Play Something We Could Love To *Sing You To Sleep*		$4		Capitol 5060
6/12/82	85	3		5 Something To Love For Again................................*Missing You All By Myself*		$4		Capitol 5116
9/25/82	76	4		6 Let's Get Crazy Again ....*Missing You All By Myself*		$4		Capitol 5154
				PHELPS, Brother — see BROTHER PHELPS				
	★269★			**PHILLIPS, Bill** '66				
				Born on 1/28/36 in Canton, North Carolina. Singer/songwriter/guitarist. Known as "Tater." Acted in the movie *The Sugarland Express*.				
				1)Put It Off Until Tomorrow 2)The Company You Keep 3)The Words I'm Gonna Have To Eat				
8/24/59	27	2		1 Sawmill...*You Are The Reason*		$15		Columbia 41416
				MEL TILLIS and BILL PHILLIPS				
2/8/60	24	4		2 Georgia Town Blues ....*Till I Get Enough Of These Blues*		$15		Columbia 41530
				MEL TILLIS and BILL PHILLIPS				
3/14/64	22	18		3 I Can Stand It (As Long As She Can) ....*Wheeling Dealing Daddy*		$10		Decca 31584
10/17/64	26	10		4 Stop Me ....*Stepping Out*		$10		Decca 31648
4/2/66	6	18		5 Put It Off Until Tomorrow *Lonely Lonely Boy*		$10		Decca 31901
				Dolly Parton (harmony vocal)				
8/13/66	8	19		6 The Company You Keep *The Lies Just Can't Be True*		$10		Decca 31996
				above 2 co-written by **Dolly Parton**				

PHILLIPS, Bill — Cont'd

DEBUT	PEAK	WKS		A-side (Chart Hit) / B-side	Pop	$	Pic	Label & Number
1/21/67	10	15	7	The Words I'm Gonna Have To Eat / *Falling Back To You*		$8		Decca 32074
7/22/67	39	7	8	I Learn Something New Everyday / *I Didn't Forget*		$8		Decca 32141
11/18/67+	25	13	9	Love's Dead End / *Oh, What It Did To Me*		$8		Decca 32207
3/15/69	54	10	10	I Only Regret / *She's An Angel*		$8		Decca 32432
10/18/69	10	14	11	Little Boy Sad / *I'm Living In Two Worlds*		$8		Decca 32565
				#17 Pop hit for Johnny Burnette in 1961				
3/28/70	43	7	12	She's Hungry Again / *You've Still Got A Place In My Heart*		$8		Decca 32638
8/22/70	46	9	13	Same Old Story, Same Old Lie / *You Can't Love Me When I'm Gone*		$8		Decca 32707
2/27/71	56	6	14	Big Rock Candy Mountain / *I Didn't Forget*		$8		Decca 32782
3/18/72	66	8	15	I Am, I Said / *Son*		$6		United Artists 50879
				#4 Pop hit for Neil Diamond in 1971				
8/11/73	91	3	16	It's Only Over Now And Then / *I've Got Yesterday*		$6		United Artists 266
6/24/78	90	3	17	Divorce Suit (You Were Named Co-Respondent) / *I've Been Loving You Too Long*		$5		Soundwaves 4570
2/3/79	89	3	18	You're Gonna Make A Cheater Out Of Me / *Temporarily Yours*		$5		Soundwaves 4579
7/7/79	85	3	19	At The Moonlite / *I'm Turning You Loose*		$5		Soundwaves 4587

PHILLIPS, Charlie '62

Born on 7/2/37 in Clovis, New Mexico. Singer/songwriter/guitarist.

DEBUT	PEAK	WKS		A-side / B-side	Pop	$	Pic	Label & Number
4/14/62	9	7	1	I Guess I'll Never Learn / *Now That It's Over*		$10		Columbia 42289
10/12/63	30	1	2	This Is The House / *Later Tonight*		$10		Columbia 42851

PHILLIPS, John '70

Born on 8/30/35 in Paris Island, South Carolina. Co-founder of The Mamas & The Papas. Formerly married to actress Michele Phillips. Father of actress MacKenzie Phillips and singer Chynna Phillips (of Wilson Phillips).

DEBUT	PEAK	WKS		A-side / B-side	Pop	$	Pic	Label & Number
7/4/70	58	7		Mississippi / *April Anne*	32	$6		Dunhill/ABC 4236

PHILLIPS, Stu '67

Born on 1/19/33 in Montreal. Singer/songwriter/guitarist. Known as "The Western Gentleman." Joined the *Grand Ole Opry* in 1967.

DEBUT	PEAK	WKS		A-side / B-side	Pop	$	Pic	Label & Number
4/30/66	39	5	1	Bracero / *Angel Of Love*		$8		RCA Victor 8771
8/20/66	32	11	2	The Great El Tigre (The Tiger) / *Another Day Has Gone*		$8		RCA Victor 8868
2/4/67	44	8	3	Walk Me To The Station / *Guess Things Happen That Way*		$8		RCA Victor 9066
6/17/67	21	14	4	Vin Rosé / *I Wish I Had Never Seen Sunshine*		$8		RCA Victor 9219
10/21/67	13	12	5	Juanita Jones / *A Castle, A Cabin*		$8		RCA Victor 9333
4/20/68	62	6	6	The Note In Box Number 9 / *Our Last Rendezvous*		$8		RCA Victor 9481
7/13/68	53	7	7	The Top Of The World / *That Completely Destroys My Plans*		$8		RCA Victor 9557
12/21/68+	68	6	8	Bring Love Back Into Our World / *Speak Softly, My Love*		$8		RCA Victor 9673

PIANO RED — see SHIRLEY, Danny

PIERCE, Webb ★6★ '55

Born on 8/8/21 in West Monroe, Louisiana. Died of heart failure on 2/24/91 (age 69). Singer/songwriter/guitarist. Hosted own radio show on KMLB in West Monroe in 1937. Served in the U.S. Army from 1940-43. Joined the *Louisiana Hayride* in 1950. Joined the *Grand Ole Opry* in 1955. Co-owner of Cedarwood music publishing company. Acted in the movies *Buffalo Guns*, *Music City USA* and *Road To Nashville*. His daughter Debbie was a member of *Chantilly*.

1)In The Jailhouse Now 2)Slowly 3)Love, Love, Love 4)I Don't Care 5)There Stands The Glass

DEBUT	PEAK	WKS		A-side / B-side	Pop	$	Pic	Label & Number
1/5/52	❶⁴	27	1	Wondering / A:❶⁴ / S:4 / J:4 *New Silver Bells*		$25		Decca 9-46364
				first recorded by the Riverside Ramblers in 1937 on Bluebird				
6/7/52	❶³	20	2	That Heart Belongs To Me / A:❶³ / J:2 / S:5 *So Used To Loving You*		$25		Decca 9-28091
10/4/52	❶⁴	23	3	Back Street Affair / A:❶⁴ / J:❶³ / S:❶² *I'll Always Take Care Of You*		$25		Decca 9-28369
1/31/53	4	7	4	I'll Go On Alone / J:4 / S:7 / A:8				
2/14/53	4	6	5	That's Me Without You / A:4 / J:4 / S:9		$25		Decca 28534
3/28/53	4	14	6	The Last Waltz / S:4 / A:5 / J:5				
4/18/53	5	6	7	I Haven't Got The Heart / J:5 / A:6		$25		Decca 28594
7/4/53	❶⁸	22	8	It's Been So Long / A:❶⁸ / S:❶⁶ / J:❶¹				
				melody is the same as "I've Got Five Dollars and It's Saturday Night" by Faron Young				
7/4/53	9	2	9	Don't Throw Your Life Away / J:9		$25		Decca 28725
10/24/53	❶¹²	27	10	There Stands The Glass / S:❶¹² / J:❶⁹ / A:❶⁶				
10/24/53+	3	17	11	I'm Walking The Dog / J:3 / A:4 / S:6		$25		Decca 28834
2/6/54	❶¹⁷	36	12	Slowly / S:❶¹⁷ / J:❶¹⁷ / A:❶¹⁵ *You Just Can't Be True*		$25		Decca 28991
6/5/54	❶²	31	13	Even Tho / A:❶² / J:2 / S:3				
6/12/54	4	18	14	Sparkling Brown Eyes / S:4 / A:4 / J:4		$25		Decca 29107
				WEBB PIERCE With Wilburn Brothers				
10/9/54	❶¹⁰	29	15	More And More / J:❶¹⁰ / S:❶⁹ / A:❶⁸				
10/9/54	4	12	16	You're Not Mine Anymore / A:4 / S:8		$25		Decca 29252
2/5/55	❶²¹	37	17	In The Jailhouse Now / J:❶²¹ / S:❶²⁰ / A:❶¹⁵				
				Wilburn Brothers (harmony vocals); written by Jimmie Rodgers; also see #96 below				
2/12/55	10	2	18	I'm Gonna Fall Out Of Love With You / A:10 / S:14		$20		Decca 29391
6/18/55	❶¹²	32	19	I Don't Care / S:❶¹² / A:❶¹² / J:❶¹²				
		6	20	Your Good For Nothing Heart / A:flip / J:flip		$20		Decca 29480
9/24/55	❶¹³	32	21	Love, Love, Love / A:❶¹³ / J:❶⁹ / S:❶⁸				
10/29/55	7	5	22	If You Were Me / A:7		$20		Decca 29662

DEBUT	PEAK	WKS	Gold	A-side	B-side	Pop	$	Label & Number
				PIERCE, Webb — Cont'd				
12/17/55+	❶⁴	25		23 Why Baby Why	A:❶⁴ / S:❶¹ / J:❶¹ *Missing You*		$20	Decca 29755
				RED SOVINE And WEBB PIERCE				
3/3/56	2⁷	21		24 Yes I Know Why/	A:2 / S:3 / J:3			
3/10/56	3	13		25 'Cause I Love You	J:3 / S:5 / J:12		$20	Decca 29805
4/21/56	5	14		26 Little Rosa	S:5 / A:5 / J:5 *Hold Everything (Till I Get Home)* [S]		$20	Decca 29876
				RED SOVINE and WEBB PIERCE				
7/21/56	7	11		27 Any Old Time/	A:7 / J:7 / S:10			
				written by Jimmie Rodgers				
		6		28 We'll Find A Way	S:flip / J:flip		$20	Decca 29974
10/13/56	10	8		29 Teenage Boogie/	S:10 / A:15			
		5		30 I'm Really Glad You Hurt Me	S:flip		$35	Decca 30045
1/5/57	3	22		31 I'm Tired/	S:3 / A:4 / J:4			
		4		32 It's My Way			$20	Decca 30155
3/30/57	❶¹	22		33 Honky Tonk Song	A:❶¹ / S:2 / J:7 *Someday*		$20	Decca 30255
4/6/57	8	9		34 Oh, So Many Years	A:8 *Can You Find It In Your Heart*		$15	Decca 30183
				KITTY WELLS and WEBB PIERCE				
4/13/57	12	2		35 Someday	A:12		$15	Decca 30255
5/27/57	7	15		36 Bye Bye, Love/	A:7 / S:8	73		
6/10/57	7	12		37 Missing You	S:3 / A:7		$15	Decca 30321
9/30/57	3	17		38 Holiday For Love/	A:3 / S:6			
11/18/57	12	1		39 Don't Do It Darlin'	A:12		$15	Decca 30419
1/20/58	12	1		40 One Week Later	A:12 *When I'm With You*		$15	Decca 30489
				WEBB PIERCE And KITTY WELLS				
5/5/58	3	17		41 Cryin' Over You	A:3 / S:12			
6/2/58	10	4		42 You'll Come Back	A:10		$15	Decca 30623
10/20/58	7	10		43 Tupelo County Jail/				
9/29/58	10	12		44 Falling Back To You	A:10 / S:18		$15	Decca 30711
1/19/59	22	3		45 I'm Letting You Go	*Sittin' Alone*		$15	Decca 30789
4/6/59	6	16		46 A Thousand Miles Ago	*What Goes On In Your Heart*		$15	Decca 30858
7/20/59	2⁹	25		47 I Ain't Never	*Shanghied*	24	$15	Decca 30923
12/21/59+	4	18		48 No Love Have I	*Whirlpool Of Love*	54	$15	Decca 31021
5/23/60	11	8		49 Is It Wrong (For Loving You)/		69		
4/11/60	17	10		50 (Doin' The) Lovers Leap		93	$12	Decca 31058
9/12/60	11	8		51 Drifting Texas Sand	*All I Need Is You*	108	$12	Decca 31118
11/14/60	4	18		52 Fallen Angel	*Truck Driver's Blues*	99	$12	Decca 31165
2/20/61	5	15		53 Let Forgiveness In	*There's More Pretty Girls Than One (Pop #118)*		$12	Decca 31197
5/29/61	3	21		54 Sweet Lips	*Last Night*		$12	Decca 31249
9/25/61	5	22		55 Walking The Streets/				
10/2/61	7	19		56 How Do You Talk To A Baby			$12	Decca 31298
2/10/62	5	16		57 Alla My Love	*You Are My Life*		$10	Decca 31347
6/2/62	7	13		58 Take Time/				
5/26/62	8	13		59 Crazy Wild Desire			$10	Decca 31380
10/6/62	5	15		60 Cow Town/				
10/13/62	19	10		61 Sooner Or Later			$10	Decca 31421
1/5/63	25	3		62 How Come Your Dog Don't Bite Nobody But Me	*So Soon*		$10	Decca 31445
				WEBB PIERCE and MEL TILLIS				
3/2/63	15	8		63 Sawmill/				
4/6/63	21	3		64 If I Could Come Back			$10	Decca 31451
6/22/63	7	15		65 Sands Of Gold	*Nobody's Darlin' But Mine*	118	$10	Decca 31488
11/9/63	9	13		66 Those Wonderful Years/				
10/26/63+	13	15		67 If The Back Door Could Talk			$10	Decca 31544
2/15/64	25	13		68 Waiting A Lifetime	*Love Come To Me*		$10	Decca 31582
5/23/64	2¹	23		69 Memory #1	*French Riviera (Pop #126)*		$10	Decca 31617
9/26/64	9	15		70 Finally	*He Made You For Me*		$10	Decca 31663
				KITTY WELLS And WEBB PIERCE				
1/30/65	26	14		71 That's Where My Money Goes/				
2/6/65	46	5		72 Broken Engagement			$10	Decca 31704
3/20/65	22	14		73 Loving You Then Losing You	*Let Me Live A Little*		$10	Decca 31737
8/14/65	13	14		74 Who Do I Think I Am/				
8/21/65	50	2		75 Hobo And The Rose			$10	Decca 31816
4/16/66	46	6		76 You Ain't No Better Than Me	*The Champ*		$10	Decca 31924
8/27/66	25	10		77 Love's Something (I Can't Understand)	*A Loner*		$10	Decca 31982
10/29/66	14	17		78 Where'd Ya Stay Last Night	*She's Twenty-One*		$8	Decca 32033
3/18/67	39	15		79 Goodbye City, Goodbye Girl	*That Same Old Street*		$8	Decca 32098
8/5/67	6	18		80 Fool Fool Fool	*Bottles And Babies*		$8	Decca 32167
1/27/68	24	13		81 Luzianna	*Somebody Please Kiss My Sweet Thing*		$8	Decca 32246
7/6/68	26	9		82 Stranger In A Strange, Strange City/				
8/3/68	74	2		83 In Another World			$8	Decca 32339
10/26/68	22	10		84 Saturday Night	*I Tried Everything To Please*		$8	Decca 32388
2/22/69	32	10		85 If I Had Last Night To Live Over	*No Tears Tonight*		$8	Decca 32438
7/5/69	14	13		86 This Thing	*Does My Memory Ever Cross Your Mind*		$8	Decca 32508
11/29/69+	38	9		87 Love Ain't Never Gonna Be No Better	*The Other Side Of You*		$8	Decca 32577
3/28/70	71	3		88 Merry-Go-Round World	*Fool's Night Out*		$8	Decca 32641
8/1/70	56	5		89 The Man You Want Me To Be	*Too Long*		$8	Decca 32694

PIERCE, Webb — Cont'd

DEBUT	PEAK	WKS		A-side / B-side	Pop	$	Pic	Label & Number
12/26/70+	73	3	90	Showing His Dollar .... *The Way We Were Back Then*		$8		Decca 32762
3/13/71	31	11	91	Tell Him That You Love Him ....*Heartaches Are For Lovers, Not For Friends*		$8		Decca 32787
9/18/71	73	2	92	Someone Stepped In (And Stole Me Blind).....................*I Miss The Little Things*		$8		Decca 32855
7/15/72	54	8	93	I'm Gonna Be A Swinger .... *Someday*		$8		Decca 32973
11/22/75	57	9	94	The Good Lord Giveth (And Uncle Sam Taketh Away) .... *Send My Love To Me*		$6		Plantation 131
3/13/76	82	5	95	I've Got Leaving On My Mind ....*Shame, Shame, Shame*		$6		Plantation 136
10/9/82	72	5	96	In The Jailhouse Now ....*Back Street Affair* [R]		$4		Columbia 03231

WILLIE NELSON & WEBB PIERCE
new version of #17 above

★337★ PILLOW, Ray '66
Born on 7/4/37 in Lynchburg, Virginia. Singer/songwriter/guitarist. Joined the *Grand Ole Opry* in 1966.
1)I'll Take The Dog 2)Thank You Ma'am 3)Mr. Do-It-Yourself

DEBUT	PEAK	WKS		A-side / B-side	Pop	$	Pic	Label & Number
2/13/65	49	4	1	Take Your Hands Off My Heart ....*Even The Bad Times Are Good*		$8		Capitol 5323
12/25/65+	17	10	2	Thank You Ma'am ....*"If" Is A Mighty Big Word*		$8		Capitol 5518
4/23/66	32	6	3	Common Colds And Broken Hearts ....*You've Got A Good Thing Going*		$8		Capitol 5597
5/14/66	9	15	4	I'll Take The Dog ....*I'd Fight The World*		$8		Capitol 5633

JEAN SHEPARD and RAY PILLOW

DEBUT	PEAK	WKS		A-side / B-side	Pop	$	Pic	Label & Number
10/8/66	26	11	5	Volkswagen ....*And I Like That Sortta Thing*		$8		Capitol 5735
11/26/66+	25	11	6	Mr. Do-It-Yourself ....*Strangers Nine To Five*		$8		Capitol 5769

JEAN SHEPARD & RAY PILLOW

DEBUT	PEAK	WKS		A-side / B-side	Pop	$	Pic	Label & Number
8/12/67	56	6	7	I Just Want To Be Alone ....*I Like A Whole Lot*		$8		Capitol 5953
12/9/67	62	2	8	Gone With The Wine ....*No Milk Today*		$8		Capitol 2030
9/14/68	51	8	9	Wonderful Day ....*If Every Man Had A Woman Like You*		$6		ABC 11114
8/23/69	38	8	10	Reconsider Me ....*The Doors Of Love*		$6		Plantation 25
2/5/72	62	3	11	Since Then ....*While I'm Gone*		$6		Mega 0055
5/13/72	66	7	12	She's Doing It To Me Again ....*Everytime*		$6		Mega 0072
1/5/74	80	8	13	Countryfied ....*I'm Doing What I Love, Loving You*		$6		Mega 1202
12/21/74+	77	4	14	Livin' In The Sunshine Of Your Love................................*The Party*		$5		ABC/Dot 17526
12/27/75	100	1	15	Roll On, Truckers ....*We've Got To Love That Other Woman Out Of Me*		$5		ABC/Dot 17589
5/13/78	97	3	16	Who's Gonna Tie My Shoes ....*Can I Have What's Left*		$6		Hilltop 130
7/21/79	82	4	17	Super Lady ....*Nighttime Masquerade*		$5		MCA 41047
7/18/81	82	3	18	One Too Many Memories ....*Friday Night Blues*		$6		First Generat. 011

PINETOPPERS, The '51
Group from Broadtop Mountain, Pennsylvania: brothers Roy and Vaughn Horton, Ray Smith, Rusty Keefer and Johnny Browers. Vocals by Trudy and Gloria Marlin (The Beaver Valley Sweethearts). Roy Horton was elected to the Country Music Hall of Fame in 1982.

DEBUT	PEAK	WKS		A-side / B-side	Pop	$	Pic	Label & Number
12/23/50+	3	13		Mockin' Bird Hill ....*J:3 / A:4 / S:5 Big Parade Polka*	10	$25		Coral 9-64061

#2 Pop hit for Patti Page in 1951

PINK, Celinda '93
Born in Tuscaloosa, Alabama; raised in Birmingham. Female singer.

DEBUT	PEAK	WKS		A-side / B-side	Pop	$	Pic	Label & Number
4/24/93	68	4		Pack Your Lies And Go ....*I've Earned The Right To Sing The Blues*		$4	∎	Step One 458

PINKARD & BOWDEN '84
Novelty duo. Pinkard was born James Pinkard on 1/16/47 in Abbeville, Louisiana. Bowden was born on 9/30/45 in Linden, Texas.

DEBUT	PEAK	WKS		A-side / B-side	Pop	$	Pic	Label & Number
3/3/84	64	8	1	Adventures In Parodies .... [N]		$4		Warner 29370

side one: Help Me Make It Through The Yard/Daddy Sang Bass/Delta Dawg/Somebody Done Somebody's Song Wrong/Drivin' My Wife Away; side two: Three Mile Island (Wolverton Mountain)/Blue Hairs Driving In My Lane/What's A W-4 (What's Forever For)

DEBUT	PEAK	WKS		A-side / B-side	Pop	$	Pic	Label & Number
9/15/84	39	9	2	Mama, She's Lazy ....*Shake A Snake* [N]		$4		Warner 29205

parody of "Mama He's Crazy" by The Judds

DEBUT	PEAK	WKS		A-side / B-side	Pop	$	Pic	Label & Number
8/16/86	92	3	3	She Thinks I Steal Cars ....*Imelda's Shoes* [N]		$4		Warner 2526

parody of "She Thinks I Still Care" by George Jones

DEBUT	PEAK	WKS		A-side / B-side	Pop	$	Pic	Label & Number
6/4/88	87	2	4	Arab, Alabama ....*Satellite Dish* [N]		$4		Warner 27909

melody based on "Good Hearted Woman" by Waylon Jennings

DEBUT	PEAK	WKS		A-side / B-side	Pop	$	Pic	Label & Number
4/15/89	79	4	5	Libyan On A Jet Plane (Leavin' On A Jet Plane) ....*Don't Pet The Dog* [N]		$4		Warner 22987

parody of "Leaving On A Jet Plane" by Peter, Paul & Mary

PIRATES OF THE MISSISSIPPI '91
Group from Montgomery, Alabama: "Wild" Bill McCorvey (vocals), Rich "Dude" Alves (guitar), Pat Severs (steel guitar), Dean Townson (bass) and Jimmy Lowe (drums).

DEBUT	PEAK	WKS		A-side / B-side	Pop	$	Pic	Label & Number
7/28/90	26	20	1	Honky Tonk Blues ....*Anything Goes*		$3	∎	Capitol 44579
11/17/90+	49	14	2	Rollin' Home				album cut
3/16/91	15	20	3	Feed Jake				album cut

above 3 from the album *Pirates Of The Mississippi* on Capitol 94389

DEBUT	PEAK	WKS		A-side / B-side	Pop	$	Pic	Label & Number
7/27/91	29	20	4	Speak Of The Devil				album cut
11/2/91	41	20	5	Fighting For You..*Talkin' 'Bout Love*		$3		Capitol 44775
2/29/92	22	20	6	Til I'm Holding You Again ....*Feed Jake*		$3		Liberty 57704
6/27/92	36	19	7	Too Much ....*Speak Of The Devil*		$3		Liberty 57767
10/10/92	56	8	8	A Street Man Named Desire ....*Mystery Ship*		$3		Liberty 57995
10/30/93	63	7	9	Dream You...				album cut

from the album *Dream You* on Liberty 80379

PITNEY, Gene '66
Born on 2/17/41 in Hartford, Connecticut; raised in Rockville, Connecticut. Singer/songwriter/guitarist. Charted 24 pop hits from 1961-70.

GEORGE & GENE George Jones & Gene Pitney:

DEBUT	PEAK	WKS		A-side / B-side	Pop	$	Pic	Label & Number
4/24/65	16	10	1	I've Got Five Dollars And It's Saturday Night ....*Wreck On The Highway*	99	$12		Musicor 1066
7/3/65	25	7	2	Louisiana Man ....*I'm A Fool To Care (Pop #115)*		$12	∎	Musicor 1097
11/20/65	50	2	3	Big Job ....*Your Old Standby*		$12	∎	Musicor 1115
1/15/66	15	12	4	Baby Ain't That Fine ....*Everybody Knows But You And Me*		$12		Musicor 1135

GENE PITNEY and MELBA MONTGOMERY

DEBUT	PEAK	WKS	Gold	A-side (Chart Hit)..B-side	Pop	$	Pic	Label & Number

George & Gene — Cont'd

DEBUT	PEAK	WKS		A-side / B-side	Pop	$	Label & Number
6/4/66	47	3		5 **That's All It Took** .... *Y'All Come*		$12	Musicor 1165

PLACE, Mary Kay   '76
Born on 8/23/47 in Tulsa, Oklahoma. Singer/composer/comedienne. Played "Loretta Haggers" on TV's *Mary Hartman, Mary Hartman* from 1976-78.

10/16/76	3	16		1 **Baby Boy** *Streets Of This Town (Ode To Femwood)*	60	$5	Columbia 10422
4/9/77	72	5		2 **Vitamin L** .... *Coke And Chips*		$5	Columbia 10510
				MARY KAY PLACE as LORETTA HAGGERS (above 2)			
11/19/77+	9	16		3 **Something To Brag About** .... *Anybody's Darlin'*		$5	Columbia 10644
				MARY KAY PLACE with Willie Nelson			

PLEASANT VALLEY BOYS — see CROW, Alvin

PLOWMAN, Linda   '71
Born on 12/31/56 in Tuscaloosa, Alabama.

| 1/30/71 | 75 | 3 | | 1 **I'm So Lonesome I Could Cry** .... *I Would* | | $7 | Janus 146 |
| 9/8/73 | 93 | 3 | | 2 **Nobody But You** .... | | $6 | Columbia 45905 |

POACHER   '78
Group from Cheshire, England, led by singer Tim Flaherty.

| 11/4/78 | 86 | 3 | | **Darling** .... *So Afraid* | | $5 | Republic 028 |

POCO   '79
Pop-folk-rock group from Los Angeles. Numerous personnel changes. Lineup in 1979: Paul Cotton (vocals, guitar), Rusty Young (steel guitar), Kim Bullard (keyboards), Charlie Harrison (bass) and Steve Chapman (drums).

| 2/10/79 | 95 | 2 | | 1 **Crazy Love** .... *Barbados* | 17 | $5 | ABC 12439 |
| 6/30/79 | 96 | 4 | | 2 **Heart Of The Night** .... *The Last Goodbye* | 20 | $4 | MCA 41023 |

POINTER, Anita — see CONLEY, Earl Thomas

POINTER SISTERS   '74
Black female vocal group from Oakland: sisters Ruth, Bonnie, June and **Anita Pointer**. Charted 27 pop hits from 1973-87.

| 7/27/74 | 37 | 16 | | **Fairytale** .... *Love In Them There Hills* | 13 | $5 | ABC/Blue Thumb 254 |

POLLARD, Chuck   '78
Born in Shreveport, Louisiana. Cousin of **Gene Wyatt**.

| 8/5/78 | 56 | 7 | | 1 **You Should Win An Oscar Every Night** .... *Wet, Wild And Warm* | | $4 | MCA 40944 |
| 11/11/78 | 71 | 5 | | 2 **The Other Side Of Jeannie** .... *Wet, Wild And Warm* | | $4 | MCA 40965 |

POMSL, Pat   '79

| 2/3/79 | 97 | 1 | | **Let My Fingers Do The Walking** .... | | $7 | ASI 1017 |

POOLE, Cheryl   '68
Born in Tyler, Texas.

8/10/68	39	10		1 **Three Playing Love** .... *I'm Not Your Woman (You're Not My Man)*		$7	Paula 309
2/1/69	70	3		2 **The Skin's Gettin' Closer To The Bone** .... *You Ain't No Friend Of Mine*		$7	Paula 1207
7/12/69	57	9		3 **Walk Among The People** .... *(I'll Always Be) Daddy's Little Girl*		$7	Paula 1214
2/14/70	70	2		4 **Everybody's Gotta Hurt** .... *You Haven't Read The Book*		$7	Paula 1219

POSEY, Sandy   '72
Born on 6/18/44 in Jasper, Alabama; raised in West Memphis, Arkansas. Charted 5 pop hits from 1966-67.
1)*Bring Him Safely Home To Me* 2)*Born To Be With You* 3)*Love Is Sometimes Easy*

10/30/71+	18	14		1 **Bring Him Safely Home To Me** *A Man In Need Of Love*		$7	Columbia 45458
5/27/72	51	11		2 **Why Don't We Go Somewhere And Love** .... *Together*		$7	Columbia 45596
10/28/72	36	8		3 **Happy, Happy Birthday Baby** .... *Thank The Lord For New York City*		$7	Columbia 45703
				#5 Pop hit for The Tune Weavers in 1957			
5/5/73	39	8		4 **Don't** .... *Thank The Lord For New York City*		$7	Columbia 45828
6/19/76	99	3		5 **Trying To Live Without You Kind Of Days** .... *Why Do We Carry On*		$6	Monument 8698
12/18/76	93	3		6 **It's Midnight (Do You Know Where Your Baby Is?)** ...... *Long Distance Kissing*		$5	Warner 8289
3/11/78	21	12		7 **Born To Be With You** .... *It's Not Too Late*		$5	Warner 8540
				#5 Pop hit for The Chordettes in 1956			
8/5/78	26	10		8 **Love, Love, Love/Chapel Of Love** .... *I Believe In Love*		$5	Warner 8610
				#30 Pop hit for The Clovers in 1956 / #1 Pop hit for The Dixie Cups in 1964			
2/10/79	26	12		9 **Love Is Sometimes Easy** .... *I Believe In Love*		$5	Warner 8731
6/30/79	82	3		10 **Try Home** .... *Love Is Sometimes Easy*		$5	Warner 8852
2/26/83	88	3		11 **Can't Get Used To Sleeping Without You** .... *You Can't Ride On My Coat Tail*		$6	Audiograph 449

POTTER, Curtis   '80
Born on 4/18/40 in Cross Plains, Texas; raised in Abilene, Texas.

5/12/79	92	3		1 **Fraulein (The Texas National Anthem)** .... *The Story Behind The Photograph*		$6	Hillside 03
				CURTIS POTTER AND A FRIEND			
				Darrell McCall (guest vocal)			
3/1/80	89	5		2 **San Antonio Medley** .... *Thank God For Country Music*		$6	Hillside 01
				CURTIS POTTER/DARRELL McCALL			

POWELL, Pati   '73

| 9/8/73 | 99 | 2 | | **Love By Appointment** .... *If You Could Do Any Better (You'd Done Been Gone)* | | $7 | Metromedia 0037 |
| | | | | PATI POWELL & BOB GALLION | | | |

POWELL, Sandy — see STREET, Mel

POWELL, Sue   '81
Born in Gallatin, Tennessee; raised in Sellersburg, Indiana. Member of **Dave & Sugar** from 1977-80. Co-host of TV's *Nashville On The Road* in 1982.

| 5/16/81 | 57 | 7 | | 1 **Midnite Flyer** .... *You Keep Coming Back To Me* | | $4 | RCA 12227 |
| 10/31/81 | 49 | 6 | | 2 **(There's No Me) Without You** .... *Delta Queen* | | $4 | RCA 12287 |

PRADO, Perez   '58

Born Damaso Perez Prado on 12/11/16 in Mantanzas, Cuba. Died on 9/14/89 (age 72). Known as "The King of The Mambo."

| 8/18/58 | **18** | 1 | ● | Patricia .... S:18 Why Wait [I] | **❶**¹ | $15 | | RCA Victor 7245 |
| | | | | PEREZ PRADO And His Orchestra | | | | |

PRAIRIE OYSTER   '92

Group from Toronto: Russell DeCarle (vocals, bass), Keith Glass (guitar), Denis Delorme (steel guitar), Joan Besen (piano), John P. Allen (fiddle) and Bruce Moffet (drums).

3/24/90	**62**	9		1 Goodbye, So Long, Hello... Different Kind Of Fire		$3		RCA 9124
6/9/90	**70**	8		2 I Don't Hurt Anymore .... But You Said		$3	▮	RCA 2510
12/21/91+	**51**	9		3 One Precious Love .... Goodbye Lonesome (Hello, Baby Doll)		$3		RCA 62108

PRESLEY, Elvis ★34★   '56

Born on 1/8/35 in Tupelo, Mississippi. Died of heart failure on 8/16/77 (age 42). Known as "The King of Rock & Roll." First recorded for Sun in 1954. Signed to RCA Records on 11/22/55. In U.S. Army from 3/24/58 to 3/5/60. Starred in 33 movies (beginning with *Love Me Tender* in 1956). NBC-TV special in 1968. Married Priscilla Beaulieu on 5/1/67; divorced on 10/11/73. Priscilla pursued acting in the 1980s with roles in TV's *Dynasty* and the *Naked Gun* movies. Their only child, Lisa Marie, was married to Michael Jackson from 1994-96. Elvis won Grammy's Lifetime Achievement Award in 1971. Inducted into the Rock and Roll Hall of Fame in 1986. Elected to the Country Music Hall of Fame in 1998.

1)Heartbreak Hotel 2)Don't Be Cruel 3)Hound Dog 4)I Forgot To Remember To Forget
5)I Want You, I Need You, I Love You

7/16/55	**5**	15		1 Baby Let's Play House/				
				#12 R&B hit for Arthur Gunter in 1955	A:5 / S:10			
		3		2 I'm Left, You're Right, She's Gone .... S:flip		$1200		Sun 217
9/17/55+	**❶**⁵	39		3 I Forgot To Remember To Forget/	J:❶⁵ / S:❶² / A:4			
12/31/55+	**11**	4		4 Mystery Train A:11		$1000		Sun 223
3/3/56	**❶**¹⁷	27	▲	5 Heartbreak Hotel/	S:❶¹⁷ / J:❶¹³ / A:❶¹²	**❶**⁸		
3/31/56	**8**	6		6 I Was The One A:8	19	$30		RCA Victor 47-6420
				also see #83 below				
6/2/56	**❶**²	20	▲	7 I Want You, I Need You, I Love You/	S:❶² / J:❶¹ / A:5	**❶**¹		
6/2/56	**13**	13		8 My Baby Left Me S:13	31	$30		RCA Victor 47-6540
				written and recorded on RCA Victor 50-0109 by Arthur "Big Boy" Crudup in 1950 ($150)				
8/4/56	**❶**¹⁰	28	▲³	9 Don't Be Cruel/	J:❶¹⁰ / S:❶⁵ / A:2	**❶**¹¹		
				10 Hound Dog .... J:❶¹⁰ / S:❶⁵ / A:6	**❶**¹¹	$30	▮	RCA Victor 47-6604
				#1 R&B hit for Big Mama Thornton in 1953				
10/20/56	**3**	18	▲²	11 Love Me Tender/	S:3 / A:4 / J:4	**❶**⁵		
				from the movie starring Presley; adapted from the 1861 tune "Aura Lee"				
		6		12 Anyway You Want Me (That's How I Will Be) .... S:flip	20	$30	▮	RCA Victor 47-6643
				picture sleeve issued with four color variations: black & white, green, light pink and dark pink				
12/29/56	**10**	3		13 Love Me .... A:10 / J:10	2²	$100	▮	RCA Victor EPA-992
				from the E.P. *Elvis, Volume 1*; the other cuts on the E.P. are "When My Blue Moon Turns To Gold Again" (Pop #19) and "Rip It Up"				
2/2/57	**3**	14	▲	14 Too Much/	J:3 / S:5 / A:6	**❶**³		
3/2/57	**8**	1		15 Playing For Keeps J:8	21	$30		RCA Victor 47-6800
4/13/57	**❶**¹	16	▲²	16 All Shook Up .... J:❶¹ / A:3 / S:3 That's When Your Heartaches Begin (Pop #58)	**❶**⁹	$30	▮	RCA Victor 47-6870
7/1/57	**❶**¹	20	▲	17 Let Me Be Your Teddy Bear/	S:❶¹ / A:4	**❶**⁷		
				also see #72 below				
9/16/57	**15**	2		18 Loving You A:15	20	$30	▮	RCA Victor 47-7000
8/19/57	**11**	2		19 Mean Woman Blues A:11		$100	▮	RCA V. EPA 2-1515
				from the E.P. *Loving You, Vol. II*; the other cuts on the E.P. are "Lonesome Cowboy," "Hot Dog" and "Got A Lot O'Livin' To Do"; #5 Pop hit for Roy Orbison in 1963; above 3 from the movie *Loving You* starring Presley				
10/14/57	**❶**¹	24	▲²	20 Jailhouse Rock/	S:❶¹ / A:3	**❶**⁷		
10/28/57	**11**	4		21 Treat Me Nice A:11	18	$30	▮	RCA Victor 47-7035
				above 2 from the movie *Jailhouse Rock* starring Presley				
2/3/58	**2**⁵	18	▲	22 Don't/	S:2 / A:3	**❶**⁵		
2/3/58	**4**	13		23 I Beg Of You .... S:4 / A:5	8	$25	▮	RCA Victor 47-7150
4/21/58	**3**	15	▲	24 Wear My Ring Around Your Neck/	S:3 / A:4	2¹		
				also see #84 below				
		2		25 Doncha' Think It's Time .... S:flip	15	$25	▮	RCA Victor 47-7240
6/30/58	**2**²	16	▲	26 Hard Headed Woman/	S:2 / A:8	**❶**²		
		3		27 Don't Ask Me Why .... S:flip	25	$25	▮	RCA Victor 47-7280
				above 2 from the movie *King Creole* starring Presley				
12/22/58	**24**	3	▲	28 One Night .... I Got Stung (Pop #8)	4	$25	▮	RCA Victor 47-7410
				#11 R&B hit for Smiley Lewis in 1956 (originally written as "One Night (Of Sin)")				
5/30/60	**27**	2	▲	29 Stuck On You .... Fame And Fortune (Pop #17)	**❶**⁴	$20	▮	RCA Victor 47-7740
				recorded 15 days after Presley's Army discharge				
12/12/60+	**22**	6	▲²	30 Are You Lonesome To-night? .... I Gotta Know (Pop #20)	**❶**⁶	$20	▮	RCA Victor 47-7810
				#4 Pop hit for Vaughn Deleath in 1927				
4/6/68	**55**	6		31 U.S. Male .... Stay Away (Pop #67)	28	$12	▮	RCA Victor 47-9465
				written and originally recorded by Jerry Reed				
6/29/68	**50**	8		32 Your Time Hasn't Come Yet, Baby .... Let Yourself Go (Pop #71)	72	$12	▮	RCA Victor 47-9547
				ELVIS PRESLEY with The Jordanaires (#14-19, 22-27, 29-32)				
				from the movie *Speedway* starring Presley				
4/19/69	**56**	2		33 Memories .... Charro	35	$10	▮	RCA Victor 47-9731
				from the NBC-TV special *Elvis*				
6/14/69	**60**	7	▲	34 In The Ghetto .... Any Day Now	3	$10	▮	RCA Victor 47-9741
8/16/69	**74**	3	●	35 Clean Up Your Own Back Yard .... The Fair Is Moving On	35	$10	▮	RCA Victor 47-9747
				from the movie *The Trouble With Girls (and how to get into it)* starring Presley				

DEBUT	PEAK	WKS	Gold	A-side (Chart Hit)..B-side	Pop	$	Pic	Label & Number
				PRESLEY, Elvis — Cont'd				
12/20/69+	13	12	▲ 36	Don't Cry Daddy..*Rubberneckin'* (Pop flip)	6	$10	■	RCA Victor 47-9768
				#34 & #36: written by Mac Davis				
2/28/70	31	10	● 37	Kentucky Rain ....*My Little Friend*	16	$8	■	RCA Victor 47-9791
				written by Eddie Rabbitt				
6/6/70	37	10	● 38	The Wonder Of You ....*Mama Liked The Roses* (Pop flip)	9	$8	■	RCA Victor 47-9835
				recorded "live" in Las Vegas; #25 Pop hit for Ray Peterson in 1959				
8/29/70	57	6	● 39	I've Lost You/	32			
		6	40	The Next Step Is Love	flip	$8	■	RCA Victor 47-9873
12/5/70	56	5	● 41	You Don't Have To Say You Love Me ....*Patch It Up* (Pop flip)	11	$8	■	RCA Victor 47-9916
				#4 Pop hit for Dusty Springfield in 1966; above 3 from the movie *Elvis-That's The Way It Is*				
1/9/71	9	13	● 42	There Goes My Everything/	flip			
				#20 Pop hit for Engelbert Humperdinck in 1967; also see #81 below				
1/9/71	23	13	43	I Really Don't Want To Know..	21	$7	■	RCA Victor 47-9960
				#11 Pop hit for Les Paul & Mary Ford in 1954				
3/27/71	55	8	44	Where Did They Go, Lord ....*Rags To Riches* (Pop flip)	33	$7	■	RCA Victor 47-9980
6/5/71	34	8	45	Life ....*Only Believe* (Pop flip)	53	$7	■	RCA Victor 47-9985
3/4/72	68	2	46	Until It's Time For You To Go ....*We Can Make The Morning*	40	$7	■	RCA Victor 74-0619
				#53 Pop hit for Neil Diamond in 1970				
9/9/72	36	13	▲ 47	It's A Matter Of Time..*Burning Love* (Pop #2)		$7	■	RCA Victor 74-0769
12/9/72+	16	13	● 48	Always On My Mind/		$7	■	RCA Victor 74-0815
		12	49	Separate Ways	20	$7		
				from the movie *Elvis on Tour*				
4/28/73	31	10	50	Fool/	flip			
		10	51	Steamroller Blues..	17	$7	■	RCA Victor 74-0910
				written and first recorded by James Taylor on his 1970 album *Sweet Baby James*; from the TV special *Aloha from Hawaii via Satellite*				
10/6/73	42	10	52	For Ol' Times Sake..*Raised On Rock* (Pop #41)	flip	$6	■	RCA V. APBO-0088
2/16/74	4	13	53	I've Got A Thing About You Baby/	39			
		13	54	Take Good Care Of Her..	flip	$6	■	RCA V. APBO-0196
				#7 Pop hit for Adam Wade in 1961				
6/8/74	6	15	55	Help Me/				
				written by Larry Gatlin				
		15	56	If You Talk In Your Sleep	17	$6	■	RCA V. APBO-0280
10/26/74+	9	14	57	It's Midnight/				
		5	58	Promised Land	14	$6	■	RCA Victor PB-10074
				#41 Pop hit for Chuck Berry in 1965				
2/8/75	14	10	59	My Boy ....*Thinking About You*	20	$6	■	RCA Victor PB-10191
				#41 Pop hit for Richard Harris in 1972				
5/17/75	11	13	60	T-R-O-U-B-L-E ....*Mr. Songman*	35	$6	■	RCA Victor PB-10278
10/18/75	33	10	61	Pieces Of My Life ....*Bringing It Back* (Pop #65)		$6	■	RCA Victor PB-10401
4/10/76	6	13	62	Hurt/	28			
				#4 Pop hit for Timi Yuro in 1961				
4/10/76	45	13	63	For The Heart	flip	$6	■	RCA Victor PB-10601
12/25/76+	❶¹	16	64	Moody Blue/	31			
		16	65	She Thinks I Still Care	flip	$6	■	RCA PB-10857
6/25/77	❶¹	17	● 66	Way Down/	18			
		17	67	Pledging My Love...		$6	■	RCA PB-10998
				#1 R&B hit for Johnny Ace in 1955				
11/19/77+	2¹	15	● 68	My Way..*America*	22	$6	■	RCA PB-11165
				from the CBS-TV special *Elvis In Concert*; based on the French standard "Comme D'Habitude"; #27 Pop hit for Frank Sinatra in 1969				
3/25/78	6	11	69	Unchained Melody/				
				#4 Pop hit for The Righteous Brothers in 1965				
		11	70	Softly, As I Leave You ....[S]	109	$6	■	RCA PB-11212
				"live" recording; Elvis narrates, with vocal by Sherrill Neilsen; #27 Pop hit for Frank Sinatra in 1964				
8/12/78	78	4	71	Puppet On A String/				
				#14 Pop hit for Presley in 1965				
		4	72	(Let Me Be Your) Teddy Bear ....[R]	105	$5	■	RCA PB-11320
				ELVIS PRESLEY with The Jordanaires (above 2)				
				same version as #17 above				
4/21/79	10	12	73	Are You Sincere/				
				#3 Pop hit for Andy Williams in 1958				
		12	74	Solitaire		$5	■	RCA PB-11533
				#17 Pop hit for the Carpenters in 1975				
8/11/79	6	13	75	There's A Honky Tonk Angel (Who Will Take Me Back In)/				
		13	76	I Got A Feelin' In My Body		$5	■	RCA PB-11679
1/17/81	❶¹	13	77	Guitar Man ....*Faded Love*	28	$5	■	RCA PB-12158
				remix by Felton Jarvis (d: 1/3/81) of Presley's #43 Pop hit from 1968; Jerry Reed (guitar)				
4/18/81	8	15	78	Lovin' Arms/				
				#61 Pop hit for Dobie Gray in 1973				
		15	79	You Asked Me To		$5		RCA PB-12205
2/27/82	73	4	80	You'll Never Walk Alone/				
				ELVIS PRESLEY with The Jordanaires				
				#90 Pop hit for Presley in 1968				
		4	81	There Goes My Everything ....[R]		$5	■	RCA PB-13058
				same version as #42 above				
11/6/82	31	12	82	The Elvis Medley ....*Always On My Mind*	71	$5	■	RCA PB-13351
				Jailhouse Rock/Teddy Bear/Hound Dog/Don't Be Cruel/Burning Love/Suspicious Minds				
5/7/83	92	2	83	I Was The One/		[R]		
				same version (with newly added overdubs) of #6 above				
		2	84	Wear My Ring Around Your Neck ....[R]		$5	■	RCA PB-13500
				same version (with newly added overdubs) of #24 above				

PRESLEY, Elvis — Cont'd

| 12/27/97 | 55 | 2 | 85 Blue Christmas .... Love Me Tender [X] | | $5 | ■ | RCA 62403-7 |

recorded in 1957

PRESTON, Eddie   '89

| 4/22/89 | 87 | 3 | 1 When Did You Stop ....Dance My Song | | $5 | | Platinum 101 |
| 9/9/89 | 71 | 4 | 2 Long Time Comin' .... | | $5 | ■ | Platinum 102 |

PRICE, Chuck   '76
Singer from Chicago.

11/2/74	75	6	1 Slow Down .... West Virginia Woman		$5		Playboy 6010
11/22/75	54	8	2 Last Of The Outlaws.................... Angels Have Days They Can't Fly		$5		Playboy 6052
4/3/76	97	2	3 Cadillac Johnson .... Trouble In Mind		$5		Playboy 6067
5/29/76	48	8	4 I Don't Want It .... Trouble In Mind		$5		Playboy 6072
10/23/76	81	3	5 Rye Whiskey ....Lucy Ain't Your Loser Lookin' Good		$5		Playboy 6087
2/26/77	91	4	6 Is Anybody Goin' To San Antone ....My Memories		$5		Playboy 6099

PRICE, David   '64
Born in Odessa, Texas. Band leader for **Red Stegall** from 1977-79.

| 2/8/64 | 29 | 8 | The World Lost A Man ....I Need A Friend | | $15 | | Rice 1001 |

tribute to John F. Kennedy; written by **Tom T. Hall**

PRICE, Denise   '82
Born Denise Davis in Russellville, Alabama.

| 12/25/82 | 94 | 3 | Two Hearts Can't Be Wrong ....Somebody Everybody's Had | | $5 | ■ | Dimension 1037 |

PRICE, Kenny ★165★   '66
Born on 5/27/31 in Florence, Kentucky. Died of a heart attack on 8/4/87 (age 56). Singer/songwriter. Regular on TV's *Hee-Haw*. Known as "The Round Mound of Sound."

1)Walking On New Grass 2)Happy Tracks 3)The Sheriff Of Boone County 4)Biloxi 5)My Goal For Today

8/20/66	7	18	1 Walking On New Grass Wasting My Time		$10		Boone 1042
12/24/66+	7	17	2 Happy Tracks The Clock		$10		Boone 1051
5/13/67	26	12	3 Pretty Girl, Pretty Clothes, Pretty Sad .... You Made Me Lie To You		$10		Boone 1056
9/9/67	24	12	4 Grass Won't Grow On A Busy Street ....Somebody Told Mary		$8		Boone 1063
12/16/67+	11	15	5 My Goal For Today ....Say Something Nice To Me		$8		Boone 1067
4/27/68	31	8	6 Going Home For The Last Time ....Blame It On Me		$8		Boone 1070
9/7/68	37	8	7 Southern Bound .... After All		$8		Boone 1075
12/7/68	59	6	8 It Don't Mean A Thing To Me .... Big Operator		$8		Boone 1081
5/10/69	64	5	9 Who Do I Know In Dallas ....I'm A Long Way From Home		$8		Boone 1085
12/6/69	62	4	10 Atlanta Georgia Stray.................................... The Clock		$7		RCA Victor 0260
1/31/70	17	12	11 Northeast Arkansas Mississippi County				
			Bootlegger....................Green, Green Grass Of Home		$7		RCA Victor 9787
7/18/70	10	14	12 Biloxi The Shortest Song In The World		$7		RCA Victor 9869
12/19/70+	8	14	13 The Sheriff Of Boone County Six String Guitar	119	$7		RCA Victor 9932
5/1/71	55	7	14 Tell Her You Love Her .... Just Plain Man		$7		RCA Victor 9973
9/18/71	38	11	15 Charlotte Fever ....There's A Song In Everything		$6		RCA Victor 1015
1/15/72	37	10	16 Super Sideman ....From Here To There		$6		RCA Victor 0617
4/29/72	44	11	17 You Almost Slipped My Mind ....Destination Anywhere		$6		RCA Victor 0686
9/16/72	24	11	18 Sea Of Heartbreak .... Smiley		$6		RCA Victor 0781
1/20/73	53	8	19 Don't Tell Me Your Troubles........ Front Of The Bus, Back Of The Church		$6		RCA Victor 0872
5/12/73	52	7	20 30 California Women .... Love's Not Hard To Take		$6		RCA Victor 0936
9/22/73	52	11	21 You're Wearin' Me Down .... The Closest Thing To Me (Is My Shadow)		$6		RCA Victor 0083
12/29/73+	29	12	22 Turn On Your Light (And Let It Shine)...... The First Song That Wasn't The Blues		$6		RCA Victor 0198
4/27/74	69	6	23 Que Pasa ....Greener Grass To Walk On		$6		RCA Victor 0256
8/31/74	42	11	24 Let's Truck Together .... Super Hillbilly		$5		RCA Victor 10039
1/4/75	67	10	25 Easy Look .... Country Blues		$5		RCA Victor 10141
5/3/75	65	8	26 Birds And Children Fly Away ....Born In Country Music (Raised On Dixieland)		$5		RCA Victor 10260
1/10/76	60	8	27 Too Big A Price To Pay ....Don't Boogie Woogie When You Say Your Prayers Tonight		$5		RCA Victor 10460
6/4/77	60	6	28 I'd Buy You Chattanooga.................................... Mortar Mixing Mama		$5		MRC 1001
9/17/77	74	5	29 Leavin' ....Boone County Weight Watchers Of America		$5		MRC 1004
12/24/77+	50	9	30 Afraid You'd Come Back .... Walkin' In That California Sunshine		$5		MRC 1007
4/8/78	74	6	31 Sunshine Man .... Sidewalk Satin Salesman		$5		MRC 1012
1/20/79	67	7	32 Hey There .... Pickin' Up The Pieces		$5		MRC 1025
			#1 Pop hit for Rosemary Clooney in 1954				
2/23/80	60	5	33 Well Rounded Traveling Man ....Everybody Needs Something		$5		Dimension 1003
9/13/80	79	4	34 She's Leavin' (And I'm Almost Gone) .... In Vain		$5		Dimension 1010

PRICE, Ray ★8★   **'56**
Born on 1/12/26 in Perryville, Texas; raised in Dallas. Singer/songwriter/guitarist. Served in the U.S. Marines from 1944-46. Began radio singing career in 1948 on KRBC in Abilene, Texas. Joined the *Big D Jamboree* in Dallas in 1949. Known as "The Cherokee Cowboy."

1)*Crazy Arms* 2)*City Lights* 3)*My Shoes Keep Walking Back To You* 4)*I Won't Mention It Again*
5)*She's Got To Be A Saint*

DEBUT	PEAK	WKS		A-side	B-side	Pop	$	Pic	Label & Number
5/17/52	3	11	1	**Talk To Your Heart** A:3 / J:6 / S:10 *I've Got To Hurry, Hurry, Hurry*			$20		Columbia 4-20913
11/8/52	4	9	2	**Don't Let The Stars Get In Your Eyes** S:4 / A:6 / J:7 *I Lost The Only Love I Knew*			$20		Columbia 4-21025
				#1 Pop hit for **Perry Como** in 1953					
3/6/54	2[2]	19	3	**I'll Be There (If You Ever Want Me)/** S:2 / A:2 / J:3					
4/10/54	6	13	4	**Release Me** J:6 / S:7			$20		Columbia 21214
				#4 Pop hit for **Engelbert Humperdinck** in 1967					
6/26/54	13	4	5	**Much Too Young To Die** S:13 / A:13 *I Love You So Much I Let You Go*			$20		Columbia 21249
10/30/54	8	13	6	**If You Don't, Somebody Else Will** S:8 / J:10 / A:14 *Oh Yes Darling!*			$20		Columbia 21315
				RAY PRICE & His Cherokee Cowboys					
1/7/56	5	11	7	**Run Boy** A:5 / J:10 / S:15 *You Never Will Be True*			$20		Columbia 21474
5/26/56	❶[20]	45	8	**Crazy Arms/** A:❶[20] / S:❶[11] / J:❶[1]					
6/9/56	7	7	9	**You Done Me Wrong** A:7			$20		Columbia 21510
11/10/56	2[2]	21	10	**I've Got A New Heartache/** A:2 / J:2 / S:3					
11/17/56	4	21	11	**Wasted Words** S:4 / A:6 / J:9			$20		Columbia 21562
6/10/57	12	4	12	**I'll Be There (When You Get Lonely)** A:12 / S:13 *Please Don't Leave Me*			$20		Columbia 40889
7/29/57	❶[4]	37	13	**My Shoes Keep Walking Back To You** A:❶[4] / S:3 *Don't Do This To Me*		63	$15		Columbia 40951
3/3/58	3	18	14	**Curtain In The Window/** A:3 / S:6					
		4	15	**It's All Your Fault**			$15		Columbia 41105
7/14/58	❶[13]	34	16	**City Lights/** A:2		71			
7/21/58	3	19	17	**Invitation To The Blues** A:3 / S:8		92	$15		Columbia 41191
1/5/59	7	19	18	**That's What It's Like To Be Lonesome** *Kissing Your Picture*			$15		Columbia 41309
5/11/59	2[1]	40	19	**Heartaches By The Number** *Wall Of Tears*			$15		Columbia 41374
				#1 Pop hit for **Guy Mitchell** in 1959					
10/12/59	❶[2]	30	20	**The Same Old Me/**					
				#51 Pop hit for **Guy Mitchell** in 1960					
11/23/59	5	15	21	**Under Your Spell Again**			$15		Columbia 41477
4/4/60	2[8]	27	22	**One More Time** *Who'll Be The First*			$15		Columbia 41590
10/3/60	5	21	23	**I Wish I Could Fall In Love Today/**					
10/24/60	23	3	24	**I Can't Run Away From Myself**			$15		Columbia 41767
3/20/61	5	21	25	**Heart Over Mind/**					
3/27/61	13	11	26	**The Twenty-Fourth Hour**			$15		Columbia 41947
10/9/61	3	23	27	**Soft Rain/**		115			
11/13/61	26	2	28	**Here We Are Again**			$12		Columbia 42132
6/2/62	12	8	29	**I've Just Destroyed The World (I'm Living In)/**					
6/2/62	22	1	30	**Big Shoes**			$12		Columbia 42310
9/22/62	5	15	31	**Pride** *I'm Walking Slow (And Thinking 'Bout Her)*			$12		Columbia 42518
2/9/63	7	20	32	**Walk Me To The Door/**					
				written by **Conway Twitty**					
3/2/63	11	16	33	**You Took Her Off My Hands (Now Please Take Her Off My Mind)**			$12		Columbia 42658
8/10/63	2[1]	21	34	**Make The World Go Away/**		100			
10/5/63	28	2	35	**Night Life**			$12	□	Columbia 42827
3/14/64	2[4]	27	36	**Burning Memories/**					
4/4/64	34	9	37	**That's All That Matters**			$12		Columbia 42971
9/5/64	7	17	38	**Please Talk To My Heart** *I Don't Know Why (I Keep Loving You)*			$10		Columbia 43086
1/9/65	38	4	39	**A Thing Called Sadness** *Here Comes My Baby Back Again*			$10		Columbia 43162
5/8/65	2[2]	24	40	**The Other Woman** *Tearful Earful*			$10		Columbia 43264
11/27/65+	11	14	41	**Don't You Ever Get Tired Of Hurting Me** *Unloved, Unwanted*			$10		Columbia 43427
				also see #83 below					
4/23/66	7	18	42	**A Way To Survive/**					
6/11/66	28	6	43	**I'm Not Crazy Yet**			$10		Columbia 43560
10/15/66	3	18	44	**Touch My Heart** *It Should Be Easier Now*			$10		Columbia 43795
3/25/67	9	17	45	**Danny Boy** *I Let My Mind Wander*		60	$8	■	Columbia 44042
7/22/67	6	18	46	**I'm Still Not Over You/**					
8/19/67	73	1	47	**Crazy**			$8		Columbia 44195
12/30/67+	8	15	48	**Take Me As I Am (Or Let Me Go)** *In The Summer Of My Life*			$8		Columbia 44374
5/4/68	11	16	49	**I've Been There Before** *Night Life*			$8		Columbia 44505
10/5/68	6	14	50	**She Wears My Ring** *Goin' Away*			$8		Columbia 44628
				#24 R&B hit for **Jimmy Sweeney** in 1962					
3/1/69	51	4	51	**Set Me Free** *Trouble*			$8		Columbia 44747
3/8/69	11	15	52	**Sweetheart Of The Year** *How Can I Write On Paper (What I Feel In My Heart)*			$8		Columbia 44761
8/16/69	14	12	53	**Raining In My Heart** *I Know Love*			$8		Columbia 44931
				#88 Pop hit for **Buddy Holly** in 1959					
11/22/69	14	11	54	**April's Fool** *Make It Rain*			$7		Columbia 45005

DEBUT	PEAK	WKS	Gold	A-side (Chart Hit)..B-side	Pop	$	Pic	Label & Number
				PRICE, Ray — Cont'd				
3/7/70	**8**	15		55 You Wouldn't Know Love *Everybody Wants To Get To Heaven*		$7		Columbia 45095
6/27/70	**❶**¹	26		56 For The Good Times/	11			
		18		57 Grazin' In Greener Pastures		$6		Columbia 45178
3/20/71	**❶**³	19		58 I Won't Mention It Again *Kiss The World Goodbye*	42	$6		Columbia 45329
8/7/71	**2**¹	17		59 I'd Rather Be Sorry *When I Loved Her*	70	$6		Columbia 45425
4/15/72	**2**¹	14		60 The Lonesomest Lonesome/	109			
4/15/72	66	14		61 That's What Leaving's About		$6		Columbia 45583
11/4/72	**❶**³	16		62 She's Got To Be A Saint *Oh, Lonesome Me*	93	$6		Columbia 45724
7/28/73	**❶**¹	16		63 You're The Best Thing That Ever Happened To Me *What Kind Of Love Is This*	82	$6		Columbia 45889
				#3 Pop hit for Gladys Knight & The Pips in 1974				
3/16/74	25	13		64 Storms Of Troubled Times *Some Things Never Change*		$6		Columbia 46015
8/17/74	15	11		65 Like A First Time Thing *You Are A Song*		$6		Columbia 10006
10/26/74+	4	15		66 Like Old Times Again *My First Day Without Her*		$6		Myrrh 146
2/8/75	3	14		67 Roses And Love Songs *The Closest Thing To Love*		$6		Myrrh 150
5/31/75	17	13		68 Farthest Thing From My Mind *All That Keeps Me Going*		$5		ABC 12095
8/9/75	31	11		69 If You Ever Change Your Mind *Just Enough To Make Me Stay*		$5		Columbia 10150
11/8/75	40	12		70 Say I Do *I'll Still Love You*		$5		ABC/Dot 17588
3/27/76	34	9		71 That's All She Wrote *I Don't Feel Nothing*		$5		ABC/Dot 17616
7/24/76	41	10		72 To Make A Long Story Short/				
7/24/76	47	10		73 We're Getting There		$5		ABC/Dot 17637
12/4/76+	14	15		74 A Mansion On The Hill *Hey, Good Lookin'*		$5		ABC/Dot 17666
3/26/77	38	9		75 Help Me *Nobody Wins*		$5		Columbia 10503
5/28/77	28	11		76 Different Kind Of Flower *Don't Let The Stars Get In Your Eyes*		$5		ABC/Dot 17690
				RAY PRICE AND THE CHEROKEE COWBOYS				
10/1/77	21	12		77 Born To Love Me *The Only Way To Say Good Morning*		$5		ABC/Dot 17718
10/28/78+	19	13		78 Feet *Let's Make A Nice Memory (Today)*		$5		Monument 267
3/3/79	30	12		79 There's Always Me *If It's All The Same To You (I'll Be Leaving In The Morning)*		$5		Monument 277
				#56 Pop hit for Elvis Presley in 1967				
6/9/79	18	13		80 That's The Only Way To Say Good Morning *All The Good Things Are Gone*		$5		Monument 283
11/24/79+	43	9		81 Misty Morning Rain *We Can't Build A Fire In The Rain*		$5		Monument 290
8/9/80	3	15		82 Faded Love *This Cold War With You*		$4		Columbia 11329
				WILLIE NELSON AND RAY PRICE				
12/6/80+	11	14		83 Don't You Ever Get Tired (Of Hurting Me) *Funny How Time Slips Away* [R]		$4		Columbia 11405
				WILLIE NELSON AND RAY PRICE				
				new version of #41 above				
3/28/81	28	13		84 Getting Over You Again *Circle Driveway*		$4		Dimension 1018
7/18/81	6	17		85 It Don't Hurt Me Half As Bad *She's The Right Kind Of A Woman*		$4		Dimension 1021
11/14/81+	9	18		86 Diamonds In The Stars *Grazin' In Greener Pastures*		$4		Dimension 1024
4/3/82	18	15		87 Forty And Fadin' *When You Gave Your Love To Me*		$4		Dimension 1031
6/5/82	19	16		88 Old Friends *When A House Is Not A Home*		$4		Columbia 02681
				ROGER MILLER & WILLIE NELSON (with Ray Price)				
8/7/82	62	7		89 Wait Till Those Bridges Are Gone *Angel In My Heart (Devil In My Mind)*		$4		Dimension 1035
12/4/82+	55	9		90 Somewhere In Texas *Gettin' Down And Gettin' High*		$4		Dimension 1038
1/15/83	70	6		91 One Fiddle, Two Fiddle/				
		6		92 San Antonio Rose		$4		Warner 29830
				RAY PRICE With Johnny Gimble & The Texas Swing Band (above 2)				
				above 2 from the movie *Honkytonk Man* starring **Clint Eastwood**				
5/7/83	72	6		93 Willie, Write Me A Song *I Love You Eyes*		$4		Warner 29691
8/27/83	70	5		94 Scotch And Soda *I Love You Eyes*		$4		Viva 29543
				#81 Pop hit for The Kingston Trio in 1962				
6/23/84	87	4		95 A New Place To Begin *Everyone Gets Crazy Now & Then*		$4		Viva 29277
9/8/84	73	6		96 Better Class Of Loser *Every Time I Sing A Love Song*		$4		Viva 29217
11/17/84	77	7		97 What Am I Gonna Do Without You *You've Been Leaving Me For Years*		$4		Viva 29147
				RAY PRICE and The Cherokee Cowboys (above 3)				
5/25/85	77	6		98 (She's Got A Hold Of Me Where It Hurts) She Won't Let Go *Memories To Burn*		$3		Step One 341
8/31/85	81	7		99 I'm Not Leaving (I'm Just Getting Out Of Your Way) *Why Don't Love Just Go Away*		$3		Step One 344
12/21/85+	67	7		100 Five Fingers *Lonely Like A Rose*		$3		Step One 350
3/15/86	60	8		101 You're Nobody Till Somebody Loves You *I'm In The Mood For Love*		$3		Step One 352
				#14 Pop hit for Russ Morgan in 1946				
6/21/86	73	5		102 All The Way *S:36 Bummin' Around*		$3		Step One 355
				#2 Pop hit for Frank Sinatra in 1957				
9/27/86	86	3		103 Please Don't Talk About Me When I'm Gone *For The Good Times*		$3		Step One 361
				#3 Pop hit for Gene Austin in 1931				
12/27/86+	55	8		104 When You Gave Your Love To Me *Forty And Fadin'*		$3		Step One 366
10/24/87	52	11		105 Just Enough Love *Why Don't Love Just Go Away (When It's All Gone)*		$3		Step One 378
3/12/88	68	5		106 Big Ole Teardrops *The Season For Missing You*		$3		Step One 383
7/9/88	55	7		107 Don't The Morning Always Come Too Soon *Come Back Home*		$3		Step One 388
12/10/88	83	4		108 I'd Do It All Over Again *Wind Beneath My Wings*		$3		Step One 393
11/18/89	79	3		109 Love Me Down To Size *I've Got A New Heartache*		$3		Step One 410
				PRICE, Toni '86				
				Singer/actress. Had a bit part in the movie *Sweet Dreams*.				
1/25/86	59	9		1 Mississippi Break Down		$6		Luv 114
9/27/86	71	6		2 How Much Do I Owe You		$6		Master 01
9/26/87	80	3		3 I Want To Be Wanted		$6		Prairie Dust 8744

PRIDE, Charley ★16★   '71

Born on 3/18/38 in Sledge, Mississippi. Black singer/songwriter/guitarist. Played baseball with the Detroit Eagles and Memphis Red Sox of the Negro American League; also played in the Pioneer League. Joined the *Grand Ole Opry* in 1993. CMA Awards: 1971 & 1972 Male Vocalist of the Year; 1971 Entertainer of the Year.

1)*Kiss An Angel Good Mornin'* 2)*I'm Just Me* 3)*Afraid Of Losing You Again*
4)*It's Gonna Take A Little Bit Longer* 5)*She's Too Good To Be True*

DEBUT	PEAK	WKS	#	A-side	B-side	Pop	$	Pic	Label & Number
12/3/66+	9	19	1	Just Between You And Me	Detroit City		$10		RCA Victor 9000
4/29/67	6	19	2	I Know One	Best Banjo Picker		$10		RCA Victor 9162
9/2/67	4	19	3	Does My Ring Hurt Your Finger	Spell Of The Freight Train		$10		RCA Victor 9281
				COUNTRY CHARLEY PRIDE (above 3)					
1/6/68	4	17	4	The Day The World Stood Still	Gone, On The Other Hand		$8		RCA Victor 9403
5/18/68	2²	15	5	The Easy Part's Over	The Right To Do Wrong		$8		RCA Victor 9514
10/5/68	4	14	6	Let The Chips Fall	She Made Me Go		$8		RCA Victor 9622
2/1/69	3	16	7	Kaw-Liga	The Little Folks	120	$7		RCA Victor 9716
				"live" recording					
6/14/69	❶¹	17	8	All I Have To Offer You (Is Me)	A Brand New Bed Of Roses	91	$7		RCA Victor 0167
11/8/69	❶³	16	9	(I'm So) Afraid Of Losing You Again	A Good Chance Of Tear-Fall Tonight	74	$7		RCA Victor 0265
3/7/70	❶²	17	10	Is Anybody Goin' To San Antone	Things Are Looking Up	70	$7		RCA Victor 9806
6/13/70	❶²	17	11	Wonder Could I Live There Anymore	Piroque Joe	87	$7		RCA Victor 9855
9/26/70	❶²	16	12	I Can't Believe That You've Stopped Loving Me	Time	71	$7		RCA Victor 9902
2/6/71	❶³	14	13	I'd Rather Love You	(In My World) You Don't Belong	79	$7		RCA Victor 9952
4/24/71	21	10	14	Let Me Live/		104			
4/24/71	70	10	15	Did You Think To Pray			$7		RCA Victor 9974
6/26/71	❶⁴	16	16	I'm Just Me	A Place For The Lonesome	94	$7		RCA Victor 9996
10/23/71	❶⁵	19	● 17	Kiss An Angel Good Mornin'	No One Could Ever Take Me From You	21	$7		RCA Victor 0550
2/19/72	2²	15	18	All His Children	You'll Still Be The One (Pride)	92	$7		RCA Victor 0624
				CHARLEY PRIDE with HENRY MANCINI					
				from the movie *Sometimes A Great Notion* starring Paul Newman					
6/3/72	❶³	16	19	It's Gonna Take A Little Bit Longer	You're Wanting Me To Stop Loving You	102	$7	■	RCA Victor 0707
10/7/72	❶³	16	20	She's Too Good To Be True	She's That Kind		$7		RCA Victor 0802
2/10/73	❶¹	14	21	A Shoulder To Cry On	I'm Learning To Love Her	101	$7		RCA Victor 0884
				written by Merle Haggard					
5/12/73	❶¹	15	22	Don't Fight The Feelings Of Love	Tennessee Girl	101	$7		RCA Victor 0942
10/13/73	❶¹	16	23	Amazing Love	Blue Ridge Mountains Turnin' Green		$7		RCA Victor 0073
4/20/74	3	14	24	We Could	Love Put A Song In My Heart		$7		RCA Victor 0257
8/24/74	3	17	25	Mississippi Cotton Picking Delta Town	Mary Go Round	70	$6		RCA Victor 10030
12/14/74+	❶¹	12	26	Then Who Am I	Completely Helpless		$6		RCA Victor 10126
3/29/75	6	14	27	I Ain't All Bad	The Hard Times Will Be The Best Times	101	$6		RCA Victor 10236
8/9/75	❶¹	14	28	Hope You're Feelin' Me (Like I'm Feelin' You)	Searching For The Morning Sun		$6		RCA Victor 10344
12/6/75+	3	14	29	The Happiness Of Having You	Right Back Missing You Again		$6		RCA Victor 10455
3/13/76	❶¹	14	30	My Eyes Can Only See As Far As You	Oklahoma Morning		$6		RCA Victor 10592
8/28/76	2²	15	31	A Whole Lotta Things To Sing About	The Hardest Part Of Livin' Loving Me		$5		RCA 10757
1/29/77	❶¹	14	32	She's Just An Old Love Turned Memory	Country Music		$5		RCA 10875
5/21/77	❶¹	14	33	I'll Be Leaving Alone	We Need Lovin'		$5		RCA 10975
9/17/77	❶¹	14	34	More To Me	Heaven Watches Over Fools Like Me		$5		RCA 11086
2/11/78	❶²	15	35	Someone Loves You Honey	Days Of Our Lives		$5		RCA 11201
6/24/78	3	15	36	When I Stop Leaving (I'll Be Gone)	I Can See The Lovin' In Your Eyes		$5		RCA 11287
10/21/78	2³	14	37	Burgers And Fries	Nothing's Prettier Than Rose Is		$5		RCA 11391
2/24/79	❶¹	15	38	Where Do I Put Her Memory	The Best In The World		$5		RCA 11477
7/14/79	❶¹	15	39	You're My Jamaica	Let Me Have A Chance To Love You (One More Time)		$5		RCA 11655
10/27/79	89	2	40	Dallas Cowboys	When I Stop Leaving (I'll Be Gone)		$6		RCA 11736
				a special edition with the Cowboys logo on a silver and blue label					
11/3/79+	2¹	15	41	Missin' You	Heartbreak Mountain		$4		RCA 11751
2/16/80	❶¹	13	42	Honky Tonk Blues	I'm So Lonesome I Could Cry		$4		RCA 11912
5/10/80	❶¹	15	43	You Win Again	There's A Little Bit Of Hank In Me		$4		RCA 12002
9/27/80	4	18	44	You Almost Slipped My Mind	Ghost-Written Love Letters		$4		RCA 12100
3/7/81	7	13	45	Roll On Mississippi	Fall Back On Me		$4		RCA 12178
8/22/81	❶²	15	46	Never Been So Loved (In All My Life)	I Call Her My Girl		$4		RCA 12294
12/26/81+	❶¹	18	47	Mountain Of Love	Love Is A Shadow		$4		RCA 13014
				#9 Pop hit for Johnny Rivers in 1964					
4/24/82	2²	18	48	I Don't Think She's In Love Anymore	Oh What A Beautiful Love Song		$4		RCA 13096
8/28/82	❶¹	17	49	You're So Good When You're Bad	I Haven't Loved This Way In Years		$4		RCA 13293
12/4/82+	❶¹	19	50	Why Baby Why	It's So Good To Be Together		$4		RCA 13397
3/5/83	7	16	51	More And More	Radio Heroes		$4		RCA 13451
6/25/83	❶¹	21	52	Night Games I Could Let Her Get Close To Me (But She Could Never Get Close To You)			$4		RCA 13542
10/15/83+	2¹	20	53	Ev'ry Heart Should Have One	Lovin' It Up (Livin' It Down)		$4		RCA 13648
6/9/84	9	20	54	The Power Of Love	Ellie		$4		RCA 13821
11/3/84	32	13	55	Missin' Mississippi	Falling In Love Again		$4		RCA 13936
4/13/85	25	13	56	Down On The Farm	S:24 / A:27 Now And Then		$4		RCA 14045

PRIDE, Charley — Cont'd

DEBUT	PEAK	WKS		A-side B-side	Pop	$		Label & Number
7/6/85	34	11		57 Let A Little Love Come In .... *Night Games*		$4		RCA 14134
1/18/86	75	5		58 The Best There Is................................ *The Tumbleweed And The Rose*		$4		RCA 14265
4/5/86	74	7		59 Love On A Blue Rainy Day .... *I Used It All On You*		$4		RCA 14296
3/21/87	14	22		60 Have I Got Some Blues For You ....S:❶[1] / A:19 *Even Knowin'*		$3		16th Avenue 70400
7/18/87	31	15		61 If You Still Want A Fool Around .... *You Took Me There*		$3		16th Avenue 70402
12/12/87+	5	23		62 Shouldn't It Be Easier Than This ....S:❶[1] *Look In Your Mirror*		$3		16th Avenue 70408
5/7/88	13	19		63 I'm Gonna Love Her On The Radio ...S:7 *Shouldn't It Be Easier Than This*		$3		16th Avenue 70414
10/15/88	49	13		64 Where Was I .... *A Whole Lot Of Lovin'*		$3		16th Avenue 70420
2/25/89	49	7		65 White Houses................................. *Shouldn't It Be Easier Than This*		$3		16th Avenue 70425
7/1/89	77	4		66 The More I Do.. *(long version)*		$3		16th Avenue 70429
11/4/89+	28	17		67 Amy's Eyes .... *I Made Love To You In My Mind*		$3		16th Avenue 70435

PROCTOR, Paul '87

12/20/86	74	4		1 Not Tonight		$6		Aurora 1003
2/21/87	79	4		2 He's Not Good Enough		$6		Aurora 1005
7/25/87	62	6		3 Ain't We Got Love		$6		19th Avenue 1009
11/19/88	96	1		4 Tied To The Wheel Of A Runaway Heart .... *Feelin' My Way Through The Dark*		$6		19th Avenue 1012

PROPHET, Ronnie '75

Born on 12/26/38 in Calumet, Quebec, Canada. Singer/songwriter/guitarist. Hosted own TV series in Canada and England.

8/23/75	26	12		1 Sanctuary .... *Wild Outlaw*		$5		RCA Victor 50027
12/27/75+	36	10		2 Shine On .... *Last Night I Felt The Whole World Changing*		$5		RCA Victor 50136
5/1/76	50	7		3 It's Enough .... *I Want To Be Touched By You*		$5		RCA Victor 50205
10/9/76	82	5		4 Big Big World		$5		RCA 50273
10/15/77	99	2		5 It Ain't Easy Lovin' Me		$5		RCA 50391

★231★ PRUETT, Jeanne '73

Born Norma Jean Bowman on 1/30/37 in Pell City, Alabama. Singer/songwriter/guitarist. Joined the *Grand Ole Opry* in 1973.
1)Satin Sheets 2)Temporarily Yours 3)Back To Back 4)I'm Your Woman 5)It's Too Late

9/18/71	66	6		1 Hold On To My Unchanging Love........................ *He's Callin' Me Baby Again*		$6		Decca 32857
3/11/72	34	12		2 Love Me .... *I'm Out Looking For You*		$6		Decca 32929
				also see #23 below				
8/5/72	64	3		3 Call On Me .... *Stay On His Mind*		$6		Decca 32977
11/4/72	60	6		4 I Forgot More Than You'll Ever Know (About Him).......... *Don't Hold Your Breath*		$6		Decca 33013
3/31/73	❶[3]	18		5 Satin Sheets *Sweet Sweetheart*	28	$5		MCA 40015
				also see #17 below				
9/15/73	8	14		6 I'm Woman *Your Memory's Comin' On*		$5		MCA 40116
3/23/74	15	14		7 You Don't Need To Move A Mountain .... *Hopefully (I'll Be Out Of My Mind)*		$5		MCA 40207
8/31/74	22	15		8 Welcome To The Sunshine (Sweet Baby Jane) ... *What My Thoughts Do All The Time*		$5		MCA 40284
1/18/75	25	12		9 Just Like Your Daddy.. *One More Time*		$5		MCA 40340
5/10/75	41	9		10 Honey On His Hands .... *One Of These Days*		$5		MCA 40395
7/26/75	24	13		11 A Poor Man's Woman ....*Momma Let Me Find Shelter (In Your Sweet Lovin' Arms)*		$5		MCA 40440
12/13/75+	77	7		12 My Baby's Gone .... *But Not Today*		$5		MCA 40490
10/2/76	41	8		13 I've Taken .... *Sweet And Warm And Right*		$5		MCA 40605
2/19/77	30	10		14 I'm Living A Lie .... *My First Pay Day*		$5		MCA 40678
5/21/77	85	4		15 She's Still All Over You...................................... *A Fancy Place To Cry*		$5		MCA 40723
2/25/78	94	3		16 I'm A Woman .... *Midnight Exchange*		$5		Mercury 55017
8/11/79	54	8		17 Please Sing Satin Sheets For Me............ *(I'm Gonna) Love All The Leavin Out Of You*		$5		IBC 0002
				final 20 seconds of recording features a refrain of #5 above				
11/24/79+	6	16		18 Back To Back *Wild Side Of Life*		$5		IBC 0005
3/15/80	5	15		19 Temporarily Yours *Ain't We Sad Today*		$5		IBC 0008
7/5/80	9	14		20 It's Too Late *I Can't Feel At Home*		$5		IBC 0010
3/14/81	81	3		21 Sad Ole Shade Of Gray .... *When I Stop Dreaming*		$5		Paid 118
6/6/81	72	4		22 I Ought To Feel Guilty .... *Who'll Turn Out The Lights (In Your World Tonight)*		$5		Paid 136
4/16/83	58	8		23 Love Me .... *Safely In The Arms Of Jesus* [R]		$4		Audiograph 454
				JEANNE PRUETT/MARTY ROBBINS new version of #2 above				
7/9/83	73	4		24 Lady Of The Eighties................... *Ain't No Way To Make A Bad Love Grow*		$4		Audiograph 467
8/22/87	81	3		25 Rented Room .... *Put Me In Your Pocket*		$5		MSR 1956

PRUITT, Lewis '60

Lead guitarist for **Carl Smith**'s band.

12/7/59+	10	21		1 Timbrook *(You'll Make) A Fool Of Me*		$25		Peach 725
6/27/60	4	17		2 Softly And Tenderly (I'll Hold You In My Arms) *Riches And Gold*		$15		Decca 31095
4/3/61	11	9		3 Crazy Bullfrog .... *The Hand That Held The Hand*		$50		Decca 31201

PRYOR, Cactus '50

Born Richard Pryor in Austin, Texas. DJ at KTBC in Austin. Member of the Country Music DJ Hall of Fame.

6/3/50	7	1		Cry Of The Dying Duck In A Thunder-Storm *A:7 Double Trouble* [N]		$25		4 Star 1459
				CACTUS PRYOR and his Pricklypears parody of "The Cry Of The Wild Goose" by **Tennessee Ernie Ford**				

PRYSOCK, Arthur '79

Born on 1/2/29 in Spartanburg, South Carolina. Died on 6/14/97 (age 68). Black singer.

9/29/79	74	5		Today I Started Loving You Again.................. *It Ain't No Big Thing (But It's Growin')*		$6		Gusto 9023
				written by **Merle Haggard**				

PUCKETT, Jerry '83

Session guitarist.

8/27/83	81	3		Heart On The Run .... *Dance Alone*		$4		Atlantic Amer. 99860

DEBUT	PEAK	WKS	Gold	A-side (Chart Hit)..B-side	Pop	$	Pic	Label & Number

PULLINS, Leroy '66
Born Carl Leroy Pullins on 11/12/40 in Elgin, Illinois. Singer/songwriter/guitarist.

| 6/25/66 | **18** | 11 | | I'm A Nut ....Knee Deep [N] | 57 | $8 | | Kapp 758 |

PUMP BOYS AND DINETTES '83
From original cast recording of the Broadway musical *Pump Boys And Dinettes*. Featuring cast members Jim Wann and Cass Morgan.

| 3/19/83 | **67** | 5 | | The Night Dolly Parton Was Almost Mine .... The Best Man | | $5 | | CBS 03549 |

PURE PRAIRIE LEAGUE '76
Country-pop-rock group from Cincinnati. Numerous personnel changes. Lineup in 1976: George Ed Powell (vocals, guitar), Larry Goshorn (guitar), Michael Connor (keyboards), Mike Reilly (bass) and Billy Hinds (drums). **Vince Gill** was lead singer from 1979-83. Charted 7 pop hits from 1975-81.

| 6/19/76 | **96** | 2 | | That'll Be The Day...I Can Only Think Of You | 106 | $5 | | RCA Victor 10679 |
| | | | | #1 Pop hit for Buddy Holly & The Crickets in 1957 | | | | |

PUTMAN, Curly '60
Born Claude Putman on 11/20/30 in Princeton, Alabama. Singer/prolific songwriter.

2/29/60	**23**	1		1 The Prison Song ....Forsaken		$20		Cherokee 504
7/8/67	**41**	9		2 My Elusive Dreams ....Hurtin' Like A Heartache	134	$7		ABC 10934
11/4/67	**67**	3		3 Set Me Free ....Hummin' A Heartache		$7		ABC 10984

PYLE, Chuck '85
Born in Pittsburgh; raised in Iowa. Singer/songwriter.

| 9/28/85 | **60** | 6 | | 1 Drifter's Wind .... (long version) | | $5 | | Urban Sound 786 |
| 1/18/86 | **81** | 6 | | 2 Breathless In The Night.. | | $5 | | Urban Sound 782 |

Q

QUIST, Jack '82
Born in Salt Lake City. Singer/songwriter.

| 9/11/82 | **52** | 9 | | 1 Memory Machine ....I'm Comin' Home | | $6 | | Memory Mach. 1015 |
| 9/9/89 | **77** | 3 | | 2 Where Does Love Go (When It Dies) .... South For The Winter | | $6 | ■ | Grudge 4756 |

R

RABBITT, Eddie ★50★ '79
Born on 11/27/41 in Brooklyn; raised in East Orange, New Jersey. Died of cancer on 5/7/98 (age 56). Singer/songwriter/guitarist.

1)*Every Which Way But Loose* 2)*On Second Thought* 3)*The Best Year Of My Life* 4)*Step By Step*
5)*I Just Want To Love You*

8/31/74	**34**	14		1 You Get To Me... Que Pasa		$6		Elektra 45895
3/22/75	**12**	17		2 Forgive And Forget... Pure Love		$6		Elektra 45237
8/30/75	**11**	14		3 I Should Have Married You .... Sweet Janine		$6		Elektra 45269
2/7/76	**❶¹**	16		4 Drinkin' My Baby (Off My Mind) .... When I Was Young		$5		Elektra 45301
6/5/76	**5**	15		5 Rocky Mountain Music/	76			
		15		6 Do You Right Tonight		$5		Elektra 45315
11/6/76+	**3**	16		7 Two Dollars In The Jukebox	I Don't Wanna Make Love (With Anyone But You)		$5		Elektra 45357
4/2/77	**2¹**	16		8 I Can't Help Myself	She Loves Me Like She Means It	77	$5		Elektra 45390
8/20/77	**6**	15		9 We Can't Go On Living Like This	You Make Love Beautiful		$5		Elektra 45418
2/18/78	**2²**	16		10 Hearts On Fire	The Girl On My Mind		$5		Elektra 45461
6/10/78	**❶¹**	14		11 You Don't Love Me Anymore	Caroline	53	$5		Elektra 45488
9/30/78	**❶¹**	14		12 I Just Want To Love You	Crossin' The Mississippi		$5		Elektra 45531
12/23/78+	**❶³**	15		13 Every Which Way But Loose	Under The Double Eagle (Steve Dorff)	30	$5		Elektra 45554
				from the movie starring Clint Eastwood				
6/16/79	**❶¹**	14		14 Suspicions	I Don't Wanna Make Love (With Anyone Else But You)	13	$5		Elektra 46053
11/3/79+	**5**	15		15 Pour Me Another Tequilla	I Will Never Let You Go Again		$5		Elektra 46558
3/15/80	**❶¹**	14		16 Gone Too Far	Loveline	82	$4		Elektra 46613
6/21/80	**❶¹**	15	●	17 Drivin' My Life Away	Pretty Lady	5	$4		Elektra 46656
				from the movie *Roadie* starring Meat Loaf				
11/8/80+	**❶¹**	17	●	18 I Love A Rainy Night	Short Road To Love	❶²	$4		Elektra 47066
8/1/81	**❶¹**	16		19 Step By Step	My Only Wish	5	$4	■	Elektra 47174
11/21/81+	**❶¹**	17		20 Someone Could Lose A Heart Tonight	Nobody Loves Me Like My Baby	15	$4		Elektra 47239
4/10/82	**2³**	16		21 I Don't Know Where To Start	Skip-A-Beat	35	$4		Elektra 47435

DEBUT	PEAK	WKS	Gold	A-side (Chart Hit)..B-side	Pop	$	Pic	Label & Number
				RABBITT, Eddie — Cont'd				
10/9/82	❶¹	19		22 You And I _All My Life, All My Love_	7	$4		Elektra 69936
				EDDIE RABBITT with CRYSTAL GAYLE				
4/2/83	❶¹	17		23 You Can't Run From Love _You Got Me Now_	55	$4		Warner 29712
9/3/83	10	18		24 You Put The Beat In My Heart _Our Love Will Survive_	81	$4		Warner 29512
12/17/83+	10	15		25 Nothing Like Falling In Love _Gone Too Far_		$4		Warner 29431
5/19/84	3	18		26 B-B-B-Burnin' Up With Love _747_		$4		Warner 29279
10/6/84+	❶¹	23		27 The Best Year Of My Life _S:❶¹ / A:❶¹ Over There_		$4		Warner 29186
2/23/85	4	19		28 Warning Sign _S:3 / A:4 Go To Sleep Big Bertha_		$4		Warner 29089
7/13/85	6	21		29 She's Comin' Back To Say Goodbye _A:5 / S:6 Dial That Telephone_		$4		Warner 28976
10/12/85	10	18		30 A World Without Love _S:10 / A:10 You Really Got A Hold On Me_		$3		RCA 14192
3/22/86	4	19		31 Repetitive Regret _S:4 / A:4 Letter From Home_		$3		RCA 14317
7/12/86	❶¹	20		32 Both To Each Other (Friends & Lovers) _S:❶¹ / A:❶¹ A World Without Love_		$3	■	RCA 14377
				EDDIE RABBITT AND JUICE NEWTON #2 Pop hit for Gloria Loring & Carl Anderson in 1986				
11/1/86+	9	20		33 Gotta Have You _A:9 / S:10 Singing In The Subway_		$3		RCA 5012
1/16/88	❶¹	20		34 I Wanna Dance With You _S:7 Gotta Have You_		$3		RCA 5238
5/28/88	❶¹	18		35 The Wanderer _S:2 Workin' Out_		$3		RCA 8306
				#2 Pop hit for Dion in 1961				
10/8/88	7	22		36 We Must Be Doin' Somethin' Right _S:9 He's A Cheater_		$3		RCA 8716
5/13/89	66	10		37 That's Why I Fell In Love With You _She's An Old Cadillac_		$3		RCA 8819
12/9/89+	❶²	26		38 On Second Thought _Only One Love In My Life_		$3		Universal 66025
4/7/90	8	21		39 Runnin' With The Wind _Feel Like A Stranger_		$3	▌	Capitol 44538
8/4/90	32	9		40 It's Lonely Out Tonite				album cut
9/29/90	11	20		41 American Boy				album cut
3/2/91	58	9		42 Tennessee Born And Bred				album cut
				above 3 from the album _Jersey Boy_ on Capitol 93882				
8/17/91	50	14		43 Hang Up The Phone				album cut
				from the album _Ten Rounds_ on Capitol 95955				
				RABBITT, Jimmy '76 Born Edward Payne in Holdenville, Oklahoma; raised in Tyler, Texas. Singer/songwriter/guitarist. Worked as a DJ in several cities.				
5/8/76	80	4		Ladies Love Outlaws _I Wish I Had Me Someone To Miss_		$5		Capitol 4257
				JIMMY RABBITT AND RENEGADE				
				RAE, Lana '72 Female singer from Oklahoma.				
2/19/72	26	14		You're My Shoulder To Lean On _Talking To The Wall_		$6		Decca 32927
				RAINES, Leon '88 Born in Mobile, Alabama.				
4/30/83	79	4		1 I'll Be Seeing You		$6		Amer. Spotlite 103
				#1 Pop hit for Bing Crosby in 1944				
7/7/84	91	2		2 Don't Give Up On Her Now _Take Me Back_		$6		Amer. Spotlite 107
11/24/84	81	3		3 Biloxi Lady _Listen To The Words_		$5		Atlantic Amer. 99700
3/9/85	83	2		4 It Happens Every Time _Drunk On Love_		$5		Atlantic Amer. 99670
12/26/87+	71	5		5 Most Of All _No Losing You_		$5		Southern Tracks 1089
				RAINFORD, Tina '77				
4/9/77	25	14		1 Silver Bird _I'm Danny's Girlfriend_		$5		Epic 50340
10/15/77	91	4		2 Big Silver Angel _Guitar Man_		$5		Epic 50455
				RAINSFORD, Willie '77 Born in Nashville. Singer/songwriter/pianist.				
3/26/77	98	2		1 No Relief In Sight _Piano Man Blues_		$7		Louisiana Hay. 7615
8/13/77	85	5		2 Cheater's Kit _She's My Woman_		$7		Louisiana Hay. 7629
				RAINWATER, Jack '77 Singer from New York City. No relation to Marvin Rainwater.				
11/12/77	96	3		All I Want Is To Love You _A Place In The Sun_		$7		Laurie 3658
				RAINWATER, Marvin '57 Born Marvin Karlton Percy on 7/2/25 in Wichita, Kansas. Singer/songwriter/guitarist. No relation to Jack Rainwater.				
4/6/57	3	28	●	1 Gonna Find Me A Bluebird/ _S:3 / A:3 / J:5 So You Think You've Got Troubles_	18			
		1		2 So You Think You've Got Troubles _S:flip_		$20		MGM 12412
4/14/58	15	3		3 Whole Lotta Woman _S:15 Baby, Don't Go_	60	$20		MGM 12609
9/15/58	11	1		4 Nothin' Needs Nothin' (Like I Need You) _A:11 (There's Always) A Need For Love_		$20		MGM 12701
7/6/59	16	6		5 Half-Breed _A Song Of Love_	66	$20		MGM 12803
				RAITT, Bonnie '80 Born on 11/8/49 in Burbank, California. Blues-rock singer/guitarist. Daugher of Broadway actor/singer John Raitt. Married actor Michael O'Keefe on 4/28/91. Charted 11 pop hits from 1977-95.				
10/4/80	42	8		Don't It Make Ya Wanna Dance _Orange Blossom Special (Mickey Gilley)_		$5	■	Full Moon 47033
				from the movie _Urban Cowboy_ starring John Travolta				
				RAKES, Pal '77 Born Palmer Rakes in Tampa, Florida. Singer/songwriter/guitarist.				
4/2/77	24	12		1 That's When The Lyin' Stops (And The Lovin' Starts) _Dirty Old Women_		$5		Warner 8340
7/30/77	31	10		2 'Til I Can't Take It Anymore _Blue Summer_		$5		Warner 8416
1/7/78	46	10		3 If I Ever Come Back _Lay It On The Line_		$5		Warner 8506
10/28/78	81	3		4 Till Then _It's Sweet Business Doing Pleasure With You_		$4		Warner 8656
				#8 Pop hit for The Mills Brothers in 1944				
3/17/79	92	3		5 You And Me And The Green Grass _Bad Deal_		$4		Warner 8765

DEBUT	PEAK	WKS	A-side / B-side	Pop	$	Pic	Label & Number
			RAKES, Pal — Cont'd				
10/29/88	71	5	6 I'm Only Lonely For You.....................................One More Time		$3		Atlantic Amer. 99276
6/24/89	73	5	7 All You're Takin' Is My Love ....I Feel A Change Comin' On		$3	■	Atlantic Amer. 99214
11/4/89	66	3	8 We Did It Once (We Can Do It Again)....................Poor Boy		$3		Atlantic 88800
			RAMBLING ROGUE — see ROSE, Fred				
			RANCH, The '97				
			Group from Australia: Keith Urban (vocals, guitar), Jerry Flowers (bass) and Peter Clarke (drums).				
9/27/97	50	13	Walkin' The Country..Clutterbilly		$3		Capitol 19699
			RANDALL, Jon '96				
			Born Jon Randall Stewart on 2/17/69 in Dallas. Former guitarist for **Emmylou Harris**. Married **Lorrie Morgan** on 11/16/96.				
7/16/94	74	3	1 This Heart...Only Game In Town		$3	▌	RCA 62833
4/6/96	18	20	2 By My Side...S:4 Candy Kisses	110	$3	▌	BNA 64512
			LORRIE MORGAN & JON RANDALL				
			RANEY, Wayne '49				
			Born on 8/17/21 in Wolf Bayou, Arkansas. Died of cancer on 1/23/93 (age 71). Singer/harmonica player.				
10/30/48	11	1	1 Lost John Boogie...................................J:11 / S:14 Jole Blon's Ghost		$30		King 719
11/20/48	13	2	2 Jack And Jill Boogie...............................J:13 Lonesome Wind Blues		$30		King 732
7/30/49	❶³	22	3 Why Don't You Haul Off And Love Me J:❶³ / S:❷¹ / A:5 Don't Know Why	22	$30		King 791
			RATTLESNAKE ANNIE '87				
			Born Rosan Gallimore on 12/26/41 in Puryear, Tennessee. Singer/songwriter/guitarist.				
5/2/87	79	3	1 Callin' Your Bluff..Goodbye To A River		$3		Columbia 07024
1/9/88	79	3	2 Somewhere South Of Macon.......................Outskirts Of Town		$3		Columbia 07634
			RAUSCH, Leon '80				
			Born Edgar Leon Rausch on 10/2/27 in Springfield, Missouri. Singer/songwriter/guitarist. Member of the **Original Texas Playboys**.				
1/17/76	99	1	1 Through The Bottom Of The Glass.................Louisana, My Home		$5		Derrick 105
8/21/76	91	5	2 She's The Trip That I've Been On.................I'll Say Your Goodbyes		$5		Derrick 107
6/10/78	89	5	3 I'm Satisfied With You		$5		Derrick 119
10/21/78	95	4	4 Let's Have A Heart To Heart Talk ......Did We Have To Come This Far To Say Goodbye		$5		Derrick 122
10/20/79	91	4	5 You Can Be Replaced.............................Put Me To The Test		$5		Derrick 124
12/15/79+	81	6	6 Palimony...Love, Love, Love		$5		Derrick 128

DEBUT	PEAK	WKS	A-side / B-side	Pop	$	Pic	Label & Number
			RAVEN, Eddy ★84★ '88				
			Born Edward Garvin Futch on 8/19/44 in Lafayette, Louisiana. Singer/songwriter/guitarist.				
			1)Joe Knows How To Live 2)Bayou Boys 3)I'm Gonna Get You 4)In A Letter To You 5)I Got Mexico				
3/16/74	63	10	1 The Last Of The Sunshine Cowboys...................Sugah Kane		$5		ABC 11421
11/23/74+	46	13	2 Ain't She Somethin' Else...........................If Is A Bird On A Chain		$5		ABC 12037
4/19/75	27	11	3 Good News, Bad News.................................Sam		$5		ABC 12083
8/2/75	68	10	4 You're My Rainy Day Woman.......................She Touched You		$5		ABC 12111
12/20/75+	34	10	5 Free To Be...Country Green		$5		ABC/Dot 17595
4/10/76	87	5	6 I Wanna Live..I Don't Wanna Talk It Over		$5		ABC/Dot 17618
8/28/76	94	3	7 The Curse Of A Woman.............................Thank God For Kids		$5		ABC/Dot 17646
12/11/76	90	4	8 I'm Losing It All.......................................Touch The Morning		$5		ABC/Dot 17663
9/2/78	71	5	9 You're A Dancer......................................She Don't Cry		$5		Monument 260
12/8/79+	44	11	10 Sweet Mother Texas.............................I Should've Called		$5		Dimension 003
3/15/80	25	11	11 Dealin' With The Devil............................She Don't Cry		$5		Dimension 1005
6/7/80	30	11	12 You've Got Those Eyes..........................Fais Do Do		$5		Dimension 1007
9/20/80	34	11	13 Another Texas Song..............................Day After Day		$5		Dimension 1011
1/24/81	23	12	14 Peace Of Mind......................................Just Leave Me Alone		$5		Dimension 1017
5/23/81	13	15	15 I Should've Called.................................Young Girl		$4		Elektra 47136
10/17/81+	11	18	16 Who Do You Know In California.................Thinking It Over		$4		Elektra 47216
2/20/82	14	18	17 A Little Bit Crazy.................................Loving Arms And Lying Eyes		$4		Elektra 47413
6/19/82	10	16	18 She's Playing Hard To Forget.................Desperate Dreams		$4		Elektra 47469
11/6/82+	25	17	19 San Antonio Nights...............................Free To Be		$4		Elektra 69929
3/17/84	❶¹	22	20 I Got Mexico..Love Burning Down		$3		RCA 13746
7/21/84	9	18	21 I Could Use Another You.........................Folks Out On The Road		$3		RCA 13839
11/10/84+	9	23	22 She's Gonna Win Your Heart......S:7 / A:7 Looking For Ways		$3		RCA 13939
4/20/85	9	21	23 Operator, Operator.......A:6 / S:10 Just For The Sake Of The Thrill		$3		RCA 14044
8/3/85	8	24	24 I Wanna Hear It From You........A:7 / S:8 Room To Run		$3		RCA 14164
12/7/85+	3	23	25 You Should Have Been Gone By Now..S:3 / A:3 We Robbed Trains		$3		RCA 14250
5/31/86	3	22	26 Sometimes A Lady..........A:3 / S:4 Just For The Sake Of The Thrill		$3		RCA 14319
11/15/86+	3	24	27 Right Hand Man............A:3 / S:6 I Got Mexico		$3		RCA 5032
3/28/87	3	21	28 You're Never Too Old For Young Love.S:8 / A:15 Other Than Montreal		$3		RCA 5128
7/25/87	❶¹	24	29 Shine, Shine, Shine.................S:12 Stay With Me		$3		RCA 5221
2/13/88	❶¹	21	30 I'm Gonna Get You.................S:2 Other Than Montreal		$3		RCA 6831
6/18/88	❶¹	21	31 Joe Knows How To Live.............S:3 Looking For Ways		$3		RCA 8303
12/3/88+	4	21	32 'Til You Cry....................Just For The Sake Of The Thrill		$3		RCA 8798

DEBUT	PEAK	WKS	Gold	A-side (Chart Hit)..B-side	Pop	$	Pic	Label & Number

RAVEN, Eddy — Cont'd

DEBUT	PEAK	WKS		A-side	B-side	Pop	$	Pic	Label & Number
4/22/89	**❶**[1]	21		33 In A Letter To You	*Risky Business*		$3		Universal 66003
8/19/89	**❶**[1]	26		34 Bayou Boys	*Angel Fire*		$3		Universal 66016
12/23/89+	6	26		35 Sooner Or Later	*Little Sheba*		$3		Capitol 44528
				first released on Universal 66029 in 1989					
4/21/90	10	21		36 Island	*A Woman's Place*		$3	▌	Capitol 44537
9/22/90	56	7		37 Zydeco Lady..					album cut
				from the album *Temporary Sanity* on Universal 76003					
3/30/91	60	7		38 Rock Me In The Rhythm Of Your Love					album cut
6/29/91	58	8		39 Too Much Candy For A Dime					album cut
				above 2 from the album *Right For The Flight* on Capitol 94258					

RAY, Mundo — see EARWOOD, Mundo

RAYBON BROS.   **'97**

Duo of brothers Marty and Tim Raybon. Marty was lead singer of **Shenandoah**.

DEBUT	PEAK	WKS		A-side	B-side	Pop	$	Pic	Label & Number
5/31/97	37	20	●	1 Butterfly Kisses .... S:2 *(instrumental)*		22	$3	▌	MCA 72016
8/16/97	64	4		2 The Way She's Lookin' .... *Tangled Up In Love*			$3		MCA 72017

RAYE, Collin ★127★   **'92**

Born Floyd Collin Wray on 8/22/59 in DeQueen, Arkansas. Singer/songwriter/guitarist. Member of **The Wrays**.

1)Love, Me 2)In This Life 3)My Kind Of Girl 4)On The Verge 5)One Boy, One Girl

DEBUT	PEAK	WKS		A-side	B-side	Pop	$	Pic	Label & Number
6/8/91	29	20		1 All I Can Be (Is A Sweet Memory) .... *Good For You*			$3		Epic 73831
10/19/91+	**❶**[3]	20		2 Love, Me	*Blue Magic*		$3		Epic 74051
2/29/92	2[1]	20		3 Every Second	*Any Old Stretch Of Blacktop*		$3		Epic 74242
7/4/92	74	1		4 It Could've Been So Good					album cut
				from the album *All I Can Be* on Epic 47468					
8/1/92	**❶**[2]	20		5 In This Life	*Blue Magic*		$3	▌	Epic 74421
12/5/92+	7	20		6 I Want You Bad (And That Ain't Good)	*Let It Be Me*		$3		Epic 74786
4/3/93	5	20		7 Somebody Else's Moon	*You Can't Take It With You*		$3		Epic 74912
8/7/93	4	20		8 That Was A River	*Big River*		$3		Epic 77118
12/11/93+	6	20		9 That's My Story	*Border And Beyond*		$3	▌	Epic 77308
4/9/94	2[1]	20		10 Little Rock	*Dreaming My Dreams With You*		$3		Epic 77436
8/6/94	8	20		11 Man Of My Word	*Nothin' A Little Love Won't Cure*		$3	▌	Epic 77632
12/3/94+	**❶**[1]	20		12 My Kind Of Girl	*Angel Of No Mercy*		$3	▌	Epic 77773
4/8/95	4	20		13 If I Were You	*A Bible And A Bus Ticket Home*		$3		Epic 77859
7/29/95	2[2]	20		14 One Boy, One Girl	S:2 *I Love Being Wrong*	87	$3	▌	Epic 77973
11/18/95+	3	20		15 Not That Different	S:5 *Sweet Miss Behavin'*	114	$3	▌	Epic 78189
11/25/95	57	11		16 What If Jesus Comes Back Like That............... *The Time Machine*			$3		Epic 78452
3/9/96	3	20		17 I Think About You	*I Volunteer*		$3		Epic 78238
7/13/96	12	20		18 Love Remains .... *I Love Being Wrong*			$3		Epic 78348
11/9/96+	21	11		19 What If Jesus Comes Back Like That...............*The Time Machine* [R]			$3		Epic 78452
2/22/97	2[2]	20		20 On The Verge					album cut
				from the album *I Think About You* on Epic 67033					
6/7/97	2[1]	20		21 What The Heart Wants					album cut
9/6/97	70	6		22 Open Arms					album cut
				#2 Pop hit for Journey in 1982					
10/25/97	51	11		23 The Gift..					album cut
				COLLIN RAYE with Jim Brickman					
12/13/97+	3	22		24 Little Red Rodeo					album cut
				above 4 from the album *The Best Of Collin Raye* on Epic 67893					

RAYE, Susan ★162★   **'72**

Born on 10/18/44 in Eugene, Oregon. Regular on TV's *Hee-Haw*. Acted in the movie *From Nashville With Music*.

1)Happy Heart 2)Pitty, Pitty, Patter 3)The Great White Horse 4)L.A. International Airport
5)Whatcha Gonna Do With A Dog Like That

DEBUT	PEAK	WKS		A-side	B-side	Pop	$	Pic	Label & Number
1/10/70	30	11		1 Put A Little Love In Your Heart .... *I've Carried This Torch Much Too Long*			$8		Capitol 2701
				#4 Pop hit for Jackie DeShannon in 1969					
2/21/70	13	11		2 We're Gonna Get Together................................*Everybody Needs Somebody*			$8	■	Capitol 2731
				BUCK OWENS & SUSAN RAYE					
5/9/70	12	12		3 Togetherness .... *Fallin' For You*			$8	■	Capitol 2791
				BUCK OWENS & SUSAN RAYE					
7/4/70	35	11		4 One Night Stand .... *She Don't Deserve You Anymore*			$8	■	Capitol 2833

DEBUT	PEAK	WKS	Gold	A-side (Chart Hit)..B-side	Pop	$	Pic	Label & Number
				RAYE, Susan — Cont'd				
8/29/70	8	13		5 The Great White Horse *Your Tender Loving Care*		$8	■	Capitol 2871
				BUCK OWENS & SUSAN RAYE				
11/14/70+	10	13		6 Willy Jones *I'll Love You Forever (If You're Sure You'll Want Me Then)*		$7		Capitol 2950
2/20/71	9	16		7 L.A. International Airport *Merry-Go-Round Of Love*	54	$7		Capitol 3035
7/17/71	6	16		8 Pitty, Pitty, Patter *I'll Be Gone*		$7	■	Capitol 3129
11/13/71+	3	14		9 (I've Got A) Happy Heart *How Long Will My Baby Be Gone*		$7	■	Capitol 3209
4/1/72	44	8		10 A Song To Sing ....*Adios, Farewell, Good-Bye, Good Luck, So Long*		$7		Capitol 3289
5/27/72	10	12		11 My Heart Has A Mind Of Its Own *You'll Never Miss The Water*		$7		Capitol 3327
				#1 Pop hit for Connie Francis in 1960				
7/15/72	13	14		12 Looking Back To See...*Cryin' Time*		$7	■	Capitol 3368
				BUCK OWENS & SUSAN RAYE				
9/30/72	16	11		13 Wheel Of Fortune ....*My Heart Skips A Beat*		$7		Capitol 3438
				#1 Pop hit for Kay Starr in 1952				
12/23/72+	17	14		14 Love Sure Feels Good In My Heart ....*I've Got You On My Mind Again*		$6		Capitol 3499
4/7/73	18	12		15 Cheating Game ....*I'll Love You Forever And Ever*		$6		Capitol 3569
6/16/73	35	8		16 The Good Old Days (Are Here Again) ....*When You Get To Heaven (I'll Be There)*		$6		Capitol 3601
				BUCK OWENS & SUSAN RAYE				
9/8/73	23	12		17 Plastic Trains, Paper Planes ....*I Won't Be Needing You*		$6		Capitol 3699
12/15/73+	57	9		18 When You Get Back From Nashville ....*Nobody's Fool But Yours*		$6		Capitol 3782
4/6/74	18	14		19 Stop The World (And Let Me Off) ....*Love's Ups And Downs*		$6		Capitol 3850
8/3/74	49	11		20 You Can Sure See It From Here.................................*I Wish I Was A Butterfly*		$6		Capitol 3927
11/23/74+	9	16		21 Whatcha Gonna Do With A Dog Like That *That Loving Feeling*		$6		Capitol 3980
5/24/75	58	7		22 Ghost Story ....*Beginner's Luck*		$6		Capitol 4063
7/5/75	20	13		23 Love Is Strange ....*Sweethearts In Heaven*		$6		Capitol 4100
				BUCK OWENS & SUSAN RAYE				
				#11 Pop hit for Mickey & Sylvia in 1957				
10/16/76	87	5		24 Ozark Mountain Lullaby...*Johnny Sunshine*		$5		United Artists 870
2/19/77	64	6		25 Mr. Heartache ....*Turn Away*		$5		United Artists 934
4/30/77	53	8		26 Saturday Night To Sunday Quiet...*My Hiding Place*		$5		United Artists 976
8/13/77	51	9		27 It Didn't Have To Be A Diamond...*My Hiding Place*		$5		United Artists 1026
11/3/84	76	5		28 Put Another Notch In Your Belt/		$7		Westexas Amer. 1
2/15/86	68	5		29 I Just Can't Take The Leaving Anymore				
				RAZORBACK — see GRAYGHOST				
				RECORD, Donnie '83				
				Born on 3/31/52 in Enid, Oklahoma. Singer/songwriter/guitarist.				
8/6/83	95	1		One More Goodbye, One More Hello		$6		BriarRose 1001
				REDDY, Helen '77				
				Born on 10/25/41 in Melbourne, Australia. Singer/actress. Charted 21 pop hits from 1971-81.				
10/22/77	98	1		Laissez Les Bontemps Rouler...*The Happy Girls (Pop #57)*		$4		Capitol 4487
				title is French for "Let The Good Times Roll"				
				RED HOTS, The '94				
				All-star group: Suzy Bogguss, Alison Krauss, Kathy Mattea and Crosby, Stills & Nash.				
10/22/94	75	1		Teach Your Children...				album cut
				#16 Pop hit for Crosby, Stills & Nash in 1970; from the album *Red Hot + Country* on Mercury 522639				
				REDMOND, Robb '77				
				Singer from Sherman Oaks, California.				
3/5/77	87	4		Lunch Time Lovers ....*Monday Morning Memory*		$7		NBC 001
				RED, WHITE & BLUE (grass) '74				
				Bluegrass group from Birmingham, Alabama: husband-and-wife Ginger (vocals, guitar) and Grant (guitar) Boatwright, Dale Whitcomb (fiddle), Dave Sebolt (bass) and Michael Barnett (drums).				
12/22/73+	71	9		July You're A Woman ....*High Ground*		$7		GRC 1009
				#100 Pop hit for Pat Boone in 1969				
				RED WILLOW BAND '79				
				Group from Beardon, South Dakota.				
6/2/79	97	1		I Wish I Had Your Arms Around Me ....*Tying The Knot*		$7		Lost 1288
				REECE, Ben '75				
9/6/75	41	12		1 Mirror, Mirror ....*She's Winning*		$5		20th Century 2227
1/3/76	87	5		2 It Don't Bother Me ....*The Things To Do Today*		$5		20th Century 2262
7/10/76	83	6		3 Even If It's Wrong...*Why'd The Last Time Have To Be The Best*		$5		Polydor 14329
11/13/76	89	4		4 Honky Tonk Fool ....*She Came To Me*		$5		Polydor 14356
				REED, Bobby '83				
				Born in Rockford, Illinois.				
3/5/83	90	2		If I Just Had My Woman...*There's Love In The Air*		$7		CBO 132

283

REED, Jerry ★74★ '71

Born Jerry Reed Hubbard on 3/20/37 in Atlanta. Singer/songwriter/guitarist/actor. Known as "The Guitar Man." Acted in several movies. Regular on TV's *Concrete Cowboys*. Formerly married to **Priscilla Mitchell**.

1)*When You're Hot, You're Hot* 2)*She Got The Goldmine* 3)*Lord, Mr. Ford* 4)*The Bird*
5)*East Bound And Down*

DEBUT	PEAK	WKS		A-side / B-side	Pop	$	Pic	Label & Number
5/20/67	53	9		1 **Guitar Man**.. *It Don't Work That Way*		$8		RCA Victor 9152
				Reed played guitar on **Elvis Presley**'s version in 1968 (#43 Pop)				
11/4/67+	15	15		2 **Tupelo Mississippi Flash**...................................... *Wabash Cannon Ball*		$8		RCA Victor 9334
4/13/68	14	15		3 **Remembering** .... *Fine On My Mind*		$8		RCA Victor 9493
				also see #28 below				
9/28/68	48	10		4 **Alabama Wild Man**.................................... *Twelve Bar Midnight*		$8		RCA Victor 9623
				also see #16 below				
1/18/69	60	6		5 **Oh What A Woman!**...................................... *Losing Your Love*		$8		RCA Victor 9701
4/5/69	20	10		6 **There's Better Things In Life**....................................... *Blues Land*		$7		RCA Victor 0124
8/30/69	11	13		7 **Are You From Dixie (Cause I'm From Dixie Too)** .... *A Worried Man*		$7		RCA Victor 0211
3/7/70	14	12		8 **Talk About The Good Times**.................................... *Alabama Jubilee*		$7		RCA Victor 9804
8/8/70	16	11		9 **Georgia Sunshine**..................................... *Swinging '69*		$7		RCA Victor 9870
10/24/70	16	18	●	10 **Amos Moses/** [N]	8			
		11		11 **The Preacher And The Bear**........................ [N]		$6		RCA Victor 9904
5/8/71	❶⁵	15		12 **When You're Hot, You're Hot** *You've Been Cryin' Again* [N]	9	$6		RCA Victor 9976
9/11/71	11	13		13 **Ko-Ko Joe**....................................... *I Feel For You*	51	$6		RCA Victor 1011
1/1/72	27	11		14 **Another Puff**....................................... *Love Man* [N]	65	$6		RCA Victor 0613
4/1/72	24	11		15 **Smell The Flowers**................................ *If It Comes To That*		$6		RCA Victor 0667
7/15/72	22	12		16 **Alabama Wild Man**....................... *Take It Easy (In Your Mind)* [R]	62	$6	■	RCA Victor 0738
				new version of #4 above				
12/23/72+	18	10		17 **You Took All The Ramblin' Out Of Me**........................... *I'm Not Playing Games*		$6		RCA Victor 0857
5/26/73	❶¹	15		18 **Lord, Mr. Ford** *Two-Timin'* [N]	68	$6		RCA Victor 0960
12/15/73+	25	10		19 **The Uptown Poker Club**.................................... *Honkin'*		$6		RCA Victor 0194
2/9/74	13	10		20 **The Crude Oil Blues**.............................. *Pickie, Pickie, Pickie* [N]	91	$6		RCA Victor 0224
5/11/74	12	14		21 **A Good Woman's Love**............................. *Everybody Needs Someone*		$6		RCA Victor 0273
10/5/74	72	6		22 **Boogie Woogie Rock And Roll**.................................. *In Between*		$6		RCA Victor 10063
12/14/74+	18	12		23 **Let's Sing Our Song**..................................... *Grab Bag*		$5		RCA Victor 10132
4/5/75	64	9		24 **Mind Your Love** .... *Struttin'*		$5		RCA Victor 10247
7/12/75	65	9		25 **The Telephone** .... *City Of New Orleans* [N]		$5		RCA Victor 10325
10/4/75	60	8		26 **You Got A Lock On Me**............................... *Reedology*	104	$5		RCA Victor 10389
7/4/76	54	8		27 **Gator**... *Good For Him*		$5		RCA Victor 10717
				from the movie starring **Burt Reynolds**				
10/9/76	57	7		28 **Remembering** .... *Babe* [R]		$5		RCA 10784
				new version of #3 above				
3/5/77	19	12		29 **Semolita**.. *The Phantom Of The Opry*		$5		RCA 10893
7/2/77	68	5		30 **With His Pants In His Hand** .... *We Called It Everything Else*		$5		RCA 11008
8/13/77	2²	16		31 **East Bound And Down/**	103			
				from the movie *Smokey & The Bandit* starring **Burt Reynolds**				
		13		32 **(I'm Just A) Redneck In A Rock And Roll Bar**.......................		$5		RCA 11056
12/24/77+	20	12		33 **You Know What**.. *Louisiana Lady*		$5		RCA 11164
				JERRY REED and SEIDINA (Reed's daughter)				
3/25/78	39	9		34 **Sweet Love Feelings** .... *You're Gonna Need Someone*		$5		RCA 11232
6/10/78	10	12		35 **(I Love You) What Can I Say/**				
		7		36 **High Rollin'**		$5		RCA 11281
				from the movie *High-Ballin'* starring Reed				
11/11/78+	14	14		37 **Gimme Back My Blues**.. *Honkin'*		$5		RCA 11407
2/24/79	18	11		38 **Second-Hand Satin Lady (And A Bargain Basement Boy)** .... *Jiffy Jam*		$5		RCA 11472
6/16/79	40	7		39 **(Who Was The Man Who Put) The Line In Gasoline**................ *Piece Of Cake* [N]		$5		RCA 11638
9/8/79	67	5		40 **Hot Stuff**....................................... *Nervous Breakdown*		$5		RCA 11698
				from the movie starring Reed				
12/1/79+	12	14		41 **Sugar Foot Rag**....................... *I Wanna Go Back Home To Georgia*		$5		RCA 11764
3/29/80	36	10		42 **Age/**				
		10		43 **Workin' At The Carwash Blues**...............................		$5		RCA 11944
				#32 Pop hit for **Jim Croce** in 1974				
7/12/80	64	6		44 **The Friendly Family Inn** .... *The Bandit*		$4		RCA 12034
8/30/80	26	12		45 **Texas Bound And Flyin'** .... *Concrete Sailor*		$4		RCA 12083
				from the movie *Smokey & The Bandit II* starring **Burt Reynolds**				
1/10/81	80	4		46 **Caffein, Nicotine, Benzedrine (And Wish Me Luck)**.. *If Love's Not Around The House*		$4		RCA 12157
5/9/81	87	3		47 **The Testimony Of Soddy Hoe** .... *Dreaming Fairy Tales*		$4		RCA 12210
7/4/81	84	2		48 **Good Friends Make Good Lovers**................. *The Devil Went Down To Georgia*		$4		RCA 12253
9/26/81	30	12		49 **Patches**.. *Stray Dogs And Stray Women*		$4		RCA 12318
				#4 Pop hit for **Clarence Carter** in 1970				
4/17/82	32	13		50 **The Man With The Golden Thumb** .... *East Bound And Down*		$4		RCA 13081
7/10/82	❶²	17		51 **She Got The Goldmine (I Got The Shaft)** *"44"* [N]	57	$4		RCA 13268
10/16/82	2³	16		52 **The Bird** *The Hobo* [N]		$4		RCA 13355
				JERRY REED and Friends				
				impressions of **Willie Nelson**'s "Whiskey River" and "On The Road Again" and **George Jones**'s "He Stopped Loving Her Today"				

REED, Jerry — Cont'd

DEBUT	PEAK	WKS		A-side / B-side	Pop	$	Pic	Label & Number
1/29/83	13	15		53 Down On The Corner .... Hard Times		$4		RCA 13422
				#3 Pop hit for Creedence Clearwater Revival in 1969				
5/21/83	16	17		54 Good Ole Boys/				
		17		55 She's Ready For Someone To Love Her		$4		RCA 13527
8/6/83	20	14		56 Hold On, I'm Comin' .... Waiting On Down The Line		$4		RCA 13580
				WAYLON JENNINGS & JERRY REED				
				#21 Pop hit for Sam & Dave in 1966				
11/12/83	58	6		57 I'm A Slave .... Nobody Ever Loved Me		$4		RCA 13663

REEVES, Del ★88★   **'65**

Born Franklin Delano Reeves on 7/14/33 in Sparta, North Carolina. Singer/songwriter/multi-instrumentalist. Joined the *Grand Ole Opry* in 1966. Hosted the *Country Carnival* TV show. Acted in the movies *Second Fiddle To A Steel Guitar, Sam Whiskey, Cotton Pickin' Chicken-Pluckers* and *Forty-Acre Feud.*

1)Girl On The Billboard 2)Good Time Charlies 3)The Belles Of Southern Bell
4)Looking At The World Through A Windshield 5)Be Glad

DEBUT	PEAK	WKS		A-side / B-side	Pop	$	Pic	Label & Number
11/6/61	9	17		1 Be Quiet Mind .... As Far As I Can See		$12		Decca 31307
10/27/62	11	11		2 He Stands Real Tall .... Empty House		$12		Decca 31417
4/27/63	13	14		3 The Only Girl I Can't Forget .... The Love She Offered Me		$10		Reprise 20158
8/8/64	41	12		4 Talking To The Night Lights .... Not Since Adam		$10		Columbia 43044
3/13/65	❶²	20		5 Girl On The Billboard .... Eyes Don't Come Crying To Me	96	$8		United Artists 824
8/14/65	4	17		6 The Belles Of Southern Bell .... Nothing To Write Home About		$8		United Artists 890
12/4/65+	9	13		7 Women Do Funny Things To Me .... My Half Of Our Past		$8		United Artists 940
4/16/66	42	7		8 One Bum Town .... Dead And Gone		$8		United Artists 50001
7/2/66	37	5		9 Gettin' Any Feed For Your Chickens ...... Plain As The Tears On My Face		$8		United Artists 50035
10/29/66	27	12		10 This Must Be The Bottom .... Laughter Keeps Running Down My Cheeks		$8		United Artists 50081
3/18/67	45	9		11 Blame It On My Do Wrong .... I Don't Have Sense Enough		$8		United Artists 50128
6/17/67	33	10		12 The Private .... Things Her Memory Makes		$8	■	United Artists 50157
10/7/67	12	18		13 A Dime At A Time .... So Much Got Lost		$8		United Artists 50210
3/9/68	56	5		14 I Just Wasted The Rest .... Our Way Of Life		$8		United Artists 50243
				DEL REEVES & BOBBY GOLDSBORO				
3/30/68	18	13		15 Wild Blood .... Lest We Forget		$8		United Artists 50270
8/17/68	5	14		16 Looking At The World Through A Windshield ...... If I Lived Here		$7		United Artists 50332
12/28/68+	3	17		17 Good Time Charlie's .... These Feet		$7		United Artists 50487
5/24/69	5	14		18 Be Glad .... Moccasin Branch		$7		United Artists 50531
10/11/69	12	11		19 There Wouldn't Be A Lonely Heart In Town ...... Little Bit Of Somethin' Else		$7		United Artists 50564
11/1/69	31	10		20 Take A Little Good Will Home .... She Thinks I Still Care		$7		United Artists 50591
				BOBBY GOLDSBORO & DEL REEVES				
2/7/70	14	12		21 A Lover's Question .... Spare Me		$7		United Artists 50622
				DEL REEVES and The Goodtime Charlies				
				#6 Pop hit for Clyde McPhatter in 1959				
5/23/70	41	11		22 Son Of A Coal Man .... The Chair That Rocked Us All		$7		United Artists 50667
5/30/70	20	12		23 Land Mark Tavern .... So Sad		$7		United Artists 50669
				DEL REEVES & PENNY DeHAVEN				
10/3/70	22	10		24 Right Back Loving You Again .... Gardenia Brown		$7		United Artists 50714
1/9/71	30	11		25 Bar Room Talk .... I'm Not Through Loving You		$7		United Artists 50743
4/10/71	33	12		26 Working Like The Devil (For The Lord) ...... Sidewalks Of Chicago		$6		United Artists 50763
7/10/71	9	12		27 The Philadelphia Fillies .... Belles Of Broadway		$6		United Artists 50802
10/23/71	31	10		28 A Dozen Pairs Of Boots .... A Rose Is Hard To Beat		$6		United Artists 50840
1/22/72	29	12		29 The Best Is Yet To Come .... Truth Can Hurt A Woman		$6		United Artists 50877
6/10/72	62	6		30 No Rings--No Strings .... Hey, Anybody Here Seen Cupid		$6		United Artists 50906
6/24/72	54	6		31 Crying In The Rain .... Time		$6		United Artists 50829
				DEL REEVES & PENNY DeHAVEN				
				#6 Pop hit for The Everly Brothers in 1962				
11/11/72	47	6		32 Before Goodbye .... Buck Jones Guitar		$6		United Artists 50964
2/24/73	54	5		33 Trucker's Paradise .... Gathering Of My Memories		$6		United Artists 51106
6/9/73	44	10		34 Mm-Mm Good .... Bridge That Wouldn't Burn		$5		United Artists 249
9/8/73	22	15		35 Lay A Little Lovin' On Me .... Lay Me To Sleep		$5		United Artists 308
2/23/74	70	8		36 What A Way To Go .... Sometimes Woman		$5		United Artists 378
5/11/74	62	7		37 Prayer From A Mobile Home .... Three Hours Late		$5		United Artists 427
9/21/74	89	4		38 She Likes Country Bands .... A Rose Is Hard To Beat		$5		United Artists 532
12/14/74+	65	8		39 Pour It All On Me .... Belles Of Broadway		$5		United Artists 564
2/15/75	65	9		40 But I Do .... One More Round Of Gin		$5		United Artists 593
				#4 Pop hit for Clarence Henry in 1961				
6/14/75	74	5		41 Puttin' In Overtime At Home .... Homemade Love		$5		United Artists 639
10/18/75	92	3		42 You Comb Her Hair Every Morning ...... Hell And Half Of Georgia		$5		United Artists 702
2/14/76	51	9		43 I Ain't Got Nobody .... I Would Like To See You Again		$5		United Artists 760
5/1/76	29	11		44 On The Rebound .... What's Our Love Coming To		$5		United Artists 797
				DEL REEVES & BILLIE JO SPEARS				
8/7/76	42	8		45 Teardrops Will Kiss The Morning Dew .... Nothing Seems To Work Anymore		$5		United Artists 832
				DEL REEVES & BILLIE JO SPEARS				
11/20/76	79	4		46 My Better Half .... Dig A Little Deeper In The Well		$5		United Artists 885
6/4/77	78	5		47 Ladies Night .... Cryin' In Arkansas Tonight		$5		United Artists 989

DEBUT	PEAK	WKS	Gold	A-side (Chart Hit) ....B-side	Pop	$	Pic	Label & Number
				REEVES, Del — Cont'd				
5/6/78	93	3	48	When My Angel Turns Into A Devil ....*How Can Anything That Feels So Good*		$5		United Artists 1191
9/2/78	79	5	49	Dig Down Deep ....*Darlin' I Love You*		$5		United Artists 1230
4/12/80	82	6	50	Take Me To Your Heart ....*What The Love Of A Lady Can Do*		$5		Koala 584
9/6/80	90	3	51	What Am I Gonna Do? ....*Night Out*		$5		Koala 594
6/6/81	67	4	52	Swinging Doors ....*Who Left The Door To Heaven Open*		$5		Koala 333
9/5/81	53	7	53	Slow Hand ....*Take Off Time*		$5		Koala 336
				#2 Pop hit for the **Pointer Sisters** in 1981				
1/23/82	67	5	54	Ain't Nobody Gonna Get My Body But You ....*Let's Think About Livin'*		$5		Koala 339
4/26/86	95	3	55	The Second Time Around		$5		Playback 1103

REEVES, Jim ★13★ '60

Born on 8/20/24 in Galloway, Texas. Died in a plane crash on 7/31/64 (age 39) in Nashville. Singer/songwriter/guitarist. Known as "Gentleman Jim." Worked as a DJ at KWKH in Shreveport, Louisiana. Joined the *Louisiana Hayride* in 1953. Joined the *Grand Ole Opry* in 1955. Acted in the movie *Kimberley Jim*. Elected to the Country Music Hall of Fame in 1967.

1)He'll Have To Go 2)Mexican Joe 3)Four Walls 4)I Guess I'm Crazy 5)Billy Bayou

DEBUT	PEAK	WKS	Gold	A-side	Pop	$	Pic	Label & Number
3/28/53	❶⁹	26	1	Mexican Joe J:❶⁹ / A:❶⁷ / S:❶⁶ *I Could Cry*		$30		Abbott 116
				JIM REEVES And The Circle O Ranch Boys				
12/5/53+	❶³	21	2	Bimbo A:❶³ / S:2 / J:2 *Gypsy Heart*		$30		Abbott 148
1/9/54	3	22	3	I Love You A:3 / J:7 / S:8 *I Want You Yes (You Want Me No)*		$30		Fabor 101
				GINNY WRIGHT/JIM REEVES				
6/26/54	15	1	4	Then I'll Stop Loving You ....A:15 *Echo Bonita*		$30		Abbott 160
10/23/54+	5	12	5	Penny Candy J:5 / A:8 *I'll Follow You*		$30		Abbott 170
4/30/55	9	1	6	Drinking Tequila J:9 *Red Eyed And Rowdy*		$30		Abbott 178
8/20/55	4	20	7	Yonder Comes A Sucker/ J:4 / A:6 / S:8		$20		RCA Victor 6200
		2	8	I'm Hurtin' Inside ....J:flip				
6/23/56	8	13	9	My Lips Are Sealed A:8 / J:8 / S:10 *Pickin' A Chicken*		$20		RCA Victor 6517
9/29/56	4	19	10	According To My Heart/ A:4 / J:8 / S:10		$20		RCA Victor 6620
		1	11	The Mother Of A Honky Tonk Girl .... S:flip				
1/12/57	3	18	12	Am I Losing You/ A:3 / J:5 / S:8		$20		RCA Victor 6749
				also see #30 below				
		5	13	Waitin' For A Train ....J:flip				
4/29/57	❶⁸	26	14	Four Walls A:❶⁸ / S:2 / J:4 *I Know And You Know*	11	$15		RCA Victor 6874
8/19/57	9	6	15	Two Shadows On Your Window/ A:9		$15		RCA Victor 6973
8/26/57	12	1	16	Young Hearts S:12 / A:14				
12/2/57+	3	18	17	Anna Marie A:3 / S:10 *Everywhere You Go*	93	$15		RCA Victor 7070
5/12/58	8	7	18	I Love You More/ A:8 / S:14		$15		RCA Victor 7171
4/21/58	10	3	19	Overnight A:10		$15		RCA Victor 7266
7/14/58	2³	22	20	Blue Boy A:2 / S:4 *Theme Of Love (I Love to Say, "I Love You")*	45	$15		RCA Victor 7380
11/10/58+	❶⁵	25	21	Billy Bayou/	95	$15		RCA Victor 7479
11/17/58+	18	7	22	I'd Like To Be..		$15		RCA Victor 7557
3/30/59	2⁴	20	23	Home *If Heartache Is The Fashion*		$15		RCA Victor 7643
7/27/59	5	16	24	Partners/		$12	●	RCA Victor 7756
8/17/59	17	7	25	I'm Beginning To Forget You..............................				
12/7/59+	❶¹⁴	34	26	He'll Have To Go *In A Mansion Stands My Love*	2³	$12		RCA Victor 7800
7/18/60	3	18	27	I'm Gettin' Better/	37			
7/25/60	6	16	28	I Know One	82	$12	■	RCA Victor 7855
10/31/60	3	25	29	I Missed Me/	44			
11/21/60	8	14	30	Am I Losing You [R]	31	$12	■	RCA Victor 7905
				new version of #12 above				
3/27/61	4	12	31	The Blizzard *Danny Boy*	62	$10		RCA Victor 7950
7/17/61	15	11	32	What Would You Do?/	73			
10/2/61	16	6	33	Stand At Your Window		$10		RCA Victor 8019
12/11/61+	2²	21	34	Losing Your Love/	89			
12/11/61+	7	16	35	(How Can I Write On Paper) What I Feel In My Heart	92	$10		RCA Victor 8080
5/26/62	2⁹	21	36	Adios Amigo/	90			
5/19/62	20	3	37	A Letter To My Heart..		$10		RCA Victor 8127
9/1/62	2³	21	38	I'm Gonna Change Everything/	95			
9/8/62	18	3	39	Pride Goes Before A Fall		$10	■	RCA Victor 8193
2/9/63	3	23	40	Is This Me? *Missing Angel*	103	$10	■	RCA Victor 8289
7/13/63	3	18	41	Guilty/	91			
7/27/63	11	18	42	Little Ole You		$10		RCA Victor 8324
1/25/64	2²	26	43	Welcome To My World/	102			
2/1/64	43	2	44	Good Morning Self..		$10		RCA Victor 8383
3/28/64	7	21	45	Love Is No Excuse *Look Who's Talking (Pop #121)*	115	$10		RCA Victor 8461
				JIM REEVES & DOTTIE WEST				
7/11/64	❶⁷	26	46	I Guess I'm Crazy *Not Until The Next Time*	82	$10		RCA Victor 8508
11/28/64+	3	19	47	I Won't Forget You *Highway To Nowhere*	93	$10		
3/6/65	❶³	23	48	This Is It *There's That Smile Again*	88	$10		

REEVES, Jim — Cont'd

DEBUT	PEAK	WKS		A-side	B-side	Pop	$	Pic	Label & Number
7/24/65	●³	21	49	Is It Really Over?	Rosa Rio	79	$8	■	RCA Victor 8625
1/8/66	2³	17	50	Snow Flake	Take My Hand Precious Lord	66	$8		RCA Victor 8719
4/2/66	●⁴	21	51	Distant Drums	Old Tige	45	$8		RCA Victor 8789
8/13/66	●¹	19	52	Blue Side Of Lonesome	It Hurts So Much (To See You Go)	59	$8		RCA Victor 8902
1/21/67	●¹	16	53	I Won't Come In While He's There	Maureen	112	$8		RCA Victor 9057
7/1/67	16	14	54	The Storm	Trying To Forget		$8		RCA Victor 9238
11/4/67+	9	17	55	I Heard A Heart Break Last Night	Golden Memories And Silver Tears		$8		RCA Victor 9343
3/9/68	9	13	56	That's When I See The Blues (In Your Pretty Brown Eyes)	I've Lived A Lot In My Time		$8		RCA Victor 9455
9/21/68	7	15	57	When You Are Gone	How Can I Write On Paper (What I Feel In My Heart)		$8		RCA Victor 9614
4/12/69	6	14	58	When Two Worlds Collide	Could I Be Falling In Love		$7		RCA Victor 0135
12/6/69+	10	14	59	Nobody's Fool/					
		13	60	Why Do I Love You (Melody of Love) [S]			$7		RCA Victor 0286
				#2 Pop hit for Billy Vaughn in 1955					
8/15/70	4	15	61	Angels Don't Lie	You Kept Me Awake Last Night		$7		RCA Victor 9880
4/10/71	16	12	62	Gypsy Feet	He Will		$7		RCA Victor 9969
1/29/72	15	14	63	The Writing's On The Wall	You're Free To Go		$7		RCA Victor 0626
7/29/72	8	16	64	Missing You	The Tie That Binds		$7		RCA Victor 0744
				#29 Pop hit for Ray Peterson in 1961					
6/2/73	12	14	65	Am I That Easy To Forget	Rosa Rio		$7		RCA Victor 0963
				#25 Pop hit for Debbie Reynolds in 1960					
4/20/74	19	14	66	I'd Fight The World	What's In It For Me		$7		RCA Victor 0255
6/21/75	54	11	67	You Belong To Me	Maureen		$6		RCA Victor 10299
				#1 Pop hit for Jo Stafford in 1952					
11/8/75	71	6	68	You'll Never Know	There's That Smile Again		$6		RCA Victor 10418
				#1 Pop hit for Dick Haymes in 1943					
2/21/76	54	9	69	I Love You Because	Is This Me?		$6		RCA Victor 10557
				#3 Pop hit for Al Martino in 1963					
4/23/77	14	13	70	It's Nothin' To Me	I Won't Forget You		$5		RCA 10956
8/27/77	23	11	71	Little Ole Dime	A Letter To My Heart		$5		RCA 11060
2/4/78	29	11	72	You're The Only Good Thing (That's Happened To Me)	When You Are Gone		$5		RCA 11187
6/23/79	10	14	73	Don't Let Me Cross Over	I've Enjoyed As Much Of This As I Can Stand		$5		RCA 11564
11/3/79+	6	15	74	Oh, How I Miss You Tonight	The Talking Walls		$5		RCA 11737
				Deborah Allen (guest vocal, above 2)					
4/12/80	10	16	75	Take Me In Your Arms And Hold Me	Missing Angel		$5		RCA 11946
				JIM REEVES/DEBORAH ALLEN					
11/22/80+	35	11	76	There's Always Me	Somewhere Along The Line		$5		RCA 12118
				#56 Pop hit for Elvis Presley in 1967					
11/7/81+	5	17	77	Have You Ever Been Lonely (Have You Ever Been Blue)	Welcome To My World		$5		RCA 12346
				JIM REEVES AND PATSY CLINE					
6/5/82	54	8	78	I Fall To Pieces	So Wrong		$5		MCA 52052
				PATSY CLINE/JIM REEVES					
1/8/83	46	9	79	The Jim Reeves Medley	He'll Have To Go		$4		RCA 13410
				Four Walls/I Missed Me/He'll Have To Go/Oh, How I Miss You Tonight					
1/21/84	70	6	80	The Image Of Me	Won't Come In While He's There		$4		RCA 13693

REEVES, John Rex   '81
Born in Panola County, Texas. Nephew of **Jim Reeves**.

DEBUT	PEAK	WKS		A-side	B-side	Pop	$	Pic	Label & Number
2/21/81	93	2	1	What Would You Do	Jamaica Farewell		$6		Soc-A-Gee 109
8/1/81	90	2	2	You're The Reason	The Next One's On Me		$6		Soc-A-Gee 110

REEVES, Ronna   '92
Born on 9/21/66 in Big Springs, Texas. Female singer.

DEBUT	PEAK	WKS		A-side	B-side	Pop	$	Pic	Label & Number
3/7/92	49	11	1	The More I Learn (The Less I Understand About Love)	If I Were You		$3	▮	Mercury 866380
7/18/92	70	4	2	What If You're Wrong	Frontier Justice		$3	▮	Mercury 866914
11/7/92	71	2	3	We Can Hold Our Own	Honky Tonk Hearts		$3		Mercury 864614
6/26/93	73	2	4	Never Let Him See Me Cry/					
9/25/93	74	2	5	He's My Weakness			$3	▮	Mercury 862260

REGAN, Bob, & Lucille Starr — see CANADIAN SWEETHEARTS, The

REGINA REGINA   '97
Vocal duo of Regina Nicks (from Houston) and Regina Leigh (from North Carolina).

DEBUT	PEAK	WKS		A-side	B-side	Pop	$	Pic	Label & Number
1/18/97	53	8		More Than I Wanted To Know	She'll Let That Telephone Ring		$3	▮	Giant 17426

★366★   REID, Mike   '91
Born on 5/24/47 in Altoona, Pennsylvania. Singer/songwriter/pianist. Pro football player with the Cincinnati Bengals from 1970-75.

DEBUT	PEAK	WKS		A-side	B-side	Pop	$	Pic	Label & Number
3/5/88	2¹	21	1	Old Folks	S:5 Earthquake		$3	■	RCA 6896
				RONNIE MILSAP & MIKE REID					
11/24/90+	●²	20	2	Walk On Faith	Turning For Home		$3	▮	Columbia 73623
3/30/91	17	20	3	Till You Were Gone	Everything To Me		$3		Columbia 73736
7/13/91	14	20	4	As Simple As That	This Road		$3		Columbia 73888
11/9/91+	23	20	5	I'll Stop Loving You	Even A Strong Man		$3		Columbia 74102
4/18/92	54	7	6	I Got A Life	Your Love Stays With Me		$3		Columbia 74286
8/29/92	45	11	7	Keep On Walkin'	Working With The Right Tools		$3		Columbia 74443
11/21/92+	43	13	8	Call Home	Working With The Right Tools		$3		Columbia 74771

REMINGTON, Rita '82
Born Rita Unruh in McPherson, Kansas.

DEBUT	PEAK	WKS		A-side	Pop	$	Pic	Label & Number
9/8/73	99	3		1 I've Never Been This Far Before .... *The Wedding Cake*		$5		Plantation 103
				female version of "You've Never Been This Far Before" by Conway Twitty				
1/14/78	86	5		2 Don't Let The Flame Burn Out ....*Midnight Man*		$5		Plantation 167
				#68 Pop hit for Jackie DeShannon in 1977				
4/8/78	100	3		3 To Each His Own .... *Rhythm Of The Rain*		$5		Plantation 171
				#1 Pop hit for Eddy Howard in 1946				
10/24/81	80	4		4 Don't We Belong In Love ....*Easier Said Than Done*		$5		Plantation 202
				RITA REMINGTON And The Smokey Valley Symphony				
3/20/82	76	5		5 The Flame .... *Blue Eyes Don't Make An Angel*		$5		Plantation 207

REMINGTONS, The '92
Trio of Jimmy Griffin (**Black Tie**), Richard Mainegra and Rick Yancey (both of Cymarron). Yancey left in 1992, replaced by Denny Henson.

DEBUT	PEAK	WKS		A-side	Pop	$	Pic	Label & Number
10/12/91+	10	20		1 A Long Time Ago *Takin' The Easy Way Out*		$3	▮	BNA 62063
2/15/92	33	20		2 I Could Love You (With My Eyes Closed) .... *Take A Little Love*		$3		BNA 62201
6/6/92	18	20		3 Two-Timin' Me ....*That's Easy For Me To Say*		$3		BNA 62276
2/6/93	52	6		4 Nobody Loves You When You're Free ....*She's All I've Got Going Now*		$3		BNA 62431
7/10/93	69	1		5 Wall Around Her Heart..*Lucky Boy*		$3		BNA 62527

RENO, Don '66
Born on 2/21/27 in Spartanburg, South Carolina. Died on 10/16/84 (age 57). Singer/banjo player. Teamed with Red Smiley as **Reno & Smiley**. Father of Dale, Don Wayne and **Ronnie Reno** (Reno Brothers).

DEBUT	PEAK	WKS		A-side	Pop	$	Pic	Label & Number
1/8/66	46	3		Soldier's Prayer In Viet Nam ....*Five By Eight* [S]		$12		Monument 912
				DON RENO & BENNY MARTIN and The Tennessee Cut Ups				

RENO, Jack ★358★ '68
Born on 11/30/35 in Bloomfield, Iowa. Singer/songwriter/guitarist. Worked as a DJ on many stations since 1958.
1)Repeat After Me 2)Hitchin' A Ride 3)I Want One

DEBUT	PEAK	WKS		A-side	Pop	$	Pic	Label & Number
12/9/67+	10	17		1 Repeat After Me *You're Gonna Have To Come And Get It*		$8		JAB 9009
5/11/68	41	11		2 How Sweet It Is (To Be In Love With You)..*Juke Box*		$8		JAB 9015
11/16/68+	19	14		3 I Want One ....*Bigger Than Love*		$6		Dot 17169
5/10/69	34	11		4 I'm A Good Man (In A Bad Frame Of Mind)............*Darling, Say It Again*		$6		Dot 17233
9/20/69	22	9		5 We All Go Crazy ....*Albuquerque*		$6		Dot 17293
4/18/70	67	3		6 That's The Way I See It........................*I've Heard That Song Before*		$6		Dot 17340
10/9/71	12	15		7 Hitchin' A Ride ....*You Are My Destiny*		$6		Target 0137
				#5 Pop hit for Vanity Fare in 1970				
1/22/72	26	14		8 Heartaches By The Numbers ....*Airline Girl*		$6		Target 0141
5/27/72	38	10		9 Do You Want To Dance.....................................*I Get Too Lonely*		$6		Target 0150
				#5 Pop hit for Bobby Freeman in 1958				
8/25/73	67	8		10 Beautiful Sunday ....*Sometimes Woman*		$5		United Artists 299
				#15 Pop hit for Daniel Boone in 1972				
2/9/74	57	10		11 Let The Four Winds Blow ....*Shackles And Chains*		$5		United Artists 374
				#15 Pop hit for Fats Domino in 1961				
8/31/74	70	7		12 Jukebox ....*Goin' Through The Motions*		$5		United Artists 502

RENO, Ronnie '83
Born on 9/28/47 in Buffalo, South Carolina. Singer/guitarist. Son of **Don Reno**. Member of **Merle Haggard**'s Strangers from 1971-78.

DEBUT	PEAK	WKS		A-side	Pop	$	Pic	Label & Number
1/22/83	86	3		1 Homemade Love ....*Hello Jesus*		$5		EMH 0010
9/24/83	76	4		2 The Letter ....*Serious Love*		$5		EMH 0024
				#1 Pop hit for The Box Tops in 1967				

RENO AND SMILEY '61
Duo of **Don Reno** and Red Smiley. Reno was born on 2/21/26 in Spartanburg, South Carolina. Died on 10/16/84. Smiley was born Arthur Lee Smiley on 5/17/25 in Asheville, North Carolina. Died on 1/2/72. Duo also recorded as **Chick And His Hot Rods**.

DEBUT	PEAK	WKS		A-side	Pop	$	Pic	Label & Number
5/29/61	14	10		1 Don't Let Your Sweet Love Die ....*Born To Lose*		$15		King 5469
8/28/61	23	5		2 Love Oh Love, Oh Please Come Home ....*Double Eagle*		$15		King 5520
9/18/61	27	2		3 Jimmy Caught The Dickens (Pushing Ernest In The Tub)...*Just Doing Rock And Roll* [N]		$10		King 5537
				CHICK AND HIS HOT RODS Backed Up With RENO AND SMILEY				

RENO BROTHERS '88
Bluegrass trio from Roanoke, Virginia: brothers Dale (b: 2/6/61), Don Wayne (b: 2/8/63) and **Ronnie Reno**. Sons of **Don Reno**.

DEBUT	PEAK	WKS		A-side	Pop	$	Pic	Label & Number
7/2/88	77	2		1 Yonder Comes A Freight Train ....*Lay Your Heartache Down*		$3		Step One 387
4/1/89	84	2		2 Love Will Never Be The Same ....*Southern Bound*		$3		Step One 398

RESTLESS HEART ★130★ '88
Group of former Nashville session musicians: **Larry Stewart** (vocals, guitar, keyboards), Dave Innis (guitar, keyboards), Greg Jennings (guitar), Paul Gregg (bass) and John Dittrich (drums). Stewart went solo in early 1992. Innis left in early 1993. The remaining three continued with two backing musicians.

1)Wheels 2)Bluest Eyes In Texas 3)Why Does It Have To Be 4)A Tender Lie 5)That Rock Won't Roll

DEBUT	PEAK	WKS		A-side	Pop	$	Pic	Label & Number
1/26/85	23	16		1 Let The Heartache Ride ....S:23 / A:23 *Few And Far Between*		$3		RCA 13969
6/1/85	10	18		2 I Want Everyone To Cry S:9 / A:10 *She's Coming Home*		$3	■	RCA 14086
10/26/85+	7	19		3 (Back To The) Heartbreak Kid S:7 / A:8 *She Danced Her Way (Into My Heart)*		$3	■	RCA 14190
3/15/86	10	20		4 Til I Loved You A:8 / S:11 *Shakin' The Night Away*		$3		RCA 14292
8/9/86	❶¹	23		5 That Rock Won't Roll S:❶¹ / A:❶¹ *You Can't Out Run The Night*		$3		RCA 14376

DEBUT	PEAK	WKS	Gold	A-side (Chart Hit) ... B-side	Pop	$	Pic	Label & Number
				RESTLESS HEART — Cont'd				
12/20/86+	❶¹	25		6 **I'll Still Be Loving You** A:❶¹ / S:7 *Victim Of The Game*	33	$3		RCA 5065
5/30/87	❶¹	25		7 **Why Does It Have To Be** (Wrong Or Right) S:5 *Hummingbird*		$3		RCA 5132
10/31/87+	❶¹	23		8 **Wheels** S:5 *New York (Hold Her Tight)*		$3	■	RCA 5280
5/21/88	❶¹	21		9 **Bluest Eyes In Texas** S:2 *Eldorado*		$3		RCA 8386
9/24/88	❶¹	23		10 **A Tender Lie** S:❶¹ *This Time*		$3		RCA 8714
2/25/89	3	18		11 **Big Dreams In A Small Town** *The Ride Of Your Life*		$3		RCA 8816
7/29/89	4	20		12 **Say What's In Your Heart** *Jenny Come Back*		$3		RCA 9034
12/16/89+	4	26		13 **Fast Movin' Train** *The Truth Hurts*		$3		RCA 9115
4/21/90	5	21		14 **Dancy's Dream** *Lady Luck*		$3		RCA 2503
9/1/90	21	16		15 **When Somebody Loves You** ... *A Little More Coal On The Fire*		$3	∎	RCA 2663
12/22/90+	16	20		16 **Long Lost Friend** *I've Never Been So Sure*		$3		RCA 2709
10/19/91+	3	20		17 **You Can Depend On Me** *Til I Loved You*		$3		RCA 62129
2/29/92	40	15		18 **Familiar Pain** *The Bluest Eyes In Texas*		$3		RCA 62054
9/12/92	9	20		19 **When She Cries** *(album snippets)*	11	$3	∎	RCA 62412
1/23/93	13	20		20 **Mending Fences** *We're Gonna Be OK*		$3		RCA 62419
5/22/93	11	20		21 **We Got The Love** ... *Meet Me On The Other Side*		$3		RCA 62510
11/6/93	72	2		22 **Big Iron Horses** ... *Born In A High Wind*		$3		RCA 62656
4/30/94	52	9		23 **Baby Needs New Shoes** ... *I'd Cross The Line*		$3	∎	RCA 62827
				REX, Tim, and Oklahoma **'81**				
11/8/80	87	3		1 **Arizona Highway**		$5		Dee Jay 103
12/13/80+	46	12		2 **Gettin' Over You** *Red Headed Lady*		$5		Dee Jay 107
4/11/81	43	10		3 **Spread My Wings** ... *Take Me Back To Oklahoma*		$5		Dee Jay 111
				REY, Ernest **'79** Son of Loretta Lynn.				
3/17/79	97	1		**Mama's Sugar** ... *Don't Feel Like The Lone Ranger*		$4		MCA 40991
				REYNOLDS, Allen **'78** Born on 8/18/38 in North Little Rock, Arkansas; raised in Memphis. Singer/songwriter/prolific producer.				
5/20/78	95	5		**Wrong Road Again** ... *Ready For The Times To Get Better*		$7		Triple I 496
				REYNOLDS, Burt **'80** Born on 2/11/36 in Waycross, Georgia. Became box-office superstar in the mid-1970s.				
10/25/80	51	7		**Let's Do Something Cheap And Superficial** ... *Pickin' Lone Star Style* from the movie *Smokey & The Bandit II* starring Reynolds	88	$4	■	MCA 51004
				RHOADS, Randy **'90**				
1/13/90	89	1		**Honey Do Weekend** ...		$6		Blue Ridge 001
				RICE, Bill **'71** Singer/songwriter/producer from Gallo, Arkansas.				
3/20/71	33	10		1 **Travelin' Minstrel Man** *Special*		$7		Capitol 3049
9/11/71	51	9		2 **Honky-Tonk Stardust Cowboy** ... *T.G.I.F. (Thank Goodness It's Forever)*		$7		Capitol 3156
4/8/72	74	2		3 **A Girl Like Her Is Hard To Find** *Here's To You, Darlin'*		$6		Epic 10833
7/1/72	63	5		4 **Something To Call Mine**		$6		Epic 10877
11/19/77	97	3		5 **All The Love We Threw Away** ... *We Can't Make It Anymore* **LOIS JOHNSON & BILL RICE**		$5		Polydor 14435
3/11/78	100	2		6 **Beggars And Choosers** ... *That's The Way It Is (With You And Me)*		$5		Polydor 14453
	★205★			**RICE, Bobby G.** **'73** Born Robert Gene Rice on 7/11/44 in Boscobel, Wisconsin. Singer/songwriter/guitarist. 1)*You Lay So Easy On My Mind* 2)*You Give Me You* 3)*Write Me A Letter* 4)*Freda Comes, Freda Goes* 5)*The Whole World's Making Love Again Tonight*				
4/25/70	32	8		1 **Sugar Shack** ... *Sweet Lil Ol' You* #1 Pop hit for Jimmy Gilmer & The Fireballs in 1963		$8		Royal American 6
8/8/70	35	11		2 **Hey Baby** ... *Hey, Hey, Santa Fe* #1 Pop hit for Bruce Channel in 1962		$8		Royal American 18
1/9/71	46	9		3 **Lover Please** ... *You're So Easy To Love* #7 Pop hit for Clyde McPhatter in 1962		$8		Royal American 27
5/22/71	20	15		4 **Mountain Of Love** ... *Five O'Clock World* #9 Pop hit for **Johnny Rivers** in 1964		$8		Royal American 32
1/1/72	33	11		5 **Suspicion** ... *The Birds And The Bees* #3 Pop hit for Terry Stafford in 1964		$8		Royal American 48
12/23/72+	3	16		6 **You Lay So Easy On My Mind** *There Ain't No Way Babe* also see #28 below		$7		Metromedia 902
5/5/73	8	15		7 **You Give Me You** *Bring Your Love To Me Softly*		$7		Metromedia 0107
9/22/73	13	14		8 **The Whole World's Making Love Again Tonight** ... *Baby, Lovin' You*		$7		Metromedia 0075
9/28/74	30	14		9 **Make It Feel Like Love Again** ... *Darlin' Forever*		$6		GRT 009
1/11/75	9	14		10 **Write Me A Letter** *Sweet Satisfying Feeling*		$6		GRT 014
5/3/75	10	14		11 **Freda Comes, Freda Goes** *Love Me Tonight*		$6		GRT 021
8/30/75	64	11		12 **I May Never Be Your Lover** (But I'll Always Be Your Friend) ... *It Was So Good While It Lasted*		$6		GRT 028
1/3/76	35	11		13 **Pick Me Up On Your Way Down** ... *Right Or Wrong*		$6		GRT 036
7/24/76	53	9		14 **You Are My Special Angel** ... *I Want To Feel It When You Feel It* same tune as "My Special Angel" by **Bobby Helms**		$6		GRT 061
11/13/76	54	9		15 **Woman Stealer** *Burning Bridges*		$6		GRT 084
7/9/77	66	7		16 **Just One Kiss Magdelena** ... *The Love She Offered You*		$6		GRT 120
7/22/78	57	6		17 **Whisper It To Me** ... *Sweet Cherry Lips*		$5		Republic 023

RICE, Bobby G. — Cont'd

DEBUT	PEAK	WKS	A-side (Chart Hit) ... B-side	Pop	$	Label & Number
11/11/78	30	10	18 The Softest Touch In Town .... *Passion*		$5	Republic 031
6/9/79	49	8	19 Oh Baby Mine (I Get So Lonely) .... *Rainbows Are Back In Style*		$5	Republic 041
			#2 Pop hit for The Four Knights in 1954			
12/1/79	67	8	20 You Make It So Easy .... *You Lay So Easy On My Mind*		$5	Sunset 102
5/3/80	53	9	21 The Man Who Takes You Home .... *Sweet Molly Brown*		$5	Sunbird 108
2/7/81	86	2	22 Livin' Together (Lovin' Apart) .... *It Was So Good While It Lasted*		$5	Sunbird 7558
10/10/81	63	5	23 Pardon My French .... *Some Lovin' Time With You*		$5	Charta 166
6/8/85	95	2	24 New Tradition .... *Those Words I Never Heard*		$5	Door Knob 230
3/8/86	70	4	25 Red Neck And Over Thirty .... *State Of The Union*		$5	Door Knob 243

WAYNE KEMP & BOBBY G. RICE

DEBUT	PEAK	WKS	A-side (Chart Hit) ... B-side	Pop	$	Label & Number
9/13/86	70	5	26 You've Taken Over My Heart .... *I'm Lookin' For Someone Lookin' For Love*		$5	Door Knob 251
6/27/87	85	2	27 Rachel's Room		$5	Door Knob 274
10/3/87	79	3	28 You Lay So Easy On My Mind .... [R]		$5	Door Knob 285
			new version of #6 above			
3/5/88	70	5	29 A Night Of Love Forgotten		$5	Door Knob 295
9/17/88	76	4	30 Clean Livin' Folk		$5	Door Knob 307

BOBBY G. RICE and PERRY LaPOINTE

RICH, Charlie ★73★   '73

Born on 12/14/32 in Colt, Arkansas. Died of an acute blood clot on 7/25/95 (age 62). Singer/songwriter/pianist. Known as "The Silver Fox." CMA Awards: 1973 Male Vocalist of the Year; 1974 Entertainer of the Year.

1)The Most Beautiful Girl 2)A Very Special Love Song 3)Behind Closed Doors 4)There Won't Be Anymore
5)Rollin' With The Flow

DEBUT	PEAK	WKS	A-side (Chart Hit) ... B-side	Pop	$	Label & Number
3/9/68	44	8	1 Set Me Free .... *I'll Just Go Away*		$7	Epic 10287
8/24/68	45	8	2 Raggedy Ann .... *Nothing In The World (To Do With Me)*		$7	Epic 10358
8/9/69	41	11	3 Life's Little Ups And Downs .... *It Takes Time*		$7	Epic 10492
2/28/70	67	5	4 Who Will The Next Fool Be .... *Stay*		$7	Sun 1110
			recorded in January 1959			
3/28/70	47	6	5 July 12, 1939 .... *I'm Flying To Nashville Tonight*	85	$7	Epic 10585
10/24/70	37	12	6 Nice 'N' Easy .... *I Can't Even Drink It Away*		$7	Epic 10662
			new version of his #131 Pop hit from 1964; #60 Pop hit for Frank Sinatra in 1964			
8/14/71	72	2	7 A Woman Left Lonely .... *Have A Heart*		$7	Epic 10745
11/27/71+	35	13	8 A Part Of Your Life .... *How Long Have You Had Him On Your Mind*		$7	Epic 10809
8/26/72	6	17	9 I Take It On Home .... *Peace On You*		$6	Epic 10867
2/10/73	❶²	20	● 10 Behind Closed Doors .... *A Sunday Kind Of Woman*	15	$5	Epic 10950
			CMA Award: Single of the Year			
7/14/73	29	11	11 Tomorrow Night .... *The Ways Of A Woman In Love*		$6	RCA Victor 0983
9/22/73	❶³	18	● 12 The Most Beautiful Girl .... *I Feel Like Going Home*	❶²	$5	Epic 11040
12/22/73+	❶²	17	13 There Won't Be Anymore .... *It's All Over Now*	18	$5	RCA Victor 0195
2/23/74	❶³	14	14 A Very Special Love Song .... *I Can't Even Drink It Away*	11	$5	Epic 11091
5/4/74	❶¹	13	15 I Don't See Me In Your Eyes Anymore .... *No Room To Dance*	47	$5	RCA Victor 0260
6/22/74	23	12	16 A Field Of Yellow Daisies .... *Party Girl*		$6	Mercury 73498
8/10/74	❶¹	15	17 I Love My Friend .... *Why, Oh Why*	24	$5	Epic 20006
9/28/74	❶¹	15	18 She Called Me Baby .... *Ten Dollars And A Clean White Shirt*	47	$5	RCA Victor 10062
12/28/74+	71	5	19 Something Just Came Over Me .... *The Best Years*		$6	Mercury 73646
2/1/75	3	12	20 My Elusive Dreams .... *Whatever Happened*	49	$5	Epic 50064
4/12/75	23	12	21 It's All Over Now .... *Big Jack*		$5	RCA Victor 10256
5/24/75	3	17	22 Every Time You Touch Me (I Get High) .... *Pass On By*	19	$5	Epic 50103
9/20/75	4	14	23 All Over Me .... *You And I*		$5	Epic 50142
12/20/75+	56	7	24 Now Everybody Knows .... *I've Got You Under My Skin*		$5	RCA Victor 10458
12/27/75+	10	13	25 Since I Fell For You .... *She*	71	$5	Epic 50182
			#4 Pop hit for Lenny Welch in 1963			
4/24/76	22	10	26 America, The Beautiful (1976) .... *Down By The Riverside*		$5	Epic 50222
9/4/76	27	9	27 Road Song .... *The Grass Is Always Greener*		$5	Epic 50268
1/8/77	24	12	28 My Mountain Dew .... *Nice 'N' Easy*		$5	RCA 10859
			all of above RCA and Mercury hits were recorded from 1963-66			
2/5/77	12	13	29 Easy Look .... *My Lady*		$5	Epic 50328
5/28/77	❶²	19	30 Rollin' With The Flow .... *To Sing A Love Song*	101	$5	Epic 50392
4/8/78	8	14	31 Puttin' In Overtime At Home .... *Ghost Of Another Man*		$4	United Artists 1193
7/1/78	10	13	32 Beautiful Woman .... *Somebody Wrote That Song For Me*		$4	Epic 50562
7/22/78	46	8	33 I Still Believe In Love .... *Wishful Thinking*		$4	United Artists 1223
10/7/78	❶¹	14	34 On My Knees .... *Mellow Melody*		$4	Epic 50616

CHARLIE RICH (with Janie Fricke)

DEBUT	PEAK	WKS	A-side (Chart Hit) ... B-side	Pop	$	Label & Number
1/6/79	3	14	35 I'll Wake You Up When I Get Home .... *Salty Dog Blues*		$4	Elektra 45553
			from the movie *Every Which Way But Loose* starring **Clint Eastwood**			
1/6/79	45	8	36 The Fool Strikes Again .... *I Loved You All The Way*		$4	United Artists 1269
3/10/79	26	11	37 I Lost My Head .... *She Knows Just How To Touch Me*		$4	United Artists 1280
5/12/79	20	13	38 Spanish Eyes .... *I Do My Swingin' At Home*		$4	Epic 50701
			#15 Pop hit for Al Martino in 1966			
8/18/79	84	4	39 Life Goes On .... *Standing Tall*		$4	United Artists 1307
11/24/79+	22	13	40 You're Gonna Love Yourself In The Morning .... *The Top Of The Stairs*		$4	United Artists 1325

DEBUT	PEAK	WKS	Gold	A-side (Chart Hit)..B-side	Pop	$	Pic	Label & Number
				RICH, Charlie — Cont'd				
3/8/80	74	5		41 I'd Build A Bridge.................................... *All You Ever Have To Do Is Touch Me*		$4		United Artists 1340
5/3/80	61	7		42 Even A Fool Would Let Go .... *Pretty People*		$4		Epic 50869
10/11/80	12	14		43 A Man Just Don't Know What A Woman Goes Through .... *Marie*		$4		Elektra 47047
2/14/81	26	11		44 Are We Dreamin' The Same Dream .... *Angelina*		$4		Elektra 47104
5/23/81	47	7		45 You Made It Beautiful .... *How Good It Used To Be*		$4		Epic 02058
				from the movie *Take This Job And Shove It* starring Art Carney				
				RICH, Debbie '89				
				Born Debra Sue Rathjen in Levenworth, Washington; raised in Napa Valley, California.				
12/3/88	87	2		1 I Ain't Gonna Take This Layin' Down		$5		Door Knob 311
2/25/89	71	4		2 Don't Be Surprised If You Get It		$5		Door Knob 318
4/22/89	74	4		3 I've Had Enough Of You		$5		Door Knob 321
9/2/89	68	5		4 Do It Again (I Think I Saw Diamonds)		$5		Door Knob 327
				RICH, Don — see ALAN, Buddy				
				RICHARDS, Earl '73				
				Born Henry Earl Sinks in Amarillo, Texas. Owned Ace of Hearts record label.				
9/6/69	39	10		1 The House Of Blue Lights .... *Hard Times A Comin'*		$7		United Artists 50561
				#9 Pop hit for Chuck Miller in 1955				
1/31/70	73	2		2 Corrine, Corrina .... *Climbing A Mountain*		$7		United Artists 50619
				#9 Pop hit for Ray Peterson in 1961				
10/10/70	57	4		3 Sunshine .... *San Francisco's Mabel Joy*		$7		United Artists 50704
1/13/73	23	12		4 Margie, Who's Watching The Baby .... *My Land*		$6		Ace of Hearts 0461
				#115 Pop hit for R.B. Greaves in 1972				
4/28/73	66	6		5 Things Are Kinda Slow At The House .... *Do My Playing At Home*		$6		Ace of Hearts 0465
7/21/73	58	11		6 The Sun Is Shining (On Everybody But Me) .... *Mother Nature's Daughter*		$6		Ace of Hearts 0470
3/2/74	83	7		7 Walkin' In Teardrops/				
12/22/73+	85	5		8 How Can I Tell Her		$6		Ace of Hearts 0477
				#22 Pop hit for Lobo in 1973				
10/18/75	91	5		9 My Babe .... *Mother Nature's Daughter*		$6		Ace of Hearts 7502
				#1 R&B hit for Little Walter in 1955				
				RICHARDS, Sue '76				
				Born Maggie Sue Wimberly in Muscle Shoals, Alabama.				
				1)Sweet Sensuous Feelings 2)Tower Of Strength 3)I Just Had You On My Mind				
3/27/71	56	8		1 Feel Free To Go .... *No Special Occasion*		$7		Epic 10709
1/12/74	48	13		2 I Just Had You On My Mind .... *Wake Up Morning*		$6		Dot 17481
7/20/74	93	5		3 Ease Me To The Ground .... *Make Me Believe It*		$6		Dot 17508
5/3/75	99	2		4 Homemade Love .... *The Painter's Brush*		$5		ABC/Dot 17547
9/6/75	32	12		5 Tower Of Strength .... *Let Me Be Your Baby Again*		$5		ABC/Dot 17572
				#5 Pop hit for Gene McDaniels in 1961				
1/17/76	25	11		6 Sweet Sensuous Feelings .... *He Plays For Me*		$5		ABC/Dot 17600
5/1/76	50	10		7 Please Tell Him That I Said Hello .... *Love Is A Rose*		$5		ABC/Dot 17622
				#84 Pop hit for Debbie Campbell in 1975				
8/21/76	70	6		8 I'll Never See Him Again .... *I've Got A Lot On My Mind*		$5		ABC/Dot 17645
11/26/77	94	3		9 Someone Loves Him .... *Livin' In A House Full Of Love*		$5		Epic 50465
7/15/78	94	4		10 Hey, What Do You Say (We Fall In Love) .... *I'll Be Wearing Blue*		$5		Epic 50546
3/10/79	85	3		11 Finders Keepers Losers Weepers		$6		MMI 1028
				STAN HITCHCOCK with Sue Richards				
				RICHEY, Kim '95				
				Born on 12/1/57 in Zanesville, Ohio. Singer/songwriter.				
6/24/95	47	12		1 Just My Luck .... *Just Like The Moon*		$3	▌	Mercury 856832
10/7/95	59	12		2 Those Words We Said .... *Let The Sun Fall Down*		$3	▌	Mercury 852300
4/20/96	66	3		3 From Where I Stand				album cut
				from the album *Kim Richey* on Mercury 526812				
5/10/97	72	2		4 I Know .... *I'm Alright*		$3	▌	Mercury 574184
				RICHIE, Lionel '87				
				Born on 6/20/49 in Tuskegee, Alabama. Black singer/songwriter/pianist. Former lead singer of the Commodores. Charted 17 pop hits from 1981-96.				
7/21/84	24	18		1 Stuck On You .... *Round And Round*	3	$4	■	Motown 1746
12/6/86+	10	15		2 Deep River Woman S:❶¹ / A:10 *Ballerina Girl (Pop #7)*	71	$3	■	Motown 1873
				LIONEL RICHIE with Alabama				
				RICHMOND, Rashell — see WHEELER, Billy Edd				
				RICKS, Steve '86				
				Born in Little Rock, Arkansas.				
6/14/86	81	4		Private Clown		$6		Southwind 8205
	★356★			**RICOCHET** '96				
				Group from Texas: Heath Wright (vocals, guitar), Teddy Carr (guitar), Junior Bryant (fiddle), Eddie Kilgallon (keyboards), Greg Cook (bass) and Jeff Bryant (drums).				
12/9/95+	5	21		1 What Do I Know S:14 *A Little Bit Of Love (Is A Dangerous Thing)*		$3	▌	Columbia 78088
4/27/96	❶²	20		2 Daddy's Money S:7 *I Wasn't Ready For You*		$3	▌	Columbia 78097
7/20/96	58	1		3 The Star Spangled Banner .... *(no B-side)*		$10		Columbia 8246 (CD)
				only available as a promo CD single				
8/17/96	9	20		4 Love Is Stronger Than Pride *I Wasn't Ready For You*		$3	▌	Columbia 78098
12/14/96	43	5		5 Let It Snow Let It Snow Let It Snow .... *(no B-side)* [X]		$10		Columbia 1296 (CD)
				#1 Pop hit for Vaughn Monroe in 1946; only available as a promo CD single				

RICOCHET — Cont'd

1/18/97	20	16		6 Ease My Troubled Mind ....Rowdy		$3	▌	Columbia 78526
5/3/97	18	20		7 He Left A Lot To Be Desired................................S:15 You Still Got It		$3	▌	Columbia 78564
9/13/97	39	13		8 Blink Of An Eye..........................Don't Forget To Feed The Jukebox (While I'm Gone)		$3		Columbia 78688
12/13/97	44	5		9 Let It Snow Let It Snow Let It Snow ....(no B-side) [X-R]		$10		Columbia 1296 (CD)
				only available as a promo CD single				

RIDDLE, Allan   '60

11/7/60	16	12		The Moon Is Crying		$20		Plaid 1001

RIDE THE RIVER   '87

Group led by singer/guitarist Danny Stockard.

2/21/87	63	5		1 You Left Her Lovin' You..		$5		Advantage 165
6/13/87	55	7		2 The First Cut Is The Deepest		$5		Advantage 169
				#21 Pop hit for Rod Stewart in 1977				
10/31/87	57	7		3 It's Such A Heartache		$5		Advantage 182
2/6/88	51	9		4 After Last Night's Storm		$5		Advantage 189

RILEY, Dan   '80

12/22/79+	78	5		Lily ....If My Tears Could Fill A Lake I'd Throw You In		$5		Armada 103

★215★   **RILEY, Jeannie C.**   '68

Born Jeanne Carolyn Stephenson on 10/19/45 in Anson, Texas. Singer/songwriter/guitarist.
1)Harper Valley P.T.A. 2)Oh, Singer 3)There Never Was A Time 4)The Girl Most Likely
5)Good Enough To Be Your Wife

8/24/68	❶³	14	●	1 Harper Valley P.T.A. Yesterday All Day Long Today	❶¹	$6		Plantation 3
				CMA Award: Single of the Year				
12/7/68+	6	15		2 The Girl Most Likely My Scrapbook	55	$6		Plantation 7
1/25/69	35	9		3 The Price I Pay To Stay ....How Can Anything So Right Be So Wrong		$6		Capitol 2378
3/29/69	5	13		4 There Never Was A Time Back To School	77	$6		Plantation 16
6/28/69	32	9		5 The Rib I'm The Woman	111	$6		Plantation 22
10/4/69	33	11		6 The Back Side Of Dallas/		$6		
10/25/69	34	8		7 Things Go Better With Love	111	$6		Plantation 29
1/31/70	7	12		8 Country Girl We Were Raised On Love	106	$6		Plantation 44
6/27/70	21	11		9 Duty Not Desire ....Holdin' On		$6		Plantation 59
12/12/70	60	4		10 My Man/		$6		
12/12/70	62	4		11 The Generation Gap		$6		Plantation 65
4/3/71	4	15		12 Oh, Singer I'll Take What's Left Of You	74	$6		Plantation 72
7/3/71	7	15		13 Good Enough To Be Your Wife Light Your Light (And Let It Shine)	97	$6		Plantation 75
10/23/71	15	13		14 Roses And Thorns ....Send Me No Tears		$6		Plantation 79
11/20/71	47	8		15 Houston Blues ....How Hard I'm Trying		$5		MGM 14310
1/15/72	12	12		16 Give Myself A Party ....Why You Been Gone So Long		$5		MGM 14341
5/20/72	30	11		17 Good Morning Country Rain ....This Is For You		$5		MGM 14382
10/28/72	57	6		18 One Night ....Without You		$5		MGM 14427
				#11 R&B hit for Smiley Lewis in 1956				
3/10/73	44	7		19 When Love Has Gone Away ....Thou Shall Not Kill		$5		MGM 14495
7/14/73	51	7		20 Hush ....Not Looking Back		$5		MGM 14554
				#4 Pop hit for Deep Purple in 1968				
11/10/73	57	9		21 Another Football Year ....Mother America		$5		MGM 14666
9/28/74	89	6		22 Plain Vanilla ....Country Child		$5		Mercury 73616
				JEANNIE C. RILEY and The Red River Symphony				
7/17/76	94	4		23 The Best I've Ever Had ....Thank You For Forgiving		$5		Warner 8226

RILEY, Larry   '81

1/17/81	90	2		1 Cheater's Last Chance.....................................How Could I Ever Stop Loving You		$7		F&L 507
5/30/81	93	2		2 Code-A-Phone		$7		F&L 509

★361★   **RIMES, LeAnn**   '96

Born Margaret LeAnn Rimes on 8/28/82 in Jackson, Mississippi; raised in Garland, Texas. Female singer. Won the 1996 Best New Artist
Grammy Award. CMA Award: 1997 Horizon Award.
1)One Way Ticket 2)Unchained Melody 3)On The Side Of Angels

5/25/96	10	20	●	1 Blue/ S:❶²⁰	26			
				song originally written for, but not recorded by, **Patsy Cline**				
3/22/97	5	20		2 The Light In Your Eyes		$3	▌	Curb 76959
7/27/96	43	10		3 Hurt Me				album cut
9/28/96	❶²	20		4 One Way Ticket (Because I Can)				album cut
				above 2 from the album Blue on Curb 77821				
12/21/96+	3	20		5 Unchained Melody/				
				#4 Pop hit for The Righteous Brothers in 1965				
12/28/96	51	3		6 Put A Little Holiday In Your Heart ....[X]		$8		Curb 1308 (CD)
				above 2 available only as a bonus CD single with the purchase of her album Blue at Target stores during the 1996 holiday season				
6/14/97	43	20	▲³	7 How Do I Live..S:❶³² (remix)	2³	$3	▌	Curb 73022
				from the movie Con Air starring Nicolas Cage				
8/23/97	48	7	●	8 You Light Up My Life................................S:2 I Believe	34	$3	▌	Curb 73027
10/11/97+	4	21		9 On The Side Of Angels				album cut
				from the album You Light Up My Life on Curb 77885				
12/27/97	71	2		10 Put A Little Holiday In Your Heart ....Unchained Melody [X-R]		$8		Curb 1308 (CD)

RISHARD, Rod   '83

8/20/83	77	5		1 You'd Better Believe It.............................. *You're The Closest I've Come*		$5		Soundwaves 4715
11/19/83	74	5		2 How Do You Tell Someone You Love .... *Friday Night Love Affair*		$5		Soundwaves 4717
3/24/84	89	3		3 The More I Go Blind..*Next Exit Out Of Love*		$5		Soundwaves 4724
7/28/84	84	3		4 Midnight Angel Of Mercy................................ *You're The Closest I've Come*		$5		Soundwaves 4734

RITTER, Tex ★140★   '45

Born Maurice Woodward Ritter on 1/12/05 in Murvaul, Texas. Died of a heart attack on 1/2/74 (age 68). Singer/guitarist/actor. Acted in several western movies from 1936-45. Co-host of *Town Hall Party* radio and TV series from 1953-60. Joined the *Grand Ole Opry* in 1965. Elected to the Country Music Hall of Fame in 1964. Father of actor John Ritter.

1)You Two-Timed Me One Time Too Often 2)I'm Wastin' My Tears On You 3)You Will Have To Pay
4)Jealous Heart 5)There's A New Moon Over My Shoulder

TEX RITTER and His Texans:

11/11/44	❶[6]	20		1 I'm Wastin' My Tears On You/	11			
11/11/44+	2[1]	22		2 There's A New Moon Over My Shoulder	21	$20		Capitol 174
12/16/44+	2[2]	23		3 Jealous Heart *We Live In Two Different Worlds*		$20		Capitol 179
8/4/45	❶[11]	20		4 You Two Timed Me One Time Too Often *Green Grow The Lilacs*		$20		Capitol 206

TEX RITTER:

12/8/45+	❶[3]	7		5 You Will Have To Pay/				
12/29/45	2[1]	3		6 Christmas Carols By The Old Corral [X]		$20		Capitol 223
5/18/46	5	6		7 Long Time Gone *I'm Gonna Leave You Like I Found You*		$20		Capitol 253
10/19/46	3	10		8 When You Leave Don't Slam The Door/				
12/7/46	3	2		9 Have I Told You Lately That I Love You		$20		Capitol 296
3/13/48	9	1		10 Rye Whiskey *Boll Weevil*		$20		Capitol Amer. 40084
6/12/48	10	7		11 Deck Of Cards S:10 / J:13 *Rounded Up In Glory* [S]		$20		Capitol Amer. 40114
6/12/48	15	1		12 Pecos Bill..J:15 *Egg-A-Bread*		$20		Capitol Amer. 40106

TEX RITTER With Andy Parker And THE PLAINSMEN
from the movie *Melody Time* starring Roy Rogers

| 7/10/48 | 5 | 7 | | 13 Rock And Rye   S:5 / J:8 *My Heart's As Cold As An Empty Jug* [N] | | $25 | | Capitol 15119 |
| 11/18/50 | 6 | 3 | | 14 Daddy's Last Letter   A:6 / S:8 *Onward Christian Soldiers* [S] | | $30 | | Capitol F1267 |

an actual letter from Private First Class John H. McCormick, a soldier killed in the Korean War

| 6/19/61 | 5 | 21 | | 15 I Dreamed Of A Hill-Billy Heaven   *The Wind And The Tree* [S] | 20 | $10 | | Capitol 4567 |
| 3/5/66 | 50 | 1 | | 16 The Men In My Little Girl's Life .... *Custody* [S] | | $7 | | Capitol 5574 |

#6 Pop hit for Mike Douglas in 1966

| 3/25/67 | 13 | 15 | | 17 Just Beyond The Moon .... *Greedy Old Dog* | | $7 | | Capitol 5839 |
| 9/30/67 | 59 | 3 | | 18 A Working Man's Prayer.................. *William Barrett Travis: A Message From The Alamo* | | $7 | | Capitol 5966 |

#79 Pop hit for Arthur Prysock in 1968

8/17/68	69	4		19 Texas .... *Stranger On Boot Hill*		$7		Capitol 2232
2/8/69	53	6		20 A Funny Thing Happened (On The Way To Miami) .... *The Governor And The Kid*		$7		Capitol 2388
7/26/69	39	10		21 Growin' Up .... *A Letter To My Sons*		$7		Capitol 2541
6/6/70	57	8		22 Green Green Valley .... *God Bless America Again*		$7		Capitol 2815
9/18/71	67	3		23 Fall Away .... *Looking Back*		$7		Capitol 3154
11/18/72	67	5		24 Comin' After Jinny .... *You Will Have To Pay For Your Yesterday*		$6		Capitol 3457
1/26/74	35	8		25 The Americans (A Canadian's Opinion) .... *He Who Is Without Sin* [S]	90	$5		Capitol 3814

RIVER ROAD   '97

Group from Louisiana: Steve Grisaffe (vocals, bass), Tony Ardoin (guitar), Charles Ventre (keyboards), Richard Comeaux (steel guitar) and Mike Burch (drums).

5/10/97	48	14		1 I Broke It, I'll Fix It .... *A Day In The Life*		$3		Capitol 19580
8/23/97	37	17		2 Nickajack .... S:23 *Tears To The Tide*		$3	▌	Capitol 19647
12/13/97+	51	10		3 Somebody Will .... *As If You Didn't Know*		$3		Capitol 19852

RIVERS, Eddie   '89

| 4/30/77 | 98 | 2 | | 1 Open Up Your Door .... *He's Still A Father In His Daughter's Eyes* | | $6 | | Charta 102 |
| 6/10/89 | 93 | 1 | | 2 You Won The Battle .... *There's No Memories Of Me (Ever Lovin' You)* | | $5 | | Charta 218 |

RIVERS, Jack   '48

Session guitarist for Gene Autry. Died on 2/11/89.

| 9/18/48 | 12 | 2 | | Dear Oakie .... J:12 *A Million Memories* | | $20 | | Capitol 15169 |

RIVERS, Johnny   '74

Born John Ramistella on 11/7/42 in New York City; raised in Baton Rouge. Singer/songwriter/guitarist. Charted 29 pop hits from 1964-78.

| 6/29/74 | 58 | 8 | | Six Days On The Road.................................... *Artists & Poets* | 106 | $6 | | Atlantic 3028 |

ROBBINS, Dennis   '92

Born in Hazelwood, North Carolina. Former member of the rock group Rockets. Lead singer/guitarist of Billy Hill.

1/17/87	63	8		1 Long Gone Lonesome Blues .... *The Mountain Man And Me*		$3		MCA 52987
10/3/87	71	9		2 Two Of A Kind (Workin' On A Full House) .... *The Church On Cumberland Road*		$3		MCA 53143
5/9/92	34	20		3 Home Sweet Home *The Only Slide I Ever Played On*		$3		Giant 18982
9/5/92	59	6		4 My Side Of Town .... *Hi O Silver*		$3		Giant 18786
1/15/94	68	4		5 Mona Lisa On Cruise Control .... *Walkin' On The Edge*		$3	▌	Giant 18294

ROBBINS, Hargus "Pig"   '79

Born on 1/18/38 in Spring City, Tennessee. Top Nashville session pianist. Blind since age four. CMA Award: 1976 Musician of the Year.

| 6/23/79 | 83 | 3 | | 1 Chunky People .... *Whatever Happened To The Girls I Knew* | | $5 | | Elektra 46037 |
| 9/1/79 | 92 | 4 | | 2 Unbreakable Hearts .... *Love, Love, Love* | | $5 | | Elektra 46512 |

DEBUT	PEAK	WKS	Gold	A-side (Chart Hit)..B-side	Pop	$	Pic	Label & Number

ROBBINS, Jenny '78

| 7/1/78 | 76 | 4 | | You've Just Found Yourself A New Woman............................*All I've Got Left* | | $6 | | El Dorado 152 |

ROBBINS, Marty ★12★ '56

Born Martin David Robinson on 9/26/25 in Glendale, Arizona. Died of heart failure on 12/8/82 (age 57). Singer/songwriter/guitarist. Father of **Ronny Robbins**. Served in the U.S. Navy from 1944-47. Hosted *Western Caravan* TV show in Phoenix in 1951. Joined the *Grand Ole Opry* in 1953. Acted in the movies *Road To Nashville* and *Guns Of A Stranger*. Hosted TV's *Marty Robbins' Spotlight* in 1977.

1)Singing The Blues 2)Don't Worry 3)Devil Woman 4)El Paso 5)A White Sport Coat

DEBUT	PEAK	WKS		A-side / B-side	Pop	$	Pic	Label & Number
12/20/52+	❶²	18	1	I'll Go On Alone A:❶²/ S:10 *You're Breaking My Heart (While You're Holding My Hand)*		$30		Columbia 21022
3/28/53	5	11	2	I Couldn't Keep From Crying J:5 / A:6 / S:6 *After You Leave*		$30		Columbia 21075
7/3/54	12	3	3	Pretty Words............................A:12 / S:14 *Your Heart's Turn To Break*		$30		Columbia 21246
11/20/54	14	1	4	Call Me Up (And I'll Come Calling On You) ....A:14 *I'm Too Big To Cry*		$30		Columbia 21291
1/8/55	14	1	5	Time Goes By..................................A:14 *It's A Pity What Money Can Do*		$30		Columbia 21324
2/12/55	7	11	6	That's All Right A:7 / S:9 *Gossip*		$40		Columbia 21351
				recorded by **Elvis Presley** in 1954				
10/1/55	9	7	7	Maybelline A:9 *This Broken Heart Of Mine*		$40		Columbia 21446
				#5 Pop hit for **Chuck Berry** in 1955				
9/22/56	❶¹³	30	8	Singing The Blues/ S:❶¹³/ J:❶¹³/ A:❶¹¹	17			
				#1 Pop hit for **Guy Mitchell** in 1956				
10/6/56	7	10	9	I Can't Quit (I've Gone Too Far) A:7		$30		Columbia 21545
2/2/57	3	15	10	Knee Deep In The Blues A:3 / S:5 / J:7				
				#16 Pop hit for **Guy Mitchell** in 1957				
3/2/57	14	2	11	The Same Two Lips............................A:14		$30		Columbia 40815
4/20/57	❶⁵	22	● 12	A White Sport Coat (And A Pink Carnation) S:❶⁵/ J:❶⁵/ A:❶¹ *Grown-Up Tears*	2¹	$25	■	Columbia 40864
9/9/57	11	3	13	Please Don't Blame Me/ S:11				
9/9/57	15	3	14	Teen-Age Dream S:15 / A:15		$25		Columbia 40969
11/25/57+	❶⁴	23	15	The Story Of My Life S:❶⁴/ A:❶⁴ *Once-A-Week Date*	15	$20	■	Columbia 41013
4/7/58	❶²	25	16	Just Married/ A:❶²/ S:3	26			
4/7/58	2²	25	17	Stairway Of Love S:2 / A:8	68	$20		Columbia 41143
8/18/58	4	10	18	She Was Only Seventeen (He Was One Year More) S:4 / A:13 *Sittin' In A Tree House*	27	$20	■	Columbia 41208
12/15/58	23	5	19	Ain't I The Lucky One............................*The Last Time I Saw My Heart*		$20		Columbia 41282
3/9/59	15	9	20	The Hanging Tree............................*The Blues Country Style*	38	$20	■	Columbia 41325
				from the movie starring Gary Cooper				
11/9/59	❶⁷	26	21	El Paso *Running Gun*	❶²	$15	■	Columbia 41511
				also see #73 below				
3/21/60	5	14	22	Big Iron *Saddle Tramp*	26	$15	■	Columbia 41589
9/26/60	26	4	23	Five Brothers *Ride, Cowboy Ride*	74	$15	■	Columbia 41771
2/6/61	❶¹⁰	19	24	Don't Worry *Like All The Other Times*	3	$15	■	Columbia 41922
6/5/61	24	4	25	Jimmy Martinez............................*Ghost Train*	51	$12	■	Columbia 42008
9/18/61	3	20	26	It's Your World *You Told Me So*	51	$12	■	Columbia 42065
2/3/62	12	13	27	Sometimes I'm Tempted ....*I Told The Brook (Pop #81)*	109	$12	■	Columbia 42246
6/2/62	12	9	28	Love Can't Wait............................*Too Far Gone*	69	$12	■	Columbia 42375
8/4/62	❶⁸	21	29	Devil Woman *April Fool's Day*	16	$12	■	Columbia 42486
12/8/62+	❶¹	14	30	Ruby Ann *Won't You Forgive*	18	$12	■	Columbia 42614
3/23/63	14	9	31	Cigarettes And Coffee Blues............................*Teenager's Dad*	93	$12		Columbia 42701
9/7/63	13	11	32	Not So Long Ago............................*I Hope You Learn A Lot*	115	$12		Columbia 42831
11/30/63+	❶³	23	33	Begging To You *Over High Mountain*	74	$12		Columbia 42890
3/7/64	15	11	34	Girl From Spanish Town............................*Kingston Girl*	106	$12		Columbia 42968
6/20/64	3	21	35	The Cowboy In The Continental Suit *Man Walks Among Us*	103	$10		Columbia 43049
10/31/64	8	17	36	One Of These Days *Up In The Air*	105	$10		Columbia 43134
4/17/65	❶¹	21	37	Ribbon Of Darkness *Little Robin*	103	$10		Columbia 43258
11/13/65	50	1	38	Old Red............................*Matilda*		$10		Columbia 43377
12/4/65+	21	10	39	While You're Dancing ....*Lonely Too Long*		$10		Columbia 43428
2/19/66	14	11	40	Count Me Out/				
3/5/66	21	7	41	Private Wilson White............................		$10		Columbia 43500
7/9/66	3	18	42	The Shoe Goes On The Other Foot Tonight *It Kind Of Reminds Me Of Me*		$10		Columbia 43680
11/19/66+	16	14	43	Mr. Shorty............................*Tall Handsome Stranger*		$10		Columbia 43870
2/4/67	16	14	44	No Tears Milady/				
2/25/67	34	11	45	Fly Butterfly Fly............................		$10		Columbia 43845
6/3/67	❶¹	16	46	Tonight Carmen *Waiting In Reno*	114	$8		Columbia 44128
9/16/67	9	14	47	Gardenias In Her Hair *In The Valley Of The Rio Grande*		$8		Columbia 44271
5/4/68	10	15	48	Love Is In The Air *I've Been Leaving Every Day*		$8		Columbia 44509
10/5/68	❶²	15	49	I Walk Alone *Lily Of The Valley*	65	$7		Columbia 44633
2/8/69	5	14	50	It's A Sin *I Feel Another Heartbreak Coming On*		$7		Columbia 44739
7/5/69	8	14	51	I Can't Say Goodbye *Hello Daily News*		$7		Columbia 44895
11/22/69+	10	13	52	Camelia *Virginia*		$7		Columbia 45024
2/21/70	❶¹	17	53	My Woman, My Woman, My Wife *Martha Ellen Jenkins*	42	$6		Columbia 45091

DEBUT	PEAK	WKS	Gold	A-side (Chart Hit)..B-side	Pop	$	Pic	Label & Number
				ROBBINS, Marty — Cont'd				
9/12/70	7	14		54 Jolie Girl *The City*	108	$6		Columbia 45215
12/19/70+	5	12		55 Padre *At Times*	113	$6		Columbia 45273
				#13 Pop hit for Toni Arden in 1958				
5/22/71	7	13		56 The Chair/	121			
		8		57 Seventeen Years..		$6		Columbia 45377
10/2/71	9	14		58 Early Morning Sunshine *Another Day Has Gone By*		$6		Columbia 45442
1/1/72	6	16		59 The Best Part Of Living *Gone With The Wind*		$6		Columbia 45520
9/9/72	32	9		60 I've Got A Woman's Love.......................... *A Little Spot In Heaven*		$6		Columbia 45668
9/23/72	11	15		61 This Much A Man *Guess I'll Just Stand Here Looking Dumb*		$7		Decca 33006
2/17/73	60	7		62 Laura (What's He Got That I Ain't Got) .... *It Kind Of Reminds Me Of Me*		$6		Columbia 45775
3/3/73	6	15		63 Walking Piece Of Heaven *Franklin, Tennessee*		$6		MCA 40012
6/23/73	40	8		64 A Man And A Train .... *Las Vegas, Nevada*		$6		MCA 40067
				from the movie *Emperor of The North Pole* starring Lee Marvin				
10/13/73	9	14		65 Love Me/				
				also see #93 below				
		11		66 Crawling On My Knees...		$6		MCA 40134
1/26/74	10	14		67 Twentieth Century Drifter *I'm Wanting To*		$6		MCA 40172
5/25/74	12	15		68 Don't You Think .... *I Couldn't Believe It Was True*		$6		MCA 40236
10/5/74	39	11		69 Two Gun Daddy................................. *Queen Of The Big Rodeo*		$6		MCA 40296
1/18/75	23	12		70 Life/				
5/31/75	76	4		71 It Takes Faith..		$6		MCA 40342
7/19/75	55	9		72 Shotgun Rider .... *These Are My Souvenirs*		$6		MCA 40425
4/17/76	❶²	16		73 El Paso City *When I'm Gone*		$5		Columbia 10305
				sequel to #21 above				
9/4/76	❶¹	14		74 Among My Souvenirs *She's Just A Drifter*		$5		Columbia 10396
				#7 Pop hit for Connie Francis in 1959				
2/5/77	4	13		75 Adios Amigo *Helen*		$5		Columbia 10472
5/21/77	10	13		76 I Don't Know Why (I Just Do) *Inspiration For A Song*	108	$5		Columbia 10536
				#12 Pop hit for Linda Scott in 1961				
10/15/77	6	15		77 Don't Let Me Touch You *Tomorrow, Tomorrow, Tomorrow*		$5		Columbia 10629
1/28/78	6	13		78 Return To Me *More Than Anything I Miss You*		$5		Columbia 10673
				#4 Pop hit for Dean Martin in 1958				
11/4/78	17	12		79 Please Don't Play A Love Song *Jenny*		$5		Columbia 10821
2/17/79	15	13		80 Touch Me With Magic .... *Confused And Lonely*		$5		Columbia 10905
6/23/79	16	12		81 All Around Cowboy *The Dreamer*		$5		Columbia 11016
10/13/79	25	10		82 Buenos Dias Argentina .... *Ballad Of A Small Man*		$5		Columbia 11102
4/12/80	37	9		83 She's Made Of Faith *Misery In My Soul*		$4		Columbia 11240
7/12/80	72	5		84 One Man's Trash (Is Another Man's Treasure) .... *I Can't Wait Until Tomorrow*		$4		Columbia 11291
11/1/80	28	12		85 An Occasional Rose................................... *Holding On To You*		$4		Columbia 11372
2/7/81	47	7		86 Completely Out Of Love .... *Another Cup Of Coffee*		$4		Columbia 11425
9/26/81	83	4		87 Jumper Cable Man *Good Hearted Woman*		$4		Columbia 02444
11/21/81	45	9		88 Teardrops In My Heart *Honeycombe*		$4		Columbia 02575
5/22/82	10	18		89 Some Memories Just Won't Die *Lover, Lover*		$4		Columbia 02854
10/2/82	24	16		90 Tie Your Dream To Mine................................... *That's All She Wrote*		$4		Columbia 03236
12/25/82+	10	17		91 Honkytonk Man *Shotgun Rag (Johnny Gimble)*		$4		Warner 29847
				from the movie starring Clint Eastwood				
3/26/83	48	9		92 Change Of Heart *Devil In A Cowboy Hat*		$4		Columbia 03789
4/16/83	58	8		93 Love Me .... *Safely In The Arms Of Jesus* [R]		$4		Audiograph 454
				JEANNE PRUETT/MARTY ROBBINS				
				new version of #65 above				
6/11/83	57	9		94 What If I Said I Love You .... *Baby That's Love*		$4		Columbia 03927
				ROBBINS, Ronny '84				
				Born Ronald Carson Robinson on 7/16/49 in Phoenix. Son of Marty Robbins.				
11/11/78	99	1		1 The Last Lie I Told Her .... *Taste The Wine*		$6		Artic 878
2/24/79	95	1		2 Why'd The Last Time Have To Be The Best .... *Where Do I Put Her Memory*		$6		Artic 8782
11/17/79	91	2		3 I Know I'm Not Your Hero Anymore................. *The I Love You's Get Further Apart*		$6		TRC 081
7/21/84	62	7		4 Those You Lose .... *We've Been Lying Here Too Long*		$4		Columbia 04506
				ROBERTS, Kenny '49				
				Born George Kingsbury on 10/14/26 in Lenoir City, Tennessee; raised in Greenfield, Massachusetts. Singer/songwriter/guitarist. Known for his yodeling.				
9/17/49	4	11		1 I Never See Maggie Alone/ *J:4 / S:5*	9			
				Roberts first recorded this with Nancy Lee for Vitacoustic 506; #13 Pop hit for Irving Aaronson in 1927				
10/8/49	15	1		2 Wedding Bells..*J:15*		$15		Coral 64012
11/19/49	14	1		3 Jealous Heart *J:14 (There's A) Bluebird On Your Windowsill*		$15		Coral 64021
5/13/50	8	4		4 Choc'late Ice Cream Cone *A:8 / J:10 Hillbilly Fever*		$15		Coral 64032
				ROBERTS, Pat '72				
				Born in Seattle. Male singer.				
10/21/72	34	12		1 Rhythm Of The Rain *Without You*		$6		Dot 17434
				#3 Pop hit for The Cascades in 1963				
3/3/73	59	8		2 Thanks For Lovin' Me .... *A Whole Lotta Lovin'*		$6		Dot 17451
7/14/73	79	4		3 Here Comes My Little Baby................................... *Love Lives Again*		$6		Dot 17465
11/3/73	81	5		4 I'm Gonna Keep Searching .... *Your Love's Been A Long Time Comin'*		$6		Dot 17478
4/6/74	77	6		5 You Got Everything That You Want .... *Love Me, Love Me*		$6		Dot 17495

ROBERTSON, Jack — '88

| 7/9/88 | 66 | 5 | | It's Not Easy .... *Cow Town Mama* | | $5 | | Soundwaves 4808 |

ROBERTSON, Texas Jim — '47
Born on 2/27/09 in Batesville, Texas. Died on 11/11/66 (age 57). Singer/guitarist.

TEXAS JIM ROBERTSON and The Panhandle Punchers:

12/28/46	5	1		1 Filipino Baby/				
2/15/47	5	1		2 Rainbow At Midnight		$15		RCA Victor 20-1975
2/28/48	8	1		3 Signed, Sealed And Delivered *Lost Deep In The Bottom Of The Sea*		$15		RCA Victor 20-2651
1/7/50	13	1		4 Slipping Around .... S:13 *Wedding Bells*		$25		RCA Victor 48-0071
				78 rpm: 21-0074				

ROBEY, Loretta — '77
Born in 1937 in Oviedo, Florida.

| 6/11/77 | 100 | 1 | | Sophisticated Country Lady.. *Lovin Cup* | | $5 | | Soundwaves 4545 |

ROBIN & CRUISER — '87
Brothers Robin and Cruiser Gordon.

| 10/24/87 | 79 | 4 | | Rings Of Gold .... *Tie Me To Your Heart Again* | | $3 | | 16th Avenue 70404 |

ROBINSON, Betty Jean — '75
Born in Hyden, Kentucky. Singer/songwriter.

4/24/71	51	10		1 All I Need Is You .... *Funny What A Pair Of Fools Will Do*		$8		Decca 32802
				CARL BELEW & BETTY JEAN ROBINSON				
11/23/74+	49	10		2 On The Way Home.. *I've Got You*		$5		MCA 40300
4/5/75	87	4		3 God Is Good .... *All I Need Is You*		$5		4 Star 1004

ROBINSON, Sharon — '87

| 12/26/87 | 86 | 4 | | Have You Hurt Any Good Ones Lately .... *Potential Strangers* | | $7 | | Nightfall 001 |

ROBISON, Carson — '48
Born on 8/4/1890 in Oswego, Kansas. Died on 3/24/57 (age 66). Singer/songwriter/guitarist. Known as "The Kansas Jaybird."

6/30/45	5	1		1 Hitler's Last Letter To Hirohito *Hirohito's Letter To Hitler* [N]		$20		Victor 20-1665
8/14/48	3	28		2 Life Gits Tee-Jus Don't It S:3 / J:3 *Wind In The Mountains* [N]	14	$20		MGM 10224
				CARSON ROBISON with His Pleasant Valley Boys				

ROCKINHORSE — '86
Group from Oakland, Minnesota, led by female singer Toni Rose.

| 8/30/86 | 68 | 6 | | 1 Have I Got A Heart For You .... | | $5 | | Long Shot 1002 |
| 12/6/86 | 86 | 3 | | 2 Let A Little Love In (Tennessee Saturday Night)........................ | | $5 | | Long Shot 1003 |

ROCKIN' SIDNEY — '85
Born Sidney Simien on 4/9/38 in Lebeau, Louisiana. Died of cancer on 2/25/98 (age 59). Black singer/songwriter/accordianist.

| 6/22/85 | 19 | 20 | | My Toot-Toot .... S:8 / A:23   *Jalapeno Lena* | | $4 | | Epic 05430 |

RODGERS, Jimmie — '55
Born on 9/8/1897 in Meridian, Mississippi. Died of tuberculosis on 5/26/33 (age 35). Singer/songwriter/guitarist. Known as "America's Blue Yodeler," "The Singing Brakeman," and "The Father of Country Music." Elected to the Country Music Hall of Fame in 1961. Inducted into the Rock and Roll Hall of Fame in 1986 as an early influence of rock and roll.

5/14/55	7	12		In The Jailhouse Now No. 2 J:7 / S:8 / A:9 *Peach Picking Time Down In Georgia*		$25		RCA Victor 6092
				JIMMIE RODGERS and the Rainbow Ranch Boys				
				recorded in 1930 on Victor 22523 ($75); new overdubbed backing includes **Chet Atkins** and **Hank Snow**				

RODGERS, Jimmie — '58
Born on 9/18/33 in Camas, Washington. Singer/guitarist/pianist. Charted 25 pop hits from 1957-67. Hosted own TV series in 1959 and 1969.
1)Oh-Oh, I'm Falling In Love Again 2)Secretly 3)Kisses Sweeter Than Wine

10/14/57	7	13	●	1 Honeycomb S:7 / A:11 *Their Hearts Were Full Of Spring*	❶⁴	$20		Roulette 4015
12/2/57	6	16	●	2 Kisses Sweeter Than Wine S:6 / A:8 *Better Loved You'll Never Be*	3	$20		Roulette 4031
3/3/58	5	11	●	3 Oh-Oh, I'm Falling In Love Again S:5 / A:15 *The Long Hot Summer* (Pop #77)	7	$20		Roulette 4045
5/19/58	5	17	●	4 Secretly/ S:5 / A:14	3			
				also see #9 below				
		9		5 Make Me A Miracle S:flip	16	$15	■	Roulette 4070
8/25/58	13	8		6 Are You Really Mine..................... S:13 *The Wizard* (Pop #45)	10	$15	■	Roulette 4090
10/29/77	67	10		7 A Good Woman Likes To Drink With The Boys .... *Everybody Needs Love*		$6		ScrimShaw 1313
2/11/78	74	5		8 Everytime I Sing A Love Song .... *Just A Little Time*		$6		ScrimShaw 1314
9/23/78	65	5		9 Secretly.. *Shovelin' Coal Missouri* [R]		$6		ScrimShaw 1318
				new version of #4 above				
3/17/79	89	4		10 Easy To Love/				
		4		11 Easy		$6		ScrimShaw 1319
				JIMMIE RODGERS & MICHELE				

RODMAN, Judy — '86
★320★
Born Judy Mae Robbins on 5/23/51 in Riverside, California; raised in Miami and Jacksonville. Singer/songwriter/guitarist. Former jingle and session singer.
1)Until I Met You 2)I'll Be Your Baby Tonight 3)Girls Ride Horses Too

3/23/85	40	14		1 I've Been Had By Love Before .... *Do You Make Love As Well As You Make Music*		$4		MTM 72050
8/10/85	33	14		2 You're Gonna Miss Me When I'm Gone .... *She Thinks That She'll Marry*		$4		MTM 72054
11/16/85+	30	17		3 I Sure Need Your Lovin'................................. A:29 *Come Next Monday*		$4		MTM 72061
4/5/86	❶¹	25		4 Until I Met You A:❶¹ / S:2 *Do You Make Love As Well As You Make Music*		$4		MTM 72065
10/4/86+	9	21		5 She Thinks That She'll Marry S:9 / A:10 *Our Love Is Fine*		$4		MTM 72076
2/21/87	7	17		6 Girls Ride Horses Too S:2 / A:7 *Heart Of A Gentleman*		$4		MTM 72083
6/20/87	5	27		7 I'll Be Your Baby Tonight S:3 *Love Comes From Inside Of You*		$4		MTM 72089
				written and first recorded by Bob Dylan on his 1968 album *John Wesley Harding*				
10/31/87+	18	21		8 I Want A Love Like That................................. S:19 *Please Don't Take My Heart*		$4		MTM 72092

DEBUT	PEAK	WKS	Gold	A-side (Chart Hit) ....B-side	Pop	$	Pic	Label & Number
				RODMAN, Judy — Cont'd				
5/21/88	43	9		9 Goin' To Work .... Please Don't Take My Heart		$4		MTM 72105
8/13/88	45	9		10 I Can Love You ....Come To Me		$4		MTM 72112

RODRIGUEZ, Johnny ★72★   '73
Born Juan Rodriguez on 12/10/51 in Sabinal, Texas. Singer/songwriter/guitarist.

1)Ridin' My Thumb To Mexico 2)That's The Way Love Goes 3)Just Get Up And Close The Door
4)You Always Come Back 5)Love Put A Song In My Heart

11/11/72+	9	18		1 **Pass Me By (If You're Only Passing Through)** *Jealous Heart*		$6		Mercury 73334
3/31/73	❶¹	16		2 **You Always Come Back (To Hurting Me)** *I Wonder Where You Are Tonight*	86	$6		Mercury 73368
8/18/73	❶²	17		3 **Ridin' My Thumb To Mexico** *Release Me*	70	$6		Mercury 73416
12/29/73+	❶¹	14		4 **That's The Way Love Goes** *I Really Don't Want To Know*		$6		Mercury 73446
3/30/74	6	14		5 **Something** *Born To Lose*	85	$6		Mercury 73471
				#1 Pop hit for The Beatles in 1969				
7/13/74	2¹	13		6 **Dance With Me (Just One More Time)** *Faded Love*		$6		Mercury 73493
10/19/74	3	13		7 **We're Over** *Oh, I Miss You*		$5		Mercury 73621
2/8/75	❶¹	12		8 **I Just Can't Get Her Out Of My Mind** *Have I Told You Lately That I Love You*		$5		Mercury 73659
5/24/75	❶¹	18		9 **Just Get Up And Close The Door** *Am I That Easy To Forget*		$5		Mercury 73682
10/4/75	❶¹	15		10 **Love Put A Song In My Heart** *Steppin' Out On You*		$5		Mercury 73715
2/28/76	3	15		11 **I Couldn't Be Me Without You** *Sometimes I Wish I Were You*		$5	■	Mercury 73769
7/10/76	2²	13		12 **I Wonder If I Ever Said Goodbye** *Louisiana*		$5		Mercury 73815
10/9/76	5	14		13 **Hillbilly Heart** *Commonly Known As The Blues*		$5		Mercury 73855
1/15/77	5	14		14 **Desperado** *There'll Always Be Honky Tonks In Texas*		$5		Mercury 73878
				first recorded by the **Eagles** on their 1973 album *Desperado*				
5/14/77	5	13		15 **If Practice Makes Perfect** *Hard Times*		$5		Mercury 73914
9/3/77	25	10		16 Eres Tu .... *You Put A Hold On Me* [F]		$5		Mercury 55004
				#9 Pop hit for Mocedades in 1974				
11/5/77	14	13		17 Savin' This Love Song For You .... *Que Te Quiero*		$5		Mercury 55012
2/25/78	7	14		18 We Believe In Happy Endings *The Immigrant*		$5		Mercury 55020
7/8/78	7	13		19 **Love Me With All Your Heart (Cuando Calienta El Sol)** *I Need It Now*		$5		Mercury 55029
				#3 Pop hit for The Ray Charles Singers in 1964				
12/16/78+	16	13		20 Alibis .... *Rest Your Love On Me*		$5		Mercury 55050
3/10/79	6	14		21 **Down On The Rio Grande** *Mexico Holiday*		$4		Epic 50671
7/7/79	17	13		22 Fools For Each Other .... *Street Walker*		$4		Epic 50735
10/20/79	16	14		23 I Hate The Way I Love It .... *Almost Persuaded*		$4		Epic 50791
				JOHNNY RODRIGUEZ and CHARLY McCLAIN				
11/24/79+	19	14		24 What'll I Tell Virginia .... *Whatever Gets Me Through The Night*		$4		Epic 50808
4/5/80	29	11		25 Love, Look At Us Now .... *Where Did It Go*		$4		Epic 50859
9/20/80	17	16		26 North Of The Border .... *When She Gets Around To Me*		$4		Epic 50932
4/11/81	22	13		27 I Want You Tonight .... *Your Love Isn't Mine Anymore*		$4		Epic 01033
8/8/81	30	11		28 Trying Not To Love You .... *Mexico Rain*		$4		Epic 02411
2/13/82	66	6		29 Born With The Blues/		$4		
12/5/81	73	7		30 It's Not The Same Old You		$4		Epic 02638
11/27/82	89	3		31 He's Not Entitled To Your Love .... *Starting All Over Again*		$4		Epic 03275
2/26/83	4	20		32 **Foolin'** *Because Of You*		$4		Epic 03598
7/9/83	6	21		33 **How Could I Love Her So Much** *Somethin' About A Jukebox*		$4		Epic 03972
11/19/83+	35	12		34 Back On Her Mind Again .... *Eleven Roses*		$4		Epic 04206
1/28/84	15	17		35 Too Late To Go Home .... *No Memories Hangin' Round*		$4		Epic 04336
5/19/84	30	15		36 Let's Leave The Lights On Tonight .... *What A Movie You'd Make*		$4		Epic 04460
8/18/84	63	7		37 First Time Burned .... *Hand Me Another Of Those*		$4		Epic 04562
10/13/84	60	8		38 Rose Of My Heart .... *Down In The Boondocks*		$4		Epic 04628
4/6/85	69	7		39 Here I Am Again .... *Full Circle*		$4		Epic 04838
12/28/85+	51	15		40 She Don't Cry Like She Used To .... *Back On Her Mind Again*		$4	■	Epic 05732
12/12/87+	12	26		41 **I Didn't (Every Chance I Had)** .... S:25 *I'm Not That Good At Goodbye*		$3		Capitol 44071
7/16/88	41	15		42 I Wanta Wake Up With You .... *Someday I'm Gonna Finish Leaving You*		$3		Capitol 44204
10/15/88	44	10		43 You Might Want To Use Me Again.................... *She Loves Austin*		$3		Capitol 44245
2/18/89	72	4		44 No Chance To Dance .... *Back To Stay*		$3		Capitol 44325
8/5/89	78	3		45 Back To Stay .... *Someday I'm Gonna Finish Leaving You*		$3		Capitol 44403
				ROE, Marlys '73				
				Female singer from Georgia.				
8/11/73	71	9		Carry Me Back .... *Somebody In Your Eyes*		$6		GRC 1002
				ROE, Tommy '87				
				Born on 5/9/42 in Atlanta. Singer/songwriter/guitarist. Charted 22 pop hits from 1962-73.				
6/9/73	73	2		1 Working Class Hero .... *Sun In My Eyes*	97	$6		MGM South 7013
5/19/79	77	3		2 **Massachusetts** .... *Just Look At Me*		$5		Warner/Curb 8800
				#11 Pop hit for the Bee Gees in 1967				
10/27/79	70	4		3 You Better Move On........................ *Just Look At Me*		$5		Warner/Curb 49085
				#24 Pop hit for Arthur Alexander in 1962				
6/21/80	87	3		4 Charlie, I Love Your Wife........................ *There Is No Sun On Sunset Boulevard*		$5		Warner/Curb 49235

DEBUT	PEAK	WKS	A-side / B-side	Pop	$	PIC	Label & Number
			ROE, Tommy — Cont'd				
11/16/85	57	11	5 Some Such Foolishness .... *Barbara Lou*		$4		Curb/MCA 52711
3/1/86	51	7	6 Radio Romance .... *Barbara Lou*		$4		Curb/MCA 52778
12/20/86+	38	14	7 Let's Be Fools Like That Again .... *Barbara Lou*		$3		Mercury 888206
5/23/87	67	5	8 Back When It Really Mattered .... *Radio Romance*		$3		Mercury 888497
			ROGERS, Dann '87				
			Nephew of **Kenny Rogers**.				
9/5/87	78	3	Just A Kid From Texas .... *We've Got To Stop Meeting This Way*		$3		MCA 53133

DEBUT	PEAK	WKS	A-side / B-side	Pop	$	PIC	Label & Number
			ROGERS, David ★154★ '72				
			Born on 3/27/36 in Atlanta. Died on 8/10/93 (age 57). Singer/songwriter/guitarist.				
			1)Need You 2)Loving You Has Changed My Life 3)Just Thank Me 4)Darlin' 5)She Don't Make Me Cry				
3/2/68	69	5	1 I'd Be Your Fool Again .... *Loser's Shoes*		$7		Columbia 44430
7/20/68	38	11	2 I'm In Love With My Wife .... *Tessie's Bar Mystery*		$7	■	Columbia 44561
11/16/68+	37	13	3 You Touched My Heart .... *Today And Tomorrow*		$7		Columbia 44668
5/17/69	59	7	4 Dearly Beloved... *The Little White Cloud That Cried*		$7		Columbia 44796
11/22/69+	23	12	5 A World Called You .... *A Picture Of You*		$7		Columbia 45007
5/9/70	46	9	6 So Much In Love With You .... *The Edge Of Your Memory*		$7		Columbia 45111
10/17/70	26	11	7 I Wake Up In Heaven .... *Baby Don't Cry*		$7		Columbia 45226
5/29/71	19	15	8 She Don't Make Me Cry .... *Bottle Do Your Thing*		$7		Columbia 45383
11/13/71+	21	13	9 Ruby You're Warm .... *Is That All San Francisco Did For You*		$7		Columbia 45478
2/26/72	9	15	10 Need You *Sweet Vibrations (Some Folks Call It Love)*		$7		Columbia 45551
			#25 Pop hit for Donnie Owens in 1958				
8/5/72	38	9	11 Goodbye .... *I'd Be Your Fool Again*		$7		Columbia 45642
11/11/72	35	11	12 All Heaven Breaks Loose .... *Completely Satisfied*		$7		Columbia 45714
4/28/73	17	12	13 Just Thank Me.. *I Wish I Was Back*		$6		Atlantic 2957
8/25/73	22	12	14 It'll Be Her... *Singin' Star*		$6		Atlantic 4005
1/5/74	9	14	15 Loving You Has Changed My Life *You Be You And I'll Be Gone*		$6		Atlantic 4012
5/25/74	21	13	16 Hey There Girl .... *Someone That I Can Forget*		$6		Atlantic 4022
9/28/74	59	7	17 I Just Can't Help Believin' .... *Now That You're A Woman*		$6		Atlantic 4204
			#9 Pop hit for **B.J. Thomas** in 1970				
4/12/75	60	8	18 It Takes A Whole Lotta Livin' In A House................................... *Since Never*		$5		United Artists 617
8/7/76	66	7	19 Whispers And Grins .... *Use Me Up*		$5		Republic 256
11/6/76	84	6	20 Mahogany Bridge .... *It's A Crying Shame (That People Change)*		$5		Republic 311
1/15/77	21	12	21 I'm Gonna Love You Right Out Of This World .... *Burning Bridges*		$5		Republic 343
4/30/77	76	4	22 The Lady And The Baby .... *That Woman Keeps This Cowboy Comin' Home*		$5		Republic 382
6/18/77	49	7	23 I Love What My Woman Does To Me		$5		Republic 001
9/3/77	47	8	24 Do You Hear My Heart Beat.............................. *They Went Together*		$5		Republic 006
11/26/77+	24	12	25 You And Me Alone... *Time For Lovin'*		$5		Republic 011
2/25/78	22	12	26 I'll Be There (When You Get Lonely) .... *Just For The Love Of It*		$5		Republic 015
5/27/78	32	10	27 Let's Try To Remember .... *That Woman Keeps This Cowboy Comin' Home*		$5		Republic 020
9/9/78	31	9	28 When A Woman Cries .... *The Power Of Positive Drinking*		$5		Republic 029
3/3/79	18	14	29 Darlin' .... *How Long Has It Been*		$5		Republic 038
7/14/79	36	8	30 You Are My Rainbow.. *If You Should Ask*		$5		Republic 042
12/15/79+	39	9	31 You're Amazing .... *Farewell Two Arms*		$5		Republic 048
5/23/81	88	3	32 Houston Blue .... *Here's To You Darling*		$6		Kari 120
11/6/82	92	2	33 Crown Prince Of The Barroom .... *Me And Ms. Chablis*		$6		Music Master 012
2/19/83	67	7	34 Hold Me... *Chuck Berry Music*		$6		Music Master 1004
6/4/83	71	5	35 You've Still Got Me		$6		Mr. Music 016
11/12/83	87	4	36 The Devil Is A Woman .... *Time For Lovin'*		$6		Mr. Music 018
3/3/84	72	4	37 I'm A Country Song..		$6		Hal Kat Kountry 2083
			ROGERS, James '89				
			Born on 12/22/49 in Chattanooga, Tennessee; raised in Fort Oglethorpe, Georgia.				
12/9/89	72	5	Something's Got A Hold On Me .... *This Is America*		$5		Soundwaves 4820
			ROGERS, Jesse '49				
			Born in Meridian, Mississippi. Hosted own NBC-TV series for children in 1949. Known as "The Western Balladeer."				
9/10/49	15	1	Wedding Bells... *J:15 Tennessee Polka*		$20		Bluebird 32-0002
			JESSE ROGERS and his '49ers				

DEBUT	PEAK	WKS	Gold	A-side (Chart Hit)..B-side	Pop	$	Pic	Label & Number

ROGERS, Kenny ★31★   '80
Born on 8/21/38 in Houston. Singer/songwriter/guitarist/actor. Member of the Kirby Stone Four and The New Christy Minstrels in the mid-1960s. Formed **The First Edition** in 1967. Went solo in 1973. Starred in the movie *Six Pack* and several TV movies including *The Gambler, Coward Of The County, Wild Horses* and *Rio Diablo*. Formerly married to Marianne Gordon of TV's *Hee-Haw*. Uncle of **Dann Rogers**. CMA 1978 & 1979 Vocal Duo of the Year (with Dottie West); 1979 Male Vocalist of the Year.

1)Coward Of The County 2)The Gambler 3)She Believes In Me 4)Islands In The Stream 5)Lucille

KENNY ROGERS AND THE FIRST EDITION:

DEBUT	PEAK	WKS	Gold	A-side / B-side	Pop	$	Pic	Label & Number
7/19/69	39	11		1 Ruby, Don't Take Your Love To Town .... *Girl Get Ahold Of Yourself*	6	$8		Reprise 0829
10/25/69	46	8		2 Ruben James .... *Sunshine*	26	$8		Reprise 0854
				some pressings show title as "Reuben James"				
7/14/73	69	6		3 Today I Started Loving You Again .... *She Thinks I Still Care*		$7		Jolly Rogers 1004
				KENNY ROGERS:				
12/13/75+	19	13		4 Love Lifted Me... *Home-Made Love*	97	$5		United Artists 746
6/26/76	46	12		5 While The Feeling's Good ....*I Would Like To See You Again*		$5		United Artists 812
10/9/76	19	13		6 Laura (What's He Got That I Ain't Got?) .... *I Wasn't Man Enough*		$5		United Artists 868
1/29/77	❶²	20	●	7 Lucille *Till I Get It Right*	5	$5		United Artists 929
				CMA Award: Single of the Year				
8/6/77	❶¹	14		8 Daytime Friends .... *We Don't Make Love Anymore*	28	$5		United Artists 1027
10/22/77	9	15		9 Sweet Music Man .... *Lying Again*	44	$5		United Artists 1095
2/18/78	❶²	17		10 Every Time Two Fools Collide .... *We Love Each Other*	101	$5		United Artists 1137
				KENNY ROGERS & DOTTIE WEST				
6/3/78	❶¹	14		11 Love Or Something Like It .... *Starting Again*	32	$5		United Artists 1210
9/2/78	2¹	14		12 Anyone Who Isn't Me Tonight .... *You And Me*		$5		United Artists 1234
				KENNY ROGERS & DOTTIE WEST				
10/28/78	❶³	16		13 The Gambler .... *Momma's Waiting*	16	$5		United Artists 1250
2/17/79	❶¹	15		14 All I Ever Need Is You *Another Somebody Done Somebody Wrong Song*	102	$5		United Artists 1276
				KENNY ROGERS & DOTTIE WEST				
				#7 Pop hit for Sonny & Cher in 1971				
4/21/79	❶²	16	●	15 She Believes In Me .... *Morgana Jones*	5	$5	■	United Artists 1273
7/7/79	3	15		16 Til I Can Make It On My Own .... *Midnight Flyer*		$5		United Artists 1299
				KENNY ROGERS & DOTTIE WEST				
9/15/79	❶²	12		17 You Decorated My Life .... *One Man's Woman*	7	$5	■	United Artists 1315
11/17/79+	❶³	15	●	18 Coward Of The County .... *I Want To Make You Smile*	3	$5	■	United Artists 1327
4/5/80	3	14		19 Don't Fall In Love With A Dreamer *Goin' Home To The Rock/Gideon Tanner*	4	$5	■	United Artists 1345
				KENNY ROGERS with Kim Carnes				
6/28/80	4	14		20 Love The World Away *Sayin' Goodbye/Requiem: Goin' Home To The Rock*	14	$5		United Artists 1359
				from the movie *Urban Cowboy* starring John Travolta				
10/11/80	❶¹	14	●	21 Lady .... *Sweet Music Man*	❶⁶	$4	■	Liberty 1380
4/4/81	❶¹	15		22 What Are We Doin' In Love *Choosin' Means Losin'* (West)	14	$4	■	Liberty 1404
				DOTTIE WEST (with Kenny Rogers)				
6/20/81	❶²	15		23 I Don't Need You .... *Without You In My Life*	3	$4	■	Liberty 1415
9/12/81	5	14		24 Share Your Love With Me .... *Greybeard*	14	$4	■	Liberty 1430
				#13 Pop hit for Aretha Franklin in 1969				
11/14/81+	9	16		25 Blaze Of Glory .... *The Good Life*	66	$4		Liberty 1441
1/30/82	5	16		26 Through The Years .... *So In Love With You*	13	$4		Liberty 1444
7/10/82	❶¹	16		27 Love Will Turn You Around .... *I Want A Son*	13	$4	■	Liberty 1471
				from the movie *Six Pack* starring Rogers				
10/16/82	3	17		28 A Love Song .... *The Fool In Me*	47	$4		Liberty 1485
1/29/83	❶¹	17		29 We've Got Tonight .... *You Are So Beautiful* (Rogers)	6	$4	■	Liberty 1492
				KENNY ROGERS and SHEENA EASTON				
				#13 Pop hit for Bob Seger in 1979				
5/7/83	13	17		30 All My Life .... *Farther I Go*	37	$4	■	Liberty 1495
7/30/83	5	18		31 Scarlet Fever *What I Learned From Loving You*	94	$4		Liberty 1503
9/3/83	❶²	23	▲	32 Islands In The Stream .... *I Will Always Love You*	❶²	$4	■	RCA 13615
				KENNY ROGERS with Dolly Parton				
11/19/83+	20	17		33 You Were A Good Friend .... *Sweet Music Man*		$4		Liberty 1511
1/14/84	3	17		34 Buried Treasure *This Woman* (Pop #23)		$4	■	RCA 13710
3/24/84	19	15		35 Together Again.. *Baby I'm A Want You*		$4		Liberty 1516
				KENNY ROGERS and Dottie West				
4/21/84	30	13		36 Eyes That See In The Dark .... *Hold Me*	79	$3		RCA 13774
6/30/84	11	19		37 Evening Star/		$3		RCA 13832
		14		38 Midsummer Nights		$3		RCA 13832
11/10/84	70	10		39 What About Me? ....*The Rest Of Last Night* (Rogers)	15	$3	■	RCA 13899
				KENNY ROGERS with KIM CARNES and JAMES INGRAM				
12/15/84	53	7		40 The Greatest Gift Of All .... *White Christmas* [X]	81	$3	■	RCA 13945
				KENNY ROGERS & DOLLY PARTON				
12/22/84+	❶¹	21		41 Crazy *S:❶¹ / A:❶¹ The Stranger*	79	$3	■	RCA 13975
4/13/85	37	12		42 Love Is What We Make It .... *A Stranger In My Place*		$3		Liberty 1524
5/25/85	❶¹	20		43 Real Love *S:❶¹ / A:❶¹ I Can't Be True*	91	$3	■	RCA 14058
				DOLLY PARTON (with Kenny Rogers)				
7/20/85	57	8		44 Twentieth Century Fool .... *It Turns Me Inside Out*		$3		Liberty 1525
10/12/85+	❶¹	22		45 Morning Desire *S:❶¹ / A:❶¹ People In Love*	72	$3	■	RCA 14194
1/18/86	47	9		46 Goodbye Marie .... *Abraham, Martin And John*		$3		Liberty 1526
2/22/86	❶¹	20		47 Tomb Of The Unknown Love *S:❶¹ / A:❶¹ One Perfect Song*		$3	■	RCA 14298

DEBUT	PEAK	WKS	Gold	A-side (Chart Hit)...B-side	Pop	$	Pic	Label & Number
				ROGERS, Kenny — Cont'd				
6/14/86	46	12		48 The Pride Is Back...S:29 *Didn't We?*		$3	■	RCA 14384
				KENNY ROGERS with NICKIE RYDER				
				tune used for a Chrysler jingle				
10/18/86	53	12		49 They Don't Make Them Like They Used To ....*Just The Thought Of Losing You*		$3	■	RCA 5016
				from the movie *Tough Guys* starring Burt Lancaster and Kirk Douglas				
12/27/86+	2²	21		50 Twenty Years Ago A:2 / S:5 *The Heart Of The Matter*		$3		RCA 5078
6/27/87	❶¹	17		51 Make No Mistake, She's Mine S:3 *You're My Love*		$3	■	RCA 5209
				RONNIE MILSAP & KENNY ROGERS				
				#51 Pop hit for Barbra Streisand & Kim Carnes in 1985				
10/10/87	2²	19		52 I Prefer The Moonlight S:5 *We're Doin' Alright*		$3		RCA 5258
3/5/88	6	16		53 The Factory S:12 *One More Day*		$3		RCA 6832
8/13/88	26	15		54 When You Put Your Heart In It ....S:25 *(instrumental) (w/Jim Horn)*		$3	■	Reprise 27812
9/3/88+	86	5		55 I Don't Call Him Daddy ....*We're Doin' Alright*		$3		RCA 8390
5/27/89	30	12		56 Planet Texas ....*When You Put Your Heart In It*		$3	■	Reprise 27690
8/26/89	8	26		57 The Vows Go Unbroken (Always True To You) *One Night*		$3		Reprise 22828
9/30/89	28	15		58 If I Ever Fall In Love Again ....*Just Another Woman In Love*		$3		Capitol 44432
				ANNE MURRAY with Kenny Rogers				
2/17/90	25	13		59 Maybe ....*If I Knew Then What I Know Now*		$3	▮	Reprise 19972
				KENNY ROGERS (with Holly Dunn)				
8/18/90	21	20		60 Love Is Strange ....*Walk Away*		$3	▮	Reprise 19760
				KENNY ROGERS and DOLLY PARTON				
				#11 Pop hit for Mickey & Sylvia in 1957				
2/2/91	69	4		61 Lay My Body Down ....*Crazy In Love*		$3		Reprise 19504
11/30/91+	11	20		62 If You Want To Find Love ....*Sunshine*		$3		Reprise 19080
				Linda Davis (backing vocal)				
12/28/96	55	2		63 Mary, Did You Know ....[X]				album cut
				KENNY ROGERS with Wynonna				
				from the album *The Gift* on Magnatone 108				
				ROGERS, Ronnie **'82**				
				Born Randall Rogers in Nashville. Singer/songwriter.				
11/21/81+	39	11		1 Gonna Take My Angel Out Tonight ....*Neon Fool*		$5		Lifesong 45094
3/20/82	37	9		2 My Love Belongs To You *Ramblers Never Change*		$5		Lifesong 45095
6/12/82	54	8		3 First Time Around ....*Stoned Little Rat*		$5		Lifesong 45116
9/25/82	86	3		4 Happy Country Birthday/				
10/16/82	86	3		5 Takin' It Back To The Hills		$5		Lifesong 45118
6/25/83	66	7		6 Inside Story ....*Dixieland Delight*		$4		Epic 03953
9/19/87	57	8		7 Good Timin' Shoes ....*Eyes Of The Young*		$3		MTM 72094
8/6/88	82	2		8 Let's Be Bad Tonight ....*Honeymoon Mornin'*		$3		MTM 72110
	★344★			**ROGERS, Roy** **'47**				
				Born Leonard Franklin Slye on 11/5/11 in Cincinnati. Died on 7/6/98 (age 86). Popular "singing cowboy" who starred in several movies. Formed the Pioneer Trio, in 1934 with Bob Nolan and Tim Spencer, which evolved into the **Sons Of The Pioneers**; group appeared in several movies. Went solo in 1937; briefly known as "Dick Weston." By 1938, known as "Roy Rogers." Married actress Dale Evans on 12/31/47; stars of *The Roy Rogers Show* TV show (1951-57) and *The Roy Rogers & Dale Evans Show* in 1962. Elected to the Country Music Hall of Fame in 1988.				
				1)*My Chickashay Gal* 2)*Blue Shadows On The Trail* 3)*A Little White Cross On The Hill*				
7/6/46	7	1		1 A Little White Cross On The Hill *I Can't Go On This Way*		$25		RCA Victor 20-1872
3/15/47	4	1		2 My Chickashay Gal *I Never Had A Chance*		$25		RCA Victor 20-2124
6/12/48	6	14		3 Blue Shadows On The Trail/ S:6 / J:7				
6/12/48	13	4		4 (There'll Never Be Another) Pecos Bill S:13		$25		RCA Victor 20-2780
				ROY ROGERS and The Sons Of The Pioneers (above 2)				
				45 rpm: 48-0035; above 2 from the movie *Melody Time* starring Rogers;				
2/4/50	8	1		5 Stampede A:8 *Church Music*		$30		RCA Victor 48-0161
				The Sons Of The Pioneers (backing vocals); 78 rpm: 21-0154				
9/26/70	35	10		6 Money Can't Buy Love ....*You And Me Against The World*		$7		Capitol 2895
1/30/71	12	11		7 Lovenworth ....*Vision At The Peace Table*		$7		Capitol 3016
6/26/71	47	11		8 Happy Anniversary ....*If I Ever Get That Close Again*		$7		Capitol 3117
2/26/72	73	4		9 These Are The Good Old Days ....*Pass It On*		$7		Capitol 3263
12/21/74+	15	13		10 Hoppy, Gene And Me ....*Good News, Bad News* [N]	65	$5		20th Century 2154
				tribute to Hopalong Cassidy, Gene Autry and Roy Rogers				
8/23/80	80	4		11 Ride Concrete Cowboy, Ride ....*Deliverance Of The Wildwood Flower*		$5		MCA 41294
				ROY ROGERS And The Sons Of The Pioneers				
				from the movie *Smokey & The Bandit II* starring **Burt Reynolds**				
11/2/91	42	10		12 Hold On Partner ....*Alive And Kickin'*		$3		RCA 62061
				ROY ROGERS & CLINT BLACK				
				ROGERS, Smokey **'49**				
				Born on 3/23/27 in Texas. Singer/songwriter/banjo player.				
1/1/49	8	4		A Little Bird Told Me J:8 *Baby Me, Baby*		$15		Capitol 15326
				#1 Pop hit for Evelyn Knight in 1949				
				ROHRS, Donnie **'81**				
				Born in 1946 in Covina, California. Singer/guitarist/pianist.				
12/16/78	95	3		1 Hey Baby		$7		Ad-Korp 1258
				#1 Pop hit for Bruce Channel in 1962				
5/2/81	85	6		2 Waltzes And Western Swing ....*Love Me Baby Tonight*		$7		Pacific Chall. 4504
				ROLAND, Adrian **'60**				
				Born in Lamarque, Texas. Died on 7/1/66.				
9/19/60	19	4		Imitation Of Love ....*It Takes More Than A While*		$20		Allstar 7207

DEBUT	PEAK	WKS	Gold	A-side (Chart Hit) .... B-side	Pop	$	Pic	Label & Number

RONE, Roger   '89

| 8/26/89 | 83 | 3 | | Holdin' On To Nothin' .... *Here I Stand* | | $6 | | True 98 |

RONICK, Holly   '89

| 11/4/89 | 86 | 2 | | Ain't No One Like Me In Tennessee .... | | $6 | ■ | Happy Man 822 |

RONSTADT, Linda ★166★   '75

Born on 7/15/46 in Tucson, Arizona. Singer/actress. Charted 35 pop hits from 1967-90. Acted in the movie *Pirates Of Penzance*. Also see Hoyt Axton.

1)When Will I Be Loved 2)To Know Him Is To Love Him 3)Blue Bayou 4)I Can't Help It 5)Telling Me Lies

3/2/74	20	12		1 Silver Threads And Golden Needles .... *Don't Cry Now*	67	$5		Asylum 11032
12/21/74+	2[1]	17		2 I Can't Help It (If I'm Still In Love With You) *You're No Good (Pop #1)*		$5		Capitol 3990
4/19/75	❶[1]	15		3 When Will I Be Loved/	2[2]			
				#8 Pop hit for The Everly Brothers in 1960				
9/13/75	54	7		4 It Doesn't Matter Anymore..	47	$5		Capitol 4050
				#13 Pop hit for Buddy Holly in 1959				
9/13/75	5	15		5 Love Is A Rose *Heat Wave (Pop #5)*	63	$5		Asylum 45282
1/3/76	11	12		6 Tracks Of My Tears/	25			
				#16 Pop hit for The Miracles in 1965				
1/3/76	12	12		7 The Sweetest Gift		$6		Asylum 45295
				LINDA RONSTADT AND EMMYLOU HARRIS				
9/4/76	27	11		8 That'll Be The Day.. *Try Me Again*	11	$5		Asylum 45340
				#1 Pop hit for Buddy Holly in 1957				
12/18/76+	6	15		9 Crazy *Someone To Lay Down Beside Me (Pop #42)*		$5		Asylum 45361
9/17/77	2[2]	19	▲	10 Blue Bayou *Old Paint*	3	$5		Asylum 45431
				#29 Pop hit for Roy Orbison in 1963				
11/12/77	81	6		11 It's So Easy .... *Lo Siento Mi Vida*	5	$5		Asylum 45438
				written by Buddy Holly				
2/18/78	46	9		12 Poor Poor Pitiful Me.................................. *Simple Man, Simple Dream*	31	$5		Asylum 45462
5/13/78	8	13		13 I Never Will Marry *Tumbling Dice (Pop #32)*		$5		Asylum 45479
9/2/78	41	8		14 Back In The U.S.A.............................. *White Rhythm & Blues*	16	$5	■	Asylum 45519
				#37 Pop hit for Chuck Berry in 1959				
12/2/78	85	5		15 Ooh Baby Baby .... *Blowing Away*	7	$5		Asylum 45546
				#16 Pop hit for The Miracles in 1965				
3/10/79	59	6		16 Love Me Tender.................................. *Just One Look (Pop #44)*		$5		Asylum 46011
3/1/80	42	8		17 Rambler Gambler .... *How Do I Make You (Pop #10)*		$4	■	Asylum 46602
10/16/82	27	12		18 Sometimes You Just Can't Win .... *Get Closer (Pop #29)*		$4	■	Asylum 69948
				LINDA RONSTADT AND JOHN DAVID SOUTHER				
1/29/83	84	3		19 I Knew You When.............................. *Talk To Me Of Mendocino*	37	$4	■	Asylum 69853
				DOLLY PARTON, LINDA RONSTADT, EMMYLOU HARRIS:				
2/21/87	❶[1]	19		20 To Know Him Is To Love Him S:❶[1] / A:❶[1] *Farther Along*		$3	■	Warner 28492
				#1 Pop hit for The Teddy Bears in 1958				
5/30/87	3	18		21 Telling Me Lies S:10 *Rosewood Casket*		$3		Warner 28371
9/26/87	5	22		22 Those Memories Of You S:10 *My Dear Companion*		$3	■	Warner 28248
3/26/88	6	18		23 Wildflowers S:13 *Hobo's Meditation*		$3		Warner 27970
4/29/95	61	9		24 Walk On.. *The Waiting*		$3	▌	Elektra 64427
				LINDA RONSTADT				

ROOFTOP SINGERS, The   '63

Folk trio from New York City: Erik Darling, Bill Svanoe and Lynne Taylor (d: 1982).

| 2/23/63 | 23 | 4 | ● | Walk Right In .... *Cool Water* | ❶[2] | $12 | ☐ | Vanguard 35017 |

ROSE, Fred   '45

Born on 8/24/1897 in Evansville, Indiana. Died of a heart attack on 12/1/54 (age 57). Singer/prolific songwriter. Formed Acuff-Rose music publishing company with Roy Acuff in 1942; they also formed the Hickory record label in 1953. Elected to the Country Music Hall of Fame in 1961. Recorded as The Rambling Rogue.

| 10/27/45 | 5 | 1 | | Tender Hearted Sue   *You're Only In My Arms (To Cry On My Shoulder)* | | $20 | | Okeh 6747 |
| | | | | **THE RAMBLING ROGUE** | | | | |

ROSE, Pam   '80

Born Pamela Rose Thacker in Chattanooga; raised in Eau Gallie, Florida. Member of Calamity Jane.

7/23/77	83	5		1 Midnight Flight .... *Sing, Feelin', Sing*		$5		Capitol 4440
11/19/77	93	3		2 Runaway Heart .... *Break Down The Walls*		$5		Capitol 4491
1/5/80	52	7		3 It's Not Supposed To Be That Way .... *We're Gonna Try It Tonight*		$4		Epic 50819
				Willie Nelson (guest vocal)				
4/19/80	60	6		4 I'm Not Through Loving You Yet............ *When Love's In Your Heart, It's In Your Eyes*		$4		Epic 50861

ROSE, Richard and Gary   '88

| 2/13/88 | 81 | 3 | | Younger Man, Older Woman.................................. *Until You're Mine* | | $3 | | Capitol 44118 |

ROSS, Charlie   '76

Born in Greenville, Mississippi. Worked as a DJ.

2/28/76	13	12		1 Without Your Love (Mr. Jordan)........................ *Sneaking Round Corners*	42	$6		Big Tree 16056
6/5/82	33	13		2 The High Cost Of Loving.................................. *She Sure Got Away With My Heart*		$5		Town House 1057
9/18/82	45	9		3 Are We In Love (Or Am I) .... *Shoot First, Ask Questions Later*		$5		Town House 1061

				ROSS, Charlie — Cont'd				
1/8/83	70	5		4 The Name Of The Game Is Cheating .... *Somebody Loves You*		$5		Town House 1063
				ROSS, Jeris '75				
				Female singer from East Alton, Illinois.				
3/11/72	75	2		1 Brand New Key .... *Baby's Thinking Leaving*		$6		Cartwheel 206
				#1 Pop hit for Melanie in 1971				
6/24/72	58	12		2 Old Fashioned Love Song .... *I Gotta Go To Memphis*		$6		Cartwheel 214
				#4 Pop hit for Three Dog Night in 1971				
12/22/73+	58	7		3 Moontan.. *People Just Like You*		$5		ABC 11397
4/26/75	17	14		4 Pictures On Paper .... *Won't You Meet Me At The Church*		$5		ABC 12064
10/11/75	66	8		5 I'd Rather Be Picked Up Here (Than Be Put Down At Home) .... *Sing A Love Song To Your Baby*		$5		ABC/Dot 17573
10/29/77	77	6		6 I Think I'll Say Goodbye .... *Rock Me*		$5		Gazelle 431
9/15/79	94	4		7 Little Bit More... *Ease Me To The Ground*		$5		Door Knob 108
				#11 Pop hit for Dr. Hook in 1976				
1/26/80	75	5		8 You Win Again .... *Rock Me*		$5		Door Knob 117
				#22 Pop hit for Fats Domino in 1962				
				ROSS, Roy — see FOLEY, Red				
				ROVERS, The '81				
				Group from Alberta, Canada: brothers Will and George Millar, their cousin Joe Millar, Jimmy Ferguson and Wilcil McDowell.				
2/28/81	45	11		1 Wasn't That A Party.............................*Matchstalk Men And Matchstalk Cats And Dogs*	37	$4		Epic 51007
3/13/82	77	4		2 Pain In My Past .... *Daddies (Bobby's Song)*		$4		Epic 02728
				ROWE, Stacey '79				
6/30/79	96	2		I Couldn't Live Without Your Love...		$7		Sabre 4510
				ROWELL, Ernie '81				
7/24/71	74	2		1 Going Back To Louisiana .... *This Bottle Hides The Weakness In Me*		$7		Prize 08
9/29/79	91	4		2 I'm Leavin' You Alone .... *He's The One*		$6		Grass 05
5/9/81	59	6		3 Music In The Mountains .... *He's The One*		$6		Grass 07
10/3/87	86	3		4 You Left My Heart For Broke		$6		Revolver 016
				ROWLAND, Dave — see DAVE & SUGAR				
				ROY, Bobbie '72				
				Born Barbara Elaine Roy on 7/27/53 in Landstuhl, Germany, where her father was in the Army. Moved to Elkins, West Virginia, in 1960.				
6/3/72	32	9		1 One Woman's Trash (Another Woman's Treasure) .... *Due To A Heartache*		$6		Capitol 3301
9/23/72	58	8		2 Leavin' On Your Mind .... *Candle In The Wind*		$6		Capitol 3428
12/16/72+	62	5		3 I Like Everything About Loving You................................ *I Wanted So To Say It*		$6		Capitol 3477
1/27/73	51	5		4 I Am Woman.. *Till I Get It Right*		$6		Capitol 3513
				#1 Pop hit for Helen Reddy in 1972				
	★237★			**ROYAL, Billy Joe** '89				
				Born on 4/3/42 in Valdosta, Georgia; raised in Marietta, Georgia. Singer/songwriter/guitarist/pianist/drummer. Charted 9 pop hits from 1965-78.				
				1)Tell It Like It Is 2)Till I Can't Take It Anymore 3)Love Has No Right				
10/26/85+	10	22		1 Burned Like A Rocket S:6 / A:11 *Lonely Loving You*		$3		Atlantic Amer. 99599
5/3/86	41	16		2 Boardwalk Angel .... S:25 *Out Of Sight And On My Mind*		$3		Atlantic Amer. 99555
8/23/86	14	24		3 I Miss You Already .... S:9 / A:17 *Another Endless Night*		$3		Atlantic Amer. 99519
2/7/87	11	26		4 Old Bridges Burn Slow .... S:❶[1] / A:11 *We've Both Got A Lot To Learn*		$3	■	Atlantic Amer. 99485
6/27/87	23	15		5 Members Only .... S:21 *Funny Face*		$3		Mercury 888680
				DONNA FARGO AND BILLY JOE ROYAL				
10/17/87+	5	23		6 I'll Pin A Note On Your Pillow S:❶[2] *A Place For The Heartache*		$3	■	Atlantic Amer. 99404
3/12/88	10	22		7 Out Of Sight And On My Mind S:❶[1] *She Don't Cry Like She Used To*		$3	■	Atlantic Amer. 99364
8/27/88	17	17		8 It Keeps Right On Hurtin' S:❶[1] *Let It Rain*		$3	■	Atlantic Amer. 99295
				#3 Pop hit for Johnny Tillotson in 1962				
2/4/89	2[2]	17		9 Tell It Like It Is *I Was Losing You*		$3	■	Atlantic Amer. 99242
				#2 Pop hit for Aaron Neville in 1967				
5/20/89	4	24		10 Love Has No Right *Cross My Heart And Hope To Try*		$3	■	Atlantic Amer. 99217
9/30/89+	2[1]	26		11 Till I Can't Take It Anymore *He Don't Know*		$3		Atlantic 88815
5/12/90	17	21		12 Searchin' For Some Kind Of Clue .... *This Too Shall Pass*		$3	❙	Atlantic 87933
9/15/90	33	20		13 Ring Where A Ring Used To Be .... *We Need To Walk*		$3	❙	Atlantic 87867
1/26/91	29	14		14 If The Jukebox Took Teardrops .... *How Could You Leave Me*		$3	❙	Atlantic 87770
3/21/92	51	8		15 I'm Okay (And Gettin' Better)		$3		album cut
				from the album *Billy Joe Royal* on Atlantic 82327				
				RUCKER, Dwight — see MALCHAK, Tim				
				RUE, Arnie '79				
				Born in Massachusetts; raised in California.				
5/5/79	56	6		1 Spare A Little Lovin' (On A Fool) .... *To Each His Own*		$5		NSD 19
11/17/79	74	4		2 Rodle-Odeo-Home .... *Yesterday's Dreams*		$5		NSD 32
				RUSHING, Jim '81				
				Born in Lubbock, Texas. Singer/songwriter.				
9/27/80	81	2		1 Dixie Dirt.. *Two Hearts Don't Always Make A Pair*		$5		Ovation 1153
12/27/80+	56	8		2 I've Loved Enough To Know .... *Two Hearts Don't Always Make A Pair*		$5		Ovation 1161

DEBUT	PEAK	WKS		A-side .... B-side	Pop	$	Pic	Label & Number
				RUSSELL, Bobby **'71**				
				Born on 4/19/41 in Nashville. Died of a heart attack on 11/19/92 (age 51). Singer/prolific songwriter. Formerly married to **Vicki Lawrence**.				
11/9/68	64	8		1 1432 Franklin Pike Circle Hero .... *Let's Talk About Them*	36	$7		Elf 90,020
3/1/69	66	3		2 Carlie .... *Ain't Society Great?*	115	$7		Elf 90,023
8/16/69	34	9		3 Better Homes And Gardens .... *Summer Sweet*		$7		Elf 90,031
7/10/71	24	13		4 Saturday Morning Confusion *Little Ole Song About Love* [N]	28	$6		United Artists 50788
8/18/73	93	3		5 Mid American Manufacturing Tycoon .... *Ships In The Night*		$5		Columbia 45901
				RUSSELL, Clifford **'83**				
				Born in Knoxville, Tennessee.				
2/12/83	97	2		She Feels Like A New Man Tonight .... *Sometimes When We Touch*		$7	■	Sugartree 0509
				RUSSELL, Jimmy **'76**				
12/18/76	99	4		You've Got To Move Two Mountains .... *It's Been So Long Darling*		$6		Charta 103
				#20 Pop hit for Marv Johnson in 1960				
	★216★			**RUSSELL, Johnny** **'73**				
				Born on 1/23/40 in Moorhead, Mississippi; raised in Fresno, California. Singer/songwriter/guitarist. Joined the *Grand Ole Opry* in 1985. Formerly married to **Beverly Heckel**.				
				1)Rednecks, White Socks And Blue Ribbon Beer 2)Catfish John 3)Hello I Love You 4)The Baptism Of Jesse Taylor 5)That's How My Baby Builds A Fire				
8/21/71	64	3		1 Mr. And Mrs. Untrue .... *I'm Stayin'*		$6		RCA Victor 1000
12/11/71+	57	9		2 What A Price .... *Listening To The Rain*		$6		RCA Victor 0570
				#22 Pop hit for **Fats Domino** in 1961				
4/1/72	59	7		3 Mr. Fiddle Man .... *Crying Takes More Practice Everyday*		$6		RCA Victor 0665
7/1/72	36	12		4 Rain Falling On Me .... *I'll Cry To That*		$6		RCA Victor 0729
11/11/72+	12	15		5 Catfish John .... *Promises Of Your Love*		$6		RCA Victor 0810
3/24/73	31	10		6 Chained .... *(Drinkin' A Beer) And Singing A Country Song*		$6		RCA Victor 0908
8/4/73	4	19		7 Rednecks, White Socks And Blue Ribbon Beer *She's A Natural Woman*		$6		RCA Victor 0021
11/10/73+	14	13		8 The Baptism Of Jesse Taylor .... *Making Plans*		$6		RCA Victor 0165
4/13/74	39	10		9 She's In Love With A Rodeo Man .... *Someday I'll Sober Up*		$6		RCA Victor 0248
9/14/74	38	10		10 She Burn't The Little Roadside Tavern Down .... *It Sure Seemed Right*		$5		RCA Victor 10038
12/21/74+	23	11		11 That's How My Baby Builds A Fire .... *Act Naturally*		$5		RCA Victor 10135
4/26/75	13	17		12 Hello I Love You .... *You Ain't Got No Class*		$5		RCA Victor 10258
10/11/75	45	10		13 Our Marriage Was A Failure .... *Catfish John*		$5		RCA Victor 10403
2/21/76	57	9		14 I'm A Trucker .... *Your Fool*		$5		RCA Victor 10563
5/22/76	45	8		15 This Man And Woman Thing .... *Over Georgia*		$5		RCA Victor 10667
12/25/76+	32	10		16 The Son Of Hickory Holler's Tramp/		$5		RCA Victor 10853
				#40 Pop hit for O.C. Smith in 1968				
		10		17 I Wonder How She's Doing Now		$5		RCA 10853
6/25/77	91	3		18 Obscene Phone Call .... *If I Want To Get It Right*		$5		RCA 10984
				Beverly Heckel (female vocal)				
12/10/77+	64	9		19 Leona .... *Your Fool*		$5		RCA 11160
5/13/78	24	12		20 You'll Be Back (Every Night In My Dreams) .... *Is Anybody Leaving San Antone*		$5		Polydor 14475
11/25/78+	29	12		21 How Deep In Love Am I? .... *Shall We Gather At The Ridge*		$4		Mercury 55045
5/19/79	57	6		22 I Might Be Awhile In New Orleans .... *Make Up My Mind*		$4		Mercury 55060
11/17/79	56	7		23 Ain't No Way To Make A Bad Love Grow .... *Keep The Change*		$4		Mercury 57008
3/15/80	57	6		24 While The Choir Sang The Hymn (I Thought Of Her) .... *Falsely Accused*		$4		Mercury 57016
6/21/80	59	7		25 We're Back In Love Again .... *Love Makes A Fool Of Us All*		$4		Mercury 57026
12/13/80+	57	9		26 Song Of The South .... *I'm Gettin' Holes In My Boots (From Climbing The Walls)*		$4		Mercury 57038
4/18/81	49	9		27 Here's To The Horses .... *Take Me To Your Heart*		$4		Mercury 57050
7/25/87	72	4		28 Butterbeans .... *Stone Country*		$4		16th Avenue 70401
				JOHNNY RUSSELL & LITTLE DAVID WILKINS				
				RUSSELL, Leon **'79**				
				Born on 4/2/41 in Lawton, Oklahoma. Rock singer/songwriter/multi-instrumentalist sessionman. Also recorded as **Hank Wilson**.				
9/29/73	57	11		1 Roll In My Sweet Baby's Arms .... *I'm So Lonesome I Could Cry (Pop flip)*	78	$6		Shelter 7336
1/12/74	68	8		2 A Six Pack To Go .... *Uncle Pen*		$6		Shelter 7338
				HANK WILSON (above 2)				
7/7/79	❶¹	13		3 Heartbreak Hotel *Sioux City Sue*		$5		Columbia 11023
				WILLIE NELSON AND LEON RUSSELL				
7/28/84	63	12		4 Good Time Charlie's Got The Blues .... *Ain't No Love In The City*		$4		Paradise 628
10/27/84	91	2		5 Wabash Cannonball .... *Tennessee Waltz*		$4		Paradise 629
				WILLIE NELSON & HANK WILSON				
				RUSTY & DOUG — see KERSHAW, Doug				
				RUUD, Nancy **'81**				
				Singer from Montana.				
7/12/80	88	3		1 A Good Love Is Like A Good Song		$6		Calico 16425
10/18/80	90	3		2 Always, Sometimes, Never .... *Am I Too Late*		$6		Calico 16493
4/4/81	87	2		3 I'm Gonna Hang Up This Heartache		$6		C&R 101
6/20/81	83	2		4 Blue As The Blue In Your Eyes		$6		C&R 102
				RYAN, Charlie **'60**				
				Born on 12/19/15 in Graceville, Minnesota; raised in Montana.				
9/5/60	14	6		Hot Rod Lincoln .... *Thru The Mill* [N-S]	33	$20		4 Star 1733
				CHARLIE RYAN and The Timberline Riders				
				first released in 1955 on Souvenir 101 ($40)				

RYAN, Jamey '67
Female singer from Texas. Regular on TV's *Hee-Haw*.

DEBUT	PEAK	WKS		A-side / B-side	Pop	$	Pic	Label & Number
8/19/67	62	3		1 You're Lookin' For A Plaything.................................*Growin' Pains*		$8		Columbia 44169
5/23/70	75	2		2 Holy Cow.................................*All A Woman Asks*		$8		Show Biz 232
				#23 Pop hit for Lee Dorsey in 1966				
8/11/73	88	2		3 Keep On Loving Me.................................*You Just Moved A Mountain*		$6		Atlantic 4001

RYAN, Tim '90
Born Tim Ryan Roullier on 2/4/64 in Montana. Singer/songwriter/guitarist.

8/4/90	42	17		1 Dance In Circles.................................*Honky Tonk Highway*		$3	▌	Epic 73372
12/22/90+	69	6		2 Breakin' All The Way.................................*A Little Love Won't Hurt A Thing*		$3	▌	Epic 73578
9/21/91	68	3		3 Seventh Direction.................................*No More Sad Songs*		$3		Epic 73959
1/18/92	65	4		4 I Will Love You Anyhow.................................*Heartache Goin' Downtown Tonight*		$3		Epic 74124
1/23/93	71	4		5 Idle Hands.................................*One Life To Live*		$3		BNA 62413

RYAN, Wesley '81

7/25/81	82	4		Nothin' To Do But Just Lie.................................*Take Good Care Of My Baby*		$5		NSD 93

RYDER, Nickie — see ROGERS, Kenny

★222★ RYLES, John Wesley '77
Born on 12/2/50 in Bastrop, Louisiana. Singer/songwriter/guitarist.
1)Once In A Lifetime Thing 2)Kay 3)Shine On Me 4)Liberated Woman 5)I've Just Been Wasting My Time

JOHN WESLEY RYLES I:

12/7/68+	9	17		1 Kay.................................*Come On Home*	83	$7		Columbia 44682
				also see #12 below				
5/17/69	55	8		2 Heaven Below.................................*A Mighty Fortress Is Our Love*		$7		Columbia 44819
12/13/69+	57	7		3 The Weakest Kind Of Man.................................*We'll Try A Little Bit Harder*		$7		Columbia 45018
5/2/70	17	10		4 I've Just Been Wasting My Time.................................*The House On The Hill*		$7		Columbia 45119
11/20/71	39	10		5 Reconsider Me.................................*Mobile*		$7		Plantation 81
				JOHN WESLEY RYLES:				
1/24/76	83	7		6 Tell It Like It Is.................................*Run Right Back*		$7		Music Mill 214
				#2 Pop hit for **Aaron Neville** in 1967				
7/10/76	72	6		7 When A Man Loves A Woman.................................*I'm Gonna Make It Without You*		$7		Music Mill 240
				#1 Pop hit for Percy Sledge in 1966				
3/26/77	18	17		8 Fool.................................*I Fought The Law*		$5		ABC/Dot 17679
8/13/77	5	16		9 Once In A Lifetime Thing.................................*Wild Rose Of Virginia*		$5		ABC/Dot 17698
12/24/77+	13	12		10 Shine On Me (The Sun Still Shines When It Rains).................................*Warming Love*		$5		ABC/Dot 17733
4/15/78	63	6		11 Easy.................................*Making Love Don't Make It Love*		$5		ABC 12348
7/15/78	50	7		12 Kay.................................*Next Time* [R]		$5		ABC 12375
				new version of #1 above				
10/7/78	45	7		13 Someday You Will.................................*That All Over Feeling*		$5		ABC 12410
12/23/78+	33	11		14 Love Ain't Made For Fools.................................*It's Raining Outside Your Door*		$5		ABC 12432
6/2/79	14	14		15 Liberated Woman.................................*She's On My Mind*		$5		MCA 41033
10/13/79	20	12		16 You Are Always On My Mind.................................*My Angel Got Her Wings Today*		$5		MCA 41124
2/23/80	24	10		17 Perfect Strangers.................................*Nothing But Love*		$4		MCA 41184
7/19/80	52	8		18 May I Borrow Some Sugar From You.................................*Let The Night Begin*		$4		MCA 41278
11/8/80	54	10		19 Cheater's Trap.................................*Two Beds - Too Bad*		$4		MCA 51033
4/4/81	80	3		20 Somewhere To Come When It Rains.................................*Your Old Love Letters*		$4		MCA 51080
7/18/81	78	3		21 Mathilda.................................*I'm Not That Crazy Anymore*		$4		MCA 51128
				#47 Pop hit for Cookie & His Cupcakes in 1959				
6/26/82	76	4		22 We've Got To Start Meeting Like This....................................		$5		Primero 1004
12/4/82	80	3		23 Just Once.................................*Hideaway*		$5		Primero 1016
				#17 Pop hit for Quincy Jones in 1981				
8/25/84	78	4		24 She Took It Too Well....................................		$4		16th Avenue 500
5/9/87	36	15		25 Midnight Blue.................................*Starting Over Again*		$4		Warner 28377
12/5/87+	20	16		26 Louisiana Rain.................................*Strong Heart*		$4		Warner 28228
6/4/88	53	7		27 Nobody Knows.................................*Freedom Feels Like Loneliness Today*		$4		Warner 27869

S

SADLER, Sammy '89
Born 8/23/67 in Memphis.

1/7/89	70	4		1 Tell It Like It Is....................................		$5		Evergreen 1088
				#2 Pop hit for **Aaron Neville** in 1967				
7/1/89	89	3		2 You Made It Easy....................................		$5		Evergreen 1093
1/13/90	86	1		3 Once In A Lifetime Thing....................................		$5		Evergreen 1106

SADLER, SSgt Barry '66
Born on 11/1/40 in Carlsbad, New Mexico. Died of heart failure on 11/5/89 (age 49). Staff Sergeant of U.S. Army Special Forces (aka Green Berets). Served in Vietnam until leg injury.

2/19/66	2²	14	●	1 The Ballad Of The Green Berets.................................*Letter From Vietnam*	❶⁵	$7	■	RCA Victor 8739
5/28/66	46	4		2 The "A" Team.................................*An Empty Glass*	28	$7	■	RCA Victor 8804

DEBUT	PEAK	WKS	A-side / notes	Pop	$	Label & Number

SAHM, Doug   '76
Born on 11/6/41 in San Antonio, Texas. Singer/songwriter/guitarist. Formed the Sir Douglas Quintet in 1965 (charted 4 pop hits from 1965-69). Formed a new Texas Tornados group with all-star lineup in 1990.

| 10/16/76 | 100 | 1 | Cowboy Peyton Place..........................*I Love The Way You Love (The Way I Love You)* | | $6 | ABC/Dot 17656 |

DOUG SAHM & THE TEXAS TORNADOS

ST. JOHN, Tommy   '83
Born on 3/23/62 in Oak Ridge, Tennessee.

1/8/83	55	9	1 The Light Of My Life (Has Gone Out Tonight)...........*Waitin' In Your Welfare Line*		$4	RCA 13405
4/16/83	78	4	2 Where'd Ya Stay Last Night ....*She Can't Make Me What I Ain't*		$4	RCA 13475
7/23/83	86	2	3 Stars On The Water ....*Wallflower*		$4	RCA 13561

ST. MARIE, Susan   '77
Niece of Tommy Overstreet.

| 11/3/73 | 91 | 4 | 1 All Or Nothing With Me ....*Lonely After You* | | $6 | Cinnamon 768 |
| 11/19/77 | 91 | 7 | 2 It's The Love In You ....*That's The Way Love Should Be* | | $6 | Pinnacle 101 |

SAMI JO   '74
Born Sami Jo Cole in Batesville, Arkansas. Female singer.

2/9/74	52	12	1 Tell Me A Lie ....*Stay Where You Are*	21	$5	MGM South 7029
7/6/74	61	9	2 It Could Have Been Me ....*Look At Us*	46	$5	MGM South 7034
1/4/75	62	9	3 I'll Believe Anything You Say ....*Lovely Daughter*		$5	MGM 14773
5/15/76	91	4	4 God Loves Us (When We All Sing Together) ....*Partly Cloudy*		$5	Polydor 14315
9/4/76	67	6	5 Take Me To Heaven ....*Let Me Laugh (To Keep From Crying)*		$5	Polydor 14341

SAMI JO COLE:

| 5/2/81 | 76 | 4 | 6 One Love Over Easy ....*You've Got My Heart In Your Hands* | | $4 | Elektra 47127 |
| 10/31/81 | 82 | 3 | 7 I Can't Help Myself (Here Comes The Feeling) ....*Carelessly* | | $4 | Elektra 47211 |

SAMONE, Stephany   '80
Born in Pleasant Grove, Texas.

| 6/7/80 | 68 | 6 | 1 Do That To Me One More Time ....*Gotta Make You Mine* | | $5 | MDJ 1004 |

#1 Pop hit for **Captain & Tennille** in 1980

| 11/22/80 | 65 | 7 | 2 Somebody's Gotta Do The Losing ....*One Day At A Time* | | $5 | MDJ 1006 |

SAMPLES, Junior   '67
Born Alvin Samples on 8/10/26 in Cumming, Georgia. Died of a heart attack on 11/13/83 (age 57). Comedian. Regular on TV's *Hee Haw*.

| 7/22/67 | 52 | 4 | World's Biggest Whopper ....*It Happened To Junior* [S] | | $10 | Chart 1460 |

Jim Morrison (interviewer)

SANDERS, Ben   '88
Singer from Dallas. Known as "The 5th Ave. Country Boy."

| 11/19/88 | 100 | 1 | I'm Leavin' You....................................*Good Advice* | | $6 | Luv 129 |

BEN SANDERS (The 5th Ave. Country Boy)

SANDERS, Debbie   '89

| 4/15/89 | 91 | 2 | No Time At All ....| | $6 | K-Ark 1050 |

SANDERS, Mack   '78
Born in Wichita, Kansas. Popular radio and TV host. Married **Sherry Bryce**; together they owned the Pilot label.

| 1/21/78 | 89 | 3 | Sweet Country Girl ....*Tonkin The Blues* | | $7 | Pilot 45101 |

★379★ SANDERS, Ray   '71
Born Raymon Sanders on 10/1/35 in St. John, Kentucky. Singer/songwriter/guitarist/actor.
1)All I Ever Need Is You 2)A World So Full Of Love 3)Lonelyville

10/31/60	18	11	1 A World So Full Of Love ....*A Little Bitty Tear*		$10	Liberty 55267
4/3/61	20	8	2 Lonelyville ....*I Haven't Gone Far Enough Yet*		$10	Liberty 55304
5/24/69	22	13	3 Beer Drinkin' Music ....*Gotta Find A Way*		$7	Imperial 66366
10/25/69	73	2	4 Three Tears (For The Sad, Hurt, And Blue) ....*Lucille*		$7	Imperial 66408
8/1/70	36	11	5 Blame It On Rosey ....*Waikiki Sand*		$6	United Artists 50689
12/26/70+	38	9	6 Judy....................................*The Wild Side Of Life*		$6	United Artists 50732
5/29/71	56	9	7 Walk All Over Georgia ....*Tonight She'll Make Me Happy*		$6	United Artists 50774
10/2/71	18	16	8 All I Ever Need Is You ....*Before I Met You*		$6	United Artists 50827

#7 Pop hit for **Sonny & Cher** in 1971

5/20/72	69	5	9 A Rose By Any Other Name (Is Still A Rose)....................*We've Gotta Learn To Help Each Other*		$6	United Artists 50886
9/9/72	67	4	10 Lucius Grinder ....*You Let My Love Live*		$6	United Artists 50933
5/5/73	75	2	11 Another Way To Say Goodbye		$6	United Artists 201
8/6/77	56	7	12 I Don't Want To Be Alone Tonight....................*The Power Of Positive Drinkin'*		$5	Republic 003
1/21/78	91	3	13 Tennessee ....*You Keep Right On Walking*		$5	Republic 013
11/29/80	93	2	14 You're A Pretty Lady, Lady ....*My Special Angel*		$6	Hillside 05

SANDERS, The   '89
Brother-and-sister team from Alaska: Dale and Vicki Sanders.

8/20/88	76	3	1 You Fit Right Into My Heart....................................		$5	Airborne 10001
2/11/89	64	7	2 Grandma's Old Wood Stove ....*Starry Lullaby*		$5	Airborne 10013
5/27/89	73	5	3 Who Needs You ....*Grandma's Old Wood Stove*		$5	Airborne 10019

SAN FERNANDO VALLEY MUSIC BAND   '79
Group from St. Paul, Minnesota. Led by Brian Murphy (vocals) and Jeff Stephens (guitar).

| 6/30/79 | 83 | 8 | Taken To The Line ....*Roll Your Own* | | $7 | C&S 017 |

SANTA FE — see CHAPMAN, Cee Cee

SARAH '88
Born in Pennsylvania; raised in California. Wife of H.L. Vogt, owner of Hub label.

DEBUT	PEAK	WKS		A-side / B-side		$		Label & Number
9/19/87	81	2		1 Lyin' Eyes ....*No Place To Run To*		$6		Hub 45
6/4/88	81	3		2 Chains ....*You Can't Hurt Me*		$6		Hub 46
				#17 Pop hit for The Cookies in 1962				
10/15/88	77	4		3 Don't Send Me Roses		$6		Hub 48

SARGEANTS, Gary '74
Born Gary Lusk in Miami. Singer/songwriter/drummer.

| 12/15/73+ | 55 | 11 | | 1 Ode To Jole Blon ....*Fair To Middlin', Lower Middle Class* | | $6 | | Mercury 73440 |
| 10/5/74 | 72 | 7 | | 2 Day Time Lover ....*Too Low To Get High* | | $6 | | Mercury 73608 |

SASKIA & SERGE '78
Husband-and-wife duo from Schagen, Holland. Saskia was born Trudy van den Berg on 4/23/47. Serge was born Ruud Schaap on 3/2/46. First recorded in 1966 as Trudy & Ruud. Changed name to Saskia & Serge in 1969.

| 1/7/78 | 88 | 5 | | Jambalaya (On The Bayou) ....*Don't Lay Your Head* | | $5 | | ABC/Hickory 54020 |

SAULS, Corkey '79
Male singer.

| 2/10/79 | 96 | 1 | | There Goes That Smile Again ....*Home Is Where I Hang My Dungarees* | | $7 | | Sand Mountain 822 |

SAVANNAH '84
Group from Brunswick, Georgia. Led by brothers Jay and Gene Willis.

10/29/83	87	5		1 Backstreet Ballet ....*It Don't Get No Better Than This*		$3		Mercury 814360
7/21/84	73	5		2 My Girl ....*Let's Get To It*		$3		Mercury 880037
				#1 Pop hit for the Temptations in 1965				

SAWMILL CREEK — see HAUSER, Bruce

SAWYER, Ray — see DR. HOOK

SAWYER BROWN ★76★ '93
Group from Nashville: Mark Miller (vocals, guitar), Bobby Randall (guitar), Gregg Hubbard (keyboards), Jim Scholten (bass) and Joe Smyth (drums). Duncan Cameron replaced Randall in 1992. CMA Award: 1985 Horizon Award.

1)Thank God For You 2)Some Girls Do 3)Step That Step 4)This Time 5)The Walk

DEBUT	PEAK	WKS		A-side / B-side	Pop	$	Pic	Label & Number
10/6/84+	16	22		1 Leona ....S:10 / A:19 *Staying Afloat*		$3		Capitol/Curb 5403
2/9/85	❶¹	21		2 Step That Step ....S:❶¹ / A:❶¹ *Feel Like Me*		$3	■	Capitol/Curb 5446
6/8/85	3	21		3 Used To Blue ....S:3 / A:3 *It's Hard To Keep A Good Love Down*		$3	■	Capitol/Curb 5477
10/5/85	5	20		4 Betty's Bein' Bad ....S:5 / A:5 *Lonely Girls*		$3	■	Capitol/Curb 5517
2/1/86	14	18		5 Heart Don't Fall Now ....S:14 / A:14 *That's A No No*		$3		Capitol/Curb 5548
5/10/86	15	16		6 Shakin' ....S:14 / A:16 *Billy Does Your Bulldog Bite*		$3		Capitol/Curb 5585
9/13/86	11	18		7 Out Goin' Cattin' ....A:11 / S:12 *The House Won't Rock*		$3	■	Capitol/Curb 5629
				SAWYER BROWN WITH "CAT" JOE BONSALL				
1/17/87	25	13		8 Gypsies On Parade ....S:21 / A:25 *Not Ready To Let You Go*		$3		Capitol/Curb 5677
5/23/87	58	9		9 Savin' The Honey For The Honeymoon ....*Lady Of The Evening*		$3		Capitol/Curb 44007
8/22/87	29	13		10 Somewhere In The Night ....S:29 *My Baby Drives A Buick*		$3	■	Capitol/Curb 44054
12/5/87+	2¹	22		11 This Missin' You Heart Of Mine ....S:13 *A Mighty Big Broom*		$3	■	Capitol/Curb 44108
4/23/88	27	13		12 Old Photographs ....*In This Town*		$3		Capitol/Curb 44143
10/1/88	11	17		13 My Baby's Gone ....S:20 *Blue Denim Soul*		$3		Capitol/Curb 44218
12/10/88	51	7		14 It Wasn't His Child ....*Falling Apart At The Heart* [X]		$3	■	Capitol/Curb 44282
2/25/89	50	9		15 Old Pair Of Shoes ....*What Am I Going To Tell My Heart*		$3		Capitol/Curb 44332
9/2/89	5	26		16 The Race Is On ....*Passin' Train*		$3		Capitol/Curb 44431
3/3/90	33	13		17 Did It For Love ....*The Heartland*		$3		Capitol/Curb 44483
5/26/90	33	13		18 Puttin' The Dark Back Into The Night				album cut
				from the album *The Boys Are Back* on Capitol/Curb 92358				
10/6/90	40	17		19 When Love Comes Callin'				album cut
				from the album *Greatest Hits* on Curb/Capitol 94259				
2/9/91	70	3		20 One Less Pony				album cut
4/6/91	68	6		21 Mama's Little Baby Loves Me				album cut
7/20/91	2¹	20		22 The Walk				album cut
				above 3 from the album *Buick* on Curb/Capitol 94260				
11/23/91+	3	20		23 The Dirt Road				album cut
3/7/92	❶¹	20		24 Some Girls Do				album cut
				above 2 from the album *The Dirt Road* on Curb/Capitol 95624				
8/8/92	5	20		25 Cafe On The Corner				album cut
11/28/92+	3	20		26 All These Years				album cut
3/27/93	5	20		27 Trouble On The Line				album cut
				above 3 from the album *Cafe On The Corner* on Curb 77574				
7/3/93	❶²	20		28 Thank God For You ....*Cafe On The Corner / (album snippets)*	117	$3	▮	Curb 76914
10/16/93+	4	20		29 The Boys And Me				album cut
2/19/94	40	11		30 Outskirts Of Town				album cut
6/25/94	5	20		31 Hard To Say				album cut
				above 3 from the album *Outskirts Of Town* on Curb 77626				
11/19/94+	2²	20		32 This Time ....*Hard To Say*		$3	▮	Curb 76930

SAWYER BROWN — Cont'd

DEBUT	PEAK	WKS	A-side	Pop	$	Pic	Label & Number
3/18/95	4	20	33 I Don't Believe In Goodbye S:25 Outskirts Of Town		$3	▌	Curb 76936
7/22/95	11	20	34 (This Thing Called) Wantin' And Havin' It All....... S:17 I Will Leave The Light On		$3	▌	Curb 76955
11/25/95+	19	20	35 'Round Here I Will Leave The Light On		$3	▌	Curb 76975
3/23/96	3	21	36 Treat Her Right/ S:10				
8/17/96	46	10	37 She's Gettin' There		$3	▌	Curb 76987
6/28/97	6	20	38 This Night Won't Last Forever/ S:9	109			
			#19 Pop hit for Michael Johnson in 1979				
3/1/97	13	20	39 Six Days On The Road S:8	117	$3	▌	Curb 73016

SAYER, Leo '78
Born Gerard Sayer on 5/21/48 in Shoreham, England. Charted 10 pop hits from 1975-81.

DEBUT	PEAK	WKS	A-side	Pop	$	Pic	Label & Number
10/21/78	63	6	Raining In My Heart No Looking Back	47	$4		Warner 8682
			#88 Pop hit for Buddy Holly in 1959				

SCARBURY, Joey '84
Born on 6/7/55 in Ontario, California. Best known for his 1981 pop hit "Theme From The Greatest American Hero (Believe It Or Not)."

DEBUT	PEAK	WKS	A-side	Pop	$	Pic	Label & Number
10/20/84	76	7	The River's Song Billy's Home		$4		RCA 13913
			from the movie The River Rat starring Tommy Lee Jones				

SCHAFFER, Norm '88

DEBUT	PEAK	WKS	A-side	Pop	$	Pic	Label & Number
3/12/88	77	4	Dallas Darlin'		$6		DSP 8712

SCHEREE '79

DEBUT	PEAK	WKS	A-side	Pop	$	Pic	Label & Number
8/25/79	94	3	I'm In Another World		$5		Compass 0027

SCHLITZ, Don '78
Born on 8/29/52 in Durham, North Carolina. Singer/prolific songwriter.

DEBUT	PEAK	WKS	A-side	Pop	$	Pic	Label & Number
5/6/78	65	7	1 The Gambler You Can't Take It With You		$4		Capitol 4576
3/31/79	91	3	2 You're The One Who Rewrote My Life Story I've Been Loved		$4		Capitol 4661

SCHMUCKER, Paul '78
Singer from Des Plaines, Illinois.

DEBUT	PEAK	WKS	A-side	Pop	$	Pic	Label & Number
11/25/78	69	6	1 The Giver You Never Game Me You		$6		Star-Fox 378
3/3/79	72	4	2 Makin' Love (Is A Beautiful Thing To Do) Country Folks		$6		Star-Fox 578
6/2/79	74	5	3 Steal Away Lonely But Never Alone		$6		Star-Fox 279
			Joni Dolson (backing vocal)				
8/11/79	83	5	4 Rainy Days And Rainbows It's Me Again		$6		Star-Fox 779
			all of above produced by Troy Shondell				

★209★ SCHNEIDER, John '84
Born on 4/8/59 in Mount Kisco, New York. Singer/songwriter/actor. Played "Bo Duke" on TV's The Dukes of Hazzard. Acted in several movies.
1)I've Been Around Enough To Know 2)You're The Last Thing I Needed Tonight 3)What's A Memory Like You

DEBUT	PEAK	WKS	A-side	Pop	$	Pic	Label & Number
6/13/81	4	17	1 It's Now Or Never Stay	14	$4	■	Scotti Brothers 02105
			adapted from the Italian song "O Sole Mio" of 1899; #1 Pop hit for Elvis Presley in 1960				
10/3/81	13	16	2 Them Good Ol' Boys Are Bad Still (Pop #69)		$4	■	Scotti Brothers 02489
5/22/82	32	9	3 Dreamin' Let Me Love You	45	$4		Scotti Brothers 02889
			#11 Pop hit for Johnny Burnette in 1960				
8/21/82	56	7	4 In The Driver's Seat They Got Nothin' On Him	72	$4		Scotti Brothers 03062
7/2/83	57	6	5 Are You Lonesome Tonight Hurts Like The Devil		$4		Scotti Brothers 03945
			JOHN SCHNEIDER AND JILL MICHAELS				
10/1/83	81	3	6 If You Believe Every Night With You		$4		Scotti Brothers 04064
7/28/84	●¹	28	7 I've Been Around Enough To Know S:●¹ / A:2 Trouble		$3		MCA 52407
1/5/85	●¹	23	8 Country Girls S:●¹ / A:●¹ The Time Of My Life		$3	■	MCA 52510
4/20/85	10	20	9 It's A Short Walk From Heaven To Hell S:7 / A:11 Honeymoon Wine		$3		MCA 52567
8/10/85	10	20	10 I'm Going To Leave You Tomorrow S:9 / A:11 I Don't Feel Much Like A Cowboy Tonight		$3	■	MCA 52648
12/14/85+	●¹	24	11 What's A Memory Like You (Doing In A Love Like This) S:●¹ / A:●¹ The One Who Got Away		$3	■	MCA 52723
5/10/86	●¹	20	12 You're The Last Thing I Needed Tonight S:●¹ / A:●¹ One More Night		$3		MCA 52827
8/30/86	5	23	13 At The Sound Of The Tone S:5 / A:5 This Time		$3		MCA 52901
12/20/86+	10	21	14 Take The Long Way Home A:10 / S:16 Better Class Of Losers		$3		MCA 52989
4/4/87	6	20	15 Love, You Ain't Seen The Last Of Me S:9 / A:24 Credit		$3		MCA 53069
7/18/87	32	15	16 When The Right One Comes Along The Gunfighter		$3		MCA 53144
11/7/87	59	6	17 If It Was Anyone But You So Good		$3		MCA 53199

SCHUTT, Dawn '89

DEBUT	PEAK	WKS	A-side	Pop	$	Pic	Label & Number
3/18/89	96	2	Take Time		$6		Master 10

SCHUYLER, Thom '83
Born on 6/10/52 in Bethlehem, Pennsylvania. Member of Schuyler, Knobloch & Overstreet.

DEBUT	PEAK	WKS	A-side	Pop	$	Pic	Label & Number
7/16/83	49	10	1 A Little At A Time The Softer I Try		$4		Capitol 5239
10/22/83	43	11	2 Brave Heart Two Way Street		$4		Capitol 5281

★386★ SCHUYLER, KNOBLOCH & OVERSTREET '87
Trio of prolific songwriters: Thom Schuyler, Fred Knobloch and Paul Overstreet. Also known as S-K-O. Overstreet replaced by Craig Bickhardt in 1987.

DEBUT	PEAK	WKS	A-side	Pop	$	Pic	Label & Number
7/12/86	9	29	1 You Can't Stop Love A:7 / S:11 Love Is The Hero		$3		MTM 72071
			S-K-O:				
12/6/86+	●¹	22	2 Baby's Got A New Baby S:●¹ / A:●¹ Bitter Pill To Swallow		$3		MTM 72081
4/18/87	16	14	3 American Me S:16 Country Heart		$3		MTM 72086

DEBUT	PEAK	WKS	Gold	A-side (Chart Hit)..B-side	Pop	$	Pic	Label & Number
				SCHUYLER, KNOBLOCH AND BICKHARDT:				
8/15/87	19	17	4	No Easy Horses .... *Too Good To Be Blue*		$3		MTM 72090
11/28/87+	24	18	5	This Old House .... S:18 *Living Without You*		$3		MTM 72100
4/23/88	8	22	6	Givers And Takers	S:14 *People Still Fall In Love*		$3		MTM 72099
10/22/88	44	11	7	Rigamarole .... *Major Repairs*		$3		MTM 72115
				SCOTT, Earl '62				
				Born Earl Batdorf on 9/9/36 in Youngstown, Ohio. Father of rock singer John Batdorf (of Batdorf & Rodney).				
11/3/62	8	10	1	Then A Tear Fell	*Save A Minute (Lose A Wife)*		$10		Kapp 854
7/27/63	23	7	2	Loose Lips..*Guess I'll Never Learn*		$8		Mercury 72110
1/4/64	30	1	3	Restless River .... *The Best I Can Give Her*		$8		Mercury 72190
1/23/65	30	14	4	I'll Wander Back To You ....*Kiss My Love Good Bye*		$7		Decca 31693
11/23/68	71	3	5	Too Rough On Me .... *Bottle In My Hand*		$7		Decca 32397
				SCOTT, Jack '74				
				Born Jack Scafone on 1/28/36 in Windsor, Ontario, Canada. Singer/songwriter/guitarist. Charted 19 pop hits from 1958-61.				
7/6/74	92	4		You're Just Gettin' Better ....*As You Take A Walk Through My Mind*		$7		Dot 17504
				SCOTT, Lang '84				
				Born in Sumter, South Carolina; raised in Harleyville, South Carolina. Married to **Linda Davis**.				
4/21/84	68	6	1	Run Your Sweet Love By Me One More Time/				
8/18/84	91	2	2	It's Been One Of Those Days................................		$4		MCA 52359
				SCRUGGS, Earl '79				
				Born on 1/6/24 in Flintville, North Carolina. Banjo player. Half of **Flatt & Scruggs** duo. His revue consisted of sons Gary (vocals, bass), Randy (guitar) and Steve (keyboards) Scruggs, with Jim Murphey (steel guitar) and Jody Maphis (drums). Steve Scruggs murdered his wife, then killed himself in September 1992.				
10/24/70	74	2	1	Nashville Skyline Rag ....*Train Number Forty-Five* [I] written and first recorded by Bob Dylan on his 1969 *Nashville Skyline* album		$7		Columbia 45218
				EARL SCRUGGS REVUE:				
7/7/79	30	11	2	I Could Sure Use The Feeling	*Drive To The Country*		$5		Columbia 10992
11/3/79	82	4	3	Play Me No Sad Songs .... *Morning After Kind Of Man*		$5		Columbia 11106
1/19/80	46	9	4	Blue Moon Of Kentucky...........................*Give Me A Sign*		$5		Columbia 11176
				TOM T. HALL & EARL SCRUGGS:				
5/22/82	77	4	5	There Ain't No Country Music On This Jukebox.........*Don't This Road Look Rough And Rocky*		$4		Columbia 02858
7/31/82	72	5	6	Song Of The South ....*Shackles And Chains*		$4		Columbia 03033
				SEA, Johnny '59				
				Born John Seay on 7/15/40 in Gulfport, Mississippi. Singer/songwriter/guitarist.				
4/20/59	13	9	1	Frankie's Man, Johnny .... *Loneliness*		$15		NRC 019
2/8/60	13	8	2	Nobody's Darling But Mine ....*My Time To Cry*		$15		NRC 049
5/23/64	27	10	3	My Baby Walks All Over Me .... *There's Another Man*	121	$8		Philips 40164
4/10/65	19	16	4	My Old Faded Rose ....*It's A Shame*		$8		Philips 40267
6/11/66	14	11	5	Day For Decision .... *Mary Rocks Him To Sleep* [S] answer to "Eve Of Destruction" by Barry McGuire	35	$7		Warner 5820
4/1/67	61	4	6	Nothin's Bad As Bein' Lonely ....*Ain't That Right*		$7		Warner 5889
3/30/68	68	2	7	Going Out To Tulsa .... *There's A Shadow Bar*		$6	■	Columbia 44423
10/19/68	32	11	8	Three Six Packs, Two Arms And A Juke Box...........*I Loved Her Fine For A Time* **JOHNNY SEAY** (above 2)		$6		Columbia 44634
				SEAL, Jim '80				
10/25/80	79	5		Bourbon Cowboy .... *From The Top To The Bottom*		$5		NSD 66
				SEALS, Brady '97				
				Born on 3/29/69 in Hamilton, Ohio. Singer/songwriter/guitarist. Former member of **Little Texas**. Related to **Johnny Duncan**, **Dan Seals** and **Troy Seals**.				
9/7/96+	32	20	1	Another You, Another Me ....S:3 *You Can Have Your Way With Me*	91	$3	▌	Reprise 17615
2/22/97	69	6	2	Still Standing Tall ....*Another You, Another Me*		$3		Reprise 17384
8/23/97	74	1	3	Natural Born Lovers .... from the album *The Truth* on Reprise 46258				album cut
				SEALS, Dan ★109★ '90				
				Born on 2/8/48 in McCamey, Texas; raised in Iraan and Rankin, Texas. Singer/songwriter/guitarist. Brother of Jim Seals (of pop duo Seals & Crofts). Member of England Dan & John Ford Coley duo (charted 9 pop hits from 1976-80). Related to **Johnny Duncan**, **Brady Seals** and **Troy Seals**. CMA Award: 1986 Vocal Duo of the Year (with **Marie Osmond**).				
				1)Love On Arrival 2)Good Times 3)You Still Move Me 4)Everything That Glitters 5)Big Wheels In The Moonlight				
4/30/83	18	17	1	Everybody's Dream Girl....................................*The Banker*		$4		Liberty 1496
8/13/83	28	14	2	After You ....*Candle In The Rain*		$4		Liberty 1504
11/19/83+	37	16	3	You Really Go For The Heart........................*On A Night Like This*		$4		Liberty 1512
2/25/84	10	21	4	God Must Be A Cowboy	*Nothin' Left To Do But Cry*		$4		Liberty 1515
7/28/84	9	23	5	(You Bring Out) The Wild Side Of Me	S:9 / A:12 *One Friend*		$3		EMI America 8220
11/24/84+	2²	21	6	My Baby's Got Good Timing	S:2 / A:2 *She Thinks I Still Care*		$3		EMI America 8245
3/30/85	9	19	7	My Old Yellow Car	S:7 / A:10 *Oh These Nights*		$3		EMI America 8261
7/6/85	❶¹	23	8	Meet Me In Montana	S:❶¹ / A:❶¹ *What Do Lonely People Do* **MARIE OSMOND (With Dan Seals)**		$3	■	Curb/Capitol 5478

308

DEBUT	PEAK	WKS	Gold	A-side (Chart Hit) .... B-side	Pop	$	Pic	Label & Number

SEALS, Dan — Cont'd

DEBUT	PEAK	WKS	A-side / B-side	Pop	$	Pic	Label & Number
10/26/85+	**❶**[1]	27	9 Bop S:❶[1] / A:❶[1] *In San Antone*	42	$3		EMI America 8289
			CMA Award: Single of the Year				
4/5/86	**❶**[1]	23	10 Everything That Glitters (Is Not Gold) S:❶[2] / A:❶[1] *So Easy To Need*		$3	■	EMI America 8311
10/25/86+	**❶**[1]	22	11 You Still Move Me S:❶[1] / A:❶[1] *I'm Still Strung Out On You*		$3		EMI America 8343
3/7/87	**❶**[1]	19	12 I Will Be There S:❶[2] / A:5 *Gonna Be Easy Now*		$3	■	EMI America 8377
6/27/87	**❶**[1]	21	13 Three Time Loser S:❶[1] *On The Front Line*		$3		EMI America 43023
10/17/87+	**❶**[1]	26	14 One Friend S:❶[1] *Bop*		$3	■	Capitol 44077
6/18/88	**❶**[1]	22	15 Addicted S:4 *Maybe I'm Missing You Now*		$3		Capitol 44130
11/12/88+	**❶**[1]	21	16 Big Wheels In The Moonlight S:22 *Factory Town*		$3		Capitol 44267
3/18/89	5	24	17 They Rage On *Factory Town*		$3		Capitol 44345
2/17/90	**❶**[3]	26	18 Love On Arrival *Those*		$3	❘	Capitol 44435
6/9/90	**❶**[2]	21	19 Good Times *Bop*		$3	❘	Capitol 44577
			#11 Pop hit for Sam Cooke in 1964				
10/13/90	49	10	20 Bordertown				album cut
2/2/91	57	6	21 Water Under The Bridge..				album cut
			above 2 from the album *On Arrival* on Capitol 91782				
11/2/91	62	10	22 Sweet Little Shoe .... *Your Blue Heart*		$3	❘	Warner 19176
4/25/92	43	13	23 Mason Dixon Line .... *Be My Angel*		$3		Warner 18986
7/25/92	51	9	24 When Love Comes Around The Bend .... *Sweet Little Shoe*		$3		Warner 18813
7/2/94	66	6	25 All Fired Up .... *Hillbilly Fever*		$3	❘	Warner 18192

SEALS, Troy   '75

Born on 11/16/38 in Big Hill, Kentucky; raised in Ohio. Singer/songwriter/guitarist. Recorded with wife **Jo Ann Campbell** as Jo Ann & Troy in the mid-1960s. Related to **Johnny Duncan**, **Brady Seals** and **Dan Seals**.

DEBUT	PEAK	WKS	A-side / B-side	Pop	$	Pic	Label & Number
8/11/73	93	4	1 I Got A Thing About You Baby .... *Coal Town Blues*		$6		Atlantic 4004
			same tune as "I've Got A Thing About You Baby" by Elvis Presley				
2/2/74	78	5	2 Star Of The Bar/				
1/19/74	96	7	3 You Can't Judge A Book By The Cover		$6		Atlantic 4013
			#48 Pop hit for Bo Diddley in 1962				
5/11/74	81	6	4 Honky-Tonkin' .... *Let Me Make The Bright Lights Shine*		$6		Atlantic 4020
7/19/75	76	7	5 Easy *I'll Take You Down To San Antonio*		$5		Columbia 10173
3/27/76	88	5	6 Sweet Dreams .... *In Our Room*		$5		Columbia 10303
4/23/77	93	2	7 Grand Ole Blues .... *One More Thrill*		$5		Columbia 10511
2/16/80	85	3	8 One Night Honeymoon .... *Wanderin' Friends Of Mine*		$4		Elektra 46573

SEARS, Dawn   '94

Female singer from East Grand Forks, Minnesota.

DEBUT	PEAK	WKS	A-side / B-side	Pop	$	Pic	Label & Number
5/7/94	62	7	Runaway Train .... *A Little At A Time*		$4	❘	Decca 54834

SEBASTIAN, John   '76

Born on 3/17/44 in New York City. Lead singer of The Lovin' Spoonful (charted 14 pop hits from 1965-69).

DEBUT	PEAK	WKS	Gold	A-side / B-side	Pop	$	Pic	Label & Number
5/15/76	93	2	●	Welcome Back .... *Warm Baby* ❶[1]		$5		Reprise 1349
				from the TV series *Welcome Back, Kotter* starring Gabriel Kaplan				

SEELY, Jeannie   ★196★   '66

Born Marilyn Jeanne Seely on 7/6/40 in Titusville, Pennsylvania; raised in Townville, Pennsylvania. Singer/songwriter. Formerly married to **Hank Cochran**. Joined the *Grand Ole Opry* in 1967.

1)Don't Touch Me 2)Wish I Didn't Have To Miss You 3)Can I Sleep In Your Arms 4)I'll Love You More
5)Lucky Ladies

DEBUT	PEAK	WKS	A-side / B-side	Pop	$	Pic	Label & Number
4/16/66	2[3]	21	1 Don't Touch Me *You Tied Tin Cans To My Heart*	85	$7		Monument 933
9/10/66	15	15	2 It's Only Love .... *Then Go Home To Her*		$7		Monument 965
12/17/66+	13	13	3 A Wanderin' Man................................ *Darling Are You Ever Coming Home*		$7		Monument 987
3/18/67	39	10	4 When It's Over.. *I'd Be Just As Lonely There*		$7		Monument 999
7/8/67	42	8	5 These Memories .... *Funny Way Of Laughin'*		$7		Monument 1011
10/28/67+	10	15	6 I'll Love You More (Than You Need) *Enough To Lie*		$7		Monument 1029
2/24/68	24	12	7 Welcome Home To Nothing .... *Maybe I Should Leave*		$7		Monument 1054
6/22/68	23	10	8 How Is He?.. *A Little Unfair*		$7		Monument 1075
3/22/69	43	11	9 Just Enough To Start Me Dreamin' .... *How Big A Fire*		$7		Decca 32452
11/15/69+	2[2]	16	10 Wish I Didn't Have To Miss You *My Tears Don't Show*		$7		Decca 32580
			JACK GREENE And JEANNIE SEELY				
3/7/70	46	6	11 Please Be My New Love .... *Have You Found It Yet*		$7		Decca 32628
12/5/70	58	5	12 Tell Me Again .... *What Kind Of Bird Is That*		$7		Decca 32757
7/17/71	71	5	13 You Don't Understand Him Like I Do .... *Another Heart For You To Break*		$7		Decca 32838
11/20/71+	42	10	14 Alright I'll Sign The Papers .... *All I Want Is You*		$7		Decca 32882
12/11/71+	15	13	15 Much Oblige .... *First Day*		$7		Decca 32898
			JACK GREENE/JEANNIE SEELY				
6/17/72	47	9	16 Pride .... *I'm Afraid I Lied*		$6		Decca 32964
8/12/72	19	12	17 What In The World Has Gone Wrong With Our Love .... *Willingly*		$6		Decca 32991
			JACK GREENE/JEANNIE SEELY				
1/20/73	72	4	18 Farm In Pennsyltucky/				
		3	19 Between The King And I		$6		Decca 33042
7/7/73	6	18	20 Can I Sleep In Your Arms *He'll Love The One He's With*		$5		MCA 40074

DEBUT	PEAK	WKS	Gold	A-side (Chart Hit)..B-side	Pop	$	Pic	Label & Number
				SEELY, Jeannie — cONT'D				
12/15/73+	11	13		21 Lucky Ladies ....*Hold Me*		$5		MCA 40162
5/18/74	37	10		22 I Miss You..*I'd Do As Much For You*		$5		MCA 40225
9/21/74	26	14		23 He Can Be Mine ....*So Was He*		$5		MCA 40287
7/19/75	59	9		24 Take My Hand ....*How Big A Fire*		$5		MCA 40428
4/17/76	96	3		25 Since I Met You Boy ....*Home To Him*		$5		MCA 40528
6/11/77	80	5		26 We're Still Hangin' In There Ain't We Jessi ....*I Don't Need Love Anymore*		$4		Columbia 10550
1/28/78	97	1		27 Take Me To Bed ....*Until You Have To*		$4		Columbia 10664
				SEEVERS, Les '69				
3/8/69	57	9		What Kind Of Magic ....*Stop, Look, Surrender*		$7		Decca 32434
				SEGER, Bob '83				
				Born on 5/6/45 in Dearborn, Michigan; raised in Detroit. Rock singer/songwriter. Charted 32 pop hits from 1968-91.				
1/22/83	15	14		Shame On The Moon......................................*House Behind A House*	2[4]	$4	■	Capitol 5187
				BOB SEGER & The Silver Bullet Band				
				SEGO BROTHERS AND NAOMI, The '64				
				Group from Macon, Georgia. Included James Sego (d: 7/24/79, age 51) and his wife Naomi.				
2/1/64	50	1		Sorry I Never Knew You...............................*Since I Got This Feeling*		$15		Songs of Faith 8032
				SEINER, Barbara '79				
3/3/79	87	3		Jealous Heart ....*Everybody Loves Somebody*		$7		Starship 109
				SELF, Ted '60				
7/4/60	20	10		Little Angel (Come Rock Me To Sleep)....................*Walk Her Down The Aisle*		$20		Plaid 115
				SELLARS, Marilyn '74				
				Born in Northfield, Minnesota. Worked as an airline stewardess.				
4/20/74	19	17		1 One Day At A Time ....*California*	37	$5		Mega 1205
12/14/74+	39	14		2 He's Everywhere ....*Good Love (I Knew I'd Find You)*		$5		Mega 1221
5/24/75	84	4		3 Gather Me ....*Red Skies Over Georgia*		$5		Mega 1230
1/24/76	91	3		4 The Door I Used To Close ....*California*		$5		Mega 1242
				SELLERS, Jason '97				
				Born on 3/4/71 in Gilmer, Texas. Formerly married to Lee Ann Womack.				
8/2/97	37	14		1 I'm Your Man ....*Divorce My Heart*		$3	■	BNA 64915
11/22/97+	46	14		2 That Does It ....*Walking In My Sleep*		$3		BNA 65322
				SEMINOLE '97				
				Duo of brothers Jimmy and Donald "Butch" Myers from Florida.				
8/16/97	69	6		She Knows Me By Heart ....*Honestly*		$3	■	Curb/Universal 56094
				SERRATT, Kenny '77				
				Born in Manila, Arkansas; raised in Dyess, Arkansas and California. Nicknamed "Country Kin."				
				1)Until The Bitter End 2)Daddy, They're Playin' A Song About You 3)Saturday Night In Dallas				
12/9/72+	56	9		1 Goodbyes Come Hard For Me.................*The Man Who Picked The Wildwood Flower*		$6		MGM 14435
				KENNY SERRATT and The Messengers:				
5/5/73	68	3		2 This Just Ain't No Good Day For Leavin'.....................*The Way I Lose My Mind*		$6		MGM 14517
9/29/73	70	13		3 Love And Honor ....*Running Kind*		$6		MGM 14636
				above 3 produced by Merle Haggard				
				KENNY SERATT:				
8/2/75	88	6		4 If I Could Have It Any Other Way ....*Not Too Old To Cry*		$5		Melodyland 6014
8/21/76	72	6		5 I've Been There Too ....*She Made Me Love You More*		$5		Hitsville 6039
2/12/77	54	8		6 Daddy, They're Playin' A Song About You ....*I Threw Away The Rose*		$5		Hitsville 6049
12/15/79	82	4		7 Never Gonna' Be A Country Star/		$5		MDJ 1001
		4		8 A Damn Good Drinking Song		$5		MDJ 1001
5/3/80	54	8		9 Saturday Night In Dallas ....*We Made Memories*		$5		MDJ 1003
9/13/80	39	8		10 Until The Bitter End		$5		MDJ 1005
				Truckin' My Way To Glory				
5/2/81	70	7		11 Sidewalks Are Grey		$5		MDJ 1008
	★371★			**SESSIONS, Ronnie** '77				
				Born on 12/7/48 in Henrietta, Oklahoma; raised in Bakersfield, California. Singer/songwriter/guitarist.				
				1)Me And Millie 2)Wiggle Wiggle 3)Juliet And Romeo				
8/5/72	36	10		1 Never Been To Spain.....................................*While I Play The Fiddle*		$6		MGM 14394
				#5 Pop hit for Three Dog Night in 1972				
11/18/72	59	6		2 Tossin' And Turnin'....................................*Knock And Ring And Tap*		$6		MGM 14445
				#1 Pop hit for Bobby Lewis in 1961				
6/23/73	66	5		3 She Feels So Good I Hate To Put Her Down...*We May Never Get This Close Again*		$6		MGM 14528
				also released as "I Just Can't Put Her Down"				
9/29/73	87	7		4 If That Back Door Could Talk ....*My Love Is Deep, My Love Is Wide*		$6		MGM 14619
10/4/75	61	10		5 Makin' Love ....*Messin' Around*		$5		MCA 40462
				#20 Pop hit for Floyd Robinson in 1959				
7/17/76	81	4		6 Support Your Local Honky Tonks ....*Showdown*		$5		MCA 40581
10/30/76+	16	17		7 Wiggle Wiggle ....*Baby, Pleae Don't Stone My Anymore*		$5		MCA 40624
4/9/77	15	13		8 Me And Millie (Stompin' Grapes And Gettin' Silly)		$5		MCA 40705
				The Losing End				
8/6/77	30	10		9 Ambush ....*Victim Of Life's Circumstances*		$5		MCA 40758
12/10/77+	57	9		10 I Like To Be With You ....*Sweet Annette*		$4		MCA 40831
3/25/78	72	7		11 Cash On The Barrelhead ....*Lucy, Ain't Your Loser Losin' Good*		$5		MCA 40875
7/15/78	96	2		12 I Never Go Around Mirrors ....*Whole Lotta Hound*		$5		MCA 40917
10/7/78	25	9		13 Juliet And Romeo ....*Poison Love*		$5		MCA 40952
6/30/79	94	3		14 Do You Want To Fly ....*Hold On To Your Hiney*		$5		MCA 41038

DEBUT	PEAK	WKS	Gold	A-side (Chart Hit)..B-side	Pop	$	Pic	Label & Number

SESSIONS, Ronnie — Cont'd

DEBUT	PEAK	WKS	A-side	B-side	$	Label & Number
12/1/79	84	5	15 Honky Tonkin' ....*Come By Here*		$5	MCA 41142
12/27/86+	78	5	16 I Bought The Shoes That Just Walked Out On Me .... *You're A Real Live Wire*		$5	Compleat 161

SEXTON, Mark   **'79**

11/24/79	97	2	Don't Say No To Me Tonight.....................................*Younger Than Tomorrow*	$6	Sun-De-Mar 79101

SHAFER, Whitey   **'81**
Born Sanger Shafer on 10/24/34 in Whitney, Texas. Singer/prolific songwriter.

12/13/80+	48	9	1 You Are A Liar ....*Like I Want To*	$4	Elektra 47063
4/11/81	67	3	2 If I Say I Love You (Consider Me Drunk)...................*I'll Break Out Again Tonight*	$4	Elektra 47117

SHAMBLIN, Michael   **'86**

3/8/86	77	3	1 Foreign Affairs	$5	F&L 548
6/7/86	83	2	2 Wishful Dreamin' ....*Livin' On Love*	$5	F&L 549

SHANE, Michael   **'89**

2/11/89	93	2	1 What's The Matter Baby	$5	Regal 1988
7/1/89	99	1	2 Broken Dreams and Memories	$5	Regal 9891

SHANNON, Bonnie   **'80**

12/20/80	88	4	Lovin' You Lightly..	$5	Door Knob 139

SHANNON, Del   **'85**
Born Charles Westover on 12/30/34 in Coopersville, Michigan. Died of a self-inflicted gunshot wound on 2/8/90 (age 55). Charted 17 pop hits from 1961-82.

3/9/85	56	6	In My Arms Again...*You Can't Forgive Me*	$5	Warner 29098

SHANNON, Guy   **'73**
Singer/songwriter/pianist.

7/7/73	69	5	1 Naughty Girl ....*Please Forgive*	$6	Cinnamon 758
10/6/73	63	11	2 Soul Deep ....*A Train That Never Runs*	$6	Cinnamon 769
			#18 Pop hit for The Box Tops in 1969		

SHARP, Kevin   **'97**
Born on 12/10/70 in Redding, California; raised in Weiser, Idaho.

9/28/96+	❶⁴	22	1 Nobody Knows		album cut
			#2 Pop hit for The Tony Rich Project in 1996		
2/8/97	3	21	2 She's Sure Taking It Well		album cut
7/26/97	4	20	3 If You Love Somebody		album cut
11/22/97+	43	13	4 There's Only You		album cut
			all of above from the album *Measure Of A Man* on Asylum 61930		

SHARP, Rosemary   **'87**
Born and in Fort Worth, Texas. Singer/songwriter.

2/28/87	85	3	1 Didn't You Go And Leave Me............................	$5	Canyon Creek 1226
8/8/87	76	4	2 Real Good Heartache.....................................	$5	Canyon Creek 0401
10/31/87	67	6	3 If You're Gonna Tell Me Lies (Tell Me Good Ones)............................	$5	Canyon Creek 0908
4/9/88	68	5	4 The Stairs ....*Until I Fall In Love Again*	$5	Canyon Creek 0210

SHARPE, Sunday   **'74**
Born in 1946 in Orlando, Florida. Female singer.

8/17/74	11	14	1 I'm Having Your Baby *It's A Beautiful Night For Love*	$5	United Artists 507
			female version of "(You're) Having My Baby" by Paul Anka		
12/21/74+	47	9	2 Mr. Songwriter ....*I Gave All I Had To Him*	$5	United Artists 571
3/29/75	48	8	3 Put Your Head On My Shoulder ....*Another Lonely Night*	$5	United Artists 602
			#2 Pop hit for Paul Anka in 1959		
2/14/76	80	5	4 Find A New Love, Girl ....*It's A Beautiful Night For Love*	$5	United Artists 758
11/6/76	18	12	5 A Little At A Time ....*Pour It In A Swinging Jug*	$5	Playboy 6090
6/18/77	62	5	6 I'm Not The One You Love (I'm The One You Make Love To) ....*Last Night's Lovin'*	$5	Playboy 5806
8/27/77	45	7	7 Hold On Tight ....*Welcome Stranger*	$5	Playboy 5813

SHATSWELL, Danny   **'78**

6/17/78	97	2	I'm A Mender ....*She's My Shelter*	$5	Mercury 55027

SHAVER, Billy Joe   **'78**
Born on 8/16/41 in Corsicana, Texas; raised in Waco, Texas. Singer/prolific songwriter.

9/15/73	88	3	1 Been To Georgia On A Fast Train ....*Old Five & Dimers Like Me*	$6	Monument 8580
3/11/78	80	5	2 You Asked Me To ....*Silver Wings Of Time*	$5	Capricorn 0286

SHAW, Brian   **'74**
Born in 1949 in Grove City, Pennsylvania. Singer/songwriter/bassist.

9/8/73	55	8	1 The Devil Is A Woman ....*Just At Dawn*	$6	RCA Victor 0058
12/15/73+	62	11	2 Good Enough To Be Your Man......................*What Loving You Means To Me*	$6	RCA Victor 0186
4/6/74	50	9	3 Friend Named Red ....*I'm Not Through Loving You*	$6	RCA Victor 0230
10/12/74	17	15	4 Here We Go Again *I'll Carry You*	$6	RCA Victor 10071
10/16/76	97	2	5 Showdown	$5	Republic 306
3/12/77	97	2	6 What Kind Of Fool (Does That Make Me)............*You Sure Were Good Last Night*	$5	Republic 360

SHAW, Ron   '78

Singer from Anaheim, California. Former member of The Hillside Singers.

DEBUT	PEAK	WKS	A-side	B-side	Pop	$	Label & Number
6/25/77	94	4	1 Hurtin' Kind Of Love .... *Like So Much Broken Glass*		$6		Pacific Chall. 1511
			also see #7 below				
7/8/78	79	7	2 Goin' Home .... *Boogie Woogie Country Girl*		$5		Pacific Chall. 1522
10/7/78	36	9	3 Save The Last Dance For Me	*If Walls Could Talk*	$5		Pacific Chall. 1631
			#1 Pop hit for The Drifters in 1960				
1/20/79	68	7	4 I Cry Instead .... *Kansas City*		$5		Pacific Chall. 1633
			#25 Pop hit for The Beatles in 1964 (as "I'll Cry Instead")				
7/28/79	93	3	5 One And One Make Three................................. *I Can't Dance*		$5		Pacific Chall. 1635
9/22/79	90	4	6 What The World Needs Now (Is Love Sweet Love) .... *Fairweather Woman*		$5		Pacific Chall. 1636
			#7 Pop hit for Jackie DeShannon in 1965				
3/22/80	91	4	7 Hurtin' Kind Of Love .... *Like So Much Broken Glass* [R]		$5		Pacific Chall. 1637
			same version as #1 above				
			RON SHAW & The Desert Wind Band:				
8/16/80	94	2	8 The Legend Of Harry And The Mountain		$5		Pacific Chall. 1638
2/7/81	78	4	9 Reachin' For Freedom		$5		Pacific Chall. 1639

SHAW, Victoria   '94

Born on 7/13/62 in New York City; raised in Los Angeles.

DEBUT	PEAK	WKS	A-side	B-side	Pop	$	Label & Number
2/25/84	61	10	1 Break My Heart .... *Forever On My Mind*		$5		MPB 5008
5/7/94	57	9	2 Cry Wolf... *Love's Not Gonna Pass Me By*		$3	∎	Reprise 18235
9/3/94	74	2	3 Tears Dry .... *Half Hearted*		$3	∎	Reprise 18111
6/10/95	58	7	4 Forgiveness .... *Bring My Baby Home*		$3	∎	Reprise 17886

SHAY, Dorothy   '47

Born Dorothy Sims in 1921 in Jacksonville, Florida. Died of a heart attack on 10/22/78 (age 57). Singer/actress. Known as "The Park Avenue Hillbilly." Acted in the movie *Comin' 'Round The Mountain*.

DEBUT	PEAK	WKS	A-side	B-side	Pop	$	Label & Number
8/16/47	4	7	Feudin' And Fightin'	*Say That We're Sweethearts Again*	4	$15	Columbia 37189
			from the Broadway musical *Laffing Room Only* starring Betty Garrett				

SHELTON, Ricky Van ★102★   '88

Born on 1/12/52 in Danville, Virginia; raised in Grit, Virginia. Singer/songwriter/guitarist. Van is his middle name. Joined the *Grand Ole Opry* in 1988. CMA Awards: 1988 Horizon Award; 1989 Male Vocalist of the Year.

1)*I'll Leave This World Loving You* 2)*Keep It Between The Lines* 3)*I've Cried My Last Tear For You*
4)*Rockin' Years* 5)*Somebody Lied*

DEBUT	PEAK	WKS	A-side	B-side	Pop	$	Label & Number
12/20/86+	24	18	1 Wild-Eyed Dream .... A:24 *Think It Over*		$4		Columbia 06542
4/18/87	7	19	2 Crime Of Passion	S:2 *Don't We All Have The Right*	$3		Columbia 07025
8/22/87	❶¹	25	3 Somebody Lied	S:❶² *Working Mans Blues*	$3		Columbia 07311
1/9/88	❶¹	23	4 Life Turned Her That Way	S:❶³ *I Don't Care*	$3		Columbia 07672
5/7/88	❶¹	20	5 Don't We All Have The Right	S:❶² *Baby, I'm Ready*	$3		Columbia 07798
9/10/88	❶²	21	6 I'll Leave This World Loving You	S:❶² *Sometimes I Cry In My Sleep*	$3		Columbia 08022
1/7/89	❶¹	16	7 From A Jack To A King	*The Picture*	$3		Columbia 08529
4/22/89	4	16	8 Hole In My Pocket	*Let Me Live With Love (And Die With You)*	$3		Columbia 68694
7/22/89	❶¹	22	9 Living Proof	*Somebody's Back In Town*	$3		Columbia 68994
11/25/89+	2²	26	10 Statue Of A Fool	*He's Got You*	$3		Columbia 73077
3/10/90	❶¹	20	11 I've Cried My Last Tear For You	*I Still Love You*	$3	∎	Columbia 73263
6/30/90	2²	21	12 I Meant Every Word He Said	*Sometimes I Cry In My Sleep*	$3		Columbia 73413
10/27/90+	4	20	13 Life's Little Ups And Downs	*Love Is Burnin'*	$3	∎	Columbia 73587
3/2/91	❶¹	20	14 Rockin' Years	*What A Heartache*	$3		Columbia 73711
			DOLLY PARTON WITH RICKY VAN SHELTON:				
5/4/91	❶¹	20	15 I Am A Simple Man	*Backroads*	$3		Columbia 73780
8/24/91	❶²	20	16 Keep It Between The Lines	*Weekend World*	$3		Columbia 73956
11/30/91+	13	20	17 After The Lights Go Out .... *Oh Heart Of Mine*		$3		Columbia 74104
3/21/92	2¹	20	18 Backroads	*Call Me Up*	$3		Columbia 74258
7/25/92	26	20	19 Wear My Ring Around Your Neck .... *Who'll Turn Out The Lights*		$3		Columbia 74418
			from the movie *Honeymoon In Vegas* starring James Caan				
10/24/92+	5	20	20 Wild Man	*If You're Ever In My Arms*	$3		Columbia 74748
3/13/93	26	20	21 Just As I Am	*Slam That Door*	$3		Columbia 74896
8/21/93	44	12	22 A Couple Of Good Years Left	*My First Reaction*	$3		Columbia 77130
1/15/94	20	20	23 Where Was I .... *If It Weren't For Me*		$3	∎	Columbia 77334
9/24/94	49	10	24 Wherever She Is	*Thanks A Lot*	$3	∎	Columbia 77653
1/28/95	62	5	25 Lola's Love.. *Been There, Done That*		$3	∎	Columbia 77792

SHENANDOAH ★118★ '90

Group from Muscle Shoals, Alabama: Marty Raybon (vocals), Jim Seales (guitar), Stan Thorn (keyboards), Ralph Ezell (bass) and Mike McGuire (drums). Seales was guitarist for the R&B group Funkadelic. McGuire married actress Teresa Blake (of TV soap *All My Children*) on 7/9/94. Rocky Thacker replaced Ezell in 1995. Thorn left in 1996.

1)Next To You, Next To Me 2)The Church On Cumberland Road 3)Two Dozen Roses 4)If Bubba Can Dance 5)Sunday In The South

DEBUT	PEAK	WKS		A-side / B-side	$	Pic	Label & Number
8/1/87	54	7	1	They Don't Make Love Like We Used To ....*Lily Of The Alley*	$4	■	Columbia 07128
12/12/87+	28	18	2	Stop The Rain...*What She Wants*	$4		Columbia 07654
4/23/88	9	24	3	She Doesn't Cry Anymore S:13 *What She Wants*	$3		Columbia 07779
10/1/88	5	21	4	Mama Knows S:5 *The Show Must Go On*	$3		Columbia 08042
1/28/89	❶²	21	5	The Church On Cumberland Road *She Doesn't Cry Anymore*	$3		Columbia 68550
5/20/89	❶¹	24	6	Sunday In The South *Changes*	$3		Columbia 68892
9/16/89	❶¹	26	7	Two Dozen Roses *Hard Country*	$3		Columbia 69061
2/17/90	6	26	8	See If I Care *Lily Of The Alley*	$3		Columbia 73237
6/9/90	❶³	21	9	Next To You, Next To Me *Daddy's Little Man*	$3	▌	Columbia 73373
10/6/90	5	20	10	Ghost In This House *She's Still Here*	$3	▌	Columbia 73520
1/19/91	7	20	11	I Got You *The Road Not Taken*	$3		Columbia 73672
5/4/91	9	20	12	The Moon Over Georgia *Can't Stop Now*	$3		Columbia 73777
9/7/91	38	11	13	When You Were Mine ....*It Ain't Love Until It Hurts*	$3		Columbia 73957
4/4/92	2¹	20	14	Rock My Baby *Wednesday Night Prayer Meeting*	$3		RCA 62199
8/8/92	28	18	15	Hey Mister (I Need This Job) ....*There Ain't No Beverly Hills In Tennessee*	$3		RCA 62290
11/28/92+	15	20	16	Leavin's Been A Long Time Comin'.............................*I Was Young Once Too*	$3		RCA 62397
6/5/93	15	20	17	Janie Baker's Love Slave *Right Where I Belong*	$3		RCA 62504
10/9/93+	3	20	18	I Want To Be Loved Like That *Just Say The Word*	$3		RCA 62642
2/12/94	❶¹	20	19	If Bubba Can Dance (I Can Too) *If It Takes Every Rib I've Got*	$3	▌	RCA 62761
6/25/94	46	11	20	I'll Go Down Loving You ....*The Blues Are Coming Over To Your House*	$3		RCA 62867
4/22/95	4	20	21	Darned If I Don't (Danged If I Do)/			
12/3/94+	7	20	22	Somewhere In The Vicinity Of The Heart **SHENANDOAH With Alison Krauss**	$3		Liberty 18484
8/5/95	24	20	23	Heaven Bound (I'm Ready) ....*Darned If I Don't (Danged If I Do)*	$3	▌	Capitol 58442
11/4/95+	40	20	24	Always Have, Always Will ....*Every Fire*	$3		Capitol 18903
2/24/96	43	12	25	All Over But The Shoutin' ....*Sunday In The South*	$3	▌	Capitol 58545

SHEPARD, Jean ★91★ '53

Born Ollie Imogene Shepard on 11/21/33 in Paul's Valley, Oklahoma; raised in Visalia, California. Singer/songwriter/bassist. Joined the *Grand Ole Opry* in 1955. Husband **Hawkshaw Hawkins** died in a plane crash on 3/5/63.

1)A Dear John Letter 2)Slippin' Away 3)A Satisfied Mind 4)Beautiful Lies 5) Forgive Me John

DEBUT	PEAK	WKS		A-side / B-side	Pop	$	Pic	Label & Number
7/25/53	❶⁶	23	1	A Dear John Letter S:❶⁶ / J:❶⁴ / A:2 *I'd Rather Die Young (Shepard)* **JEAN SHEPARD with FERLIN HUSKEY** #44 Pop hit for **Pat Boone** in 1960	4	$25		Capitol 2502
10/10/53	4	7	2	Forgive Me John S:4 / J:6 / A:8 *My Wedding Ring (Shepard)* **JEAN SHEPARD with FERLIN HUSKEY**		$25		Capitol 2586
6/25/55	4	22	3	A Satisfied Mind/				
7/16/55	13	1	4	Take Possession *A:13*		$25		Capitol 3118
10/8/55	4	19	5	Beautiful Lies/ S:4 / J:4 / A:12				
10/22/55	10	3	6	I Thought Of You *A:10*		$25		Capitol 3222
12/22/58	18	2	7	I Want To Go Where No One Knows Me ....*Just Another Girl*		$20		Capitol 4068
4/20/59	30	1	8	Have Heart, Will Love *I'll Take The Blame*		$20		Capitol 4129
5/30/64	5	24	9	Second Fiddle (To An Old Guitar) *Two Little Boys*		$10		Capitol 5169
1/9/65	38	11	10	A Tear Dropped By ....*He Plays The Bongo (I Play The Banjo)*		$10		Capitol 5304
6/5/65	30	7	11	Someone's Gotta Cry *Don't Take Advantage Of Me*		$10		Capitol 5392
3/5/66	13	16	12	Many Happy Hangovers To You.................*Our Past Is In My Way*		$10		Capitol 5585
5/14/66	9	15	13	I'll Take The Dog *I'd Fight The World* **JEAN SHEPARD and RAY PILLOW**		$8		Capitol 5633
7/16/66	10	18	14	If Teardrops Were Silver *Outstanding In Your Field*		$8		Capitol 5681
11/26/66+	25	11	15	Mr. Do-It-Yourself........................*Strangers Nine To Five* **JEAN SHEPARD & RAY PILLOW**		$8		Capitol 5769
1/28/67	12	15	16	Heart, We Did All That We Could...................*My Momma Didn't Raise No Fools*		$8		Capitol 5822
5/27/67	17	12	17	Your Forevers (Don't Last Very Long) ....*Coming Or Going*		$8		Capitol 5899
9/30/67	40	8	18	I Don't See How I Can Make It.........................*Enough Heart To Hurt*		$8		Capitol 5983
2/10/68	52	6	19	An Old Bridge ....*My New Darlin'*		$8		Capitol 2073
6/15/68	36	8	20	A Real Good Woman ....*The Trouble With Girls*		$8		Capitol 2180
10/5/68	62	8	21	Everyday's A Happy Day For Fools ....*My World Is You*		$7		Capitol 2273
5/3/69	69	4	22	I'm Tied Around Your Finger ....*You're Calling Me Sweetheart Again*		$7		Capitol 2425

SHEPARD, Jean — Cont'd

DEBUT	PEAK	WKS		A-side / B-side	Pop	$		Label & Number
9/6/69	18	11		23 Seven Lonely Days .... *Invisible Tears*		$7		Capitol 2585
1/3/70	8	14		24 Then He Touched Me *Only Mama That'll Walk The Line*		$7		Capitol 2694
4/25/70	23	11		25 A Woman's Hand.................................... *What Went Wrong*		$7		Capitol 2779
8/15/70	22	12		26 I Want You Free .... *Be Nice To Everybody*		$7		Capitol 2847
11/7/70	12	14		27 Another Lonely Night.................*Your Name's Become A Household Word*		$7		Capitol 2941
2/20/71	24	10		28 With His Hand In Mine............................*Just Plain Lonely*		$6		Capitol 3033
9/18/71	55	2		29 Just As Soon As I Get Over Loving You ....*My Name Is Woman*		$6		Capitol 3153
1/8/72	55	8		30 Safe In These Lovin' Arms Of Mine ....*The Closest Thing To Perfect*		$6		Capitol 3238
6/3/72	68	4		31 Virginia .... *We Go Good Together*		$6		Capitol 3315
8/19/72	46	10		32 Just Like Walkin' In The Sunshine ....*Candlelighted World*		$6		Capitol 3395
6/9/73	4	18		33 Slippin' Away *Think I'll Go Somewhere And Cry Myself To Sleep*	81	$5		United Artists 248
11/24/73+	36	11		34 Come On Phone .... *Are You Sincere?*		$5		United Artists 317
2/23/74	13	13		35 At The Time .... *Love Came Pouring Down*		$5		United Artists 384
6/29/74	17	12		36 I'll Do Anything It Takes (To Stay With You) ....*Safe In The Love Of My Man*		$5		United Artists 442
10/26/74+	14	13		37 Poor Sweet Baby....................................*I'm Not That Good At Goodbye*		$5		United Artists 552
2/22/75	16	13		38 The Tip Of My Fingers ....*Bright Lights And Country Music*		$5		United Artists 591
8/30/75	49	10		39 I'm A Believer (In A Whole Lot Of Lovin')........................*I Think I'll Wait Til Tomorrow*		$5		United Artists 701
12/20/75+	44	9		40 Another Neon Night ....*Another Somebody Done Somebody Wrong Song*		$5		United Artists 745
4/10/76	49	8		41 Mercy .... *Wife Of A Hard Working Man*		$5		United Artists 776
6/26/76	41	10		42 Ain't Love Good .... *I Can't Imagine*		$5		United Artists 818
12/4/76+	74	7		43 I'm Giving You Denver ....*He Loves Everything He Gets His Hands On*		$5		United Artists 899
4/16/77	82	5		44 Hardly A Day Goes By ....*Lovin' You Comes So Easy*		$5		United Artists 956
4/15/78	85	6		45 The Real Thing................................... *Break My Mind*		$5		Scorpion 157

SHEPPARD, T.G. ★54★   '81
Born William Browder on 7/20/42 in Alamo, Tennessee. Singer/songwriter/guitarist. Invented his stage name; initials do not signify "The German Sheppard" or "The Good Sheppard," as commonly thought.

1)Last Cheater's Waltz 2)I'll Be Coming Back For More 3)Party Time 4)Tryin' To Beat The Morning Home
5)I Loved 'Em Every One

DEBUT	PEAK	WKS		A-side / B-side	Pop	$		Label & Number
11/30/74+	❶[1]	19		1 Devil In The Bottle *Rollin' With The Flow*	54	$5		Melodyland 6002
4/12/75	❶[1]	15		2 Tryin' To Beat The Morning Home *I'll Be Satisfied*	95	$5		Melodyland 6006
8/16/75	14	16		3 Another Woman..........................*I Can't Help Myself (Sugar Pie, Honey Bunch)*		$5		Melodyland 6016
12/27/75+	7	15		4 Motels And Memories *Pigskin Charade*	102	$5		Melodyland 6028
5/29/76	14	13		5 Solitary Man .... *Shame*	100	$5		Hitsville 6032
				#21 Pop hit for **Neil Diamond** in 1970				
9/18/76	8	14		6 Show Me A Man *We Just Live Here (We Don't Love Here Anymore)*		$5		Hitsville 6040
12/25/76+	37	8		7 May I Spend Every New Years With You ....*I'll Always Remember That Song*		$5		Hitsville 6048
3/5/77	20	10		8 Lovin' On ....*I'll Always Remember That Song*		$5		Hitsville 6053
11/12/77+	13	14		9 Mister D.J. .... *Easy To Love (So Hard To Leave)*		$4		Warner/Curb 8490
2/18/78	13	13		10 Don't Ever Say Good-Bye................*She Pretended We Were Married*		$4		Warner/Curb 8525
5/27/78	5	13		11 When Can We Do This Again *Jenny, Don't Worry 'Bout The Kid*		$4		Warner/Curb 8593
9/23/78	7	11		12 Daylight *Never Ending Crowded Circle*		$4		Warner/Curb 8678
12/16/78+	8	14		13 Happy Together *That's All She Wrote*		$4		Warner/Curb 8721
				#1 Pop hit for the Turtles in 1967				
4/21/79	4	13		14 You Feel Good All Over *I Wish That I Could Hurt That Way Again*		$4		Warner/Curb 8808
8/4/79	❶[2]	14		15 Last Cheater's Waltz *You Do It To Me Every Time*		$4		Warner/Curb 49024
12/1/79+	❶[2]	15		16 I'll Be Coming Back For More *(She Wanted To Live) Faster Than I Could Dream*		$4		Warner/Curb 49110
4/5/80	6	16		17 Smooth Sailin' *I Came Home To Make Love To You*		$4		Warner/Curb 49214
8/2/80	❶[1]	15		18 Do You Wanna Go To Heaven *How Far Our Love Goes*		$4		Warner/Curb 49515
12/6/80+	❶[1]	13		19 I Feel Like Loving You Again *Let The Little Bird Fly*		$4		Warner/Curb 49615
3/14/81	❶[1]	15		20 I Loved 'Em Every One *I Could Never Dream The Way You Feel*	37	$4		Warner/Curb 49690
7/18/81	❶[1]	16		21 Party Time *You Waltzed Yourself Right Into My Life*		$4		Warner/Curb 49761
11/21/81+	❶[1]	19		22 Only One You *We Belong In Love Tonight*	68	$4		Warner/Curb 49858
4/3/82	❶[1]	16		23 Finally *All My Cloudy Days Are Gone*	58	$4		Warner/Curb 50041
9/4/82	❶[1]	19		24 War Is Hell (On The Homefront Too) *In Another Minute*		$4		Warner/Curb 29934
11/20/82+	❶[1]	20		25 Faking Love *Reno And Me*		$4		Warner/Curb 29854
				T.G. SHEPPARD AND KAREN BROOKS				
4/9/83	12	15		26 Without You .... *Where Did We Go Right?*		$4		Warner/Curb 29695
				#1 Pop hit for Nilsson in 1972				
10/15/83+	❶[1]	21		27 Slow Burn *First Things First*		$4		Warner/Curb 29469
2/18/84	12	15		28 Make My Day ....*How Lucky We Are* [N]	62	$4		Warner/Curb 29343
				T.G. SHEPPARD with CLINT EASTWOOD from the movie *Sudden Impact* starring Clint Eastwood				
6/2/84	3	21		29 Somewhere Down The Line *It's A Bad Night For Good Girls*		$4		Warner/Curb 29369
9/29/84	57	9		30 Home Again .... *Dream On*		$4		Elektra 69697
				JUDY COLLINS with T.G. Sheppard				
11/10/84+	4	22		31 One Owner Heart *A:4 / S:5 I Could Get Used To This*		$4		Warner/Curb 29167
3/9/85	10	17		32 You're Going Out Of My Mind *S:10 / A:12 Heat Lightning*		$4		Warner/Curb 29071

SHEPPARD, T.G. — Cont'd

DEBUT	PEAK	WKS	#	A-side	B-side	Pop	$	Pic	Label & Number
5/11/85	21	18	33	Fooled Around And Fell In Love	A:18 / S:23 Banging My Heart		$3	■	Columbia 04890
				#3 Pop hit for Elvin Bishop in 1976					
9/7/85	8	20	34	Doncha?	S:5 / A:9 Hunger For You		$3		Columbia 05591
12/28/85+	9	18	35	In Over My Heart	S:8 / A:9 A Great Work Of Art		$3		Columbia 05747
5/17/86	❶¹	23	36	Strong Heart	S:❶¹ / A:❶¹ What You Gonna Do About Her		$3		Columbia 05905
10/11/86+	2²	26	37	Half Past Forever (Till I'm Blue In The Heart)	S:2 / A:2 The Bad Thing About Good Love		$3		Columbia 06347
3/21/87	2¹	20	38	You're My First Lady	S:5 / A:13 Paintin' The Town Blue		$3		Columbia 06999
9/5/87	2¹	24	39	One For The Money	S:2 Come To Me		$3		Columbia 07312
9/24/88	48	7	40	Don't Say It With Diamonds (Say It With Love)	There's A Lot Of Heart		$3		Columbia 08029
11/26/88+	14	20	41	You Still Do	Something Worth Waiting For		$3		Columbia 08119
3/30/91	63	6	42	Born In A High Wind	(long version)		$3		Curb/Capitol 79565

SHERLEY, Glen   **'71**
Born in Oklahoma; raised in California. Died of a self-inflicted gunshot on 5/11/78. Singer/songwriter/guitarist.

DEBUT	PEAK	WKS		A-side	B-side	Pop	$	Pic	Label & Number
7/10/71	63	4		Greystone Chapel	Dialogue / Looking Back In Anger		$6		Mega 0027
				recorded "live" at Folsom Prison on 1/31/71; first recorded by Johnny Cash on his 1968 Johnny Cash At Folsom Prison album					

SHIBLEY, Arkie   **'51**
Born in 1915 in Van Buren, Arkansas. His Mountain Dew Boys consisted of Leon Kelly, Jack Hays and Phil Fregon.

DEBUT	PEAK	WKS		A-side	B-side	Pop	$	Pic	Label & Number
12/30/50+	5	7		Hot Rod Race	A:5 / J:6 I'm Living Alone With An Old Love [N]		$75		Gilt-Edge 5021
				ARKIE SHIBLEY and his Mountain Dew Boys					

SHINER, Mervin   **'49**
Born on 2/20/21 in Bethlehem, Pennsylvania. Singer/songwriter/guitarist.

DEBUT	PEAK	WKS	#	A-side	B-side	Pop	$	Pic	Label & Number
10/8/49	5	11	1	Why Don't You Haul Off And Love Me	J:5 / S:11 Soft Lips		$20		Decca 46178
4/1/50	6	3	2	Peter Cottontail	A:6 / S:7 Floppy	8	$25		Decca 9-46221
				MURV SHINER:					
5/27/67	73	4	3	Big Brother	Big Shot, The Pool Shark		$8		MGM 13704
1/4/69	50	10	4	Too Hard To Say I'm Sorry	Tecumseh Valley		$7		MGM 14007

SHIRLEY, Danny   **'84**
Born on 8/12/56 in Chattanooga, Tennessee. Lead singer of Confederate Railroad.

DEBUT	PEAK	WKS	#	A-side	B-side	Pop	$	Pic	Label & Number
10/20/84	72	5	1	Love And Let Love			$7		Amor 1002
2/16/85	93	5	2	Yo Yo (The Right String, But The Wrong Yo Yo)			$10		Amor 1006
				DANNY SHIRLEY & "PIANO RED"					
				#10 R&B hit for Piano Red in 1951					
8/29/87	82	3	3	Deep Down (Everybody Wants To Be From Dixie)			$6		Amor 2001
12/5/87	81	2	4	Going To California			$6		Amor 2002
2/20/88	76	7	5	I Make The Living (She Makes The Living Worthwhile)			$6		Amor 2004

SHIRLEY & SQUIRRELY   **'76**
Studio group assembled by producer Bob Milsap.

DEBUT	PEAK	WKS		A-side	B-side	Pop	$	Pic	Label & Number
6/5/76	28	11		Hey Shirley (This Is Squirely)	(instrumental) [N]	48	$6		GRT 054

SHONDELL, Troy   **'88**
Born on 5/14/44 in Fort Wayne, Indiana. Singer/multi-instrumentalist. Charted 3 pop hits from 1961-62.

DEBUT	PEAK	WKS	#	A-side	B-side	Pop	$	Pic	Label & Number
10/6/79	95	2	1	Still Loving You	Doctor Love		$7		Star-Fox 77
11/8/80	83	4	2	(Sittin' Here) Lovin' You	(Here I Am) Single Again		$7		TeleSonic 804
5/14/88	79	2	3	(I'm Looking For Some) New Blue Jeans			$7		AVM 14

SHOOTERS, The   **'89**
Group from Muscle Shoals, Alabama: Walt Aldridge (vocals), Barry Billings (guitar), Chalmers Davis (keyboards), Gary Baker (bass; Baker & Myers) and Michael Dillon (drums).

DEBUT	PEAK	WKS	#	A-side	B-side	Pop	$	Pic	Label & Number
1/24/87	21	15	1	They Only Come Out At Night	A:21 Remote Control		$3		Epic 06623
6/6/87	41	11	2	'Til The Old Wears Off	Some Fools Were Made To Be Broken		$3		Epic 07131
9/26/87	34	13	3	Tell It To Your Teddy Bear	Dancing Alone		$3		Epic 07367
1/30/88	31	15	4	I Taught Her Everything She Knows About Love	I'll Cry Instead		$3		Epic 07684
10/22/88+	13	21	5	Borderline	She's Steppin' Out		$3		Epic 08082
3/4/89	17	19	6	If I Ever Go Crazy	Leave And Learn		$3		Epic 68587
7/15/89	39	9	7	You Just Can't Lose 'Em All	If I Were You		$3		Epic 68955

SHOPPE, The   **'81**
Group from Dallas: Mark Cathey and Kevin Bailey (vocals), Roger Ferguson (guitar), Clarke Wilcox (banjo), Mike Caldwell (harmonica), Jack Wilcox (bass) and Lou Chavez (drums).

DEBUT	PEAK	WKS	#	A-side	B-side	Pop	$	Pic	Label & Number
4/19/80	76	5	1	Three Way Love	Livin' In Your Lovin'		$6		Rainbow Sound 8019
8/30/80	78	4	2	Star Studded Nights	The South's Gonna Rise Again		$6		Rainbow Sound 8022
2/21/81	33	10	3	Doesn't Anybody Get High On Love Anymore	Paralyzed		$5		NSD 80
5/23/81	61	7	4	Dream Maker	Up To My Heart In Love		$5		NSD 90
11/17/84	74	5	5	If You Think I Love You Now			$6		Amer. Country 2
2/16/85	79	6	6	Hurts All Over			$6		Amer. Country 3
9/14/85	56	8	7	Holdin' The Family Together	The Sky Is Falling		$4		MTM 72056
12/21/85+	47	11	8	While The Moon's In Town	There's A Fire Inside		$4		MTM 72063

SHRUM, Walter   **'45**

DEBUT	PEAK	WKS		A-side	B-side	Pop	$	Pic	Label & Number
10/6/45	3	1		Triflin' Gal	You Two-Timed Me Once Too Often		$40		Coast 2010
				WALTER SHRUM and his Colorado Hillbillies					

SHURFIRE   **'87**

DEBUT	PEAK	WKS	#	A-side	B-side	Pop	$	Pic	Label & Number
7/4/87	54	7	1	Bringin' The House Down	My Heart's In Louisiana		$5		AIR 173
11/21/87	49	9	2	Roll The Dice	I Want Some		$5		AIR 180
3/12/88	57	6	3	First In Line			$5		AIR 181

SHYLO '77
Vocal trio from Texas: Danny Hogan, Ronny Scaife and Perry York.

2/14/76	75	8		1 Dog Tired Of Cattin' Around..Heartbeat		$5		Columbia 10267
6/12/76	75	7		2 Livin' On Love Street · Beyond The Sun		$5		Columbia 10343
9/25/76	86	5		3 Ol' Man River (I've Come To Talk Again).. Showdown		$5		Columbia 10398
1/8/77	63	8		4 Drinkin' My Way Back Home .... Didn't Get No Lovin'		$5		Columbia 10456
5/28/77	87	4		5 (I'm Coming Home To You) Dixie.............................. Whiskey Fever		$5		Columbia 10534
12/17/77+	91	5		6 Gotta Travel On.. The Drifter		$5		Columbia 10647
3/10/79	79	6		7 Freckles .... Wait Until Dark		$5		Columbia 10918
9/15/79	92	2		8 I'm Puttin' My Love Inside You .... What Kind Of Dance Is That		$5		Columbia 11048
5/22/82	89	3		9 Crime In The Sheets .... (I Wish You'd) Love Me Alone		$4		Mercury 76151

SIDE OF THE ROAD GANG '76
Group from Dallas.

8/14/76	98	2		Suitcase Life .... Sittin' By The Side Of The Road		$5		Capitol 4298

SIERRA '83
Vocal group from Virginia: E.J. Harris (lead), William Arney (tenor), Rodney Painter (baritone) and David Mangum (bass).

2/5/83	58	8		1 Keep On Playin' That Country Music		$7		Musicom 52701
5/14/83	87	3		2 I'd Do It In A Heart Beat		$7		Musicom 52702
11/5/83	93	2		3 Old Fashioned Lovin'		$7		Cardinal 052
3/17/84	70	6		4 Branded Man .... Northern Lights		$6		Awesome 101
6/23/84	68	6		5 Love Is The Reason .... I'd Do It In A Heartbeat		$6		Awesome 106
2/9/85	68	6		6 The Almighty Lover .... How Many Angels		$6		Awesome 110

SILVER CITY BAND '77
Group from Memphis.

10/1/77	99	2		1 If You Really Want Me To I'll Go .... Georgia Girl		$5		Columbia 10601
7/29/78	95	2		2 I'm Still Missing You .... Valentine Partner		$5		Columbia 10759

SILVER CREEK '81
Group led by singer/songwriter Roger Ivie.

9/12/81	94	2		1 You And Me And Tennessee..		$6		Cardinal 8102
				ROGER IVIE And SILVERCREEK				
11/21/81	64	7		2 Lonely Women		$6		Cardinal 8103

SIMMONS, Gene '77
Born in 1933 in Tupelo, Mississippi. Known as "Jumpin' Gene." Not to be confused with the lead singer of Kiss. Hit the pop charts with "Haunted House" in 1964.

9/10/77	88	3		Why Didn't I Think Of That .... Tennessee Party Time		$7		Deltune 1201

SIMON, Carly '78
Born on 6/25/45 in New York City. Singer/songwriter. Charted 23 pop hits from 1971-89. Won the 1971 Best New Artist Grammy Award. Married to James Taylor from 1972-83.

9/9/78	33	10		Devoted To You .... Boys In The Trees	36	$5		Elektra 45506
				CARLY SIMON and JAMES TAYLOR				

SIMON & VERITY '85
British vocal duo.

2/16/85	78	4		1 We've Still Got Love .... In Love And Out Of Danger		$4		EMI America 8257
5/18/85	91	3		2 Your Eyes .... In Love And Out Of Danger		$4		EMI America 8264

SIMPSON, Red '72
Born Joseph Simpson on 3/6/34 in Higley, Arizona. Singer/songwriter/guitarist.

4/2/66	38	4		1 Roll Truck Roll .... Runaway Truck		$8		Capitol 5577
6/4/66	39	3		2 The Highway Patrol .... Big Mack		$8		Capitol 5637
12/24/66+	41	8		3 Diesel Smoke, Dangerous Curves .... I'm Gonna Write Momma For Money		$8		Capitol 5783
12/4/71+	4	17		4 I'm A Truck · Where Love Used To Be		$7		Capitol 3236
4/22/72	62	5		5 Country Western Truck Drivin' Singer .... You're The First		$7		Capitol 3298
6/30/73	63	5		6 Awful Lot To Learn About Truck Drivin' .... You Still Got A Hold On Me		$6		Capitol 3616
9/18/76	92	4		7 Truck Driver's Heaven .... It Ain't Even Halloween		$5		Warner 8259
				same tune as "I Dreamed Of A Hillbilly Heaven" by **Eddie Dean**				
10/27/79	99	2		8 The Flying Saucer Man And The Truck Driver .... I Miss You A Little		$10		K.E.Y. 108

SINATRA, Nancy — see TILLIS, Mel

SINGLETARY, Daryle '97
Born on 3/10/71 in Cairo, Georgia. Singer/songwriter.

4/8/95	39	13		1 I'm Living Up To Her Low Expectations .... My Heart's Too Broke		$3	∎	Giant 17902
7/29/95	2[1]	20		2 I Let Her Lie · S:21 Ordinary Heroes		$3	∎	Giant 17818
12/9/95+	4	20		3 Too Much Fun				album cut
				from the album Daryle Singletary on Giant 24606				
5/11/96	50	10		4 Workin' It Out .... What Am I Doing There		$3	∎	Giant 17650
10/12/96+	2[1]	23		5 Amen Kind Of Love				album cut
				from the album All Because Of You on Giant 24660				
3/15/97	48	10		6 The Used To Be's .... That's What I Get For Thinkin'		$3		Giant 17399
7/26/97	68	3		7 Even The Wind				album cut
				from the album All Because Of You on Giant 24660				
11/8/97+	28	20		8 The Note .... S:9 I Let Her Lie	90	$3	∎	Giant 17268

★342★ SINGLETON, Margie   '64

Born Margaret Ebey on 10/5/35 in Coushatta, Louisiana. Singer/songwriter/guitarist. Formerly married to music executive Shelby Singleton. Married Leon Ashley in 1965.

1)Keeping Up With The Joneses 2)Old Records 3)Waltz Of The Angels

DEBUT	PEAK	WKS		A-side / B-side	Pop	$	Pic	Label & Number
8/3/59	25	5		1 Nothin' But True Love .... *It's Better To Know*		$20		Starday 443
2/1/60	12	14		2 The Eyes Of Love .... *Angel Hands*		$20		Starday 472
9/18/61	15	3		3 Did I Ever Tell You .... *Not Even Friends*		$15		Mercury 71856
				GEORGE JONES & MARGIE SINGLETON				
6/16/62	11	10		4 Waltz Of The Angels .... *Talk About Lovin'*		$15		Mercury 71955
				GEORGE JONES & MARGIE SINGLETON				
12/28/63+	11	14		5 Old Records .... *How Do You Celebrate Goodbye*		$12		Mercury 72213
3/14/64	5	23		6 Keeping Up With The Joneses/				
3/28/64	40	6		7 No Thanks, I Just Had One..........		$12	■	Mercury 72237
				MARGIE SINGLETON And FARON YOUNG (above 2)				
12/5/64	38	8		8 Another Woman's Man - Another Man's Woman .... *Honky Tonk Happy*		$12		Mercury 72312
				FARON YOUNG AND MARGIE SINGLETON				
9/9/67	39	8		9 Ode To Billie Joe .... *Big Boys Don't Need Mamas*		$10		Ashley 2011
11/11/67	54	7		10 Hangin' On .... *Four O'Clock*		$10		Ashley 2015
				LEON ASHLEY & MARGIE SINGLETON				
3/2/68	52	8		11 Wandering Mind .... *Your Conscience Sends Me Flowers*		$10		Ashley 2050
5/11/68	55	6		12 You'll Never Be Lonely Again .... *Parting Of The Ways*		$10		Ashley 3000
				LEON ASHLEY - MARGIE SINGLETON				

SKAGGS, Ricky ★80★   '86

Born on 7/18/54 in Cordell, Kentucky. Singer/songwriter/mandolin player. Played mandolin from age five. Member of the Clinch Mountain Boys (1969) and **The Country Gentlemen** (1974). Married **Sharon White** in 1981. Joined the *Grand Ole Opry* in 1982. CMA Awards: 1982 Horizon Award; 1982 Male Vocalist of the Year; 1985 Entertainer of the Year; 1987 Vocal Duo of the Year (with Sharon White).

1)Cajun Moon 2)Lovin' Only Me 3)Uncle Pen 4)I Wouldn't Change You If I Could 5)Highway 40 Blues

DEBUT	PEAK	WKS		A-side / B-side	Pop	$	Pic	Label & Number
4/19/80	86	4		1 I'll Take The Blame .... *Could You Love Me One More Time*		$8		Sugar Hill 3706
5/2/81	16	16		2 Don't Get Above Your Raising .... *Low And Lonely*		$4		Epic 02034
9/12/81	9	17		3 You May See Me Walkin' .... *So Round, So Firm, So Fully Packed*		$4		Epic 02499
1/23/82	❶¹	23		4 Crying My Heart Out Over You .... *Lost To A Stranger*		$4		Epic 02692
5/29/82	❶¹	18		5 I Don't Care .... *If That's The Way You Feel*		$4		Epic 02931
9/18/82	❶¹	17		6 Heartbroke .... *Don't Think I'll Cry*		$4		Epic 03212
12/25/82+	❶¹	20		7 I Wouldn't Change You If I Could .... *One Way Rider*		$4		Epic 03482
4/30/83	❶¹	19		8 Highway 40 Blues .... *Don't Let Your Sweet Love Die*		$4		Epic 03812
8/13/83	2¹	19		9 You've Got A Lover .... *Let's Love The Bad Times Away*		$4		Epic 04044
12/3/83+	❶¹	20		10 Don't Cheat In Our Hometown .... *Children Go*		$4		Sugar Hill/Epic 04245
3/24/84	❶¹	18		11 Honey (Open That Door) .... *She's More To Be Pitied*		$4		Sugar Hill/Epic 04394
7/21/84	❶¹	19		12 Uncle Pen .... S:7 / A:20 *I'm Head Over Heels In Love*		$4		Sugar Hill/Epic 04527
				written by **Bill Monroe**				
11/3/84+	2¹	22		13 Something In My Heart .... S:❶¹ / A:3 *Baby, I'm In Love With You*		$4		Epic 04668
3/23/85	❶¹	19		14 Country Boy .... S:❶¹ / A:❶¹ *Wheel Hoss*		$4		Epic 04831
9/14/85	7	23		15 You Make Me Feel Like A Man .... S:7 / A:8 *Rendezvous*		$4		Epic 05585
1/11/86	❶¹	20		16 Cajun Moon .... S:❶¹ / A:❶¹ *Rockin' The Boat*		$4		Epic 05748
5/24/86	10	18		17 I've Got A New Heartache .... S:7 / A:10 *She Didn't Say Why*		$4		Epic 05898
10/4/86	4	20		18 Love's Gonna Get You Someday .... S:3 / A:4 *Walkin' In Jerusalem*		$4		Epic 06327
2/14/87	30	11		19 I Wonder If I Care As Much .... S:19 / A:30 *Raisin' The Dickens*		$4		Epic 06650
				made the Pop charts as a flip side by **The Everly Brothers** in 1957				
5/2/87	10	23		20 Love Can't Ever Get Better Than This .... S:5 *Daddy Was A Hardworking, Honest Man*		$4		Epic 07060
				RICKY SKAGGS & SHARON WHITE				
10/17/87+	18	20		21 I'm Tired .... S:12 *San Antonio Rose*		$4		Epic 07416
2/27/88	33	13		22 (Angel On My Mind) That's Why I'm Walkin' .... S:16 *Lord, She Sure Is Good At Lovin' Me*		$4		Epic 07721
				same tune as "Why I'm Walkin'" by Stonewall Jackson				
6/11/88	17	16		23 Thanks Again .... S:11 *If You Don't Believe The Bible*		$4		Epic 07924
10/15/88	30	15		24 Old Kind Of Love .... S:19 *Woman You Won't Break Mine*		$4		Epic 08063
4/8/89	❶¹	21		25 Lovin' Only Me .... *Home Is Wherever You Are*		$3		Epic 68693
8/5/89	5	26		26 Let It Be You .... *The Fields Of Home*		$3		Epic 68995
12/9/89+	13	26		27 Heartbreak Hurricane .... *Casting My Shadow In The Road*		$3		Epic 73078
4/21/90	20	16		28 Hummingbird .... *Kentucky Thunder*		$3	▌	Epic 73312
9/1/90	25	20		29 He Was On To Somethin' (So He Made You) .... *When I Love*		$3	▌	Epic 73496
8/17/91	37	18		30 Life's Too Long (To Live Like This) .... *Lonesome For You*		$3		Epic 73947
12/21/91+	12	20		31 Same Ol' Love .... *My Father's Son*		$3	▌	Epic 74147
5/16/92	43	10		32 From The Word Love .... *You Can't Take It With You When You Go*		$3		Epic 74311
11/25/95+	57	14		33 Solid Ground				album cut
4/20/96	45	11		34 Cat's In The Cradle				album cut
				#1 Pop hit for Harry Chapin in 1974; above 2 from the album *Solid Ground* on Atlantic 82834				

★355★

SKINNER, Jimmie '58
Born on 4/27/09 in Blue Lick, Ohio. Died of a heart attack on 10/27/79 (age 70). Singer/songwriter/guitarist. Worked as a DJ in Tennessee and Ohio.
1)I Found My Girl In The USA 2)Dark Hollow 3)What Makes A Man Wander

DEBUT	PEAK	WKS		A-side / B-side		$		Label & Number
4/30/49	15	1		1 Tennessee Border ....S:15 Candy Kisses		$30		Radio Artist 244
11/4/57+	5	17		2 I Found My Girl In The USA A:5 / S:9 Carroll County Blues		$15		Mercury 71192
				answer to "Fraulein" by Bobby Helms and "Geisha Girl" by Hank Locklin				
3/24/58	8	8		3 What Makes A Man Wander A:8 / S:14 We've Got Things In Common		$15		Mercury 71256
1/19/59	7	10		4 Dark Hollow/				
1/12/59	21	8		5 Walkin' My Blues Away		$15		Mercury 71387
8/3/59	17	11		6 John Wesley Hardin ....Misery Loves Company		$15		Mercury 71470
1/18/60	14	11		7 Riverboat Gambler ....Married To A Friend		$15		Mercury 71539
5/16/60	21	4		8 Lonesome Road Blues ....Two Squares Away		$15		Mercury 71606
8/29/60	13	8		9 Reasons To Live ....I'm A Lot More Lonesome Now		$15		Mercury 71663
12/19/60	30	1		10 Careless Love ....I'll Weaken And Call		$15		Mercury 71704

SKIP AND LINDA '82
Duo of Skip Eaton and Linda Davis.

DEBUT	PEAK	WKS		A-side / B-side		$		Label & Number
8/21/82	63	7		1 If You Could See You Through My Eyes ....The Clown		$5		MDJ 68178
10/23/82	73	5		2 I Just Can't Turn Temptation Down ....Don't Surrender Your Love		$5		MDJ 68179
12/18/82	89	4		3 This Time..		$5		MDJ 68180

S-K-O — see SCHUYLER, KNOBLOCH & OVERSTREET

SKY KINGS, The '96
All-star trio: John Cowan (New Grass Revival), Bill Lloyd (Foster & Lloyd) and Rusty Young (Poco).

DEBUT	PEAK	WKS		A-side / B-side		$	Pic	Label & Number
4/20/96	52	7		Picture Perfect ....That's How You Learn About Love		$3	▌	Warner 17663

SLATER, David '88
Born on 11/22/62 in Dallas.

DEBUT	PEAK	WKS		A-side / B-side		$		Label & Number
3/26/88	36	13		1 I'm Still Your Fool ....I've Met My Match		$3		Capitol 44129
6/25/88	30	17		2 The Other Guy Rest Assured		$3		Capitol 44184
				#11 Pop hit for the Little River Band in 1983				
10/22/88	63	8		3 We Were Meant To Be Lovers ....Losin' My Louisiana Blues		$3		Capitol 44257
				#31 Pop hit for Photoglo in 1980				
5/13/89	65	6		4 She Will..The Story Of Us		$3		Capitol 44359
9/23/89	75	3		5 Whatcha Gonna Do About Her ....Be With Me		$3		Capitol 44433

SLEDD, Patsy '74
Born Patricia Randolph on 1/29/44 in Falcon, Missouri. Singer/songwriter/pianist.

DEBUT	PEAK	WKS		A-side / B-side		$	Pic	Label & Number
9/9/72	68	6		1 Nothing Can Stop My Loving You ....Don't Fight The Feeling		$6		Mega 0085
1/5/74	33	12		2 Chip Chip Don't Fight The Feeling		$5		Mega 1203
				#10 Pop hit for Gene McDaniels in 1962				
12/7/74+	72	9		3 See Saw ....We Gotta Lotta Love		$5		Mega 1217
				#25 Pop hit for The Moonglows in 1956				
2/7/76	90	5		4 The Cowboy And The Lady ....This Is It		$5		Mega 1244
11/28/87	79	3		5 Don't Stay If You Don't Love Me ....My Diamond Is Only A Stone		$5	■	Showtime 1007

SLEWFOOT '86
Group from Myrtle Beach, South Carolina.

DEBUT	PEAK	WKS		A-side / B-side		$		Label & Number
9/13/86	85	3		Nice To Be With You ....Better Than This		$5		Step One 360
				#4 Pop hit for Gallery in 1972				

SLIGO STUDIO BAND '81
Group from Norfolk, Virginia.

DEBUT	PEAK	WKS		A-side / B-side		$		Label & Number
4/18/81	94	2		You're The Reason ....She Offered Her Honor		$7		GBS 708

SLOANE, Rene — see MITCHELL, Price

SLYE, Carrie '83
Born on 2/28/60 in Grants, New Mexico; raised in Gurden, Arkansas.

DEBUT	PEAK	WKS		A-side / B-side		$		Label & Number
7/23/83	78	4		Ease The Fever		$7		Friday 42683

SMALLWOOD, Laney '78
Singer/actress. Also recorded as Laney Hicks.

DEBUT	PEAK	WKS		A-side / B-side		$		Label & Number
7/1/78	57	6		1 That "I Love You, You Love Me Too" Love Song ....I'm Sure To Cry		$5		Monument 255
12/19/81	92	3		2 Until The Nights ....I Love The Way You Love Me		$5		Monument 21001
				CHARLIE McCOY & LANEY SMALLWOOD				
				written and first recorded by Billy Joel on his 1978 52nd Street album				
4/16/83	74	4		3 The State Of Our Union ....Just Doin' Nothin' With You (Is Really Somethin')		$5		Monument 03518
				CHARLIE McCOY & LANEY HICKS				

SMART, Jimmy '61
Born in Terrell, Texas.

DEBUT	PEAK	WKS		A-side / B-side		$		Label & Number
10/10/60	18	2		1 Broken Dream ....It's Too Late For Me		$25		Allstar 7211
3/13/61	16	7		2 Shorty ....In My Dreams		$20		Plaid 1004

SMILEY, Red — see RENO & SMILEY

SMITH, Andy Lee '89
Female singer.

DEBUT	PEAK	WKS		A-side / B-side		$	Pic	Label & Number
11/11/89	71	3		Invitation To The Blues...		$5	■	615 1024

SMITH, Arthur "Guitar Boogie"   '49
Born on 4/1/21 in Clinton, South Carolina. Songwriter/guitarist.

9/25/48	9	2		1 Banjo Boogie J:9 Have A Little Fun [I]		$25		MGM 10229
12/25/48+	8	7		2 Guitar Boogie/ J:8 [I]				
				above 2 tunes revised in 1959 as "Guitar Boogie Shuffle" by The Virtues				
1/1/49	8	4		3 Boomerang J:8 [I]		$25		MGM 10293
				ARTHUR "Guitar Boogie" SMITH and His Cracker-Jacks (above 3)				
10/19/63	29	3		4 Tie My Hunting Dog Down, Jed ....Guitar Hop [N]		$15		Starday 642
				parody of "Tie Me Kangaroo Down, Sport" by Rolf Harris				

SMITH, Bobby   '81
Born in 1946 in Balch Springs, Texas.

5/7/77	70	8		1 Do You Wanna Make Love .... Too Turned On		$6		Autumn 398
				#5 Pop hit for Peter McCann in 1977				
8/22/81	30	11		2 Just Enough Love (For One Woman) Goin' In Circles		$4		Liberty 1417
11/28/81+	40	10		3 Too Many Hearts In The Fire................ You Hit Me Right Where I Love		$4		Liberty 1439
2/20/82	47	9		4 And Then Some....................................Everytime I Do		$4		Liberty 1452
10/2/82	68	5		5 It's Been One Of Those Days ....Loving You Could Never Be Better		$4		Liberty 1480

SMITH, Cal ★159★   '75
Born Calvin Grant Shofner on 4/7/32 in Gans, Oklahoma; raised in Oakland, California. Singer/guitarist.

1)It's Time To Pay The Fiddler 2)The Lord Knows I'm Drinking 3)Country Bumpkin
4)I've Found Someone Of My Own 5)Between Lust And Watching TV

1/28/67	58	10		1 The Only Thing I Want................................. Stranger In The House		$7		Kapp 788
8/19/67	61	2		2 I'll Never Be Lonesome With You......................If I Had My Life To Live Over		$7		Kapp 834
2/24/68	60	5		3 Destination Atlanta G.A...........................Did She Ask About Me		$7		Kapp 884
6/22/68	58	7		4 Jacksonville................................ I Love You A Thousand Ways		$7		Kapp 913
10/5/68	35	7		5 Drinking Champagne..............................Honky Tonk Blues		$7		Kapp 938
6/14/69	51	8		6 It Takes All Night Long ....Daddy's Arms		$7		Kapp 994
9/27/69	55	4		7 You Can't Housebreak A Tomcat ....At The Sight Of You		$7		Kapp 2037
1/3/70	47	2		8 Heaven Is Just A Touch Away .... I Overlooked An Orchid		$7		Kapp 2059
4/25/70	70	2		9 The Difference Between Going And Really Gone .... My Happiness Goes Off		$7		Kapp 2076
1/16/71	58	7		10 That's What It's Like To Be Lonesome ....The Only Girl In The Game		$6		Decca 32768
5/6/72	4	15		11 I've Found Someone Of My Own The Lights Of The Living		$6		Decca 32959
				#5 Pop hit for Free Movement in 1971				
9/16/72	58	8		12 For My Baby .... A Handful Of Stars		$6		Decca 33003
				#28 Pop hit for Brook Benton in 1961				
12/16/72+	❶[1]	17		13 The Lord Knows I'm Drinking Sweet Things I Remember About You	64	$6		Decca 33040
5/26/73	25	11		14 I Can Feel The Leavin' Coming On/				
		7		15 I've Loved You All Over The World...............................		$5		MCA 40061
10/13/73	63	9		16 Bleep You/				
		7		17 An Hour And A Six-Pack...		$5		MCA 40136
3/9/74	❶[1]	15		18 Country Bumpkin It's Not The Miles You Traveled		$5		MCA 40191
				CMA Award: Single of the Year				
8/3/74	11	13		19 Between Lust And Watching TV..........................Some Kind Of A Woman		$5		MCA 40265
12/7/74+	❶[1]	16		20 It's Time To Pay The Fiddler Love Is The Foundation		$5		MCA 40335
4/26/75	13	13		21 She Talked A Lot About Texas ....Baby's Gone		$5		MCA 40394
10/25/75	12	14		22 Jason's Farm .... You Slip Into My Mind		$5		MCA 40467
2/14/76	33	10		23 Thunderstorms.........................19 Years And 1800 Miles		$5		MCA 40517
6/5/76	43	9		24 MacArthur's Hand .... Sunday Morning Christian		$5		MCA 40563
10/9/76	38	10		25 Woman Don't Try To Sing My Song .... I Play A Man		$5		MCA 40618
1/22/77	15	14		26 I Just Came Home To Count The Memories........Feelin' The Weight Of My Chains		$5		MCA 40671
4/30/77	23	10		27 Come See About Me .... The In Crowd		$5		MCA 40714
9/24/77	53	8		28 Helen ....I'm Forty Now		$5		MCA 40789
12/17/77+	51	9		29 Throwin' Memories On The Fire ....Tabernacle Tom		$5		MCA 40839
2/25/78	73	4		30 I'm Just A Farmer...................The Ghost Of Jim Bob Wilson		$5		MCA 40864
6/24/78	68	5		31 Bits And Pieces Of Life ....Leona		$5		MCA 40911
1/6/79	71	6		32 The Rise And Fall Of The Roman Empire .... Oklahoma Sunshine		$5		MCA 40982
4/14/79	91	2		33 One Little Skinny Rib .... I Fed Her Love		$5		MCA 41001
11/3/79	92	2		34 The Room At The Top Of The Stairs ....Happy Anniversary		$5		MCA 41128
10/30/82	68	6		35 Too Many Irons In The Fire ....Honky Tonk Girl		$5		Soundwaves 4686
				BILLY PARKER and CAL SMITH				
9/6/86	75	5		36 King Lear .... Country Bumpkin'		$5		Step One 358

SMITH, Carl ★25★   '51

Born on 3/15/27 in Maynardwalle, Tennessee. Singer/songwriter/guitarist. Began singing on radio station WROL in Knoxville. Served in the U.S. Navy from 1945-47. Played bass in Skeets Williamson's band. Formerly married to **June Carter**; their daughter is **Carlene Carter**. Married **Goldie Hill** in 1957.

1)Let Old Mother Nature Have Her Way 2)Hey Joe! 3)Don't Just Stand There 4)Loose Talk
5)Are You Teasing Me

DEBUT	PEAK	WKS		A-side	B-side	Pop	$	Pic	Label & Number
6/2/51	2[1]	20	1	Let's Live A Little	A:2 / S:3 / J:3 There's Nothing As Sweet As My Baby		$25		Columbia 4-20796
8/4/51	4	17	2	Mr. Moon/	A:4 / J:5 / S:8				
8/4/51	8	3	3	If Teardrops Were Pennies	J:8 / A:9 / S:9		$25		Columbia 4-20825
10/27/51	❶[8]	33	4	Let Old Mother Nature Have Her Way	J:❶[8] / S:❶[6] / A:❶[3] Me And My Broken Heart		$25		Columbia 4-20862
3/1/52	❶[8]	24	5	(When You Feel Like You're In Love) Don't Just Stand There	A:❶[8] / S:❶[5] / J:❶[3] The Little Girl In My Home Town		$25		Columbia 4-20893
5/24/52	❶[1]	19	6	Are You Teasing Me/	A:❶[1] / S:2 / J:2				
5/31/52	5	10	7	It's A Lovely, Lovely World	A:5 / S:8 / J:9		$25		Columbia 4-20922
10/25/52	6	6	8	Our Honeymoon	A:6 / J:6 / S:7 Sing Her A Love Song		$25		Columbia 4-21008
1/31/53	9	1	9	That's The Kind Of Love I'm Looking For	J:9 My Lonely Heart's Runnin' Wild		$20		Columbia 21051
5/9/53	4	6	10	Orchids Mean Goodbye/	J:4 / A:7 / S:7				
5/2/53	7	3	11	Just Wait 'Til I Get You Alone	A:7 / J:7 / S:9		$20		Columbia 21087
7/4/53	2[2]	10	12	Trademark/	S:2 / J:5 / A:6				
7/18/53	6	1	13	Do I Like It?	A:6		$20		Columbia 21119
7/25/53	❶[8]	26	14	Hey Joe!	J:❶[8] / A:❶[4] / S:❶[2] Darlin' Am I The One		$20		Columbia 21129
11/7/53	7	6	15	Satisfaction Guaranteed	S:7 / A:7 / J:8 Who'll Buy My Heartaches		$20		Columbia 21166
2/13/54	7	4	16	Dog-Gone It, Baby, I'm In Love	A:7 / S:8 What Am I Going To Do With You?		$20		Columbia 21197
5/1/54	2[1]	16	17	Back Up Buddy	A:2 / S:4 / J:4 If You Tried As Hard To Love Me		$20		Columbia 21226
8/7/54	4	11	18	Go, Boy, Go	S:4 / A:7 / J:9 If You Saw Her Through My Eyes		$20		Columbia 21266
11/6/54+	❶[7]	32	19	Loose Talk/	S:❶[7] / A:❶[6] / J:❶[4]				
11/6/54+	5	10	20	More Than Anything Else In The World	A:5 / S:15		$20		Columbia 21317
1/22/55	5	16	21	Kisses Don't Lie	S:5 / J:7 / A:8				
1/29/55	13	2	22	No, I Don't Believe I Will	S:13 / A:15		$20		Columbia 21340
4/23/55	12	3	23	Wait A Little Longer Please, Jesus	A:12 Works Of The Lord		$20		Columbia 21368
5/14/55	3	25	24	There She Goes/	A:3 / S:5 / J:8				
				#26 Pop hit for **Jerry Wallace** in 1961					
5/14/55	11	7	25	Old Lonesome Times	S:11 / A:13		$20		Columbia 21382
10/15/55	11	4	26	Don't Tease Me	A:11 / S:13 I Just Dropped In To Say Goodbye		$20		Columbia 21429
12/3/55+	6	14	27	You're Free To Go/	S:6 / J:6 / A:7				
12/3/55+	7	15	28	I Feel Like Cryin'	S:7 / J:9 / A:11		$20		Columbia 21462
3/31/56	11	3	29	I've Changed	A:11 / S:14 If You Do Dear		$20		Columbia 21493
6/23/56	4	23	30	You Are The One/	A:4 / J:5 / S:6				
8/4/56	6	6	31	Doorstep To Heaven	S:6		$20		Columbia 21522
10/13/56	6	12	32	Before I Met You/	J:6 / A:7 / S:9				
				CARL SMITH with The Tunesmiths (above 3)					
10/20/56	9	10	33	Wicked Lies	S:9		$20		Columbia 21552
3/2/57	15	1	34	You Can't Hurt Me Anymore	S:15 That's The Way I Like You The Best		$20		Columbia 40823
9/16/57	2[2]	13	35	Why, Why	A:2 / S:7 Emotions		$15		Columbia 40984
3/3/58	6	14	36	Your Name Is Beautiful	A:6 / S:9 You're So Easy To Love	80	$15		Columbia 41092
12/15/58	28	1	37	Walking The Slow Walk	A Love Was Born		$15		Columbia 41243
1/19/59	15	11	38	The Best Years Of Your Life	Mr. Moon		$15		Columbia 41290
6/1/59	19	3	39	It's All My Heartache	I'll Kiss The Past Goodbye		$12		Columbia 41344
7/20/59	5	12	40	Ten Thousand Drums	The Tall, Tall Gentleman	43	$12	■	Columbia 41417
12/14/59	24	4	41	Tomorrow Night	I'll Walk With You		$12		Columbia 41489
3/21/60	30	1	42	Make The Waterwheel Roll	Past		$12		Columbia 41557
6/20/60	28	2	43	Cut Across Shorty	Why Did You Come My Way		$12		Columbia 41642
2/20/61	29	2	44	You Make Me Live Again	I Don't Hurt Now (As Much As I Used To)		$12		Columbia 41819
7/10/61	11	9	45	Kisses Never Lie	Why Can't You Be Satisfied With Me		$12		Columbia 42042
1/13/62	11	15	46	Air Mail To Heaven/					
1/27/62	24	2	47	Things That Mean The Most			$12		Columbia 42222
5/12/62	16	7	48	The Best Dressed Beggar (In Town)	I Used To Be		$12		Columbia 42349
4/20/63	28	1	49	Live For Tomorrow	Let's Talk This Thing Over		$12		Columbia 42686
8/24/63	17	8	50	In The Back Room Tonight	Take My Love With You, Too		$12		Columbia 42768
12/21/63+	16	11	51	Triangle/					
11/9/63+	23	5	52	I Almost Forgot Her Today			$12		Columbia 42858
2/22/64	17	14	53	The Pillow That Whispers	Sweet Little Country Girl		$12		Columbia 42949
6/20/64	15	20	54	Take My Ring Off Your Finger	The Ballad Of Hershel Lawson		$10		Columbia 43033
10/17/64	14	15	55	Lonely Girl/					
12/12/64+	26	9	56	When It's Over			$10		Columbia 43124
2/13/65	32	11	57	She Called Me Baby	My Friends Are Gonna Be Strangers		$10		Columbia 43200
6/26/65	33	8	58	Be Good To Her/					
6/12/65	42	3	59	Keep Me Fooled			$10		Columbia 43266
10/16/65	36	6	60	Let's Walk Away Strangers	Ain't Love A Hurting Thing		$10		Columbia 43361

SMITH, Carl — Cont'd

DEBUT	PEAK	WKS		A-side / B-side	Pop	$	Pic	Label & Number
3/12/66	45	4		61 Why Do I Keep Doing This To Us/				
3/19/66	49	1		62 Why Can't You Feel Sorry For Me...		$10		Columbia 43485
9/17/66	42	5		63 Man With A Plan .... You Mean Ol' Moon		$10		Columbia 43753
12/3/66+	52	8		64 You Better Be Better To Me/				
1/14/67	65	3		65 It's Only A Matter Of Time		$10		Columbia 43866
5/13/67	54	7		66 I Should Get Away Awhile (From You)/				
4/22/67	68	3		67 Mighty Day		$8		Columbia 44034
8/26/67	10	18		68 Deep Water .... I Really Don't Want To Know		$8		Columbia 44233
1/13/68	18	11		69 Foggy River .... When Will The Rainbow Follow The Rain		$8		Columbia 44396
5/18/68	43	9		70 You Ought To Hear Me Cry .... I Used Up My Last Chance Last Night		$8		Columbia 44486
9/21/68	48	5		71 There's No More Love .... (Remember Me) I'm The One Who Loves You		$8		Columbia 44620
1/4/69	25	13		72 Faded Love And Winter Roses .... Until I Looked At You		$8		Columbia 44702
4/26/69	18	13		73 Good Deal, Lucille .... Never Gonna Cry No More		$8		Columbia 44816
8/16/69	14	12		74 I Love You Because .... Mister, Come And Get Your Wife		$8		Columbia 44939
12/6/69+	35	8		75 Heartbreak Avenue .... It's Nice To See You Once Again		$8		Columbia 45031
3/14/70	18	10		76 Pull My String And Wind Me Up .... It's All Right		$8		Columbia 45086
7/11/70	46	8		77 Pick Me Up On Your Way Down/				
		4		78 Bonaparte's Retreat		$7		Columbia 45177
10/3/70	20	12		79 How I Love Them Old Songs .... Little Crop Of Cotton Tops		$7		Columbia 45225
2/13/71	44	10		80 Don't Worry 'Bout The Mule (Just Load The Wagon) .... Darling Days		$7		Columbia 45293
6/5/71	43	8		81 Lost It On The Road .... I'm Wound Up Tight (Now Turn Me Loose)		$6		Columbia 45382
9/11/71	21	13		82 Red Door .... You Walked In My Sleep Last Night		$6		Columbia 45436
12/11/71+	34	12		83 Don't Say You're Mine .... Country Soul Man		$6		Columbia 45497
5/13/72	46	11		84 Mama Bear .... Before My Time		$6		Columbia 45558
8/5/72	54	9		85 If This Is Goodbye .... If You Saw Her		$6		Columbia 45648
9/29/73	76	6		86 I Need Help .... Yesterday Is Gone		$6		Columbia 45923
1/25/75	67	9		87 The Way I Lose My Mind .... Happy Birthday My Darlin'		$5		Hickory/MGM 337
11/15/75	97	2		88 Roly Poly............................ Remembered By Someone (Remembered By Me)		$5		Hickory/MGM 357
5/29/76	97	3		89 If You Don't, Somebody Else Will .... It's Gonna Be One Of Those Days		$5		Hickory/MGM 371
12/11/76	98	4		90 A Way With Words .... Till I Stop Needing You		$5		ABC/Hickory 54004
4/9/77	96	4		91 Show Me A Brick Wall .... It's Teardrop Time		$5		ABC/Hickory 54009
9/3/77	84	4		92 This Kinda Love Ain't Meant For Sunday School........ There Stands The Glass		$5		ABC/Hickory 54016
2/4/78	81	4		93 This Lady Loving Me .... Loose Talk		$5		ABC/Hickory 54022

SMITH, Connie ★70★   '64

Born Constance June Meador on 8/14/41 in Elkhart, Indiana; raised in Hinton, West Virginia, and Warner, Ohio. Singer/songwriter. Joined the *Grand Ole Opry* in 1971. Acted in the movies *Las Vegas Hillbillies*, *Road To Nashville* and *Second Fiddle To A Steel Guitar*. Married Marty Stuart on 7/8/97.

1)Once A Day 2)Ain't Had No Lovin' 3)Just One Time 4)The Hurtin's All Over 5)Cincinnati, Ohio

DEBUT	PEAK	WKS		A-side / B-side	Pop	$	Pic	Label & Number
9/26/64	❶[8]	28		1 Once A Day The Threshold	101	$10		RCA Victor 8416
1/23/65	4	24		2 Then And Only Then/	116			
2/6/65	25	17		3 Tiny Blue Transistor Radio..		$10		RCA Victor 8489
6/5/65	9	16		4 I Can't Remember Senses	130	$10		RCA Victor 8551
9/25/65	4	19		5 If I Talk To Him I Don't Have Anyplace To Go		$10		RCA Victor 8663
2/12/66	4	17		6 Nobody But A Fool (Would Love You) I'll Never Get Over Loving You		$10		RCA Victor 8746
6/11/66	2[2]	17		7 Ain't Had No Lovin' Five Fingers To Spare		$10		RCA Victor 8842
10/15/66	3	19		8 The Hurtin's All Over Invisible Tears		$10		RCA Victor 8964
3/11/67	10	15		9 I'll Come Runnin' It's Now Or Never		$10		RCA Victor 9108
6/24/67	4	15		10 Cincinnati, Ohio Don't Feel Sorry For Me		$10	■	RCA Victor 9214
10/28/67	5	15		11 Burning A Hole In My Mind Only For Me		$10		RCA Victor 9335
1/27/68	7	14		12 Baby's Back Again It Only Hurts For A Little While		$10		RCA Victor 9413
5/18/68	10	15		13 Run Away Little Tears Let Me Help You Work It Out		$10		RCA Victor 9513
9/28/68	20	11		14 Cry, Cry, Cry The Hurt Goes On		$10		RCA Victor 9624
3/1/69	13	14		15 Ribbon Of Darkness A Lonely Woman		$8		RCA Victor 0101
7/5/69	20	11		16 Young Love .... Something Pretty		$8		RCA Victor 0181
				CONNIE SMITH AND NAT STUCKEY				
				#1 Pop hit for Tab Hunter in 1957				
11/8/69	6	15		17 You And Your Sweet Love I Can't Get Used To Being Lonely		$8		RCA Victor 0258
3/14/70	59	4		18 If God Is Dead (Who's That Living In My Soul)............... His Love Takes Care Of Me		$8		RCA Victor 9805
				NAT STUCKEY AND CONNIE SMITH				
5/16/70	5	15		19 I Never Once Stopped Loving You The Son Shines Down On Me		$7		RCA Victor 9832
9/12/70	14	11		20 Louisiana Man .... Alone With You		$7		RCA Victor 9887
1/2/71	11	14		21 Where Is My Castle .... Clinging To A Saving Hand		$7		RCA Victor 9938
5/8/71	2[2]	17		22 Just One Time Don't Walk Away	119	$7		RCA Victor 9981
10/16/71	14	15		23 I'm Sorry If My Love Got In Your Way.......................... Plenty Of Time		$7		RCA Victor 0535
3/4/72	5	15		24 Just For What I Am I'd Still Want To Serve Him Today		$7		RCA Victor 0655
8/5/72	7	15		25 If It Ain't Love (Let's Leave It Alone) Living Without You		$7		RCA Victor 0752
12/23/72+	8	14		26 Love Is The Look You're Looking For My Ecstasy		$7		RCA Victor 0860

DEBUT	PEAK	WKS	Gold	A-side (Chart Hit)...B-side	Pop	$	Pic	Label & Number
				SMITH, Connie — Cont'd				
3/31/73	21	12		27 You've Got Me (Right Where You Want Me) .... *A Picture Of Me (Without You)*		$6		Columbia 45816
6/23/73	23	10		28 Dream Painter .... *Once A Day*		$7		RCA Victor 0971
11/10/73+	10	14		29 Ain't Love A Good Thing .... *I Still Feel The Same About You*		$6		Columbia 45954
3/23/74	35	11		30 Dallas .... *That's The Way Love Goes*		$6		Columbia 46008
6/29/74	13	13		31 I Never Knew (What That Song Meant Before) ....*Did We Have To Come This Far (To Say Goodbye)*		$6		Columbia 46058
11/16/74+	13	12		32 I've Got My Baby On My Mind .... *Why Don't You Love Me*		$5		Columbia 10051
2/22/75	30	10		33 I Got A Lot Of Hurtin' Done Today ....*Back In The Country*		$5		Columbia 10086
5/17/75	15	13		34 Why Don't You Love Me .... *Loving You (Has Changed My Whole Life)*		$5		Columbia 10135
10/4/75	29	11		35 The Song We Fell In Love To .... *One Little Reason*		$5		Columbia 10210
1/31/76	10	15		36 ('Til) I Kissed You .... *Ridin' On A Rainbow*		$5		Columbia 10277
6/5/76	31	10		37 So Sad (To Watch Good Love Go Bad) .... *Constantly* #7 Pop hit for The Everly Brothers in 1960		$5		Columbia 10345
8/28/76	13	14		38 I Don't Wanna Talk It Over Anymore .... *You Crossed My Mind A Thousand Times Today*		$5		Columbia 10393
3/26/77	42	8		39 The Latest Shade Of Blue ....*I'm All Wrapped Up In You*		$5		Columbia 10501
5/28/77	58	7		40 Coming Around .... *You And Love And I*		$5		Monument 219
11/5/77+	14	15		41 I Just Want To Be Your Everything .... *Scrapbook* #1 Pop hit for Andy Gibb in 1977		$5		Monument 231
2/25/78	34	10		42 Lovin' You Baby ....*All Of A Sudden*		$5		Monument 241
5/27/78	68	6		43 There'll Never Be Another For Me ....*The Wayward Wind*		$5		Monument 252
11/4/78	68	5		44 Smooth Sailin'................................... *Loving You Has Sure Been Good To Me*		$5		Monument 266
4/7/79	88	3		45 Lovin' You, Lovin' Me/				
		3		46 Ten Thousand And One		$5		Monument 281
6/23/79	93	2		47 Don't Say Love .... *I Don't Want To Be Free*		$5		Monument 284
7/27/85	71	6		48 A Far Cry From You .... *Don't Touch (The Pain's Not Dry)*		$4	■	Epic 05414
				SMITH, Darden **'88** Born on 3/11/62 in Brenham, Texas.				
2/20/88	56	8		1 Little Maggie .... *Place In Time*		$3		Epic 07709
5/28/88	59	6		2 Day After Tomorrow... *God's Will*		$3		Epic 07906
				SMITH, David **'79** Singer from Dallas.				
10/20/79	64	5		Heroes And Idols (Don't Come Easy) .... *Loraine Phillips*		$5		MDJ 1004
				SMITH, Dennis **'80**				
3/1/80	94	2		California Calling .... *Get It Together*		$7		Adonda 79021
				SMITH, Jerry **'69** Session pianist. Also recorded as **Papa Joe's Music Box**.				
5/17/69	44	10		1 Truck Stop .... *My Happiness* [I]	71	$7		ABC 11162
8/16/69	63	5		2 Sweet 'N' Sassy .... *Sunrise Serenade* [I]		$7		ABC 11230
12/20/69	62	3		3 Papa Joe's Thing...*Jean* [I] **PAPA JOE'S MUSIC BOX**		$7		ABC 11246
6/6/70	44	9		4 Drivin' Home .... *Louisiana Blues* [I]	125	$6		Decca 32679
10/3/70	60	7		5 Steppin' Out ....*Closing Time* [I]		$6		Decca 32730
				SMITH, Kate **'48** Born on 5/1/07 in Greenville, Virginia. Died on 6/17/86 (age 79). Popular soprano. Hosted own radio and TV shows. Charted 9 pop hits from 1940-48.				
10/30/48	10	1		Foggy River .... *S:10 Cool Water*		$12		MGM 30059
				SMITH, Logan **'74** Male singer/songwriter.				
1/19/74	63	11		Little Man................................ *Down On The Farm* [N]		$7		Brand X 6
				SMITH, Lou **'60**				
8/15/60	9	17		1 Cruel Love .... *Close To My Heart*		$20		KRCO 105
4/17/61	21	5		2 I'm Wondering .... *Aching Breaking Heart*		$20		Salvo 2862

SMITH, Margo ★175★   **'78**
Born Betty Lou Miller on 4/9/42 in Dayton, Ohio. Singer/songwriter/actress.

1)Don't Break The Heart That Loves You 2)It Only Hurts For A Little While 3)Little Things Mean A Lot 4)Still A Woman 5)Take My Breath Away

DEBUT	PEAK	WKS	Gold	A-side	B-side	$	Label & Number
4/5/75	8	18		1 There I Said It	*Hurt Me Twice*	$6	20th Century 2172
9/13/75	30	12		2 Paper Lovin' .... *He Don't Love Here*		$6	20th Century 2222
12/20/75+	51	8		3 Meet Me Later .... *Baby's Hurtin'*		$6	20th Century 2255
5/29/76	10	14		4 Save Your Kisses For Me .... *I'm About To Do It Again* #27 Pop hit for The Brotherhood Of Man in 1976		$5	Warner 8213
10/2/76	7	16		5 Take My Breath Away .... *When Where And Why*		$5	Warner 8261
3/12/77	12	12		6 Love's Explosion .... *So Close Again*		$5	Warner 8339
6/25/77	23	10		7 My Weakness .... *I'd Rather Have A Heart Abused*		$5	Warner 8399
8/20/77	43	8		8 So Close Again .... *Saturday Night At The General Store* **MARGO SMITH & NORRO WILSON**		$5	Warner 8427

DEBUT	PEAK	WKS	Gold	A-side (Chart Hit)..B-side	Pop	$	Pic	Label & Number
				SMITH, Margo — Cont'd				
12/17/77+	❶²	18		9 **Don't Break The Heart That Loves You** *Apt. #4, Sixth Street In Cincinnati*	104	$5		Warner 8508
				#1 Pop hit for **Connie Francis** in 1962				
4/29/78	❶¹	15		10 **It Only Hurts For A Little While** *Lookout Mountain*		$5		Warner 8555
				#11 Pop hit for The Ames Brothers in 1956				
9/9/78	3	14		11 **Little Things Mean A Lot** *Make Love The Way We Used To*		$5		Warner 8653
				#1 Pop hit for Kitty Kallen in 1954				
1/20/79	7	13		12 **Still A Woman** *Tennessee Sandman*		$5		Warner 8726
5/5/79	10	13		13 **If I Give My Heart To You** *We'd Better Love It Over*		$5		Warner 8806
				#3 Pop hit for Doris Day in 1954				
9/8/79	27	9		14 **Baby My Baby** .... *The Belle Of Buttercup Lane*		$4		Warner 49038
12/8/79+	13	13		15 **The Shuffle Song** .... *Move Over Juanita*		$4		Warner 49109
7/5/80	43	9		16 **My Guy** .... *If You Remember Me*		$4		Warner 49250
				#1 Pop hit for Mary Wells in 1964				
10/11/80	52	7		17 **He Gives Me Diamonds, You Give Me Chills** .... *Every Little Bit Hurts*		$4		Warner 49569
12/20/80+	12	14		18 **Cup Of Tea** .... *Goodbye*		$4		Warner 49626
				REX ALLEN, JR. AND MARGO SMITH				
4/25/81	72	4		19 **My Heart Cries For You** .... *Borrowed Angel*		$4		Warner 49701
				#2 Pop hit for Guy Mitchell in 1951				
6/13/81	26	12		20 **While The Feeling's Good** .... *Watered Down Love*		$4		Warner 49738
				REX ALLEN, JR. & MARGO SMITH				
5/8/82	64	7		21 **Either You're Married Or You're Single** .... *Where The Heart Leads*		$5		AMI 1304
8/21/82	70	5		22 **Could It Be I Don't Belong Here Anymore** .... *Ridin' High*		$5		AMI 1309
12/10/83	78	4		23 **Wedding Bells**		$5		Moon Shine 3019
1/28/84	63	7		24 **Please Tell Him That I Said Hello**		$5		Moon Shine 3021
				#84 Pop hit for Debbie Campbell in 1975				
6/22/85	82	2		25 **All I Do Is Dream Of You**		$7		Bermuda Dunes 106
8/10/85	63	8		26 **Everyday People**		$7		Bermuda Dunes 110
				MARGO SMITH AND TOM GRANT				
4/23/88	77	4		27 **Echo Me** .... *Love Letters In The Sand*		$7		Playback 1300
				SMITH, Rick **'76**				
				Born in Louisville, Kentucky.				
9/11/76	99	2		1 **The Way I Loved Her** .... *Catchin' The 9:45*		$5		Cin Kay 110
10/23/76	58	7		2 **Daddy How'm I Doin'** .... *The Blues Was Here To Stay*		$5		Cin Kay 114
				SMITH, Russell **'89**				
				Born Howard Russell Smith on 6/17/49 in Nashville. Former lead singer of the **Amazing Rhythm Aces**.				
2/4/84	74	6		1 **Where Did We Go Right** .... *Hesitation*		$4		Capitol 5293
5/14/88	53	8		2 **Three Piece Suit** .... *Not Made Of Stone*		$3		Epic 07789
7/23/88	49	8		3 **Betty Jean** .... *Not Made Of Stone*		$3		Epic 07972
3/18/89	37	14		4 **I Wonder What She's Doing Tonight** *This Little Town*		$3		Epic 68615
7/22/89	61	8		5 **Anger And Tears** .... *The Colorado Side*		$3		Epic 68964

SMITH, Sammi ★143★ **'71**

Born Jewel Fay Smith on 8/5/43 in Orange, California; raised in Oklahoma. Female singer/songwriter.

1)Help Me Make It Through The Night 2)Today I Started Loving You Again 3)Then You Walk In
4)I've Got To Have You 5)Cheatin's A Two Way Street

DEBUT	PEAK	WKS	Gold	A-side (Chart Hit) B-side	Pop	$	Pic	Label & Number
1/27/68	69	2		1 **So Long, Charlie Brown, Don't Look For Me Around** .... *Turn Around*		$7		Columbia 44370
6/8/68	53	7		2 **Why Do You Do Me Like You Do** .... *22 Road Markers To A Mile*		$7		Columbia 44523
8/16/69	58	6		3 **Brownville Lumberyard** .... *Shadows Of Your Mind*		$7		Columbia 44905
9/5/70	25	13		4 **He's Everywhere** .... *This Room For Rent*		$6	■	Mega 0001
12/19/70+	❶³	20	●	5 **Help Me Make It Through The Night** *When Michael Calls*	8	$6		Mega 0015
				CMA Award: Single of the Year				
5/15/71	10	14		6 **Then You Walk In** *Willie*	118	$6		Mega 0026
9/18/71	27	12		7 **For The Kids** .... *Saunders' Ferry Lane*		$6		Mega 0039
1/1/72	38	10		8 **Kentucky** .... *The Marionette*		$6		Mega 0056
4/22/72	36	8		9 **Girl In New Orleans** .... *Isn't It Sad*		$6		Mega 0068
6/17/72	13	15		10 **I've Got To Have You** .... *Jimmy's In Georgia*	77	$6		Mega 0079
12/23/72+	51	8		11 **The Toast Of '45** .... *Tony*		$6		Mega 0097
5/19/73	62	8		12 **I Miss You Most When You're Here** .... *Billy Jacks*		$6		Mega 0109
9/29/73	44	12		13 **City Of New Orleans** .... *Don't Blow No Smoke On Me*		$6		Mega 0118
				#18 Pop hit for Arlo Guthrie in 1972				
1/19/74	16	12		14 **The Rainbow In Daddy's Eyes** .... *Birmingham Mistake*		$5		Mega 1204
6/1/74	75	7		15 **Never Been To Spain** .... *It's Not Easy*		$5		Mega 1210
				#5 Pop hit for Three Dog Night in 1972				
9/7/74	26	13		16 **Long Black Veil** .... *Paste Me On Some Feathers*		$5		Mega 1214
2/1/75	33	11		17 **Cover Me** .... *He Makes It Hard To Say Goodbye*		$5		Mega 1222
9/13/75	9	15		18 **Today I Started Loving You Again** *Fine As Wine*		$5		Mega 1236
12/20/75+	81	7		19 **Huckelberry Pie** .... *I Won't Sing No Love Songs Anymore*		$5		Elektra 45292
				EVEN STEVENS/SAMMI SMITH				
1/10/76	51	6		20 **My Window Faces The South** .... *Before The Next Teardrop Falls*		$5		Mega 1246

DEBUT	PEAK	WKS	Gold	A-side (Chart Hit) .... B-side	Pop	$	Plc	Label & Number

SMITH, Sammi — Cont'd

DEBUT	PEAK	WKS	A-side	B-side	$	Label & Number
2/21/76	43	9	21 As Long As There's A Sunday	Children	$5	Elektra 45300
5/29/76	60	6	22 I'll Get Better	Rabbitt Tracks	$5	Elektra 45320
7/17/76	29	11	23 Sunday School To Broadway	Good Mornin' Sunshine, Goodbye	$5	Elektra 45334
7/31/76	71	6	24 Just You 'N' Me	Walking In The Sunshine	$5	Zodiac 1005
			#4 Pop hit for Chicago in 1973			
2/5/77	19	12	25 Loving Arms	I Just Wanted To Sing	$5	Elektra 45374
5/14/77	27	11	26 I Can't Stop Loving You	De Grazia's Song	$5	Elektra 45398
			#1 Pop hit for Ray Charles in 1962			
9/17/77	23	11	27 Days That End In "Y"	Hallelujah For Beer	$5	Elektra 45429
4/29/78	48	8	28 It Just Won't Feel Like Cheating (With You)	I Ain't Got Time To Rock No Babies	$5	Elektra 45476
8/5/78	73	4	29 Norma Jean	Lookin' For Lovin'	$5	Elektra 45504
3/10/79	16	14	30 What A Lie	It's Not My Way	$7	Cyclone 100
7/21/79	27	11	31 The Letter	It's A Day For Sad Song	$7	Cyclone 104
			#1 Pop hit for The Box Tops in 1967			
11/29/80+	36	13	32 I Just Want To Be With You	I've Never Loved You More Than I Do Now	$5	Sound Factory 425
3/7/81	16	13	33 Cheatin's A Two Way Street	The Legend Of Wooley Swamp	$5	Sound Factory 427
8/8/81	34	11	34 Sometimes I Cry When I'm Alone	Once Or Twice	$5	Sound Factory 446
3/27/82	69	5	35 Gypsy And Joe		$5	Sound Factory 433
7/20/85	76	4	36 You Just Hurt My Last Feeling	Lying In My Arms	$5	Step One 342
3/1/86	80	4	37 Love Me All Over	Don't Let It Happen Again	$5	Step One 351

SMITH, Warren   **'60**

Born on 2/7/33 in Humphreys County, Mississippi. Died of a heart attack on 1/30/80 (age 46). Rockabilly singer/songwriter.

DEBUT	PEAK	WKS	A-side	B-side	$	Label & Number
9/5/60	5	17	1 I Don't Believe I'll Fall In Love Today	Cave In	$15	Liberty 55248
2/20/61	7	15	2 Odds And Ends (Bits And Pieces)	A Whole Lot Of Nothin'	$15	Liberty 55302
9/11/61	23	3	3 Why, Baby, Why	Why I'm Walking	$15	Liberty 55361
			WARREN SMITH and SHIRLEY COLLIE			
9/11/61	26	3	4 Call Of The Wild	Old Lonesome Feeling	$15	Liberty 55336
11/2/63	25	4	5 That's Why I Sing In A Honky Tonk/			
1/11/64	41	2	6 Big City Ways		$15	Liberty 55615
8/1/64	41	8	7 Blue Smoke	Judge And Jury	$15	Liberty 55699

SMOKIN' ARMADILLOS   **'96**

Group from Bakersfield, California: Rick Russell (vocals), Josh Graham and Scott Meeks (guitars), Jason Theiste (fiddle), Aaron Casida (bass) and Darin Kirkindoll (drums).

DEBUT	PEAK	WKS	A-side	B-side	$	Plc	Label & Number
1/13/96	53	10	1 Let Your Heart Lead Your Mind	Miracle Man	$3	▌	MCG/Curb 76976
5/11/96	68	4	2 Thump Factor	S:21 Miracle Man	$3	▌	MCG/Curb 76989

SNODGRASS, Elmer   **'60**

Worked as a DJ on WAKE in Bakersfield, California.

DEBUT	PEAK	WKS	A-side	B-side	$	Label & Number
1/18/60	20	10	1 Until Today	Sidelines	$15	Decca 31048
			ELMER SNODGRASS AND THE MUSICAL PIONEERS			
1/30/61	25	1	2 What A Terrible Feeling	Heartaches Over You	$15	Decca 31145

SNOW, Hank ★22★   **'50**

Born Clarence Eugene Snow on 5/9/14 in Brooklyn, Nova Scotia, Canada. Singer/songwriter/guitarist. Hosted own radio shows on CNHS in Halifax, CBC in Montreal and CKCW in Mocton, Canada. Joined the *Grand Ole Opry* in 1950. Backing group: The Rainbow Ranch Boys. Known as "The Singing Ranger." Elected to the Country Music Hall of Fame in 1979.

1)I'm Moving On 2)I Don't Hurt Anymore 3)The Rhumba Boogie 4)The Golden Rocket
5)I've Been Everywhere

HANK SNOW, The Singing Ranger and his Rainbow Ranch Boys:

DEBUT	PEAK	WKS	A-side	B-side	$	Label & Number
12/31/49	10	1	1 Marriage Vow	S:10 The Star Spangled Waltz	$30	RCA Victor 48-0056
			78 rpm: 21-0062			
7/1/50	❶²¹	44	2 I'm Moving On	S:❶²¹ / A:❶¹⁸ / J:❶¹⁴ With This Ring I Thee Wed	$25	RCA Victor 48-0328
			also see #78 below			
11/25/50+	❶²	23	3 The Golden Rocket	S:❶² / A:❶¹ / J:2 Paving The Highway With Tears	$25	RCA Victor 48-0400
3/3/51	❶⁸	27	4 The Rhumba Boogie	S:❶⁸ / J:❶⁵ / A:❶² You Pass Me By	$25	RCA Victor 48-0431
5/12/51	2¹	14	5 Down The Trail Of Achin' Hearts/	J:2 / A:7 / S:7		
4/21/51	4	11	6 Bluebird Island	S:4 / J:7	$25	RCA Victor 48-0441
			HANK SNOW (The Singing Ranger) with ANITA CARTER and the Rainbow Ranch Boys (above 2)			
9/15/51	6	6	7 Unwanted Sign Upon Your Heart	S:6 / A:9 Your Locket Is My Broken Heart	$25	RCA Victor 48-0498
12/15/51+	4	9	8 Music Makin' Mama From Memphis	J:4 / A:5 / S:6 The Highest Bidder	$20	RCA Victor 47-4346
4/5/52	2³	18	9 The Gold Rush Is Over	J:2 / A:4 / S:4 Why Do You Punish Me (For Loving You)	$20	RCA Victor 47-4522
7/5/52	2¹	14	10 Lady's Man/	S:2 / J:5 / A:6		
7/26/52	8	3	11 Married By The Bible, Divorced By The Law	J:8 / S:10	$20	RCA Victor 47-4733
9/27/52	3	11	12 I Went To Your Wedding	J:3 / A:4 / S:4 The Boogie Woogie Flying Cloud	$20	RCA Victor 47-4909
12/27/52+	3	16	13 (Now And Then, There's) A Fool Such As I/	A:3 / J:3 / S:4	$20	
			#2 Pop hit for Elvis Presley in 1959			
12/13/52+	4	10	14 The Gal Who Invented Kissin'	S:4 / J:5 / A:9		RCA Victor 5034
4/4/53	9	9	15 Honeymoon On A Rocket Ship	S:9 / A:9 / J:⁹ There Wasn't An Organ At Our Wedding	$20	RCA Victor 5155
6/6/53	3	11	16 Spanish Fire Ball	S:3 / J:4 / A:5 Between Fire And Water	$20	RCA Victor 5296
10/3/53	10	1	17 For Now And Always	A:10 A Message From The Tradewinds	$20	RCA Victor 5380

DEBUT	PEAK	WKS	Gold	A-side (Chart Hit) .... B-side	Pop	$	Pic	Label & Number
				SNOW, Hank — Cont'd				
11/28/53	6	6	18	When Mexican Joe Met Jole Blon _S:8 / J:9 No Longer A Prisoner_		$20		RCA Victor 5490
5/29/54	❶20	41	19	I Don't Hurt Anymore _S:❶20 / J:❶20 / A:❶18 My Arabian Baby_		$20		RCA Victor 5698
12/4/54	10	6	20	That Crazy Mambo Thing/ _J:10 / S:11_				
1/1/55	15	1	21	The Next Voice You Hear .... _S:15_		$15		RCA Victor 5912
12/25/54+	❶2	16	22	Let Me Go, Lover! _A:❶2 / J:2 / S:3 I've Forgotten You_		$15		RCA Victor 5960
				#1 Pop hit for Joan Weber in 1955				
4/2/55	15	1	23	Silver Bell .... _S:15 The Old Spinning Wheel_ [I]		$15		RCA Victor 5995
				HANK SNOW and CHET ATKINS				
4/9/55	3	27	24	Yellow Roses/ _S:3 / A:3 / J:3_				
4/16/55	3	17	25	Would You Mind? _A:3 / J:4_		$15		RCA Victor 6057
7/23/55	7	8	26	Cryin', Prayin', Waitin', Hopin'/ _J:7 / S:9 / A:10_				
7/23/55	7	2	27	I'm Glad I Got To See You Once Again _J:7 / S:12_		$15		RCA Victor 6154
11/5/55	5	9	28	Born To Be Happy/ _J:5 / A:10 / S:14_				
11/5/55	5	8	29	Mainliner (The Hawk With Silver Wings) _J:5 / S:8_		$15		RCA Victor 6269
2/4/56	5	10	30	These Hands/ _J:5 / A:6 / S:8_				
2/18/56	11	4	31	I'm Moving In .... _S:11_		$15		RCA Victor 6379
8/4/56	4	22	32	Conscience I'm Guilty/ _J:4 / S:8 / A:9_				
8/4/56	5	4	33	Hula Rock _J:5_		$20		RCA Victor 6578
12/15/56+	7	9	34	Stolen Moments _J:7 / S:8 / A:9 Two Won't Care_		$15		RCA Victor 6715
				HANK SNOW:				
7/22/57	4	19	35	Tangled Mind/ _A:4 / S:9_				
7/22/57	8	14	36	My Arms Are A House _A:8 / S:13_		$15		RCA Victor 6955
3/31/58	15	1	37	Whispering Rain .... _A:15 / S:18 I Wish I Was The Moon_		$15		RCA Victor 7154
6/23/58	7	9	38	Big Wheels _A:7 / S:18 I'm Hurting All Over_		$15		RCA Victor 7233
11/3/58	16	5	39	A Woman Captured Me .... _My Lucky Friend_		$15		RCA Victor 7325
3/16/59	19	6	40	Doggone That Train .... _Father Time And Mother Love_		$15		RCA Victor 7448
6/1/59	6	11	41	Chasin' A Rainbow _I Heard My Heart Break Last Night_		$15		RCA Victor 7524
				HANK SNOW and The Rainbow Ranch Boys				
10/19/59	3	20	42	The Last Ride _The Party Of The Second Part_		$15		RCA Victor 7586
4/11/60	22	5	43	Rockin', Rollin' Ocean .... _Walkin' And Talkin'_	87	$15		RCA Victor 7702
7/18/60	9	15	44	Miller's Cave _The Change Of The Tide_	101	$15		RCA Victor 7748
5/15/61	5	20	45	Beggar To A King _Poor Little Jimmie_		$12		RCA Victor 7869
10/9/61	11	9	46	The Restless One _I Know_		$12		RCA Victor 7933
6/2/62	15	10	47	You Take The Future (And I'll Take The Past) .... _Dog Bone_		$12		RCA Victor 8009
9/15/62	❶2	22	48	I've Been Everywhere _Ancient History_	68	$12		RCA Victor 8072
4/27/63	9	11	49	The Man Who Robbed The Bank At Santa Fe _You're Losing Your Baby_		$12	■	RCA Victor 8151
10/26/63	2³	22	50	Ninety Miles An Hour (Down A Dead End Street) _Blue Roses_	124	$12		RCA Victor 8239
4/11/64	11	15	51	Breakfast With The Blues/		$12		RCA Victor 8334
				also see #79 below				
7/4/64	21	12	52	I Stepped Over The Line		$12		RCA Victor 8334
2/13/65	7	19	53	The Wishing Well (Down In The Well) _Human_		$12		RCA Victor 8488
10/30/65	28	5	54	The Queen Of Draw Poker Town .... _Tears In The Trade Winds_		$10		RCA Victor 8655
12/25/65+	18	14	55	I've Cried A Mile .... _Crazy Little Train (Of Love)_		$10		RCA Victor 8713
5/7/66	22	11	56	The Count Down .... _Isle Of Sicily_		$10		RCA Victor 8808
12/10/66+	21	14	57	Hula Love .... _A Letter From Viet Nam (To Mother)_		$10		RCA Victor 9012
				#9 Pop hit for Buddy Knox in 1957				
5/13/67	18	14	58	Down At The Pawn Shop .... _Listen_		$10		RCA Victor 9188
9/23/67	20	15	59	Learnin' A New Way Of Life .... _Wild Flower_		$10		RCA Victor 9300
2/24/68	69	3	60	Who Will Answer? (Aleluya No. 1)/				
				#19 Pop hit for Ed Ames in 1968				
4/6/68	70	5	61	I Just Wanted To Know (How the Wind Was Blowing)		$10		RCA Victor 9433
6/8/68	20	13	62	The Late And Great Love (Of My Heart) .... _Born For You_		$10		RCA Victor 9523
12/28/68+	16	16	63	The Name Of The Game Was Love .... _The Gypsy And Me_		$8		RCA Victor 9685
5/31/69	26	9	64	Rome Wasn't Built In A Day .... _Like A Bird_		$8		RCA Victor 0151
11/1/69	53	5	65	That's When The Hurtin' Sets In .... _I'm Movin'_		$8		RCA Victor 0251
7/11/70	52	7	66	Vanishing Breed .... _What More Can I Say_		$8		RCA Victor 9856
11/7/70	57	5	67	Come The Morning .... _Francesca_		$8		RCA Victor 9907
4/21/73	71	3	68	North To Chicago .... _Friend_		$7		RCA Victor 0915
2/9/74	❶1	15	69	Hello Love _Until The End Of Time_		$7		RCA Victor 0215
6/29/74	36	11	70	That's You And Me .... _Brand On My Heart_		$7		RCA Victor 0307
11/16/74+	26	11	71	Easy To Love .... _Just A Faded Petal From A Beautiful Bouquet_		$6		RCA Victor 10108
3/22/75	47	10	72	Merry-Go-Round Of Love .... _My Filipino Rose_		$6		RCA Victor 10225
8/2/75	79	6	73	Hijack .... _The Last Ride_		$6		RCA Victor 10338
11/29/75	95	2	74	Colorado Country Morning .... _I Keep Dreaming Of You All The Time_		$6		RCA Victor 10439
5/29/76	87	4	75	Who's Been Here Since I've Been Gone .... _That's When He Dropped The World In My Hands_		$6		RCA Victor 10681
11/27/76	98	1	76	You're Wondering Why .... _Somewhere Someone Is Waiting For You_		$5		RCA 10804
7/16/77	81	4	77	Trouble In Mind .... _Trying To Get My Baby Off My Mind_		$5		RCA 11021
9/24/77	80	4	78	I'm Still Movin' On .... _I'm Gonna Bid My Blues Goodbye_		$5		RCA 11080
				sequel to #2 above				
12/3/77	96	2	79	Breakfast With The Blues .... _I've Done At Least One Thing_ [R]		$5		RCA 11153
				new version of #51 above				
7/1/78	93	4	80	Nevertheless .... _Don't Rock The Boat_		$5		RCA 11276
10/7/78	93	4	81	Ramblin' Rose .... _Red Roses_		$5		RCA 11377
				#2 Pop hit for Nat King Cole in 1962				

SNOW, Hank — Cont'd

DEBUT	PEAK	WKS	A-side / B-side	Pop	$	Pic	Label & Number
3/31/79	80	3	82 The Mysterious Lady From St. Martinique.....................Get On My Love Train		$5		RCA 11487
7/21/79	91	3	83 A Good Gal Is Hard To Find...I Wish My Heart Could Talk		$5		RCA 11622
11/10/79	98	2	84 It Takes Too Long...6 String Tennessee Flattop		$5		RCA 11734
2/16/80	78	4	85 Hasn't It Been Good Together.....................................It Was Love		$5		RCA 11891
			HANK SNOW AND KELLY FOXTON				

SNUFF   '82
Group from Virginia: Jim Bowling (vocals), Robbie House and Chuck Larson (guitars), Cecil Hooker (fiddle), C. Scott Trabue (bass) and Michael Johnson (drums).

| 8/7/82 | 71 | 6 | (So This Is) Happy Hour...It Must Be Love | | $4 | | Elektra/Curb 69996 |

SNYDER, Jimmy   '70

2/14/70	30	9	1 The Chicago Story...Take Her Flowers		$6		Wayside 009
			written by Tom T. Hall				
8/16/80	71	7	2 Just To Prove My Love To You.....................Kiss Your Love Goodbye		$6		e.i.o. 1126

SNYDER, Rick   '88

| 7/23/88 | 66 | 4 | Losing Somebody You Love...I Know The Feeling | | $3 | | Capitol 44185 |

SOLID GOLD BAND   '82
Group from Galina, Kansas: Jim Rowland, John Green, Mike Bartlett, Tyler Ogle and Buddy Burr.

11/28/81+	47	9	1 Cherokee Country...It's Just Your Memory		$5		NSD 110
2/20/82	65	6	2 I Never Had The One That I Wanted/				
		6	3 Bandera, Texas...		$5		NSD 121
7/17/82	68	6	4 Country Fiddles.........................The Sun Shines Bright In Oklahoma		$5		NSD 138

SOME OF CHET'S FRIENDS   '67
Group of RCA recording artists: Eddy Arnold, Bobby Bare, Don Bowman, Jim Ed Brown, Archie Campbell, Floyd Cramer, Skeeter Davis, Jimmy Dean, George Hamilton IV, Homer & Jethro, Waylon Jennings, Hank Locklin, John D. Loudermilk, Willie Nelson, Norma Jean, Jerry Reed, Connie Smith, Hank Snow, Porter Wagoner and Dottie West.

| 6/24/67 | 38 | 9 | Chet's Tune...Country Gentleman | | $8 | ■ | RCA Victor 9229 |
| | | | tribute to Chet Atkins | | | | |

SONNIER, Jo-el   '88
Born Joel Sonnier on 10/2/46 in Rayne, Louisiana. Cajun singer/songwriter/accordianist. Once known as "The Cajun Valentino."
1)No More One More Time 2)Tear-Stained Letter 3)If Your Heart Should Ever Roll This Way Again

10/4/75	78	7	1 I've Been Around Enough To Know.........................A Brighter Shade Of Blue		$5		Mercury 73702
3/6/76	99	1	2 Always Late (With Your Kisses).........................Knock, Knock, Knock		$5		Mercury 73754
6/5/76	100	1	3 He's Still All Over You.........................Am I Just Your Friend		$5		Mercury 73796
11/28/87+	39	14	4 Come On Joe...Say You Love Me		$3		RCA 5282
2/20/88	7	22	5 No More One More Time S:14 Louisiana 1927		$3		RCA 6895
7/16/88	9	19	6 Tear-Stained Letter S:12 Say You Love Me		$3		RCA 8304
11/19/88+	35	12	7 Rainin' In My Heart...Baby Hold On		$3		RCA 8726
			#34 Pop hit for Slim Harpo in 1961				
5/6/89	47	10	8 (Blue, Blue, Blue) Blue, Blue.........................I've Got Dreams To Remember		$3		RCA 8918
10/28/89+	24	17	9 If Your Heart Should Ever Roll This Way Again..............You Done Me Wrong		$3		RCA 9014
4/7/90	65	6	10 The Scene Of The Crime...Evangeline Special		$3		RCA 9123

SONS OF THE DESERT   '97
Group from Waco, Texas: brothers Drew (vocals) and Tim (guitar) Womack, Scott Saunders (keyboards), Doug Virden (bass) and Brian Westrum (drums).

| 3/8/97 | 10 | 21 | 1 Whatever Comes First   S:22 Drive Away | | $3 | ▌ | Epic 78542 |
| 8/30/97 | 33 | 17 | 2 Hand Of Fate...Burned In My Mind | | $3 | | Epic 78663 |

SONS OF THE PIONEERS   ★292★   '45
Originally a trio consisting of Bob Nolan (d: 6/15/80, age 72), Leonard "Roy Rogers" Slye (d: 7/6/98, age 86) and Tim Spencer (d: 6/26/74, age 65). Formed in 1934 and first called the Pioneers; recorded for Decca in 1934. Brothers Karl (guitar; d: 9/20/61, age 52) and Hugh (fiddle; d: 3/17/80, age 76) Farr were added in 1936. Group appeared in several western movies. Rogers and Spencer left in 1937, replaced by Lloyd Perryman (d: 5/31/77, age 60) and Pat Brady. Spencer returned shortly thereafter. Group elected to the Country Music Hall of Fame in 1980.
1)Stars And Stripes On Iwo Jima 2)Teardrops In My Heart 3)Cool Water

10/6/45	4	2	1 Stars And Stripes On Iwo Jima Cool Water		$20		RCA Victor 20-1724
6/29/46	6	1	2 No One To Cry To Grievin' My Heart Out For You		$20		RCA Victor 20-1868
2/15/47	5	1	3 Baby Doll The Letter Marked Unclaimed		$20		RCA Victor 20-2086
3/8/47	4	1	4 Cool Water Tumbling Tumbleweeds		$20		Decca 46027
			originally released in 1941 on Decca 5939; also see #10 below				
7/12/47	5	1	5 Cigareetes, Whusky, And Wild, Wild Women/ My Best To You				
			#15 Pop hit for Red Ingle in 1948				
2/19/49	12	1	6 My Best To You J:12		$20		RCA Victor 20-2199
7/26/47	4	2	7 Teardrops In My Heart You Don't Know What Lonesome Is		$20		RCA Victor 20-2276
6/12/48	6	14	8 Blue Shadows On The Trail/ S:6 / J:7				
6/12/48	13	4	9 (There'll Never Be Another) Pecos Bill.........................S:13		$25		RCA Victor 20-2780
			ROY ROGERS and The Sons Of The Pioneers				
			45 rpm: 48-0035; above 2 from the movie Melody Time starring Rogers				
8/21/48	11	1	10 Tumbling Tumbleweeds J:11 Cowboy Camp Meetin'		$20		RCA Victor 20-1904
			original version released in 1934 on Decca 5047				
9/4/48	7	11	11 Cool Water S:7 / J:11 Tumbling Tumbleweeds [R]		$20		Decca 46027
			also see #4 above				
9/10/49	10	1	12 Room Full Of Roses J:10 Riders In The Sky	26	$20		RCA Victor 21-0065
			45 rpm: 48-0060				
8/23/80	80	4	13 Ride Concrete Cowboy, Ride.........................Deliverance Of The Wildwood Flower		$5		MCA 41294
			ROY ROGERS And The Sons Of The Pioneers				
			from the movie Smokey & The Bandit II starring Burt Reynolds				

SOSEBEE, Tommy '53
Born Bud Thomas Sosebee on 5/23/23 in Duncan, South Carolina. Died on 10/23/67 (age 44). Known as "The Voice Of The Hills."

| 3/14/53 | 7 | 2 | | **Till I Waltz Again With You**   A:7 *All Night Boogie* | | $25 | | Coral 60916 |
| | | | | #1 Pop hit for Teresa Brewer in 1953 | | | | |

SOUTH, Joe '61
Born Joe Souter on 2/28/40 in Atlanta. Singer/songwriter/guitarist.

8/28/61	16	6		1 **You're The Reason** .... *Juke Box*	87	$20		Fairlane 21006
				JOE SOUTH and The Believers:				
10/4/69	27	9		2 **Don't It Make You Want To Go Home** .... *Hearts Desire*	41	$7		Capitol 2592
1/31/70	56	5		3 **Walk A Mile In My Shoes** .... *Shelter*	12	$7		Capitol 2704

SOUTHER, J.D. '82
Born John David Souther in Detroit; raised in Amarillo, Texas. Singer/songwriter.

12/1/79+	60	10		1 **You're Only Lonely** .... *Songs Of Love*	7	$4		Columbia 11079
10/16/82	27	12		2 **Sometimes You Just Can't Win** ... *Get Closer (Pop #29)*		$4	■	Asylum 69948
				LINDA RONSTADT AND JOHN DAVID SOUTHER				

SOUTHERN ASHE '81
Group from Columbus, Georgia.

| 8/15/81 | 80 | 3 | | **Paradise** .... *Loving On A Three-Way Street* | | $5 | | Soundwaves 4641 |

SOUTHERN PACIFIC ★255★ '88
Group from Los Angeles: Tim Goodman (vocals, guitar), John McFee (guitar, fiddle; The Doobie Brothers), Kurt Howell (keyboards), Stu Cook (bass; Creedence Clearwater Revival) and Keith Knudsen (drums; The Doobie Brothers). Goodman replaced by David Jenkins (formerly with Pablo Cruise) in 1986. Jenkins left in early 1989. Group disbanded in 1991.
1)New Shade Of Blue 2)Any Way The Wind Blows 3)Honey I Dare You

6/1/85	60	6		1 **Someone's Gonna Love Me Tonight**................. *The Blaster*		$3		Warner 29020
8/3/85	14	19		2 **Thing About You** .... S:13 / A:14 *Reno Bound*		$3		Warner 28943
				Emmylou Harris (guest vocal); written and first recorded by Tom Petty on his 1981 album *Hard Promises*				
11/16/85+	18	19		3 **Perfect Stranger** ....A:17 / S:18 *Bluebird Wine*		$3		Warner 28870
4/19/86	9	17		4 **Reno Bound** A:8 / S:9 *Someone's Gonna Love Me Tonight*		$3		Warner 28722
8/9/86	17	17		5 **A Girl Like Emmylou** .... A:17 / S:19 *Hearts Desire*		$3		Warner 28647
12/6/86+	37	13		6 **Killbilly Hill** .... *Bluegrass Blues*		$3		Warner 28554
3/21/87	26	14		7 **Don't Let Go Of My Heart** .... S:26 *What's It Gonna Take*		$3		Warner 28408
4/9/88	14	18		8 **Midnight Highway** .... S:18 *What's It Gonna Take*		$3	■	Warner 27952
8/6/88	2²	24		9 **New Shade Of Blue** S:11 *Just Hang On*		$3		Warner 27790
12/10/88+	5	19		10 **Honey I Dare You** *Trail Of Tears*		$3	■	Warner 27691
5/27/89	4	19		11 **Any Way The Wind Blows** *Reno Bound*		$3	■	Warner 22965
				from the movie *Pink Cadillac* starring Clint Eastwood				
12/2/89+	26	18		12 **Time's Up** ....*Memphis Queen*		$3		Warner 22714
				SOUTHERN PACIFIC and CARLENE CARTER				
4/7/90	31	14		13 **I Go To Pieces** .... *Beyond Love*		$3		Warner 19860
				#9 Pop hit for Peter and Gordon in 1965				
8/11/90	32	16		14 **Reckless Heart** .... *Side Saddle*		$3	▮	Warner 19871

SOUTHERN REIGN '88
Group led by singers Patsy McKeehan and Jeff Crocker.

11/1/86	80	3		1 **The Auction**		$5		Regal 1
1/10/87	62	7		2 **15 to 33** .... *Sugary Sam*		$5		Regal 2
5/2/87	79	4		3 **Summer On The Mississippi**....................................		$5		Regal 3
9/19/87	61	6		4 **Cheap Motels (And One Night Stands)**..........*Summer On The Mississippi*		$4		Step One 377
5/28/88	60	5		5 **Please Don't Leave Me Now** *I Don't Think I Want To Love You Anymore*		$4		Step One 385
10/15/88	80	3		6 **There's A Telephone Ringing (In An Empty House)**.......*Excuse Me For Loving You*		$4		Step One 391

SOVINE, Red ★160★ '66
Born Woodrow Wilson Sovine on 7/17/18 in Charleston, West Virginia. Died as a result of a car crash (which occurred when he had a heart attack while driving) on 4/4/80 (age 61). Singer/songwriter/guitarist. Joined the *Grand Ole Opry* in 1954. Father of **Roger Sovine**. Once known as "The Old Syrup Sopper."

1)Giddyup Go 2)Why Baby Why 3)Teddy Bear 4)Little Rosa 5)Hold Everything

3/26/55	14	2		1 **Are You Mine** .... S:14 *Ko Ko Mo (I Love You So)*		$20		Decca 29411
				RED SOVINE - GOLDIE HILL				
12/17/55+	❶⁴	25		2 **Why Baby Why** A:❶⁴ / S:❶¹ / J:❶¹ *Missing You*		$20		Decca 29755
				RED SOVINE and WEBB PIERCE				
3/24/56	15	1		3 **If Jesus Came To Your House** ....A:15 *I Got Religion (The Old Time Way)*		$20		Decca 29825
4/21/56	5	14		4 **Little Rosa/** S:5 / A:5 / J:5 [S]		$20		Decca 29876
				RED SOVINE and WEBB PIERCE				
5/19/56	5	8		5 **Hold Everything (Till I Get Home)** J:5		$20		
1/11/64	22	12		6 **Dream House For Sale**...................... *King Of The Open Road* [S]		$10		Starday 650
11/20/65+	❶⁶	22		7 **Giddyup Go** *Kiss And The Keys* [S]	82	$10		Starday 737
4/30/66	47	2		8 **Long Night** .... *Too Much*		$10		Starday 757
11/12/66	44	8		9 **Class Of 49** ....*I Hope My Wife Don't Find Out*		$10		Starday 779
2/18/67	17	12		10 **I Didn't Jump The Fence** ....*Don't Let My Glass Run Dry*		$10		Starday 794

DEBUG	PEAK	WKS	Gold	A-side (Chart Hit)...B-side	Pop	$	Pic Label & Number

SOVINE, Red — Cont'd

DEBUT	PEAK	WKS		A-side / B-side	Pop	$	Label & Number
7/29/67	9	16		11 Phantom 309/ [S]			Starday 811
				also see #22 below			
7/1/67	33	10		12 In Your Heart		$8	Starday 811
12/9/67+	33	13		13 Tell Maude I Slipped .... Not Like It Was With You		$8	Starday 823
7/20/68	63	2		14 Loser Making Good.. Good Enough For Nothing		$8	Starday 842
10/12/68	61	6		15 Normally, Norma Loves Me .... Live And Let Live And Be Happy		$8	Starday 852
8/2/69	62	7		16 Who Am I .... Three Hearts In A Tangle		$8	Starday 872
4/18/70	52	10		17 I Know You're Married But I Love You Still............... Money, Marbles And Chalk		$8	Starday 889
7/25/70	54	7		18 Freightliner Fever.. Mr. Sunday Sun		$8	Starday 896
7/6/74	16	16		19 It'll Come Back .... Down Through The Years		$6	Chart 5220
				label shows title as "I'll Come Back"; also see #31 below			
11/2/74	58	9		20 Can I Keep Him Daddy .... Red's So Fine		$6	Chart 5230
8/30/75	91	4		21 Daddy's Girl .... Daisy's Chain		$6	Chart 7507
				RED SOVINE AND THE GIRLS			
12/27/75+	47	10		22 Phantom 309 .... I Didn't Jump The Fence [R-S]		$5	Starday 101
				same version as #11 above			
6/19/76	**❶**[3]	13	●	23 Teddy Bear .... Daddy [S]	40	$5	Starday 142
9/18/76	45	5		24 Little Joe... Cold Love To Go [S]	102	$5	Starday 144
12/11/76	96	2		25 Last Goodbye... Lonely Arms Of Mine [S]		$5	Starday 147
2/19/77	98	2		26 Just Gettin' By .... I'm Gonna Move		$5	Starday 148
12/3/77	92	5		27 Woman Behind The Man Behind The Wheel .... Jealous Heart		$5	Gusto 169
3/11/78	70	5		28 Lay Down Sally... The King's Last Concert		$5	Gusto 180
5/27/78	77	5		29 The Days Of Me And You.................................. I'd Love To Make Love To You		$5	Gusto 188
4/12/80	74	5		30 The Little Family Soldier.................... I Didn't Know She Was Loving Me Goodbye [S]		$5	Gusto 9028
7/12/80	89	3		31 It'll Come Back...Love Is [R]		$5	Gusto 9030
				new version of #19 above			

SOVINE, Roger   **'68**
Born in Eleanor, West Virginia. Son of **Red Sovine**.

| 5/4/68 | 47 | 8 | | 1 Culman, Alabam .... Savannah Georgia Vagrant | | $7 | Imperial 66291 |
| 11/8/69 | 68 | 5 | | 2 Little Bitty Nitty Gritty Dirt Town .... Son | | $7 | Imperial 66398 |

SPACEK, Sissy   **'83**
Born Mary Elizabeth Spacek on 12/25/49 in Quitman, Texas. Singer/actress. Won Academy Award portraying **Loretta Lynn** in the movie *Coal Miner's Daughter.*

4/26/80	24	11		1 Coal Miner's Daughter .... I'm A Honky Tonk Girl		$4	■ MCA 41221
				from the movie starring Spacek			
8/20/83	15	17		2 Lonely But Only For You .... Old Home Town	110	$4	■ Atlantic Amer. 99847
1/21/84	57	9		3 If I Can Just Get Through The Night.............................. Honky Tonkin'		$4	Atlantic Amer. 99801
5/5/84	79	3		4 If You Could Only See Me Now .... Have I Told You Lately That I Love You		$4	Atlantic Amer. 99773

SPEARS, Billie Jo ★131★   **'75**
Born Billie Jean Spears on 1/14/37 in Beaumont, Texas. Singer/songwriter.

1)Blanket On The Ground 2)Mr. Walker, It's All Over 3)What I've Got In Mind 4)Misty Blue 5)If You Want Me

11/30/68+	48	10		1 He's Got More Love In His Little Finger .... A Woman Of The World		$7	Capitol 2331
4/19/69	4	13		2 Mr. Walker, It's All Over	Tips And Tables	80	$6	Capitol 2436
9/13/69	43	7		3 Stepchild .... Softly And Tenderly		$6	Capitol 2593
12/20/69+	40	10		4 Daddy, I Love You .... Look Out Your Window		$6	Capitol 2690
7/25/70	17	14		5 Marty Gray.. True Love		$6	Capitol 2844
11/28/70	30	9		6 I Stayed Long Enough .... Come On Home		$6	Capitol 2964
				written by **Tammy Wynette**			
3/20/71	23	12		7 It Could 'A Been Me... Break Away		$6	Capitol 3055
2/12/72	68	3		8 Souvenirs And California Mem'rys .... What A Love I Have In You		$6	Capitol 3258
10/5/74	80	5		9 See The Funny Little Clown .... All I Want Is You		$5	United Artists 549
				#9 Pop hit for **Bobby Goldsboro** *in 1964*			
2/1/75	**❶**[1]	17		10 Blanket On The Ground	Come On Home	78	$5	United Artists 584
7/12/75	20	14		11 Stay Away From The Apple Tree .... Before Your Time		$5	United Artists 653
11/1/75+	20	15		12 Silver Wings And Golden Rings .... Then Give Him Back To Me		$5	United Artists 712
2/28/76	5	16		13 What I've Got In Mind	Everytime Two Fools Collide		$5	United Artists 764
5/1/76	29	11		14 On The Rebound .... What's Our Love Coming To		$5	United Artists 797
				DEL REEVES & BILLIE JO SPEARS			
6/19/76	5	16		15 Misty Blue	Let's Try To Wake It Up Again		$5	United Artists 813
				#3 Pop hit for **Dorothy Moore** *in 1976*			
8/7/76	42	8		16 Teardrops Will Kiss The Morning Dew.............. Nothing Seems To Work Anymore		$5	United Artists 832
				DEL REEVES & BILLIE JO SPEARS			
10/23/76	18	12		17 Never Did Like Whiskey .... No Other Man		$5	United Artists 880
1/29/77	11	13		18 I'm Not Easy .... Too Far Gone		$5	United Artists 935
5/7/77	8	13		19 If You Want Me	Don't Ever Let Go Of Me		$5	United Artists 985
8/20/77	18	13		20 Too Much Is Not Enough .... The End Of Me		$5	United Artists 1041
1/14/78	18	11		21 Lonely Hearts Club .... His Little Something On The Side		$5	United Artists 1127
4/15/78	17	12		22 I've Got To Go .... There's More To A Tear (Than Meets The Eye)		$5	United Artists 1190

DEBUT	PEAK	WKS	Gold	A-side (Chart Hit) ....B-side	Pop	$	Pic	Label & Number
				SPEARS, Billie Jo — Cont'd				
8/12/78	16	12		23 '57 Chevrolet .... *The Lovin' Kind*		$5		United Artists 1229
11/11/78+	24	13		24 Love Ain't Gonna Wait For Us .... *Say It Again*		$5		United Artists 1251
2/24/79	60	6		25 Yesterday .... *The Miracle Of Love*		$5		United Artists 1274
				#1 Pop hit for The Beatles in 1965				
4/21/79	21	11		26 I Will Survive.............................. *Rainy Days And Stormy Nights*		$5		United Artists 1292
				#1 Pop hit for Gloria Gaynor in 1979				
8/4/79	23	12		27 Livin' Our Love Together .... *You*		$5		United Artists 1309
11/3/79+	21	14		28 Rainy Days And Stormy Nights .... *Everyday I Have To Cry*		$5		United Artists 1326
2/23/80	15	13		29 Standing Tall .... *Freedom Song*		$5		United Artists 1336
6/28/80	39	9		30 Natural Attraction .... *You Could Know As Much About A Stranger*		$5		United Artists 1358
1/10/81	13	13		31 Your Good Girl's Gonna Go Bad .... *(I Never Promised You A) Rose Garden*		$4		Liberty 1395
5/2/81	58	5		32 What The World Needs Now Is Love.. *Snowbird*		$4		Liberty 1409
				#7 Pop hit for Jackie DeShannon in 1965				
1/7/84	39	13		33 Midnight Blue/				
4/7/84	51	8		34 Midnight Love		$5		Parliament 1801
				SPEARS, Bobby — see CASSADY, Linda				
				SPEEGLE, David '89				
				Singer/guitarist from Tampa, Florida.				
12/9/89	83	4		Tie Me Up (Hold Me Down) .... *Dim Lights And Candles*		$6		Bitter Creek 07789
				SPEEKS, Ronnie '81				
1/17/81	93	2		Baby Loved Me............................... *You Almost Slipped My Mind*		$5		Dimension 1014
				SPELLING ON THE STONE '89				
				Song refers to the spelling of **Elvis Presley**'s middle name on his grave stone. The artist has never been identified.				
12/24/88+	82	4		Spelling On The Stone		$5		Curb 10522
				first released on LS 53 in 1988 ($10)				
				SPENCER, Teddy '88				
8/20/88	82	3		Grass Is Greener		$5		Oak 1052
				SPITZ, Michele '81				
7/25/81	93	2		Old Fashioned Lover (In A Brand New Love Affair)..................... *If You Ever Need Me Again*		$5		50 States 83
				SPRINGER, Roger '92				
5/23/92	69	2		The Right One Left.. *Honky Tonk Ways*		$3		MCA 54250
				SPRINGER BROTHERS '80				
2/2/80	87	5		1 What's A Nice Girl Like You (Doin' In A Love Like This) ...... *Twice As Strong*		$4		Elektra 46575
5/10/80	89	2		2 Cathy's Clown .... *No Fair Fallin In Love*		$4		Elektra 46622
				#1 Pop hit for The Everly Brothers in 1960				
				SPRINGFIELD, Bobby Lee '87				
				Born in 1953 in Amarillo, Texas. Singer/prolific songwriter.				
3/26/83	86	3		1 A Different Woman Every Night......................... *Young And Hungry*		$5		Kat Family 03562
				BOBBY SPRINGFIELD				
6/13/87	75	5		2 Hank Drank .... *Wild Cat*		$4		Epic 07110
9/5/87	66	5		3 Chain Gang .... *Wild Cat*		$4		Epic 07310
				SPRINGFIELDS, The '62				
				British folk trio: Dusty Springfield (charted 19 pop hits from 1964-88), with brother Tom Springfield and Tim Feild.				
8/25/62	16	10		Silver Threads And Golden Needles .... *Aunt Rhody*	20	$12		Philips 40038
				SPURZZ '80				
				Group from Nashville. Member Tony Ingram later joined **Atlanta**.				
8/23/80	76	4		Cowboy Stomp! .... *Night Club*		$4		Epic 50911
				STACK, Billy '78				
2/25/78	82	5		1 Love Can Make The Children Sing................................ *The Big Time*		$5		Caprice 2045
6/24/78	100	1		2 Boogiewoogieitis .... *Rainbow Rider*		$5		Caprice 2048
5/12/79	83	3		3 No Greater Love .... *She Wanted So Bad To Be Good*		$5		Caprice 2058
				STAFF, Bobbi '66				
				Born in 1946 in Kingston, North Carolina. Female singer.				
6/25/66	31	6		Chicken Feed.. *I Didn't Cry Today*		$10		RCA Victor 8833
				STAFFORD, Jim '74				
				Born on 1/16/44 in Eloise, Florida. Singer/songwriter/multi-instrumentalist. Co-hosted TV's *Those Amazing Animals* from 1980-81. Formerly married to **Bobbie Gentry**.				
3/2/74	66	8	●	1 Spiders & Snakes.. *Undecided*	3	$5		MGM 14648
5/18/74	64	7		2 My Girl Bill... *L.A. Mamma* [N]	12	$5		MGM 14718
8/17/74	57	6		3 Wildwood Weed .... *The Last Chant* [N]	7	$5		MGM 14737
1/10/81	65	6		4 Cow Patti.. *Texas Guitar Swing* [N]	102	$4		Viva/Warner 49611
				from the movie *Any Which Way You Can* starring **Clint Eastwood**				
11/20/82	61	8		5 What Mama Don't Know .... *That's What Little Kids Do* [N]		$4		Town House 1062
2/4/84	67	9		6 Little Bits And Pieces .... *Banjo Billy* [N]		$4		Columbia 04339
				STAFFORD, Jo '47				
				Born on 11/12/20 in Coalinga, California. Female singer. Charted 78 pop hits from 1944-57. Married orchestra leader Paul Weston. Also see **Red Ingle**.				
9/20/47	5	2		Feudin' And Fightin' .... *Love And The Weather* [N]	6	$12		Capitol 443
				Paul Weston (orch.); from the Broadway musical *Laffing Room Only* starring Betty Garrett				

STAFFORD, Terry '74
Born in Hollis, Oklahoma; raised in Amarillo, Texas. Died on 3/17/96. Male singer/songwriter. Charted the pop hit "Suspicion" in 1964.

12/1/73+	31	14		1 Amarillo By Morning/				
8/25/73	35	12		2 Say, Has Anybody Seen My Sweet Gypsy Rose...................		$6		Atlantic 4006
				#3 Pop hit for Tony Orlando & Dawn in 1973				
3/23/74	24	13		3 Captured _It Sure Is Bad To Love Her_		$6		Atlantic 4015
8/24/74	69	6		4 Stop If You Love Me .... _We've Grown Close_		$6		Atlantic 4026
3/12/77	94	4		5 It Sure Is Bad To Love Her................		$6		Casino 113
2/18/89	89	3		6 Lonestar Lonesome		$6		Player 134

STALEY, Karen '89
Singer/songwriter.

12/24/88+	86	4		1 So Good To Be In Love .... _Keep Walkin' On_		$3		MCA 53470
5/13/89	85	2		2 Now And Then .... _Looks Like Rain_		$3		MCA 53632

STAMPLEY, Joe ★53★ '73
Born on 6/6/43 in Springhill, Louisiana. Singer/songwriter/pianist. CMA Award: 1980 Vocal Duo of the Year (with **Moe Bandy**).

1)Soul Song 2)All These Things 3)Just Good Ol' Boys 4)Roll On Big Mama 5)I'm Still Loving You

2/20/71	74	2		1 Take Time To Know Her .... _I Live To Love You_		$6		Dot 17363
				#11 Pop hit for Percy Sledge in 1968				
2/12/72	75	2		2 Hello Operator................ _Hello Charlie_		$6		Dot 17400
6/17/72	9	17		3 If You Touch Me (You've Got To Love Me) _All The Praises_		$6		Dot 17421
11/11/72+	❶¹	15		4 Soul Song _Not Too Long Ago_	37	$6	☐	Dot 17442
3/24/73	7	14		5 Bring It On Home (To Your Woman) _You Make Life Easy_		$6		Dot 17452
8/18/73	12	16		6 Too Far Gone _The Night Time And My Baby_		$6		Dot 17469
12/8/73+	3	17		7 I'm Still Loving You _The Weatherman_		$6		Dot 17485
5/4/74	11	13		8 How Lucky Can One Man Be .... _Can You Imagine How I Feel_		$6		Dot 17502
9/14/74	5	16		9 Take Me Home To Somewhere _Hall Of Famous Losers_		$6		Dot 17522
1/18/75	8	11		10 Penny _Backtrackin'_		$5		ABC/Dot 17537
3/1/75	❶¹	14		11 Roll On Big Mama _Love's Running Through My Veins_		$5		Epic 50075
5/10/75	41	11		12 Unchained Melody................ _Dallas Alice_		$5		ABC/Dot 17551
				#4 Pop hit for The Righteous Brothers in 1965				
6/7/75	11	13		13 Dear Woman .... _Get On My Love Train_		$5		Epic 50114
8/30/75	70	8		14 Cry Like A Baby .... _Try A Little Tenderness_		$5		ABC/Dot 17575
				#2 Pop hit for The Box Tops in 1968				
9/20/75	12	13		15 Billy, Get Me A Woman .... _She Has Love_		$5		Epic 50147
12/20/75+	25	10		16 She's Helping Me Get Over Loving You .... _Ray Of Sunshine_		$5		Epic 50179
1/3/76	61	8		17 You Make Life Easy .... _Clinging Vine_		$5		ABC/Dot 17599
3/13/76	43	8		18 Sheik Of Chicago .... _Whiskey Talkin'_		$5		Epic 50199
4/24/76	❶¹	16		19 All These Things _My Louisiana Woman_		$5		ABC/Dot 17624
				#97 Pop hit for The Uniques in 1966; also see #44 below				
5/22/76	43	9		20 Was It Worth It .... _Live It Up_		$5		Epic 50224
7/24/76	16	11		21 The Night Time And My Baby................ _The Most Beautiful Girl_		$5		ABC/Dot 17642
8/7/76	18	14		22 Whiskey Talkin' _Darlin' Raise The Shade_		$5		Epic 50259
10/30/76	12	12		23 Everything I Own .... _Dallas Alice_		$5		ABC/Dot 17654
				#5 Pop hit for Bread in 1972				
12/25/76+	11	15		24 There She Goes Again .... _You Lift Me Up_		$5		Epic 50316
4/2/77	26	12		25 She's Long Legged .... _The Better Part Of Me_		$5		Epic 50361
7/2/77	15	13		26 Baby, I Love You So .... _Pour The Wine_		$5		Epic 50410
10/22/77	14	13		27 Everyday I Have To Cry Some .... _What Would I Do Then_		$5		Epic 50453
				#45 Pop hit for Arthur Alexander in 1975				
3/18/78	6	16		28 Red Wine And Blue Memories _Houston Treat My Lady Good_		$5		Epic 50517
7/15/78	6	14		29 If You've Got Ten Minutes (Let's Fall In Love) _If This Is Freedom_		$5		Epic 50575
11/4/78+	5	12		30 Do You Ever Fool Around _Please Don't Throw Our Love Away_		$5		Epic 50626
4/28/79	12	14		31 I Don't Lie .... _Draggin' Main_		$5		Epic 50694
7/14/79	❶¹	16		32 Just Good Ol' Boys _Make A Little Love Each Day_		$5		Columbia 11027
				MOE BANDY & JOE STAMPLEY				
9/1/79	9	14		33 Put Your Clothes Back On _I Could Be Persuaded_		$5		Epic 50754
11/17/79+	7	14		34 Holding The Bag _When It Comes To Cowgirls (We Just Can't Say No)_		$5		Columbia 11147
				MOE BANDY & JOE STAMPLEY				
3/15/80	17	12		35 After Hours .... _I'm Afraid To Know You That Well_		$5		Epic 50854
4/12/80	11	15		36 Tell Ole I Ain't Here, He Better Get On Home .... _Only The Names Have Been Changed_		$5		Columbia 11244
				MOE BANDY & JOE STAMPLEY				
6/28/80	32	11		37 Haven't I Loved You Somewhere Before .... _Whiskey Fever_		$5		Epic 50893
10/4/80	18	15		38 There's Another Woman .... _No Love At All_		$5		Epic 50934
1/24/81	9	15		39 I'm Gonna Love You Back To Loving Me Again _Back On The Road Again_		$5		Epic 50972
3/14/81	10	15		40 Hey Joe (Hey Moe) _Two Beers Away_		$4		Columbia 60508
				MOE BANDY & JOE STAMPLEY				
5/23/81	18	15		41 Whiskey Chasin' .... _The Jukebox Never Plays Home Sweet Home_		$4		Epic 02097

DEBUT	PEAK	WKS	Gold	A-side (Chart Hit) .... B-side	Pop	$	Pic	Label & Number
				STAMPLEY, Joe — Cont'd				
8/1/81	12	14		42 Honky Tonk Queen .... Partners In Rhyme		$4		Columbia 02198
				MOE BANDY & JOE STAMPLEY				
12/5/81+	41	10		43 Let's Get Together And Cry/		$4		Epic 02533
10/24/81	62	5		44 All These Things .... [R]		$4		
				new version of #19 above				
3/20/82	18	17		45 I'm Goin' Hurtin' .... The Fool		$4		Epic 02791
7/17/82	30	12		46 I Didn't Know You Could Break A Broken Heart .... I Just Can't Get Over You		$4		Epic 03016
10/16/82+	25	15		47 Backslidin' .... I'm Willing To Try		$4		Epic 03290
2/19/83	24	14		48 Finding You .... I'm Just Crazy Enough		$4		Epic 03558
6/18/83	12	18		49 Poor Side Of Town .... It's Over		$4		Epic 03966
				#1 Pop hit for Johnny Rivers in 1966				
10/29/83+	8	20		50 Double Shot (Of My Baby's Love) .... Penny		$4		Epic 04173
				#17 Pop hit for the Swingin' Medallions in 1966				
2/11/84	29	16		51 Brown Eyed Girl .... A Winner Never Quits		$4		Epic 04366
				#10 Pop hit for Van Morrison in 1967				
5/5/84	39	10		52 Memory Lane .... Could It Wait Until Forever		$4		Epic 04446
				JOE STAMPLEY and JESSICA BOUCHER				
6/2/84	8	16		53 Where's The Dress .... Wildlife Sanctuary [N]		$4		Columbia 04477
				MOE BANDY & JOE STAMPLEY				
10/13/84	36	10		54 The Boy's Night Out .... Alive And Well		$4	■	Columbia 04601
				MOE BANDY and JOE STAMPLEY				
1/26/85	48	10		55 Daddy's Honky Tonk .... Wild And Crazy Guys		$4		Columbia 04756
				MOE BANDY and JOE STAMPLEY				
4/20/85	58	8		56 Still On A Roll .... He's Back In Texas		$4		Columbia 04843
				MOE BANDY and JOE STAMPLEY				
7/6/85	67	7		57 When Something Is Wrong With My Baby .... Say It Like You Mean It		$4		Epic 05405
				#42 Pop hit for Sam & Dave in 1967				
9/21/85	47	10		58 I'll Still Be Loving You .... Heart Troubles		$4		Epic 05592
2/1/86	72	6		59 When You Were Blue And I Was Green .... There's No You Left In Us Anymore		$4		Epic 05758
7/30/88	56	6		60 Cry Baby		$5		Evergreen 1075
5/20/89	89	3		61 You Sure Got This Ol' Redneck Feelin' Blue		$5		Evergreen 1081
8/12/89	59	9		62 If You Don't Know Me By Now		$5		Evergreen 1100
				#3 Pop hit for Harold Melvin & The Bluenotes in 1972; #1 Pop hit for Simply Red in 1989				
				STANLEY BROTHERS '60				
				Bluegrass duo of Carter (b: 8/27/25 in McClure, Virginia; d: 12/1/66) and brother Ralph (b: 2/25/27 in Stratton, Virginia) Stanley. Formed The Clinch Mountain Boys in 1946.				
3/21/60	17	12		How Far To Little Rock .... Heaven Seems So Near [N]		$15		King 5306
				STARCHER, Buddy '66				
				Born Oby Edgar Starcher on 3/16/06 in Ripley, West Virginia. Singer/songwriter/DJ.				
2/12/49	8	1		1 I'll Still Write Your Name In The Sand .... J:8 Darling What More Can I Do		$20		4 Star 1145
4/9/66	2¹	15		2 History Repeats Itself .... Sniper's Hill [S]	39	$10		Boone 1038
				an accounting of "coincidental" parallels between the careers and deaths of Presidents Lincoln and Kennedy				
				STARK, Donna '80				
6/7/80	92	2		Why Don't You Believe Me .... I'm So Lonesome And So Blue		$6		RCI 2344
				#1 Pop hit for Joni James in 1952				
				STARLAND VOCAL BAND '76				
				Group from Washington, D.C.: two husband-and-wife teams: Bill Danoff and Kathy "Taffy" Nivert, with John Carroll and Margot Chapman.				
7/17/76	94	2	●	Afternoon Delight .... Starland	❶²	$5		Windsong 10588
				STARR, Kay '50				
				Born Katherine Starks on 7/21/22 in Dougherty, Oklahoma; raised in Dallas and Memphis. Charted 40 pop hits from 1948-62. Acted in the movies Make Believe Ballroom and When You're Smiling.				
9/16/50	2¹	16		1 I'll Never Be Free/ .... A:2 / J:2 / S:4	3			
8/26/50	5	6		2 Ain't Nobody's Business But My Own .... A:5 / J:10	22	$25		Capitol F1124
				KAY STARR and TENNESSEE ERNIE (above 2)				
	★399★			**STARR, Kenny** '76				
				Born Kenneth Trebbe on 9/21/52 in Topeka, Kansas; raised in Burlingame, Kansas. Singer/guitarist.				
				1)The Blind Man In The Bleachers 2)Hold Tight 3)Tonight I'll Face The Man				
4/7/73	56	6		1 That's A Whole Lotta Lovin' (You Give Me) .... Carol		$5		MCA 40023
10/20/73	97	4		2 Ev'ryday Woman .... My Lovin' Time With You		$5		MCA 40124
3/1/75	89	3		3 Put Another Notch In Your Belt .... Where Love Begins		$5		MCA 40350
				written by Mac Davis				
11/8/75+	2²	15		4 The Blind Man In The Bleachers .... Texas Proud	58	$5		MCA 40474
				#18 Pop hit for David Geddes in 1975				
3/13/76	26	10		5 Tonight I'll Face The Man (Who Made It Happen) .... I Can't See In The Dark		$5		MCA 40524
7/4/76	73	5		6 The Calico Cat/				
8/21/76	75	3		7 Victims		$5		MCA 40580
11/13/76	58	8		8 I Just Can't (Turn My Habit Into Love) .... The Upper Hand		$5		MCA 40637
2/12/77	43	8		9 Me And The Elephant .... Smooth Talkin' Guy		$5		MCA 40672
8/27/77	64	7		10 Old Time Lovin' .... Hobo On The Freight Train To Heaven		$5		MCA 40769
11/19/77+	25	14		11 Hold Tight .... Rockin' Robin		$5		MCA 40817
4/22/78	72	5		12 The Rest Of My Life .... Tuffy		$5		MCA 40880
7/1/78	70	6		13 Slow Drivin' .... Watchin' The River Run		$5		MCA 40922
				STARR, Penny — see DeHAVEN, Penny				
				STARR, Ringo — see OWENS, Buck				

DEBUT	PEAK	WKS	Gold A-side (Chart Hit)...B-side	Pop	$	Pic Label & Number

STATLER, Darrell   '69
Born on 12/27/40 in Llano, Texas. Singer/prolific songwriter.

| 9/6/69 | 40 | 7 | Blue Collar Job ....*I'm Barely Gettin' By* | | $7 | Dot 17275 |

STATLER BROTHERS, The ★38★   '78

Vocal group from Staunton, Virginia: brothers Don (lead) and Harold (bass) Reid, Philip Balsley (baritone) and **Lew DeWitt** (tenor). Worked with **Johnny Cash** from 1963-71. Jimmy Fortune replaced DeWitt in 1983. DeWitt died of Crohn's disease on 8/15/90 (age 52). Group hosts own variety show on TNN. CMA Awards: 1972, 1973, 1974, 1975, 1976, 1977, 1979, 1980 & 1984 Vocal Group of the Year.

1)*Do You Know You Are My Sunshine* 2)*Too Much On My Heart* 3)*Elizabeth* 4)*My Only Love*
5)*Flowers On The Wall*

9/25/65+	2⁴	27	1 Flowers On The Wall *Billy Christian*	4	$8	Columbia 43315
6/18/66	30	11	2 The Right One ....*Is That What You'd Have Me Do*		$8	Columbia 43624
11/26/66+	37	10	3 That'll Be The Day ....*Makin' Rounds*		$8	Columbia 43868
5/13/67	10	14	4 Ruthless *Do You Love Me Tonight*		$8	Columbia 44070
9/2/67	10	14	5 You Can't Have Your Kate And Edith, Too *Walking In The Sunshine*		$8	Columbia 44245
4/27/68	60	3	6 Jump For Joy ....*Take A Bow, Rufus Humfry*		$8	Columbia 44480
1/4/69	60	3	7 I'm The Boy/			
10/19/68	75	2	8 Sissy..		$8	Columbia 44608
11/21/70+	9	17	9 Bed Of Rose's *The Last Goodbye*	58	$6	Mercury 73141
4/24/71	19	13	10 New York City ....*This Part Of The World*		$6	Mercury 73194
8/21/71	13	14	11 Pictures.......................................*Making Memories*		$6	Mercury 73229
12/11/71+	23	13	12 You Can't Go Home ....*Second Thoughts*		$6	Mercury 73253
3/11/72	2⁴	15	13 Do You Remember These *Since Then*	105	$6	Mercury 73275
8/19/72	6	15	14 The Class Of '57 *Every Time I Trust A Gal*		$6	Mercury 73315
2/3/73	20	11	15 Monday Morning Secretary ....*A Special Song For Wanda*		$6	Mercury 73360
6/9/73	29	9	16 Woman Without A Home ....*I'll Be Your Baby Tonight*		$6	Mercury 73392
9/15/73	26	12	17 Carry Me Back................................*I Wish I Could Be*		$6	Mercury 73415
1/12/74	22	11	18 Whatever Happened To Randolph Scott.....................*The Strand*		$6	Mercury 73448
6/8/74	31	13	19 Thank You World ....*The Blackwood Brothers By The Statler Brothers*		$6	Mercury 73485
11/9/74+	15	14	20 Susan When She Tried *She's Too Good*		$6	Mercury 73625
3/1/75	31	11	21 All American Girl ....*A Few Old Memories*		$6	Mercury 73665
6/21/75	3	19	22 I'll Go To My Grave Loving You *You've Been Like A Mother To Me*	93	$6	Mercury 73687
1/3/76	39	9	23 How Great Thou Art .... *Noah Found Grace In The Eyes Of The Lord*		$6	Mercury 73732
4/17/76	13	13	24 Your Picture In The Paper ....*All The Times*		$6	Mercury 73785
10/2/76	10	14	25 Thank God I've Got You *Hat And Boots*		$6	Mercury 73846
1/15/77	10	13	26 The Movies *You Could Be Coming To Me*		$6	Mercury 73877
4/30/77	8	13	27 I Was There *Somebody New Will Be Coming Along*		$6	Mercury 73906
8/13/77	18	12	28 Silver Medals And Sweet Memories .... *The Regular Saturday Nite Card Game*		$5	Mercury 55000
12/3/77+	17	13	29 Some I Wrote...*Carried Away*		$5	Mercury 55013
3/18/78	❶²	17	30 Do You Know You Are My Sunshine *You're The First*		$5	Mercury 55022
8/5/78	3	14	31 Who Am I To Say *I Dreamed About You*		$5	Mercury 55037
11/18/78+	5	15	32 The Official Historian On Shirley Jean Berrell *The Best That I Can Do*		$5	Mercury 55048
3/31/79	7	12	33 How To Be A Country Star *A Little Farther Down The Road*		$5	Mercury 55057
7/7/79	11	13	34 Here We Are Again ....*Mr. Autry*		$5	Mercury 55066
10/27/79	10	13	35 Nothing As Original As You *Counting My Memories*		$5	Mercury 57007
1/19/80	8	14	36 (I'll Even Love You) Better Than I Did Then *Almost In Love*		$5	Mercury 57012
7/12/80	5	16	37 Charlotte's Web *One Less Day To Go*		$5	Mercury 57031
			from the movie *Smokey & The Bandit II* starring **Burt Reynolds**			
11/8/80+	13	14	38 Don't Forget Yourself...................*We Got Paid By Cash*		$5	Mercury 57037
3/28/81	35	9	39 In The Garden .... *How Are Things In Clay, Kentucky?*		$5	Mercury 57048
			popular hymn written in 1912			
6/13/81	5	18	40 Don't Wait On Me *Chet Atkins' Hand*		$5	Mercury 57051
			also see #64 below			
10/24/81+	12	16	41 Years Ago..*Dad*		$5	Mercury 57059
3/13/82	3	18	42 You'll Be Back (Every Night In My Dreams) *We Ain't Even Started Yet*		$5	Mercury 76142
7/3/82	7	16	43 Whatever *Do You Know You Are My Sunshine*		$5	Mercury 76162
10/23/82+	17	16	44 A Child Of The Fifties .... *(I'll Love You) All Over Again*		$5	Mercury 76184
4/16/83	2¹	19	45 Oh Baby Mine (I Get So Lonely) *I'm Dyin' A Little Each Day*		$4	Mercury 811488
			#2 Pop hit for The Four Knights in 1954			
8/13/83	9	17	46 Guilty *I Never Want To Kiss You Goodbye*		$4	Mercury 812988
12/10/83+	❶¹	23	47 Elizabeth *The Class Of '57*		$4	Mercury 814881
4/21/84	3	21	48 Atlanta Blue *If It Makes Any Difference*		$4	■ Mercury 818700
8/18/84	8	23	49 One Takes The Blame S:6 / A:8 *Give It Your Best*		$3	Mercury 880130
12/8/84+	❶¹	20	50 My Only Love S:❶¹ / A:❶¹ *(Let's Just) Take One Night At A Time*		$3	Mercury 880411
4/20/85	3	20	51 Hello Mary Lou S:3 / A:3 *Remembering You*		$3	Mercury 880685
			#9 Pop hit for **Ricky Nelson** in 1961			
8/24/85	❶¹	25	52 Too Much On My Heart S:❶² / A:❶¹ *Her Heart Or Mine*		$3	Mercury 884016
1/11/86	8	21	53 Sweeter And Sweeter S:7 / A:9 *Amazing Grace*		$3	Mercury 884317
5/17/86	5	24	54 Count On Me S:3 / A:5 *Will You Be There?*		$3	■ Mercury 884721

DEBUT	PEAK	WKS	Gold	A-side (Chart Hit) .... B-side	Pop	$	Pic	Label & Number
				STATLER BROTHERS, The — Cont'd				
9/27/86	36	12		55 Only You .... We Got The Mem'ries		$3		Mercury 888042
				#5 Pop hit for The Platters in 1955				
12/13/86+	7	21		56 Forever .... S:❶² / A:7 More Like Daddy Than Me		$3		Mercury 888219
6/13/87	10	20		57 I'll Be The One .... S:9 De Ja-Vu		$3		Mercury 888650
10/31/87	42	13		58 Maple Street Mem'ries ....Jesus Showed Me So		$3		Mercury 870920
2/20/88	15	23		59 The Best I Know How ....S:19 I Lost My Heart To You		$3		Mercury 870164
6/11/88	27	19		60 Am I Crazy? ....S:29 Beyond Romance		$3		Mercury 870442
10/15/88+	12	22		61 Let's Get Started If We're Gonna Break My Heart.....................S:14 Guilty		$3		Mercury 870681
2/18/89	36	10		62 Moon Pretty Moon .... I'll Be The One		$3		Mercury 872604
5/13/89	6	20		63 More Than A Name On A Wall .... Atlanta Blue		$3		Mercury 874196
10/7/89	67	5		64 Don't Wait On Me .... (long version) [R]		$3		Mercury 891014
				"live" version of #40 above				
11/18/89	56	7		65 A Hurt I Can't Handle .... Don't Wait On Me		$3		Mercury 876112
7/28/90	54	8		66 Small Small World .... My Music, My Memories And You		$3	∎	Mercury 875498
	★262★			**STEAGALL, Red** '76				
				Born Russell Steagall on 12/22/37 in Gainesville, Texas. Singer/songwriter/guitarist.				
				1)Lone Star Beer And Bob Wills Music 2)Someone Cares For You 3)Somewhere My Love 4)Truck Drivin' Man				
				5)Hard Hat Days And Honky Tonk Nights				
1/15/72	31	11		1 Party Dolls And Wine......................Middle Tennessee Country Boy's Blues		$6		Capitol 3244
				RED STEGALL				
11/25/72+	22	12		2 Somewhere, My Love .... Give Me One More Chance		$6		Capitol 3461
				#9 Pop hit for Ray Conniff & The Singers in 1966				
4/14/73	51	5		3 True Love ....Something Nice And Easy		$6		Capitol 3562
				#3 Pop hit for Bing Crosby & Grace Kelly in 1956				
7/14/73	41	8		4 If You've Got The Time .... Ol' Helen		$6		Capitol 3651
10/6/73	87	7		5 The Fiddle Man .... Neon Playboy		$6		Capitol 3724
1/26/74	93	5		6 This Just Ain't My Day (For Lettin' Darlin' Down)........... Little Old Heartbreaker You		$6		Capitol 3797
3/2/74	54	10		7 I Gave Up Good Mornin' Darling .... Ballad Of Billy's Lady		$6		Capitol 3825
7/20/74	52	9		8 Finer Things In Life .... Tight Levis And Yellow Ribbons		$6		Capitol 3913
10/26/74+	17	17		9 Someone Cares For You .... Throw Away Heart		$6		Capitol 3965
3/22/75	62	9		10 She Worshipped Me .... April's Paintings		$6		Capitol 4042
2/28/76	11	15		11 Lone Star Beer And Bob Wills Music I've Never Been This Loved Before		$5		ABC/Dot 17610
6/19/76	29	11		12 Truck Drivin' Man.................................... Neons And Nylons		$5		ABC/Dot 17634
9/25/76	45	9		13 Rosie (Do You Wanna Talk It Over)................ The Walls Of This Old Honky Tonk		$5		ABC/Dot 17653
12/25/76+	59	8		14 Her L-O-V-E's Gone .... Take Me Back To Texas		$5		ABC/Dot 17670
3/12/77	53	8		15 I Left My Heart In San Francisco .... Texas Red		$5		ABC/Dot 17684
				#19 Pop hit for Tony Bennett in 1962				
8/13/77	90	4		16 Freckles Brown .... My Adobe Hacienda		$5		ABC/Dot 17709
11/12/77	72	8		17 The Devil Ain't A Lonely Woman's Friend.......... The Rain Don't Stop In Oklahoma		$5		ABC/Dot 17726
3/11/78	63	9		18 Hang On Feelin'/		$5		
			4	19 Bob's Got A Swing Band In Heaven				ABC 12337
				tribute to Bob Wills				
9/22/79	41	9		20 Goodtime Charlie's Got The Blues .... Songs About People In Love		$4		Elektra 46527
2/9/80	31	9		21 3 Chord Country Song .... Jackson Hole, Wyoming		$4		Elektra 46590
5/10/80	49	8		22 Dim The Lights And Pour The Wine.................... He Ain't Got Nothin' On Me		$4		Elektra 46633
8/23/80	30	12		23 Hard Hat Days And Honky Tonk Nights .... Last Call For Alcohol		$4		Elektra 47014
				STEARNS, June '68				
				Born Agnes June Stearns on 4/5/39 in Albany, New York. Singer/guitarist.				
				1)Jackson Ain't A Very Big Town 2)Tyin' Strings 3)Empty House				
4/27/68	47	12		1 Empty House .... I'm The Queen (Of My Lonely Little World)		$7		Columbia 44483
9/14/68	57	5		2 Where He Stops Nobody Knows .... I Cry Myself Awake		$7		Columbia 44575
10/19/68	21	8		3 Jackson Ain't A Very Big Town The True And Lasting Kind		$7		Columbia 44656
				JOHNNY DUNCAN AND JUNE STEARNS				
1/4/69	53	6		4 Walking Midnight Road .... Plastic Saddle		$7		Columbia 44695
3/15/69	74	3		5 Back To Back (We're Strangers)................... If That's The Only Way		$7		Columbia 44752
				JOHNNY DUNCAN AND JUNE STEARNS				
6/7/69	70	4		6 What Makes You So Different ....Trouble In Mind		$7		Columbia 44852
12/27/69	58	4		7 Drifting Too Far (From Your Arms)...................He Was A Carpenter		$7		Columbia 45042
9/26/70	41	6		8 Tyin' Strings ....Don't Trouble Trouble		$6		Decca 32726
6/12/71	57	8		9 Sweet Baby On My Mind .... How's My Ex Treating You		$6		Decca 32828
10/16/71	56	8		10 Your Kind Of Lovin' .... Another		$6		Decca 32876
				STEEL, Ric '88				
12/5/87+	57	9		1 The Radio Song .... Third Times The Charm		$6		Panache 1001
6/18/88	59	7		2 Whose Baby Are You..		$6		Panache 1002
				STEELE, Jeffrey '97				
				Born on 8/27/61 in Burbank, California; raised in North Hollywood. Former lead singer of Boy Howdy.				
3/22/97	60	4		A Girl Like You .... My Greatest Love		$3		Curb 73012
				STEELE, Larry '66				
1/15/66	43	3		1 I Ain't Crying Mister .... Ramblin Man		$8		K-Ark 659
4/6/68	75	2		2 Hard Times .... The Apple Or The Pair		$8		K-Ark 802
				LARRY STEELE and THE WRANGLERS				
11/9/74	90	5		3 Daylight Losing Time................................ Watermelon Man		$8		Air Stream 004

STEFFIN SISTERS   '89
Vocal group of sisters from West Monroe, Louisiana: Jenny, Marianne, Beth and Kathy Steffin.

| 5/27/89 | 88 | 2 | | I Still Need You .... *Guitar Fiddlin' Joe* | | $6 | ■ | Windward 7 |

★348★   **STEGALL, Keith**   '85
Born Robert Keith Stegall on 11/1/54 in Wichita Falls, Texas. Singer/songwriter/guitarist/pianist. Acted in the movies *Killing At Hell's Gate* and *Country Gold*.
    1)Pretty Lady 2)California 3)Whatever Turns You On

3/1/80	58	6		1 The Fool Who Fooled Around .... *Keep On Playing That Country Music*		$4		Capitol 4835
2/21/81	55	7		2 Anything That Hurts You (Hurts Me) .... *She's Nobody's Baby But Mine*		$4		Capitol 4967
9/12/81	65	5		3 Won't You Be My Baby .... *Keep On Playing That Country Music*		$4		Capitol 5034
3/13/82	64	5		4 In Love With Loving You .... *Hurry On Home*		$4		EMI America 8107
5/12/84	25	16		5 I Want To Go Somewhere .... *The Cowboy Thing To Do*		$3		Epic 04442
9/22/84	19	21		6 Whatever Turns You On .... S:11 / A:21 *Daylight Lovin' Time*		$3	■	Epic 04590
2/16/85	13	18		7 California .... S:13 / A:18 *Straight Shooter*		$3		Epic 04771
6/15/85	10	22		8 Pretty Lady .... A:9 / S:12 *These Tears*		$3	■	Epic 04934
11/2/85	45	10		9 Feed The Fire .... *Marylee*		$3		Epic 05643
3/1/86	36	13		10 I Think I'm In Love .... *Sweet Love Bandit*		$3		Epic 05815
11/15/86	52	9		11 Ole Rock And Roller (With A Country Heart) .... *On A Good Night*		$3		Epic 06418
1/27/96	43	13		12 1969/				
5/18/96	75	1		13 Fifty-Fifty		$3	▮	Mercury 852618

STENMARK-MUELLER BAND   '87
Duo from Salt Lake City: K.J. Stenmark and LynnDee Mueller.

| 11/14/87 | 95 | 1 | | Lover To Lover .... | | $7 | | Envelope 7004 |

STEPHENS, Ott   '63
Born on 9/21/41 in Ringold, Georgia. Male singer/guitarist.

1/19/63	15	7		1 Robert E. Lee .... *Never Tired Of Loving You*		$15		Chancellor 107
6/13/64	23	15		2 Be Quiet Mind .... *Hard Luck Story*		$12		Reprise 0272
6/12/65	36	12		3 Enough Man For You .... *Never Tired Of Loving You*		$10		Chart 1205

STEVENS, Even   '75
Born in Lewiston, Ohio; raised in Cincinnati. Singer/prolific songwriter.

6/21/75	38	13		1 Let The Little Boy Dream .... *Josie's Comin' Home*		$5		Elektra 45254
12/20/75+	81	7		2 Huckelberry Pie .... *I Won't Sing No Love Songs Anymore*		$5		Elektra 45292
				EVEN STEVENS/SAMMI SMITH				
10/15/77	97	1		3 The King Of Country Music Meets The Queen Of Rock & Roll .... *I'm From Outer Space*		$5		Elektra 45430
				EVEN STEVENS & SHERRY GROOMS				

STEVENS, Geraldine   '69
Born Geraldine Ann Pasquale on 2/17/46 in Chicago. Better known as Dodie Stevens. Charted the pop hit "Pink Shoe Laces" in 1959.

| 9/13/69 | 57 | 3 | | Billy, I've Got To Go To Town .... *It's Not Their Heartache, It's Mine* | 117 | $8 | | World Pacific 77927 |
| | | | | answer to "Ruby, Don't Take Your Love To Town" by **Kenny Rogers** | | | | |

STEVENS, Jeff, and The Bullets   '87
Family trio from Alum Creek, West Virginia; brothers Jeff (vocals, guitar) and Warren (bass) Stevens, with cousin Terry Dotson (drums).

12/27/86+	69	8		1 Darlington County .... *Tamed By Love*		$3		Atlantic Amer. 99494
				written and first recorded by Bruce Springsteen on his 1984 *Born In The U.S.A.* album				
3/28/87	61	6		2 You're In Love Alone .... *Tamed By Love*		$3		Atlantic Amer. 99475
7/18/87	53	8		3 Geronimo's Cadillac .... *Tamed By Love*		$3		Atlantic Amer. 99433
				#37 Pop hit for Michael Murphey in 1972				
4/22/89	70	5		4 Johnny Lucky And Suzi 66 .... *Change Of Heart*		$3	■	Atlantic Amer. 99259

STEVENS, Lee J.   '89

| 1/14/89 | 92 | 2 | | You'll Be The First To Know .... | | $5 | | Regal 01 |

STEVENS, Ray   **★170★**   '75
Born Harold Ray Ragsdale on 1/24/39 in Clarksdale, Georgia. Singer/songwriter/comedian. Hosted own TV show in 1970. Also recorded as Henhouse Five Plus Too.
    1)Misty 2)The Streak 3)Shriner's Convention 4)You Are So Beautiful 5)Turn Your Radio On

11/1/69	55	6		1 Sunday Mornin' Comin' Down .... *The Minority*	81	$8		Monument 1163
12/27/69+	63	2		2 Have A Little Talk With Myself .... *The Little Woman*	123	$8		Monument 1171
5/2/70	39	6	●	3 Everything Is Beautiful .... *A Brighter Day*	❶²	$6		Barnaby 2011
12/4/71+	17	13		4 Turn Your Radio On .... *Loving You On Paper*	63	$6		Barnaby 2048
7/14/73	37	11		5 Nashville .... *Golden Age*		$6		Barnaby 5020
4/13/74	3	13	●	6 The Streak .... *You've Got The Music Inside* [N]	❶³	$6		Barnaby 600
11/30/74+	37	10		7 Everybody Needs A Rainbow .... *Inside*		$6		Barnaby 610
3/22/75	3	17		8 Misty .... *Sunshine*	14	$6		Barnaby 614
				#12 Pop hit for Johnny Mathis in 1959				
9/27/75	38	11		9 Indian Love Call .... *Piece Of Paradise*	68	$6		Barnaby 616
				#3 Pop hit for Paul Whiteman in 1925				
1/3/76	48	8		10 Young Love .... *Deep Purple*	93	$6		Barnaby 618
				#1 Pop hit for Tab Hunter in 1957				

DEBUT	PEAK	WKS	Gold	A-side (Chart Hit) ....B-side	Pop	$	Pic	Label & Number
				STEVENS, Ray — Cont'd				
5/1/76	16	13		11 You Are So Beautiful .... *One Man Band*	101	$5		Warner 8198
				#5 Pop hit for Joe Cocker in 1975				
8/7/76	27	10		12 Honky Tonk Waltz .... *Om*		$5		Warner 8237
1/8/77	39	7		13 In The Mood .... *Classical Cluck* [N]	40	$5		Warner 8301
				HENHOUSE FIVE PLUS TOO				
				#1 Pop hit for Glenn Miller in 1940				
2/19/77	81	6		14 Get Crazy With Me .... *Dixie Hummingbird*		$5		Warner 8318
6/11/77	44	9		15 Dixie Hummingbird .... *Feel The Music*		$5		Warner 8393
8/12/78	36	10		16 Be Your Own Best Friend .... *With A Smile*		$5		Warner 8603
4/14/79	85	3		17 I Need Your Help Barry Manilow .... *Daydream Romance* [N]	49	$5	■	Warner 8785
2/9/80	7	12		18 Shriner's Convention *You're Never Goin' To Tampa With Me* [N]	101	$4		RCA 11911
9/13/80	20	13		19 Night Games.......................... *Let's Do It Right This Time*		$4		RCA 12069
2/14/81	33	10		20 One More Last Chance .... *I Believe You Love Me*		$4		RCA 12170
2/6/82	35	10		21 Written Down In My Heart .... *Country Boy, Country Club Girl*		$4		RCA 13038
5/22/82	63	7		22 Where The Sun Don't Shine....... *Why Don't We Go Somewhere And Love*		$4		RCA 13207
2/11/84	64	8		23 My Dad .... *Me*		$4		Mercury 818057
12/8/84+	20	14		24 Mississippi Squirrel Revival .... S:12 / A:28 *Ned Nostril* [N]		$3		MCA 52492
3/23/85	74	6		25 It's Me Again, Margaret .... *Joggin'* [N]		$3		MCA 52548
9/14/85	45	14		26 The Haircut Song .... *Punk Country Love* [N]		$3		MCA 52657
1/25/86	50	10		27 The Ballad Of The Blue Cyclone .... S:26 *Vacation Bible School* [N]		$3		MCA 52771
9/13/86	70	7		28 People's Court............. *Dudley Dorite (Of The Highway Patrol)* [N]		$3		MCA 52924
11/1/86	63	6		29 Southern Air .... S:27 *The Camping Trip* [N]		$3		MCA 52906
				Jerry Clower and **Minnie Pearl** (guest vocals)				
5/9/87	41	9		30 Would Jesus Wear A Rolex .... S:15 *Cool Down Willard* [N]		$3		MCA 53101
10/8/88	88	2		31 The Day I Tried To Teach Charlene MacKenzie How To Drive .... *I Don't Need None Of That* [N]		$3		MCA 53423
7/6/91	62	10		32 Working For The Japanese .... [N]				album cut
3/14/92	72	2		33 Power Tools.. [N]				album cut
				above 2 from the album *#1 With A Bullet* on Curb/Capitol 95914				

STEWART, Gary ★191★　　　　　'75

Born on 5/28/45 in Letcher County, Kentucky. Singer/songwriter/pianist.

1)She's Actin' Single 2)Out Of Hand 3)Drinkin' Thing 4)Your Place Or Mine 5)You're Not The Woman You Use To Be

DEBUT	PEAK	WKS		A-side	B-side	$	Pic	Label & Number
11/17/73	63	7		1 Ramblin' Man.. *Williamson County*		$6		RCA Victor 0144
				#2 Pop hit for The Allman Brothers Band in 1973				
6/1/74	10	18		2 Drinkin' Thing *I See The Want To In Your Eyes*		$5		RCA Victor 0281
10/19/74+	4	16		3 Out Of Hand *Draggin' Shackles*		$5		RCA Victor 10061
3/8/75	❶¹	13		4 She's Actin' Single (I'm Drinkin' Doubles) *Williamson County*		$5		RCA Victor 10222
6/21/75	15	15		5 You're Not The Woman You Use To Be............ *I Owe It All To Mama*		$5		MCA 40414
10/11/75	20	12		6 Flat Natural Born Good-Timin' Man .... *This Old Heart Won't Let Go*		$5	■	RCA Victor 10351
1/31/76	23	13		7 Oh, Sweet Temptation .... *Hank Western*		$5		RCA Victor 10550
5/22/76	15	14		8 In Some Room Above The Street .... *Easy People*		$5		RCA Victor 10680
11/20/76+	11	13		9 Your Place Or Mine .... *Lord, What A Woman*		$4		RCA 10833
5/21/77	16	12		10 Ten Years Of This .... *I Ain't Living Long Like This*		$4		RCA 10957
10/22/77	26	13		11 Quits.. *Dancing Eyes*		$4		RCA 11131
3/11/78	16	12		12 Whiskey Trip .... *Williamson County*		$4		RCA 11224
7/22/78	36	8		13 Single Again .... *Little Junior*		$4		RCA 11297
11/25/78+	41	9		14 Stone Wall (Around Your Heart) .... *I Got Mine*		$4		RCA 11416
4/14/79	66	5		15 Shady Streets .... *Everything A Good Little Girl Needs*		$4		RCA 11534
7/14/79	75	3		16 Mazelle .... *One More*		$4		RCA 11623
6/14/80	48	9		17 Cactus And A Rose .... *Staring Each Other Down*		$4		RCA 11960
9/27/80	66	4		18 Are We Dreamin' The Same Dream/				RCA 12081
		4		19 　Roarin'		$4		
4/11/81	72	4		20 Let's Forget That We're Married .... *Honky Tonk Man*		$4		RCA 12203
11/7/81	36	11		21 She's Got A Drinking Problem .... *Memories Swim In Whiskey*		$4		RCA 12343
4/10/82	41	11		22 Brotherly Love.. *Firewater Friends*		$4	■	RCA 13049
				GARY STEWART/DEAN DILLON				
7/24/82	83	4		23 She Sings Amazing Grace .... *Cold Turkey*		$4		RCA 13261
1/8/83	47	12		24 Those Were The Days.......................... *Drinkin' Thing*		$4		RCA 13401
				GARY STEWART AND DEAN DILLON				
4/16/83	71	4		25 Smokin' In The Rockies .... *Hard Time For Lovers*		$4		RCA 13472
				GARY STEWART & DEAN DILLON				
4/14/84	75	7		26 Hey, Bottle Of Whiskey.................. *Roadhouse Romances*		$5		Red Ash 8403
8/11/84	64	7		27 I Got A Bad Attitude................................ *Life's A Game*		$5		Red Ash 8406
10/1/88	63	7		28 Brand New Whiskey....................................		$5		Hightone 506
12/3/88+	64	9		29 An Empty Glass		$5		Hightone 507
3/18/89	77	3		30 Rainin', Rainin', Rainin'		$5		Hightone 509

STEWART, Larry '93
Born on 3/3/59 in Paducah, Kentucky. Lead singer of **Restless Heart** from 1986-91.

3/6/93	5	20		1 Alright Already — *The Boy Down The Road*		$3		RCA 62474
7/3/93	34	17		2 I'll Cry Tomorrow .... *Brittany*		$3		RCA 62546
11/6/93	62	6		3 We Can Love .... *When You Come Back To Me*		$3		RCA 62696
8/20/94	43	11		4 Heart Like A Hurricane .... *(remix)*		$3	■	Columbia 77638
12/3/94+	46	16		5 Losing Your Love .... *One Track Mind*		$3	■	Columbia 77753
4/8/95	56	9		6 Rockin' The Rock .... *I'm Not Through Lovin' You*		$3	■	Columbia 77857
7/6/96	46	15		7 Why Can't You .... *I'm Not Through Lovin' You*		$3	■	Columbia 78307
1/25/97	70	4		8 Always A Woman				album cut

from the album *Why Can't You* on Columbia 67410

STEWART, Lisa '92
Born on 8/6/68 in Louisville, Mississippi. Became co-host of TNN's *This Week In Country Music* in 1997.

10/31/92	61	7		1 Somebody's In Love .... *Is It Love*		$3		BNA 62311
3/20/93	72	3		2 Drive Time .... *Don't Touch Me*		$3	■	BNA 62441

STEWART, Vernon '63
1/12/63	17	6		The Way It Feels To Die .... *You're Not All Here*		$15		Chart 501

STEWART, Wynn ★156★ '67
Born Wynnford Stewart on 6/7/34 in Morrisville, Missouri. Died of a heart attack on 7/17/85 (age 51). Singer/songwriter/guitarist.

1)It's Such A Pretty World Today 2)Wishful Thinking 3)Love's Gonna Happen To Me 4)After The Storm
5)'Cause I Have You

7/21/56	14	1		1 The Waltz Of The Angels .... A:14 *Why Do I Love You So*		$20		Capitol 3408
12/28/59+	5	22		2 Wishful Thinking — *Uncle Tom Got Caught*		$15		Challenge 9061
5/30/60	26	2		3 Wrong Company .... *We'll Never Love Again*		$15		Challenge 9071
				WYNN STEWART AND JAN HOWARD				
12/25/61	18	7		4 Big, Big Love .... *One More Memory*		$15		Challenge 9121
11/24/62	27	3		5 Another Day, Another Dollar .... *Donna On My Mind*		$15		Challenge 9164
11/21/64	30	15		6 Half Of This, Half Of That .... *The Happy Part Of Town*		$8		Capitol 5271
10/16/65	43	7		7 I Keep Forgettin' That I Forgot About You .... *My Rosalie*		$8	■	Capitol 5485
2/25/67	❶²	22		8 It's Such A Pretty World Today — *Ol' What's Her Name*		$8		Capitol 5831
				#1 Easy Listening hit for Andy Russell in 1967				
7/15/67	9	16		9 'Cause I Have You/				
8/5/67	68	3		10 That's The Only Way To Cry		$8	■	Capitol 5937
				WYNN STEWART And The Tourists:				
11/11/67+	7	16		11 Love's Gonna Happen To Me — *Waltz Of The Angels*		$7	■	Capitol 2012
4/20/68	10	13		12 Something Pretty — *Built-In Love*		$7	■	Capitol 2137
8/24/68	16	11		13 In Love .... *My Own Little World*		$7	■	Capitol 2240
12/14/68+	29	11		14 Strings .... *Happy Blues*		$7		Capitol 2341
4/5/69	20	12		15 Let The Whole World Sing It With Me .... *Who Are You?*		$7		Capitol 2421
7/26/69	19	10		16 World-Wide Travelin' Man .... *Cry Baby*		$6		Capitol 2549
11/15/69	47	9		17 Yours Forever .... *Goin' Steady*		$6		Capitol 2657
4/11/70	55	4		18 You Don't Care What Happens To Me .... *Young As Spring*		$6		Capitol 2751
				WYNN STEWART:				
9/12/70	13	13		19 It's A Beautiful Day .... *Prisoner On The Run*		$6		Capitol 2888
1/2/71	32	10		20 Heavenly .... *You're No Secret Of Mine*		$6		Capitol 3000
5/1/71	55	6		21 Baby, It's Yours .... *I Was The First One To Know*		$6		Capitol 3080
9/18/71	53	5		22 Hello Little Rock .... *You Can't Take It With You*		$6		Capitol 3157
11/11/72	49	8		23 Paint Me A Rainbow .... *I Know They'll Make Room For You*		$5		RCA Victor 0819
7/14/73	51	9		24 Love Ain't Worth A Dime Unless It's Free .... *Me And My Jesus Would Know*		$5		RCA Victor 0004
10/27/73	62	9		25 It's Raining In Seattle .... *If I Were You (And I Wish I Was)*		$5		RCA Victor 0114
6/14/75	80	9		26 Lonely Rain .... *Just Now Thought Of You*		$5		Playboy 6035
7/31/76	8	14		27 After The Storm — *Don't Monkey With My Widow*		$5		Playboy 6080
11/20/76+	19	11		28 Sing A Sad Song .... *It's Such A Pretty World Today*		$5		Playboy 6091
12/23/78+	37	11		29 Eyes Big As Dallas .... *Such A Perfect Day For Making Love*		$6		WIN 126
6/9/79	59	5		30 Could I Talk You Into Loving Me Again .... *I Was Raised Down On The Farm*		$6		WIN 127
8/24/85	98	1		31 Wait Till I Get My Hands On You .... *Would You Want The World To End*		$7		Pretty World 001

STONE, Cliffie, And His Orchestra '48
Born Clifford Snyder on 3/1/17 in Burbank, California. Died of a heart attack on 1/16/98 (age 80). Singer/songwriter/bassist/bandleader. Popular radio/TV personality in Los Angeles, hosting *Hollywood Barn Dance*, *Lucky Stars* and *Dinner Bell Roundup* (later known as *Hometown Jamboree*). Worked as an A&R executive for Capitol Records. Elected to the Country Music Hall of Fame in 1989.

3/15/47	4	1		1 Silver Stars, Purple Sage, Eyes Of Blue — *If You Knew Susie*		$15		Capitol 354
3/6/48	4	8		2 Peepin' Thru The Keyhole (Watching Jole Blon) — *Wabash Blues*		$20		Capitol Amer. 40083
				CLIFFIE STONE And His Barn Dance Band				
8/28/48	11	3		3 When My Blue Moon Turns To Gold Again .. J:11 *Take It Any Way You Can Get It*		$15		Capitol 15108
				#19 Pop hit for Elvis Presley in 1956				
10/15/66	30	7		4 Little Pink Mack .... *That'll Be The Day*		$12		Tower 269
				KAY ADAMS with The Cliffie Stone Group				

STONE, Doug ★155★   '92
Born Douglas Brooks on 6/19/56 in Marietta, Georgia. Singer/songwriter/guitarist. Changed name to avoid confusion with Garth Brooks. Starred in the 1995 movie *Gordy*.

1)A Jukebox With A Country Song 2)In A Different Light 3)Too Busy Being In Love

DEBUT	PEAK	WKS		A-side / B-side	Pop	$	Pic	Label & Number
3/10/90	4	25		1 I'd Be Better Off (In A Pine Box) *It's A Good Thing I Don't Love You Anymore*		$3	▮	Epic 73246
7/14/90	6	21		2 Fourteen Minutes Old *High Weeds And Rust*		$3	▮	Epic 73425
11/10/90+	5	20		3 These Lips Don't Know How To Say Goodbye *We Always Agree On Love*		$3	▮	Epic 73570
3/16/91	❶¹	20		4 In A Different Light *Turn This Thing Around*		$3		Epic 73741
7/20/91	4	20		5 I Thought It Was You *(For Every Inch I've Laughed) I've Cried A Mile*		$3		Epic 73895
11/16/91+	❶²	20		6 A Jukebox With A Country Song *Remember The Ride*		$3		Epic 74089
3/21/92	3	20		7 Come In Out Of The Pain *The Feeling Never Goes Away*		$3		Epic 74259
7/11/92	4	20		8 Warning Labels *Left, Leavin', Goin' Or Gone*		$3		Epic 74399
11/7/92+	❶¹	20		9 Too Busy Being In Love *The Workin' End Of A Hoe*		$3		Epic 74761
2/27/93	6	20		10 Made For Lovin' You *She's Got A Future In The Movies*		$3		Epic 74885
6/19/93	❶¹	20		11 Why Didn't I Think Of That *This Empty House*		$3		Epic 77025
10/23/93+	2²	20		12 I Never Knew Love *This Empty House*	81	$3	▮	Epic 77228
2/26/94	4	20		13 Addicted To A Dollar *That's A Lie*		$3	▮	Epic 77375
6/18/94	6	20		14 More Love *She Used To Love Me A Lot*		$3	▮	Epic 77549
10/29/94+	7	20		15 Little Houses *I'd Be Better Off (In A Pine Box)*		$3		Epic 77716
3/4/95	13	20		16 Faith In Me, Faith In You......................S:25 *Enough About Me (Let's Talk About You)*		$3		Columbia 77837
6/24/95	41	11		17 Sometimes I Forget...*You Won't Outlive Me*		$3	▮	Columbia 77945
9/23/95+	12	20		18 Born In The Dark...*Down On My Knees*		$3		Columbia 78039

STONEMANS, The   '66
Family group from Monorat, Virginia: Ernest "Pop" (autoharp, guitar), Scotty (fiddle), Van (guitar), Donna (mandolin), Roni (banjo) and Jim (bass). All shared vocals. Roni was a regular on TV's *Hee-Haw*. "Pop" died on 6/14/68 (age 75). Scotty died on 3/4/73 (age 40). CMA Award: 1967 Vocal Group of the Year.

DEBUT	PEAK	WKS		A-side / B-side	Pop	$	Pic	Label & Number
6/4/66	40	3		1 Tupelo County Jail *Spell Of The Freight Train*		$8		MGM 13466
10/8/66	21	11		2 The Five Little Johnson Girls *Goin' Back To Bowling Green*		$8		MGM 13557
3/25/67	40	12		3 Back To Nashville, Tennessee...*Bottle Of Wine*		$8		MGM 13667
8/5/67	49	7		4 West Canterbury Subdivision Blues ....*The Three Cent Opera*		$8		MGM 13755
7/20/68	41	8		5 Christopher Robin ....*The Love I Left Behind*		$7		MGM 13945

STOREY, Lewis   '86
Born in Casa Grande, Arizona.

DEBUT	PEAK	WKS		A-side / B-side	Pop	$	Pic	Label & Number
2/8/86	48	8		1 Ain't No Tellin'...*Flo's Inn*		$3	▮	Epic 05786
5/17/86	60	6		2 Katie, Take Me Dancin'...*Friday Fool's Parade*		$3		Epic 05890

STORIE, James   '88

DEBUT	PEAK	WKS		A-side / B-side	Pop	$	Pic	Label & Number
10/22/88	100	1		Lost Highway...*Whispering Pines*		$7		GMC 1001

STOVALL, Vern   '67
Born on 10/3/28 in Altus, Oklahoma; raised in Vian, Oklahoma. Also see **Phil Baugh**.

DEBUT	PEAK	WKS		A-side / B-side	Pop	$	Pic	Label & Number
9/23/67	58	8		Dallas ....*Movin' Round*		$10		Longhorn 581

STRAIT, George ★15★   '90
Born on 5/18/52 in Poteet, Texas; raised in Pearsall, Texas. Singer/songwriter/guitarist. Served in the U.S. Army from 1972-74. Graduated from Southwest Texas State with a degree in agriculture. Formed the Ace In The Hole band in 1975. Starred in the movie *Pure Country*. CMA Awards: 1985, 1986, 1996, 1997 & 1998 Male Vocalist of the Year; 1989 & 1990 Entertainer of the Year.

1)Love Without End, Amen 2)One Night At A Time 3)I've Come To Expect It From You 4)Check Yes Or No
5)Carrying Your Love With Me

DEBUT	PEAK	WKS		A-side / B-side	Pop	$	Pic	Label & Number
5/16/81	6	18		1 Unwound *She's Playing Hell Trying To Get Me To Heaven*		$4		MCA 51104
9/12/81	16	17		2 Down And Out...*Blame It On Mexico*		$4		MCA 51170
1/30/82	3	22		3 If You're Thinking You Want A Stranger (There's One Coming Home) *Her Goodbye Hit Me In The Heart*		$4		MCA 51228
6/19/82	❶¹	18		4 Fool Hearted Memory *The Steal Of The Night*		$4		MCA 52066
				from the movie *The Soldier* starring Klaus Kinski				
10/9/82+	6	19		5 Marina Del Rey *I Can't See Texas From Here*		$4		MCA 52120
2/12/83	4	17		6 Amarillo By Morning *Lover In Disguise*		$4		MCA 52162
6/11/83	❶¹	23		7 A Fire I Can't Put Out *Honky Tonk Crazy*		$3		MCA 52225
10/8/83+	❶¹	23		8 You Look So Good In Love *A Little Heaven's Rubbing Off On Me*		$3		MCA 52279
2/11/84	❶¹	23		9 Right Or Wrong *Fifteen Years Going Up (And One Night Coming Down)*		$3		MCA 52337
6/2/84	❶¹	21		10 Let's Fall To Pieces Together *You're The Cloud I'm On (When I'm High)*		$3		MCA 52392
9/29/84+	❶¹	23		11 Does Fort Worth Ever Cross Your Mind S:❶¹ / A:❶¹ *Love Comes From The Other Side Of Town*		$3		MCA 52458
2/2/85	5	20		12 The Cowboy Rides Away S:4 / A:5 *Any Old Time*		$3		MCA 52526

DEBUT	PEAK	WKS	Gold	A-side (Chart Hit)..B-side	Pop	$	Pic	Label & Number
				STRAIT, George — Cont'd				
6/1/85	5	18		13 **The Fireman** S:4 / A:5 *What Did You Expect Me To Do*		$3		MCA 52586
9/21/85	❶¹	22		14 **The Chair** S:❶¹ / A:❶¹ *In Too Deep*		$3	■	MCA 52667
1/18/86	4	21		15 **You're Something Special To Me** S:4 / A:4 *Dance Time In Texas*		$3		MCA 52764
5/17/86	❶¹	22		16 **Nobody In His Right Mind Would've Left Her** S:❶¹ / A:❶¹ *You Still Get To Me*		$3		MCA 52817
9/13/86	❶¹	22		17 **It Ain't Cool To Be Crazy About You** S:❶¹ / A:❶¹ *Rhythm Of The Road*		$3		MCA 52914
1/17/87	❶¹	21		18 **Ocean Front Property** S:❶⁴ / A:❶¹ *My Heart Won't Wander Very Far From You*		$3		MCA 53021
5/2/87	❶¹	16		19 **All My Ex's Live In Texas** S:❶² / A:25 *I'm All Behind You Now*		$3		MCA 53087
8/22/87	❶¹	18		20 **Am I Blue** S:❶³ *Someone's Walkin' Around Upstairs*		$3		MCA 53165
2/6/88	❶¹	19		21 **Famous Last Words Of A Fool** S:❶² *It's Too Late Now*		$3		MCA 53248
5/21/88	❶¹	19		22 **Baby Blue** S:❶² *Back To Bein' Me*		$3		MCA 53340
9/17/88	❶¹	20		23 **If You Ain't Lovin' (You Ain't Livin')** S:❶² *Is It That Time Again*		$3		MCA 53400
1/21/89	❶¹	18		24 **Baby's Gotten Good At Goodbye** *Bigger Man Than Me*		$3		MCA 53486
4/29/89	❶¹	20		25 **What's Going On In Your World** *Let's Get Down To It*		$3		MCA 53648
8/12/89	❶¹	21		26 **Ace In The Hole** *Oh Me, Oh My Sweet Baby*		$3		MCA 53693
12/2/89+	8	26		27 **Overnight Success/**				
3/24/90	67	5		28 **Hollywood Squares**...		$3		MCA 53755
4/28/90	❶⁵	21		29 **Love Without End, Amen** *Too Much Of Too Little*		$3		MCA 53820
8/11/90	4	21		30 **Drinking Champagne** *We're Supposed To Do That Now And Then*		$3		MCA 79070
11/3/90	❶⁵	20		31 **I've Come To Expect It From You** *Stranger In My Arms*		$3		MCA 53969
3/23/91	❶²	20		32 **If I Know Me** *Home In San Antone*		$3		MCA 54052
6/15/91	❶³	20		33 **You Know Me Better Than That** *Baby Blue*		$3		MCA 54127
10/5/91	3	20		34 **The Chill Of An Early Fall** *Her Only Bad Habit Is Me*		$3		MCA 54180
1/18/92	24	20		35 **Lovesick Blues** *Is It Already Time*		$3		MCA 54318
4/18/92	5	20		36 **Gone As A Girl Can Get** *Faults And All*		$3		MCA 54379
7/11/92	3	20		37 **So Much Like My Dad** *Wonderland Of Love*		$3		MCA 54439
10/3/92	❶²	20		38 **I Cross My Heart** *You're Right I'm Wrong*		$3		MCA 54478
11/14/92	70	3		39 **Overnight Male**...				album cut
				from the album *Pure Country* on MCA 10651				
1/2/93	❶¹	20		40 **Heartland** *Baby Your Baby*		$3		MCA 54563
5/1/93	6	20		41 **When Did You Stop Loving Me** *Where The Sidewalk Ends*		$3		MCA 54642
				above 4 from the movie *Pure Country* starring Strait				
8/21/93	❶²	20		42 **Easy Come, Easy Go** *She Lays It All On The Line*	71	$3	▌	MCA 54717
12/4/93+	3	20		43 **I'd Like To Have That One Back** *That's Where My Baby Feels At Home*	109	$3	▌	MCA 54767
1/22/94	8	20		44 **Lovebug** *Just Look At Me*	114	$3	▌	MCA 54819
6/25/94	4	20		45 **The Man In Love With You** *We Must Be Loving Right*	112	$3	▌	MCA 54854
10/8/94	❶¹	20		46 **The Big One** *No One But You*		$3	▌	MCA 54938
12/24/94+	❶¹	20		47 **You Can't Make A Heart Love Somebody** *What Am I Waiting For*	111	$3	▌	MCA 54964
3/25/95	3	20		48 **Adalida** *Down Louisiana Way*		$3	▌	MCA 55019
6/24/95	7	20		49 **Lead On** *I Met A Friend Of Yours Today*		$3		MCA 55064
9/23/95	❶⁴	20		50 **Check Yes Or No** – *Fly Me To The Moon*		$3		MCA 55127
				CMA Award: Single of the Year				
12/23/95+	5	20		51 **I Know She Still Loves Me** *Unwound*		$3		MCA 55163
12/30/95	73	1		52 **Santa Claus Is Coming To Town**.....................................[X]				album cut
				Christmas standard written in 1934; from the album *Merry Christmas Strait To You* on MCA 5800				
4/6/96	❶²	20		53 **Blue Clear Sky** *I Ain't Never Seen No One Like You*		$3		MCA 55187
5/18/96	❶³	20		54 **Carried Away** *Do The Right Thing*		$3		MCA 55204
8/24/96	4	20		55 **I Can Still Make Cheyenne** *Need I Say More*		$3		MCA 55248
12/21/96+	19	13		56 **King Of The Mountain**... *I'd Just As Soon Go*		$3		MCA 55288
2/8/97	69	6		57 **Do The Right Thing**...				album cut
				from the album *Blue Clear Sky* on MCA 11428				
3/15/97	❶⁵	20		58 **One Night At A Time** S:2 *Won't You Come Home (And Talk To A Stranger)*	59	$3	▌	MCA 55321
5/3/97	❶⁴	21		59 **Carrying Your Love With Me** *I've Got A Funny Feeling*		$3		MCA 72007
5/3/97	70	1		60 **Won't You Come Home (And Talk To A Stranger)**...............				album cut
5/3/97	71	1		61 **Round About Way**...				album cut
				above 2 from the album *Carrying Your Love With Me* on MCA 11584				
9/6/97	3	20		62 **Today My World Slipped Away** *Round About Way*		$3		MCA 72019
12/27/97	58	2		63 **Merry Christmas Strait To You**.......................................[X]				album cut
12/27/97	69	2		64 **Santa Claus Is Coming To Town**..................................[X-R]				album cut
				above 2 from the album *Merry Christmas Strait To You* on MCA 5800				

STREET, Mel   ★197★   '73

Born King Malachi Street on 10/21/33 in Grundy, West Virginia. Died of a self-inflicted gunshot on 10/21/78 (age 45). Singer/songwriter/guitarist.

1)Lovin' On Back Streets   2)Borrowed Angel   3)If I Had A Cheating Heart
4)I Met A Friend Of Your's Today   5)Walk Softly On The Bridges

DEBUT	PEAK	WKS		A-side / B-side	Pop	$	Pic	Label & Number
5/27/72	7	17		1 **Borrowed Angel** *House Of Pride*		$7		Royal American 64
11/4/72+	5	16		2 **Lovin' On Back Streets** *Who'll Turn Out The Lights*		$6		Metromedia 901
3/17/73	11	15		3 **Walk Softly On The Bridges** .... *Spoiled Lonely Man*		$6		Metromedia 906
7/28/73	38	10		4 **The Town Where You Live**.............................. *Body Man*		$6		Metromedia 0018

DEBUT	PEAK	WKS	Gold	A-side (Chart Hit)..B-side	Pop	$	Pic	Label & Number

STREET, Mel — Cont'd

DEBUT	PEAK	WKS		A-side / B-side	Pop	$	Pic	Label & Number
11/10/73+	11	13		5 Lovin' On Borrowed Time .... Moonshine Man		$6		Metromedia 0143
5/11/74	15	15		6 You Make Me Feel More Like A Man .... Green River		$6		GRT 002
11/2/74+	16	13		7 Forbidden Angel .... Don't Lead Me On		$6		GRT 012
3/1/75	13	14		8 Smokey Mountain Memories .... Let's Put Out The Fire		$6		GRT 017
6/28/75	17	14		9 Even If I Have To Steal .... Country Pride		$6		GRT 025
10/11/75	23	11		10 (This Ain't Just Another) Lust Affair .... Strange Empty World		$6		GRT 030
2/7/76	32	10		11 The Devil In Your Kisses (And The Angel In Your Eyes) .... Baby Don't Save Your Love For A Rainy Day		$6		GRT 043
6/12/76	10	14		12 I Met A Friend Of Your's Today She Boogies When He's Gone		$6		GRT 057
10/23/76	24	13		13 Looking Out My Window Through The Pain .... Virginia's Song		$6		GRT 083
3/19/77	56	7		14 Rodeo Bum .... Guilty As Sin		$6		GRT 116
6/25/77	19	12		15 Barbara Don't Let Me Be The Last To Know .... My Friend The Jukebox		$5		Polydor 14399
9/24/77	15	12		16 Close Enough For Lonesome .... If This Is Having A Good Time		$5		Polydor 14421
1/14/78	9	13		17 If I Had A Cheating Heart Memory Eraser		$5		Polydor 14448
4/22/78	24	10		18 Shady Rest .... She's No Honky Tonk Angel		$5		Polydor 14468
10/21/78	68	5		19 Just Hangin' On .... The Easy Lovin' Kind		$5		Mercury 55043
10/6/79	17	11		20 The One Thing My Lady Never Puts Into Words .... Borrowed Angel		$5		Sunset 100
1/26/80	30	10		21 Tonight Let's Sleep On It Baby .... Muddy Mississippi		$5		Sunbird 103
11/1/80	36	12		22 Who'll Turn Out The Lights .... Lust Affair		$5		Sunbird 7555
10/31/81	48	8		23 Slip Away .... Let's Put Out The Fire		$5		Sunbird 7568

MEL STREET & SANDY POWELL

STREETFEET   **'83**

| 2/12/83 | 78 | 4 | | Where Do You Go .... | | $6 | | Triple T 2001 |

STREETS — see NIGHTSTREETS

STREISAND, Barbra   **'78**

Born on 4/24/42 in Brooklyn. Popular singer/actress/director/producer. Starred in several movies and Broadway shows. Charted 42 pop hits from 1964-96. Married to actor Elliott Gould from 1963-71. Married actor James Brolin on 7/1/98. Won Grammy's Lifetime Achievement Award in 1995.

| 11/25/78 | 70 | 8 | ● | You Don't Bring Me Flowers .... (instrumental) | **0**² | $4 | | Columbia 10840 |

BARBRA & NEIL

STRODE, Lance   **'89**

| 4/8/89 | 92 | 1 | | Dangerous Ground .... | | $7 | | Bootstrap 0416 |

STROMAN, Gene   **'87**

Born on 2/19/61 in Terrell, Texas.

| 1/17/87 | 53 | 8 | | 1 Goodbye Song .... I'm Not That Crazy | | $3 | | Capitol 5662 |
| 8/15/87 | 74 | 5 | | 2 I Don't Feel Much Like A Cowboy Tonight .... Too Many Rivers | | $3 | | Capitol 44015 |

STRUNK, Jud   **'73**

Born Justin Strunk on 6/11/36 in Jamestown, New York; raised in Farmington, Maine. Died in a plane crash on 10/15/81 (age 45). Singer/songwriter/banjo player. Regular on TV's *Laugh-In*.

2/24/73	33	14		1 Daisy A Day .... The Searchers	14	$6		MGM 14463
7/21/73	86	4		2 Next Door Neighbor's Kid .... I'd Prefer To Do It All Again		$6		MGM 14572
8/9/75	51	6		3 The Biggest Parakeets In Town .... I Wasn't Wrong About You [N]	50	$5		Melodyland 6015
2/7/76	88	5		4 Pamela Brown .... They're Tearing Down A Town		$5		Melodyland 6027

STUART, Marty ★161★   **'92**

Born John Marty Stuart on 9/30/58 in Philadelphia, Mississippi. Singer/songwriter/guitarist. Toured with Lester Flatt (**Flatt & Scruggs**) and Nashville Grass from age 13. Toured with the **Johnny Cash** Band from 1979-85. Once married to Cash's daughter Cindy. Married **Connie Smith** on 7/8/97. Joined the *Grand Ole Opry* in 1992.

1)The Whiskey Ain't Workin' 2)Tempted 3)This One's Gonna Hurt You 4)Burn Me Down 5)Little Things

12/28/85+	19	18		1 Arlene .... S:13 / A:22 Midnight Moonlight		$4	■	Columbia 05724
5/31/86	59	6		2 Honky Tonker .... Anyhow I Love You		$4		Columbia 05897
8/9/86	39	12		3 All Because Of You .... Maria (Love To See You Again)		$4		Columbia 06230
11/22/86	59	8		4 Do You Really Want My Lovin' .... Heart Of Stone		$4		Columbia 06425
3/19/88	56	7		5 Mirrors Don't Lie .... Freight Train Boogie		$4		Columbia 07729
6/4/88	66	6		6 Matches .... Old Hat		$4		Columbia 07914
8/19/89	32	12		7 Cry Cry Cry .... The Wild One		$3		MCA 53687
11/18/89+	42	11		8 Don't Leave Her Lonely Too Long .... The Coal Mine Blues		$3		MCA 53751
4/28/90	8	21		9 Hillbilly Rock Western Girls		$3		MCA 79001
9/1/90	20	20		10 Western Girls .... Me And Billy The Kid		$3		MCA 79068
12/22/90+	8	20		11 Little Things Paint The Town Tonight		$3		MCA 53975
4/20/91	12	20		12 Till I Found You .... Half A Heart		$3		MCA 54065
8/17/91	5	20		13 Tempted I'm Blue, I'm Lonesome		$3		MCA 54145
11/23/91+	2¹	20		14 The Whiskey Ain't Workin' Bible Belt		$3		Warner 19097

TRAVIS TRITT Featuring Marty Stuart

| 2/8/92 | 7 | 20 | | 15 Burn Me Down   Blue Train | | $3 | | MCA 54253 |
| 6/6/92 | 7 | 20 | | 16 This One's Gonna Hurt You (For A Long, Long Time)   The King Of Dixie | | $3 | | MCA 54405 |

MARTY STUART AND TRAVIS TRITT

| 9/12/92 | 18 | 20 | | 17 Now That's Country .... Me & Hank & Jumpin' Jack Flash | | $3 | | MCA 54477 |

STUART, Marty — Cont'd

DEBUT	PEAK	WKS		A-side / B-side		$	Pic	Label & Number
12/12/92+	24	20		18 High On A Mountain Top .... *You And Me*		$3		MCA 54538
4/17/93	38	15		19 Hey Baby .... *Down Home*		$3		MCA 54607
1/22/94	26	19		20 Kiss Me, I'm Gone .... *Marty Stuart Visits The Moon*		$3	▮	MCA 54777
6/25/94	54	8		21 Love And Luck .... *Oh What A Silent Night*		$3	▮	MCA 54840
9/24/94	68	5		22 That's What Love's About .... *Shake Your Hips*		$3	▮	MCA 54915
4/1/95	58	8		23 The Likes Of Me .... *You Can Walk All Over Me*		$3		MCA 55010
6/24/95	46	18		24 If I Ain't Got You .... *Wheels*		$3		MCA 55069
4/20/96	23	20		25 Honky Tonkin's What I Do Best .... *Me & Hank & Jumpin' Jack Flash*		$3		MCA 55197
				MARTY STUART & TRAVIS TRITT				
8/17/96	50	10		26 Thanks To You .... *Country Girls*		$3		MCA 55226
10/26/96+	26	20		27 You Can't Stop Love .... *The Mississippi Mudcat And Sister Cheryl Crow*		$3		MCA 55270

STUBBY AND THE BUCCANEERS — see CAPTAIN STUBBY

STUCKEY, Nat ★134★   '66
Born Nathaniel Stuckey on 12/17/34 in Cass County, Texas. Died of cancer on 8/24/88 (age 53). Singer/songwriter/guitarist. Worked as a DJ in Texas and Louisiana.

1)Sweet Thang 2)Sweet Thang And Cisco 3)Plastic Saddle 4)Take Time To Love Her
5)She Wakes Me With A Kiss Every Morning

DEBUT	PEAK	WKS		A-side / B-side		$	Pic	Label & Number
9/10/66	4	18		1 Sweet Thang *Paralyze My Mind*		$10	▮	Paula 243
1/7/67	17	13		2 Oh! Woman .... *On The Other Hand*		$10		Paula 257
4/15/67	27	12		3 All My Tomorrows/		$10		Paula 267
4/29/67	67	3		4 You're Puttin' Me On..		$10		Paula 267
9/2/67	41	8		5 Adorable Women .... *I Knew Her When*		$10		Paula 276
12/23/67+	17	14		6 My Can Do Can't Keep Up With My Want To .... *If There's No Other Way*		$10		Paula 287
5/18/68	63	5		7 Leave This One Alone .... *I Never Knew*		$10		Paula 300
10/12/68	9	16		8 Plastic Saddle *Woman Of Hurt*		$8		RCA Victor 9631
2/15/69	13	11		9 Joe And Mabel's 12th Street Bar And Grill .... *Loving You*		$8		RCA Victor 9720
6/7/69	15	13		10 Cut Across Shorty .... *Understand Little Man*		$8		RCA Victor 0163
7/5/69	20	11		11 Young Love .... *Something Pretty*		$8		RCA Victor 0181
				CONNIE SMITH AND NAT STUCKEY #1 Pop hit for Tab Hunter in 1957				
10/4/69	8	11		12 Sweet Thang And Cisco *Son Of A Bum*		$8		RCA Victor 0238
1/10/70	33	10		13 Sittin' In Atlanta Station .... *Don't Wait For Me*		$8		RCA Victor 9786
3/14/70	59	4		14 If God Is Dead (Who's That Living In My Soul) .... *His Love Takes Care Of Me*		$8		RCA Victor 9805
				NAT STUCKEY AND CONNIE SMITH				
5/16/70	31	8		15 Old Man Willis .... *Beauty Of A Bar*		$7		RCA Victor 9833
9/5/70	31	9		16 Whiskey, Whiskey .... *What Am I Doing In L.A.?*		$7		RCA Victor 9884
12/12/70+	11	15		17 She Wakes Me With A Kiss Every Morning (And She Loves Me To Sleep Every Night) .... *The Devil Made Me Do That*		$7		RCA Victor 9929
4/24/71	24	12		18 Only A Woman Like You .... *Half The Love*		$7		RCA Victor 9977
9/4/71	17	13		19 I'm Gonna Act Right .... *Chained*		$7		RCA Victor 1010
12/11/71+	16	14		20 Forgive Me For Calling You Darling .... *He's Got The Whole World In His Hands*		$7		RCA Victor 0590
4/22/72	26	12		21 Is It Any Wonder That I Love You .... *Got It Comin' Day*		$7		RCA Victor 0687
8/19/72	18	13		22 Don't Pay The Ransom .... *There's Still You*		$7		RCA Victor 0761
2/3/73	10	14		23 Take Time To Love Her *Carry Me Back*		$7		RCA Victor 0879
6/16/73	22	12		24 I Used It All On You .... *I Know The Feelin'*		$7		RCA Victor 0973
10/20/73	14	12		25 Got Leaving On Her Mind .... *Now Lonely Is Only A Word*		$6		RCA Victor 0115
2/23/74	31	11		26 You Never Say You Love Me Anymore .... *The Man That I Am*		$6		RCA Victor 0222
6/1/74	42	13		27 It Hurts To Know The Feeling's Gone .... *Plans For The Future*		$6		RCA Victor 0288
11/9/74	36	12		28 You Don't Have To Go Home .... *I Sure Do Enjoy Loving You*		$6		RCA Victor 10090
7/5/75	85	7		29 Boom Boom Barroom Man .... *Ain't Nothing Bad About Feelin Good*		$6		RCA Victor 10307
2/28/76	13	13		30 Sun Comin' Up .... *Honky Tonk Dreams*		$5		MCA 40519
6/12/76	46	10		31 The Way He's Treated You .... *At Least One Time*		$5		MCA 40568
9/4/76	42	9		32 That's All She Ever Said Except Goodbye .... *After The Lovin' Has Passed*		$5		MCA 40608
12/11/76+	48	8		33 The Shady Side Of Charlotte .... *They'd Love To Be Children Again*		$5		MCA 40658
7/23/77	63	6		34 Buddy, I Lied .... *Don't You Believe Her*		$5		MCA 40752
10/29/77	62	6		35 I'm Coming Home To Face The Music .... *Linda On My Mind*		$5		MCA 40808
3/18/78	66	6		36 That Lucky Old Sun (Just Rolls Around Heaven All Day) .... *I'm Coming Home* #1 Pop hit for Frankie Laine in 1949		$5		MCA 40855
7/8/78	26	10		37 The Days Of Sand And Shovels .... *Mexican Divorce* #34 Pop hit for Bobby Vinton in 1969		$5		MCA 40923

SUDDERTH, Anna   '80
DEBUT	PEAK	WKS		A-side / B-side		$	Pic	Label & Number
5/10/80	90	4		Not A Day Goes By		$7		Verite 801

SULLIVAN, Gene   '58
Born on 11/16/14 in Carbon Hill, Alabama. Died on 10/24/84 (age 69). Member of **Wiley & Gene**.

DEBUT	PEAK	WKS		A-side / B-side		$	Pic	Label & Number
12/9/57+	9	8		Please Pass The Biscuits A:9 / S:16 *Wash Your Feet Before Going To Bed* [N]		$15		Columbia 40971

SULLIVAN, Phil   '59
DEBUT	PEAK	WKS		A-side / B-side		$	Pic	Label & Number
6/8/59	26	6		Hearts Are Lonely .... *Rich Man-Po' Boy*		$15		Starday 437

SUMMER, Scott '79
Born in Fort Smith, Kansas.

DEBUT	PEAK	WKS		A-side / B-side	Pop	$	Pic	Label & Number
2/3/79	80	4		1 Flip Side Of Today .... *I'm In Love*		$5		Con Brio 146
5/26/79	92	3		2 I Don't Wanna Want You .... *Old Fashioned Lady*		$5		Con Brio 152

★334★ SUN, Joe '78
Born James Joseph Paulson on 9/25/43 in Rochester, Minnesota. Singer/songwriter/guitarist. Worked as a DJ in Florida and Wisconsin.
1)Old Flames 2)High And Dry 3)I'd Rather Go On Hurtin'

DEBUT	PEAK	WKS		A-side / B-side	Pop	$	Pic	Label & Number
6/24/78	14	16		1 Old Flames (Can't Hold A Candle To You) *I'll Find It Where I Can*		$5		Ovation 1107
11/4/78	20	12		2 High And Dry .... *Midnight Train Of Memories*		$5		Ovation 1117
3/24/79	27	11		3 On Business For The King/				Ovation 1122
		11		4 Blue Ribbon Blues		$5		Ovation 1122
9/15/79	20	11		5 I'd Rather Go On Hurtin' .... *I'm Still Crazy About You*		$5		Ovation 1127
12/8/79+	34	11		6 Out Of Your Mind .... *Mysteries Of Life (My First Truckin' Song)*		$5		Ovation 1137
1/26/80	48	7		7 What I Had With You .... *I Gotta Get Back The Feeling*		$5		Ovation 1138
				SHEILA ANDREWS with Joe Sun				
3/22/80	23	12		8 Shotgun Rider .... *Little Bit Of Push*	71	$5		Ovation 1141
8/16/80	21	11		9 Bombed, Boozed, And Busted .... *I'll Find It Where I Can*		$5		Ovation 1152
12/27/80+	43	11		10 Ready For The Times To Get Better .... *Bottom Line*		$5		Ovation 1162
3/20/82	40	9		11 Holed Up In Some Honky Tonk .... *Boys In The Back Of The Bus*		$4		Elektra 47417
6/19/82	57	7		12 Fraulein .... *I Ain't Honky Tonkin' No More*		$4		Elektra 47467
				JOE SUN WITH SHOTGUN				
10/2/82	85	2		13 You Make Me Want To Sing .... *Midnight Train Of Memories*		$4		Elektra 69954
7/14/84	73	5		14 Bad For Me		$4		AMI 1319
1/26/85	77	3		15 Why Would I Want To Forget		$4		AMI 1321

SUNSHINE RUBY '53
Born Ruby Bateman in 1940 in Texas.

DEBUT	PEAK	WKS		A-side / B-side	Pop	$	Pic	Label & Number
6/20/53	4	1		Too Young To Tango A:4 *Hearts Weren't Meant To Be Broken*		$10		RCA Victor 5250
				Sonny James (fiddle); written by Sheb Wooley				

SUPER GRIT COWBOY BAND '82
Group from North Carolina. Led by singers/guitarists Curtis Wright and Bill Ellis. Don Cox was once a member.

DEBUT	PEAK	WKS		A-side / B-side	Pop	$	Pic	Label & Number
8/1/81	71	6		1 If You Don't Know Me By Now .... *This Ol' Highway Song*		$6		Hoodswamp 8002
10/24/81	64	6		2 Carolina By The Sea .... *Can't Play For Real*		$6		Hoodswamp 8003
3/6/82	83	3		3 Semi Diesel Blues .... *Sweet Lady*		$6		Hoodswamp 8004
7/10/82	48	9		4 She Is The Woman *Roar Of The Crowd*		$6		Hoodswamp 8005
4/23/83	79	4		5 I Bought The Shoes (That Just Walked Out On Me)		$6		Hoodswamp 8006

★325★ SUPERNAW, Doug '93
Born on 9/26/60 in Houston. Singer/songwriter/guitarist.
1)I Don't Call Him Daddy 2)Not Enough Hours In The Night 3)Reno

DEBUT	PEAK	WKS		A-side / B-side	Pop	$	Pic	Label & Number
2/20/93	50	13		1 Honky Tonkin' Fool .... *You're Gonna Bring Back Cheatin' Songs*		$3		BNA 62432
5/22/93	4	20		2 Reno *Daddy's Girl*		$3		BNA 62537
10/2/93	❶²	20		3 I Don't Call Him Daddy *I Would Have Loved You All Night Long*		$3		BNA 62638
2/5/94	23	20		4 Red And Rio Grande .... *Five Generations Of Rock County Wilsons*		$3		BNA 62757
7/2/94	55	9		5 State Fair .... *He Went To Paris*		$3		BNA 62851
9/3/94	60	7		6 You Never Even Call Me By My Name .... *State Fair*		$3	∎	BNA 62938
1/14/95	16	20		7 What'll You Do About Me .... *Wishin' Her Well*		$3	∎	BNA 64214
10/14/95+	3	21		8 Not Enough Hours In The Night S:13 *We're All Here*		$3	∎	Giant 17764
3/9/96	51	10		9 She Never Looks Back .... S:21 *What In The World*		$3	∎	Giant 17687
6/8/96	53	9		10 You Still Got Me				album cut
				from the album *You Still Got Me* on Giant 24639				
10/12/96	69	1		11 Long Tall Texan				album cut
				THE BEACH BOYS Featuring Doug Supernaw				
				#51 Pop hit for Murry Kellum in 1963; from the album *Stars And Stripes Vol. 1* on River North 1205				

SUTTON, Glenn '79
Born Royce Glenn Sutton on 9/28/37 in Hodge, Louisiana; raised in Henderson, Texas. Singer/prolific songwriter. Formerly married to Lynn Anderson.

DEBUT	PEAK	WKS		A-side / B-side	Pop	$	Pic	Label & Number
1/6/79	55	5		1 The Football Card .... *The Ballad Of The Blue Cyclone* [N]	46	$5		Mercury 55052
9/15/79	73	4		2 Red Neck Disco .... *Hip! Hip! Hip! Horray, For The E.R.A.* [N]		$5		Mercury 57001
10/11/86	74	4		3 I'll Go Steppin' Too .... *Hulk-A-Mania*		$3		Mercury 884974

SWAMPWATER '71
Group led by guitarist Floyd "Gib" Guilbeau (later played fiddle with the Burrito Brothers).

DEBUT	PEAK	WKS		A-side / B-side	Pop	$	Pic	Label & Number
6/12/71	72	2		Take A City Bride .... *It's Your Game, Mary Jane*		$7		King 6376

★300★ SWAN, Billy '74
Born on 5/12/42 in Cape Girardeau, Missouri. Singer/songwriter/pianist. Member of Black Tie.
1)I Can Help 2)Everything's The Same 3)I'm Into Lovin' You

DEBUT	PEAK	WKS		A-side / B-side	Pop	$	Pic	Label & Number
10/12/74	❶²	14	●	1 I Can Help *Ways Of A Woman In Love*	❶²	$6		Monument 8621
8/30/75	17	14		2 Everything's The Same (Ain't Nothing Changed) .... *Overnite Thing*	91	$6		Monument 8661
3/20/76	45	9		3 Just Want To Taste Your Wine .... *Love You Baby - To The Bone*		$6		Monument 8682
				BILLY SWAN with The Jordanaires				
9/11/76	75	5		4 You're The One .... *Ms. Misery*		$6		Monument 8706
				co-written by Buddy Holly and Waylon Jennings				
12/11/76	95	2		5 Shake, Rattle And Roll .... *I Got It For You*		$5		Columbia 10443
				#7 Pop hit for Bill Haley & His Comets in 1954				
6/24/78	30	15		6 Hello! Remember Me .... *Never Go Lookin' Again*		$5		A&M 2046
12/2/78	97	3		7 No Way Around It (It's Love) .... *Forever In Your Love*		$5		A&M 2103

SWAN, Billy — Cont'd

DEBUT	PEAK	WKS		A-side	B-side		$		Label & Number
4/4/81	18	13	8	Do I Have To Draw A Picture	I Want To Change Your Life		$4		Epic 51000
7/25/81	18	13	9	I'm Into Lovin' You	Not Far From Forty		$4		Epic 02196
11/28/81+	19	14	10	Stuck Right In The Middle Of Your Love	Soft Touch		$4		Epic 02601
4/10/82	32	13	11	With Their Kind Of Money And Our Kind Of Love	Lay Down And Love Me Tonight		$4		Epic 02841
10/9/82	56	9	12	Your Picture Still Loves Me (And I Still Love You)	Give Your Lovin' To Me		$4		Epic 03226
1/29/83	39	10	13	Rainbows And Butterflies	Only Be You		$4		Epic 03505
6/4/83	67	8	14	Yes	I Can't Stop Writing Love Songs		$4		Epic 03917
4/26/86	45	10	15	You Must Be Lookin' For Me	Three Chord Rock And Roll		$3		Mercury 884668
2/7/87	63	6	16	I'm Gonna Get You	Three Chord Rock And Roll		$3		Mercury 888320

SWEAT, Isaac Payton   '78
Born in 1945 in Port Arthur, Texas; raised in Nederland, Texas. Died on 6/23/90.

9/9/78	91	4		Shed So Many Tears	All This Ol' Wailin'		$5		Gusto 9010

SWEET, Rachel   '76
Born in 1963 in Akron, Ohio. Singer/actress. Charted the pop hit "Everlasting Love" (with Rex Smith) in 1981.

6/19/76	96	4		We Live In Two Different Worlds	Paper Airplane		$6		Derrick 1000

★286★ SWEETHEARTS OF THE RODEO   '87
Duo of sisters from Manhattan Beach, California: Janis (guitar, vocals) and Kristine (vocals) Oliver. Janis was married to **Vince Gill** from 1980-97.

1)Chains Of Gold 2)Midnight Girl/Sunset Town 3)Blue To The Bone

4/5/86	21	15	1	Hey Doll Baby ....S:12 / A:25 *Everywhere I Turn*			$3	■	Columbia 05824
				#8 R&B hit for The Clovers in 1956					
7/26/86	7	22	2	Since I Found You	S:7 / A:7 *Chosen Few*		$3		Columbia 06166
11/29/86+	4	22	3	Midnight Girl/Sunset Town	S:3 / A:4 *I Can't Resist*		$3		Columbia 06525
4/4/87	4	17	4	Chains Of Gold	S:3 / A:17 *Gotta Get Away*		$3		Columbia 07023
9/12/87	10	18	5	Gotta Get Away	S:11 *Since I Found You*		$3		Columbia 07314
4/2/88	5	20	6	Satisfy You	S:2 *One Time, One Night*		$3		Columbia 07757
8/6/88	5	20	7	Blue To The Bone	S:0¹ *You Never Talk Sweet*		$3		Columbia 07985
12/3/88+	9	22	8	I Feel Fine	S:29 *Until I Stop Dancing*		$3		Columbia 08504
				#1 Pop hit for The Beatles in 1964					
4/15/89	39	11	9	If I Never See Midnight Again	Gone Again		$3		Columbia 68684
1/13/90	25	15	10	This Heart	So Sad (To Watch Good Love Go Bad)		$3		Columbia 73213
8/24/91	63	4	11	Hard-Headed Man	Sisters		$3		Columbia 73907
11/9/91	74	1	12	Devil And Your Deep Blue Eyes	Be Good To Me		$3		Columbia 74064

SWEETWATER   '81
Gospel-based group led by Willie Wynn of **The Tennesseans**. Member **Darrell Holt** went solo in 1987.

10/17/81	75	4	1	I'd Throw It All Away/					
8/8/81	84	4	2	Antioch Church House Choir			$6		Faucet 1592

SWING SHIFT BAND, The   '88
Group features Buddy Emmons and **Ray Pennington**.

11/12/88	76	3		(Turn Me Loose And) Let Me Swing	Loose Tights		$4		Step One 392

SYLVIA   ★172★   '82
Born Sylvia Kirby on 12/9/56 in Kokomo, Indiana. Singer/songwriter.

1)Nobody 2)Drifter 3)Fallin' In Love 4)Like Nothing Ever Happened 5)I Never Quite Got Back

10/13/79	36	10	1	You Don't Miss A Thing	Cry Baby Cry		$4		RCA 11735
4/26/80	35	11	2	It Don't Hurt To Dream	No News Is Good News		$4		RCA 11958
9/6/80	10	16	3	Tumbleweed	Anytime, Anyplace		$4		RCA 12077
1/17/81	❶¹	14	4	Drifter	Missin' You		$4	■	RCA 12164
4/25/81	7	16	5	The Matador	Cry Baby Cry		$4	■	RCA 12214
9/12/81	8	15	6	Heart On The Mend	Rainbow Rider		$4		RCA 12302
1/16/82	12	15	7	Sweet Yesterday	I Feel Cheated		$4		RCA 13020
6/5/82	❶¹	24	● 8	Nobody	I'll Make It Right With You	15	$3		RCA 13223
10/30/82+	2²	20	9	Like Nothing Ever Happened	Drifter		$3		RCA 13330
2/19/83	57	11	10	The Wayward Wind	Shenandoah		$3		RCA 13441
				JAMES GALWAY WITH SYLVIA					
				#1 Pop hit for Gogi Grant in 1956					
5/7/83	5	18	11	Snapshot	Tonight I'm Gettin' Friendly With The Blues		$3		RCA 13501
8/27/83	18	17	12	The Boy Gets Around	Who's Kidding Who		$3		RCA 13589
12/3/83+	3	19	13	I Never Quite Got Back (From Loving You)	So Complete		$3		RCA 13689
4/7/84	24	14	14	Victims Of Goodbye	Unguarded Moments		$3	■	RCA 13755
7/7/84	36	13	15	Love Over Old Times	I Just Don't Have The Heart		$3		RCA 13838
2/16/85	2²	22	16	Fallin' In Love	S:2 / A:2 *True Blue*		$3		RCA 13997
6/29/85	9	18	17	Cry Just A Little Bit	A:8 / S:9 *Only The Shadows Know*		$3		RCA 14107
				#67 hit for Shakin' Stevens in 1984					

DEBUT	PEAK	WKS	Gold	A-side (Chart Hit)..B-side	Pop	$	Pic	Label & Number
				SYLVIA — Cont'd				
11/16/85+	9	25		18 I Love You By Heart .... A:9 / S:10 *Eyes Like Mine*		$3		RCA 14217
				SYLVIA & MICHAEL JOHNSON				
7/5/86	33	15		19 Nothin' Ventured Nothin' Gained .... *Come To Me*		$3		RCA 14375
5/16/87	66	6		20 Straight From My Heart .... *Makes You Wanna Slow Down*		$3		RCA 5127
				SYLVIE & HER SILVER DOLLAR BAND '89				
				Group from Miami.				
7/1/89	95	2		Where You Gonna Hang Your Hat...*Warm Like A Fire*		$6		Playback 75711

T

DEBUT	PEAK	WKS	Gold	A-side	Pop	$	Pic	Label & Number
				TACKETT, Marlow '82				
				Born in Dorton, Kentucky. Male singer/songwriter/guitarist.				
1/19/80	95	2		1 Would You Know Love ....*South Bound Train*		$7		Palace 1006
4/26/80	93	2		2 Midnight Fire		$7		Palace 1008
11/15/80	92	3		3 Ride That Bull (Big Bertha) ....*Would You Know Love?*		$6		Kari 114
7/10/82	67	6		4 Ever-Lovin' Woman ....*Hang In There Teardrop*		$4		RCA 13255
10/23/82	54	9		5 634-5789 ....*She Couldn't Take It Anymore*		$4		RCA 13347
				#13 Pop hit for Wilson Pickett in 1966				
4/23/83	67	6		6 I Know My Way To You By Heart..*Big Old Teardrops*		$4		RCA 13471
8/6/83	56	8		7 I Spent The Night In The Heart Of Texas ....*Way Back When*		$4		RCA 13579
				TAFF, Russ '95				
				Born in Farmersville, California. Contemporary Christian singer/songwriter.				
1/14/95	53	9		1 Love Is Not A Thing ....*Once In A Lifetime*		$3	▌	Reprise 18029
4/1/95	51	10		2 One And Only Love...*Home To You*		$3	▌	Reprise 17918
7/29/95	66	4		3 Bein' Happy ....*Heart Like Yours*		$3	▌	Reprise 17801
				TALBERT, Bubba '83				
				Born in 1949 in Blanchard, Louisiana.				
4/9/83	81	3		1 Easy Catch..*Where Do We Go From Here?*		$6	■	Ranger 5734
7/23/83	77	3		2 Downright Broke My Heart		$6		Ranger 702
				TALL, Tom '55				
				Born Tommie Lee Guthrie on 12/17/37 in Amarillo, Texas.				
1/1/55	2³	26		1 Are You Mine A:2 / J:4 / S:5 *I've Got Somebody New*		$30		Fabor 117
				GINNY WRIGHT/TOM TALL				
1/4/64	25	1		2 Bad, Bad Tuesday ....*Oohin' And Aahin'*		$15		Petal 1210
				TALLEY, James '76				
				Born on 11/9/44 in Mehan, Oklahoma.				
3/13/76	75	8		1 Tryin' Like The Devil ....*Nothin' But The Blues*		$5		Capitol 4218
7/24/76	61	9		2 Are They Gonna Make Us Outlaws Again ....*Forty Hours*		$5		Capitol 4297
4/23/77	83	4		3 Alabama Summertime ....*When The Fiddler Packs His Case*		$5		Capitol 4410
				TAMMY JO '80				
				Female singer Tammy Jo Whitehead.				
3/15/80	88	3		1 I Go To Pieces ....*Don't Be Angry*		$5		Ridgetop 00880
				#9 Pop hit for Peter & Gordon in 1965				
6/14/80	76	4		2 Love Talking/		$5		
		4		3 Wishing Well		$5		Ridgetop 00980
				TANNER, Fargo '75				
				Born in Little Rock, Arkansas; raised in Dallas. Male singer.				
6/7/75	69	11		Don't Drop It ....*I Go Crazy (But I Can't Let You Go)*		$6		Avco 612
				TAPP, Demetriss '73				
				Female singer from North Carolina.				
9/15/73	97	3		Skinny Dippin' ....*Just Let Me Make Believe*		$6		ABC 11383
				TATE, Michael '81				
3/7/81	93	2		Mexican Girl ....*True Love*		$5		Oak 47102
				TAYLOR, Carmol '76				
				Born on 9/5/31 in Brilliant, Alabama. Died of cancer on 12/5/86 (age 55). Male singer/prolific songwriter.				
6/28/75	48	11		1 Back In The U.S.A. ....*I'd Like To Sleep Til I Get Over You*		$5		Elektra 45255
				#37 Pop hit for Chuck Berry in 1959				
10/4/75	91	5		2 Who Will I Be Loving Now ....*So Fine*		$5		Elektra 45277
2/14/76	35	12		3 Play The Saddest Song On The Juke Box........................*I'd Like To Sleep*		$5		Elektra 45299
5/8/76	23	11		4 I Really Had A Ball Last Night *Good Cheatin' Songs*		$5		Elektra 45312
9/18/76	53	6		5 That Little Difference ....*Love What's Left Of Me*		$5		Elektra 45342
1/8/77	87	5		6 Neon Women ....*Crying Steel Guitar*		$5		Elektra 45367
				CARMOL TAYLOR & STELLA PARTON				
1/22/77	100	1		7 What Would I Do Then? ....*You're Looking At A Happy Man*		$5		Elektra 45366
7/23/77	80	5		8 Good Cheatin' Songs ....*I Don't Want My Country Funky*		$5		Elektra 45409
				TAYLOR, Chet '79				
8/4/79	92	2		Barefoot Angel ....*Bet My Soul*		$6		Vista 108

TAYLOR, Chip   '75
Born James Wesley Voigt 1940 in Westchester County, New York. Singer/songwriter. Brother of actor Jon Voigt.

DEBUT	PEAK	WKS	A-side	B-side	Pop	$	Pic	Label & Number
1/4/75	80	6	1 Me As I Am	*Comin' From Behind*		$5		Warner 8050
5/17/75	28	10	2 Early Sunday Morning	*Shickshinny*		$5		Warner 8090
9/13/75	61	7	3 Big River	*John Tucker's On The Wagon Again*		$5		Warner 8128
1/10/76	92	4	4 Circle Of Tears	*You're Alright, Charlie*		$5		Warner 8159
1/8/77	93	4	5 Hello Atlanta	*Farmer's Daughter*		$5		Columbia 10446

CHIP TAYLOR (With Ghost Train)

TAYLOR, Frank   '63

DEBUT	PEAK	WKS	A-side	B-side	Pop	$	Pic	Label & Number
6/1/63	28	1	Snow White Cloud	*Send Her Back To Me*		$15		Parkway 869

TAYLOR, James   '86
Born on 3/12/48 in Boston. Singer/songwriter/guitarist. Charted 22 pop hits from 1970-97. Married to **Carly Simon** from 1972-83. Brother of Livingston Taylor.

DEBUT	PEAK	WKS	A-side	B-side	Pop	$	Pic	Label & Number
7/16/77	88	3	1 Bartender's Blues	*Handy Man* (Pop #4)		$5		Columbia 10557
9/9/78	33	10	2 Devoted To You	*Boys In The Trees*	36	$5		Elektra 45506
			CARLY SIMON and JAMES TAYLOR					
12/7/85+	26	16	3 Everyday	S:25 / A:27 *Limousine Driver*	61	$4	■	Columbia 05681
			written by Buddy Holly					
3/15/86	80	9	4 Only One	*Mona*		$4	■	Columbia 05785

TAYLOR, Jim   '79

DEBUT	PEAK	WKS	A-side	B-side	Pop	$	Pic	Label & Number
8/5/78	100	1	1 I'll Still Need You Mary Ann	*I'm Still Waiting For You*		$7		Checkmate 3069
12/9/78+	68	10	2 Leave It To Love	*Too Many Tears Have Fallen*		$7		Checkmate 3106

TAYLOR, Judy   '82
Born in Murfreesboro, Tennessee.

DEBUT	PEAK	WKS	A-side	B-side	Pop	$	Pic	Label & Number
1/9/82	84	3	1 A Married Man	*I Wish That I Could Hurt That Way Again*		$4		Warner 49859
5/22/82	79	4	2 A Step In The Right Direction	*He Picked Me Up When You Let Me Down*		$4		Warner 50061
9/25/82	70	4	3 The End Of The World	*He Picked Me Up When You Let Me Down*		$4		Warner 29913

TAYLOR, Les   '91
Born on 12/27/48 in Oneida, Kentucky; raised in London, Kentucky. Member of **Exile** from 1979-89.

DEBUT	PEAK	WKS	A-side	B-side	Pop	$	Pic	Label & Number
11/25/89	46	11	1 Shoulda, Coulda, Woulda Loved You	*A Southern Breeze*		$3		Epic 73063
4/28/90	58	10	2 Knowin' You Were Leavin'	*A Southern Breeze*		$3		Epic 73264
3/9/91	44	12	3 I Gotta Mind To Go Crazy	*For The Rest Of Your Life*		$3	▮	Epic 73712
7/27/91	50	9	4 The Very First Lasting Love	*Lonely Weekends*		$3		Epic 73904

SHELBY LYNNE WITH LES TAYLOR

TAYLOR, Livingston   '88
Born on 11/21/50 in Boston. Singer/songwriter/guitarist. Brother of **James Taylor**.

DEBUT	PEAK	WKS	A-side	B-side	Pop	$	Pic	Label & Number
10/22/88	94	2	Loving Arms	*(pop version)*		$4	■	Critique 99275

LIVINGSTON TAYLOR (with Leah Kunkel)

TAYLOR, Mary   '68
Singer/songwriter. Regular on TV's *Hee Haw* from 1969-70.

DEBUT	PEAK	WKS	A-side	B-side	Pop	$	Pic	Label & Number
1/7/67	72	4	1 Don't Waste Your Time	*We Fooled 'Em Again*		$7		Capitol 5776
6/22/68	44	8	2 If I Don't Like The Way You Love Me	*It Takes So Many*		$6		Dot 17104
11/23/68	51	7	3 Feed Me One More Lie	*I'll Be Better Off*		$6		Dot 17168

TAYLOR, R. Dean   '83
Born in 1939 in Toronto. Charted a pop hit in 1970 with "Indiana Wants Me."

DEBUT	PEAK	WKS	A-side	B-side	Pop	$	Pic	Label & Number
1/15/83	90	2	Let's Talk It Over			$6		Strummer 3748

TAYLOR-GOOD, Karen   '82
Born Karen Berke in El Paso, Texas.

1)Diamond In The Rough 2)Tenderness Place 3)Up On Your Love

KAREN TAYLOR:

DEBUT	PEAK	WKS	A-side	B-side	Pop	$	Pic	Label & Number
3/6/82	38	11	1 Diamond In The Rough	*Doesn't Daddy Love Me Anymore*		$5		Mesa 1111
7/24/82	67	7	2 Country Boy's Song	*One Man Woman*		$5		Mesa 1112

KAREN TAYLOR-GOOD:

DEBUT	PEAK	WKS	A-side	B-side	Pop	$	Pic	Label & Number
11/20/82	62	9	3 I'd Rather Be Doing Nothing With You	*Sinking Kind Of Feeling*		$5		Mesa 1113
3/5/83	42	11	4 Tenderness Place	*When The Churchbell Stops Ringing*		$5		Mesa 1114
8/27/83	62	7	5 Don't Call Me	*Begging To You*		$5		Mesa 1115
1/7/84	62	10	6 Handsome Man	*Welcome To The World*		$5		Mesa 1116
9/8/84	66	7	7 We Just Gotta Dance	*I'd Rather Be Doing Nothing With You*		$5		Mesa 1117
4/6/85	61	7	8 Starlite	*Words Are Cheap*		$5		Mesa 1118
10/5/85	57	8	9 Up On Your Love	*Afraid To Go To Sleep*		$5		Mesa 1119
5/10/86	79	4	10 Come In Planet Earth (Are You Listenin')			$5		Mesa 2011

TENNESSEANS, The   '78
Group formed by Willie Wynn (later with **Sweetwater**). Included Tony King who was later with **Matthews, Wright & King**.

DEBUT	PEAK	WKS	A-side	B-side	Pop	$	Pic	Label & Number
12/2/78	81	5	Nineteen-Sixty Something Songwriter Of The Year	*I Can Heal You*		$5		Capitol 4645

TENNESSEE EXPRESS   '81
Vocal group from Nashville.

DEBUT	PEAK	WKS	A-side	B-side	Pop	$	Pic	Label & Number
8/15/81	31	11	1 Big Like A River	*Now*		$4		RCA 12277
12/12/81	75	4	2 Little Things	*How Much I Love You*		$4		RCA 12362
			#13 Pop hit for **Bobby Goldsboro** in 1965					
4/3/82	70	4	3 The Arms Of A Stranger	*Someone Just Like You*		$4		RCA 13078
7/24/82	78	5	4 Operator/			$4		RCA 13265
			#22 Pop hit for **Manhattan Transfer** in 1975					
		5	5 Let Me In And Let Me Love You			$4		RCA 13265

DEBUT	PEAK	WKS	Gold	A-side (Chart Hit)..B-side	Pop	$	Pic	Label & Number
				TENNESSEE EXPRESS — Cont'd				
2/5/83	62	7		6 How Long Will It Take.................................. *Lead Me Into Love*		$4		RCA 13423
6/4/83	65	6		7 Cotton Fields .... *Good For Nothing*		$4		RCA 13526
				#13 Pop hit for The Highwaymen in 1962				
				TENNESSEE PULLEYBONE **'73**				
				Group consisted of Smig Smith (vocals), Dave Gillon, Ham Hamilton and Bones Kaelin.				
9/8/73	75	4		The Door's Always Open............................... *Swinging Doors*		$6		JMI 25
				TENNESSEE TORNADO — see FOSTER, Jerry				
				TENNESSEE VALLEY BOYS **'84**				
				Vocal group: Rick Baird, Jimmy Ponder, James Fulbright and Dan Britton. Assembled by Wally Fowler (b: 2/15/17; d: 6/3/94). Fowler also created the Oak Ridge Quartet (which evolved into the **Oak Ridge Boys**).				
4/14/84	57	10		Lo And Behold .... *It's Gonna Take Time*		$7		Nashwood 12684
				WALLY FOWLER'S TENNESSEE VALLEY BOYS				
				TERRY, Al **'54**				
				Born Allison Joseph Theriot on 1/14/22 in Kaplan, Louisiana. Singer/songwriter/guitarist.				
4/24/54	8	5		1 Good Deal, Lucille *A:8 / J:8* *Say A Prayer For Me*		$30		Hickory 1003
2/29/60	28	1		2 Watch Dog .... *Passing The Blues Around*		$25		Hickory 1111
				TERRY, Gordon **'70**				
				Born on 10/7/31 in Decatur, Alabama. Singer/songwriter/fiddler.				
5/30/70	62	5		The Ballad Of J.C. ....*Untanglin' My Mind* [N]		$7		Capitol 2792
				tribute to **Johnny Cash** to the tune of "The Ballad Of New Orleans"				
				TEXAS PLAYBOYS — see ORIGINAL TEXAS PLAYBOYS				
				TEXAS VOCAL COMPANY **'83**				
				Vocal trio from Dallas: Sandy Skinner, Dick Root and Dave Roth.				
4/30/83	65	5		1 Two Hearts .... *You Did It Again*		$4		RCA 13504
10/8/83	82	3		2 It Had To Be You .... *Backsliding*		$4		RCA 13566
★247★				**THOMAS, B.J.** **'83**				
				Born Billy Joe Thomas on 8/7/42 in Hugo, Oklahoma; raised in Rosenberg, Texas. Singer/songwriter. Charted 26 pop hits from 1966-83.				
				1)Whatever Happened To Old Fashioned Love 2)Another Somebody Done Somebody Wrong Song 3)New Looks From An Old Lover				
2/22/75	❶¹	16	●	1 (Hey Won't You Play) Another Somebody Done Somebody Wrong Song *City Boys*	❶¹	$5		ABC 12054
10/4/75	37	10		2 Help Me Make It (To My Rockin' Chair) .... *We Are Happy Together*	64	$5		ABC 12121
5/14/77	98	1		3 Home Where I Belong................................ *Hallelujah*		$5		Myrrh 166
1/28/78	25	13		4 Everybody Loves A Rain Song .... *Dusty Roads*	43	$4		MCA 40854
2/10/79	86	3		5 We Could Have Been The Closest Of Friends .... *In My Heart*		$4		MCA 40986
4/18/81	27	11		6 Some Love Songs Never Die .... *There Ain't No Love*		$4		MCA 51087
8/8/81	22	12		7 I Recall A Gypsy Woman............................ *The Lovin' Kind*		$4		MCA 51151
2/12/83	❶¹	21		8 Whatever Happened To Old Fashioned Love *I Just Sing*	93	$4		Cleveland Int'l 03492
7/9/83	❶¹	21		9 New Looks From An Old Lover *You Keep The Man In Me Happy*		$4		Columbia 03985
11/26/83+	3	21		10 Two Car Garage *Beautiful World*		$4		Cleveland Int'l 04237
4/14/84	10	19		11 The Whole World's In Love When You're Lonely *We're Here To Love*		$4		Cleveland Int'l 04431
8/4/84	14	18		12 Rock And Roll Shoes.................. *S:14 / A:21* *Then I'll Be Over You*		$3		Columbia 04531
				RAY CHARLES (with B.J. THOMAS)				
10/20/84+	17	19		13 The Girl Most Likely To .... *S:17 / A:17* *From This Moment On*		$4		Cleveland Int'l 04608
11/9/85	61	11		14 The Part Of Me That Needs You Most .... *Northern Lights*		$3		Columbia 05647
				#98 Pop hit for Jay Black in 1980				
2/22/86	62	7		15 America Is .... *Broken Toys*		$3	■	Columbia 05771
10/4/86	59	6		16 Night Life .... *Make The World Go Away*		$3		Columbia 06314
				THOMAS, Darrell **'79**				
				Born in 1952 in Melcher, Iowa.				
5/19/79	99	3		Waylon, Sing To Mama................................ *The Conquered King*		$7		Ozark Opry 101
				THOMAS, Dick **'45**				
				Born Richard Thomas Goldhahn on 9/4/15 in Philadelphia. Singer/fiddler/accordionist/actor. Acted in several western movies.				
9/29/45	❶⁴	23		1 Sioux City Sue *Tumbling Tumbleweeds*	16	$20		National 5007
12/8/45	4	1		2 Honestly *Half-Way To Montana*		$20		National 5008
				DICK THOMAS And His Nashville Ramblers:				
9/25/48	13	1		3 The Beaut From Butte .... *J:13* *Two Car Garage*		$15		Decca 46132
2/12/49	12	1		4 The Sister Of Sioux City Sue .... *J:12 / S:14* *Charlotte Belle (Carolina Waltz)*		$15		Decca 46147
				THOMAS, Jeff **'87**				
1/17/87	85	3		Hollywood's Dream..		$5		Revolver 014

THOMPSON, Hank ★39★   '52

Born Henry William Thompson on 9/3/25 in Waco, Texas. Singer/songwriter/guitarist. Backing group: The Brazos Valley Boys. Elected to the Country Music Hall of Fame in 1989.

1)The Wild Side Of Life 2)Rub-A-Dub-Dub 3)Wake Up, Irene 4)Squaws Along The Yukon
5)Humpty Dumpty Heart

HANK THOMPSON and His Brazos Valley Boys:

DEBUT	PEAK	WKS	#	A-side	B-side	Pop	$	Label & Number
1/31/48	2²	38	1	Humpty Dumpty Heart	J:2 / S:3 Today		$20	Capitol Amer. 40065
9/4/48	12	2	2	Yesterday's Mail	J:12		$20	Capitol 15132
10/16/48	7	10	3	Green Light	J:7 / S:8 You Remembered Me		$20	Capitol 15187
				also see #21 below				
2/5/49	10	1	4	What Are We Gonna Do About The Moonlight	J:10		$20	Capitol 15132
2/5/49	14	1	5	I Find You Cheatin' On Me/	S:14			
2/12/49	15	1	6	You Broke My Heart (In Little Bitty Pieces)	J:15		$20	Capitol 15345
10/1/49	6	7	7	Whoa Sailor	J:6 / S:8 Swing Wide Your Gates Of Love		$20	Capitol 40218
10/1/49	10	1	8	Soft Lips/	J:10			
11/5/49	15	1	9	The Grass Looks Greener Over Yonder	J:15		$20	Capitol 40211
3/15/52	❶15	30	10	The Wild Side Of Life	S:❶15 / J:❶15 / A:❶8 Cryin' In The Deep Blue Sea		$25	Capitol F1942
6/28/52	3	15	11	Waiting In The Lobby Of Your Heart	J:3 / S:5 / A:7 Don't Make Me Cry Again		$25	Capitol F2063
12/13/52	10	1	12	The New Wears Off Too Fast	J:10 You're Walking On My Heart		$25	Capitol F2269
3/28/53	9	2	13	No Help Wanted	J:9 / A:10 / S:10 I'd Have Never Found Somebody New		$25	Capitol 2376
5/23/53	❶3	20	14	Rub-A-Dub-Dub	J:❶3 / A:2 / S:5 I'll Sign My Heart Away		$25	Capitol 2445
9/19/53	8	4	15	Yesterday's Girl	S:8 / A:8 John Henry		$25	Capitol 2553
12/12/53+	❶2	19	16	Wake Up, Irene	J:❶2 / S:3 / A:4 Go Cry Your Heart Out		$25	Capitol 2646
				answer to "Goodnight, Irene" by Red Foley & Ernest Tubb				
5/22/54	9	1	17	A Fooler, A Faker/	J:9 / S:15			
5/8/54	10	2	18	Breakin' The Rules	S:10		$20	Capitol 2758
7/3/54	9	12	19	Honky-Tonk Girl/	S:9 / J:10 / A:11			
				also see #72 below				
7/17/54	10	4	20	We've Gone Too Far	S:10 / A:15		$20	Capitol 2823
10/16/54	3	20	21	The New Green Light	J:3 / S:7 / A:8 A Lonely Heart Knows		$20	Capitol 2920
				new version of #3 above				
2/26/55	12	4	22	If Lovin' You Is Wrong/	S:12 / A:14			
3/12/55	13	2	23	Annie Over	S:13		$20	Capitol 3030
6/4/55	5	9	24	Wildwood Flower/	J:5 / S:8 / A:13 [I]			
				HANK THOMPSON and His Brazos Valley Boys with MERLE TRAVIS				
6/4/55	7	8	25	Breakin' In Another Heart	S:7		$20	Capitol 3106
8/20/55	6	11	26	Most Of All	A:6 / S:11 Simple Simon		$20	Capitol 3188
12/10/55	5	7	27	Don't Take It Out On Me/	S:5 / J:9 / A:13			
			5	28	Honey, Honey Bee Ball	S:flip / J:flip		$20	Capitol 3275
3/24/56	4	22	29	The Blackboard Of My Heart/	A:4 / S:6 / J:6			
3/24/56	14	5	30	I'm Not Mad, Just Hurt	S:14		$20	Capitol 3347
2/23/57	13	4	31	Rockin' In The Congo/	S:13			
				also see #78 below				
		2	32	I Was The First One	S:flip		$30	Capitol 3623
10/14/57	14	2	33	Tears Are Only Rain	A:14 Under The Double Eagle		$20	Capitol 3781
6/9/58	11	3	34	How Do You Hold A Memory	A:11 Li'l Liza Jane		$20	Capitol 3950
8/18/58	2⁴	22	35	Squaws Along The Yukon	Gathering Flowers		$20	Capitol 4017
12/1/58+	7	23	36	I've Run Out Of Tomorrows/				
2/2/59	26	3	37	You're Going Back To Your Old Ways Again			$20	Capitol 4085
5/11/59	13	10	38	Anybody's Girl/				
6/29/59	25	1	39	Total Strangers			$20	Capitol 4182
11/9/59+	22	10	40	I Didn't Mean To Fall In Love	I Guess I'm Getting Over You		$20	Capitol 4269
3/21/60	10	16	41	A Six Pack To Go	What Made Her Change	102	$20	Capitol 4334
8/1/60	14	14	42	She's Just A Whole Lot Like You	There My Future Goes	99	$20	Capitol 4386
5/29/61	7	11	43	Oklahoma Hills/				
5/29/61	25	2	44	Teach Me How To Lie			$20	Capitol 4556
9/18/61	12	10	45	Hangover Tavern	Give The World A Smile		$20	Capitol 4605
9/7/63	23	1	46	I Wasn't Even In The Running	The More In Love Your Heart Is		$15	Capitol 4968
9/28/63	22	5	47	Too In Love	Blackboard Of My Heart		$15	Capitol 5008
1/11/64	45	2	48	Twice As Much	Reaching For The Moon		$15	Capitol 5071
8/14/65	42	2	49	Then I'll Start Believing In You	In The Back Of Your Mind		$15	Capitol 5422
10/22/66	15	14	50	Where Is The Circus	Love Walked Out Long Before She Did		$10	Warner 5858
2/4/67	16	13	51	He's Got A Way With Women	Let The Four Winds Choose		$10	Warner 5886
				HANK THOMPSON:				
7/13/68	7	15	52	On Tap, In The Can, Or In The Bottle	If I Lose You Tomorrow		$8	Dot 17108
10/26/68+	5	15	53	Smoky The Bar	Clubs, Spades, Diamonds, And Hearts		$8	Dot 17163
3/8/69	47	9	54	I See Them Everywhere	Today		$8	Dot 17207
7/12/69	46	9	55	The Pathway Of My Life	At Certain Times		$8	Dot 17262
10/18/69	60	6	56	Oklahoma Home Brew	Let's Get Drunk And Be Somebody		$8	Dot 17307
5/9/70	54	5	57	But That's All Right	Take It All Away		$8	Dot 17347

DEBUT	PEAK	WKS	Gold	A-side (Chart Hit)...B-side	Pop	$	Pic	Label & Number
				THOMPSON, Hank — Cont'd				
10/10/70	69	4		58 One Of The Fortunate Few ....*I'm Afraid I Lied*		$8		Dot 17354
3/6/71	15	14		59 Next Time I Fall In Love (I Won't)..................*Big Boat Across Oklahoma*		$7		Dot 17365
7/17/71	18	16		60 The Mark Of A Heel ....*Promise Her Anything*		$7		Dot 17385
12/4/71+	11	14		61 I've Come Awful Close ....*Teardrops On The Rocks*		$7		Dot 17399
4/29/72	16	12		62 Cab Driver...*Gloria*		$7		Dot 17410
				#23 Pop hit for **The Mills Brothers** in 1968				
9/23/72	53	8		63 Glow Worm...................*You're Nobody Till Somebody Loves You*		$7		Dot 17430
				#1 Pop hit for **The Mills Brothers** in 1952				
3/17/73	70	2		64 Roses In The Wine ....*That's Why I Sing In A Honky Tonk*		$7		Dot 17447
9/1/73	48	9		65 Kindly Keep It Country ....*Jill's Jack In The Box*		$7		Dot 17470
2/2/74	8	15		66 The Older The Violin, The Sweeter The Music ......*A Six Pack To Go*		$7		Dot 17490
7/13/74	10	16		67 Who Left The Door To Heaven Open ......*When My Blue Moon Turns To Gold Again*		$7		Dot 17512
1/25/75	29	10		68 Mama Don't 'Low ....*Wait A Little Longer Baby*		$6		ABC/Dot 17535
6/28/75	70	8		69 That's Just My Truckin' Luck ....*After You Have Made Me Over*		$6		ABC/Dot 17556
3/6/76	72	6		70 Asphalt Cowboy............................*Fifteen Miles To Clarksville*		$6		ABC/Dot 17612
9/4/76	86	3		71 Big Band Days...*Forgive Me*		$6		ABC/Dot 17649
1/15/77	91	4		72 Honky Tonk Girl ....*Another Shot Of Toddy* [R]		$6		ABC/Dot 17673
				new version of #19 above				
5/21/77	92	2		73 Just An Old Flame ....*Don't Get Around Much Anymore*		$6		ABC/Dot 17695
10/21/78	92	3		74 I'm Just Gettin' By ....*I Hear The South Callin' Me*		$5		ABC 12409
3/3/79	88	3		75 Dance With Me Molly ....*Point Of No Return*		$5		ABC 12447
8/25/79	29	12		76 I Hear The South Callin' Me ....*Through The Bottom Of The Glass*		$4		MCA 41079
2/2/80	32	9		77 Tony's Tank-Up, Drive-In Cafe ....*Point Of No Return*		$4		MCA 41176
12/19/81+	82	5		78 Rockin' In The Congo ....*The Convict And The Rose* [R]		$8	■	Churchill 7779
				new version of #31 above				
7/23/83	82	5		79 Once In A Blue Moon ....*Let's Stop What We Started*		$5	■	Churchill 94026
				THOMPSON, J.W. **'80**				
				Born in Alexandria, Louisiana. Male singer/songwriter.				
9/15/79	90	2		1 The Visitor ....*When You're Honky Tonkin'*		$5		Southern Star 309
10/4/80	56	9		2 Halftime ....*Jesus Loves Cowboys The Same*		$5		NSD 62
1/24/81	72	4		3 Two Out Of Three Ain't Bad ....*Bubbles In My Beer*		$5		NSD 75
10/22/83	97	1		4 We've Got A Good Thing Goin' ....*Makin' Love With A Married Man*		$6		USA Country 1001
7/14/84	91	2		5 Hello Josephine		$6		Century 21 109
				THOMPSON, Sue **'74**				
				Born Eva Sue McKee on 7/19/26 in Nevada, Missouri; raised in San Jose, California. Singer/guitarist. Married to **Hank Penny** from 1953-63. Charted 7 pop hits from 1961-65.				
				1)*Good Old Fashioned Country Love* 2)*Oh, How Love Changes* 3)*I Think They Call It Love*				
				DON GIBSON & SUE THOMPSON:				
8/28/71	50	8		1 The Two Of Us Together ....*Oh Yes, I Love You*		$8		Hickory 1607
4/22/72	71	3		2 Did You Ever Think ....*Love's Garden*		$8		Hickory 1629
8/12/72	37	11		3 I Think They Call It Love.....................*Over There's The Door*		$8		Hickory 1646
11/18/72	72	5		4 Candy And Roses ....*A Full Time Job*		$8		Hickory 1652
				SUE THOMPSON:				
12/23/72	64	5		5 Cause I Love You ....*My Tears Don't Show*		$8		Hickory 1654
3/17/73	52	6		6 Go With Me ....*The Two Of Us Together*		$8		Hickory 1665
9/15/73	53	9		7 Warm Love ....*Fly The Friendly Skies With Jesus*		$6		Hickory/MGM 303
8/10/74	31	12		8 Good Old Fashioned Country Love ....*Ages And Ages Ago*		$6		Hickory/MGM 324
7/19/75	36	11		9 Oh, How Love Changes ....*Sweet And Tender Times*		$6		Hickory/MGM 350
9/6/75	50	9		10 Big Mable Murphy ....*Big Daddy*		$6		Hickory/MGM 354
				SUE THOMPSON:				
2/21/76	95	3		11 Never Naughty Rosie ....*He Cheats On Me*		$6		Hickory/MGM 364
				SUE THOMPSON:				
4/3/76	98	2		12 Get Ready-Here I Come ....*Once More*		$6		Hickory/MGM 367
				THOMPSON BROTHERS BAND, The **'97**				
				Group from Norwell, Massachusetts: Andy (vocals) and Matt (drums) Thompson, with Mike Whitty (bass).				
11/15/97	56	8		Drive Me Crazy ....*Back On The Farm*		$3		RCA 64998
				THORNTON, Marsha **'90**				
				Born on 10/22/64 in Killen, Alabama.				
9/23/89	62	7		1 Deep Water ....*Don't Tell Me What To Do*		$3		MCA 53711
1/6/90	59	10		2 A Bottle Of Wine And Patsy Cline ....*Don't Tell Me What To Do*		$3		MCA 53762
2/16/91	73	2		3 Maybe The Moon Will Shine ....*A Far Cry From You*		$3		MCA 53995
				THRASHER BROTHERS **'82**				
				Vocal group of brothers Joe (lead), Jim (tenor) and Andy (baritone) Thrasher, with John Gresham (bass) and Roger Hallmark (guitar, banjo, fiddle). Joe's son, Neil, formed **Thrasher Shiver** duo.				
12/15/79+	72	5		1 A Message To Khomeini ....*Maharishi* [N]		$6		Vulcan 10004
				ROGER HALLMARK and The Thrasher Brothers				
3/7/81	83	2		2 Lovers Love ....*Wouldn't It Make A Good Country Song*		$4		MCA 51049
2/6/82	62	5		3 Best Of Friends ....*The Captain & The Delta Queen*		$4		MCA 51227
				from the TV series *Simon & Simon* starring Gerald McRaney and Jameson Parker				
9/11/82	60	6		4 Still The One ....*Long Tall Texan*		$4		MCA 52093
				#5 Pop hit for **Orleans** in 1976				
1/15/83	81	4		5 Wherever You Are ....*Heart To Heart*		$4		MCA 52153
12/10/83	80	8		6 Whatcha Got Cookin' In Your Oven Tonight...........*Southern Swing*		$4		MCA 52297

THRASHER SHIVER '97
Duo of Neil Thrasher and Kelly Shiver. Neil's father, Joe, was lead singer of the **Thrasher Brothers**.

8/10/96	65	6		1 Goin', Goin', Gone				album cut
2/22/97	49	10		2 Be Honest				album cut
				above 2 from the album *Thrasher Shiver* on Asylum 61929				

THREE SUNS, The '50
Instrumental trio from Philadelphia: brothers Al (guitar; d: 1965) and Morty (accordion; d: 7/20/90), with cousin Artie Dunn (organ; d: 1989).

2/4/50	7	4		Beyond The Sunset A:7 *The Game Of Broken Hearts*		$30		RCA Victor 47-3105
				THE THREE SUNS with ROSALIE ALLEN and ELTON BRITT				
				78 rpm: 20-3599; #71 Pop hit for **Pat Boone** in 1959				

THROCKMORTON, Sonny '79
Born James Fron Throckmorton on 4/2/41 in Carlsbad, New Mexico. Singer/prolific songwriter.

9/4/76	76	6		1 Rosie .... *Troublesome Waters*		$6	■	Starcrest 073
12/25/76+	73	7		2 Lovin' You, Lovin' Me ....*I Don't Know How To Tell Her (She Don't Love Me Anymore)*		$6		Starcrest 094
9/16/78	54	8		3 I Wish You Could Have Turned My Head (And Left My Heart Alone) ....*She Sure Makes Leavin' Look Easy*		$4		Mercury 55039
2/3/79	47	8		4 Smooth Sailin'/		$4		Mercury 55051
		8		5 Last Cheater's Waltz		$4		Mercury 55051
7/14/79	66	6		6 Can't You Hear That Whistle Blow........................*I Feel Like Loving You Again*		$4		Mercury 55061
4/5/80	89	3		7 Friday Night Blues ....*It Always Rains On Me*		$4		Mercury 57018
12/12/81	77	5		8 A Girl Like You ....*I've Broken My Own Heart*		$4		MCA 51214

THUNDERKLOUD, Billy, & The Chieftones '75
Vocal group of Native Americans from British Columbia: Vincent "Billy Thunderkloud" Clifford, Jack Wolf, Barry Littlestar and Richard Grayowl.

5/17/75	16	12		1 What Time Of Day *When Love Is Right*	92	$5		20th Century 2181
10/25/75	37	11		2 Pledging My Love ....*I Will Love You Until I Die*		$5		20th Century 2239
				#17 Pop hit for Johnny Ace in 1955				
5/29/76	74	5		3 Indian Nation (The Lament of the Cherokee Reservation Indian) ....*I'm Going Right To Where I Do Wrong*		$5		Polydor 14321
				#1 Pop hit for The Raiders in 1971				
8/7/76	47	8		4 Try A Little Tenderness ....*A Natural Feelin' For You*		$5		Polydor 14338
				#25 Pop hit for Otis Redding in 1967				
12/11/76	77	6		5 It's Alright ....*The Wanderer*		$5		Polydor 14362

TIBOR BROTHERS, The '76
Vocal group of brothers from Hebron, North Dakota: Francis, Gerard, Harvey, Kurt and Larry Tibor.

4/17/76	95	3		It's So Easy Lovin' You ....*Movin' Along*		$5		Ariola America 7615

TIERNY, Patti '73

9/22/73	90	4		Cryin' Eyes ....*Jody's Face*		$6		MGM 14561

TILLIS, Mel ★28★ '72
Born Lonnie Melvin Tillis on 8/8/32 in Tampa, Florida; raised in Pahokee, Florida. Singer/songwriter/guitarist/actor. Acted in the movies *W.W. & The Dixie Dancekings*, *Smokey & The Bandit II*, *Uphill All The Way* and *Murder In Music City*. Owned several music publishing companies. Backing band: The Statesiders. Father of **Pam Tillis**. Known for his stuttering speech. CMA Award: 1976 Entertainer of the Year.

1)I Ain't Never 2)Good Woman Blues 3)Coca Cola Cowboy 4)I Believe In You 5)Southern Rains

11/10/58	24	4		1 The Violet And A Rose ....*No Song To Sing*		$15		Columbia 41189
1/5/59	28	4		2 Finally ....*The Brooklyn Bridge*		$15		Columbia 41277
8/24/59	27	2		3 Sawmill ....*You Are The Reason*		$15		Columbia 41416
				MEL TILLIS and BILL PHILLIPS				
				also see #33 below				
2/8/60	24	4		4 Georgia Town Blues ....*Till I Get Enough Of These Blues*		$15		Columbia 41530
				MEL TILLIS and BILL PHILLIPS				
1/5/63	25	3		5 How Come Your Dog Don't Bite Nobody But Me ....*So Soon*		$10		Decca 31445
				WEBB PIERCE and MEL TILLIS				
7/3/65	14	16		6 Wine ....*Buried Alive*		$12		RIC 158
10/15/66	17	14		7 Stateside ....*Home Is Where The Hurt Is*		$8		Kapp 772
2/18/67	11	19		8 Life Turned Her That Way ....*If I Could Only Start Over*	128	$8	■	Kapp 804
7/15/67	20	14		9 Goodbye Wheeling ....*At The Sight Of You*		$8		Kapp 837
12/16/67	71	3		10 Survival Of The Fittest ....*The Old Gang's Gone*		$8		Kapp 867
1/13/68	26	12		11 All Right (I'll Sign The Papers) ....*Helpless, Hopeless Fool*		$8		Kapp 881
5/11/68	17	15		12 Something Special ....*You Name It*		$8		Kapp 905
10/5/68	31	7		13 Destroyed By Man ....*I Haven't Seen Mary In Years*		$8		Kapp 941
12/21/68+	10	17		14 Who's Julie ....*Give Me One More Day*		$8		Kapp 959
4/19/69	13	15		15 Old Faithful..*Sorrow Overtakes The Wine*		$8		Kapp 986
				MEL TILLIS And The Statesiders:				
8/16/69	9	15		16 These Lonely Hands Of Mine *Cover Mama's Flowers*		$6		Kapp 2031
1/17/70	10	11		17 She'll Be Hanging 'Round Somewhere *Where Love Has Died*		$6		Kapp 2072
4/25/70	3	17		18 Heart Over Mind *Lingering Memories*		$6		Kapp 2086
7/25/70	5	14		19 Heaven Everyday *How Do You Drink The Wine*		$6		MGM 14148
10/17/70	25	11		20 To Lonely, Too Long ....*Memories Made This House*		$6		Kapp 2103
11/7/70	8	13		21 Commercial Affection *I Thought About You*		$6		MGM 14176

DEBUT	PEAK	WKS	Gold	A-side (Chart Hit)...B-side	Pop	$	Pic	Label & Number
				TILLIS, Mel, And The Statesiders — Cont'd				
1/30/71	**4**	15		22 The Arms Of A Fool _Veil Of White Lace_	114	$6		MGM 14211
5/8/71	**56**	9		23 One Drink .... _I Could Never Be Ashamed Of You_		$6		Kapp 2121
6/5/71	**8**	15		24 Take My Hand _Life's Little Surprises_	110	$6		MGM 14255
				MEL TILLIS AND SHERRY BRYCE with The Statesiders				
7/31/71	**8**	16		25 Brand New Mister Me _Brand New Wrapper_		$6		MGM 14275
10/30/71	**9**	14		26 Living And Learning _Tangled Vines_		$6		MGM 14303
				MEL TILLIS & SHERRY BRYCE				
1/1/72	**14**	13		27 Untouched .... _I Went A Ramblin'_		$6		MGM 14329
4/8/72	**38**	10		28 Anything's Better Than Nothing..................... _Then It Will Be All Over_		$6		MGM 14365
				MEL TILLIS & SHERRY BRYCE And The Statesiders				
5/6/72	**12**	11		29 Would You Want The World To End .... _Things Have Changed A Lot_		$6		MGM 14372
8/12/72	**❶²**	15		30 I Ain't Never _Burden Of Love_		$6		MGM 14418
12/9/72+	**3**	16		31 Neon Rose _It's My Love (And I'm Gonna Give It)_		$6		MGM 14454
4/28/73	**21**	13		32 Thank You For Being You.. _Over The Hill_		$6		MGM 14522
8/25/73	**2¹**	17		33 Sawmill _Mama's Gonna Pray_ [R]		$6		MGM 14585
				new version of #3 above				
11/17/73+	**26**	13		34 Let's Go All The Way Tonight.. _In The Vine_		$6		MGM 14660
				MEL TILLIS & SHERRY BRYCE & The Statesiders				
1/12/74	**2¹**	18		35 Midnight, Me And The Blues _Modern Home Magazine_		$6		MGM 14689
4/13/74	**11**	14		36 Don't Let Go .... _Why Not Do The Things (They Think We've Done)_		$6		MGM 14714
				MEL TILLIS & SHERRY BRYCE And The Statesiders				
				#13 Pop hit for Roy Hamilton in 1958				
5/18/74	**3**	16		37 Stomp Them Grapes _Hang My Picture In Your Heart_		$5		MGM 14720
10/5/74	**3**	14		38 Memory Maker _Second Best_		$5		MGM 14744
1/4/75	**14**	13		39 You Are The One.. _I See Heaven In You_		$5		MGM 14776
				MEL TILLIS & SHERRY BRYCE And The Statesiders				
2/1/75	**7**	16		40 Best Way I Know How _Honey Dew Melon_		$5		MGM 14782
5/17/75	**32**	13		41 Mr. Right And Mrs. Wrong .... _Just Two Strangers Passing In The Night_		$5		MGM 14803
				MEL TILLIS AND SHERRY BRYCE And The Statesiders				
6/14/75	**4**	16		42 Woman In The Back Of My Mind _Kissing Your Picture (Is So Cold)_		$5		MGM 14804
11/1/75+	**16**	14		43 Lookin' For Tomorrow (And Findin' Yesterdays) .... _Tennessee Banjo Man_		$5		MGM 14835
3/20/76	**15**	10		44 Mental Revenge.. _My Bad Girl Treats Me Good_		$5		MGM 14846
				MEL TILLIS:				
5/29/76	**11**	13		45 Love Revival .... _Gator Bar_		$5		MCA 40559
10/2/76	**❶²**	16		46 Good Woman Blues _You Can't Trust A Crazy Man_		$5		MCA 40627
1/15/77	**❶¹**	14		47 Heart Healer _It's Just Not That Easy To Say_		$5		MCA 40667
4/23/77	**9**	13		48 Burning Memories _Golden Nugget Gambling Casino_		$5		MCA 40710
8/13/77	**3**	16		49 I Got The Hoss _It's Been A Long Time_		$5		MCA 40764
12/24/77+	**4**	16		50 What Did I Promise Her Last Night _Woman, You Should Be In Movies_		$5		MCA 40836
5/13/78	**❶¹**	14		51 I Believe In You _She Don't Trust You Daddy_		$5		MCA 40900
9/9/78	**4**	13		52 Ain't No California _What Comes Natural To A Fool_		$5		MCA 40946
1/13/79	**2³**	14		53 Send Me Down To Tucson/				
				from the movie _Every Which Way But Loose_ starring **Clint Eastwood**				
		14		54 Charlie's Angel		$5		MCA 40983
6/16/79	**❶¹**	15		55 Coca Cola Cowboy _Cottonmouth_		$5		MCA 41041
				from the movie _Every Which Way But Loose_ starring **Clint Eastwood**				
9/29/79	**6**	14		56 Blind In Love _Black Jack, Water Back_		$4		Elektra 46536
1/19/80	**6**	13		57 Lying Time Again _Fooled Around And Fell In Love_		$4		Elektra 46583
4/26/80	**3**	16		58 Your Body Is An Outlaw _Rain On My Parade_		$4		Elektra 46628
8/30/80	**9**	13		59 Steppin' Out _Whiskey Chasin'_		$4		Elektra 47015
12/13/80+	**❶¹**	16		60 Southern Rains _Forgive Me For Giving You The Blues_		$4		Elektra 47082
4/4/81	**8**	13		61 A Million Old Goodbyes _Louisiana Lonely_		$4		Elektra 47116
7/11/81	**23**	12		62 Texas Cowboy Night .... _After The Lovin'_		$4		Elektra 47157
				MEL TILLIS & NANCY SINATRA				
9/5/81	**10**	16		63 One-Night Fever _Time Has Treated You Well_		$4		Elektra 47178
12/26/81+	**43**	8		64 Play Me Or Trade Me/				
		8		65 Where Would I Be		$4		Elektra 47247
				MEL TILLIS & NANCY SINATRA (above 2)				
2/27/82	**36**	9		66 It's A Long Way To Daytona .... _Always You, Always Me_		$4		Elektra 47412
5/29/82	**37**	9		67 The One That Got Away .... _Why Ain't Life The Way It's S'posed To Be_		$4		Elektra 47453
9/25/82	**17**	15		68 Stay A Little Longer _Dream Of Me_		$4		Elektra 69963
3/12/83	**10**	20		69 In The Middle Of The Night _Even At Her Worst (She's Still The Best)_		$3		MCA 52182
8/6/83	**49**	10		70 A Cowboy's Dream .... _After All This Time_		$3		MCA 52247
10/29/83	**53**	10		71 She Meant Forever When She Said Goodbye .... _Try It Again_		$3		MCA 52285
4/28/84	**10**	22		72 New Patches _Almost Like You Never Went Away_		$3		MCA 52373
10/27/84	**47**	12		73 Slow Nights .... _Midnight Love_		$3		MCA 52474
				MEL TILLIS WITH GLEN CAMPBELL				
6/1/85	**37**	12		74 You Done Me Wrong... _Another Heart Down_		$3		RCA 14061
9/7/85	**61**	7		75 California Road .... _One More Time_		$3		RCA 14175
3/5/88	**31**	14		76 You'll Come Back (You Always Do) .... _Try It Again_		$3		Mercury 870192
11/4/89	**67**	4		77 City Lights .... _Who's Julie_		$5		Radio 001

349

TILLIS, Pam ★142★   '92
Born on 7/24/57 in Plant City, Florida. Daughter of **Mel Tillis**. Married to Bob DiPiero of **Billy Hill**. CMA Award: 1994 Female Vocalist of the Year.

1)Mi Vida Loca 2)When You Walk In The Room 3)Maybe It Was Memphis 4)Shake The Sugar Tree
5)In Between Dances

DEBUT	PEAK	WKS		A-side / B-side	Pop	$	Pic	Label & Number
11/10/84	71	5		1 Goodbye Highway .... Somebody Else's		$4		Warner 29155
1/25/86	55	8		2 Those Memories Of You .... Drawn To The Fire		$4		Warner 28806
7/5/86	67	4		3 I Thought I'd About Had It With Love .... Drawn To The Fire		$4		Warner 28676
2/21/87	68	6		4 I Wish She Wouldn't Treat You That Way .... Drawn To The Fire		$4		Warner 28444
5/16/87	71	6		5 There Goes My Love .... Drawn To The Fire		$4		Warner 28346
12/1/90+	5	20		6 Don't Tell Me What To Do _Melancholy Child_		$3		Arista 2129
4/6/91	6	20		7 One Of Those Things _Already Fallen_		$3		Arista 2203
8/17/91	11	20		8 Put Yourself In My Place .... I've Seen Enough To Know		$3		Arista 12268
12/14/91+	3	20		9 Maybe It Was Memphis _Draggin' My Chains_		$3	▮	Arista 12371
4/11/92	21	20		10 Blue Rose Is .... Ancient History		$3		Arista 12408
8/22/92	3	20		11 Shake The Sugar Tree _Maybe It Was Memphis_		$3		Arista 12454
1/2/93	4	20		12 Let That Pony Run _Fine, Fine, Very Fine Love_		$3	▮	Arista 12506
5/1/93	11	20		13 Cleopatra, Queen Of Denial _Homeward Looking Angel_		$3	▮	Arista 12552
8/28/93	16	20		14 Do You Know Where Your Man Is ...... We've Tried Everything Else		$3	▮	Arista 12606
3/26/94	5	20		15 Spilled Perfume _'Til All The Lonely's Gone_		$3	▮	Arista 12676
8/6/94	2¹	20		16 When You Walk In The Room _'Til All The Lonely's Gone_		$3	▮	Arista 12726
				#35 Pop hit for The Searchers in 1964				
11/19/94+	❶²	20		17 Mi Vida Loca (My Crazy Life) _Ancient History_		$3		Arista 12759
3/11/95	16	12		18 I Was Blown Away .... Calico Plains		$3		Arista 12802
6/3/95	3	20		19 In Between Dances _They Don't Break'em Like They Used To_		$3		Arista 12833
10/7/95+	6	20		20 Deep Down _Tequila Mockingbird_		$3	▮	Arista 12878
1/27/96	8	20		21 The River And The Highway _All Of This Love_		$3		Arista 12958
6/8/96	14	20		22 It's Lonely Out There .... You Can't Have A Good Time Without Me		$3		Arista 10505
10/12/96	62	4		23 Betty's Got A Bass Boat .... Mandolin Rain		$3		Arista 13045
4/26/97	4	20		24 All The Good Ones Are Gone/				
9/6/97	5	21		25 Land Of The Living		$3		Arista 13084

TILLMAN, Floyd ★304★   '44
Born on 12/8/14 in Ryan, Oklahoma; raised in Post, Texas. Singer/songwriter/guitarist. Elected to the Country Music Hall of Fame in 1984.
1)They Took The Stars Out Of Heaven 2)Drivin' Nails In My Coffin 3)Each Night At Nine

FLOYD TILLMAN and His Favorite Playboys:

DEBUT	PEAK	WKS		A-side / B-side	Pop	$	Pic	Label & Number
1/8/44	❶¹	13		1 They Took The Stars Out Of Heaven _Why Do You Treat Me This Way_		$15		Decca 6090
12/30/44	4	8		2 Each Night At Nine/				
12/16/44	5	3		3 G.I. Blues		$15		Decca 6104

FLOYD TILLMAN:

DEBUT	PEAK	WKS		A-side / B-side	Pop	$	Pic	Label & Number
8/3/46	2¹	7		4 Drivin' Nails In My Coffin _Some Other World_		$12		Columbia 36998
7/10/48	5	19		5 I Love You So Much, It Hurts _J:5 / S:6 I'll Take What I Can Get_		$12		Columbia 20430
1/29/49	14	1		6 Please Don't Pass Me By .... S:14 Cold Cold Woman		$12		Columbia 20496
7/2/49	5	12		7 Slipping Around _S:5 / A:6 / J:8 You Made Me Live, Love And Die_		$12		Columbia 20581
10/8/49	6	8		8 I'll Never Slip Around Again _S:6 / J:8 This Cold War With You_		$12		Columbia 20615
12/31/49+	4	3		9 I Gotta Have My Baby Back _A:4 It Had To Be That Way_		$12		Columbia 20641
12/19/60	29	1		10 It Just Tears Me Up .... The Song Of Music		$15		Liberty 55280

TILLOTSON, Johnny   '62
Born on 4/20/39 in Jacksonville, Florida; raised in Palatka, Florida. Acted in the movie _Just For Fun_. Charted 26 pop hits from 1958-65.

DEBUT	PEAK	WKS		A-side / B-side	Pop	$	Pic	Label & Number
6/23/62	4	13		1 It Keeps Right On A-Hurtin' _She Gave Sweet Love To Me_	3	$12		Cadence 1418
9/8/62	11	10		2 Send Me The Pillow You Dream On ....../........ What'll I Do (Pop #106)	17	$12		Cadence 1424
11/11/67+	48	10		3 You're The Reason .... Countin' My Teardrops		$8		MGM 13829
2/17/68	63	6		4 I Can Spot A Cheater .... It Keeps Right On A Hurtin'		$8		MGM 13888
6/18/77	99	1		5 Toy Hearts .... Just An Ordinary Man		$6		United Artists 986
3/31/84	91	2		6 Lay Back (In The Arms Of Someone) .... What's Another Year		$6		Reward 04346

TILTON, Sheila   '76
Born in 1951 in Kailua, Hawaii.

DEBUT	PEAK	WKS		A-side / B-side	Pop	$	Pic	Label & Number
7/10/76	23	13		Half As Much .... I'll Be Whatever You Say		$5		Con Brio 110
				#1 Pop hit for Rosemary Clooney in 1952				

TINY TIM   '88
Born Herbert Khaury on 4/12/30 in New York City. Died of heart failure on 11/30/96 (age 66). Novelty singer/ukulele player. Charted a pop hit in 1968 with "Tip-Toe Thru' The Tulips With Me."

DEBUT	PEAK	WKS		A-side / B-side	Pop	$	Pic	Label & Number
4/16/88	70	5		Leave Me Satisfied .... I Wanna' Get Crazy With You		$6		NLT 1993

★214★

TIPPIN, Aaron '92
Born on 7/3/58 in Pensacola, Florida; raised in Travelers Rest, South Carolina. Singer/songwriter/guitarist.
1)There Ain't Nothin' Wrong With The Radio 2)That's As Close As I'll Get To Loving You
3)I Wouldn't Have It Any Other Way

DEBUT	PEAK	WKS	A-side / B-side	Pop	$	Pic	Label & Number
11/3/90+	6	20	1 You've Got To Stand For Something — Up Against You		$3	▌	RCA 2664
4/6/91	40	19	2 I Wonder How Far It Is Over You — You Should See Me Missing You		$3		RCA 2747
8/24/91	54	11	3 She Made A Memory Out Of Me — The Sky's Got The Blues		$3		RCA 62015
2/15/92	❶³	20	4 There Ain't Nothin' Wrong With The Radio — I Miss Misbehavin'		$3		RCA 62181
6/20/92	5	20	5 I Wouldn't Have It Any Other Way — What I Can't Live Without		$3		RCA 62241
10/24/92	38	13	6 I Was Born With A Broken Heart — Read Between The Lines		$3		RCA 62338
1/30/93	7	20	7 My Blue Angel — The Sound Of Your Goodbye (Sticks And Stones)		$3		RCA 62430
6/26/93	7	20	8 Working Man's Ph.D. — When Country Took The Throne		$3		RCA 62520
10/23/93+	17	20	9 The Call Of The Wild — Nothin' In The World		$3	▌	RCA 62657
2/12/94	47	10	10 Honky-Tonk Superman — Let's Talk About You		$3	▌	RCA 62755
4/23/94	30	20	11 Whole Lotta Love On The Line — I Promised You The World		$3		RCA 62832
10/8/94+	15	20	12 I Got It Honest — Lookin' Back At Myself		$3	▌	RCA 62947
2/25/95	39	11	13 She Feels Like A Brand New Man Tonight — Lovin' Me Into An Early Grave		$3		RCA 64272
9/2/95	❶²	21	14 That's As Close As I'll Get To Loving You — S:3 She Feels Like A Brand New Man Tonight	101	$3	▌	RCA 64392
2/3/96	22	16	15 Without Your Love — Country Boy's Toolbox		$3	▌	RCA 64471
6/1/96	51	11	16 Everything I Own — She Made A Man Out Of A Mountain Of Stone		$3		RCA 64544
10/19/96	69	2	17 How's The Radio Know — I Can Help		$3		RCA 64640
2/15/97	50	7	18 That's What Happens When I Hold You — Whole Lotta Love On The Line		$3		RCA 64770
4/26/97	65	4	19 A Door				album cut

from the album *Greatest Hits...And Then Some* on RCA 67427

TODD, Dick '67

DEBUT	PEAK	WKS	A-side / B-side	Pop	$	Pic	Label & Number
9/2/67	52	6	Big Wheel Cannonball — Return Of The Double Eagle		$8		Decca 32168

DICK TODD With The **Appalachian Wildcats**
new lyrical version of **Roy Acuff**'s "Wabash Cannonball"

TOLIVER, Tony '97
Born in Texas. Singer/songwriter/pianist.

DEBUT	PEAK	WKS	A-side / B-side	Pop	$	Pic	Label & Number
8/10/96	71	6	1 Bettin' Forever For You — Louisiana Lonely		$3	▌	Rising Tide 56040
1/18/97	67	2	2 He's On The Way Home — Swinging Doors		$3		Rising Tide 56042

TOMMY & DONNA '88

DEBUT	PEAK	WKS	A-side / B-side	Pop	$	Pic	Label & Number
11/26/88	72	6	Take It Slow With Me		$6		Oak 1067

TOMORROW'S WORLD '90
All-star collaboration in honor of Earth Day: **Lynn Anderson, Butch Baker, Shane Barmby, Billy Hill, Suzy Bogguss, Kix Brooks, T. Graham Brown, The Burch Sisters, Holly Dunn, Foster & Lloyd, Vince Gill, William Lee Golden, Highway 101, Shelby Lynne, Johnny Rodriguez, Dan Seals, Les Taylor, Pam Tillis, Mac Wiseman** and **Kevin Welch**.

DEBUT	PEAK	WKS	A-side / B-side	Pop	$	Pic	Label & Number
5/5/90	74	1	Tomorrow's World — (instrumental)		$3		Warner 4069

TOMPALL — see GLASER BROTHERS

TOPEL & WARE '87
Duo of Michael Topel and James Ware.

DEBUT	PEAK	WKS	A-side / B-side	Pop	$	Pic	Label & Number
10/24/87	93	3	Change Of Heart		$6		RCI 2406

TOROK, Mitchell '53
Born on 10/28/29 in Houston. Singer/songwriter/guitarist.

DEBUT	PEAK	WKS	A-side / B-side	Pop	$	Pic	Label & Number
8/22/53	❶²	24	1 Caribbean — J:❶² / S:4 / A:5 Weep Away		$30		Abbott 140

an alternate recording by Torok became a #27 Pop hit in 1959 on Guyden 2018 ($15)

DEBUT	PEAK	WKS	A-side / B-side	Pop	$	Pic	Label & Number
1/23/54	9	3	2 Hootchy Kootchy Henry (From Hawaii) — J:9 Gigolo		$30		Abbott 150
2/18/67	73	3	3 Instant Love — I Let The Hurts Put Me In The Driver's Seat		$10		Reprise 0541

TOUCH OF COUNTRY '88

DEBUT	PEAK	WKS	A-side / B-side	Pop	$	Pic	Label & Number
11/12/88	85	3	1 I Won't Be Seeing Her No More — Long Talk With Myself		$5		OL 127
7/15/89	87	3	2 Did I Leave My Heart At Your House		$5	■	OL 130

TRACTORS, The '94
Country-rock group from Tulsa, Oklahoma: Casey Van Beek (vocals), Steve Ripley (guitar), Walt Richmond (keyboards), Ron Getman (bass) and Jamie Oldaker (drums).

DEBUT	PEAK	WKS	A-side / B-side	Pop	$	Pic	Label & Number
8/27/94	11	20	1 Baby Likes To Rock It — Tulsa Shuffle		$3		Arista 12717
12/17/94	41	4	2 The Santa Claus Boogie — Swingin' Home For Christmas [X]	91	$3	▌	Arista 12771
12/31/94+	50	11	3 Tryin' To Get To New Orleans — Doreen		$3		Arista 12784
12/16/95	43	5	4 Santa Claus Is Comin' (In A Boogie Woogie Choo Choo Train) — Santa Looked A Lot Like Daddy [X]		$3		Arista 12923
12/23/95	63	3	5 The Santa Claus Boogie — Swingin' Home For Christmas [X-R]		$3	▌	Arista 12771
10/4/97	75	1	6 The Last Time		$3		album cut

#9 Pop hit for The Rolling Stones in 1965; from the album *Stone Country* on Beyond Music 3055

DEBUT	PEAK	WKS	A-side / B-side	Pop	$	Pic	Label & Number
12/27/97	65	3	7 Santa Claus Is Comin' (In A Boogie Woogie Choo Choo Train) — Santa Looked A Lot Like Daddy [X-R]		$3		Arista 12923

TRADER-PRICE '89
Vocal group from Burns Flat, Oklahoma: brothers Dan, Chris and Erick Trader-Price, with Don Bell.

DEBUT	PEAK	WKS	A-side / B-side	Pop	$	Pic	Label & Number
8/12/89	55	7	1 Sad Eyes — Who's Gonna Know		$3		Universal 66022

#1 Pop hit for Robert John in 1979

DEBUT	PEAK	WKS	A-side / B-side	Pop	$	Pic	Label & Number
12/23/89+	64	4	2 Lately Rose — Hideaway		$3		Universal 66031

TRAMMELL, Bobby Lee '72

Born in Jonesboro, Arkansas.

DEBUT	PEAK	WKS	Gold	A-side / B-side	Pop	$	Pic	Label & Number
5/27/72	52	9		Love Isn't Love (Till You Give It Away) .... *Tell Me That You Love Me*		$7		Souncot 1135

★297★ TRASK, Diana '74

Born on 6/23/40 in Warburton, Australia. Singer/pianist.

1)Lean It All On Me 2)Say When 3)When I Get My Hands On You

DEBUT	PEAK	WKS	Gold	A-side / B-side	Pop	$	Pic	Label & Number
6/22/68	70	4		1 Lock, Stock And Tear Drops .... *Precious Time*		$7		Dial 4077
11/23/68	59	6		2 Hold What You've Got .... *This Heart Was Made For Lovin'*		$6		Dot 17160
				#5 Pop hit for Joe Tex in 1965				
8/30/69	58	4		3 Children .... *The Staying Kind*		$6		Dot 17286
11/29/69+	37	7		4 I Fall To Pieces .... *Long Ago Is Gone*	114	$6		Dot 17316
3/28/70	38	9		5 Beneath Still Waters .... *Heartbreak Hotel*		$6		Dot 17342
7/31/71	59	9		6 The Chokin' Kind .... *Let's Keep Her Free (America)*		$6		Dot 17384
				#13 Pop hit for Joe Simon in 1969				
1/22/72	30	14		7 We've Got To Work It Out Between Us .... *I Keep It Hid*		$6		Dot 17404
7/15/72	33	12		8 It Meant Nothing To Me .... *How Much Have I Hurt Thee*		$6		Dot 17424
3/3/73	15	13		9 Say When .... *Old Southern Cotton Town*		$6		Dot 17448
7/7/73	20	13		10 It's A Man's World (If You Had A Man Like Mine) .... *World Of The Missing*		$6		Dot 17467
12/8/73+	16	15		11 When I Get My Hands On You .... *Shadow Of My Man*		$6		Dot 17486
3/30/74	13	13		12 Lean It All On Me .... *The King*	101	$6		Dot 17496
8/17/74	32	10		13 (If You Wanna Hold On) Hold On To Your Man .... *Loneliness*		$6		Dot 17520
1/11/75	21	14		14 Oh Boy .... *Alone Again Naturally*		$5		ABC/Dot 17536
6/28/75	82	5		15 There Has To Be A Loser .... *Sunshine*		$5		ABC/Dot 17555
11/29/75	99	2		16 Cry .... *I Can Take A Little Heartache*		$5		ABC/Dot 17587
				#1 Pop hit for Johnnie Ray in 1951				
6/13/81	62	6		17 This Must Be My Ship		$6		Kari 121
9/19/81	74	3		18 Stirrin' Up Feelings .... *Give My Heart A Break*		$6		Kari 123

★210★ TRAVIS, Merle '46

Born on 11/29/17 in Rosewood, Kentucky. Died on 10/20/83 (age 65). Singer/songwriter/guitarist. Father of **Tom Bresh**. Acted in the movie *From Here To Eternity*. Regular on TV's *Hometown Jamboree* and *Town Hall Party*. Elected to the Country Music Hall of Fame in 1977.

1)Divorce Me C.O.D. 2)So Round, So Firm, So Fully Packed 3)Cincinnati Lou

DEBUT	PEAK	WKS	Gold	A-side / B-side	Pop	$	Pic	Label & Number
6/8/46	2⁴	11		1 Cincinnati Lou/				
6/15/46	3	9		2 No Vacancy		$20		Capitol 258
9/21/46	❶¹⁴	23		3 Divorce Me C.O.D./				
1/11/47	5	2		4 Missouri		$20		Capitol 290
1/25/47	❶¹⁴	22		5 So Round, So Firm, So Fully Packed *Sweet Temptation*		$20		Capitol 349
5/17/47	4	3		6 Steel Guitar Rag/		$20		Capitol 384
5/24/47	4	4		7 Three Times Seven				
11/1/47	4	2		8 Fat Gal/		$20		Capitol Amer. 40026
3/20/48	7	1		9 Merle's Boogie Woogie				
8/28/48	11	3		10 Crazy Boogie .... J:11 / S:12 *I'm A Natural Born Gamblin' Man*		$20		Capitol 15143
2/5/49	13	1		11 What A Shame .... J:13 *Dapper Dan*		$20		Capitol 15317
6/4/55	5	9		12 Wildwood Flower J:5 / S:8 / A:13 *Breakin' In Another Heart* [I]		$20		Capitol 3106
				HANK THOMPSON and His Brazos Valley Boys with MERLE TRAVIS				
7/30/66	44	4		13 John Henry, Jr. .... *That Same Ol' Natural Urge*		$10		Capitol 5657

TRAVIS, Randy ★65★ '90

Born **Randy Traywick** on 5/4/59 in Marshville, North Carolina. Singer/songwriter/guitarist/actor. Married his manager, Lib Hatcher, on 5/31/91. Joined the *Grand Ole Opry* in 1986. Acted in several movies. CMA Awards: 1986 Horizon Award; 1987 & 1988 Male Vocalist of the Year.

1)Hard Rock Bottom Of Your Heart 2)Forever And Ever, Amen 3)Look Heart, No Hands 4)I Told You So 5)It's Just A Matter Of Time

DEBUT	PEAK	WKS	Gold	A-side / B-side	Pop	$	Pic	Label & Number
1/6/79	91	4		1 She's My Woman .... *(instrumental)*		$20		Paula 431
				RANDY TRAYWICK				
8/31/85	67	12		2 On The Other Hand .... *Can't Stop Now*		$4		Warner 28962
12/28/85+	6	24		3 1982 S:4 / A:7 *Reasons I Cheat*		$3		Warner 28828
4/26/86	❶¹	23		4 On The Other Hand S:❶² / A:❶¹ *Can't Stop Now* [R]		$3		Warner 28962
8/16/86	❶¹	21		5 Diggin' Up Bones S:❶¹ / A:❶¹ *There'll Always Be A Honky Tonk Somewhere*		$3		Warner 28649
12/13/86+	2²	21		6 No Place Like Home A:2 / S:4 *Send My Body*		$3		Warner 28525
4/25/87	❶³	22		7 Forever And Ever, Amen S:❶² / A:16 *Promises*		$3	■	Warner 28384
				CMA Award: Single of the Year				
8/29/87	❶¹	22		8 I Won't Need You Anymore (Always And Forever) S:❶¹ *Tonight I'm Walkin' Out On The Blues*		$3		Warner 28246
12/12/87+	❶¹	19		9 Too Gone Too Long S:3 *My House*		$3	■	Warner 28286
4/9/88	❶²	18		10 I Told You So S:❶² *Good Intentions*		$3	■	Warner 27969
7/30/88	❶¹	17		11 Honky Tonk Moon S:❶² *Young Guns*		$3	■	Warner 27833
11/19/88+	❶¹	18		12 Deeper Than The Holler S:2 *It's Out Of My Hands*		$3	■	Warner 27689
3/11/89	❶¹	17		13 Is It Still Over? *Here In My Heart*		$3	■	Warner 27551
7/1/89	17	15		14 Promises .... *Written In Stone*		$3		Warner 22917

DEBUT	PEAK	WKS	A-side (Chart Hit) ... B-side	Pop	$	Pic	Label & Number
			TRAVIS, Randy — Cont'd				
9/23/89	**❶**¹	26	15 **It's Just A Matter Of Time** _This Day Was Made For Me And You_		$3	■	Warner 22841
			#3 Pop hit for Brook Benton in 1959				
1/27/90	**❶**⁴	26	16 **Hard Rock Bottom Of Your Heart** _When Your World Was Turning For Me_		$3		Warner 19935
5/12/90	**2**²	21	17 **He Walked On Water** _Card Carryin' Fool_		$3	▮	Warner 19878
9/8/90	**8**	20	18 **A Few Ole Country Boys** _Smokin' The Hive_		$3	▮	Warner 19586
			RANDY TRAVIS & GEORGE JONES				
2/2/91	**3**	20	19 **Heroes And Friends** _Shopping For Dresses_		$3		Warner 19469
5/4/91	**3**	20	20 **Point Of Light** _Waiting On The Light To Change_		$3	▮	Warner 19283
8/24/91	**49**	8	21 **We're Strangers Again** ...._If You Were The Friend_		$3	▮	Epic 73958
			TAMMY WYNETTE with Randy Travis				
9/28/91	**❶**¹	20	22 **Forever Together** _This Day Was Made For Me And You_		$3		Warner 19158
12/21/91+	**2**³	20	23 **Better Class Of Losers** _I'm Gonna Have A Little Talk_		$3		Warner 19069
4/4/92	**20**	20	24 **I'd Surrender All** .... _Let Me Try_		$3		Warner 18943
8/15/92	**❶**¹	20	25 **If I Didn't Have You** _I Told You So_		$3		Warner 18792
11/21/92+	**❶**²	20	26 **Look Heart, No Hands** _The Heart To Climb The Mountain_		$3		Warner 18709
4/10/93	**21**	20	27 **An Old Pair Of Shoes**.._Promises_		$3		Warner 18616
9/4/93	**46**	8	28 **Cowboy Boogie**				album cut
			from the album _Wind In The Wire_ on Warner 45319				
12/25/93+	**65**	6	29 **Wind In The Wire** _Down At The Old Corral_		$3		Warner 18274
3/12/94	**2**¹	20	30 **Before You Kill Us All** _The Box_		$3	▮	Warner 18208
6/11/94	**❶**¹	20	31 **Whisper My Name** _Oscar The Angel_		$3	▮	Warner 18153
10/22/94	**5**	20	32 **This Is Me** _Gonna Walk That Line_		$3	▮	Warner 18062
2/11/95	**7**	20	33 **The Box** _Honky Tonk Side Of Town_		$3		Warner 17970
6/15/96	**24**	17	34 **Are We In Trouble Now** _Nobody's Home_		$3		Warner 17619
10/5/96	**25**	20	35 **Would I** ...._Don't Take Your Love Away From Me_		$3		Warner 17494
2/22/97	**60**	4	36 **Price To Pay** .... _I Wish It Would Rain_		$3		Warner 17382
4/26/97	**51**	15	37 **King Of The Road**...				album cut
			from the album _Full Circle_ on Warner 46328				
	★280★		**TREVINO, Rick** '97				
			Born on 5/16/71 in Austin, Texas. Singer/songwriter/guitarist.				
			1)Running Out Of Reasons To Run 2)Learning As You Go 3)She Can't Say I Didn't Cry				
9/18/93	**44**	20	1 **Just Enough Rope** .... _A Quarter At A Time_		$3	▮	Columbia 77159
2/12/94	**35**	19	2 **Honky Tonk Crowd**............_Un Momento Alla (For A Moment There)_		$3	▮	Columbia 77373
6/4/94	**3**	20	3 **She Can't Say I Didn't Cry** _She Just Left Me Lounge_		$3	▮	Columbia 77535
10/8/94+	**5**	20	4 **Doctor Time** _What I'll Know Then_		$3	▮	Columbia 77708
2/11/95	**43**	12	5 **Looking For The Light** ...._Life Can Turn On A Dime_		$3	▮	Columbia 77820
5/6/95	**6**	20	6 **Bobbie Ann Mason** _S:6 San Antonio Rose To You_		$3	▮	Columbia 77903
9/9/95	**45**	11	7 **Save This One For Me**				album cut
			from the album _Looking For The Light_ on Columbia 66771				
6/1/96	**2**²	20	8 **Learning As You Go** _I'm Here For You_		$3		Columbia 78329
10/26/96+	**❶**¹	22	9 **Running Out Of Reasons To Run** _See Rock City_		$3	▮	Columbia 78331
3/22/97	**7**	22	10 **I Only Get This Way With You**				album cut
9/27/97	**44**	8	11 **See Rock City**...				album cut
			above 2 from the album _Learning As You Go_ on Columbia 67452				
			TREVOR, Van '66				
			Born on 11/12/40 in Lewiston, Maine. Singer/songwriter/producer.				
4/23/66	**22**	18	1 **Born To Be In Love With You** _It's So Good To Be Loved_		$15		Band Box 367
11/19/66+	**27**	13	2 **Our Side** .... _When You've Lost Your Baby_		$15		Band Box 371
9/9/67	**26**	15	3 **You've Been So Good To Me** .... _Sunday Morning_		$8		Date 1565
4/27/68	**31**	11	4 **Take Me Along With You** ...._Guitar_		$8		Date 1594
2/1/69	**42**	9	5 **The Things That Matter** ...._Band Of Gold_		$6		Royal American 280
5/10/69	**56**	7	6 **A Man Away From Home** ...._I've Got Today To Live For_		$6		Royal American 283
6/13/70	**42**	8	7 **Luziana River** .... _Sweet Diana_		$6		Royal American 9
1/23/71	**54**	6	8 **Wish I Was Home Instead** ...._Did I Have A Good Time_		$6		Royal American 23
			TRIBBLE, Mark '89				
5/6/89	**86**	2	**Lay Me Down Carolina**...		$6		Paloma 5
			TRINITY, Bobby '77				
8/27/77	**95**	2	**I Love Everything I Get My Hands On**		$7		GRT 128
			TRINITY LANE '88				
			Trio of singer/songwriters: **Tom Grant**, Allen Estes and Sharon Anderson.				
4/23/88	**75**	4	1 **For A Song**.._Don't Put It Past My Heart_		$3		Curb 10507
8/13/88	**70**	3	2 **Someday, Somenight** ...._Indian Eyes_		$3		Curb 10511
11/5/88	**90**	2	3 **Ready To Take That Ride** ...._How Can I Pull Myself Together_		$3		Curb 10515
			TRIPP, Allen '82				
			Born in Fort Worth, Texas.				
3/20/82	**39**	11	**Love Is** ...._Lady Sorrow_		$6		Nashville 1001

TRITT, Travis ★97★ '91

Born James Travis Tritt on 2/9/63 in Marietta, Georgia. Singer/songwriter/guitarist. Joined the *Grand Ole Opry* in 1992. Married model Theresa Nelson on 4/12/97. CMA Award: 1991 Horizon Award.

1)Anymore 2)Can I Trust You With My Heart 3)Help Me Hold On 4)Foolish Pride 5)Here's A Quarter

DEBUT	PEAK	WKS		A-side	B-side	Pop	$	Pic	Label & Number
9/2/89	9	26	1	Country Club	Sign Of The Times		$3		Warner 22882
2/24/90	❶¹	26	2	Help Me Hold On	All I'll Ever Be		$3	▮	Warner 19918
6/16/90	2¹	21	3	I'm Gonna Be Somebody	The Road Home		$3	▮	Warner 19797
9/22/90	28	18	4	Put Some Drive In Your Country...	If I Were A Drinker		$3	▮	Warner 19715
2/16/91	3	20	5	Drift Off To Dream	Son Of The New South		$3		Warner 19431
6/1/91	2¹	20	6	Here's A Quarter (Call Someone Who Cares)	If Hell Had A Jukebox		$3		Warner 19310
9/14/91	❶²	20	7	Anymore	It's All About To Change		$3		Warner 19190
11/23/91+	2¹	20	8	The Whiskey Ain't Workin'	Bible Belt		$3		Warner 19097
				TRAVIS TRITT Featuring Marty Stuart					
3/7/92	4	20	9	Nothing Short Of Dying/					
5/9/92	72	3	10	Bible Belt			$3		Warner 18984
				TRAVIS TRITT featuring Little Feat					
				from the movie *My Cousin Vinny* starring Joe Pesci					
6/6/92	7	20	11	This One's Gonna Hurt You (For A Long, Long Time)	The King Of Dixie		$3		MCA 54405
				MARTY STUART AND TRAVIS TRITT					
8/29/92	5	20	12	Lord Have Mercy On The Working Man	(album version)		$3		Warner 18779
				Brooks & Dunn, T. Graham Brown, George Jones, Little Texas, Dana McVicker, Tanya Tucker and Porter Wagoner (guest vocals)					
12/5/92+	❶²	20	13	Can I Trust You With My Heart	A Hundred Years From Now		$3		Warner 18669
12/12/92+	13	20	14	T-R-O-U-B-L-E...	Leave My Girl Alone	108	$3		Warner 18496
7/17/93	11	20	15	Looking Out For Number One	Blue Collar Man		$3	▮	Warner 18463
10/30/93+	21	22	16	Take It Easy	I Wish I Could Go Back Home		$3		Warner 18240
				#12 Pop hit for the **Eagles** in 1972					
10/30/93	30	17	17	Worth Every Mile..					album cut
				from the album *T-R-O-U-B-L-E* on Warner 45058					
4/23/94	❶¹	20	18	Foolish Pride	No Vacation From The Blues	112	$3	▮	Warner 18180
8/6/94	22	16	19	Ten Feet Tall And Bulletproof................................	(acoustic version)		$3	▮	Warner 18104
11/26/94+	11	20	20	Between An Old Memory And Me..........................	Wishful Thinking		$3	▮	Warner 18003
4/15/95	2¹	20	21	Tell Me I Was Dreaming					album cut
				from the album *Ten Feet Tall And Bulletproof* on Warner 45603					
8/19/95	7	20	22	Sometimes She Forgets/					
1/20/96	51	8	23	Only You (And You Alone)			$3		Warner 17792
				#5 Pop hit for The Platters in 1955					
4/20/96	23	20	24	Honky Tonkin's What I Do Best	Me & Hank & Jumpin' Jack Flash		$3		MCA 55197
				MARTY STUART & TRAVIS TRITT					
7/27/96	3	20	25	More Than You'll Ever Know	S:6 Still In Love With You	110	$3	▮	Warner 17606
11/23/96+	6	20	26	Where Corn Don't Grow/					
4/19/97	24	20	27	She's Going Home With Me					Warner 17451
1/25/97	29	20	● 28	Here's Your Sign (Get The Picture)............ S:❶⁸	Things Have Changed (Engvall) [C]	43	$3	▮	Warner 17491
				BILL ENGVALL with Travis Tritt					
7/26/97	18	20	29	Helping Me Get Over You					album cut
				TRAVIS TRITT Featuring Lari White					
11/22/97+	23	20	30	Still In Love With You.....................................					album cut
				above 2 from the album *The Restless Kind* on Warner 46304					

TUBB, Ernest ★17★ '49

Born on 2/9/14 in Crisp, Texas. Died of emphysema on 9/6/84 (age 70). Singer/songwriter/guitarist. Known as "The Texas Troubadour." Joined the *Grand Ole Opry* in 1943. Acted in the movies *Fighting Buckaroo, Hollywood Barn Dance, Ridin' West* and *Jamboree*. Broadcast from his own Ernest Tubb Record Shop in Nashville beginning in 1947. Elected to the Country Music Hall of Fame in 1965. Father of **Justin Tubb**.

1)Soldier's Last Letter 2)It's Been So Long Darling 3)Goodnight Irene 4)Rainbow At Midnight
5)Slipping Around

DEBUT	PEAK	WKS		A-side	B-side	Pop	$	Pic	Label & Number
1/8/44	2³	17	1	Try Me One More Time	That's When It's Comin' Home To You	15	$20		Decca 6093
5/27/44	❶⁴	29	2	Soldier's Last Letter/		16			
6/3/44	4	3	3	Yesterday's Tears		23	$20		Decca 6098
3/31/45	3	14	4	Tomorrow Never Comes/			$20		Decca 6106
3/17/45	6	1	5	Keep My Mem'ry In Your Heart					
8/4/45	3	8	6	Careless Darlin'	Are You Waiting Just For Me		$20		Decca 6110
11/17/45	❶⁴	13	7	It's Been So Long Darling	Should I Come Back Home To You		$20		Decca 6112
11/16/46+	❶²	20	8	Rainbow At Midnight	I Don't Blame You		$20		Decca 46018
11/16/46	2⁴	12	9	Filipino Baby/			$20		Decca 46019
12/21/46	5	2	10	Drivin' Nails In My Coffin			$20		

DEBUT	PEAK	WKS	Gold	A-side (Chart Hit)..B-side	Pop	$	Pic	Label & Number
				TUBB, Ernest — Cont'd				
5/17/47	4	6		11 Don't Look Now (But Your Broken Heart Is Showing)/				
6/28/47	5	1		12 So Round, So Firm, So Fully Packed		$20		Decca 46040
7/19/47	4	1		13 I'll Step Aside · · · · · · *There's Gonna Be Some Changes Made Around Here*		$20		Decca 46041
5/15/48	5	14		14 Seaman's Blues · · · · · · S:5 / J:8 *Waiting For A Train*		$20		Decca 46119
7/17/48	15	1		15 You Nearly Lose Your Mind .... J:15 *I Ain't Goin' Honky Tonkin' Anymore*		$20		Decca 46125
8/7/48	5	13		16 Forever Is Ending Today/ · · · · · · S:5 / J:6	30		*	
9/4/48	9	6		17 That Wild And Wicked Look In Your Eye · · · · · · J:9		$20		Decca 46134
12/11/48+	2¹	17		18 Have You Ever Been Lonely? (Have You Ever Been Blue)/ · · · · · · J:2 / S:9				
12/11/48+	5	17		19 Let's Say Goodbye Like We Said Hello · · · · · · S:5 / J:6		$20		Decca 46144
3/19/49	4	9		20 Till The End Of The World/ · · · · · · J:4 / S:11				
5/7/49	15	1		21 Daddy, When Is Mommy Coming Home J:15		$20		Decca 46150
4/9/49	2¹	16		22 I'm Bitin' My Fingernails And Thinking Of You/ · · · · · · J:2 / S:4	30			
				ANDREWS SISTERS and ERNEST TUBB with The Texas Troubadors				
4/16/49	6	5		23 Don't Rob Another Man's Castle · · · · · · J:6 / S:10		$20		Decca 24592
				ERNEST TUBB and ANDREWS SISTERS with The Texas Troubadors				
5/28/49	6	4		24 Mean Mama Blues · · · · · · J:6 *Yesterday's Tears*		$20		Decca 46162
7/30/49	❶¹	20		25 Slipping Around/ · · · · · · J:❶¹ / S:4	17			
9/17/49	10	3		26 My Tennessee Baby · · · · · · J:10		$20		Decca 46173
9/3/49	6	10		27 My Filipino Rose/ · · · · · · J:6 / S:11				
9/3/49	8	8		28 Warm Red Wine · · · · · · S:8 / J:9		$20		Decca 46175
12/3/49	❶¹	6		29 Blue Christmas/ · · · · · · J:❶¹ / A:2 / S:2 [X]	23			
				Christmas standard popularized by Elvis Presley in 1957; also see #43 and #48 below				
12/24/49	7	1		30 White Christmas · · · · · · J:7 / S:15 [X]		$20		Decca 46186
				#1 Pop hit for Bing Crosby in 1942				
12/31/49+	2²	10		31 Tennessee Border No. 2/ · · · · · · S:2 / J:2				
				RED FOLEY and ERNEST TUBB				
1/21/50	7	2		32 Don't Be Ashamed Of Your Age · · · · · · J:7 / A:9		$20		Decca 46200
				ERNEST TUBB and RED FOLEY				
2/4/50	2¹	17		33 Letters Have No Arms/ · · · · · · J:2 / A:3 / S:5 *I'll Take A Back Seat For You*				
2/25/50	8	1		34 I'll Take A Back Seat For You · · · · · · J:8		$20		Decca 46207
2/25/50	2¹	20		35 I Love You Because/ · · · · · · J:2 / S:4 / A:6				
				#3 Pop hit for Al Martino in 1963				
3/18/50	8	2		36 Unfaithful One · · · · · · J:8		$20		Decca 46213
6/24/50	3	15		37 Throw Your Love My Way · · · · · · A:3 / J:4 / S:5				
8/5/50	9	4		38 Give Me A Little Old Fashioned Love · · · · · · J:9		$25		Decca 9-46243
8/12/50	❶³	15		39 Goodnight Irene/ · · · · · · J:❶³ / S:❶² / A:2	10			
				RED FOLEY-ERNEST TUBB with The Sunshine Trio				
				#1 Pop hit for Gordon Jenkins & The Weavers in 1950				
9/2/50	9	2		40 Hillbilly Fever No. 2 · · · · · · J:9		$25		Decca 9-46255
				ERNEST TUBB-RED FOLEY				
10/28/50	10	2		41 You Don't Have To Be A Baby To Cry · · · · · · J:10 *G-I-R-L Spells Trouble*		$25		Decca 9-46257
				#3 Pop hit for The Caravelles in 1963				
11/4/50	5	9		42 (Remember Me) I'm The One Who Loves You · · · · · · J:5 / S:7 *I Need Attention Bad*		$25		Decca 9-46269
				#32 Pop hit for Dean Martin in 1965				
12/30/50	9	1		43 Blue Christmas · · · · · · A:9 / J:10 *White Christmas* [X-R]		$25		Decca 9-46186
5/19/51	9	1		44 The Strange Little Girl · · · · · · J:9 *Kentucky Waltz*		$25		Decca 9-46311
				RED FOLEY and ERNEST TUBB with Anita Kerr Singers				
6/2/51	9	3		45 Don't Stay Too Long · · · · · · A:9 *If You Want Some Lovin'*		$25		Decca 9-46296
9/15/51	6	2		46 Hey La La · · · · · · J:6 *Precious Little Baby*		$25		Decca 9-46338
12/15/51	7	2		47 Driftwood On The River · · · · · · J:7 *I'm Stepping Out Of The Picture*		$25		Decca 9-46377
12/29/51	5	1		48 Blue Christmas · · · · · · A:5 *White Christmas* [X-R]		$25		Decca 9-46186
2/2/52	5	9		49 Too Old To Cut The Mustard · · · · · · S:5 / J:8 / A:10 *I'm In Love With Molly*		$25		Decca 9-46387
				ERNEST TUBB And RED FOLEY				
2/9/52	3	11		50 Missing In Action · · · · · · S:3 / A:5 / J:9 *A Heartsick Soldier On Heartbreak Ridge*		$20		Decca 9-46389
5/17/52	9	2		51 Somebody's Stolen My Honey · · · · · · J:9 / S:10 *My Mother Must Have Been A Girl Like You*		$20		Decca 9-28067
9/13/52	5	11		52 Fortunes In Memories · · · · · · J:5 / A:7 *So Many Times*		$20		Decca 9-28310
4/18/53	7	2		53 No Help Wanted #2 · · · · · · S:7 / J:9 *You're A Real Good Friend*		$20		Decca 28634
				ERNEST TUBB - RED FOLEY				
12/12/53	9	2		54 Divorce Granted · · · · · · J:9 *Counterfeit Kisses*		$20		Decca 28869
10/16/54	11	5		55 Two Glasses, Joe .... S:11 *Journey's End*		$20		Decca 29220
9/17/55	7	11		56 The Yellow Rose Of Texas · · · · · · A:7 / S:13 *A Million Miles From Here*		$15		Decca 29633
				#1 Pop hit for Mitch Miller in 1955				
12/17/55	7	4		57 Thirty Days (To Come Back Home) · · · · · · J:7 / A:10 *Answer The Phone*		$15		Decca 29731
				#2 R&B hit for Chuck Berry in 1955				
7/8/57	8	2		58 Mister Love · · · · · · A:8 *Leave Me*		$15		Decca 30305
				ERNEST TUBB and THE WILBURN BROTHERS				
4/28/58	13	4		59 House Of Glass ....A:13 *Heaven Help Me*		$15		Decca 30549
5/26/58	9	10		60 Hey, Mr. Bluebird · · · · · · A:9 / S:14 *How Do We Know*		$15		Decca 30610
				ERNEST TUBB And THE WILBURN BROTHERS				
10/20/58	8	11		61 Half A Mind/		$15		Decca 30685
10/20/58	21	1		62 The Blues		$15		
1/5/59	19	3		63 What Am I Living For .... *Goodbye Sunshine Hello Blues*		$15		Decca 30759
5/4/59	12	13		64 I Cried A Tear .... *I'd Rather Be*		$15		Decca 30872
				#6 Pop hit for LaVern Baker in 1959				
9/28/59	14	14		65 Next Time ....*What I Know About Her*		$15		Decca 30952
9/5/60	16	7		66 Ev'rybody's Somebody's Fool .... *Let The Little Girl Dance*		$12		Decca 31119

DEBUT	PEAK	WKS	Gold	A-side (Chart Hit)..B-side	Pop	$	Pic	Label & Number
				TUBB, Ernest — Cont'd				
6/5/61	16	9		67 Thoughts Of A Fool...*Don't Just Stand There*		$12		Decca 31241
11/13/61	14	11		68 Through That Door...............................*What Will You Tell Them?*		$12		Decca 31300
8/18/62	16	9		69 I'm Looking High And Low For My Baby/				
9/8/62	30	1		70 Show Her Lots Of Gold..		$12		Decca 31399
6/22/63	28	1		71 Mr. Juke Box ....*Walking The Floor Over You*		$12		Decca 31476
9/28/63 ·	3	23		72 Thanks A Lot ....*The Way That You're Living*		$10		Decca 31526
5/30/64	26	17		73 Be Better To Your Baby ....*Think Of Me, Thinking Of You*		$10		Decca 31614
7/25/64	11	23		74 Mr. And Mrs. Used To Be ....*Love Was Right Here All The Time*		$10		Decca 31643
				ERNEST TUBB AND LORETTA LYNN				
12/26/64+	15	17		75 Pass The Booze.....................*(A Memory) That's All You'll Ever Be To Me*		$10		Decca 31706
3/6/65	29	12		76 Do What You Do Well ....*Turn Around Walk Away*		$10		Decca 31742
7/24/65	24	11		77 Our Hearts Are Holding Hands ....*We're Not Kids Anymore*		$10		Decca 31793
				ERNEST TUBB AND LORETTA LYNN				
10/23/65	34	7		78 Waltz Across Texas..*Lots Of Luck*		$10		Decca 31824
				also see #90 below				
1/1/66	48	2		79 It's For God, And Country, And You Mom (That's Why I'm				
				Fighting In Viet Nam) ....*After The Boy Gets The Girl*		$10		Decca 31861
4/2/66	32	9		80 Till My Getup Has Gotup And Gone ....*Just One More*		$10		Decca 31908
				ERNEST TUBB and His Texas Troubadours (above 3)				
10/15/66	16	16		81 Another Story................*There's No Room In My Heart (For The Blues)*		$10		Decca 32022
2/25/67	45	9		82 Sweet Thang ....*Beautiful, Unhappy Home*		$10		Decca 32091
				ERNEST TUBB AND LORETTA LYNN				
2/3/68	55	5		83 Too Much Of Not Enough ....*Nothing Is Better Than You*		$8		Decca 32237
7/20/68	69	2		84 I'm Gonna Make Like A Snake ....*Mama, Who Was That Man?*		$8		Decca 32315
				written by Loretta Lynn				
3/15/69	43	7		85 Saturday Satan Sunday Saint ....*Tommy's Doll*		$8		Decca 32448
6/14/69	18	10		86 Who's Gonna Take The Garbage Out.............*Somewhere Between*		$8		Decca 32496
				ERNEST TUBB And LORETTA LYNN				
7/21/73	93	2		87 I've Got All The Heartaches I Can Handle ....*The Texas Troubadour*		$6		MCA 40056
12/17/77+	79	7		88 Sometimes I Do/				
		7		89 Half My Heart's In Texas..		$7		1st Generation 001
6/2/79	56	6		90 Waltz Across Texas...............................*Jealous Loving Heart* [R]		$6		Cachet 4501
				ERNEST TUBB and Friends				
				Willie Nelson (guest vocal); new version of #78 above				
10/13/79	31	9		91 Walkin' The Floor Over You ....*Let's Say Good-Bye Like We Said Hello*		$6		Cachet 4507
				ERNEST TUBB & FRIENDS				
				Charlie Daniels and Merle Haggard (guest vocals); Tubb's classic hit, first recorded in 1941 on Decca 5958 ($20)				
				TUBB, Justin				**'54**
				Born on 8/20/35 in San Antonio, Texas. Died of a stomach aneurysm on 1/24/98 (age 62). Singer/songwriter/guitarist. Son of **Ernest Tubb.** Joined the *Grand Ole Opry* in 1955.				
7/3/54	4	21		1 Looking Back To See ....*J:4 / A:5 / S:5 I Miss You So*		$20		Decca 29145
				GOLDIE HILL - JUSTIN TUBB				
1/8/55	11	2		2 Sure Fire Kisses ....*A:11 / S:13 Fickle Heart*		$20		Decca 29349
				JUSTIN TUBB - GOLDIE HILL				
2/19/55	8	7		3 I Gotta Go Get My Baby ....*A:8 Chuga-Chuga, Chica-Mauga (Choo-Choo Train)*		$20		Decca 29401
4/13/63	6	16		4 Take A Letter, Miss Gray ....*Here I Sit A-Waitin'*		$10	■	Groove 0017
10/2/65	23	9		5 Hurry, Mr. Peters ....*We've Got A Lot In Common*		$8		RCA Victor 8659
				JUSTIN TUBB & LORENE MANN				
				answer to "Yes, Mr. Peters" by Roy Drusky & Priscilla Mitchell				
7/30/66	44	2		6 We've Gone Too Far, Again ....*Together But Still Alone*		$8		RCA Victor 8834
				JUSTIN TUBB & LORENE MANN				
2/25/67	63	7		7 But Wait There's More ....*The Second Thing I'm Gonna Do*		$8		RCA Victor 9082
				TUCKER, Jerry Lee				**'88**
11/12/88	93	2		Livin' In Shadows		$6		Oak 1057
				TUCKER, Jimmy				**'80**
5/19/79	98	2		1 I'm Gonna Move to The Country (And Get Away To It All)........................		$5		Gar-Pax 2715
12/8/79	85	4		2 (You've Got That) Fire Goin' Again ....*Somebody Loves Me*		$5		NSD 35
4/5/80	82	3		3 The Reading Of The Will ....*It's Not Easy Lovin' You*		$5		NSD 40
				TUCKER, La Costa — see LA COSTA				
				TUCKER, Rick				**'89**
1/21/89	83	3		Honey I'm Just Walking Out The Door		$5		Oak 1066

TUCKER, Tanya ★30★   '73

Born on 10/10/58 in Seminole, Texas; raised in Wilcox, Arizona. Singer/songwriter/actress. Sister of **LaCosta**. Acted in the movies *Jeremiah Johnson* and *Hard Country*. CMA Award: 1991 Female Vocalist of the Year.

1)What's Your Mama's Name 2)Would You Lay With Me 3)Lizzie And The Rainman 4)Strong Enough To Bend
5)Just Another Love

DEBUT	PEAK	WKS		A-side	B-side	Pop	$	Pic	Label & Number
5/13/72	6	17	1	**Delta Dawn**	*I Love The Way He Loves Me*	72	$5	■	Columbia 45588
				#1 Pop hit for **Helen Reddy** in 1973					
11/18/72+	5	15	2	**Love's The Answer/**			$5		Columbia 45721
		13	3	**The Jamestown Ferry**			$5		
3/24/73	❶¹	17	4	**What's Your Mama's Name**	*Rainy Girl*	86	$5		Columbia 45799
7/21/73	❶¹	16	5	**Blood Red And Goin' Down**	*The Missing Piece Of Puzzle*	74	$5		Columbia 45892
1/12/74	❶¹	17	6	**Would You Lay With Me (In A Field Of Stone)**	*No Man's Land*	46	$5		Columbia 45991
6/8/74	4	14	7	**The Man That Turned My Mama On**	*Satisfied With Missing You*	86	$5		Columbia 46047
1/4/75	18	11	8	**I Believe The South Is Gonna Rise Again**	*Old Dan Tucker's Daughter*		$5		Columbia 10069
4/26/75	❶¹	15	9	**Lizzie And The Rainman**	*Traveling Salesman*	37	$5		MCA 40402
6/14/75	18	15	10	**Spring**	*Bed Of Roses*		$5		Columbia 10127
8/23/75	❶¹	15	11	**San Antonio Stroll**	*The Serenade That We Played*		$5		MCA 40444
11/8/75	23	10	12	**Greener Than The Grass (We Laid On)**	*Guess I'll Have To Love Him More*		$5		Columbia 10236
12/13/75+	4	15	13	**Don't Believe My Heart Can Stand Another You**	*Depend On You*		$5		MCA 40497
4/17/76	3	14	14	**You've Got Me To Hold On To**	*Ain't That A Shame*		$5		MCA 40540
8/7/76	❶¹	15	15	**Here's Some Love**	*Pride Of Franklin County*	82	$5		MCA 40598
12/25/76+	12	12	16	**Ridin' Rainbows**	*Short Cut*		$5		MCA 40650
4/16/77	7	14	17	**It's A Cowboy Lovin' Night**	*Wings*		$5		MCA 40708
7/23/77	40	8	18	**You Are So Beautiful**	*Almost Persuaded*		$5		Columbia 10577
				#5 Pop hit for Joe Cocker in 1975					
8/13/77	16	11	19	**Dancing The Night Away**	*Let's Keep It That Way*		$5		MCA 40755
6/10/78	86	3	20	**Save Me**	*Slippin' Away*	105	$5	■	MCA 40902
11/25/78+	5	15	21	**Texas (When I Die)**	*Not Fade Away (Pop #70)*		$5	■	MCA 40976
4/7/79	18	13	22	**I'm The Singer, You're The Song**	*Lover Goodbye (Pop #103)*		$4		MCA 41005
8/23/80	10	14	23	**Pecos Promenade**	*The King Of Country Music*		$4		MCA 41305
				from the movie *Smokey & The Bandit II* starring **Burt Reynolds**					
9/27/80	59	6	24	**Dream Lover**	*Bronco*		$4		MCA 41323
				TANYA TUCKER AND GLEN CAMPBELL					
				#2 Pop hit for **Bobby Darin** in 1959					
12/20/80+	4	15	25	**Can I See You Tonight**	*Let Me Count The Ways*		$4		MCA 51037
4/11/81	85	4	26	**Why Don't We Just Sleep On It Tonight**	*It's Your World*		$4		Capitol 4986
				GLEN CAMPBELL and TANYA TUCKER					
4/25/81	40	8	27	**Love Knows We Tried**	*Somebody (Trying To Tell You Something)*		$4		MCA 51096
7/4/81	50	7	28	**Should I Do It**	*Lucky Enough For Two*		$4		MCA 51131
				#13 Pop hit for the **Pointer Sisters** in 1982					
10/17/81	83	4	29	**Rodeo Girls**	*Halfway To Heaven*		$4		MCA 51184
11/27/82+	10	23	30	**Feel Right/**			$4		Arista 0677
10/16/82	77	4	31	**Cry**			$4		Arista 1053
4/23/83	41	12	32	**Changes**	*Too Long*		$4		Arista 9046
7/23/83	22	15	33	**Baby I'm Yours**	*I Don't Want You To Go*		$4		
				#11 Pop hit for Barbara Lewis in 1965					
2/15/86	3	25	34	**One Love At A Time**	S:3 / A:4 *Fool, Fool Heart*		$3	■	Capitol 5533
7/12/86	❶¹	24	35	**Just Another Love**	S:❶¹ / A:❶¹ *You Could Change My Mind*		$3	■	Capitol 5604
11/8/86+	2¹	23	36	**I'll Come Back As Another Woman**	S:❶¹ / A:2 *Somebody To Care*		$3		Capitol 5652
3/28/87	8	25	37	**It's Only Over For You**	S:❶¹ / A:23 *Girls Like Me*		$3		Capitol 5694
7/25/87	2²	25	38	**Love Me Like You Used To**	S:❶² *If I Didn't Love You*		$3	■	Capitol 44036
11/21/87+	❶¹	24	39	**I Won't Take Less Than Your Love**	S:2 *Heartbreaker*		$3		Capitol 44100
				TANYA TUCKER WITH PAUL DAVIS & PAUL OVERSTREET					
4/2/88	❶¹	20	40	**If It Don't Come Easy**	S:5 *I'll Tennessee You In My Dreams*		$3		Capitol 44142
7/16/88	❶¹	23	41	**Strong Enough To Bend**	S:5 *Back On My Feet*		$3		Capitol 44188
12/3/88+	2¹	19	42	**Highway Robbery**	*Lonesome Town*		$3		Capitol 44271
4/1/89	4	19	43	**Call On Me**	*Daddy And Home*		$3		Capitol 44348
7/22/89	27	15	44	**Daddy And Home**	*Playing For Keeps*		$3		Capitol 44401
10/28/89+	2²	26	45	**My Arms Stay Open All Night**	*Love Me Like You Used To*		$3		Capitol 44469
3/24/90	3	23	46	**Walking Shoes**	*This Heart Of Mine*		$3	❙	Capitol 44520
6/23/90	6	21	47	**Don't Go Out**			$3	❙	Capitol 44586
				TANYA TUCKER with T. Graham Brown					
10/20/90+	6	20	48	**It Won't Be Me**					album cut
2/23/91	12	20	49	**Oh What It Did To Me**					album cut
				above 2 from the album *Tennessee Woman* on Capitol 91821					
6/22/91	2¹	20	50	**Down To My Last Teardrop**					album cut
				from the album *What Do I Do With Me* on Capitol 95562					
10/12/91+	2¹	20	51	**(Without You) What Do I Do With Me**	*Oh What It Did To Me*		$3		Capitol 44774
2/15/92	3	20	52	**Some Kind Of Trouble**	*Oh What It Did To Me*		$3		Liberty 57703
5/30/92	4	20	53	**If Your Heart Ain't Busy Tonight**	*Down To My Last Teardrop*		$3		Liberty 57768

TUCKER, Tanya — Cont'd

DEBUT	PEAK	WKS		A-side / B-side	Pop	$	Pic	Label & Number
9/26/92	2[1]	20		54 Two Sparrows In A Hurricane / *Danger Ahead*		$3		Liberty 56825
1/16/93	2[2]	20		55 It's A Little Too Late / *Cadillac Ranch*	112	$3	▪	Liberty 56953
4/17/93	4	20		56 Tell Me About It / *What Do They Know*		$3		Liberty 56985
				TANYA TUCKER with Delbert McClinton				
10/9/93	2[1]	20		57 Soon / *Sneaky Moon*		$3		Liberty 17594
11/20/93	75	2		58 Already Gone				album cut
				#32 Pop hit for the **Eagles** in 1974; from the album *Common Thread* on Giant 24531				
1/15/94	11	20		59 We Don't Have To Do This.. *Silence Is King*		$3		Liberty 17803
5/28/94	4	20		60 Hangin' In / *Let The Good Times Roll*		$3		Liberty 17908
9/17/94	20	19		61 You Just Watch Me .... *I Love You Anyway*		$3		Liberty 18135
2/11/95	27	15		62 Between The Two Of Them ....*Love Will*		$3		Liberty 18485
5/27/95	40	11		63 Find Out What's Happenin'		$3		album cut
				from the album *Fire To Fire* on Liberty 28943				
3/1/97	9	20		64 Little Things .... S:9 *Two Sparrows In A Hurricane*	114	$3	▪	Capitol 58630
7/19/97	45	11		65 Ridin' Out The Heartache ....*I Don't Believe That's How You Feel*		$3		Capitol 19628

★360★				**TURNER, Grant**		'64		

Born Jesse Granderson Turner on 5/17/12 in Abilene, Texas. Died on 10/19/91 (age 79). Dean of the *Grand Ole Opry* announcers from 1945. Elected to the Country Music Hall of Fame in 1981.

10/24/64	48	1		The Bible In Her Hand .... *Lord Don't Let Me Down*		$15		Chart 1130

★360★				**TURNER, Mary Lou**		'76		

Born on 6/13/47 in Hazard, Kentucky; raised in Dayton, Ohio.

1)Sometimes 2)That's What Made Me Love You 3)Where Are You Going, Billy Boy

7/6/74	94	2		1 All That Keeps Me Goin' .... *I'll Always Be Your Woman If You'll Always Be My Man*		$5		MCA 40244
1/25/75	85	7		2 Come On Home .... *Tomorrow*		$5		MCA 40343
11/29/75+	❶[1]	16		3 Sometimes / *Circle In A Triangle*		$5		MCA 40488
				BILL ANDERSON and MARY LOU TURNER				
3/27/76	7	12		4 That's What Made Me Love You / *Can We Still Be Friends*		$5		MCA 40533
				BILL ANDERSON and MARY LOU TURNER				
6/12/76	25	12		5 It's Different With You .... *Old Habits Are Hard To Break*		$5		MCA 40566
10/2/76	30	10		6 Love It Away .... *Must You Throw Dirt In My Face*		$5		MCA 40620
2/5/77	40	9		7 Cheatin' Overtime................................... *I Never Have The Time*		$5		MCA 40674
6/4/77	93	3		8 The Man Still Turns Me On .... *Maybe It's Time To Start*		$5		MCA 40727
7/16/77	18	12		9 Where Are You Going, Billy Boy....................... *Sad Ole Shade Of Gray*		$5		MCA 40753
				BILL ANDERSON and MARY LOU TURNER				
12/10/77+	73	7		10 He Picked Me Up When You Let Me Down .... *Man Can't Live By Bed Alone*		$5		MCA 40828
1/28/78	25	10		11 I'm Way Ahead Of You .... *Just Enough To Make Me Want It All*		$5		MCA 40852
				BILL ANDERSON & MARY LOU TURNER				
8/4/79	78	4		12 Yours And Mine .... *You Can't Remember, And I Can't Forget*		$5	■	Churchill 7741
10/20/79	81	4		13 Caught With My Feelings Down/				
		2		14 You Can't Remember And I Can't Forget		$5		Churchill 7744
2/9/80	91	2		15 I Wanna Love You Tonight .... *If You Cross That Bridge*		$5		Churchill 7751

				TURNER, Zeb		'51		

Born William Edward Grishaw on 6/23/15 in Lynchburg, Virginia. Singer/songwriter/guitarist.

| 9/17/49 | 11 | 1 | | 1 Tennessee Boogie................................ J:11 *A Drunkard's Confession* | | $25 | | King 790 |
| 4/21/51 | 8 | 2 | | 2 Chew Tobacco Rag .... J:8 / A:9 *No More Nothin'* | | $30 | | King 45-950 |

				TURNER NICHOLS		'94		

Duo of South Carolina native Zack Turner and Missouri native Tim Nichols. Formed songwriting partnership in 1988.

| 8/14/93 | 51 | 13 | | 1 Moonlight Drive-In .... *Anything* | | $3 | | BNA 62577 |
| 12/11/93+ | 49 | 11 | | 2 She Loves To Hear Me Rock .... *Harleys And Horses* | | $3 | | BNA 62708 |

				TUTTLE, Wesley		'45		

Born on 12/30/17 in Lamar, Colorado. Singer/songwriter/guitarist. Acted in several western movies. Married actress Marilyn Myers.

				WESLEY TUTTLE And His Texas Stars:				
10/6/45	❶[4]	14		1 With Tears In My Eyes / *Too Little Too Late*		$15		Capitol 216
3/9/46	3	4		2 Detour/				
				#5 Pop hit for **Patti Page** in 1951				
3/16/46	5	2		3 I Wish I Had Never Met Sunshine		$15		Capitol 233
7/20/46	4	5		4 Tho' I Tried (I Can't Forget You) / *When You Cry (You Cry Alone)*		$15		Capitol 267
11/20/54	15	1		5 Never.. S:15 *Friendly Love*		$20		Capitol 2850
				MARILYN & WESLEY TUTTLE				

★243★				**TWAIN, Shania**		'97		

Pronounced: shu-NYE-uh. Born Eileen Regina Edwards on 8/28/65 in Windsor, Ontario; raised in Timmins, Ontario. Adopted the name Shania which means "I'm on my way" in the Ojibwa Indian language. Married rock producer Robert John "Mutt" Lange on 12/28/93.

1)Love Gets Me Every Time 2)I'm Outta Here! 3)You Win My Love

3/27/93	55	18		1 What Made You Say That .... *Crime Of The Century*		$3	▪	Mercury 864992
7/3/93	55	11		2 Dance With The One That Brought You .... *When He Leaves You*		$3	▪	Mercury 862346
5/13/95 ●	❶[2]	20		3 Any Man Of Mine/ S:❶[10]	31			
1/14/95	11	20		4 Whose Bed Have Your Boots Been Under?................................	87	$3	▪	Mercury 856448
11/18/95+	❶[2]	20		5 (If You're Not In It For Love) I'm Outta Here!/ S:❶[1]	74			
8/12/95	14	20		6 The Woman In Me (Needs The Man In You)	90	$3	▪	Mercury 852206
2/24/96	❶[2]	20		7 You Win My Love S:2 *Home Ain't Where His Heart Is (Anymore)*	108	$3	▪	Mercury 852138
5/11/96	❶[1]	20		8 No One Needs To Know / *Leaving Is The Only Way Out*		$3		Mercury 852986
8/10/96	28	14		9 Home Ain't Where His Heart Is (Anymore)........................ S:19 *Whose Bed Have Your Boots Been Under?*		$3	▪	Mercury 578384

DEBUT	PEAK	WKS	Gold	A-side (Chart Hit)...B-side	Pop	$	Pic	Label & Number
				TWAIN, Shania — Cont'd				
11/30/96+	48	9		10 God Bless The Child .... S:❶[1] *If It Don't Take Two*	75	$3	∎	Mercury 578748
10/4/97	❶[5]	20	●	11 Love Gets Me Every Time S:2 *(remix)*	25	$3	∎	Mercury 568062
11/15/97+	6	32		12 From This Moment On				album cut
				SHANIA TWAIN with Bryan White				
11/15/97+	6	20		13 Don't Be Stupid (You Know I Love You) S:2 *If It Don't Take Two*	40	$3	∎	Mercury 568242
11/15/97	66	2		14 Honey, I'm Home				album cut
11/15/97	70	1		15 Man! I Feel Like A Woman!				album cut
11/15/97	74	1		16 Come On Over				album cut
				above 3 from the album *Come On Over* on Mercury 536003				
				TWISTER ALLEY **'93**				
				Group from area of Arkansas known as "Twister Alley": Shellee Morris (vocals), Amy Hitt, Steve Goins, Lance Blythe, Randy Loyd and Kevin King.				
11/6/93	61	7		1 Nothing In Common But Love .... *Redneck Ways (In The U.S.A.)*		$3	∎	Mercury 862846
3/12/94	70	4		2 Young Love				album cut
				#1 Pop hit for Tab Hunter in 1957; from the album *Twister Alley* on Mercury 514927				

				TWITTY, Conway ★4★ **'70**				
				Born Harold Lloyd Jenkins on 9/1/33 in Friars Point, Mississippi; raised in Helena, Arkansas. Died of an abdominal aneurysm on 6/5/93 (age 59). Singer/songwriter/guitarist. Father of **Joni Lee** and **Jesseca James**. Uncle of **Larry Jenkins**. Changed name in 1957 (borrowed from Conway, Arkansas and Twitty, Texas). Acted in the movies *Sexpot Goes To College* and *College Confidential*. Charted 20 pop hits from 1957-76. Owned the Twitty City tourist complex in Hendersonville, Tennessee. CMA Awards: 1972, 1973, 1974 & 1975 Vocal Duo of the Year (with **Loretta Lynn**).				
				1)Hello Darlin' 2)You've Never Been This Far Before 3)Happy Birthday Darlin' 4)She Needs Someone To Hold Her 5)Touch The Hand				
3/26/66	18	12		1 Guess My Eyes Were Bigger Than My Heart .... *Honky Tonk Man*		$8		Decca 31897
9/17/66	36	10		2 Look Into My Teardrops .... *If You Were Mine To Lose*		$8		Decca 31983
2/18/67	21	14		3 I Don't Want To Be With Me .... *Before I'll Set Her Free*		$8		Decca 32081
7/8/67	32	12		4 Don't Put Your Hurt In My Heart .... *Walk Me To The Door*		$8		Decca 32147
12/9/67	61	4		5 Funny (But I'm Not Laughing) .... *Working Girl*		$8		Decca 32208
3/23/68	5	18		6 The Image Of Me *Dim Lights, Thick Smoke (And Loud, Loud Music)*		$7		Decca 32272
8/17/68	❶[1]	17		7 Next In Line *I'm Checking Out*		$7		Decca 32361
12/28/68+	2[2]	17		8 Darling, You Know I Wouldn't Lie *Table In The Corner*		$7		Decca 32424
5/10/69	❶[1]	17		9 I Love You More Today *Bad Girl*		$7		Decca 32481
9/20/69	❶[1]	14		10 To See My Angel Cry *I Did The Best I Could (With What I Had)*		$7		Decca 32546
1/3/70	3	14		11 That's When She Started To Stop Loving You *I'll Get Over Losing You*		$7		Decca 32599
4/25/70	❶[4]	20		12 Hello Darlin' *Girl At The Bar*	60	$7		Decca 32661
10/10/70	❶[1]	18		13 Fifteen Years Ago *Up Comes The Bottle (Down Goes The Man)*	81	$7		Decca 32742
2/6/71	❶[2]	14		14 After The Fire Is Gone *The One I Can't Live Without*	56	$7		Decca 32776
				CONWAY TWITTY/LORETTA LYNN				
2/6/71	59	6		15 What Am I Living For .... *I'll Try*		$7		MGM 14205
				#26 Pop hit for Twitty in 1960 on MGM 12886				
3/20/71	❶[1]	17		16 How Much More Can She Stand *Just Like A Stranger*	105	$7		Decca 32801
7/17/71	4	14		17 I Wonder What She'll Think About Me Leaving *Heartache Just Walked In*	112	$7		Decca 32842
				written by Merle Haggard				
9/11/71	50	10		18 What A Dream .... *Long Black Train*		$7		MGM 14274
				#106 Pop hit for Twitty in 1960 on MGM 12918				
10/2/71	❶[1]	17		19 Lead Me On *Four Glass Walls*		$7		Decca 32873
				LORETTA LYNN AND CONWAY TWITTY				
12/4/71+	4	16		20 I Can't See Me Without You *I Didn't Lose Her (I Threw Her Away)*		$7		Decca 32895
4/1/72	❶[1]	15		21 (Lost Her Love) On Our Last Date *I'll Never Make It Home Tonight*	112	$7		Decca 32945
7/29/72	❶[1]	15		22 I Can't Stop Loving You *Since She's Not With The One She Loves*		$7		Decca 32988
12/2/72+	❶[2]	15		23 She Needs Someone To Hold Her (When She Cries) *This Road That I Walk*		$7		Decca 33033
3/31/73	2[1]	14		24 Baby's Gone *Dim Lonely Places*		$6		MCA 40027
6/23/73	❶[1]	14		25 Louisiana Woman, Mississippi Man *Living Together Alone*		$6		MCA 40079
				LORETTA LYNN/CONWAY TWITTY				
7/21/73	❶[3]	19		26 You've Never Been This Far Before *You Make It Hard*	22	$6		MCA 40094
1/19/74	❶[1]	15		27 There's A Honky Tonk Angel (Who'll Take Me Back In) *Don't Let It Go To Your Heart*		$6		MCA 40173
5/11/74	3	15		28 I'm Not Through Loving You Yet *Before Your Time*		$6		MCA 40224
6/15/74	❶[1]	15		29 As Soon As I Hang Up The Phone *A Lifetime Before*		$6		MCA 40251
				LORETTA LYNN/CONWAY TWITTY				
8/24/74	❶[2]	17		30 I See The Want To In Your Eyes *Girl From Tupelo*		$6		MCA 40282
1/11/75	❶[1]	14		31 Linda On My Mind *She's Just Not Over You Yet*	61	$6		MCA 40339
5/24/75	❶[2]	13		32 Touch The Hand/ *Don't Cry Joni*		$6		MCA 40407
8/16/75	4	13		33 Don't Cry Joni *Touch The Hand*	63	$6		
				Joni Lee (guest vocal)				
6/21/75	❶[1]	16		34 Feelins' *You Done Lost Your Baby*		$6		MCA 40420
				LORETTA LYNN/CONWAY TWITTY				
12/6/75+	❶[1]	14		35 This Time I've Hurt Her More Than She Loves Me *She Did-It Did-I Didn't*		$6		MCA 40492
4/3/76	❶[1]	13		36 After All The Good Is Gone *I Got A Good Thing Going*		$6		MCA 40534
6/19/76	3	12		37 The Letter *God Bless America Again*		$6		MCA 40572
				LORETTA LYNN/CONWAY TWITTY				
8/21/76	❶[1]	13		38 The Games That Daddies Play *There's More Love In The Arms You're Leaving*		$6		MCA 40601

DEBUT	PEAK	WKS	Gold	A-side (Chart Hit)..B-side	Pop	$	Pic	Label & Number
				TWITTY, Conway — Cont'd				
11/20/76+	●¹	14		39 I Can't Believe She Gives It All To Me _I Can't Help It If She Can't Stop Loving Me_		$6		MCA 40649
3/5/77	●¹	16		40 Play, Guitar Play _One In A Million_		$6		MCA 40682
6/4/77	2³	14		41 I Can't Love You Enough _The Bed I'm Dreaming On_		$6		MCA 40728
				LORETTA LYNN/CONWAY TWITTY				
7/23/77	●¹	15		42 I've Already Loved You In My Mind _I've Changed My Mind_		$6		MCA 40754
10/29/77	3	15		43 Georgia Keeps Pulling On My Ring _Talkin' 'Bout You_		$6		MCA 40805
2/18/78	16	10		44 The Grandest Lady Of Them All _I'm Used To Losing You_		$6		MCA 40857
6/24/78	6	11		45 From Seven Till Ten/				
		9		46 You're The Reason Our Kids Are Ugly		$6		MCA 40920
				LORETTA LYNN/CONWAY TWITTY (above 2)				
7/15/78	2¹	14		47 Boogie Grass Band _That's All She Wrote_		$6		MCA 40929
11/18/78+	3	15		48 Your Love Had Taken Me That High _My Woman Knows_		$5		MCA 40963
3/17/79	●¹	14		49 Don't Take It Away _Draggin' Chains_		$5		MCA 41002
7/14/79	●¹	15		50 I May Never Get To Heaven _Grand Ole Blues_		$5		MCA 41059
10/27/79	●³	14		51 Happy Birthday Darlin' _Heavy Tears_		$5		MCA 41135
11/10/79+	9	14		52 You Know Just What I'd Do/				
		14		53 The Sadness Of It All		$5		MCA 41141
				CONWAY TWITTY/LORETTA LYNN (above 2)				
2/2/80	●¹	13		54 I'd Love To Lay You Down _She Thinks I Still Care_		$4		MCA 41174
5/10/80	5	15		55 It's True Love _Hit The Road Jack_		$4		MCA 41232
				CONWAY TWITTY & LORETTA LYNN				
6/28/80	6	13		56 I've Never Seen The Likes Of You _Soulful Woman_		$4		MCA 41271
10/18/80+	3	17		57 A Bridge That Just Won't Burn _You'll Be Back (Every Night In My Dreams)_		$4		MCA 51011
1/31/81	7	15		58 Lovin' What Your Lovin' Does To Me _Silent Partner_		$4		MCA 51050
				CONWAY TWITTY & LORETTA LYNN				
2/21/81	●¹	14		59 Rest Your Love On Me/				
		12		60 I Am The Dreamer (You Are The Dream)		$4		MCA 51059
5/30/81	2²	18		61 I Still Believe In Waltzes _Oh Honey - Oh Babe_		$4		MCA 51114
				CONWAY TWITTY & LORETTA LYNN				
7/11/81	●¹	16		62 Tight Fittin' Jeans _I Made You A Woman_		$4		MCA 51137
10/31/81+	●¹	18		63 Red Neckin' Love Makin' Night _Hearts_		$4		MCA 51199
1/30/82	●¹	17		64 The Clown _The Boy Next Door_		$4	■	Elektra 47302
4/24/82	●²	16		65 Slow Hand _When Love Was Something Else_		$4		Elektra 47443
				#2 Pop hit for the **Pointer Sisters** in 1981				
5/8/82	69	7		66 Over Thirty (Not Over The Hill) _Love Salvation_		$4		MCA 52032
9/18/82	2²	18		67 We Did But Now You Don't _A Good Love Died Tonight_		$4		Elektra 69964
12/25/82+	●¹	19		68 The Rose _It's Only Make Believe_		$4	■	Elektra 69854
				#3 Pop hit for Bette Midler in 1980				
4/2/83	44	11		69 We Had It All _Cheatin' Fire_		$4		MCA 52154
5/28/83	2²	21		70 Lost In The Feeling _You've Never Been This Far Before_		$3		Warner 29636
				Ricky Skaggs (backing vocal)				
9/24/83	6	19		71 Heartache Tonight _Hello Darlin'_		$3		Warner 29505
				#1 Pop hit for the **Eagles** in 1979				
12/24/83+	7	18		72 Three Times A Lady _I Think I'm In Love_		$3		Warner 29395
				#1 Pop hit for the Commodores in 1978				
4/14/84	●¹	19		73 Somebody's Needin' Somebody _(Lying Here With) Linda On My Mind_		$3		Warner 29308
7/28/84	●¹	19		74 I Don't Know A Thing About Love (The Moon Song) _S:●¹ / A:●¹ Don't Cry Joni_		$3		Warner 29227
				Joni Lee (guest vocal)				
11/10/84+	●¹	21		75 Ain't She Somethin' Else _A:●¹ / S:2 The Games That Daddies Play_		$3		Warner 29137
3/16/85	●¹	20		76 Don't Call Him A Cowboy _S:●¹ / A:●¹ After All The Good Is Gone_		$3		Warner 29057
7/6/85	3	19		77 Between Blue Eyes And Jeans _S:3 / A:3 Baby's Gone_		$3		Warner 28966
10/26/85	19	18		78 The Legend And The Man _S:16 / A:21 (I Can't Believe) She Gives It All To Me_		$3		Warner 28866
3/1/86	26	14		79 You'll Never Know How Much I Needed You Today _A:24 / S:29 Fifteen Years Ago_		$3		Warner 28772
6/7/86	●¹	21		80 Desperado Love _S:●² / A:●¹ I Can't See Me Without You_		$3		Warner 28692
10/18/86+	2¹	25		81 Fallin' For You For Years _A:2 / S:3 I'll Try_		$3		Warner 28577
3/7/87	2²	23		82 Julia _S:3 / A:4 Everybody Needs A Hero_		$3		MCA 53034
7/11/87	2¹	24		83 I Want To Know You Before We Make Love _S:2 Snake Boots_		$3		MCA 53134
11/14/87+	6	23		84 That's My Job _S:8 Lonelytown_		$3		MCA 53200
4/9/88	7	19		85 Goodbye Time _S:11 Your Loving Side_		$3		MCA 53276
8/6/88	9	19		86 Saturday Night Special _S:8 If You Were Mine To Lose_		$3		MCA 53373
11/26/88+	4	23		87 I Wish I Was Still In Your Dreams _S:30 If You Were Mine To Lose_		$3		MCA 53456
4/22/89	2¹	25		88 She's Got A Single Thing In Mind _Too White To Sing The Blues_		$3		MCA 53633
8/26/89	19	15		89 House On Old Lonesome Road _Nobody Can Fill Your Shoes_		$3		MCA 53688
12/9/89+	51	12		90 Who's Gonna Know _Private Part Of My Heart_		$3		MCA 53759
4/14/90	30	14		91 Fit To Be Tied Down _When You're Cool (The Sun Shines All The Time)_		$3		MCA 79000
9/8/90	2²	20		92 Crazy In Love _Heart's Breakin' All Over Town_		$3		MCA 79067
1/5/91	3	20		93 I Couldn't See You Leavin' _Just The Thought Of Losing You_		$3		MCA 53983
5/4/91	57	9		94 One Bridge I Didn't Burn _I'm Tired Of Being Something_		$3		MCA 54077
8/24/91	22	20		95 She's Got A Man On Her Mind _You Put It There_		$3		MCA 54186
12/7/91+	56	9		96 Who Did They Think He Was _Let The Pretty Lady Dance_		$3		MCA 54281
8/14/93	62	5		97 I'm The Only Thing (I'll Hold Against You) _Final Touches_		$3		MCA 54716

TWO HEARTS '85
Duo of sisters from Burbank, Oklahoma: Jama and Cathy Bowen.

11/23/85	63	8		1 Two Hearts Can't Be Wrong		$5	■	MDJ 5831
8/2/86	77	5		2 Feel Like I'm Falling For You .... *All Wrapped Up In Your Love*		$5	■	MDJ 5832

TYLER, Bonnie '78
Born Gaynor Hopkins on 6/8/53 in Swansea, Wales. Pop singer.

4/15/78	10	15	●	1 It's A Heartache .... *It's About Time*	3	$5		RCA 11249
2/24/79	86	3		2 My Guns Are Loaded .... *Baby I Just Love You*	107	$5		RCA 11468

TYLER, Kris '98
Female singer from Omaha, Nebraska. Worked as a TV news producer at KNXV in Phoenix.

4/12/97	68	5		1 Keeping Your Kisses .... *Rockin' Horse*		$3	▌	Rising Tide 56045
11/8/97+	45	16		2 What A Woman Knows .... *A Thousand Tears Ago*		$3	▌	Rising Tide 56051

TYLER, "T" Texas '48
★352★

Born David Luke Myrick on 6/20/16 in Mena, Arkansas. Died of cancer on 1/28/72 (age 55). Singer/songwriter/guitarist. Known as "The Man With A Million Friends." Acted in the movie *Horseman of The Sierras*. Hosted own *Range Round-Up* TV series in Los Angeles.

1)Deck Of Cards 2)Courtin' In The Rain 3)My Bucket's Got A Hole In It

8/24/46	5	1		1 Filipino Baby .... *You Were Only Teasing Me*		$20		4 Star 1009
				"T" TEXAS TYLER and his Oklahoma Melody Boys				
4/10/48	2¹	13		2 Deck Of Cards .... S:2 / J:3 *Ida Red* [S]		$20		4 Star 1228
7/3/48	10	2		3 Dad Gave My Dog Away .... S:10 / J:13 *Beautiful Life*		$20		4 Star 1248
9/25/48	9	4		4 Memories Of France/ J:9		$20		
11/13/48	11	1		5 Honky Tonk Gal J:11		$20		4 Star 1249
11/26/49	4	5		6 My Bucket's Got A Hole In It .... J:4 / A:8 *Cry-Baby Heart*		$20		4 Star 1383
4/18/53	5	15		7 Bumming Around .... S:5 / J:5 *Jealous Love*		$20		Decca 28579
7/17/54	3	19		8 Courtin' In The Rain .... A:3 / J:4 *Old Blue*		$20		4 Star 1660
				T. TEXAS TYLER and His Band				

TYNDALL, Lynne '88
Born in Owensboro, Kentucky; raised in Nashville.

11/14/87	67	5		1 Lovin' The Blue		$5		Evergreen 1060
5/14/88	62	6		2 This Is Me Leaving		$5		Evergreen 1071
11/5/88	83	4		3 Love's Slippin' Up On Me		$5		Evergreen 1079
6/10/89	74	3		4 I Promise		$5		Evergreen 1091

U

ULISSE, Donna '91
Born in Hampton, Virginia.

2/2/91	75	3		1 Things Are Mostly Fine .... *Legend In My Heart*		$3	▌	Atlantic 87862
4/13/91	66	5		2 When Was The Last Time .... *Legend In My Heart*		$3		Atlantic 87739

USA FOR AFRICA '85
All-star colaboration (USA: United Support of Artists) for starving people in Africa. Includes **Ray Charles**, **Kim Carnes**, **Willie Nelson**, **Lionel Richie** and **Kenny Rogers**.

4/20/85	76	6	▲⁴	We Are The World .... *Grace*	❶⁴	$3	■	Columbia 04839

V

VALENTINO '81
Born Valentino Enrique Hernandez on 2/13/60 in Toledo, Ohio.

8/1/81	62	6		She Took The Place Of You .... *You Belong To My Heart*		$4		RCA 12269

VANCE, Vince, & The Valiants '97
Vocal group from New Orleans.

12/25/93	55	3		1 All I Want For Christmas Is You .... [X]				album cut
12/24/94	52	3		2 All I Want For Christmas Is You .... [X-R]				album cut
12/23/95	52	3		3 All I Want For Christmas Is You .... [X-R]				album cut
12/28/96	49	3		4 All I Want For Christmas Is You .... [X-R]				album cut
12/27/97	43	3		5 All I Want For Christmas Is You .... [X-R]				album cut
				all of above are the same version; from the album *All I Want For Christmas Is You* on Waldoxy 9289				

VAN DYKE, Bruce '89

5/6/89	94	1		1 It's All In The Touch		$5		Aria 51688
8/26/89	73	4		2 Hard-Headed Heart		$5	■	Aria 51689

VAN DYKE, Leroy ★246★ '61
Born on 10/4/29 in Spring Fork, Missouri. Singer/songwriter/guitarist. Acted in the movie *What Am I Bid.*
1)Walk On By 2)If A Woman Answers 3)Auctioneer

DEBUT	PEAK	WKS		A-side	B-side	Pop	$	Pic	Label & Number
1/5/57	9	2		1 Auctioneer A:9 / J:10 *I Fell In Love With A Pony-Tail*		19	$15		Dot 15503
9/4/61	❶19	37		2 Walk On By *My World Is Caving In*		5	$10		Mercury 71834
3/31/62	3	12		3 If A Woman Answers (Hang Up The Phone) *A Broken Promise*		35	$10		Mercury 71926
12/29/62	16	7		4 Black Cloud *Five Steps*			$10		Mercury 72057
1/11/64	50	1		5 Happy To Be Unhappy *Now I Lay Me Down*			$10		Mercury 72198
				written by Bobby Bare					
2/29/64	45	3		6 Night People *Baby (Where Can You Be)*			$10	■	Mercury 72232
1/9/65	40	5		7 Anne Of A Thousand Days *Poor Guy*			$10		Mercury 72360
10/15/66	34	9		8 Roses From A Stranger *Before I Change My Mind*			$8		Warner 5841
4/15/67	66	4		9 I've Never Been Loved *Less Of Me*			$8		Warner 7001
1/6/68	23	11		10 Louisville *There's Always Tomorrow*			$8		Warner 7155
8/31/68	69	5		11 You May Be Too Much For Memphis, Baby *Road Of Love*			$7		Kapp 931
11/1/69	56	4		12 Crack In My World *We'll Try A Little Bit Harder*			$7		Kapp 2054
6/13/70	63	7		13 An Old Love Affair, Now Showing *Belle*			$7		Kapp 2091
12/12/70	71	2		14 Mister Professor *People Gonna Turn You Off*			$6		Decca 32756
9/18/71	62	5		15 I Get Lonely When It Rains *Party Girl*			$6		Decca 32866
3/25/72	69	6		16 I'd Rather Be Wantin' Love *My Mind Is On You*			$6		Decca 32933
4/26/75	79	6		17 Unfaithful Fools *What Will You Do Now, Mrs. Jones?*			$5		ABC 12070
12/20/75+	75	7		18 Who's Gonna Run The Truck Stop In Tuba City When I'm Gone? *There Ain't No Roses In My Bed*			$5		ABC/Dot 17597
4/23/77	77	6		19 Texas Tea *Las Vegas Girl*			$5		ABC/Dot 17691

VANWARMER, Randy '88
Born Randall Van Wormer on 3/30/55 in Indian Hills, Colorado. Singer/songwriter/guitarist.

DEBUT	PEAK	WKS		A-side	B-side	Pop	$	Pic	Label & Number
6/30/79	71	6	●	1 Just When I Needed You Most *Your Light*		4	$5		Bearsville 0334
2/20/88	53	8		2 I Will Hold You *I'll Be On The Next Dream Home*			$3		16th Avenue 70407
8/20/88	72	4		3 Where The Rocky Mountains Touch The Morning Sun *That's What Your Smile Does For Me*			$3		16th Avenue 70418

VASSY, Kin '82
Born Charles Kindred Vassy. Died of cancer on 6/23/94 (age 50). Former member of **The First Edition**.

DEBUT	PEAK	WKS		A-side	B-side	Pop	$	Pic	Label & Number
10/13/79	85	5		1 Do I Ever Cross Your Mind *Sometimes Love Is Better When It's Gone*			$5		ia 501
3/8/80	67	6		2 Makes Me Wonder If I Ever Said Goodbye *Fort Worth Featherbed*			$5		ia 502
7/5/80	88	4		3 There's Nobody Like You *Nite Out*			$5		ia 505
				above 2 produced by Kenny Rogers; also released on United Artists 1368 in 1980					
5/16/81	39	10		4 Likin' Him And Lovin' You *Hell And High Water*			$4		Liberty 1407
8/15/81	48	8		5 Sneakin' Around *Lonely Hearts*			$4		Liberty 1427
12/12/81+	21	14		6 When You Were Blue And I Was Green *A Honky Tonk Heart*			$4		Liberty 1440
5/1/82	78	4		7 Cast The First Stone *Lonely Hearts*			$4		Liberty 1458
8/21/82	59	8		8 Women In Love *Hell And High Water*			$4		Liberty 1469
1/22/83	80	4		9 Tryin' To Love Two *All For The Love Of A Girl*			$4		Liberty 1488
				#10 Pop hit for William Bell in 1977					

VAUGHN, Sammy '78

DEBUT	PEAK	WKS		A-side	B-side	Pop	$	Pic	Label & Number
8/19/78	67	5		1 This Time Around			$6		Oak 1007
2/10/79	98	1		2 Sunshine			$5		Alpine 100

VAUGHN, Sharon '74

DEBUT	PEAK	WKS		A-side	B-side	Pop	$	Pic	Label & Number
4/27/74	39	11		1 Until The End Of Time *Someone To Give My Love To*			$6		Cinnamon 793
				NARVEL FELTS and SHARON VAUGHN					
8/10/74	96	4		2 Never A Night Goes By			$6		Cinnamon 799
12/6/75	99	2		3 You And Me, Me And You *The Time I've Had With You*			$5		ABC/Dot 17590

VAUS, Steve '92

DEBUT	PEAK	WKS		A-side	B-side	Pop	$	Pic	Label & Number
8/8/92	68	2		We Must Take America Back *Never Had A Chance*			$3	▌	RCA 62308

VEACH, Gail '87

DEBUT	PEAK	WKS		A-side	B-side	Pop	$	Pic	Label & Number
8/1/87	86	2		1 Would You Catch Me Baby (If I Fall For You)			$6		Prairie Dust 128
4/16/88	93	1		2 Deepest Shade Of Blue			$6		Choice 101

VEGA, Ray '96
Born on 7/28/61 in Los Angeles; raised in El Paso, Texas. Singer/songwriter. Member of **The Vega Brothers**.

DEBUT	PEAK	WKS		A-side	B-side	Pop	$	Pic	Label & Number
11/16/96	56	12		Remember When *Maria*			$3		BNA 64652

VEGA BROTHERS, The '86
Duo of brothers from El Paso, Texas: Robert and **Ray Vega**.

DEBUT	PEAK	WKS		A-side	B-side	Pop	$	Pic	Label & Number
4/19/86	54	6		Heartache The Size Of Texas *New Woman*			$4		MCA 52777

VERA, Billy '87
Born William McCord on 5/28/44 in Riverside, California; raised in Westchester County, New York. Singer/songwriter. Acted in the movies *Buckaroo Banzai* and *The Doors.*

DEBUT	PEAK	WKS		A-side	B-side	Pop	$	Pic	Label & Number
1/24/87	42	13	●	1 At This Moment *I Can Take Care Of Myself*		❶2	$4		Rhino 74403
				BILLY VERA & THE BEATERS					
				recorded "live" in 1981					
4/25/87	93	2		2 She Ain't Johnnie *My Girl Josephine*			$4		Macola 9812
				originally released on Midland Int'l. 44295 in 1977					

VERNON, Kenny '70
Born on 7/19/40 in Jackson, Tennessee. Singer/songwriter/guitarist.

DEBUT	PEAK	WKS		A-side / B-side	Pop	$	Label & Number
10/1/66	48	2		1 It Makes You Happy (To Know You Make Me Blue) .. *Too Much Loving Turned Her Bad*		$10	Caravan 123

LaWANDA LINDSEY & KENNY VERNON:

1/4/69	58	9		2 Eye To Eye.. *Looking Over Our Shoulders*		$7	Chart 1063
3/21/70	27	14		3 Pickin' Wild Mountain Berries .... *We Don't Deserve Each Other*		$6	Chart 5055
				#27 Pop hit for Peggy Scott & Jo Jo Benson in 1968			
9/19/70	51	9		4 Let's Think About Where We're Going .... *Puzzles Of My Mind*		$6	Chart 5090
2/27/71	42	9		5 The Crawdad Song .... *Wrong Number*		$6	Chart 5114

KENNY VERNON:

6/17/72	56	8		6 That'll Be The Day.. *I'd Go Right Back Again*		$5	Capitol 3331
				#1 Pop hit for Buddy Holly in 1957			
1/13/73	55	6		7 Feel So Fine .... *Would You Settle For Roses*		$5	Capitol 3506
6/9/73	66	3		8 Lady .... *What Kind Of Mood (Will She Be In Tonight)*		$5	Capitol 3590
1/5/74	74	8		9 What Was Your Name Again? .... *Have I Ever Lied To You*		$5	Capitol 3785

VICKERY, Mack '77
Born on 6/8/38 in Town Creek, Alabama; raised in Adrianne, Michigan. Singer/prolific songwriter. Also recorded as **Atlanta James**.

6/8/74	95	3		1 That Kind Of Fool.. *Starting All Over Again*		$6	MCA 40233

ATLANTA JAMES

5/28/77	49	7		2 Ishabilly .... *Think It Over*		$5	Playboy 5800
9/24/77	94	2		3 Here's To The Horses .... *When It Counted, You Could Never Count On Me*		$5	Playboy 5814

VINCENT, Gene '56
Born Vincent Eugene Craddock on 2/11/35 in Norfolk, Virginia. Died of an ulcer on 10/12/71 (age 36). Rock and roll singer/songwriter/guitarist.

7/7/56	5	17		Be-Bop-A-Lula S:5 / J:5 / A:9 *Woman Love*	7	$40	Capitol 3450

GENE VINCENT and His Blue Caps

VINCENT, Rick '93
Born in San Bernadino; raised in Bakersfield, California.

12/12/92+	39	15		1 The Best Mistakes I Ever Made..			album cut
5/22/93	69	4		2 Ain't Been A Train Through Here In Years			album cut
				above 2 from the album *A Wanted Man* on Curb 77586			

VINTON, Bobby '70
Born Stanley Robert Vinton on 4/16/35 in Canonsburg, Pennsylvania. Charted 47 pop hits from 1962-80. Hosted own TV variety series from 1975-76.

2/28/70	27	9		1 My Elusive Dreams *Over And Over*	46	$6	■ Epic 10576
12/15/79	86	5		2 Make Believe It's Your First Time................... *I Remember Loving You*	78	$5	Tapestry 002
7/2/83	87	3		3 You Are Love .... *Ghost Of Another Man*		$5	Larc 81019
11/24/84	91	3		4 Bed Of Roses .... *I Know A Goodbye*		$5	Tapestry 4009
12/24/88+	63	7		5 The Last Rose .... *Sealed With A Kiss*		$3	Curb 10512
7/22/89	70	5		6 Please Tell Her That I Said Hello .... *Getting Used To Being Loved Again*		$3	Curb 10541
				#84 Pop hit for Debbie Campbell in 1975			
11/11/89	64	8		7 It's Been One Of Those Days...................... *(Now And Then There's) A Fool Such As I*		$3	Curb 10560

VON, Vicki Rae '87
Born in Marshalltown, Iowa; raised in Ankeny, Iowa.

4/11/87	52	10		1 Not Tonight I've Got A Heartache................... *It's All Over But The Lying*		$3	Atlantic Amer. 99471
7/25/87	53	9		2 Torn-Up .... *Hold Me Like You've Never Had Me*		$3	Atlantic Amer. 99442

WADE, Norman '79
Born in Columbus, Georgia.

11/17/79	97	2		I'm A Long Gone Daddy .... *Arms Of Someone Else*		$6	NSD 29

WAGONEERS '88
Group from Austin, Texas: Monte Warden (vocals, guitar), Brent Wilson (guitar), Craig Allan Pettigrew (bass) and Thomas Lewis (drums).

6/25/88	43	9		1 I Wanna Know Her Again .... *Stout And High*		$4	A&M 1215
9/10/88	52	6		2 Every Step Of The Way.. *It'll Take Some Time*		$4	A&M 1230
1/14/89	66	5		3 Help Me Get Over You .... *Please Don't Think I'm Guilty*		$4	A&M 1261
6/24/89	53	7		4 Sit A Little Closer .... *Spare Time*		$4	A&M 1435

WAGONER, Porter ★33★   '55

Born on 8/12/27 in West Plains, Missouri. Singer/songwriter/guitarist. Joined the *Grand Ole Opry* in 1957. Hosted own TV series from 1960-79. Co-host of TNN's *Opry Backstage*. CMA Awards: 1968 Vocal Group of the Year (with **Dolly Parton**); 1970 & 1971 Vocal Duo of the Year (with Dolly Parton).

1)*A Satisfied Mind* 2)*Misery Loves Company* 3)*Please Don't Stop Loving Me*
  4)*The Carroll County Accident* 5)*Making Plans*

DEBUT	PEAK	WKS	A-side	B-side	Pop	$	Label & Number
10/30/54+	7	12	1 Company's Comin'	A:7 *Tricks Of The Trade*		$20	RCA Victor 5848
5/28/55	❶⁴	33	2 A Satisfied Mind	A:❶⁴ / S:2 / J:2 *Itchin' For My Baby*		$15	RCA Victor 6105
12/3/55+	3	22	3 Eat, Drink, And Be Merry (Tomorrow You'll Cry)	S:3 / J:3 / A:5 *Let's Squiggle*		$15	RCA Victor 6289
3/31/56	8	11	4 What Would You Do? (If Jesus Came To Your House)	S:8 / A:14 *How Can You Refuse Him Now*		$15	RCA Victor 6421
5/26/56	14	4	5 Uncle Pen .... A:14 *How I've Tried* written by Bill Monroe			$15	RCA Victor 6494
11/17/56	11	2	6 Tryin' To Forget The Blues .... A:11 *I've Known You From Somewhere*			$15	RCA Victor 6598
8/19/57	11	3	7 I Thought I Heard You Calling My Name .... A:11 *Pay Day*			$15	RCA Victor 6964
5/4/59	29	1	8 Me And Fred And Joe And Bill .... *Out Of Sight Out Of Mind*			$12	RCA Victor 7457
1/18/60	26	4	9 The Girl Who Didn't Need Love .... *Your Kind Of People*			$12	RCA Victor 7638
10/31/60	26	1	10 Falling Again/				
10/31/60	30	1	11 An Old Log Cabin For Sale			$12	RCA Victor 7770
3/6/61	10	13	12 Your Old Love Letters	*Heartbreak Affair*		$12	RCA Victor 7837
1/13/62	❶²	29	13 Misery Loves Company	*I Cried Again*		$12	RCA Victor 7967
6/23/62	10	10	14 Cold Dark Waters	*Ain't It Awful*		$12	RCA Victor 8026
12/8/62+	7	15	15 I've Enjoyed As Much Of This As I Can Stand	*One Way Ticket To The Blues*		$12	RCA Victor 8105
6/22/63	20	7	16 My Baby's Not Here (In Town Tonight)/				
7/20/63	29	1	17 In The Shadows Of The Wine			$12	RCA Victor 8178
1/18/64	19	12	18 Howdy Neighbor Howdy .... *Find Out*			$12	RCA Victor 8257
4/25/64	5	23	19 Sorrow On The Rocks	*The Life Of The Party*		$12	RCA Victor 8338
10/10/64	11	25	20 I'll Go Down Swinging .... *Country Music Has Gone To Town*			$12	RCA Victor 8432
5/1/65	21	8	21 I'm Gonna Feed You Now .... *The Bride's Bouquet* also see #73 below			$12	RCA Victor 8524
7/31/65	4	19	22 Green, Green Grass Of Home	*Dooley*		$10	RCA Victor 8622
			#11 Pop hit for Tom Jones in 1967				
12/25/65+	3	17	23 Skid Row Joe	*Love Your Neighbor*		$10	RCA Victor 8723
5/7/66	21	12	24 I Just Came To Smell The Flowers .... *I'm A Long Way From Home*			$10	RCA Victor 8800
11/5/66	48	4	25 Ole Slew-Foot.. *Let Me In* also see # 72 below			$10	RCA Victor 8977
1/28/67	2¹	19	26 The Cold Hard Facts Of Life	*You Can't Make A Heel Toe The Mark*		$10	RCA Victor 9067
7/15/67	15	16	27 Julie .... *Try Being Lonely* written by Waylon Jennings			$10	RCA Victor 9243
12/2/67+	7	17	28 The Last Thing On My Mind	*Love Is Worth Living*		$10	RCA Victor 9369
			PORTER WAGONER/DOLLY PARTON				
12/16/67+	24	12	29 Woman Hungry..............................*Out Of The Silence (Came A Song)*			$10	RCA Victor 9379
4/13/68	7	16	30 Holding On To Nothin'	*Just Between You And Me*		$10	RCA Victor 9490
			PORTER WAGONER and DOLLY PARTON				
6/8/68	16	14	31 Be Proud Of Your Man .... *Wino*			$10	RCA Victor 9530
7/27/68	5	13	32 We'll Get Ahead Someday/				
10/5/68	51	6	33 Jeannie's Afraid Of The Dark			$10	RCA Victor 9577
			PORTER WAGONER & DOLLY PARTON (above 2)				
11/9/68+	2⁴	21	34 The Carroll County Accident	*Sorrow Overtakes The Wine*	92	$8	RCA Victor 9651
3/8/69	9	14	35 Yours Love	*Malena*		$8	RCA Victor 0104
			DOLLY PARTON/PORTER WAGONER				
6/14/69	3	15	36 Big Wind	*Tennessee Stud*		$8	RCA Victor 0168
6/21/69	16	11	37 Always, Always..................................*No Reason To Hurry Home*			$8	RCA Victor 0172
			PORTER WAGONER and DOLLY PARTON				
10/25/69	5	16	38 Just Someone I Used To Know	*My Hands Are Tied*		$8	RCA Victor 0247
			PORTER WAGONER and DOLLY PARTON				
11/15/69	21	11	39 When You're Hot You're Hot .... *The Answer Is Love*			$8	RCA Victor 0267
2/14/70	9	15	40 Tomorrow Is Forever	*Mendy Never Sleeps*		$8	RCA Victor 9799
			PORTER WAGONER AND DOLLY PARTON				
3/14/70	41	5	41 You Got-ta Have A License .... *Fairchild*			$8	RCA Victor 9802
4/4/70	43	9	42 Little Boy's Prayer .... *Roses Out Of Season*			$8	RCA Victor 9811
8/1/70	7	15	43 Daddy Was An Old Time Preacher Man	*A Good Understanding*		$8	RCA Victor 9875
			PORTER WAGONER AND DOLLY PARTON				
9/26/70	41	9	44 Jim Johnson .... *One More Dime*			$8	RCA Victor 9895
1/2/71	18	16	45 The Last One To Touch Me .... *The Alley*			$8	RCA Victor 9939
2/27/71	7	13	46 Better Move It On Home	*Two Of A Kind*		$8	RCA Victor 9958
			PORTER WAGONER AND DOLLY PARTON				
5/8/71	15	13	47 Charley's Picture .... *Simple As I Am*	116	$8	RCA Victor 9979
6/26/71	14	12	48 The Right Combination...................................*The Pain Of Loving You*	106	$8	RCA Victor 9994
			PORTER WAGONER AND DOLLY PARTON				
8/28/71	11	14	49 Be A Little Quieter .... *Watching*			$7	RCA Victor 1007

WAGONER, Porter — Cont'd

DEBUT	PEAK	WKS	A-side / B-side	Pop	$	Label & Number
11/13/71+	11	13	50 Burning The Midnight Oil ....*More Than Words Can Tell*		$7	RCA Victor 0565
			PORTER WAGONER AND DOLLY PARTON			
2/26/72	8	14	51 What Ain't To Be, Just Might Happen *Little Bird*		$7	RCA Victor 0648
4/8/72	9	14	52 Lost Forever In Your Kiss *The Fog Has Lifted*		$7	RCA Victor 0675
			PORTER WAGONER AND DOLLY PARTON			
8/5/72	14	13	53 A World Without Music ....*Denise Mayree*		$7	RCA Victor 0753
9/2/72	14	13	54 Together Always ....*Love's All Over*		$7	RCA Victor 0773
			PORTER WAGONER AND DOLLY PARTON			
11/11/72	16	12	55 Katy Did ....*Darlin' Debra Jean*		$7	RCA Victor 0820
3/3/73	30	9	56 We Found It ....*Love Have Mercy On Us*		$7	RCA Victor 0893
			PORTER WAGONER AND DOLLY PARTON			
4/21/73	54	7	57 Lightening The Load................................*Tomorrow Is Forever*		$7	RCA Victor 0923
6/23/73	3	17	58 If Teardrops Were Pennies *Come To Me*		$7	RCA Victor 0981
			PORTER WAGONER AND DOLLY PARTON			
7/14/73	37	9	59 Wake Up, Jacob ....*Stella, Dear Sweet Stella*		$7	RCA Victor 0013
12/15/73+	43	12	60 George Leroy Chickashea...........................*Cassie*		$7	RCA Victor 0187
3/30/74	46	9	61 Tore Down/			
		9	62 Nothing Between		$7	RCA Victor 0233
7/27/74	15	9	63 Highway Headin' South ....*Freida*		$7	RCA Victor 0328
8/3/74	❶[1]	17	64 Please Don't Stop Loving Me *Sounds Of Nature*		$7	RCA Victor 10010
			PORTER WAGONER & DOLLY PARTON			
12/14/74+	19	12	65 Carolina Moonshiner ....*Not A Cloud In The Sky*		$6	RCA Victor 10124
7/12/75	5	17	66 Say Forever You'll Be Mine *How Can I (Help You Forgive Me)*		$6	RCA Victor 10328
			PORTER WAGONER & DOLLY PARTON			
11/8/75	96	2	67 Indian Creek ....*Thank You For The Happiness*		$6	RCA Victor 10411
5/15/76	8	14	68 Is Forever Longer Than Always *If You Say I Can*		$6	RCA Victor 10652
			PORTER WAGONER AND DOLLY PARTON			
11/13/76	66	5	69 When Lea Jane Sang ....*Storm Of Love*		$5	RCA 10803
10/15/77	76	5	70 I Haven't Learned A Thing...................*Hand Me Down My Walking Cane*		$5	RCA 10974
			Merle Haggard (guest vocal)			
1/7/78	64	6	71 Mountain Music.............................*A Natural Wonder*		$5	RCA 11186
11/18/78+	31	11	72 Ole Slew-Foot/ [R]			
			new version of #25 above			
		11	73 I'm Gonna Feed 'Em Now ....[R]		$5	RCA 11411
			new version of #21 above			
3/17/79	34	8	74 I Want To Walk You Home.......................*Old Love Letters*		$5	RCA 11491
8/11/79	32	9	75 Everything I've Always Wanted ....*No Bed Of Roses*		$5	RCA 11671
12/22/79+	64	7	76 Hold On Tight ....*Someone Just Like You*		$5	RCA 11771
5/24/80	84	4	77 Is It Only Cause You're Lonely ....*When She Was Mine*		$5	RCA 11998
6/21/80	2[2]	17	78 Making Plans *Beneath The Sweet Magnolia Tree*		$5	RCA 11983
			PORTER WAGONER AND DOLLY PARTON			
11/8/80+	12	14	79 If You Go, I'll Follow You...........................*Hide Me Away*		$5	RCA 12119
			PORTER WAGONER & DOLLY PARTON			
11/13/82	53	8	80 Turn The Pencil Over.........................*Texas Moonbeam Waltz*		$4	Warner 29875
			from the movie *Honkytonk Man* starring Clint **Eastwood**			
3/5/83	35	14	81 This Cowboy's Hat...................*She Don't Have A License To Drive Me Up The Wall*		$4	Warner 29772

WAKELY, Jimmy ★114★ **'49**

Born on 2/16/14 in Mineola, Arkansas; raised in Oklahoma. Died on 9/25/82 (age 68). Singer/songwriter/guitarist/pianist. Regular on **Gene Autry**'s *Melody Ranch* radio show in the early 1940s. Known as "The Melody Kid." Starred in several western movies. Hosted own radio show from 1952-57. Co-hosted TV's *Five Star Jubilee* in 1961.

1)*Slipping Around* 2)*One Has My Name* 3)*I Love You So Much It Hurts* 4)*I'll Never Slip Around Again* 5)*Let's Go To Church*

DEBUT	PEAK	WKS	A-side / B-side	Pop	$	Label & Number
4/15/44	2[1]	4	1 I'm Sending You Red Roses *A Tiny Little Voice In A Tiny Little Prayer*		$15	Decca 6095
4/3/48	9	6	2 Signed, Sealed And Delivered *S:9 / J:9 Easy To Please*		$15	Capitol Amer. 40088
9/4/48	❶[11]	32	3 One Has My Name (The Other Has My Heart) *S:❶[11] / J:❶[7] You're The Sweetest Rose In Texas*	10	$15	Capitol 15162
10/30/48+	❶[5]	28	4 I Love You So Much It Hurts *J:❶[5] / S:❶[4] I Don't Want Your Sympathy*	21	$15	Capitol 15243
			#8 Pop hit for **The Mills Brothers** in 1949			
11/13/48+	8	5	5 Mine All Mine *J:8 Walkin' The Sidewalks Of Shame*		$15	Capitol 15236
2/5/49	10	1	6 Forever More *J:10 Think Of Me Thinking Of You*		$15	Capitol 15333
2/19/49	9	6	7 Till The End Of The World *S:9 / J:15 Moon Over Montana*		$15	Capitol 15368
5/14/49	4	9	8 I Wish I Had A Nickel/ *J:4 / S:10*			
6/18/49	10	3	9 Someday You'll Call My Name *J:10*		$15	Capitol 40153
8/6/49	14	2	10 Tellin' My Troubles To My Old Guitar ....*J:14 Try To Understand*		$15	Capitol 40187
			MARGARET WHITING and JIMMY WAKELY:			
9/10/49	❶[17]	28	● 11 Slipping Around/ *S:❶[17] / J:❶[12] / A:2*	❶[3]		
9/10/49	6	8	12 Wedding Bells *J:6 / S:7*	30	$15	Capitol 40224
11/5/49	2[3]	13	13 I'll Never Slip Around Again *S:2 / J:2 / A:10 Six Times A Week And Twice On Sunday*	8	$15	Capitol 40246
2/11/50	2[1]	9	14 Broken Down Merry-Go-Round/ *S:2 / J:3 / A:5*	12		
2/11/50	3	7	15 The Gods Were Angry With Me *S:3 / J:4*	17	$20	Capitol F800

WAKELY, Jimmy — Cont'd

DEBUT	PEAK	WKS		A-side / B-side	Pop	$	Pic	Label & Number
4/8/50	**7**	3		16 Peter Cottontail *A:7 Mr. Easter Bunny*	26	$20		Capitol F929
				JIMMY WAKELY				
4/22/50	**2**[1]	10		17 Let's Go To Church (Next Sunday Morning) *S:2 / A:6 / J:6 Why Do You Say Those Things (That Hurt Me So)*	13	$20		Capitol F960
9/23/50	**10**	1		18 Mona Lisa *A:10 Steppin' Out*		$20		Capitol F1151
				JIMMY WAKELY				
				#1 Pop hit for Nat "King" Cole in 1950; from the movie *Captain Carey, U.S.A.* starring Alan Ladd				
11/18/50	**6**	1		19 A Bushel And A Peck *S:6 / J:10 Beyond The Reef*	6	$20		Capitol F1234
				from the Broadway musical *Guys and Dolls* starring Robert Alda				
1/20/51	**7**	1		20 My Heart Cries For You *S:7 / A:10 Music By The Angels*	12	$20		Capitol F1328
				JIMMY WAKELY				
3/17/51	**5**	12		21 Beautiful Brown Eyes *S:5 / J:5 / A:9 At The Close Of A Long Long Day*	12	$20		Capitol F1393
				JIMMY WAKELY and the LES BAXTER CHORUS				
6/2/51	**7**	2		22 When You And I Were Young Maggie Blues *J:7 Till We Meet Again*	20	$20		Capitol F1500
12/8/51	**5**	5		23 I Don't Want To Be Free *J:5 Let's Live A Little*		$20		Capitol F1816

WALKER, Billy ★62★   '62

Born on 1/14/29 in Ralls, Texas. Singer/songwriter/guitarist. Regular on *Big D Jamboree* radio show in Dallas as "The Masked Singer" in 1949. Joined the *Grand Ole Opry* in 1960. Acted in the movies *Second Fiddle To A Steel Guitar* and *Red River Round Up*. Known as "The Tall Texan."

1)Charlie's Shoes 2)A Million And One 3)Cross The Brazos At Waco 4)Bear With Me A Little Longer
5)Sing Me A Love Song To Baby

DEBUT	PEAK	WKS		A-side / B-side	Pop	$	Pic	Label & Number
6/26/54	**8**	13		1 Thank You For Calling *A:8 / S:12 Pretend You Just Don't Know Me*		$20		Columbia 21256
6/24/57	**12**	6		2 On My Mind Again .... *A:12 Viva La Matador!*		$15		Columbia 40920
11/7/60	**19**	8		3 I Wish You Love .... *Gotta Find A Way*		$12		Columbia 41763
10/16/61	**23**	2		4 Funny How Time Slips Away .... *Joey's Back In Town*		$12		Columbia 42050
				#22 Pop hit for Jimmy Elledge in 1962				
3/3/62	**❶**[2]	23		5 Charlie's Shoes *Wild Colonial Boy*		$12		Columbia 42287
9/1/62	**5**	12		6 Willie The Weeper *Beggin' For Trouble*		$12		Columbia 42492
8/17/63	**21**	12		7 Heart, Be Careful *Storm Of Love*		$10	■	Columbia 42794
12/28/63+	**22**	14		8 The Morning Paper ....*Coming Back For More*		$10		Columbia 42891
4/25/64	**7**	24		9 Circumstances/		$8		Columbia 43010
5/9/64	**43**	4		10 It's Lonesome		$8		
10/10/64	**2**[2]	22		11 Cross The Brazos At Waco *Down To My Last Cigarette*	128	$8	□	Columbia 43120
4/10/65	**8**	18		12 Matamoros *I'm Nothing To You*		$8		Columbia 43223
8/21/65	**16**	13		13 If It Pleases You/				
9/25/65	**45**	2		14 I'm So Miserable Without You		$8		Columbia 43327
6/4/66	**49**	2		15 The Old French Quarter (In New Orleans) .... *How Do You Ask?*		$7	■	Monument 932
6/25/66	**2**[4]	21		16 A Million And One *Close To Linda*		$7		Monument 943
11/12/66+	**3**	17		17 Bear With Me A Little Longer *It's Beginning To Hurt*		$7		Monument 980
3/4/67	**10**	15		18 Anything Your Heart Desires *I Gotta Get Me Feelin' Better*		$7		Monument 997
7/1/67	**18**	12		19 In Del Rio .... *Wish I Could Love That Much Again*		$7		Monument 1013
9/23/67	**11**	13		20 I Taught Her Everything She Knows .... *I Treat Her Like A Baby*		$7		Monument 1024
3/2/68	**18**	14		21 Sundown Mary .... *Oh, Matilda*		$7		Monument 1055
7/13/68	**8**	10		22 Ramona *One Inch Off The Ground*		$7		Monument 1079
				#1 Pop hit for both Gene Austin and Paul Whiteman in 1928				
11/2/68	**20**	10		23 Age Of Worry .... *Is This Desire*		$7		Monument 1098
2/8/69	**20**	13		24 From The Bottle To The Bottom .... *She*		$7		Monument 1123
				BILLY WALKER and The Tennessee Walkers				
5/10/69	**12**	12		25 Smoky Places ....*Elusive Butterfly*		$7		Monument 1140
				#12 Pop hit for The Corsairs in 1962				
9/6/69	**37**	7		26 Better Homes And Gardens .... *If You See My Baby*		$7		Monument 1154
12/6/69+	**9**	14		27 Thinking 'Bout You, Babe *Invisible Tears*		$7		Monument 1174
3/21/70	**23**	11		28 Darling Days...............................*Pretend You Don't See Me*		$7		Monument 1189
6/27/70	**3**	18		29 When A Man Loves A Woman (The Way That I Love You) *She's As Close As I Can Get (To Loving You)*		$6		MGM 14134
10/24/70	**3**	15		30 She Goes Walking Through My Mind *It's Your Fault I'm Cheating*		$6		MGM 14173
1/23/71	**3**	14		31 I'm Gonna Keep On Keep On Lovin' You *It's A Long Way Down From Riches To Rags*		$6		MGM 14210
5/8/71	**28**	10		32 It's Time To Love Her .... *She's Feeling Like A New Man Tonight*		$6		MGM 14239
				from the movie *Lookin' Good* starring Robert Blake				
7/24/71	**22**	12		33 Don't Let Him Make A Memory Out Of Me ....*A Fool And His Love*		$6		MGM 14268
11/13/71	**25**	10		34 Traces Of A Woman .... *You Gave Me A Mountain*		$6		MGM 14305
5/27/72	**24**	11		35 Gone (Our Endless Love) .... *All I Have To Offer You Is Me*		$6		MGM 14377
				BILLY WALKER with The Mike Curb Congregation				
10/7/72	**3**	14		36 Sing Me A Love Song To Baby *The Day I Was Out & He Was In*		$6		MGM 14422
3/3/73	**34**	9		37 My Mind Hangs On To You .... *Charlie's Shoes*		$6		MGM 14488
7/14/73	**52**	8		38 The Hand Of Love... *Ranada*		$6		MGM 14565
11/10/73	**96**	3		39 Too Many Memories .... *Margarita*		$6		MGM 14669
1/19/74	**39**	10		40 I Changed My Mind......................................*Heart Be Careful*		$6		MGM 14693
				written by Conway Twitty				
5/18/74	**74**	7		41 How Far Our Love Goes .... *Love Me Back To Heaven (One More Time)*		$6		MGM 14717

WALKER, Billy — Cont'd

DEBUT	PEAK	WKS		A-side / B-side		$	Label & Number
9/7/74	73	9		42 Fine As Wine .... *The Honky Tonks Are Calling Me Again*		$6	MGM 14742
3/22/75	10	18		43 Word Games .... *I Can't Say No If She Keeps Saying Yes*		$5	RCA Victor 10205
8/30/75	25	13		44 If I'm Losing You .... *I'd Love To Feel You Loving Me Again*		$5	RCA Victor 10345
12/20/75+	19	13		45 Don't Stop In My World (If You Don't Mean To Stay) .... *Honky Tonkitis*		$5	RCA Victor 10466
4/17/76	41	9		46 (Here I Am) Alone Again............................... *When The Song Is Gone (The Music Dies)*		$5	RCA Victor 10613
7/31/76	67	6		47 Love You All To Pieces .... *Sierra Nevada*		$5	RCA Victor 10729
11/27/76+	48	9		48 Instead Of Givin' Up (I'm Givin' In) .... *Curtains On The Windows*		$5	RCA 10821
7/2/77	100	1		49 (If You Can) Why Can't I ....*The Magic Touch*		$5	Casino 124
8/20/77	86	6		50 It Always Brings Me Back Around To You		$5	MRC 1003
10/22/77	64	9		51 Ringgold Georgia.................................. *Have I Told You Lately That I Loved You*		$5	MRC 1005
				BILLY WALKER AND BRENDA KAYE PERRY			
1/14/78	57	7		52 Carlena And José Gomez..................................... *Every Cheatin' Thing She Knows*		$5	MRC 1009
5/6/78	92	2		53 It's Not Over Till It's Over .... *Don't Let The Morning Sun Shine Shame On You*		$5	MRC 1014
8/26/78	82	4		54 You're A Violin That Never Has Been Played................ *Broken Pieces Of Love*		$5	Scorpion 0552
3/24/79	72	5		55 Lawyers .... *Why (Don't Ask Me Why)*		$5	Caprice 2056
6/23/79	69	6		56 Sweet Lovin' Things/			
		6		57 Rainbow And Roses		$5	Caprice 2057
9/29/79	70	6		58 A Little Bit Short On Love (A Little Bit Long On Tears) .... *I'm Gonna Leave You Tomorrow*		$5	Caprice 2059
2/9/80	48	8		59 You Turn My Love Light On .... *Love Is Free*		$5	Caprice 2060
7/12/80	74	5		60 Let Me Be The One.......................................*If We Take Our Time*		$5	Paid 102
				BILLY WALKER & BARBARA FAIRCHILD			
12/20/80+	70	7		61 Bye Bye Love/			
10/11/80	79	3		62 Love's Slipping Through Our Fingers (Leaving Time On Our Hands)		$5	Paid 107
				BILLY WALKER & BARBARA FAIRCHILD (above 2)			
4/2/83	93	2		63 One Away From One Too Many......................... *Looking Through The Eyes Of Love*		$5	Dimension 1042
12/7/85	81	5		64 Coffee Brown Eyes		$6	Tall Texan 59
7/30/88	79	3		65 Wild Texas Rose		$6	Tall Texan 60

★220★ WALKER, Charlie   **'58**

Born on 11/2/26 in Copeville, Texas. Singer/songwriter/guitarist. Worked as a DJ in the early '50s. Joined the *Grand Ole Opry* in 1967. Acted in the movie *Country Music*.
   *1)Pick Me Up On Your Way Down 2)Wild As A Wildcat 3)Don't Squeeze My Sharmon 4)Only You, Only You
   5)Who Will Buy The Wine*

DEBUT	PEAK	WKS		A-side / B-side		$	Label & Number
1/28/56	9	2		1 Only You, Only You *J:9 Can't Get There From Here*		$20	Decca 29715
10/20/58	2⁴	22		2 Pick Me Up On Your Way Down *Two Empty Arms*		$15	Columbia 41211
6/8/59	16	9		3 I'll Catch You When You Fall .... *I Don't Mind Saying*		$12	Columbia 41388
10/26/59	22	2		4 When My Conscience Hurts The Most................... *Bow Down Your Head And Cry*		$12	Columbia 41467
5/16/60	11	16		5 Who Will Buy The Wine .... *I Go Anywhere*		$12	Columbia 41633
2/6/61	25	3		6 Facing The Wall.......................*I Walked Out On Heaven (When I Walked Out On You)*		$12	Columbia 41820
11/28/64+	17	16		7 Close All The Honky Tonks ....*Truck Driving Man*		$10	Epic 9727
6/5/65	8	18		8 Wild As A Wildcat *Out Of A Honky Tonk*		$8	Epic 9799
12/4/65+	39	7		9 He's A Jolly Good Fellow .... *Memory Killer*		$8	Epic 9852
3/19/66	37	3		10 The Man In The Little White Suit... *Fraulein*		$8	Epic 9875
10/15/66	56	2		11 Daddy's Coming Home (Next Week)/			
10/29/66	65	5		12 I'm Gonna Hang Up My Gloves		$7	Epic 10063
				written by Merle Haggard			
1/28/67	38	11		13 The Town That Never Sleeps .... *The Way To Say Goodbye*		$7	Epic 10118
6/10/67	8	15		14 Don't Squeeze My Sharmon *You Lied To Me*		$7	Epic 10174
11/4/67	33	10		15 I Wouldn't Take Her To A Dogfight .... *Tonight, We're Calling It A Day*		$7	Epic 10237
3/30/68	54	7		16 Truck Drivin' Cat With Nine Wives .... *Sweetheart Of The Year*		$7	Epic 10295
8/3/68	31	11		17 San Diego .... *When My Conscience Hurts The Most*		$7	Epic 10349
3/1/69	52	10		18 Honky-Tonk Season .... *Too Many Nights In Too Many Arms*		$7	Epic 10426
8/23/69	44	9		19 Moffett, Oklahoma .... *You're From Texas*		$7	Epic 10499
2/21/70	56	6		20 Honky Tonk Women .... *Rosie Bokay*		$7	Epic 10565
				#1 Pop hit for The Rolling Stones in 1969			
6/27/70	52	7		21 Let's Go Fishin' Boys (The Girls Are Bitin') .... *You're All Dressed Up*		$6	Epic 10610
6/5/71	71	2		22 My Baby Used To Be That Way .... *Before I Found The Wine*		$6	Epic 10722
8/5/72	74	3		23 I Don't Mind Goin' Under (If It'll Get Me Over You)................... *Honky Tonk Heart*		$5	RCA Victor 0730
1/13/73	65	7		24 Soft Lips And Hard Liquor ....*It's Better Than Going Home Alone*		$5	RCA Victor 0870
8/17/74	66	8		25 Odds And Ends (Bits And Pieces)........................... *Society's Got Us*		$5	Capitol 3922

WALKER, Cindy   **'44**

Born in Mexia, Texas. Singer/prolific songwriter. Inducted into the Country Music Hall of Fame in 1997.

DEBUT	PEAK	WKS		A-side / B-side		$	Label & Number
11/4/44	5	1		When My Blue Moon Turns To Gold Again *Pins And Needles (In My Heart)*		$15	Decca 6103
				#19 Pop hit for **Elvis Presley** in 1956			

WALKER, Clay ★182★   '97
Born Ernest Clayton Walker on 8/19/69 in Beaumont, Texas. Singer/songwriter/guitarist.

1)Rumor Has It 2)This Woman And This Man 3)Live Until I Die

DEBUT	PEAK	WKS		A-side	B-side	Pop	$	Pic	Label & Number
7/10/93	❶¹	20	1	What's It To You	*Where Do I Fit In The Picture*	73	$3	■	Giant 18450
10/30/93+	❶¹	20	2	Live Until I Die	*The Silence Speaks For Itself*	107	$3	■	Giant 18332
2/26/94	11	20	3	Where Do I Fit In The Picture	*Money Can't Buy (The Love We Had)*		$3		Giant 18210
4/30/94	67	3	4	White Palace			$3		album cut
				from the album Clay Walker on Giant 24511					
6/11/94	❶¹	20	5	Dreaming With My Eyes Open	*Money Can't Buy (The Love We Had)*		$3		Giant 18139
9/24/94	❶¹	20	6	If I Could Make A Living	*Down By The Riverside*	121	$3	■	Giant 18068
1/14/95	❶²	20	7	This Woman And This Man	*Lose Your Memory*		$3		Giant 17995
5/6/95	16	20	8	My Heart Will Never Know S:10	*Money Ain't Everything*		$3	■	Giant 17887
9/16/95	2²	20	9	Who Needs You Baby	S:4 *Where Were You*	120	$3	■	Giant 17771
1/13/96	2¹	20	10	Hypnotize The Moon	S:❶³ *A Cowboy's Toughest Ride*	105	$3	■	Giant 17704
5/25/96	5	20	11	Only On Days That End In "Y"					album cut
9/28/96	18	19	12	Bury The Shovel					album cut
				above 2 from the album Hypnotize The Moon on Giant 24640					
2/1/97	❶²	20	13	Rumor Has It					album cut
				from the album Rumor Has It on Giant 24674					
4/26/97	18	20	14	One, Two, I Love You	*Country Boy And City Girl*		$3		Giant 17351
8/9/97	4	20	15	Watch This					album cut
				from the album Rumor Has It on Giant 24674					
12/20/97+	2¹	27	16	Then What?	S:4 *Country Boy And City Girl*	65	$3	■	Giant 17262

WALKER, Jerry Jeff   '76
Born Ronald Clyde Crosby on 3/16/42 in Oneonta, New York. Singer/songwriter/guitarist.

DEBUT	PEAK	WKS		A-side	B-side	Pop	$	Pic	Label & Number
12/6/75+	54	7	1	Jaded Lover	*I Love You*		$5		MCA 40487
7/24/76	88	5	2	It's A Good Night For Singing/			$5		
		5	3	Dear John Letter Lounge			$5		MCA 40570
8/6/77	93	4	4	Mr. Bojangles	*Don't It Make You Wanna Dance?*		$5		MCA 40760
				new version of his #77 Pop hit from 1968					
8/29/81	82	3	5	Got Lucky Last Night	*Maybe Mexico*		$5		SouthCoast 51146
7/8/89	70	6	6	I Feel Like Hank Williams Tonight	*Mr. Bojangles*		$5		Tried & True 1692
10/14/89	62	6	7	The Pickup Truck Song	*(longer version)*		$5		Tried & True 1695
12/9/89+	63	6	8	Trashy Women....................................	*I Feel Like Hank Williams Tonight*		$5		Tried & True 1698

WALKER, Kathy — see BLIXSETH, Tim / LEE, T L

WALKER, Wiley — see WILEY & GENE

WALLACE, Jerry ★148★   '72
Born on 12/15/28 in Guilford, Missouri; raised in Glendale, Arizona. Singer/songwriter/guitarist. Charted 13 pop hits from 1958-72.

*1)If You Leave Me Tonight I'll Cry 2)Do You Know What It's Like To Be Lonesome 3)Don't Give Up On Me
4)My Wife's House 5)To Get To You*

DEBUT	PEAK	WKS		A-side	B-side	Pop	$	Pic	Label & Number
10/9/65	23	11	1	Life's Gone And Slipped Away	*Twelve Little Roses*		$10		Mercury 72461
4/9/66	45	2	2	Diamonds And Horseshoes	*Will The Pain Fade Away*		$10		Mercury 72529
7/9/66	43	7	3	Wallpaper Roses	*The Son Of A Green Beret*		$10		Mercury 72589
10/15/66	44	7	4	Not That I Care..........................	*Release Me (And Let Me Love Again)*		$10		Mercury 72619
11/25/67+	36	13	5	This One's On The House..........................	*A New Sun Risin'*		$8		Liberty 56001
5/18/68	69	3	6	Another Time, Another Place, Another World	*That's What Fools Are For*		$8		Liberty 56028
9/14/68	22	10	7	Sweet Child Of Sunshine	*Our House On Paper*		$8		Liberty 56059
4/5/69	69	6	8	Son..........................	*Temptation (Make Me Go Home)*		$8		Liberty 56095
10/11/69	71	2	9	Swiss Cottage Place	*With Ageing*		$8		Liberty 56130
5/9/70	74	2	10	Even The Bad Times Are Good..........................	*For All We Know*		$8		Liberty 56155
				new version of his #114 Pop hit from 1964					
2/13/71	22	14	11	After You/					
2/13/71	51	14	12	She'll Remember			$7		Decca 32777
8/21/71	19	14	13	The Morning After	*I Can't Take It Any More*		$7		Decca 32859
1/1/72	12	22	14	To Get To You	*Time*	48	$7		Decca 32914
7/22/72	❶²	17	15	If You Leave Me Tonight I'll Cry	*What's He Doin' In My World*	38	$7		Decca 32989
				popularized due to play on TV's Night Gallery (the episode titled "The Tune In Dan's Cafe")					
12/2/72	66	7	16	Thanks To You For Lovin' Me	*Funny How Time Slips Away*		$7		United Artists 50971
12/9/72+	2¹	15	17	Do You Know What It's Like To Be Lonesome	*Where Did He Come From?*		$7		Decca 33036

WALLACE, Jerry — Cont'd

DEBUT	PEAK	WKS	A-side / B-side	Pop	$	Label & Number
4/14/73	21	12	18 Sound Of Goodbye/			
		12	19 The Song Nobody Sings		$6	MCA 40037
8/25/73	3	16	20 Don't Give Up On Me *You Look Like Forever*		$6	MCA 40111
2/9/74	18	12	21 Guess Who .... *All I Ever Want From You (Is You)*		$6	MCA 40183
6/15/74	9	14	22 My Wife's House *A Better Way To Say I Love You*		$6	MCA 40248
11/16/74+	20	12	23 I Wonder Whose Baby (You Are Now)..................*Make Hay While The Sun Shines*		$6	MCA 40321
3/8/75	32	12	24 Comin' Home To You .... *River St. Marie*		$5	MGM 14788
7/19/75	41	9	25 Wanted Man .... *Your Love*		$5	MGM 14809
11/1/75	70	6	26 Georgia Rain .... *In The Garden*		$5	MGM 14832
7/2/77	26	13	27 I Miss You Already .... *At The End Of A Rainbow*		$5	BMA 002
11/12/77+	28	12	28 I'll Promise You Tomorrow .... *You're On The Run*		$5	BMA 005
2/18/78	24	11	29 At The End Of A Rainbow .... *Looking For A Memory*		$5	BMA 006
			#7 Pop hit for Earl Grant in 1958			
6/3/78	64	6	30 My Last Sad Song .... *Out Wickenburg Way*		$5	BMA 008
10/14/78	38	8	31 I Wanna Go To Heaven .... *After You*		$5	4 Star 1035
3/3/79	67	5	32 Yours Love .... *There She Goes*		$5	4 Star 1036
12/1/79+	68	8	33 You've Still Got Me .... *Now That Sandy's Gone*		$5	Door Knob 116
4/5/80	56	7	34 Cling To Me .... *Paper Madonna*		$5	Door Knob 127
10/4/80	80	5	35 If I Could Set My Love To Music .... *Cling To Me*		$5	Door Knob 134

WALLACE, Ron   '95

Singer/guitarist from Independence, Missouri.

DEBUT	PEAK	WKS	A-side / B-side	Pop	$	Pic	Label & Number
9/2/95	65	6	I'm Listening Now .... *Don't Get Mad*		$3	▌	Columbia 78021

WALSH, David   '85

Born in Syracuse, New York.

DEBUT	PEAK	WKS	A-side / B-side	Pop	$	Label & Number
7/27/85	91	2	1 Alice, Rita and Donna .... *Music Man*		$5	Charta 196
10/26/85	84	3	2 Tired Of The Same Old Thing .... *Sweet Lydia's Biscuits*		$5	Charta 198
10/29/88	97	1	3 All The Things We Are Not............................. *Two Sides To Lonesome*		$5	Charta 212
2/18/89	84	3	4 Somewhere In Canada................................*She's The Newest Broken Heart*		$5	Charta 215

WARD, Chris   '96

Born in 1960 in New York City. Male singer/songwriter/guitarist.

DEBUT	PEAK	WKS	A-side / B-side	Pop	$	Pic	Label & Number
8/17/96	68	2	Fall Reaching................................. *Somewhere Between Goodbye And Gone*		$3	▌	Giant 17601

WARD, Dale   '68

Male singer. Charted a pop hit in 1964 ("Letter From Sherry").

DEBUT	PEAK	WKS	A-side / B-side	Pop	$	Label & Number
11/9/68	74	2	If Loving You Means Anything .... *River Of Regret*		$7	Monument 1094

WARD, Jacky   ★212★   '78

Born on 11/18/46 in Groveton, Texas. Male singer/guitarist.
1)A Lover's Question 2)That's The Way A Cowboy Rocks And Rolls 3)Save Your Heart For Me
4)Wisdom Of A Fool 5)Fools Fall In Love

DEBUT	PEAK	WKS	A-side / B-side	Pop	$	Label & Number
6/10/72	39	10	1 Big Blue Diamond .... *Just Hanging On*		$7	Target 0146
7/14/73	88	3	2 Dream Weaver .... *Biggest Piece Of Me*		$6	Mega 0112
4/19/75	50	12	3 Stealin' .... *I Can't Stand The Pain*		$5	Mercury 73667
11/1/75+	38	13	4 Dance Her By Me (One More Time) .... *Just Because*		$5	Mercury 73716
4/17/76	92	4	5 She'll Throw Stones At You .... *One Pillow Between Us*		$5	Mercury 73783
9/4/76	24	12	6 I Never Said It Would Be Easy .... *Nobody's Perfect*		$5	Mercury 73826
2/5/77	31	12	7 Texas Angel .... *Just Out Of Reach*		$5	Mercury 73880
6/25/77	69	6	8 Why Not Tonight .... *The Feelin's Right*		$5	Mercury 73918
9/10/77	9	19	9 Fools Fall In Love *Big Blue Diamond*		$5	Mercury 55003
			#10 R&B hit for The Drifters in 1957			
2/4/78	3	15	10 A Lover's Question *She Belongs To Me*	106	$5	Mercury 55018
			#6 Pop hit for Clyde McPhatter in 1959			
5/20/78	20	12	11 Three Sheets In The Wind/			
		11	12 I'd Really Love To See You Tonight		$6	Mercury 55026
			JACKY WARD & REBA McENTIRE (above 2)			
			#2 Pop hit for England Dan & John Ford Coley in 1976			
8/5/78	24	10	13 I Want To Be In Love .... *Hey Friend*		$5	Mercury 55038
11/4/78	11	13	14 Rhythm Of The Rain .... *From Me To You*		$5	Mercury 55047
			#3 Pop hit for The Cascades in 1963			
2/17/79	8	14	15 Wisdom Of A Fool *One Day And A Night*		$5	Mercury 55055
7/7/79	26	11	16 That Makes Two Of Us.................................. *Good Friends*		$6	Mercury 55054
			JACKY WARD/REBA McENTIRE			
9/22/79	14	12	17 You're My Kind Of Woman .... *Rainbow*		$5	Mercury 57004
1/5/80	32	10	18 I'd Do Anything For You .... *Ain't It Just Like Me*		$5	Mercury 57013
5/24/80	8	16	19 Save Your Heart For Me *It Doesn't Matter Anymore*		$5	Mercury 57022
9/13/80	7	15	20 That's The Way A Cowboy Rocks And Rolls *I Learned All About Cheatin' From You*		$5	Mercury 57032
1/24/81	13	14	21 Somethin' On The Radio .... *Let Me Be Your Man*		$5	Mercury 57044
3/20/82	32	11	22 Travelin' Man .... *Save A Little Love*		$4	Asylum 47424
			#1 Pop hit for Ricky Nelson in 1961			
7/3/82	57	7	23 Take The Mem'ry When You Go .... *Get Rhythm*		$4	Asylum 47468
3/5/83	85	3	24 The Night's Almost Over .... *Black And White Rainbows*		$4	Warner 69844
1/9/88	83	3	25 Can't Get To You From Here		$5	Electric 105

WARINER, Steve ★56★ '86

Born on 12/25/54 in Noblesville, Indiana. Singer/songwriter/guitarist. Bassist with **Dottie West** from 1971-74. Joined the *Grand Ole Opry* in 1996. Also see *Jed Zeppelin* and *Nicolette Larson*.

1)What If I Said 2)You Can Dream Of Me 3)Some Fools Never Learn 4)I Got Dreams 5)Lynda

DEBUT	PEAK	WKS	A-side	B-side	Pop	$	Pic	Label & Number
4/22/78	63	7	1 I'm Already Taken	Daytime Dreamer		$5	■	RCA 11173
8/19/78	76	3	2 So Sad (To Watch Good Love Go Bad)	Atlanta/My Greatest Loss		$5		RCA 11336
			#7 Pop hit for The Everly Brothers in 1960					
1/27/79	94	2	3 Marie	One Song In Everybody		$5		RCA 11447
11/10/79	49	10	4 Forget Me Not/					
8/4/79	60	7	5 Beside Me			$5		RCA 11658
7/5/80	41	10	6 The Easy Part's Over	It's Your Move		$4		RCA 12029
11/15/80+	7	17	7 Your Memory	Vince		$4		RCA 12139
4/11/81	6	18	8 By Now	Beverly (Take Care of Your Baby)		$4		RCA 12204
9/26/81	❶¹	18	9 All Roads Lead To You	Here We Are	107	$4		RCA 12307
3/6/82	15	18	10 Kansas City Lights	The Easy Part's Over		$4		RCA 13072
9/4/82	30	11	11 Don't It Break Your Heart	We'll Never Know		$4		RCA 13308
11/27/82+	27	17	12 Don't Plan On Sleepin' Tonight	Your Memory		$4		RCA 13395
5/7/83	23	13	13 Don't Your Mem'ry Ever Sleep At Night	Well, Hello Again		$4		RCA 13515
8/13/83	5	18	14 Midnight Fire	You Turn It All Around		$4		RCA 13588
12/10/83+	4	20	15 Lonely Women Make Good Lovers	I Can Hear Kentucky Calling Me		$4		RCA 13691
4/7/84	12	18	16 Why Goodbye	Don't You Give Up On Love		$4		RCA 13768
9/22/84	49	10	17 Don't You Give Up On Love	When Is It All Gonna End		$4		RCA 13862
12/15/84+	3	25	18 What I Didn't Do	S:3 / A:3 Your Love Has Got A Hold On Me		$3	■	MCA 52506
4/6/85	8	20	19 Heart Trouble	A:8 / S:9 As Long As Love's Been Around		$3		MCA 52562
7/27/85	❶¹	22	20 Some Fools Never Learn	S:❶¹ / A:❶¹ You Can't Cut Me Any Deeper		$3		MCA 52644
11/16/85+	❶¹	22	21 You Can Dream Of Me	A:❶¹ / S:2 I Let A Keeper Get Away		$3	■	MCA 52721
3/15/86	❶¹	24	22 Life's Highway	S:❶¹ / A:❶¹ She's Crazy For Leaving		$3		MCA 52786
8/16/86	4	19	23 Starting Over Again	S:3 / A:4 She's Leaving Me All Over Town		$3		MCA 52837
12/27/86+	❶¹	24	24 Small Town Girl	A:❶¹ / S:9 When It Rains		$3		MCA 53006
4/25/87	❶¹	23	25 The Weekend	S:8 / A:30 Fastbreak		$3		MCA 53068
5/30/87	6	28	26 The Hand That Rocks The Cradle	S:11 Arkansas		$3		MCA 53108
			GLEN CAMPBELL with Steve Wariner					
9/5/87	❶¹	23	27 Lynda	S:2 There's Always A First Time		$3		MCA 53160
2/20/88	2¹	18	28 Baby I'm Yours	S:4 All That Matters		$3		MCA 53287
6/18/88	2²	21	29 I Should Be With You	S:7 Caught Between Your Duty And Your Dream		$3		MCA 53347
10/15/88+	6	24	30 Hold On (A Little Longer)	S:15 Runnin'		$3		MCA 53419
3/4/89	❶¹	22	31 Where Did I Go Wrong	Piano Texas Girl		$3		MCA 53504
7/1/89	❶¹	21	32 I Got Dreams	The Loser Wins		$3		MCA 53665
10/21/89+	5	26	33 When I Could Come Home To You	Do You Want To Make Something Of It		$3		MCA 53738
3/17/90	7	24	34 The Domino Theory	I Wanna Go Back		$3	▮	MCA 53733
7/21/90	8	20	35 Precious Thing	She's In Love		$3	▮	MCA 53854
11/10/90+	17	20	36 There For Awhile	Why Do The Heroes Die So Young		$3		MCA 53936
9/28/91+	6	20	37 Leave Him Out Of This	Like A River To The Sea		$3		Arista 12349
2/8/92	3	20	38 The Tips Of My Fingers	When Will I Let Go		$3		Arista 12393
5/30/92	9	20	39 A Woman Loves	Everything's Gonna Be Alright		$3		Arista 12426
9/12/92	32	15	40 Crash Course In The Blues	My, How The Time Don't Fly		$3		Arista 12461
2/20/93	30	14	41 Like A River To The Sea	On My Heart Again		$3		Arista 12510
7/3/93	8	20	42 If I Didn't Love You	The Same Mistake Again		$3	▮	Arista 12578
11/13/93+	24	18	43 Drivin' And Cryin'	Drive		$3		Arista 12609
4/9/94	18	20	44 It Won't Be Over You	Missing You		$3		Arista 12672
9/17/94	63	4	45 Drive	The Same Mistake Again		$3		Arista 12744
5/27/95	72	3	46 Get Back	The Long And Winding Road (John Berry)		$3	▮	Liberty 58411
			#1 Pop hit for The Beatles in 1969					
11/8/97+	❶¹	23	47 What If I Said	Daddy Can You See Me	59	$3	▮	Warner 17263
			ANITA COCHRAN with Steve Wariner					

WARNER, Virgil '67

Born in Phoenix.

9/9/67	51	7	1 Here We Go Again	Hangin' On		$7		LHI 17018
2/24/68	65	4	2 Storybook Children	Lady Bird		$7		LHI 1204
			VIRGIL WARNER & SUZI JANE HOKUM (above 2)					
			#54 Pop hit for Billy Vera & Judy Clay in 1968					

WARNES, Jennifer '79

Born in Seattle; raised in Orange County, California. Pop singer/actress.

2/19/77	17	15	1 Right Time Of The Night	Daddy Don't Go	6	$5		Arista 0223
6/30/79	10	16	2 I Know A Heartache When I See One	Frankie In The Rain	19	$4		Arista 0430
1/12/80	84	3	3 Don't Make Me Over	I'm Restless	67	$4		Arista 0455

WARNES, Jennifer — Cont'd

DEBUT	PEAK	WKS		A-side / B-side	Pop	$	Plc	Label & Number
2/23/80	76	5		4 **Lost The Good Thing**.................... *Three Lines*		$5		Regency 45002
				STEVE GILLETTE (with Jennifer Warnes)				
2/6/82	57	7		5 **Could It Be Love**.................... *I'm Restless*	47	$4		Arista 0611
2/28/87	86	4		6 **Ain't No Cure For Love**.................... *Famous Blue Raincoat*		$4	■	Cypress 661111

WARREN, Kelly '79
Born in Lamesa, Texas. Female singer/actress.

1/6/79	85	5		1 **One Man's Woman**.................... *If I Could Just Find My Way (Back To You)*		$5		RCA 11428
11/17/79	69	4		2 **Don't Touch Me**.................... *Never Been To Spain*		$6		Jeremiah 1002
				JERRY NAYLOR/KELLI WARREN				

WASHINGTON, Jon '88
British singer/songwriter/actor.

10/22/88	73	3		1 **One Dance Love Affair**....................		$5		Door Knob 310
1/28/89	73	3		2 **Two Hearts**.................... *Lady Of The Evening*		$5		Door Knob 315

WATERS, Chris '80
Born Christopher Dunn in San Antonio, Texas. Singer/songwriter. Brother of **Holly Dunn**.

11/29/80	82	3		1 **My Lady Loves Me (Just As I Am)**.................... *Nobody's Fool*		$5		Rio 1001
3/7/81	89	2		2 **It's Like Falling In Love (Over And Over Again)**.................... *Long As I Can See The Light*		$5		Rio 1002

WATERS, Joe '82
Born in Chillicothe, Ohio. Singer/songwriter. Known as "Appalachia Joe."

9/26/81	85	3		1 **Livin' In The Light Of Her Love**.................... *Wild Honey Mountain Girl*		$7		New Colony 6811
12/12/81+	47	10		2 **Some Day My Ship's Comin' In**.................... *Jubilee*		$7	■	New Colony 6812
4/17/82	75	4		3 **The Queen Of Hearts Loves You**.................... *Love Can Be Fatal*		$7		New Colony 6813
12/17/83+	74	6		4 **Harvest Moon**.................... *Sweet Georgia Clay (I'll Be Home Someday)*		$7	■	New Colony 6814
5/26/84	90	2		5 **Rise Above It All**.................... *Pay The Price For Love*		$7		New Colony 6815

WATSON, B.B. '91
Born Haskill Watson on 7/10/53 in Tyler, Texas; raised in La Porte, Texas. B.B. stands for Bad Boy.

8/10/91	23	21		1 **Light At The End Of The Tunnel**.................... *Honkytonk The Town Tonight*		$3	▌	BNA 62039
2/1/92	43	12		2 **Lover Not A Fighter**.................... *Bottle Of Whiskey*		$3		BNA 62195

WATSON, Clyde '77

8/27/77	99	2		**The Touch Of Her Fingers**.................... *Trouble*		$6		Groovy 100

WATSON, Doc & Merle '73
Father-and-son duo. Arthel "Doc" Watson was born on 3/2/23 in Deep Gap, North Carolina. Blind singer/songwriter/guitarist/banjo player. Merle was born on 2/8/49 in North Carolina. Died in a tractor accident on 10/23/85 (age 36). Singer/banjo player.

7/21/73	71	7		1 **Bottle Of Wine**.................... *Corrina, Corrina*		$6		United Artists 276
				#9 Pop hit for The Fireballs in 1968				
9/2/78	88	5		2 **Don't Think Twice, It's All Right**.................... *Under The Double Eagle*		$5		United Artists 1231
				#9 Pop hit for Peter, Paul & Mary in 1963				

WATSON, Gene ★68★ '82
Born Gary Gene Watson on 10/11/43 in Palestine, Texas; raised in Paris, Texas. Singer/songwriter/guitarist.

1)Fourteen Carat Mind 2)You're Out Doing What I'm Here Doing Without 3)Paper Rosie
4)Love In The Hot Afternoon 5)Should I Come Home

1/25/75	87	7		1 **Bad Water**.................... *I'll Run Right Back To You*		$8		Resco 630
				#58 Pop hit for The Raeletts in 1971				
5/24/75	3	19		2 **Love In The Hot Afternoon** *Through The Eyes Of Love*		$5		Capitol 4076
				first released on Resco 634 in 1975 ($8)				
10/11/75	5	15		3 **Where Love Begins** *Long Enough To Care*		$5		Capitol 4143
2/14/76	10	15		4 **You Could Know As Much About A Stranger** *Harvest Time*		$5		Capitol 4214
6/12/76	20	12		5 **Because You Believed In Me**.................... *When My World Left Town*		$5		Capitol 4279
9/25/76	52	9		6 **Her Body Couldn't Keep You (Off My Mind)**.................... *If I'm A Fool For Leaving*		$5		Capitol 4331
1/29/77	3	17		7 **Paper Rosie** *That Tone Of Voice*		$5		Capitol 4378
8/13/77	11	15		8 **The Old Man And His Horn** *Just At Dawn*		$5		Capitol 4458
12/3/77+	8	16		9 **I Don't Need A Thing At All** *Hey Barnum And Bailey*		$5		Capitol 4513
4/8/78	11	14		10 **Cowboys Don't Get Lucky All The Time**.................... *I'd Love To Live With You Again*		$4		Capitol 4556
8/26/78	8	14		11 **One Sided Conversation** *I Know What It's Like In Her Arms*		$4		Capitol 4616
2/17/79	5	16		12 **Farewell Party** *I Don't Know How To Tell Her (She Don't Love Me Anymore)*		$4		Capitol 4680
6/9/79	5	15		13 **Pick The Wildwood Flower** *Mama Sold Roses*		$4		Capitol 4723
9/15/79	3	13		14 **Should I Come Home (Or Should I Go Crazy)** *Beautiful You*		$4		Capitol 4772
1/5/80	4	14		15 **Nothing Sure Looked Good On You** *The Beer At Dorsey's Bar*		$4		Capitol 4814
4/12/80	18	13		16 **Bedroom Ballad** *After The Party*		$4		Capitol 4854
8/2/80	15	12		17 **Raisin' Cane In Texas** *A Cold Day In July*		$4		Capitol 4898
11/1/80	13	14		18 **No One Will Ever Know** *Down And Out This Way Again*		$4		Capitol 4940
2/7/81	33	8		19 **Any Way You Want Me** *Those Eyes That Lie To Me*		$4		Warner 49648
				from the movie *Any Which Way You Can* starring **Clint Eastwood**				
2/28/81	17	13		20 **Between This Time And The Next Time**.................... *I'm Tellin' Me A Lie*		$3		MCA 51039
6/20/81	23	13		21 **Maybe I Should Have Been Listening**.................... *I'm Gonna Kill You*		$3		MCA 51127

DEBUT	PEAK	WKS	Gold	A-side (Chart Hit)	B-side	Pop	$	Pic	Label & Number
				WATSON, Gene — Cont'd					
10/3/81+	❶¹	19		22 Fourteen Carat Mind	Lonely Me		$3		MCA 51183
2/27/82	9	18		23 Speak Softly (You're Talking To My Heart)	'Til Melinda Comes Around		$3		MCA 52009
7/3/82	8	18		24 This Dream's On Me	This Torch That I Carry For You		$3		MCA 52074
11/6/82+	5	21		25 What She Don't Know Won't Hurt Her	Fightin' Fire With Fire		$3		MCA 52131
3/19/83	2¹	19		26 You're Out Doing What I'm Here Doing Without	You're Just Another Beer Drinkin' Song		$3		MCA 52191
7/23/83	9	18		27 Sometimes I Get Lucky And Forget	You Put Out An Old Flame Last Night		$3		MCA 52243
11/26/83+	10	17		28 Drinkin' My Way Back Home	My Memories Of You		$3		MCA 52309
3/31/84	10	17		29 Forever Again	Growing Apart		$3		MCA 52356
6/30/84	33	14		30 Little By Little	The Ballad Of Richard Lindsey		$3		MCA 52410
10/13/84+	7	27		31 Got No Reason Now For Goin' Home	S:6 / A:6 A Memory Away		$3		Curb/MCA 52457
3/2/85	43	10		32 One Hell Of A Heartache	Sailing Home To Me		$3		Curb/MCA 52533
6/22/85	24	17		33 Cold Summer Day In Georgia	A:21 / S:24 The Note		$3		Epic 05407
10/19/85+	5	21		34 Memories To Burn	S:4 / A:5 Get Along Little Doggie		$3		Epic 05633
3/1/86	32	15		35 Carmen	The New York Times		$3		Epic 05817
7/5/86	50	8		36 Bottle Of Tears	Stranger In Our House Tonight		$3		Epic 06057
9/13/86	29	14		37 Everything I Used To Do	S:23 / A:29 I Saved Your Place		$3		Epic 06290
3/14/87	43	13		38 Honky Tonk Crazy	Starting New Memories Today		$3		Epic 06987
8/15/87	28	16		39 Everybody Needs A Hero	S:23 When She Touches Me		$3		Epic 07308
11/12/88+	5	22		40 Don't Waste It On The Blues	I Picked A San Antonio Rose		$3		Warner 27692
3/18/89	20	14		41 Back In The Fire	Just How Little I Know		$3		Warner 27532
7/22/89	24	24		42 The Jukebox Played Along	Somewhere Over You		$3		Warner 22912
11/25/89+	41	16		43 The Great Divide	Ain't No Fun To Be Alone In San Antone		$3		Warner 22751
2/23/91	61	7		44 At Last					album cut
6/1/91	67	5		45 You Can't Take It With You When You Go					album cut
				above 2 from the album *At Last* on Warner 26329					
1/2/93	66	5		46 One And One And One	She's No Lady		$3		Broadland 192
1/25/97	44	18		47 Change Her Mind					album cut
6/7/97	73	1		48 No Goodbyes					album cut
				above 2 from the album *The Good Ole Days* on Step One 104					

WAYLON & JESSI — see JENNINGS, Waylon / COLTER, Jessi

WAYLON & WILLIE — see JENNINGS, Waylon / NELSON, Willie

WAYNE, Bobby '71
Born Robert Wayne Edrington in Childress, Texas. Guitarist with **Merle Haggard**'s Strangers.

| 2/6/71 | 61 | 7 | | Harold's Super Service | I Can't Stand Me | | $6 | | Capitol 3025 |

WAYNE, Nancy '74

5/25/74	55	12		1 The Back Door Of Heaven	The Greatest Show On Earth		$5		20th Century 2086
10/5/74	34	11		2 Gone	'Til I Can't Take It Anymore		$5		20th Century 2124
4/26/75	80	7		3 I Wanna Kiss You	Cold Carolina Morning		$5		20th Century 2184

WEATHERLY, Jim '75
Born on 3/17/43 in Pontotoc, Mississippi. Singer/prolific songwriter.

2/1/75	9	13		1 I'll Still Love You	My First Day Without Her	87	$5		Buddah 444
7/12/75	58	8		2 It Must Have Been The Rain	Mississippi		$5		Buddah 467
7/23/77	27	10		3 All That Keeps Me Going	I Hope It Never Rains Like That Again		$5		ABC 12288
11/3/79	32	11		4 Smooth Sailin'	Let Me Love It Away		$4		Elektra 46547
2/16/80	34	9		5 Gift From Missouri	All I Need To Know		$4		Elektra 46592
10/11/80	82	3		6 Safe In The Arms Of Your Love (Cold in The Streets)	All I Need To Know		$4		Elektra 47027

WEAVERS, The '51
Highly influential folk group: Pete Seeger, Veronica "Ronnie" Gilbert, Lee Hays and Fred Kellerman. Backed by Hamilton Henry "Terry" Gilkyson. Hays died on 8/26/81 (age 68).

6/2/51	8	2	●	On Top Of Old Smoky	J:8 Across The Wide Missouri	2⁸	$20		Decca 9-27515
				THE WEAVERS and TERRY GILKYSON					
				Vic Schoen (orch.); adaptation of a tradtional Southern Highlands folk song					

WEBB, Jay Lee '69
Born Willie Lee Webb on 2/12/37 in Van Lear, Kentucky. Died of cancer on 7/31/96 (age 59). Brother of **Loretta Lynn**, **Crystal Gayle** and **Peggy Sue**; distant cousin of **Patty Loveless**.

2/11/67	37	6		1 I Come Home A-Drinkin' (To A Worn-Out Wife Like You)	Since You Made A Wreck Out Of Me		$8		Decca 32087
				JACK WEBB					
				answer to **Loretta Lynn**'s "Don't Come Home A'Drinkin'"					
2/1/69	21	13		2 She's Lookin' Better By The Minute	The House Where Losers Go		$7		Decca 32430
11/27/71	69	5		3 The Happiness Of Having You	Don't Blow Your Horn, Gabe		$7		Decca 32887

WEBB, June '58
Born on 9/22/34 in L'Anse, Michigan.

| 11/3/58 | 29 | 3 | | A Mansion On The Hill | Friendly Enemy | | $20 | | Hickory 1086 |

WEBSTER, Chase '70
Born in Franklin, Tennessee. Singer/songwriter.

| 6/20/70 | 68 | 2 | | Moody River | Turn Out The Lights | | $10 | | Show Biz 233 |
| | | | | #1 Pop hit for **Pat Boone** in 1961 (written by Webster) | | | | | |

DEBUT	PEAK	WKS	Gold	A-side (Chart Hit) ....B-side	Pop	$	Pic	Label & Number

WEISSBERG, Eric   '73
Prominent session musician. Former member of The Tarriers.

2/3/73	5	12	●	1 Dueling Banjos *End Of A Dream* [I]	2^4	$6		Warner 7659
				ERIC WEISSBERG & STEVE MANDELL				
				tune written in 1955 as "Feuding Banjos" by Arthur "Guitar Boogie" Smith; from the movie *Deliverance* starring Burt Reynolds				
3/29/75	91	4		2 Yakety Yak ....*Meadow Muffins*		$6		Epic 50072
				ERIC WEISSBERG & DELIVERANCE				
				#1 Pop hit for The Coasters in 1958				

WELCH, Ernie   '89
Singer from Decatur, Alabama.

| 5/20/89 | 96 | 1 | | Who Have You Got To Lose.. | | $6 | | Duck Tape 021 |

WELCH, Kevin   '90
Born on 8/17/55 in Los Angeles. Singer/prolific songwriter.

1/21/89	41	10		1 Stay November ....*I Am No Drifter*		$3		Warner 27647
4/29/89	64	6		2 I Came Straight To You ....*Hello, I'm Gone*		$3		Warner 22972
5/26/90	39	11		3 Till I See You Again ....*A Letter To Dustin*		$3	▌	Reprise 19873
10/20/90	49	11		4 Praying For Rain ....*The Mother Road*		$3	▌	Reprise 19585
3/2/91	54	10		5 True Love Never Dies ....*Some Kind Of Paradise*		$3		Reprise 19440

WELK, Lawrence   '45
Born on 3/11/03 in Strasburg, North Dakota. Died of pneumonia on 5/17/92 (age 89). Polka bandleader/accordian player. Band's style labeled as "champagne music." Hosted own TV series from 1955-82. Charted 28 pop hits from 1944-65.

9/8/45	❶[1]	14		1 Shame On You/	13			
11/10/45	3	2		2 At Mail Call Today		$20		Decca 18698
				LAWRENCE WELK AND HIS ORCHESTRA with RED FOLEY (above 2)				

WELLER, Freddy ★147★   '69
Born Wilton Frederick Weller on 9/9/47 in Atlanta. Singer/songwriter/guitarist. Member of Paul Revere & The Raiders from 1967-71.

    1)Games People Play 2)The Promised Land 3)Indian Lake 4)Another Night Of Love
    5)These Are Not My People

4/12/69	2^2	17		1 Games People Play *Home*		$6		Columbia 44800
				#12 Pop hit for Joe South in 1969				
7/26/69	5	15		2 These Are Not My People *You Never Knew Julie*	113	$6		Columbia 44916
11/22/69+	25	10		3 Down In The Boondocks ....*Amarillo, Texas*		$6		Columbia 45026
				#9 Pop hit for Billy Joe Royal in 1965				
4/11/70	75	2		4 I Shook The Hand.....................................*We Gotta All Get Together*		$6		Columbia 45087
12/12/70+	3	18		5 The Promised Land *Goodnight Sandy*	125	$6		Columbia 45276
				written by Chuck Berry				
6/12/71	3	14		6 Indian Lake *(I'd Do It All) Over You*	108	$6		Columbia 45388
				#10 Pop hit for The Cowsills in 1968				
9/25/71	5	15		7 Another Night Of Love *Always Something Special*		$6		Columbia 45451
2/19/72	26	12		8 Ballad Of A Hillbilly Singer.........................*Good Old-Fashioned Music*		$6		Columbia 45542
6/24/72	17	12		9 The Roadmaster...*Who Do You Love*		$6		Columbia 45624
11/18/72+	11	13		10 She Loves Me (Right Out Of My Mind) ....*There's An Angel On My Shoulder*		$6		Columbia 45723
4/21/73	8	14		11 Too Much Monkey Business *It Sure Feels Good (To Be Loved Again)*		$5		Columbia 45827
				written by Chuck Berry				
8/18/73	13	13		12 The Perfect Stranger....................................*Betty Ann And Shirley Cole*		$5		Columbia 45902
12/15/73+	11	15		13 I've Just Got To Know (How Loving You Would Be).................*Georgia Girl*		$5		Columbia 45968
5/18/74	21	14		14 Sexy Lady ....*Bobby Crabtree's Grave*		$5		Columbia 46040
9/14/74	16	15		15 You're Not Getting Older (You're Getting Better) ....*Are We Makin' Love?*		$5		Columbia 10016
5/24/75	64	8		16 Love You Back To Georgia ....*Show Me The Way To Your Love*		$5		ABC/Dot 17554
9/20/75	52	9		17 Stone Crazy ....*Still Making Love To You*		$5		ABC/Dot 17577
3/20/76	42	9		18 Ask Any Old Cheater Who Knows ....*A Legend In My Home*		$5		Columbia 10300
7/4/76	44	9		19 Liquor, Love And Life ....*Celia Brown*		$5		Columbia 10352
10/9/76	56	8		20 Room 269 ....*I Drank Myself Sober*		$5		Columbia 10411
3/5/77	79	6		21 Strawberry Curls ....*When You Were Mine*		$5		Columbia 10482
5/28/77	41	9		22 Merry-Go-Round ....*One Man Show*		$5		Columbia 10539
9/10/77	44	9		23 Nobody Cares But You.......................................*Love Doctor*		$5		Columbia 10598
2/25/78	93	4		24 Let Me Fall Back In Your Arms ....*Snuff Queens*		$5		Columbia 10682
7/8/78	32	9		25 Bar Wars ....*One Of The Mysteries Of Love*		$5		Columbia 10769
10/21/78	23	12		26 Love Got In The Way ....*You Win Again*		$5		Columbia 10837
1/27/79	27	11		27 Fantasy Island ....*Take A Little Bit*		$5		Columbia 10890
5/19/79	40	8		28 Nadine ....*Too Many Memories*		$5		Columbia 10973
				#23 Pop hit for Chuck Berry in 1964				
8/11/79	44	9		29 That Run-Away Woman Of Mine ....*Atlanta*		$4		Columbia 11044
11/24/79+	33	11		30 Go For The Night ....*Two Makes One Wonderful Love*		$4		Columbia 11149
3/22/80	66	5		31 A Million Old Goodbyes ....*Sleep With Me*		$4		Columbia 11221
5/17/80	45	8		32 Lost In Austin ....*Explosion!*		$4		Columbia 11266

WELLMAN, Tiny   '88
Born Paul Wellman in Flatwoods, Kentucky.

| 6/25/88 | 85 | 2 | | Nothing Left To Lose.. | | $6 | | Lee Ann 7342 |

WELLS, Kitty ★35★ '52

Born Ellen Muriel Deason on 8/30/19 in Nashville. Singer/songwriter/guitarist. Married **Johnny Wright** in 1937. Mother of **Bobby Wright** and **Ruby Wright**. Elected to the Country Music Hall of Fame in 1976. Won Grammy's Lifetime Achievement Award in 1991. Known as "The Queen of Country Music."

1)It Wasn't God Who Made Honky Tonk Angels 2)Heartbreak U.S.A. 3)One By One 4)Makin' Believe
5)You And Me

DEBUT	PEAK	WKS	A-side / B-side	Pop	$	Label & Number
7/19/52	❶⁶	18	1 It Wasn't God Who Made Honky Tonk Angels S:❶⁶ / J:❶⁵ / A:2 *I Don't Want Your Money, I Want Your Time*		$25	Decca 9-28232
			answer to "The Wild Side Of Life" by **Hank Thompson**; also see #81 below			
3/7/53	6	4	2 Paying For That Back Street Affair S:6 / J:9 *Crying Steel Guitar Waltz*		$20	Decca 28578
			answer to "Back Street Affair" by **Webb Pierce**			
9/12/53	8	2	3 Hey Joe J:8 *My Cold Cold Heart Is Melted Now*		$20	Decca 28797
			answer to "Hey Joe!" by **Carl Smith**			
1/23/54	9	1	4 Cheatin's A Sin J:9 *I Gave My Wedding Dress Away*		$20	Decca 28931
4/3/54	8	1	5 Release Me J:8 *After Dark*		$20	Decca 29023
5/22/54	❶¹	41	6 One By One/ J:❶¹ / A:2 / S:2		$20	Decca 29065
7/10/54	12	1	7 I'm A Stranger In My Home.....................A:12 / S:15			
			KITTY WELLS and RED FOLEY (above 2)			
12/4/54	14	1	8 Thou Shalt Not Steal ....S:14 *I Hope My Divorce Is Never Granted*		$20	Decca 29313
2/26/55	3	16	9 As Long As I Live/ J:3 / S:7 / A:8		$20	Decca 29390
			RED FOLEY And KITTY WELLS			
2/26/55	6	17	10 Make Believe ('Til We Can Make It Come True) J:6 / S:7 / A:14			
			KITTY WELLS And RED FOLEY			
3/12/55	2¹⁵	28	11 Makin' Believe/ S:2 / A:2 / J:2		$20	Decca 29419
4/9/55	7	11	12 Whose Shoulder Will You Cry On A:7			
7/30/55	9	13	13 There's Poison In Your Heart/ J:9 / S:11		$20	Decca 29577
9/24/55	12	1	14 I'm In Love With You....................A:12			
12/17/55+	7	8	15 Lonely Side Of Town/ S:3 / J:7		$20	Decca 29728
12/24/55	7	9	16 I've Kissed You My Last Time S:7 / A:10			
1/28/56	3	31	17 You And Me/ S:3 / A:3 / J:6		$20	Decca 29740
		6	18 No One But You ....S:flip / J:flip			
			RED FOLEY and KITTY WELLS (above 2)			
5/12/56	11	5	19 How Far Is Heaven ....A:11 / S:15 *Dust On The Bible*		$20	Decca 29823
			KITTY WELLS With Carol Sue (her daughter)			
7/7/56	3	34	20 Searching (For Someone Like You)/ J:3 / A:4 / S:4		$20	Decca 29956
9/22/56	13	1	21 I'd Rather Stay Home A:13			
12/1/56+	6	13	22 Repenting/ J:6 / S:9 / A:11		$20	Decca 30094
		7	23 I'm Counting On You ....S:flip / J:flip			
4/6/57	8	9	24 Oh' So Many Years A:8 *Can You Find It In Your Heart*		$15	Decca 30183
			KITTY WELLS and WEBB PIERCE			
6/3/57	7	9	25 Three Ways (To Love You) A:7 / S:15 *A Change Of Heart*		$15	Decca 30288
9/23/57	10	6	26 (I'll Always Be Your) Fraulein S:10 / A:13 *What I Believe Dear*		$15	Decca 30415
			answer to "Fraulein" by **Bobby Helms**			
1/20/58	12	1	27 One Week Later ....A:12 *When I'm With You*		$15	Decca 30489
			WEBB PIERCE and KITTY WELLS			
3/3/58	3	19	28 I Can't Stop Loving You/ A:3 / S:8		$15	Decca 30551
		11	29 She's No Angel ....S:flip			
7/7/58	7	14	30 Jealousy A:7 / S:11 *I Can't Help Wondering*	78	$15	Decca 30662
10/6/58	15	11	31 Touch And Go Heart/		$15	Decca 30736
11/10/58	16	7	32 He's Lost His Love For Me			
2/16/59	5	14	33 Mommy For A Day/		$15	Decca 30804
3/9/59	18	2	34 All The Time....................			
7/6/59	12	10	35 Your Wild Life's Gonna Get You Down ....*You'll Never Be Mine Again*		$15	Decca 30890
11/9/59+	5	25	36 Amigo's Guitar *Lonely Is A Word*		$15	Decca 30987
4/18/60	5	22	37 Left To Right *Memory Of Love*		$15	Decca 31065
9/5/60	16	9	38 Carmel By The Sea ....*The Man I Used To Know*		$15	Decca 31123
12/19/60	26	3	39 I Can't Tell My Heart That ....*When Do You Love Me*		$15	Decca 31164
			KITTY WELLS And ROY DRUSKY			
3/6/61	19	10	40 The Other Cheek/		$12	Decca 31192
3/20/61	29	2	41 Fickle Fun....................			
5/29/61	❶⁴	23	42 Heartbreak U.S.A./		$12	Decca 31246
6/26/61	20	5	43 There Must Be Another Way To Live			
12/4/61+	10	12	44 Day Into Night/		$12	Decca 31313
1/6/62	21	3	45 Our Mansion Is A Prison Now			
3/3/62	5	14	46 Unloved Unwanted *Au Revoir (Goodbye)*		$12	Decca 31349
8/4/62	8	11	47 Will Your Lawyer Talk To God *The Big Let Down*		$12	Decca 31392
11/3/62	7	13	48 We Missed You *Wicked World*		$10	Decca 31422
3/30/63	13	9	49 Cold And Lonely (Is The Forecast For Tonight) ....*Is It Asking Too Much*		$10	Decca 31457
8/17/63	22	6	50 I Gave My Wedding Dress Away/		$10	Decca 31501
8/3/63	29	2	51 A Heartache For A Keepsake....................			

DEBUT	PEAK	WKS	Gold	A-side (Chart Hit)..B-side	Pop	$	Pic	Label & Number
				WELLS, Kitty — Cont'd				
2/1/64	7	25		52 **This White Circle On My Finger** *(I Didn't Have To) Break Up Someone's Home*		$10		Decca 31580
5/30/64	4	25		53 **Password/**				
6/20/64	34	4		54 **I've Thought Of Leaving You**..................................		$10		Decca 31622
9/26/64	9	15		55 **Finally** *He Made You For Me*		$10		Decca 31663
				KITTY WELLS And WEBB PIERCE				
12/26/64+	8	15		56 **I'll Repossess My Heart** *Kill Him With Kindness*		$10		Decca 31705
4/17/65	4	17		57 **You Don't Hear/**				
3/20/65	27	14		58 **Six Lonely Hours**..................................		$10		Decca 31749
8/14/65	9	16		59 **Meanwhile, Down At Joe's** *Leavin' Town Tonight*		$10		Decca 31817
2/5/66	15	13		60 **A Woman Half My Age** *When Your Little High Horse Runs Down*		$10		Decca 31881
7/23/66	14	13		61 **It's All Over (But The Crying)** *... You Left Your Mark On Me*		$10		Decca 31957
10/29/66	49	9		62 **Only Me And My Hairdresser Know/**				
10/15/66	52	9		63 **A Woman Never Forgets**..................................		$8		Decca 32024
2/18/67	34	16		64 **Love Makes The World Go Around** *.................. I'm Just Not Smart*		$8		Decca 32088
5/6/67	43	11		65 **Happiness Means You/**				
6/3/67	60	5		66 **Hello Number One**..................................		$8		Decca 32126
				KITTY WELLS AND RED FOLEY (above 2)				
8/12/67	28	13		67 **Queen Of Honky Tonk Street**.................................*Wasting My Time*		$8		Decca 32163
12/30/67+	63	4		68 **Living As Strangers** *Loved And Wanted*		$8		Decca 32223
				KITTY WELLS AND RED FOLEY				
1/27/68	35	10		69 **My Big Truck Drivin' Man** *... You Want Her Not Me*		$8		Decca 32247
5/11/68	54	8		70 **We'll Stick Together** *Heartbreak Waltz*		$8		Decca 32294
				KITTY WELLS And JOHNNY WRIGHT				
7/27/68	52	8		71 **Gypsy King** *When Hearts Grow Hard And Cold*		$8		Decca 32343
11/16/68	47	7		72 **Happiness Hill** *You're No Angel Yourself*		$8		Decca 32389
1/18/69	74	2		73 **Have I Told You Lately That I Love You?** *... We Need One More Chance*		$8		Decca 32427
				KITTY WELLS And RED FOLEY				
5/17/69	61	5		74 **Guilty Street**.................................*Shape Up Or Get Out*		$8	■	Decca 32455
8/15/70	71	4		75 **Your Love Is The Way** *It's Written All Over Your Face*		$8		Decca 32700
4/17/71	72	2		76 **They're Stepping All Over My Heart**.................*Your Old Love Letters*		$8		Decca 32795
7/24/71	49	9		77 **Pledging My Love** *... Thank You For Loving Me*		$8		Decca 32840
				#17 Pop hit for Johnny Ace in 1955				
4/1/72	72	3		78 **Sincerely** *...................................... J. J. Sneed*		$8		Decca 32931
				#1 Pop hit for The McGuire Sisters in 1955				
9/27/75	94	3		79 **Anybody Out There Wanna Be A Daddy** *...... Somewhere Down The Road*		$6		Capricorn 0240
8/25/79	75	6		80 **Thank You For The Roses** *... Loving You Was All I Ever Needed*		$7		Ruboca 122
10/6/79	60	6		81 **The Wild Side Of Life** *... I Don't Believe I'll Fall In Love Today*		$4		Mercury 57006
				RAYBURN ANTHONY WITH KITTY WELLS				
				WELLS, Mike '75				
				Born in 1964 in New Jersey.				
2/22/75	54	9		1 **Sing A Love Song, Porter Wagoner** *...................................... Detour*		$5		Playboy 6029
2/7/76	77	7		2 **Wild World** *The Lady And The Tramp*		$5		Playboy 6061
				#11 Pop hit for Cat Stevens in 1971				
				WELLS, Ruby — see JOHNNIE & JACK				
				WENCE, Bill '80				
				Born on 7/2/42 in Salinas, California. Worked as a DJ on several stations.				
9/15/79	92	4		1 **Quicksand**..................................		$6		Rustic 1003
1/26/80	85	4		2 **Break Away**..................................		$6		Rustic 1005
6/7/80	63	6		3 **I Wanna Do It Again** *... Quicksand*		$6		Rustic 1009
9/27/80	85	4		4 **Night Lies**..................................		$6		Rustic 1012

WEST, Dottie ★52★ '78
Born Dorothy Marie Marsh on 10/11/32 in McMinnville, Tennessee. Died in a car crash on 9/4/91 (age 58). Singer/songwriter/guitarist. Mother of **Shelly West**. Joined the *Grand Ole Opry* in 1964. Acted in the movies *Second Fiddle To A Steel Guitar* and *There's A Still On The Hill*. CMA Awards: 1978 & 1979 Vocal Duo of the Year (with **Kenny Rogers**).

1)*Every Time Two Fools Collide* 2)*All I Ever Need Is You* 3)*A Lesson In Leavin'* 4)*What Are We Doin' In Love* 5)*Are You Happy Baby?*

DEBUT	PEAK	WKS		A-side/B-side	Pop	$	Pic	Label & Number
11/30/63	29	2		1 **Let Me Off At The Corner** *... I Wish You Wouldn't Do That*		$12		RCA Victor 8225
3/28/64	7	21		2 **Love Is No Excuse** *Look Who's Talking (Pop #121)*	115	$10		RCA Victor 8324
				JIM REEVES & DOTTIE WEST				
8/22/64	10	15		3 **Here Comes My Baby** *(How Can I Face) These Heartaches Alone*		$10		RCA Victor 8374
2/27/65	32	8		4 **Didn't I**.................................*In It's Own Little Way*		$10		RCA Victor 8467
5/22/65	30	10		5 **Gettin' Married Has Made Us Strangers** *... It Just Takes Practice*		$10		RCA Victor 8525
8/21/65	32	5		6 **No Sign Of Living** *... Night Life*		$10		RCA Victor 8615
12/4/65+	22	14		7 **Before The Ring On Your Finger Turns Green** *... Wear Away*		$10		RCA Victor 8702
3/12/66	5	21		8 **Would You Hold It Against Me** *You're The Only World I Know*		$10		RCA Victor 8770
8/13/66	24	10		9 **Mommy, Can I Still Call Him Daddy** *... Suffertime*		$10		RCA Victor 8900
				DOTTIE WEST With Dale West (her son)				
12/17/66+	17	13		10 **What's Come Over My Baby** *... How Many Lifetimes Will It Take?*		$10		RCA Victor 9011
3/18/67	8	16		11 **Paper Mansions** *Someone's Gotta Cry*		$10		RCA Victor 9118
8/26/67	13	14		12 **Like A Fool**.................................*Everything's A Wreck (Since You're Gone)*		$10		RCA Victor 9267

DEBUT	PEAK	WKS	Gold	A-side (Chart Hit)..B-side	Pop	$	Pic	Label & Number
				WEST, Dottie — Cont'd				
12/16/67+	24	12		13 Childhood Places .... *No One*		$10		RCA Victor 9377
4/27/68	15	12		14 Country Girl .... *That's Where Our Love Must Be*		$10		RCA Victor 9497
9/7/68	19	12		15 Reno .... *My Heart Has Changed Its Mind*		$10		RCA Victor 9604
2/22/69	2¹	17		16 Rings Of Gold *Final Examination*		$8		RCA Victor 9715
				DOTTIE WEST & DON GIBSON				
7/12/69	32	10		17 Sweet Memories .... *How's The World Treating You*		$8		RCA Victor 0178
				DOTTIE WEST And DON GIBSON				
10/4/69	47	6		18 Clinging To My Baby's Hand ....*Don't Say A Word*		$8		RCA Victor 0239
12/13/69+	7	13		19 There's A Story (Goin' 'Round) *Lock, Stock, And Teardrops*		$8		RCA Victor 0291
				DOTTIE WEST AND DON GIBSON				
2/7/70	45	8		20 I Heard Our Song ....*Makin' Memories*		$8		RCA Victor 9792
7/18/70	46	10		21 Til I Can't Take It Anymore ....*I Love You Because*		$8		RCA Victor 9867
				DOTTIE WEST & DON GIBSON				
8/1/70	37	10		22 It's Dawned On Me You're Gone .... *Love's Farewell*		$7		RCA Victor 9872
10/31/70	21	12		23 Forever Yours .... *The Cold Hand Of Fate*		$7		RCA Victor 9911
1/30/71	29	11		24 Slowly .... *Sweet Thang*		$6		RCA Victor 9947
				JIMMY DEAN AND DOTTIE WEST				
3/6/71	48	8		25 Careless Hands....................................... *Only One Thing Left To Do*		$6		RCA Victor 9957
5/29/71	53	8		26 Lonely Is ....*Cancel Tomorrow*		$6		RCA Victor 9982
9/11/71	51	8		27 Six Weeks Every Summer (Christmas Every Other Year) .... *Wish I Didn't Love You Anymore*		$6		RCA Victor 1012
6/3/72	52	9		28 I'm Only A Woman .... *Baby I Tried*		$6		RCA Victor 0711
12/2/72+	28	11		29 If It's All Right With You....................................*Special Memory*	97	$6		RCA Victor 0828
4/28/73	44	9		30 Just What I've Been Looking For..............*Everything's A Wreck (Since You're Gone)*		$6		RCA Victor 0930
				Larry Gatlin (backing vocal)				
9/15/73	2¹	15		31 Country Sunshine *Wish I Didn't Love You Anymore*	49	$6		RCA Victor 0072
3/30/74	8	14		32 Last Time I Saw Him *Everybody Bring A Song*		$6		RCA Victor 0231
				#14 Pop hit for Diana Ross in 1974				
7/13/74	21	13		33 House Of Love .... *Love As Long As We Can*		$6		RCA Victor 0321
12/14/74+	35	10		34 Lay Back Lover .... *Good Lovin' You*		$6		RCA Victor 10125
5/10/75	65	10		35 Rollin' In Your Sweet Sunshine .... *Carolina Cousins*		$6		RCA Victor 10269
3/27/76	68	7		36 Here Come The Flowers .... *He's Not For You*		$6		RCA Victor 10553
6/26/76	91	5		37 If I'm A Fool For Loving You ....*Home Made Love*		$6		RCA Victor 10699
11/13/76+	19	15		38 When It's Just You And Me .... *We Love Each Other*		$5		United Artists 898
3/19/77	28	12		39 Every Word I Write .... *We Love Each Other*		$5		United Artists 946
7/9/77	30	10		40 Tonight You Belong To Me........................... *Tiny Fingers*		$5		United Artists 1010
				#4 Pop hit for Patience & Prudence in 1956				
10/8/77	57	8		41 That's All I Wanted To Know .... *Who's Gonna Love Me Now*		$5		United Artists 1084
2/18/78	❶²	17		42 Every Time Two Fools Collide *We Love Each Other*	101	$5		United Artists 1137
				KENNY ROGERS & DOTTIE WEST				
6/10/78	17	12		43 Come See Me And Come Lonely .... *Decorate Your Conscience*		$5		United Artists 1209
9/2/78	2¹	14		44 Anyone Who Isn't Me Tonight *You And Me*		$5		United Artists 1234
				KENNY ROGERS & DOTTIE WEST				
12/2/78+	49	9		45 Reaching Out To Hold You............................. *My Two Empty Arms*		$5		United Artists 1257
2/17/79	❶¹	15		46 All I Ever Need Is You *Another Somebody Done Somebody Wrong Song*	102	$5		United Artists 1276
				KENNY ROGERS & DOTTIE WEST				
				#7 Pop hit for Sonny & Cher in 1971				
7/7/79	3	15		47 Til I Can Make It On My Own *Midnight Flyer*		$5		United Artists 1299
				KENNY ROGERS & DOTTIE WEST				
10/20/79	12	15		48 You Pick Me Up (And Put Me Down) .... *We've Got Tonite*		$5		United Artists 1324
2/9/80	❶¹	15		49 A Lesson In Leavin' *Love's So Easy For Two*	73	$5		United Artists 1339
6/7/80	13	14		50 Leavin's For Unbelievers .... *Blue As I Want To*		$5		United Artists 1352
12/13/80+	❶¹	16		51 Are You Happy Baby? *Right Or Wrong*		$4	■	Liberty 1392
4/4/81	❶¹	15		52 What Are We Doin' In Love *Choosin' Means Losin' (West)*	14	$4		Liberty 1404
				DOTTIE WEST (with Kenny Rogers)				
7/11/81	16	14		53 (I'm Gonna) Put You Back On The Rack .... *Sorry Seems To Be The Hardest Word*		$4		Liberty 1419
9/19/81	80	4		54 Once You Were Mine.................... *Dream Baby (How Long Must I Dream)*		$4		RCA 12284
11/7/81+	16	14		55 It's High Time .... *Don't Be Kind*		$4	■	Liberty 1436
2/20/82	26	13		56 You're Not Easy To Forget .... *Something's Missin'*		$4		Liberty 1451
9/11/82	29	11		57 She Can't Get My Love Off The Bed .... *Hurt*		$4	■	Liberty 1479
12/18/82+	63	7		58 If It Takes All Night .... *Try To Win A Friend*		$4	■	Liberty 1490
6/18/83	40	11		59 Tulsa Ballroom .... *The Woman In Love With You*		$4		Liberty 1500
3/24/84	19	15		60 Together Again .... *Baby I'm A Want You*		$4		Liberty 1516
				KENNY ROGERS and Dottie West				
9/15/84	77	7		61 What's Good For The Goose (Is Good For The Gander) .... *Tell Me Again*		$4		Permian 82006
12/1/84	67	8		62 Let Love Come Lookin' For You .... *Blue Fiddle Waltz*		$4		Permian 82007
5/25/85	53	8		63 We Know Better Now ....*Let Love Come Lookin' For You*		$4		Permian 82010
				WEST, Jim **'80**				
11/3/79	95	2		1 Honky Tonk Disco		$6		Macho 002
12/15/79	92	4		2 Can't Love On Lies		$6		Macho 003
				JIM WEST with Carol Chase				
12/20/80	79	5		3 Slip Away		$6		Macho 008
3/14/81	83	3		4 Lovin' Night................................. *Dancin' Round And Round*		$6		Macho 009
				Stephanie Winslow (backing vocal)				

DEBUT	PEAK	WKS	Gold	A-side (Chart Hit) ... B-side	Pop	$	Pic	Label & Number
	★206★			**WEST, Shelly** '81				

Born on 5/23/58 in Cleveland; raised in Nashville. Singer/songwriter/guitarist. Daughter of **Dottie West**. Married to **Allen Frizzell** from 1977-85. Formed a singing partnership with Allen's brother, **David Frizzell**. CMA Awards: 1981 & 1982 Vocal Duo of the Year (with David Frizzell).

1)You're The Reason God Made Oklahoma 2)José Cuervo 3)I Just Came Here To Dance 4)Flight 309 To Tennessee 5)Another Honky-Tonk Night On Broadway

DAVID FRIZZELL & SHELLY WEST:

DEBUT	PEAK	WKS	Gold	A-side	Pop	$	Pic	Label & Number
1/17/81	❶[1]	17		1 **You're The Reason God Made Oklahoma** — *That's Where Lovers Go Wrong*		$4		Warner 49650

from the movie *Any Which Way You Can* starring **Clint Eastwood**

DEBUT	PEAK	WKS	Gold	A-side	Pop	$	Pic	Label & Number
6/20/81	9	15		2 **A Texas State Of Mind** — *Let's Duet*		$4		Warner 49745
10/10/81	16	16		3 **Husbands And Wives** ... *Yours For The Asking*		$4		Warner 49825
2/6/82	8	18		4 **Another Honky-Tonk Night On Broadway** — *Three Act Play*		$4		Warner 50007
7/17/82	4	18		5 **I Just Came Here To Dance** — *Our Day Will Come*		$4		Warner 29980
12/4/82+	43	11		6 **Please Surrender** ... *Being A Man, Being A Woman*		$4		Warner 29850

from the movie *Honkytonk Man* starring **Clint Eastwood**

SHELLY WEST:

DEBUT	PEAK	WKS	Gold	A-side	Pop	$	Pic	Label & Number
2/12/83	❶[1]	23		7 **José Cuervo** — *Country Lullabye*		$4		Warner 29778
3/26/83	52	10		8 **Cajun Invitation** ... *Yesterday's Lovers*		$4		Warner 29756

FRIZZELL & WEST

DEBUT	PEAK	WKS	Gold	A-side	Pop	$	Pic	Label & Number
7/2/83	4	18		9 **Flight 309 To Tennessee** — *Sexy Song*		$3		Viva 29597
9/3/83	71	4		10 **Pleasure Island** ... *Betcha Can't Cry Just One*		$3		Viva 29544

FRIZZELL & WEST

DEBUT	PEAK	WKS	Gold	A-side	Pop	$	Pic	Label & Number
11/5/83+	10	18		11 **Another Motel Memory** — *Suite Sixteen*		$3		Viva 29461
2/4/84	20	17		12 **Silent Partners** ... *Confidential*		$3		Viva 29404

FRIZZELL & WEST

DEBUT	PEAK	WKS	Gold	A-side	Pop	$	Pic	Label & Number
3/10/84	56	7		13 **Now I Lay Me Down To Cheat** ... *Let's Make A Little Love Tonight*		$3		Viva 29353
6/2/84	34	14		14 **Somebody Buy This Cowgirl A Beer** ... *Small Talk*		$3		Viva 29265
9/15/84	13	20		15 **It's A Be Together Night** ... *Straight From The Heart*		$3		Viva 29187

FRIZZELL & WEST

DEBUT	PEAK	WKS	Gold	A-side	Pop	$	Pic	Label & Number
1/19/85	21	16		16 **Now There's You** ... S:18 / A:21 *I'll Still Be Loving You*		$3		Viva 29106
4/13/85	60	8		17 **Do Me Right** ... *Easy, Soft And Slow*		$3		Viva 29048

FRIZZELL & WEST

DEBUT	PEAK	WKS	Gold	A-side	Pop	$	Pic	Label & Number
6/15/85	46	10		18 **Don't Make Me Wait On The Moon** ... *Let's Stay The Way We Are Tonight*		$3		Warner 28997
9/7/85	64	7		19 **I'll Dance The Two Step** ... *Why Must The Ending Be So Sad*		$3		Warner 28909
3/15/86	54	5		20 **What Would You Do** ... *Why Must The Ending Be So Sad*		$3		Warner 28769
9/6/86	55	10		21 **Love Don't Come Any Better Than This** ... *My Heart Feels Like Dancing Again*		$3		Warner 28648

WEST, Speedy — see ORVILLE & IVY

WESTERN FLYER '96

Group from Texas: Danny Myrick (vocals), Steve Charles, Chris Marion, Roger Helton, T.J. Klay and Bruce Gust. Named after the brand of bicycle.

DEBUT	PEAK	WKS	Gold	A-side	Pop	$	Pic	Label & Number
7/23/94	61	9		1 **Western Flyer** ... *I Would Give Anything*		$3		Step One 479
10/29/94	62	8		2 **She Should've Been Mine** ... *I Would Give Anything*		$3		Step One 485
7/22/95	71	3		3 **Friday Night Stampede** ... *album cut*				
11/11/95	74	1		4 **His Memory** ... *album cut*				

above 2 from the album *Western Flyer* on Step One 85

DEBUT	PEAK	WKS	Gold	A-side	Pop	$	Pic	Label & Number
8/3/96	32	20		5 **What Will You Do With M-E** S:24 *(album version)*		$3	∎	Step One 507

WESTERN UNION BAND, The '88

DEBUT	PEAK	WKS	Gold	A-side	Pop	$	Pic	Label & Number
7/9/88	76	3		1 **Bed Of Roses** ... *L.A. Freeway*		$6		Shawn-Del 2201
10/8/88	81	3		2 **Rising Cost Of Loving You** ... *So Much Love*		$6		Shawn-Del 2202

WHEELER, Billy Edd '65

Born on 12/9/32 in Whitesville, West Virginia. Singer/songwriter/guitarist.

DEBUT	PEAK	WKS	Gold	A-side	Pop	$	Pic	Label & Number
11/28/64+	3	24		1 **Ode To The Little Brown Shack Out Back** — *Sister Sara* [N]	50	$8		Kapp 617

recorded "live" at The Mountain State Art & Craft Fair in Ripley, West Virginia

DEBUT	PEAK	WKS	Gold	A-side	Pop	$	Pic	Label & Number
8/24/68	63	5		2 **I Ain't The Worryin' Kind** ... *It's More Than Honey (That I'm After)*		$8		Kapp 928
5/3/69	51	6		3 **West Virginia Woman** ... *One Step*		$7		United Artists 50507
9/13/69	62	7		4 **Fried Chicken And A Country Tune** ... *The Coon Hunters*		$7		United Artists 50579
7/29/72	71	3		5 **200 Lbs. O' Slingin' Hound** ... *The Hoedown*		$6		RCA Victor 0739
11/17/79	94	2		6 **Duel Under The Snow** ... *Ode To The Little Brown Shack Out Back*		$7		Radio Cinema 001
6/20/81	55	6		7 **Daddy** ... *Long Arm Of The Law (Wheeler)*		$5		NSD 94

BILLY EDD WHEELER with Rashell Richmond

WHEELER, Karen '74

Born on 3/12/47 in Sikeston, Missouri. Singer/songwriter/guitarist. Daughter of **Onie Wheeler**.

DEBUT	PEAK	WKS	Gold	A-side	Pop	$	Pic	Label & Number
7/8/72	67	4		1 **The First Time For Us** ... *A Special Day*		$6		Chart 5166
3/9/74	31	12		2 **Born To Love And Satisfy** ... *A Woman In Love*		$5	∎	RCA Victor 0223
9/21/74	97	3		3 **What Can I Do (To Make You Happy)** ... *You're Smothering Me*		$5		RCA Victor 10034

WHEELER, Onie '73

Born on 11/10/21 in Senath, Missouri. Died onstage at the *Grand Ole Opry* on 5/27/84 (age 62). Singer/songwriter/harmonica player. Father of **Karen Wheeler**.

DEBUT	PEAK	WKS	Gold	A-side	Pop	$	Pic	Label & Number
2/3/73	53	10		**John's Been Shucking My Corn** ... *Make 'Em All Go Home* [N]		$7		Royal American 76

WHIPPLE, Sterling '78

Born in Eugene, Oregon. Singer/songwriter.

DEBUT	PEAK	WKS	Gold	A-side	Pop	$	Pic	Label & Number
4/15/78	26	9		1 **Dirty Work** ... *Don't Give Up On Me*		$4		Warner 8552
10/14/78	25	10		2 **Then You'll Remember** ... *Nice Guys Always Finish Last*		$4		Warner 8632
3/24/79	84	4		3 **Love Is Hours In The Making** ... *What Do You Do With Your Hands*		$4		Warner 8747

DEBUT	PEAK	WKS		A-side	B-side	Pop	$	Pic	Label & Number
				WHISPERING WILL '79					
2/24/79	89	2		Double W .... [N]			$6		Vista 104
				parody of "Double S" by **Bill Anderson**					
				WHITE, Bill '78					
				Born in 1934. Brother of **Ann J. Morton** and **Jim Mundy**.					
7/15/78	79	3		Unbreakable Hearts .... *Lovely Love*			$6		Prairie Dust 7625
				WHITE, Brian '88					
5/21/88	70	4		It's Too Late To Love You Now			$6		Oak 1050
	★277★			**WHITE, Bryan** '96					
				Born on 2/17/74 in Lawton, Oklahoma; raised in Oklahoma City. Singer/guitarist. CMA Award: 1996 Horizon Award.					
				1)So Much For Pretending 2)Sittin' On Go 3)Rebecca Lynn					
10/8/94	48	9		1 Eugene You Genius .... *Going, Going, Gone*			$3	∎	Asylum 64510
12/24/94+	24	20		2 Look At Me Now .... *Helpless Heart*			$3	∎	Asylum 64489
5/13/95	❶¹	20		3 Someone Else's Star	S:5 *This Town*	112	$3	∎	Asylum 64435
10/7/95+	❶¹	20		4 Rebecca Lynn	S:7 *Nothing Less Than Love*	114	$3	∎	Asylum 64360
3/2/96	4	20		5 I'm Not Supposed To Love You Anymore	S:2 *Blindhearted*	101	$3	∎	Asylum 64313
6/29/96	❶²	20		6 So Much For Pretending	S:6 *On Any Given Night*	119	$3	∎	Asylum 64267
10/19/96+	15	20		7 That's Another Song					album cut
3/1/97	❶¹	20		8 Sittin' On Go					album cut
				above 2 from the album *Between Now And Forever* on Asylum 61880					
8/2/97	4	20		9 Love Is The Right Place	S:7 *Between Now And Forever*	101	$3	∎	Asylum 64152
11/15/97+	6	32		10 From This Moment On					album cut
				SHANIA TWAIN with Bryan White					
				from the album *Come On Over* on Mercury 536003					
11/29/97+	16	20		11 One Small Miracle					album cut
				from the album *The Right Place* on Asylum 62047					
				WHITE, Charley '79					
6/30/79	86	2		Rocket 'Til The Cows Come Home .... *My Babe* [N]			$7		NSD 22
				WHITE, Danny '83					
				Born Wilford Daniel White on 2/9/52 in Mesa, Arizona. Pro football quarterback with the Dallas Cowboys from 1976-88.					
2/5/83	85	2		You're A Part Of Me .... *Let It Be Me*			$6		Grand Prix 2
				DANNY WHITE & LINDA NAIL					
				WHITE, JJ — see JJ					
				WHITE, Joy '93					
				Born in Turrell, Arkansas; raised in Mishawaka, Indiana.					
10/24/92	68	3		1 Little Tears .... *Maybe In Mayberry*			$3		Columbia 74412
1/30/93	45	14		2 True Confessions .... *Let's Talk About Love Again*			$3		Columbia 74845
6/12/93	71	3		3 Cold Day In July .... *Bittersweet End*			$3		Columbia 74952
7/9/94	73	5		4 Wild Love... *You Were Right From Your Side*			$3	∎	Columbia 77565
				JOY LYNN WHITE					
	★376★			**WHITE, Lari** '94					
				Pronounced: Laurie. Born on 5/13/65 in Dunedin, Florida.					
2/13/93	44	12		1 What A Woman Wants .... *Good Good Love*			$3		RCA 62420
5/15/93	47	16		2 Lead Me Not .... *Anything Goes*			$3		RCA 62511
9/11/93	68	4		3 Lay Around And Love On You .... *Don't Leave Me Lonely*			$3		RCA 62622
4/9/94	10	20		4 That's My Baby	*Where The Lights Are Low*		$3	∎	RCA 62764
9/3/94	5	20		5 Now I Know	*It's Love*		$3	∎	RCA 62896
1/21/95	10	20		6 That's How You Know (When You're In Love)	*If I'm Not Already Crazy*		$3		RCA 64233
12/16/95+	20	20		7 Ready, Willing And Able .... *Don't Fence Me In*			$3	∎	RCA 64455
5/18/96	52	7		8 Wild At Heart .... *Do It Again*			$3		RCA 64520
7/26/97	18	20		9 Helping Me Get Over You					album cut
				TRAVIS TRITT Featuring Lari White					
				from the album *The Restless Kind* on Warner 46304					
				WHITE, L.E., And Lola Jean Dillon '77					
				White was born in Knoxville, Tennessee. Played fiddle in **Bill Monroe**'s band. Father of **Michael White**.					
6/18/77	73	7		1 Home, Sweet Home .... *It's Almost As Cold Outside* [N]			$6		Epic 50389
11/26/77	90	3		2 You're The Reason Our Kids Are Ugly .... *The Vacation* [N]			$6		Epic 50474
				WHITE, Mack '74					
				Born in Dothan, Georgia.					
12/1/73+	34	14		1 Too Much Pride .... *By The Circle On Your Finger*			$6		Commercial 1314
4/27/74	66	7		2 Sweet And Tender Feeling .... *Thou Shalt Not Steal*			$6		Commercial 1315
10/19/74	75	10		3 Ain't It All Worth Living For .... *Thou Shalt Not Steal*			$5		Playboy 6016
2/28/76	35	13		4 Let Me Be Your Friend .... *That Woman Of Mine*			$6		Commercial 1317
8/21/76	34	10		5 Take Me As I Am (Or Let Me Go)	*By The Circle On Your Finger*		$6		Commercial 1319
11/27/76	68	8		6 A Stranger To Me .... *That Woman Of Mine*			$6		Commercial 1320
3/25/78	77	6		7 Just Out Of Reach .... *You Can Have Her*			$6		Commercial 00033
				#24 Pop hit for **Solomon Burke** in 1961					
7/15/78	83	3		8 Goodbyes Don't Come Easy			$6		Commercial 00040
2/27/82	88	3		9 Kiss The Hurt Away			$6		Commercial 121

WHITE, Michael '92

Born in Knoxville, Tennessee; raised in Nashville. Singer/songwriter. Son of L.E. White.

DEBUT	PEAK	WKS		A-side / B-side	Pop	$	Pic	Label & Number
12/21/91+	32	18		1 Professional Fool .... *Hard Headed Broken Hearted*		$3	∎	Reprise 19128
6/27/92	43	11		2 Familiar Ground .... *Me Or The Misery*		$3		Reprise 18881
11/7/92	63	4		3 She Likes To Dance .... *(dance mix)*		$3		Reprise 18694

WHITE, Roger '67

| 10/14/67 | 57 | 4 | | Mystery Of Tallahatchie Bridge .... *Wild Roses* | 123 | $12 | | Big A 103 |

answer to "Ode To Billie Joe" by **Bobbie Gentry**

WHITE, Sharon — see SKAGGS, Ricky / WHITES, The

WHITE, Tony Joe '83

Born on 7/23/43 in Goodwill, Louisiana. Singer/songwriter. Best known for his 1969 pop hit "Polk Salad Annie."

| 11/1/80 | 91 | 2 | | 1 Mama Don't Let Your Cowboys Grow Up To Be Babies .... *Disco Blues* | | $5 | | Casablanca 2304 |

Waylon Jennings (guest vocal); parody of "Mammas Don't Let Your Babies Grow Up To Be Cowboys" by **Waylon & Willie**

| 11/26/83 | 55 | 10 | | 2 The Lady In My Life .... *We Belong Together* | | $4 | | Columbia 04134 |
| 3/3/84 | 85 | 3 | | 3 We Belong Together .... *Naughty Lady* | | $4 | | Columbia 04356 |

WHITEHEAD, Benny '73

Singer/songwriter from Dallas.

| 1/27/73 | 61 | 5 | | Blue Eyed Jane .... *So Long Gone* | | $6 | | Reprise 1131 |

★266★ WHITES, The '83

Family trio from Abilene, Texas: H.S. "Buck" White (guitar, mandolin, piano), with daughters Cheryl (bass) and **Sharon White** (guitar). All share vocals. Sharon married **Ricky Skaggs**. Group joined the *Grand Ole Opry* in 1984.

1)Hangin' Around 2)I Wonder Who's Holding My Baby Tonight 3)Pins And Needles

6/20/81	66	4		1 Send Me The Pillow You Dream On .... *West Virginia Memories*		$4		Capitol 5004
8/28/82	10	17		2 You Put The Blue In Me .... *Old River*		$3		Elektra/Curb 69980
12/25/82+	9	19		3 Hangin' Around .... *West Virginia Mem'ries*		$3		Elektra/Curb 69855
4/30/83	9	18		4 I Wonder Who's Holding My Baby Tonight .... *Follow The Leader*		$4		Warner/Curb 29659
9/10/83	25	14		5 When The New Wears Off Of Our Love .... *Blue Letters*		$3		Warner/Curb 29513
12/17/83+	10	19		6 Give Me Back That Old Familiar Feeling .... *Pipeliner Blues*		$3		Warner/Curb 29411
5/12/84	14	17		7 Forever You .... *(Our Own) Jole' Blon*		$3		MCA/Curb 52381
8/25/84	10	22		8 Pins And Needles .... S:8 / A:12 *Move It On Over*		$3		MCA/Curb 52432
3/9/85	12	17		9 If It Ain't Love (Let's Leave It Alone) .... S:11 / A:16 *I Don't Care*		$3		MCA/Curb 52535
6/29/85	27	15		10 Hometown Gossip .... A:25 / S:27 *No One Has To Tell Me (What Love Is)*		$3		MCA/Curb 52615
11/2/85	33	14		11 I Don't Want To Get Over You .... *Down In Louisiana*		$3		MCA/Curb 52697
5/24/86	36	12		12 Love Won't Wait .... A:35 *Daddy's Hands*		$3		MCA/Curb 52825
11/8/86+	30	16		13 It Should Have Been Easy .... A:30 *Love Won't Wait*		$3		MCA/Curb 52953
3/7/87	58	7		14 There Ain't No Binds .... *Mama's Rockin' Chair*		$3		MCA/Curb 53038
4/8/89	82	2		15 Doing It By The Book		$4		Canaan 689357

WHITE WATER JUNCTION '84

| 10/27/84 | 97 | 1 | | Sleeping Back To Back .... | | $5 | | Jungle Rogue 1004 |

★257★ WHITING, Margaret '49

Born on 7/22/24 in Detroit; raised in Hollywood. Charted 36 pop hits from 1945-67.

1)Slipping Around 2)I'll Never Slip Around Again 3)Let's Go To Church (Next Sunday Morning)

MARGARET WHITING and JIMMY WAKELY:

9/10/49	❶[17]	28	●	1 Slipping Around/ .... S:❶[17] / J:❶[12] / A:2	❶[3]			
9/10/49	6	8		2 Wedding Bells .... J:6 / S:7	30	$15		Capitol 40224 (78)
11/5/49	2[3]	13		3 I'll Never Slip Around Again .... S:2 / J:2 / A:10 *Six Times A Week And Twice On Sunday*	8	$15		Capitol 40246 (78)
2/11/50	2[1]	9		4 Broken Down Merry-Go-Round/ .... S:2 / J:3 / A:5	12			
2/11/50	3	7		5 The Gods Were Angry With Me .... S:3 / J:4	17	$20		Capitol F800
4/22/50	2[1]	10		6 Let's Go To Church (Next Sunday Morning) .... S:2 / A:6 / J:6 *Why Do You Say Those Things (That Hurt Me So)*	13	$20		Capitol F960
11/18/50	6	1		7 A Bushel And A Peck .... S:6 / J:10 *Beyond The Reef*	6	$20		Capitol F1234

from the Broadway musical *Guys And Dolls* starring Robert Alda

| 6/2/51 | 7 | 2 | | 8 When You And I Were Young Maggie Blues .... J:7 *Till We Meet Again* | 20 | $20 | | Capitol F1500 |
| 12/8/51 | 5 | 5 | | 9 I Don't Want To Be Free .... J:5 *Let's Live A Little* | | $20 | | Capitol F1816 |

WHITLEY, Keith ★164★ '88

Born Jesse Keith Whitley on 7/1/55 in Sandy Hook, Kentucky. Died of alcohol abuse on 5/9/89 (age 33). Singer/songwriter/guitarist. Married **Lorrie Morgan** in 1986.

1)When You Say Nothing At All 2)I'm No Stranger To The Rain 3)Don't Close Your Eyes

| 9/29/84 | 59 | 9 | | 1 Turn Me To Love .... *Pick Me Up On Your Way Down* | | $3 | | RCA 13810 |

Patty Loveless (harmony vocal)

2/23/85	76	7		2 A Hard Act To Follow .... *Don't Our Love Look Natural*		$3		RCA 13996
9/14/85	57	10		3 I've Got The Heart For You .... *I Gotta Get Drunk*		$3		RCA 14173
11/2/85+	14	20		4 Miami, My Amy .... S:13 / A:14 *I've Got The Heart For You*		$3		RCA 14285
6/21/86	9	26		5 Ten Feet Away .... A:8 / S:9 *Nobody In His Right Mind Would've Left Her*		$3		RCA 14363
11/8/86+	9	23		6 Homecoming '63 .... A:9 / S:20 *On The Other Hand*		$3		RCA 5013

DEBUT	PEAK	WKS	Gold	A-side (Chart Hit)..B-side	Pop	$	Pic	Label & Number
				WHITLEY, Keith — Cont'd				
3/14/87	10	16		7 Hard Livin' *A:14 / S:15 Quittin' Time*		$3		RCA 5116
8/29/87	36	17		8 Would These Arms Be In Your Way .... *Someone New*		$3	■	RCA 5237
11/14/87+	16	21		9 Some Old Side Road .... *Light At The End Of The Tunnel*		$3		RCA 5326
4/30/88	❶¹	23		10 Don't Close Your Eyes *S:5 Lucky Dog*		$3		RCA 6901
9/17/88	❶²	22		11 When You Say Nothing At All *S:5 Lucky Dog*		$3		RCA 8637
1/21/89	❶²	22		12 I'm No Stranger To The Rain *A Day In The Life*		$3		RCA 8797
				CMA Award: Single of the Year				
6/24/89	❶¹	19		13 I Wonder Do You Think Of Me *Brother Jukebox*		$3		RCA 8940
10/14/89+	❶¹	26		14 It Ain't Nothin' *Heartbreak Highway*		$3		RCA 9059
3/3/90	3	26		15 I'm Over You *Tennessee Courage*		$3		RCA 9122
7/28/90	13	20		16 'Til A Tear Becomes A Rose .... *Lady's Choice*		$3		RCA 2619
				KEITH WHITLEY AND LORRIE MORGAN				
9/7/91	2¹	20		17 Brotherly Love *Backbone Job*		$3		RCA 62037
				KEITH WHITLEY & EARL THOMAS CONLEY				
12/21/91+	15	20		18 Somebody's Doin' Me Right .... *Would These Arms Be In Your Way*		$3		RCA 62166
11/4/95	75	1		19 Wherever You Are Tonight .... *Tell Me Something I Don't Know*		$3	▌	BNA 64424

WHITMAN, Slim ★128★   '52

Born Otis Dewey Whitman on 1/20/24 in Tampa, Florida. Singer/songwriter/guitarist/yodeller. Regular on the *Louisiana Hayride* in 1950. Once known as "The Smilin' Star Duster."

1)Indian Love Call 2)Secret Love 3)Keep It A Secret 4)Rose-Marie 5)Singing Hills

DEBUT	PEAK	WKS	Gold	A-side	Pop	$	Pic	Label & Number
5/17/52	10	1		1 Love Song Of The Waterfall *A:10 My Love Is Going Stale*		$25		Imperial 45-8134
				SLIM WHITMAN (The Smilin' Star Duster)				
7/5/52	2³	24	●	2 Indian Love Call *S:2 / J:2 / A:3 China Doll*	9	$25		Imperial 45-8156
12/6/52+	3	13		3 Keep It A Secret/ *A:3 / J:3 / S:5*		$25		Imperial 45-8169
12/20/52	10	1		4 My Heart Is Broken In Three *J:10*		$25		
11/14/53	8	5		5 North Wind *S:8 / A:8 / J:8 Darlin' Don't Cry*		$25		Imperial 8208
1/23/54	2¹	18	●	6 Secret Love *A:2 / S:3 / J:3 Why*		$25		Imperial 8223
				#1 Pop hit for Doris Day in 1954; from the movie *Calamity Jane* starring Doris Day				
5/1/54	4	23	●	7 Rose-Marie *J:4 / S:5 / A:7 We Stood At The Altar*		$25		Imperial 8236
11/6/54	4	3		8 Singing Hills *J:4 I Hate To See You Cry*		$25		Imperial 8267
1/15/55	11	2		9 Cattle Call .... *S:11 When I Grow Too Old To Dream*		$25		Imperial 8281
7/3/61	30	1		10 The Bells That Broke My Heart .... *I'd Climb The Highest Mountain*		$15		Imperial 5746
2/29/64	48	1		11 Tell Me Pretty Words .... *Only You And You Alone*		$10		Imperial 66012
10/30/65	8	17		12 More Than Yesterday *La Golondrina*		$10		Imperial 66130
3/12/66	17	12		13 The Twelfth Of Never .... *Straight From Heaven*		$10		Imperial 66153
				#9 Pop hit for Johnny Mathis in 1957				
7/16/66	49	2		14 I Remember You .... *A Travelin' Man*	134	$10		Imperial 66181
				#5 Pop hit for Frank Ifield in 1962; also see #36 below				
12/3/66	54	6		15 One Dream .... *Jerry*		$10		Imperial 66212
3/11/67	56	8		16 What's This World A-Comin' To .... *You Bring Out The Best In Me*		$10		Imperial 66226
7/22/67	61	6		17 I'm A Fool .... *North Wind*		$10		Imperial 66248
11/18/67	65	5		18 The Keeper Of The Key .... *Broken Wings*		$10		Imperial 66262
3/16/68	17	14		19 Rainbows Are Back In Style .... *How Could I Not Love You*		$10		Imperial 66283
8/10/68	22	11		20 Happy Street .... *My Heart Is In The Roses*		$10		Imperial 66311
11/30/68+	43	8		21 Livin' On Lovin' (And Lovin' Livin' With You) .... *Heaven Says Hello*		$10		Imperial 66337
4/19/69	43	4		22 My Happiness .... *Promises*		$10		Imperial 66358
				#2 Pop hit for Connie Francis in 1959				
7/12/69	61	5		23 Irresistible .... *Flower Of Love*		$10		Imperial 66384
4/18/70	27	12		24 Tomorrow Never Comes .... *Come Take My Hand*		$10		Imperial 66441
8/8/70	26	12		25 Shutters And Boards .... *I Pretend*		$8		United Artists 50697
				#24 Pop hit for Jerry Wallace in 1963				
12/12/70+	7	14		26 Guess Who *From Heaven To Heartache*	121	$8		United Artists 50731
				#31 Pop hit for Jesse Belvin in 1959				
5/1/71	6	15		27 Something Beautiful (To Remember) *Jerry*		$7		United Artists 50775
8/14/71	21	13		28 It's A Sin To Tell A Lie .... *That's Enough For Me*		$7		United Artists 50806
				#7 Pop hit for Somethin' Smith & The Redheads in 1955				
12/11/71+	56	7		29 Loveliest Night Of The Year .... *Near You*		$7		United Artists 50852
				#3 Pop hit for Mario Lanza in 1951				
10/21/72	51	7		30 (It's No) Sin .... *It Takes A Lot Of Tenderness*		$7		United Artists 50952
				#1 Pop hit for Eddy Howard in 1951				
3/3/73	73	4		31 Hold Me .... *So Close To Home*		$6		United Artists 178
7/14/73	88	5		32 Where The Lilacs Grow .... *Something Beautiful (To Remember)*		$6		United Artists 269
4/20/74	82	5		33 It's All In The Game .... *Make Believe*		$6		United Artists 402
				#1 Pop hit for Tommy Edwards in 1958				
8/9/80	15	12		34 When .... *Since You Went Away*		$5		Cleveland Int'l 50912
11/22/80	69	5		35 That Silver-Haired Daddy Of Mine .... *If I Could Only Dream*		$5		Cleveland Int'l 50946
				#7 Pop hit for Gene Autry & Jimmy Long in 1935				
2/7/81	44	8		36 I Remember You .... *Where Do I Go From Here* [R]		$5		Cleveland Int'l 50971
				new version of #14 above				

				WHITMAN, Slim — Cont'd				
8/15/81	54	7		37 Can't Help Falling In Love With You .... *Oh My Darlin' (I Love You)*		$5		Cleveland Int'l 02402
				#2 Pop hit for **Elvis Presley** in 1962				

WHITTAKER, Roger   **'83**
Born on 3/22/36 in Nairobi, Kenya. British singer. Best known for his 1975 pop hit "The Last Farewell."

| 12/17/83 | 91 | 4 | | I Love You Because ....*Eternally* | | $5 | | Main Street 93016 |

WICHITA LINEMEN, The   **'79**
Vocal group from Wichita, Kansas. Led by Greg Stevens.

12/24/77	100	2		1 Everyday Of My Life		$6		Linemen 773
10/20/79	93	4		2 You're A Pretty Lady, Lady ....*Magic Hands*		$6		Linemen 10838
				THE WICHITA LINEMEN featuring Greg Stevens				

WICKHAM, Lewie   **'70**

| 3/28/70 | 36 | 10 | | 1 Little Bit Late ....*Endless Love Affair* [N] | | $7 | | Starday 888 |
| 7/8/78 | 59 | 7 | | 2 $60 Duck ....*Truckers Lament* [N] | | $4 | | MCA 40928 |

WICKLINE   **'84**
Group from Fox Island, Washington. Led by husband-and-wife team of Bob and Lynda Wickline.

3/28/81	90	3		1 Do Fish Swim?		$6		Cascade Mt. 2325
9/10/83	85	3		2 True Love's Getting Pretty Hard To Find		$6		Cascade Mt. 3030
2/4/84	78	7		3 Ski Bumpus/Banjo Fantasy II.......................*Powder Winter* [I]		$6		Cascade Mt. 4045
				WICKLINE BAND Featuring Scott Gavin				

WIER, Rusty   **'87**
Male singer/songwriter/guitarist from Austin, Texas.

4/25/87	74	4		1 Close Your Eyes.......................................*Kum-Bak Bar & Grill*		$6		Black Hat 102
				written by **James Taylor**				
8/15/87	70	5		2 (Lover Of The) Other Side Of The Hill...............*I Kept Thinkin' About You*		$6		Black Hat 103

WIGGINS, John & Audrey   **'94**
Brother-and-sister duo from Waynesville, North Carolina. John was born on 12/13/62. Audrey was born on 12/26/67.

4/30/94	47	11		1 Falling Out Of Love ....*Memory Making Night*		$3	∎	Mercury 858476
8/13/94	22	20		2 Has Anybody Seen Amy.............................*Memory Making Night*		$3	∎	Mercury 858920
11/26/94	*58*	9		3 She's In The Bedroom Crying ....*New Mexico*		$3	∎	Mercury 856296
4/5/97	49	12		4 Somewhere In Love ....*I Can Sleep When I'm Dead*		$3		Mercury 574300

WIGGINS, "Little" Roy — see MORGAN, George

WILBOURN, Bill, & Kathy Morrison   **'70**
Wilbourn worked as a DJ from Aliceville, Alabama.

7/20/68	65	5		1 The Lovers ....*Your Gentle Way Of Loving Me*		$6		United Artists 50310
1/11/69	44	6		2 Him And Her ....*You're Driving Me Out Of My Mind*		$6		United Artists 50474
6/28/69	52	7		3 Lovin' Season ....*Model Couple*		$6		United Artists 50537
				#81 Pop hit for **Gene & Debbe** in 1968				
5/9/70	34	12		4 A Good Thing *That's The Way I Want It To Be*		$6		United Artists 50660
10/31/70	65	6		5 Look How Far We've Come.........................*The Hand That Feeds You*		$6		United Artists 50718

WILBURN BROTHERS ★126★   **'67**
Duo from Hardy, Arkansas: brothers Doyle (b: 7/7/30; d: 10/16/82) and Teddy (b: 11/30/31) Wilburn. Regulars on the *Louisiana Hayride* from 1948-51. Joined the *Grand Ole Opry* in 1953. Doyle was once married to **Margie Bowes**. Also see **Webb Pierce**.

1)Hurt Her Once For Me 2)Trouble's Back In Town 3)Sparkling Brown Eyes 4)Which One Is To Blame
5)Roll Muddy River

6/12/54	**4**	18		1 Sparkling Brown Eyes *S:4 / A:4 / J:4 Even Tho*		$25		Decca 29107
				WEBB PIERCE With Wilburn Brothers				
6/11/55	**13**	2		2 I Wanna Wanna Wanna ....*A:13 My Heart Or My Mind*		$20		Decca 29459
1/21/56	**13**	3		3 You're Not Play Love ....*A:13 Look Around (Take A Look At Me)*		$20		Decca 29747
8/11/56	**10**	8		4 I'm So In Love With You ....*A:10 Deep Elem Blues*		$20		Decca 29887
12/1/56	**6**	11		5 Go Away With Me ....*A:6 Great Big Love*		$15		Decca 30087
7/8/57	**8**	2		6 Mister Love *A:8 Leave Me*		$15		Decca 30305
				ERNEST TUBB and THE WILBURN BROTHERS				
5/26/58	**9**	10		7 Hey, Mr. Bluebird *A:9 / S:14 How Do We Know*		$15		Decca 30610
				ERNEST TUBB And THE WILBURN BROTHERS				
1/5/59	**4**	19		8 Which One Is To Blame/				
1/19/59	**18**	4		9 The Knoxville Girl		$15		Decca 30787
5/18/59	**6**	19		10 Somebody's Back In Town *I Love Everybody*		$15		Decca 30871
10/26/59	**9**	13		11 A Woman's Intuition *A Town That Never Sleeps*		$15		Decca 30968
12/19/60	27	2		12 The Best Of All My Heartaches ....*Someone Else's Love*		$12		Decca 31152
7/31/61	14	6		13 Blue Blue Day ....*No Legal Right*		$12		Decca 31276
5/12/62	**4**	22		14 Trouble's Back In Town *Young But True Love*	101	$12		Decca 31363
11/17/62	21	5		15 The Sound Of Your Footsteps ....*Day After Day*		$12		Decca 31425
5/11/63	**4**	13		16 Roll Muddy River *Not That I Care*		$12		Decca 31464
9/14/63	**10**	13		17 Tell Her So *Here Comes A Million Memories*		$12		Decca 31520
2/29/64	34	4		18 Hangin' Around ....*Never Alone*		$12		Decca 31578
11/14/64+	19	15		19 I'm Gonna Tie One On Tonight...........................*Making Plans*		$10		Decca 31674
5/29/65	30	12		20 I Had One Too Many ....*Left Out*		$10		Decca 31764

DEBUT	PEAK	WKS	Gold	A-side (Chart Hit)	B-side	Pop	$	Pic	Label & Number
				WILBURN BROTHERS — Cont'd					
9/18/65	5	20		21 It's Another World	My Day Won't Be Complete		$10		Decca 31819
2/5/66	8	17		22 Someone Before Me	Something About You		$10		Decca 31894
7/9/66	13	14		23 I Can't Keep Away From You	I'm Not Gonna Dress Up		$10		Decca 31974
11/12/66+	3	20		24 Hurt Her Once For Me/					
2/11/67	70	3		25 Just To Be Where You Are			$8		Decca 32038
4/29/67	13	14		26 Roarin' Again	Go Mena Si (I'm Sorry)		$8		Decca 32117
9/9/67	24	14		27 Goody, Goody Gumdrop	You're Standing In The Way		$8		Decca 32169
10/26/68	43	8		28 We Need A Lot More Happiness	If You're With Me		$8		Decca 32386
3/15/69	38	11		29 It Looks Like The Sun's Gonna Shine	Make My Heart Die Away		$8		Decca 32449
1/31/70	37	8		30 Little Johnny From Down The Street	Which Side's The Wrong Side		$8		Decca 32608
3/4/72	47	9		31 Arkansas	Santa Fe Rolls Royce		$8		Decca 32921
				WILCOX, Harlow **'69** Top session guitarist from Norman, Oklahoma.					
9/20/69	42	13		Groovy Grubworm	Moose Trot [I]	30	$8	■	Plantation 28
				HARLOW WILCOX and The Oakies					
				WILD CHOIR **'86** Group from Nashville: **Gail Davies**, Pete Pendras, Denny Bixby, Larry Chaney and Bob Mummert.					
6/14/86	51	13		1 Next Time	Love Back		$3		RCA 14337
10/25/86	40	13		2 Heart To Heart	I Don't Wanta Hold Your Hand		$3		RCA 5011
				WILD CHOIR FEATURING GAIL DAVIES					
				WILD ROSE **'89** Female group: Pamela Gadd (vocals), Wanda Vick (guitar), Pam Perry (mandolin), Kathy Mac (bass) and Nancy Given Prout (drums). Prout married Brian Prout of **Diamond Rio.**					
9/16/89	15	17		1 Breaking New Ground	Home Sweet Highway		$3		Universal 66018
1/13/90	38	15		2 Go Down Swingin'	Wild Rose		$3		Universal 66033
6/8/91	73	2		3 Straight And Narrow					album cut
				from the album *Straight And Narrow* on Capitol 94255					
				WILEY and GENE **'46** Duo of Wiley Walker and **Gene Sullivan**. Walker was born on 11/17/11 in Laurel Hill, Florida. Died on 5/17/66 (age 54). Sullivan was born on 11/16/14 in Carbon Hill, Alabama. Died on 10/24/84 (age 69).					
1/5/46	2¹	1		Make Room In Your Heart For A Friend	Forgive Me		$15		Columbia 36869
	★324★			**WILKINS, Little David** **'75** Born in Parsons, Tennessee. 1)One Monkey Don't Stop No Show 2)Whoever Turned You On, Forgot To Turn You Off 3)The Good Night Special					
3/22/69	54	7		1 Just Blow In His Ear	Government Inspected		$7		Plantation 11
				DAVID WILKINS					
6/23/73	63	4		2 Love In The Back Seat	To My One And Only		$5		MCA 40034
9/22/73	41	12		3 Too Much Hold Back	You Can't Stop Me From Loving You		$5		MCA 40115
3/30/74	50	9		4 Georgia Keeps Pulling On My Ring	Run It By Me One More Time		$5		MCA 40200
10/26/74	77	8		5 Not Tonight	My Love For You		$5		MCA 40299
12/28/74+	14	15		6 Whoever Turned You On, Forgot To Turn You Off	Butterbeans		$5		MCA 40345
7/19/75	11	14		7 One Monkey Don't Stop No Show	Make Me Stop Loving Her		$5		MCA 40427
1/31/76	18	15		8 The Good Night Special	Let's Do Something (Even If It's Wrong)		$5		MCA 40510
7/4/76	75	5		9 Disco-Tex/					
		4		10 Half The Way In, Half The Way Out			$5		MCA 40579
11/20/76	88	5		11 The Greatest Show On Earth	King Of All The Taverns		$5		MCA 40646
1/22/77	21	12		12 He'll Play The Music (But You Can't Make Him Dance)	He Cries Like A Baby		$5		MCA 40668
6/18/77	60	8		13 Is Everybody Ready	Makin' Love In Waltz Time		$5		MCA 40734
10/22/77	21	14		14 Agree To Disagree	Her Old Stomping Ground		$4		Playboy 5822
3/4/78	68	6		15 Don't Stop The Music (You're Playing My Song)	The Only Good Part Of Leaving		$4		Playboy 5825
8/5/78	74	5		16 Motel Rooms	If There's An Easy Way For Love To Die		$4		Epic 50571
7/12/86	79	3		17 Lady In Distress			$5		Jere 1003
7/25/87	72	4		18 Butterbeans	Stone Country		$4		16th Avenue 70401
				JOHNNY RUSSELL & LITTLE DAVID WILKINS					
				WILLCOX, Pete **'82** Singer/actor. Elvis Presley impersonator. Played "The King" on the TV's *The Last Precinct.*					
4/24/82	75	5		The King			$7		M&M 503
				WILLET, Slim **'52** Born Winston Lee Moore on 12/1/19 in Dublin, Texas. Died of a heart attack on 7/1/66 (age 46). Singer/songwriter.					
9/27/52	❶¹	23		Don't Let The Stars (Get In Your Eyes)	A:❶¹ / S:2 / J:2 Hadacol Corners		$25		4 Star 1614 (45)
				SLIM WILLET With The Brush Cutters					
				WILLIAMS, Becky **'88**					
7/9/88	75	4		Tie Me Up (Hold Me Down)			$5	■	Country Pride 0011
				WILLIAMS, Beth **'87** Born in Puerto Rico; raised in Texas.					
9/27/86	82	3		1 Wrong Train	Blue Tonight		$5		BGM 71086
11/29/86	64	7		2 These Eyes			$5		BGM 92486
3/28/87	58	6		3 Man At The Backdoor	The Way I Do		$5		BGM 13087

DEBUT	PEAK	WKS	Gold	A-side (Chart Hit)..B-side	Pop	$	Pic	Label & Number

WILLIAMS, Cootie   **'44**
Born Charles Melvin Williams on 7/24/08 in Mobile, Alabama. Died on 9/15/85 (age 77). Jazz trumpeter.

| 7/8/44 | 4 | 6 | | **Red Blues** *Things Ain't What They Used To Be* | 18 | $40 | | Hit 7084 |

COOTIE WILLIAMS and his Orchestra
Eddie "Cleanhead" Vinson (vocal); issued on Majestic 7084 as "Cherry Red-Blues"

WILLIAMS, Diana   **'76**
Born in Nashville.

| 8/28/76 | 53 | 6 | | **Teddy Bear's Last Ride** .... *If You Cared Enough To Cry* [S] | 66 | $4 | | Capitol 4317 |

answer to "Teddy Bear" by **Red Sovine**

WILLIAMS, Don ★32★   **'80**
Born on 5/27/39 in Floydada, Texas. Singer/songwriter/guitarist. Member of the Pozo-Seco Singers from 1964-71. Acted in the movies *W.W. & The Dixie Dancekings* and *Smokey & The Bandit II*. CMA Award: 1978 Male Vocalist of the Year.

1)I Believe In You 2)Lord, I Hope This Day Is Good 3)You're My Best Friend
4)Some Broken Hearts Never Mend 5)Till The Rivers All Run Dry

12/16/72+	14	16		1 **The Shelter Of Your Eyes** .... *Playin' Around*		$7		JMI 12
5/5/73	12	16		2 **Come Early Morning/**				
7/28/73	33	11		3 **Amanda**		$7		JMI 24
11/17/73+	13	14		4 **Atta Way To Go** .... *I Recall A Gypsy Woman*		$7		JMI 32
3/2/74	5	15		5 **We Should Be Together** *Millers Cave*		$7		JMI 36
6/29/74	62	7		6 **Down The Road I Go** .... *She's In Love With A Rodeo Man*		$7		JMI 42
7/6/74	❶¹	17		7 **I Wouldn't Want To Live If You Didn't Love Me** *Fly Away*		$6		Dot 17516
12/14/74+	4	15		8 **The Ties That Bind** *Goodbye Isn't Really Good At All*		$5		ABC/Dot 17531
				#37 Pop hit for Brook Benton in 1960				
4/12/75	❶¹	17		9 **You're My Best Friend** *Where Are You*		$5		ABC/Dot 17550
8/16/75	❶¹	16		10 **(Turn Out The Light And) Love Me Tonight** *Reason To Be*		$5		ABC/Dot 17568
1/31/76	❶¹	16		11 **Till The Rivers All Run Dry** *Don't You Think It's Time*		$5		ABC/Dot 17604
6/12/76	❶¹	14		12 **Say It Again** *I Don't Want The Money*		$5		ABC/Dot 17631
10/16/76	2²	15		13 **She Never Knew Me** *Ramblin'*	103	$5		ABC/Dot 17658
3/12/77	❶¹	16		14 **Some Broken Hearts Never Mend** *I'll Forgive But I'll Never Forget*	108	$5		ABC/Dot 17683
9/3/77	❶¹	15		15 **I'm Just A Country Boy** *It's Gotta Be Magic*	110	$5		ABC/Dot 17717
2/11/78	7	14		16 **I've Got A Winner In You** *Overlookin' And Underthinkin'*		$5		ABC 12332
7/1/78	3	15		17 **Rake And Ramblin' Man** *Too Many Tears*		$5		ABC 12373
11/4/78+	❶¹	16		18 **Tulsa Time** *When I'm With You*	106	$5		ABC 12425
				#30 Pop hit for Eric Clapton in 1980				
3/17/79	3	15		19 **Lay Down Beside Me** *I Would Like To See You Again*		$4		MCA 12458
				also released on ABC 12458 in 1979				
8/4/79	❶¹	14		20 **It Must Be Love** *Not A Chance*		$4		MCA 41069
12/8/79+	❶¹	16		21 **Love Me Over Again** *Circle Driveway*		$4		MCA 41155
2/16/80	97	2		22 **Could You Ever Really Love A Poor Boy** .... *Livingston Saturday Night*		$7		Phono 2693
3/29/80	2³	15		23 **Good Ole Boys Like Me** *We're All The Way*		$4		MCA 41205
8/23/80	❶²	16		24 **I Believe In You** *It Only Rains On Me*	24	$4		MCA 41304
2/21/81	6	16		25 **Falling Again** *I Keep Putting Off Getting Over You*		$4		MCA 51065
7/4/81	4	15		26 **Miracles** *I Don't Want To Love You*		$4		MCA 51134
9/19/81	3	17		27 **If I Needed You** *Ashes By Now*		$4		Warner 49809
				EMMYLOU HARRIS & DON WILLIAMS				
11/21/81+	❶¹	20		28 **Lord, I Hope This Day Is Good** *Smooth Talking Baby*		$4		MCA 51207
4/17/82	3	16		29 **Listen To The Radio** *Only Love*		$4		MCA 52037
8/21/82	3	17		30 **Mistakes** *Fool, Fool Heart*		$4		MCA 52097
12/11/82+	❶¹	20		31 **If Hollywood Don't Need You** *Help Yourselves To Each Other*		$4		MCA 52152
4/16/83	❶¹	18		32 **Love Is On A Roll** *I'll Take Your Love Anytime*		$4		MCA 52205
7/30/83	2¹	19		33 **Nobody But You** *If Love Gets There Before I Do*		$4		MCA 52245
12/3/83+	❶¹	19		34 **Stay Young** *Pressure Makes Diamonds*		$4		MCA 52310
5/19/84	❶¹	20		35 **That's The Thing About Love** *I'm Still Looking For You*		$4		MCA 52389
9/1/84	11	21		36 **Maggie's Dream** .... A:10 / S:11 *Leavin'*		$4		MCA 52448
1/5/85	2¹	20		37 **Walkin' A Broken Heart** S:2 / A:2 *True Blue Hearts*		$4		MCA 52514
10/12/85	20	19		38 **It's Time For Love** .... S:20 / A:20 *I'll Never Need Another You*		$4		MCA 52692
1/18/86	3	22		39 **We've Got A Good Fire Goin'** S:2 / A:2 *Shot Full Of Love*		$3	■	Capitol 5526
5/31/86	❶¹	22		40 **Heartbeat In The Darkness** A:❶¹ / S:2 *The Light In Your Eyes*		$3		Capitol 5588
10/18/86+	3	22		41 **Then It's Love** A:3 / S:4 *It's About Time*		$3		Capitol 5638
2/7/87	9	21		42 **Senorita** A:9 / S:13 *Send Her Roses*		$3		Capitol 5683
6/6/87	4	26		43 **I'll Never Be In Love Again** S:❶² *Send Her Roses*		$3		Capitol 44019
10/24/87+	9	26		44 **I Wouldn't Be A Man** S:18 *The Light In Your Eyes*		$3	■	Capitol 44066
3/12/88	5	23		45 **Another Place, Another Time** S:16 *Running Out Of Reasons To Run*		$3		Capitol 44131
8/13/88	7	24		46 **Desperately** S:22 *You Love Me Through It All*		$3		Capitol 44216
1/7/89	5	21		47 **Old Coyote Town** *You Love Me Through It All*		$3		Capitol 44274
4/22/89	4	24		48 **One Good Well** *Flowers Won't Grow (In Gardens Of Stone)*		$3		RCA 8867
9/16/89	4	26		49 **I've Been Loved By The Best** *Won't You Love Me Like You Love Me*		$3		RCA 9017
1/27/90	4	26		50 **Just As Long As I Have You** *Why Get Up*		$3		RCA 9119

WILLIAMS, Don — Cont'd

DEBUT	PEAK	WKS		A-side / B-side		$		Label & Number
6/16/90	22	21		51 Maybe That's All It Takes.................................... *We're All The Way*		$3		RCA 2507
9/15/90	2²	20		52 Back In My Younger Days *Diamonds To Dust*		$3		RCA 2677
1/19/91	4	20		53 True Love *Learn To Let It Go*		$3		RCA 2745
5/18/91	7	20		54 Lord Have Mercy On A Country Boy *Jamaica Farewell*		$3		RCA 2820
2/15/92	72	3		55 Too Much Love..................................... *Back On The Street Again*		$3		RCA 62180
6/6/92	73	2		56 It's Who You Love .... *The Old Trail*		$3		RCA 62240

WILLIAMS, Hank ★41★   '50

Born Hiram King Williams on 9/17/23 in Mount Olive, Alabama. Died of alcohol/drug abuse on 1/1/53 (age 29). Singer/songwriter/guitarist. Hosted own radio show on WSFA in Montgomery; billed as "The Singing Kid." Formed his own band, **The Drifting Cowboys,** as a teenager. Married Audrey Sheppard in 1944; their son is **Hank Williams, Jr.**. First recorded for Sterling in 1946. Regular on the *Louisiana Hayride* from 1948-49, with the *Grand Ole Opry* from 1949-52. In 1952, divorced Audrey, was fired from the Opry in August and married Billie Jean Jones Eshlimar (**Billie Jean Horton**) who later married **Johnny Horton**. Elected to the Country Music Hall of Fame in 1961. Also recorded as Luke The Drifter. Won Grammy's Lifetime Achievement Award in 1987. Inducted into the Rock and Roll Hall of Fame in 1987 as a forefather of rock 'n' roll.

   1)Lovesick Blues 2)Jambalaya (On The Bayou) 3)Kaw-Liga 4)Why Don't You Love Me 5)Hey, Good Lookin'

HANK WILLIAMS With His Drifting Cowboys:

DEBUT	PEAK	WKS		A-side / B-side	Pop	$		Label & Number
8/9/47	4	3		1 Move It On Over *(Last Night) I Heard You Crying In Your Sleep*		$75		MGM 10033
7/3/48	14	1		2 Honky Tonkin'.. *J:14 I'll Be A Bachelor 'Til I Die* first released in 1947 on Sterling 210 ($300)		$50		MGM 10171
7/24/48	6	3		3 I'm A Long Gone Daddy *J:8 Blues Come Around*		$40		MGM 10212
3/5/49	12	2		4 Mansion On The Hill................... *J:12 I Can't Get You Off Of My Mind*		$40		MGM 10328
3/5/49	❶16	42	●	5 Lovesick Blues/ *S:❶16 / J:❶10*	24			
7/9/49	6	2		6 Never Again (Will I Knock On Your Door) *J:6*		$40		MGM 10352
5/14/49	2²	29		7 Wedding Bells *S:2 / J:2 I've Just Told Mama Goodbye*		$40		MGM 10401
7/23/49	5	11		8 Mind Your Own Business *J:5 / S:6 There'll Be No Tear-Drops Tonight*		$30		MGM 10461
10/1/49	4	9		9 You're Gonna Change (Or I'm Gonna Leave)/ *S:4 / J:8*				
10/8/49	12	3		10 Lost Highway *S:12 / J:14*		$30		MGM 10506
11/26/49	2¹	12		11 My Bucket's Got A Hole In It *S:2 / J:2 / A:5 I'm So Lonesome I Could Cry*		$30		MGM 10560
2/18/50	5	5		12 I Just Don't Like This Kind Of Livin' *S:5 / J:5 / A:8 May You Never Be Alone*		$40		MGM K10609
3/25/50	❶8	21		13 Long Gone Lonesome Blues/ *A:❶8 / S:❶5 / J:❶4*				
4/15/50	9	1		14 My Son Calls Another Man Daddy *J:9*		$40		MGM K10645
5/27/50	❶10	25		15 Why Don't You Love Me *A:❶10 / S:❶6 / J:❶5 A House Without Love* also see #41 below		$40		MGM K10696
10/7/50	5	6		16 They'll Never Take Her Love From Me/ *A:5*				
10/14/50	9	1		17 Why Should We Try Anymore *S:9*		$40		MGM K10760
11/18/50	❶1	15		18 Moanin' The Blues/ *A:❶1 / S:2 / J:3*				
11/18/50	9	4		19 Nobody's Lonesome For Me *A:❶1 / S:2 / J:4*		$40		MGM K10832
3/17/51	❶1	46	●	20 Cold, Cold Heart/ *A:❶1 / S:2 / J:4*				
3/3/51	8	4		21 Dear John *J:8 / S:10*		$40		MGM K10904
6/9/51	2²	13		22 I Can't Help It (If I'm Still In Love With You)/ *A:2 / J:3 / S:6*				
5/26/51	3	10		23 Howlin' At The Moon *J:3 / S:4 / A:6*		$40		MGM K10961
7/14/51	❶8	25		24 Hey, Good Lookin' *A:❶8 / S:2 / J:2 My Heart Would Know*		$30		MGM K11000
10/20/51	4	18		25 Crazy Heart/ *J:4 / A:6 / S:7*				
10/20/51	9	2		26 Lonesome Whistle *A:9*		$30		MGM K11054
12/22/51+	4	15		27 Baby, We're Really In Love *A:4 / J:4 / S:8 I'd Still Want You*		$30		MGM K11100
3/1/52	2¹	12		28 Honky Tonk Blues *J:2 / S:7 / A:10 I'm Sorry For You, My Friend*		$30		MGM K11160
5/3/52	2²	16		29 Half As Much *S:2 / J:4 / A:7 Let's Turn Back The Years*		$30		MGM K11202
8/16/52	❶14	29	●	30 Jambalaya (On The Bayou) *S:❶14 / A:❶14 / J:❶12 Window Shopping*	20	$30		MGM K11283
10/11/52	2¹	12		31 Settin' The Woods On Fire/ *A:2 / J:4 / S:5*				
11/15/52	10	1		32 You Win Again *J:10*		$30		MGM K11318
12/20/52+	❶1	13		33 I'll Never Get Out Of This World Alive *S:❶1 / J:4 / A:7 I Could Never Be Ashamed Of You*		$30		MGM 11366
2/21/53	❶13	19		34 Kaw-Liga/ *S:❶13 / A:❶8 / J:❶8*				
2/21/53	❶6	23		35 Your Cheatin' Heart *A:❶8 / J:❶2 / S:2*		$30		MGM 11416
5/16/53	❶4	13		36 Take These Chains From My Heart *S:❶4 / J:2 / A:3 Ramblin' Man*		$30		MGM 11479
7/25/53	4	9		37 I Won't Be Home No More *S:4 / J:4 / A:5 My Love For You (Has Turned To Hate)*		$30		MGM 11533
10/10/53	7	2		38 Weary Blues From Waitin' *S:7 / J:7 / A:9 I Can't Escape From You*		$30		MGM 11574
4/30/55	9	3		39 Please Don't Let Me Love You *J:9 Faded Love And Winter Roses*		$25		MGM 11928

HANK WILLIAMS:

DEBUT	PEAK	WKS		A-side / B-side	Pop	$		Label & Number
6/11/66	43	4		40 I'm So Lonesome I Could Cry .... *You Win Again* recorded in 1949 (B-side of #11 above); features new instrumental backing	109	$10		MGM 13489
10/9/76	61	7		41 Why Don't You Love Me .... *Ramblin' Man* [R] same version as #15 above		$5		MGM 14849
2/4/89	7	14		42 There's A Tear In My Beer *You Brought Me Down To Earth* **HANK WILLIAMS, JR.** with Hank Williams, Sr. Hank Sr.'s vocals dubbed in from a vinyl record		$3	■	Warner/Curb 27584

WILLIAMS, Hank Jr. ★14★ '70

Born Randall Hank Williams on 5/26/49 in Shreveport, Louisiana; raised in Nashville. Singer/songwriter/guitarist. Son of **Hank Williams**. Injured in a mountain climbing accident on 8/8/75 in Montana, returned to performing in 1977. Starred in movie *A Time To Sing*. His father gave him the nickname "Bocephus." Also recorded as **Luke The Drifter, Jr.** CMA Awards: 1987 & 1988 Entertainer of the Year.

1)*All For The Love Of Sunshine* 2)*Mind Your Own Business* 3)*Eleven Roses* 4)*I'm For Love* 5)*Born To Boogie*

DEBUT	PEAK	WKS		A-side (Chart Hit) / B-side	Pop	$	Pic	Label & Number
2/8/64	5	19	1	**Long Gone Lonesome Blues** — *Doesn't Anybody Know My Name*	67	$12	■	MGM 13208
7/25/64	42	6	2	**Guess What, That's Right, She's Gone** ....*Goin' Steady With The Blues*		$12	■	MGM 13253
12/26/64+	46	5	3	**Endless Sleep**............................*My Bucket's Got A Hole In It*	90	$12		MGM 13278
				#5 Pop hit for Jody Reynolds in 1958				
5/28/66	5	19	4	**Standing In The Shadows** — *It's Written All Over Your Face*		$10		MGM 13504
12/24/66+	43	13	5	**I Can't Take It No Longer**.....................*You Can Hear A Tear Drop*		$10		MGM 13640
6/17/67	60	4	6	**I'm In No Condition** ....*I'm Gonna Break Your Heart*		$10		MGM 13730
8/26/67	46	8	7	**Nobody's Child**.............................*Next Best Thing To Nothing*		$10		MGM 13782
1/13/68	31	11	8	**I Wouldn't Change A Thing About You (But Your Name)**.................................*No Meaning And No End*		$10		MGM 13857
6/1/68	51	6	9	**The Old Ryman**...................*I Wonder Where You Are Tonight*		$10		MGM 13922
8/31/68	3	16	10	**It's All Over But The Crying** — *Rock In My Shoe*		$8		MGM 13968
				from the movie *A Time to Sing* starring Williams				
11/9/68	39	8	11	**I Was With Red Foley (The Night He Passed Away)**..................*On Trial*		$8		MGM 14002
				LUKE THE DRIFTER, JR.				
1/18/69	14	12	12	**Custody**.................................*My Home Town Circle "R"*		$8		MGM 14020
				LUKE THE DRIFTER, JR.				
2/22/69	16	10	13	**A Baby Again**...*Swim Across A Tear*		$8		MGM 14024
5/3/69	3	14	14	**Cajun Baby** — *My Heart Won't Let Me Go*	107	$7		MGM 14047
				also see #82 below				
7/5/69	37	8	15	**Be Careful Of Stones That You Throw**...............*Book Of Memories*		$7		MGM 14062
				LUKE THE DRIFTER, JR. #31 Pop hit for Dion in 1963				
9/13/69	4	14	16	**I'd Rather Be Gone** — *Try Try Again*		$7		MGM 14077
1/3/70	36	8	17	**Something To Think About**.....................*(There Must Be) A Better Way To Live*		$7		MGM 14095
				LUKE THE DRIFTER, JR.				
3/7/70	12	13	18	**I Walked Out On Heaven** ....*Your Love's One Thing (I Ain't Forgot)*		$7		MGM 14107
5/23/70	36	9	19	**It Don't Take But One Mistake** ....*Goin' Home*		$7		MGM 14120
				LUKE THE DRIFTER, JR.				
7/4/70	23	12	20	**Removing The Shadow** ....*Party People*		$7		MGM 14136
				HANK WILLIAMS, JR. and LOIS JOHNSON				
8/1/70	❶²	15	21	**All For The Love Of Sunshine** — *Ballad Of The Moonshine*		$7		MGM 14152
				HANK WILLIAMS, JR. With THE MIKE CURB CONGREGATION from the movie *Kelly's Heroes* starring Clint Eastwood				
10/3/70	12	13	22	**So Sad (To Watch Good Love Go Bad)**.................*Let's Talk It Over Again*		$7		MGM 14164
				HANK WILLIAMS, JR. & LOIS JOHNSON #7 Pop hit for The Everly Brothers in 1960				
12/19/70+	3	15	23	**Rainin' In My Heart** — *A-EEE*	108	$7		MGM 14194
				HANK WILLIAMS, JR. With THE MIKE CURB CONGREGATION #34 Pop hit for Slim Harpo in 1961				
4/24/71	6	14	24	**I've Got A Right To Cry** — *Jesus Loved The Devil Out Of Me*	102	$7		MGM 14240
8/21/71	18	14	25	**After All They All Used To Belong To Me** ....*Happy Kind Of Sadness*		$7		MGM 14277
12/18/71+	7	14	26	**Ain't That A Shame** — *The End Of A Bad Day*		$7		MGM 14317
				HANK WILLIAMS, JR. with The Mike Curb Congregation #1 R&B hit for Fats Domino in 1955				
4/1/72	14	14	27	**Send Me Some Lovin'**.................*What We Used To Hang On To (Is Gone)*		$7		MGM 14356
				HANK WILLIAMS, JR. & LOIS JOHNSON				
4/29/72	❶²	16	28	**Eleven Roses** — *Richmond Valley Breeze*		$7		MGM 14371
9/16/72	3	16	29	**Pride's Not Hard To Swallow** — *Hamburger Steak, Holiday Inn*		$7		MGM 14421
11/18/72+	22	11	30	**Whole Lotta Loving** ....*Why Should We Try Anymore*		$7		MGM 14443
				HANK WILLIAMS, JR. & LOIS JOHNSON #6 Pop hit for Fats Domino in 1959				
2/24/73	23	13	31	**After You** ....*Knoxville Courthouse Blues*		$6		MGM 14486
6/16/73	12	14	32	**Hank** ....*Grandpa Shepherd*		$6		MGM 14550
10/20/73	4	18	33	**The Last Love Song** — *Country Music-Those Tear Jerking Songs*		$6		MGM 14656
3/9/74	13	12	34	**Rainy Night In Georgia** ....*Country Music In My Soul*		$6		MGM 14700
				#4 Pop hit for Brook Benton in 1970				
7/6/74	7	13	35	**I'll Think Of Something** — *Country Music Lover*		$6		MGM 14731
11/2/74	19	12	36	**Angels Are Hard To Find**.....................*Getting Over You*		$6		MGM 14755
				also see #93 below				
4/12/75	26	10	37	**Where He's Going, I've Already Been/**				
		4	38	**The Kind Of Woman I Got**.........................		$6		MGM 14794
7/5/75	29	13	39	**The Same Old Story**...............................*Country Love*		$6		MGM 14813
11/8/75	19	13	40	**Stoned At The Jukebox** ....*There's A Devil In The Bottle*		$6		MGM 14833
4/10/76	38	9	41	**Living Proof** ....*Brothers Of The Road*		$6		MGM 14845
4/9/77	27	12	42	**Mobile Boogie** ....*She's The Star (On The Stage Of My Mind)*		$5		Warner/Curb 8361
8/20/77	59	7	43	**I'm Not Responsible/**		$5		
		5	44	**(Honey, Won't You) Call Me**..............................		$5		Warner/Curb 8410

WILLIAMS, Hank Jr. — Cont'd

DEBUT	PEAK	WKS	A-side (Chart Hit) / B-side	Pop	$	Pic	Label & Number
10/1/77	47	9	45 One Night Stands .... *I'm Not Responsible*		$5		Warner/Curb 8451
1/7/78	38	9	46 Feelin' Better........... *Once And For All*		$5		Warner/Curb 8507
5/13/78	76	4	47 You Love The Thunder........... *I Just Ain't Been Able* written and first recorded by Jackson Browne on his 1978 *Running On Empty* album		$5		Warner/Curb 8564
8/12/78	15	12	48 I Fought The Law........... *It's Different With You* #9 Pop hit for the Bobby Fuller Four in 1966		$5		Warner/Curb 8641
11/25/78	54	6	49 Old Flame, New Fire .... *Payin' On Time*		$5		Warner/Curb 8715
3/31/79	49	6	50 To Love Somebody .... *We Can Work It All Out* #17 Pop hit for the **Bee Gees** in 1967		$4		Elektra/Curb 46018
6/9/79	4	15	51 Family Tradition *Paying On Time*	104	$4		Elektra/Curb 46046
10/6/79	2²	14	52 Whiskey Bent And Hell Bound *O.D.'d In Denver*		$4		Elektra/Curb 46535
2/9/80	5	13	53 Women I've Never Had *Tired Of Being Johnny B. Good*		$4		Elektra/Curb 46593
5/17/80	12	12	54 Kaw-Liga *The American Way*		$4		Elektra/Curb 46636
8/30/80	6	13	55 Old Habits *Won't It Be Nice*		$4		Elektra/Curb 47016
2/7/81	❶¹	13	56 Texas Women *You Can't Find Many Kissers*		$4		Elektra/Curb 47102
5/30/81	❶¹	14	57 Dixie On My Mind *Ramblin' Man*		$4		Elektra/Curb 47137
9/5/81	❶¹	19	58 All My Rowdy Friends (Have Settled Down) *Everytime I Hear That Song*		$4		Elektra/Curb 47191
1/23/82	2³	20	59 A Country Boy Can Survive *Weatherman*		$4		Elektra/Curb 47257
6/5/82	❶¹	15	60 Honky Tonkin' *High And Pressurized*		$4		Elektra/Curb 47462
10/9/82	5	16	61 The American Dream/				
		16	62 If Heaven Ain't A Lot Like Dixie		$4		Elektra/Curb 69960
1/29/83	4	18	63 Gonna Go Huntin' Tonight *Twodot Montana*		$4		Elektra/Curb 69846
6/4/83	6	16	64 Leave Them Boys Alone *The Girl On The Front Row At Fort Worth* **Waylon Jennings** and **Ernest Tubb** (guest vocals)		$4		Warner/Curb 29633
10/1/83	5	21	65 Queen Of My Heart *She Had Me*		$4		Warner/Curb 29500
10/22/83	15	16	66 The Conversation *Fancy Free* **WAYLON JENNINGS** with **Hank Williams, Jr.**		$4		RCA 13631
2/18/84	3	18	67 Man Of Steel *Now I Know How George Feels*		$4		Warner/Curb 29382
6/16/84	5	18	68 Attitude Adjustment *Knoxville Courthouse Blues*		$4		Warner/Curb 29253
10/6/84	10	19	69 All My Rowdy Friends Are Coming Over Tonight S:8 / A:14 *Video Blues* opening theme for ABC's *Monday Night Football* (with new lyrics)		$4		Warner/Curb 29184
1/19/85	10	18	70 Major Moves S:8 / A:9 *Mr. Lincoln*		$4		Warner/Curb 29095
5/11/85	❶¹	23	71 I'm For Love S:❶¹ / A:❶¹ *Lawyers, Guns And Money*		$4		Warner/Curb 29022
8/31/85	14	17	72 Two Old Cats Like Us........... S:13 / A:17 *Little Hotel Room* **RAY CHARLES** (with **Hank Williams, Jr.**)		$3		Columbia 05575
9/7/85	4	20	73 This Ain't Dallas S:4 / A:4 *I Really Like Girls*		$3		Warner/Curb 28912
2/22/86	❶¹	18	74 Ain't Misbehavin' S:❶¹ / A:❶¹ *I've Been Around* #17 Pop hit for Fats Waller in 1929		$3		Warner/Curb 28794
6/14/86	2²	21	75 Country State Of Mind S:❶¹ / A:2 *Fat Friends*		$3		Warner/Curb 28691
10/11/86	❶²	19	76 Mind Your Own Business S:❶² / A:❶² *My Name Is Bocephus* **Reba McEntire**, **Willie Nelson**, **Tom Petty** and **Reverend Ike** (guest vocals)		$3		Warner/Curb 28581
2/21/87	31	11	77 When Something Is Good (Why Does It Change) ....S:26 *Loving Instructor*		$3		Warner/Curb 28452
6/13/87	❶¹	20	78 Born To Boogie S:❶² *What It Boils Down To*		$3		Warner/Curb 28369
10/10/87+	4	21	79 Heaven Can't Be Found S:4 *The Doctor's Song*		$3	■	Warner/Curb 28227
2/20/88	2¹	21	80 Young Country S:❶¹ *Buck Naked* **Butch Baker**, **T. Graham Brown**, **Steve Earle**, **Highway 101**, **Dana McVicker**, **Marty Stuart** and **Keith Whitley** (guest vocals)		$3	■	Warner/Curb 28120
6/25/88	8	15	81 If The South Woulda Won S:4 *Wild Streak*		$3	■	Warner/Curb 27862
8/27/88	52	7	82 Cajun Baby .... *I Wanna Hold You* [R] **DOUG KERSHAW** with **HANK WILLIAMS, JR.** new version of #14 above		$4		BGM 81588
9/24/88	21	20	83 That Old Wheel S:17 *Tennessee Flat Top Box* **JOHNNY CASH** with **Hank Williams, Jr.**		$3		Mercury 870688
11/5/88+	14	15	84 Early In The Morning And Late At Night ....S:8 *I'm Just A Man*		$3	■	Warner/Curb 27722
2/4/89	7	14	85 There's A Tear In My Beer *You Brought Me Down To Earth* **HANK WILLIAMS, JR.** with **Hank Williams, Sr.** Hank Sr.'s vocals dubbed in from a vinyl record		$3	■	Warner/Curb 27584
7/8/89	6	20	86 Finders Are Keepers *What You Don't Know (Won't Hurt You)*		$3		Warner/Curb 22945
2/10/90	15	18	87 Ain't Nobody's Business *Big Mamou*		$3		Warner/Curb 19957
5/19/90	10	21	88 Good Friends, Good Whiskey, Good Lovin' *Family Tradition*		$3	▮	Warner/Curb 19872
9/1/90	62	6	89 Man To Man .... *Whiskey Bent And Hell Bound*		$3	▮	Warner/Curb 19818
9/15/90	27	6	90 Don't Give Us A Reason .... *U.S.A. Today*		$3	▮	Warner/Curb 19542
1/5/91	39	13	91 I Mean I Love You .... *Stoned At The Jukebox*		$3		Warner/Curb 19463
5/4/91	26	19	92 If It Will It Will *Won't It Be Nice*		$3		Warner/Curb 19352
8/17/91	59	8	93 Angels Are Hard To Find ....*Hollywood Honeys* [R] new version of #36 above		$3		Warner/Curb 19193
2/8/92	54	11	94 Hotel Whiskey *The Count Song*		$3		Capricorn/Curb 19023
5/23/92	55	8	95 Come On Over To The Country........... *Wild Weekend*		$3		Capricorn/Curb 18923
2/20/93	62	8	96 Everything Comes Down To Money And Love........... *S.O.B. I'm Tired*		$3		Capricorn/Curb 18614
12/24/94+	62	6	97 I Ain't Goin' Peacefully........... *Greeted In Enid* / (album snippets)		$3	▮	MCG/Curb 76932
4/22/95	74	2	98 Hog Wild S:26 *Wild Thing*		$3	▮	MCG/Curb 76948

WILLIAMS, Jason D.   **'89**
Singer/pianist from El Dorado, Arkansas.

DEBUT	PEAK	WKS	A-side (Chart Hit) / B-side	Pop	$	Pic	Label & Number
5/20/89	71	5	1 Where There's Smoke........... *Tore Up Over You*		$3		RCA 8869
9/23/89	70	4	2 Waitin' On Ice........... *Get Out You Big Roll Daddy*		$3		RCA 9026

DEBUT	PEAK	WKS	Gold	A-side (Chart Hit) .... B-side	Pop	$	Pic	Label & Number

WILLIAMS, Johnny   '72

| 5/6/72 | 68 | 5 | | He Will Break Your Heart .... *If Loving You Means Anything* | 104 | $7 | | Epic 10845 |

#7 Pop hit for Jerry Butler in 1960

WILLIAMS, Lawton   '62
Born on 7/29/22 in Troy, Tennessee. Singer/prolific songwriter.

| 10/23/61+ | 13 | 25 | | 1 Anywhere There's People .... *Plowed Ground* | | $12 | | Mercury 71867 |
| 9/19/64 | 40 | 4 | | 2 Everything's O.K. On The LBJ .... *Don't Look Down* | | $10 | | RCA Victor 8407 |

WILLIAMS, Leona   '78
Born Leona Belle Helton on 1/7/43 in Vienna, Missouri. Singer/songwriter/guitarist. Married to **Merle Haggard** from 1978-83. Married **Dave Kirby** in 1978.

5/31/69	66	5		1 Once More .... *I Narrowed This Triangle (Down To Two)*		$6		Hickory 1532
8/21/71	52	9		2 Country Girl With Hot Pants On .... *Babe, Just For You*		$6		Hickory 1606
9/22/73	93	3		3 Your Shoeshine Girl ...... *Since I'm Not With The One I Love (I'll Love The One I'm With)*		$6		Hickory/MGM 304
10/28/78	8	12		4 The Bull And The Beaver *I'm Gettin' High*		$5		MCA 40962

MERLE HAGGARD/LEONA WILLIAMS

2/17/79	92	2		5 The Baby Song/				
		2		6 Call Me Crazy Lady		$5		MCA 40988
4/4/81	54	8		7 I'm Almost Ready .... *The End Of The World*		$4		Elektra 47114

#34 Pop hit for Pure Prairie League in 1980

| 11/14/81 | 84 | 3 | | 8 Always Late With Your Kisses .... *Startin' Today* | | $4 | | Elektra 47217 |
| 5/28/83 | 42 | 14 | | 9 We're Strangers Again .... *Sally Let Your Bangs Hang Down* | | $4 | | Mercury 812214 |

MERLE HAGGARD & LEONA WILLIAMS

WILLIAMS, Lois   '69

| 9/20/69 | 74 | 3 | | A Girl Named Sam .... *We've Got Another Chance* [N] | | $7 | | Starday 877 |

answer to "A Boy Named Sue" by Johnny Cash

WILLIAMS, Otis   '71
Born on 6/2/36 in Cincinnati. Black singer. Former leader of The Charms. Not to be confused with the same-named member of The Temptations.

| 5/8/71 | 72 | 2 | | I Wanna Go Country .... *Rocky Top* | | $10 | | Stop 388 |

OTIS WILLIAMS and The Midnight Cowboys

WILLIAMS, Paul   '81
Born on 9/19/40 in Omaha. Singer/prolific songwriter. Acted in several movies.

| 12/12/81 | 93 | 4 | | Making Believe .... *Oh How I Miss You Tonight* | | $5 | | Paid 146 |

WILLIAMS, Tex ★151★   '47
Born Sollie Paul Williams on 8/23/17 in Ramsey, Illinois. Died of cancer on 10/11/85 (age 68). Singer/songwriter/guitarist. Acted in many western movies. Worked as a singer with **Spade Cooley**'s band. Hosted own *Ranch Party* TV series in 1958.

1)Smoke! Smoke! Smoke! 2)Never Trust A Woman 3)Don't Telephone-Don't Telegraph
4)That's What I Like About The West 5)Suspicion

TEX WILLIAMS And His Western Caravan:

| 11/30/46 | 4 | 2 | | 1 The California Polka *Rose Of The Alamo* | | $15 | | Capitol 302 |
| 7/5/47 | ❶16 | 23 | ● | 2 Smoke! Smoke! Smoke! (That Cigarette) [N] | ❶6 | $15 | | Capitol Amer. 40001 |

also see #19 below

| 10/4/47 | 4 | 8 | | 3 That's What I Like About The West *Downtown Poker Club* | | $15 | | Capitol Amer. 40031 |

new version of "That's What I Like About The South" by Phil Harris

12/13/47	2⁸	15		4 Never Trust A Woman *What It Means To Be Blue*		$15		Capitol Amer. 40054
2/14/48	2²	11		5 Don't Telephone - Don't Telegraph (Tell A Woman) *Blue As A Heart Ache*		$15		Capitol Amer. 40081
5/15/48	4	12		6 Suspicion *S:4 / J:4 Flo From St. Joe Mo*		$12		Capitol 40109
6/19/48	5	15		7 Banjo Polka *J:5 / S:11 Pretty Red Lights*		$12		Capitol 15101
6/26/48	6	8		8 Who? Me?/ *S:6 / J:11*		$12		Capitol 15113
7/31/48	15	1		9 Foolish Tears *J:15*				
9/11/48	6	5		10 Talking Boogie/ *J:6 / S:12*		$12		Capitol 15175
11/13/48	13	3		11 Just A Pair Of Blue Eyes *J:13 / S:14*				
11/20/48	5	8		12 Life Gits Tee-Jus, Don't It? *J:5 / S:9 Big Hat Polka* [N]	27	$12		Capitol 15271
10/22/49	11	2		13 (There's A) Bluebird On Your Windowsill *J:11 / S:12 A Letter Asking For My Broken Heart*		$12		Capitol 40225

TEX WILLIAMS:

5/29/65	26	11		14 Too Many Tigers .... *Winter Snow*		$8		Boone 1028
10/2/65	30	9		15 Big Tennessee .... *My Last Two Tens*		$8		Boone 1032
1/8/66	18	8		16 Bottom Of A Mountain .... *Tears Are Only Rain*		$8		Boone 1036
9/24/66	44	2		17 Another Day, Another Dollar In The Hole .... *The Big Man*		$8		Boone 1044
6/17/67	57	5		18 Black Jack County .... *Ain't Gonna Walk Your Dog*		$8		Boone 1059
2/17/68	32	10		19 Smoke, Smoke, Smoke - '68 .... *The Lonely One* [R]		$8		Boone 1069

new version of #2 above

6/29/68	45	7		20 Here's To You And Me .... *If Not For You There Could Go Me*		$8		Boone 1072
9/19/70	50	9		21 It Ain't No Big Thing .... *I Never Knew What Doing Was (Til I Got Done By You)*		$7		Monument 1216
8/28/71	29	14		22 The Night Miss Nancy Ann's Hotel For Single Girls Burned Down .... *If It's All The Same To You* [N]		$7		Monument 8503
1/22/72	67	4		23 Everywhere I Go (He's Already Been There) .... *Pretty In Blue*		$7		Monument 8533

WILLIAMS, Tex — Cont'd

| 6/29/74 | 70 | 8 | 24 | **Those Lazy, Hazy, Crazy Days Of Summer**.....................*Nowhere West Virginia* | | $6 | | Granite 507 |

#6 Pop hit for **Nat King Cole** in 1963

WILLIAMS, Tucker '80

Singer from Dallas.

| 1/19/80 | 96 | 2 | | **Donna-Earth Angel (Medley)** .... *Honey Love* | | $7 | | Yatahey 999 |

"Donna" was a #2 Pop hit for Ritchie Valens in 1959; "Earth Angel" was a #1 R&B hit for The Penguins in 1955

WILLIAMS BROS. '63

Duo of brothers Jimmy and Bobby Williams.

| 6/15/63 | 28 | 1 | | **Bad Old Memories** ....*The Last Time* | | $20 | | Del-Mar 1008 |

WILLING, Foy '44

Born Foy Willingham in 1915 in Bosque County, Texas. Died on 7/24/78 (age 63). Singer/songwriter/guitarist. Acted in several western movies.

FOY WILLING And His Riders Of The Purple Sage:

| 7/15/44 | 3 | 5 | 1 | **Texas Blues** *Hang Your Head In Shame* | | $15 | | Capitol 162 |
| 3/16/46 | 6 | 1 | 2 | **Detour** *Someone Won't Your Heart Little Darlin'* | | $15 | | Decca 9000 |

#5 Pop hit for **Patti Page** in 1951

| 12/14/46 | 4 | 1 | 3 | **Have I Told You Lately (That I Love You)** *Cool Water* | | $15 | | Majestic 6000 |
| 6/19/48 | 14 | 2 | 4 | **Anytime** ....J:14 *I'm Waltzing With A Broken Heart* | | $15 | | Capitol Amer. 40108 |

#2 Pop hit for Eddie Fisher in 1952

| 1/1/49 | 15 | 1 | 5 | **Brush Those Tears From Your Eyes** .... S:15 *Rose Of Ol' Pawnee* | | $15 | | Capitol 15290 |

WILLIS, Andra '73

Female singer/actress. Regular on TV's *The Lawrence Welk Show* from 1967-69.

2/24/73	56	7	1	**Down Home Lovin' Woman** ....*Cryin' Cause You're Gone*		$6		Capitol 3525
8/4/73	85	5	2	**Til I Can't Take It Anymore** ....*After You*		$6		Capitol 3666
4/19/75	63	9	3	**Baby** ....*I'd Like To Be*		$6		Capitol 4044

TENNESSEE ERNIE FORD & ANDRA WILLIS

WILLIS, Hal '64

Born Leonard Francis Gauthier in Roslyn, Quebec, Canada.

| 10/31/64 | 5 | 16 | 1 | **The Lumberjack** *Dig Me A Hole* | 120 | $12 | | Sims 207 |
| 7/30/66 | 45 | 5 | 2 | **Doggin' In The U.S. Mail** ....*The Battle Of Viet Nam* | | $12 | | Sims 288 |

WILLIS, Kelly '91

Born on 10/1/68 in Virginia. Female singer. Acted in the movie *Bob Roberts*.

4/27/91	51	9	1	**Baby Take A Piece Of My Heart** ....*Standing By The River*		$3		MCA 54050
7/31/93	72	2	2	**Whatever Way The Wind Blows** ....*World Without You*		$3		MCA 54678
10/16/93	63	5	3	**Heaven's Just A Sin Away**...*Get Real*		$3	∎	MCA 54733

WILLIS BROTHERS, The '64

Trio of brothers: Guy (guitar), Skeeter (fiddle) and Vic (accordian) Willis. Guy was born James Willis on 7/5/15 in Alex, Arkansas. Died on 4/13/81 (age 65). Skeeter was born Charles Willis on 12/20/17 in Coalton, Oklahoma. Died of cancer in 1976 (age 58). Vic was born Richard Willis on 5/31/22 in Schulter, Oklahoma. Died in a car crash on 1/15/95 (age 72). Trio joined the *Grand Ole Opry* in 1946.

9/5/64	9	20	1	**Give Me 40 Acres (To Turn This Rig Around)** *Gonna Buy Me A Juke Box*		$10		Starday 681
6/12/65	41	8	2	**A Six Foot Two By Four**.......................................*Strange Old Town* [N]		$10		Starday 713
2/25/67	14	15	3	**Bob** ....*Show Her Lots Of Gold*		$8		Starday 796
7/29/67	62	3	4	**Somebody Knows My Dog** ....*The End Of The Road*		$8		Starday 812

WILLOUGHBY, Larry '84

Singer/songwriter/guitarist. Cousin of **Rodney Crowell**.

11/12/83	65	5	1	**Heart On The Line (Operator, Operator)**...*Stone Cold*		$4		Atlantic Amer. 99826
2/4/84	55	8	2	**Building Bridges**...		$4		Atlantic Amer. 99797
6/23/84	82	3	3	**Angel Eyes** ....*The Devil's On The Loose*		$4		Atlantic Amer. 99759

WILLS, Bob ★99★ '46

Born James Robert Wills on 3/6/05 in Kosse, Texas. Died of a stroke on 5/13/75 (age 70). Singer/songwriter/fiddle player. Formed the Texas Playboys in 1933. Band featured **Tommy Duncan** (vocals) and **Leon McAuliffe** (steel guitar). Hosted own radio show on KVOO in Tulsa from 1934-58. Acted in several western movies. Known as "The King of Western Swing." Brother of **Johnnie Lee Wills**. Elected to the Country Music Hall of Fame in 1968. His band recorded as the **Original Texas Playboys** in 1977. Tommy Duncan performs the vocals on all songs below (unless noted).

1)New Spanish Two Step 2)Silver Dew On The Blue Grass Tonight 3)Smoke On The Water
4)Stars And Stripes On Iwo Jima 5)Sugar Moon

BOB WILLS and his Texas Playboys:

| 1/8/44 | 3 | 1 | 1 | **New San Antonio Rose** | 11 | $25 | | Okeh 5694 |

vocal version of his classic hit from 1941

| 9/9/44 | 2⁵ | 11 | 2 | **We Might As Well Forget It/** | 11 | | | |

Leon Huff (vocal)

| 9/23/44 | 2² | 17 | 3 | **You're From Texas** | 14 | $25 | | Okeh 6722 |

Leon McAuliffe (vocal); from the movie *A Tornado In The Saddle* starring Wills

3/24/45	❶²	15	4	**Smoke On The Water/**				
3/24/45	3	18	5	**Hang Your Head In Shame**		$25		Okeh 6736
6/16/45	❶¹	11	6	**Stars And Stripes On Iwo Jima/**				
7/21/45	5	4	7	**You Don't Care What Happens To Me**		$25		Okeh 6742
11/17/45	❶³	14	8	**Silver Dew On The Blue Grass Tonight/**				
11/3/45+	2¹	8	9	**Texas Playboy Rag** [I]		$20		Columbia 36841
12/29/45+	❶¹	5	10	**White Cross On Okinawa** *Empty Chair At The Christmas Table*		$20		Columbia 36881

WILLS, Bob — Cont'd

DEBUT	PEAK	WKS	A-side / B-side	Pop	$	Label & Number
5/4/46	❶¹⁶	23	11 **New Spanish Two Step/**	20		
			vocal version of his 1935 instrumental "Spanish Two Step" on Vocalion 03230			
5/11/46	3	18	12 **Roly-Poly**		$20	Columbia 36966
11/30/46	2²	8	13 **Stay A Little Longer/**		$20	
11/30/46	4	1	14 **I Can't Go On This Way**		$20	Columbia 37097
3/29/47	5	1	15 **I'm Gonna Be Boss From Now On** _There's A Big Rock In The Road_		$20	Columbia 37205
			Jesse Ashlock (vocal)			
5/17/47	❶¹	6	16 **Sugar Moon** _Brain Cloudy Blues_		$20	Columbia 37313
7/12/47	4	1	17 **Bob Wills Boogie** _Rose Of Old Pawnee_ [I]		$20	Columbia 37357
1/31/48	4	17	18 **Bubbles In My Beer** _Spanish Fandango_		$20	MGM 10116
7/3/48	8	2	19 **Keeper Of My Heart** J:8 _I'll Have Somebody Else_		$20	MGM 10175
7/24/48	15	1	20 **Texarkana Baby** S:15 _New Texas Playboy Rag_		$20	Columbia 38179
9/18/48	10	1	21 **Thorn In My Heart** J:10 _Neath Hawaiian Palms_		$20	MGM 10236
1/21/50	10	1	22 **Ida Red Likes The Boogie** J:10 _A King Without A Queen_		$25	MGM K10570
			Tiny Moore (vocal); also see #26 below			
11/4/50	8	5	23 **Faded Love** A:8 _Boot Heel Drag_		$25	MGM K10786
			Rusty McDonald and The Playboy Trio (vocals)			
8/8/60	5	17	24 **Heart To Heart Talk** _What's The Matter With The Mill_		$15	Liberty 55260
1/23/61	26	1	25 **The Image Of Me** _Goodbye Liza Jane_		$15	Liberty 55264
			BOB WILLS with **TOMMY DUNCAN** and **The Texas Playboys** (above 2)			
10/16/76	99	1	26 **Ida Red** _Don't Let The Deal Go Down_		$6	Capitol 4332
			Leon Rausch (vocal); "live" recording; also see #22 above			

★281★ WILLS, David '75
Born on 10/23/51 in Pulaski, Tennessee. Singer/songwriter/guitarist.
1)From Barrooms To Bedrooms 2)There's A Song On The Jukebox 3)The Eyes Of A Stranger
4)Miss Understanding 5)The Barmaid

DEBUT	PEAK	WKS	A-side / B-side	$	Label & Number
11/16/74+	10	18	1 **There's A Song On The Jukebox** _I Can't Even Drink It Away_	$6	Epic 50036
3/29/75	10	13	2 **From Barrooms To Bedrooms** _I'll Be More Than Happy (To Set You Free)_	$6	Epic 50090
7/12/75	31	11	3 **The Barmaid** _Make Me Hate You_	$6	Epic 50118
11/1/75	35	9	4 **She Deserves My Very Best** _Lady Of The Evening_	$6	Epic 50154
2/7/76	47	8	5 **Queen Of The Starlight Ballroom** _Long Tall Sally_	$6	Epic 50188
5/22/76	55	7	6 **Woman** _Paint Me A Picture_	$6	Epic 50228
			#14 Pop hit for Peter & Gordon in 1966		
8/21/76	66	6	7 **(I'm Just Pouring Out) What She Bottled Up In Me** _The Happy Hour_	$6	Epic 50260
5/21/77	52	9	8 **The Best Part Of My Days (Are My Nights With You)** _I'm Gonna Save It For My Baby_	$5	United Artists 988
9/17/77	91	4	9 **Cheatin' Turns Her On** _I'm Gonna Save It For My Baby_	$5	United Artists 1042
11/19/77	82	5	10 **Do You Wanna Make Love** _The Fool Strikes Again_	$4	United Artists 1097
			#5 Pop hit for Peter McCann in 1977		
7/15/78	70	6	11 **You Snap Your Fingers (And I'm Back In Your Hands)** _To Make A Long Story Short_	$4	United Artists 1196
2/17/79	50	7	12 **I'm Being Good** _Women Have A Feeling ('Bout These Things)_	$4	United Artists 1271
10/6/79	82	4	13 **Endless** _One, Two, Three, We Were Lovers_	$4	United Artists 1319
5/31/80	91	5	14 **She's Hangin' In There (I'm Hangin' Out)** _Take It Back_	$4	United Artists 1350
9/27/80	65	6	15 **The Light Of My Life (Has Gone Out Again Tonight)** _Marriage On The Rocks_	$4	United Artists 1375
3/12/83	52	7	16 **Those Nights, These Days** _Tennessee Moon_	$3	RCA 13460
6/18/83	19	16	17 **The Eyes Of A Stranger** _Give Her Heart A Break_	$3	RCA 13541
11/12/83+	26	15	18 **Miss Understanding** _First To Make It Last_	$3	RCA 13653
2/25/84	31	11	19 **Lady In Waiting** _First Time Feeling_	$3	RCA 13737
11/24/84	69	7	20 **Macon Love** _Racin' Down The Highway_	$3	RCA 13940
10/8/88	85	3	21 **Paper Thin Walls** _Honey Baby_	$3	Epic 08043

WILLS, Johnnie Lee '50
Born on 9/2/12 in Jewett, Texas. Died on 10/25/84 (age 72). Singer/fiddle player. Brother of **Bob Wills**.
JOHNNIE LEE WILLS And His Boys:

DEBUT	PEAK	WKS	A-side / B-side	Pop	$	Label & Number
1/28/50	2⁵	11	1 **Rag Mop** S:2 / J:2 / A:3 _Near Me_	9	$20	Bullet 696 (78)
			#1 Pop hit for the Ames Brothers in 1950			
4/1/50	7	2	2 **Peter Cotton Tail** J:7 / A:8 _Shattered Dreams_		$20	Bullet 700 (78)

WILLS, Mark '97
Born on 8/8/73 in Cleveland, Tennessee; raised in Blue Ridge, Georgia. Singer/songwriter/guitarist.

DEBUT	PEAK	WKS	A-side / B-side	$	Pic	Label & Number
6/8/96	6	20	1 **Jacob's Ladder/** S:13			
10/12/96	33	18	2 **High Low And In Between**	$3	▌	Mercury 578004
3/1/97	5	21	3 **Places I've Never Been** _Ace Of Hearts_	$3		Mercury 574150

WILLS, Tommy '79
Jazz saxophonist.

DEBUT	PEAK	WKS	A-side / B-side	$	Label & Number
1/13/79	100	1	**Wildwood Flower** _Ram-Bunk-Shush_	$7	Golden Moon 004
			Marti Maes (vocal)		

WILSON, Benny '85
Born in Young Harris, Georgia. Singer/songwriter.

DEBUT	PEAK	WKS	A-side / B-side	$	Label & Number
2/2/85	50	9	1 **Acres Of Diamonds** _I Just Don't Love You, That's All_	$3	Columbia 04724
3/22/86	78	8	2 **If You Wanna Talk Love** _Where The Light Comes From_	$3	Columbia 05829

WILSON, Coleman '61
Born in Young Harris, Georgia.

DEBUT	PEAK	WKS	A-side / B-side	$	Label & Number
7/31/61	23	5	**Passing Zone Blues** _Flat-Footed Mama_	$20	King 5512

WILSON, Hank — see RUSSELL, Leon

WILSON, Jim   '55
Born in Bowling Green, Kentucky. Popular DJ in Texas.

7/23/55	8	9		Daddy, You Know What? A:8 *Plans For Divorce*		$20		Mercury 70635

includes a short narration by Wilson's daughter June

WILSON, Larry Jon   '76
Singer/songwriter from Swainsboro, Georgia.

4/24/76	74	7		Think I Feel A Hitchhike Coming On ....*Drowning In the Mainstream*		$6		Monument 8692

WILSON, Meri   '77
Born in Japan; raised in Marietta, Georgia. Female singer/songwriter.

6/18/77	50	8	●	Telephone Man ....*Itinerary* [N]	18	$5		GRT 127

WILSON, Norro   '70
Born Norris Wilson on 4/4/38 in Scottsville, Kentucky. Singer/prolific songwriter.
1)Do It To Someone You Love 2)Everybody Needs Lovin' 3)Ain't It Good

1/11/69	68	7		1 Only You ....*Hey Mister*		$8		Smash 2192
				#5 Pop hit for The Platters in 1955				
4/5/69	44	8		2 Love Comes But Once In A Lifetime ....*All The Time*		$8		Smash 2210
9/13/69	56	8		3 Shame On Me ....*Let Me Go Back*		$8		Smash 2236
7/4/70	20	13		4 Do It To Someone You Love *No One Will Ever Know*		$7		Mercury 73077
11/28/70	53	9		5 Old Enough To Want To (Fool Enough To Try)...................*State Line Daddy*		$7		Mercury 73125
11/18/72+	28	12		6 Everybody Needs Lovin'...*The Strange Little Girl*		$6		RCA Victor 0824
3/31/73	64	4		7 Darlin' Raise The Shade ....*Keep Me From Blowing Away*		$6		RCA Victor 0909
9/8/73	35	11		8 Ain't It Good (To Feel This Way).................................*It's All In The Game*		$6		RCA Victor 0062
7/6/74	96	2		9 Loneliness (Can Break A Good Man Down) ....*I Want To Hold You In My Arms*		$6		Capitol 3886
8/20/77	43	8		10 So Close Again ....*Saturday Night At The General Store*		$5		Warner 8427
				MARGO SMITH & NORRO WILSON				

WILSON, Tim   '93
Comedian from Columbus, Georgia.

3/27/93	70	2		Garth Brooks Has Ruined My Life ....*Help Me Find Jimmy Hoffa* [N]		$4	▮	Southern Tracks 0035

WINGS — see McCARTNEY, Paul

★289★ WINSLOW, Stephanie   '79
Born on 8/27/56 in Yankton, South Dakota. Singer/fiddle player. Formerly married to Ray Ruff (owner of the Oak record label).
1)Say You Love Me 2)Crying 3)Anything But Yes Is Still A No

9/29/79	10	11		1 Say You Love Me *Oh, Mister*		$5		Warner/Curb 49074
				#11 Pop hit for Fleetwood Mac in 1976				
1/12/80	14	10		2 Crying ....*Try*		$5		Warner/Curb 49146
				#2 Pop hit for Roy Orbison in 1961				
4/5/80	38	6		3 I Can't Remember ....*Don't Go*		$5		Warner/Curb 49201
6/21/80	36	10		4 Try It On ....*Me Without You*		$5		Warner/Curb 49257
9/20/80	35	9		5 Baby, I'm A Want You ....*Pretend*		$5		Warner/Curb 49557
				#3 Pop hit for Bread in 1971				
12/13/80+	25	13		6 Anything But Yes Is Still A No ....*Cold Cold Heart*		$5		Warner/Curb 49628
3/21/81	36	7		7 Hideaway Healing ....*Will This Be The Last Time*		$4		Warner/Curb 49693
6/27/81	39	9		8 I've Been A Fool/		$4		Warner/Curb 49753
		9		9 Sometimes When We Touch...................................				
				#3 Pop hit for Dan Hill in 1978				
10/10/81	29	10		10 When You Walk In The Room..........................*Somebody To Love*		$5		Warner/Curb 49831
				#35 Pop hit for The Searchers in 1964				
5/1/82	43	10		11 Slippin' And Slidin'.......................................*Another Night*		$5		Primero 1003
				#33 Pop hit for Little Richard in 1956				
6/26/82	40	10		12 Don't We Belong In Love ....*Another Night*		$5		Primero 1007
9/18/82	69	5		13 In Between Lovers...*Try*		$5		Primero/Curb 1012
5/14/83	61	6		14 Nobody Else For Me ....*Another Night*		$5		Oak 1056
9/3/83	25	15		15 Kiss Me Darling ....*Another Night*		$4		Curb/MCA 52291
1/7/84	29	12		16 Dancin' With The Devil ....*I Don't Want To Talk About It*		$4		Curb/MCA 52327
4/7/84	42	9		17 Baby, Come To Me ....*Kisses Like Fire*		$4		Curb/MCA 52372
				#1 Pop hit for Patti Austin with **James Ingram** in 1983				

WINTERMUTE, Joann   '89
Female singer/songwriter from Dallas.

3/11/89	82	3		1 Two Old Flames One Cheatin' Fire ....*My Heart Just Doesn't Know*		$5		Canyon Creek 1225
5/27/89	81	3		2 I Wouldn't Trade Your Love....................................		$5		Door Knob 324
8/19/89	78	3		3 How I Love You In The Morning..............................		$5		Door Knob 330

WINTERS, Don   '61
Born on 4/17/29 in Tampa, Florida.

7/3/61	10	10		1 Too Many Times/				
7/17/61	27	2		2 Shake Hands With A Loser		$12		Decca 31253

WISEMAN, Mac   '59
Born Malcolm Wiseman on 5/23/25 in Cremora, Virginia. Bluegrass singer/songwriter/banjo player.

5/28/55	10	2		1 The Ballad Of Davy Crockett A:10 *Danger Heartbreak Ahead*		$20		Dot 1240
8/10/59	5	20		2 Jimmy Brown The Newsboy *I've Got No Use For The Women*		$15		Dot 15946
9/21/63	12	8		3 Your Best Friend And Me ....*When The Moon Comes Over The Mountain*		$8		Capitol 5011
11/9/68	54	7		4 Got Leavin' On Her Mind ....*She Simply Left*		$7		MGM 13986
12/6/69+	38	9		5 Johnny's Cash And Charley's Pride.............*Mama, Put My Little Shoes Away* [N]		$6		RCA Victor 0283

WISEMAN, Mac — Cont'd

DEBUT	PEAK	WKS	A-side / B-side	Pop	$	Label & Number
3/18/78	78	5	6 Never Going Back Again .... *Goodbye Mexico Rose*		$6	Churchill 7706
5/12/79	69	4	7 My Blue Heaven .... *If I Could Be With You/It Must Be True*		$6	Churchill 7735

MAC WISEMAN and WOODY HERMAN

7/7/79	88	3	8 Scotch And Soda .... *Dancing Bear*		$6	Churchill 7738
			#81 Pop hit for The Kingston Trio in 1962			
10/13/79	95	3	9 Shackles And Chains .... *Midnight Flyer*		$6	CMH 1522

OSBORNE BROS. & MAC WISEMAN

WOFFORD, E.D.   '78

7/1/78	77	4	Baby, I Need Your Lovin'................ *Why Not Try Lovin' Me*		$5	MC/Curb 5012
			#3 Pop hit for Johnny Rivers in 1967			

WOLF, Gary   '83
Born in 1948 in Richmond, Kentucky.

7/17/82	51	9	1 Love Never Dies *Ages And Pages Ago*		$3	Columbia 02986
10/30/82	64	7	2 The Perfect Picture (To Fit My Frame Of Mind) .... *If I Could Only Go Back To Goodbye*		$3	Columbia 03272
2/19/83	62	7	3 Livin' On Memories .... *Lone Wolf*		$3	Columbia 03493
7/7/84	63	8	4 You Bring The Heartache (I'll Bring The Wine) .... *Call On Me*		$3	Mercury 822244
3/23/85	73	3	5 It's My Life .... *First Things First*		$3	Mercury 880564

WOLFPACK, The   '82
All-star trio: Kenny Earl, Narvel Felts and Lobo.

5/8/82	88	3	Bull Smith Can't Dance The Cotton-Eyed Joe ..... *I Don't Want To Want You* [N]		$6	Lobo 6

WOMACK, Lee Ann   '98
Born on 8/19/66 in Jacksonville, Texas. Formerly married to Jason Sellers.

3/15/97	23	20	1 Never Again, Again .... *S:9 (album snippets)*	124	$3	▌	Decca 55320
6/21/97	2[1]	20	2 The Fool *Trouble's Here*		$3		Decca 72009
11/1/97+	2[1]	22	3 You've Got To Talk To Me *A Man With 18 Wheels*		$3		Decca 72023

WOOD, Bobby   '64
Singer/pianist from Memphis.

10/31/64	46	2	That's All I Need To Know .... *This Time*	130	$12	Joy 288

WOOD, Danny   '80
Born in Grand Prairie, Texas. Singer/songwriter/guitarist.

10/23/76	92	4	1 If This Is Freedom (I Want Out) .... *I Won't Be Sleepin' Alone*		$5	London 242
4/2/77	93	2	2 I Need Somethin' Easy Tonight .... *Permanent Thing*		$5	London 248
6/21/80	30	10	3 A Heart's Been Broken *All The Kind Young Strangers*		$4	RCA 11968
12/6/80+	37	12	4 It Took Us All Night Long To Say Goodbye .... *Crazy Dreams*		$4	RCA 12123
3/21/81	58	7	5 Fool's Gold .... *Where Were You (When I Came Home Last Night)*		$4	RCA 12181

WOOD, Del   '51
Born Polly Adelaide Hendricks on 2/22/20 in Nashville. Died on 10/3/89 (age 69). Female pianist. Joined the *Grand Ole Opry* in 1953.

9/8/51	5	12	Down Yonder *J:5 / A:7 / S:9 Mine, All Mine* [I]	4	$25	Tennessee 775
			#5 Pop hit for Ernest Hare & Billy Jones in 1921			

WOOD, Jeff   '97
Born on 5/10/68 in Oklahoma City. Singer/songwriter.

11/2/96+	44	18	1 You Just Get One			album cut
3/15/97	55	10	2 Use Mine			album cut
6/7/97	63	8	3 You Call That A Mountain			album cut
			all of above from the album *Between The Earth And The Stars* on Imprint 10006			

WOOD, Nancy   '81
Born Renate Kern in Germany; exchange student who lived in Janesville, Michigan. Host of *Nancy's Country Drive-In* radio series in Germany.

10/10/81	79	4	Imagine That .... *Turn Your Love Light On*		$6	Montage 1202

WOODRUFF, Bob   '94
Born on 3/14/61 in Suffern, New York.

2/26/94	70	3	1 Hard Liquor, Cold Women, Warm Beer .... *The Year We Tried To Kill The Pain*		$3	▌	Asylum 64575
5/21/94	74	1	2 Bayou Girl .... *Poisoned At The Well*		$3		Asylum 64553

BOB WOUDRUFF

WOODS, Gene   '60
Singer from Chattanooga, Tennessee.

10/10/60	7	13	The Ballad Of Wild River *Afraid*		$25	HAP 1004

WOODY, Bill   '79
Born in 1959 in Jacksonville, Florida; raised in North Carolina.

4/21/79	65	9	1 Just Between Us .... *I Love You*		$4	MCA 54043
8/4/79	88	4	2 Love Wouldn't Leave Us Alone .... *Organized Noise*		$4	MCA 41070

WOOLERY, Chuck   '77
Born in Ashland, Kentucky. Hosted TV's *Wheel Of Fortune* and *Love Connection*.

7/9/77	78	5	1 Painted Lady .... *Growing Up In A Country Way*		$5	Warner 8381
7/12/80	94	2	2 The Greatest Love Affair .... *Heroes And Lovers* [S]		$4	Epic 50897

WOOLEY, Amy   '82
Born in Cleveland.

7/31/82	51	9	If My Heart Had Windows .... *Burned By Love*		$4	MCA 52084

★331★ WOOLEY, Sheb '62

Born Shelby Wooley on 4/10/21 in Erick, Oklahoma. Singer/songwriter/actor. Played "Pete Nolan" on the TV series *Rawhide*. Also made comical recordings under pseudonym **Ben Colder**. Acted in the movies *High Noon*, *Rocky Mountain*, *Giant* and *Hoosiers*. Wrote *Hee Haw*'s theme song.

1)That's My Pa 2)Almost Persuaded No. 2 3)Don't Go Near The Eskimos

1/13/62	❶¹	17		1 That's My Pa *Meet Mr. Lonely* [N]	51	$10		MGM 13046
12/29/62	18	1		2 Don't Go Near The Eskimos ....*Louisiana Trapper* [N]	62	$10		MGM 13104
				BEN COLDER				
				parody of "Don't Go Near The Indians" by Rex Allen				
3/2/63	30	2		3 Hello Wall No. 2 ....*Shudders And Screams* [N]	131	$10		MGM 13122
				BEN COLDER				
				parody of "Hello Walls" by Faron Young				
7/18/64	33	10		4 Blue Guitar ....*Natchez Landing*		$10		MGM 13241
5/21/66	34	9		5 I'll Leave The Singin' To The Bluebirds ....*Buba Hoo Boba Dee*		$8		MGM 13477
9/24/66	6	15		6 Almost Persuaded No. 2 *Packets Of Pencils* [N]	58	$8		MGM 13590
				BEN COLDER				
				parody of "Almost Persuaded" by David Houston				
10/15/66	70	2		7 Tonight's The Night My Angel's Halo Fell ....*Anchors Aweigh*		$8		MGM 13556
6/29/68	22	12		8 Tie A Tiger Down ....*Make 'Em Laugh*		$8		MGM 13938
10/26/68	24	6		9 Harper Valley P.T.A. (Later That Same Day)....................*Folsom Prison Blues* [N]	67	$8		MGM 13997
				BEN COLDER				
				parody of "Harper Valley P.T.A." by Jeannie C. Riley				
1/4/69	65	3		10 Little Green Apples No. 2.................................*It's Such A Pretty World Tonight* [N]		$8		MGM 14015
				BEN COLDER				
				parody of "Little Green Apples" by Roger Miller				
1/11/69	52	9		11 I Remember Loving You ....*That Girl (Next Door)*		$8		MGM 14005
10/25/69	63	7		12 The One Man Band ....*You Still Turn Me On*		$8		MGM 14085
2/13/71	50	6		13 Fifteen Beers Ago ....*Sunday Mornin' Comin' Down* [N]		$8		MGM 14209
				BEN COLDER				
				parody of "Fifteen Years Ago" by Conway Twitty				

★375★ WOPAT, Tom '87

Born on 9/9/51 in Lodi, Wisconsin. Singer/songwriter/actor. Played "Luke Duke" on TV's *The Dukes of Hazzard*. Host of TNN's *Prime Time Country* in 1996.

1)The Rock And Roll Of Love 2)A Little Bit Closer 3)Susannah

4/19/86	39	13		1 True Love (Never Did Run Smooth)........................A:37 *Some Day, Some Night*		$3		EMI America 8316
8/16/86	44	11		2 I Won't Let You Down ....*Wheels*		$3		EMI America 8334
12/20/86+	16	19		3 The Rock And Roll Of Love A:15 / S:24 *A Good Woman's Love*		$3		EMI America 8364
5/9/87	28	14		4 Put Me Out Of My Misery ....*Daylight Loving Time*		$3		EMI America 43010
8/29/87	20	17		5 Susannah ....*Cars*		$3		EMI America 43034
1/9/88	18	17		6 A Little Bit Closer ....*Bad Thing About Good Love*		$3		EMI-Manhattan 50112
6/11/88	40	10		7 Hey Little Sister ....*A Letter In The Fire*		$3		Capitol 44144
10/8/88	29	16		8 Not Enough Love ....*A Letter In The Fire*		$3		Capitol 44243
6/29/91	46	15		9 Too Many Honky Tonks (On My Way Home) ....*I've Been There*		$3	∎	Epic 73862
11/23/91	51	11		10 Back To The Well ....*Always A Blue Moon*		$3		Epic 74063

WORK, Jimmy '55

Born in 1924 in Akron, Ohio; raised in Dukedom, Tennessee. Singer/songwriter/guitarist.

2/19/55	5	13		1 Making Believe J:5 / A:7 / S:11 *Just Like Downtown*		$20		Dot 1221
7/2/55	6	4		2 That's What Makes The Juke Box Play J:6 *Don't Give Me A Reason To Wonder Why*		$20		Dot 1245

★326★ WORTH, Marion '60

Born Mary Ann Ward on 7/4/30 in Birmingham, Alabama. Singer/songwriter/guitarist. Joined the *Grand Ole Opry* in 1963.

1)That's My Kind Of Love 2)I Think I Know 3)Are You Willing, Willie

10/19/59+	12	20		1 Are You Willing, Willie ....*This Heart Of Mine*		$25		Cherokee 503
5/23/60	5	15		2 That's My Kind Of Love *I Lost Johnny*		$20		Guyden 2033
11/14/60	7	23		3 I Think I Know *Tomorrow At A Quarter Till Nine*		$15	∎	Columbia 41799
5/22/61	21	1		4 There'll Always Be Sadness ....*I'm Not At All Sorry For You*		$15		Columbia 41972
2/2/63	14	5		5 Shake Me I Rattle (Squeeze Me I Cry) ....*Tennessee Teardrops*	42	$15	∎	Columbia 42640
6/8/63	18	3		6 Crazy Arms...*Lovers' Lane*		$15		Columbia 42703
4/11/64	33	13		7 You Took Him Off My Hands (Now You Took Take Him Off My Mind) ....*He Loves Me, He Loves Me Not*		$15		Columbia 42992
5/9/64	23	17		8 Slipping Around ....*I Love You So Much It Hurts*		$15		Columbia 43020
				MARION WORTH AND GEORGE MORGAN				
10/24/64	25	6		9 The French Song ....*Kentucky Waltz*		$10		Columbia 43119
				#54 Pop hit for Lucille Starr in 1964				
12/11/65+	32	6		10 I Will Not Blow Out The Light ....*Twenty-One Days Of Darkness*		$10		Columbia 43405
11/4/67	64	6		11 A Woman Needs Love....................................*I've Got That Sad And Lonely Feeling*		$8		Decca 32195
3/30/68	45	10		12 Mama Sez ....*Then I'll Be Over You*		$8		Decca 32278

WRAYS, The '87

Group from Oregon: Bubba Wray, Jim Covert, Lynn Phillips, and Joe Dale Cleghorn. Bubba became better known as **Collin Raye**.

THE WRAY BROTHERS BAND:

3/19/83	88	3		1 Reason To Believe		$6		CIS 3011
				#19 Pop hit for Rod Stewart in 1993				
4/6/85	93	4		2 Until We Meet Again		$6		Sasparilla 0003

THE WRAYS:

5/10/86	71	5		3 I Don't Want To Know Your Name ....*Here's To The Men Who Can Cry*		$3		Mercury 884621
6/6/87	48	10		4 You Lay A Lotta Love On Me..*Until We Meet Again*		$3		Mercury 888542

WREN, Larry   '77

| 5/21/77 | 98 | 3 | | 1 Lie To Me/ | | | | |
| | | 3 | | 2 It's Saturday Night.. | | $6 | | 50 States 51 |

WRIGHT, B.J.   '80
Born in Gallatin, Tennessee. Male singer.

10/21/78	96	4		1 Memory Bound ....Don't Say Love		$5		Soundwaves 4577
3/24/79	93	2		2 Leaning On Each Other ....California Rose		$5		Soundwaves 4581
7/28/79	61	5		3 I've Got A Right To Be Wrong ....Free At Last		$5		Soundwaves 4589
12/22/79+	87	6		4 Nobody's Darlin' But Mine ....(Somewhere There's A) Rainbow Over Texas		$5		Soundwaves 4593
				#19 Pop hit for **Jimmie Davis** in 1937				
5/3/80	36	11		5 J.R. Memory Bound		$5		Soundwaves 4604
				title refers to "J.R. Ewing" (Larry Hagman) of TV's *Dallas*				
8/2/80	73	5		6 Lost Love Affair..You're Drivin' Me Crazy		$5		Soundwaves 4610
12/27/80+	81	6		7 I Know An Ending (When It Comes)...............................Baby Blue		$5		Soundwaves 4624

★315★   **WRIGHT, Bobby**   '71
Born John Robert Wright on 3/30/42 in Charleston, West Virginia. Singer/songwriter/guitarist/actor. Son of **Johnny Wright** and **Kitty Wells**; brother of **Ruby Wright**. Played "Willy Moss" on TV's *McHale's Navy*.
   1)Here I Go Again 2)Seasons In The Sun 3)Lovin' Someone On My Mind 4)Upstairs In The Bedroom
     5)Lay Some Happiness On Me

4/29/67	44	12		1 Lay Some Happiness On Me...........................How Much Lonelier Can Lonely Be		$6		Decca 32107
				#55 Pop hit for **Dean Martin** in 1967				
12/2/67	67	3		2 That See Me Later Look ....Nail My Shoes To The Floor		$6		Decca 32193
10/5/68	70	4		3 Old Before My Time ....Shutting Out The Light		$6		Decca 32367
5/17/69	40	10		4 Upstairs In The Bedroom ....My Home Away From Home		$6		Decca 32464
11/1/69	70	2		5 Sing A Song About Love ....If You Don't Swing - Don't Ring		$6		Decca 32564
3/8/70	61	4		6 Take Me Back To The Goodtimes, Sally ....Something Called Happiness		$6		Decca 32633
8/1/70	47	9		7 Hurry Home To Me ....My Home Away From Home		$6		Decca 32705
4/24/71	74	2		8 If You Want Me To I'll Go ....Rain Falling On Me		$6		Decca 32792
7/10/71	13	16		9 Here I Go Again ....If You Don't Swing...Don't Ring		$6		Decca 32839
12/25/71+	54	8		10 Search Your Heart ....I'll Walk On Water		$6		Decca 32903
8/12/72	60	5		11 Just Because I'm Still In Love With You..................Pledging My Love		$6		Decca 32985
1/27/73	75	1		12 If Not For You ....Searching (For Someone Like You)		$6		Decca 33034
				#25 Pop hit for **Olivia Newton-John** in 1971				
10/20/73	39	11		13 Lovin' Someone On My Mind............................This Time		$5		ABC 11390
2/23/74	24	12		14 Seasons In The Sun ....Live And Let Live		$5		ABC 11418
				#1 Pop hit for **Terry Jacks** in 1974				
6/22/74	56	10		15 Everybody Needs A Rainbow ....I'll Surely Fall In Love With You		$5		ABC 11443
10/5/74	55	11		16 Baby's Gone ....Love Look (At Us Now)		$5		ABC 12028
				written by **Bobby Goldsboro** and **Roy Orbison**; #84 Pop hit for **Gene Thomas** in 1964				
3/8/75	75	7		17 I Just Came Home To Count The Memories.. No One Has Ever Loved Me Like You		$5		ABC 12062
1/8/77	79	6		18 Neon Lady ....'57 Chevrolet		$4		United Artists 913
9/24/77	97	1		19 Playing With The Baby's Mama		$4		United Artists 1051
10/21/78	100	3		20 Takin' A Chance ....I Don't Know How To Tell Her		$4		United Artists 1238
7/28/79	77	3		21 I'm Turning You Loose ....Going Home		$4		United Artists 1300

WRIGHT, Chely   '97
Born on 10/25/70 in Kansas City. Female singer/guitarist.

6/25/94	58	10		1 He's A Good Ole Boy..............................Go On And Go		$3	▌	Polydor 853056
10/22/94	48	14		2 Till I Was Loved By You ....He Don't Do Bars Anymore		$3	▌	Polydor 853810
2/4/95	56	8		3 Sea Of Cowboy Hats ....Nobody But A Fool		$3	▌	Polydor 851430
10/21/95	66	7		4 Listenin' To The Radio ....Till All Her Tears Are Dry		$3	▌	Polydor 577282
2/10/96	41	15		5 The Love That We Lost...................Gotta Get Good At Givin' Again		$3	▌	Polydor 577936
7/19/97	14	20		6 Shut Up And Drive S:11 *(album snippets)*	112	$3	▌	MCA 72012
11/29/97+	39	15		7 Just Another Heartache ....Feelin' Single And Seein' Double		$3		MCA 72025

WRIGHT, Curtis   '89
Born on 6/6/55 in Huntington, Pennsylvania. Singer/songwriter. Former member of the **Super Grit Cowboy Band** and **Orrall & Wright**.

11/11/89	38	13		1 She's Got A Man On Her Mind		$5		Airborne 75746
7/11/92	59	7		2 Hometown Radio..				album cut
1/2/93	53	10		3 If I Could Stop Lovin' You				album cut
				above 2 from the album *Curtis Wright* on Liberty 97825				

WRIGHT, Ginny   '55
Born in Twin City, Georgia.

1/9/54	3	22		1 I Love You A:3 / J:7 / S:8 *I Want You Yes (You Want Me No)*		$30		Fabor 101
				GINNY WRIGHT/JIM REEVES				
1/1/55	2³	26		2 Are You Mine A:2 / J:4 / S:5 *I've Got Somebody New*		$30		Fabor 117
				GINNY WRIGHT/TOM TALL				

★353★   **WRIGHT, Johnny**   '65
Born on 5/13/14 in Mount Juliet, Tennessee; raised in Nashville. Singer/songwriter/fiddle player. Member of **Johnnie & Jack** duo. Married **Kitty Wells** in 1938. Father of **Bobby Wright** and **Ruby Wright**.
   1)Hello Vietnam 2)Walkin', Talkin', Cryin', Barely Beatin' Broken Heart 3)Blame It On The Moonlight

5/2/64	22	15		1 Walkin', Talkin', Cryin', Barely Beatin' Broken				
				Heart ....They're All Going Home But One		$8		Decca 31593
				JOHNNY WRIGHT And The Tennessee Mountain Boys				
1/2/65	37	5		2 Don't Give Up The Ship ....Guitar Lessons		$8		Decca 31679
5/8/65	28	11		3 Blame It On The Moonlight ....Rest In Peace		$8		Decca 31740
8/28/65	❶³	21		4 Hello Vietnam Mexico City		$8		Decca 31821

DEBUT	PEAK	WKS	Gold	A-side (Chart Hit)..B-side	Pop	$	Pic	Label & Number
				WRIGHT, Johnny — Cont'd				
12/18/65+	31	10		5 Keep The Flag Flying .... *You're Over There (And I'm Over Here)*		$8		Decca 31875
6/4/66	31	6		6 Nickels, Quarters And Dimes .... *Is Love Worth All The Heartaches*		$8		Decca 31927
10/15/66	53	7		7 I'm Doing This For Daddy .... *Racing Man*		$8		Decca 32002
12/31/66+	50	11		8 Mama's Little Jewel .... *Nothing From Nothing*		$8		Decca 32061
8/12/67	66	5		9 American Power .... *Settle Back Down To Earth*		$8		Decca 32162
12/16/67	69	4		10 Music To Cry By .... *Cheaters Can't Win*		$8		Decca 32216
5/11/68	54	8		11 We'll Stick Together .... *Heartbreak Waltz*		$8		Decca 32294
				KITTY WELLS And JOHNNY WRIGHT				
11/30/68	66	5		12 (They Always Come Out) Smellin' Like A Rose .... *One Little Taco*		$8		Decca 32402
				WRIGHT, Justin **'89**				
				Born in Springfield, Illinois in 1961; raised in Phoenix.				
2/4/89	91	2		Settin' At The Kitchen Table		$6		Bear 195
				WRIGHT, Lee **'79**				
				Male singer.				
12/23/78+	86	4		1 Capricorn Kings .... *Wait 'Til Morning*		$6		Prairie Dust 7628
7/6/85	90	4		2 The Eyes Have It		$6		Prairie Dust 5185
				WRIGHT, Michelle **'92**				
				Born on 7/1/61 in Morpeth, Ontario, Canada.				
6/2/90	32	21		1 New Kind Of Love .... *As Far As Lonely Goes*		$3		Arista 2002
10/13/90	72	5		2 Woman's Intuition .... *As Far As Lonely Goes*		$3		Arista 2090
5/11/91	73	2		3 All You Really Wanna Do .... *The Longest Night*		$3		Arista 2208
4/4/92	10	20		4 Take It Like A Man *Guitar Talk*		$3		Arista 12406
7/25/92	43	19		5 One Time Around .... *A Little More Comfortable*		$3		Arista 12444
10/31/92	31	17		6 He Would Be Sixteen .... *The Change*		$3		Arista 12480
2/27/93	55	7		7 The Change .... *If I'm Ever Over You*		$3		Arista 12528
7/30/94	57	8		8 One Good Man .... *Where Do We Go From Here*		$3	∎	Arista 12727
7/13/96	50	10		9 Nobody's Girl .... *I'm Not Afraid*		$3	∎	Arista 13023
				WRIGHT, Randy **'84**				
				Born on 9/11/56 in Troy, Missouri. Singer/songwriter/drummer.				
11/5/83	86	3		1 There's Nobody Lovin' At Home .... *Times Like This*		$4		MCA 52273
5/12/84	77	4		2 If You're Serious About Cheating .... *Times Like This*		$4		MCA 52358
				WRIGHT, Ruby **'64**				
				Born on 10/27/39 in Nashville. Daughter of **Kitty Wells** and **Johnny Wright**; sister of **Bobby Wright**.				
9/5/64	13	13		1 Dern Ya .... *Such A Silly Notion* [N]	103	$15		RIC 126
				answer to "Dang Me" by Roger Miller				
11/5/66	72	2		2 A New Place To Hang Your Hat .... *A Kick In The Conscience*		$10		Epic 10055
5/27/67	69	7		3 (I Can Find) A Better Deal Than That .... *Everytime, All The Time*		$10		Epic 10150
				WRIGHT, Sonny **'79**				
				Born Nathan Edward Wright on 2/2/43 in Flagler, Colorado. Married to **Peggy Sue**.				
10/22/77	100	1		1 If This Is What Love's All About .... *Someone I Can't Say No To*		$5		Door Knob 038
				PEGGY SUE & SONNY WRIGHT				
11/10/79	86	5		2 Gently Hold Me .... *If This Is What Love's All About*		$5		Door Knob 113
				PEGGY SUE & SONNY WRIGHT				
4/26/80	91	4		3 Molly (And The Texas Rain) .... *It Wasn't Me Who Said I Owned A Gold Mine*		$5		Door Knob 128
				WRIGHT BROTHERS, The **'81**				
				Vocal trio from Bedford, Indiana: brothers Tom and Tim Wright, with Karl Hinkle. John McDowell replaced Hinkle in early 1984.				
10/31/81	35	12		1 Family Man .... *Engine Engine Number Nine*		$4		Warner 49837
4/3/82	42	11		2 When You Find Her, Keep Her .... *Let The Little Bird Fly*		$4		Warner 50033
9/4/82	40	8		3 Made In The U.S.A. .... *Words Of Love*		$4		Warner 29926
1/8/83	68	5		4 So Easy To Love .... *We Don't Know Why*		$4		Warner 29839
3/31/84	33	13		5 Southern Women .... *Love's Slippin' Up On Me*		$3		Mercury 818653
8/11/84	46	11		6 So Close .... *Radio Lover*		$3		Mercury 880055
11/3/84	57	9		7 Eight Days A Week .... *She's A Diamond*		$3		Mercury 880316
				#1 Pop hit for The Beatles in 1965				
3/30/85	48	10		8 Fire In The Sky .... *Pride*		$3		Mercury 880596
9/10/88	85	3		9 Come On Rain		$4		Airborne 10006
				WYATT, Gene **'68**				
				Died in 1979 (age 42). Cousin of **Chuck Pollard**.				
3/23/68	74	2		1 I Stole The Flowers .... *I'm A One Woman Man*		$10		Mercury 41032
8/17/68	69	3		2 I Just Ain't Got (As Much As He's Got Going For Me) .... *Chains Around My Mind*		$10		Paula 308
				WYATT, Nina **'88**				
1/30/88	76	3		1 Richer Now With You .... *You're Not Playing Love By The Rules*		$5		Charta 207
8/20/88	88	2		2 After The Passion Leaves .... *Love Finally Got The Best Of Me*		$5		Charta 210
				WYATT BROTHERS **'87**				
12/27/86+	79	5		Wyatt Liquor		$7		Wyatt 103

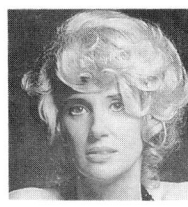

WYNETTE, Tammy ★26★ '67

Born Virginia Wynette Pugh on 5/5/42 in Itawamba County, Mississippi. Died of a blood clot on 4/6/98 (age 55). Married to **George Jones** from 1969-75. Married her manager George Richey (brother of **Wyley McPherson**) on 7/6/78. Known as "The First Lady of Country Music." Elected to the Country Music Hall of Fame in 1998. CMA Awards: 1968, 1969 & 1970 Female Vocalist of the Year.

1)*I Don't Wanna Play House* 2)*D-I-V-O-R-C-E* 3)*Stand By Your Man* 4)*He Loves Me All The Way* 5)*My Elusive Dreams*

DEBUT	PEAK	WKS	A-side B-side	Pop	$	Pic	Label & Number
12/10/66+	44	9	1 Apartment #9 .... *I'm Not Mine To Give*		$12		Epic 10095
3/18/67	3	21	2 Your Good Girl's Gonna Go Bad *Send Me No Roses*		$10		Epic 10134
7/15/67	❶²	18	3 My Elusive Dreams *Marriage On The Rocks* DAVID HOUSTON and TAMMY WYNETTE	89	$10		Epic 10194
8/26/67	❶³	20	4 I Don't Wanna Play House *Soakin' Wet*		$10		Epic 10211
1/6/68	❶¹	17	5 Take Me To Your World *Good*		$10		Epic 10269
1/20/68	11	14	6 It's All Over .... *Together We Stand (Divided We Fall)* DAVID HOUSTON & TAMMY WYNETTE		$10		Epic 10274
5/18/68	❶³	17	7 D-I-V-O-R-C-E *Don't Make Me Now*	63	$10		Epic 10315
10/19/68	❶³	21	8 Stand By Your Man *I Stayed Long Enough*	19	$10		Epic 10398
4/12/69	❶²	14	9 Singing My Song *Too Far Gone*	75	$10	■	Epic 10462
8/30/69	❶²	16	10 The Ways To Love A Man *Still Around*	81	$10		Epic 10512
1/31/70	2³	14	11 I'll See Him Through *Enough Of A Woman*	100	$10		Epic 10571
5/23/70	❶³	16	12 He Loves Me All The Way *Our Last Night Together*	97	$10		Epic 10612
9/12/70	❶²	15	13 Run, Woman, Run *My Daddy Doll*	92	$10		Epic 10653
11/28/70+	5	13	14 The Wonders You Perform *Gentle Shepherd*	104	$10		Epic 10687
3/6/71	2³	15	15 We Sure Can Love Each Other *Fun*	103	$10		Epic 10707
7/17/71	❶²	15	16 Good Lovin' (Makes It Right) *I Love You, Mr. Jones*	111	$10		Epic 10759
12/25/71+	9	13	17 Take Me *We Go Together* TAMMY WYNETTE & GEORGE JONES		$10		Epic 10815
1/1/72	❶¹	14	18 Bedtime Story *Reach Out Your Hand*	86	$10		Epic 10818
5/20/72	2²	14	19 Reach Out Your Hand *Love's The Answer*		$10		Epic 10856
7/8/72	6	15	20 The Ceremony *The Great Divide* TAMMY WYNETTE & GEORGE JONES		$10		Epic 10881
9/16/72	❶¹	14	21 My Man *Things I Love To Do*		$10		Epic 10909
11/25/72+	38	9	22 Old Fashioned Singing .... *We Love To Sing About Jesus* GEORGE JONES & TAMMY WYNETTE		$10		Epic 10923
12/30/72+	❶¹	15	23 'Til I Get It Right *The Bridge Of Love*	106	$10		Epic 10940
4/7/73	❶¹	17	24 Kids Say The Darndest Things *I Wish I Had A Mommy Like You*	72	$10		Epic 10969
4/7/73	32	9	25 Let's Build A World Together .... *Touching Shoulders* GEORGE JONES AND TAMMY WYNETTE		$10		Epic 10963
9/1/73	❶²	17	26 We're Gonna Hold On *My Elusive Dreams* GEORGE JONES & TAMMY WYNETTE		$8		Epic 11031
12/29/73+	❶²	15	27 Another Lonely Song *The Only Time I'm Really Me*		$8		Epic 11079
2/9/74	15	13	28 (We're Not) The Jet Set .... *Crawdad Song* GEORGE JONES and TAMMY WYNETTE		$8		Epic 11083
7/27/74	8	12	29 We Loved It Away *Ain't Love Been Good* GEORGE JONES & TAMMY WYNETTE		$8		Epic 11151
8/17/74	4	16	30 Woman To Woman *Love Me Forever*		$7		Epic 50008
2/15/75	4	16	31 (You Make Me Want To Be) A Mother *I'm Not A Has-Been (I Just Never Was)*		$7		Epic 50071
5/17/75	25	13	32 God's Gonna Get'cha (For That) .... *Those Were The Good Times* GEORGE JONES AND TAMMY WYNETTE		$7		Epic 50099
9/20/75	13	13	33 I Still Believe In Fairy Tales .... *Your Memory's Gone To Rest*		$7		Epic 50145
2/14/76	❶¹	15	34 'Til I Can Make It On My Own *Love Is Something Good For Everybody*	84	$7		Epic 50196
6/5/76	❶¹	15	35 Golden Ring *We're Putting It Back Together* GEORGE JONES and TAMMY WYNETTE		$7		Epic 50235
8/21/76	❶²	16	36 You And Me *When Love Was All We Had*	101	$7		Epic 50264
12/11/76+	❶²	16	37 Near You *Tattletale Eyes* GEORGE JONES and TAMMY WYNETTE #1 Pop hit for Francis Craig in 1947		$7		Epic 50314
3/19/77	6	14	38 (Let's Get Together) One Last Time *Hardly A Day Goes By*		$7		Epic 50349
7/16/77	5	13	39 Southern California *Keep The Change* GEORGE JONES and TAMMY WYNETTE		$7		Epic 50418
10/8/77	6	15	40 One Of A Kind *Loving You, I Do*		$6		Epic 50450
4/22/78	26	11	41 I'd Like To See Jesus (On The Midnight Special) .... *Love Doesn't Always Come (On The Night It's Needed)*		$6		Epic 50538
7/15/78	3	15	42 Womanhood *50 Words Or Less*		$6		Epic 50574
2/10/79	6	13	43 They Call It Making Love *Let Me Be Me*		$6		Epic 50661
6/9/79	7	14	44 No One Else In The World *Mama, Your Little Girl Fell*		$6		Epic 50722
3/1/80	2¹	14	45 Two Story House *It Sure Was Good* GEORGE JONES and TAMMY WYNETTE		$6		Epic 50849
4/19/80	17	14	46 He Was There (When I Needed You) .... *Only The Names Have Been Changed*		$6		Epic 50868
8/9/80	17	13	47 Starting Over .... *I'll Be Thinking Of You*		$6		Epic 50915
9/6/80	19	11	48 A Pair Of Old Sneakers .... *We'll Talk About It Later* GEORGE JONES and TAMMY WYNETTE		$6		Epic 50930

WYNETTE, Tammy — Cont'd

DEBUT	PEAK	WKS	Gold	A-side / B-side	Pop	$	Pic	Label & Number
3/21/81	21	12		49 Cowboys Don't Shoot Straight (Like They Used To) ...... *You Brought Me Back*		$5		Epic 51011
9/5/81	18	14		50 Crying In The Rain...*Bring Back My Baby To Me*		$5		Epic 02439
				#6 Pop hit for **The Everly Brothers** in 1962				
3/27/82	8	17		51 Another Chance *What's It Like To Be A Woman*		$5		Epic 02770
8/14/82	16	16		52 You Still Get To Me In My Dreams ....*If I Didn't Have A Heart*		$5		Epic 03064
12/11/82+	19	15		53 A Good Night's Love..................................*I'm Going On With Everything Gone*		$5		Epic 03384
4/23/83	46	9		54 I Just Heard A Heart Break (And I'm So Afraid It's Mine) ....*Back To The Wall*		$4		Epic 03811
7/9/83	63	7		55 Unwed Fathers................................*I'm So Afraid That I'd Live Through It*		$4		Epic 03971
10/1/83	63	6		56 Still In The Ring ....*Midnight Love*		$4		Epic 04101
6/2/84	40	15		57 Lonely Heart ....*(I'm Not) A Candle In The Wind*		$4		Epic 04467
2/23/85	6	22		58 Sometimes When We Touch *A:5 / S:6 You're Gonna Be The Last One*		$3		Columbia 04782
				MARK GRAY and TAMMY WYNETTE				
				#3 Pop hit for Dan Hill in 1978				
7/13/85	48	9		59 You Can Lead A Heart To Love (But You Can't Make It Fall) ....*He Talks To Me*		$3		Epic 05399
8/30/86	53	8		60 Alive And Well ....*I'll Be Thinking Of You*		$3		Epic 06263
8/1/87	12	19		61 Your Love *S:7 I Wasn't Meant To Live My Life Alone*		$3		Epic 07226
				Ricky Skaggs (harmony vocal)				
12/5/87+	16	20		62 Talkin' To Myself Again ....*S:15 A Slow Burning Fire*		$3		Epic 07635
				The O'Kanes (harmony vocals)				
5/7/88	25	15		63 Beneath A Painted Sky ....*S:24 Some Things Will Never Change*		$3		Epic 07788
				Emmylou Harris (harmony vocal)				
2/18/89	51	11		64 Next To You...................................*When A Girl Becomes A Wife*		$3		Epic 68570
5/27/89	66	6		65 Thank The Cowboy For The Ride ....*We Called It Everything But Quits*		$3		Epic 68894
10/7/89	63	5		66 While The Feeling's Good ....*Our Wedding Band*		$3		Curb 10559
				WAYNE NEWTON (with Tammy Wynette)				
9/1/90	57	8		67 Let's Call It A Day Today ....*When A Girl Becomes A Wife*		$3	▌	Epic 73427
2/2/91	56	8		68 What Goes With Blue ....*I Love My Man*		$3	▌	Epic 46238
8/24/91	49	8		69 We're Strangers Again ....*If You Were The Friend*		$3	▌	Epic 73958
				TAMMY WYNETTE with Randy Travis				
12/25/93+	68	2		70 Silver Threads And Golden Needles ....*Let Her Fly*		$3	▌	Columbia 77294
				PARTON/WYNETTE/LYNN				
10/8/94	67	9		71 Girl Thang...........................				album cut
				TAMMY WYNETTE With Wynonna				
				from the album *Without Walls* on Epic 52481				
7/1/95	69	4		72 One ....*Golden Ring*		$3		MCA 55048
				GEORGE JONES AND TAMMY WYNETTE				

WYNONNA ★173★   '92

Born Christina Ciminella on 5/30/64 in Ashland, Kentucky. Singer/songwriter/guitarist. Half of **The Judds** duo with her mother, Naomi, from 1983-91. Sister of actress Ashley Judd.

1)No One Else On Earth 2)I Saw The Light 3)To Be Loved By You

DEBUT	PEAK	WKS	Gold	A-side / B-side	Pop	$	Pic	Label & Number
				WYNONNA JUDD:				
2/15/92	❶[1]	20		1 She Is His Only Need *No One Else On Earth*		$3		Curb/MCA 54320
5/9/92	❶[3]	20		2 I Saw The Light *When I Reach The Place I'm Goin'*		$3		Curb/MCA 54407
8/15/92	❶[4]	20		3 No One Else On Earth *(album version)*	83	$3	▌	Curb/MCA 54449
12/5/92+	4	20		4 My Strongest Weakness *What It Takes*	119	$3	▌	Curb/MCA 54516
4/3/93	3	20		5 Tell Me Why *A Little Bit Of Love*	77	$3	▌	Curb/MCA 54606
5/15/93	2[1]	20		6 A Bad Goodbye *The Hard Way*	43	$3	▌	RCA 62503
				CLINT BLACK (with Wynonna)				
7/17/93	3	20		7 Only Love *Just Like New*	102	$3	▌	Curb/MCA 54689
10/30/93+	6	20		8 Is It Over Yet *That Was Yesterday*		$3		Curb/MCA 54754
12/25/93	61	1		9 Let's Make A Baby King...[X]				album cut
				from the album *Tell Me Why* on Curb/MCA 10822				
2/19/94	2[1]	20		10 Rock Bottom *Girls With Guitars*		$3	▌	Curb/MCA 54809
6/4/94	10	20		11 Girls With Guitars *I Just Drove By*		$3	▌	Curb/MCA 54875
10/8/94	67	9		12 Girl Thang......................................				album cut
				TAMMY WYNETTE With Wynonna				
				from the album *Without Walls* on Epic 52481				
				WYNONNA:				
1/6/96	❶[1]	20		13 To Be Loved By You *Freebird*		$3	▌	Curb/MCA 55084
4/27/96	14	20		14 Heaven Help My Heart.........................*(album version)*		$3		Curb/MCA 55194
8/31/96	44	10		15 My Angel Is Here *Change The World*		$3		Curb/MCA 55252
11/16/96	55	6		16 Somebody To Love You ....*(club mix)*		$3		Curb/MCA 55286
12/28/96	55	2		17 Mary, Did You Know...[X]				album cut
				KENNY ROGERS With Wynonna				
				from the album *The Gift* on Magnatone 108				
10/4/97	13	20		18 When Love Starts Talkin'.........................*S:9 The Other Side*	98	$3	▌	Curb/Universal 56095
12/13/97+	14	20		19 Come Some Rainy Day				album cut
				from the album *The Other Side* on Curb/Universal 53061				

DEBUT	PEAK	WKS	Gold	A-side (Chart Hit)..B-side	Pop	$	Pic	Label & Number

WYRICK, Jim   '83
Born in Maynardville, Tennessee.

2/26/83	85	2		The Memory..*First To Be The Last*		$5		NSD 157

JIM WYRICK and Union Gold

Y

YANKOVIC, Frankie, & His Yanks   '49
Born on 7/28/15 in Davis, West Virginia; raised in Cleveland. Died on 10/14/98 (age 83). Accordionist/polka bandleader. Known as "America's Polka King."

5/8/48	7	1		1 Just Because	*A Night In May*	9	$10		Columbia 12359
1/1/49	13	1		2 The Iron Range...S:13 *Linda's Lullaby* [I]			$10		Columbia 12381
4/30/49	7	7	●	3 Blue Skirt Waltz	S:7 / J:10 *Charlie Was A Boxer*	12	$10		Columbia 12394

FRANKIE YANKOVIC & HIS YANKS with THE MARLIN SISTERS

YARBROUGH, Bob   '71
Born in 1940 in Chattanooga, Tennessee.

5/22/71	38	12		1 You're Just More A Woman...........................*In The Palm Of My Hand*		$8		Sugar Hill 013
4/17/76	85	5		2 50 Ways To Leave Your Lover.................*You Only Look Me Up When You're Down*		$6		Music Mill 186

BOB YARBOROUGH
#1 Pop hit for Paul Simon in 1976

YATES, Billy   '97
Born on 3/13/63 in Doniphan, Missouri.

5/10/97	69	3		1 I Smell Smoke...*Goodbye Makes The Saddest Sound*		$3	▮	Almo Sounds 89010
5/24/97	36	16		2 Flowers..				album cut
				from the album *Billy Yates* on Almo Sounds 80015				
10/4/97	69	1		3 When The Walls Come Tumblin' Down...........................*Broken Hearted Me*		$3		Almo Sounds 89013

YATES, Jenny   '87

4/25/87	80	3		A Whole Month Of Sundays...*Holding Out For Love*		$3		Mercury 888428

YATES, Lori   '88
Born in Toronto.

11/12/88	77	5		1 Scene Of The Crime...*Cowboy*		$3	▪	Columbia 08055
3/25/89	78	4		2 Promises, Promises...*Heart In A Suitcase*		$3		Columbia 68596

YEARWOOD, Trisha   ★137★   '91
Born Patricia Lynn Yearwood on 9/19/64 in Monticello, Georgia. Singer/songwriter. Married Robert Reynolds of **The Mavericks** on 5/21/94. CMA Awards: 1997 & 1998 Female Vocalist of the Year.

1)She's In Love With The Boy 2)Thinkin' About You 3)XXX's And OOO's 4)Believe Me Baby
5)In Another's Eyes

5/18/91	❶²	20		1 She's In Love With The Boy	*Victim Of The Game*		$3		MCA 54076
9/14/91	4	20		2 Like We Never Had A Broken Heart	*The Whisper Of Your Heart*		$3		MCA 54172
12/21/91+	8	20		3 That's What I Like About You	*When Goodbye Was A Word*		$3		MCA 54270
3/28/92	4	20		4 The Woman Before Me	*You Done Me Wrong (And That Ain't Right)*		$3		MCA 54362
8/8/92	5	20		5 Wrong Side Of Memphis	*Lonesome Dove*		$3		MCA 54414
11/7/92+	2¹	20		6 Walkaway Joe	*You Don't Have To Move That Mountain*		$3		MCA 54495
				TRISHA YEARWOOD with Don Henley					
3/6/93	12	20		7 You Say You Will..*Hearts In Armor*		$3		MCA 54600
6/12/93	19	20		8 Down On My Knees.......................................*For Reasons I've Forgotten*		$3		MCA 54670
10/16/93	2¹	20		9 The Song Remembers When	*Oh Lonesome You*	82	$3	▮	MCA 54734
2/5/94	21	20		10 Better Your Heart Than Mine.........................*Hard Promises To Keep*		$3	▮	MCA 54786
6/4/94	72	2		11 I Fall To Pieces..*(album version)*		$3	▮	MCA 54836
				AARON NEVILLE AND TRISHA YEARWOOD					
7/9/94	❶²	20		12 XXX's And OOO's (An American Girl)	*One In A Row*	114	$3	▮	MCA 54898
12/17/94	60	4		13 It Wasn't His Child...*Reindeer Boogie* [X]		$3		MCA 54940
1/14/95	❶²	20		14 Thinkin' About You	*Fairytale*	120	$3	▮	MCA 54973
4/29/95	23	15		15 You Can Sleep While I Drive...............S:19 *Two Days From Knowing*		$3	▮	MCA 55025
				written and first recorded by Melissa Etheridge on her 1989 *Brave And Crazy* album					
8/5/95	9	20		16 I Wanna Go Too Far	*The Restless Kind*		$3		MCA 55078
12/2/95+	59	8		17 On A Bus To St. Cloud..*O Mexico*		$3		MCA 55141
7/13/96	❶²	20		18 Believe Me Baby (I Lied)	*Little Hercules*		$3		MCA 55211
11/9/96+	3	20		19 Everybody Knows	*A Lover Is Forever*		$3		MCA 55250
3/1/97	36	13		20 I Need You...*Hello, I'm Gone*		$3		MCA 55308
6/7/97	2¹	20		21 How Do I Live	S:3 *(remix)*	23	$3	▮	MCA 72015
				from the movie *Con Air* starring Nicolas Cage					
8/23/97	2²	20		22 In Another's Eyes	*I Want To Live Again*		$3		MCA 72021
				TRISHA YEARWOOD AND GARTH BROOKS					

YOAKAM, Dwight ★113★   '89

Born on 10/23/56 in Pikeville, Kentucky. Singer/songwriter/guitarist/actor. Member of the **Buzzin' Cousins**. Acted in the movie *Sling Blade*.

1)*I Sang Dixie* 2)*Streets Of Bakersfield* 3)*Ain't That Lonely Yet* 4)*Fast As You*
5)*A Thousand Miles From Nowhere*

DEBUT	PEAK	WKS		A-side / B-side	Pop	$	Label & Number
3/1/86	3	24	1	Honky Tonk Man — S:3 / A:4 *Miner's Prayer*		$3	Reprise 28793
7/12/86	4	21	2	Guitars, Cadillacs — S:3 / A:4 *I'll Be Gone*		$3	■ Reprise 28688
11/15/86	31	15	3	It Won't Hurt — S:22 / A:30 *Bury Me*		$3	Reprise 28565
4/11/87	7	16	4	Little Sister — S:4 / A:21 *This Drinkin' Will Kill Me*		$3	■ Reprise 28432
				#5 Pop hit for **Elvis Presley** in 1961			
7/25/87	8	19	5	Little Ways — S:4 *Readin', Rightin', Rt. 23*		$3	■ Reprise 28310
11/14/87+	6	19	6	Please, Please Baby — S:6 *Throughout All Time*		$3	Reprise 28174
3/5/88	9	22	7	Always Late With Your Kisses — S:5 *1,000 Miles*		$3	■ Reprise 27994
7/16/88	❶¹	18	8	Streets Of Bakersfield — S:❶³ *One More Time*		$3	■ Reprise 27964
				DWIGHT YOAKAM & BUCK OWENS			
11/12/88+	❶¹	21	9	I Sang Dixie — S:18 *Floyd County*		$3	■ Reprise 27715
3/4/89	5	19	10	I Got You — *South Of Cincinnati*		$3	Reprise 27567
6/24/89	46	7	11	Buenas Noches From A Lonely Room (She Wore Red Dresses) — *What I Don't Know*		$3	Reprise 22944
9/30/89	35	10	12	Long White Cadillac — *Little Ways*		$3	■ Reprise 22799
10/20/90+	11	20	13	Turn It On, Turn It Up, Turn Me Loose — *Since I Started Drinkin' Again*		$3	▌ Reprise 19543
3/2/91	5	20	14	You're The One — *If There Was A Way*		$3	Reprise 19405
8/10/91	15	21	15	Nothing's Changed Here — *Sad, Sad Music*		$3	Reprise 19256
12/21/91+	7	20	16	It Only Hurts When I Cry — *Let's Work Together*		$3	Reprise 19148
4/25/92	18	20	17	The Heart That You Own — *Dangerous Man*		$3	Reprise 18966
8/8/92	47	10	18	Send A Message To My Heart — *Takes A Lot To Rock You*		$3	Reprise 18846
				DWIGHT YOAKAM & PATTY LOVELESS			
10/24/92	35	20	19	Suspicious Minds — *Burning Love*		$3	Epic Sound. 74753
				#1 Pop hit for **Elvis Presley** in 1969; from the movie *Honeymoon In Vegas* starring James Caan			
3/13/93	2³	20	20	Ain't That Lonely Yet — *A Thousand Miles From Nowhere*	101	$3	▌ Reprise 18590
6/26/93	2¹	20	21	A Thousand Miles From Nowhere — *Ain't That Lonely Yet*		$3	▌ Reprise 18528
7/3/93+	2¹	20	22	Fast As You — *Home For Sale*	70	$3	▌ Reprise 18341
				originally charted as an album cut for 3 weeks (#72); re-entered on 10/2/93			
2/19/94	14	20	23	Try Not To Look So Pretty — *Wild Ride*		$3	▌ Reprise 18239
7/2/94	22	20	24	Pocket Of A Clown			album cut
				from the album *This Time* on Reprise 45241			
10/14/95	20	20	25	Nothing/ — S:19			
2/3/96	51	8	26	Gone (That'll Be Me)		$3	▌ Reprise 17734
4/20/96	59	5	27	Sorry You Asked?			album cut
				from the album *Gone* on Reprise 46051			
7/12/97	47	10	28	Claudette			album cut
				written by **Roy Orbison**; from the album *Under The Covers* on Reprise 46690			
12/27/97	60	2	29	Santa Claus Is Back In Town...[X]			album cut
				from the album *Come On Christmas* on Warner 46683			

YOUNG, Cole   '83

DEBUT	PEAK	WKS		A-side / B-side	$	Label & Number
7/23/83	72	5		Just Give Me One More Night — *I'd Keep My Heart In Line*	$5	Evergreen 1008

YOUNG, Faron ★21★   '58

Born on 2/25/32 in Shreveport, Louisiana. Died of a self-inflicted gunshot on 12/10/96 (age 64). Singer/songwriter/guitarist/actor. Joined the *Louisiana Hayride* in 1951. Served in the U.S. Army from 1952-54. Known as "The Young Sheriff." Acted in several movies. Founder and one-time publisher of the *Music City News* magazine.

1)*Alone With You* 2)*Hello Walls* 3)*Country Girl* 4)*Live Fast, Love Hard, Die Young*
5)*It's Four In The Morning*

DEBUT	PEAK	WKS		A-side / B-side	$	Label & Number
1/10/53	2¹	18	1	Goin' Steady — A:2 / J:7 / S:10 *Just Out Of Reach (Of My Two Open Arms)*	$25	Capitol 2299
				also see #66 below		
6/6/53	5	5	2	I Can't Wait (For The Sun To Go Down) — A:5 *What's The Use To Love You*	$25	Capitol 2461
9/4/54	8	9	3	A Place For Girls Like You — A:8 / S:13 *In The Chapel In The Moonlight*	$25	Capitol 2859
11/20/54+	2³	27	4	If You Ain't Lovin' (You Ain't Livin') — A:2 / J:2 / S:3 *If That's The Fashion*	$20	Capitol 2953
4/2/55	❶³	22	5	Live Fast, Love Hard, Die Young/ — A:❶³ / J:2 / S:3	$20	Capitol 3056
		12	6	Forgive Me, Dear — J:flip		
8/13/55	2⁴	28	7	All Right/ — A:2 / J:3 / S:4	$20	Capitol 3169
8/6/55	11	9	8	Go Back You Fool — S:11		
11/19/55+	5	13	9	It's A Great Life (If You Don't Weaken)/ — A:5 / J:6 / S:7	$20	Capitol 3258
		1	10	For The Love Of A Woman Like You — J:flip		
4/14/56	3	10	11	You're Still Mine/ — A:3 / S:5	$15	Capitol 3369
4/7/56	4	16	12	I've Got Five Dollars And It's Saturday Night — S:4 / J:4 / A:10		

DEBUT	PEAK	WKS	Gold	A-side / B-side	Pop	$	Pic	Label & Number
				YOUNG, Faron — Cont'd				
6/23/56	2¹	33		13 Sweet Dreams/ A:2 / J:4 / S:5				
		3		14 Until I Met You .... J:flip		$15		Capitol 3443
11/10/56	9	6		15 Turn Her Down/ A:9 / S:13				
		1		16 I'll Be Satisfied With Love .... S:flip		$15		Capitol 3549
2/23/57	5	13		17 I Miss You Already (And You're Not Even Gone)/ A:5 / S:8				
		1		18 I'm Gonna Live Some Before I Die ...... S:flip		$15		Capitol 3611
5/20/57	15	1		19 The Shrine Of St. Cecilia .... A:15 He Was There	96	$15		Capitol 3696
8/5/57	12	1		20 Love Has Finally Come My Way ....A:12 Moonlight Mountain		$15		Capitol 3753
6/23/58	❶¹³	29		21 Alone With You/ A:❶¹³ / S:2	51			
6/30/58	10	2		22 Every Time I'm Kissing You A:10		$15		Capitol 3982
10/20/58	9	17		23 That's The Way I Feel/				
10/27/58	22	5		24 I Hate Myself....................................		$15		Capitol 4050
2/2/59	16	9		25 A Long Time Ago/				
1/26/59	20	10		26 Last Night At A Party		$15		Capitol 4113
4/13/59	14	8		27 That's The Way It's Gotta Be .... We're Talking It Over		$15		Capitol 4164
7/20/59	❶⁴	32		28 Country Girl/				
7/27/59	27	6		29 I Hear You Talkin'		$15		Capitol 4233
11/16/59+	4	21		30 Riverboat/	83			
11/16/59+	10	18		31 Face To The Wall		$15		Capitol 4291
4/11/60	5	17		32 Your Old Used To Be I'll Be Alright (In The Morning)		$15		Capitol 4351
10/24/60	21	5		33 There's Not Any Like You Left .... Is She All You Thought She'd Be		$15		Capitol 4410
12/26/60+	20	7		34 Forget The Past/				
1/16/61	28	3		35 A World So Full Of Love		$15		Capitol 4463
3/20/61	❶⁹	23		36 Hello Walls/	12			
5/15/61	28	2		37 Congratulations..............................		$15		Capitol 4533
				above 2 written by Willie Nelson				
10/2/61	8	17		38 Backtrack I Can't Find The Time	89	$15	■	Capitol 4616
3/24/62	7	13		39 Three Days I Let It Slip Away		$15	■	Capitol 4696
6/16/62	4	19		40 The Comeback Over Lonely And Under Kissed		$15		Capitol 4754
12/22/62+	9	10		41 Down By The River Safely In Love Again		$15		Capitol 4868
3/2/63	4	16		42 The Yellow Bandana How Much I Must Have Loved You	114	$12		Mercury 72085
6/8/63	14	7		43 Nightmare/				
6/1/63	30	1		44 I've Come To Say Goodbye		$12		Mercury 72114
10/26/63	13	7		45 We've Got Something In Common .... Think About The Good Old Days		$12		Mercury 72167
12/21/63+	10	14		46 You'll Drive Me Back (Into Her Arms Again) What Will I Tell My Darling		$12		Mercury 72201
3/14/64	5	23		47 Keeping Up With The Joneses/				
3/28/64	40	6		48 No Thanks, I Just Had One		$12	■	Mercury 72237
				MARGIE SINGLETON And FARON YOUNG (above 2)				
8/1/64	23	6		49 Rhinestones/				
7/25/64	48	2		50 Old Courthouse		$12		Mercury 72271
10/3/64	11	16		51 My Friend On The Right .... The World's Greatest Love		$12		Mercury 72313
12/5/64	38	8		52 Another Woman's Man - Another Man's Woman ....Honky Tonk Happy		$12		Mercury 72312
				FARON YOUNG AND MARGIE SINGLETON				
1/30/65	10	18		53 Walk Tall The Weakness Of A Man		$10		Mercury 72375
8/7/65	34	6		54 Nothing Left To Lose .... Dingaka (The Witch Doctor)		$10		Mercury 72440
11/27/65+	14	13		55 My Dreams................................. You Had A Call		$10		Mercury 72490
10/15/66	7	16		56 Unmitigated Gall Some Of Your Memories (Hurt Me All Of The Time)		$10		Mercury 72617
4/8/67	48	8		57 I Guess I Had Too Much To Dream Last Night...I Just Don't Know How To Say No		$10		Mercury 72656
10/28/67+	14	16		58 Wonderful World Of Women All I Can Stand		$8		Mercury 72728
3/9/68	14	16		59 She Went A Little Bit Farther Stay, Love		$8	■	Mercury 72774
8/3/68	8	16		60 I Just Came To Get My Baby Missing You Was All I Did Today		$8		Mercury 72827
3/1/69	25	19		61 I've Got Precious Memories .... You Stayed Just Long Enough		$8		Mercury 72889
7/12/69	2²	16		62 Wine Me Up That's Where My Baby Feels At Home		$8		Mercury 72936
11/1/69	4	14		63 Your Time's Comin' Painted Girls And Wine		$8		Mercury 72983
2/7/70	6	14		64 Occasional Wife The Guns Of Johnny Rondo		$7		Mercury 73018
5/30/70	4	16		65 If I Ever Fall In Love (With A Honky Tonk Girl) A Bunch Of Young Ideas		$7		Mercury 73065
10/10/70	5	12		66 Goin' Steady That's My Way [R]		$7		Mercury 73112
				new version of #1 above				
3/27/71	6	17		67 Step Aside Seems Like I'm Always Leaving		$7		Mercury 73191
8/7/71	9	14		68 Leavin' And Sayin' Goodbye She Was The Color Of Love		$7		Mercury 73220
12/4/71+	❶²	20		69 It's Four In The Morning It's Not The Miles	92	$7		Mercury 73250
7/22/72	5	16		70 This Little Girl Of Mine It Hurts So Good		$7		Mercury 73308
2/3/73	15	11		71 She Fights That Lovin' Feeling .... I'm In Love With Everything		$7		Mercury 73359
7/21/73	9	16		72 Just What I Had In Mind All At Once It's Forever		$7		Mercury 73403
3/9/74	8	14		73 Some Kind Of A Woman Again Today		$7		Mercury 73464
7/13/74	20	12		74 The Wrong In Loving You .... Almost Dawn In Denver		$7		Mercury 73500
11/30/74+	23	12		75 Another You .... God's Been Good To Me		$6		Mercury 73633
7/19/75	16	13		76 Here I Am In Dallas .... Too Much Of Not Enough Of You		$6		Mercury 73692
12/13/75+	21	12		77 Feel Again .... Some Old Rainy Mornin'		$6		Mercury 73731
4/10/76	33	10		78 I'd Just Be Fool Enough .... What You See Is What You Get		$6		Mercury 73782
10/9/76	30	11		79 (The Worst You Ever Gave Me Was) The Best I Ever Had ....You Get The Feelin'		$6		Mercury 73847
7/9/77	25	11		80 Crutches .... The Last Goodbye		$6		Mercury 73925

YOUNG, Faron — Cont'd

DEBUT	PEAK	WKS		A-side / B-side		$		Label & Number
2/25/78	38	10	81	Loving Here And Living There And Lying In Between .... *City Lights*		$6		Mercury 55019
4/7/79	67	6	82	The Great Chicago Fire .... *Old Songs*		$5		MCA 41004
9/22/79	69	6	83	That Over Thirty Look/		$5		MCA 41046
7/14/79	70	5	84	Second Hand Emotion		$5		MCA 41046
2/16/80	56	7	85	(If I'd Only Known) It Was The Last Time.................................. *Free And Easy*		$4		MCA 41177
8/30/80	72	4	86	Tearjoint .... *I May Lose You Tomorrow*		$4		MCA 41292
4/25/81	88	2	87	Until The Bitter End... *Motel With No Phone*		$4		MCA 51088
9/10/88	100	2	88	Stop And Take The Time .... *Misty Morning Rain*		$5		Step One 390
2/4/89	87	2	89	Here's To You .... *You're Just Another Drinking Song*		$5		Step One 397

YOUNG, Neil '85

Born on 11/12/45 in Toronto. Rock singer/songwriter/guitarist. Member of **Crosby, Stills, Nash & Young**. Charted 11 pop hits from 1970-83. Inducted into the Rock and Roll Hall of Fame in 1995.

DEBUT	PEAK	WKS		A-side / B-side		$		Label & Number
10/5/85	33	18		Get Back To The Country .... A:29 *Misfits*		$4		Geffen 28883

YOUNG, Roger '79

Singer from Yuma, Arizona.

DEBUT	PEAK	WKS		A-side / B-side		$		Label & Number
8/18/79	85	3		Skip A Rope		$6		Dessa 79-2

YOUNG, Steve '77

Born on 7/12/42 in Newnan, Georgia. Singer/songwriter.

DEBUT	PEAK	WKS		A-side / B-side		$		Label & Number
2/5/77	84	5		It's Not Supposed To Be That Way .... *Lonesome, On'ry And Mean*		$5		RCA 10868
				written by Willie Nelson				

YOUNGER, James & Michael '82

Duo of brothers from Edinburg, Texas: James and Michael Williams.

1)Nothing But The Radio On 2)There's No Substitute For You 3)Lovers On The Rebound

YOUNGER BROTHERS:

DEBUT	PEAK	WKS		A-side / B-side		$		Label & Number
4/24/82	68	5	1	Lonely Hearts.. *A Taste Of The Wind*		$4		MCA 52030
7/3/82	19	15	2	Nothing But The Radio On *A Taste Of The Wind*		$4		MCA 52076
12/11/82+	48	12	3	There's No Substitute For You.................................. *Here Comes The Tempter*		$4		MCA 52148
3/5/83	50	8	4	Somewhere Down The Line..*Blame It On Mexico*		$4		MCA 52183

JAMES & MICHAEL YOUNGER:

DEBUT	PEAK	WKS		A-side / B-side		$		Label & Number
6/4/83	54	10	5	A Taste Of The Wind .... *Lost In The Feeling*		$4		MCA 52222
9/17/83	48	9	6	Lovers On The Rebound.. *Here Comes The Tempter*		$4		MCA 52263
12/24/83+	65	8	7	Shoot First, Ask Questions Later .... *Thinking 'Bout Leaving*		$4		MCA 52317
6/29/85	82	5	8	My Special Angel.. *In South Texas*		$5		Permian 82011
4/5/86	67	7	9	Back On The Radio Again .... *Women Like Her Are In Dreams*		$5		AIR 102
9/27/86	65	7	10	She Wants To Marry A Cowboy		$5		AIR 106

YOUNGER BROTHERS BAND '84

Group from Leola, Pennsylvania. Led by Terry Gehman.

DEBUT	PEAK	WKS		A-side / B-side		$		Label & Number
9/8/84	92	2		Making Love To Dixie.. *I Don't Want To Be Your Friend*		$6		ERP 04094

Z

ZACA CREEK '89

Group of brothers from Santa Ynez, California: Gates (vocals), Scot (guitar), Jeff (keyboards) and James (bass) Foss.

DEBUT	PEAK	WKS		A-side / B-side		$		Label & Number
9/23/89	38	11	1	Sometimes Love's Not A Pretty Thing .... *Rock Me Back*		$3		Columbia 69062
12/23/89+	58	6	2	Ghost Town... *Time's Up*		$3		Columbia 73096
3/13/93	70	3	3	Broken Heartland				album cut
				from the album *Broken Heartland* on Giant 24491				

ZADORA, Pia '80

Born Pia Schipani on 5/4/56 in New York City. Actress/singer. Starred in several movies.

DEBUT	PEAK	WKS		A-side / B-side		$		Label & Number
4/28/79	76	3	1	Bedtime Stories/				
3/31/79	98	1	2	Tell Him		$4		Warner/Curb 8766
				#4 Pop hit for The Exciters in 1963				
8/25/79	65	5	3	I Know A Good Thing When I Feel It .... *Trouble*		$4		Warner/Curb 49065
1/12/80	55	5	4	Baby It's You.................................. *Roses Ain't Red (I Don't Love You)*		$4		Warner/Curb 49148
				#8 Pop hit for The Shirelles in 1962				

ZEILER, Gayle '82

Born in Gilroy, California. Ethel of **Ethel & The Shameless Hussies**.

DEBUT	PEAK	WKS		A-side / B-side		$		Label & Number
1/30/82	78	4		No Place To Hide		$7		Equa 670

SONG TITLE SECTION

Lists, alphabetically, all A-side titles in the Artist Section. The artist's name is listed with each title along with the highest position attained and the year the song peaked on the chart.

Some titles show the letter **F** as a position, indicating that the title was listed as a flip side and did not chart on its own.

A song with more than one charted version is listed once, with the artists' names listed below in chronological order. Many songs that have the same title, but are different tunes, are listed separately, with the most popular title listed first. This will make it easy to determine which songs are the same composition, the number of charted versions of a particular song, and which of these was the most popular.

Cross references have been used throughout to aid in finding a title.

Please keep the following in mind when searching for titles:

Titles such as "I.O.U.," "P.T. 109," and "S.O.S." will be found at the beginning of their respective letters; however, titles such as "D-I-V-O-R-C-E" and "T-R-O-U-B-L-E," which are spellings of words, are listed with their regular spellings.

Two-word titles that have the <u>exact</u> same spelling as one-word titles are listed together alphabetically. ("Honky-Tonk Man" is listed directly before "Honkytonk Man.")

Titles that are <u>identical</u>, except for an apostrophized word in one of the titles, are shown together. ("Fallin' For You" appears immediately above "Falling For You.")

A

A-11
26/65   *Johnny Paycheck*
54/89   *Buck Owens*
85/76 **"A" My Name Is Alice** *Marie Osmond*
46/66 **"A" Team** *SSgt Barry Sadler*
Abilene
1/63   *George Hamilton IV*
24/77   *Sonny James*
Above And Beyond
3/60   *Buck Owens*
1/89   *Rodney Crowell*
16/81 **Acapulco** *Johnny Duncan*
89/79 **Accentuate The Positive** *Tommy O'Day*
16/60 **Accidently On Purpose** *George Jones*
4/56 **According To My Heart** *Jim Reeves*
1/89 **Ace In The Hole** *George Strait*
9/92 **Aces** *Suzy Bogguss*
5/62 **Aching, Breaking Heart** *George Jones*
Achy Breaky Heart
1/92   *Billy Ray Cyrus*
71/92   *Alvin & The Chipmunks*
50/85 **Acres Of Diamonds** *Benny Wilson*
86/90 **Across The Room From You**
    Phil Cohron
Act Naturally
1/63   *Buck Owens*
27/89   *Buck Owens & Ringo Starr*
3/95 **Adalida** *George Strait*
1/88 **Addicted** *Dan Seals*
4/94 **Addicted To A Dollar** *Doug Stone*
2/62 **Adios Amigo** *Jim Reeves*
4/77 **Adios Amigo** *Marty Robbins*
41/67 **Adorable Women** *Nat Stuckey*
64/84 **Adventures In Parodies**
    Pinkard & Bowden
14/49 **Afraid** *Rex Allen with Jerry Byrd*
22/73 **Afraid I'll Want To Love Her One More**
    Time *Billy "Crash" Craddock*
    Afraid Of Losing You Again ..see: (I'm
    So)
50/78 **Afraid You'd Come Back** *Kenny Price*
4/84 **After All** *Ed Bruce*
43/87 **After All** *Patty Loveless*
1/76 **After All The Good Is Gone**
    Conway Twitty
    (After All These Years) ..see: I Still
    Love You
18/71 **After All They All Used To Belong To**
    Me *Hank Williams, Jr.*
1/89 **After All This Time** *Rodney Crowell*
6/70 **After Closing Time** *David Houston &*
    Barbara Mandrell
17/80 **After Hours** *Joe Stampley*
51/88 **After Last Night's Storm** *Ride The River*
79/88 **After Lovin' You** *Melissa Kay*
7/62 **After Loving You** *Eddy Arnold*
10/77 **(After Sweet Memories) Play Born To**
    Lose Again *Dottsy*
75/81 **After Texas** *Roy Head*
32/77 **After The Ball** *Johnny Cash*
    After The Fire Is Gone
1/71   *Conway Twitty & Loretta Lynn*
17/74   *Willie Nelson & Tracy Nelson*
70/82 **After The Glitter Fades** *Stevie Nicks*
19/83 **After The Great Depression**
    Razzy Bailey
10/83 **After The Last Goodbye** *Gus Hardin*
13/92 **After The Lights Go Out**
    Ricky Van Shelton
16/82 **After The Love Slips Away**
    Earl Thomas Conley
40/77 **After The Lovin'** *Engelbert Humperdinck*
88/88 **After The Passion Leaves** *Nina Wyatt*
65/70 **After The Preacher's Gone** *Peggy Sue*
8/76 **After The Storm** *Wynn Stewart*
82/82 **After Tonight** *Deborah Allen*
22/71 **After You** *Jerry Wallace*
23/73 **After You** *Hank Williams, Jr.*

28/83 **After You** *Dan Seals*
    Afternoon Delight
9/76   *Johnny Carver*
94/76   *Starland Vocal Band*
19/65 **Again** *Don Gibson*
66/92 **Against The Grain** *Garth Brooks*
36/80 **Age** *Jerry Reed*
20/68 **Age Of Worry** *Billy Walker*
21/77 **Agree To Disagree** *Little David Wilkins*
69/93 **Ain't Been A Train Through Here In**
    Years *Rick Vincent*
1/93 **Ain't Going Down (Til The Sun Comes**
    Up) *Garth Brooks*
55/69 **Ain't Gonna Worry** *Leon Ashley*
65/83 **Ain't Gonna Worry My Mind**
    Richard Leigh
15/96 **Ain't Got Nothin' On Us**
    John Michael Montgomery
68/68 **Ain't Got The Time** *Tom T. Hall*
23/63 **Ain't Got Time For Nothin'** *Bob Gallion*
19/68 **Ain't Got Time To Be Unhappy**
    Bob Luman
2/66 **Ain't Had No Lovin'** *Connie Smith*
23/58 **Ain't I The Lucky One** *Marty Robbins*
    Ain't It All Worth Living For
15/72   *Tompall/Glaser Brothers*
75/74   *Mack White*
14/73 **Ain't It Amazing, Gracie** *Buck Owens*
97/76 **Ain't It Good To Be In Love Again**
    Vicky Fletcher
35/73 **Ain't It Good (To Feel This Way)**
    Norro Wilson
51/85 **Ain't It Just Like Love** *Billy Burnette*
77/78 **Ain't Life Hell**
    Hank Cochran & Willie Nelson
10/74 **Ain't Love A Good Thing** *Connie Smith*
41/76 **Ain't Love Good** *Jean Shepard*
1/86 **Ain't Misbehavin'** *Hank Williams, Jr.*
17/90 **Ain't Necessarily So** *Willie Nelson*
4/78 **Ain't No California** *Mel Tillis*
86/87 **Ain't No Cure For Love** *Jennifer Warnes*
74/76 **Ain't No Heartbreak** *Dorsey Burnette*
4/82 **Ain't No Money** *Rosanne Cash*
86/89 **Ain't No One Like Me In Tennessee**
    Holly Ronick
48/86 **Ain't No Tellin'** *Lewis Storey*
7/83 **Ain't No Trick (It Takes Magic)**
    Lee Greenwood
56/79 **Ain't No Way To Make A Bad Love**
    Grow *Johnny Russell*
67/82 **Ain't Nobody Gonna Get My Body But**
    You *Del Reeves*
15/90 **Ain't Nobody's Business**
    Hank Williams, Jr.
5/50 **Ain't Nobody's Business But My Own**
    Kay Starr & Tennessee Ernie
10/72 **Ain't Nothin' Shakin' (But The Leaves**
    On The Trees) *Billy "Crash" Craddock*
88/88 **Ain't She Shinin' Tonight** *Jim Moore*
    Ain't She Somethin' Else
46/75   *Eddy Raven*
1/85   *Conway Twitty*
7/72 **Ain't That A Shame** *Hank Williams, Jr.*
2/93 **Ain't That Lonely Yet** *Dwight Yoakam*
68/77 **Ain't That Lovin' You Baby**
    David Houston
53/86 **Ain't That Peculiar** *New Grass Revival*
75/83 **Ain't That The Way It Goes** *Dave Kemp*
62/87 **Ain't We Got Love** *Paul Proctor*
82/83 **Ain't Your Memory Got No Pride At All**
    Ray Charles
11/62 **Air Mail To Heaven** *Carl Smith*
37/83 **Air That I Breathe** *Rex Allen, Jr.*
    Alabam
1/60   *Cowboy Copas*
61/68   *Guy Mitchell*
3/51 **Alabama Jubilee** *Red Foley*
83/77 **Alabama Summertime** *James Talley*
    Alabama Wild Man
48/68   *Jerry Reed*
22/72   *Jerry Reed*
1/93 **Alibis** *Tracy Lawrence*

    Alibis
16/79   *Johnny Rodriguez*
81/84   *Lane Brody*
20/81 **Alice Doesn't Love Here Anymore**
    Bobby Goldsboro
69/82 **Alice In Dallas (Sweet Texas)**
    Wyvon Alexander
91/85 **Alice, Rita and Donna** *David Walsh*
18/75 **Alimony** *Bobby Bare*
34/88 **Alive And Well** *Gatlin Bros.*
    Alive And Well
53/86   *Tammy Wynette*
81/87   *Nisha Jackson*
7/46 **All Alone In This World Without You**
    Eddy Arnold
21/59 **All-American Boy** *Grandpa Jones*
57/85 **All American Country Boy** *Con Hunley*
31/75 **All American Girl** *Statler Brothers*
37/70 **All American Husband** *Peggy Sue*
23/75 **All-American Man** *Johnny Paycheck*
84/83 **All-American Redneck** *Randy Howard*
16/79 **All Around Cowboy** *Marty Robbins*
67/74 **All Around Cowboy Of 1964** *Buddy Alan*
64/84 **All Around The Water Tank**
    Mel McDaniel
39/86 **All Because Of You** *Marty Stuart*
64/70 **All Day Sucker** *Liz Anderson*
66/94 **All Fired Up** *Dan Seals*
9/69 **All For The Love Of A Girl** *Claude King*
1/70 **All For The Love Of Sunshine**
    Hank Williams, Jr.
    All Grown Up
8/58   *Johnny Horton*
26/63   *Johnny Horton*
35/72 **All Heaven Breaks Loose** *David Rogers*
72/69 **All Heaven Broke Loose** *Hugh X. Lewis*
72/84 **All Heaven Is About To Break Loose**
    Zella Lehr
2/72 **All His Children**
    Charley Pride/Henry Mancini
29/91 **All I Can Be (Is A Sweet Memory)**
    Collin Raye
3/76 **All I Can Do** *Dolly Parton*
82/85 **All I Do Is Dream Of You** *Margo Smith*
27/97 **All I Do Is Love Her** *James Bonamy*
    All I Ever Need Is You
18/71   *Ray Sanders*
1/79   *Kenny Rogers & Dottie West*
67/72 **All I Had To Do** *Jim Ed Brown*
    All I Have To Do Is Dream
1/58   *Everly Brothers*
6/70   *Bobbie Gentry & Glen Campbell*
79/75   *Nitty Gritty Dirt Band*
85/81   *Nancy Montgomery*
1/69 **All I Have To Offer You (Is Me)**
    Charley Pride
11/49 **All I Need Is Some More Lovin'**
    George Morgan
51/71 **All I Need Is You** *Carl Belew & Betty*
    Jean Robinson
8/95 **All I Need To Know** *Kenny Chesney*
52/84 **All I Wanna Do (Is Make Love To You)**
    Bandana
21/79 **All I Want And Need Forever**
    Vern Gosdin
    All I Want For Christmas Is You
55/93   *Vince Vance & The Valiants*
52/94   *Vince Vance & The Valiants*
52/95   *Vince Vance & The Valiants*
49/96   *Vince Vance & The Valiants*
43/97   *Vince Vance & The Valiants*
5/96 **All I Want Is A Life** *Tim McGraw*
96/77 **All I Want Is To Love You**
    Jack Rainwater
84/78 **All I Want To Do In Life** *Jack Clement*
67/71 **All I Want To Do Is Say I Love You**
    Brian Collins
30/82 **All I'm Missing Is You** *Eddy Arnold*
60/88 **All In My Mind** *Cali McCord*
13/73 **All In The Name Of Love** *Narvel Felts*
74/91 **All In The Name Of Love**
    Bellamy Brothers
11/92 **All Is Fair In Love And War**
    Ronnie Milsap

9/74	**Bring Back Your Love To Me**
	Don Gibson
11/90	**Bring Back Your Love To Me**
	Earl Thomas Conley
18/72	**Bring Him Safely Home To Me**
	Sandy Posey
20/80	**Bring It On Home** *Big Al Downing*
1/76	**Bring It On Home To Me** *Mickey Gilley*
7/73	**Bring It On Home (To Your Woman)**
	Joe Stampley
68/69	**Bring Love Back Into Our World**
	Stu Phillips
13/69	**Bring Me Sunshine** *Willie Nelson*
80/85	**Bring On The Sunshine** *Dennis Bottoms*
25/66	**Bring Your Heart Home** *Jimmy Newman*
	Bring Your Sweet Self Back To Me
	..see: (Honey, Baby, Hurry!)
54/87	**Bringin' The House Down** *Shurfire*
23/75	**Bringing It Back** *Brenda Lee*
43/65	**Bringing Mary Home**
	Country Gentlemen
64/82	**Bringing Out The Fool In Me**
	Gary Goodnight
15/73	**Broad-Minded Man** *Jim Ed Brown*
62/93	**Broken** *Andy Childs*
94/76	**Broken Bones** *Tommy Cash*
1/77	**Broken Down In Tiny Pieces**
	Billy "Crash" Craddock
2/50	**Broken Down Merry-Go-Round**
	Margaret Whiting & Jimmy Wakely
18/60	**Broken Dream** *Jimmy Smart*
99/89	**Broken Dreams and Memories**
	Michael Shane
46/65	**Broken Engagement** *Webb Pierce*
1/79	**Broken Hearted Me** *Anne Murray*
70/93	**Broken Heartland** *Zaca Creek*
5/76	**Broken Lady** *Larry Gatlin*
10/92	**Broken Promise Land** *Mark Chesnutt*
9/80	**Broken Trust** *Brenda Lee*
1/98	**Broken Wing** *Martina McBride*
64/77	**Brooklyn** *Cody Jameson*
51/78	**Brother** *DeWayne Orender*
	Brother Juke-Box
96/77	*Don Everly*
1/91	*Mark Chesnutt*
75/70	**Brother River** *Johnny Darrell*
77/76	**Brother Shelton** *Brenda Lee*
	Brotherly Love
53/89	*Moe Bandy*
2/91	*Keith Whitley & Earl Thomas Conley*
41/82	**Brotherly Love**
	Gary Stewart & Dean Dillon
29/84	**Brown Eyed Girl** *Joe Stampley*
3/70	**Brown Eyed Handsome Man**
	Waylon Jennings
58/69	**Brownville Lumberyard** *Sammi Smith*
41/73	**Brush Arbor Meeting** *Brush Arbor*
15/49	**Brush Those Tears From Your Eyes**
	Foy Willing
16/95	**Bubba Hyde** *Diamond Rio*
4/92	**Bubba Shot The Jukebox**
	Mark Chesnutt
	Bubbles In My Beer
4/48	*Bob Wills*
68/71	*Ray Pennington*
1/65	**Buckaroo** *Buck Owens*
14/78	**Bucket To The South** *Ava Barber*
63/77	**Buddy, I Lied** *Nat Stuckey*
46/89	**Buenas Noches From A Lonely Room**
	(She Wore Red Dresses)
	Dwight Yoakam
25/79	**Buenos Dias Argentina** *Marty Robbins*
58/68	**Buffalo Nickel** *Rusty Draper*
16/93	**Bug, The** *Mary-Chapin Carpenter*
99/77	**Bugle Ann** *Wayne Carson*
12/63	**Building A Bridge** *Claude King*
	Building Bridges
55/84	*Larry Willoughby*
72/85	*Nicolette Larson*
30/79	**Building Memories** *Sonny James*
8/78	**Bull And The Beaver**
	Merle Haggard/Leona Williams
66/80	**Bull Rider** *Johnny Cash*

88/82	**Bull Smith Can't Dance The**
	Cotton-Eyed Joe *Wolfpack*
	Bumming Around
5/53	*Jimmie Dean*
5/53	*"T" Texas Tyler*
31/76	**Bump Bounce Boogie**
	Asleep At The Wheel
4/52	**Bundle Of Southern Sunshine**
	Eddy Arnold
2/78	**Burgers And Fries** *Charley Pride*
3/84	**Buried Treasure** *Kenny Rogers*
97/78	**Burn Atlanta Down** *Bobby Barnett*
80/84	**Burn Georgia Burn (There's A Fire In**
	Your Soul) *Butch Baker*
7/92	**Burn Me Down** *Marty Stuart*
4/92	**Burn One Down** *Clint Black*
10/86	**Burned Like A Rocket** *Billy Joe Royal*
71/87	**Burned Out** *Tina Danièlle*
3/89	**Burnin' A Hole In My Heart** *Skip Ewing*
1/89	**Burnin' Old Memories** *Kathy Mattea*
31/75	**Burnin' Thing** *Mac Davis*
	Burning
37/75	*Ferlin Husky*
88/77	*Marie Owens*
5/67	**Burning A Hole In My Mind**
	Connie Smith
	Burning Bridges
18/67	*Glen Campbell*
79/81	*Bill Nash*
	Burning Memories
2/64	*Ray Price*
9/77	*Mel Tillis*
10/62	**Burning Of Atlanta** *Claude King*
11/72	**Burning The Midnight Oil** *Porter*
	Wagoner & Dolly Parton
78/80	**Burning Up Your Memory**
	Peggy Forman
55/68	**Bury The Bottle With Me** *Dick Curless*
18/96	**Bury The Shovel** *Clay Walker*
21/71	**Bus Fare To Kentucky** *Skeeter Davis*
6/50	**Bushel And A Peck** *Margaret Whiting &*
	Jimmy Wakely
22/75	**Busiest Memory In Town** *Dickey Lee*
	Busted
13/63	*Johnny Cash with The Carter Family*
6/82	*John Conlee*
8/52	**Busybody** *Pee Wee King*
	But Alabama ..see: (Nothing Left
	Between Us)
	But For Love
19/69	*Eddy Arnold*
54/79	*Jerry Naylor*
65/75	**But I Do** *Del Reeves*
83/87	**But I Never Do** *Brenda Cole*
35/94	**But I Will** *Faith Hill*
30/82	**But It's Cheating** *Family Brown*
26/80	**But Love Me** *Janie Fricke*
68/89	**But, She Loves Me** *Roy Clark*
54/70	**But That's All Right** *Hank Thompson*
	But Tonight I'm Gonna Love You
72/74	*Harrison Jones*
91/77	*Daniel*
63/67	**But Wait There's More** *Justin Tubb*
	But You Know I Love You
2/69	*Bill Anderson*
1/81	*Dolly Parton*
16/60	**But You Use To** *Laverne Downs*
65/89	**But You Will** *Razzy Bailey*
72/87	**Butterbeans** *Johnny Russell & Little*
	David Wilkins
47/75	**Butterfly** *Eddy Arnold*
22/76	**Butterfly For Bucky** *Bobby Goldsboro*
	Butterfly Kisses
37/97	*Raybon Bros.*
45/97	*Bob Carlisle*
66/97	*Jeff Carson*
4/88	**Button Off My Shirt** *Ronnie Milsap*
6/48	**Buttons And Bows** *Gene Autry*
18/96	**By My Side** *Lorrie Morgan & Jon Randall*
6/81	**By Now** *Steve Wariner*
	By The Time I Get To Phoenix
2/68	*Glen Campbell*
40/71	*Glen Campbell/Anne Murray (medley)*

46/68	**By The Time You Get To Phoenix**
	Wanda Jackson
65/94	**By The Way She's Lookin'** *Jesse Hunter*
96/79	**Bye, Bye, Baby** *Dan Dickey*
	Bye Bye Love
1/57	*Everly Brothers*
7/57	*Webb Pierce*
70/81	*Billy Walker & Barbara Fairchild*

C

23/77	**C.B. Savage** *Rod Hart*
83/76	**C.B. Widow** *Linda Cassady*
10/83	**C.C. Waterback**
	George Jones/Merle Haggard
	C'est La Vie ..see: (You Never Can Tell)
16/72	**Cab Driver** *Hank Thompson*
98/79	**Cabello Diablo (Devil Horse)**
	Chris LeDoux
78/76	**Cabin High (In The Blue Ridge**
	Mountains) *Don King*
9/59	**Cabin In The Hills** *Flatt & Scruggs*
48/80	**Cactus And A Rose** *Gary Stewart*
97/76	**Cadillac Johnson** *Chuck Price*
18/93	**Cadillac Ranch** *Chris LeDoux*
3/92	**Cadillac Style** *Sammy Kershaw*
5/92	**Cafe On The Corner** *Sawyer Brown*
80/81	**Caffein, Nicotine, Benzedrine**
	Jerry Reed
26/95	**Cain's Blood** *4 Runner*
	Cajun Baby
3/69	*Hank Williams, Jr.*
52/88	*Doug Kershaw/Hank Williams Jr.*
52/83	**Cajun Invitation**
	David Frizzell & Shelly West
93/81	**Cajun Lady** *Ralph May*
1/86	**Cajun Moon** *Ricky Skaggs*
16/62	**Cajun Queen** *Jimmy Dean*
23/68	**Cajun Stripper** *Jim Ed Brown*
68/88	**Calendar Blues** *Jill Jordan*
73/76	**Calico Cat** *Kenny Starr*
11/48	**Calico Rag** *Al Dexter*
13/85	**California** *Keith Stegall*
45/79	**California** *Glen Campbell*
51/89	**California Blue** *Roy Orbison*
65/73	**California Blues (Blue Yodel No. 4)**
	Compton Brothers
94/80	**California Calling** *Dennis Smith*
45/69	**California Cotton Fields** *Dallas Frazier*
11/69	**California Girl (And The Tennessee**
	Square) *Tompall/Glaser Brothers*
68/70	**California Grapevine** *Freddie Hart*
99/73	**California Is Just Mississippi** *Billy Mize*
31/77	**California Lady** *Randy Barlow*
43/76	**California Okie** *Buck Owens*
4/46	**California Polka** *Tex Williams*
61/85	**California Road** *Mel Tillis*
77/85	**California Sleeping** *Loy Blanton*
70/68	**California Sunshine** *Rusty Draper*
20/67	**California Up Tight Band**
	Flatt & Scruggs
96/89	**California Wine** *Mark Murphey*
19/76	**Call, The** *Anne Murray*
71/97	**Call, The** *Little Texas*
	Call Her Your Sweetheart
9/52	*Eddy Arnold*
28/66	*Frank Ifield*
	Call Home
52/86	*Glen Campbell*
43/93	*Mike Reid*
	Call Me ..see: (Honey, Won't You)
64/87	**Call Me A Fool** *Dana McVicker*
F/79	**Call Me Crazy Lady** *Leona Williams*
82/82	**Call Me Friend** *Vince Anthony*
46/70	**Call Me Gone** *Stan Hitchcock*
9/63	**Call Me Mr. Brown** *Skeets McDonald*

416

11/57	**Don't Laugh** *Louvin Brothers*
83/82	**Don't Lead Me On** *Wyvon Alexander*
42/90	**Don't Leave Her Lonely Too Long**
	Marty Stuart
67/83	**Don't Leave Me Lonely Loving You**
	Randy Barlow
44/64	**Don't Leave Me Lonely Too Long**
	Kathy Dee
11/74	**Don't Let Go** *Mel Tillis & Sherry Bryce*
26/87	**Don't Let Go Of My Heart**
	Southern Pacific
33/64	**Don't Let Her Know** *Buck Owens*
30/63	**Don't Let Her See Me Cry** *Lefty Frizzell*
22/71	**Don't Let Him Make A Memory Out Of**
	Me *Billy Walker*
83/86	**Don't Let It Go To Your Heart**
	Bonnie Nelson
	Don't Let Me Cross Over
1/62	*Carl Butler & Pearl*
9/69	*Jerry Lee Lewis & Linda Gail Lewis*
10/79	*Jim Reeves*
6/77	**Don't Let Me Touch You** *Marty Robbins*
86/77	**Don't Let My Love Stand In Your Way**
	Jim Glaser
1/92	**Don't Let Our Love Start Slippin' Away**
	Vince Gill
86/76	**Don't Let Smokey Mountain Smoke**
	Get In Your Eyes *Osborne Brothers*
24/67	**Don't Let That Doorknob Hit You**
	Norma Jean
86/78	**Don't Let The Flame Burn Out**
	Rita Remington
15/75	**Don't Let The Good Times Fool You**
	Melba Montgomery
37/73	**Don't Let The Green Grass Fool You**
	O.B. McClinton
	Don't Let The Stars Get In Your Eyes
1/52	*Skeets McDonald*
1/52	*Slim Willet*
4/52	*Ray Price*
8/53	*Red Foley*
	(also see: I Let)
16/71	**(Don't Let The Sun Set On You) Tulsa**
	Waylon Jennings
14/61	**Don't Let Your Sweet Love Die**
	Reno & Smiley
4/45	**Don't Live A Lie** *Gene Autry*
12/82	**Don't Look Back** *Gary Morris*
61/80	**Don't Look Back** *Dickey Lee*
11/81	**Don't Look Now (But We Just Fell In**
	Love) *Eddy Arnold*
4/47	**Don't Look Now (But Your Broken**
	Heart Is Showing) *Ernest Tubb*
17/97	**Don't Love Make A Diamond Shine**
	Tracy Byrd
1/84	**Don't Make It Easy For Me**
	Earl Thomas Conley
60/69	**Don't Make Love** *Mac Curtis*
51/95	**Don't Make Me Feel At Home**
	Wesley Dennis
F/57	**Don't Make Me Go** *Johnny Cash*
84/80	**Don't Make Me Over** *Jennifer Warnes*
46/85	**Don't Make Me Wait On The Moon**
	Shelly West
29/78	**Don't Make No Promises (You Can't**
	Keep) *Don King*
41/68	**Don't Monkey With Another Monkey's**
	Monkey *Johnny Paycheck*
18/72	**Don't Pay The Ransom** *Nat Stuckey*
27/83	**Don't Plan On Sleepin' Tonight**
	Steve Wariner
23/63	**Don't Pretend** *Bobby Edwards*
49/80	**Don't Promise Me Anything (Do It)**
	Brenda Lee
4/76	**Don't Pull Your Love (medley)**
	Glen Campbell
47/67	**Don't Put Your Hands On Me**
	Lorene Mann
32/67	**Don't Put Your Hurt In My Heart**
	Conway Twitty
25/89	**Don't Quit Me Now** *James House*
	Don't Rob Another Man's Castle
1/49	*Eddy Arnold*
6/49	*Ernest Tubb & Andrews Sisters*

1/91	**Don't Rock The Jukebox** *Alan Jackson*
15/77	**Don't Say Goodbye** *Rex Allen, Jr.*
48/88	**Don't Say It With Diamonds (Say It**
	With Love) *T.G. Sheppard*
93/79	**Don't Say Love** *Connie Smith*
97/79	**Don't Say No To Me Tonight**
	Mark Sexton
51/87	**Don't Say No Tonight** *Mason Dixon*
76/83	**Don't Say You Love Me (Just Love Me**
	Again) *Mike Campbell*
34/72	**Don't Say You're Mine** *Carl Smith*
55/83	**Don't Send Me No Angels** *Wayne Kemp*
77/88	**Don't Send Me Roses** *Sarah*
2/72	**Don't She Look Good** *Bill Anderson*
8/67	**Don't Squeeze My Sharmon**
	Charlie Walker
62/88	**Don't Start The Fire** *Marcia Lynn*
2/52	**Don't Stay Away (Till Love Grows**
	Cold) *Lefty Frizzell*
79/87	**Don't Stay If You Don't Love Me**
	Patsy Sledd
86/79	**Don't Stay On Your Side Of The Bed**
	Tonight *Ann J. Morton*
9/51	**Don't Stay Too Long** *Ernest Tubb*
10/95	**Don't Stop** *Wade Hayes*
14/76	**Don't Stop Believin'** *Olivia Newton-John*
19/76	**Don't Stop In My World (If You Don't**
	Mean To Stay) *Billy Walker*
43/75	**Don't Stop Loving Me** *Don Gibson*
45/74	**Don't Stop Now** *Sherry Bryce*
10/57	**Don't Stop The Music** *George Jones*
68/78	**Don't Stop The Music (You're Playing**
	My Song) *Little David Wilkins*
27/64	**Don't Take Advantage Of Me**
	Bonnie Owens
17/70	**Don't Take All Your Loving** *Don Gibson*
4/97	**Don't Take Her She's All I Got**
	Tracy Byrd
	Don't Take It Away
67/75	*Jody Miller*
1/79	*Conway Twitty*
5/55	**Don't Take It Out On Me**
	Hank Thompson
61/83	**Don't Take Much** *Peter Isaacson*
69/77	**Don't Take My Sunshine Away**
	Ava Barber
1/94	**Don't Take The Girl** *Tim McGraw*
1/59	**Don't Take Your Guns To Town**
	Johnny Cash
59/88	**Don't Talk To Me** *Libby Hurley*
11/55	**Don't Tease Me** *Carl Smith*
2/48	**Don't Telephone - Don't Telegraph**
	(Tell A Woman) *Tex Williams*
55/85	**Don't Tell Me Love Is Kind**
	Almost Brothers
5/91	**Don't Tell Me What To Do** *Pam Tillis*
	Don't Tell Me Your Troubles
5/59	*Don Gibson*
53/73	*Kenny Price*
10/74	**Don't Tell (That Sweet Ole Lady Of**
	Mine) *Johnny Carver*
1/76	**Don't The Girls All Get Prettier At**
	Closing Time *Mickey Gilley*
55/88	**Don't The Morning Always Come Too**
	Soon *Ray Price*
88/78	**Don't Think Twice, It's All Right**
	Doc & Merle Watson
5/77	**Don't Throw It All Away** *Dave & Sugar*
54/91	**Don't Throw Me In The Briarpatch**
	Keith Palmer
9/53	**Don't Throw Your Life Away**
	Webb Pierce
5/89	**Don't Toss Us Away** *Patty Loveless*
	Don't Touch Me
2/66	*Jeannie Seely*
12/66	*Wilma Burgess*
69/79	*Jerry Naylor/Kelli Warren*
96/79	*Brenda Joyce*
20/87	**Don't Touch Me There** *Charly McClain*
68/96	**Don't Touch My Hat** *Lyle Lovett*
97/79	**Don't Treat Me Like A Stranger**
	Randy Gurley
1/86	**Don't Underestimate My Love For You**
	Lee Greenwood

	Don't Wait On Me
5/81	*Statler Brothers*
67/89	*Statler Brothers*
23/69	**Don't Wake Me I'm Dreaming**
	Warner Mack
86/77	**Don't Want To Take A Chance (On**
	Loving You) *Ann J. Morton*
5/89	**Don't Waste It On The Blues**
	Gene Watson
72/67	**Don't Waste Your Time** *Mary Taylor*
	Don't We All Have The Right
F/70	*Roger Miller*
1/88	*Ricky Van Shelton*
	Don't We Belong In Love
80/81	*Rita Remington*
40/82	*Stephanie Winslow*
62/67	**Don't Wipe The Tears That You Cry For**
	Him (On My Good White Shirt)
	Tommy Collins
	Don't Worry
1/61	*Marty Robbins*
96/78	*Glenda Griffith*
73/96	**Don't Worry Baby** *Beach Boys*
	Featuring Lorrie Morgan
1/82	**Don't Worry 'Bout Me Baby** *Janie Fricke*
	Don't Worry 'Bout The Mule (Just Load
	The Wagon)
41/68	*Glenn Barber*
44/71	*Carl Smith*
9/89	**Don't You** *Forester Sisters*
8/85	**Doncha?** *T.G. Sheppard*
62/91	**Don't You Even (Think About Leavin')**
	Dean Dillon
	Don't You Ever Get Tired Of Hurting Me
11/66	*Ray Price*
92/77	*Connie Cato*
11/81	*Willie Nelson & Ray Price*
1/89	*Ronnie Milsap*
77/78	**Don't You Feel It Now** *Betty Martin*
49/84	**Don't You Give Up On Love**
	Steve Wariner
1/83	**Don't You Know How Much I Love You**
	Ronnie Milsap
12/74	**Don't You Think** *Marty Robbins*
71/78	**Don't You Think It's Time**
	Tommy Jennings
F/58	**Doncha' Think It's Time** *Elvis Presley*
5/78	**Don't You Think This Outlaw Bit's**
	Done Got Out Of Hand
	Waylon Jennings
23/83	**Don't Your Mem'ry Ever Sleep At Night**
	Steve Wariner
	Doncha ..see: Don't You
96/80	**Donna-Earth Angel (Medley)**
	Tucker Williams
6/86	**Doo-Wah Days** *Mickey Gilley*
70/70	**Doogie Ray** *George Kent*
1/75	**Door, The** *George Jones*
65/97	**Door, A** *Aaron Tippin*
	Door I Used To Close
28/76	*Roy Head*
91/76	*Marilyn Sellars*
	Door Is Always Open
75/73	*Tennessee Pulleybone*
70/75	*Lois Johnson*
1/76	*Dave & Sugar*
88/75	**Door Number Three** *Jimmy Buffett*
6/56	**Doorstep To Heaven** *Carl Smith*
34/64	**Double Life** *Joe Carson*
30/78	**Double S** *Bill Anderson*
	(also see: Double W)
8/84	**Double Shot (Of My Baby's Love)**
	Joe Stampley
13/49	**Double Talkin' Woman** *Earl Nunn*
89/79	**Double W** *Whispering Will*
16/81	**Down And Out** *George Strait*
65/86	**Down At The Mall** *Tom T. Hall*
18/67	**Down At The Pawn Shop** *Hank Snow*
36/77	**Down At The Pool** *Johnny Carver*
4/47	**Down At The Roadside Inn** *Al Dexter*
2/91	**Down At The Twist And Shout**
	Mary-Chapin Carpenter
9/63	**Down By The River** *Faron Young*
28/97	**Down Came A Blackbird** *Lila McCann*

52/67	**Down, Down, Came The World**
	Bobby Barnett
1/91	**Down Home** *Alabama*
56/73	**Down Home Lovin' Woman** *Andra Willis*
10/95	**Down In Flames** *BlackHawk*
38/70	**Down In New Orleans** *Buddy Alan*
	Down In Tennessee
12/86	*John Anderson*
23/95	*Mark Chesnutt*
	Down In The Boondocks
37/69	*Penny DeHaven*
25/70	*Freddy Weller*
45/68	**Down In The Flood** *Flatt & Scruggs*
42/85	**Down In The Florida Keys** *Tom T. Hall*
68/88	**Down In The Orange Grove**
	John Anderson
41/80	**Down In The Quarter** *Tommy Overstreet*
81/88	**Down On Market Street** *Lorie Ann*
19/93	**Down On My Knees** *Trisha Yearwood*
82/88	**Down On The Bayou** *Ogden Harless*
13/83	**Down On The Corner** *Jerry Reed*
94/79	**Down On The Corner At A Bar Called**
	Kelly's *Johnny Paycheck*
2/94	**Down On The Farm** *Tim McGraw*
25/85	**Down On The Farm** *Charley Pride*
6/79	**Down On The Rio Grande**
	Johnny Rodriguez
6/89	**Down That Road Tonight**
	Nitty Gritty Dirt Band
58/88	**Down The Road** *Charly McClain*
70/90	**Down The Road** *Mac McAnally*
62/74	**Down The Road I Go** *Don Williams*
33/85	**Down The Road Mountain Pass**
	Dan Fogelberg
59/78	**Down The Roads Of Daddy's Dreams**
	Darrell McCall
2/51	**Down The Trail Of Achin' Hearts**
	Hank Snow with Anita Carter
16/79	**Down To Earth Woman** *Kenny Dale*
2/81	**Down To My Last Broken Heart**
	Janie Fricke
2/91	**Down To My Last Teardrop**
	Tanya Tucker
91/77	**Down To My Pride** *Linda Hargrove*
41/74	**Down To The End Of The Wine**
	Jack Blanchard & Misty Morgan
18/63	**Down To The River** *Rose Maddox*
5/51	**Down Yonder** *Del Wood*
32/73	**Downfall Of Me** *Sonny James*
64/79	**Downhill Stuff** *John Denver*
77/83	**Downright Broke My Heart**
	Bubba Talbert
36/84	**Downtown** *Dolly Parton*
31/71	**Dozen Pairs Of Boots** *Del Reeves*
37/97	**Dozen Red Roses** *Tammy Graham*
29/70	**Drag 'Em Off The Interstate, Sock It To**
	'Em, J.P. Blues *Dick Curless*
95/80	**Draggin' Leather** *Mitch Goodson*
11/59	**Draggin' The River** *Ferlin Husky*
45/72	**Draggin' The River** *Warner Mack*
87/81	**Draw Me A Line** *Ray Griff*
	Dream ..see: **All I Have To Do Is**
	Dream Baby (How Long Must I Dream)
50/70	*Bob Regan & Lucille Starr*
7/71	*Glen Campbell*
9/83	*Lacy J. Dalton*
22/64	**Dream House For Sale** *Red Sovine*
	Dream Lover
5/71	*Billy "Crash" Craddock*
59/79	*Rick Nelson*
59/80	*Tanya Tucker & Glen Campbell*
88/86	*Rick Nelson*
94/84	**Dream Lover** *Susie Brading*
	Dream Maker
61/81	*Shoppe*
69/83	*Tommy Overstreet*
47/73	**Dream Me Home** *Mac Davis*
40/79	**Dream Never Dies** *Bill Anderson*
7/81	**Dream Of Me** *Vern Gosdin*
7/79	**Dream On** *Oak Ridge Boys*
18/84	**Dream On Texas Ladies** *Rex Allen, Jr.*
23/73	**Dream Painter** *Connie Smith*
80/80	**Dream Street Rose** *Gordon Lightfoot*
88/73	**Dream Weaver** *Jacky Ward*

63/93	**Dream You** *Pirates Of The Mississippi*
32/82	**Dreamin'** *John Schneider*
32/79	**Dreamin's All I Do** *Earl Thomas Conley*
10/75	**Dreaming My Dreams With You**
	Waylon Jennings
1/94	**Dreaming With My Eyes Open**
	Clay Walker
100/78	**Dreamland** *Gordon Lightfoot*
9/86	**Dreamland Express** *John Denver*
46/81	**Dreams Can Come In Handy** *Cindy Hurt*
15/82	**Dreams Die Hard** *Gary Morris*
35/77	**Dreams Of A Dreamer** *Darrell McCall*
3/68	**Dreams Of The Everyday Housewife**
	Glen Campbell
8/73	**Drift Away** *Narvel Felts*
3/91	**Drift Off To Dream** *Travis Tritt*
1/81	**Drifter** *Sylvia*
60/85	**Drifter's Wind** *Chuck Pyle*
48/80	**Driftin Away** *Miki Mori*
8/67	**Drifting Apart** *Warner Mack*
96/78	**Drifting Lovers** *Charlie McCoy*
11/60	**Drifting Texas Sand** *Webb Pierce*
58/69	**Drifting Too Far (From Your Arms)**
	June Stearns
7/51	**Driftwood On The River** *Ernest Tubb*
F/70	**Drink Boys, Drink** *Jim Ed Brown*
59/69	**Drink Canada Dry** *Bobby Barnett*
25/80	**Drink It Down, Lady** *Rex Allen, Jr.*
3/97	**Drink, Swear, Steal & Lie**
	Michael Peterson
2/85	**Drinkin' And Dreamin'** *Waylon Jennings*
17/80	**Drinkin' And Drivin'** *Johnny Paycheck*
8/86	**Drinkin' My Baby Goodbye**
	Charlie Daniels Band
1/76	**Drinkin' My Baby (Off My Mind)**
	Eddie Rabbitt
	Drinkin' My Way Back Home
63/77	*Shylo*
10/84	*Gene Watson*
70/80	**Drinkin' Them Long Necks** *Roy Head*
10/74	**Drinkin' Thing** *Gary Stewart*
	Drinking Champagne
35/68	*Cal Smith*
4/90	*George Strait*
9/55	**Drinking Tequila** *Jim Reeves*
79/78	**Drinking Them Beers** *Tompall Glaser*
20/73	**Drinking Wine Spo-Dee O'Dee**
	Jerry Lee Lewis
63/94	**Drive** *Steve Wariner*
56/97	**Drive Me Crazy**
	Thompson Brothers Band
	Drive South
63/90	*Forester Sister & The Bellamy Brothers*
2/93	*Suzy Bogguss*
72/93	**Drive Time** *Lisa Stewart*
24/94	**Drivin' And Cryin'** *Steve Wariner*
44/70	**Drivin' Home** *Jerry Smith*
1/80	**Drivin' My Life Away** *Eddie Rabbitt*
	Drivin' Nails In My Coffin
2/46	*Floyd Tillman*
5/46	*Ernest Tubb*
26/84	**Drivin' Wheel** *Emmylou Harris*
68/93	**Driving You Out Of My Mind**
	Marshall Tucker Band
17/76	**Dropkick Me, Jesus** *Bobby Bare*
	Dropping Out Of Sight
32/67	*Jimmy Newman*
35/81	*Bobby Bare*
96/79	**Drown In The Flood** *Lois Kaye*
39/85	**Drowning In Memories**
	T. Graham Brown
25/61	**Drunk Again** *Lattie Moore*
	(Drunk On Arrival) ..see: D.O.A.
94/79	**Duel Under The Snow** *Billy Edd Wheeler*
5/73	**Dueling Banjos** *Eric Weissberg & Steve*
	Mandell
	(Dukes Of Hazzard) ..see: Theme From
	The
15/90	**Dumas Walker** *Kentucky Headhunters*
24/67	**Dumb Blonde** *Dolly Parton*
1/95	**Dust On The Bottle** *David Lee Murphy*
44/69	**Dusty Road** *Norma Jean*
21/70	**Duty Not Desire** *Jeannie C. Riley*
93/84	**Dying To Believe** *Jack Greene*

E

27/69	**Each And Every Part Of Me**
	Bobby Lewis
5/45	**Each Minute Seems A Million Years**
	Eddy Arnold
4/60	**Each Moment ('Spent With You)**
	Ernest Ashworth
4/44	**Each Night At Nine** *Floyd Tillman*
16/69	**Each Time** *Johnny Bush*
22/91	**Eagle, The** *Waylon Jennings*
53/94	**Eagle Over Angel** *Brother Phelps*
33/91	**Eagle When She Flies** *Dolly Parton*
35/70	**Early In The Morning** *Mac Curtis*
14/89	**Early In The Morning And Late At Night**
	Hank Williams, Jr.
79/75	**Early Morning Love** *Sammy Johns*
9/66	**Early Morning Rain** *George Hamilton IV*
9/71	**Early Morning Sunshine** *Marty Robbins*
28/75	**Early Sunday Morning** *Chip Taylor*
	Earth Angel ..see: Donna
93/74	**Ease Me To The Ground** *Sue Richards*
80/77	**Ease My Mind On You** *Marie Owens*
20/97	**Ease My Troubled Mind** *Ricochet*
78/83	**Ease The Fever** *Carrie Slye*
	Easier
61/83	*Sandy Croft*
91/84	*Sandy Croft*
20/93	**Easier Said Than Done** *Radney Foster*
87/81	**Easier To Go**
	Gene Kennedy & Karen Jeglum
2/77	**East Bound And Down** *Jerry Reed*
	Easy
45/79	*Bobby Hood*
F/79	*Jimmie Rodgers & Michele*
63/78	**Easy** *John Wesley Ryles*
76/75	**Easy** *Troy Seals*
89/78	**Easy** *Barry Kaye*
69/95	**Easy As One, Two, Three** *John Bunzow*
2/75	**Easy As Pie** *Billy "Crash" Craddock*
81/83	**Easy Catch** *Bubba Talbert*
1/93	**Easy Come, Easy Go** *George Strait*
14/64	**Easy Come-Easy Go** *Bill Anderson*
68/86	**Easy Does It** *Tim Malchak*
12/78	**Easy From Now On** *Emmylou Harris*
	Easy Look
67/75	*Kenny Price*
12/77	*Charlie Rich*
1/71	**Easy Loving** *Freddie Hart*
26/60	**Easy Money** *James O'Gwynn*
32/83	**Easy On The Eye** *Gatlin Bros.*
1/52	**Easy On The Eyes** *Eddy Arnold*
	Easy Part's Over
2/68	*Charley Pride*
41/80	*Steve Wariner*
57/87	**Easy To Find** *Girls Next Door*
26/75	**Easy To Love** *Hank Snow*
89/79	**Easy To Love** *Jimmie Rodgers*
5/86	**Easy To Please** *Janie Fricke*
3/56	**Eat, Drink, And Be Merry (Tomorrow**
	You'll Cry) *Porter Wagoner*
	Ebony Eyes
25/61	*Everly Brothers*
89/79	*Orion*
77/88	**Echo Me** *Margo Smith*
2/49	**Echo Of Your Footsteps** *Eddy Arnold*
1/53	**Eddy's Song** *Eddy Arnold*
2/63	**8 X 10** *Bill Anderson*
57/84	**Eight Days A Week** *Wright Brothers*
43/64	**Eight Years (And Two Children Later)**
	Claude Gray
1/88	**Eighteen Wheels And A Dozen Roses**
	Kathy Mattea
93/75	**18 Yellow Roses** *C.L. Goodson*
7/87	**80's Ladies** *K.T. Oslin*
64/82	**Either You're Married Or You're Single**
	Margo Smith
1/59	**El Paso** *Marty Robbins*
1/76	**El Paso City** *Marty Robbins*

61/86	**Good And Lonesome** *Lowes*
57/90	**Good As Gone** *Joe Barnhill*
4/97	**Good As I Was To You** *Lorrie Morgan*
80/77	**Good Cheatin' Songs** *Carmol Taylor*
25/63	**Good Country Song** *Hank Cochran*
	Good Deal, Lucille
8/54	*Al Terry*
18/69	*Carl Smith*
62/74	**Good Enough To Be Your Man** *Brian Shaw*
7/71	**Good Enough To Be Your Wife** *Jeannie C. Riley*
81/77	**Good Evening Henry** *Peggy Sue*
10/90	**Good Friends, Good Whiskey, Good Lovin'** *Hank Williams, Jr.*
84/81	**Good Friends Make Good Lovers** *Jerry Reed*
91/79	**Good Gal Is Hard To Find** *Hank Snow*
58/94	**Good Girls Go To Heaven** *Charlie Floyd*
29/87	**Good God, I Had It Good** *Pake McEntire*
	Good Hearted Woman
3/72	*Waylon Jennings*
1/76	*Waylon & Willie*
57/75	**Good Lord Giveth (And Uncle Sam Taketh Away)** *Webb Pierce*
53/85	**Good Love Died Tonight** *Leon Everette*
	Good Love Is Like A Good Song
23/73	*Bob Luman*
88/80	*Nancy Ruud*
1/71	**Good Lovin' (Makes It Right)** *Tammy Wynette*
21/80	**Good Lovin' Man** *Gail Davies*
27/71	**Good Man** *June Carter Cash*
55/70	**Good Morning** *Leapy Lee*
30/72	**Good Morning Country Rain** *Jeannie C. Riley*
	Good Morning, Dear
67/68	*Frank Ifield*
71/68	*Don Gibson*
	Good Morning Loving
61/74	*Larry Kingston*
91/75	*Larry Kingston*
43/64	**Good Morning Self** *Jim Reeves*
37/77	**Good 'N' Country** *Kathy Barnes*
9/73	**Good News** *Jody Miller*
27/75	**Good News, Bad News** *Eddy Raven*
51/84	**Good Night For Falling In Love** *Hillary Kanter*
18/76	**Good Night Special** *Little David Wilkins*
19/83	**Good Night's Love** *Tammy Wynette*
	(Good Ol' Boys) ..see: Good Ole Boys, & Theme From The Dukes Of Hazzard
47/97	**Good Ol' Fashioned Love** *Tracy Byrd*
15/81	**Good Ol' Girls** *Sonny Curtis*
81/82	**Good Old Days** *Cristy Lane*
35/73	**Good Old Days (Are Here Again)** *Buck Owens & Susan Raye*
31/74	**Good Old Fashioned Country Love** *Don Gibson & Sue Thompson*
55/77	**Good Old Fashioned Saturday Night Honky Tonk Barroom Brawl** *Vernon Oxford*
16/83	**Good Ole Boys** *Jerry Reed*
2/80	**Good Ole Boys Like Me** *Don Williams*
1/94	**Good Run Of Bad Luck** *Clint Black*
34/70	**Good Thing** *Bill Wilbourn & Kathy Morrison*
2/73	**Good Things** *David Houston*
	Good Time ..also see: Goodtime
3/69	**Good Time Charlie's** *Del Reeves*
1/90	**Good Times** *Dan Seals*
	Good Times
44/68	*Willie Nelson*
25/81	*Willie Nelson*
57/87	**Good Timin' Shoes** *Ronnie Rogers*
1/76	**Good Woman Blues** *Mel Tillis*
67/77	**Good Woman Likes To Drink With The Boys** *Jimmie Rodgers*
12/74	**Good Woman's Love** *Jerry Reed*
	Good Year For The Roses
2/71	*George Jones*
56/94	*George Jones With Alan Jackson*

	Goodbye
73/71	*David Frizzell*
19/74	*Rex Allen, Jr.*
22/79	*Eddy Arnold*
38/72	**Goodbye** *David Rogers*
39/67	**Goodbye City, Goodbye Girl** *Webb Pierce*
86/80	**Goodbye Eyes** *Pebble Daniel*
24/84	**Goodbye Heartache** *Louise Mandrell*
70/92	**Goodbye Highway** *Darryl & Don Ellis*
71/84	**Goodbye Highway** *Pam Tillis*
75/71	**Goodbye Jukebox** *Bobby Lord*
12/63	**Goodbye Kisses** *Cowboy Copas*
22/59	**Goodbye Little Darlin'** *Johnny Cash*
32/89	**Goodbye Lonesome, Hello Baby Doll** *Lonesome Strangers*
	Goodbye Marie
17/81	*Bobby Goldsboro*
47/86	*Kenny Rogers*
93/77	**Goodbye My Friend** *Engelbert Humperdinck*
11/94	**Goodbye Says It All** *BlackHawk*
62/90	**Goodbye, So Long, Hello** *Prairie Oyster*
53/87	**Goodbye Song** *Gene Stroman*
72/67	**Goodbye Swingers** *Glen Garrison*
7/88	**Goodbye Time** *Conway Twitty*
20/67	**Goodbye Wheeling** *Mel Tillis*
8/87	**Goodbyes All We've Got Left** *Steve Earle*
56/73	**Goodbyes Come Hard For Me** *Kenny Serratt*
83/78	**Goodbyes Don't Come Easy** *Mack White*
91/74	**Goodbyes Don't Come Easy** *Warner Mack*
62/64	**Goodie Wagon** *Billy Large*
	Goodnight Irene
1/50	*Red Foley-Ernest Tubb*
5/50	*Moon Mullican* (also see: Wake Up, Irene)
53/76	**Goodnight My Love** *Randy Barlow*
6/96	**Goodnight Sweetheart** *David Kersh*
3/54	**Goodnight, Sweetheart, Goodnight** *Johnnie & Jack*
	Goodtime Charlie's Got The Blues
63/72	*Danny O'Keefe*
41/79	*Red Steagall*
63/84	*Leon Russell*
83/79	**Goody Goody** *Rebecca Lynn*
24/67	**Goody, Goody Gumdrop** *Wilburn Brothers*
10/89	**Gospel According To Luke** *Skip Ewing*
	Got Leaving On Her Mind
54/68	*Mac Wiseman*
14/73	*Nat Stuckey*
82/81	**Got Lucky Last Night** *Jerry Jeff Walker*
	Got My Heart Set On You
1/86	*John Conlee*
72/86	*Mason Dixon*
7/85	**Got No Reason Now For Goin' Home** *Gene Watson*
1/72	**Got The All Overs For You (All Over Me)** *Freddie Hart*
10/87	**Gotta Get Away** *Sweethearts Of The Rodeo*
41/69	**Gotta Get To Oklahoma ('Cause California's Gettin' To Me)** *Hagers*
4/46	**Gotta Get Together With My Gal** *Elton Britt*
9/87	**Gotta Have You** *Eddie Rabbitt*
12/86	**Gotta Learn To Love Without You** *Michael Johnson*
4/78	**Gotta' Quit Lookin' At You Baby** *Dave & Sugar*
	Gotta Travel On
5/59	*Billy Grammer*
15/59	*Bill Monroe*
91/78	*Shylo*
70/93	**Graceland** *Willie Nelson*
69/67	**Grain Of Salt** *Penny Starr*
93/77	**Grand Ole Blues** *Troy Seals*
97/73	**Grand Ole Opry Song** *Nitty Gritty Dirt Band Feat. Jimmy Martin*

	Grand Tour
1/74	*George Jones*
38/93	*Aaron Neville*
16/78	**Grandest Lady Of Them All** *Conway Twitty*
	Grandma Got Run Over By A Reindeer
92/83	*Elmo 'N Patsy*
64/97	*Elmo & Patsy*
1/72	**Grandma Harp** *Merle Haggard*
	(Grandma's Diary) ..see: Johnny, My Love
64/89	**Grandma's Old Wood Stove** *Sanders*
9/81	**Grandma's Song** *Gail Davies*
1/86	**Grandpa (Tell Me 'Bout The Good Old Days)** *Judds*
23/96	**Grandpa Told Me So** *Kenny Chesney*
82/88	**Grass Is Greener** *Teddy Spencer*
15/49	**Grass Looks Greener Over Yonder** *Hank Thompson*
24/67	**Grass Won't Grow On A Busy Street** *Kenny Price*
71/96	**Gravitational Pull** *Chris LeDoux*
F/70	**Grazin' In Greener Pastures** *Ray Price*
83/76	**(Great American) Classic Cowboy** *Penny DeHaven*
	Great Balls Of Fire
1/58	*Jerry Lee Lewis*
F/79	*Dolly Parton*
67/79	**Great Chicago Fire** *Faron Young*
12/74	**Great Divide** *Roy Clark*
41/90	**Great Divide** *Gene Watson*
32/66	**Great El Tigre (The Tiger)** *Stu Phillips*
8/75	**Great Expectations** *Buck Owens*
58/73	**Great Filling Station Holdup** *Jimmy Buffett*
10/48	**Great Long Pistol** *Jerry Irby*
63/74	**Great Mail Robbery** *Rex Allen, Jr.*
46/68	**Great Pretender** *Lamar Morris*
8/70	**Great White Horse** *Buck Owens & Susan Raye*
53/84	**Greatest Gift Of All** *Kenny Rogers & Dolly Parton*
94/80	**Greatest Love Affair** *Chuck Woolery*
3/92	**Greatest Man I Never Knew** *Reba McEntire*
22/64	**Greatest One Of All** *Melba Montgomery*
88/76	**Greatest Show On Earth** *Little David Wilkins*
	Green Berets ..see: Ballad Of
78/73	**Green Door** *Mayf Nutter*
95/81	**Green Eyed Girl** *Sean Morton Downey*
	Green Eyes
37/82	*Tom Carlile*
62/87	*Danny Davis/The Nashville Brass/ Dona Mason*
82/85	**Green Eyes** *Jesseca James*
4/65	**Green, Green Grass Of Home** *Porter Wagoner*
57/70	**Green Green Valley** *Tex Ritter*
7/48	**Green Light** *Hank Thompson*
11/67	**Green River** *Waylon Jennings*
53/73	**Green Snakes On The Ceiling** *Johnny Bush*
90/77	**Greenback Shuffle** *King Edward IV & The Knights*
26/61	**Greener Pastures** *Stonewall Jackson*
23/75	**Greener Than The Grass (We Laid On)** *Tanya Tucker*
49/68	**Greenwich Village Folk Song Salesman** *Jim & Jesse*
63/71	**Greystone Chapel** *Glen Sherley*
4/46	**Grievin' My Heart Out For You** *Jimmie Davis*
9/59	**Grin And Bear It** *Jimmy Newman*
	(Grits And Groceries) ..see: If I Don't Love You
42/69	**Groovy Grubworm** *Harlow Wilcox*
39/69	**Growin' Up** *Tex Ritter*
	(Grundy County Auction Incident) ..see: Sold
16/90	**Guardian Angels** *Judds*
19/71	**Guess Away The Blues** *Don Gibson*
18/66	**Guess My Eyes Were Bigger Than My Heart** *Conway Twitty*

4/55	**Hearts Of Stone** *Red Foley*
2/78	**Hearts On Fire** *Eddie Rabbitt*
60/81	**Hearts (Our Hearts)** *Susie Allanson*
100/77	**Heat Is On** *Tricia Johns*
55/69	**Heaven Below** *John Wesley Ryles*
24/95	**Heaven Bound (I'm Ready)** *Shenandoah*
85/77	**Heaven Can Be Anywhere (Twin Pines Theme)** *Charlie Daniels Band*
4/88	**Heaven Can't Be Found** *Hank Williams, Jr.*
5/70	**Heaven Everyday** *Mel Tillis*
14/96	**Heaven Help My Heart** *Wynonna*
18/68	**Heaven Help The Working Girl** *Norma Jean*
14/96	**Heaven In My Woman's Eyes** *Tracy Byrd*
98/78	**Heaven Is Being Good To Me** *Dick Moebakken* (also see: Old Rivers)
47/70	**Heaven Is Just A Touch Away** *Cal Smith*
3/72	**Heaven Is My Woman's Love** *Tommy Overstreet*
73/85	**Heaven Knows** *Audie Henry*
88/80	**Heaven On A Freight Train** *Max D. Barnes*
66/73	**Heaven On Earth** *Sonny James*
16/89	**Heaven Only Knows** *Emmylou Harris*
1/68	**Heaven Says Hello** *Sonny James*
F/79	**Heaven Was A Drink Of Wine** *Merle Haggard*
	Heaven's Just A Sin Away
1/77	*Kendalls*
63/93	*Kelly Willis*
32/71	**Heavenly** *Wynn Stewart*
8/82	**Heavenly Bodies** *Earl Thomas Conley*
11/70	**Heavenly Sunshine** *Ferlin Husky*
38/66	**Heck Of A Fix In 66** *Jim Nesbitt*
53/77	**Helen** *Cal Smith*
1/86	**Hell And High Water** *T. Graham Brown*
	Hell Yes I Cheated
95/77	*James Pastell*
82/82	*Jim Owen*
93/77	**Hello Atlanta** *Chip Taylor*
52/95	**Hello Cruel World** *George Ducas*
39/80	**Hello Daddy, Good Morning Darling** *Mel McDaniel*
1/70	**Hello Darlin'** *Conway Twitty*
4/61	**Hello Fool** *Ralph Emery* (also see: Hello Walls)
13/75	**Hello I Love You** *Johnny Russell*
26/70	**Hello, I'm A Jukebox** *George Kent*
91/84	**Hello Josephine** *J.W. Thompson*
14/75	**Hello Little Bluebird** *Donna Fargo*
53/71	**Hello Little Rock** *Wynn Stewart*
1/74	**Hello Love** *Hank Snow*
	Hello Mary Lou
14/70	*Bobby Lewis*
3/85	*Statler Brothers*
4/78	**Hello Mexico (And Adios Baby To You)** *Johnny Duncan*
60/67	**Hello Number One** *Kitty Wells & Red Foley*
75/72	**Hello Operator** *Joe Stampley*
	Hello Out There
8/62	*Carl Belew*
28/74	*LaWanda Lindsey*
30/78	**Hello! Remember Me** *Billy Swan*
79/74	**Hello Summertime** *Bobby Goldsboro*
94/79	**Hello Texas** *Brian Collins*
90/78	**Hello, This Is Anna** *O.B. McClinton Feat. Peggy Jo Adams*
57/78	**Hello, This Is Joannie (The Telephone Answering Machine Song)** *Paul Evans*
	Hello Trouble
5/63	*Orville Couch*
62/74	*LaWanda Lindsey*
11/89	*Desert Rose Band*
1/65	**Hello Vietnam** *Johnny Wright*
30/63	**Hello Wall No. 2** *Ben Colder*
1/61	**Hello Walls** *Faron Young* (also see: Hello Fool)

14/73	**Hello We're Lonely** *Patti Page & Tom T. Hall*
29/81	**Hello Woman** *Doug Kershaw*
56/92	**Help, I'm White And I Can't Get Down** *Geezinslaws*
	Help Me
6/74	*Elvis Presley*
38/77	*Ray Price*
66/89	**Help Me Get Over You** *Wagoneers*
1/90	**Help Me Hold On** *Travis Tritt*
	Help Me Make It Through The Night
1/71	*Sammi Smith*
4/80	*Willie Nelson*
37/75	**Help Me Make It (To My Rockin' Chair)** *B.J. Thomas*
	Help Yourself To Me
47/75	*Roy Head*
97/75	*Debra Barber*
18/97	**Helping Me Get Over You** *Travis Tritt*
	Helpless
19/64	*Joe Carson*
73/68	*Dal Perkins*
62/88	**Henrietta** *Mel McDaniel*
7/54	**Hep Cat Baby** *Eddy Arnold*
67/69	**Her And The Car And The Mobile Home** *Dave Kirby*
52/76	**Her Body Couldn't Keep You (Off My Mind)** *Gene Watson*
92/80	**Her Cheatin Heart (Made A Drunken Fool Of Me)** *Jerry Naill*
96/81	**Her Empty Pillow (Lying Next To Mine)** *Jimmy McMillan*
59/77	**Her L-O-V-E's Gone** *Red Steagall*
7/97	**Her Man** *Gary Allan*
96/75	**Her Memory's Gonna Kill Me** *Jim Alley*
3/76	**Her Name Is...** *George Jones*
59/71	**Here Come The Elephants** *Johnny Bond*
68/76	**Here Come The Flowers** *Dottie West*
2/68	**Here Comes Heaven** *Eddy Arnold*
1/71	**Here Comes Honey Again** *Sonny James*
10/64	**Here Comes My Baby** *Dottie West*
79/73	**Here Comes My Little Baby** *Pat Roberts*
	Here Comes Santa Claus (Down Santa Claus Lane)
5/47	*Gene Autry*
4/48	*Gene Autry*
8/49	*Gene Autry*
88/82	**Here Comes That Feelin' Again** *Ralph May*
32/80	**Here Comes That Feeling Again** *Don King*
15/74	**Here Comes That Girl Again** *Tommy Overstreet*
65/89	**(Here Comes) That Old Familiar Feeling** *Lisa Childress*
80/76	**Here Comes That Rainy Day Feeling Again** *Connie Cato*
10/76	**Here Comes The Freedom Train** *Merle Haggard*
9/78	**Here Comes The Hurt Again** *Mickey Gilley*
85/88	**Here Comes The Night** *Dolly Hartt*
22/95	**Here Comes The Rain** *Mavericks*
4/68	**Here Comes The Rain, Baby** *Eddy Arnold*
15/78	**Here Comes The Reason I Live** *Ronnie McDowell*
73/73	**Here Comes The Sun** *Lloyd Green*
38/73	**Here Comes The World Again** *Johnny Bush*
4/95	**Here I Am** *Patty Loveless*
	Here I Am Again
3/72	*Loretta Lynn*
69/85	*Johnny Rodriguez*
41/76	**(Here I Am) Alone Again** *Billy Walker*
	Here I Am Drunk Again
13/60	*Clyde Beavers*
11/76	*Moe Bandy*
16/75	**Here I Am In Dallas** *Faron Young*
	Here I Go Again
13/71	*Bobby Wright*
83/84	*Cheryl Handy*
77/79	**Here I Go Again** *Dorsey Burnette*
20/78	**Here In Love** *Dottsy*

3/90	**Here In The Real World** *Alan Jackson*
7/55	**Here Today And Gone Tomorrow** *Browns*
2/91	**Here We Are** *Alabama*
11/79	**Here We Are Again** *Statler Brothers*
26/61	**Here We Are Again** *Ray Price*
17/74	**Here We Go Again** *Brian Shaw*
	Here We Go Again
51/67	*Virgil Warner & Suzi Jane Hokum*
66/72	*Johnny Duncan*
65/82	*Roy Clark*
95/73	**Here With You** *Bobby Lewis*
1/77	**Here You Come Again** *Dolly Parton*
2/91	**Here's A Quarter (Call Someone Who Cares)** *Travis Tritt*
42/70	**Here's A Toast To Mama** *Charlie Louvin*
1/76	**Here's Some Love** *Tanya Tucker*
64/97	**Here's The Deal** *Jeff Carson*
60/79	**Here's To All The Too Hard Working Husbands** *David Houston*
	Here's To The Horses
94/77	*Mack Vickery*
49/81	*Johnny Russell*
88/77	**Here's To The Next Time** *Billy Larkin*
87/89	**Here's To You** *Faron Young*
45/68	**Here's To You And Me** *Tex Williams*
29/97	**Here's Your Sign (Get The Picture)** *Bill Engvall*
41/73	**Herman Schwartz** *Stonewall Jackson*
14/54	**Hernando's Hideaway** *Homer & Jethro*
77/83	**Hero, The** *Lee Dresser*
4/91	**Heroes** *Paul Overstreet*
3/91	**Heroes And Friends** *Randy Travis*
64/79	**Heroes And Idols (Don't Come Easy)** *David Smith*
54/85	**Hey** *Hillary Kanter*
	Hey Baby
35/70	*Bobby G. Rice*
95/78	*Donnie Rohrs*
7/82	*Anne Murray*
38/93	**Hey Baby** *Marty Stuart*
2/83	**Hey Bartender** *Johnny Lee*
2/89	**Hey Bobby** *K.T. Oslin*
75/84	**Hey, Bottle Of Whiskey** *Gary Stewart*
5/94	**Hey Cinderella** *Suzy Bogguss*
15/68	**Hey Daddy** *Charlie Louvin*
33/77	**Hey Daisy (Where Have All The Good Times Gone)** *Tom Bresh*
21/86	**Hey Doll Baby** *Sweethearts Of The Rodeo*
	Hey, Good Lookin'
1/51	*Hank Williams*
74/92	*Mavericks*
58/89	**Hey Heart** *Dean Dillon*
1/53	**Hey Joe!** *Carl Smith*
8/53	**Hey Joe** *Kitty Wells*
10/81	**Hey Joe (Hey Moe)** *Moe Bandy & Joe Stampley*
6/51	**Hey La La** *Ernest Tubb*
51/85	**Hey Lady** *Narvel Felts*
13/68	**Hey Little One** *Glen Campbell*
40/88	**Hey Little Sister** *Tom Wopat*
3/74	**Hey Loretta** *Loretta Lynn*
13/63	**Hey Lucille!** *Claude King*
19/76	**Hey, Lucky Lady** *Dolly Parton*
9/58	**Hey, Mr. Bluebird** *Ernest Tubb & The Wilburn Brothers*
8/53	**Hey, Mr. Cotton Picker** *Tennessee Ernie*
28/92	**Hey Mister (I Need This Job)** *Shenandoah*
22/58	**Hey Sheriff** *Rusty & Doug*
28/76	**Hey Shirley (This Is Squirrely)** *Shirley & Squirrely*
67/79	**Hey There** *Kenny Price*
21/74	**Hey There Girl** *David Rogers*
65/70	**Hey There Johnny** *Mayf Nutter*
94/78	**Hey, What Do You Say (We Fall In Love)** *Sue Richards*
1/75	**(Hey Won't You Play) Another Somebody Done Somebody Wrong Song** *B.J. Thomas*
100/78	**Hey You** *Bobby Havens*
9/65	**Hicktown** *Tennessee Ernie Ford*

429

	I Go To Pieces
88/80	*Tammy Jo*
39/88	*Dean Dillon*
76/88	*Trisha Lynn*
31/90	*Southern Pacific*
64/84	**I Got A Bad Attitude** *Gary Stewart*
58/92	**I Got A Date** *Forester Sisters*
F/79	**I Got A Feelin' In My Body** *Elvis Presley*
54/92	**I Got A Life** *Mike Reid*
30/75	**I Got A Lot Of Hurtin' Done Today** *Connie Smith*
45/93	**I Got A Love** *Matthews, Wright & King*
8/84	**I Got A Million Of 'Em** *Ronnie McDowell*
93/73	**I Got A Thing About You Baby** *Troy Seals*
40/71	**I Got A Woman** *Bob Luman*
1/89	**I Got Dreams** *Steve Wariner*
43/91	**I Got It Bad** *Matraca Berg*
15/95	**I Got It Honest** *Aaron Tippin*
1/84	**I Got Mexico** *Eddy Raven*
4/59	**I Got Stripes** *Johnny Cash*
3/77	**I Got The Hoss** *Mel Tillis*
56/87	**I Got The One I Wanted** *Nielsen White Band*
93/79	**I Got Western Pride** *Ray Frushay*
4/68	**I Got You** *Waylon Jennings & Anita Carter*
5/89	**I Got You** *Dwight Yoakam*
7/91	**I Got You** *Shenandoah*
88/79	**I Gotta Get Back The Feeling** *Sheila Andrews*
	I Gotta Get Drunk (And I Shore Do Dread It)
27/63	*Joe Carson*
55/76	*Willie Nelson*
8/55	**I Gotta Go Get My Baby** *Justin Tubb*
	I Gotta Have My Baby Back
4/50	*Floyd Tillman*
10/50	*Red Foley*
73/67	*Glen Campbell*
15/56	**I Gotta Know** *Wanda Jackson*
44/91	**I Gotta Mind To Go Crazy** *Les Taylor*
72/87	**I Grow Old Too Fast (And Smart Too Slow)** *Johnny Paycheck*
82/89	**I Guess By Now** *Big Al Downing*
48/67	**I Guess I Had Too Much To Dream Last Night** *Faron Young*
55/88	**I Guess I Just Missed You** *Canyon*
9/62	**I Guess I'll Never Learn** *Charlie Phillips*
	I Guess I'm Crazy
13/55	*Tommy Collins*
1/64	*Jim Reeves*
1/84	**I Guess It Never Hurts To Hurt Sometimes** *Oak Ridge Boys*
14/93	**I Guess You Had To Be There** *Lorrie Morgan*
72/76	**I Guess You Never Loved Me Anyway** *Randy Cornor*
5/86	**I Had A Beautiful Time** *Merle Haggard*
63/87	**I Had A Heart** *Darlene Austin*
5/79	**I Had A Lovely Time** *Kendalls*
33/82	**I Had It All** *Fred Knoblock*
60/86	**I Had My Heart Set On You** *Emmylou Harris*
30/65	**I Had One Too Many** *Wilburn Brothers*
4/44	**I Hang My Head And Cry** *Gene Autry*
	I Hate Goodbyes
25/73	*Bobby Bare*
40/77	*Lois Johnson*
22/58	**I Hate Myself** *Faron Young*
16/79	**I Hate The Way I Love It** *Johnny Rodriguez & Charly McClain*
78/79	**I Hate The Way Our Love Is** *Jimmy Peters & Lynda K. Lance*
10/73	**I Hate You** *Ronnie Milsap*
17/81	**I Have A Dream** *Cristy Lane*
26/77	**I Have A Dream, I Have A Dream** *Roy Clark*
	I Have Loved You Girl (But Not Like This Before)
87/75	*Earl Thomas Conley*
2/83	*Earl Thomas Conley*
90/80	**I Have To Break The Chains That Bind Me** *Gary Goodnight*

17/97	**I Have To Surrender** *Ty Herndon*
7/88	**I Have You** *Glen Campbell*
5/53	**I Haven't Got The Heart** *Webb Pierce*
76/77	**I Haven't Learned A Thing** *Porter Wagoner*
54/67	**I Hear It Now** *Browns*
17/66	**I Hear Little Rock Calling** *Ferlin Husky*
83/88	**I Hear The South** *Vassar Clements*
29/79	**I Hear The South Callin' Me** *Hank Thompson*
91/78	**I Hear You Coming Back** *Brent Burns*
27/59	**I Hear You Talkin'** *Faron Young*
9/68	**I Heard A Heart Break Last Night** *Jim Reeves*
93/79	**I Heard A Song Today** *Tommy O'Day*
12/49	**I Heard About You** *Bud Hobbs*
33/65	**I Heard From A Memory Last Night** *Jim Edward Brown*
71/84	**I Heard It On The Radio** *Robin Lee*
45/70	**I Heard Our Song** *Dottie West*
	(I Heard That) Lonesome Whistle ..see: Lonesome Whistle
4/57	**I Heard The Bluebirds Sing** *Browns*
6/74	**I Honestly Love You** *Olivia Newton-John*
59/68	**I Hope I Like Mexico Blues** *Dallas Frazier*
36/70	**I Hope So** *Willie Nelson*
49/72	**I Hope You're Havin' Better Luck Than Me** *Crystal Gayle*
10/84	**I Hurt For You** *Deborah Allen*
69/68	**I Just Ain't Got (As Much As He's Got Going For Me)** *Gene Wyatt*
16/89	**I Just Called To Say Goodbye Again** *Larry Boone*
77/85	**I Just Came Back (To Break My Heart Again)** *Bruce Hauser/Sawmill Creek Band*
4/82	**I Just Came Here To Dance** *David Frizzell & Shelly West*
	I Just Came Home To Count The Memories
75/75	*Bobby Wright*
15/77	*Cal Smith*
7/82	*John Anderson*
	I Just Came In Here (To Let A Little Hurt Out)
51/77	*Peggy Sue*
96/89	*Sandy Ellwanger*
8/68	**I Just Came To Get My Baby** *Faron Young*
21/66	**I Just Came To Smell The Flowers** *Porter Wagoner*
1/75	**I Just Can't Get Her Out Of My Mind** *Johnny Rodriguez*
	I Just Can't Help Believing
36/70	*David Frizzell*
59/74	*David Rogers*
48/65	**I Just Can't Let You Say Goodbye** *Willie Nelson*
21/88	**I Just Can't Say No To You** *Moe Bandy*
63/95	**I Just Can't Stand To Be Unhappy** *Bobbie Cryner*
5/79	**I Just Can't Stay Married To You** *Cristy Lane*
68/86	**I Just Can't Take The Leaving Anymore** *Susan Raye*
58/76	**I Just Can't (Turn My Habit Into Love)** *Kenny Starr*
73/82	**I Just Can't Turn Temptation Down** *Skip & Linda*
40/72	**I Just Couldn't Let Her Walk Away** *Dorsey Burnette*
51/66	**I Just Couldn't See The Forest (For The Trees)** *Lefty Frizzell*
11/82	**I Just Cut Myself** *Ronnie McDowell*
92/75	**I Just Don't Give A Damn** *George Jones*
5/50	**I Just Don't Like This Kind Of Livin'** *Hank Williams*
1/79	**I Just Fall In Love Again** *Anne Murray*
28/76	**I Just Got A Feeling** *La Costa*
10/53	**(I Just Had A Date) A Lover's Quarrel** *George Morgan*

	I Just Had You On My Mind
48/74	*Sue Richards*
21/78	*Dottsy*
22/80	*Billy "Crash" Craddock*
46/83	**I Just Heard A Heart Break** *Tammy Wynette*
63/76	**I Just Love Being A Woman** *Barbara Fairchild*
45/96	**I Just Might Be** *Lorrie Morgan*
78/79	**I Just Need A Coke (To Get The Whiskey Down)** *Lenny Gault*
11/81	**I Just Need You For Tonight** *Billy "Crash" Craddock*
17/74	**I Just Started Hatin' Cheatin' Songs Today** *Moe Bandy*
43/79	**I Just Wanna Feel The Magic** *Bobby Borchers*
56/67	**I Just Want To Be Alone** *Ray Pillow*
36/81	**I Just Want To Be With You** *Sammi Smith*
14/78	**I Just Want To Be Your Everything** *Connie Smith*
1/78	**I Just Want To Love You** *Eddie Rabbitt*
97/78	**I Just Want To Love You** *DeAnne Horn*
70/68	**I Just Wanted To Know (How The Wind Was Blowing)** *Hank Snow*
1/94	**I Just Wanted To Know** *Mark Chesnutt*
59/78	**I Just Wanted You To Know** *Ronnie McDowell*
56/68	**I Just Wasted The Rest** *Del Reeves & Bobby Goldsboro*
1/78	**I Just Wish You Were Someone I Love** *Larry Gatlin with Brothers & Friends*
89/79	**I Just Wonder Where He Could Be Tonight** *Hilka & Jebry Lee Briley*
1/81	**I Keep Coming Back** *Razzy Bailey*
14/68	**I Keep Coming Back For More** *Dave Dudley*
43/65	**I Keep Forgettin' That I Forgot About You** *Wynn Stewart*
	I Kissed You ..see: ('Til)
48/73	**I Knew Jesus (Before He Was A Star)** *Glen Campbell*
37/88	**I Knew Love** *Nanci Griffith*
64/91	**I Knew My Day Would Come** *Vern Gosdin*
91/78	**I Knew The Mason** *Chapin Hartford*
84/83	**I Knew You When** *Linda Ronstadt*
86/76	**I Knew You When** *Jerry Foster*
59/70	**I Knew You'd Be Leaving** *Peggy Little*
72/97	**I Know** *Kim Richey*
100/78	**I Know** *DeAnne Horn*
65/79	**I Know A Good Thing When I Feel It** *Pia Zadora*
10/79	**I Know A Heartache When I See One** *Jennifer Warnes*
81/81	**I Know An Ending (When It Comes)** *B.J. Wright*
4/70	**I Know How** *Loretta Lynn*
1/88	**I Know How He Feels** *Reba McEntire*
74/67	**I Know How To Do It** *Bobby Braddock*
91/79	**I Know I'm Not Your Hero Anymore** *Ronny Robbins*
56/86	**I Know Love** *Everly Brothers*
67/83	**I Know My Way To You By Heart** *Marlow Tackett*
	I Know One
6/60	*Jim Reeves*
6/67	*Charley Pride*
5/96	**I Know She Still Loves Me** *George Strait*
96/77	**I Know The Feeling** *Jerry Green*
35/85	**I Know The Way To You By Heart** *Vern Gosdin*
89/88	**I Know There's A Heart In There Somewhere** *Chris Austin*
21/89	**I Know What I've Got** *J.C. Crowley*
1/87	**I Know Where I'm Going** *Judds*
13/92	**I Know Where Love Lives** *Hal Ketchum*
	I Know You're Married (But I Love You Still)
29/66	*Bill Anderson & Jan Howard*
52/70	*Red Sovine*

434

449

M

2/64	**Memory #1** *Webb Pierce*
10/81	**Memphis** *Fred Knoblock*
79/84	**Memphis In May** *Darrell McCall*
7/80	**Men** *Charly McClain*
8/91	**Men** *Forester Sisters*
	Men In My Little Girl's Life
16/66	Archie Campbell
50/66	Tex Ritter
60/94	**Men Will Be Boys** *Billy Dean*
88/89	**Men With Broken Hearts** *Charley Hager*
13/93	**Mending Fences** *Restless Heart*
8/61	**Mental Cruelty**
	Buck Owens & Rose Maddox
14/68	**Mental Journey** *Leon Ashley*
	Mental Revenge
12/67	Waylon Jennings
15/76	Mel Tillis
2/93	**Mercury Blues** *Alan Jackson*
49/76	**Mercy** *Jean Shepard*
7/48	**Merle's Boogie Woogie** *Merle Travis*
58/97	**Merry Christmas Strait To You**
	George Strait
41/77	**Merry-Go-Round** *Freddy Weller*
47/75	**Merry-Go-Round Of Love** *Hank Snow*
71/70	**Merry-Go-Round World** *Webb Pierce*
72/80	**Message To Khomeini**
	Thrasher Brothers
93/81	**Mexican Girl** *Michael Tate*
1/53	**Mexican Joe** *Jim Reeves*
61/77	**Mexican Love Songs** *Linda Hargrove*
94/85	**Mexico** *Backtrack/John Hunt*
4/44	**Mexico Joe** *Ivie Anderson*
85/80	**Mexico Winter** *Bobby Hood*
4/74	**Mi Esposa Con Amor (To My Wife With**
	Love) *Sonny James*
1/95	**Mi Vida Loca (My Crazy Life)** *Pam Tillis*
14/86	**Miami, My Amy** *Keith Whitley*
93/73	**Mid American Manufacturing Tycoon**
	Bobby Russell
4/78	**Middle Age Crazy** *Jerry Lee Lewis*
41/79	**Middle-Age Madness**
	Earl Thomas Conley
86/75	**Middle Of A Memory** *Eddy Arnold*
1/53	**Midnight** *Red Foley*
16/77	**Midnight Angel** *Barbara Mandrell*
84/84	**Midnight Angel Of Mercy** *Rod Rishard*
36/87	**Midnight Blue** *John Wesley Ryles*
39/84	**Midnight Blue** *Billie Jo Spears*
76/82	**Midnight Cabaret** *Wyvon Alexander*
43/80	**Midnight Choir** *Gatlin Bros.*
5/83	**Midnight Fire** *Steve Wariner*
93/80	**Midnight Fire** *Marlow Tackett*
83/77	**Midnight Flight** *Pam Rose*
	Midnight Flyer
74/73	Osborne Brothers
94/79	Charlie McCoy
4/87	**Midnight Girl/Sunset Town**
	Sweethearts Of The Rodeo
1/81	**Midnight Hauler** *Razzy Bailey*
14/88	**Midnight Highway** *Southern Pacific*
3/92	**Midnight In Montgomery** *Alan Jackson*
59/79	**Midnight Lace** *Big Al Downing*
51/84	**Midnight Love** *Billie Jo Spears*
93/82	**Midnight Magic** *Gary Buck*
64/74	**Midnight Man** *Marty Mitchell*
2/74	**Midnight, Me And The Blues** *Mel Tillis*
7/73	**Midnight Oil** *Barbara Mandrell*
6/80	**Midnight Rider** *Willie Nelson*
9/82	**Midnight Rodeo** *Leon Everette*
43/89	**Midnight Train** *Charlie Daniels Band*
87/77	**Midnight Train To Georgia**
	Eddie Middleton
57/81	**Midnite Flyer** *Sue Powell*
85/87	**Midnite Rock** *Indiana*
F/84	**Midsummer Nights** *Kenny Rogers*
68/67	**Mighty Day** *Carl Smith*
47/91	**Miles Across The Bedroom** *Gary Morris*
38/77	**Miles And Miles Of Texas**
	Asleep At The Wheel
8/52	**Milk Bucket Boogie** *Red Foley*
	Miller's Cave
9/60	Hank Snow
4/64	Bobby Bare
2/66	**Million And One** *Billy Walker*

39/83	**Million Light Beers Ago** *David Frizzell*
	Million Old Goodbyes
66/80	Freddy Weller
8/81	Mel Tillis
13/63	**Million Years Or So** *Eddy Arnold*
12/68	**Milwaukee, Here I Come**
	George Jones & Brenda Carter
51/93	**Mind Of Her Own** *John Berry*
64/75	**Mind Your Love** *Jerry Reed*
	Mind Your Own Business
5/49	Hank Williams
35/64	Jimmy Dean
1/86	Hank Williams, Jr.
8/49	**Mine All Mine** *Jimmy Wakely*
79/84	**Minstrel, The** *Mike Dekle*
69/78	**Minstrel Man** *Rebecca Lynn*
24/66	**Minute Men (Are Turning In Their**
	Graves) *Stonewall Jackson*
9/63	**Minute You're Gone** *Sonny James*
4/81	**Miracles** *Don Williams*
3/91	**Mirror Mirror** *Diamond Rio*
41/75	**Mirror, Mirror** *Ben Reece*
49/89	**Mirror Mirror** *Barbara Mandrell*
56/88	**Mirrors Don't Lie** *Marty Stuart*
12/82	**Mis'ry River** *Terri Gibbs*
3/80	**Misery And Gin** *Merle Haggard*
	Misery Loves Company
1/62	Porter Wagoner
F/80	Ronnie Milsap
2/81	**Miss Emily's Picture** *John Conlee*
55/72	**Miss Pauline** *Billy Bob Bowman*
26/84	**Miss Understanding** *David Wills*
32/84	**Missin' Mississippi** *Charley Pride*
65/88	**Missin' Texas** *Kim Grayson*
3/52	**Missing In Action** *Ernest Tubb*
2/80	**Missin' You** *Charley Pride*
	Missing You
7/57	Webb Pierce
8/72	Jim Reeves
54/96	**Missing You** *Mavericks*
79/90	**Missing You** *Marcy Bros.*
1/50	**Mississippi** *Red Foley*
19/79	**Mississippi** *Charlie Daniels Band*
31/76	**Mississippi** *Barbara Fairchild*
	Mississippi
58/70	John Phillips
75/78	Jack Paris
59/86	**Mississippi Break Down** *Toni Price*
3/74	**Mississippi Cotton Picking Delta Town**
	Charley Pride
15/95	**Mississippi Moon** *John Anderson*
20/85	**Mississippi Squirrel Revival**
	Ray Stevens
14/71	**Mississippi Woman** *Waylon Jennings*
20/75	**Mississippi You're On My Mind**
	Stoney Edwards
5/47	**Missouri** *Merle Travis*
3/82	**Mistakes** *Don Williams*
	Mister ..see: Mr.
3/75	**Misty** *Ray Stevens*
	Misty Blue
4/66	Wilma Burgess
3/67	Eddy Arnold
5/76	Billie Jo Spears
37/72	**Misty Memories** *Brenda Lee*
77/86	**Misty Mississippi** *Rusty Budde*
43/80	**Misty Morning Rain** *Ray Price*
	Misunderstanding ..see: Miss
	Understanding
44/73	**Mm-Mm Good** *Del Reeves*
	Moanin' The Blues
1/50	Hank Williams
87/89	Vicki Bird
65/82	**Moanin The Blues** *Kenny Dale*
60/81	**Mobile Bay** *Johnny Cash*
27/77	**Mobile Boogie** *Hank Williams, Jr.*
64/81	**Moccasin Man** *Dave Kirby*
	Mockin' Bird Hill
3/51	Pinetoppers
7/51	Les Paul & Mary Ford
9/77	Donna Fargo
94/74	**Mockingbird** *Terri Lane & Jimmy Nall*
75/86	**Modern Day Cowboy** *Jay Clark*
92/89	**Modern Day Cowboy** *John Marriott*

51/85	**Modern Day Marriages** *Razzy Bailey*
1/85	**Modern Day Romance**
	Nitty Gritty Dirt Band
44/69	**Moffett, Oklahoma** *Charlie Walker*
5/64	**Molly** *Eddy Arnold & The Needmore*
	Creek Singers
53/69	**Molly** *Jim Glaser*
91/80	**Molly (And The Texas Rain)**
	Sonny Wright
10/48	**Molly Darling** *Eddy Arnold*
28/75	**Molly (I Ain't Gettin' Any Younger)**
	Dorsey Burnette
	Mom And Dad's Waltz
2/51	Lefty Frizzell
21/61	Patti Page
43/79	**Moment By Moment** *Narvel Felts*
24/66	**Mommy, Can I Still Call Him Daddy**
	Dottie West
5/59	**Mommy For A Day** *Kitty Wells*
	Mona Lisa
4/50	Moon Mullican
10/50	Jimmy Wakely
11/81	Willie Nelson
2/84	**Mona Lisa Lost Her Smile**
	David Allan Coe
68/94	**Mona Lisa On Cruise Control**
	Dennis Robbins
20/73	**Monday Morning Secretary**
	Statler Brothers
13/88	**Money** *K.T. Oslin*
15/57	**Money** *Brownie*
35/70	**Money Can't Buy Love** *Roy Rogers*
74/89	**Money Don't Make A Man A Lover**
	Dawnett Faucett
48/65	**Money Greases The Wheels**
	Ferlin Husky
1/93	**Money In The Bank** *John Anderson*
	Money, Marbles And Chalk
12/49	Stubby & The Buccaneers
15/49	Patti Page
15/60	**Money To Burn** *George Jones*
11/72	**Monkey That Became President**
	Tom T. Hall
	Monsters' Holiday ..see: (It's A)
95/74	**Montgomery Mable** *Merle Kilgore*
54/92	**Month Of Sundays** *Vern Gosdin*
42/68	**Moods Of Mary** *Tompall/Glaser Brothers*
1/77	**Moody Blue** *Elvis Presley*
68/70	**Moody River** *Chase Webster*
16/60	**Moon Is Crying** *Allan Riddle*
1/87	**Moon Is Still Over Her Shoulder**
	Michael Johnson
9/91	**Moon Over Georgia** *Shenandoah*
36/89	**Moon Pretty Moon** *Statler Brothers*
	(Moon Song) ..see: I Don't Know A
	Thing About Love
72/80	**Moonlight And Magnolia** *Buck Owens*
51/93	**Moonlight Drive-In** *Turner Nichols*
18/90	**Moonshadow Road** *T. Graham Brown*
58/74	**Moontan** *Jeris Ross*
76/87	**Moonwalkin'** *Don Malena*
77/87	**Moon Walking** *Bonnie Leigh*
26/72	**More About John Henry** *Tom T. Hall*
	More And More
1/54	Webb Pierce
7/83	Charley Pride
77/89	**More I Do** *Charley Pride*
95/79	**More I Get The More I Want**
	Becky Hobbs
89/84	**More I Go Blind** *Rod Rishard*
49/92	**More I Learn (The Less I Understand**
	About Love) *Ronna Reeves*
6/94	**More Love** *Doug Stone*
61/82	**More Nights** *Lane Brody*
51/80	**More Than A Bedroom Thing**
	Bill Anderson
6/89	**More Than A Name On A Wall**
	Statler Brothers
5/55	**More Than Anything Else In The World**
	Carl Smith
47/89	**More Than Enough** *Glen Campbell*
41/97	**More Than Everything** *Rhett Akins*
84/87	**More Than Friendly Persuasion**
	Bonnie Nelson

New Blue Jeans ..see: (I'm Looking For Some)
18/82 **New Cut Road** *Bobby Bare*
1/89 **New Fool At An Old Game** *Reba McEntire*
3/54 **New Green Light** *Hank Thompson*
39/68 **New Heart** *Ernest Ashworth*
New Jolie Blonde (New Pretty Blonde)
1/47   *Red Foley*
2/47   *Moon Mullican*
43/77 **New Kid In Town** *Eagles*
32/90 **New Kind Of Love** *Michelle Wright*
25/67 **New Lips** *Roy Drusky*
1/83 **New Looks From An Old Lover** *B.J. Thomas*
51/88 **New Never Wore Off My Sweet Baby** *Dean Dillon*
28/69 **New Orleans** *Anthony Armstrong Jones*
10/84 **New Patches** *Mel Tillis*
87/84 **New Place To Begin** *Ray Price*
72/66 **New Place To Hang Your Hat** *Ruby Wright*
New Pretty Blonde ..see: New Jolie Blonde
79/88 **New River** *Heartland*
26/59 **New River Train** *Bobby Helms*
3/44 **New San Antonio Rose** *Bob Wills*
2/88 **New Shade Of Blue** *Southern Pacific*
64/86 **New Shade Of Blue** *Perry LaPointe*
1/46 **New Spanish Two Step** *Bob Wills*
5/46 **New Steel Guitar Rag** *Bill Boyd*
95/85 **New Tradition** *Bobby G. Rice*
64/93 **New Way Home** *K.T. Oslin*
17/82 **New Way Out** *Karen Brooks*
2/91 **New Way (To Light Up An Old Flame)** *Joe Diffie*
10/52 **New Wears Off Too Fast** *Hank Thompson*
62/82 **New Will Never Wear Off Of You** *Crash Craddock*
73/73 **New York Callin' Miami** *Kent Fox*
19/71 **New York City** *Statler Brothers*
83/81 **New York Cowboy** *Nashville Superpickers*
26/63 **New York Town** *Flatt & Scruggs*
18/80 **New York Wine And Tennessee Shine** *Dave & Sugar*
17/79 **Next Best Feeling** *Mary K. Miller*
86/73 **Next Door Neighbor's Kid** *Jud Strunk*
1/68 **Next In Line** *Conway Twitty*
9/57 **Next In Line** *Johnny Cash*
55/98 **Next Step** *Jim Collins*
F/70 **Next Step Is Love** *Elvis Presley*
16/92 **Next Thing Smokin'** *Joe Diffie*
14/59 **Next Time** *Ernest Tubb*
51/86 **Next Time** *Wild Choir*
15/71 **Next Time I Fall In Love (I Won't)** *Hank Thompson*
92/87 **Next Time I Marry** *Victoria Hallman*
51/89 **Next To You** *Tammy Wynette*
Next To You
78/85   *Craig Dillingham*
74/86   *Tommy Overstreet*
1/90 **Next To You, Next To Me** *Shenandoah*
15/55 **Next Voice You Hear** *Hank Snow*
37/70 **Nice 'N' Easy** *Charlie Rich*
85/86 **Nice To Be With You** *Slewfoot*
37/97 **Nickajack** *River Road*
80/83 **Nickel's Worth Of Heaven** *Brian Collins*
31/66 **Nickels, Quarters And Dimes** *Johnny Wright*
26/59 **Night** *Jimmy Martin*
77/75 **Night Atlanta Burned** *Chet Atkins*
67/83 **Night Dolly Parton Was Almost Mine** *Pump Boys & Dinettes*
81/77 **Night Flying** *Roy Drusky*
1/83 **Night Games** *Charley Pride*
20/80 **Night Games** *Ray Stevens*
43/87 **Night Hank Williams Came To Town** *Johnny Cash*
58/85 **Night Has A Heart Of It's Own** *Lacy J. Dalton*
9/95 **Night Is Fallin' In My Heart** *Diamond Rio*
85/80 **Night Lies** *Bill Wence*

Night Life
28/63   *Ray Price*
31/68   *Claude Gray*
20/80   *Danny Davis/Willie Nelson/ The Nashville Brass*
59/86   *B.J. Thomas*
F/86   *Roy Clark*
29/71 **Night Miss Nancy Ann's Hotel For Single Girls Burned Down** *Tex Williams*
70/88 **Night Of Love Forgotten** *Bobby G. Rice*
45/64 **Night People** *Leroy Van Dyke*
Night The Lights Went Out In Georgia
36/73   *Vicki Lawrence*
12/92   *Reba McEntire*
Night They Drove Old Dixie Down
71/70   *Buckaroos*
33/71   *Alice Creech*
16/76 **Night Time And My Baby** *Joe Stampley*
2/78 **Night Time Magic** *Larry Gatlin*
83/79 **Night Time Music Man** *Judy Argo*
85/83 **Night's Almost Over** *Jacky Ward*
F/72 **Night's Not Over Yet** *Roy Drusky*
20/90 **Night's Too Long** *Patty Loveless*
14/63 **Nightmare** *Faron Young*
4/86 **Nights** *Ed Bruce*
27/78 **Nights Are Forever Without You** *Buck Owens*
84/89 **Nights Are Never Long Enough With You** *Sylvia, Forrest*
48/97 **Nights Like These** *Lynns*
93/83 **Nights Like Tonight** *Austin O'Neal*
95/82 **Nights Out At The Days End** *Owen Brothers*
89/85 **Nightshift** *Nashville Nightshift*
1/81 **9 To 5** *Dolly Parton*
41/67 **Ninety Days** *Jimmy Dean*
2/63 **Ninety Miles An Hour** *Hank Snow*
13/59 **Ninety-Nine** *Bill Anderson*
7/81 **1959** *John Anderson*
43/96 **1969** *Keith Stegall*
81/78 **Nineteen-Sixty Something Songwriter Of The Year** *Tennesseans*
6/86 **1982** *Randy Travis*
58/84 **1984** *Craig Dillingham*
9,999,999 Tears
3/76   *Dickey Lee*
75/89   *Tammy Lucas*
76/78 **Ninth Of September** *Jim Chesnut*
39/81 **No Aces** *Patti Page*
8/68 **No Another Time** *Lynn Anderson*
72/69 **No Blues Is Good News** *George Jones*
72/89 **No Chance To Dance** *Johnny Rodriguez*
1/74 **No Charge** *Melba Montgomery*
1/94 **No Doubt About It** *Neal McCoy*
19/87 **No Easy Horses** *Schuyler, Knobloch & Bickhardt*
49/83 **No Fair Fallin' In Love** *Jan Gray*
3/93 **No Future In The Past** *Vince Gill*
No Gettin' Over Me ..see: (There's)
73/97 **No Goodbyes** *Gene Watson*
83/79 **No Greater Love** *Billy Stack*
60/73 **No Headstone On My Grave** *Jerry Lee Lewis*
No Help Wanted
1/53   *Carlisles*
9/53   *Hank Thompson*
7/53 **No Help Wanted #2** *Ernest Tubb*
13/55 **No, I Don't Believe I Will** *Carl Smith*
2/44 **No Letter Today** *Ted Daffan*
No Love At All
15/70   *Lynn Anderson*
80/80   *Jan Gray*
No Love Have I
4/60   *Webb Pierce*
26/78   *Gail Davies*
67/92   *Holly Dunn*
3/95 **No Man's Land** *John Michael Montgomery*
1/90 **No Matter How High** *Oak Ridge Boys*
17/79 **No Memories Hangin' Round** *Rosanne Cash/Bobby Bare*
26/94 **No More Cryin'** *McBride & The Ride*
19/73 **No More Hanging On** *Jerry Lee Lewis*

No More One More Time
71/87   *Judy Byram*
7/88   *Jo-el Sonnier*
15/71 **No Need To Worry** *Johnny Cash & June Carter*
1/96 **No News** *Lonestar*
8/78 **No, No, No (I'd Rather Be Free)** *Rex Allen, Jr.*
F/56 **No One But You** *Kitty Wells & Red Foley*
79/87 **No One Can Touch Me** *Carla Monday*
14/55 **No One Dear But You** *Johnnie & Jack*
7/79 **No One Else In The World** *Tammy Wynette*
1/92 **No One Else On Earth** *Wynonna*
6/86 **No One Mends A Broken Heart Like You** *Barbara Mandrell*
1/96 **No One Needs To Know** *Shania Twain*
6/46 **No One To Cry To** *Sons Of The Pioneers*
97/89 **No One To Talk To But The Blues** *Maripat*
No One Will Ever Know
42/66   *Frank Ifield*
13/80   *Gene Watson*
10/67 **No One's Gonna Hurt You Anymore** *Bill Anderson*
78/87 **No Ordinary Memory** *Bill Anderson*
93/80 **No Ordinary Woman** *Byron Gallimore*
2/87 **No Place Like Home** *Randy Travis*
78/82 **No Place To Hide** *Gayle Zeiler*
No Relief In Sight
98/77   *Willie Rainsford*
20/82   *Con Hunley*
62/72 **No Rings--No Strings** *Del Reeves*
57/82 **No Room To Cry** *Mike Campbell*
32/65 **No Sign Of Living** *Dottie West*
58/92 **No Sir** *Darryl & Don Ellis*
10/78 **No Sleep Tonight** *Randy Barlow*
93/84 **No Survivors** *Peter Isaacson*
16/67 **No Tears Milady** *Marty Robbins*
72/78 **No Tell Motel** *David Houston*
40/64 **No Thanks, I Just Had One** *Margie Singleton & Faron Young*
No Thinkin' Thing ..see: (This Ain't)
91/89 **No Time At All** *Debbie Sanders*
3/93 **No Time To Kill** *Clint Black*
3/46 **No Vacancy** *Merle Travis*
97/76 **No Way Around It (It's Love)** *Billy Swan*
70/92 **No Way Jose** *Ray Kennedy*
49/85 **No Way José** *David Frizzell*
53/96 **No Way Out** *Suzy Bogguss*
69/82 **No Way Out** *Johnny Paycheck*
53/80 **No Way To Drown A Memory** *Stoney Edwards*
70/95 **No Yesterday** *Billy Montana*
1/82 **Nobody** *Sylvia*
4/66 **Nobody But A Fool (Would Love You)** *Connie Smith*
2/83 **Nobody But You** *Don Williams*
43/69 **Nobody But You** *Buckaroos*
93/73 **Nobody But You** *Linda Plowman*
44/77 **Nobody Cares But You** *Freddy Weller*
61/83 **Nobody Else For Me** *Stephanie Winslow*
49/85 **Nobody Ever Gets Enough Love** *Con Hunley*
1/85 **Nobody Falls Like A Fool** *Earl Thomas Conley*
Nobody In His Right Mind Would've Left Her
25/81   *Dean Dillon*
1/86   *George Strait*
1/97 **Nobody Knows** *Kevin Sharp*
53/88 **Nobody Knows** *John Wesley Ryles*
84/89 **Nobody Knows Me** *Lyle Lovett*
1/79 **Nobody Likes Sad Songs** *Ronnie Milsap*
68/81 **Nobody Loves Anybody Anymore** *Kris Kristofferson*
1/84 **Nobody Loves Me Like You Do** *Anne Murray (with Dave Loggins)*
52/93 **Nobody Loves You When You're Free** *Remingtons*
26/87 **Nobody Should Have To Love This Way** *Crystal Gayle*
82/88 **Nobody There But Me** *Willie Nelson*

3/85	**Nobody Wants To Be Alone**
	Crystal Gayle
68/70	**Nobody Wants To Hear It Like It Is**
	Jack Barlow
2/93	**Nobody Wins** *Radney Foster*
5/73	**Nobody Wins** *Brenda Lee*
22/88	**Nobody's Angel** *Crystal Gayle*
46/67	**Nobody's Child** *Hank Williams, Jr.*
	Nobody's Darling But Mine
13/60	*Johnny Sea*
87/80	*B.J. Wright*
10/70	**Nobody's Fool** *Jim Reeves*
24/81	**Nobody's Fool** *Deborah Allen*
11/62	**Nobody's Fool But Yours** *Buck Owens*
50/96	**Nobody's Girl** *Michelle Wright*
13/94	**Nobody's Gonna Rain On Our Parade**
	Kathy Mattea
1/90	**Nobody's Home** *Clint Black*
9/50	**Nobody's Lonesome For Me**
	Hank Williams
2/90	**Nobody's Talking** *Exile*
8/69	**None Of My Business** *Henson Cargill*
73/78	**Norma Jean** *Sammi Smith*
2/92	**Norma Jean Riley** *Diamond Rio*
61/68	**Normally, Norma Loves Me** *Red Sovine*
37/81	**North Alabama** *Dave Kirby*
42/72	**North Carolina** *Dallas Frazier*
17/80	**North Of The Border** *Johnny Rodriguez*
1/61	**North To Alaska** *Johnny Horton*
71/73	**North To Chicago** *Hank Snow*
8/53	**North Wind** *Slim Whitman*
56/82	**North Wind** *Jim & Jesse/Charlie Louvin*
17/70	**Northeast Arkansas Mississippi**
	County Bootlegger *Kenny Price*
71/94	**Not** *Bellamy Brothers*
90/80	**Not A Day Goes By** *Anna Sudderth*
1/95	**Not A Moment Too Soon** *Tim McGraw*
43/88	**Not A Night Goes By** *Tim Malchak*
76/85	**Not Another Heart Song** *Tom Jones*
2/90	**Not Counting You** *Garth Brooks*
3/96	**Not Enough Hours In The Night**
	Doug Supernaw
29/88	**Not Enough Love** *Tom Wopat*
62/80	**Not Exactly Free** *O.B. McClinton*
69/89	**Not Fade Away** *Trish Lynn*
70/89	**Not Like This** *Tim Malchak*
24/64	**Not My Kind Of People**
	Stonewall Jackson
87/84	**Not On The Bottom Yet** *Boxcar Willie*
1/95	**Not On Your Love** *Jeff Carson*
65/95	**Not So Different After All**
	Brother Phelps
13/63	**Not So Long Ago** *Marty Robbins*
3/96	**Not That Different** *Collin Raye*
44/66	**Not That I Care** *Jerry Wallace*
74/86	**Not Tonight** *Paul Proctor*
77/74	**Not Tonight** *Little David Wilkins*
52/87	**Not Tonight I've Got A Heartache**
	Vicki Rae Von
15/92	**Not Too Much To Ask** *Mary-Chapin*
	Carpenter with Joe Diffie
7/63	**Not What I Had In Mind** *George Jones*
68/92	**Not With My Heart You Don't**
	Paulette Carlson
28/98	**Note, The** *Daryle Singletary*
62/68	**Note In Box Number 9** *Stu Phillips*
1/98	**Nothin' But The Taillights** *Clint Black*
20/93	**Nothin' But The Wheel** *Patty Loveless*
25/59	**Nothin' But True Love** *Margie Singleton*
	Nothin' But You
70/83	*Steve Earle & The Dukes*
51/91	*Robin Lee*
26/97	**Nothin' Less Than Love** *Buffalo Club*
11/58	**Nothin' Needs Nothin' (Like I Need**
	You) *Marvin Rainwater*
35/76	**Nothin' Takes The Place Of You**
	Asleep At The Wheel
64/92	**Nothin' To Do (And All Night To Do It)**
	Billy Burnette
82/81	**Nothin' To Do But Just Lie**
	Wesley Ryan
33/86	**Nothin' Ventured Nothin' Gained** *Sylvia*
61/67	**Nothin's Bad As Bein' Lonely**
	Johnny Sea

20/95	**Nothing** *Dwight Yoakam*
10/79	**Nothing As Original As You**
	Statler Brothers
26/82	**Nothing Behind You, Nothing In Sight**
	John Conlee
F/74	**Nothing Between** *Porter Wagoner*
19/82	**Nothing But The Radio On**
	James & Michael Younger
91/79	**Nothing But Time** *Helen Hudson*
12/86	**Nothing But Your Love Matters**
	Gatlin Bros.
37/85	**Nothing Can Hurt Me Now** *Gail Davies*
68/72	**Nothing Can Stop My Loving You**
	Patsy Sledd
7/73	**Nothing Ever Hurt Me (Half As Bad As**
	Losing You) *George Jones*
1/89	**Nothing I Can Do About It Now**
	Willie Nelson
61/93	**Nothing In Common But Love**
	Twister Alley
87/84	**(Nothing Left Between Us) But**
	Alabama *Gordon Dee*
34/65	**Nothing Left To Lose** *Faron Young*
85/88	**Nothing Left To Lose** *Tiny Wellman*
10/84	**Nothing Like Falling In Love**
	Eddie Rabbitt
4/92	**Nothing Short Of Dying** *Travis Tritt*
4/80	**Nothing Sure Looked Good On You**
	Gene Watson
39/68	**Nothing Takes The Place Of Loving**
	You *Stonewall Jackson*
15/91	**Nothing's Changed Here**
	Dwight Yoakam
63/90	**Nothing's Gonna Bother Me Tonight**
	Forester Sisters
3/90	**Nothing's News** *Clint Black*
1/86	**Now And Forever (You And Me)**
	Anne Murray
85/89	**Now And Then** *Karen Staley*
	(also see: I Still Long To Hold You)
	(Now And Then There's) A Fool Such
	As I ..see: Fool Such As I
56/76	**Now Everybody Knows** *Charlie Rich*
68/68	**Now I Can Live Again** *Mickey Gilley*
5/94	**Now I Know** *Lari White*
56/84	**Now I Lay Me Down To Cheat**
	Shelly West
62/82	**Now I Lay Me Down To Cheat**
	David Allan Coe
26/93	**Now I Pray For Rain** *Neal McCoy*
69/86	**Now I've Got A Heart Of Gold**
	Sonny Curtis
71/91	**Now It Belongs To You** *Mark O'Connor*
83/86	**Now She's In Paris** *Dave Holladay*
98/73	**Now That It's Over** *Brush Arbor*
38/81	**Now That The Feeling's Gone**
	Billy "Crash" Craddock
17/91	**Now That We're Alone** *Rodney Crowell*
43/96	**Now That's All Right With Me**
	Mandy Barnett
18/92	**Now That's Country** *Marty Stuart*
21/85	**Now There's You** *Shelly West*
	Now You See 'Em, Now You Don't
19/78	*Roy Head*
70/88	*Marty Haggard*
64/87	**Now You're Talkin'** *Mel McDaniel*
66/93	**Now You're Talkin'** *Dixiana*
7/92	**Nowhere Bound** *Diamond Rio*
20/87	**Nowhere Road** *Steve Earle*
54/97	**Nowhere, USA** *Dean Miller*
51/89	**#1 Heartache Place** *Larry Gatlin & The*
	Gatlin Brothers
41/65	**Number One Heel** *Bonnie Owens*
	#1 With A Heartache
66/75	*Billy Larkin*
94/78	*La Costa*
11/80	**Numbers** *Bobby Bare*
94/77	**Nyquil Blues** *Alvin Crow*

O

	O Holy Night
55/95	*John Berry*
74/96	*Martina McBride*
63/97	*John Berry*
67/97	*Martina McBride*
18/94	**O What A Thrill** *Mavericks*
3/47	**Oakie Boogie** *Jack Guthrie*
91/77	**Obscene Phone Call** *Johnny Russell*
28/80	**Occasional Rose** *Marty Robbins*
6/70	**Occasional Wife** *Faron Young*
1/87	**Ocean Front Property** *George Strait*
29/61	**Ocean Of Tears** *Billie Jean Horton*
	Odds And Ends (Bits And Pieces)
7/61	*Warren Smith*
66/74	*Charlie Walker*
21/71	**Ode To A Half A Pound Of Ground**
	Round *Tom T. Hall*
	Ode To Billie Joe
17/67	*Bobbie Gentry*
39/67	*Margie Singleton*
	(also see: Mystery Of Tallahatchie
	Bridge)
55/74	**Ode To Jole Blon** *Gary Sargeants*
3/65	**Ode To The Little Brown Shack Out**
	Back *Billy Edd Wheeler*
91/89	**Of All The Foolish Things To Do**
	Ross Lewis
22/97	**Of Course I'm Alright** *Alabama*
38/67	**Off And On** *Charlie Louvin*
F/76	**Off And Running** *Maury Finney*
5/79	**Official Historian On Shirley Jean**
	Berrell *Statler Brothers*
	(Oh Baby Mine) I Get So Lonely
1/54	*Johnnie & Jack*
49/79	*Bobby G. Rice*
2/83	*Statler Brothers*
21/75	**Oh Boy** *Diana Trask*
38/84	**Oh Carolina** *Vince Gill*
10/86	**Oh Darlin'** *O'Kanes*
12/82	**Oh Girl** *Con Hunley*
25/70	**Oh Happy Day** *Glen Campbell*
9/87	**Oh Heart** *Baillie & The Boys*
70/74	**Oh, How Happy** *Sherry Bryce*
79/89	**Oh How I Love You (Como Te Quiero)**
	Tony Perez
6/80	**Oh, How I Miss You Tonight**
	Jim Reeves
65/70	**Oh How I Waited** *Ron Lowry*
36/75	**Oh, How Love Changes**
	Don Gibson & Sue Thompson
48/88	**Oh Jenny** *Billy Montana*
	Oh Lonesome Me
1/58	*Don Gibson*
13/61	*Johnny Cash*
64/66	*Bobbi Martin*
63/70	*Stonewall Jackson*
92/76	*Loggins & Messina*
8/90	*Kentucky Headhunters*
78/86	**Oh Louisiana** *Jim & Jesse*
40/71	**Oh, Love Of Mine** *Johnny & Jonie Mosby*
5/93	**Oh Me, Oh My, Sweet Baby**
	Diamond Rio
42/64	**Oh No!** *Browns*
76/82	**Oh, No** *Randy Parton*
	Oh-Oh, I'm Falling In Love Again
5/58	*Jimmie Rodgers*
29/73	*Eddy Arnold*
	Oh Pretty Woman
13/70	*Arlene Harden (Lovin' Man)*
89/89	*Roy Orbison & Friends*
4/71	**Oh, Singer** *Jeannie C. Riley*
8/57	**Oh, So Many Years**
	Kitty Wells & Webb Pierce
	Oh, Such A Stranger
68/68	*Frank Ifield*
61/73	*Don Gibson*
23/76	**Oh, Sweet Temptation** *Gary Stewart*
97/76	**Oh Those Texas Women** *Gene Davis*

5/88 **Oh What A Love** *Nitty Gritty Dirt Band*
56/87 **Oh What A Night** *Mel McDaniel*
60/69 **Oh What A Woman!** *Jerry Reed*
12/91 **Oh What It Did To Me** *Tanya Tucker*
4/47 **(Oh Why, Oh Why, Did I Ever Leave)**
Wyoming *Dick Jurgens*
17/67 **Oh! Woman** *Nat Stuckey*
55/73 **Oh Woman** *Jack Barlow*
57/86 **Oh Yes I Can** *Tari Hensley*
1/69 **Okie From Muskogee** *Merle Haggard*
9/86 **Oklahoma Borderline** *Vince Gill*
49/82 **Oklahoma Crude** *Corbin/Hanner Band*
46/84 **Oklahoma Heart** *Becky Hobbs*
Oklahoma Hills
1/45 *Jack Guthrie*
7/61 *Hank Thompson*
60/69 **Oklahoma Home Brew** *Hank Thompson*
15/72 **Oklahoma Sunday Morning**
Glen Campbell
86/76 **Oklahoma Sunshine** *Pat Boone*
13/90 **Oklahoma Swing** *Vince Gill*
9/48 **Oklahoma Waltz** *Johnny Bond*
Ol' Man River ..see: Old Man River
70/68 **Old Before My Time** *Bobby Wright*
38/73 **Old Betsy Goes Boing, Boing, Boing**
Hummers
48/86 **Old Blue Yodeler** *Razzy Bailey*
52/68 **Old Bridge** *Jean Shepard*
11/87 **Old Bridges Burn Slow** *Billy Joe Royal*
30/66 **Old Brush Arbors** *George Jones*
4/93 **Old Country** *Mark Chesnutt*
48/64 **Old Courthouse** *Faron Young*
5/89 **Old Coyote Town** *Don Williams*
1/73 **(Old Dogs-Children And) Watermelon**
Wine *Tom T. Hall*
1/95 **Old Enough To Know Better**
Wade Hayes
53/70 **Old Enough To Want To (Fool Enough**
To Try) *Norro Wilson*
13/69 **Old Faithful** *Mel Tillis*
49/73 **Old Faithful** *Tony Booth*
86/81 **Old Familiar Feeling** *Wyvon Alexander*
83/81 **Old Fangled Country Songs** *Kenny O.*
F/78 **Old Fashioned Love** *Kendalls*
58/72 **Old Fashioned Love Song** *Jeris Ross*
93/81 **Old Fashioned Lover (In A Brand New**
Love Affair) *Michele Spitz*
93/83 **Old Fashioned Lovin'** *Sierra*
38/73 **Old Fashioned Singing**
George Jones & Tammy Wynette
1/81 **Old Flame** *Alabama*
5/86 **Old Flame** *Juice Newton*
46/89 **Old Flame, New Fire** *Burch Sisters*
54/78 **Old Flame, New Fire** *Hank Williams, Jr.*
Old Flames (Can't Hold A Candle To
You)
14/78 *Joe Sun*
86/78 *Brian Collins*
1/80 *Dolly Parton*
5/92 **Old Flames Have New Names**
Mark Chesnutt
2/88 **Old Folks** *Ronnie Milsap & Mike Reid*
49/66 **Old French Quarter (In New Orleans)**
Billy Walker
19/82 **Old Friends** *Roger Miller/*
Willie Nelson/Ray Price
6/80 **Old Habits** *Hank Williams, Jr.*
2/85 **Old Hippie** *Bellamy Brothers*
19/74 **Old Home Filler-Up An' Keep**
On-A-Truckin' Cafe *C.W. McCall*
44/82 **Old Home Town** *Glen Campbell*
30/88 **Old Kind Of Love** *Ricky Skaggs*
34/77 **Old King Kong** *George Jones*
20/60 **Old Lamplighter** *Browns*
30/60 **Old Log Cabin For Sale** *Porter Wagoner*
11/55 **Old Lonesome Times** *Carl Smith*
63/70 **Old Love Affair, Now Showing**
Leroy Van Dyke
11/77 **Old Man And His Horn** *Gene Watson*
1/74 **Old Man From The Mountain**
Merle Haggard
63/88 **Old Man No One Loves** *George Jones*

Old Man River
86/76 *Shylo*
22/83 *Mel McDaniel*
31/70 **Old Man Willis** *Nat Stuckey*
Old Man's Back In Town
48/92 *Garth Brooks*
59/97 *Garth Brooks*
74/84 **Old Memories Are Hard To Lose**
Kimberly Springs
90/75 **Old Memory (Got In My Eye)**
Ferlin Husky
7/59 **Old Moon** *Betty Foley*
21/93 **Old Pair Of Shoes** *Randy Travis*
50/89 **Old Pair Of Shoes** *Sawyer Brown*
Old Photographs
81/84 *Sam Neely*
27/88 *Sawyer Brown*
11/64 **Old Records** *Margie Singleton*
50/65 **Old Red** *Marty Robbins*
3/62 **Old Rivers** *Walter Brennan*
(also see: Heaven Is Being Good To
Me)
51/68 **Old Ryman** *Hank Williams, Jr.*
5/86 **Old School** *John Conlee*
8/63 **Old Showboat** *Stonewall Jackson*
9/80 **Old Side Of Town** *Tom T. Hall*
9/51 **Old Soldiers Never Die** *Gene Autry*
64/95 **Old Stuff** *Garth Brooks*
26/77 **Old Time Feeling** *Johnny Cash &*
June Carter Cash
64/77 **Old Time Lovin'** *Kenny Starr*
97/74 **Old Time Sunshine Song** *Roy Acuff*
21/86 **Old Violin** *Johnny Paycheck*
Old Wives' Tale ..see: (Just An)
3/52 **Older And Bolder** *Eddy Arnold*
8/74 **Older The Violin, The Sweeter The**
Music *Hank Thompson*
1/81 **Older Women** *Ronnie McDowell*
52/86 **Ole Rock And Roller** *Keith Stegall*
Ole Slew-Foot
48/66 *Porter Wagoner*
31/79 *Porter Wagoner*
59/96 **On A Bus To St. Cloud** *Trisha Yearwood*
2/96 **On A Good Night** *Wade Hayes*
23/87 **On And On** *Anne Murray*
27/79 **On Business For The King** *Joe Sun*
5/90 **On Down The Line** *Patty Loveless*
1/78 **On My Knees** *Charlie Rich with*
Janie Fricke
12/57 **On My Mind Again** *Billy Walker*
20/95 **On My Own** *Reba McEntire*
1/90 **On Second Thought** *Eddie Rabbitt*
7/68 **On Tap, In The Can, Or In The Bottle**
Hank Thompson
9/74 **On The Cover Of The Music City News**
Buck Owens
76/81 **On The Inside** *Patti Page*
On The Other Hand
67/85 *Randy Travis*
1/86 *Randy Travis*
44/67 **On The Other Hand** *Charlie Louvin*
29/76 **On The Rebound** *Del Reeves & Billie Jo*
Spears
6/93 **On The Road** *Lee Roy Parnell*
1/80 **On The Road Again** *Willie Nelson*
4/98 **On The Side Of Angels** *LeAnn Rimes*
69/91 **On The Surface** *Rosanne Cash*
2/97 **On The Verge** *Collin Raye*
49/75 **On The Way Home** *Betty Jean Robinson*
49/84 **On The Wings Of A Nightingale**
Everly Brothers
85/83 **On The Wings Of My Victory**
Glen Campbell
8/51 **On Top Of Old Smoky** *Weavers*
4/67 **Once** *Ferlin Husky*
1/64 **Once A Day** *Connie Smith*
68/87 **Once A Fool, Always A Fool** *Jeff Dugan*
91/75 **Once Again I Go To Sleep With Lovin'**
On My Mind *Melody Allen*
87/90 **Once And For Always** *Gary Dale Parker*
60/96 **Once I Was The Light Of Your Life**
Stephanie Bentley
1/86 **Once In A Blue Moon**
Earl Thomas Conley

34/79 **Once In A Blue Moon** *Zella Lehr*
82/83 **Once In A Blue Moon** *Hank Thompson*
Once In A Lifetime Thing
5/77 *John Wesley Ryles*
86/90 *Sammy Sadler*
85/86 **Once In A Very Blue Moon** *Nanci Griffith*
53/94 **Once In A While** *Billy Dean*
Once More
8/58 *Roy Acuff*
13/58 *Osborne Brothers & Red Allen*
66/69 *Leona Williams*
2/70 **Once More With Feeling**
Jerry Lee Lewis
42/70 **Once More With Feeling** *Willie Nelson*
3/93 **Once Upon A Lifetime** *Alabama*
80/86 **Once Upon A Time** *Bobby Blue*
Once You Get The Feel Of It
42/83 *Con Hunley*
79/88 *Marshall Tucker Band*
75/97 **Once You Learn** *Noel Haggard*
80/81 **Once You Were Mine** *Dottie West*
3/74 **Once You've Had The Best**
George Jones
69/95 **One** *George Jones & Tammy Wynette*
95/78 **One A.M. Alone** *Dave Dudley*
27/63 **One Among The Many** *Ned Miller*
66/93 **One And One And One** *Gene Watson*
93/79 **One And One Make Three** *Ron Shaw*
51/95 **One And Only Love** *Russ Taff*
93/83 **One Away From One Too Many**
Billy Walker
85/80 **One Bar At A Time** *Stoney Edwards*
61/85 **One Big Family** *Heart Of Nashville*
2/95 **One Boy, One Girl** *Collin Raye*
57/91 **One Bridge I Didn't Burn** *Conway Twitty*
42/66 **One Bum Town** *Del Reeves*
1/54 **One By One** *Kitty Wells & Red Foley*
95/75 **One By One** *Jimmy Elledge*
73/88 **One Dance Love Affair** *Jon Washington*
One Day At A Time
19/74 *Marilyn Sellars*
1/80 *Cristy Lane*
8/74 **One Day At A Time** *Don Gibson*
72/82 **One Day Since Yesterday**
Colleen Camp
23/64 **One Dozen Roses (And Our Love)**
George Morgan
54/66 **One Dream** *Slim Whitman*
10/65 **One Dyin' And A Buryin'** *Roger Miller*
2/95 **One Emotion** *Clint Black*
70/83 **One Fiddle, Two Fiddle** *Ray Price*
75/82 **One Fine Morning** *Corbin/Hanner Band*
74/88 **One Fire Between Us** *Judy Byram*
2/87 **One For The Money** *T.G. Sheppard*
1/88 **One Friend** *Dan Seals*
74/92 **One Good Love** *Nitty Gritty Dirt Band*
57/94 **One Good Man** *Michelle Wright*
71/80 **One Good Reason** *Melissa Lewis*
4/89 **One Good Well** *Don Williams*
17/61 **One Grain Of Sand** *Eddy Arnold*
One Has My Name (The Other Has My
Heart)
1/48 *Jimmy Wakely*
11/48 *Eddie Dean*
8/49 *Bob Eberly*
3/69 *Jerry Lee Lewis*
43/85 **One Hell Of A Heartache** *Gene Watson*
One Hell Of A Woman ..see: (You
Better Be)
6/91 **One Hundred And Two** *Judds*
14/71 **One Hundred Children** *Tom T. Hall*
1/86 **100% Chance Of Rain** *Gary Morris*
3/86 **One I Loved Back Then (The Corvette**
Song) *George Jones*
58/75 **One I Sing My Love Songs To**
Tommy Cash
11/64 **One If For Him, Two If For Me**
David Houston
1/80 **One In A Million** *Johnny Lee*
73/78 **One In A Million** *Nate Harvell*
19/66 **One In A Row** *Willie Nelson*
50/89 **One In Your Heart One On Your Mind**
Charly McClain
1/49 **One Kiss Too Many** *Eddy Arnold*

82/78 **Promises** *Eric Clapton*
15/67 **Promises And Hearts (Were Made To Break)** *Stonewall Jackson*
4/68 **Promises, Promises** *Lynn Anderson*
78/89 **Promises, Promises** *Lori Yates*
58/66 **Proof Is In The Kissing** *Charlie Louvin*
3/93 **Prop Me Up Beside The Jukebox (If I Die)** *Joe Diffie*
47/78 **Proud Lady** *Bob Luman*
Proud Mary
22/69   *Anthony Armstrong Jones*
56/73   *Brush Arbor*
22/75 **Proud Of You Baby** *Bob Luman*
91/80 **Prove It To You One More Time Again** *Kris Kristofferson*
74/82 **Pull My String** *Rich Landers*
18/70 **Pull My String And Wind Me Up** *Carl Smith*
28/68 **Punish Me Tomorrow** *Carl Butler & Pearl*
78/78 **Puppet On A String** *Elvis Presley*
71/95 **Pure Bred Redneck** *Cooter Brown*
1/74 **Pure Love** *Ronnie Milsap*
28/66 **Pursuing Happiness** *Norma Jean*
11/65 **Pushed In A Corner** *Ernest Ashworth*
Put A Little Holiday In Your Heart
51/96   *LeAnn Rimes*
71/97   *LeAnn Rimes*
30/70 **Put A Little Love In Your Heart** *Susan Raye*
23/76 **Put A Little Lovin' On Me** *Bobby Bare*
60/89 **Put A Quarter In The Jukebox** *Buck Owens*
21/75 **Put Another Log On The Fire** *Tompall*
Put Another Notch In Your Belt
89/75   *Kenny Starr*
76/84   *Susan Raye*
Put It Off Until Tomorrow
6/66   *Bill Phillips*
9/80   *Kendalls*
77/78 **Put It On Me** *Louise Mandrell*
43/76 **Put Me Back Into Your World** *Eddy Arnold*
30/73 **Put Me Down Softly** *Dickey Lee*
99/78 **Put Me Out Of My Memory** *Johnny Bush*
28/87 **Put Me Out Of My Misery** *Tom Wopat*
28/90 **Put Some Drive In Your Country** *Travis Tritt*
55/88 **Put Us Together Again** *Goldens*
Put You Back On The Rack ..see: (I'm Gonna)
25/64 **Put Your Arms Around Her** *Norma Jean*
9/79 **Put Your Clothes Back On** *Joe Stampley*
1/82 **Put Your Dreams Away** *Mickey Gilley*
Put Your Hand In The Hand
61/71   *Beth Moore*
67/71   *Anne Murray*
48/75 **Put Your Head On My Shoulder** *Sunday Sharpe*
44/69 **Put Your Lovin' Where Your Mouth Is** *Peggy Little*
11/91 **Put Yourself In My Place** *Pam Tillis*
4/90 **Put Yourself In My Shoes** *Clint Black*
Puttin' In Overtime At Home
74/75   *Del Reeves*
8/78   *Charlie Rich*
33/90 **Puttin' The Dark Back Into The Night** *Sawyer Brown*
68/82 **Pyramid Of Cans** *Mundo Earwood*
85/80 **Pyramid Song** *J.C. Cunningham*

69/74 **Que Pasa** *Kenny Price*
28/65 **Queen Of Draw Poker Town** *Hank Snow*

462

14/81 **Queen Of Hearts** *Juice Newton*
75/82 **Queen Of Hearts Loves You** *Joe Waters*
28/67 **Queen Of Honky Tonk Street** *Kitty Wells*
2/93 **Queen Of Memphis** *Confederate Railroad*
7/93 **Queen Of My Double Wide Trailer** *Sammy Kershaw*
5/83 **Queen Of My Heart** *Hank Williams, Jr.*
77/76 **Queen Of New Orleans** *Earl Thomas Conley*
83/75 **Queen Of Temptation** *Brian Collins*
5/65 **Queen Of The House** *Jody Miller* (also see: King Of The Road)
Queen Of The Silver Dollar
29/73   *Doyle Holly*
25/76   *Dave & Sugar*
47/76 **Queen Of The Starlight Ballroom** *David Wills*
92/79 **Quicksand** *Bill Wence*
3/50 **Quicksilver** *Elton Britt & Rosalie Allen*
64/68 **Quiet Kind** *Mac Curtis*
36/87 **Quietly Crazy** *Ed Bruce*
26/90 **Quit While I'm Behind** *Jennifer McCarter & The McCarters*
3/71 **Quits** *Bill Anderson*
26/77 **Quits** *Gary Stewart*
7/90 **Quittin' Time** *Mary-Chapin Carpenter*
55/86 **Quittin' Time** *Con Hunley*

R

Race Is On
3/64   *George Jones*
5/89   *Sawyer Brown*
85/87 **Rachel's Room** *Bobby G. Rice*
39/88 **Radio, The** *Vince Gill*
62/94 **Radio Active** *Bryan Austin*
1/85 **Radio Heart** *Charly McClain*
19/84 **Radio Land** *Michael Murphey*
62/89 **Radio Lover** *George Jones*
51/86 **Radio Romance** *Tommy Roe*
53/90 **Radio Romance** *Canyon*
57/88 **Radio Song** *Ric Steel*
Rag Mop
2/50   *Johnnie Lee Wills*
90/78   *Drifting Cowboys*
19/78 **Ragamuffin Man** *Donna Fargo*
15/61 **Ragged But Right** *Moon Mullican*
31/74 **Ragged Old Flag** *Johnny Cash*
45/68 **Raggedy Ann** *Charlie Rich* (also see: You've Been Quite A Doll)
76/82 **Ragin' Cajun** *Charlie Daniels Band*
5/47 **Ragtime Cowboy Joe** *Eddy Howard*
52/74 **Railroad Lady** *Lefty Frizzell*
87/75 **Rain** *Kris Kristofferson & Rita Coolidge*
36/72 **Rain Falling On Me** *Johnny Russell*
63/72 **Rain-Rain** *Lois Johnson*
58/95 **Rain Through The Roof** *Billy Montana*
F/79 **Rainbow And Roses** *Billy Walker*
Rainbow At Midnight
5/46   *Carlisle Brothers*
1/47   *Ernest Tubb*
5/47   *Texas Jim Robertson*
28/70 **Rainbow Girl** *Bobby Lord*
16/74 **Rainbow In Daddy's Eyes** *Sammi Smith*
75/74 **Rainbow In My Hand** *Doyle Holly*
8/49 **Rainbow In My Heart** *George Morgan*
99/77 **Rainbow In Your Eyes** *Jan & Malcolm*
77/89 **Rainbow Of Our Own** *Shane Barmby*
4/81 **Rainbow Stew** *Merle Haggard*
39/83 **Rainbows And Butterflies** *Billy Swan*
90/77 **Rainbows And Horseshoes** *R.C. Bannon*
20/66 **Rainbows And Roses** *Roy Drusky*
17/68 **Rainbows Are Back In Style** *Slim Whitman*

33/74 **Raindrops** *Narvel Felts*
55/83 **Rainin' Down In Nashville** *Tom Carlile*
59/81 **Rainin' In My Eyes** *Miki Mori*
77/89 **Rainin', Rainin', Rainin'** *Gary Stewart*
Rainin' In My Heart
3/71   *Hank Williams, Jr.*
35/89   *Jo-el Sonnier*
Raining In My Heart
14/69   *Ray Price*
63/78   *Leo Sayer*
4/77 **Rains Came** *Freddy Fender*
47/75 **Rainy Day People** *Gordon Lightfoot*
2/75 **Rainy Day Woman** *Waylon Jennings*
83/79 **Rainy Days And Rainbows** *Paul Schmucker*
21/80 **Rainy Days And Stormy Nights** *Billie Jo Spears*
13/74 **Rainy Night In Georgia** *Hank Williams, Jr.*
15/80 **Raisin' Cane In Texas** *Gene Watson*
3/78 **Rake And Ramblin' Man** *Don Williams*
42/80 **Rambler Gambler** *Linda Ronstadt*
2/77 **Ramblin' Fever** *Merle Haggard*
29/67 **Ramblin' Man** *Ray Pennington*
Ramblin' Man
63/73   *Gary Stewart*
79/73   *Jimmy Payne*
94/79 **Ramblin' Music Man** *Charlie McCoy*
Ramblin' Rose
37/77   *Johnny Lee*
93/78   *Hank Snow*
8/68 **Ramona** *Billy Walker*
1/73 **Rated "X"** *Loretta Lynn*
1/44 **Ration Blues** *Louis Jordan*
Raunchy
6/58   *Bill Justis*
11/58   *Ernie Freeman*
80/78 **Rave On** *Jerry Naylor*
3/73 **Ravishing Ruby** *Tom T. Hall*
52/77 **Raymond's Place** *Ray Griff*
2/72 **Reach Out Your Hand** *Tammy Wynette*
61/73 **Reach Out Your Hand And Touch Me** *Sonny James*
78/81 **Reachin' For Freedom** *Ron Shaw/Desert Wind Band*
49/79 **Reaching Out To Hold You** *Dottie West*
38/87 **Read Between The Lines** *Lynn Anderson*
4/86 **Read My Lips** *Marie Osmond*
82/80 **Reading Of The Will** *Jimmy Tucker*
Ready For The Times To Get Better
1/78   *Crystal Gayle*
43/81   *Joe Sun*
72/87 **Ready Or Not** *Don Malena*
90/88 **Ready To Take That Ride** *Trinity Lane*
20/96 **Ready, Willing And Able** *Lari White*
38/80 **Real Buddy Holly Story** *Sonny Curtis*
20/80 **Real Cowboy (You Say You're)** *Billy "Crash" Craddock*
67/86 **Real Good** *Bobby Bare*
9/88 **Real Good Feel Good Song** *Mel McDaniel*
76/87 **Real Good Heartache** *Rosemary Sharp*
52/94 **Real Good Way To Wind Up Lonesome** *James House*
36/68 **Real Good Woman** *Jean Shepard*
1/85 **Real Love** *Dolly Parton (with Kenny Rogers)*
69/89 **Real Old-Fashioned Broken Heart** *Bama Band*
30/67 **Real Thing** *Billy Grammer*
79/79 **Real Thing** *O.B. McClinton*
85/78 **Real Thing** *Jean Shepard*
Reason To Believe
75/69   *Suzi Jane Hokum*
88/83   *Wray Brothers Band*
Reason Why I'm Here
97/77   *Joni Lee*
85/78   *Mike Lunsford*
13/60 **Reasons To Live** *Jimmie Skinner*
6/83 **Reasons To Quit** *Merle Haggard & Willie Nelson*
1/96 **Rebecca Lynn** *Bryan White*
24/61 **Rebel - Johnny Yuma** *Johnny Cash*

4/95	**Safe In The Arms Of Love**	
	Martina McBride	
44/85	**Safe In The Arms Of Love** *Robin Lee*	
82/80	**Safe In The Arms Of Your Love (Cold**	
	In The Streets) *Jim Weatherly*	
55/72	**Safe In These Lovin' Arms Of Mine**	
	Jean Shepard	
1/64	**Saginaw, Michigan** *Lefty Frizzell*	
	Sail Away	
98/77	*Sam Neely*	
2/79	*Oak Ridge Boys*	
16/79	**Sail On** *Tom Grant*	
63/85	**Sailing Home To Me** *Loy Blanton*	
16/59	**Sailor Man** *Johnnie & Jack*	
19/59	**Sal's Got A Sugar Lip** *Johnny Horton*	
51/75	**Sally G** *Paul McCartney & Wings*	
20/62	**Sally Was A Good Old Girl**	
	Hank Cochran	
98/79	**Salt On The Wound** *Jerry Fuller*	
8/52	**Salty Dog Rag** *Red Foley*	
8/70	**Salute To A Switchblade** *Tom T. Hall*	
87/79	**Salute To The Duke** *Paul Ott*	
40/77	**Sam** *Olivia Newton-John*	
	Sam Hill	
11/64	*Claude King*	
45/64	*Merle Haggard*	
1/67	**Sam's Place** *Buck Owens*	
12/92	**Same Ol' Love** *Ricky Skaggs*	
83/81	**Same Old Boy** *Gary Gentry*	
1/59	**Same Old Me** *Ray Price*	
28/91	**Same Old Star** *McBride & The Ride*	
29/75	**Same Old Story** *Hank Williams, Jr.*	
46/70	**Same Old Story, Same Old Lie**	
	Bill Phillips	
65/73	**Same Old Way** *Stan Hitchcock*	
5/82	**Same Ole Me** *George Jones*	
8/49	**Same Sweet Girl** *Hank Locklin*	
14/57	**Same Two Lips** *Marty Robbins*	
47/66	**Sammy** *David Houston*	
50/67	**San Antonio** *Willie Nelson*	
89/80	**San Antonio Medley**	
	Curtis Potter/Darrell McCall	
25/83	**San Antonio Nights** *Eddy Raven*	
	San Antonio Rose	
8/61	*Floyd Cramer*	
F/83	*Ray Price*	
	San Antonio Stroll	
1/75	*Tanya Tucker*	
F/76	*Maury Finney*	
31/68	**San Diego** *Charlie Walker*	
	San Francisco Is A Lonely Town	
46/69	*Ben Peters*	
86/79	*Nick Nixon*	
26/75	**Sanctuary** *Ronnie Prophet*	
7/63	**Sands Of Gold** *Webb Pierce*	
F/79	**Santa Barbara** *Ronnie Milsap*	
	Santa Claus Boogie	
41/94	*Tractors*	
63/95	*Tractors*	
60/97	**Santa Claus Is Back In Town**	
	Dwight Yoakam	
	Santa Claus Is Comin' (In A Boogie	
	Woogie Choo Choo Train)	
43/95	*Tractors*	
65/97	*Tractors*	
	Santa Claus Is Coming To Town	
73/95	*George Strait*	
69/97	*George Strait*	
5/88	**Santa Fe** *Bellamy Brothers*	
70/95	**Santa Got Lost In Texas** *Jeff Carson*	
50/95	**Santa I'm Right Here** *Toby Keith*	
56/97	**Santa Looked A Lot Like Daddy**	
	Garth Brooks	
57/70	**Santo Domingo** *Buddy Alan*	
57/79	**Sarah's Eyes** *Vern Gosdin*	
1/73	**Satin Sheets** *Jeanne Pruett*	
17/73	**Satisfaction** *Jack Greene*	
7/53	**Satisfaction Guaranteed** *Carl Smith*	

	Satisfied Mind	
1/55	*Porter Wagoner*	
3/55	*Red Foley*	
4/55	*Jean Shepard*	
25/73	*Roy Drusky*	
41/76	*Bob Luman*	
84/83	*Con Hunley*	
	Satisfy Me And I'll Satisfy You	
83/74	*Josie Brown*	
53/91	*Clinton Gregory*	
5/88	**Satisfy You** *Sweethearts Of The Rodeo*	
24/71	**Saturday Morning Confusion**	
	Bobby Russell	
22/68	**Saturday Night** *Webb Pierce*	
54/80	**Saturday Night In Dallas** *Kenny Seratt*	
9/88	**Saturday Night Special** *Conway Twitty*	
53/77	**Saturday Night To Sunday Quiet**	
	Susan Raye	
43/69	**Saturday Satan Sunday Saint**	
	Ernest Tubb	
6/83	**Save Me** *Louise Mandrell*	
86/78	**Save Me** *Tanya Tucker*	
12/85	**Save The Last Chance** *Johnny Lee*	
	Save The Last Dance For Me	
100/76	*Bennie Lindsey*	
36/78	*Ron Shaw*	
4/79	*Emmylou Harris*	
26/79	*Jerry Lee Lewis*	
3/84	*Dolly Parton*	
11/62	**Save The Last Dance For Me**	
	Buck Owens	
45/95	**Save This One For Me** *Rick Trevino*	
8/80	**Save Your Heart For Me** *Jacky Ward*	
10/76	**Save Your Kisses For Me** *Margo Smith*	
3/86	**Savin' My Love For You** *Pake McEntire*	
58/87	**Savin' The Honey For The Honeymoon**	
	Sawyer Brown	
14/77	**Savin' This Love Song For You**	
	Johnny Rodriguez	
	Sawmill	
27/59	*Mel Tillis & Bill Phillips*	
15/63	*Webb Pierce*	
2/73	*Mel Tillis*	
21/94	**Sawmill Road** *Diamond Rio*	
85/80	**Say A Long Goodbye** *Mary K. Miller*	
5/75	**Say Forever You'll Be Mine**	
	Porter Wagoner & Dolly Parton	
35/73	**Say, Has Anybody Seen My Sweet**	
	Gypsy Rose *Terry Stafford*	
38/96	**Say I** *Alabama*	
40/75	**Say I Do** *Ray Price*	
1/76	**Say It Again** *Don Williams*	
31/91	**Say It's Not True** *Lionel Cartwright*	
8/68	**Say It's Not You** *George Jones*	
78/89	**Say The Part About I Love You**	
	Lorie Ann	
4/89	**Say What's In Your Heart**	
	Restless Heart	
15/73	**Say When** *Diana Trask*	
F/84	**Say When** *Johnny Lee*	
37/97	**Say Yes** *Burnin' Daylight*	
	Say You Love Me	
93/76	*Lynda K. Lance*	
10/79	*Stephanie Winslow*	
	Say You Love Me Again ..see: (I Wanna	
	Hear You)	
57/83	**Say You'll Stay** *Wayne Massey*	
1/77	**Say You'll Stay Until Tomorrow**	
	Tom Jones	
2/77	**Saying Hello, Saying I Love You,**	
	Saying Goodbye	
	Jim Ed Brown/Helen Cornelius	
5/83	**Scarlet Fever** *Kenny Rogers*	
7/60	**Scarlet Ribbons (For Her Hair)** *Browns*	
66/74	**Scarlet Water** *Johnny Duncan*	
58/91	**Scars** *Ray Kennedy*	
90/89	**Scars** *Johnny Paycheck*	
65/90	**Scene Of The Crime** *Jo-el Sonnier*	
77/88	**Scene Of The Crime** *Lori Yates*	
	Scotch And Soda	
88/79	*Mac Wiseman*	
70/83	*Ray Price*	
27/58	**Scotland** *Bill Monroe*	

8/81	**Scratch My Back (And Whisper in My**	
	Ear) *Razzy Bailey*	
	Sea Cruise	
94/77	*Everett Peek*	
50/80	*Billy "Crash" Craddock*	
56/95	**Sea Of Cowboy Hats** *Chely Wright*	
	Sea Of Heartbreak	
2/61	*Don Gibson*	
24/72	*Kenny Price*	
33/79	*Lynn Anderson*	
39/89	*Ronnie McDowell*	
83/88	**Sealed With A Kiss** *Leah Marr*	
5/48	**Seaman's Blues** *Ernest Tubb*	
43/77	**Search, The** *Freddie Hart*	
54/72	**Search Your Heart** *Bobby Wright*	
82/76	**Searchin' For A Rainbow**	
	Marshall Tucker Band	
17/90	**Searchin' For Some Kind Of Clue**	
	Billy Joe Royal	
	Searching (For Someone Like You)	
3/56	*Kitty Wells*	
45/75	*Melba Montgomery*	
75/87	*Lanier McKuhen*	
24/74	**Seasons In The Sun** *Bobby Wright*	
	Seasons Of My Heart	
9/56	*Jimmy Newman*	
10/60	*Johnny Cash*	
90/79	**Second Best (Is Too Far Down The**	
	Line) *Don Deal*	
18/62	**Second Choice** *Stonewall Jackson*	
50/73	**Second Cup Of Coffee**	
	George Hamilton IV	
24/59	**Second Fiddle** *Buck Owens*	
5/64	**Second Fiddle (To An Old Guitar)**	
	Jean Shepard	
70/79	**Second Hand Emotion** *Faron Young*	
7/84	**Second Hand Heart** *Gary Morris*	
3/63	**Second Hand Rose** *Roy Drusky*	
18/79	**Second-Hand Satin Lady (And A**	
	Bargain Basement Boy) *Jerry Reed*	
15/60	**Second Honeymoon** *Johnny Cash*	
95/86	**Second Time Around** *Del Reeves*	
5/86	**Second To No One** *Rosanne Cash*	
60/72	**Second Tuesday In December**	
	Jack Blanchard & Misty Morgan	
	Secret Love	
2/54	*Slim Whitman*	
47/73	*Tony Booth*	
1/75	*Freddy Fender*	
	Secretly	
5/58	*Jimmie Rodgers*	
65/78	*Jimmie Rodgers*	
47/81	**Secrets** *Mac Davis*	
6/90	**See If I Care** *Shenandoah*	
44/97	**See Rock City** *Rick Trevino*	
F/69	**See Ruby Fall** *Johnny Cash*	
72/75	**See Saw** *Patsy Sledd*	
	See The Big Man Cry	
7/65	*Charlie Louvin*	
85/76	*Bobby Wayne Loftis*	
80/74	**See The Funny Little Clown**	
	Billie Jo Spears	
51/96	**See Ya** *Confederate Railroad*	
41/79	**See You In September** *Debby Boone*	
18/76	**See You On Sunday** *Glen Campbell*	
16/72	**Seed Before The Rose**	
	Tommy Overstreet	
50/93	**Seeds** *Kathy Mattea*	
2/90	**Seein' My Father In Me** *Paul Overstreet*	
	Seeing Is Believing	
96/74	*Jan Howard*	
55/80	*Donna Fargo*	
2/75	**Seeker, The** *Dolly Parton*	
83/76	**Seems Like I Can't Live With You, But I**	
	Can't Live Without You *Price Mitchell*	
81/90	**Selfish Man** *Dwayne Crews*	
83/82	**Semi Diesel Blues**	
	Super Grit Cowboy Band	
2/92	**Seminole Wind** *John Anderson*	
19/77	**Semolita** *Jerry Reed*	
79/73	**Send A Little Love My Way**	
	Anne Murray	
47/92	**Send A Message To My Heart**	
	Dwight Yoakam & Patty Loveless	

466

64/86 **Slow Motion** *Malchak & Rucker*
47/84 **Slow Nights** *Mel Tillis with*
    Glen Campbell
36/89 **Slow Passin' Time** *Anne Murray*
17/62 **Slow Poison** *Johnny & Jack*
    Slow Poke
1/51   *Pee Wee King*
7/52   *Hawkshaw Hawkins*
76/82 **Slow Texas Dancing** *Donna Hazard*
85/79 **Slow Tunes And Promises** *Bobby Hood*
    Slowly
1/54   *Webb Pierce*
29/71   *Jimmy Dean & Dottie West*
37/81   *Kippi Brannon*
75/89 **Slowly But Surely** *Marie Osmond*
46/93 **Small Price** *Gibson/Miller Band*
54/90 **Small Small World** *Statler Brothers*
35/68 **Small Time Laboring Man**
    George Jones
89/79 **Small Time Picker** *Bobby Wayne Loftis*
44/97 **Small Town** *John Anderson*
1/87 **Small Town Girl** *Steve Wariner*
2/91 **Small Town Saturday Night**
    Hal Ketchum
24/72 **Smell The Flowers** *Jerry Reed*
    Smellin' Like A Rose ..see: (They Always Come Out)
15/74 **Smile For Me** *Lynn Anderson*
39/72 **Smile, Somebody Loves You**
    Linda Gail Lewis
13/60 **Smiling Bill McCall** *Johnny Cash*
24/59 **Smoke Along The Track**
    Stonewall Jackson
84/82 **Smoke Gets In Your Eyes** *Narvel Felts*
44/96 **Smoke In Her Eyes** *Ty England*
    Smoke On The Water
1/44   *Red Foley*
1/45   *Bob Wills*
7/45   *Boyd Heath*
    Smoke! Smoke! Smoke! (That Cigarette)
1/47   *Tex Williams*
32/68   *Tex Williams ('68)*
97/73   *Commander Cody*
78/78   *Tom Bresh*
89/82   *Sammy Davis, Jr.*
8/49 **Smokey Mountain Boogie**
    Tennessee Ernie
    Smokey Mountain Memories
13/75   *Mel Street*
F/82   *Earl Thomas Conley*
71/83 **Smokin' In The Rockies**
    Gary Stewart & Dean Dillon
1/80 **Smoky Mountain Rain** *Ronnie Milsap*
12/69 **Smoky Places** *Billy Walker*
5/69 **Smoky The Bar** *Hank Thompson*
    Smooth Sailin'
68/78   *Connie Smith*
47/79   *Sonny Throckmorton*
6/80   *T.G. Sheppard*
32/79 **Smooth Sailin'** *Jim Weatherly*
43/85 **Smooth Sailing (Rock In The Road)**
    Mark Gray
94/79 **Smooth Southern Highway** *Don Cox*
77/76 **Snap, Crackle And Pop** *Johnny Carver*
    Snap Your Fingers
40/71   *Dick Curless*
12/74   *Don Gibson*
1/87   *Ronnie Milsap*
5/83 **Snapshot** *Sylvia*
48/81 **Sneakin' Around** *Kin Vassy*
16/67 **Sneaking 'Cross The Border**
    Harden Trio
69/74 **Sneaky Snake** *Tom T. Hall*
2/66 **Snow Flake** *Jim Reeves*
28/63 **Snow White Cloud** *Frank Taylor*
10/70 **Snowbird** *Anne Murray*
46/84 **So Close** *Wright Brothers*
72/83 **So Close** *Backroads*
43/77 **So Close Again**
    Margo Smith & Norro Wilson
4/56 **So Doggone Lonesome** *Johnny Cash*
68/83 **So Easy To Love** *Wright Brothers*
64/88 **So Far Not So Good** *Jeff Chance*

22/82 **So Fine** *Oak Ridge Boys*
68/78 **So Good** *Jewel Blanch*
27/78 **So Good, So Rare, So Fine** *Freddie Hart*
86/89 **So Good To Be In Love** *Karen Staley*
F/77 **So Good Woman** *Waylon Jennings*
2/95 **So Help Me Girl** *Joe Diffie*
22/62 **So How Come (No One Loves Me)**
    Don Gibson
43/69 **So Long** *Bobby Helms*
69/68 **So Long, Charlie Brown, Don't Look For Me Around** *Sammi Smith*
1/44 **So Long Pal** *Al Dexter*
14/55 **So Lovely, Baby** *Rusty & Doug*
16/59 **So Many Times** *Roy Acuff*
    So Many Ways
28/73   *Eddy Arnold*
33/77   *David Houston*
45/66 **So Much For Me, So Much For You**
    Liz Anderson
1/96 **So Much For Pretending** *Bryan White*
46/70 **So Much In Love With You**
    David Rogers
3/92 **So Much Like My Dad** *George Strait*
    So Round, So Firm, So Fully Packed
1/47   *Merle Travis*
3/47   *Johnny Bond*
5/47   *Ernest Tubb*
    So Sad (To Watch Good Love Go Bad)
12/70   *Hank Williams, Jr. & Lois Johnson*
31/76   *Connie Smith*
76/78   *Steve Wariner*
28/83   *Emmylou Harris*
19/59 **So Soon** *Jimmy Newman*
71/82 **(So This Is) Happy Hour** *Snuff*
20/71 **So This Is Love** *Tommy Cash*
41/86 **So This Is Love** *Charly McClain*
14/62 **So Wrong** *Patsy Cline*
F/57 **So You Think You've Got Troubles**
    Marvin Rainwater
58/79 **Soap** *O.B. McClinton*
13/78 **Soft Lights And Hard Country Music**
    Moe Bandy
97/78 **Soft Lights And Slow Sexy Music**
    Jody Miller
10/49 **Soft Lips** *Hank Thompson*
65/73 **Soft Lips And Hard Liquor**
    Charlie Walker
3/61 **Soft Rain** *Ray Price*
8/72 **Soft, Sweet And Warm** *David Houston*
30/78 **Softest Touch In Town** *Bobby G. Rice*
74/69 **Softly And Tenderly** *Lois Johnson*
4/60 **Softly And Tenderly (I'll Hold You In My Arms)** *Lewis Pruitt*
F/78 **Softly, As I Leave You** *Elvis Presley*
69/73 **Sold American** *Kinky Friedman*
29/76 **Sold Out Of Flagpoles** *Johnny Cash*
1/95 **Sold (The Grundy County Auction Incident)** *John Michael Montgomery*
71/91 **Soldier Boy** *Donna Fargo*
51/80 **Soldier Of Fortune** *Tom T. Hall*
54/86 **Soldier Of Love** *Billy Burnette*
15/59 **Soldier's Joy** *Hawkshaw Hawkins*
    Soldier's Last Letter
1/44   *Ernest Tubb*
3/71   *Merle Haggard*
46/66 **Soldier's Prayer In Viet Nam**
    Don Reno & Benny Martin
57/96 **Solid Ground** *Ricky Skaggs*
F/79 **Solitaire** *Elvis Presley*
    (also see: I'm Getting Good At Missing You)
28/69 **Solitary** *Don Gibson*
14/76 **Solitary Man** *T.G. Sheppard*
1/77 **Some Broken Hearts Never Mend**
    Don Williams
47/82 **Some Day My Ship's Comin' In**
    Joe Waters
10/81 **Some Days Are Diamonds (Some Days Are Stone)** *John Denver*
45/82 **Some Days It Rains All Night Long**
    Terri Gibbs
1/85 **Some Fools Never Learn** *Steve Wariner*

    Some Gave All
72/92   *Billy Ray Cyrus*
52/93   *Billy Ray Cyrus*
1/92 **Some Girls Do** *Sawyer Brown*
22/86 **Some Girls Have All The Luck**
    Louise Mandrell
8/91 **Some Guys Have All The Love**
    Little Texas
25/84 **Some Hearts Get All The Breaks**
    Charly McClain
81/86 **Some Hearts Get All The Breaks**
    Roger Miller
17/78 **Some I Wrote** *Statler Brothers*
8/74 **Some Kind Of A Woman** *Faron Young*
3/92 **Some Kind Of Trouble** *Tanya Tucker*
68/91 **Some Kinda Woman** *Linda Davis*
27/81 **Some Love Songs Never Die**
    B.J. Thomas
10/82 **Some Memories Just Won't Die**
    Marty Robbins
61/82 **Some Never Stand A Chance**
    Family Brown
20/82 **Some Of My Best Friends Are Old Songs** *Louise Mandrell*
72/85 **Some Of Shelly's Blues**
    Maines Brothers Band
28/73 **Some Old California Memory**
    Henson Cargill
16/88 **Some Old Side Road** *Keith Whitley*
54/73 **Some Roads Have No Ending**
    Warner Mack
57/85 **Some Such Foolishness** *Tommy Roe*
13/96 **Some Things Are Meant To Be**
    Linda Davis
83/81 **Some You Win, Some You Lose** *Orion*
34/84 **Somebody Buy This Cowgirl A Beer**
    Shelly West
4/85 **Somebody Else's Fire** *Janie Fricke*
5/93 **Somebody Else's Moon** *Collin Raye*
10/76 **Somebody Hold Me (Until She Passes By)** *Narvel Felts*
69/97 **Somebody Knew** *Rhett Akins*
62/67 **Somebody Knows My Dog**
    Willis Brothers
20/81 **Somebody Led Me Away** *Loretta Lynn*
1/87 **Somebody Lied** *Ricky Van Shelton*
1/66 **Somebody Like Me** *Eddy Arnold*
66/93 **Somebody Like That** *Glen Campbell*
67/88 **Somebody Loses, Somebody Wins**
    Rosie Flores
21/72 **Somebody Loves Me** *Johnny Paycheck*
8/76 **Somebody Loves You** *Crystal Gayle*
9/93 **Somebody New** *Billy Ray Cyrus*
84/87 **Somebody Ought To Tell Him That She's Gone** *Ogden Harless*
    Somebody Paints The Wall
62/89   *Josh Logan*
8/93   *Tracy Lawrence*
16/62 **Somebody Save Me** *Ferlin Husky*
1/85 **Somebody Should Leave**
    Reba McEntire
22/97 **Somebody Slap Me** *John Anderson*
1/76 **Somebody Somewhere** *Loretta Lynn*
6/79 **Somebody Special** *Donna Fargo*
55/96 **Somebody To Love You** *Wynonna*
18/63 **Somebody Told Somebody**
    Rose Maddox
59/77 **Somebody Took Her Love (And Never Gave It Back)** *Jimmie Peters*
9/86 **Somebody Wants Me Out Of The Way**
    George Jones
    Somebody Will
57/95   *Terry McBride & The Ride*
51/98   *River Road*
52/69 **Somebody's Always Leaving**
    Stonewall Jackson
7/83 **Somebody's Always Saying Goodbye**
    Anne Murray
    Somebody's Back In Town
6/59   *Wilburn Brothers*
81/84   *Chris Hillman*
2/51 **Somebody's Been Beatin' My Time**
    Eddy Arnold

474

476

5/81	**Today All Over Again** *Reba McEntire*
	Today I Started Loving You Again
69/73	*Kenny Rogers*
9/75	*Sammi Smith*
74/79	*Arthur Prysock*
43/86	*Emmylou Harris*
	Today My World Slipped Away
10/83	*Vern Gosdin*
3/97	*George Strait*
38/73	**Today Will Be The First Day Of The Rest Of My Life** *LaWanda Lindsey*
3/92	**Today's Lonely Fool** *Tracy Lawrence*
45/71	**Today's Teardrops** *Bobby Lewis*
21/78	**Toe To Toe** *Freddie Hart*
	Together Again
1/64	*Buck Owens*
1/76	*Emmylou Harris*
19/84	*Kenny Rogers & Dottie West*
92/88	**Together Alone** *Ogden Harless*
14/72	**Together Always** *Porter Wagoner & Dolly Parton*
	Togetherness
24/68	*Freddie Hart*
12/70	*Buck Owens & Susan Raye*
30/85	**Tokyo, Oklahoma** *John Anderson*
36/70	**Tom Green County Fair** *Roger Miller*
1/86	**Tomb Of The Unknown Love** *Kenny Rogers*
5/65	**Tombstone Every Mile** *Dick Curless*
9/70	**Tomorrow Is Forever** *Porter Wagoner & Dolly Parton*
	Tomorrow Never Comes
3/45	*Ernest Tubb*
27/70	*Slim Whitman*
	Tomorrow Night
24/59	*Carl Smith*
29/73	*Charlie Rich*
11/71	**Tomorrow Night In Baltimore** *Roger Miller*
74/90	**Tomorrow's World** *Tomorrow's World*
5/78	**Tonight** *Barbara Mandrell*
1/67	**Tonight Carmen** *Marty Robbins*
4/93	**Tonight I Climbed The Wall** *Alan Jackson*
26/76	**Tonight I'll Face The Man (Who Made It Happen)** *Kenny Starr*
31/66	**Tonight I'm Coming Home** *Buddy Cagle*
	Tonight I'm Feeling You (All Over Again)
65/80	*"Blackjack" Jack Grayson*
38/82	*Jack Grayson*
19/84	**Tonight I'm Here With Someone Else** *Karen Brooks*
66/88	**Tonight In America** *David Lynn Jones*
30/80	**Tonight Let's Sleep On It Baby** *Mel Street*
10/72	**Tonight My Baby's Coming Home** *Barbara Mandrell*
89/88	**Tonight She Went Crazy Without Me** *Mike Lunsford*
6/79	**Tonight She's Gonna Love Me (Like There Was No Tomorrow)** *Razzy Bailey*
12/74	**Tonight Someone's Falling In Love** *Johnny Carver*
20/94	**(Tonight We Just Might) Fall In Love Again** *Hal Ketchum*
26/86	**Tonight We Ride** *Michael Murphey*
69/69	**Tonight We're Calling It A Day** *Hugh X. Lewis*
30/77	**Tonight You Belong To Me** *Dottie West*
65/85	**Tonight's The Night** *Carlette*
28/78	**Tonight's The Night (It's Gonna Be Alright)** *Roy Head*
70/66	**Tonight's The Night My Angel's Halo Fell** *Sheb Wooley*
32/80	**Tony's Tank-Up, Drive-In Cafe** *Hank Thompson*
60/76	**Too Big A Price To Pay** *Kenny Price*
1/93	**Too Busy Being In Love** *Doug Stone*
3/90	**Too Cold At Home** *Mark Chesnutt*

	Too Far Gone
72/67	*Canadian Sweethearts*
12/73	*Joe Stampley*
73/79	*Emmylou Harris*
13/79	*Emmylou Harris*
85/76	**Too Far Gone (To Care What You Do To Me)** *Gary S. Paxton*
88/79	**Too Fast For Rapid City** *Sheila Andrews*
1/88	**Too Gone Too Long** *Randy Travis*
89/83	**Too Good To Be Through** *Dave Lemmon*
47/85	**Too Good To Say No To** *Leon Everette*
4/84	**Too Good To Stop Now** *Mickey Gilley*
50/69	**Too Hard To Say I'm Sorry** *Murv Shiner*
10/83	**Too Hot To Sleep** *Louise Mandrell*
22/63	**Too In Love** *Hank Thompson*
42/86	**Too Late** *Kendalls*
15/84	**Too Late To Go Home** *Johnny Rodriguez*
9/64	**Too Late To Try Again** *Carl Butler & Pearl*
88/74	**Too Late To Turn Back Now** *Four Guys*
	Too Late To Worry Too Blue To Cry
1/44	*Al Dexter*
3/44	*Texas Jim Lewis*
6/75	*Ronnie Milsap*
62/97	**Too Little Too Much** *Nikki Nelson*
28/81	**Too Long Gone** *Vern Gosdin*
40/82	**Too Many Hearts In The Fire** *Bobby Smith*
46/91	**Too Many Honky Tonks (On My Way Home)** *Tom Wopat*
68/82	**Too Many Irons In The Fire** *Billy Parker & Cal Smith*
1/81	**Too Many Lovers** *Crystal Gayle*
21/73	**Too Many Memories** *Bobby Lewis*
96/73	**Too Many Memories** *Billy Walker*
29/78	**Too Many Nights Alone** *Bobby Bare*
5/87	**Too Many Rivers** *Forester Sisters*
74/73	**Too Many Ties That Bind** *Jan Howard*
26/65	**Too Many Tigers** *Tex Williams*
2/86	**Too Many Times** *Earl Thomas Conley & Anita Pointer*
10/61	**Too Many Times** *Don Winters*
3/57	**Too Much** *Elvis Presley*
36/92	**Too Much** *Pirates Of The Mississippi*
58/91	**Too Much Candy For A Dime** *Eddy Raven*
4/96	**Too Much Fun** *Daryle Singletary*
62/91	**Too Much Fun** *Forester Sisters*
41/73	**Too Much Hold Back** *Little David Wilkins*
1/86	**Too Much Is Not Enough** *Bellamy Brothers/The Forester Sisters*
18/77	**Too Much Is Not Enough** *Billie Jo Spears*
72/92	**Too Much Love** *Don Williams*
8/73	**Too Much Monkey Business** *Freddy Weller*
25/89	**Too Much Month At The End Of The Money** *Billy Hill*
45/69	**Too Much Of A Man (To Be Tied Down)** *Arlene Harden*
55/68	**Too Much Of Not Enough** *Ernest Tubb*
28/67	**Too Much Of You** *Lynn Anderson*
1/85	**Too Much On My Heart** *Statler Brothers*
34/74	**Too Much Pride** *Mack White*
19/60	**Too Much To Lose** *Carl Belew*
84/81	**Too Much, Too Little, Too Late** *Mary Bailey*
13/57	**Too Much Water** *George Jones*
	Too Old To Cut The Mustard
5/52	*Ernest Tubb & Red Foley*
6/52	*Carlisles*
29/72	*Buck Owens & Buddy Alan*
46/87	**Too Old To Grow Up Now** *Pake McEntire*
13/80	**Too Old To Play Cowboy** *Razzy Bailey*
71/68	**Too Rough On Me** *Earl Scott*
4/53	**Too Young To Tango** *Sunshine Ruby*
	Took It Like A Man, Cried Like A Baby
42/82	*Cedar Creek*
68/88	*Kevin Pearce*
2/73	**Top Of The World** *Lynn Anderson*
53/68	**Top Of The World** *Stu Phillips*

46/74	**Tore Down** *Porter Wagoner*
3/77	**Torn Between Two Lovers** *Mary MacGregor*
71/72	**Torn From The Pages Of Life** *Stonewall Jackson*
53/87	**Torn-Up** *Vicki Rae Von*
59/72	**Tossin' And Turnin'** *Ronnie Sessions*
25/59	**Total Strangers** *Hank Thompson*
1/85	**Touch A Hand, Make A Friend** *Oak Ridge Boys*
5/88	**Touch And Go Crazy** *Lee Greenwood*
15/58	**Touch And Go Heart** *Kitty Wells*
	Touch Me
7/62	*Willie Nelson*
62/77	*Howdy Glenn*
54/86	**Touch Me** *Bandana*
	Touch Me (I'll Be Your Fool Once More)
18/79	*Big Al Downing*
4/83	*Tom Jones*
1/86	**Touch Me When We're Dancing** *Alabama*
15/79	**Touch Me With Magic** *Marty Robbins*
3/66	**Touch My Heart** *Ray Price*
99/77	**Touch Of Her Fingers** *Clyde Watson*
1/75	**Touch The Hand** *Conway Twitty*
6/73	**Touch The Morning** *Don Gibson*
	(Touch The Wind) ..see: Eres Tu
6/72	**Touch Your Woman** *Dolly Parton*
3/71	**Touching Home** *Jerry Lee Lewis*
92/74	**Touching Me, Touching You** *Vicky Fletcher*
43/85	**Touchy Situation** *Razzy Bailey*
82/80	**Tough Act To Follow** *Billy Parker*
67/95	**Tougher Than The Rest** *Chris LeDoux*
	Tower Of Strength
32/75	*Sue Richards*
33/79	*Narvel Felts*
16/68	**Town That Broke My Heart** *Bobby Bare*
38/67	**Town That Never Sleeps** *Charlie Walker*
38/73	**Town Where You Live** *Mel Street*
12/49	**Toy Heart** *Bill Monroe*
99/77	**Toy Hearts** *Johnny Tillotson*
48/74	**Toy Telephone** *Johnny Bush*
75/76	**Tra-La-La-La Suzy** *Price Mitchell*
30/72	**Traces** *Sonny James*
25/71	**Traces Of A Woman** *Billy Walker*
29/74	**Traces Of Life** *Lonzo & Oscar*
11/76	**Tracks Of My Tears** *Linda Ronstadt*
2/53	**Trademark** *Carl Smith*
69/96	**Trail Of Tears** *Billy Ray Cyrus*
	Train Medley
95/80	*Boxcar Willie*
61/83	*Boxcar Willie*
7/57	**Train Of Love** *Johnny Cash*
6/87	**Train Of Memories** *Kathy Mattea*
74/71	**Train Train (Carry Me Away)** *Murry Kellum*
57/88	**Trains Make Me Lonesome** *Marty Haggard*
20/89	**Trainwreck Of Emotion** *Lorrie Morgan*
14/48	**Tramp On The Street** *Carlisles*
	Trashy Women
63/90	*Jerry Jeff Walker*
10/93	*Confederate Railroad*
52/72	**Travelin' Light** *George Hamilton IV*
29/59	**Travelin' Man** *Red Foley*
32/82	**Travelin' Man** *Jacky Ward*
44/66	**Travelin' Man** *Dick Curless*
20/73	**Traveling Man** *Dolly Parton*
42/72	**Travelin' Minstrel Band** *Carter Family*
33/71	**Travelin' Minstrel Man** *Bill Rice*
51/67	**Traveling Shoes** *Guy Mitchell*
6/51	**Travellin' Blues** *Lefty Frizzell*
6/58	**Treasure Of Love** *George Jones*
3/96	**Treat Her Right** *Sawyer Brown*
12/71	**Treat Him Right** *Barbara Mandrell*
62/74	**Treat Me Like A Lady** *Sherry Bryce*
18/91	**Treat Me Like A Stranger** *Baillie & The Boys*
11/57	**Treat Me Nice** *Elvis Presley*
16/64	**Triangle** *Carl Smith*
	(Tribute To Luther Perkins) ..see: Cashin' In

68/93	**Two Steps In The Right Direction**
	Roger Ballard
2/80	**Two Story House**
	George Jones & Tammy Wynette
18/92	**Two-Timin' Me** *Remingtons*
39/86	**Two Too Many** *Holly Dunn*
85/84	**Two Will Be One** *Kenny Dale*
41/91	**Tyin' Strings** *June Stearns*
58/95	**Tyler** *Davis Daniel*

U

55/68	**U.S. Male** *Elvis Presley*
9/75	**U.S. Of A** *Donna Fargo*
8/58	**Uh-Huh--mm** *Sonny James*
F/57	**Uh, Uh, No** *George Jones*
1/91	**Unanswered Prayers** *Garth Brooks*
58/88	**Unattended Fire** *Razzy Bailey*
29/73	**Unbelievable Love** *Jim Ed Brown*
51/93	**Unbreakable Heart** *Carlene Carter*
	Unbreakable Hearts
79/78	*Bill White*
92/79	*Hargus "Pig" Robbins*
	Unchained Melody
41/75	*Joe Stampley*
6/78	*Elvis Presley*
26/91	*Ronnie McDowell*
3/97	*LeAnn Rimes*
49/76	**Uncle Hiram And The Homemade Beer**
	Dick Feller
	Uncle Pen
14/56	*Porter Wagoner*
1/84	*Ricky Skaggs*
4/77	**Uncloudy Day** *Willie Nelson*
27/91	**Unconditional Love** *Glen Campbell*
44/87	**Unconditional Love** *New Grass Revival*
18/62	**Under Cover Of The Night** *Dave Dudley*
66/83	**Under Loved And Over Lonely**
	Katy Moffatt
24/88	**Under The Boardwalk** *Lynn Anderson*
72/90	**Under The Gun** *Suzy Bogguss*
2/61	**Under The Influence Of Love**
	Buck Owens
54/93	**Under This Old Hat** *Chris LeDoux*
	Under Your Spell Again
4/59	*Buck Owens*
5/59	*Ray Price*
39/71	*Waylon Jennings & Jessi Colter*
65/76	*Barbara Fairchild*
93/89	*Shelby Lynne*
28/78	**Undercover Lovers** *Stella Parton*
88/80	**Undercover Man** *Liz Lyndell*
26/64	**Understand Your Gal** *Margie Bowes*
1/64	**Understand Your Man** *Johnny Cash*
10/68	**Undo The Right** *Johnny Bush*
67/73	**Uneasy Rider** *Charlie Daniels*
23/72	**Unexpected Goodbye** *Glenn Barber*
79/75	**Unfaithful Fools** *Leroy Van Dyke*
8/50	**Unfaithful One** *Ernest Tubb*
32/83	**Unfinished Business** *Lloyd David Foster*
18/63	**Unkind Words** *Kathy Dee*
14/48	**Unloved And Unclaimed** *Roy Acuff*
5/62	**Unloved Unwanted** *Kitty Wells*
7/66	**Unmitigated Gall** *Faron Young*
4/94	**Untanglin' My Mind** *Clint Black*
10/55	**Untied** *Tommy Collins*
54/85	**Until I Fall In Love Again** *Marie Osmond*
1/86	**Until I Met You** *Judy Rodman*
57/77	**Until I Met You** *Tom Bresh*
F/56	**Until I Met You** *Faron Young*
68/72	**Until It's Time For You To Go**
	Elvis Presley
1/69	**Until My Dreams Come True**
	Jack Greene

	Until The Bitter End
39/80	*Kenny Seratt*
88/81	*Faron Young*
39/74	**Until The End Of Time**
	Narvel Felts & Sharon Vaughn
77/85	**Until The Music Is Gone** *Becky Chase*
50/78	**Until The Next Time** *Billy Parker*
92/81	**Until The Nights** *Charlie McCoy &*
	Laney Smallwood
20/60	**Until Today** *Elmer Snodgrass*
42/79	**Until Tonight** *Juice Newton*
93/85	**Until We Meet Again**
	Wray Brothers Band
73/80	**Until You** *Terry Bradshaw*
4/88	**Untold Stories** *Kathy Mattea*
14/72	**Untouched** *Mel Tillis*
6/51	**Unwanted Sign Upon Your Heart**
	Hank Snow
	Unwed Fathers
63/83	*Tammy Wynette*
56/85	*Gail Davies*
6/81	**Unwound** *George Strait*
9/89	**Up And Gone** *McCarters*
57/85	**Up On Your Love** *Karen Taylor-Good*
41/66	**Up This Hill And Down**
	Osborne Brothers
	Up To Heaven ..see: (You Lift Me)
28/75	**Uproar** *Anne Murray*
10/95	**Upstairs Downtown** *Toby Keith*
40/69	**Upstairs In The Bedroom** *Bobby Wright*
25/74	**Uptown Poker Club** *Jerry Reed*
94/81	**Urban Cowboys, Outlaws, Cavaleers**
	James Marvell
7/67	**Urge For Going** *George Hamilton IV*
55/97	**Use Mine** *Jeff Wood*
48/97	**Used To Be's** *Daryle Singletary*
3/85	**Used To Blue** *Sawyer Brown*

V

53/97	**Valentine** *Martina McBride With*
	Jim Brickman
15/69	**Vance** *Roger Miller*
52/70	**Vanishing Breed** *Hank Snow*
7/76	**Vaya Con Dios** *Freddy Fender*
30/77	**Vegas** *Bobby & Jeannie Bare*
56/95	**Veil Of Tears** *Hal Ketchum*
9/83	**Velvet Chains** *Gary Morris*
5/82	**Very Best Is You** *Charly McClain*
50/91	**Very First Lasting Love**
	Shelby Lynne & Les Taylor
1/74	**Very Special Love Song** *Charlie Rich*
40/84	**Victim Of Life's Circumstances**
	Vince Gill
34/82	**Victim Or A Fool** *Rodney Crowell*
75/76	**Victims** *Kenny Starr*
24/84	**Victims Of Goodbye** *Sylvia*
10/96	**Vidalia** *Sammy Kershaw*
12/66	**Viet Nam Blues** *Dave Dudley*
21/67	**Vin Rosé** *Stu Phillips*
	Violet And A Rose
24/58	*Mel Tillis*
10/62	*"Little" Jimmy Dickens*
36/64	*Wanda Jackson*
73/76	**Virgil And The $300 Vacation**
	Cledus Maggard
68/72	**Virginia** *Jean Shepard*
22/77	**Virginia, How Far Will You Go**
	Dickey Lee
90/79	**Visitor, The** *J.W. Thompson*
72/77	**Vitamin L** *Mary Kay Place*
26/60	**Volkswagen** *Ray Pillow*
22/63	**Volunteer, The** *Autry Inman*
8/89	**Vows Go Unbroken (Always True To**
	You) *Kenny Rogers*

W

72/87	**W. Lee O'Daniel (And The Light Crust**
	Dough Boys) *Johnny Cash*
	Wabash Cannonball
52/67	*Dick Todd*
27/70	*Dick Curless*
63/70	*Danny Davis/The Nashville Brass*
97/76	*Charlie McCoy*
91/84	*Willie Nelson & Hank Wilson*
50/66	**Waco** *Lorne Greene*
12/55	**Wait A Little Longer Please, Jesus**
	Carl Smith
98/85	**Wait Till I Get My Hands On You**
	Wynn Stewart
62/82	**Wait Till Those Bridges Are Gone**
	Ray Price
70/77	**Waitin' At The End Of Your Run**
	Ava Barber
	Waitin' For A Train ..see: Waiting For A
	Train
39/92	**Waitin' For The Deal To Go Down**
	Dixiana
12/58	**Waitin' In School** *Ricky Nelson*
1/66	**Waitin' In Your Welfare Line**
	Buck Owens
70/89	**Waitin' On Ice** *Jason D. Williams*
69/87	**Waitin' Up** *George Highfill*
25/64	**Waiting A Lifetime** *Webb Pierce*
	Waiting For A Train (All Around The
	Watertank)
F/57	*Jim Reeves*
11/71	*Jerry Lee Lewis*
72/76	**Waiting For The Tables To Turn**
	Wayne Kemp
50/89	**Waiting Here For You** *Gail Davies*
3/52	**Waiting In The Lobby Of Your Heart**
	Hank Thompson
14/74	**Wake Me Into Love**
	Bud Logan & Wilma Burgess
63/80	**Wake Me Up** *Louise Mandrell*
21/70	**Wake Me Up Early In The Morning**
	Bobby Lord
1/54	**Wake Up, Irene** *Hank Thompson*
	(also see: Goodnight Irene)
37/73	**Wake Up, Jacob** *Porter Wagoner*
1/57	**Wake Up Little Susie** *Everly Brothers*
2/91	**Walk, The** *Sawyer Brown*
56/70	**Walk A Mile In My Shoes** *Joe South*
56/71	**Walk All Over Georgia** *Ray Sanders*
57/69	**Walk Among The People** *Cheryl Poole*
48/77	**Walk Away With Me** *Randy Barlow*
56/82	**Walk Me 'Cross The River** *Jerri Kelly*
28/87	**Walk Me In The Rain** *Girls Next Door*
7/63	**Walk Me To The Door** *Ray Price*
44/67	**Walk Me To The Station** *Stu Phillips*
2/90	**Walk On** *Reba McEntire*
30/83	**Walk On** *Karen Brooks*
61/95	**Walk On** *Linda Ronstadt*
74/87	**Walk On Boy** *Ogden Harless*
	Walk On By
1/61	*Leroy Van Dyke*
98/79	*Robert Gordon*
43/80	*Donna Fargo*
73/87	*Perry LaPointe*
55/88	*Asleep At The Wheel*
1/91	**Walk On Faith** *Mike Reid*
5/68	**Walk On Out Of My Mind**
	Waylon Jennings
9/61	**Walk Out Backwards** *Bill Anderson*
71/93	**Walk Outside The Lines**
	Marshall Tucker Band
	Walk Right Back
76/77	*LaWanda Lindsey*
4/78	*Anne Murray*
	Walk Right In
23/63	*Rooftop Singers*
92/77	*Dr. Hook*
7/76	**Walk Softly** *Billy "Crash" Craddock*

482

485

58/85	**Wino The Clown** *Bill Anderson*	
87/78	**Wipe You From My Eyes (Gettin' Over You)** *King Edward IV & The Knights*	
8/79	**Wisdom Of A Fool** *Jacky Ward*	
62/98	**Wish, The** *Blake & Brian*	
2/70	**Wish I Didn't Have To Miss You** *Jack Greene & Jeannie Seely*	
2/94	**Wish I Didn't Know Now** *Toby Keith*	
60/72	**Wish I Was A Little Boy Again** *LaWanda Lindsey*	
54/71	**Wish I Was Home Instead** *Van Trevor*	
61/66	**Wish Me A Rainbow** *Hugh X. Lewis*	
2/81	**Wish You Were Here** *Barbara Mandrell*	
83/86	**Wishful Dreamin'** *Michael Shamblin*	
22/84	**Wishful Drinkin'** *Atlanta*	
83/80	**Wishful Drinkin'** *Diane Pfeifer*	
5/60	**Wishful Thinking** *Wynn Stewart*	
32/79	**Wishing I Had Listened To Your Song** *Bobby Borchers*	
F/80	**Wishing Well** *Tammy Jo*	
7/65	**Wishing Well (Down In The Well)** *Hank Snow*	
56/91	**With Body And Soul** *Kentucky Headhunters*	
24/71	**With His Hand In Mine** *Jean Shepard*	
68/77	**With His Pants In His Hand** *Jerry Reed*	
5/85	**With Just One Look In Your Eyes** *Charly McClain with Wayne Massey*	
10/78	**With Love** *Rex Allen, Jr.*	
1/67	**With One Exception** *David Houston*	
3/68	**With Pen In Hand** *Johnny Darrell*	
1/45	**With Tears In My Eyes** *Wesley Tuttle*	
32/82	**With Their Kind Of Money And Our Kind Of Love** *Billy Swan*	
31/91	**With This Ring** *T. Graham Brown*	
7/83	**With You** *Charly McClain*	
33/86	**With You** *Vince Gill*	
74/72	**Within My Loving Arms** *Kenni Huskey*	
11/84	**Without A Song** *Willie Nelson*	
50/88	**Without A Trace** *Marie Osmond*	
78/81	**Without Love** *Johnny Cash*	
	Without You	
79/79	Susie Allanson	
12/83	T.G. Sheppard	
50/76	**Without You** *Jessi Colter*	
92/81	**Without You** *Buck Owens* (also see: There's No Me)	
2/92	**(Without You) What Do I Do With Me** *Tanya Tucker*	
10/56	**Without Your Love** *Bobby Lord*	
22/96	**Without Your Love** *Aaron Tippin*	
13/76	**Without Your Love (Mr. Jordan)** *Charlie Ross*	
1/84	**Woke Up In Love** *Exile*	
12/75	**Wolf Creek Pass** *C.W. McCall*	
1/62	**Wolverton Mountain** *Claude King* (also see: I'm The Girl On)	
55/76	**Woman** *David Wills*	
2/71	**Woman Always Knows** *David Houston*	
4/92	**Woman Before Me** *Trisha Yearwood*	
92/77	**Woman Behind The Man Behind The Wheel** *Red Sovine*	
16/58	**Woman Captured Me** *Hank Snow*	
38/76	**Woman Don't Try To Sing My Song** *Cal Smith*	
58/73	**Woman Ease My Mind** *Claude Gray*	
15/66	**Woman Half My Age** *Kitty Wells*	
24/68	**Woman Hungry** *Porter Wagoner*	
9/57	**Woman I Need** *Johnny Horton*	
1/89	**Woman In Love** *Ronnie Milsap*	
4/67	**Woman In Love** *Bonnie Guitar*	
3/81	**Woman In Me** *Crystal Gayle*	
14/95	**Woman In Me (Needs The Man In You)** *Shania Twain*	
74/81	**Woman In My Heart** *Bobby Hood*	
4/75	**Woman In The Back Of My Mind** *Mel Tillis*	
48/69	**Woman In Your Life** *Wilma Burgess*	
	Woman Left Lonely	
72/71	Charlie Rich	
F/71	Patti Page	
54/97	**Woman Like You** *Matt King*	
17/70	**Woman Lives For Love** *Wanda Jackson*	
9/92	**Woman Loves** *Steve Wariner*	
64/67	**Woman Needs Love** *Marion Worth*	
52/66	**Woman Never Forgets** *Kitty Wells*	
58/86	**Woman Of The 80's** *Donna Fargo*	
1/69	**Woman Of The World (Leave My World Alone)** *Loretta Lynn*	
35/75	**Woman On My Mind** *David Houston*	
	Woman (Sensuous Woman)	
1/72	Don Gibson	
21/94	Mark Chesnutt	
54/76	**Woman Stealer** *Bobby G. Rice*	
4/74	**Woman To Woman** *Tammy Wynette*	
4/78	**Woman To Woman** *Barbara Mandrell*	
29/73	**Woman Without A Home** *Statler Brothers*	
20/69	**Woman Without Love** *Johnny Darrell*	
43/75	**Woman, Woman** *Jim Glaser*	
12/84	**Woman Your Love** *Moe Bandy*	
	Woman's Hand	
66/69	Barbara Fairchild	
23/70	Jean Shepard	
9/59	**Woman's Intuition** *Wilburn Brothers*	
72/90	**Woman's Intuition** *Michelle Wright*	
59/69	**Woman's Side Of Love** *Lynda K. Lance*	
6/96	**Woman's Touch** *Toby Keith*	
16/82	**Woman's Touch** *Tom Jones*	
70/79	**Woman's Touch** *Glenn Barber*	
80/89	**Woman's Way** *Mundo Earwood*	
3/78	**Womanhood** *Tammy Wynette*	
57/91	**Women** *Bandit Brothers*	
74/81	**Women** *Wyvon Alexander*	
9/66	**Women Do Funny Things To Me** *Del Reeves*	
4/82	**Women Do Know How To Carry On** *Waylon Jennings*	
18/80	**Women Get Lonely** *Charly McClain*	
5/80	**Women I've Never Had** *Hank Williams, Jr.*	
	Women In Love	
59/82	Kin Vassy	
55/85	Bill Medley	
65/81	**Won't You Be My Baby** *Keith Stegall*	
	Won't You Come Home (And Talk To A Stranger)	
61/69	Wayne Kemp	
70/97	George Strait	
1/70	**Wonder Could I Live There Anymore** *Charley Pride*	
37/70	**Wonder Of You** *Elvis Presley*	
39/75	**Wonder When My Baby's Comin' Home** *Barbara Mandrell*	
51/68	**Wonderful Day** *Ray Pillow*	
66/89	**Wonderful Tonight** *Butch Baker*	
14/68	**Wonderful World Of Women** *Faron Young*	
1/52	**Wondering** *Webb Pierce*	
6/70	**Wonders Of The Wine** *David Houston*	
5/71	**Wonders You Perform** *Tammy Wynette*	
41/64	**Wooden Soldier** *Hank Locklin*	
10/75	**Word Games** *Billy Walker*	
8/79	**Words** *Susie Allanson*	
12/94	**Words By Heart** *Billy Ray Cyrus*	
63/73	**Words Don't Come Easy** *David Frizzell*	
73/72	**Words Don't Fit The Picture** *Willie Nelson*	
10/67	**Words I'm Gonna Have To Eat** *Bill Phillips*	
55/90	**Work Song** *Corbin/Hanner*	
	Workin' At The Car Wash Blues	
27/74	Tony Booth	
F/80	Jerry Reed	
40/95	**Workin' For The Weekend** *Ken Mellons*	
86/83	**Workin' In A Coalmine** *Bob Jenkins*	
21/64	**Workin' It Out** *Flatt & Scruggs*	
50/96	**Workin' It Out** *Daryle Singletary*	
	Workin' Man Blues	
1/69	Merle Haggard	
48/95	Jed Zeppelin	
4/88	**Workin' Man (Nowhere To Go)** *Nitty Gritty Dirt Band*	
69/92	**Workin' Man's Dollar** *Chris LeDoux*	
30/80	**Workin' My Way To Your Heart** *Dickey Lee*	
37/73	**Workin' On A Feelin'** *Tommy Cash*	
73/73	**Working Class Hero** *Tommy Roe*	
16/86	**Working Class Man** *Lacy J. Dalton*	
75/94	**Working Elf Blues** *Daron Norwood*	
62/91	**Working For The Japanese** *Ray Stevens*	
F/81	**Working Girl** *Dolly Parton*	
33/71	**Working Like The Devil (For The Lord)** *Del Reeves*	
7/85	**Working Man** *John Conlee*	
16/77	**Working Man Can't Get Nowhere Today** *Merle Haggard*	
7/93	**Working Man's Ph.D.** *Aaron Tippin*	
59/67	**Working Man's Prayer** *Tex Ritter*	
7/86	**Working Without A Net** *Waylon Jennings*	
28/92	**Working Woman** *Rob Crosby*	
23/70	**World Called You** *David Rogers*	
90/77	**World Famous Holiday Inn** *Buck Owens*	
10/66	**World Is Round** *Roy Drusky*	
29/64	**World Lost A Man** *David Price*	
	World Needs A Melody	
32/71	Red Lane	
35/72	Carter Family with Johnny Cash	
1/74	**World Of Make Believe** *Bill Anderson*	
1/68	**World Of Our Own** *Sonny James*	
	World So Full Of Love	
18/60	Ray Sanders	
28/61	Faron Young	
66/68	**World The Way I Want It** *Tom T. Hall*	
19/69	**World-Wide Travelin' Man** *Wynn Stewart*	
10/85	**World Without Love** *Eddie Rabbitt*	
14/72	**World Without Music** *Porter Wagoner*	
52/67	**World's Biggest Whopper** *Junior Samples*	
6/84	**World's Greatest Lover** *Bellamy Brothers*	
18/79	**World's Most Perfect Woman** *Ronnie McDowell*	
46/66	**World's Worse Loser** *George Jones*	
5/96	**Worlds Apart** *Vince Gill*	
47/64	**Worst Of Luck** *Bobby Barnett*	
30/76	**(Worst You Ever Gave Me Was) The Best I Ever Had** *Faron Young*	
30/93	**Worth Every Mile** *Travis Tritt*	
73/96	**Worth The Fall** *Brett James*	
25/96	**Would I** *Randy Travis*	
41/87	**Would Jesus Wear A Rolex** *Ray Stevens*	
36/87	**Would These Arms Be In Your Way** *Keith Whitley*	
91/75	**Would You Be My Lady** *David Allan Coe*	
13/58	**Would You Care** *Browns*	
6/82	**Would You Catch A Falling Star** *John Anderson*	
86/87	**Would You Catch Me Baby (If I Fall For You)** *Gail Veach*	
5/66	**Would You Hold It Against Me** *Dottie West*	
95/80	**Would You Know Love** *Marlow Tackett*	
1/74	**Would You Lay With Me (In A Field Of Stone)** *Tanya Tucker*	
3/55	**Would You Mind?** *Hank Snow*	
92/73	**Would You Still Love Me** *Ben Peters*	
1/72	**Would You Take Another Chance On Me** *Jerry Lee Lewis*	
21/73	**Would You Walk With Me Jimmy** *Arlene Harden*	
12/72	**Would You Want The World To End** *Mel Tillis*	
72/85	**Wouldn't It Be Great** *Loretta Lynn*	
3/62	**Wound Time Can't Erase** *Stonewall Jackson*	
18/84	**Wounded Hearts** *Mark Gray*	
77/86	**Wrap Me Up In Your Love** *J.D. Martin*	
12/77	**Wrap Your Love All Around Your Man** *Lynn Anderson*	
38/73	**Wrap Your Love Around Me** *Melba Montgomery*	
46/72	**Wrapped Around Her Finger** *George Jones*	
50/76	**Wreck Of The Edmund Fitzgerald** *Gordon Lightfoot*	
8/61	**Wreck On The Highway** *Wilma Lee & Stoney Cooper*	

9/75 **Write Me A Letter** *Bobby G. Rice*
16/66 **Write Me A Picture** *George Hamilton IV*
6/44 **Write Me Sweetheart** *Roy Acuff*
Writing On The Wall
96/88   *Kenny Carr*
31/89   *George Jones*
15/72 **Writing's On The Wall** *Jim Reeves*
35/82 **Written Down In My Heart** *Ray Stevens*
5/90 **Wrong** *Waylon Jennings*
26/60 **Wrong Company**
   Wynn Stewart & Jan Howard
6/74 **Wrong Ideas** *Brenda Lee*
20/74 **Wrong In Loving You** *Faron Young*
14/65 **Wrong Number** *George Jones*
37/96 **Wrong Place, Wrong Time**
   Mark Chesnutt
Wrong Road Again
6/75   *Crystal Gayle*
95/78   *Allen Reynolds*
5/92 **Wrong Side Of Memphis**
   Trisha Yearwood
76/78 **Wrong Side Of The Rainbow**
   Jim Chesnut
49/68 **Wrong Side Of The World**
   Hugh X. Lewis
Wrong Train
82/86   *Beth Williams*
83/89   *Judy Lindsey*
65/93 **Wrong's What I Do Best** *George Jones*
1/77 **Wurlitzer Prize (I Don't Want To Get Over You)** *Waylon Jennings*
79/87 **Wyatt Liquor** *Wyatt Brothers*
Wyoming ..see: (Oh Why, Oh Why, Did I Ever Leave)

1/94 **XXX's And OOO's (An American Girl)**
   Trisha Yearwood

3/77 **Y'All Come Back Saloon**
   Oak Ridge Boys
4/65 **Yakety Axe** *Chet Atkins*
91/75 **Yakety Yak**
   Eric Weissberg & Deliverance
17/59 **Yankee, Go Home** *Goldie Hill*
17/92 **Yard Sale** *Sammy Kershaw*
69/95 **Yeah Buddy** *Jeff Carson*
1/71 **Year That Clayton Delaney Died**
   Tom T. Hall
Yearning
10/57   *George Jones & Jeanette Hicks*
22/61   *Benny Barnes*
1/80 **Years** *Barbara Mandrell*
2/85 **Years After You** *John Conlee*
12/82 **Years Ago** *Statler Brothers*
48/96 **Years From Here** *Baker & Myers*
4/63 **Yellow Bandana** *Faron Young*
59/67 **Yellow Haired Woman** *Claude King*
30/81 **Yellow Pages** *Roger Bowling*
5/73 **Yellow Ribbon** *Johnny Carver*
49/72 **Yellow River** *Compton Brothers*
1/84 **Yellow Rose**
   Johnny Lee with Lane Brody
7/55 **Yellow Rose Of Texas** *Ernest Tubb*
1/89 **Yellow Roses** *Dolly Parton*
3/55 **Yellow Roses** *Hank Snow*

67/83 **Yes** *Billy Swan*
83/75 **Yes** *Connie Cato*
75/71 **Yes, Dear, There Is A Virginia**
   Glenn Barber
2/56 **Yes I Know Why** *Webb Pierce*
6/66 **(Yes) I'm Hurting** *Don Gibson*
12/78 **Yes Ma'am** *Tommy Overstreet*
Yes Ma'm (I [He] Found Her [Me] In A Honky Tonk)
67/73   *Glenn Barber*
98/82   *Dixie Harrison*
1/65 **Yes, Mr. Peters** *Roy Drusky & Priscilla Mitchell*
   (also see: Hurry, Mr. Peters)
83/77 **Yes She Do, No She Don't** *Alvin Crow & The Pleasant Valley Boys*
60/79 **Yesterday** *Billie Jo Spears*
86/89 **Yesterday Is Too Far Away**
   Burch Denny
50/76 **Yesterday Just Passed My Way Again**
   Don Everly
10/80 **Yesterday Once More** *Moe Bandy*
9/69 **Yesterday, When I Was Young**
   Roy Clark
8/53 **Yesterday's Girl** *Hank Thompson*
9/77 **Yesterday's Gone** *Vern Gosdin*
40/69 **Yesterday's Letters** *Bobby Lord*
12/48 **Yesterday's Mail** *Hank Thompson*
11/63 **Yesterday's Memories** *Eddy Arnold*
57/81 **Yesterday's News (Just Hit Home Today)** *Johnny Paycheck*
99/88 **Yesterday's Rain** *Joy Ford*
4/44 **Yesterday's Tears** *Ernest Tubb*
Yesterday's Wine
62/71   *Willie Nelson*
1/82   *Merle Haggard/George Jones*
7/90 **Yet** *Exile*
25/80 **Yippy Cry Yi** *Rex Allen, Jr.*
YoYo Man ..see: (I'm A)
93/85 **Yo Yo (The Right String, But The Wrong Yo Yo)**
   Danny Shirley & "Piano Red"
44/65 **Yodel, Sweet Molly** *Ira Louvin*
Yonder Comes A Freight Train
56/68   *Jim & Jesse*
77/88   *Reno Brothers*
4/55 **Yonder Comes A Sucker** *Jim Reeves*
1/87 **You Again** *Forester Sisters*
19/89 **You Ain't Down Home** *Jann Browne*
6/89 **You Ain't Going Nowhere** *Chris Hillman & Roger McGuinn*
13/72 **You Ain't Gonna Have Ol' Buck To Kick Around No More** *Buck Owens*
5/79 **You Ain't Just Whistlin' Dixie**
   Bellamy Brothers
57/97 **You Ain't Lonely Yet** *Big House*
2/95 **You Ain't Much Fun** *Toby Keith*
46/66 **You Ain't No Better Than Me**
   Webb Pierce
2/66 **You Ain't Woman Enough** *Loretta Lynn*
You All ..also see: Y'All
7/54 **You All Come** *Arlie Duff*
You Almost Slipped My Mind
44/72   *Kenny Price*
4/80   *Charley Pride*
1/73 **You Always Come Back (To Hurting Me)** *Johnny Rodriguez*
37/76 **You Always Look Your Best (Here In My Arms)** *George Jones*
5/92 **You And Forever And Me** *Little Texas*
1/82 **You And I** *Eddie Rabbitt with Crystal Gayle*
You And Me
1/76   *Tammy Wynette*
92/77   *Lloyd Green*
3/56 **You And Me** *Red Foley & Kitty Wells*
   (also see: Now And Forever)
15/70 **You And Me Against The World**
   Bobby Lord
24/78 **You And Me Alone** *David Rogers*
94/81 **You And Me And Tennessee**
   Silver Creek
92/79 **You And Me And The Green Grass**
   Pal Rakes

99/75 **You And Me, Me And You**
   Sharon Vaughn
4/95 **You And Only You** *John Berry*
91/89 **You And The Horse (That You Rode In On)** *Patsy Cole*
8/97 **You And You Alone** *Vince Gill*
6/69 **You And Your Sweet Love**
   Connie Smith
48/81 **You Are A Liar** *Whitey Shafer*
85/84 **You Are A Miracle**
   Maines Brothers Band
87/83 **You Are Love** *Bobby Vinton*
72/88 **You Are My Angel** *Billy Parker*
12/64 **You Are My Flower** *Flatt & Scruggs*
10/86 **You Are My Music, You Are My Song**
   Charly McClain with Wayne Massey
36/79 **You Are My Rainbow** *David Rogers*
You Are My Special Angel ..see: My Special Angel
69/77 **You Are My Sunshine** *Duane Eddy*
1/68 **You Are My Treasure** *Jack Greene*
You Are So Beautiful
16/76   *Ray Stevens*
40/77   *Tanya Tucker*
93/78 **You Are Still The One** *Linda Hargrove*
97/83 **You Are The Music In Time With My Heart** *Joy Ford*
4/56 **You Are The One** *Carl Smith*
14/75 **You Are The One**
   Mel Tillis & Sherry Bryce
85/86 **You Are The Rock (And I'm A Rolling Stone)** *Carl Jackson*
11/76 **You Are The Song (Inside Of Me)**
   Freddie Hart
34/78 **You Are The Sunshine Of My Life**
   Marty Mitchell
86/84 **You Are What Love Means To Me**
   Craig Bickhardt
You Ask Me To
8/73   *Waylon Jennings*
80/78   *Billy Joe Shaver*
F/81   *Elvis Presley*
You, Babe
59/72   *Lefty Frizzell*
23/89   *Merle Haggard*
67/93 **You Baby You** *Highway 101*
20/67 **You Beat All I Ever Saw** *Johnny Cash*
You Belong To Me
54/75   *Jim Reeves*
93/89   *T.C. Brandon*
58/74 **You Bet Your Sweet, Sweet Love**
   Kenny O'Dell
52/67 **You Better Be Better To Me** *Carl Smith*
79/77 **(You Better Be) One Hell Of A Woman**
   Glenn Barber
49/80 **You Better Hurry Home (Somethin's Burnin')** *Connie Cato*
You Better Move On
10/71   *Billy "Crash" Craddock*
70/79   *Tommy Roe*
18/81   *George Jones & Johnny Paycheck*
2/54 **You Better Not Do That** *Tommy Collins*
28/68 **You Better Sit Down Kids** *Roy Drusky*
2/95 **You Better Think Twice** *Vince Gill*
49/66 **You Better Watch Your Friends**
   Jim Nesbitt
72/88 **You Blossom Me** *Bertie Higgins*
97/75 **You Bring Out The Best In Me**
   Brenda Pepper
66/85 **You Bring Out The Lover In Me**
   Zella Lehr
9/84 **(You Bring Out) The Wild Side Of Me**
   Dan Seals
63/84 **You Bring The Heartache (I'll Bring The Wine)** *Gary Wolf*
15/49 **You Broke My Heart (In Little Bitty Pieces)** *Hank Thompson*
95/79 **You Broke My Heart So Gently (It Almost Didn't Break)** *Sandra Kaye*
You Call Everybody Darling
71/73   *Lamar Morris*
69/91   *K.T. Oslin*
63/97 **You Call That A Mountain** *Jeff Wood*

489

TOP ARTISTS

Kings & Queens Of Country (The Top 400 Artists)

Top 25 Artists By Decade

Top Artist Achievements
  Most Chart Hits
  Most Top 40 Hits
  Most Top 10 Hits
  Most #1 Hits
  Most Weeks At The #1 Position
  Most Crossover Hits

  Most Consecutive #1 Hits
  Most Consecutive Top 10 Hits
  Artists With Longest Chart Careers
  Artists With Longest Span Between Chart Hits
  Top Artists Who Never Hit #1
  Artist's First Hit Is Their Biggest Hit
  One-Hit Wonders

TOP 400 ARTISTS

This section ranks the Top 400 country artists from 1944-1997. Each artist's accumulated point total is shown to the right of their name. This ranking includes all titles that peaked <u>prior</u> to 1998.

A picture of each Top 200 artist is shown next to their listing in the artist section of this book.

Headings And Special Symbols:

Old Rank: Artist ranking in *Top Country Singles 1944-1993*

New Rank: Artist ranking in *Top Country Singles 1944-1997*

● = **Deceased Solo Artist**

■ = **Deceased Group Member**
Each square indicates a deceased member.

★ = **Hot Artist**
Artist had significant chart activity since the previous edition with an increase of at least 200 points or an increase in ranking of at least 40 positions.

✪ = **Super Hot Artist**
Artist had significant chart activity since the previous edition with an increase of at least 400 points or an increase in ranking of at least 100 positions.

— = Artist did not rank in the Top 400 of the previous edition.

POINT SYSTEM

Points are awarded according to the following formula:

1. Each artist's charted singles are given points based on their highest charted position:

#1	=	100 points for its first week at #1, plus 10 points for each additional week at #1
#2	=	90 points for its first week at #2, plus 5 points for each additional week at #2
#3	=	80 points for its first week at #3, plus 3 points for each additional week at #3
#4-5	=	70 points
#6-10	=	60 points
#11-20	=	50 points
#21-30	=	45 points
#31-40	=	40 points
#41-50	=	35 points
#51-60	=	30 points
#61-70	=	25 points
#71-80	=	20 points
#81-90	=	15 points
#91-100	=	10 points

2. Total weeks charted are added in.

In the case of a tie, the artist listed first is determined by the following tie-breaker rules:

1) Most charted singles
2) Most Top 40 singles
3) Most Top 10 singles

When two or more artists combine for a hit single, such as Faith Hill and Tim McGraw, the full point value is given to each artist. Duos, such as Brooks & Dunn, are considered regular recording teams, and their points are not shared by either artist individually.

Old Rank	New Rank		Points
(1)	1.	Eddy Arnold	12,571
(2)	★2.	George Jones	11,406
(3)	3.	Johnny Cash	9,533
(4)	4.	Conway Twitty ●	9,083
(5)	5.	Merle Haggard	8,952
(6)	6.	Webb Pierce ●	7,925
(8)	7.	Dolly Parton	7,869
(7)	8.	Ray Price	7,708
(9)	9.	Willie Nelson	7,654
(10)	10.	Buck Owens	7,447
(11)	11.	Waylon Jennings	7,275
(12)	12.	Marty Robbins ●	7,226
(13)	13.	Jim Reeves ●	6,808
(14)	14.	Hank Williams, Jr.	6,745
(40)	✪15.	George Strait	6,417
(15)	16.	Charley Pride	6,412
(16)	17.	Ernest Tubb ●	6,399
(17)	18.	Loretta Lynn	6,239
(18)	19.	Sonny James	6,170
(33)	✪20.	Alabama	6,152
(20)	21.	Faron Young ●	6,060
(19)	22.	Hank Snow	6,053
(21)	23.	Ronnie Milsap	5,937
(37)	✪24.	Reba McEntire	5,933
(22)	25.	Carl Smith	5,841
(23)	26.	Tammy Wynette ●	5,785
(24)	27.	Bill Anderson	5,576
(25)	28.	Mel Tillis	5,340
(26)	29.	Red Foley ●	5,311
(36)	✪30.	Tanya Tucker	5,218
(28)	31.	Kenny Rogers	5,207
(27)	32.	Don Williams	5,191
(29)	33.	Porter Wagoner	5,172
(30)	34.	Elvis Presley ●	5,152
(31)	35.	Kitty Wells	5,079
(32)	36.	Don Gibson	5,045
(34)	37.	Glen Campbell	4,941
(35)	38.	The Statler Brothers ■	4,788
(38)	39.	Hank Thompson	4,733
(39)	40.	Crystal Gayle	4,517
(41)	41.	Hank Williams ●	4,380
(42)	42.	Jerry Lee Lewis	4,335
(43)	43.	David Houston ●	4,230
(44)	44.	Oak Ridge Boys ■	4,191
(45)	45.	Bobby Bare	4,180
(46)	46.	Barbara Mandrell	4,177
(47)	47.	Mickey Gilley	4,056
(91)	✪48.	Garth Brooks	3,982
(48)	49.	Lynn Anderson	3,981
(49)	50.	Eddie Rabbitt ●	3,975
(50)	51.	Anne Murray	3,896
(51)	52.	Dottie West ●	3,838
(52)	53.	Joe Stampley	3,806
(53)	54.	T.G. Sheppard	3,711
(54)	55.	Emmylou Harris	3,670
(55)	56.	Steve Wariner	3,625
(73)	✪57.	John Anderson	3,620
(56)	58.	Bellamy Brothers	3,522
(57)	59.	Tom T. Hall	3,496
(103)	✪60.	Vince Gill	3,484
(139)	✪61.	Alan Jackson	3,481
(58)	62.	Billy Walker	3,478
(59)	63.	Earl Thomas Conley	3,477
(60)	64.	Moe Bandy	3,467
(75)	✪65.	Randy Travis	3,455
(61)	66.	Ferlin Husky	3,310
(62)	67.	Johnny Paycheck	3,236
(65)	68.	Gene Watson	3,227
(63)	69.	Freddie Hart	3,179
(64)	70.	Connie Smith	3,173
(135)	✪71.	Clint Black	3,146
(66)	72.	Johnny Rodriguez	3,130
(67)	73.	Charlie Rich ●	3,074
(68)	74.	Jerry Reed	3,066
(69)	75.	Larry Gatlin & The Gatlin Brothers	3,001
(106)	✪76.	Sawyer Brown	2,995
(70)	77.	Janie Fricke	2,978
(71)	78.	Lefty Frizzell ●	2,930
(72)	79.	Jim Ed Brown	2,923
(74)	80.	Ricky Skaggs	2,902
(136)	✪81.	Patty Loveless	2,810
(76)	82.	Vern Gosdin	2,805
(77)	83.	Billy "Crash" Craddock	2,772
(78)	84.	Eddy Raven	2,747
(79)	85.	John Conlee	2,741
(80)	86.	Lee Greenwood	2,689
(81)	87.	Stonewall Jackson	2,681
(83)	88.	Del Reeves	2,641
(82)	89.	Roy Drusky	2,633
(102)	✪90.	Kathy Mattea	2,615
(84)	91.	Jean Shepard	2,582
(85)	92.	Roger Miller ●	2,579
(86)	93.	Dave Dudley	2,569
(87)	94.	Charly McClain	2,538
(88)	95.	Donna Fargo	2,502
(89)	96.	The Judds	2,466
(165)	✪97.	Travis Tritt	2,442
(92)	98.	Roy Clark	2,422
(90)	99.	Bob Wills ●	2,413
(93)	100.	Ronnie McDowell	2,405
(234)	✪101.	Brooks & Dunn	2,400
(99)	102.	Ricky Van Shelton	2,379
(94)	103.	George Hamilton IV	2,314
(95)	104.	Skeeter Davis	2,313
(96)	105.	Mel McDaniel	2,280
(97)	106.	Jack Greene	2,265
(212)	✪107.	Mark Chesnutt	2,261
(168)	✪108.	Lorrie Morgan	2,255
(101)	109.	Dan Seals	2,250
(98)	110.	Johnny Duncan	2,248
(100)	111.	The Kendalls	2,225
(223)	✪112.	Joe Diffie	2,211
(137)	✪113.	Dwight Yoakam	2,167

Old Rank	New Rank		Points
(104)	114.	Jimmy Wakely ●—	2,166
(279)	✪115.	Tracy Lawrence	2,141
(105)	116.	Rosanne Cash	2,135
(107)	117.	"Tennessee" Ernie Ford ●—	2,111
(160)	✪118.	Shenandoah	2,105
(108)	119.	Nitty Gritty Dirt Band	2,100
(109)	120.	Gary Morris	2,097
(110)	121.	Johnny Lee	2,092
(111)	122.	Gene Autry ●—	2,036
(112)	123.	Hank Locklin	2,019
(113)	124.	Jimmy Newman	2,017
(114)	125.	George Morgan ●—	2,005
(115)	126.	Wilburn Brothers ■—	1,994
(289)	✪127.	Collin Raye	1,994
(116)	128.	Slim Whitman	1,986
(117)	129.	Al Dexter ●—	1,986
(123)	130.	Restless Heart	1,980
(118)	131.	Billie Jo Spears	1,978
(119)	132.	Tommy Overstreet	1,975
(120)	133.	Ed Bruce	1,968
(121)	134.	Nat Stuckey ●—	1,964
(122)	135.	Exile	1,947
(124)	136.	Narvel Felts	1,922
(257)	✪137.	Trisha Yearwood	1,907
(125)	138.	Razzy Bailey	1,898
(127)	139.	Michael Martin Murphey	1,896
(126)	140.	Tex Ritter ●—	1,891
(128)	141.	Bob Luman ●—	1,877
(243)	✪142.	Pam Tillis	1,819
(129)	143.	Sammi Smith	1,809
(130)	144.	Rex Allen, Jr.	1,791
(132)	145.	Brenda Lee	1,789
—	✪146.	John Michael Montgomery	1,784
(131)	147.	Freddy Weller	1,769
(133)	148.	Jerry Wallace	1,756
(224)	✪149.	Mary Chapin Carpenter	1,736
(134)	150.	Claude King	1,724
(138)	151.	Tex Williams ●—	1,700
(140)	152.	Juice Newton	1,683
(275)	✪153.	Diamond Rio	1,682
(141)	154.	David Rogers ●—	1,675
(216)	✪155.	Doug Stone	1,667
(142)	156.	Wynn Stewart ●—	1,660
(143)	157.	The Forester Sisters	1,636
(144)	158.	Jan Howard	1,634
(145)	159.	Cal Smith	1,624
(146)	160.	Red Sovine ●—	1,611
(202)	★161.	Marty Stuart	1,609
(147)	162.	Susan Raye	1,601
(148)	163.	Lacy J. Dalton	1,589
(151)	164.	Keith Whitley ●—	1,558
(149)	165.	Kenny Price ●—	1,553
(156)	166.	Linda Ronstadt	1,551
—	✪167.	Tim McGraw	1,551
(150)	168.	Mac Davis	1,545
(152)	169.	Warner Mack	1,533
(153)	170.	Ray Stevens	1,526

Old Rank	New Rank		Points
(154)	171.	Dickey Lee	1,522
(155)	172.	Sylvia	1,522
(263)	✪173.	Wynonna	1,519
(332)	✪174.	Sammy Kershaw	1,512
(157)	175.	Margo Smith	1,504
(158)	176.	Jimmy Dean	1,500
(159)	177.	Wanda Jackson	1,497
(161)	178.	David Frizzell	1,493
(162)	179.	John Denver ●—	1,480
(174)	180.	Rodney Crowell	1,474
(163)	181.	Charlie Louvin	1,455
—	✪182.	Clay Walker	1,452
(164)	183.	Highway 101	1,449
(166)	184.	Melba Montgomery	1,439
(167)	185.	Louise Mandrell	1,436
(170)	186.	Holly Dunn	1,432
(169)	187.	The Everly Brothers	1,397
(181)	188.	Dave & Sugar	1,391
(171)	189.	Leon Everette	1,390
(172)	190.	Freddy Fender	1,387
(173)	191.	Gary Stewart	1,384
(175)	192.	Barbara Fairchild	1,381
(329)	✪193.	Little Texas	1,381
(176)	194.	Gail Davies	1,378
(177)	195.	The Browns	1,373
(178)	196.	Jeannie Seely	1,366
(179)	197.	Mel Street ●—	1,365
(180)	198.	Patsy Cline ●—	1,352
(182)	199.	Jody Miller	1,338
(183)	200.	Johnny Carver	1,332
(184)	201.	Ernest Ashworth	1,327
(185)	202.	T. Graham Brown	1,326
(191)	203.	Charlie Daniels Band	1,321
—	✪204.	Neal McCoy	1,321
(186)	205.	Bobby G. Rice	1,316
(187)	206.	Shelly West	1,302
—	✪207.	Toby Keith	1,300
(188)	208.	David Allan Coe	1,297
(190)	209.	John Schneider	1,293
(189)	210.	Merle Travis ●—	1,290
(357)	✪211.	Lee Roy Parnell	1,286
(193)	212.	Jacky Ward	1,268
(192)	213.	Claude Gray	1,264
(322)	✪214.	Aaron Tippin	1,255
(194)	215.	Jeannie C. Riley	1,253
(195)	216.	Johnny Russell	1,247
(196)	217.	Tompall & The Glaser Brothers	1,242
(197)	218.	Cowboy Copas ●—	1,242
(200)	219.	Marie Osmond	1,241
(198)	220.	Charlie Walker	1,236
—	✪221.	Tracy Byrd	1,231
(199)	222.	John Wesley Ryles	1,225
(274)	✪223.	Billy Dean	1,224
(233)	★224.	Suzy Bogguss	1,222
(201)	225.	Con Hunley	1,217
(205)	226.	Paul Overstreet	1,216

Old Rank	New Rank		Points
(203)	227.	Johnny Horton ....●	1,206
(204)	228.	Cristy Lane	1,202
(206)	229.	Flatt & Scruggs ....■...	1,197
(207)	230.	The Desert Rose Band	1,195
(208)	231.	Jeanne Pruett	1,194
(214)	232.	K.T. Oslin	1,170
(209)	233.	Helen Cornelius	1,163
(210)	234.	Bobby Goldsboro	1,155
(211)	235.	Norma Jean	1,155
(213)	236.	Bobby Lewis	1,146
(215)	237.	Billy Joe Royal	1,135
—	✪238.	Faith Hill...............................	1,097
(217)	239.	Jim Glaser	1,089
—	✪240.	John Berry	1,081
(218)	241.	"Little" Jimmy Dickens	1,080
—	✪242.	Martina McBride	1,076
—	✪243.	Shania Twain	1,076
(219)	244.	Randy Barlow	1,062
(220)	245.	Johnnie & Jack ....■...	1,047
(221)	246.	Leroy Van Dyke	1,042
(222)	247.	B.J. Thomas	1,029
(293)	★248.	Hal Ketchum	1,010
(225)	249.	Olivia Newton-John	996
(318)	★250.	Billy Ray Cyrus	993
(227)	251.	Johnny Bush	989
(226)	252.	Pee Wee King	989
(228)	253.	Dick Curless ....●	976
(229)	254.	Buddy Alan	972
(230)	255.	Southern Pacific	968
—	✪256.	BlackHawk	957
(231)	257.	Margaret Whiting	953
(232)	258.	Tommy Cash	946
(235)	259.	Elton Britt ....●	939
(236)	260.	Ray Griff	930
(237)	261.	Mundo Earwood	926
(238)	262.	Red Steagall	922
(239)	263.	Patti Page	903
(240)	264.	Susie Allanson	903
(241)	265.	Roy Acuff ....●	898
(242)	266.	The Whites	898
(244)	267.	Carl Butler & Pearl ....■ ■...	888
(245)	268.	Roy Head	887
(246)	269.	Bill Phillips	887
(306)	★270.	Mark Collie	880
(253)	271.	Bobby Helms ....●	879
(248)	272.	Tom Jones	877
(249)	273.	Henson Cargill	865
(250)	274.	Don King	864
(251)	275.	Rose Maddox ....●	861
(252)	276.	Liz Anderson	859
—	✪277.	Bryan White	849
(254)	278.	Bonnie Guitar	843
(255)	279.	Johnny Darrell ....●	842
—	✪280.	Rick Trevino	839
(256)	281.	David Wills	837
(258)	282.	Johnny and Jonie Mosby	836
—	✪283.	Confederate Railroad	833

Old Rank	New Rank		Points
(259)	284.	Glenn Barber	829
(261)	285.	The Louvin Brothers ....■	825
(262)	286.	Sweethearts Of The Rodeo	822
(264)	287.	Wayne Kemp	817
(265)	288.	Lionel Cartwright	816
(266)	289.	Stephanie Winslow	811
(303)	290.	The Carlisles	805
(267)	291.	Lois Johnson	804
(310)	292.	Sons Of The Pioneers...■ ■ ■ ■ ■ ■...	804
(268)	293.	Baillie And The Boys	803
(269)	294.	Jessi Colter	797
(284)	295.	Asleep At The Wheel	796
(260)	296.	Arlene Harden	796
(270)	297.	Diana Trask	794
(271)	298.	Kenny Dale	792
(272)	299.	Jack Blanchard & Misty Morgan ...	792
(273)	300.	Billy Swan	783
(276)	301.	Dean Dillon	779
(316)	302.	McBride & The Ride	772
(277)	303.	Carl Perkins ....●	770
(278)	304.	Floyd Tillman	770
(247)	305.	Deborah Allen	760
(281)	306.	Wilma Burgess	755
(282)	307.	C.W. McCall	753
(283)	308.	Michael Johnson	752
(338)	309.	Carlene Carter	751
(285)	310.	Tommy Collins	747
(286)	311.	Debby Boone	740
(331)	312.	Skip Ewing	738
(287)	313.	Ray Charles	734
(288)	314.	Johnny Bond ....●	731
(290)	315.	Bobby Wright	725
(291)	316.	Moon Mullican ....●	722
(292)	317.	Mark Gray	717
—	✪318.	David Lee Murphy	716
—	✪319.	Kenny Chesney	711
(294)	320.	Judy Rodman	709
(296)	321.	Dottsy	692
(297)	322.	Zella Lehr	687
(295)	323.	Ted Daffan ....●	687
(298)	324.	Little David Wilkins	685
—	✪325.	Doug Supernaw	685
(299)	326.	Marion Worth	680
(300)	327.	Stella Parton	677
(301)	328.	La Costa	673
(302)	329.	Larry Boone	667
(280)	330.	June Carter	667
(304)	331.	Sheb Wooley	664
(325)	332.	Lyle Lovett	662
—	✪333.	Ty Herndon	662
(305)	334.	Joe Sun	659
(307)	335.	Hoyt Axton	657
(308)	336.	Jim Nesbitt	655
(309)	337.	Ray Pillow	654
(321)	338.	Robin Lee	650
(311)	339.	R.C. Bannon	648

Old Rank	New Rank		Points
(312)	340.	Sherry Bryce	646
(313)	341.	Terri Gibbs	644
(314)	342.	Margie Singleton	637
(315)	343.	Peggy Sue	635
(317)	344.	Roy Rogers ●	634
—	✪345.	Wade Hayes	633
(319)	346.	Osborne Brothers	630
(320)	347.	Ned Miller	630
(350)	348.	Keith Stegall	621
(323)	349.	Billy Parker	619
(324)	350.	Bobby Borchers	614
(326)	351.	Tony Booth	610
(327)	352.	"T" Texas Tyler ●	610
(328)	353.	Johnny Wright	608
(330)	354.	Spade Cooley ●	606
(333)	355.	Jimmie Skinner ●	604
—	✪356.	Ricochet	601
(334)	357.	Big Al Downing	599
(335)	358.	Jack Reno	599
(336)	359.	Foster & Lloyd	599
(337)	360.	Mary Lou Turner	597
—	✪361.	LeAnn Rimes	597
(339)	362.	Hawkshaw Hawkins ●	589
(340)	363.	Becky Hobbs	588
(341)	364.	Charlie McCoy	584
—	✪365.	Rhett Akins	582
(342)	366.	Mike Reid	577
(343)	367.	Burl Ives ●	576
(344)	368.	The O'Kanes	575
—	✪369.	Lonestar	571
—	★370.	Chris LeDoux	567

Old Rank	New Rank		Points
(345)	371.	Ronnie Sessions	567
(346)	372.	Dorsey Burnette ●	567
(347)	373.	Penny DeHaven	564
(348)	374.	Kris Kristofferson	564
(349)	375.	Tom Wopat	563
—	✪376.	Lari White	554
(351)	377.	Jimmy Buffett	551
—	✪378.	Terri Clark	550
(353)	379.	Ray Sanders	547
(354)	380.	Carl Belew ●	545
(355)	381.	Hugh X. Lewis	543
(356)	382.	Stoney Edwards ●	542
(352)	383.	Wilma Lee & Stoney Cooper ■	542
—	✪384.	The Mavericks	539
(358)	385.	Leon Ashley	533
(359)	386.	Schuyler, Knobloch & Overstreet	533
(360)	387.	LaWanda Lindsey	532
—	✪388.	David Ball	532
—	✪389.	Deana Carter	532
(371)	390.	The Kentucky Headhunters	529
(361)	391.	Mason Dixon	527
(362)	392.	Sonny Curtis	525
(363)	393.	Bill Monroe ●	522
(364)	394.	Darrell McCall	521
(365)	395.	Ricky Nelson ●	521
(366)	396.	Lane Brody	520
(367)	397.	Bandana	519
(368)	398.	Brian Collins	515
(369)	399.	Kenny Starr	509
—	400.	Doug Kershaw	507

TOP 25 ARTISTS BY DECADE

FORTIES ('44-'49)

		Points
1.	Eddy Arnold	3,587
2.	Ernest Tubb	2,612
3.	Bob Wills	2,143
4.	Al Dexter	1,986
5.	Red Foley	1,746
6.	Gene Autry	1,741
7.	Jimmy Wakely	1,415
8.	Tex Ritter	1,344
9.	Tex Williams	1,203
10.	Merle Travis	1,172
11.	Hank Williams	1,032
12.	Sons Of The Pioneers	780
13.	Elton Britt	703
14.	Ted Daffan	687
15.	Floyd Tillman	651
16.	Spade Cooley	606
17.	Hank Thompson	597
18.	Cowboy Copas	594
19.	George Morgan	579
20.	Roy Acuff	570
21.	Margaret Whiting	469
22.	"T" Texas Tyler	426
23.	Bill Monroe	420
24.	Jimmie Davis	415
25.	"Tennessee" Ernie Ford	413

FIFTIES ('50-'59)

		Points
1.	Webb Pierce	5,041
2.	Eddy Arnold	4,422
3.	Hank Snow	3,913
4.	Carl Smith	3,519
5.	Red Foley	3,433
6.	Hank Williams	3,203
7.	Johnny Cash	2,648
8.	Elvis Presley	2,628
9.	Kitty Wells	2,528
10.	Ernest Tubb	2,503
11.	Ray Price	2,290
12.	Hank Thompson	2,267
13.	Faron Young	2,192
14.	Jim Reeves	2,175
15.	Marty Robbins	2,020
16.	Lefty Frizzell	1,901
17.	"Tennessee" Ernie Ford	1,365
18.	Ferlin Husky	1,210
19.	The Everly Brothers	1,070
20.	Johnnie & Jack	993
21.	George Jones	988
22.	Don Gibson	932
23.	Jimmy Newman	811
24.	Johnny Horton	789
25.	The Browns	769

SIXTIES ('60-'69)

		Points
1.	Buck Owens	4,804
2.	George Jones	4,097
3.	Jim Reeves	3,374
4.	Johnny Cash	3,014
5.	Eddy Arnold	2,783
6.	Marty Robbins	2,601
7.	Webb Pierce	2,559
8.	Bill Anderson	2,552
9.	Ray Price	2,410
10.	Faron Young	2,398
11.	Kitty Wells	2,363
12.	Sonny James	2,341
13.	Porter Wagoner	2,235
14.	Stonewall Jackson	2,031
15.	Loretta Lynn	1,943
16.	Roy Drusky	1,892
17.	David Houston	1,880
18.	Don Gibson	1,830
19.	Merle Haggard	1,760
20.	Roger Miller	1,705
21.	Billy Walker	1,683
22.	Carl Smith	1,671
23.	Bobby Bare	1,605
24.	George Hamilton IV	1,594
25.	Skeeter Davis	1,542

SEVENTIES ('70-'79)

		Points
1.	Conway Twitty	4,274
2.	Merle Haggard	3,588
3.	Charley Pride	3,377
4.	Dolly Parton	3,305
5.	Loretta Lynn	3,236
6.	Tammy Wynette	3,203
7.	Mel Tillis	3,187
8.	George Jones	3,070
9.	Waylon Jennings	3,022
10.	Sonny James	2,851
11.	Johnny Cash	2,771
12.	Charlie Rich	2,665
13.	Lynn Anderson	2,628
14.	Willie Nelson	2,617
15.	Tom T. Hall	2,566
16.	Freddie Hart	2,394
17.	Jerry Lee Lewis	2,341
18.	Bill Anderson	2,279
19.	Billy "Crash" Craddock	2,249
20.	David Houston	2,246
21.	Hank Williams, Jr.	2,245
22.	Joe Stampley	2,228
23.	Don Gibson	2,215
24.	Glen Campbell	2,160
25.	Ronnie Milsap	2,091

EIGHTIES ('80-'89)

		Points
1.	Willie Nelson	3,888
2.	Conway Twitty	3,517
3.	Merle Haggard	3,465
4.	Kenny Rogers	3,397
5.	Alabama	3,368
6.	Ronnie Milsap	3,278
7.	Oak Ridge Boys	3,036
8.	Hank Williams, Jr.	2,977
9.	Earl Thomas Conley	2,862
10.	Dolly Parton	2,861
11.	George Strait	2,854
12.	Reba McEntire	2,840
13.	Don Williams	2,829
14.	Crystal Gayle	2,805
15.	Waylon Jennings	2,790
16.	Bellamy Brothers	2,720
17.	George Jones	2,667
18.	Steve Wariner	2,507
19.	T.G. Sheppard	2,498
20.	Ricky Skaggs	2,432
21.	Janie Fricke	2,426
22.	Mickey Gilley	2,420
23.	The Statler Brothers	2,350
24.	Emmylou Harris	2,344
25.	Lee Greenwood	2,296

NINETIES ('90-'97)

		Points
1.	Garth Brooks	3,770
2.	George Strait	3,563
3.	Alan Jackson	3,434
4.	Clint Black	2,901
5.	Reba McEntire	2,737
6.	Vince Gill	2,711
7.	Alabama	2,704
8.	Brooks & Dunn	2,400
9.	Travis Tritt	2,356
10.	Mark Chesnutt	2,261
11.	Joe Diffie	2,211
12.	Tracy Lawrence	2,141
13.	Patty Loveless	2,015
14.	Collin Raye	1,994
15.	Trisha Yearwood	1,907
16.	Randy Travis	1,906
17.	Lorrie Morgan	1,892
18.	Sawyer Brown	1,837
19.	John Michael Montgomery	1,784
20.	Tanya Tucker	1,778
21.	Diamond Rio	1,682
22.	Pam Tillis	1,670
23.	Doug Stone	1,667
24.	Mary Chapin Carpenter	1,578
25.	Tim McGraw	1,551

TOP ARTIST ACHIEVEMENTS

MOST CHART HITS

1. George Jones 159
2. Eddy Arnold 145
3. Johnny Cash 135
4. Willie Nelson 114
5. Ray Price 109
6. Merle Haggard 103
7. Dolly Parton 103
8. Hank Williams, Jr. 98
9. Conway Twitty 97
10. Webb Pierce 96
11. Waylon Jennings 96
12. Marty Robbins 94
13. Carl Smith 93
14. Ernest Tubb 91
15. Buck Owens 90
16. Faron Young 89
17. Hank Snow 85
18. Elvis Presley 85
19. Don Gibson 82
20. Porter Wagoner 81
21. Kitty Wells 81
22. Jim Reeves 80
23. Bill Anderson 80
24. Hank Thompson 79
25. Loretta Lynn 77
26. Mel Tillis 77
27. Glen Campbell 75

MOST TOP 40 HITS

1. George Jones 141
2. Eddy Arnold 128
3. Johnny Cash 104
4. Merle Haggard 90
5. Dolly Parton 89
6. Waylon Jennings 89
7. Conway Twitty 88
8. Webb Pierce 84
9. Marty Robbins 83
10. Ray Price 82
11. Ernest Tubb 82
12. Willie Nelson 80
13. Faron Young 79
14. Hank Williams, Jr. 78
15. Buck Owens 75
16. Jim Reeves 73
17. Loretta Lynn 69
18. Carl Smith 69
19. Mel Tillis 68
20. Elvis Presley 66
21. Hank Snow 65
22. Porter Wagoner 65
23. Don Gibson 65
24. Sonny James 64
25. Kitty Wells 64
26. Reba McEntire 63
27. Red Foley 61

MOST TOP 10 HITS

1. Eddy Arnold 92
2. George Jones 78
3. Conway Twitty 75
4. Merle Haggard 71
5. Ernest Tubb 58
6. Red Foley 56
7. Webb Pierce 54
8. Dolly Parton 54
9. Waylon Jennings 53
10. George Strait 53
11. Johnny Cash 52
12. Charley Pride 52
13. Jim Reeves 51
14. Loretta Lynn 51
15. Alabama 49
16. Ronnie Milsap 49
17. Buck Owens 47
18. Marty Robbins 47
19. Ray Price 46
20. Reba McEntire 45
21. Don Williams 45
22. Sonny James 43
23. Hank Snow 43
24. Hank Williams, Jr. 42
25. Willie Nelson 41
26. Faron Young 41
27. Tanya Tucker 40

MOST #1 HITS

1. Conway Twitty 40
2. Merle Haggard 38
3. Ronnie Milsap 35
4. George Strait 32
5. Alabama 32
6. Charley Pride 29
7. Eddy Arnold 28
8. Dolly Parton 24
9. Sonny James 23
10. Buck Owens 21
11. Willie Nelson 20
12. Reba McEntire 20
13. Tammy Wynette 20
14. Kenny Rogers 20
15. Crystal Gayle 18
16. Earl Thomas Conley 18
17. Don Williams 17
18. Garth Brooks 17
19. Oak Ridge Boys 17
20. Mickey Gilley 17
21. Eddie Rabbitt 17
22. Waylon Jennings 16
23. Marty Robbins 16
24. Loretta Lynn 16

MOST WEEKS AT THE #1 POSITION

1. Eddy Arnold 145
2. Webb Pierce 111
3. Buck Owens 82
4. Hank Williams 82
5. Johnny Cash 69
6. Sonny James 66
7. Marty Robbins 63
8. Jim Reeves 58
9. George Strait 58
10. Merle Haggard 57
11. Hank Snow 56
12. Conway Twitty 52
13. Elvis Presley 50
14. Charley Pride 49
15. Ray Price 47
16. Ronnie Milsap 47
17. Al Dexter 47
18. Alabama 40
19. Red Foley 40
20. Tammy Wynette 37
21. Lefty Frizzell 36
22. Dolly Parton 33
23. Waylon Jennings 33
24. Jimmy Wakely 33

MOST CROSSOVER HITS

1. Elvis Presley 61
2. Johnny Cash 52
3. Eddy Arnold 37
4. Glen Campbell 37
5. Kenny Rogers 32
6. Marty Robbins 31
7. Anne Murray 28
8. Jim Reeves 27
9. Dolly Parton 24
10. Sonny James 21
11. John Denver 21
12. Buck Owens 19
13. Roger Miller 19
14. Willie Nelson 17
15. Charley Pride 16
16. Tammy Wynette 16
17. Mac Davis 16
18. Waylon Jennings 15
19. Ronnie Milsap 15
20. Don Gibson 15
21. Jerry Lee Lewis 15
22. Olivia Newton-John 15
23. Eddie Rabbitt 14

MOST CONSECUTIVE #1 HITS

1. 21 **Alabama** (1980-87)
2. 16 **Earl Thomas Conley** (1983-89)
3. 16 **Sonny James** (1967-71)
4. 15 **Buck Owens** (1963-67)
5. 11 **George Strait** (1986-89)
6. 11 **Conway Twitty** (1974-77)
7. 10 **Ronnie Milsap** (1980-83)
8. 9 **Merle Haggard** (1973-76)
9. 9 **Webb Pierce** (1953-56)
10. 9 **Dan Seals** (1985-89)
11. 8 **Eddy Arnold** (1948-49)
12. 8 **The Judds** (1984-87)
13. 8 **T.G. Sheppard** (1980-83)

Excludes Christmas hits, re-issues, B-sides, and duos (unless they add to the streak).

MOST CONSECUTIVE TOP 10 HITS

1. 67 **Eddy Arnold** (1945-56)
2. 65 **Merle Haggard** (1966-85)
3. 56 **Red Foley** (1945-56)
4. 48 **Ronnie Milsap** (1974-92)
5. 42 **Alabama** (1980-94)
6. 38 **Charley Pride** (1971-84)
7. 37 **Webb Pierce** (1952-58)
8. 36 **Conway Twitty** (1968-77)
9. 35 **Buck Owens** (1962-72)
10. 34 **Waylon Jennings** (1973-85)
11. 33 **Hank Williams** (1949-55)
12. 32 **Eddie Rabbitt** (1976-88)
13. 31 **George Strait** (1982-91)
14. 31 **Ernest Tubb** (1949-53)

Excludes Christmas hits, re-issues, B-sides, and duos (unless they add to the streak).

ARTISTS WITH LONGEST CHART CAREERS

Dates		Artist (Years/Months/Weeks)
7/6/46	- 1/4/92	**Roy Rogers** (45/6/0)
2/12/44	- 6/24/89	**Roy Acuff** (45/4/2)
7/16/55	- 1/3/98	**Elvis Presley** (42/5/3)
10/29/55	- 1/31/98	**George Jones** (42/3/0)
8/9/47	- 5/6/89	**Hank Williams** (41/9/0)
4/6/57	- 1/3/98	**Brenda Lee** (40/9/0)
3/30/57	- 1/4/97	**Bobby Helms** (39/9/1)
6/30/45	- 4/23/83	**Eddy Arnold** (37/9/3)
5/17/52	- 12/2/89	**Ray Price** (37/6/2)
1/10/53	- 2/11/89	**Faron Young** (36/1/0)
1/8/44	- 12/8/79	**Ernest Tubb** (35/11/0)
1/31/48	- 8/20/83	**Hank Thompson** (35/6/3)

ARTISTS WITH LONGEST SPAN BETWEEN CHART HITS

Dates		Artist (Years/Months/Weeks)
9/10/49	- 8/23/80	**Sons Of The Pioneers** (30/11/2)
8/22/70	- 12/28/96	**Bobby Helms** (23/4/1)
12/9/67	- 8/22/92	**Geezinslaw Brothers** (24/8/2)
3/20/61	- 9/29/84	**The Everly Brothers** (23/6/1)
2/4/50	- 9/26/70	**Roy Rogers** (20/7/3)
9/15/58	- 5/7/77	**Duane Eddy** (18/7/3)
10/9/48	- 10/15/66	**Cliffie Stone** (18/0/1)
5/27/50	- 5/4/68	**Elton Britt** (17/11/1)
4/25/64	- 2/13/82	**Gary Buck** (17/9/3)
8/27/49	- 3/4/67	**June Carter** (17/6/1)
2/12/49	- 4/9/66	**Buddy Starcher** (17/2/0)

TOP ARTISTS WHO NEVER HIT #1

	Artist Rank	
1.	104	**Skeeter Davis**
2.	124	**Jimmy Newman**
3.	126	**Wilburn Brothers**
4.	128	**Slim Whitman**
5.	132	**Tommy Overstreet**
6.	134	**Nat Stuckey**
7.	136	**Narvel Felts**
8.	141	**Bob Luman**
9.	144	**Rex Allen, Jr.**
10.	145	**Brenda Lee**
11.	147	**Freddy Weller**

To qualify, artist must rank in the Top 150.

ARTIST'S FIRST HIT IS THEIR BIGGEST HIT

Donna Fargo	Jean Shepard
Red Foley	Connie Smith
George Morgan	Kitty Wells
Marie Osmond	Shelly West
Jeannie C. Riley	Trisha Yearwood

To qualify, an artist's first hit has to have reached #1 and has to be ranked as their biggest hit. The artist must also have a minimum of 20 hits.

ONE-HIT WONDERS

1. **The Davis Sisters**
   ....I Forgot More Than You'll Ever Know (1^8/'53)
2. **Leon Payne**...................... I Love You Because (1^2/'50)
3. **Slim Willet**
   ....Don't Let The Stars (Get In Your Eyes) (1^1/'52)

The above artists' only chart hit reached the #1 position.

CHART FACTS & FEATS

A unique compilation of interesting and unusual Country singles chart accomplishments.

All-Time Top 100 #1 Hits 1944-1997

Top 25 #1 Hits By Decade

Singles Of Longevity

MVPs

Songs With Longest Titles

Songs With Most Charted Versions

Top Country Labels

Country Music Association Awards
    Single of the Year
    Song of the Year

Country Music Hall Of Fame

Christmas Singles 1944-1997

Label Abbreviations

ALL-TIME TOP 100 #1 HITS
1944-1997

PK YR	WKS CHR	WKS T40	WKS T10	WKS @ #1	RANK	TITLE	ARTIST
50	44	44	44	21	1.	I'm Moving On	Hank Snow
47	46	46	41	21	2.	I'll Hold You In My Heart (Till I Can Hold You In My Arms)	Eddy Arnold
55	37	37	34	21	3.	In The Jailhouse Now	Webb Pierce
56	45	45	41	20	4.	Crazy Arms	Ray Price
54	41	41	40	20	5.	I Don't Hurt Anymore	Hank Snow
48	54	54	53	19	6.	Bouquet Of Roses	Eddy Arnold
61	37	37	29	19	7.	Walk On By	Leroy Van Dyke
54	36	36	32	17	8.	Slowly	Webb Pierce
49	28	28	27	17	9.	Slipping Around	Margaret Whiting & Jimmy Wakely
56	27	27	26	17	10.	Heartbreak Hotel	Elvis Presley
49	42	42	40	16	11.	Lovesick Blues	Hank Williams
46	29	29	29	16	12.	Guitar Polka	Al Dexter
63	30	30	24	16	13.	Love's Gonna Live Here	Buck Owens
46	23	23	23	16	14.	New Spanish Two Step	Bob Wills
47	23	23	23	16	15.	Smoke! Smoke! Smoke! (That Cigarette)	Tex Williams
51	31	31	31	15	16.	Slow Poke	Pee Wee King
52	30	30	30	15	17.	The Wild Side Of Life	Hank Thompson
60	36	36	30	14	18.	Please Help Me, I'm Falling	Hank Locklin
60	34	34	29	14	19.	He'll Have To Go	Jim Reeves
52	29	29	29	14	20.	Jambalaya (On The Bayou)	Hank Williams
51	25	25	25	14	21.	The Shot Gun Boogie	"Tennessee" Ernie Ford
46	23	23	23	14	22.	Divorce Me C.O.D.	Merle Travis
47	22	22	22	14	23.	So Round, So Firm, So Fully Packed	Merle Travis
44	30	30	30	13	24.	So Long Pal	Al Dexter
55	32	32	28	13	25.	Love, Love, Love	Webb Pierce
56	30	30	28	13	26.	Singing The Blues	Marty Robbins
44	27	27	27	13	27.	Smoke On The Water	Red Foley
58	34	34	25	13	28.	City Lights	Ray Price
58	29	29	20	13	29.	Alone With You	Faron Young
50	20	20	20	13	30.	Chattanoogie Shoe Shine Boy	Red Foley
53	19	19	19	13	31.	Kaw-Liga	Hank Williams
55	32	32	28	12	32.	I Don't Care	Webb Pierce
51	28	28	28	12	33.	Always Late (With Your Kisses)	Lefty Frizzell
53	27	27	27	12	34.	There Stands The Glass	Webb Pierce
60	34	34	26	12	35.	Alabam	Cowboy Copas
49	31	31	26	12	36.	Don't Rob Another Man's Castle	Eddy Arnold
48	32	32	31	11	37.	One Has My Name (The Other Has My Heart)	Jimmy Wakely
51	27	27	27	11	38.	I Want To Be With You Always	Lefty Frizzell
51	24	24	24	11	39.	I Wanna Play House With You	Eddy Arnold
51	23	23	23	11	40.	There's Been A Change In Me	Eddy Arnold
62	24	24	22	11	41.	Don't Let Me Cross Over	Carl Butler & Pearl
45	20	20	20	11	42.	You Two Timed Me One Time Too Often	Tex Ritter
60	36	36	30	10	43.	Wings Of A Dove	Ferlin Husky
54	29	29	27	10	44.	More And More	Webb Pierce
56	28	28	25	10	45.	Don't Be Cruel / Hound Dog	Elvis Presley
50	32	25	25	10	46.	Why Don't You Love Me	Hank Williams
57	27	27	21	10	47.	Gone	Ferlin Husky
58	23	23	19	10	48.	Ballad Of A Teenage Queen	Johnny Cash
55	21	21	18	10	49.	Sixteen Tons	"Tennessee" Ernie Ford
59	21	21	18	10	50.	The Battle Of New Orleans	Johnny Horton

508

PK YR	WKS CHR	WKS T40	WKS T10	WKS @ #1	RANK	TITLE	ARTIST
61	19	19	18	10	51.	Don't Worry	Marty Robbins
59	19	19	17	10	52.	The Three Bells	The Browns
48	39	39	37	9	53.	Anytime	Eddy Arnold
45	31	31	31	9	54.	Shame On You	Spade Cooley
53	26	26	26	9	55.	Mexican Joe	Jim Reeves
62	26	26	21	9	56.	Wolverton Mountain	Claude King
57	24	24	20	9	57.	Young Love	Sonny James
61	23	23	18	9	58.	Hello Walls	Faron Young
66	25	24	13	9	59.	Almost Persuaded	David Houston
51	33	33	33	8	60.	Let Old Mother Nature Have Her Way	Carl Smith
48	32	32	27	8	61.	Just A Little Lovin' (Will Go A Long, Long Way)	Eddy Arnold
51	27	27	27	8	62.	The Rhumba Boogie	Hank Snow
58	34	34	26	8	63.	Oh Lonesome Me	Don Gibson
53	26	26	26	8	64.	Hey Joe!	Carl Smith
53	26	26	26	8	65.	I Forgot More Than You'll Ever Know	The Davis Sisters
57	26	26	25	8	66.	Four Walls	Jim Reeves
51	25	25	25	8	67.	Hey, Good Lookin'	Hank Williams
52	24	24	24	8	68.	(When You Feel Like You're In Love) Don't Just Stand There	Carl Smith
45	22	22	22	8	69.	At Mail Call Today	Gene Autry
53	22	22	22	8	70.	It's Been So Long	Webb Pierce
50	21	21	21	8	71.	Long Gone Lonesome Blues	Hank Williams
58	24	24	20	8	72.	Guess Things Happen That Way	Johnny Cash
57	22	22	20	8	73.	Wake Up Little Susie	The Everly Brothers
64	28	27	19	8	74.	Once A Day	Connie Smith
62	21	21	14	8	75.	Devil Woman	Marty Robbins
55	32	32	29	7	76.	Loose Talk	Carl Smith
61	32	32	24	7	77.	Tender Years	George Jones
64	26	26	22	7	78.	My Heart Skips A Beat	Buck Owens
59	26	26	22	7	79.	El Paso	Marty Robbins
62	27	27	21	7	80.	Mama Sang A Song	Bill Anderson
57	26	26	21	7	81.	Bye Bye Love	The Everly Brothers
45	21	21	21	7	82.	I'm Losing My Mind Over You	Al Dexter
63	27	27	20	7	83.	Still	Bill Anderson
63	26	26	19	7	84.	Ring Of Fire	Johnny Cash
64	26	24	18	7	85.	I Guess I'm Crazy	Jim Reeves
66	23	21	15	7	86.	There Goes My Everything	Jack Greene
66	19	18	13	7	87.	Waitin' In Your Welfare Line	Buck Owens
56	43	43	39	6	88.	I Walk The Line	Johnny Cash
53	23	23	23	6	89.	A Dear John Letter	Jean Shepard with Ferlin Huskey
53	23	23	23	6	90.	Your Cheatin' Heart	Hank Williams
44	20	20	20	6	91.	I'm Wastin' My Tears On You	Tex Ritter
62	23	23	19	6	92.	She Thinks I Still Care	George Jones
45	19	19	19	6	93.	Oklahoma Hills	Jack Guthrie
64	27	27	18	6	94.	I Don't Care (Just As Long As You Love Me)	Buck Owens
52	18	18	18	6	95.	It Wasn't God Who Made Honky Tonk Angels	Kitty Wells
64	22	22	17	6	96.	Understand Your Man	Johnny Cash
64	25	22	15	6	97.	Dang Me	Roger Miller
59	20	20	15	6	98.	Don't Take Your Guns To Town	Johnny Cash
44	15	15	15	6	99.	Straighten Up And Fly Right	King Cole Trio
66	22	21	14	6	100.	Giddyup Go	Red Sovine

The rankings of the Top 100 #1 Hits are based on the most weeks a record held the No. 1 position. Ties are broken in this order: total weeks in the Top 10, total weeks in the Top 40; and, finally, total weeks charted.

TOP 25 #1 HITS BY DECADE
1944-1949

PK YR	WKS CHR	WKS T40	WKS T10	WKS @ #1	RANK	TITLE	ARTIST
47	46	46	41	21	1.	I'll Hold You In My Heart (Till I Can Hold You In My Arms)	Eddy Arnold
48	54	54	53	19	2.	Bouquet Of Roses	Eddy Arnold
49	28	28	27	17	3.	Slipping Around	Margaret Whiting & Jimmy Wakely
49	42	42	40	16	4.	Lovesick Blues	Hank Williams
46	29	29	29	16	5.	Guitar Polka	Al Dexter
46	23	23	23	16	6.	New Spanish Two Step	Bob Wills
47	23	23	23	16	7.	Smoke! Smoke! Smoke! (That Cigarette)	Tex Williams
46	23	23	23	14	8.	Divorce Me C.O.D.	Merle Travis
47	22	22	22	14	9.	So Round, So Firm, So Fully Packed	Merle Travis
44	30	30	30	13	10.	So Long Pal	Al Dexter
44	27	27	27	13	11.	Smoke On The Water	Red Foley
49	31	31	26	12	12.	Don't Rob Another Man's Castle	Eddy Arnold
48	32	32	31	11	13.	One Has My Name (The Other Has My Heart)	Jimmy Wakely
45	20	20	20	11	14.	You Two Timed Me One Time Too Often	Tex Ritter
48	39	39	37	9	15.	Anytime	Eddy Arnold
45	31	31	31	9	16.	Shame On You	Spade Cooley
48	32	32	27	8	17.	Just A Little Lovin' (Will Go A Long, Long Way)	Eddy Arnold
45	22	22	22	8	18.	At Mail Call Today	Gene Autry
45	21	21	21	7	19.	I'm Losing My Mind Over You	Al Dexter
44	20	20	20	6	20.	I'm Wastin' My Tears On You	Tex Ritter
45	19	19	19	6	21.	Oklahoma Hills	Jack Guthrie
44	15	15	15	6	22.	Straighten Up And Fly Right	King Cole Trio
47	38	38	38	5	23.	It's A Sin	Eddy Arnold
49	28	28	26	5	24.	I Love You So Much It Hurts	Jimmy Wakely
46	13	13	13	5	25.	Wine, Women And Song	Al Dexter

1950-1959

PK YR	WKS CHR	WKS T40	WKS T10	WKS @ #1	RANK	TITLE	ARTIST
50	44	44	44	21	1.	I'm Moving On	Hank Snow
55	37	37	34	21	2.	In The Jailhouse Now	Webb Pierce
56	45	45	41	20	3.	Crazy Arms	Ray Price
54	41	41	40	20	4.	I Don't Hurt Anymore	Hank Snow
54	36	36	32	17	5.	Slowly	Webb Pierce
56	27	27	26	17	6.	Heartbreak Hotel	Elvis Presley
51	31	31	31	15	7.	Slow Poke	Pee Wee King
52	30	30	30	15	8.	The Wild Side Of Life	Hank Thompson
52	29	29	29	14	9.	Jambalaya (On The Bayou)	Hank Williams
51	25	25	25	14	10.	The Shot Gun Boogie	"Tennessee" Ernie Ford
55	32	32	28	13	11.	Love, Love, Love	Webb Pierce
56	30	30	28	13	12.	Singing The Blues	Marty Robbins
58	34	34	25	13	13.	City Lights	Ray Price
58	29	29	20	13	14.	Alone With You	Faron Young
50	20	20	20	13	15.	Chattanoogie Shoe Shine Boy	Red Foley
53	19	19	19	13	16.	Kaw-Liga	Hank Williams
55	32	32	28	12	17.	I Don't Care	Webb Pierce
51	28	28	28	12	18.	Always Late (With Your Kisses)	Lefty Frizzell
53	27	27	27	12	19.	There Stands The Glass	Webb Pierce
51	27	27	27	11	20.	I Want To Be With You Always	Lefty Frizzell
51	24	24	24	11	21.	I Wanna Play House With You	Eddy Arnold
51	23	23	23	11	22.	There's Been A Change In Me	Eddy Arnold
54	29	29	27	10	23.	More And More	Webb Pierce
56	28	28	25	10	24.	Don't Be Cruel / Hound Dog	Elvis Presley
50	25	25	25	10	25.	Why Don't You Love Me	Hank Williams

TOP 25 #1 HITS BY DECADE
1960-1969

PK YR	WKS CHR	WKS T40	WKS T10	WKS @ #1	RANK	TITLE	ARTIST
61	37	37	29	19	1.	Walk On By	Leroy Van Dyke
63	30	30	24	16	2.	Love's Gonna Live Here	Buck Owens
60	36	36	30	14	3.	Please Help Me, I'm Falling	Hank Locklin
60	34	34	29	14	4.	He'll Have To Go	Jim Reeves
60	34	34	26	12	5.	Alabam	Cowboy Copas
62	24	24	22	11	6.	Don't Let Me Cross Over	Carl Butler & Pearl
60	36	36	30	10	7.	Wings Of A Dove	Ferlin Husky
61	19	19	18	10	8.	Don't Worry	Marty Robbins
62	26	26	21	9	9.	Wolverton Mountain	Claude King
61	23	23	18	9	10.	Hello Walls	Faron Young
66	25	24	13	9	11.	Almost Persuaded	David Houston
64	28	27	19	8	12.	Once A Day	Connie Smith
62	21	21	14	8	13.	Devil Woman	Marty Robbins
61	32	32	24	7	14.	Tender Years	George Jones
64	26	26	22	7	15.	My Heart Skips A Beat	Buck Owens
62	27	27	21	7	16.	Mama Sang A Song	Bill Anderson
63	27	27	20	7	17.	Still	Bill Anderson
63	26	26	19	7	18.	Ring Of Fire	Johnny Cash
64	26	24	18	7	19.	I Guess I'm Crazy	Jim Reeves
66	23	21	15	7	20.	There Goes My Everything	Jack Greene
66	19	18	13	7	21.	Waitin' In Your Welfare Line	Buck Owens
62	23	23	19	6	22.	She Thinks I Still Care	George Jones
64	27	27	18	6	23.	I Don't Care (Just As Long As You Love Me)	Buck Owens
64	22	22	17	6	24.	Understand Your Man	Johnny Cash
64	25	22	15	6	25.	Dang Me	Roger Miller

1970-1979

PK YR	WKS CHR	WKS T40	WKS T10	WKS @ #1	RANK	TITLE	ARTIST
72	19	18	12	6	1.	My Hang-Up Is You	Freddie Hart
77	18	14	10	6	2.	Luckenbach, Texas (Back to the Basics of Love)	Waylon Jennings
75	15	13	8	6	3.	Convoy	C.W. McCall
71	19	18	13	5	4.	Kiss An Angel Good Mornin'	Charley Pride
70	20	19	12	5	5.	Rose Garden	Lynn Anderson
77	19	14	10	5	6.	Here You Come Again	Dolly Parton
71	15	13	10	5	7.	When You're Hot, You're Hot	Jerry Reed
70	20	18	10	4	8.	Hello Darlin'	Conway Twitty
70	17	16	10	4	9.	Baby, Baby (I Know You're A Lady)	David Houston
71	16	15	10	4	10.	Empty Arms	Sonny James
71	16	14	9	4	11.	I'm Just Me	Charley Pride
70	15	14	9	4	12.	Don't Keep Me Hangin' On	Sonny James
77	18	15	8	4	13.	Don't It Make My Brown Eyes Blue	Crystal Gayle
78	16	12	8	4	14.	Mammas Don't Let Your Babies Grow Up To Be Cowboys	Waylon & Willie
73	17	14	7	4	15.	If We Make It Through December	Merle Haggard
77	20	13	7	4	16.	Heaven's Just A Sin Away	The Kendalls
70	14	13	7	4	17.	It's Just A Matter Of Time	Sonny James
71	24	22	13	3	18.	Easy Loving	Freddie Hart
71	20	18	12	3	19.	Help Me Make It Through The Night	Sammy Smith
71	19	17	12	3	20.	I Won't Mention It Again	Ray Price
72	23	17	10	3	21.	The Happiest Girl In The Whole U.S.A.	Donna Fargo
73	19	16	10	3	22.	You've Never Been This Far Before	Conway Twitty
72	16	15	10	3	23.	Carolyn	Merle Haggard
70	16	14	9	3	24.	Endlessly	Sonny James
70	16	14	9	3	25.	He Loves Me All The Way	Tammy Wynette

TOP 25 #1 HITS BY DECADE
1980-1989

PK YR	WKS CHR	WKS T40	WKS T10	WKS @ #1	RANK	TITLE	ARTIST
80	15	9	8	3	1.	Coward Of The County	Kenny Rogers
80	15	13	7	3	2.	My Heart	Ronnie Milsap
80	14	10	7	3	3.	Lookin' For Love	Johnny Lee
87	22	13	6	3	4.	Forever And Ever, Amen	Randy Travis
85	22	14	8	2	5.	Have Mercy	The Judds
83	23	15	7	2	6.	Islands In The Stream	Kenny Rogers with Dolly Parton
83	22	15	7	2	7.	Houston (Means I'm One Day Closer To You)	Larry Gatlin & The Gatlin Brothers
84	22	15	7	2	8.	Why Not Me	The Judds
85	23	14	7	2	9.	Lost In The Fifties Tonight (In The Still Of The Night)	Ronnie Milsap
88	22	14	7	2	10.	When You Say Nothing At All	Keith Whitley
86	19	14	7	2	11.	Mind Your Own Business	Hank Williams, Jr.
84	20	13	7	2	12.	To All The Girls I've Loved Before	Julio Iglesias & Willie Nelson
80	16	12	7	2	13.	I Believe In You	Don Williams
80	14	10	7	2	14.	My Heroes Have Always Been Cowboys	Willie Nelson
89	26	24	6	2	15.	A Woman In Love	Ronnie Milsap
88	21	15	6	2	16.	I'll Leave This World Loving You	Ricky Van Shelton
82	21	15	6	2	17.	Always On My Mind	Willie Nelson
87	23	14	6	2	18.	Somewhere Tonight	Highway 101
89	22	14	6	2	19.	I'm No Stranger To The Rain	Keith Whitley
88	20	14	6	2	20.	Eighteen Wheels And A Dozen Roses	Kathy Mattea
80	16	13	6	2	21.	One In A Million	Johnny Lee
81	16	11	6	2	22.	Love In The First Degree	Alabama
81	15	11	6	2	23.	(There's) No Gettin' Over Me	Ronnie Milsap
81	15	11	6	2	24.	Never Been So Loved (In All My Life)	Charley Pride
81	15	10	6	2	25.	I Don't Need You	Kenny Rogers

1990-1997

PK YR	WKS CHR	WKS T40	WKS T10	WKS @ #1	RANK	TITLE	ARTIST
97	20	20	13	6	1.	It's Your Love	Tim McGraw & Faith Hill
90	21	20	11	5	2.	Love Without End, Amen	George Strait
97	20	20	10	5	3.	One Night At A Time	George Strait
90	20	19	10	5	4.	I've Come To Expect It From You	George Strait
97	20	20	9	5	5.	Love Gets Me Every Time	Shania Twain
95	20	19	9	5	6.	I Like It, I Love It	Tim McGraw
92	20	16	9	5	7.	Achy Breaky Heart	Billy Ray Cyrus
95	20	18	11	4	8.	Check Yes Or No	George Strait
90	20	19	10	4	9.	Jukebox In My Mind	Alabama
97	21	16	10	4	10.	Carrying Your Love With Me	George Strait
90	26	22	9	4	11.	Hard Rock Bottom Of Your Heart	Randy Travis
90	20	19	9	4	12.	Friends In Low Places	Garth Brooks
97	22	16	9	4	13.	Nobody Knows	Kevin Sharp
93	20	16	9	4	14.	Chattahoochee	Alan Jackson
92	20	19	8	4	15.	What She's Doing Now	Garth Brooks
94	20	19	8	4	16.	Pickup Man	Joe Diffie
94	20	18	8	4	17.	I Swear	John Michael Montgomery
92	20	17	8	4	18.	No One Else On Earth	Wynonna
92	20	16	8	4	19.	Boot Scootin' Boogie	Brooks & Dunn
94	20	18	7	4	20.	Wink	Neal McCoy
94	20	17	7	4	21.	Wild One	Faith Hill
96	20	20	10	3	22.	My Maria	Brooks & Dunn
96	20	19	10	3	23.	Little Bitty	Alan Jackson
92	20	18	10	3	24.	Don't Let Our Love Start Slippin' Away	Vince Gill
92	20	17	10	3	25.	Love, Me	Collin Raye

SINGLES OF LONGEVITY

Singles with 32 or more total weeks charted.

PK YR	PK WKS	PK POS	WKS CHR	RANK	TITLE	ARTIST
48	19	1	54	1.	Bouquet Of Roses	Eddy Arnold
57	4	1	52	2.	Fraulein	Bobby Helms
47	21	1	46	3.	I'll Hold You In My Heart (Till I Can Hold You In My Arms)	Eddy Arnold
61	2	1	46*	4.	I Fall To Pieces	Patsy Cline
51	1	1	46	5.	Cold, Cold Heart	Hank Williams
56	20	1	45	6.	Crazy Arms	Ray Price
50	21	1	44	7.	I'm Moving On	Hank Snow
56	6	1	43	8.	I Walk The Line	Johnny Cash
49	16	1	42	9.	Lovesick Blues	Hank Williams
98	6	1	42	10.	Just To See You Smile	Tim McGraw
54	20	1	41	11.	I Don't Hurt Anymore	Hank Snow
54	1	1	41	12.	One By One	Kitty Wells & Red Foley
49	1	1	40	13.	Tennessee Saturday Night	Red Foley
59	1	2	40	14.	Heartaches By The Number	Ray Price
48	9	1	39	15.	Anytime	Eddy Arnold
56	5	1	39	16.	I Forgot To Remember To Forget	Elvis Presley
48	2	3	39*	17.	Tennessee Waltz	Pee Wee King
57	2	4	39	18.	Geisha Girl	Hank Locklin
47	5	1	38	19.	It's A Sin	Eddy Arnold
48	2	2	38	20.	Humpty Dumpty Heart	Hank Thompson
55	21	1	37	21.	In The Jailhouse Now	Webb Pierce
61	19	1	37	22.	Walk On By	Leroy Van Dyke
57	4	1	37	23.	My Shoes Keep Walking Back To You	Ray Price
54	1	1	37	24.	I Really Don't Want To Know	Eddy Arnold
54	17	1	36	25.	Slowly	Webb Pierce
60	14	1	36	26.	Please Help Me, I'm Falling	Hank Locklin
60	10	1	36	27.	Wings Of A Dove	Ferlin Husky
50	4	1	36	28.	I'll Sail My Ship Alone	Moon Mullican
63	1	1	36	29.	Talk Back Trembling Lips	Ernest Ashworth
58	1	9	36	30.	Is It Wrong (For Loving You)	Warner Mack
86	1	1	35*	31.	On The Other Hand	Randy Travis
58	2	5	35	32.	Send Me The Pillow You Dream On	Hank Locklin
60	14	1	34	33.	He'll Have To Go	Jim Reeves
58	13	1	34	34.	City Lights	Ray Price
60	12	1	34	35.	Alabam	Cowboy Copas
58	8	1	34	36.	Oh Lonesome Me	Don Gibson
61	1	2	34	37.	The Window Up Above	George Jones
56	1	3	34	38.	Searching (For Someone Like You)	Kitty Wells
51	8	1	33	39.	Let Old Mother Nature Have Her Way	Carl Smith
55	4	1	33	40.	A Satisfied Mind	Porter Wagoner
56	1	2	33	41.	Sweet Dreams	Faron Young
55	13	1	32	42.	Love, Love, Love	Webb Pierce
55	12	1	32	43.	I Don't Care	Webb Pierce
48	11	1	32	44.	One Has My Name (The Other Has My Heart)	Jimmy Wakely
50	10	1	32*	45.	Why Don't You Love Me	Hank Williams
48	8	1	32	46.	Just A Little Lovin' (Will Go A Long, Long Way)	Eddy Arnold
55	7	1	32	47.	Loose Talk	Carl Smith
61	7	1	32	48.	Tender Years	George Jones
59	4	1	32	49.	Country Girl	Faron Young
51	3	1	32	50.	I Love You A Thousand Ways	Lefty Frizzell
53	3	1	32	51.	Let Me Be The One	Hank Locklin
50	2	1	32	52.	I Love You Because	Leon Payne
96	1	5	32	53.	It's Midnight Cinderella	Garth Brooks
98	1	6	32	54.	From This Moment On	Shania Twain With Bryan White

* Singles which charted more than once. To qualify, the recharted hit must be the original vocal and not a re-recording.

MVP'S (Most Valuable Platters)

Following is a list of all records in this book valued at $40 or more.

Year	Value	Title	Artist...Label & Number
55	$1200	1. **Baby Let's Play House / I'm Left, You're Right, She's Gone**	*Elvis Presley*...Sun 217
55	$1000	2. **I Forgot To Remember To Forget / Mystery Train**	*Elvis Presley*...Sun 223
60	$500	3. **I'm A Honky Tonk Girl**	*Loretta Lynn*...Zero 107
56	$100	4. **Love Me**	*Elvis Presley*...RCA Victor EPA-992
57	$100	5. **Mean Woman Blues**	*Elvis Presley*...RCA Victor EPA 2-1515
56	$75	6. **Without Your Love**	*Bobby Lord*...Columbia 21539
50	$75	7. **Hot Rod Race**	*Arkie Shibley*...Gilt-Edge 5021
47	$75	8. **Move It On Over**	*Hank Williams*...MGM 10033
45	$60	9. **Each Minute Seems A Million Years**	*Eddy Arnold*...Bluebird 33-0527
56	$60	10. **Dixie Fried / I'm Sorry, I'm Not Sorry**	*Carl Perkins*...Sun 249
44	$50	11. **Mexico Joe**	*Ivie Anderson*...Exclusive 3113
48	$50	12. **'Fore Day In The Morning**	*Roy Brown*...DeLuxe 3198
49	$50	13. **Sittin' On The Doorstep**	*Woody Carter*...Macy's 100
56	$50	14. **Blue Suede Shoes**	*Carl Perkins*...Sun 234
56	$50	15. **Boppin' The Blues**	*Carl Perkins*...Sun 243
57	$50	16. **Your True Love**	*Carl Perkins*...Sun 261
61	$50	17. **Crazy Bullfrog**	*Lewis Pruitt*...Decca 31201
48	$50	18. **Honky Tonkin'**	*Hank Williams*...MGM 10171
53	$40	19. **Tennessee Wig Walk**	*Bonnie Lou*...King 1237
53	$40	20. **Seven Lonely Days**	*Bonnie Lou*...King 1192
56	$40	21. **So Doggone Lonesome / Folsom Prison Blues**	*Johnny Cash*...Sun 232
55	$40	22. **Cry! Cry! Cry!**	*Johnny Cash*...Sun 221
47	$40	23. **Jole Blon**	*Harry Choates*...Modern Mountain 511
56	$40	24. **The Fool**	*Sanford Clark*...Dot 15481
45	$40	25. **There's A New Moon Over My Shoulder**	*Jimmie Davis*...Decca 6105
44	$40	26. **Is It Too Late Now / There's A Chill On The Hill Tonight**	*Jimmie Davis*...Decca 6100
46	$40	27. **Grievin' My Heart Out For You**	*Jimmie Davis*...Decca 18756
48	$40	28. **One Has My Name (The Other Has My Heart)**	*Eddie Dean*...Crystal 132
44	$40	29. **I Learned A Lesson, I'll Never Forget**	*5 Red Caps*...Beacon 7120
53	$40	30. **Crying In The Chapel**	*Darrell Glenn*...Valley 105
54	$40	31. **You Can't Have My Love**	*Wanda Jackson & Billy Gray*...Decca 29140
58	$40	32. **Pink Pedal Pushers**	*Carl Perkins*...Columbia 41131
55	$40	33. **That's All Right**	*Marty Robbins*...Columbia 21351
55	$40	34. **Maybelline**	*Marty Robbins*...Columbia 21446
45	$40	35. **Triflin' Gal**	*Walt Shrum*...Coast 2010
56	$40	36. **Be-Bop-A-Lula**	*Gene Vincent*...Capitol 3450
44	$40	37. **Red Blues**	*Cootie Williams*...Hit 7084
50	$40	38. **Why Don't You Love Me**	*Hank Williams*...MGM K10696
50	$40	39. **Long Gone Lonesome Blues / My Son Calls Another Man Daddy**	*Hank Williams*...MGM K10645
51	$40	40. **Cold, Cold Heart / Dear John**	*Hank Williams*...MGM K10904
50	$40	41. **Moanin' The Blues / Nobody's Lonesome For Me**	*Hank Williams*...MGM K10832
49	$40	42. **Wedding Bells**	*Hank Williams*...MGM 10401
51	$40	43. **I Can't Help It (If I'm Still In Love With You) / Howlin' At The Moon**	*Hank Williams*...MGM K10961
50	$40	44. **They'll Never Take Her Love From Me / Why Should We Try Anymore**	*Hank Williams*...MGM K10760
50	$40	45. **I Just Don't Like This Kind Of Livin'**	*Hank Williams*...MGM 10609
48	$40	46. **I'm A Long Gone Daddy**	*Hank Williams*...MGM 10212
49	$40	47. **Never Again (Will I Knock On Your Door)**	*Hank Williams*...MGM 10352
49	$40	48. **Mansion On The Hill**	*Hank Williams*...MGM 10328

SONGS WITH LONGEST TITLES

	# of Char.		Artist
1.	78	She Wakes Me With A Kiss Every Morning (And She Loves Me To Sleep Every Night)	Nat Stuckey
2.	76	It's For God, And Country, And You Mom (That's Why I'm Fighting In Viet Nam)	Ernest Tubb
3.	70	I Wouldn't Live in New york City (If They Gave Me The Whole Dang Town)	Buck Owens
4.	69	If You Think I'm Crazy Now (You Should Have Seen Me When I Was A Kid)	Bobby Bare
5.	67	If You're Gonna Play In Texas (You Gotta Have A Fiddle In The Band)	Alabama
6.	67	Lyin', Cheatin', Woman Chasin', Honky Tonkin', Whiskey Drinkin' You	Loretta Lynn
7.	66	I'm Just An Old Chuck Of Coal (But I'm Gonna Be A Diamond Someday)	John Anderson
8.	66	Don't Wipe The Tears That You Cry For Him (On My Good White Shirt)	Tommy Collins
9.	66	It's The Bible Against The Bottle (In The Battle For Daddy's Soul)	Earl Thomas Conley
10.	65	There Won't Be No Country Music (There Won't Be No Rock 'N' Roll)	C.W. McCall

SONGS WITH MOST CHARTED VERSIONS

	Total Versions		Songwriter(s)
1.	8	I Love You Because	Leon Payne
2.	7	Making Believe	Jimmy Work
3.	7	Slipping Around	Floyd Tillman
4.	7	Sweet Dreams	Don Gibson
5.	7	Why Baby Why	Luther Dixon/Larry Harrison
6.	6	Candy Kisses	George Morgan
7.	6	I Fall To Pieces	Hank Cochran/Harlan Howard
8.	6	Lovesick Blues	Hank Williams
9.	6	My Elusive Dreams	Curly Putman/Billy Sherrill
10.	6	Oh Lonesome Me	Don Gibson
11.	6	Satisfied Mind	Red Hayes/Jack Rhodes
12.	6	Tennessee Waltz	Redd Stewart/Pee Wee King
13.	6	Wild Side Of Life	William Warren/Arlie A. Carter
14.	6	You're The Reason	Bobby Edwards/Mildred Imes/Fred Henley/Terry Fell

TOP COUNTRY LABELS

		Total Hits			Total Hits
1.	RCA	2,190	21.	Reprise	97
2.	Columbia	1,546	22.	Soundwaves	89
3.	Capitol	1,420	23.	BNA	87
4.	MCA	1,181	24.	Sun	71
5.	Epic	888	25.	Polydor	67
6.	Decca	801	26.	Starday	65
7.	Mercury	772	27.	Chart	64
8.	Warner	771	28.	Giant	61
9.	Curb	498	29.	Asylum	56
10.	Dot	320	30.	King	55
11.	United Artists	319	31.	Imperial	53
12.	ABC	315	32.	Step One	52
13.	MGM	305	33.	MTM	51
14.	Elektra	234	34.	GRT	49
15.	Liberty	207	35.	Ovation	48
16.	Arista	192	36.	Republic	48
17.	Atlantic	153	37.	Kapp	47
18.	Hickory	140	38.	Playboy	46
19.	Monument	132	39.	Evergreen	45
20.	Door Knob	100	40.	Mega	44

COUNTRY MUSIC ASSOCIATION AWARDS

Single of the Year — Song of the Year

SINGLE OF THE YEAR Title...Artist(s)	YEAR	SONG OF THE YEAR Title...Songwriter(s)
There Goes My Everything...*Jack Greene*	1967	There Goes My Everything...*Dallas Frazier*
Harper Valley P.T.A....*Jeannie C. Riley*	1968	Honey...*Bobby Russell*
A Boy Named Sue...*Johnny Cash*	1969	The Carroll County Accident...*Bob Ferguson*
Okie From Muskogee...*Merle Haggard*	1970	Sunday Morning Coming Down...*Kris Kristofferson*
Help Me Make It Through The Night...*Sammi Smith*	1971	Easy Loving...*Freddie Hart*
The Happiest Girl In The Whole U.S.A....*Donna Fargo*	1972	Easy Loving...*Freddie Hart*
Behind Closed Doors...*Charlie Rich*	1973	Behind Closed Doors...*Kenny O'Dell*
Country Bumpkin...*Cal Smith*	1974	Country Bumpkin...*Don Wayne*
Before The Next Teardrop Falls...*Freddy Fender*	1975	Back Home Again...*John Denver*
Good Hearted Woman... *Waylon Jennings & Willie Nelson*	1976	Rhinestone Cowboy...*Larry Weiss*
Lucille...*Kenny Rogers*	1977	Lucille...*Roger Bowling & Hal Bynum*
Heaven's Just A Sin Away...*The Kendalls*	1978	Don't It Make My Brown Eyes Blue...*Richard Leigh*
The Devil Went Down To Georgia... *Charlie Daniels Band*	1979	The Gambler...*Don Schlitz*
He Stopped Loving Her Today...*George Jones*	1980	He Stopped Loving Her Today... *Bobby Braddock & Curly Putman*
Elvira...*Oak Ridge Boys*	1981	He Stopped Loving Her Today... *Bobby Braddock & Curly Putman*
Always On My Mind...*Willie Nelson*	1982	Always On My Mind... *Johnny Christopher, Wayne Carson & Mark James*
Swingin'...*John Anderson*	1983	Always On My Mind... *Johnny Christopher, Wayne Carson & Mark James*
A Little Good News...*Anne Murray*	1984	The Wind Beneath My Wings... *Larry Henley & Jeff Silbar*
Why Not Me...*The Judds*	1985	God Bless The USA...*Lee Greenwood*
Bop...*Dan Seals*	1986	On The Other Hand...*Paul Overstreet & Don Schlitz*
Forever And Ever, Amen...*Randy Travis*	1987	Forever And Ever, Amen... *Paul Overstreet & Don Schlitz*
Eighteen Wheels And A Dozen Roses...*Kathy Mattea*	1988	80's Ladies...*K.T. Oslin*
I'm No Stranger To The Rain...*Keith Whitley*	1989	Chiseled In Stone...*Max D. Barnes & Vern Gosdin*
When I Call Your Name...*Vince Gill*	1990	Where've You Been...*Jon Vezner & Don Henry*
Friends In Low Places...*Garth Brooks*	1991	When I Call Your Name...*Vince Gill & Tim DuBois*
Achy Breaky Heart...*Billy Ray Cyrus*	1992	Look At Us...*Vince Gill & Max D. Barnes*
Chattahoochee...*Alan Jackson*	1993	I Still Believe In You...*Vince Gill & John Barlow Jarvis*
I Swear...*John Michael Montgomery*	1994	Chattahoochee...*Alan Jackson & Jim McBride*
When You Say Nothing At All... *Alison Krauss & Union Station*	1995	Independence Day...*Gretchen Peters*
Check Yes Or No...*George Strait*	1996	Go Rest High On That Mountain...*Vince Gill*
Strawberry Wine...*Deana Carter*	1997	Strawberry Wine...*Matraca Berg & Gary Harrison*
Holes In The Floor Of Heaven...*Steve Wariner*	1998	Holes In The Floor Of Heaven... *Billy Kirsch & Steve Wariner*

COUNTRY MUSIC HALL OF FAME

YEAR	INDUCTEE(S)	YEAR	INDUCTEE(S)
1961	Jimmie Rodgers Fred Rose Hank Williams	1980	Johnny Cash Connie B. Gay Original Sons of the Pioneers
1962	Roy Acuff	1981	Vernon Dalhart Grant Turner
1963	(elections held but no candidate received enough votes)	1982	Lefty Frizzell Roy Horton Marty Robbins
1964	Tex Ritter	1983	"Little" Jimmy Dickens
1965	Ernest Tubb	1984	Ralph Peer Floyd Tillman
1966	Eddy Arnold James R. Denny George D. Hay Uncle Dave Macon	1985	Lester Flatt & Earl Scruggs
1967	Red Foley J.L. (Joe) Frank Jim Reeves Stephen H. Sholes	1986	Whitey Ford (The Duke Of Paducah) Wesley H. Rose
1968	Bob Wills	1987	Rod Brasfield
1969	Gene Autry	1988	Loretta Lynn Roy Rogers
1970	Original Carter Family (A.P., Maybelle, Sara) Bill Monroe	1989	Jack Stapp Cliffie Stone Hank Thompson
1971	Arthur Edward Satherley	1990	"Tennessee" Ernie Ford
1972	Jimmie Davis	1991	Boudleaux & Felice Bryant
1973	Chet Atkins Patsy Cline	1992	George Jones Frances Preston
1974	Owen Bradley Frank "Pee Wee" King	1993	Willie Nelson
1975	Minnie Pearl	1994	Merle Haggard
1976	Paul Cohen Kitty Wells	1995	Roger Miller Jo Walker-Meador
1977	Merle Travis	1996	Patsy Montana Buck Owens Ray Price
1978	Grandpa Jones	1997	Harlan Howard Brenda Lee Cindy Walker
1979	Hubert Long Hank Snow	1998	George Morgan Elvis Presley E.W. "Bud" Wendell Tammy Wynette

Titles in bold type made the Top 10; the peak position/peak year is shown below each title. The complete chart data for each of these songs may be found in the Artist Section.

ALABAMA
1. Christmas In Dixie
   #35/'82; #47/'97
2. Angels Among Us
   #51/'93; #28/'94
3. The Blessings
   #72/'96

ALLAN, Gary
Please Come Home For Christmas
#70/'96

ANDERSON, John
Christmas Time
#57/'94

ARNOLD, Eddy
1. **Will Santy Come To Shanty Town /**
   #5/'49
2. **C-H-R-I-S-T-M-A-S**
   #7/'49
3. Christmas Can't Be Far Away
   #12/'54

AUTRY, Gene
1. **Here Comes Santa Claus (Down Santa Claus Lane)**
   #5/'47; #4/'48; #8/'49
2. **Rudolph, The Red-Nosed Reindeer**
   #1(1)/'49; #5/'50
3. **Frosty The Snow Man**
   #4/'50

BELLAMY BROTHERS
It's So Close To Christmas (And I'm So Far From Home)
#62/'81

BERRY, John
O Holy Night
#55/'95; #63/'97

BLACK, Clint
1. Til' Santa's Gone (Milk And Cookies)
   #58/'95; #65/'96; #40/'97
2. The Kid
   #71/'95

BLACKHAWK
We Three Kings (Star Of Wonder)
#75/'97

BOYD, Jimmy
I Saw Mommy Kissing Santa Claus
#7/'52

BROOKS, Garth
1. The Old Man's Back In Town
   #48/'92; #59/'97
2. White Christmas
   #70/'94
3. Santa Looked A Lot Like Daddy
   #56/'97

BROWN, Jim Ed/Helen Cornelius
Fall Softly Snow
#91/'77

CARSON, Jeff
Santa Got Lost In Texas
#70/'95

CARTER, Carlene
Rockin' Little Christmas
#66/'94

CASH, Johnny
The Little Drummer Boy
#24/'59

CHESNUTT, Mark
What Child Is This
#75/'96

DENVER, John
Please, Daddy
#69/'73

DIFFIE, Joe
Leroy The Redneck Reindeer
#33/'95; #46/'96; #54/'97

ELMO & PATSY
Grandma Got Run Over By A Reindeer
#92/'83; #64/'97

EWING, Skip
Christmas Carol
#68/'95; #60/'97

FOXWORTHY, Jeff
1. Redneck 12 Days Of Christmas
   #18/'95; #39/'96; #39/'97
2. 'Twas The Night After Christmas
   #67/'96

GILL, Vince
1. Have Yourself A Merry Little Christmas
   #52/'93; #54/'94; #64/'97
2. It Won't Be The Same This Year
   #74/'94

HAGGARD, Merle
If We Make It Through December
#1(4)/'73

HARRIS, Emmylou
Light Of The Stable
#99/'75

HELMS, Bobby
Jingle Bell Rock
#13/'57; #60/'96

JACKSON, Alan
1. I Only Want You For Christmas
   #41/'91; #48/'95; #48/'97
2. Honky Tonk Christmas
   #53/'93; #59/'94
3. Rudolph The Red-Nosed Reindeer
   #56/'96
4. A Holly Jolly Christmas
   #51/'97

JUDDS, The
Silver Bells
#68/'97

KEITH, Toby
Santa I'm Right Here
#50/'95

KERSHAW, Sammy
Christmas Time's A Comin'
#50/'94; #53/'97

LEE, Brenda
Rockin' Around The Christmas Tree
#62/'97

LONESTAR
I'll Be Home For Christmas
#75/'96

LUMAN, Bob
A Christmas Tribute
#92/'77

MANDRELL, Louise/R.C. Bannon
Christmas Is Just A Song For Us
This Year
#35/'82

McBRIDE, Martina
O Holy Night
#74/'96; #67/'97

McENTIRE, Reba
The Christmas Song (Chestnuts
Roasting On An Open Fire)
#63/'96

MORGAN, Lorrie
1. My Favorite Things
#64/'93
2. Sleigh Ride
#67/'95; #64/'96

MULLINS, Dee
Remember Bethlehem
#71/'70

NITTY GRITTY DIRT BAND
Colorado Christmas
#93/'83

NORWOOD, Daron
The Working Elf Blues
#75/'94

PARNELL, Lee Roy
Please Come Home For
Christmas
#71/'96

PARTON, Dolly
1. **Hard Candy Christmas**
#8/'82; #73/'97
2. The Greatest Gift Of All
Kenny Rogers & Dolly Parton
#53/'84

PRESLEY, Elvis
Blue Christmas
#55/'97

RICOCHET
Let It Snow Let It Snow Let It
Snow
#43/'96; #44/'97

RIMES, LeAnn
Put A Little Holiday In Your Heart
#51/'96; #71/'97

RITTER, Tex
**Christmas Carols By The Old
Corral**
#2(1)/'45

ROGERS, Kenny
1. The Greatest Gift Of All
Kenny Rogers & Dolly Parton
#53/'84
2. Mary, Did You Know
Kenny Rogers with Wynonna
#55/'96

SAWYER BROWN
It Wasn't His Child
#51/'88

STRAIT, George
1. Santa Claus Is Coming To Town
#73/'95; #69/'97
2. Merry Christmas Strait To You
#58/'97

TRACTORS, The
1. The Santa Claus Boogie
#41/'94; #63/'95
2. Santa Claus Is Comin' (In A
Boogie Woogie Choo Choo
Train)
#43/'95; #65/'97

TUBB, Ernest
1. **Blue Christmas /**
#1(1)/'49; #9/'50; #5/'51
2. **White Christmas**
#7/'49

VANCE, Vince, & The Valiants
All I Want For Christmas Is You
#55/'93; #52/'94; #52/'95;
#49/'96; #43/'97

WYNONNA
1. Let's Make A Baby King
#61/'93
2. Mary, Did You Know
Kenny Rogers with Wynonna
#55/'96

YEARWOOD, Trisha
It Wasn't His Child
#60/'94

YOAKAM, Dwight
Santa Claus Is Back In Town
#60/'97

LABEL ABBREVIATIONS

ABC-Para.	ABC-Paramount
Air Int'l.	Air International
Amer. Country	American Country
Amer. Spotlite..........	American Spotlite
America Sm. or America/Sm.	
...... America Smash or America/Smash	
Artists Of Am.	Artists Of America
Associated Art.	Associated Artists
Atlantic Amer.	Atlantic America
Bakersfield I. ..Bakersfield International	
Capitol Amer.	Capitol Americana
Cascade Mt.	Cascade Mountain
Cleveland Int'l ..	Cleveland International
Country Int'l.	Country International
Country Show.	
....	Country Showcase America
Curb/EMI Amer.	Curb/EMI America
Eagle Int'l.	Eagle International
Epic Sound.	Epic Soundtrax
First Generat.	First Generation
Grind. Switch	Grinder's Switch
Jack O'Diam.	Jack O'Diamonds
Louisiana Hay.	Louisiana Hayride
Memory Mach.	Memory Machine
Nashville Amer.	Nashville America
Pacific Chall.	Pacific Challenger
RCA V.	RCA Victor
Southern Bis.	Southern Biscuit
SSS Int'l.	SSS International
Traveler Ent.	Traveler Enterprises
Westexas Amer.	Westexas America

#1 HITS

This section lists, in chronological order, all 1,340 songs which hit #1 on *Billboard's* Country singles charts from 1944 through 1997.

From May 15, 1948 through October 13, 1958, when *Billboard* published more than one weekly Country singles chart, the chart designation and #1 weeks on each chart are listed beneath the record title. The chart designations are:

> BS: Best Sellers
> JY: Jockeys
> JB: Juke Box

The date shown is the earliest date that a record hit #1 on any of the Country singles charts. The weeks column lists the total weeks at #1, from whichever chart it achieved its highest total. This total is not a combined total from the various Country singles charts.

Because of the multiple charts used for this research, some dates are duplicated, as certain #1 hits may have peaked on the same week on different charts. *Billboard* also showed ties at #1 on some of these charts; therefore, the total weeks for each year may calculate out to more than 52.

Billboard has not published an issue for the last week of the year since 1976. For the years 1976 through 1991, *Billboard* considered the charts listed in the last published issue of the year to be "frozen" and all chart positions remained the same for the unpublished week. This frozen chart data is included in our tabulations. Since 1992, *Billboard* has compiled a Country singles chart for the last week of the year, even though an issue is not published. This chart is only available through *Billboard's* computerized information network (BIN) or by mail. Our tabulations include this unpublished chart data.

See the introduction pages of this book for more details on researching the Country singles charts.

> **DATE:** Date single first peaked at the #1 position
> **WKS:** Total weeks single held the #1 position
> ↕: Indicates single hit #1, dropped down, and then returned to the #1 spot

> The top hit of each year is boxed out for quick reference. The top hit is determined by most weeks at the #1 position, followed by total weeks in the Top 10, Top 40, and total weeks charted.

#1 HITS

1944

	DATE	WKS	
1.	1/8	5↕	**Pistol Packin' Mama** *Bing Crosby & the Andrews Sisters*
2.	2/5	3	**Pistol Packin' Mama** *Al Dexter*
3.	2/26	3↕	**Ration Blues** *Louis Jordan*
4.	3/11	1	**Rosalita** *Al Dexter*
5.	3/18	1	**They Took The Stars Out Of Heaven** *Floyd Tillman*
6.	3/25	13↕	**So Long Pal** *Al Dexter*
7.	4/1	2↕	**Too Late To Worry** *Al Dexter*
8.	6/10	6↕	**Straighten Up And Fly Right** *King Cole Trio*
9.	7/29	5	**Is You Is Or Is You Ain't (Ma' Baby)** *Louis Jordan*
10.	9/2	4	**Soldier's Last Letter** *Ernest Tubb*
11.	9/23	13	**Smoke On The Water** *Red Foley*
12.	12/23	6	**I'm Wastin' My Tears On You** *Tex Ritter*

1945

	DATE	WKS	
1.	2/3	7↕	**I'm Losing My Mind Over You** *Al Dexter*
2.	3/17	1	**There's A New Moon Over My Shoulder** *Jimmie Davis*
3.	3/31	9↕	**Shame On You** *Spade Cooley*
4.	4/14	2↕	**Smoke On The Water** *Bob Wills*
5.	5/19	8↕	**At Mail Call Today** *Gene Autry*
6.	7/7	1	**Stars And Stripes On Iwo Jima** *Bob Wills*
7.	7/28	6↕	**Oklahoma Hills** *Jack Guthrie*
8.	8/25	11↕	**You Two Timed Me One Time Too Often** *Tex Ritter*
9.	10/27	4↕	**With Tears In My Eyes** *Wesley Tuttle*
10.	11/24	4↕	**Sioux City Sue** *Dick Thomas*
11.	11/24	1	**Shame On You** *Lawrence Welk Orchestra with Red Foley*
12.	12/8	4↕	**It's Been So Long Darling** *Ernest Tubb*
13.	12/15	3↕	**Silver Dew On The Blue Grass Tonight** *Bob Wills*

1946

	DATE	WKS	
1.	1/5	3↕	**You Will Have To Pay** *Tex Ritter*
2.	1/5	1	**White Cross On Okinawa** *Bob Wills*
3.	2/2	16↕	**Guitar Polka** *Al Dexter*
4.	5/18	16↕	**New Spanish Two Step** *Bob Wills*
5.	9/14	5↕	**Wine, Women And Song** *Al Dexter*
6.	10/12	14↕	**Divorce Me C.O.D.** *Merle Travis*

1947

	DATE	WKS	
1.	1/18	2↕	**Rainbow At Midnight** *Ernest Tubb*
2.	2/8	14	**So Round, So Firm, So Fully Packed** *Merle Travis*
3.	5/17	2↕	**New Jolie Blonde (New Pretty Blonde)** *Red Foley*
4.	5/24	1	**What Is Life Without Love** *Eddy Arnold*

1947 (cont'd)

5.	6/7	1	**Sugar Moon** *Bob Wills*
6.	6/14	5	**It's A Sin** *Eddy Arnold*
7.	7/19	16↕	**Smoke! Smoke! Smoke! (That Cigarette)** *Tex Williams*
8.	11/1	21↕	**I'll Hold You In My Heart (Till I Can Hold You In My Arms)** *Eddy Arnold*

1948

	DATE	WKS	
1.	4/3	9	**Anytime** *Eddy Arnold* JB: 9 / BS: 3

2.	6/5	19↕	**Bouquet Of Roses** *Eddy Arnold* BS: 19↕ / JB: 18↕
3.	6/5	3↕	**Texarkana Baby** *Eddy Arnold* JB: 3↕ / BS: 1
4.	9/18	8↕	**Just A Little Lovin' (Will Go A Long, Long Way)** *Eddy Arnold* JB: 8↕ / BS: 4↕
5.	11/13	11↕	**One Has My Name (The Other Has My Heart)** *Jimmy Wakely* BS: 11↕ / JB: 7↕
6.	12/25	1	**A Heart Full Of Love (For A Handful of Kisses)** *Eddy Arnold* BS: 1

1949

	DATE	WKS	
1.	1/22	5↕	**I Love You So Much It Hurts** *Jimmy Wakely* JB: 5↕ / BS: 4↕
2.	3/5	12↕	**Don't Rob Another Man's Castle** *Eddy Arnold* JB: 12↕ / BS: 6↕
3.	3/19	1	**Tennessee Saturday Night** *Red Foley* JB: 1
4.	4/2	3↕	**Candy Kisses** *George Morgan* BS: 3↕
5.	5/7	16↕	**Lovesick Blues** *Hank Williams* BS: 16↕ / JB: 10↕
6.	6/18	3↕	**One Kiss Too Many** *Eddy Arnold* JB: 3↕

7.	7/30	4	**I'm Throwing Rice (At The Girl That I Love)** *Eddy Arnold* BS: 4 / JB: 3↕
8.	9/10	3↕	**Why Don't You Haul Off And Love Me** *Wayne Raney* JB: 3↕ / BS: 2↕
9.	9/24	1	**Slipping Around** *Ernest Tubb* JB: 1
10.	10/8	17	**Slipping Around** *Margaret Whiting & Jimmy Wakely* BS: 17 / JB: 12↕

11.	12/10	4	**Mule Train** *Tennessee Ernie* JY: 4

#1 HITS

1949 (cont'd)

12. 1/7 **1** **Rudolph, The Red-Nosed Reindeer**
Gene Autry
JY: 1

13. 1/7 **1** **Blue Christmas** *Ernest Tubb*
JB: 1

DATE	WKS	**1950**

1. 1/14 **2↕** **I Love You Because** *Leon Payne*
JY: 2↕

2. 1/14 **1** **Blues Stay Away From Me**
Delmore Brothers
JB: 1

3. 1/21 **13** **Chattanoogie Shoe Shine Boy**
Red Foley
JB: 13 / JY: 13↕ / BS: 12

4. 1/28 **1** **Take Me In Your Arms And Hold Me**
Eddy Arnold
JB: 1

5. 4/22 **8↕** **Long Gone Lonesome Blues**
Hank Williams
JY: 8↕ / BS: 5↕ / JB: 4

6. 5/27 **4↕** **Birmingham Bounce** *Red Foley*
BS: 4↕ / JB: 3↕

7. 6/17 **10** **Why Don't You Love Me** *Hank Williams*
JY: 10 / BS: 6↕ / JB: 5

8. 6/17 **4** **I'll Sail My Ship Alone** *Moon Mullican*
JB: 4 / BS: 1

9. 7/15 **1** **Mississippi** *Red Foley*
JB: 1

10. 8/19 **21↕** **I'm Moving On** *Hank Snow*
BS: 21↕ / JY: 18↕ / JB: 14

11. 8/26 **3** **Goodnight Irene** *Red Foley-Ernest Tubb*
JB: 3 / BS: 2

12. 12/23 **3** **If You've Got The Money I've Got The Time** *Lefty Frizzell*
JB: 3

13. 12/30 **1** **Moanin' The Blues** *Hank Williams*
JY: 1

DATE	WKS	**1951**

1. 1/6 **3↕** **I Love You A Thousand Ways**
Lefty Frizzell
JY: 3↕

2. 1/6 **2** **The Golden Rocket** *Hank Snow*
BS: 2 / JY: 1

3. 1/13 **14** **The Shot Gun Boogie** *Tennessee Ernie*
JB: 14 / BS: 3↕ / JY: 1

4. 2/10 **11↕** **There's Been A Change In Me**
Eddy Arnold
JY: 11↕ / BS: 4↕

5. 3/31 **8↕** **The Rhumba Boogie** *Hank Snow*
BS: 8↕ / JB: 5 / JY: 2↕

6. 5/12 **1** **Cold, Cold Heart** *Hank Williams*
JY: 1

7. 5/19 **3** **Kentucky Waltz** *Eddy Arnold*
JB: 3 / BS: 3↕

8. 5/26 **11** **I Want To Be With You Always**
Lefty Frizzell
JY: 11 / BS: 6↕ / JB: 5

1951 (cont'd)

9. 7/14 **11** **I Wanna Play House With You**
Eddy Arnold
JB: 11 / BS: 6↕

10. 8/11 **8↕** **Hey, Good Lookin'** *Hank Williams*
JY: 8↕

11. 9/1 **12↕** **Always Late (With Your Kisses)**
Lefty Frizzell
BS: 12↕ / JY: 6↕ / JB: 6

12. 11/3 **15↕** **Slow Poke** *Pee Wee King*
JB: 15↕ / BS: 14 / JY: 9↕

13. 12/22 **8↕** **Let Old Mother Nature Have Her Way**
Carl Smith
JB: 8↕ / BS: 6 / JY: 3↕

DATE	WKS	**1952**

1. 2/2 **3↕** **Give Me More, More, More (Of Your Kisses)** *Lefty Frizzell*
JY: 3↕ / JB: 3↕

2. 3/1 **4** **Wondering** *Webb Pierce*
JY: 4

3. 3/29 **8↕** **(When You Feel Like You're In Love) Don't Just Stand There** *Carl Smith*
JY: 8↕ / BS: 5↕ / JB: 3↕

4. 5/3 **1** **Easy On The Eyes** *Eddy Arnold*
BS: 1

5. 5/10 **15** **The Wild Side Of Life** *Hank Thompson*
BS: 15 / JB: 15 / JY: 8↕

6. 7/12 **3↕** **That Heart Belongs To Me** *Webb Pierce*
JY: 3↕

7. 7/19 **1** **Are You Teasing Me** *Carl Smith*
JY: 1

8. 8/16 **4↕** **A Full Time Job** *Eddy Arnold*
JY: 4↕

9. 8/23 **6** **It Wasn't God Who Made Honky Tonk Angels** *Kitty Wells*
BS: 6 / JB: 5

10. 9/6 **14↕** **Jambalaya (On The Bayou)**
Hank Williams
BS: 14↕ / JY: 14↕ / JB: 12↕

11. 12/6 **4↕** **Back Street Affair** *Webb Pierce*
JY: 4↕ / JB: 3 / BS: 2↕

12. 12/6 **1** **Don't Let The Stars (Get In Your Eyes)**
Slim Willet
JY: 1

13. 12/27 **3** **Don't Let The Stars Get In Your Eyes**
Skeets McDonald
JB: 3

DATE	WKS	**1953**

1. 1/10 **1** **Midnight** *Red Foley*
BS: 1

2. 1/24 **2↕** **I'll Go On Alone** *Marty Robbins*
JY: 2↕

3. 1/24 **1** **I'll Never Get Out Of This World Alive**
Hank Williams
BS: 1

4. 1/31 **4** **No Help Wanted** *The Carlisles*
JB: 4 / JY: 4↕

5. 1/31 **3** **Eddy's Song** *Eddy Arnold*
BS: 3

#1 HITS

1953 (cont'd)

6.   2/7   3   **I Let The Stars Get In My Eyes**
Goldie Hill
JB: 3

7.   2/21   13   **Kaw-Liga** *Hank Williams*
BS: 13 / JY: 8 / JB: 8↕

8.   4/11   6↕   **Your Cheatin' Heart** *Hank Williams*
JY: 6↕ / JB: 2↕

9.   5/9   9↕   **Mexican Joe** *Jim Reeves*
JB: 9↕ / JY: 7↕ / BS: 6↕

10.   6/6   4↕   **Take These Chains From My Heart**
Hank Williams
BS: 4↕

11.   7/11   8↕   **It's Been So Long** *Webb Pierce*
JY: 8↕ / BS: 6 / JB: 1

12.   8/1   3↕   **Rub-A-Dub-Dub** *Hank Thompson*
JB: 3↕

13.   8/22   8↕   **Hey Joe!** *Carl Smith*
JB: 8↕ / JY: 4↕ / BS: 2↕

14.   8/29   6↕   **A Dear John Letter**
Jean Shepard & Ferlin Huskey
BS: 6↕ / JB: 4↕

15.   10/17   8↕   **I Forgot More Than You'll Ever Know**
The Davis Sisters
JY: 8↕ / BS: 6↕ / JB: 2↕

16.   11/21   12↕   **There Stands The Glass** *Webb Pierce*
BS: 12↕ / JB: 9↕ / JY: 6↕

17.   12/12   2   **Caribbean** *Mitchell Torok*
JB: 2

18.   12/19   3↕   **Let Me Be The One** *Hank Locklin*
JY: 3↕ / JB: 2↕

1954

	DATE	WKS	
1.	1/9	3↕	**Bimbo** *Jim Reeves* JY: 3↕
2.	2/20	17	**Slowly** *Webb Pierce* BS: 17 / JB: 17↕ / JY: 15
3.	2/20	2	**Wake Up, Irene** *Hank Thompson* JB: 2
4.	5/15	1	**I Really Don't Want To Know** *Eddy Arnold* JB: 1
5.	6/12	2	**(Oh Baby Mine) I Get So Lonely** *Johnnie & Jack* JY: 2
6.	6/19	20	**I Don't Hurt Anymore** *Hank Snow* BS: 20 / JB: 20↕ / JY: 18↕
7.	7/3	2	**Even Tho** *Webb Pierce* JY: 2
8.	7/31	1	**One By One** *Kitty Wells & Red Foley* JB: 1
9.	11/6	10↕	**More And More** *Webb Pierce* JB: 10↕ / BS: 9 / JY: 8↕

1955

	DATE	WKS	
1.	1/8	7	**Loose Talk** *Carl Smith* BS: 7 / JY: 6↕ / JB: 4
2.	1/29	2	**Let Me Go, Lover!** *Hank Snow* JY: 2
3.	2/26	21	**In The Jailhouse Now** *Webb Pierce* JB: 21 / BS: 20 / JY: 15

1955 (cont'd)

4.   6/18   3   **Live Fast, Love Hard, Die Young**
Faron Young
JY: 3

5.   7/9   4   **A Satisfied Mind** *Porter Wagoner*
JY: 4

6.   7/16   12   **I Don't Care** *Webb Pierce*
BS: 12 / JY: 12 / JB: 12

7.   10/8   2   **The Cattle Call** *Eddy Arnold*
BS: 2

8.   10/22   13↕   **Love, Love, Love** *Webb Pierce*
JY: 13↕ / JB: 9↕ / BS: 8

9.   10/22   2   **That Do Make It Nice** *Eddy Arnold*
JB: 2

10.   12/17   10   **Sixteen Tons** *Tennessee Ernie Ford*
BS: 10 / JB: 7↕ / JY: 3↕

1956

	DATE	WKS	
1.	2/11	4↕	**Why Baby Why** *Red Sovine & Webb Pierce* JY: 4↕ / BS: 1 / JB: 1
2.	2/25	5	**I Forgot To Remember To Forget** *Elvis Presley* JB: 5 / BS: 2
3.	3/17	17	**Heartbreak Hotel** *Elvis Presley* BS: 17 / JB: 13↕ / JY: 12
4.	3/17	2	**I Don't Believe You've Met My Baby** *The Louvin Brothers* JY: 2
5.	4/7	3	**Blue Suede Shoes** *Carl Perkins* JB: 3
6.	6/23	20↕	**Crazy Arms** *Ray Price* JY: 20↕ / BS: 11↕ / JB: 1
7.	7/14	2	**I Want You, I Need You, I Love You** *Elvis Presley* BS: 2 / JB: 1
8.	7/21	6↕	**I Walk The Line** *Johnny Cash* JB: 6↕ / JY: 1
9.	9/15	10	**Don't Be Cruel/** JB: 10 / BS: 5 / JY: 2
10.		10	**Hound Dog** *Elvis Presley* JB: 10 / BS: 5
11.	11/10	13	**Singing The Blues** *Marty Robbins* BS: 13 / JB: 13 / JY: 11↕

1957

	DATE	WKS	
1.	2/2	9	**Young Love** *Sonny James* JY: 9 / BS: 7 / JB: 3
2.	3/2	5↕	**There You Go** *Johnny Cash* JB: 5↕
3.	4/6	10	**Gone** *Ferlin Husky* BS: 10 / JY: 9 / JB: 5↕
4.	5/13	1	**All Shook Up** *Elvis Presley* JB: 1
5.	5/20	5	**A White Sport Coat (And A Pink** **Carnation)** *Marty Robbins* BS: 5 / JB: 5 / JY: 1
6.	5/20	1	**Honky Tonk Song** *Webb Pierce* JY: 1
7.	5/27	8↕	**Four Walls** *Jim Reeves* JY: 8↕

#1 HITS

1957 (cont'd)

6/17/57: Billboard's last "Juke Box" chart.

8.	7/15	7	**Bye Bye Love** *The Everly Brothers*
			JY: 7 / BS: 7
9.	8/5	1	**Let Me Be Your Teddy Bear** *Elvis Presley*
			BS: 1
10.	9/9	2	**Whole Lot Of Shakin' Going On**
			Jerry Lee Lewis
			BS: 2
11.	9/16	4↕	**Fraulein** *Bobby Helms*
			JY: 4↕ / BS: 3
12.	9/16	4↕	**My Shoes Keep Walking Back To You**
			Ray Price
			JY: 4↕
13.	10/14	8↕	**Wake Up Little Susie** *The Everly Brothers*
			JY: 8↕ / BS: 7
14.	12/2	1	**Jailhouse Rock** *Elvis Presley*
			BS: 1
15.	12/9	4	**My Special Angel** *Bobby Helms*
			BS: 4 / JY: 1

1958

	DATE	WKS	
1.	1/6	4	**The Story Of My Life** *Marty Robbins*
			BS: 4 / JY: 4
2.	1/6	2	**Great Balls Of Fire** *Jerry Lee Lewis*
			BS: 2
3.	2/3	10	**Ballad Of A Teenage Queen**
			Johnny Cash
			JY: 10 / BS: 8
4.	4/14	8↕	**Oh Lonesome Me** *Don Gibson*
			BS: 8↕ / JY: 8↕
5.	5/26	2↕	**Just Married** *Marty Robbins*
			JY: 2↕
6.	6/2	3	**All I Have To Do Is Dream**
			The Everly Brothers
			BS: 3 / JY: 1
7.	6/23	8	**Guess Things Happen That Way**
			Johnny Cash
			BS: 8 / JY: 3↕
8.	7/21	13	**Alone With You** *Faron Young*
			JY: 13
9.	8/25	2	**Blue Blue Day** *Don Gibson*
			BS: 2
10.	9/8	6	**Bird Dog** *The Everly Brothers*
			BS: 6

10/13/58: Billboard's last "Best Sellers" and "Jockeys" charts (replaced with one all-encompassing "Hot C&W Sides" chart).

| 11. | 10/20 | 13 | **City Lights** *Ray Price* |

1959

	DATE	WKS	
1.	1/19	5	**Billy Bayou** *Jim Reeves*
2.	2/23	6	**Don't Take Your Guns To Town**
			Johnny Cash
3.	4/6	1	**When It's Springtime In Alaska (It's Forty Below)** *Johnny Horton*
4.	4/13	5	**White Lightning** *George Jones*

1959 (cont'd)

5.	5/18	10	**The Battle Of New Orleans** *Johnny Horton*
6.	7/27	5	**Waterloo** *Stonewall Jackson*
7.	8/31	10	**The Three Bells** *The Browns*
8.	11/9	4	**Country Girl** *Faron Young*
9.	12/7	2	**The Same Old Me** *Ray Price*
10.	12/21	7	**El Paso** *Marty Robbins*

1960

	DATE	WKS	
1.	2/8	14	**He'll Have To Go** *Jim Reeves*
2.	5/16	14	**Please Help Me, I'm Falling** *Hank Locklin*
3.	8/22	12	**Alabam** *Cowboy Copas*
4.	11/14	10↕	**Wings Of A Dove** *Ferlin Husky*

1961

	DATE	WKS	
1.	1/9	5	**North To Alaska** *Johnny Horton*
2.	2/27	10	**Don't Worry** *Marty Robbins*
3.	5/8	9	**Hello Walls** *Faron Young*
4.	7/10	4	**Heartbreak U.S.A.** *Kitty Wells*
5.	8/7	2	**I Fall To Pieces** *Patsy Cline*
6.	8/21	7↕	**Tender Years** *George Jones*
7.	9/25	19↕	**Walk On By** *Leroy Van Dyke*
8.	11/20	2	**Big Bad John** *Jimmy Dean*

1962

	DATE	WKS	
1.	3/10	2↕	**Misery Loves Company** *Porter Wagoner*
2.	3/17	1	**That's My Pa** *Sheb Wooley*
3.	3/31	5↕	**She's Got You** *Patsy Cline*
4.	4/28	2↕	**Charlie's Shoes** *Billy Walker*
5.	5/19	6	**She Thinks I Still Care** *George Jones*
6.	6/30	9	**Wolverton Mountain** *Claude King*
7.	9/1	8	**Devil Woman** *Marty Robbins*
8.	10/27	7↕	**Mama Sang A Song** *Bill Anderson*

11/3/62: The 'W' signifying "Western" is dropped from chart title. Chart now designated only as "Hot Country Singles."

| 9. | 11/10 | 2↕ | **I've Been Everywhere** *Hank Snow* |
| 10. | 12/29 | 11↕ | **Don't Let Me Cross Over** *Carl Butler & Pearl* |

1963

	DATE	WKS	
1.	1/5	1	**Ruby Ann** *Marty Robbins*
2.	1/19	3↕	**The Ballad Of Jed Clampett** *Flatt & Scruggs*
3.	4/13	7↕	**Still** *Bill Anderson*
4.	5/4	4↕	**Lonesome 7-7203** *Hawkshaw Hawkins*
5.	6/15	4↕	**Act Naturally** *Buck Owens*
6.	7/27	7	**Ring Of Fire** *Johnny Cash*
7.	9/14	4	**Abilene** *George Hamilton IV*
8.	10/12	1	**Talk Back Trembling Lips** *Ernest Ashworth*
9.	10/19	16	**Love's Gonna Live Here** *Buck Owens*

#1 HITS

#1 HITS

1968 (cont'd)

21.	11/23	3	**Stand By Your Man** *Tammy Wynette*
22.	12/14	1	**Born To Be With You** *Sonny James*
23.	12/21	2	**Wichita Lineman** *Glen Campbell*

	DATE	WKS	**1969**
1.	1/4	6	**Daddy Sang Bass** *Johnny Cash*
2.	2/15	2	**Until My Dreams Come True** *Jack Greene*
3.	3/1	1	**To Make Love Sweeter For You** *Jerry Lee Lewis*
4.	3/8	3	**Only The Lonely** *Sonny James*
5.	3/29	2	**Who's Gonna Mow Your Grass** *Buck Owens*
6.	4/12	1	**Woman Of The World (Leave My World Alone)** *Loretta Lynn*
7.	4/19	3	**Galveston** *Glen Campbell*
8.	5/10	1	**Hungry Eyes** *Merle Haggard*
9.	5/17	2	**My Life (Throw It Away If I Want To)** *Bill Anderson*
10.	5/31	2	**Singing My Song** *Tammy Wynette*
11.	6/14	3	**Running Bear** *Sonny James*
12.	7/5	2	**Statue Of A Fool** *Jack Greene*
13.	7/19	1	**I Love You More Today** *Conway Twitty*
14.	7/26	2	**Johnny B. Goode** *Buck Owens*
15.	8/9	1	**All I Have To Offer You (Is Me)** *Charley Pride*
16.	8/16	1	**Workin' Man Blues** *Merle Haggard*
17.	8/23	5	**A Boy Named Sue** *Johnny Cash*
18.	9/27	1	**Tall Dark Stranger** *Buck Owens*
19.	10/4	3	**Since I Met You, Baby** *Sonny James*
20.	10/25	2	**The Ways To Love A Man** *Tammy Wynette*
21.	11/8	1	**To See My Angel Cry** *Conway Twitty*
22.	11/15	4	**Okie From Muskogee** *Merle Haggard*
23.	12/13	3	**(I'm So) Afraid Of Losing You Again** *Charley Pride*

	DATE	WKS	**1970**
1.	1/3	4	**Baby, Baby (I Know You're A Lady)** *David Houston*
2.	1/31	2	**A Week In A Country Jail** *Tom T. Hall*
3.	2/14	4	**It's Just A Matter Of Time** *Sonny James*
4.	3/14	3	**The Fightin' Side Of Me** *Merle Haggard*
5.	4/4	2	**Tennessee Bird Walk** *Jack Blanchard & Misty Morgan*
6.	4/18	2	**Is Anybody Goin' To San Antone** *Charley Pride*
7.	5/2	1	**My Woman My Woman, My Wife** *Marty Robbins*
8.	5/9	1	**The Pool Shark** *Dave Dudley*
9.	5/16	3	**My Love** *Sonny James*
10.	6/6	4	**Hello Darlin'** *Conway Twitty*
11.	7/4	3	**He Loves Me All The Way** *Tammy Wynette*
12.	7/25	2	**Wonder Could I Live There Anymore** *Charley Pride*

1970 (cont'd)

13.	8/8	4	**Don't Keep Me Hangin' On** *Sonny James*
14.	9/5	2	**All For The Love Of Sunshine** *Hank Williams, Jr. With The Mike Curb Congregation*
15.	9/19	1	**For The Good Times** *Ray Price*
16.	9/26	2	**There Must Be More To Love Than This** *Jerry Lee Lewis*
17.	10/10	2	**Sunday Morning Coming Down** *Johnny Cash*
18.	10/24	2	**Run, Woman, Run** *Tammy Wynette*
19.	11/7	2	**I Can't Believe That You've Stopped Loving Me** *Charley Pride*
20.	11/21	1	**Fifteen Years Ago** *Conway Twitty*
21.	11/28	3	**Endlessly** *Sonny James*
22.	12/19	1	**Coal Miner's Daughter** *Loretta Lynn*
23.	12/26	5	**Rose Garden** *Lynn Anderson*

	DATE	WKS	**1971**
1.	1/30	1	**Flesh And Blood** *Johnny Cash*
2.	2/6	1	**Joshua** *Dolly Parton*
3.	2/13	3	**Help Me Make It Through The Night** *Sammi Smith*
4.	3/6	3	**I'd Rather Love You** *Charley Pride*
5.	3/27	2	**After The Fire Is Gone** *Conway Twitty & Loretta Lynn*
6.	4/10	4	**Empty Arms** *Sonny James*
7.	5/8	1	**How Much More Can She Stand** *Conway Twitty*
8.	5/15	3	**I Won't Mention It Again** *Ray Price*
9.	6/5	2	**You're My Man** *Lynn Anderson*
10.	6/19	5	**When You're Hot, You're Hot** *Jerry Reed*
11.	7/24	1	**Bright Lights, Big City** *Sonny James*
12.	7/31	4	**I'm Just Me** *Charley Pride*
13.	8/28	2	**Good Lovin' (Makes It Right)** *Tammy Wynette*
14.	9/11	3↕	**Easy Loving** *Freddie Hart*
15.	9/18	2	**The Year That Clayton Delaney Died** *Tom T. Hall*
16.	10/16	3	**How Can I Unlove You** *Lynn Anderson*
17.	11/6	1	**Here Comes Honey Again** *Sonny James*
18.	11/13	1	**Lead Me On** *Conway Twitty And Loretta Lynn*
19.	11/20	2	**Daddy Frank (The Guitar Man)** *Merle Haggard*
20.	12/4	5	**Kiss An Angel Good Mornin'** *Charley Pride*

	DATE	WKS	**1972**
1.	1/8	1	**Would You Take Another Chance On Me** *Jerry Lee Lewis*
2.	1/15	3	**Carolyn** *Merle Haggard*
3.	2/5	2	**One's On The Way** *Loretta Lynn*
4.	2/19	2	**It's Four In The Morning** *Faron Young*
5.	3/4	1	**Bedtime Story** *Tammy Wynette*
6.	3/11	6	**My Hang-Up Is You** *Freddie Hart*

#1 HITS

1972 (cont'd)

7.	4/22	3	**Chantilly Lace** *Jerry Lee Lewis*
8.	5/13	2	**Grandma Harp** *Merle Haggard*
9.	5/27	1	**(Lost Her Love) On Our Last Date** *Conway Twitty*
10.	6/3	3	**The Happiest Girl In The Whole U.S.A.** *Donna Fargo*
11.	6/24	1	**That's Why I Love You Like I Do** *Sonny James*
12.	7/1	2	**Eleven Roses** *Hank Williams, Jr.*
13.	7/15	1	**Made In Japan** *Buck Owens*
14.	7/22	3	**It's Gonna Take A Little Bit Longer** *Charley Pride*
15.	8/12	2	**Bless Your Heart** *Freddie Hart & The Heartbeats*
16.	8/26	2↕	**If You Leave Me Tonight I'll Cry** *Jerry Wallace*
17.	9/2	1	**Woman (Sensuous Woman)** *Don Gibson*
18.	9/16	1	**When The Snow Is On The Roses** *Sonny James*
19.	9/23	1	**I Can't Stop Loving You** *Conway Twitty*
20.	9/30	2	**I Ain't Never** *Mel Tillis*
21.	10/14	3	**Funny Face** *Donna Fargo*
22.	11/4	1	**It's Not Love (But It's Not Bad)** *Merle Haggard*
23.	11/11	1	**My Man** *Tammy Wynette*
24.	11/18	3	**She's Too Good To Be True** *Charley Pride*
25.	12/9	3	**Got The All Overs For You (All Over Me)** *Freddie Hart & The Heartbeats*
26.	12/30	3	**She's Got To Be A Saint** *Ray Price*

	DATE	WKS	1973
1.	1/20	1	**Soul Song** *Joe Stampley*
2.	1/27	1	**(Old Dogs-Children And) Watermelon Wine** *Tom T. Hall*
3.	2/3	2	**She Needs Someone To Hold Her (When She Cries)** *Conway Twitty*
4.	2/17	1	**I Wonder If They Ever Think Of Me** *Merle Haggard*
5.	2/24	1	**Rated "X"** *Loretta Lynn*
6.	3/3	1	**The Lord Knows I'm Drinking** *Cal Smith*
7.	3/10	1	**'Til I Get It Right** *Tammy Wynette*
8.	3/17	2	**Teddy Bear Song** *Barbara Fairchild*
9.	3/31	1	**Keep Me In Mind** *Lynn Anderson*
10.	4/7	1	**Super Kind Of Woman** *Freddie Hart & The Heartbeats*
11.	4/14	1	**A Shoulder To Cry On** *Charley Pride*
12.	4/21	1	**Superman** *Donna Fargo*
13.	4/28	2	**Behind Closed Doors** *Charlie Rich*
14.	5/12	1	**Come Live With Me** *Roy Clark*
15.	5/19	1	**What's Your Mama's Name** *Tanya Tucker*
16.	5/26	3↕	**Satin Sheets** *Jeanne Pruett*
17.	6/9	1	**You Always Come Back (To Hurting Me)** *Johnny Rodriguez*

1973 (cont'd)

18.	6/16	1	**Kids Say The Darndest Things** *Tammy Wynette*
19.	6/30	1	**Don't Fight The Feelings Of Love** *Charley Pride*
20.	7/7	1	**Why Me** *Kris Kristofferson*
21.	7/14	2	**Love Is The Foundation** *Loretta Lynn*
22.	7/28	1	**You Were Always There** *Donna Fargo*
23.	8/4	1	**Lord, Mr. Ford** *Jerry Reed*
24.	8/11	1	**Trip To Heaven** *Freddie Hart & The Heartbeats*
25.	8/18	1	**Louisiana Woman, Mississippi Man** *Loretta Lynn/Conway Twitty*
26.	8/25	2	**Everybody's Had The Blues** *Merle Haggard*
27.	9/8	3	**You've Never Been This Far Before** *Conway Twitty*
28.	9/29	1	**Blood Red And Goin' Down** *Tanya Tucker*
29.	10/6	1	**You're The Best Thing That Ever Happened To Me** *Ray Price*
30.	10/13	2	**Ridin' My Thumb To Mexico** *Johnny Rodriguez*
31.	10/27	2	**We're Gonna Hold On** *George Jones & Tammy Wynette*
32.	11/10	2	**Paper Roses** *Marie Osmond*
33.	11/24	3	**The Most Beautiful Girl** *Charlie Rich*
34.	12/15	1	**Amazing Love** *Charley Pride*
35.	12/22	4	**If We Make It Through December** *Merle Haggard*

	DATE	WKS	1974
1.	1/19	2	**I Love** *Tom T. Hall*
2.	2/2	1	**Jolene** *Dolly Parton*
3.	2/9	1	**World Of Make Believe** *Bill Anderson*
4.	2/16	1	**That's The Way Love Goes** *Johnny Rodriguez*
5.	2/23	2	**Another Lonely Song** *Tammy Wynette*
6.	3/9	2	**There Won't Be Anymore** *Charlie Rich*
7.	3/23	1	**There's A Honky Tonk Angel (Who'll Take Me Back In)** *Conway Twitty*
8.	3/30	2	**Would You Lay With Me (In A Field Of Stone)** *Tanya Tucker*
9.	4/6	3	**A Very Special Love Song** *Charlie Rich*
10.	4/27	1	**Hello Love** *Hank Snow*
11.	5/4	1	**Things Aren't Funny Anymore** *Merle Haggard*
12.	5/11	1	**Is It Wrong (For Loving You)** *Sonny James*
13.	5/18	1	**Country Bumpkin** *Cal Smith*
14.	5/25	1	**No Charge** *Melba Montgomery*
15.	6/1	1	**Pure Love** *Ronnie Milsap*
16.	6/8	1	**I Will Always Love You** *Dolly Parton*
17.	6/15	1	**I Don't See Me In Your Eyes Anymore** *Charlie Rich*
18.	6/22	1	**This Time** *Waylon Jennings*
19.	6/29	1	**Room Full Of Roses** *Mickey Gilley*
20.	7/6	2	**He Thinks I Still Care** *Anne Murray*
21.	7/20	1	**Marie Laveau** *Bobby Bare*

#1 HITS

1974 (cont'd)

22.	7/27	1	**You Can't Be A Beacon (If Your Light Don't Shine)** *Donna Fargo*
23.	8/3	2	**Rub It In** *Billy "Crash" Craddock*
24.	8/17	1	**As Soon As I Hang Up The Phone** *Loretta Lynn/Conway Twitty*
25.	8/24	1	**Old Man From The Mountain** *Merle Haggard*
26.	8/31	1	**The Grand Tour** *George Jones*
27.	9/7	2	**Please Don't Tell Me How The Story Ends** *Ronnie Milsap*
28.	9/21	1	**I Wouldn't Want To Live If You Didn't Love Me** *Don Williams*
29.	9/28	1	**I'm A Ramblin' Man** *Waylon Jennings*
30.	10/5	1	**I Love My Friend** *Charlie Rich*
31.	10/12	1	**Please Don't Stop Loving Me** *Porter Wagoner & Dolly Parton*
32.	10/19	2	**I See The Want To In Your Eyes** *Conway Twitty*
33.	11/2	1	**I Overlooked An Orchid** *Mickey Gilley*
34.	11/9	1	**Love Is Like A Butterfly** *Dolly Parton*
35.	11/16	1	**Country Is** *Tom T. Hall*
36.	11/23	1	**Trouble In Paradise** *Loretta Lynn*
37.	11/30	1	**Back Home Again** *John Denver*
38.	12/7	1	**She Called Me Baby** *Charlie Rich*
39.	12/14	2	**I Can Help** *Billy Swan*
40.	12/28	1	**What A Man, My Man Is** *Lynn Anderson*

DATE	WKS	**1975**	
1.	1/4	1	**The Door** *George Jones*
2.	1/11	1	**Ruby, Baby** *Billy "Crash" Craddock*
3.	1/18	1	**Kentucky Gambler** *Merle Haggard*
4.	1/25	1	**(I'd Be) A Legend In My Time** *Ronnie Milsap*
5.	2/1	1	**City Lights** *Mickey Gilley*
6.	2/8	1	**Then Who Am I** *Charley Pride*
7.	2/15	1	**Devil In The Bottle** *T.G. Sheppard*
8.	2/22	1	**I Care** *Tom T. Hall*
9.	3/1	1	**It's Time To Pay The Fiddler** *Cal Smith*
10.	3/8	1	**Linda On My Mind** *Conway Twitty*
11.	3/15	2	**Before The Next Teardrop Falls** *Freddy Fender*
12.	3/29	1	**The Bargain Store** *Dolly Parton*
13.	4/5	1	**I Just Can't Get Her Out Of My Mind** *Johnny Rodriguez*
14.	4/12	2	**Always Wanting You** *Merle Haggard*
15.	4/26	1	**Blanket On The Ground** *Billie Jo Spears*
16.	5/3	1	**Roll On Big Mama** *Joe Stampley*
17.	5/10	1	**She's Actin' Single (I'm Drinkin' Doubles)** *Gary Stewart*
18.	5/17	1	**(Hey Won't You Play) Another Somebody Done Somebody Wrong Song** *B.J. Thomas*
19.	5/24	1	**I'm Not Lisa** *Jessi Colter*
20.	5/31	1	**Thank God I'm A Country Boy** *John Denver*
21.	6/7	1	**Window Up Above** *Mickey Gilley*
22.	6/14	1	**When Will I Be Loved** *Linda Ronstadt*
23.	6/21	1	**You're My Best Friend** *Don Williams*

1975 (cont'd)

24.	6/28	1	**Tryin' To Beat The Morning Home** *T.G. Sheppard*
25.	7/5	1	**Lizzie And The Rainman** *Tanya Tucker*
26.	7/12	1	**Movin' On** *Merle Haggard*
27.	7/19	2	**Touch The Hand** *Conway Twitty*
28.	8/2	1	**Just Get Up And Close The Door** *Johnny Rodriguez*
29.	8/9	2	**Wasted Days And Wasted Nights** *Freddy Fender*
30.	8/23	3↕	**Rhinestone Cowboy** *Glen Campbell*
31.	9/6	1	**Feelins'** *Loretta Lynn/Conway Twitty*
32.	9/20	2	**Daydreams About Night Things** *Ronnie Milsap*
33.	10/4	2	**Blue Eyes Crying In The Rain** *Willie Nelson*
34.	10/18	1	**Hope You're Feelin' Me (Like I'm Feelin' You)** *Charley Pride*
35.	10/25	1	**San Antonio Stroll** *Tanya Tucker*
36.	11/1	1	**(Turn Out The Light And) Love Me Tonight** *Don Williams*
37.	11/8	1	**I'm Sorry** *John Denver*
38.	11/15	1	**Are You Sure Hank Done It This Way** *Waylon Jennings*
39.	11/22	1	**Rocky** *Dickey Lee*
40.	11/29	1	**It's All In The Movies** *Merle Haggard*
41.	12/6	1	**Secret Love** *Freddy Fender*
42.	12/13	1	**Love Put A Song In My Heart** *Johnny Rodriguez*
43.	12/20	6	**Convoy** *C.W. McCall*

DATE	WKS	**1976**	
1.	1/31	1	**This Time I've Hurt Her More Than She Loves Me** *Conway Twitty*
2.	2/7	1	**Sometimes** *Bill Anderson & Mary Lou Turner*
3.	2/14	1	**The White Knight** *Cledus Maggard & The Citizen's Band*
4.	2/21	3	**Good Hearted Woman** *Waylon & Willie*
5.	3/13	1	**The Roots Of My Raising** *Merle Haggard*
6.	3/20	1	**Faster Horses (The Cowboy And The Poet)** *Tom T. Hall*
7.	3/27	1	**Til The Rivers All Run Dry** *Don Williams*
8.	4/3	1	**You'll Lose A Good Thing** *Freddy Fender*
9.	4/10	1	**'Til I Can Make It On My Own** *Tammy Wynette*
10.	4/17	1	**Drinkin' My Baby (Off My Mind)** *Eddie Rabbitt*
11.	4/24	1	**Together Again** *Emmylou Harris*
12.	5/1	1	**Don't The Girls All Get Prettier At Closing Time** *Mickey Gilley*
13.	5/8	1	**My Eyes Can Only See As Far As You** *Charley Pride*
14.	5/15	1	**What Goes On When The Sun Goes Down** *Ronnie Milsap*
15.	5/22	1	**After All The Good Is Gone** *Conway Twitty*

#1 HITS

1976 (cont'd)

16.	5/29	2	**One Piece At A Time** *Johnny Cash*
17.	6/12	1	**I'll Get Over You** *Crystal Gayle*
18.	6/19	2	**El Paso City** *Marty Robbins*
19.	7/4	1	**All These Things** *Joe Stampley*
20.	7/10	1	**The Door Is Always Open** *Dave & Sugar*
21.	7/17	3	**Teddy Bear** *Red Sovine*
22.	8/7	1	**Golden Ring** *George Jones & Tammy Wynette*
23.	8/14	1	**Say It Again** *Don Williams*
24.	8/21	1	**Bring It On Home To Me** *Mickey Gilley*
25.	8/28	2	**(I'm A) Stand By My Woman Man** *Ronnie Milsap*
26.	9/11	2	**I Don't Want To Have To Marry You** *Jim Ed Brown/Helen Cornelius*
27.	9/25	1	**If You've Got The Money I've Got The Time** *Willie Nelson*
28.	10/2	1	**Here's Some Love** *Tanya Tucker*
29.	10/9	1	**The Games That Daddies Play** *Conway Twitty*
30.	10/16	2	**You And Me** *Tammy Wynette*
31.	10/30	1	**Among My Souvenirs** *Marty Robbins*
32.	11/6	1	**Cherokee Maiden** *Merle Haggard*
33.	11/13	2	**Somebody Somewhere (Don't Know What He's Missin' Tonight)** *Loretta Lynn*
34.	11/27	2	**Good Woman Blues** *Mel Tillis*
35.	12/11	2	**Thinkin' Of A Rendezvous** *Johnny Duncan*
36.	12/25	2	**Sweet Dreams** *Emmylou Harris*

1977

	DATE	WKS	
1.	1/8	1	**Broken Down In Tiny Pieces** *Billy "Crash" Craddock*
2.	1/15	1	**You Never Miss A Real Good Thing (Till He Says Goodbye)** *Crystal Gayle*
3.	1/22	1	**I Can't Believe She Gives It All To Me** *Conway Twitty*
4.	1/29	1	**Let My Love Be Your Pillow** *Ronnie Milsap*
5.	2/5	2	**Near You** *George Jones & Tammy Wynette*
6.	2/19	1	**Moody Blue** *Elvis Presley*
7.	2/26	1	**Say You'll Stay Until Tomorrow** *Tom Jones*
8.	3/5	1	**Heart Healer** *Mel Tillis*
9.	3/12	1	**She's Just An Old Love Turned Memory** *Charley Pride*
10.	3/19	2	**Southern Nights** *Glen Campbell*
11.	4/2	2	**Lucille** *Kenny Rogers*
12.	4/16	1	**It Couldn't Have Been Any Better** *Johnny Duncan*
13.	4/23	1	**She's Got You** *Loretta Lynn*
14.	4/30	1	**She's Pulling Me Back Again** *Mickey Gilley*
15.	5/7	1	**Play, Guitar Play** *Conway Twitty*
16.	5/14	1	**Some Broken Hearts Never Mend** *Don Williams*

1977 (cont'd)

17.	5/21	6	**Luckenbach, Texas (Back to the Basics of Love)** *Waylon Jennings*
18.	7/2	1	**That Was Yesterday** *Donna Fargo*
19.	7/9	1	**I'll Be Leaving Alone** *Charley Pride*
20.	7/16	3	**It Was Almost Like A Song** *Ronnie Milsap*
21.	8/6	2	**Rollin' With The Flow** *Charlie Rich*
22.	8/20	1	**Way Down** *Elvis Presley*
23.	8/27	4	**Don't It Make My Brown Eyes Blue** *Crystal Gayle*
24.	9/24	1	**I've Already Loved You In My Mind** *Conway Twitty*
25.	10/1	1	**Daytime Friends** *Kenny Rogers*
26.	10/8	4	**Heaven's Just A Sin Away** *The Kendalls*
27.	11/5	1	**I'm Just A Country Boy** *Don Williams*
28.	11/12	1	**More To Me** *Charley Pride*
29.	11/19	2	**The Wurlitzer Prize (I Don't Want To Get Over You)** *Waylon Jennings*
30.	12/3	5	**Here You Come Again** *Dolly Parton*

1978

	DATE	WKS	
1.	1/7	2	**Take This Job And Shove It** *Johnny Paycheck*
2.	1/21	1	**What A Difference You've Made In My Life** *Ronnie Milsap*
3.	1/28	2	**Out Of My Head And Back In My Bed** *Loretta Lynn*
4.	2/11	1	**I Just Wish You Were Someone I Love** *Larry Gatlin with Brothers & Friends*
5.	2/18	2	**Don't Break The Heart That Loves You** *Margo Smith*
6.	3/4	4	**Mammas Don't Let Your Babies Grow Up To Be Cowboys** *Waylon & Willie*
7.	4/1	1	**Ready For The Times To Get Better** *Crystal Gayle*
8.	4/8	2	**Someone Loves You Honey** *Charley Pride*
9.	4/22	2	**Every Time Two Fools Collide** *Kenny Rogers & Dottie West*
10.	5/6	2	**It's All Wrong, But It's All Right** *Dolly Parton*
11.	5/20	1	**She Can Put Her Shoes Under My Bed (Anytime)** *Johnny Duncan*
12.	5/27	2	**Do You Know You Are My Sunshine** *The Statler Brothers*
13.	6/10	1	**Georgia On My Mind** *Willie Nelson*
14.	6/17	1	**Two More Bottles Of Wine** *Emmylou Harris*
15.	6/24	1	**I'll Be True To You** *The Oak Ridge Boys*
16.	7/1	1	**It Only Hurts For A Little While** *Margo Smith*
17.	7/8	1	**I Believe In You** *Mel Tillis*
18.	7/15	3	**Only One Love In My Life** *Ronnie Milsap*
19.	8/5	1	**Love Or Something Like It** *Kenny Rogers*

#1 HITS

1978 (cont'd)

20.	8/12	1	**You Don't Love Me Anymore** *Eddie Rabbitt*
21.	8/19	2	**Talking In Your Sleep** *Crystal Gayle*
22.	9/2	1	**Blue Skies** *Willie Nelson*
23.	9/9	3	**I've Always Been Crazy** *Waylon Jennings*
24.	9/30	3	**Heartbreaker** *Dolly Parton*
25.	10/21	1	**Tear Time** *Dave & Sugar*
26.	10/28	1	**Let's Take The Long Way Around The World** *Ronnie Milsap*
27.	11/4	3	**Sleeping Single In A Double Bed** *Barbara Mandrell*
28.	11/25	1	**Sweet Desire** *The Kendalls*
29.	12/2	1	**I Just Want To Love You** *Eddie Rabbitt*
30.	12/9	1	**On My Knees** *Charlie Rich with Janie Fricke*
31.	12/16	3	**The Gambler** *Kenny Rogers*

DATE	WKS	1979	
1.	1/6	1	**Tulsa Time** *Don Williams*
2.	1/13	1	**Lady Lay Down** *John Conlee*
3.	1/20	1	**I Really Got The Feeling** *Dolly Parton*
4.	1/27	2	**Why Have You Left The One You Left Me For** *Crystal Gayle*
5.	2/10	3	**Every Which Way But Loose** *Eddie Rabbitt*
6.	3/3	3	**Golden Tears** *Dave & Sugar*
7.	3/24	3	**I Just Fall In Love Again** *Anne Murray*
8.	4/14	1	**(If Loving You Is Wrong) I Don't Want To Be Right** *Barbara Mandrell*
9.	4/21	1	**All I Ever Need Is You** *Kenny Rogers & Dottie West*
10.	4/28	1	**Where Do I Put Her Memory** *Charley Pride*
11.	5/5	1	**Backside Of Thirty** *John Conlee*
12.	5/12	1	**Don't Take It Away** *Conway Twitty*
13.	5/19	3	**If I Said You Have A Beautiful Body Would You Hold It Against Me** *Bellamy Brothers*
14.	6/9	2	**She Believes In Me** *Kenny Rogers*
15.	6/23	1	**Nobody Likes Sad Songs** *Ronnie Milsap*
16.	6/30	3	**Amanda** *Waylon Jennings*
17.	7/21	1	**Shadows In The Moonlight** *Anne Murray*
18.	7/28	2	**You're The Only One** *Dolly Parton*
19.	8/11	1	**Suspicions** *Eddie Rabbitt*
20.	8/18	1	**Coca Cola Cowboy** *Mel Tillis*
21.	8/25	1	**The Devil Went Down To Georgia** *Charlie Daniels Band*
22.	9/1	1	**Heartbreak Hotel** *Willie Nelson & Leon Russell*
23.	9/8	1	**I May Never Get To Heaven** *Conway Twitty*
24.	9/15	1	**You're My Jamaica** *Charley Pride*
25.	9/22	1	**Just Good Ol' Boys** *Moe Bandy & Joe Stampley*
26.	9/29	1	**It Must Be Love** *Don Williams*

1979 (cont'd)

27.	10/6	2	**Last Cheater's Waltz** *T.G. Sheppard*
28.	10/20	2	**All The Gold In California** *Larry Gatlin & The Gatlin Brothers*
29.	11/3	2	**You Decorated My Life** *Kenny Rogers*
30.	11/17	2	**Come With Me** *Waylon Jennings*
31.	12/1	1	**Broken Hearted Me** *Anne Murray*
32.	12/8	1	**I Cheated Me Right Out Of You** *Moe Bandy*
33.	12/15	3	**Happy Birthday Darlin'** *Conway Twitty*

DATE	WKS	1980	
1.	1/5	3	**Coward Of The County** *Kenny Rogers*
2.	1/26	2	**I'll Be Coming Back For More** *T.G. Sheppard*
3.	2/9	1	**Leaving Louisiana In The Broad Daylight** *The Oak Ridge Boys*
4.	2/16	1	**Love Me Over Again** *Don Williams*
5.	2/23	1	**Years** *Barbara Mandrell*
6.	3/1	1	**I Ain't Living Long Like This** *Waylon Jennings*
7.	3/8	2	**My Heroes Have Always Been Cowboys** *Willie Nelson*
8.	3/22	1	**Why Don't You Spend The Night** *Ronnie Milsap*
9.	3/29	1	**I'd Love To Lay You Down** *Conway Twitty*
10.	4/5	1	**Sugar Daddy** *Bellamy Brothers*
11.	4/12	1	**Honky Tonk Blues** *Charley Pride*
12.	4/19	1	**It's Like We Never Said Goodbye** *Crystal Gayle*
13.	4/26	1	**A Lesson In Leavin'** *Dottie West*
14.	5/3	1	**Are You On The Road To Lovin' Me Again** *Debby Boone*
15.	5/10	1	**Beneath Still Waters** *Emmylou Harris*
16.	5/17	1	**Gone Too Far** *Eddie Rabbitt*
17.	5/24	1	**Starting Over Again** *Dolly Parton*
18.	5/31	3	**My Heart** *Ronnie Milsap*
19.	6/21	1	**One Day At A Time** *Cristy Lane*
20.	6/28	1	**Trying To Love Two Women** *The Oak Ridge Boys*
21.	7/5	1	**He Stopped Loving Her Today** *George Jones*
22.	7/12	1	**You Win Again** *Charley Pride*
23.	7/19	1	**True Love Ways** *Mickey Gilley*
24.	7/26	1	**Bar Room Buddies** *Merle Haggard & Clint Eastwood*
25.	8/2	1	**Dancin' Cowboys** *Bellamy Brothers*
26.	8/9	1	**Stand By Me** *Mickey Gilley*
27.	8/16	1	**Tennessee River** *Alabama*
28.	8/23	1	**Drivin' My Life Away** *Eddie Rabbitt*
29.	8/30	1	**Cowboys And Clowns** *Ronnie Milsap*
30.	9/6	3	**Lookin' For Love** *Johnny Lee*
31.	9/27	1	**Old Flames Can't Hold A Candle To You** *Dolly Parton*
32.	10/4	1	**Do You Wanna Go To Heaven** *T.G. Sheppard*
33.	10/11	1	**Loving Up A Storm** *Razzy Bailey*
34.	10/18	2	**I Believe In You** *Don Williams*

#1 HITS

1980 (cont'd)

35.	11/1	1	**Theme From The Dukes Of Hazzard (Good Ol' Boys)** *Waylon Jennings*
36.	11/8	1	**On The Road Again** *Willie Nelson*
37.	11/15	1	**Could I Have This Dance** *Anne Murray*
38.	11/22	1	**Lady** *Kenny Rogers*
39.	11/29	1	**If You Ever Change Your Mind** *Crystal Gayle*
40.	12/6	1	**Smoky Mountain Rain** *Ronnie Milsap*
41.	12/13	1	**Why Lady Why** *Alabama*
42.	12/20	1	**That's All That Matters** *Mickey Gilley*
43.	12/27	2	**One In A Million** *Johnny Lee*

	DATE	WKS	## 1981
1.	1/10	1	**I Think I'll Just Stay Here And Drink** *Merle Haggard*
2.	1/17	1	**I Love A Rainy Night** *Eddie Rabbitt*
3.	1/24	1	**9 To 5** *Dolly Parton*
4.	1/31	1	**I Feel Like Loving You Again** *T.G. Sheppard*
5.	2/7	1	**I Keep Coming Back** *Razzy Bailey*
6.	2/14	1	**Who's Cheatin' Who** *Charly McClain*
7.	2/21	1	**Southern Rains** *Mel Tillis*
8.	2/28	1	**Are You Happy Baby?** *Dottie West*
9.	3/7	1	**Do You Love As Good As You Look** *The Bellamy Brothers*
10.	3/14	1	**Guitar Man** *Elvis Presley*
11.	3/21	1	**Angel Flying Too Close To The Ground** *Willie Nelson*
12.	3/28	1	**Texas Women** *Hank Williams, Jr.*
13.	4/4	1	**Drifter** *Sylvia*
14.	4/11	1	**You're The Reason God Made Oklahoma** *David Frizzell & Shelly West*
15.	4/18	1	**Old Flame** *Alabama*
16.	4/25	1	**A Headache Tomorrow (Or A Heartache Tonight)** *Mickey Gilley*
17.	5/2	1	**Rest Your Love On Me** *Conway Twitty*
18.	5/9	1	**Am I Losing You** *Ronnie Milsap*
19.	5/16	1	**I Loved 'Em Every One** *T.G. Sheppard*
20.	5/23	1	**Seven Year Ache** *Rosanne Cash*
21.	5/30	1	**Elvira** *The Oak Ridge Boys*
22.	6/6	1	**Friends** *Razzy Bailey*
23.	6/13	1	**What Are We Doin' In Love** *Dottie West (with Kenny Rogers)*
24.	6/20	1	**But You Know I Love You** *Dolly Parton*
25.	6/27	1	**Blessed Are The Believers** *Anne Murray*
26.	7/4	1	**I Was Country When Country Wasn't Cool** *Barbara Mandrell*
27.	7/11	1	**Fire & Smoke** *Earl Thomas Conley*
28.	7/18	2	**Feels So Right** *Alabama*
29.	8/1	1	**Dixie On My Mind** *Hank Williams, Jr.*
30.	8/8	1	**Too Many Lovers** *Crystal Gayle*
31.	8/15	2	**I Don't Need You** *Kenny Rogers*
32.	8/29	2	**(There's) No Gettin' Over Me** *Ronnie Milsap*
33.	9/12	1	**Older Women** *Ronnie McDowell*
34.	9/19	1	**You Don't Know Me** *Mickey Gilley*

1981 (cont'd)

35.	9/26	1	**Tight Fittin' Jeans** *Conway Twitty*
36.	10/3	1	**Midnight Hauler** *Razzy Bailey*
37.	10/10	1	**Party Time** *T.G. Sheppard*
38.	10/17	1	**Step By Step** *Eddie Rabbitt*
39.	10/24	2	**Never Been So Loved (In All My Life)** *Charley Pride*
40.	11/7	1	**Fancy Free** *The Oak Ridge Boys*
41.	11/14	1	**My Baby Thinks He's A Train** *Rosanne Cash*
42.	11/21	1	**All My Rowdy Friends (Have Settled Down)** *Hank Williams, Jr.*
43.	11/28	1	**My Favorite Memory** *Merle Haggard*
44.	12/5	1	**Bet Your Heart On Me** *Johnny Lee*
45.	12/12	1	**Still Doin' Time** *George Jones*
46.	12/19	1	**All Roads Lead To You** *Steve Wariner*
47.	12/26	2	**Love In The First Degree** *Alabama*

	DATE	WKS	## 1982
1.	1/9	1	**Fourteen Carat Mind** *Gene Watson*
2.	1/16	1	**I Wouldn't Have Missed It For The World** *Ronnie Milsap*
3.	1/23	1	**Red Neckin' Love Makin' Night** *Conway Twitty*
4.	1/30	1	**The Sweetest Thing (I've Ever Known)** *Juice Newton*
5.	2/6	1	**Lonely Nights** *Mickey Gilley*
6.	2/13	1	**Someone Could Lose A Heart Tonight** *Eddie Rabbitt*
7.	2/20	1	**Only One You** *T.G. Sheppard*
8.	2/27	1	**Lord, I Hope This Day Is Good** *Don Williams*
9.	3/6	1	**You're The Best Break This Old Heart Ever Had** *Ed Bruce*
10.	3/13	1	**Blue Moon With Heartache** *Rosanne Cash*
11.	3/20	1	**Mountain Of Love** *Charley Pride*
12.	3/27	1	**She Left Love All Over Me** *Razzy Bailey*
13.	4/3	1	**Bobbie Sue** *The Oak Ridge Boys*
14.	4/10	1	**Big City** *Merle Haggard*
15.	4/17	1	**The Clown** *Conway Twitty*
16.	4/24	1	**Crying My Heart Out Over You** *Ricky Skaggs*
17.	5/1	1	**Mountain Music** *Alabama*
18.	5/8	2	**Always On My Mind** *Willie Nelson*
19.	5/22	2	**Just To Satisfy You** *Waylon & Willie*
20.	6/5	1	**Finally** *T.G. Sheppard*
21.	6/12	1	**For All The Wrong Reasons** *The Bellamy Brothers*
22.	6/19	2	**Slow Hand** *Conway Twitty*
23.	7/3	1	**Any Day Now** *Ronnie Milsap*
24.	7/10	1	**Don't Worry 'Bout Me Baby** *Janie Fricke*
25.	7/17	1	**'Till You're Gone** *Barbara Mandrell*
26.	7/24	1	**Take Me Down** *Alabama*
27.	7/31	1	**I Don't Care** *Ricky Skaggs*
28.	8/7	1	**Honky Tonkin'** *Hank Williams, Jr.*
29.	8/14	1	**I'm Gonna Hire A Wino To Decorate Our Home** *David Frizzell*

#1 HITS

1982 (cont'd)

30.	8/21	1	**Nobody** *Sylvia*
31.	8/28	1	**Fool Hearted Memory** *George Strait*
32.	9/4	1	**Love Will Turn You Around** *Kenny Rogers*
33.	9/11	2	**She Got The Goldmine (I Got The Shaft)** *Jerry Reed*
34.	9/25	1	**What's Forever For** *Michael Murphey*
35.	10/2	1	**Put Your Dreams Away** *Mickey Gilley*
36.	10/9	1	**Yesterday's Wine** *Merle Haggard/George Jones*
37.	10/16	1	**I Will Always Love You** *Dolly Parton*
38.	10/23	1	**He Got You** *Ronnie Milsap*
39.	10/30	1	**Close Enough To Perfect** *Alabama*
40.	11/6	1	**You're So Good When You're Bad** *Charley Pride*
41.	11/13	1	**Heartbroke** *Ricky Skaggs*
42.	11/20	1	**War Is Hell (On The Homefront Too)** *T.G. Sheppard*
43.	11/27	1	**It Ain't Easy Bein' Easy** *Janie Fricke*
44.	12/4	1	**You And I** *Eddie Rabbitt with Crystal Gayle*
45.	12/11	1	**Redneck Girl** *The Bellamy Brothers*
46.	12/18	1	**Somewhere Between Right And Wrong** *Earl Thomas Conley*
47.	12/25	2	**Wild And Blue** *John Anderson*

	DATE	WKS	1983
1.	1/8	1	**Can't Even Get The Blues** *Reba McEntire*
2.	1/15	1	**Going Where The Lonely Go** *Merle Haggard*
3.	1/22	1	**(Lost His Love) On Our Last Date** *Emmylou Harris*
4.	1/29	1	**Talk To Me** *Mickey Gilley*
5.	2/5	1	**Inside** *Ronnie Milsap*
6.	2/12	1	**'Til I Gain Control Again** *Crystal Gayle*
7.	2/19	1	**Faking Love** *T.G. Sheppard & Karen Brooks*
8.	2/26	1	**Why Baby Why** *Charley Pride*
9.	3/5	1	**If Hollywood Don't Need You** *Don Williams*
10.	3/12	1	**The Rose** *Conway Twitty*
11.	3/19	1	**I Wouldn't Change You If I Could** *Ricky Skaggs*
12.	3/26	1	**Swingin'** *John Anderson*
13.	4/2	1	**When I'm Away From You** *Bellamy Brothers*
14.	4/9	1	**We've Got Tonight** *Kenny Rogers & Sheena Easton*
15.	4/16	1	**Dixieland Delight** *Alabama*
16.	4/23	1	**American Made** *The Oak Ridge Boys*
17.	4/30	1	**You're The First Time I've Thought About Leaving** *Reba McEntire*
18.	5/7	1	**Jose Cuervo** *Shelly West*
19.	5/14	1	**Whatever Happened To Old Fashioned Love** *B.J. Thomas*
20.	5/21	1	**Common Man** *John Conlee*

1983 (cont'd)

21.	5/28	1	**You Take Me For Granted** *Merle Haggard*
22.	6/4	1	**Lucille (You Won't Do Your Daddy's Will)** *Waylon Jennings*
23.	6/11	1	**Our Love Is On The Faultline** *Crystal Gayle*
24.	6/18	1	**You Can't Run From Love** *Eddie Rabbitt*
25.	6/25	1	**Fool For Your Love** *Mickey Gilley*
26.	7/2	1	**Love Is On A Roll** *Don Williams*
27.	7/9	1	**Highway 40 Blues** *Ricky Skaggs*
28.	7/16	1	**The Closer You Get** *Alabama*
29.	7/23	1	**Pancho And Lefty** *Willie Nelson & Merle Haggard*
30.	7/30	1	**I Always Get Lucky With You** *George Jones*
31.	8/6	1	**Your Love's On The Line** *Earl Thomas Conley*
32.	8/13	1	**He's A Heartache (Looking For A Place To Happen)** *Janie Fricke*
33.	8/20	1	**Love Song** *The Oak Ridge Boys*
34.	8/27	1	**You're Gonna Ruin My Bad Reputation** *Ronnie McDowell*
35.	9/3	1	**A Fire I Can't Put Out** *George Strait*
36.	9/10	1	**I'm Only In It For The Love** *John Conlee*
37.	9/17	1	**Night Games** *Charley Pride*
38.	9/24	1	**Baby, What About You** *Crystal Gayle*
39.	10/1	1	**New Looks From An Old Lover** *B.J. Thomas*
40.	10/8	1	**Don't You Know How Much I Love You** *Ronnie Milsap*
41.	10/15	1	**Paradise Tonight** *Charly McClain & Mickey Gilley*
42.	10/22	1	**Lady Down On Love** *Alabama*
43.	10/29	2	**Islands In The Stream** *Kenny Rogers with Dolly Parton*
44.	11/12	1	**Somebody's Gonna Love You** *Lee Greenwood*
45.	11/19	1	**One Of A Kind Pair Of Fools** *Barbara Mandrell*
46.	11/26	1	**Holding Her And Loving You** *Earl Thomas Conley*
47.	12/3	1	**A Little Good News** *Anne Murray*
48.	12/10	1	**Tell Me A Lie** *Janie Fricke*
49.	12/17	1	**Black Sheep** *John Anderson*
50.	12/24	2	**Houston (Means I'm One Day Closer To You)** *Larry Gatlin & The Gatlin Brothers*

	DATE	WKS	1984
1.	1/7	1	**You Look So Good In Love** *George Strait*
2.	1/14	1	**Slow Burn** *T.G. Sheppard*
3.	1/21	1	**In My Eyes** *John Conlee*
4.	1/28	1	**The Sound Of Goodbye** *Crystal Gayle*
5.	2/4	1	**Show Her** *Ronnie Milsap*

#1 HITS

1984 (cont'd)

#	Date	Wks	Title / Artist
6.	2/11	1	**That's The Way Love Goes** *Merle Haggard*
7.	2/18	1	**Don't Cheat In Our Hometown** *Ricky Skaggs*
8.	2/25	1	**Stay Young** *Don Williams*
9.	3/3	1	**Woke Up In Love** *Exile*
10.	3/10	1	**Going, Going, Gone** *Lee Greenwood*
11.	3/17	1	**Elizabeth** *The Statler Brothers*
12.	3/24	1	**Roll On (Eighteen Wheeler)** *Alabama*
13.	3/31	1	**Let's Stop Talkin' About It** *Janie Fricke*
14.	4/7	1	**Don't Make It Easy For Me** *Earl Thomas Conley*
15.	4/14	1	**Thank God For The Radio** *The Kendalls*
16.	4/21	1	**The Yellow Rose** *Johnny Lee with Lane Brody*
17.	4/28	1	**Right Or Wrong** *George Strait*
18.	5/5	1	**I Guess It Never Hurts To Hurt Sometimes** *The Oak Ridge Boys*
19.	5/12	2	**To All The Girls I've Loved Before** *Julio Iglesias & Willie Nelson*
20.	5/26	1	**As Long As I'm Rockin' With You** *John Conlee*
21.	6/2	1	**Honey (Open That Door)** *Ricky Skaggs*
22.	6/9	1	**Someday When Things Are Good** *Merle Haggard*
23.	6/16	1	**I Got Mexico** *Eddy Raven*
24.	6/23	1	**When We Make Love** *Alabama*
25.	6/30	1	**I Can Tell By The Way You Dance (You're Gonna Love Me Tonight)** *Vern Gosdin*
26.	7/7	1	**Somebody's Needin' Somebody** *Conway Twitty*
27.	7/14	1	**I Don't Want To Be A Memory** *Exile*
28.	7/21	1	**Just Another Woman In Love** *Anne Murray*
29.	7/28	1	**Angel In Disguise** *Earl Thomas Conley*
30.	8/4	1	**Mama He's Crazy** *The Judds*
31.	8/11	1	**That's The Thing About Love** *Don Williams*
32.	8/18	1	**Still Losing You** *Ronnie Milsap*
33.	8/25	1	**Long Hard Road (The Sharecropper's Dream)** *Nitty Gritty Dirt Band*
34.	9/1	1	**Let's Fall To Pieces Together** *George Strait*
35.	9/8	1	**Tennessee Homesick Blues** *Dolly Parton*
36.	9/15	1	**You're Gettin' To Me Again** *Jim Glaser*
37.	9/22	1	**Let's Chase Each Other Around The Room** *Merle Haggard*
38.	9/29	1	**Turning Away** *Crystal Gayle*
39.	10/6	1	**Everyday** *The Oak Ridge Boys*
40.	10/13	1	**Uncle Pen** *Ricky Skaggs*
41.	10/20	1	**I Don't Know A Thing About Love (The Moon Song)** *Conway Twitty*
42.	10/27	1	**If You're Gonna Play In Texas (You Gotta Have A Fiddle In The Band)** *Alabama*
43.	11/3	1	**City Of New Orleans** *Willie Nelson*

1984 (cont'd)

#	Date	Wks	Title / Artist
44.	11/10	1	**I've Been Around Enough To Know** *John Schneider*
45.	11/17	1	**Give Me One More Chance** *Exile*
46.	11/24	1	**You Could've Heard A Heart Break** *Johnny Lee*
47.	12/1	1	**Your Heart's Not In It** *Janie Fricke*
48.	12/8	1	**Chance Of Lovin' You** *Earl Thomas Conley*
49.	12/15	1	**Nobody Loves Me Like You Do** *Anne Murray (with Dave Loggins)*
50.	12/22	2	**Why Not Me** *The Judds*

1985

#	Date	Wks	Title / Artist
1.	1/5	1	**Does Fort Worth Ever Cross Your Mind** *George Strait*
2.	1/12	1	**The Best Year Of My Life** *Eddie Rabbitt*
3.	1/19	1	**How Blue** *Reba McEntire*
4.	1/26	1	**(There's A) Fire In The Night** *Alabama*
5.	2/2	1	**A Place To Fall Apart** *Merle Haggard (with Janie Fricke)*
6.	2/9	1	**Ain't She Somethin' Else** *Conway Twitty*
7.	2/16	1	**Make My Life With You** *Oak Ridge Boys*
8.	2/23	1	**Baby's Got Her Blue Jeans On** *Mel McDaniel*
9.	3/2	1	**Baby Bye Bye** *Gary Morris*
10.	3/9	1	**My Only Love** *The Statler Brothers*
11.	3/16	1	**Crazy For Your Love** *Exile*
12.	3/23	1	**Seven Spanish Angels** *Ray Charles with Willie Nelson*
13.	3/30	1	**Crazy** *Kenny Rogers*
14.	4/6	1	**Country Girls** *John Schneider*
15.	4/13	1	**Honor Bound** *Earl Thomas Conley*
16.	4/20	1	**I Need More Of You** *Bellamy Brothers*
17.	4/27	1	**Girls Night Out** *The Judds*
18.	5/4	1	**There's No Way** *Alabama*
19.	5/11	1	**Somebody Should Leave** *Reba McEntire*
20.	5/18	1	**Step That Step** *Sawyer Brown*
21.	5/25	1	**Radio Heart** *Charly McClain*
22.	6/1	1	**Don't Call Him A Cowboy** *Conway Twitty*
23.	6/8	1	**Natural High** *Merle Haggard*
24.	6/15	1	**Country Boy** *Ricky Skaggs*
25.	6/22	1	**Little Things** *The Oak Ridge Boys*
26.	6/29	1	**She Keeps The Home Fires Burning** *Ronnie Milsap*
27.	7/6	1	**She's A Miracle** *Exile*
28.	7/13	1	**Forgiving You Was Easy** *Willie Nelson*
29.	7/20	1	**Dixie Road** *Lee Greenwood*
30.	7/27	1	**Love Don't Care (Whose Heart It Breaks)** *Earl Thomas Conley*
31.	8/3	1	**Forty Hour Week (For A Livin')** *Alabama*
32.	8/10	1	**I'm For Love** *Hank Williams, Jr.*
33.	8/17	1	**Highwayman** *Waylon Jennings/Willie Nelson/Johnny Cash/Kris Kristofferson*
34.	8/24	1	**Real Love** *Dolly Parton (with Kenny Rogers)*

#1 HITS

1985 (cont'd)

35.	8/31	1	**Love Is Alive** *The Judds*
36.	9/7	1	**I Don't Know Why You Don't Want Me**
			Rosanne Cash
37.	9/14	1	**Modern Day Romance**
			Nitty Gritty Dirt Band
38.	9/21	1	**I Fell In Love Again Last Night**
			The Forester Sisters
39.	9/28	2	**Lost In The Fifties Tonight (In The Still**
			Of The Night) *Ronnie Milsap*
40.	10/12	1	**Meet Me In Montana**
			Marie Osmond with Dan Seals
41.	10/19	1	**You Make Me Want To Make You Mine**
			Juice Newton
42.	10/26	1	**Touch A Hand, Make A Friend**
			The Oak Ridge Boys
43.	11/2	1	**Some Fools Never Learn** *Steve Wariner*
44.	11/9	1	**Can't Keep A Good Man Down**
			Alabama
45.	11/16	1	**Hang On To Your Heart** *Exile*
46.	11/23	1	**I'll Never Stop Loving You** *Gary Morris*
47.	11/30	1	**Too Much On My Heart**
			The Statler Brothers
48.	12/7	1	**I Don't Mind The Thorns (If You're The**
			Rose) *Lee Greenwood*
49.	12/14	1	**Nobody Falls Like A Fool**
			Earl Thomas Conley
50.	12/21	1	**The Chair** *George Strait*
51.	12/28	2	**Have Mercy** *The Judds*

DATE	WKS	**1986**	
1.	1/11	1	**Morning Desire** *Kenny Rogers*
2.	1/18	1	**Bop** *Dan Seals*
3.	1/25	1	**Never Be You** *Rosanne Cash*
4.	2/1	1	**Just In Case** *The Forester Sisters*
5.	2/8	1	**Hurt** *Juice Newton*
6.	2/15	1	**Makin' Up For Lost Time (The Dallas**
			Lovers' Song)
			Crystal Gayle & Gary Morris
7.	2/22	1	**There's No Stopping Your Heart**
			Marie Osmond
8.	3/1	1	**You Can Dream Of Me** *Steve Wariner*
9.	3/8	1	**Think About Love** *Dolly Parton*
10.	3/15	1	**I Could Get Used To You** *Exile*
11.	3/22	1	**What's A Memory Like You (Doing In**
			A Love Like This) *John Schneider*
12.	3/29	1	**Don't Underestimate My Love For You**
			Lee Greenwood
13.	4/5	1	**100% Chance Of Rain** *Gary Morris*
14.	4/12	1	**She And I** *Alabama*
15.	4/19	1	**Cajun Moon** *Ricky Skaggs*
16.	4/26	1	**Now And Forever (You And Me)**
			Anne Murray
17.	5/3	1	**Once In A Blue Moon**
			Earl Thomas Conley
18.	5/10	1	**Grandpa (Tell Me 'Bout The Good Old**
			Days) *The Judds*
19.	5/17	1	**Ain't Misbehavin'** *Hank Williams, Jr.*

1986 (cont'd)

20.	5/24	1	**Tomb Of The Unknown Love**
			Kenny Rogers
21.	5/31	1	**Whoever's In New England**
			Reba McEntire
22.	6/7	1	**Happy, Happy Birthday Baby**
			Ronnie Milsap
23.	6/14	1	**Life's Highway** *Steve Wariner*
24.	6/21	1	**Mama's Never Seen Those Eyes**
			The Forester Sisters
25.	6/28	1	**Living In The Promiseland**
			Willie Nelson
26.	7/5	1	**Everything That Glitters (Is Not Gold)**
			Dan Seals
27.	7/12	1	**Hearts Aren't Made To Break (They're**
			Made To Love) *Lee Greenwood*
28.	7/19	1	**Until I Met You** *Judy Rodman*
29.	7/26	1	**On The Other Hand** *Randy Travis*
30.	8/2	1	**Nobody In His Right Mind Would've**
			Left Her *George Strait*
31.	8/9	1	**Rockin' With The Rhythm Of The Rain**
			The Judds
32.	8/16	1	**You're The Last Thing I Needed**
			Tonight *John Schneider*
33.	8/23	1	**Strong Heart** *T.G. Sheppard*
34.	8/30	1	**Heartbeat In The Darkness** *Don Williams*
35.	9/6	1	**Desperado Love** *Conway Twitty*
36.	9/13	1	**Little Rock** *Reba McEntire*
37.	9/20	1	**Got My Heart Set On You** *John Conlee*
38.	9/27	1	**In Love** *Ronnie Milsap*
39.	10/4	1	**Always Have Always Will** *Janie Fricke*
40.	10/11	1	**Both To Each Other (Friends &**
			Lovers) *Eddie Rabbitt & Juice Newton*
41.	10/18	1	**Just Another Love** *Tanya Tucker*
42.	10/25	1	**Cry** *Crystal Gayle*
43.	11/1	1	**It'll Be Me** *Exile*
44.	11/8	1	**Diggin' Up Bones** *Randy Travis*
45.	11/15	1	**That Rock Won't Roll** *Restless Heart*
46.	11/22	1	**You're Still New To Me**
			Marie Osmond with Paul Davis
47.	11/29	1	**Touch Me When We're Dancing**
			Alabama
48.	12/6	1	**It Ain't Cool To Be Crazy About You**
			George Strait
49.	12/13	1	**Hell And High Water** *T. Graham Brown*
50.	12/20	1	**Too Much Is Not Enough**
			Bellamy Brothers
51.	12/27	2	**Mind Your Own Business**
			Hank Williams, Jr.

DATE	WKS	**1987**	
1.	1/10	1	**Give Me Wings** *Michael Johnson*
2.	1/17	1	**What Am I Gonna Do About You**
			Reba McEntire
3.	1/24	1	**Cry Myself To Sleep** *The Judds*
4.	1/31	1	**You Still Move Me** *Dan Seals*
5.	2/7	1	**Leave Me Lonely** *Gary Morris*
6.	2/14	1	**How Do I Turn You On** *Ronnie Milsap*
7.	2/21	1	**Straight To The Heart** *Crystal Gayle*

#1 HITS

1987 (cont'd)

8.	2/28	1	**I Can't Win For Losin' You** *Earl Thomas Conley*
9.	3/7	1	**Mornin' Ride** *Lee Greenwood*
10.	3/14	1	**Baby's Got A New Baby** *S-K-O*
11.	3/21	1	**I'll Still Be Loving You** *Restless Heart*
12.	3/28	1	**Small Town Girl** *Steve Wariner*
13.	4/4	1	**Ocean Front Property** *George Strait*
14.	4/11	1	**"You've Got" The Touch** *Alabama*
15.	4/18	1	**Kids Of The Baby Boom** *Bellamy Brothers*
16.	4/25	1	**Rose In Paradise** *Waylon Jennings*
17.	5/2	1	**Don't Go To Strangers** *T. Graham Brown*
18.	5/9	1	**The Moon Is Still Over Her Shoulder** *Michael Johnson*
19.	5/16	1	**To Know Him Is To Love Him** *Dolly Parton, Linda Ronstadt, Emmylou Harris*
20.	5/23	1	**Can't Stop My Heart From Loving You** *The O'Kanes*
21.	5/30	1	**It Takes A Little Rain (To Make Love Grow)** *The Oak Ridge Boys*
22.	6/6	1	**I Will Be There** *Dan Seals*
23.	6/13	3	**Forever And Ever, Amen** *Randy Travis*
24.	7/4	1	**That Was A Close One** *Earl Thomas Conley*
25.	7/11	1	**All My Ex's Live In Texas** *George Strait*
26.	7/18	1	**I Know Where I'm Going** *The Judds*
27.	7/25	1	**The Weekend** *Steve Wariner*
28.	8/1	1	**Snap Your Fingers** *Ronnie Milsap*
29.	8/8	1	**One Promise Too Late** *Reba McEntire*
30.	8/15	1	**A Long Line Of Love** *Michael Martin Murphey*
31.	8/22	1	**Why Does It Have To Be (Wrong Or Right)** *Restless Heart*
32.	8/29	1	**Born To Boogie** *Hank Williams, Jr.*
33.	9/5	1	**She's Too Good To Be True** *Exile*
34.	9/12	1	**Make No Mistake, She's Mine** *Ronnie Milsap & Kenny Rogers*
35.	9/19	1	**This Crazy Love** *The Oak Ridge Boys*
36.	9/26	1	**Three Time Loser** *Dan Seals*
37.	10/3	1	**You Again** *The Forester Sisters*
38.	10/10	1	**The Way We Make A Broken Heart** *Rosanne Cash*
39.	10/17	1	**Fishin' In The Dark** *Nitty Gritty Dirt Band*
40.	10/24	1	**Shine, Shine, Shine** *Eddy Raven*
41.	10/31	1	**Right From The Start** *Earl Thomas Conley*
42.	11/7	1	**Am I Blue** *George Strait*
43.	11/14	1	**Maybe Your Baby's Got The Blues** *The Judds*
44.	11/21	1	**I Won't Need You Anymore (Always And Forever)** *Randy Travis*
45.	11/28	1	**Lynda** *Steve Wariner*
46.	12/5	1	**Somebody Lied** *Ricky Van Shelton*
47.	12/12	1	**The Last One To Know** *Reba McEntire*
48.	12/19	1	**Do Ya'** *K.T. Oslin*
49.	12/26	2	**Somewhere Tonight** *Highway 101*

1988

	DATE	WKS	
1.	1/9	1	**I Can't Get Close Enough** *Exile*
2.	1/16	1	**One Friend** *Dan Seals*
3.	1/23	1	**Where Do The Nights Go** *Ronnie Milsap*
4.	1/30	1	**Goin' Gone** *Kathy Mattea*
5.	2/6	1	**Wheels** *Restless Heart*
6.	2/13	1	**Tennessee Flat Top Box** *Rosanne Cash*
7.	2/20	1	**Twinkle, Twinkle Lucky Star** *Merle Haggard*
8.	2/27	1	**I Won't Take Less Than Your Love** *Tanya Tucker*
9.	3/5	1	**Face To Face** *Alabama*
10.	3/12	1	**Too Gone Too Long** *Randy Travis*
11.	3/19	1	**Life Turned Her That Way** *Ricky Van Shelton*
12.	3/26	1	**Turn It Loose** *The Judds*
13.	4/2	1	**Love Will Find Its Way To You** *Reba McEntire*
14.	4/9	1	**Famous Last Words Of A Fool** *George Strait*
15.	4/16	1	**I Wanna Dance With You** *Eddie Rabbitt*
16.	4/23	1	**I'll Always Come Back** *K.T. Oslin*
17.	4/30	1	**It's Such A Small World** *Rodney Crowell & Rosanne Cash*
18.	5/7	1	**Cry, Cry, Cry** *Highway 101*
19.	5/14	1	**I'm Gonna Get You** *Eddy Raven*
20.	5/21	2	**Eighteen Wheels And A Dozen Roses** *Kathy Mattea*
21.	6/4	1	**What She Is (Is A Woman In Love)** *Earl Thomas Conley*
22.	6/11	2	**I Told You So** *Randy Travis*
23.	6/25	1	**He's Back And I'm Blue** *The Desert Rose Band*
24.	7/2	1	**If It Don't Come Easy** *Tanya Tucker*
25.	7/9	1	**Fallin' Again** *Alabama*
26.	7/16	1	**If You Change Your Mind** *Rosanne Cash*
27.	7/23	1	**Set 'Em Up Joe** *Vern Gosdin*
28.	7/30	1	**Don't We All Have The Right** *Ricky Van Shelton*
29.	8/6	1	**Baby Blue** *George Strait*
30.	8/13	1	**Don't Close Your Eyes** *Keith Whitley*
31.	8/20	1	**Bluest Eyes In Texas** *Restless Heart*
32.	8/27	1	**The Wanderer** *Eddie Rabbitt*
33.	9/3	1	**I Couldn't Leave You If I Tried** *Rodney Crowell*
34.	9/10	1	**(Do You Love Me) Just Say Yes** *Highway 101*
35.	9/17	1	**Joe Knows How To Live** *Eddy Raven*
36.	9/24	1	**Addicted** *Dan Seals*
37.	10/1	1	**We Believe In Happy Endings** *Earl Thomas Conley with Emmylou Harris*
38.	10/8	1	**Honky Tonk Moon** *Randy Travis*
39.	10/15	1	**Streets Of Bakersfield** *Dwight Yoakam & Buck Owens*
40.	10/22	1	**Strong Enough To Bend** *Tanya Tucker*
41.	10/29	1	**Gonna Take A Lot Of River** *The Oak Ridge Boys*
42.	11/5	1	**Darlene** *T. Graham Brown*

#1 HITS

1988 (cont'd)

43.	11/12	1	**Runaway Train** *Rosanne Cash*
44.	11/19	2	**I'll Leave This World Loving You** *Ricky Van Shelton*
45.	12/3	1	**I Know How He Feels** *Reba McEntire*
46.	12/10	1	**If You Ain't Lovin' (You Ain't Livin')** *George Strait*
47.	12/17	1	**A Tender Lie** *Restless Heart*
48.	12/24	2	**When You Say Nothing At All** *Keith Whitley*

DATE	WKS	**1989**

1.	1/7	1	**Hold Me** *K.T. Oslin*
2.	1/14	1	**Change Of Heart** *The Judds*
3.	1/21	1	**She's Crazy For Leavin'** *Rodney Crowell*
4.	1/28	1	**Deeper Than The Holler** *Randy Travis*
5.	2/4	1	**What I'd Say** *Earl Thomas Conley*
6.	2/11	1	**Song Of The South** *Alabama*
7.	2/18	1	**Big Wheels In The Moonlight** *Dan Seals*
8.	2/25	1	**I Sang Dixie** *Dwight Yoakam*
9.	3/4	1	**I Still Believe In You** *The Desert Rose Band*
10.	3/11	1	**Don't You Ever Get Tired (Of Hurting Me)** *Ronnie Milsap*
11.	3/18	1	**From A Jack To A King** *Ricky Van Shelton*
12.	3/25	1	**New Fool At An Old Game** *Reba McEntire*
13.	4/1	1	**Baby's Gotten Good At Goodbye** *George Strait*
14.	4/8	2	**I'm No Stranger To The Rain** *Keith Whitley*
15.	4/22	2	**The Church On Cumberland Road** *Shenandoah*
16.	5/6	1	**Young Love** *The Judds*
17.	5/13	1	**Is It Still Over?** *Randy Travis*
18.	5/20	1	**If I Had You** *Alabama*
19.	5/27	1	**After All This Time** *Rodney Crowell*
20.	6/3	1	**Where Did I Go Wrong** *Steve Wariner*
21.	6/10	1	**A Better Man** *Clint Black*
22.	6/17	1	**Love Out Loud** *Earl Thomas Conley*
23.	6/24	1	**I Don't Want To Spoil The Party** *Rosanne Cash*
24.	7/1	1	**Come From The Heart** *Kathy Mattea*
25.	7/8	1	**Lovin' Only Me** *Ricky Skaggs*
26.	7/15	1	**In A Letter To You** *Eddy Raven*
27.	7/22	1	**What's Going On In Your World** *George Strait*
28.	7/29	1	**Cathy's Clown** *Reba McEntire*
29.	8/5	1	**Why'd You Come In Here Lookin' Like That** *Dolly Parton*
30.	8/12	1	**Timber, I'm Falling In Love** *Patty Loveless*
31.	8/19	1	**Sunday In The South** *Shenandoah*
32.	8/26	1	**Are You Ever Gonna Love Me** *Holly Dunn*
33.	9/2	1	**I'm Still Crazy** *Vern Gosdin*

1989 (cont'd)

34.	9/9	1	**I Wonder Do You Think Of Me** *Keith Whitley*
35.	9/16	1	**Nothing I Can Do About It Now** *Willie Nelson*
36.	9/23	1	**Above And Beyond** *Rodney Crowell*
37.	9/30	1	**Let Me Tell You About Love** *The Judds*
38.	10/7	1	**I Got Dreams** *Steve Wariner*
39.	10/14	1	**Killin' Time** *Clint Black*
40.	10/21	1	**Living Proof** *Ricky Van Shelton*
41.	10/28	1	**High Cotton** *Alabama*
42.	11/4	1	**Ace In The Hole** *George Strait*
43.	11/11	1	**Burnin' Old Memories** *Kathy Mattea*
44.	11/18	1	**Bayou Boys** *Eddy Raven*
45.	11/25	1	**Yellow Roses** *Dolly Parton*
46.	12/2	1	**It's Just A Matter Of Time** *Randy Travis*
47.	12/9	1	**If Tomorrow Never Comes** *Garth Brooks*
48.	12/16	1	**Two Dozen Roses** *Shenandoah*
49.	12/23	2	**A Woman In Love** *Ronnie Milsap*

DATE	WKS	**1990**

| 1. | 1/6 | 1 | **Who's Lonely Now** *Highway 101* |
| 2. | 1/13 | 1 | **It Ain't Nothin'** *Keith Whitley* |

1/20/90: Billboard begins compiling Country chart through their BDS system (a computerized airplay monitoring system).

| 3. | 1/20 | 3 | **Nobody's Home** *Clint Black* |
| 4. | 2/10 | 1 | **Southern Star** *Alabama* |

2/17/90: Chart renamed "Hot Country Singles & Tracks"

5.	2/17	2	**On Second Thought** *Eddie Rabbitt*
6.	3/3	1	**No Matter How High** *Oak Ridge Boys*
7.	3/10	1	**Chains** *Patty Loveless*
8.	3/17	4	**Hard Rock Bottom Of Your Heart** *Randy Travis*
9.	4/14	1	**Five Minutes** *Lorrie Morgan*
10.	4/21	3	**Love On Arrival** *Dan Seals*
11.	5/12	1	**Help Me Hold On** *Travis Tritt*
12.	5/19	2	**Walkin' Away** *Clint Black*
13.	6/2	1	**I've Cried My Last Tear For You** *Ricky Van Shelton*
14.	6/9	5	**Love Without End, Amen** *George Strait*
15.	7/14	3	**The Dance** *Garth Brooks*
16.	8/4	2	**Good Times** *Dan Seals*
17.	8/18	3	**Next To You, Next To Me** *Shenandoah*
18.	9/8	4	**Jukebox In My Mind** *Alabama*
19.	10/6	4	**Friends In Low Places** *Garth Brooks*
20.	11/3	1	**You Lie** *Reba McEntire*
21.	11/10	1	**Home** *Joe Diffie*
22.	11/17	1	**You Really Had Me Going** *Holly Dunn*
23.	11/24	2	**Come Next Monday** *K.T. Oslin*
24.	12/8	5	**I've Come To Expect It From You** *George Strait*

#1 HITS

	DATE	WKS	
1.	1/12	2	**Unanswered Prayers** *Garth Brooks*
2.	1/26	1	**Forever's As Far As I'll Go** *Alabama*
3.	2/2	1	**Daddy's Come Around** *Paul Overstreet*
4.	2/9	2	**Brother Jukebox** *Mark Chesnutt*
5.	2/23	2	**Walk On Faith** *Mike Reid*
6.	3/9	2	**I'd Love You All Over Again** *Alan Jackson*
7.	3/23	2	**Loving Blind** *Clint Black*
8.	4/6	1	**Two Of A Kind, Workin' On A Full House** *Garth Brooks*
9.	4/13	3	**Down Home** *Alabama*
10.	5/4	1	**Rockin' Years** *Dolly Parton with Ricky Van Shelton*
11.	5/11	2	**If I Know Me** *George Strait*
12.	5/25	1	**In A Different Light** *Doug Stone*
13.	6/1	2	**Meet In The Middle** *Diamond Rio*
14.	6/15	1	**If The Devil Danced (In Empty Pockets)** *Joe Diffie*
15.	6/22	2	**The Thunder Rolls** *Garth Brooks*
16.	7/6	3	**Don't Rock The Jukebox** *Alan Jackson*
17.	7/27	1	**I Am A Simple Man** *Ricky Van Shelton*
18.	8/3	2	**She's In Love With The Boy** *Trisha Yearwood*
19.	8/17	3	**You Know Me Better Than That** *George Strait*
20.	9/7	2	**Brand New Man** *Brooks & Dunn*
21.	9/21	1	**Leap Of Faith** *Lionel Cartwright*
22.	9/28	2	**Where Are You Now** *Clint Black*
23.	10/12	2	**Keep It Between The Lines** *Ricky Van Shelton*
24.	10/26	2	**Anymore** *Travis Tritt*
25.	11/9	1	**Someday** *Alan Jackson*
26.	11/16	2	**Shameless** *Garth Brooks*
27.	11/30	1	**Forever Together** *Randy Travis*
28.	12/7	2	**For My Broken Heart** *Reba McEntire*
29.	12/21	2	**My Next Broken Heart** *Brooks & Dunn*

	DATE	WKS	
1.	1/4	3	**Love, Me** *Collin Raye*
2.	1/25	1	**Sticks And Stones** *Tracy Lawrence*
3.	2/1	2	**A Jukebox With A Country Song** *Doug Stone*
4.	2/15	4	**What She's Doing Now** *Garth Brooks*
5.	3/14	1	**Straight Tequila Night** *John Anderson*
6.	3/21	1	**Dallas** *Alan Jackson*
7.	3/28	2	**Is There Life Out There** *Reba McEntire*
8.	4/11	1	**She Is His Only Need** *Wynonna*
9.	4/18	3	**There Ain't Nothin' Wrong With The Radio** *Aaron Tippin*
10.	5/9	2	**Neon Moon** *Brooks & Dunn*
11.	5/23	1	**Some Girls Do** *Sawyer Brown*
12.	5/30	5	**Achy Breaky Heart** *Billy Ray Cyrus*
13.	7/4	3	**I Saw The Light** *Wynonna*
14.	7/25	1	**The River** *Garth Brooks*
15.	8/1	4	**Boot Scootin' Boogie** *Brooks & Dunn*
16.	8/29	1	**I'll Think Of Something** *Mark Chesnutt*
17.	9/5	2	**I Still Believe In You** *Vince Gill*

1992 (cont'd)

18.	9/19	2	**Love's Got A Hold On You** *Alan Jackson*
19.	10/3	2	**In This Life** *Collin Raye*
20.	10/17	1	**If I Didn't Have You** *Randy Travis*
21.	10/24	4	**No One Else On Earth** *Wynonna*
22.	11/21	2	**I'm In A Hurry (And Don't Know Why)** *Alabama*
23.	12/5	2	**I Cross My Heart** *George Strait*
24.	12/19	1	**She's Got The Rhythm (And I Got The Blues)** *Alan Jackson*
25.	12/26	3	**Don't Let Our Love Start Slippin' Away** *Vince Gill*

	DATE	WKS	
1.	1/16	1	**Somewhere Other Than The Night** *Garth Brooks*
2.	1/23	2	**Look Heart, No Hands** *Randy Travis*
3.	2/6	1	**Too Busy Being In Love** *Doug Stone*
4.	2/13	2	**Can I Trust You With My Heart** *Travis Tritt*
5.	2/27	3	**What Part Of No** *Lorrie Morgan*
6.	3/20	1	**Heartland** *George Strait*
7.	3/27	2	**When My Ship Comes In** *Clint Black*
8.	4/10	2	**The Heart Won't Lie** *Reba McEntire & Vince Gill*
9.	4/24	1	**She Don't Know She's Beautiful** *Sammy Kershaw*
10.	5/1	2	**Alibis** *Tracy Lawrence*
11.	5/15	3	**I Love The Way You Love Me** *John Michael Montgomery*
12.	6/5	2	**Should've Been A Cowboy** *Toby Keith*
13.	6/19	2	**Blame It On Your Heart** *Patty Loveless*
14.	7/3	1	**That Summer** *Garth Brooks*
15.	7/10	1	**Money In The Bank** *John Anderson*
16.	7/17	4	**Chattahoochee** *Alan Jackson*
17.	8/14	1	**It Sure Is Monday** *Mark Chesnutt*
18.	8/21	1	**Why Didn't I Think Of That** *Doug Stone*
19.	8/28	1	**Can't Break It To My Heart** *Tracy Lawrence*
20.	9/4	2	**Thank God For You** *Sawyer Brown*
21.	9/18	2↕	**Ain't Going Down (Til The Sun Comes Up)** *Garth Brooks*
22.	9/25	1	**Holdin' Heaven** *Tracy Byrd*
23.	10/9	1	**One More Last Chance** *Vince Gill*
24.	10/16	1	**What's It To You** *Clay Walker*
25.	10/23	2	**Easy Come, Easy Go** *George Strait*
26.	11/6	1	**Does He Love You** *Reba McEntire*
27.	11/13	1	**She Used To Be Mine** *Brooks & Dunn*
28.	11/20	1	**Almost Goodbye** *Mark Chesnutt*
29.	11/27	1	**Reckless** *Alabama*
30.	12/4	1	**American Honky-Tonk Bar Association** *Garth Brooks*
31.	12/11	1	**My Second Home** *Tracy Lawrence*
32.	12/18	2	**I Don't Call Him Daddy** *Doug Supernaw*

#1 HITS

1995 (cont'd)

1994

	DATE	WKS	
1.	1/1	4	**Wild One** *Faith Hill*
2.	1/29	1	**Live Until I Die** *Clay Walker*
3.	2/5	4	**I Swear** *John Michael Montgomery*
4.	3/5	1	**I Just Wanted You To Know** *Mark Chesnutt*
5.	3/12	1	**Tryin' To Get Over You** *Vince Gill*
6.	3/19	2	**No Doubt About It** *Neal McCoy*
7.	4/2	2	**My Love** *Little Texas*
8.	4/16	2	**If The Good Die Young** *Tracy Lawrence*
9.	4/30	1	**Piece Of My Heart** *Faith Hill*
10.	5/7	1	**A Good Run Of Bad Luck** *Clint Black*
11.	5/14	1	**If Bubba Can Dance (I Can Too)** *Shenandoah*
12.	5/21	1	**Your Love Amazes Me** *John Berry*
13.	5/28	2	**Don't Take The Girl** *Tim McGraw*
14.	6/11	1	**That Ain't No Way To Go** *Brooks & Dunn*
15.	6/18	4	**Wink** *Neal McCoy*
16.	7/16	1	**Foolish Pride** *Travis Tritt*
17.	7/23	3	**Summertime Blues** *Alan Jackson*
18.	8/13	2	**Be My Baby Tonight** *John Michael Montgomery*
19.	8/27	1	**Dreaming With My Eyes Open** *Clay Walker*
20.	9/3	1	**Whisper My Name** *Randy Travis*
21.	9/10	2	**XXX's And OOO's (An American Girl)** *Trisha Yearwood*
22.	9/24	2	**Third Rock From The Sun** *Joe Diffie*
23.	10/8	1	**Who's That Man** *Toby Keith*
24.	10/15	2	**She's Not The Cheatin' Kind** *Brooks & Dunn*
25.	10/29	3	**Livin' On Love** *Alan Jackson*
26.	11/19	1	**Shut Up And Kiss Me** *Mary Chapin Carpenter*
27.	11/26	1	**If I Could Make A Living** *Clay Walker*
28.	12/3	1	**The Big One** *George Strait*
29.	12/10	1	**If You've Got Love** *John Michael Montgomery*
30.	12/17	4	**Pickup Man** *Joe Diffie*

1995

	DATE	WKS	
1.	1/14	2	**Not A Moment Too Soon** *Tim McGraw*
2.	1/28	1	**Gone Country** *Alan Jackson*
3.	2/4	2	**Mi Vida Loca (My Crazy Life)** *Pam Tillis*
4.	2/18	1	**My Kind Of Girl** *Collin Raye*
5.	2/25	2	**Old Enough To Know Better** *Wade Hayes*
6.	3/11	1	**You Can't Make A Heart Love Somebody** *George Strait*
7.	3/18	2	**This Woman And This Man** *Clay Walker*
8.	4/1	2	**Thinkin' About You** *Trisha Yearwood*
9.	4/15	1	**The Heart Is A Lonely Hunter** *Reba McEntire*
10.	4/22	3:	**I Can Love You Like That** *John Michael Montgomery*
11.	4/29	1	**Little Miss Honky Tonk** *Brooks & Dunn*
12.	5/20	1	**Gonna Get A Life** *Mark Chesnutt*

1995 (cont'd)

	DATE	WKS	
13.	5/27	1	**What Mattered Most** *Ty Herndon*
14.	6/3	3	**Summer's Comin'** *Clint Black*
15.	6/24	1	**Texas Tornado** *Tracy Lawrence*
16.	7/1	3	**Sold (The Grundy County Auction Incident)** *John Michael Montgomery*
17.	7/22	2	**Any Man Of Mine** *Shania Twain*
18.	8/5	1	**I Don't Even Know Your Name** *Alan Jackson*
19.	8/12	1	**I Didn't Know My Own Strength** *Lorrie Morgan*
20.	8/19	2	**You're Gonna Miss Me When I'm Gone** *Brooks & Dunn*
21.	9/2	1	**Not On Your Love** *Jeff Carson*
22.	9/9	1	**Someone Else's Star** *Bryan White*
23.	9/16	5	**I Like It, I Love It** *Tim McGraw*
24.	10/21	1	**She's Every Woman** *Garth Brooks*
25.	10/28	2	**Dust On The Bottle** *David Lee Murphy*
26.	11/11	4	**Check Yes Or No** *George Strait*
27.	12/9	2	**Tall, Tall Trees** *Alan Jackson*
28.	12/23	2	**That's As Close As I'll Get To Loving You** *Aaron Tippin*

1996

	DATE	WKS	
1.	1/6	1	**Rebecca Lynn** *Bryan White*
2.	1/13	3	**It Matters To Me** *Faith Hill*
3.	2/3	2	**(If You're Not In It For Love) I'm Outta Here!** *Shania Twain*
4.	2/17	3	**Bigger Than The Beatles** *Joe Diffie*
5.	3/2	1	**Wild Angels** *Martina McBride*
6.	3/9	1	**I'll Try** *Alan Jackson*
7.	3/16	1	**The Beaches Of Cheyenne** *Garth Brooks*
8.	3/23	2	**You Can Feel Bad** *Patty Loveless*
9.	4/6	1	**To Be Loved By You** *Wynonna*
10.	4/13	3	**No News** *Lonestar*
11.	5/4	2	**You Win My Love** *Shania Twain*
12.	5/18	3	**My Maria** *Brooks & Dunn*
13.	6/8	2	**Blue Clear Sky** *George Strait*
14.	6/22	3	**Time Marches On** *Tracy Lawrence*
15.	7/13	1	**No One Needs To Know** *Shania Twain*
16.	7/20	1	**Daddy's Money** *Ricochet*
17.	8/3	1	**Don't Get Me Started** *Rhett Akins*
18.	8/10	3	**Carried Away** *George Strait*
19.	8/31	2	**She Never Lets It Go To Her Heart** *Tim McGraw*
20.	9/14	1	**Guys Do It All The Time** *Mindy McCready*
21.	9/21	2	**So Much For Pretending** *Bryan White*
22.	10/5	1	**Living In A Moment** *Ty Herndon*
23.	10/12	2	**Believe Me Baby (I Lied)** *Trisha Yearwood*
24.	10/26	1	**Like The Rain** *Clint Black*
25.	11/16	1	**Lonely Too Long** *Patty Loveless*
26.	11/23	2	**Strawberry Wine** *Deana Carter*
27.	12/7	3	**Little Bitty** *Alan Jackson*
28.	12/28	2	**One Way Ticket (Because I Can)** *LeAnn Rimes*

#1 HITS

	DATE	WKS	
1.	1/11	4	**Nobody Knows** *Kevin Sharp*
2.	2/8	2	**It's A Little Too Late** *Mark Chesnutt*
3.	2/22	1	**A Man This Lonely** *Brooks & Dunn*
4.	3/1	1	**Running Out Of Reasons To Run** *Rick Trevino*
5.	3/8	1	**Me Too** *Toby Keith*
6.	3/15	2	**We Danced Anyway** *Deana Carter*
7.	3/29	1	**How Was I To Know** *Reba McEntire*
8.	4/5	1	**(This Ain't) No Thinkin' Thing** *Trace Adkins*
9.	4/12	2	**Rumor Has It** *Clay Walker*
10.	4/26	5	**One Night At A Time** *George Strait*
11.	5/31	1	**Sittin' On Go** *Bryan White*
12.	6/7	6	**It's Your Love** *Tim McGraw & Faith Hill*
13.	7/19	4	**Carrying Your Love With Me** *George Strait*
14.	8/16	2	**Come Cryin' To Me** *Lonestar*
15.	8/30	3	**She's Got It All** *Kenny Chesney*
16.	9/20	1	**There Goes** *Alan Jackson*
17.	9/27	3	**How Your Love Makes Me Feel** *Diamond Rio*
18.	10/18	1	**How Do I Get There** *Deana Carter*
19.	10/25	2	**Everywhere** *Tim McGraw*
20.	11/8	5	**Love Gets Me Every Time** *Shania Twain*
21.	12/13	1	**From Here To Eternity** *Michael Peterson*
22.	12/20	3	**Longneck Bottle** *Garth Brooks*

THE CHARTS FROM

When the talk turns to music, more people turn to Joel Whitburn's Record Research Collection than to any other reference source.

That's because these are the **only** books that get right to the bottom of *Billboard's* major charts, with **complete, fully accurate chart data on every record ever charted**. So they're quoted with confidence by DJ's, music show hosts, program directors, collectors and other music enthusiasts worldwide.

Each book lists every record's significant chart data, such as peak position, debut date, peak date, weeks charted, label, record number and much more, all conveniently arranged for fast, easy reference. Most books also feature artist biographies, record notes, RIAA Platinum/Gold Record certifications, top artist and record achievements, all-time artist and record rankings, a chronological listing of all #1 hits, and additional in-depth chart information.

TOP POP SINGLES 1955-1996
Over 22,000 pop singles — every "Hot 100" hit — arranged by artist. Features thousands of artist biographies and countless titles notes. Also, for the first time, includes the B-side title of every "Hot 100" hit, doubling the number of titles listed in any previous edition. 912 pages. $79.95 Hardcover / $69.95 Softcover.

POP ANNUAL 1955-1994
A year-by-year ranking, based on chart performance, of over 20,000 pop hits. 880 pages. $69.95 Hardcover / $59.95 Softcover.

POP HITS 1940-1954
Compiled strictly from *Billboard* and divided into two easy-to-use sections — one lists all the hits artist-by-artist and the other year-by-year. Filled with artist bios, title notes, and many special sections. 414 pages. Hardcover. $44.95.

POP MEMORIES 1890-1954
Unprecedented in depth and dimension. An artist-by-artist, title-by-title chronicle of the 65 formative years of recorded popular music. Fascinating facts and statistics on over 1,600 artists and 12,000 recordings, compiled directly from America's popular music charts, surveys and record listings. 660 pages. Hardcover. $59.95.

TOP POP ALBUMS 1955-1996
An artist-by-artist history of the over 18,300 albums that ever appeared on *Billboard's* pop albums charts, with a complete A-Z listing below each artist of <u>every</u> track from <u>every</u> charted album by that artist. 1,056 pages. Hardcover. $89.95.

TOP POP ALBUM TRACKS 1955-1992
An all-inclusive, alphabetical index of every song track from every charted music album, with the artist's name and the album's chart debut year. 544 pages. Hardcover. $34.95.

TOP POP ALBUM TRACKS 1993-1996
A 3 1/2-year supplement to the above Tracks book — alphabetically indexes over 21,000 tracks from the more than 1,600 albums that have appeared on *The Billboard 200* pop albums charts since 1992. 88 pages. Softcover. $14.95.

BILLBOARD HOT 100/POP SINGLES CHARTS:

THE EIGHTIES 1980-1989
THE SEVENTIES 1970-1979
THE SIXTIES 1960-1969
Three complete collections of the actual weekly "Hot 100" charts from each decade; black-and-white reproductions at 70% of original size. Over 550 pages each. Deluxe Hardcover. $79.95 each.

POP CHARTS 1955-1959
Reproductions of every weekly pop singles chart *Billboard* published from 1955 through 1959 ("Best Sellers," "Jockeys," "Juke Box," "Top 100" and "Hot 100"). 496 pages. Deluxe Hardcover. $59.95.

BILLBOARD POP ALBUM CHARTS 1965-1969
The greatest of all album eras...straight off the pages of *Billboard*! Every weekly *Billboard* pop albums chart, shown in its entirety, from 1965 through 1969. Black-and-white reproductions at 70% of original size. 496 pages. Deluxe Hardcover. $59.95.

TOP COUNTRY SINGLES 1944-1997
The complete history of the most genuine of American musical genres, with an artist-by-artist listing of every "Country" single ever charted. 544 pages. Hardcover. $64.95.

COUNTRY ANNUAL 1944-1997
A year-by-year ranking, based on chart performance, of over 16,000 Country hits. 704 pages. Hardcover. $64.95.

TOP TO BOTTOM!

Record To Ever Appear On Every Major Billboard Chart.

TOP R&B SINGLES 1942-1995
Revised edition of our R&B bestseller — loaded with new features! Every "Soul," "Black," "Urban Contemporary" and "Rhythm & Blues" charted single, listed by artist. 704 pages. Hardcover. $64.95.

TOP COUNTRY ALBUMS 1964-1997
First edition! A music industry first and a Record Research exclusive — features an artist-by-artist listing of every album to appear on *Billboard's* Top Country Albums chart from its first appearance in 1964 through September, 1997. 304 pages. Hardcover. $49.95.

TOP ADULT CONTEMPORARY 1961-1993
America's leading listener format is covered hit by hit in this fact-packed volume. Lists, artist by artist, the complete history of *Billboard's* "Easy Listening" and "Adult Contemporary" charts. 368 pages. Hardcover. $39.95.

ROCK TRACKS
Two artist-by-artist listings of the over 3,700 titles that appeared on *Billboard's* "Album Rock Tracks" chart from March, 1981 through August, 1995 and the over 1,200 titles that appeared on *Billboard's* "Modern Rock Tracks" chart from September, 1988 through August, 1995. 288 pages. Softcover. $34.95.

BUBBLING UNDER SINGLES AND ALBUMS 1998 Edition
All "Bubbling Under The Hot 100" (1959-1997) and "Bubbling Under The Top Pop Albums" (1970-1985) charts covered in full and organized artist by artist. Also features a photo section of every EP that hit *Billboard's* "Best Selling Pop EP's" chart (1957-1960). 416 pages. Softcover. $49.95.

BILLBOARD TOP 10 CHARTS 1958-1997
A complete listing of each weekly Top 10 chart, along with each week's "Highest Debut" and "Biggest Mover" from the entire "Hot 100" chart, and more! 780 pages. Hardcover. $39.95.

BILLBOARD TOP 1000 x 5 1996 Edition
Includes five complete separate rankings — from #1 through #1000 — of the all-time top charted hits of Pop & Hot 100 Singles 1955-1996, Pop Singles 1940-1954, Adult Contemporary Singles 1961-1996, R&B Singles 1942-1996, and Country Singles 1944-1996. 288 pages. Softcover. $29.95.

DAILY #1 HITS 1940-1992
A desktop calendar of a half-century of #1 pop records. Lists one day of the year per page of every record that held the #1 position on the pop singles charts on that day for each of the past 53+ years. 392 pages. Spiral-bound softcover. $24.95.

BILLBOARD #1s 1950-1991
A week-by-week listing of every #1 single and album from *Billboard's* Pop, R&B, Country and Adult Contemporary charts. 336 pages. Softcover. $24.95.

MUSIC YEARBOOKS 1997/1996/1995/1994/1993
A complete review of '97, '96, '95, '94 or '93 charted music — as well as a superb supplemental update of our Record Research Pop Singles and Albums, Country Singles, R&B Singles, Adult Contemporary Singles, and Bubbling Under Singles books. Various page lengths. Softcover. 1997, 1996 & 1995 editions $34.95 each / 1994 & 1993 editions $29.95 each.

MUSIC & VIDEO YEARBOOKS 1992/1991/1990
Comprehensive, yearly updates on *Billboard's* major singles, albums and videocassettes charts. Various page lengths. Softcover. $29.95 each.

For complete book descriptions and ordering information, call, write, fax or e-mail today.

RECORD RESEARCH INC.
P.O. Box 200
Menomonee Falls, WI 53052-0200   U.S.A.
Phone: 414-251-5408
Fax: 414-251-9452
E-mail: record@execpc.com

We're On The Internet — If you'd like to place an order electronically, simply use the convenient order form on our Web Site: **http://www.recordresearch.com**.

The *RECORD RESEARCH* Collection

	Book Title	Quantity	Price	Total
1.	Billboard Pop Charts 1955-1959 (hardcover)	_____	$59.95	_____
2.	Billboard Hot 100 Charts - The Sixties (hardcover)	_____	$79.95	_____
3.	Billboard Hot 100 Charts - The Seventies (hardcover)	_____	$79.95	_____
4.	Billboard Hot 100 Charts - The Eighties (hardcover)	_____	$79.95	_____
5.	Billboard Pop Album Charts 1965-1969 (hardcover)	_____	$59.95	_____
6.	Top Pop Albums 1955-1996 (hardcover)	_____	$89.95	_____
7.	Top Pop Album Tracks 1955-1992 (hardcover)	_____	$34.95	_____
8.	Top Pop Album Tracks 1993-1996 (softcover)	_____	$14.95	_____
9.	Top Pop Singles 1955-1996 (hardcover)	_____	$79.95	_____
10.	Top Pop Singles 1955-1996 (softcover)	_____	$69.95	_____
11.	Pop Hits 1940-1954 (hardcover)	_____	$44.95	_____
12.	Pop Annual 1955-1994 (hardcover)	_____	$69.95	_____
13.	Pop Annual 1955-1994 (softcover)	_____	$59.95	_____
14.	Top Country Singles 1944-1997 (hardcover)	_____	$64.95	_____
15.	Country Annual 1944-1997 (hardcover)	_____	$64.95	_____
16.	Top R&B Singles 1942-1995 (hardcover)	_____	$64.95	_____
17.	Pop Memories 1890-1954 (hardcover)	_____	$59.95	_____
18.	Bubbling Under Singles And Albums 1998 Edition (softcover)	_____	$49.95	_____
19.	Top Country Albums 1964-1997 (hardcover)	_____	$49.95	_____
20.	Top Adult Contemporary 1961-1993 (hardcover)	_____	$39.95	_____
21.	Top 10 Charts 1958-1997 (hardcover)	_____	$39.95	_____
22.	Rock Tracks (softcover)	_____	$34.95	_____
23.	Billboard Top 1000 x 5 1996 Edition (softcover)	_____	$29.95	_____
24.	Daily #1 Hits 1940-1992 (softcover)	_____	$24.95	_____
25.	Billboard #1s 1950-1991 (softcover)	_____	$24.95	_____
26.	Music Yearbooks (softcover) ....$34.95 each			_____

☐ 1997　　☐ 1996　　☐ 1995

27.	Music Yearbooks (softcover) ....$29.95 each			_____

☐ 1994　　☐ 1993

28.	Music & Video Yearbooks (softcover) ....$29.95 each			_____

☐ 1992　　☐ 1991　　☐ 1990

Shipping & Handling (see below) ...... _____

Wisconsin Residents Only (add 5.1% sales tax)...... _____

SHIPPING & HANDLING:

If your order subtotals:	U.S.	Foreign
Up to $20.00	$4.50	$4.50
$20.01 - $50.00	$6.00	$6.00
$50.01 - $80.00	$7.50	$7.50
$80.01 - $130.00	$8.50	$10.00
$130.01 - $180.00	$9.00	$12.50
$180.01 - $230.00	$10.00	$16.00
$230.01 - $300.00	$11.50	$21.00
Over $300.00	$13.00	$25.00

TOTAL PAYMENT ....$_____

PAYMENT METHOD:

☐ MasterCard　　　　☐ Check

☐ VISA　　　　　　　☐ Money Order

☐ American Express

Credit Card
Expiration Date: _____ / _____
　　　　　　　　　　Mo.　　　　Yr.

U.S. orders shipped via UPS (please give complete street address). Foreign orders shipped via surface mail; allow 8-12 weeks for delivery. Must be paid in U.S. dollars and drawn on a U.S. bank. Call for special air shipping information/rates.

Credit Card #　__ __ __ __　　__ __ __ __　　__ __ __ __　　__ __ __ __

Signature _____

To charge your order by phone, call **414-251-5408** or fax **414-251-9452** (office hours: 8 a.m.-noon & 1-5 p.m. CST) or e-mail to: **record@execpc.com** or mail to: **Record Research Inc., P.O. Box 200, Menomonee Falls, WI 53052-0200 U.S.A.**

Name _____

Company Name _____

Address _____ Apt/Suite # _____

City _____ State/Province _____

ZIP/Postal Code_____ Country _____